MW00355783

## EDITORIAL BOARD

**ROBERT C. CLARK**
DIRECTING EDITOR
Distinguished Service Professor and Austin Wakeman Scott
Professor of Law and Former Dean of the Law School
Harvard University

**DANIEL A. FARBER**
Sho Sato Professor of Law and Director, Environmental Law Program
University of California at Berkeley

**HEATHER K. GERKEN**
J. Skelly Wright Professor of Law
Yale University

**SAMUEL ISSACHAROFF**
Bonnie and Richard Reiss Professor of Constitutional Law
New York University

**HERMA HILL KAY**
Barbara Nachtrieb Armstrong Professor of Law and
Former Dean of the School of Law
University of California at Berkeley

**HAROLD HONGJU KOH**
Sterling Professor of International Law and
Former Dean of the Law School
Yale University

**SAUL LEVMORE**
William B. Graham Distinguished Service Professor of Law and
Former Dean of the Law School
University of Chicago

**THOMAS W. MERRILL**
Charles Evans Hughes Professor of Law
Columbia University

**ROBERT L. RABIN**
A. Calder Mackay Professor of Law
Stanford University

**CAROL M. ROSE**
Gordon Bradford Tweedy Professor Emeritus of Law and Organization and
Professorial Lecturer in Law
Yale University
Lohse Chair in Water and Natural Resources
University of Arizona

UNIVERSITY CASEBOOK SERIES®

# PRIVACY AND DATA PROTECTION LAW

WILLIAM MCGEVERAN, CIPP/US
Associate Professor and Solly Robins Distinguished Research Fellow
University of Minnesota Law School

FOUNDATION PRESS

The publisher is not engaged in rendering legal or other professional advice, and this publication is not a substitute for the advice of an attorney. If you require legal or other expert advice, you should seek the services of a competent attorney or other professional.

*University Casebook Series* is a trademark registered in the U.S. Patent and Trademark Office.

© 2016 William McGeveran

Printed in the United States of America

**ISBN:** 978-1-63460-264-8

*To Shooey, McG, and Tiger*

# PREFACE

Privacy and data protection law have long been fun topics to study and teach. They are constantly changing; they involve sophisticated issues related to technology, culture, and regulation; they require complex policy tradeoffs and core questions of government power; and they affect daily life for everyone. More recently, however, privacy became a more serious business. As a growing and evolving set of laws has come into force, every large institution has faced the prospect of serious liability. Mishandling personal data can also harm reputation and operational capacity. Thus a whole new legal practice has emerged to counsel clients about privacy risk and compliance—and to help them when things go wrong.

This casebook responds to that new need. It prepares law students for opportunities in a rapidly growing field, whether as privacy specialists or as attorneys with expertise about data that will be vital in every area—from policing to health care to financial services, and from human resources to marketing. The book emphasizes the meat-and-potatoes topics for practicing privacy lawyers. It focuses on the role of the modern regulatory state in the enforcement of privacy law. Significant attention to data security, consumer protection law, and international data protection rules is woven throughout. The book also considers key privacy issues raised by law enforcement and national security interests, and the interplay between public-sector and private-sector restrictions.

The organization of the book follows the layered structure of privacy and data protection law. Part One lays the foundations of earlier constitutional and tort law and the emergence of newer administrative regulation. Part Two traces the life cycle of data from the perspective of an organization, starting with its collection and continuing through its use, storage, and eventual disclosure. Finally, Part Three reviews the numerous sectoral privacy laws that are so important in the United States, applying the principles from the first two Parts to specific types of organizations or functions.

Finally, the realities of contemporary privacy practice also guide the approach of this book. In addition to reading traditional case excerpts, students will grapple with complicated regulatory text and foreign court rulings. "Focus" notes illuminate important but knotty topics such as EU regulation of cross-border data transfers or workplace monitoring of employees' smartphones. "Practice" notes present exercises and problems for students to apply what they learn. Case studies explore modern privacy challenges such as online behavioral tracking, big data, payment card security, and social media.

To help keep up to date in this fast moving area, a web site accompanies this book, found at www.mcgeveranprivacy.com. The site will provide updates as the law changes, and password-protected materials for professors including a Teacher's Manual and sample syllabi and materials.

A note on editing: almost all of the excerpted materials have been abridged. In statutory and regulatory excerpts, but not in others, the omissions are noted with ellipses. Text in brackets was added by me. I altered punctuation where it was confusing, especially in non-US sources with different conventions, but otherwise left the original wording unchanged.

WILLIAM MCGEVERAN

St. Paul, Minnesota
May 2016

# ACKNOWLEDGMENTS

It turns out writing a casebook alone is a major undertaking. Fortunately, I received assistance from many quarters (although remaining mistakes are my responsibility, naturally).

Most excerpts in the book come from material in the public domain or they are reproduced pursuant to doctrines of fair use or fair dealing. I acknowledge with thanks the following copyright permissions:

- American Law Institute. Restatement of Torts, Restatement (Second) of Torts, copyright 1938, 1965, 1977, 1979. Reprinted with permission of the American Law Institute.
- Quotations of public sector materials from the United Kingdom, the Republic of Ireland, and the European Union are used in accordance with PSI General License Number 2005/08/01.
- The PCI Security Standards Council granted permission to use excerpts and an image from *PCI Security Standards Council, PCI DSS Quick Reference Guide: Understanding the Payment Card Industry.* © 2014 PCI Security Standards Council, LLC 401 Edgewater Place Suite 600 Wakefield, MA USA 01880 www.pcisecuritystandards.org. Used with permission.
- The International Association of Privacy Professionals granted permission to use excerpts from Peter P. Swire & Kenesa Ahmad, *Foundations of Information Privacy and Data Protection* (2012).
- LexisNexis Corporate Law Advisory granted permission to use an excerpt from David Katz, *Contracting in a World of Data Breaches and Insecurity: Managing Third-Party Vendor Engagements* (May 2, 2013). (Disclaimer: The views and opinions expressed in this article do not reflect the views, opinions or policies of the organizations the sources represent.)

I leaned heavily on support from my splendid student research assistants Chelsea Lemke, Hannah Nelson, and Paul Overbee. Many students in my privacy classes at the University of Minnesota chimed in with questions, suggestions, and typo-spotting, and I also learned from those to whom I taught privacy law at University College Dublin Sutherland School of Law and the University of Notre Dame Law School London Programme. I was lucky to work with my eagle-eyed assistant, Victoria Jackson, and the invaluable reference mavens at the University of Minnesota Law Library, particularly Connie Lenz and Mary Rumsey. The editorial and production staff at Foundation Press has been wonderful, especially my editor, Tessa Boury.

The engaged and friendly community of privacy law scholars helped me incubate the ideas embodied in this book and I am grateful to all of them, and particularly to Woody Hartzog, Andrea Matwyshyn, and Neil Richards for specific useful suggestions. I also benefitted from conversations with many privacy practitioners I have met along the way, through the International Association of Privacy Professionals, the Future of Privacy Forum, and the large and active group of privacy professionals in the Twin Cities.

My father, William A. McGeveran, Jr., came out of retirement as a reference book editor to review chapters for me. Happily, he and my mother, Nancy McGeveran (an English professor) raised me to write grammatically, so there weren't too many terrible paragraphs to revise. I am so grateful to both of them. Finally and most importantly, I simply could not have done this without the encouragement, patience, and support of my wife, Elizabeth.

# SUMMARY OF CONTENTS



## PART 1. FOUNDATIONS



## PART 2. THE LIFE CYCLE OF DATA

## PART 3. SECTOR-SPECIFIC REGULATION

# TABLE OF CONTENTS

## PART 2. THE LIFE CYCLE OF DATA

## PART 3. SECTOR-SPECIFIC REGULATION

# TABLE OF CASES

The principal cases are in bold type.

UNIVERSITY CASEBOOK SERIES®

# PRIVACY AND DATA PROTECTION LAW

# PART 1

# FOUNDATIONS

When he spoke to law students, the late Justice Antonin Scalia often remarked that they were studying entire areas of law that didn't exist when he was in law school. He frequently offered labor and employment law and environmental law as two examples of these novel fields. Privacy and data protection law are much newer than these. Before the 1960s, a coherent law of privacy was not even a real concept. Many of the rules examined in this book came into being in the 1990s or later. Even now, as privacy-related issues make national news every day, major law firms organize privacy practice groups, and the International Association of Privacy Professionals grows at a rapid pace, there are still some lawyers who might not recognize privacy law as a subject area capable of clear definition. Those lawyers are mistaken, and the next decade will prove it.

But law seldom materializes from thin air. In its early stages, labor and employment law adapted contract law that had long governed some workplace relationships. Environmental law similarly drew upon concepts such as nuisance and easements from tort and property law. So, too, privacy and data protection law have precedents found in basic first-year law courses, particularly constitutional law and torts. Even these forms of proto-privacy law underwent significant change starting in the 1960s, but they formed the base on which later developments built.

Part One begins with constitutional law [Chapter 1] and tort law [Chapter 2], showing how each began grappling with the privacy issues created by new technology early in the twentieth century, and then gradually transformed into more modern shape. Both of these types of law remain in force, but their primary importance comes from their doctrinal and thematic influence on statutes and regulations that came later and that dominate practical privacy and data protection law today. Their influence is clearly seen in the two primary models for newer types of privacy rules, covered in the two subsequent chapters: one rooted in consumer protection concepts [Chapter 3] and the other in what Europeans have long called "data protection"—an understanding of an individual's prerogative to control personal information, rooted in human rights [Chapter 4]. Together, these four chapters illuminate the foundations of all the narrower and more detailed statutes and regulations that make up contemporary privacy and data protection law.

## CHAPTER 1

# CONSTITUTIONAL LAW

The word "privacy" does not appear in the United States Constitution. Yet concepts of private information and decisionmaking are woven through the entire document, and courts have developed a substantial jurisprudence of constitutional privacy. This is most evident in the Fourth Amendment, which forbids "unreasonable searches and seizures" by the government. Indeed, the oldest and largest body of privacy law in the US arose in the context of criminal prosecutions, where defendants routinely challenge the use of evidence allegedly gathered in violation of the Fourth Amendment. As we shall see, courts also derived privacy rules from other portions of the United States Constitution. Some state constitutions incorporate additional privacy rules beyond the federal provisions, and many constitutions in other countries confer more expansive and more explicit privacy rights.

These rules are vital to the protection of individual privacy rights against government infringement, and thus central to the study of privacy law. This book also begins with them because they are some of the oldest and most heavily litigated privacy rules. It is not a comprehensive examination; other law school courses cover many of these rules in much greater depth, particularly courses on criminal procedure or free speech rights. But the principles and intuitions embodied in these cases permeate all the rest of the law of privacy. Starting here establishes themes that will recur throughout the course.

## A. THE FOURTH AMENDMENT

### 1. FOUNDATIONS

### Olmstead v. United States

277 U.S. 438 (1928)

■ MR. CHIEF JUSTICE TAFT delivered the opinion of the Court.

The petitioners were convicted in the District Court for the Western District of Washington of a conspiracy to violate the National Prohibition Act by unlawfully possessing, transporting and importing intoxicating liquors and maintaining nuisances, and by selling intoxicating liquors. Seventy-two others, in addition to the petitioners, were indicted. Some were not apprehended, some were acquitted, and others pleaded guilty.

The evidence in the records discloses a conspiracy of amazing magnitude to import, possess, and sell liquor unlawfully. It involved the employment of not less than 50 persons, of two sea-going vessels for the transportation of liquor to British Columbia, of smaller vessels for coastwise transportation to the state of Washington, the purchase and use of a branch beyond the suburban limits of Seattle, with a large underground cache for storage and a number of smaller caches in that city, the maintenance of a central office manned with operators, and the employment of executives, salesmen, deliverymen dispatchers, scouts, bookkeepers, collectors, and an attorney. In a bad month sales amounted to $176,000; the aggregate for a year must have exceeded $2,000,000.

Olmstead was the leading conspirator and the general manager of the business. He made a contribution of $10,000 to the capital; 11 others contributed $1,000 each. The profits were divided, one-half to Olmstead and the remainder to the other 11. Of the several offices in Seattle, the chief one was in a large office building. In this there were three telephones on three different lines. There were telephones in an office of the manager in his own home, at the homes of his associates, and at other places in the city. Communication was had frequently with Vancouver, British Columbia. Times were fixed for the deliveries of the 'stuff' to places along Puget Sound near Seattle, and from there the liquor was removed and deposited in the caches already referred to. One of the chief men was always on duty at the main office to receive orders by the telephones and to direct their filling by a corps of men stationed in another room—the "bull pen." The call numbers of the telephones were given to those known to be likely customers. At times the sales amounted to 200 cases of liquor per day.

The information which led to the discovery of the conspiracy and its nature and extent was largely obtained by intercepting messages on the telephones of the conspirators by four federal prohibition officers. Small wires were inserted along the ordinary telephone wires from the residences of four of the petitioners and those leading from the chief office. The insertions were made without trespass upon any property of the defendants. They were made in the basement of the large office building. The taps from house lines were made in the streets near the houses.

The gathering of evidence continued for many months. Conversations of the conspirators, of which refreshing stenographic notes were currently made, were testified to by the government witnesses. They revealed the large business transactions of the partners and their subordinates. Men at the wires heard the orders given for liquor by customers and the acceptances; they became auditors of the conversations between the partners. All this disclosed the conspiracy charged in the indictment. Many of the intercepted conversations were not merely reports, but parts of the criminal acts. The evidence also disclosed the difficulties to which the conspirators were subjected, the reported news of the capture of vessels, the arrest of their men, and the seizure of cases of liquor in garages and other places. It showed the dealing by Olmstead, the chief conspirator, with members of the Seattle police, the messages to them which secured the release of arrested members of the conspiracy, and also direct promises to officers of payments as soon as opportunity offered.

The Fourth Amendment provides:

> The right of the people to be secure in their persons, houses, papers, and effects, against unreasonable searches and seizures, shall not be violated, and no warrants shall issue, but upon probable cause, supported by oath or affirmation, and particularly describing the place to be searched, and the persons or things to be seized.

And the Fifth:

> No person . . . shall be compelled in any criminal case to be a witness against himself.

There is no room in the present case for applying the Fifth Amendment, unless the Fourth Amendment was first violated. There was no evidence of compulsion to induce the defendants to talk over their many telephones. They were continually and voluntarily transacting business without knowledge of the interception. Our consideration must be confined to the Fourth Amendment.

[The Fourth Amendment] shows that the search is to be of material things—the person, the house, his papers, or his effects. The description of the warrant necessary to make the proceeding lawful is that it must specify the place to be searched and the person or things to be seized.

The Fourth Amendment may have proper application to a sealed letter in the mail, because of the constitutional provision for the Postoffice Department and the relations between the government and those who pay to secure protection of their sealed letters. *See* Revised Statutes, §§ 3978–3988, whereby Congress monopolizes the carriage of letters and excludes from that business everyone else, and section 3929 (39 U.S.C. § 259), which forbids any postmaster or other person to open any letter not addressed to himself. It is plainly within the words of the amendment to say that the unlawful rifling by a government agent of a sealed letter is a search and seizure of the sender's papers of effects. The letter is a paper, an effect, and in the custody of a government that forbids carriage, except under its protection.

The United States takes no such care of telegraph or telephone messages as of mailed sealed letters. The amendment does not forbid what was done here. There was no searching. There was no seizure. The evidence was secured by the use of the sense of hearing and that only. There was no entry of the houses or offices of the defendants.

By the invention of the telephone 50 years ago, and its application for the purpose of extending communications, one can talk with another at a far distant place. The language of the amendment cannot be extended and expanded to include telephone wires, reaching to the whole world from the defendant's house or office. The intervening wires are not part of his house or office, any more than are the highways along which they are stretched.

Congress may, of course, protect the secrecy of telephone messages by making them, when intercepted, inadmissible in evidence in federal criminal trials, by direct legislation, and thus depart from the common law of evidence. But the courts may not adopt such a policy by attributing an enlarged and unusual meaning to the Fourth Amendment. The reasonable view is that one who installs in his house a telephone instrument with connecting wires intends to project his voice to those quite outside, and that the wires beyond his house, and messages while passing over them, are not within the protection of the Fourth Amendment. Here those who intercepted the projected voices were not in the house of either party to the conversation.

Neither the cases we have cited nor any of the many federal decisions brought to our attention hold the Fourth Amendment to have been violated as against a defendant, unless there has been an official search and seizure of his person or such a seizure of his papers or his tangible material effects or an actual physical invasion of his house or curtilage for the purpose of making a seizure.

We think, therefore, that the wire tapping here disclosed did not amount to a search or seizure within the meaning of the Fourth Amendment.

Affirmed.

■ MR. JUSTICE BRANDEIS (dissenting).

The defendants were convicted of conspiring to violate the National Prohibition Act. Before any of the persons now charged had been arrested or indicted, the telephones by means of which they habitually communicated with one another and with others had been tapped by federal officers. To this end, a lineman of long experience in wire tapping was employed, on behalf of the government and at its expense. He tapped eight telephones, some in the homes of the persons charged, some in their offices. Acting on behalf of the government and in their official capacity, at least six other prohibition agents listened over the tapped wires and reported the messages taken. Their operations extended over a period of nearly five months. The typewritten record of the notes of conversations overheard occupies 775 typewritten pages. By objections seasonably made and persistently renewed, the defendants objected to the admission of the evidence obtained by wire tapping, on the ground that the government's wire tapping constituted an unreasonable search and seizure, in violation of the Fourth Amendment, and that the use as evidence of the conversations overheard compelled the defendants to be witnesses against themselves, in violation of the Fifth Amendment.

The government makes no attempt to defend the methods employed by its officers. Indeed, it concedes that, if wire tapping can be deemed a search and seizure within the Fourth Amendment, such wire tapping as was practiced in the case at bar was an unreasonable search and seizure, and that the evidence thus obtained was inadmissible. But it relies on the language of the amendment, and it claims that the protection given thereby cannot properly be held to include a telephone conversation.

"We must never forget," said Mr. Chief Justice Marshall in *McCulloch v. Maryland*, 4 Wheat. 316, 407 4 L. Ed. 579, "that it is a Constitution we are expounding." Since then this court has repeatedly sustained the exercise of power by Congress, under various clauses of that instrument, over objects of which the fathers could not have dreamed. We have likewise held that general limitations on the powers of government, like those embodied in the due process clauses of the Fifth and Fourteenth Amendments, do not forbid the United States or the states from meeting modern conditions by regulations which a century ago, or even half a century ago, probably would have been rejected as arbitrary and oppressive. Clauses guaranteeing to the individual protection against specific abuses of power, must have a similar capacity of adaptation to a changing world. It was with reference to such a clause that this court said in *Weems v. United States*, 217 U. S. 349, 373, 30 S. Ct. 544, 551 (54 L. Ed. 793, 19 Ann. Cas. 705):

> Legislation, both statutory and constitutional, is enacted, it is true, from an experience of evils, but its general language should not, therefore, be necessarily confined to the form that evil had theretofore taken. Time works changes, brings into existence new conditions and purposes. Therefore a principle to be vital must be capable of wider application than the mischief which gave it birth. This is peculiarly true of Constitutions. They are not ephemeral enactments, designed to meet passing occasions.

When the Fourth and Fifth Amendments were adopted, "the form that evil had theretofore taken" had been necessarily simple. Force and violence were then the only means known to man by which a government could directly effect self-incrimination. It could compel the individual to testify—a compulsion effected, if need be, by torture. It could secure possession of his papers and other articles incident to his private life—a seizure effected, if need be, by breaking and entry. Protection against such invasion of "the sanctities of a man's home and the privacies of life" was provided in the Fourth and Fifth Amendments by specific language. But "time works changes, brings into existence new conditions and purposes." Subtler and more far-reaching means of invading privacy have become available to the government. Discovery and invention have made it possible for the government, by means far more effective than stretching upon the rack, to obtain disclosure in court of what is whispered in the closet.

The progress of science in furnishing the government with means of espionage is not likely to stop with wire tapping. Ways may some day be developed by which the government, without removing papers from secret drawers, can reproduce them in court, and by which it will be enabled to expose to a jury the most intimate occurrences of the home. Advances in the psychic and related sciences may bring means of exploring unexpressed beliefs, thoughts and emotions.

In *Ex parte Jackson*, 96 U.S. 727 (1877), it was held that a sealed letter intrusted to the mail is protected by the amendments. The mail is a public service furnished by the government. The telephone is a public service furnished by its authority. There is, in essence, no difference between the sealed letter and the private telephone message.

The evil incident to invasion of the privacy of the telephone is far greater than that involved in tampering with the mails. Whenever a telephone line is tapped, the privacy of the persons at both ends of the line is invaded, and all conversations between them upon any subject, and although proper, confidential, and privileged, may be overheard. Moreover, the tapping of one man's telephone line involves the tapping of the telephone of every other person whom he may call, or who may call him. As a means of espionage, writs of assistance and general warrants are but puny instruments of tyranny and oppression when compared with wire tapping.

Time and again this court, in giving effect to the principle underlying the Fourth Amendment, has refused to place an unduly literal construction upon it.

Unjustified search and seizure violates the Fourth Amendment, whatever the character of the paper; whether the paper when taken by the federal officers was in the home, in an office, or elsewhere; whether the taking was effected by force, by fraud, or in the orderly process of a court's procedure [citing cases for each situation]. From these decisions, it follows necessarily that the amendment is violated by the officer's reading the paper without a physical seizure, without his even touching it, and that use, in any criminal proceeding, of the contents of the paper so examined—as where they are testified to by a federal officer who thus saw the document or where, through knowledge so obtained, a copy has been procured elsewhere—any such use constitutes a violation of the Fifth Amendment.

The protection guaranteed by the amendments is much broader in scope. The makers of our Constitution undertook to secure conditions favorable to the pursuit of happiness. They recognized the significance of man's spiritual nature, of his feelings and of his intellect. They knew that only a part of the pain, pleasure and satisfactions of life are to be found in material things. They sought to protect Americans in their beliefs, their thoughts, their emotions and their sensations. They conferred, as against the government, the right to be let alone—the most comprehensive of rights and the right most valued by civilized men. To protect, that right, every unjustifiable intrusion by the government upon the privacy of the individual, whatever the means employed, must be deemed a violation of the Fourth Amendment. And the use, as evidence in a criminal proceeding, of facts ascertained by such intrusion must be deemed a violation of the Fifth.

Applying to the Fourth and Fifth Amendments the established rule of construction, the defendants' objections to the evidence obtained by wire tapping must, in my opinion, be sustained. It is, of course, immaterial where the physical connection with the telephone wires leading into the defendants' premises was made. And it is also immaterial that the intrusion was in aid of law enforcement. Experience should teach us to be most on our guard to protect liberty when the government's purposes are beneficent. Men born to freedom are naturally alert to repel invasion of their liberty by evil-minded rulers. The greatest dangers to liberty lurk in insidious encroachment by men of zeal, well-meaning but without understanding.

[Additional dissents by Justices Holmes, Butler, and Stone are omitted.]

## NOTES

1. ***Privacy and Trespass.*** An important theme illustrated in this case comes up again and again in privacy jurisprudence to this day: the connection between privacy rights and property rights. The majority drew a sharp contrast between privacy interests in tangible possessions within the home ("papers" and "effects") and privacy of conversations projected through telephone wires outside the home. This approach connects privacy to a vision of property often summarized in the aphorism that "a man's home is his castle," used by venerable English commentators such as Sir Edward Coke and Sir William Blackstone.

In some subsequent cases the degree of "unauthorized physical encroachment" on private property became an extremely important aspect of the analysis. So, in *Goldman v. United States*, 316 U.S. 129 (1942), the Court found no violation of the Fourth Amendment when federal agents listened to conversations in an office by using a bugging device placed against the adjoining wall in the room next door, because there had been no trespass into the office itself. Compare the facts in *Silverman v. United States*, 365 U.S. 505 (1961), where police officers investigating a gambling operation headquartered in a row house got permission from the owners of the row house next door to use it for surveillance. They used a "spike mike" that they inserted "into a crevice extending several inches into the party wall" until it hit a heating duct. The officers could then hear conversations throughout the targeted row house because the occupants' voices echoed through the heating system. While the *Silverman* Court recognized "the Fourth Amendment implications of these and other frightening paraphernalia which the vaunted marvels of an electronic age may visit upon human society," it disposed of the case based on the "unauthorized physical penetration" of the spike mike from one row house to the other—a violation of the Fourth Amendment based on *Olmstead* and its progeny. Watch for this theme in other cases, both in constitutional law and in other forms of privacy law.

2. ***Privacy and Technology.*** Another important theme animating *Olmstead* is the interplay between the law and developing technology. The invention of the telegraph, and especially the telephone, had revolutionized interpersonal communication by the 1920s, when *Olmstead* was decided—much as digital technological developments like the internet have changed it more recently. How should interpretation of constitutional provisions like the Fourth Amendment adapt to disruptive technological change? Notice that both the majority and the Brandeis dissent rely on analogies between newer electronic technology and more traditional (and familiar) modes of communication through the mail—in support of opposite conclusions. Courts and other decisionmakers often use such historical analogies to grapple with new technology. What are the benefits and pitfalls of doing so?

3. ***The Roles of Courts, Congress, and Agencies.*** Chief Justice Taft explicitly stated that Congress could enact legislation regulating wiretapping by law enforcement. Six years after *Olmstead*, Congress did just that. As part of the Communications Act of 1934, a comprehensive statute that created the Federal Communications Commission and transformed regulation of both telephone and radio, Congress also considered wiretapping. Section 605 of the new law restricted wiretapping without a warrant, and later court decisions determined that evidence gathered from unauthorized wiretapping could not be used in federal court. Under the new law, the wiretap evidence against Olmstead in this case would have been barred. However, Section 605 was deficient in other ways. It regulated only wiretapping and not, for example, the bugs in *Goldman* and *Silverman*. It did not affect state wiretapping laws, many of which were weaker and allowed the use of wiretap evidence in state court. Later, the discovery of large-scale FBI wiretapping operations in the 1950s and 1960s exposed other flaws in the law. The federal wiretapping statute has been comprehensively overhauled twice, and Congress considered further changes in recent years. [For more about these wiretapping statutes, see Chapter 5.] Meanwhile, the Department of Justice issues its own internal rules concerning the use of electronic surveillance in investigations and prosecutions under its authority. We will see continued debate about the best means to protect privacy in law enforcement operations. Should courts applying constitutional law be the primary regulator? Or should privacy be maintained mainly through provisions in statutes, such as Section 605, or through internal regulations like the DOJ's guidelines? Or through some combination?

4. ***Excluding Illegally Gathered Evidence.*** This excerpt omits the Court's lengthy discussion of a separate argument made by the petitioners about the legality of the federal agents' actions under a 1909 Washington statute that made wiretapping a misdemeanor. Olmstead argued that the federal government's use of legally prohibited methods automatically violated the Fourth Amendment. In their dissents, Justices Brandeis and Holmes energetically agreed with him on this point. The majority opinion rejected the argument, in part for the technical reason that it was outside the scope of the writ of certiorari granted in the case (a limitation the Supreme Court often has ignored, both then and now). Chief Justice Taft also addressed the argument on its merits:

> A standard which would forbid the reception of evidence, if obtained by other than nice ethical conduct by government officials, would make society suffer and give criminals greater immunity than has been known heretofore. In the absence of controlling legislation by Congress, those who realize the difficulties in bringing offenders to justice may well deem it wise that the exclusion of evidence should be confined to cases where rights under the Constitution would be violated by admitting it.

The same rule remains in effect today: gathering information in violation of state law such as trespass does not violate the Fourth Amendment automatically. In the years since *Olmstead*, however, the Supreme Court and Congress have created multiple "exclusionary rules" to penalize gathering information in violation of specified privacy restrictions. Under these rules, the information cannot be used as evidence in a criminal prosecution. Is this the best response to overreaching by law enforcement? The disagreement in *Olmstead* also highlights the inevitable tension between upholding privacy rights and "bringing offenders to justice." Not surprisingly, we will see this tension repeatedly.

5. ***The Fifth Amendment.*** The *Olmstead* opinion mentions but then sets aside the Fifth Amendment. The Fifth Amendment generates additional constitutional privacy law, but it is limited in important ways. It applies only to statements and actions that are compelled by the government, incriminating to the individual, and "testimonial" in nature. These limitations leave room for the government to gather a great deal of information: from taking a criminal defendant's blood sample, to mandating the production of documents, to requiring people to fill out tax returns. *See, e.g., United States v. Hubbell*, 530 U.S. 27, 34–38 (2000). At times the privilege against self-incrimination still implicates privacy interests, however. For example, some courts have held that the Fifth Amendment may bar the government from compelling a criminal defendant to reveal the password for an encrypted computer hard drive. *See, e.g., In Re Grand Jury Subpoena Duces Tecum Dated March 25, 2011*, 670 F.3d 1335 (11th Cir. 2012).

## Katz v. United States

389 U.S. 347 (1967)

■ MR. JUSTICE STEWART delivered the opinion of the Court.

The petitioner was convicted in the District Court for the Southern District of California under an eight-count indictment charging him with transmitting wagering information by telephone from Los Angeles to Miami and Boston in violation of a federal statute. At trial the Government was permitted, over the petitioner's objection, to introduce evidence of the petitioner's end of telephone conversations, overheard by FBI agents who had attached an electronic listening and recording device to the outside of the public telephone booth from which he had placed his calls. In affirming his conviction, the Court of Appeals rejected the contention that the recordings had been obtained in violation of the Fourth Amendment, because "[t]here was no physical entrance into the area occupied by [the petitioner]." We granted certiorari in order to consider the constitutional questions thus presented.

The petitioner had phrased those questions as follows:

> A. Whether a public telephone booth is a constitutionally protected area so that evidence obtained by attaching an electronic listening recording device to the top of such a booth is obtained in violation of the right to privacy of the user of the booth.
>
> B. Whether physical penetration of a constitutionally protected area is necessary before a search and seizure can be said to be violative of the Fourth Amendment to the United States Constitution.

We decline to adopt this formulation of the issues. In the first place the correct solution of Fourth Amendment problems is not necessarily promoted by incantation of the phrase "constitutionally protected area." Secondly, the Fourth Amendment cannot be translated into a general constitutional "right to privacy." That Amendment protects individual privacy against certain kinds of governmental intrusion, but its protections go further, and often have nothing to do with privacy at all.

[The] effort to decide whether or not a given "area," viewed in the abstract, is "constitutionally protected" deflects attention from the problem presented by this case. For the Fourth Amendment protects people, not places. What a person knowingly exposes to the public, even in his own home or office, is not a subject of Fourth Amendment protection. But what he seeks to preserve as private, even in an area accessible to the public, may be constitutionally protected.

The Government stresses the fact that the telephone booth from which the petitioner made his calls was constructed partly of glass, so that he was as visible after he entered it as he would have been if he had remained outside. But what he sought to exclude when he entered the booth was not the intruding eye—it was the uninvited ear. He did not shed his right to do so simply because he made his calls from a place where he might be seen. No less than an individual in a business office, in a friend's apartment, or in a taxicab [citing cases for each], a person in a telephone booth may rely upon the protection of the Fourth Amendment. One who occupies it, shuts the door behind him, and pays the toll that permits him to place a call is surely entitled to assume that the words he utters into the mouthpiece will not be broadcast to the world. To read the Constitution more narrowly is to ignore the vital role that the public telephone has come to play in private communication.

The Government contends, however, that the activities of its agents in this case should not be tested by Fourth Amendment requirements, for the surveillance technique they employed involved no physical penetration of the telephone booth from which the petitioner placed his calls. It is true that the absence of such penetration was at one time thought to foreclose further Fourth Amendment inquiry, for that Amendment was thought to limit only searches and seizures of tangible property [citing *Olmstead* and *Goldman*]. [A]lthough a closely divided Court supposed in *Olmstead* that surveillance without any trespass and without the seizure of any material object fell outside the ambit of the Constitution, we have since departed from the narrow view on which that decision rested. Indeed, we have expressly held that the Fourth Amendment governs not only the seizure of tangible items, but extends as well to the recording of oral statements overheard without any technical trespass under local property law [citing *Silverman*]. Once this much is acknowledged, and once it is recognized that the Fourth Amendment protects people—and not simply "areas"—against unreasonable searches and seizures it becomes clear that the reach of that Amendment cannot turn upon the presence or absence of a physical intrusion into any given enclosure.

We conclude that the underpinnings of *Olmstead* and *Goldman* have been so eroded by our subsequent decisions that the "trespass" doctrine there enunciated can no longer be regarded as controlling. The Government's activities in electronically listening to and recording the petitioner's words violated the privacy upon which he justifiably relied while using the telephone booth and thus constituted a "search and seizure" within the meaning of the Fourth Amendment. The fact that the electronic device employed to achieve that end did not happen to penetrate the wall of the booth can have no constitutional significance.

The question remaining for decision, then, is whether the search and seizure conducted in this case complied with constitutional standards. In that regard, the Government's position is that its agents acted in an entirely defensible manner: They did not begin their electronic surveillance until investigation of the petitioner's activities had established a strong probability that he was using the telephone in question to transmit gambling information to persons in other States, in violation of federal law. Moreover, the surveillance was limited, both in scope and in duration, to the specific purpose of establishing the contents of the petitioner's unlawful telephonic communications. The agents confined their surveillance to the brief periods during which he used the telephone booth, and they took great care to overhear only the conversations of the petitioner himself.

Accepting this account of the Government's actions as accurate, it is clear that this surveillance was so narrowly circumscribed that a duly authorized magistrate, properly notified of the need for such investigation, specifically informed of the basis on which it was to proceed, and clearly apprised of the precise intrusion it would entail, could constitutionally have authorized, with appropriate safeguards, the very limited search and seizure that the Government asserts in fact took place.

The Government urges that, because its agents relied upon the decisions in *Olmstead* and *Goldman*, and because they did no more here than they might properly have done with prior judicial sanction, we should retroactively validate their conduct. That we cannot do. It is apparent that the agents in this case acted with restraint. Yet the inescapable fact is that this restraint was imposed by the agents themselves, not by a judicial officer. They were not required, before commencing the search, to present their estimate of probable cause for detached scrutiny by a neutral magistrate. They were not compelled, during the conduct of the search itself, to observe precise limits established in advance by a specific court order. Nor were they directed, after the search had been completed, to notify the authorizing magistrate in detail of all that had been seized. In the absence of such safeguards, this Court has never sustained a search upon the sole ground that officers reasonably expected to find evidence of a particular crime and voluntarily confined their activities to the least intrusive means consistent with that end.

Judgment reversed.

■ MR. JUSTICE HARLAN, concurring.

I join the opinion of the Court, which I read to hold only (a) that an enclosed telephone booth is an area where, like a home, and unlike a field, a person has a constitutionally protected reasonable expectation of privacy; (b) that electronic as well as physical intrusion into a place that is in this sense private may constitute a violation of the Fourth Amendment; and (c) that the invasion of a constitutionally protected area by federal authorities is, as the Court has long held, presumptively unreasonable in the absence of a search warrant.

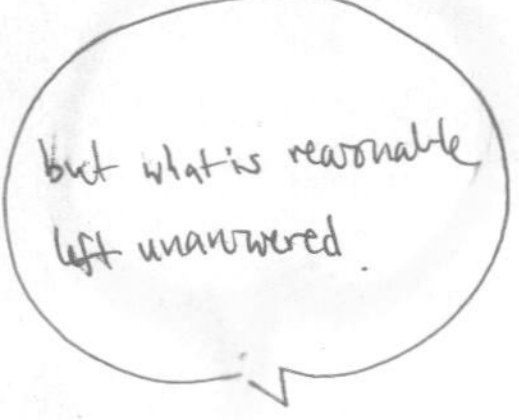


As the Court's opinion states, "the Fourth Amendment protects people, not places." The question, however, is what protection it affords to those people. Generally, as here, the answer to that question requires reference to a "place." My understanding of the rule that has emerged from prior decisions is that there is a twofold requirement, first that a person have exhibited an actual (subjective) expectation of privacy and, second, that the expectation be one that society is prepared to recognize as "reasonable." Thus a man's home is, for most purposes, a place where he expects privacy, but objects, activities, or statements that he exposes to the "plain view" of outsiders are not "protected" because no intention to keep them to himself has been exhibited. On the other hand, conversations in the open would not be protected against being overheard, for the expectation of privacy under the circumstances would be unreasonable.

The critical fact in this case is that "[o]ne who occupies [a telephone booth], shuts the door behind him, and pays the toll that permits him to place a call is surely entitled to assume" that his conversation is not being intercepted. The point is not that the booth is "accessible to the public" at other times, but that it is a temporarily private place whose momentary occupants' expectations of freedom from intrusion are recognized as reasonable.

In *Silverman*, we held that eavesdropping accomplished by means of an electronic device that penetrated the premises occupied by petitioner was a violation of the Fourth Amendment. That case established that interception of conversations reasonably intended to be private could constitute a "search and seizure," and that the examination or taking of physical property was not required. In *Silverman* we found it unnecessary to re-examine *Goldman*, which had held that electronic surveillance accomplished without the physical penetration of petitioner's premises by a tangible object did not violate the Fourth Amendment. This case requires us to reconsider *Goldman*, and I agree that it should now be overruled. Its limitation on Fourth Amendment protection is, in the present day, bad physics as well as bad law, for reasonable expectations of privacy may be defeated by electronic as well as physical invasion.

Finally, I do not read the Court's opinion to declare that no interception of a conversation one-half of which occurs in a public telephone booth can be reasonable in the absence of a warrant. As elsewhere under the Fourth Amendment, warrants are the general rule, to which the legitimate needs of law enforcement may demand specific exceptions. It will be time enough to consider any such exceptions when an appropriate occasion presents itself, and I agree with the Court that this is not one.

[Concurrences by Justices Douglas and White are omitted.]

■ MR. JUSTICE BLACK, dissenting.

If I could agree with the Court that eavesdropping carried on by electronic means (equivalent to wiretapping) constitutes a "search" or "seizure," I would be happy to join the Court's opinion.

My basic objection is twofold: (1) I do not believe that the words of the Amendment will bear the meaning given them by today's decision, and (2) I do not believe that it is the proper role of this Court to rewrite the Amendment in order "to bring it into harmony with the times" and thus reach a result that many people believe to be desirable.

While I realize that an argument based on the meaning of words lacks the scope, and no doubt the appeal, of broad policy discussions and philosophical discourses on such nebulous subjects as privacy, for me the language of the Amendment is the crucial place to look in construing a written document such as our Constitution. The Fourth Amendment says that

> The right of the people to be secure in their persons, houses, papers, and effects, against unreasonable searches and seizures,

> shall not be violated, and no Warrants shall issue, but upon probable cause, supported by Oath or affirmation, and particularly describing the place to be searched, and the persons or things to be seized.

The first clause protects "persons, houses, papers, and effects, against unreasonable searches and seizures." These words connote the idea of tangible things with size, form, and weight, things capable of being searched, seized, or both. The second clause of the Amendment still further establishes its Framers' purpose to limit its protection to tangible things by providing that no warrants shall issue but those "particularly describing the place to be searched, and the persons or things to be seized." A conversation overheard by eavesdropping, whether by plain snooping or wiretapping, is not tangible and, under the normally accepted meanings of the words, can neither be searched nor seized. How can one "describe" a future conversation, and, if one cannot, how can a magistrate issue a warrant to eavesdrop one in the future? It is argued that information showing what is expected to be said is sufficient to limit the boundaries of what later can be admitted into evidence; but does such general information really meet the specific language of the Amendment which says "particularly describing"? Rather than using language in a completely artificial way, I must conclude that the Fourth Amendment simply does not apply to eavesdropping.

Since I see no way in which the words of the Fourth Amendment can be construed to apply to eavesdropping, that closes the matter for me. In interpreting the Bill of Rights, I willingly go as far as a liberal construction of the language takes me, but I simply cannot in good conscience give a meaning to words which they have never before been thought to have and which they certainly do not have in common ordinary usage. I will not distort the words of the Amendment in order to "keep the Constitution up to date" or "to bring it into harmony with the times." It was never meant that this Court have such power, which in effect would make us a continuously functioning constitutional convention.

The Fourth Amendment protects privacy only to the extent that it prohibits unreasonable searches and seizures of "persons, houses, papers, and effects." No general right is created by the Amendment so as to give this Court the unlimited power to hold unconstitutional everything which affects privacy.

For these reasons I respectfully dissent.

## NOTES

1. ***The Reasonable Expectation of Privacy.*** It may not stand out when reading the decision for the first time, but by far the most important and enduring aspect of *Katz* comes from Justice Harlan's concurrence. He articulated a test for the "reasonable expectation of privacy" that has become a key question in Fourth Amendment privacy cases. Note that his test

proceeds in two steps, asking first whether the person actually held a "subjective" expectation of privacy and then whether it is an expectation that "society is prepared to recognize as 'reasonable.'" In spite of its pervasive influence—or perhaps because of that influence—the test is widely criticized. Many later judges and commentators have pointed out the inherent circularity of a "reasonable expectations" measure: naturally individuals' expectations are shaped by what the law allows, but the law claims to adhere to individuals' expectations. It is also fair to ask whether the second prong of the test merely restates the ultimate question. Isn't the court just trying to figure out what counts as "unreasonable" under the Fourth Amendment? Notwithstanding these critiques, the notion of "expectations" has become a cornerstone, not just of Fourth Amendment jurisprudence, but of all privacy law.

2. ***Privacy and Trespass, Again.*** In *Katz*, the justices were responding quite directly to the trespass-based vision of privacy they attribute to the decision in *Olmstead*. The opinion for the Court declared that "the Fourth Amendment protects people, not places." But isn't Justice Harlan correct that critical facts distinguishing one situation from another still will turn on "place" much of the time—because we reasonably expect some locations to be more private than others? On the other hand, privacy in a glass-enclosed public telephone booth does not seem to turn on any ownership of property, so did *Katz* indeed shift away from a Blackstonian vision to some degree?

3. ***Warrants.*** Note that all of the disagreement in *Katz* concerned the requirement that law enforcement officers secure a valid warrant for their wiretapping. The majority indicated that, had they asked for one, the investigators in this case probably should have been granted a warrant to do exactly what they did. In fact, most major Fourth Amendment decisions do not constrain what the authorities may do, but rather which activities require judicial permission first, in the form of a search warrant. To secure such a warrant, the Fourth Amendment requires that the authorities describe the scope of the intended search with particularity and demonstrate "probable cause" that the target of the search committed (or is preparing to commit) a certain criminal offense. The *Katz* opinion emphasized that, while the officers chose to limit their intrusion on the defendant's privacy in various ways, "this restraint was imposed by the agents themselves, not by a judicial officer." Consider the Court's reasons for insisting upon such judicial oversight, and see if you can come up with others yourself. In practice, courts grant the overwhelming majority of applications for warrants. Does this show that warrants are ineffective in protecting individual privacy rights?

4. ***Black's Dissent.*** Justice Black is famous for his strict textualist reading of constitutional provisions, including the Bill of Rights. Is he correct that the *Katz* majority departs dramatically from the Fourth Amendment's language? If so, is that appropriate? The Federal Rules of Evidence were not codified until 1975, and before then, evidence rules came from judicially derived common law. Suppose *Katz*, decided in 1967, had reached the same conclusion about excluding wiretap evidence under this common-law

authority (or, for that matter, did so later through judicial interpretation of the Rules of Evidence). Would that address Justice Black's objections? What are the benefits and drawbacks of invoking constitutional law to draw lines about privacy rather than relying on other legal sources?

5. ***Different Rules for National Security?*** Omitted concurrences by Justices Douglas and White took up an issue tangential to this case but crucial in future ones: whether the same warrant requirements apply in cases involving national security. Justice White opined, "We should not require the warrant procedure and the magistrate's judgment if the President of the United States or his chief legal officer, the Attorney General, has considered the requirements of national security and authorized electronic surveillance as reasonable." Justice Douglas called White's view "a wholly unwarranted green light for the Executive Branch to resort to electronic eavesdropping without a warrant." Douglas argued that, because the President and Attorney General are responsible for protecting national security, "they are not detached, disinterested, and neutral as a court or magistrate must be." Obviously the same dispute persists today [see Chapter 9].

6. ***The State Action Requirement.*** This is as good a place as any to recognize a potentially obvious but still crucial restriction on the sweep of constitutional privacy rules in the United States: they typically apply to the government alone. Under the state action doctrine, the requirements of the Bill of Rights may extend to certain seemingly private entities or activities that are highly influenced by government, or to government enforcement of private arrangements that would run afoul of the Constitution. But these are complex exceptions to a simple general rule: restrictions in the US Constitution apply to the government alone. As we will see, there are numerous other sources of privacy regulation applicable to private entities, but in the US the Constitution seldom figures among them. In contrast, legal systems in other countries often create "positive" constitutional rights that citizens may enforce against other private parties.

---

## Focus

### Development of Fourth Amendment Doctrine

Building on the foundations of Justice Harlan's "reasonable expectations" test, courts have constructed a complex edifice of Fourth Amendment law. A few brief highlights of these doctrines follow.

1. ***Exigent Circumstances.*** Obviously courts do not require police officers chasing a gun-wielding bank robber fleeing the scene of a crime to stop what they are doing and secure a warrant. Various "exigent circumstances" such as this "hot pursuit" scenario have yielded complex doctrine. In general, for instance, law enforcement officers may conduct searches pursuant to a lawful arrest (such as frisking the suspect) and may engage in sweeps of an area when doing so is necessary to protect themselves.

2. ***Exclusionary Rules.*** Ordinarily, when a court determines that information was gathered in violation of the Fourth or Fifth Amendment, prosecutors are barred from using it against the defendant. Moreover, if evidence that was gathered

wrongfully then prompts authorities to seek and secure additional evidence, that latter evidence also will be excluded under the "fruit of the poisonous tree" doctrine—whether or not seizure of the latter evidence was otherwise unlawful. Exclusionary rules are intended both to protect the privacy interests of the defendant and to create meaningful incentives for the government to limit its collection of information without a warrant. But as Chief Justice Taft noted in *Olmstead*, they surely allow guilty people to escape conviction. Note that many, probably most, Fourth and Fifth Amendment privacy cases arise as disputes over the admissibility of evidence in criminal prosecutions.

3. ***Perception and Plain View.*** Many Fourth Amendment cases turn on the ability of a law enforcement officer to perceive something that later turns out to be incriminating evidence. Under the "plain view doctrine," there is no reasonable expectation of privacy when officers can see or hear something from a location where they are lawfully present. This principle can even limit privacy protection in the home, where the expectation of privacy is generally the strongest. So, for example, there probably would be no such expectation involving an argument loud enough to be heard from the street outside a home, the smell of marijuana smoke in the public hallway outside an apartment door, or stolen property visible through the uncurtained window of a house. A similar "plain feel doctrine" means no warrant is necessary to confiscate contraband or a weapon touched during an otherwise permissible frisk. Likewise, under the "open fields" doctrine there usually is no reasonable expectation of privacy in outdoor areas beyond the "curtilage" immediately surrounding a home.

4. ***Technological Enhancement.*** Doctrines governing situations like plain view and curtilage can become more complex when officers use technological means to perceive more than they could with their unaided senses. A number of cases have allowed warrantless aerial or satellite surveillance of property that could not have been seen from the ground. Other cases permit the use of trained dogs to sniff for contraband without a warrant. In contrast, courts have shown some hesitation to extend the plain view doctrine to situations where a view was available only by relying on a high-powered telescope or similar equipment.

In a famous case involving the use of a thermal sensor to detect heat emanating from a residence (and thus indicating the presence of high-intensity lamps to grow marijuana), the Supreme Court held that a warrant was required. The opinion by Justice Scalia emphasized that the technology gathered information about the interior of a home, and that " '[a]t the very core' of the Fourth Amendment 'stands the right of a man to retreat into his own home and there be free from unreasonable governmental intrusion.' " *Kyllo v. United States*, 533 U.S. 27, 31 (2001) (quoting *Silverman v. United States*, 365 U.S. 505, 511 (1961)). Its holding elaborated on the technological erosion of privacy in the home:

> [I]n the case of the search of the interior of homes—the prototypical and hence most commonly litigated area of protected privacy—there is a ready criterion, with roots deep in the common law, of the minimal expectation of privacy that *exists*, and that is acknowledged to be *reasonable*. To withdraw protection of this minimum expectation would be to permit police technology to erode the privacy guaranteed by the Fourth Amendment. We think that obtaining by sense-enhancing technology any information regarding the interior of the home that could not otherwise have been obtained without physical intrusion into a constitutionally protected area," *Silverman*, 365 U.S. at 512, constitutes a search at least where (as here) the technology in question is not in general public use. This assures preservation of that degree of privacy against government that existed when the Fourth Amendment was adopted.

*Id.* at 34. The *Kyllo* dissent objected that the interception of heat emanating *outside* the home was not a search of the *inside* of the home. Does this resemble Chief Justice Taft's comments in *Olmstead* about a "telephone instrument with connecting wires" that will "project [the defendant's] voice to those quite outside" the home? The dissenters also criticized the *Kyllo* majority's reliance on the "general public use" of technology:

> [T]he contours of [the majority's] new rule are uncertain because its protection apparently dissipates as soon as the relevant technology is 'in general public use.' Yet how much use is general public use is not even hinted at by the Court's opinion, which makes the somewhat doubtful assumption that the thermal imager used in this case does not satisfy that criterion. In any event, putting aside its lack of clarity, this criterion is somewhat perverse because it seems likely that the threat to privacy will grow, rather than recede, as the use of intrusive equipment becomes more readily available.

*Id.* at 47 (Stevens, J., dissenting). In this context, it is perhaps noteworthy that Amazon and eBay offer multiple thermal imaging cameras for sale to the public for a few thousand dollars each. The evolution of reasonable expectations in response to technological change presents challenges throughout all of privacy law, as we shall see repeatedly.

5. ***The Third Party Doctrine.*** Especially significant exclusions from Fourth Amendment protection arise when individuals reveal information to others. Under the "third party doctrine," an individual no longer reasonably expects information to remain private once a third party knows it and might disclose it further. The original disclosure functions something like a waiver, voiding Fourth Amendment protections over that information. This reasoning first applied to criminal informants who revealed confidences they heard from the target of an investigation. Similarly, courts held that one resident of a home can consent to its search by law enforcement without approval from other residents. Later, this waiver rationale extended to many types of institutional third parties. The Supreme Court ruled that law enforcement needed no warrant to obtain individual financial transaction records held by banks or lists of a person's dialed telephone numbers held by telecommunications companies. In both cases, the Court concluded the customers must have realized that the service provider retained data about their activities, and that it presumably could share that information with others including the government, eliminating any reasonable expectation of privacy. Both cases have led to many routine investigative techniques outside the warrant requirement, and also to statutory responses [see Chapters 5, 13, and 14].

A colorful example of the third party doctrine occurred when police in California arranged, without a warrant, for a neighborhood trash collector to hand over plastic garbage bags left for collection at the curb by residents of a particular home suspected of selling illegal drugs. Investigators went through the bags and found evidence of drug use, which they then used as the basis to apply for a search warrant of the home, generating much more evidence that formed the basis of a criminal prosecution. The defendants challenged the warrant because they argued the underlying information was gathered from the trash bags in violation of the Fourth Amendment, and so the evidence gathered under the warrant was fruit of the poisonous tree. The Supreme Court disagreed:

> [R]espondents exposed their garbage to the public sufficiently to defeat their claim to Fourth Amendment protection. It is common knowledge that plastic garbage bags left on or at the side of a public street are readily accessible to animals, children, scavengers, snoops, and other members

of the public. Moreover, respondents placed their refuse at the curb for the express purpose of conveying it to a third party, the trash collector, who might himself have sorted through respondents' trash or permitted others, such as the police, to do so. Accordingly, having deposited their garbage in an area particularly suited for public inspection and, in a manner of speaking, public consumption, for the express purpose of having strangers take it, respondents could have had no reasonable expectation of privacy in the inculpatory items that they discarded.

*California v. Greenwood*, 486 U.S. 35, 40–41 (1988).

6. ***Special Needs Doctrine***. Courts apply more lenient standards to certain searches conducted for administrative purposes or other governmental "special needs." Under these standards, for example, the Supreme Court has permitted routine inspections without warrants to enforce housing, mine safety, and welfare regulations. Security screening checks at locations such as airports also fall under the special needs doctrine. Significant monitoring in government workplaces [see Chapter 11] and student searches in public schools [see Chapter 15] are also permitted by this doctrine. The measures adopted still must be reasonable under the circumstances, but the resulting balance takes account of the importance of the government's interest as well.

---

## 2. CONTEMPORARY CHALLENGES

### United States v. Jones

132 S. Ct. 945 (2012)

■ JUSTICE SCALIA delivered the opinion of the Court.

We decide whether the attachment of a Global-Positioning-System (GPS) tracking device to an individual's vehicle, and subsequent use of that device to monitor the vehicle's movements on public streets, constitutes a search or seizure within the meaning of the Fourth Amendment.

#### I

In 2004 respondent Antoine Jones, owner and operator of a nightclub in the District of Columbia, came under suspicion of trafficking in narcotics and was made the target of an investigation by a joint FBI and Metropolitan Police Department task force. Officers employed various investigative techniques, including visual surveillance of the nightclub, installation of a camera focused on the front door of the club, and a pen register and wiretap covering Jones's cellular phone.

Based in part on information gathered from these sources, in 2005 the Government applied to the United States District Court for the District of Columbia for a warrant authorizing the use of an electronic tracking device on the Jeep Grand Cherokee registered to Jones's wife. A warrant issued, authorizing installation of the device in the District of Columbia and within 10 days.

On the 11th day, and not in the District of Columbia but in Maryland, agents installed a GPS tracking device on the undercarriage of the Jeep while it was parked in a public parking lot. Over the next 28 days, the Government used the device to track the vehicle's movements, and once had to replace the device's battery when the vehicle was parked in a different public lot in Maryland. By means of signals from multiple satellites, the device established the vehicle's location within 50 to 100 feet, and communicated that location by cellular phone to a Government computer. It relayed more than 2,000 pages of data over the 4-week period.

GPS-derived locational data [was introduced at] trial, which connected Jones to the alleged conspirators' stash house that contained $850,000 in cash, 97 kilograms of cocaine, and 1 kilogram of cocaine base. The jury returned a guilty verdict, and the District Court sentenced Jones to life imprisonment.

The United States Court of Appeals for the District of Columbia Circuit reversed the conviction because of admission of the evidence obtained by warrantless use of the GPS device which, it said, violated the Fourth Amendment. The D.C. Circuit denied the Government's petition for rehearing en banc, with four judges dissenting. We granted certiorari.

## II

### A

It is important to be clear about what occurred in this case: The Government physically occupied private property for the purpose of obtaining information. We have no doubt that such a physical intrusion would have been considered a "search" within the meaning of the Fourth Amendment when it was adopted.

The text of the Fourth Amendment reflects its close connection to property, since otherwise it would have referred simply to "the right of the people to be secure against unreasonable searches and seizures"; the phrase "in their persons, houses, papers, and effects" would have been superfluous.

Consistent with this understanding, our Fourth Amendment jurisprudence was tied to common-law trespass, at least until the latter half of the 20th century. Thus, in *Olmstead v. United States*, we held that wiretaps attached to telephone wires on the public streets did not constitute a Fourth Amendment search because "[t]here was no entry of the houses or offices of the defendants."

Our later cases, of course, have deviated from that exclusively property-based approach. In *Katz v. United States* we said that "the Fourth Amendment protects people, not places," and found a violation in attachment of an eavesdropping device to a public telephone booth. Our later cases have applied the analysis of Justice Harlan's concurrence in that case, which said that a violation occurs when government officers violate a person's "reasonable expectation of privacy."

The Government contends that the Harlan standard shows that no search occurred here, since Jones had no "reasonable expectation of privacy" in the area of the Jeep accessed by Government agents (its underbody) and in the locations of the Jeep on the public roads, which were visible to all. But we need not address the Government's contentions, because Jones's Fourth Amendment rights do not rise or fall with the *Katz* formulation. At bottom, we must assure preservation of that degree of privacy against government that existed when the Fourth Amendment was adopted. For most of our history the Fourth Amendment was understood to embody a particular concern for government trespass upon the areas ("persons, houses, papers, and effects") it enumerates. *Katz* did not repudiate that understanding.

**B**

The concurrence begins by accusing us of applying "18th-century tort law." That is a distortion. What we apply is an 18th-century guarantee against unreasonable searches, which we believe must provide at a minimum the degree of protection it afforded when it was adopted. The concurrence does not share that belief. It would apply exclusively *Katz*'s reasonable-expectation-of-privacy test, even when that eliminates rights that previously existed.

The concurrence faults our approach for "present[ing] particularly vexing problems" in cases that do not involve physical contact, such as those that involve the transmission of electronic signals. We entirely fail to understand that point. For unlike the concurrence, which would make *Katz* the exclusive test, we do not make trespass the exclusive test. Situations involving merely the transmission of electronic signals without trespass would remain subject to *Katz* analysis.

In fact, it is the concurrence's insistence on the exclusivity of the *Katz* test that needlessly leads us into "particularly vexing problems" in the present case. This Court has to date not deviated from the understanding that mere visual observation does not constitute a search. We accordingly held that "[a] person traveling in an automobile on public thoroughfares has no reasonable expectation of privacy in his movements from one place to another." [quoting *United States v. Knotts*, 460 U.S. 276, 281 (1983)] Thus, even assuming that the concurrence is correct to say that "[t]raditional surveillance" of Jones for a 4-week period "would have required a large team of agents, multiple vehicles, and perhaps aerial assistance," our cases suggest that such visual observation is constitutionally permissible. It may be that achieving the same result through electronic means, without an accompanying trespass, is an unconstitutional invasion of privacy, but the present case does not require us to answer that question.

And answering it affirmatively leads us needlessly into additional thorny problems. The concurrence posits that "relatively short-term monitoring of a person's movements on public streets" is okay, but that "the use of longer term GPS monitoring in investigations of most offenses" is no good. That introduces yet another novelty into our jurisprudence. There is no precedent for the proposition that whether a search has occurred depends on the nature of the crime being investigated. And even accepting that novelty, it remains unexplained why a 4-week investigation is "surely" too long and why a drug-trafficking conspiracy involving substantial amounts of cash and narcotics is not an "extraordinary offens[e]" which may permit longer observation. What of a 2-day monitoring of a suspected purveyor of stolen electronics? Or of a 6-month monitoring of a suspected terrorist? We may have to grapple with these "vexing problems" in some future case where a classic trespassory search is not involved and resort must be had to *Katz* analysis; but there is no reason for rushing forward to resolve them here.

The judgment of the Court of Appeals for the D.C. Circuit is affirmed.

■ JUSTICE SOTOMAYOR, concurring.

I join the Court's opinion because I agree that a search within the meaning of the Fourth Amendment occurs, at a minimum, "[w]here, as here, the Government obtains information by physically intruding on a constitutionally protected area." [T]he trespassory test applied in the majority's opinion reflects an irreducible constitutional minimum: When the Government physically invades personal property to gather information, a search occurs. The reaffirmation of that principle suffices to decide this case.

Nonetheless, as Justice ALITO notes, physical intrusion is now unnecessary to many forms of surveillance. With increasing regularity, the Government will be capable of duplicating the monitoring undertaken in this case by enlisting factory- or owner-installed vehicle tracking devices or GPS-enabled smartphones. In cases of electronic or other novel modes of surveillance that do not depend upon a physical invasion on property, the majority opinion's trespassory test may provide little guidance. But "[s]ituations involving merely the transmission of electronic signals without trespass would *remain* subject to *Katz* analysis." As Justice ALITO incisively observes, the same technological advances that have made possible nontrespassory surveillance techniques will also affect the *Katz* test by shaping the evolution of societal privacy expectations. Under that rubric, I agree with Justice ALITO that, at the very least, "longer term GPS monitoring in investigations of most offenses impinges on expectations of privacy."

In cases involving even short-term monitoring, some unique attributes of GPS surveillance relevant to the *Katz* analysis will require particular attention. GPS monitoring generates a precise, comprehensive record of a person's public movements that reflects a wealth of detail about her familial, political, professional, religious, and sexual associations. The Government can store such records and efficiently mine them for information years into the future. And because GPS monitoring is cheap in comparison to conventional surveillance techniques and, by design, proceeds surreptitiously, it evades the ordinary checks that constrain abusive law enforcement practices: "limited police resources and community hostility." *Illinois v. Lidster*, 540 U.S. 419, 426 (2004).

Awareness that the Government may be watching chills associational and expressive freedoms. And the Government's unrestrained power to assemble data that reveal private aspects of identity is susceptible to abuse. The net result is that GPS monitoring—by making available at a relatively low cost such a substantial quantum of intimate information about any person whom the Government, in its unfettered discretion, chooses to track—may alter the relationship between citizen and government in a way that is inimical to democratic society.

I would take these attributes of GPS monitoring into account when considering the existence of a reasonable societal expectation of privacy in the sum of one's public movements.

More fundamentally, it may be necessary to reconsider the premise that an individual has no reasonable expectation of privacy in information voluntarily disclosed to third parties. This approach is ill suited to the digital age, in which people reveal a great deal of information about themselves to third parties in the course of carrying out mundane tasks. People disclose the phone numbers that they dial or text to their cellular providers; the URLs that they visit and the e-mail addresses with which they correspond to their Internet service providers; and the books, groceries, and medications they purchase to online retailers. Perhaps, as Justice ALITO notes, some people may find the "tradeoff" of privacy for convenience "worthwhile," or come to accept this "diminution of privacy" as "inevitable," and perhaps not. I for one doubt that people would accept without complaint the warrantless disclosure to the Government of a list of every Web site they had visited in the last week, or month, or year. But whatever the societal expectations, they can attain constitutionally protected status only if our Fourth Amendment jurisprudence ceases to treat secrecy as a prerequisite for privacy. I would not assume that all information voluntarily disclosed to some member of the public for a limited purpose is, for that reason alone, disentitled to Fourth Amendment protection.

Resolution of these difficult questions in this case is unnecessary, however, because the Government's physical intrusion on Jones' Jeep supplies a narrower basis for decision. I therefore join the majority's opinion.

■ JUSTICE ALITO, with whom JUSTICE GINSBURG, JUSTICE BREYER, and JUSTICE KAGAN join, concurring in the judgment.

This case requires us to apply the Fourth Amendment's prohibition of unreasonable searches and seizures to a 21st-century surveillance technique, the use of a Global Positioning System (GPS) device to monitor a vehicle's movements for an extended period of time. Ironically, the

Court has chosen to decide this case based on 18th-century tort law. By attaching a small GPS device to the underside of the vehicle that respondent drove, the law enforcement officers in this case engaged in conduct that might have provided grounds in 1791 for a suit for trespass to chattels. And for this reason, the Court concludes, the installation and use of the GPS device constituted a search.

This holding, in my judgment, is unwise. It strains the language of the Fourth Amendment; it has little if any support in current Fourth Amendment case law; and it is highly artificial.

I would analyze the question presented in this case by asking whether respondent's reasonable expectations of privacy were violated by the long-term monitoring of the movements of the vehicle he drove.

[T]he Court's reasoning largely disregards what is really important (the *use* of a GPS for the purpose of long-term tracking) and instead attaches great significance to something that most would view as relatively minor (attaching to the bottom of a car a small, light object that does not interfere in any way with the car's operation). Attaching such an object is generally regarded as so trivial that it does not provide a basis for recovery under modern tort law.

[T]he Court's reliance on the law of trespass will present particularly vexing problems in cases involving surveillance that is carried out by making electronic, as opposed to physical, contact with the item to be tracked. For example, suppose that the officers in the present case had followed respondent by surreptitiously activating a stolen vehicle detection system that came with the car when it was purchased. Would the sending of a radio signal to activate this system constitute a trespass to chattels? Trespass to chattels has traditionally required a physical touching of the property. In recent years, courts have wrestled with the application of this old tort in cases involving unwanted electronic contact with computer systems, and some have held that even the transmission of electrons that occurs when a communication is sent from one computer to another is enough. But may such decisions be followed in applying the Court's trespass theory? Assuming that what matters under the Court's theory is the law of trespass as it existed at the time of the adoption of the Fourth Amendment, do these recent decisions represent a change in the law or simply the application of the old tort to new situations?

The *Katz* expectation-of-privacy test avoids the problems and complications noted above, but it is not without its own difficulties. It involves a degree of circularity, and judges are apt to confuse their own expectations of privacy with those of the hypothetical reasonable person to which the *Katz* test looks. In addition, the *Katz* test rests on the assumption that this hypothetical reasonable person has a well-developed and stable set of privacy expectations. But technology can change those expectations. Dramatic technological change may lead to periods in which popular expectations are in flux and may ultimately produce significant changes in popular attitudes. New technology may provide increased convenience or security at the expense of privacy, and many people may find the tradeoff worthwhile. And even if the public does not welcome the diminution of privacy that new technology entails, they may eventually reconcile themselves to this development as inevitable.

On the other hand, concern about new intrusions on privacy may spur the enactment of legislation to protect against these intrusions. This is what ultimately happened with respect to wiretapping. After *Katz*, Congress did not leave it to the courts to develop a body of Fourth Amendment case law governing that complex subject. Instead, Congress promptly enacted a comprehensive statute, and since that time, the regulation of wiretapping has been governed primarily by statute and not by case law. In an ironic sense, although *Katz* overruled *Olmstead*, Chief Justice Taft's suggestion in the latter case that the regulation of wiretapping was a matter better left for Congress has been borne out.

Recent years have seen the emergence of many new devices that permit the monitoring of a person's movements. In some locales, closed-circuit television video monitoring is becoming ubiquitous. On toll roads, automatic toll collection systems create a precise record of the movements of motorists who choose to make use of that convenience. Many motorists purchase cars that are equipped with devices that permit a central station to ascertain the car's location at any time so that roadside assistance may be provided if needed and the car may be found if it is stolen.

Perhaps most significant, cell phones and other wireless devices now permit wireless carriers to track and record the location of users—and as of June 2011, it has been reported, there were more than 322 million wireless devices in use in the United States. For older phones, the accuracy of the location information depends on the density of the tower network, but new "smart phones," which are equipped with a GPS device, permit more precise tracking. For example, when a user activates the GPS on such a phone, a provider is able to monitor the phone's location and speed of movement and can then report back real-time traffic conditions after combining ("crowdsourcing") the speed of all such phones on any particular road. Similarly, phone-location-tracking services are offered as "social" tools, allowing consumers to find (or to avoid) others who enroll in these services. The availability and use of these and other new devices will continue to shape the average person's expectations about the privacy of his or her daily movements.

In the pre-computer age, the greatest protections of privacy were neither constitutional nor statutory, but practical. Traditional surveillance for any extended period of time was difficult and costly and therefore rarely undertaken. The surveillance at issue in this case—constant monitoring of the location of a vehicle for four weeks—would have required a large team of agents, multiple vehicles, and perhaps aerial assistance. Only an investigation of unusual importance could have justified such an expenditure of law enforcement resources. Devices like the one used in the present case, however, make long-term monitoring relatively easy and cheap. In circumstances involving dramatic technological change, the best solution to privacy concerns may be legislative. A legislative body is well situated to gauge changing public attitudes, to draw detailed lines, and to balance privacy and public safety in a comprehensive way.

To date, however, Congress and most States have not enacted statutes regulating the use of GPS tracking technology for law enforcement purposes. The best that we can do in this case is to apply existing Fourth Amendment doctrine and to ask whether the use of GPS tracking in a particular case involved a degree of intrusion that a reasonable person would not have anticipated.

Under this approach, relatively short-term monitoring of a person's movements on public streets accords with expectations of privacy that our society has recognized as reasonable. But the use of longer term GPS monitoring in investigations of most offenses impinges on expectations of privacy. For such offenses, society's expectation has been that law enforcement agents and others would not—and indeed, in the main, simply could not—secretly monitor and catalogue every single movement of an individual's car for a very long period. In this case, for four weeks, law enforcement agents tracked every movement that respondent made in the vehicle he was driving. We need not identify with precision the point at which the tracking of this vehicle became a search, for the line was surely crossed before the 4-week mark. Other cases may present more difficult questions. But where uncertainty exists with respect to whether a certain period of GPS surveillance is long enough to constitute a Fourth Amendment search, the police may always seek a warrant. We also need not consider whether prolonged GPS monitoring in the context of investigations involving extraordinary offenses would similarly intrude on a constitutionally protected sphere of privacy. In such cases, long-term tracking might have been mounted using previously available techniques.

For these reasons, I conclude that the lengthy monitoring that occurred in this case constituted a search under the Fourth Amendment. I therefore agree with the majority that the decision of the Court of Appeals must be affirmed.

## Riley v. California

134 S. Ct. 2473 (2014)

■ CHIEF JUSTICE ROBERTS delivered the opinion of the Court.

These two cases raise a common question: whether the police may, without a warrant, search digital information on a cell phone seized from an individual who has been arrested.

## I

### A

In the first case, petitioner David Riley was stopped by a police officer for driving with expired registration tags. In the course of the stop, the officer also learned that Riley's license had been suspended. The officer impounded Riley's car, pursuant to department policy, and another officer conducted an inventory search of the car. Riley was arrested for possession of concealed and loaded firearms when that search turned up two handguns under the car's hood.

An officer searched Riley incident to the arrest and found items associated with the "Bloods" street gang. He also seized a cell phone from Riley's pants pocket. According to Riley's uncontradicted assertion, the phone was a "smart phone," a cell phone with a broad range of other functions based on advanced computing capability, large storage capacity, and Internet connectivity. The officer accessed information on the phone and noticed that some words (presumably in text messages or a contacts list) were preceded by the letters "CK"—a label that, he believed, stood for "Crip Killers," a slang term for members of the Bloods gang.

At the police station about two hours after the arrest, a detective specializing in gangs further examined the contents of the phone. The detective testified that he "went through" Riley's phone "looking for evidence, because . . . gang members will often video themselves with guns or take pictures of themselves with the guns." Although there was "a lot of stuff" on the phone, particular files that "caught [the detective's] eye" included videos of young men sparring while someone yelled encouragement using the moniker "Blood." The police also found photographs of Riley standing in front of a car they suspected had been involved in a shooting a few weeks earlier.

Riley was ultimately charged, in connection with that earlier shooting, with firing at an occupied vehicle, assault with a semiautomatic firearm, and attempted murder. The State alleged that Riley had committed those crimes for the benefit of a criminal street gang, an aggravating factor that carries an enhanced sentence. Prior to trial, Riley moved to suppress all evidence that the police had obtained from his cell phone. He contended that the searches of his phone violated the Fourth Amendment, because they had been performed without a warrant and were not otherwise justified by exigent circumstances. The trial court rejected that argument. At Riley's trial, police officers testified about the photographs and videos found on the phone, and some of the photographs were admitted into evidence. Riley was convicted on all three counts and received an enhanced sentence of 15 years to life in prison. [Riley's appeals in California state court were unsuccessful.]

## B

In the second case, a police officer performing routine surveillance observed respondent Brima Wurie make an apparent drug sale from a car. Officers subsequently arrested Wurie and took him to the police station. At the station, the officers seized two cell phones from Wurie's person. The one at issue here was a "flip phone," a kind of phone that is flipped open for use and that generally has a smaller range of features than a smart phone. Five to ten minutes after arriving at the station, the officers noticed that the phone was repeatedly receiving calls from a source identified as "my house" on the phone's external screen. A few minutes later, they opened the phone and saw a photograph of a woman and a baby set as the phone's wallpaper. They pressed one button on the phone to access its call log, then another button to determine the phone number associated with the "my house" label. They next used an online phone directory to trace that phone number to an apartment building.

When the officers went to the building, they saw Wurie's name on a mailbox and observed through a window a woman who resembled the woman in the photograph on Wurie's phone. They secured the apartment while obtaining a search warrant and, upon later executing the warrant, found and seized 215 grams of crack cocaine, marijuana, drug paraphernalia, a firearm and ammunition, and cash.

Wurie was charged with distributing crack cocaine, possessing crack cocaine with intent to distribute, and being a felon in possession of a firearm and ammunition. He moved to suppress the evidence obtained from the search of the apartment, arguing that it was the fruit of an unconstitutional search of his cell phone. The District Court denied the motion. Wurie was convicted on all three counts and sentenced to 262 months in prison.

A divided panel of the First Circuit reversed the denial of Wurie's motion to suppress and vacated Wurie's convictions for possession with intent to distribute and possession of a firearm as a felon. The court held that cell phones are distinct from other physical possessions that may be searched incident to arrest without a warrant, because of the amount of personal data cell phones contain and the negligible threat they pose to law enforcement interests.

## II

As [its] text makes clear, the ultimate touchstone of the Fourth Amendment is "reasonableness." Our cases have determined that, where a search is undertaken by law enforcement officials to discover evidence of criminal wrongdoing, reasonableness generally requires the obtaining of a judicial warrant. Such a warrant ensures that the inferences to support a search are drawn by a neutral and detached magistrate instead of being judged by the officer engaged in the often competitive enterprise of ferreting out crime. In the absence of a warrant, a search is reasonable only if it falls within a specific exception to the warrant requirement.

The two cases before us concern the reasonableness of a warrantless search incident to a lawful arrest. In 1914, this Court first acknowledged in dictum "the right on the part of the Government, always recognized under English and American law, to search the person of the accused when legally arrested to discover and seize the fruits or evidences of crime." *Weeks v. United States*, 232 U.S. 383, 392 (1914). Since that time, it has been well accepted that such a search constitutes an exception to the warrant requirement. Indeed, the label "exception" is something of a misnomer in this context, as warrantless searches incident to arrest occur with far greater frequency than searches conducted pursuant to a warrant.

Although the existence of the exception for such searches has been recognized for a century, its scope has been debated for nearly as long. That debate has focused on the extent to which officers may search property found on or near the arrestee. Three related precedents set forth the rules governing such searches:

The first, *Chimel v. California*, 395 U.S. 752 (1969), laid the groundwork for most of the existing search incident to arrest doctrine. Police officers in that case arrested Chimel inside his home and proceeded to search his entire three-bedroom house, including the attic and garage. In particular rooms, they also looked through the contents of drawers.

The Court crafted the following rule for assessing the reasonableness of a search incident to arrest:

> When an arrest is made, it is reasonable for the arresting officer to search the person arrested in order to remove any weapons that the latter might seek to use in order to resist arrest or effect his escape. Otherwise, the officer's safety might well be endangered, and the arrest itself frustrated. In addition, it is entirely reasonable for the arresting officer to search for and seize any evidence on the arrestee's person in order to prevent its concealment or destruction. . . . There is ample justification, therefore, for a search of the arrestee's person and the area 'within his immediate control'—construing that phrase to mean the area from within which he might gain possession of a weapon or destructible evidence.

The extensive warrantless search of Chimel's home did not fit within this exception, because it was not needed to protect officer safety or to preserve evidence.

Four years later, in *United States v. Robinson*, 414 U.S. 218 (1973), the Court applied the *Chimel* analysis in the context of a search of the arrestee's person. A police officer had arrested Robinson for driving with a revoked license. The officer conducted a patdown search and felt an object that he could not identify in Robinson's coat pocket. He removed the object, which turned out to be a crumpled cigarette package, and opened it. Inside were 14 capsules of heroin.

The Court of Appeals concluded that the search was unreasonable because Robinson was unlikely to have evidence of the crime of arrest on his person, and because it believed that extracting the cigarette package and opening it could not be justified as part of a protective search for weapons. This Court reversed, rejecting the notion that "case-by-case adjudication" was required to determine "whether or not there was present one of the reasons supporting the authority for a search of the person incident to a lawful arrest." As the Court explained, "[t]he authority to search the person incident to a lawful custodial arrest, while based upon the need to disarm and to discover evidence, does not depend on what a court may later decide was the probability in a particular arrest situation that weapons or evidence would in fact be found upon the person of the suspect." Instead, a "custodial arrest of a suspect based on probable cause is a reasonable intrusion under the Fourth Amendment; that intrusion being lawful, a search incident to the arrest requires no additional justification."

The Court thus concluded that the search of Robinson was reasonable even though there was no concern about the loss of evidence, and the arresting officer had no specific concern that Robinson might be armed. In doing so, the Court did not draw a line between a search of Robinson's person and a further examination of the cigarette pack found during that search. It merely noted that, "[h]aving in the course of a lawful search come upon the crumpled package of cigarettes, [the officer] was entitled to inspect it." A few years later, the Court clarified that this exception was limited to "personal property immediately associated with the person of the arrestee." *United States v. Chadwick*, 433 U.S. 1 (1977) (200-pound, locked footlocker could not be searched incident to arrest).

The search incident to arrest trilogy concludes with [*Arizona v. Gant*, 556 U.S. 332 (2009)], which analyzed searches of an arrestee's vehicle. *Gant*, like *Robinson*, recognized that the *Chimel* concerns for officer safety and evidence preservation underlie the search incident to arrest exception. As a result, the Court concluded that *Chimel* could authorize police to search a vehicle "only when the arrestee is unsecured and within reaching distance of the passenger compartment at the time of the search." *Gant* added, however, an independent exception for a warrantless search of a vehicle's passenger compartment "when it is 'reasonable to believe evidence relevant to the crime of arrest might be found in the vehicle.'" That exception stems not from *Chimel*, the Court explained, but from "circumstances unique to the vehicle context."

### III

These cases require us to decide how the search incident to arrest doctrine applies to modern cell phones, which are now such a pervasive and insistent part of daily life that the proverbial visitor from Mars might conclude they were an important feature of human anatomy. A smart phone of the sort taken from Riley was unheard of ten years ago; a significant majority of American adults now own such phones. Even less sophisticated phones like Wurie's, which have already faded in popularity since Wurie was arrested in 2007, have been around for less than 15 years. Both phones are based on technology nearly inconceivable just a few decades ago, when *Chimel* and *Robinson* were decided.

Absent more precise guidance from the founding era, we generally determine whether to exempt a given type of search from the warrant requirement by assessing, on the one hand, the degree to which it intrudes upon an individual's privacy and, on the other, the degree to which it is needed for the promotion of legitimate governmental interests. Such a balancing of interests supported the search incident to arrest exception in *Robinson*, and a mechanical application of *Robinson* might well support the warrantless searches at issue here.

But while *Robinson*'s categorical rule strikes the appropriate balance in the context of physical objects, neither of its rationales has much force with respect to digital content on cell phones. On the government interest side, *Robinson* concluded that the two risks identified in *Chimel*—harm to officers and destruction of evidence—are present in all custodial arrests. There are no comparable risks when the search is of digital data. In addition, *Robinson* regarded any privacy interests retained by an individual after arrest as significantly diminished by the fact of the arrest itself. Cell phones, however, place vast quantities of personal information literally in the hands of individuals. A search of the information on a cell phone bears little resemblance to the type of brief physical search considered in *Robinson*.

We therefore decline to extend *Robinson* to searches of data on cell phones, and hold instead that officers must generally secure a warrant before conducting such a search.

## A

We first consider each *Chimel* concern in turn. In doing so, we do not overlook *Robinson*'s admonition that searches of a person incident to arrest, "while based upon the need to disarm and to discover evidence," are reasonable regardless of "the probability in a particular arrest situation that weapons or evidence would in fact be found." Rather than requiring the "case-by-case adjudication" that *Robinson* rejected, we ask instead whether application of the search incident to arrest doctrine to this particular category of effects would "untether the rule from the justifications underlying the *Chimel* exception," [citing *Gant*].

### 1

Digital data stored on a cell phone cannot itself be used as a weapon to harm an arresting officer or to effectuate the arrestee's escape. Law enforcement officers remain free to examine the physical aspects of a phone to ensure that it will not be used as a weapon—say, to determine whether there is a razor blade hidden between the phone and its case.

Once an officer has secured a phone and eliminated any potential physical threats, however, data on the phone can endanger no one.

Perhaps the same might have been said of the cigarette pack seized from Robinson's pocket. Once an officer gained control of the pack, it was unlikely that Robinson could have accessed the pack's contents. But unknown physical objects may always pose risks, no matter how slight, during the tense atmosphere of a custodial arrest. The officer in *Robinson* testified that he could not identify the objects in the cigarette pack but knew they were not cigarettes. Given that, a further search was a reasonable protective measure. No such unknowns exist with respect to digital data. As the First Circuit explained, the officers who searched Wurie's cell phone "knew exactly what they would find therein: data. They also knew that the data could not harm them."

**2**

The United States and California focus primarily on the second *Chimel* rationale: preventing the destruction of evidence.

Both Riley and Wurie concede that officers could have seized and secured their cell phones to prevent destruction of evidence while seeking a warrant. That is a sensible concession. And once law enforcement officers have secured a cell phone, there is no longer any risk that the arrestee himself will be able to delete incriminating data from the phone.

The United States and California argue that information on a cell phone may nevertheless be vulnerable to two types of evidence destruction unique to digital data—remote wiping and data encryption. Remote wiping occurs when a phone, connected to a wireless network, receives a signal that erases stored data. This can happen when a third party sends a remote signal or when a phone is preprogrammed to delete data upon entering or leaving certain geographic areas (so-called "geofencing"). Encryption is a security feature that some modern cell phones use in addition to password protection. When such phones lock, data becomes protected by sophisticated encryption that renders a phone all but "unbreakable" unless police know the password.

As an initial matter, these broader concerns about the loss of evidence are distinct from *Chimel*'s focus on a defendant who responds to arrest by trying to conceal or destroy evidence within his reach. With respect to remote wiping, the Government's primary concern turns on the actions of third parties who are not present at the scene of arrest. And data encryption is even further afield. There, the Government focuses on the ordinary operation of a phone's security features, apart from *any* active attempt by a defendant or his associates to conceal or destroy evidence upon arrest.

We have also been given little reason to believe that either problem is prevalent. The briefing reveals only a couple of anecdotal examples of remote wiping triggered by an arrest.

Moreover, in situations in which an arrest might trigger a remote-wipe attempt or an officer discovers an unlocked phone, it is not clear that the ability to conduct a warrantless search would make much of a difference. The need to effect the arrest, secure the scene, and tend to other pressing matters means that law enforcement officers may well not be able to turn their attention to a cell phone right away. Cell phone data would be vulnerable to remote wiping from the time an individual anticipates arrest to the time any eventual search of the phone is completed, which might be at the station house hours later. Likewise, an officer who seizes a phone in an unlocked state might not be able to begin his search in the short time remaining before the phone locks and data becomes encrypted.

In any event, as to remote wiping, law enforcement is not without specific means to address the threat. Remote wiping can be fully prevented by disconnecting a phone from the network. There are at least two simple ways to do this: First, law enforcement officers can turn the phone off or remove its battery. Second, if they are concerned about encryption or other potential problems, they can leave a phone powered on and place it in an enclosure that isolates the phone from radio waves. Such devices are commonly called "Faraday bags," after the English scientist Michael Faraday. They are essentially sandwich bags made of aluminum foil: cheap, lightweight, and easy to use. They may not be a complete answer to the problem, but at least for now they provide a reasonable response. In fact, a number of law enforcement agencies around the country already encourage the use of Faraday bags.

To the extent that law enforcement still has specific concerns about the potential loss of evidence in a particular case, there remain more targeted ways to address those concerns. If the police are truly confronted with a "now or never" situation—for example, circumstances suggesting that a defendant's phone will be the target of an imminent remote-wipe attempt—they may be able to rely on exigent circumstances to search the phone immediately.

### B

The search incident to arrest exception rests not only on the heightened government interests at stake in a volatile arrest situation, but also on an arrestee's reduced privacy interests upon being taken into police custody. Put simply, a patdown of Robinson's clothing and an inspection of the cigarette pack found in his pocket constituted only minor additional intrusions compared to the substantial government authority exercised in taking Robinson into custody.

The fact that an arrestee has diminished privacy interests does not mean that the Fourth Amendment falls out of the picture entirely. Not every search is acceptable solely because a person is in custody. *Chimel* refused to "characteriz[e] the invasion of privacy that results from a top-to-bottom search of a man's house as 'minor.' " Because a search of the arrestee's entire house was a substantial invasion beyond the arrest itself, the Court concluded that a warrant was required.

*Robinson* is the only decision from this Court applying *Chimel* to a search of the contents of an item found on an arrestee's person. Lower courts applying *Robinson* and *Chimel*, however, have approved searches of a variety of personal items carried by an arrestee. *See, e.g., United States v. Carrion*, 809 F.2d 1120, 1123, 1128 (5th Cir. 1987) (billfold and address book); *United States v. Watson*, 669 F.2d 1374, 1383–1384 (11th Cir. 1982) (wallet); *United States v. Lee*, 501 F.2d 890, 892 (D.C. Cir. 1974) (purse).

The United States asserts that a search of all data stored on a cell phone is "materially indistinguishable" from searches of these sorts of physical items. That is like saying a ride on horseback is materially indistinguishable from a flight to the moon. Both are ways of getting from point A to point B, but little else justifies lumping them together. Modern cell phones, as a category, implicate privacy concerns far beyond those implicated by the search of a cigarette pack, a wallet, or a purse. A conclusion that inspecting the contents of an arrestee's pockets works no substantial additional intrusion on privacy beyond the arrest itself may make sense as applied to physical items, but any extension of that reasoning to digital data has to rest on its own bottom.

1

Cell phones differ in both a quantitative and a qualitative sense from other objects that might be kept on an arrestee's person. The term "cell phone" is itself misleading shorthand; many of these devices are in fact minicomputers that also happen to have the capacity to be used as a telephone. They could just as easily be called cameras, video players, rolodexes, calendars, tape recorders, libraries, diaries, albums, televisions, maps, or newspapers.

One of the most notable distinguishing features of modern cell phones is their immense storage capacity. Before cell phones, a search of a person was limited by physical realities and tended as a general matter to constitute only a narrow intrusion on privacy. Most people cannot lug around every piece of mail they have received for the past several months, every picture they have taken, or every book or article they have read—nor would they have any reason to attempt to do so. And if they did, they would have to drag behind them a trunk of the sort held to require a search warrant in *Chadwick* rather than a container the size of the cigarette package in *Robinson*.

But the possible intrusion on privacy is not physically limited in the same way when it comes to cell phones. The current top-selling smart phone has a standard capacity of 16 gigabytes (and is available with up to 64 gigabytes). Sixteen gigabytes translates to millions of pages of text, thousands of pictures, or hundreds of videos. Cell phones couple that capacity with the ability to store many different types of information:

Even the most basic phones that sell for less than $20 might hold photographs, picture messages, text messages, Internet browsing history, a calendar, a thousand-entry phone book, and so on. We expect that the gulf between physical practicability and digital capacity will only continue to widen in the future.

The storage capacity of cell phones has several interrelated consequences for privacy. First, a cell phone collects in one place many distinct types of information—an address, a note, a prescription, a bank statement, a video—that reveal much more in combination than any isolated record. Second, a cell phone's capacity allows even just one type of information to convey far more than previously possible. The sum of an individual's private life can be reconstructed through a thousand photographs labeled with dates, locations, and descriptions; the same cannot be said of a photograph or two of loved ones tucked into a wallet. Third, the data on a phone can date back to the purchase of the phone, or even earlier. A person might carry in his pocket a slip of paper reminding him to call Mr. Jones; he would not carry a record of all his communications with Mr. Jones for the past several months, as would routinely be kept on a phone.

Finally, there is an element of pervasiveness that characterizes cell phones but not physical records. Prior to the digital age, people did not typically carry a cache of sensitive personal information with them as they went about their day. Now it is the person who is not carrying a cell phone, with all that it contains, who is the exception. According to one poll, nearly three-quarters of smart phone users report being within five feet of their phones most of the time, with 12% admitting that they even use their phones in the shower. A decade ago police officers searching an arrestee might have occasionally stumbled across a highly personal item such as a diary. But those discoveries were likely to be few and far between. Today, by contrast, it is no exaggeration to say that many of the more than 90% of American adults who own a cell phone keep on their person a digital record of nearly every aspect of their lives—from the mundane to the intimate. Allowing the police to scrutinize such records on a routine basis is quite different from allowing them to search a personal item or two in the occasional case.

Although the data stored on a cell phone is distinguished from physical records by quantity alone, certain types of data are also qualitatively different. An Internet search and browsing history, for example, can be found on an Internet-enabled phone and could reveal an individual's private interests or concerns—perhaps a search for certain symptoms of disease, coupled with frequent visits to WebMD. Data on a cell phone can also reveal where a person has been. Historic location information is a standard feature on many smart phones and can reconstruct someone's specific movements down to the minute, not only around town but also within a particular building. *See United States v. Jones*, 132 S. Ct. 945, 955 (2012) (Sotomayor, J., concurring).

Mobile application software on a cell phone, or "apps," offer a range of tools for managing detailed information about all aspects of a person's life. There are apps for Democratic Party news and Republican Party news; apps for alcohol, drug, and gambling addictions; apps for sharing prayer requests; apps for tracking pregnancy symptoms; apps for planning your budget; apps for every conceivable hobby or pastime; apps for improving your romantic life. There are popular apps for buying or selling just about anything, and the records of such transactions may be accessible on the phone indefinitely. There are over a million apps available in each of the two major app stores; the phrase "there's an app for that" is now part of the popular lexicon. The average smart phone user has installed 33 apps, which together can form a revealing montage of the user's life.

In 1926, Learned Hand observed (in an opinion later quoted in *Chimel*) that it is "a totally different thing to search a man's pockets and use against him what they contain, from ransacking his house for everything which may incriminate him." United States v. Kirschenblatt, 16 F.2d 202, 203 (2nd Cir. 1926). If his pockets contain a cell phone, however, that is no longer true. Indeed, a cell phone search would typically expose to the government far *more* than the most exhaustive search of a house: A phone not only contains in digital form many sensitive records previously found in the home; it also contains a broad array of private information never found in a home in any form—unless the phone is.

2

To further complicate the scope of the privacy interests at stake, the data a user views on many modern cell phones may not in fact be stored on the device itself. Treating a cell phone as a container whose contents may be searched incident to an arrest is a bit strained as an initial matter. But the analogy crumbles entirely when a cell phone is used to access data located elsewhere, at the tap of a screen. That is what cell phones, with increasing frequency, are designed to do by taking advantage of "cloud computing." Cloud computing is the capacity of Internet-connected devices to display data stored on remote servers rather than on the device itself. Cell phone users often may not know whether particular information is stored on the device or in the cloud, and it generally makes little difference. Moreover, the same type of data may be stored locally on the device for one user and in the cloud for another.

The United States concedes that the search incident to arrest exception may not be stretched to cover a search of files accessed remotely—that is, a search of files stored in the cloud. Such a search would be like finding a key in a suspect's pocket and arguing that it allowed law enforcement to unlock and search a house. But officers searching a phone's data would not typically know whether the information they are viewing was stored locally at the time of the arrest or has been pulled from the cloud.

Although the Government recognizes the problem, its proposed solutions are unclear. It suggests that officers could disconnect a phone from the network before searching the device—the very solution whose feasibility it contested with respect to the threat of remote wiping. Alternatively, the Government proposes that law enforcement agencies "develop protocols to address" concerns raised by cloud computing. Probably a good idea, but the Founders did not fight a revolution to gain the right to government agency protocols. The possibility that a search might extend well beyond papers and effects in the physical proximity of an arrestee is yet another reason that the privacy interests here dwarf those in *Robinson.*

### C

Apart from their arguments for a direct extension of *Robinson,* the United States and California offer various fallback options for permitting warrantless cell phone searches under certain circumstances. Each of the proposals is flawed and contravenes our general preference to provide clear guidance to law enforcement through categorical rules.

The United States proposes a rule that would restrict the scope of a cell phone search to those areas of the phone where an officer reasonably believes that information relevant to the crime, the arrestee's identity, or officer safety will be discovered. This approach would impose few meaningful constraints on officers. The proposed categories would sweep in a great deal of information, and officers would not always be able to discern in advance what information would be found where.

We also reject the United States' suggestion that officers should always be able to search a phone's call log, as they did in Wurie's case. The Government relies on *Smith v. Maryland,* 442 U.S. 735 (1979), which held that no warrant was required to use a pen register at telephone company premises to identify numbers dialed by a particular caller. The Court in that case, however, concluded that the use of a pen register was not a "search" at all under the Fourth Amendment. There is no dispute here that the officers engaged in a search of Wurie's cell phone. Moreover, call logs typically contain more than just phone numbers; they include any identifying information that an individual might add, such as the label "my house" in Wurie's case.

Finally, at oral argument California suggested a different limiting principle, under which officers could search cell phone data if they could have obtained the same information from a pre-digital counterpart. But the fact that a search in the pre-digital era could have turned up a photograph or two in a wallet does not justify a search of thousands of photos in a digital gallery. The fact that someone could have tucked a paper bank statement in a pocket does not justify a search of every bank statement from the last five years. And to make matters worse, such an analogue test would allow law enforcement to search a range of items contained on a phone, even though people would be unlikely to carry such a variety of information in physical form. In Riley's case, for example, it is implausible that he would have strolled around with video tapes, photo albums, and an address book all crammed into his pockets. But because each of those items has a pre-digital analogue, police under California's proposal would be able to search a phone for all of those items—a significant diminution of privacy.

In addition, an analogue test would launch courts on a difficult line-drawing expedition to determine which digital files are comparable to physical records. Is an e-mail equivalent to a letter? Is a voicemail equivalent to a phone message slip? It is not clear how officers could make these kinds of decisions before conducting a search, or how courts would apply the proposed rule after the fact. An analogue test would "keep defendants and judges guessing for years to come." *Sykes v. United States,* 131 S. Ct. 2267, 2287 (2011) (Scalia, J., dissenting) (discussing the Court's analogue test under the Armed Career Criminal Act).

## IV

We cannot deny that our decision today will have an impact on the ability of law enforcement to combat crime. Cell phones have become important tools in facilitating coordination and communication among members of criminal enterprises, and can provide valuable incriminating information about dangerous criminals. Privacy comes at a cost.

Our holding, of course, is not that the information on a cell phone is immune from search; it is instead that a warrant is generally required before such a search, even when a cell phone is seized incident to arrest. Our cases have historically recognized that the warrant requirement is an important working part of our machinery of government, not merely an inconvenience to be somehow 'weighed' against the claims of police efficiency.

Moreover, even though the search incident to arrest exception does not apply to cell phones, other case-specific exceptions may still justify a warrantless search of a particular phone. One well-recognized exception applies when "the exigencies of the situation" make the needs of law enforcement so compelling that a warrantless search is objectively reasonable under the Fourth Amendment. Such exigencies could include the need to prevent the imminent destruction of evidence in individual cases, to pursue a fleeing suspect, and to assist persons who are seriously injured or are threatened with imminent injury. In *Chadwick*, for example, the Court held that the exception for searches incident to arrest did not justify a search of the trunk at issue, but noted that "if officers have reason to believe that luggage contains some immediately dangerous instrumentality, such as explosives, it would be foolhardy to transport it to the station house without opening the luggage."

In light of the availability of the exigent circumstances exception, there is no reason to believe that law enforcement officers will not be able to address some of the more extreme hypotheticals that have been suggested: a suspect texting an accomplice who, it is feared, is preparing to detonate a bomb, or a child abductor who may have information about the child's location on his cell phone. The defendants here recognize—indeed, they stress—that such fact-specific threats may justify a warrantless search of cell phone data. The critical point is that, unlike the search incident to arrest exception, the exigent circumstances exception requires a court to examine whether an emergency justified a warrantless search in each particular case.

Modern cell phones are not just another technological convenience. With all they contain and all they may reveal, they hold for many Americans "the privacies of life." The fact that technology now allows an individual to carry such information in his hand does not make the information any less worthy of the protection for which the Founders fought. Our answer to the question of what police must do before searching a cell phone seized incident to an arrest is accordingly simple—get a warrant.

■ JUSTICE ALITO, concurring in part and concurring in the judgment.

While I agree with the holding of the Court, I would reconsider the question presented here if either Congress or state legislatures, after assessing the legitimate needs of law enforcement and the privacy interests of cell phone owners, enact legislation that draws reasonable distinctions based on categories of information or perhaps other variables.

The regulation of electronic surveillance provides an instructive example. After this Court held that electronic surveillance constitutes a search even when no property interest is invaded, *see Katz v. United States,* 389 U.S. 347, 353–359 (1967), Congress responded by enacting Title III of the Omnibus Crime Control and Safe Streets Act of 1968. Since that time, electronic surveillance has been governed primarily, not by decisions of this Court, but by the statute, which authorizes but imposes detailed restrictions on electronic surveillance. [For more on this statute, see Chapter 5.]

Many forms of modern technology are making it easier and easier for both government and private entities to amass a wealth of information about the lives of ordinary Americans, and at the same time, many ordinary Americans are choosing to make public much information that was seldom revealed to outsiders just a few decades ago.

In light of these developments, it would be very unfortunate if privacy protection in the 21st century were left primarily to the federal courts using the blunt instrument of the Fourth Amendment. Legislatures, elected by the people, are in a better position than we are to assess and respond to the changes that have already occurred and those that almost certainly will take place in the future.

## NOTES

1. ***Keeping Pace with Technology.*** Like *Olmstead* and many other major Supreme Court privacy cases, *Jones* and *Riley* force the judiciary to apply old rules to new technology. Just as judges do in any case, the Court tries to analogize the new situation to those covered by existing precedents. How well do these analogies work in these two cases? Where do they fall short? What can we learn from the fact that, by the time the Supreme Court decided Wurie's case in its *Riley* opinion, the type of flip phone at issue in his case was almost obsolete? Continue to watch for the ways courts handle new technology throughout this course.

2. ***Quantity and Quality.*** Carefully examine the discussion of the arrestees' privacy interests in the contents of their cell phones in Part III.B of *Riley*. What exactly are the "qualitative" and the "quantitative" differences between the information in cell phones and other search cases? Likewise, in *Jones*, notice how the justices grapple with the question of why access to *a larger amount* of location data from GPS—what Justice Sotomayor calls a "substantial quantum of intimate information"—entirely changes the character of the privacy interests. Are these changes of degree or kind? Does it matter?

3. ***The Return of Trespass?*** Concepts of trespass are important, yet again, in *Jones*. Justice Scalia hearkens back to *Olmstead* as a basis for ruling that the placement of the GPS tracker on an automobile required a warrant. Is this a departure from *Katz*? Is it "unwise," as Justice Alito's concurrence argues? Or are trespass and the reasonable expectation of privacy cumulative tests, as Justice Sotomayor indicates? Does all this mean the declaration in *Katz* that "the Fourth Amendment protects people, not places" turned out to be wrong?

4. ***Warrants.*** Like *Katz*, both *Jones* and *Riley* emphasize that their decisions do not ban the challenged law enforcement practice, but mandate that law enforcement secure a warrant first. Again, the main effect of this requirement is to interpose the requirement of probable cause and judicial review. In *Jones*, there was a warrant, but officers did not adhere to its requirements and the government conceded this made the GPS tracking effectively warrantless. If the FBI and D.C. police had simply obeyed the conditions of the warrant in *Jones*, would the various Justices' concerns be assuaged? Why or why not? Based on what the *Riley* Court says about the arrests of Riley and Wurie, would officers have been able to secure warrants for the cell phones in those cases?

5. ***Location Data.*** GPS is just one example of new technology that allows third parties to collect location data much more easily than in the past. Other examples include sophisticated license plate readers, automated passes used to pay highway tolls or transit fares, and sometimes even tiny short-range transmitters called RFID tags that are embedded in many physical items. When is this data private? Is it especially sensitive? Carefully

think through the arguments, and avoid simply concluding that the availability of some type of data feels "creepy." In what circumstance can you articulate privacy harms from location data? How do these distinctions arise in *Jones*?

**6.** ***Commercial Availability of Technology.*** Today it is easy to find "GPS spy trackers" advertised online for less than $300. Some even allow users to log in to an iPhone app for real-time location information about a vehicle carrying the device. How would the *Kyllo* rule about the general availability of technology apply to the use of GPS in *Jones*?

**7.** ***Legislatures and Courts.*** Justice Alito's concurrence in *Riley* expresses the hope that Congress might legislate to redefine the scope of police investigative powers in light of new technology. Would law enforcement location tracking and cell phone searches be handled by statute better than they are by constitutional rules? What are the advantages and drawbacks of each?

---

## Practice

Cloud Computing and the Fourth Amendment

Suppose Officer Krupke approaches CloudLocker, a provider of "cloud computing" services—the storage of personal files on remote computer servers, often in a way that is not immediately apparent through the user interface. Krupke explains that he is investigating David Riley concerning his possible involvement in a gang-related drive-by shooting, and he believes Riley may have stored incriminating documents in a CloudLocker account. CloudLocker voluntarily provides Krupke with access to Riley's files. Those files include videos of young men sparring while someone yelled encouragement using a gang moniker and photographs of Riley standing in front of a car that Krupke suspects was used in the shooting. His suspicions confirmed, Krupke included this information in an application for a search warrant for Riley's apartment, where police found much more incriminating evidence. In the subsequent prosecution, Riley sought to exclude all the evidence from his CloudLocker account and his apartment, arguing that the search of his CloudLocker documents violated the Fourth Amendment. Assume that the case is now before the Supreme Court. Based on what you have read, and limiting your analysis to constitutional issues, what are the best arguments for and against Riley's position?

---

## B. THE FIRST AMENDMENT

Privacy rules usually control what information one person or entity can communicate about another. For this reason, the First Amendment's protection of speech and press freedoms often arises as a limit on privacy regulation, one which we will see often. [In particular, see Chapter 8.] This section discusses a different role for the First Amendment, as a possible *source* of privacy restrictions. Sometimes, courts and scholars have suggested, the state must respect a need for privacy or anonymity in order to safeguard the values protected by the First Amendment.

## Stanley v. Georgia

394 U.S. 557 (1969)

■ MR. JUSTICE MARSHALL delivered the opinion of the Court.

An investigation of appellant's alleged bookmaking activities led to the issuance of a search warrant for appellant's home. Under authority of this warrant, federal and state agents secured entrance. They found very little evidence of bookmaking activity, but while looking through a desk drawer in an upstairs bedroom, one of the federal agents, accompanied by a state officer, found three reels of eight-millimeter film. Using a projector and screen found in an upstairs living room, they viewed the films. The state officer concluded that they were obscene and seized them. Since a further examination of the bedroom indicated that appellant occupied it, he was charged with possession of obscene matter and placed under arrest. He was later indicted for "knowingly hav(ing) possession of . . . obscene matter" in violation of Georgia law. Appellant was tried before a jury and convicted. The Supreme Court of Georgia affirmed.

Appellant raises several challenges to the validity of his conviction. We find it necessary to consider only one. Appellant argues here, and argued below, that the Georgia obscenity statute, insofar as it punishes mere private possession of obscene matter, violates the First Amendment, as made applicable to the States by the Fourteenth Amendment. For reasons set forth below, we agree that the mere private possession of obscene matter cannot constitutionally be made a crime.

It is now well established that the Constitution protects the right to receive information and ideas. This right to receive information and ideas, regardless of their social worth, is fundamental to our free society. Moreover, in the context of this case—a prosecution for mere possession of printed or filmed matter in the privacy of a person's own home—that right takes on an added dimension. For also fundamental is the right to be free, except in very limited circumstances, from unwanted governmental intrusions into one's privacy.

> The makers of our Constitution undertook to secure conditions favorable to the pursuit of happiness. They recognized the significance of man's spiritual nature, of his feelings and of his intellect. They knew that only a part of the pain, pleasure and satisfactions of life are to be found in material things. They sought to protect Americans in their beliefs, their thoughts, their emotions and their sensations. They conferred, as against the government, the right to be let alone—the most comprehensive of rights and the right most valued by civilized man.

*Olmstead v. United States*, 277 U.S. 438, 478 (1928) (Brandeis, J., dissenting).

These are the rights that appellant is asserting in the case before us. He is asserting the right to read or observe what he pleases—the right to satisfy his intellectual and emotional needs in the privacy of his own home. He is asserting the right to be free from state inquiry into the contents of his library. Georgia contends that appellant does not have these rights, that there are certain types of materials that the individual may not read or even possess. Georgia justifies this assertion by arguing that the films in the present case are obscene. But we think that mere categorization of these films as 'obscene' is insufficient justification for such a drastic invasion of personal liberties guaranteed by the First and Fourteenth Amendments. Whatever may be the justifications for other statutes regulating obscenity, we do not think they reach into the privacy of one's own home. If the First Amendment means anything, it means that a State has no business telling a man, sitting alone in his own house, what books he may read or what films he may watch. Our whole constitutional heritage rebels at the thought of giving government the power to control men's minds.

And yet, in the face of these traditional notions of individual liberty, Georgia asserts the right to protect the individual's mind from the effects of obscenity. We are not certain that this argument amounts to anything more than the assertion that the State has the right to control the moral content of a person's thoughts. To some, this may be a noble purpose, but it is wholly inconsistent with the philosophy of the First Amendment.

We hold that the First and Fourteenth Amendments prohibit making mere private possession of obscene material a crime. As we have said, the States retain broad power to regulate obscenity; that power simply does not extend to mere possession by the individual in the privacy of his own home. Accordingly, the judgment of the court below is reversed and the case is remanded for proceedings not inconsistent with this opinion.

## NOTES

1. ***The Fourth Amendment in* Stanley.** While the outcome of *Stanley* was unanimous, four justices signed a concurrence written by Justice Stewart that preferred a narrower decision based only on the Fourth Amendment. These justices argued that the nature of the films could not be determined without viewing them, and that this examination exceeded the authority granted by a warrant to search for evidence of gambling offenses. With some acid, the concurrence regrets that "the Court today disregards this preliminary issue in its hurry to move on to newer constitutional frontiers." Why do you suppose Justice Marshall based the decision on the First Amendment? Was he right to do so? What if a label on the outside of the tape canister had made it clear that the contents were pornographic? What if the police had reason to believe that the suspect concealed gambling records on film reels falsely labeled as pornography?

2. ***Home, Again.*** By this point, the paramount importance of the home as a bastion of privacy in the law should be getting familiar. Justice Marshall underscored several times that the films were in the defendant's home, writing at one point "a State has no business telling a man, *sitting alone in his own house*, what books he may read or what films he may watch." Should the logic of *Stanley* extend to other locations? What about hotel rooms? The trunk of an automobile? A pocketbook or briefcase? What about information that is stored on a server through a cloud-based computer platform?

3. ***Intellectual Privacy.*** Neil Richards has suggested that *Stanley* is an example of a concept he calls "intellectual privacy":

> Intellectual privacy is the ability, whether protected by law or social circumstances, to develop ideas and beliefs away from the unwanted gaze or interference of others. Surveillance or interference can warp the integrity of our freedom of thought and can skew the way we think, with clear repercussions for the content of our subsequent speech or writing. The ability to freely make up our minds and to develop new ideas thus depends upon a substantial measure of intellectual privacy. In this way, intellectual privacy is a cornerstone of meaningful First Amendment liberties.

Neil M. Richards, *Intellectual Privacy*, 87 TEX. L. REV. 387, 389 (2008). Notice two key steps to Richards' argument. First, scrutiny from the authorities encourages conformity in the way we think and act. This is an old notion, brought vividly to life by the all-seeing telescreens in George Orwell's *1984*. (You may also be familiar with the related notion of the Panopticon, first advanced by Jeremy Bentham and later developed by Michel Foucault.) Second, because that scrutiny can distort our own intellectual formation, it is antithetical to the values of the First Amendment. Keep these principles in mind as we consider the harms of surveillance or disclosure that privacy law attempts to mitigate.

4. ***Intellectual Privacy in the Private Sector.*** The First Amendment constrains government actors. Most states also have laws strongly protecting the confidentiality of borrower records in public libraries from all disclosures, including inquiries by authorities. But private entities know a great deal about our reading and viewing habits. How much do the concerns articulated in *Stanley* or by Richards apply to social media platforms or services like Netflix or Amazon? Even though these private companies are not constrained by the US Constitution, do the values of the First Amendment support greater privacy regulation through other means? [For an example of legislation aimed at this problem, see Chapter 14.] Or is there something unique about government knowledge of our reading and thinking?

5. ***Books and Films as Investigative Evidence.*** The holding of *Stanley* forbids Georgia from making the possession of obscene films a crime. But what if a suspect's reading or viewing habits provide evidence of some other criminal activity? In *Tattered Cover, Inc. v. City of Thornton*, 44 P.3d

1044 (Colo. 2002), the Colorado Supreme Court considered a bookstore's challenge to a search warrant that sought records of purchases made by a particular suspect; the police had good reason to believe the store had sold him a how-to book about setting up a methamphetamine lab. The court determined that the warrant should be judged by a balancing test considering both law enforcement and privacy interests and concluded, "[B]ecause of the strength of other evidence at the City's disposal and because of the substantial chilling effects that are likely to result from execution of the warrant, we hold that the City has failed to demonstrate that its need for this evidence is sufficiently compelling to outweigh the harmful effects of the search warrant." In its decision, based on the state constitution, the court underscored the intellectual privacy interests at stake:

> Without the right to receive information and ideas, the protection of speech under the United States and Colorado Constitutions would be meaningless. It makes no difference that one can voice whatever view one wishes to express if others are not free to listen to these thoughts. The converse also holds true. Everyone must be permitted to discover and consider the full range of expression and ideas available in our "marketplace of ideas."
>
> Bookstores are places where a citizen can explore ideas, receive information, and discover myriad perspectives on every topic imaginable. When a person buys a book at a bookstore, he engages in activity protected by the First Amendment because he is exercising his right to read and receive ideas and information. Any governmental action that interferes with the willingness of customers to purchase books, or booksellers to sell books, thus implicates First Amendment concerns.

In many other cases, however, this balance allows the warrant, especially if the issuing court has taken precautions to minimize harm to First Amendment interests. The US Supreme Court put it this way in a case involving a warrant to seize photographs of a campus protest from the offices of a student newspaper:

> [T]he prior cases do no more than insist that the courts apply the warrant requirements with particular exactitude when First Amendment interests would be endangered by the search. As we see it, no more than this is required where the warrant requested is for the seizure of criminal evidence reasonably believed to be on the premises occupied by a newspaper. Properly administered, the preconditions for a warrant—probable cause, specificity with respect to the place to be searched and the things to be seized, and overall reasonableness—should afford sufficient protection against the harms that are assertedly threatened by warrants for searching newspaper offices.

*Zurcher v. Stanford Daily*, 436 U.S. 547, 565 (1978).

# McIntyre v. Ohio Elections Commission

514 U.S. 334 (1995)

■ JUSTICE STEVENS delivered the opinion of the Court.

The question presented is whether an Ohio statute that prohibits the distribution of anonymous campaign literature is a "law . . . abridging the freedom of speech" within the meaning of the First Amendment.

## I

On April 27, 1988, Margaret McIntyre distributed leaflets to persons attending a public meeting at the Blendon Middle School in Westerville, Ohio. At this meeting, the superintendent of schools planned to discuss an imminent referendum on a proposed school tax levy. The leaflets expressed Mrs. McIntyre's opposition to the levy. There is no suggestion that the text of her message was false, misleading, or libelous. She had composed and printed it on her home computer and had paid a professional printer to make additional copies. Some of the handbills identified her as the author; others merely purported to express the views of "CONCERNED PARENTS AND TAX PAYERS." Except for the help provided by her son and a friend, who placed some of the leaflets on car windshields in the school parking lot, Mrs. McIntyre acted independently.

While Mrs. McIntyre distributed her handbills, an official of the school district, who supported the tax proposal, advised her that the unsigned leaflets did not conform to the Ohio election laws. Undeterred, Mrs. McIntyre appeared at another meeting on the next evening and handed out more of the handbills.

Five months later, the same school official filed a complaint with the Ohio Elections Commission charging that Mrs. McIntyre's distribution of unsigned leaflets violated § 3599.09(A) of the Ohio Code. The commission agreed and imposed a fine of $100. [Mrs. McIntyre, and later her estate, pursued appeals of the decision through the Ohio Supreme Court and on to the U.S. Supreme Court].

## II

Ohio maintains that the statute under review is a reasonable regulation of the electoral process. The State does not suggest that all anonymous publications are pernicious or that a statute totally excluding them from the marketplace of ideas would be valid. This is a wise (albeit implicit) concession, for the anonymity of an author is not ordinarily a sufficient reason to exclude her work product from the protections of the First Amendment.

Anonymous pamphlets, leaflets, brochures and even books have played an important role in the progress of mankind. Great works of literature have frequently been produced by authors writing under assumed names. Despite readers' curiosity and the public's interest in identifying the creator of a work of art, an author generally is free to decide whether or not to disclose his or her true identity. The decision in favor of anonymity may be motivated by fear of economic or official retaliation, by concern about social ostracism, or merely by a desire to preserve as much of one's privacy as possible. Whatever the motivation may be, at least in the field of literary endeavor, the interest in having anonymous works enter the marketplace of ideas unquestionably outweighs any public interest in requiring disclosure as a condition of entry. Accordingly, an author's decision to remain anonymous, like other decisions concerning omissions or additions to the content of a publication, is an aspect of the freedom of speech protected by the First Amendment.

## III

We must, therefore, decide whether and to what extent the First Amendment's protection of anonymity encompasses documents intended to influence the electoral process.

[T]he speech in which Mrs. McIntyre engaged—handing out leaflets in the advocacy of a politically controversial viewpoint—is the essence of First Amendment expression. That this advocacy occurred in the heat of a controversial referendum vote only strengthens the protection afforded to Mrs. McIntyre's expression: Urgent, important, and effective speech can be no less protected than impotent speech, lest the right to speak be relegated to those instances when it is least needed. No form of speech is entitled to greater constitutional protection than Mrs. McIntyre's.

## IV

[T]he State argues that, even under the strictest standard of review, the disclosure requirement in § 3599.09(A) is justified by two important and legitimate state interests. Ohio judges its interest in preventing fraudulent and libelous statements and its interest in providing the electorate with relevant information to be sufficiently compelling to justify the anonymous speech ban.

Insofar as the interest in informing the electorate means nothing more than the provision of additional information that may either buttress or undermine the argument in a document, we think the identity of the speaker is no different from other components of the document's content that the author is free to include or exclude. The simple interest in providing voters with additional relevant information does not justify a state requirement that a writer make statements or disclosures she would otherwise omit. Moreover, in the case of a handbill written by a private citizen who is not known to the recipient, the name and address of the author add little, if anything, to the reader's ability to evaluate the document's message. Thus, Ohio's informational interest is plainly insufficient to support the constitutionality of its disclosure requirement.

The state interest in preventing fraud and libel stands on a different footing. We agree with Ohio's submission that this interest carries special weight during election campaigns when false statements, if credited, may have serious adverse consequences for the public at large. Ohio does not, however, rely solely on § 3599.09(A) to protect that interest. Its Election Code includes detailed and specific prohibitions against making or disseminating false statements during political campaigns. We recognize that a State's enforcement interest might justify a more limited identification requirement, but Ohio has shown scant cause for inhibiting the leafletting at issue here.

Under our Constitution, anonymous pamphleteering is not a pernicious, fraudulent practice, but an honorable tradition of advocacy and of dissent. Anonymity is a shield from the tyranny of the majority. *See generally* J. Mill, *On Liberty and Considerations on Representative Government* 1, 3–4 (R. McCallum ed. 1947). It thus exemplifies the purpose behind the Bill of Rights, and of the First Amendment in particular: to protect unpopular individuals from retaliation—and their ideas from suppression—at the hand of an intolerant society. The right to remain anonymous may be abused when it shields fraudulent conduct. But political speech by its nature will sometimes have unpalatable consequences, and, in general, our society accords greater weight to the value of free speech than to the dangers of its misuse. Ohio has not shown that its interest in preventing the misuse of anonymous election-related speech justifies a prohibition of all uses of that speech. The State may, and does, punish fraud directly. But it cannot seek to punish fraud indirectly by indiscriminately outlawing a category of speech, based on its content, with no necessary relationship to the danger sought to be prevented. One would be hard pressed to think of a better example of the pitfalls of Ohio's blunderbuss approach than the facts of the case before us.

■ JUSTICE GINSBURG, concurring.

In for a calf is not always in for a cow. The Court's decision finds unnecessary, overintrusive, and inconsistent with American ideals the State's imposition of a fine on an individual leafleteer who, within her local community, spoke her mind, but sometimes not her name. We do not thereby hold that the State may not in other, larger circumstances require the speaker to disclose its interest by disclosing its identity.

■ JUSTICE THOMAS, concurring in the judgment.

Instead of asking whether "an honorable tradition" of anonymous speech has existed throughout American history, or what the "value" of anonymous speech might be, we should determine whether the phrase "freedom of speech, or of the press," as originally understood, protected anonymous political leafletting. I believe that it did.

Unfortunately, we have no record of discussions of anonymous political expression either in the First Congress, which drafted the Bill of Rights, or in the state ratifying conventions. Thus, our analysis must focus on the practices and beliefs held by the Founders concerning anonymous political articles and pamphlets.

There is little doubt that the Framers engaged in anonymous political writing. The essays in the Federalist Papers, published under the pseudonym of "Publius," are only the most famous example of the outpouring of anonymous political writing that occurred during the ratification of the Constitution. Of course, the simple fact that the Framers engaged in certain conduct does not necessarily prove that they forbade its prohibition by the government. In this case, however, the historical evidence indicates that Founding-era Americans opposed attempts to require that anonymous authors reveal their identities on the ground that forced disclosure violated the "freedom of the press." [Justice Thomas provided an extensive historical review of the widespread use of pseudonyms in the Founding Era.]

I cannot join the majority's analysis because it deviates from our settled approach to interpreting the Constitution and because it superimposes its modern theories concerning expression upon the constitutional text.

While, like Justice SCALIA, I am loath to overturn a century of practice shared by almost all of the States, I believe the historical evidence from the framing outweighs recent tradition.

■ JUSTICE SCALIA, with whom THE CHIEF JUSTICE joins, dissenting.

[T]he Court invalidates a species of protection for the election process that exists, in a variety of forms, in every State except California, and that has a pedigree dating back to the end of the 19th century. Preferring the views of the English utilitarian philosopher John Stuart Mill to the considered judgment of the American people's elected representatives from coast to coast, the Court discovers a hitherto unknown right-to-be-unknown while engaging in electoral politics. I dissent from this imposition of free-speech imperatives that are demonstrably not those of the American people today, and that there is inadequate reason to believe were those of the society that begat the First Amendment or the Fourteenth.

## I

The question posed by the present case is not the easiest sort to answer for those who adhere to the Court's (and the society's) traditional view that the Constitution bears its original meaning and is unchanging.

In the present case, *absent other indication,* I would be inclined to agree with the concurrence [of Justice Thomas] that a society which used anonymous political debate so regularly would not regard as constitutional even moderate restrictions made to improve the election process. (I would, however, want further evidence of common practice in 1868, since I doubt that the Fourteenth Amendment time-warped the post-Civil War States back to the Revolution.)

But there *is* other indication, of the most weighty sort: the widespread and longstanding traditions of our people. Principles of liberty fundamental enough to have been embodied within constitutional guarantees are not readily erased from the Nation's consciousness. A governmental practice that has become general throughout the United States, and particularly one that has the validation of long, accepted usage, bears a strong presumption of constitutionality. And that is what we have before us here.

## II

The foregoing analysis suffices to decide this case for me. Where the meaning of a constitutional text (such as "the freedom of speech") is unclear, the widespread and long-accepted practices of the American people are the best indication of what fundamental beliefs it was intended to enshrine. Even if I were to close my eyes to practice, however, and were to be guided exclusively by deductive analysis from our case law, I would reach the same result.

Three basic questions must be answered to decide this case. Two of them are readily answered by our precedents; the third is readily answered by common sense and by a decent regard for the practical judgment of those more familiar with elections than we are. The first question is whether protection of the election process justifies limitations upon speech that cannot constitutionally be imposed generally. Our cases plainly answer that question in the affirmative—indeed, they suggest that no justification for regulation is more compelling than protection of the electoral process.

The second question relevant to our decision is whether a "right to anonymity" is such a prominent value in our constitutional system that even protection of the electoral process cannot be purchased at its expense. The answer, again, is clear: no. Several of our cases have held that *in peculiar circumstances* the compelled disclosure of a person's identity would unconstitutionally deter the exercise of First Amendment associational rights. But those cases did not acknowledge any general right to anonymity, or even any right on the part of *all* citizens to ignore the particular laws under challenge. Rather, they recognized a right to an *exemption* from otherwise valid disclosure requirements on the part of someone who could show a "reasonable probability" that the compelled disclosure would result in "threats, harassment, or reprisals from either Government officials or private parties." Anonymity can still be enjoyed by those who require it, without utterly destroying useful disclosure laws. The record in this case contains not even a hint that Mrs. McIntyre feared "threats, harassment, or reprisals"; indeed, she placed her name on some of her fliers and meant to place it on all of them.

It may take decades to work out the shape of this newly expanded right-to-speak-incognito, even in the elections field. And in other areas, of course, a whole new boutique of wonderful First Amendment litigation opens its doors. Must a parade permit, for example, be issued to a group that refuses to provide its identity, or that agrees to do so only under assurance that the identity will not be made public? Must a municipally owned theater that is leased for private productions book anonymously sponsored presentations? Must a government periodical that has a "letters to the editor" column disavow the policy that most newspapers have against the publication of anonymous letters? Must a public university that makes its facilities available for a speech by Louis Farrakhan or David Duke refuse to disclose the on-campus or off-campus group that has sponsored or paid for the speech? Must a municipal "public-access" cable channel permit anonymous (and masked) performers? The silliness that follows upon a generalized right to anonymous speech has no end.

The third and last question relevant to our decision is whether the prohibition of anonymous campaigning is effective in protecting and enhancing democratic elections. In answering this question no, the Justices of the majority set their own views—on a practical matter that bears closely upon the real-life experience of elected politicians and *not* upon that of unelected judges—up against the views of 49 state legislatures and the Federal Congress. We might also add to the list on the other side the legislatures of foreign democracies: Australia, Canada, and England, for example, all have prohibitions upon anonymous campaigning. How is it, one must wonder, that all of these elected legislators, from around the country and around the world, could not see what six Justices of this Court see so clearly that they are willing to require the entire Nation to act upon it: that requiring identification of the source of campaign literature does not improve the quality of the campaign?

I do not know where the Court derives its perception that "anonymous pamphleteering is not a pernicious, fraudulent practice, but an honorable tradition of advocacy and of dissent." I can imagine no reason why an anonymous leaflet is any more honorable, as a general matter, than an anonymous phone call or an anonymous letter. It facilitates wrong by eliminating accountability, which is ordinarily the very purpose of the anonymity. There are of course exceptions, and where anonymity is needed to avoid "threats, harassment, or reprisals" the First Amendment will require an exemption from the Ohio law. But to strike down the Ohio law in its general application—and similar laws of 49 other States and the Federal Government—on the ground that all anonymous communication is in our society traditionally sacrosanct, seems to me a distortion of the past that will lead to a coarsening of the future.

## NOTES

1. ***Mrs. McIntyre's Limited Legacy.*** Overall, *McIntyre* has not unleashed the flood of litigation feared by Justice Scalia. A more accurate prediction came from Justice Ginsburg's statement, "In for a calf is not always in for a cow." A few years later, the Court did rely heavily on *McIntyre* to invalidate "a village ordinance making it a misdemeanor to engage in door-to-door advocacy without first registering with the mayor and receiving a

permit." *Watchtower Bible & Tract Soc'y v. Village of Stratton*, 536 U.S. 150, 153 (2002). More recently, however, the Supreme Court has seldom cited the decision. Lower courts have recognized a right to anonymous speech in some cases; for example, they have invalidated laws that prohibited the use of online pseudonyms, *see, e.g., ACLU v. Miller*, 977 F. Supp. 1228 (N.D. Ga. 1997), and laws that required registered sex offenders to report their online user names and passwords to the government, *see, e.g., Doe v. Harris*, 772 F.3d 563 (9th Cir. 2014). But in other situations, even including consideration of other election-related disclosure laws, courts have read *McIntyre* narrowly or disregarded it altogether.

2. ***Harms.*** Probably the key difference between the majority opinion and Justice Scalia's dissent is the view of each concerning relevant harms from disclosure requirements. The majority opinion's reasoning rests largely on the danger that society will lose the benefits of speech if disclosure requirements have a chilling effect on speakers, but it is less concerned with the reasons a speaker might feel chilled. ("The decision in favor of anonymity may be motivated by fear of economic or official retaliation, by concern about social ostracism, or merely by a desire to preserve as much of one's privacy as possible.") Justice Scalia would limit First Amendment protection to a previously recognized category of cases where the speaker can show a "reasonable probability" that the compelled disclosures will subject those identified to "threats, harassment, or reprisals." Historically, the Supreme Court limited such protection against "threats, harassment, and reprisals" to highly unpopular minority views, such as supporters of integration in the segregated south of the 1950s, as in *NAACP v. Alabama*, 357 U.S. 449 (1958), or members of a socialist party that could demonstrate a history of harassment, as in *Brown v. Socialist Workers '74 Campaign Comm. (Ohio)*, 459 U.S. 87 (1982). How does each of these articulations of harm interpret the First Amendment's role as a source of privacy rules? *See* William McGeveran, *Mrs. McIntyre's Persona: Bringing Privacy Theory to Election Law*, 19 WM. & MARY BILL OF RIGHTS J. 859 (2011); William McGeveran, *Mrs. McIntyre's Checkbook: Privacy Costs of Political Contribution Disclosure*, 6 U. PENN. J. CONST. L. 1 (2003).

3. ***Proving Harms.*** It can be difficult to prove "threats, harassment, and reprisals." Donors to the campaign for a 2008 California ballot initiative to ban gay marriage sought to prevent disclosure of their identities under applicable election law, and presented anecdotal evidence of death threats, boycotts, and vandalism. The district court noted that the initiative had succeeded, so its donors were not an isolated and vulnerable minority in the political process, and therefore did not qualify for any exemption from disclosure. The exemption, the court concluded, is reserved for "groups seeking to further ideas historically and pervasively rejected and vilified by both this country's government and its citizens." *ProtectMarriage.com v. Bowen*, 599 F. Supp. 2d 1197, 1215 (E.D. Cal. 2009). A subsequent Supreme Court case concerned the release of names of people who signed a petition to put an initiative on the ballot in Washington State to revoke a same-sex union law. The Court held that a particularized showing of harm was necessary to be shielded from such disclosure. Dueling concurrences in that

case differed about the standard of proof necessary to secure the exemption. Justice Alito warned that "the as-applied exemption becomes practically worthless if speakers cannot obtain the exemption quickly and well in advance of speaking. . . . Additionally, speakers must be able to obtain an as-applied exemption without clearing a high evidentiary hurdle." *Doe v. Reed*, 561 U.S. 186, 204 (2010) (Alito, J., concurring). Justice Sotomayor's concurrence, on the other hand, argued that courts should be "deeply skeptical" of claims of chilling effects in such cases. *Id.* at 215 (Sotomayor, J., concurring). Justice Stevens went further, stating that a court should "demand strong evidence" of "a significant threat of harassment . . . that cannot be mitigated by law enforcement measures." *Id.* at 218–19 (Stevens, J., concurring in part and concurring in the judgment). What should be the standard of proof? Could Mrs. McIntyre have qualified for the exemption under each of these standards?

4. ***Widespread Enactments and Privacy.*** Justice Scalia highlighted the widespread adoption of disclosure laws like the one at issue in *McIntyre* and concluded that courts should defer to state legislatures by finding such requirements constitutional. Should courts take cues about society's reasonable expectations of privacy from enactments of elected officials? Are there reasons to defer to legislatures in some circumstances and not others?

## C. SUBSTANTIVE DUE PROCESS

### Griswold v. Connecticut

381 U.S. 479 (1965)

■ MR. JUSTICE DOUGLAS delivered the opinion of the Court.

Appellant Griswold is Executive Director of the Planned Parenthood League of Connecticut. Appellant Buxton is a licensed physician and a professor at the Yale Medical School who served as Medical Director for the League at its Center in New Haven—a center open and operating from November 1 to November 10, 1961, when appellants were arrested.

They gave information, instruction, and medical advice to married persons as to the means of preventing conception. They examined the wife and prescribed the best contraceptive device or material for her use. Fees were usually charged, although some couples were serviced free.

The statutes whose constitutionality is involved in this appeal are §§ 53–32 and 54–196 of the General Statutes of Connecticut (1958 rev.). The former provides:

> Any person who uses any drug, medicinal article or instrument for the purpose of preventing conception shall be fined not less than fifty dollars or imprisoned not less than sixty days nor more than one year or be both fined and imprisoned.

Section 54–196 provides:

> Any person who assists, abets, counsels, causes, hires or commands another to commit any offense may be prosecuted and punished as if he were the principal offender.

The appellants were found guilty as accessories and fined $100 each, against the claim that the accessory statute as so applied violated the Fourteenth Amendment.

Coming to the merits, we are met with a wide range of questions that implicate the Due Process Clause of the Fourteenth Amendment.

[The Court then reviewed precedents finding that parents have constitutional rights to make certain educational choices for their children, and that publicizing membership in the NAACP or refusing bar admission to former Communist Party members infringed First Amendment freedom of association.]

The foregoing cases suggest that specific guarantees in the Bill of Rights have penumbras, formed by emanations from those guarantees that help give them life and substance. Various guarantees create zones of privacy. The right of association contained in the penumbra of the First Amendment is one, as we have seen. The Third Amendment in its prohibition against the quartering of soldiers "in any house" in time of peace without the consent of the owner is another facet of that privacy. The Fourth Amendment explicitly affirms the "right of the people to be secure in their persons, houses, papers, and effects, against unreasonable searches and seizures." The Fifth Amendment in its Self-Incrimination Clause enables the citizen to create a zone of privacy which government may not force him to surrender to his detriment. The Ninth Amendment provides: "The enumeration in the Constitution, of certain rights, shall not be construed to deny or disparage others retained by the people."

We have had many controversies over these penumbral rights of "privacy and repose." These cases bear witness that the right of privacy which presses for recognition here is a legitimate one.

The present case, then, concerns a relationship lying within the zone of privacy created by several fundamental constitutional guarantees. And it concerns a law which, in forbidding the use of contraceptives rather than regulating their manufacture or sale, seeks to achieve its goals by means having a maximum destructive impact upon that relationship. Such a law cannot stand in light of the familiar principle, so often applied by this Court, that a governmental purpose to control or prevent activities constitutionally subject to state regulation may not be achieved by means which sweep unnecessarily broadly and thereby invade the area of protected freedoms. Would we allow the police to search the sacred precincts of marital bedrooms for telltale signs of the use of contraceptives? The very idea is repulsive to the notions of privacy surrounding the marriage relationship.

We deal with a right of privacy older than the Bill of Rights—older than our political parties, older than our school system. Marriage is a coming together for better or for worse, hopefully enduring, and intimate to the degree of being sacred. It is an association that promotes a way of life, not causes; a harmony in living, not political faiths; a bilateral loyalty, not commercial or social projects. Yet it is an association for as noble a purpose as any involved in our prior decisions.

Reversed.

■ MR. JUSTICE BLACK, with whom MR. JUSTICE STEWART joins, dissenting.

One of the most effective ways of diluting or expanding a constitutionally guaranteed right is to substitute for the crucial word or words of a constitutional guarantee another word or words, more or less flexible and more or less restricted in meaning. This fact is well illustrated by the use of the term "right of privacy" as a comprehensive substitute for the Fourth Amendment's guarantee against "unreasonable searches and seizures." "Privacy" is a broad, abstract and ambiguous concept which can easily be shrunken in meaning but which can also, on the other hand, easily be interpreted as a constitutional ban against many things other than searches and seizures. For these reasons I get nowhere in this case by talk about a constitutional "right [of] privacy" as an emanation from one or more constitutional provisions. I like my privacy as well as the next one, but I am nevertheless compelled to admit that government has a right to invade it unless prohibited by some specific constitutional provision. For these reasons I cannot agree with the Court's judgment and the reasons it gives for holding this Connecticut law unconstitutional.

■ MR. JUSTICE STEWART, whom MR. JUSTICE BLACK joins, dissenting.

Since 1879 Connecticut has had on its books a law which forbids the use of contraceptives by anyone. I think this is an uncommonly silly law. As a practical matter, the law is obviously unenforceable, except in the oblique context of the present case. As a philosophical matter, I believe the use of contraceptives in the relationship of marriage should be left to personal and private choice, based upon each individual's moral, ethical, and religious beliefs. As a matter of social policy, I think professional counsel about methods of birth control should be available to all, so that each individual's choice can be meaningfully made. But we are not asked in this case to say whether we think this law is unwise, or even asinine. We are asked to hold that it violates the United States Constitution. And that I cannot do.

In the course of its opinion the Court refers to no less than six Amendments to the Constitution: the First, the Third, the Fourth, the Fifth, the Ninth, and the Fourteenth. But the Court does not say which of these Amendments, if any, it thinks is infringed by this Connecticut law.

As to the First, Third, Fourth, and Fifth Amendments, I can find nothing in any of them to invalidate this Connecticut law, even assuming that all those Amendments are fully applicable against the States. It has not even been argued that this is a law "respecting an establishment of religion, or prohibiting the free exercise thereof." And surely, unless the solemn process of constitutional adjudication is to descend to the level of a play on words, there is not involved here any abridgment of "the freedom of speech, or of the press; or the right of the people peaceably to assemble, and to petition the Government for a redress of grievances." No soldier has been quartered in any house. There has been no search, and no seizure. Nobody has been compelled to be a witness against himself.

What provision of the Constitution, then, does make this state law invalid? The Court says it is the right of privacy "created by several fundamental constitutional guarantees." With all deference, I can find no such general right of privacy in the Bill of Rights, in any other part of the Constitution, or in any case ever before decided by this Court.

[Concurrences by Justices Goldberg and White are omitted.]

## NOTES

1. ***The Extensive Legacy of* Griswold.** Some of the Supreme Court's most politically controversial decisions in the last 50 years concern the constitutional right to privacy articulated in *Griswold*. Perhaps most famously, the Court leaned heavily on *Griswold*'s derivation of a constitutional privacy right as the basis for a right to have an abortion in *Roe v. Wade*, 410 U.S. 113, 152–53 (1973). Later cases made many additional refinements in the constitutional law of abortion. *See, e.g.*, *Gonzales v. Carhart*, 550 U.S. 124 (2007); *Planned Parenthood v. Casey*, 505 U.S. 833 (1992). But the core holding of *Roe* itself, finding a right to privacy that extends to abortion, remains in force. Abortion is not the only social issue the Court has examined through the prism of privacy. The Court also relied on privacy when it struck down sodomy laws in *Lawrence v. Texas*, 539 U.S. 558 (2003). But it rejected an effort to overturn bans on assisted suicide based on a right to privacy. *See Washington v. Glucksberg*, 521 U.S. 702 (1997).

2. ***Which Amendment?*** The *Griswold* decision is extraordinarily vague about the precise constitutional source of the right to privacy it enunciates. A separate concurrence, written by Justice Goldberg and signed by Chief Justice Warren and Justice Brennan, suggested that the right to privacy articulated in the majority could be housed in the Ninth Amendment, which reads, "The enumeration in the Constitution, of certain rights, shall not be construed to deny or disparage others retained by the people." The lower court in *Roe v. Wade* also held this view, but more recently it has fallen by the wayside in most constitutional decisions. The *Roe* majority concentrated on the Due Process Clause of the Fourteenth Amendment as the source of the right to privacy first discussed in *Griswold*, thus initiating a body of doctrine often called "substantive due process."

3. ***Home, Family, Sexuality.*** Note how strongly Justice Douglas emphasizes the potential intrusiveness of Connecticut's law on activities within the home. To this familiar privacy argument he adds the sanctity of private family life, particularly marriage. He is less explicit about the impact of the Connecticut law on individuals' sexual life, although that clearly also plays a role in the Court's reasoning. These intuitions do a great deal of the work in the opinion. You will see repeated reliance on the presumptive privacy of home, family, and sexuality throughout your study of privacy law. How well can you articulate the justifications for each?

4. ***The Dark Side of Intimate Privacy.*** Domestic violence advocates long protested that misguided notions about the privacy of marital and sexual relations led law enforcement authorities to disregard or downplay physical abuse by intimate partners. *See, e.g.*, Reva B. Siegel, *'The Rule of Love': Wife Beating as a Prerogative and Privacy*, 105 YALE L.J. 2117 (1996). Increasingly, largely in response to years of activism and education, police officers now intervene in domestic violence situations and prosecutors pursue charges. The shift toward much greater government involvement in this previously "private" setting, right alongside less involvement in matters like contraception and abortion, demonstrates that understandings of privacy tradeoffs are culturally contingent and change with time—potentially in either direction, toward more privacy or less. How does that notion relate to the idea of evolving expectations of privacy under the Fourth Amendment?

## Whalen v. Roe

429 U.S. 589 (1977)

■ MR. JUSTICE STEVENS delivered the opinion of the Court.

The constitutional question presented is whether the State of New York may record, in a centralized computer file, the names and addresses of all persons who have obtained, pursuant to a doctor's prescription, certain drugs for which there is both a lawful and an unlawful market.

The District Court enjoined enforcement of the portions of the New York State Controlled Substances Act of 1972 which require such recording on the ground that they violate appellees' constitutionally protected rights of privacy. We noted probable jurisdiction of the appeal by the Commissioner of Health and now reverse.

Many drugs have both legitimate and illegitimate uses. In response to a concern that such drugs were being diverted into unlawful channels, in 1970 the New York Legislature created a special commission to evaluate the State's drug-control laws. The commission found the existing laws deficient in several respects. There was no effective way to prevent the use of stolen or revised prescriptions, to prevent unscrupulous pharmacists from repeatedly refilling prescriptions, to prevent users from obtaining prescriptions from more than one doctor, or to prevent doctors from over-prescribing, either by authorizing an excessive amount in one prescription or by giving one patient multiple prescriptions. In drafting new legislation to correct such defects, the commission consulted with enforcement officials in California and Illinois where central reporting systems were being used effectively.

The new New York statute classified potentially harmful drugs in five schedules. Drugs, such as heroin, which are highly abused and have no recognized medical use, are in Schedule I; they cannot be prescribed. Schedules II through V include drugs which have a progressively lower potential for abuse but also have a recognized medical use. Our concern is limited to Schedule II which includes the most dangerous of the legitimate drugs.

With an exception for emergencies, the Act requires that all prescriptions for Schedule II drugs be prepared by the physician in triplicate on an official form. The completed form identifies the prescribing physician; the dispensing pharmacy; the drug and dosage; and the name, address, and age of the patient. One copy of the form is retained by the physician, the second by the pharmacist, and the third is forwarded to the New York State Department of Health in Albany. A prescription made on an official form may not exceed a 30-day supply, and may not be refilled.

The District Court found that about 100,000 Schedule II prescription forms are delivered to a receiving room at the Department of Health in Albany each month. They are sorted, coded, and logged and then taken to another room where the data on the forms is recorded on magnetic tapes for processing by a computer. Thereafter, the forms are returned to the receiving room to be retained in a vault for a five-year period and then destroyed as required by the statute. The receiving room is surrounded by a locked wire fence and protected by an alarm system. The computer tapes containing the prescription data are kept in a locked cabinet. When the tapes are used, the computer is run "off-line," which means that no terminal outside of the computer room can read or record any information. Public disclosure of the identity of patients is expressly prohibited by the statute and by a Department of Health regulation. Willful violation of these prohibitions is a crime punishable by up to one year in prison and a $2,000 fine. At the time of trial there were 17 Department of Health employees with access to the files; in addition, there were 24 investigators with authority to investigate cases of overdispensing which might be identified by the computer. Twenty months after the effective date of the Act, the computerized data had only been used in two investigations involving alleged overuse by specific patients.

A few days before the Act became effective, this litigation was commenced by a group of patients regularly receiving prescriptions for Schedule II drugs, by doctors who prescribe such drugs, and by two associations of physicians. After various preliminary proceedings, a three-judge District Court conducted a one-day trial. Appellees offered evidence tending to prove that persons in need of treatment with

Schedule II drugs will from time to time decline such treatment because of their fear that the misuse of the computerized data will cause them to be stigmatized as "drug addicts."

The District Court held that "the doctor-patient relationship intrudes on one of the zones of privacy accorded constitutional protection" and that the patient-identification provisions of the Act invaded this zone with "a needlessly broad sweep," and enjoined enforcement of the provisions of the Act which deal with the reporting of patients' names and addresses.

### I

The New York statute challenged in this case represents a considered attempt to deal with a problem. It is manifestly the product of an orderly and rational legislative decision. It was recommended by a specially appointed commission which held extensive hearings on the proposed legislation, and drew on experience with similar programs in other States. There surely was nothing unreasonable in the assumption that the patient-identification requirement might aid in the enforcement of laws designed to minimize the misuse of dangerous drugs. For the requirement could reasonably be expected to have a deterrent effect on potential violators as well as to aid in the detection or investigation of specific instances of apparent abuse. At the very least, it would seem clear that the State's vital interest in controlling the distribution of dangerous drugs would support a decision to experiment with new techniques for control. If in this case experience teaches that the patient-identification requirement results in the foolish expenditure of funds to acquire a mountain of useless information the legislative process remains available to terminate the unwise experiment. It follows that the legislature's enactment of the patient-identification requirement was a reasonable exercise of New York's broad police powers. The District Court's finding that the necessity for the requirement had not been proved is not, therefore, a sufficient reason for holding the statutory requirement unconstitutional.

### II

Appellees contend that the statute invades a constitutionally protected "zone of privacy." The cases sometimes characterized as protecting "privacy" have in fact involved at least two different kinds of interests. One is the individual interest in avoiding disclosure of personal matters, and another is the interest in independence in making certain kinds of important decisions. Appellees argue that both of these interests are impaired by this statute. The mere existence in readily available form of the information about patients' use of Schedule II drugs creates a genuine concern that the information will become publicly known and that it will adversely affect their reputations. This concern makes some patients reluctant to use, and some doctors reluctant to prescribe, such drugs even when their use is medically indicated. It follows, they argue, that the making of decisions about matters vital to the care of their health is inevitably affected by the statute. Thus, the statute threatens to impair both their interest in the nondisclosure of private information and also their interest in making important decisions independently.

We are persuaded, however, that the New York program does not, on its face, pose a sufficiently grievous threat to either interest to establish a constitutional violation.

Public disclosure of patient information can come about in three ways. Health Department employees may violate the statute by failing, either deliberately or negligently, to maintain proper security. A patient or a doctor may be accused of a violation and the stored data may be offered in evidence in a judicial proceeding. Or, thirdly, a doctor, a pharmacist, or the patient may voluntarily reveal information on a prescription form.

The third possibility existed under the prior law and is entirely unrelated to the existence of the computerized data bank. Neither of the other two possibilities provides a proper ground for attacking the statute as invalid on its face. There is no support in the record, or in the experience of the two States that New York has emulated, for an assumption that the security provisions of the statute will be administered improperly. And the remote possibility that judicial supervision of the evidentiary use of particular items of stored information will provide inadequate protection against unwarranted disclosures is surely not a sufficient reason for invalidating the entire patient-identification program.

Even without public disclosure, it is, of course, true that private information must be disclosed to the authorized employees of the New York Department of Health. Such disclosures, however, are not significantly different from those that were required under the prior law. Nor are they meaningfully distinguishable from a host of other unpleasant invasions of privacy that are associated with many facets of health care. Unquestionably, some individuals' concern for their own privacy may lead them to avoid or to postpone needed medical attention. Nevertheless, disclosures of private medical information to doctors, to hospital personnel, to insurance companies, and to public health agencies are often an essential part of modern medical practice even when the disclosure may reflect unfavorably on the character of the patient. Requiring such disclosures to representatives of the State having responsibility for the health of the community, does not automatically amount to an impermissible invasion of privacy.

Appellees also argue, however, that even if unwarranted disclosures do not actually occur, the knowledge that the information is readily available in a computerized file creates a genuine concern that causes some persons to decline needed medication. The record supports the conclusion that some use of Schedule II drugs has been discouraged by that concern; it also is clear, however, that about 100,000 prescriptions for such drugs were being filled each month prior to the entry of the

District Court's injunction. Clearly, therefore, the statute did not deprive the public of access to the drugs.

Nor can it be said that any individual has been deprived of the right to decide independently, with the advice of his physician, to acquire and to use needed medication. Although the State no doubt could prohibit entirely the use of particular Schedule II drugs, it has not done so.

We hold that neither the immediate nor the threatened impact of the patient-identification requirements in the New York State Controlled Substances Act of 1972 on either the reputation or the independence of patients for whom Schedule II drugs are medically indicated is sufficient to constitute an invasion of any right or liberty protected by the Fourteenth Amendment.

IV

A final word about issues we have not decided. We are not unaware of the threat to privacy implicit in the accumulation of vast amounts of personal information in computerized data banks or other massive government files. The collection of taxes, the distribution of welfare and social security benefits, the supervision of public health, the direction of our Armed Forces, and the enforcement of the criminal laws all require the orderly preservation of great quantities of information, much of which is personal in character and potentially embarrassing or harmful if disclosed. The right to collect and use such data for public purposes is typically accompanied by a concomitant statutory or regulatory duty to avoid unwarranted disclosures. Recognizing that in some circumstances that duty arguably has its roots in the Constitution, nevertheless New York's statutory scheme, and its implementing administrative procedures, evidence a proper concern with, and protection of, the individual's interest in privacy. We therefore need not, and do not, decide any question which might be presented by the unwarranted disclosure of accumulated private data whether intentional or unintentional or by a system that did not contain comparable security provisions. We simply hold that this record does not establish an invasion of any right or liberty protected by the Fourteenth Amendment.

■ MR. JUSTICE BRENNAN, concurring.

I write only to express my understanding of the opinion of the Court, which I join.

The information disclosed by the physician under this program is made available only to a small number of public health officials with a legitimate interest in the information. As the record makes clear, New York has long required doctors to make this information available to its officials on request, and that practice is not challenged here. Such limited reporting requirements in the medical field are familiar and are not generally regarded as an invasion of privacy. Broad dissemination by state officials of such information, however, would clearly implicate constitutionally protected privacy rights, and would presumably be justified only by compelling state interests.

What is more troubling about this scheme, however, is the central computer storage of the data thus collected. Obviously, as the State argues, collection and storage of data by the State that is in itself legitimate is not rendered unconstitutional simply because new technology makes the State's operations more efficient. However, as the example of the Fourth Amendment shows, the Constitution puts limits not only on the type of information the State may gather, but also on the means it may use to gather it. The central storage and easy accessibility of computerized data vastly increase the potential for abuse of that information, and I am not prepared to say that future developments will not demonstrate the necessity of some curb on such technology.

In this case, as the Court's opinion makes clear, the State's carefully designed program includes numerous safeguards intended to forestall the danger of indiscriminate disclosure. Given this serious and, so far as the record shows, successful effort to prevent abuse and limit access to the personal information at issue, I cannot say that the statute's provisions for computer storage, on their face, amount to a deprivation of constitutionally protected privacy interests, any more than the more traditional reporting provisions.

■ MR. JUSTICE STEWART, concurring.

Mr. Justice BRENNAN's concurring opinion states that "[b]road dissemination by state officials of [the information collected by New York State] . . . would clearly implicate constitutionally protected privacy rights. . . ." The only possible support in his opinion for this statement is its earlier reference to two footnotes in the Court's opinion. The footnotes, however, cite to only two Court opinions, and those two cases do not support the proposition advanced by Mr. Justice BRENNAN.

The first case referred to, *Griswold v. Connecticut*, held that a State cannot constitutionally prohibit a married couple from using contraceptives in the privacy of their home. Whatever the ratio decidendi of *Griswold*, it does not recognize a general interest in freedom from disclosure of private information.

The other case referred to, *Stanley v. Georgia*, held that an individual cannot constitutionally be prosecuted for possession of obscene materials in his home. Although *Stanley* makes some reference to privacy rights, the holding there was simply that the First Amendment as made applicable to the States by the Fourteenth protects a person's right to read what he chooses in circumstances where that choice poses no threat to the sensibilities or welfare of others.

Upon the understanding that nothing the Court says today is contrary to the above views, I join its opinion and judgment.

## NOTES

1. ***Is There a Constitutional Right?*** Does *Whalen* determine whether the constitution guarantees a right to data privacy? If so, how broad is it? The majority opinion is vague at best, and the dueling concurrences of Justices Brennan and Stewart complicate this analysis. The Supreme Court itself has never done anything to clarify that fundamental question. In two later cases, it assumed the existence of a constitutional right concerning government information collection, but then held that whatever its scope, any such assumed right was not violated in the situation under review. *See NASA v. Nelson*, 131 S. Ct. 746 (2010) (upholding federal government background checks for private contractors) [see Chapter 11]; *Nixon v. Administrator of Gen. Servs.*, 433 U.S. 425 (1977) (rejecting former President Nixon's assertion of constitutional privacy rights in certain of his communications while in office).

The federal circuit courts are even more indeterminate. Most circuits recognize a constitutional right to information privacy in some form, but its breadth differs significantly from one circuit to the next. While the Third Circuit, for example, applies a multifactor test to *Whalen* claims [see Note 2], the Eighth Circuit views any *Whalen* right very narrowly, *see Cooksey v. Boyer*, 289 F.3d 513 (8th Cir. 2002) (suggesting disclosures "must be either a shocking degradation or an egregious humiliation" to implicate *Whalen*). The D.C. Circuit has expressed "grave doubts as to the existence of a constitutional right of privacy in the nondisclosure of personal information." *AFL–CIO v. Dept. of Housing & Urban Dev.*, 118 F.3d 786 (D.C. Cir. 1997); *see also J.P. v. DeSanti*, 653 F.2d 1080, 1088 (6th Cir. 1981) (criticizing "courts [that] have uncritically picked up that part of *Whalen* pertaining to nondisclosure and have created a rule that the courts must balance a governmental intrusion on this 'right' of privacy against the government's interest in the intrusion.").

2. ***Factors for Evaluation.*** Probably the most fully elaborated recognition of a constitutional right to information privacy comes in the Third Circuit. Courts there consider multiple factors when evaluating challenges to government data collection under the *Whalen*-based right, including:

> the type of record requested, the information it does or might contain, the potential for harm in any subsequent nonconsensual disclosure, the injury from disclosure to the relationship in which the record was generated, the adequacy of safeguards to prevent unauthorized disclosure, the degree of need for access, and whether there is an express statutory mandate, articulated public policy, or other recognizable public interest militating toward access.

*Behar v. Pennsylvania Dept. of Transp.*, 791 F. Supp. 2d 383, 398 (M.D. Pa. 2011) (quoting *United States v. Westinghouse Elec. Corp.*, 638 F.2d 570, 578 (3d Cir. 1980)). If you were a judge sitting in another circuit, would you recommend adoption of this "*Westinghouse* test" by your court?

3. ***Data Security and the Constitution.*** In addition to being amusingly out of date with its references to "magnetic tapes" and its definition of "off-line," the discussion of procedures for the government's handling of prescription data appears central to the Court's holding. There is even less evident concern in the United States Constitution for data *security* than for the broader notion of data *privacy*. How does this Court view their interconnection? If New York had taken fewer security precautions when dealing with the data in *Whalen*, would the outcome have differed? What if the security had been extremely lax? What if there were evidence it had been breached? Might whatever right emerges from *Whalen* amount to a right to have personal data stored by the government securely?

4. ***Drugs.*** How much of the result in *Whalen* was driven by a change in societal and governmental views about the regulation of narcotics? The drugs included in the database at issue in *Whalen* are now considered very serious indeed, including opium and its derivatives, cocaine, and amphetamines. When the case was decided in 1977, attitudes toward such "hard" drugs were pivoting from the permissive 1960s to the widespread "just say no" messages of the 1980s and the beginning of the federal government's "war on drugs." If the database had held information related to some other topic, is it possible the justices might have ruled differently?

5. ***Decisional Privacy and Informational Privacy.*** Until recently, most (though not all) privacy scholars considered the interests protected in cases like *Griswold* and *Roe* quite distinct from core "information privacy" law. The *Whalen* majority echoes this view when it states, "The cases sometimes characterized as protecting 'privacy' have in fact involved at least two different kinds of interests." A minority view, particularly among feminist scholars, always criticized this division. *See, e.g.*, Ruth Gavison, *Privacy and the Limits of Law*, 89 YALE L.J. 421 (1980). More recently, as notions of personal autonomy have become increasingly important in understanding privacy law across the board, the assumption of a binary split between "informational" and "decisional" cases has eroded significantly. In his influential taxonomy of privacy interests, Daniel Solove classifies the latter as a form of privacy he calls "decisional interference." *See* Daniel J. Solove, *A Taxonomy of Privacy*, 154 U. PA. L. REV. 477, 557–62 (2006). In what sense are cases like *Griswold* and *Whalen* both "privacy" cases? In what sense are they distinct from one another? How do they each compare to eavesdropping cases such as *Katz*? Does answering these questions help to derive a workable universal definition of "privacy"? *See* Neil Richards, *The Information Privacy Law Project*, 94 GEO. L.J. 1087, 1105–16 (2006).

## D. OTHER CONSTITUTIONAL SYSTEMS

So far we have considered only cases arising under the United States Constitution. For several major reasons, constitutional cases in other countries often differ significantly from those decided under our federal constitution. The US Constitution is the oldest national written constitution in use today and is among the most difficult to amend. Consequently, it says little about the modern concept of privacy. As we have seen, this means that any protection for privacy must be derived from its other provisions. Most democracies in the world operate under constitutions written within the last 100 years, many of which date from just the last few decades. These more recent documents almost always provide explicit privacy rights. Often these rights are modeled closely on the United Nations' Universal Declaration of Human Rights.

## UNIVERSAL DECLARATION OF HUMAN RIGHTS

### ARTICLE 12

No one shall be subjected to arbitrary interference with his privacy, family, home or correspondence, nor to attacks upon his honour and reputation. Everyone has the right to the protection of the law against such interference or attacks.

## EUROPEAN CONVENTION ON HUMAN RIGHTS

### ARTICLE 8

1. Everyone has the right to respect for his private and family life, his home and his correspondence.

2. There shall be no interference by a public authority with the exercise of this right except such as is in accordance with the law and is necessary in a democratic society in the interests of national security, public safety or the economic well-being of the country, for the prevention of disorder or crime, for the protection of health or morals, or for the protection of the rights and freedoms of others.

## CHARTER OF FUNDAMENTAL RIGHTS OF THE EUROPEAN UNION

### ARTICLES 7 AND 8

**Article 7: Respect for private and family life**

Everyone has the right to respect for his or her private and family life, home and communications.

**Article 8: Protection of personal data**

1. Everyone has the right to the protection of personal data concerning him or her.

2. Such data must be processed fairly for specified purposes and on the basis of the consent of the person concerned or some other legitimate basis laid down by law. Everyone has the right of access to data which has been collected concerning him or her, and the right to have it rectified.

3. Compliance with these rules shall be subject to control by an independent authority.

## Focus

European Constitutional Documents

The complexity of European constitutional law has filled many large books, and cannot be given full treatment here. Every privacy lawyer does need to understand certain basic principles, however. Any company that operates abroad—which, thanks to the internet and expanding conceptions of jurisdiction, could be many companies—needs to pay attention to the "human rights" conception of privacy found in the majority of fully industrialized countries outside the US.

The three constitutional documents excerpted above have overlapping but not identical scope. The Universal Declaration of Human Rights, adopted in 1948 by the newly-created United Nations in the immediate aftermath of World War II, is not a binding treaty with any enforcement mechanism. It is, however, the founding document of international human rights law and a linchpin of customary international law. It profoundly influenced most subsequent constitutions—which is to say, most of those now in effect around the world.

The European Convention on Human Rights, by contrast, is a treaty. It first came into effect in 1953 and was among those heavily influenced by the Declaration. It has now been ratified by 47 European nations (called "contracting states"), including virtually every country on the continent. The Convention created the European Court of Human Rights (ECHR), which sits in Strasbourg, France. An individual, a group, or another country may file an application in that court accusing a contracting state of violating the Convention's human rights guarantees. It is a treaty obligation to implement judgments issued by the ECHR (although there are also nonbinding advisory opinions). ECHR decisions on privacy rights are influential in many national courts both in Europe and on other continents, because so many recent constitutions share the European Convention's lineage tracing back to the Declaration.

Finally, the Charter is a document of the European Union (EU), a distinct multinational organization layered on top of other European institutions. The EU is primarily an economic entity allowing free trade and movement between its 28 member countries. Most EU law is promulgated in the form of "directives" and "regulations," which bear more resemblance to statutes than to constitutional documents. [For more on these, see Chapter 4.] All EU members are also obliged to ratify the Convention, which, along with the jurisprudence of the ECHR, is very influential in EU legislative and judicial processes. The Charter is much newer; it became effective in 2009 under the Treaty of Lisbon. Many of the rights contained in the Charter stem directly from the Convention, and where that is so they are to have the same meaning and scope. Rights guaranteed in the Charter can be enforced through the Court of Justice of the European Union (CJEU), headquartered in Luxembourg.

Review the privacy rights articulated in the Declaration, the Convention, and the Charter. How do they compare to one another? The cases that follow—one decided by the ECHR under the Convention and one by the CJEU under the Charter—illustrate some of the similarities and differences. As you will notice immediately, these decisions also epitomize a European style of judicial drafting rather different from what most American law students typically encounter.

## S. and Marper v. The United Kingdom

[2008] ECHR 1581

1. The case originated in two applications against the United Kingdom of Great Britain and Northern Ireland lodged with the [European Court of Human Rights] under Article 34 of the Convention for the Protection of Human Rights and Fundamental Freedoms ("the Convention") by two British nationals, Mr. S. ("the first applicant") and Mr. Michael Marper ("the second applicant"), on 16 August 2004. The President of the Grand Chamber acceded to the first applicant's request not to have his name disclosed.

3. The applicants complained under Articles 8 and 14 that the authorities had continued to retain their fingerprints and cellular samples and DNA profiles after the criminal proceedings against them had ended with an acquittal or had been discontinued.

9. The applicants were born in 1989 and 1963 respectively and live in Sheffield.

10. The first applicant, Mr. S., was arrested on 19 January 2001 at the age of eleven and charged with attempted robbery. His fingerprints and DNA samples were taken. He was acquitted on 14 June 2001.

11. The second applicant, Mr. Michael Marper, was arrested on 13 March 2001 and charged with harassment of his partner. His fingerprints and DNA samples were taken. Before a pre-trial review took place, he and his partner had become reconciled, and the charge was not pressed. On 11 June 2001, the Crown Prosecution Service served a notice of discontinuance on the applicant's solicitors, and on 14 June the case was formally discontinued.

12. Both applicants asked for their fingerprints and DNA samples to be destroyed, but in both cases the police refused. The applicants applied for judicial review of the police decisions not to destroy the fingerprints and samples. [Appeals in the UK court system, up through the House of Lords, were unsuccessful.]

[The Court described at length the British proceedings, relevant law in the United Kingdom, and relevant European law.]

45. According to the information provided by the parties or otherwise available to the Court, a majority of the Council of Europe member States allow the compulsory taking of fingerprints and cellular samples in the context of criminal proceedings. At least 20 member States make provision for the taking of DNA information and storing it on national data bases or in other forms (Austria, Belgium, the Czech Republic, Denmark, Estonia, Finland, France, Germany, Greece, Hungary, Ireland, Italy, Latvia, Luxembourg, the Netherlands, Norway, Poland, Spain, Sweden and Switzerland). This number is steadily increasing.

46. In most of these countries (including Austria, Belgium, Finland, France, Germany, Hungary, Ireland, Italy, Luxembourg, the Netherlands, Norway, Poland, Spain and Sweden), the taking of DNA information in the context of criminal proceedings is not systematic but limited to some specific circumstances and/or to more serious crimes, notably those punishable by certain terms of imprisonment.

47. The United Kingdom is the only member State expressly to permit the systematic and indefinite retention of DNA profiles and cellular samples of persons who have been acquitted or in respect of whom criminal proceedings have been discontinued.

[The Court then described law and practice in Canada and various international law sources.]

## ALLEGED VIOLATION OF ARTICLE 8 OF THE CONVENTION

58. The applicants complained under Article 8 of the Convention about the retention of their fingerprints, cellular samples and DNA profiles pursuant to section 64 (1A) of the [United Kingdom's] Police and Criminal Evidence Act 1984 ("the PACE").

### A. Existence of an interference with private life

59. The Court will first consider whether the retention by the authorities of the applicants' fingerprints, DNA profiles and cellular samples constitutes an interference in their private life.

#### (a) General principles

66. The Court recalls that the concept of "private life" is a broad term not susceptible to exhaustive definition. It covers the physical and psychological integrity of a person. It can therefore embrace multiple aspects of the person's physical and social identity. Elements such as, for example, gender identification, name and sexual orientation and sexual life fall within the personal sphere protected by Article 8. Beyond a person's name, his or her private and family life may include other means of personal identification and of linking to a family. Information about the person's health is an important element of private life. The Court furthermore considers that an individual's ethnic identity must be regarded as another such element (see in particular Article 6 of the Data Protection Convention which lists personal data revealing racial origin as a special category of data along with other sensitive information about an individual). Article 8 protects in addition a right to personal development, and the right to establish and develop relationships with other human beings and the outside world. The concept of private life moreover includes elements relating to a person's right to their image.

67. The mere storing of data relating to the private life of an individual amounts to an interference within the meaning of Article 8. The subsequent use of the stored information has no bearing on that finding. However, in determining whether the personal information retained by the authorities involves any of the private-life aspects

mentioned above, the Court will have due regard to the specific context in which the information at issue has been recorded and retained, the nature of the records, the way in which these records are used and processed and the results that may be obtained.

**(b) Application of the principles to the present case**

**(i) Cellular samples and DNA profiles**

70. In [*Van der Velden v. The Netherlands*], the Court considered that, given the use to which cellular material in particular could conceivably be put in the future, the systematic retention of that material was sufficiently intrusive to disclose interference with the right to respect for private life. The Government criticised that conclusion on the ground that it speculated on the theoretical future use of samples and that there was no such interference at present.

71. The Court maintains its view that an individual's concern about the possible future use of private information retained by the authorities is legitimate and relevant to a determination of the issue of whether there has been an interference. Indeed, bearing in mind the rapid pace of developments in the field of genetics and information technology, the Court cannot discount the possibility that in the future the private-life interests bound up with genetic information may be adversely affected in novel ways or in a manner which cannot be anticipated with precision today. Accordingly, the Court does not find any sufficient reason to depart from its finding in the *Van der Velden* case.

72. In addition to the highly personal nature of cellular samples, the Court notes that they contain much sensitive information about an individual, including information about his or her health. Moreover, samples contain a unique genetic code of great relevance to both the individual and his relatives.

73. Given the nature and the amount of personal information contained in cellular samples, their retention per se must be regarded as interfering with the right to respect for the private lives of the individuals concerned. That only a limited part of this information is actually extracted or used by the authorities through DNA profiling and that no immediate detriment is caused in a particular case does not change this conclusion.

75. The Court observes that the profiles contain substantial amounts of unique personal data. In the Court's view, the DNA profiles' capacity to provide a means of identifying genetic relationships between individuals is in itself sufficient to conclude that their retention interferes with the right to the private life of the individuals concerned.

76. The Court further notes that it is not disputed by the Government that the processing of DNA profiles allows the authorities to assess the likely ethnic origin of the donor and that such techniques are in fact used in police investigations. The possibility the DNA profiles

create for inferences to be drawn as to ethnic origin makes their retention all the more sensitive and susceptible of affecting the right to private life.

77. In view of the foregoing, the Court concludes that the retention of both cellular samples and DNA profiles discloses an interference with the applicants' right to respect for their private lives, within the meaning of Article 8 § 1 of the Convention.

**(ii) Fingerprints**

78. It is common ground that fingerprints do not contain as much information as either cellular samples or DNA profiles.

[The Court went on to examine prior precedents concerning retention of fingerprints, photographs, and voice samples.]

86. In the instant case, the Court notes furthermore that the applicants' fingerprints were initially taken in criminal proceedings and subsequently recorded on a nationwide database with the aim of being permanently kept and regularly processed by automated means for criminal-identification purposes. It is accepted in this regard that, because of the information they contain, the retention of cellular samples and DNA profiles has a more important impact on private life than the retention of fingerprints. However, the Court considers that, while it may be necessary to distinguish between the taking, use and storage of fingerprints, on the one hand, and samples and profiles, on the other, in determining the question of justification, the retention of fingerprints constitutes an interference with the right to respect for private life.

**B. Justification for the interference**

[The Court summarized the parties' arguments about whether the challenged policies were permitted under paragraph 2 of Article 8 and then turned to its own analysis.]

**(a) In accordance with the law**

95. The Court recalls its well established case-law that the wording "in accordance with the law" requires the impugned measure both to have some basis in domestic law and to be compatible with the rule of law, which is expressly mentioned in the preamble to the Convention and inherent in the object and purpose of Article 8. The law must thus be adequately accessible and foreseeable, that is, formulated with sufficient precision to enable the individual—if need be with appropriate advice—to regulate his conduct. For domestic law to meet these requirements, it must afford adequate legal protection against arbitrariness and accordingly indicate with sufficient clarity the scope of discretion conferred on the competent authorities and the manner of its exercise.

96. The level of precision required of domestic legislation—which cannot in any case provide for every eventuality—depends to a considerable degree on the content of the instrument in question, the field it is designed to cover and the number and status of those to whom it is addressed.

97. The Court agrees with the Government that the retention of the applicants' fingerprint and DNA records had a clear basis in the domestic law. There is also clear evidence that these records are retained in practice save in exceptional circumstances.

98. As regards the conditions attached to and arrangements for the storing and use of this personal information, section 64 [of the UK statute] is far less precise. It provides that retained samples and fingerprints must not be used by any person except for purposes related to the prevention or detection of crime, the investigation of an offence or the conduct of a prosecution.

99. The Court agrees with the applicants that at least the first of these purposes is worded in rather general terms and may give rise to extensive interpretation. It reiterates that it is as essential, in this context, as in telephone tapping, secret surveillance and covert intelligence-gathering, to have clear, detailed rules governing the scope and application of measures, as well as minimum safeguards concerning, inter alia, duration, storage, usage, access of third parties, procedures for preserving the integrity and confidentiality of data and procedures for its destruction, thus providing sufficient guarantees against the risk of abuse and arbitrariness [citing cases]. The Court notes, however, that these questions are in this case closely related to the broader issue of whether the interference was necessary in a democratic society. In view of its analysis in paragraphs 105–126 below, the Court does not find it necessary to decide whether the wording of section 64 meets the "quality of law" requirements within the meaning of Article 8 § 2 of the Convention.

### (b) Legitimate aim

100. The Court agrees with the Government that the retention of fingerprint and DNA information pursues the legitimate purpose of the detection, and therefore, prevention of crime.

### (c) Necessary in a democratic society

#### (i) General principles

101. An interference will be considered "necessary in a democratic society" for a legitimate aim if it answers a "pressing social need" and, in particular, if it is proportionate to the legitimate aim pursued and if the reasons adduced by the national authorities to justify it are "relevant and sufficient." While it is for the national authorities to make the initial assessment in all these respects, the final evaluation of whether the interference is necessary remains subject to review by the Court for conformity with the requirements of the Convention.

102. A margin of appreciation must be left to the competent national authorities in this assessment. The breadth of this margin varies and depends on a number of factors including the nature of the Convention right in issue, its importance for the individual, the nature of the interference and the object pursued by the interference. The margin will

tend to be narrower where the right at stake is crucial to the individual's effective enjoyment of intimate or key rights. Where a particularly important facet of an individual's existence or identity is at stake, the margin allowed to the State will be restricted. Where, however, there is no consensus within the Member States of the Council of Europe, either as to the relative importance of the interest at stake or as to how best to protect it, the margin will be wider.

103. The protection of personal data is of fundamental importance to a person's enjoyment of his or her right to respect for private and family life, as guaranteed by Article 8 of the Convention. The domestic law must afford appropriate safeguards to prevent any such use of personal data as may be inconsistent with the guarantees of this Article. The need for such safeguards is all the greater where the protection of personal data undergoing automatic processing is concerned, not least when such data are used for police purposes. The domestic law should notably ensure that such data are relevant and not excessive in relation to the purposes for which they are stored; and preserved in a form which permits identification of the data subjects for no longer than is required for the purpose for which those data are stored (see Article 5 of the Data Protection Convention and the preamble thereto). The domestic law must also afford adequate guarantees that retained personal data was efficiently protected from misuse and abuse (see notably Article 7 of the Data Protection Convention). The above considerations are especially valid as regards the protection of special categories of more sensitive data (see Article 6 of the Data Protection Convention) and more particularly of DNA information, which contains the person's genetic make-up of great importance to both the person concerned and his or her family.

104. The interests of the data subjects and the community as a whole in protecting the personal data, including fingerprint and DNA information, may be outweighed by the legitimate interest in the prevention of crime (see Article 9 of the Data Protection Convention). However, the intrinsically private character of this information calls for the Court to exercise careful scrutiny of any State measure authorising its retention and use by the authorities without the consent of the person concerned.

**(ii) Application of these principles to the present case**

105. The Court finds it to be beyond dispute that the fight against crime, and in particular against organised crime and terrorism, which is one of the challenges faced by today's European societies, depends to a great extent on the use of modern scientific techniques of investigation and identification.

106. However, while it recognises the importance of such information in the detection of crime, the Court must delimit the scope of its examination. The question is not whether the retention of fingerprints, cellular samples and DNA profiles may in general be regarded as justified under the Convention. The only issue to be

considered by the Court is whether the retention of the fingerprint and DNA data of the applicants, as persons who had been suspected, but not convicted, of certain criminal offences, was justified under Article 8, paragraph 2 of the Convention.

117. While neither the statistics nor the examples provided by the Government in themselves establish that the successful identification and prosecution of offenders could not have been achieved without the permanent and indiscriminate retention of the fingerprint and DNA records of all persons in the applicants' position, the Court accepts that the extension of the database has nonetheless contributed to the detection and prevention of crime.

118. The question, however, remains whether such retention is proportionate and strikes a fair balance between the competing public and private interests.

119. In this respect, the Court is struck by the blanket and indiscriminate nature of the power of retention in England and Wales. The material may be retained irrespective of the nature or gravity of the offence with which the individual was originally suspected or of the age of the suspected offender; fingerprints and samples may be taken—and retained—from a person of any age, arrested in connection with a recordable offence, which includes minor or non-imprisonable offences. The retention is not time-limited; the material is retained indefinitely whatever the nature or seriousness of the offence of which the person was suspected. Moreover, there exist only limited possibilities for an acquitted individual to have the data removed from the nationwide database or the materials destroyed; in particular, there is no provision for independent review of the justification for the retention according to defined criteria, including such factors as the seriousness of the offence, previous arrests, the strength of the suspicion against the person and any other special circumstances.

120. The Court acknowledges that the level of interference with the applicants' right to private life may be different for each of the three different categories of personal data retained. The retention of cellular samples is particularly intrusive given the wealth of genetic and health information contained therein. However, such an indiscriminate and open-ended retention regime as the one in issue calls for careful scrutiny regardless of these differences.

125. In conclusion, the Court finds that the blanket and indiscriminate nature of the powers of retention of the fingerprints, cellular samples and DNA profiles of persons suspected but not convicted of offences, as applied in the case of the present applicants, fails to strike a fair balance between the competing public and private interests and that the respondent State has overstepped any acceptable margin of appreciation in this regard. Accordingly, the retention at issue constitutes a disproportionate interference with the applicants' right to respect for private life and cannot be regarded as necessary in a

democratic society. This conclusion obviates the need for the Court to consider the applicants' criticism regarding the adequacy of certain particular safeguards, such as too broad an access to the personal data concerned and insufficient protection against the misuse or abuse of such data.

126. Accordingly, there has been a violation of Article 8 of the Convention in the present case.

## Digital Rights Ireland Ltd. v. Minister for Communications, Marine and Natural Resources

ECLI:EU:C:2014:238 (2014) (Grand Chamber, CJEU)

1. These requests for a preliminary ruling concern the validity of Directive 2006/24/EC of the European Parliament and of the Council of 15 March 2006 on the retention of data generated or processed in connection with the provision of publicly available electronic communications services or of public communications networks and amending Directive 2002/58/EC.

2. The request made by the High Court (Case C–293/12) concerns proceedings between (i) Digital Rights Ireland Ltd. ("Digital Rights") and (ii) the Minister for Communications, Marine and Natural Resources, the Minister for Justice, Equality and Law Reform, the Commissioner of the Garda Síochána, Ireland and the Attorney General, regarding the legality of national legislative and administrative measures concerning the retention of data relating to electronic communications.

3. The request made by the Verfassungsgerichtshof (Constitutional Court) (Case C–594/12) concerns constitutional actions brought before that court by the Kärntner Landesregierung (Government of the Province of Carinthia) and by Mr. Seitlinger, Mr. Tschohl and 11,128 other applicants regarding the compatibility with the Federal Constitutional Law (Bundes-Verfassungsgesetz) of the law transposing Directive 2006/24 into Austrian national law.

**Consideration of the questions referred**

23. [T]he referring courts are essentially asking the Court to examine the validity of Directive 2006/24 in the light of Articles 7, 8 and 11 of the Charter.

***The relevance of Articles 7, 8 and 11 of the Charter with regard to the question of the validity of Directive 2006/24***

25. The obligation, under Article 3 of Directive 2006/24, on providers of publicly available electronic communications services or of public communications networks to retain data for the purpose of making them accessible, if necessary, to the competent national authorities raises questions relating to respect for private life and communications under Article 7 of the Charter, the protection of personal data under

Article 8 of the Charter and respect for freedom of expression under Article 11 of the Charter.

26. In that regard, it should be observed that the data which providers of publicly available electronic communications services or of public communications networks must retain, pursuant to Articles 3 and 5 of Directive 2006/24, include data necessary to trace and identify the source of a communication and its destination, to identify the date, time, duration and type of a communication, to identify users' communication equipment, and to identify the location of mobile communication equipment, data which consist, inter alia, of the name and address of the subscriber or registered user, the calling telephone number, the number called and an IP address for Internet services. Those data make it possible, in particular, to know the identity of the person with whom a subscriber or registered user has communicated and by what means, and to identify the time of the communication as well as the place from which that communication took place. They also make it possible to know the frequency of the communications of the subscriber or registered user with certain persons during a given period.

27. Those data, taken as a whole, may allow very precise conclusions to be drawn concerning the private lives of the persons whose data has been retained, such as the habits of everyday life, permanent or temporary places of residence, daily or other movements, the activities carried out, the social relationships of those persons and the social environments frequented by them.

28. In such circumstances, even though the directive does not permit the retention of the content of the communication or of information consulted using an electronic communications network, it is not inconceivable that the retention of the data in question might have an effect on the use, by subscribers or registered users, of the means of communication covered by that directive and, consequently, on their exercise of the freedom of expression guaranteed by Article 11 of the Charter.

29. The retention of data for the purpose of possible access to them by the competent national authorities, as provided for by Directive 2006/24, directly and specifically affects private life and, consequently, the rights guaranteed by Article 7 of the Charter. Furthermore, such a retention of data also falls under Article 8 of the Charter because it constitutes the processing of personal data within the meaning of that article and, therefore, necessarily has to satisfy the data protection requirements arising from that article.

***Interference with the rights laid down in Articles 7 and 8 of the Charter***

32. By requiring the retention of the data listed in Article 5(1) of Directive 2006/24 and by allowing the competent national authorities to access those data, Directive 2006/24 derogates from the system of

protection of the right to privacy established by Directives 95/46 and 2002/58 [the Data Protection Directive and a narrower directive concerning privacy in electronic communications networks] with regard to the processing of personal data in the electronic communications sector, directives which provided for the confidentiality of communications and of traffic data as well as the obligation to erase or make those data anonymous where they are no longer needed for the purpose of the transmission of a communication, unless they are necessary for billing purposes and only for as long as so necessary.

33. To establish the existence of an interference with the fundamental right to privacy, it does not matter whether the information on the private lives concerned is sensitive or whether the persons concerned have been inconvenienced in any way.

34. As a result, the obligation imposed by Directive 2006/24 on providers of publicly available electronic communications services or of public communications networks to retain, for a certain period, data relating to a person's private life and to his communications constitutes in itself an interference with the rights guaranteed by Article 7 of the Charter.

35. Furthermore, the access of the competent national authorities to the data constitutes a further interference with that fundamental right. Accordingly, Articles 4 and 8 of Directive 2006/24 laying down rules relating to the access of the competent national authorities to the data also constitute an interference with the rights guaranteed by Article 7 of the Charter.

36. Likewise, Directive 2006/24 constitutes an interference with the fundamental right to the protection of personal data guaranteed by Article 8 of the Charter because it provides for the processing of personal data.

37. It must be stated that the interference caused by Directive 2006/24 with the fundamental rights laid down in Articles 7 and 8 of the Charter is wide-ranging, and it must be considered to be particularly serious. Furthermore, the fact that data are retained and subsequently used without the subscriber or registered user being informed is likely to generate in the minds of the persons concerned the feeling that their private lives are the subject of constant surveillance.

***Justification of the interference with the rights guaranteed by Articles 7 and 8 of the Charter***

42. It is apparent from the case-law of the Court that the fight against international terrorism in order to maintain international peace and security constitutes an objective of general interest. The same is true of the fight against serious crime in order to ensure public security. Furthermore, it should be noted, in this respect, that Article 6 of the Charter lays down the right of any person not only to liberty, but also to security.

44. It must therefore be held that the retention of data for the purpose of allowing the competent national authorities to have possible access to those data, as required by Directive 2006/24, genuinely satisfies an objective of general interest.

45. In those circumstances, it is necessary to verify the proportionality of the interference found to exist.

46. In that regard, according to the settled case-law of the Court, the principle of proportionality requires that acts of the EU institutions be appropriate for attaining the legitimate objectives pursued by the legislation at issue and do not exceed the limits of what is appropriate and necessary in order to achieve those objectives.

48. In the present case, in view of the important role played by the protection of personal data in the light of the fundamental right to respect for private life and the extent and seriousness of the interference with that right caused by Directive 2006/24, the EU legislature's discretion is reduced, with the result that review of that discretion should be strict.

49. As regards the question of whether the retention of data is appropriate for attaining the objective pursued by Directive 2006/24, it must be held that, having regard to the growing importance of means of electronic communication, data which must be retained pursuant to that directive allow the national authorities which are competent for criminal prosecutions to have additional opportunities to shed light on serious crime and, in this respect, they are therefore a valuable tool for criminal investigations. Consequently, the retention of such data may be considered to be appropriate for attaining the objective pursued by that directive.

51. As regards the necessity for the retention of data required by Directive 2006/24, it must be held that the fight against serious crime, in particular against organised crime and terrorism, is indeed of the utmost importance in order to ensure public security and its effectiveness may depend to a great extent on the use of modern investigation techniques. However, such an objective of general interest, however fundamental it may be, does not, in itself, justify a retention measure such as that established by Directive 2006/24 being considered to be necessary for the purpose of that fight.

54. Consequently, the EU legislation in question must lay down clear and precise rules governing the scope and application of the measure in question and imposing minimum safeguards so that the persons whose data have been retained have sufficient guarantees to effectively protect their personal data against the risk of abuse and against any unlawful access and use of that data [citing, *inter alia, Marper*].

55. The need for such safeguards is all the greater where, as laid down in Directive 2006/24, personal data are subjected to automatic

processing and where there is a significant risk of unlawful access to those data [citing, *inter alia, Marper*].

56. As for the question of whether the interference caused by Directive 2006/24 is limited to what is strictly necessary, it should be observed that the directive requires the retention of all traffic data concerning fixed telephony, mobile telephony, Internet access, Internet e-mail and Internet telephony. It therefore applies to all means of electronic communication, the use of which is very widespread and of growing importance in people's everyday lives. Furthermore, the directive covers all subscribers and registered users. It therefore entails an interference with the fundamental rights of practically the entire European population.

57. In this respect, it must be noted, first, that Directive 2006/24 covers, in a generalised manner, all persons and all means of electronic communication as well as all traffic data without any differentiation, limitation or exception being made in the light of the objective of fighting against serious crime.

58. Directive 2006/24 affects, in a comprehensive manner, all persons using electronic communications services, but without the persons whose data are retained being, even indirectly, in a situation which is liable to give rise to criminal prosecutions. It therefore applies even to persons for whom there is no evidence capable of suggesting that their conduct might have a link, even an indirect or remote one, with serious crime. Furthermore, it does not provide for any exception, with the result that it applies even to persons whose communications are subject, according to rules of national law, to the obligation of professional secrecy.

59. Moreover, whilst seeking to contribute to the fight against serious crime, Directive 2006/24 does not require any relationship between the data whose retention is provided for and a threat to public security and, in particular, it is not restricted to a retention in relation (i) to data pertaining to a particular time period and/or a particular geographical zone and/or to a circle of particular persons likely to be involved, in one way or another, in a serious crime, or (ii) to persons who could, for other reasons, contribute, by the retention of their data, to the prevention, detection or prosecution of serious offences.

60. Secondly, not only is there a general absence of limits in Directive 2006/24 but Directive 2006/24 also fails to lay down any objective criterion by which to determine the limits of the access of the competent national authorities to the data and their subsequent use for the purposes of prevention, detection or criminal prosecutions concerning offences that, in view of the extent and seriousness of the interference with the fundamental rights enshrined in Articles 7 and 8 of the Charter, may be considered to be sufficiently serious to justify such an interference. On the contrary, Directive 2006/24 simply refers, in Article

1(1), in a general manner to serious crime, as defined by each Member State in its national law.

61. Furthermore, Directive 2006/24 does not contain substantive and procedural conditions relating to the access of the competent national authorities to the data and to their subsequent use. Article 4 of the directive, which governs the access of those authorities to the data retained, does not expressly provide that that access and the subsequent use of the data in question must be strictly restricted to the purpose of preventing and detecting precisely defined serious offences or of conducting criminal prosecutions relating thereto; it merely provides that each Member State is to define the procedures to be followed and the conditions to be fulfilled in order to gain access to the retained data in accordance with necessity and proportionality requirements.

62. In particular, Directive 2006/24 does not lay down any objective criterion by which the number of persons authorised to access and subsequently use the data retained is limited to what is strictly necessary in the light of the objective pursued. Above all, the access by the competent national authorities to the data retained is not made dependent on a prior review carried out by a court or by an independent administrative body whose decision seeks to limit access to the data and their use to what is strictly necessary for the purpose of attaining the objective pursued and which intervenes following a reasoned request of those authorities submitted within the framework of procedures of prevention, detection or criminal prosecutions. Nor does it lay down a specific obligation on Member States designed to establish such limits.

63. Thirdly, so far as concerns the data retention period, Article 6 of Directive 2006/24 requires that those data be retained for a period of at least six months, without any distinction being made between the categories of data set out in Article 5 of that directive on the basis of their possible usefulness for the purposes of the objective pursued[,] or according to the persons concerned.

64. Furthermore, that period is set at between a minimum of 6 months and a maximum of 24 months, but it is not stated that the determination of the period of retention must be based on objective criteria in order to ensure that it is limited to what is strictly necessary.

65. It follows from the above that Directive 2006/24 does not lay down clear and precise rules governing the extent of the interference with the fundamental rights enshrined in Articles 7 and 8 of the Charter. It must therefore be held that Directive 2006/24 entails a wide-ranging and particularly serious interference with those fundamental rights in the legal order of the EU, without such an interference being precisely circumscribed by provisions to ensure that it is actually limited to what is strictly necessary.

66. Moreover, as far as concerns the rules relating to the security and protection of data retained by providers of publicly available

electronic communications services or of public communications networks, it must be held that Directive 2006/24 does not provide for sufficient safeguards, as required by Article 8 of the Charter, to ensure effective protection of the data retained against the risk of abuse and against any unlawful access and use of that data. In the first place, Article 7 of Directive 2006/24 does not lay down rules which are specific and adapted to (i) the vast quantity of data whose retention is required by that directive, (ii) the sensitive nature of that data and (iii) the risk of unlawful access to that data, rules which would serve, in particular, to govern the protection and security of the data in question in a clear and strict manner in order to ensure their full integrity and confidentiality. Furthermore, a specific obligation on Member States to establish such rules has also not been laid down.

67. Article 7 of Directive 2006/24, read in conjunction with Article 4(1) of Directive 2002/58 and the second subparagraph of Article 17(1) of Directive 95/46, does not ensure that a particularly high level of protection and security is applied by those providers by means of technical and organisational measures, but permits those providers in particular to have regard to economic considerations when determining the level of security which they apply, as regards the costs of implementing security measures. In particular, Directive 2006/24 does not ensure the irreversible destruction of the data at the end of the data retention period.

68. In the second place, it should be added that that directive does not require the data in question to be retained within the European Union, with the result that it cannot be held that the control, explicitly required by Article 8(3) of the Charter, by an independent authority of compliance with the requirements of protection and security, as referred to in the two previous paragraphs, is fully ensured. Such a control, carried out on the basis of EU law, is an essential component of the protection of individuals with regard to the processing of personal data.

69. Having regard to all the foregoing considerations, it must be held that, by adopting Directive 2006/24, the EU legislature has exceeded the limits imposed by compliance with the principle of proportionality in the light of Articles 7, 8 and 52(1) of the Charter.

70. In those circumstances, there is no need to examine the validity of Directive 2006/24 in the light of Article 11 of the Charter.

71. Consequently, Directive 2006/24 is invalid.

## NOTES

1. ***The Limited Role of European Courts.*** In some ways the Convention and the Charter have a more limited role than constitutions in the US. European governance structures must give individual member nations more deference than states enjoy in modern American federalism, for example. The *Marper* court discusses this sliding-scale "margin of

appreciation" in paragraph 102 of the opinion. Nevertheless, the Court's decision in *Marper* is binding on the UK government by virtue of its obligations under the Convention. The result in *Digital Rights Ireland* effectively strikes down an EU directive. Subsequent proceedings in Ireland and Austria will determine whether the data retention rules challenged in each of those countries can be upheld when the government can no longer defend them by arguing that they are required by a binding directive. In each of these cases, however, the national courts will continue to refer to both the Convention and the Charter when determining the scope of privacy rights.

2. ***Positive Liberties.*** The Bill of Rights in the United States Constitution is a charter of negative liberties—prohibitions against certain actions by the government that intrude on individual freedom. Many other constitutions, including the Convention and the Charter, also confer some positive liberties—rights that the government must affirmatively protect, such as rights to housing or education. As we shall see, this understanding affects constitutional privacy rights, because sometimes courts outside the US not only forbid the government from intruding on privacy, but also require the government to have laws against intrusions on one private party's privacy by another private party. For example, in *Von Hannover v. Germany*, 2004–III Eur. Ct. H.R. 294, before the European Court of Human Rights, Princess Caroline of Monaco invoked Article 8 of the European Convention to challenge a magazine's publication of paparazzi photographs of herself and her children. This could never be a constitutional claim in the US, although of course it might be brought as a tort claim [see Chapter 2].

3. ***The Data Protection Convention.*** In addition to the general protection of privacy under Article 8, the *Marper* decision also refers to the Data Protection Convention of 1981, a separate treaty that spells out privacy rights related to personal information in more detail. There are multiple treaties on narrower topics that come into play in privacy-related decisions in Europe—never mind the additional layers of EU and national law.

4. ***The First Invalid Directive.*** The *Digital Rights Ireland* decision marked the first time the CJEU invalidated an EU directive, on any topic, because it was unconstitutional. Here, the unconstitutionality was anchored in the requirements of the EU Charter, but those are so similar to the requirements of the European Convention and other constitutional documents that the analysis likely could have played out the same way. Yet in the past, the CJEU had primarily targeted national law, not EU law. If you were a European official charged with drafting a new directive for data retention that would be consistent with *Digital Rights Ireland*, how would you do so?

5. ***Abstract Analysis and Case-Specific Analysis.*** Compare the reasoning in *Marper* and *Digital Rights Ireland* to US Fourth Amendment cases, like *Katz* and *Jones*. While US cases are grounded in a specific factual setting, cases referred to EU-level courts are often framed as abstract legal analyses, based on the questions posed by national courts. Is one of them structurally superior to the other? Or is the difference based on the nature of political organization on each side of the Atlantic?

Strict scrutiny

6. ***Proportionality and Strict Scrutiny***. In the US, courts often examine laws related to certain suspect classifications such as race under a standard of strict scrutiny. The analysis demands that a law advance a legitimate government interest, that it be narrowly tailored to achieve that interest, and that it be the least restrictive means for doing so. How does the proportionality analysis in *Marper* and *Digital Rights Ireland* compare to strict scrutiny?

7. ***The* Digital Rights Ireland *Decision and the USA Freedom Act.*** In the US, Congress recently established new requirements for retention of many of the same types of data covered by Directive 2006/24 as a key provision of surveillance law reforms. The USA Freedom Act, passed in June 2015, revoked the authority claimed by the National Security Agency and other federal intelligence agencies to collect vast quantities of data about phone calls on an ongoing daily basis. Instead, it required telecommunications companies to make that data available in response to requests authorized by a special foreign intelligence surveillance court. Providers must retain the data for two years. [For more on this statute and the surrounding dispute, see Chapter 9.] Is this exactly the same law *Digital Rights Ireland* struck down for Europe? If not, how does it differ?

---

## Practice

### DNA Databases in Two Constitutional Systems

A recent US Supreme Court decision, *Maryland v. King*, 133 S. Ct. 1958 (2013), upheld a Maryland law concerning the collection and retention of DNA samples from arrestees. The decision described the Maryland law as follows:

> The Act authorizes Maryland law enforcement authorities to collect DNA samples from "an individual who is charged with . . . a crime of violence or an attempt to commit a crime of violence; or . . . burglary or an attempt to commit burglary." Maryland law defines a crime of violence to include murder, rape, first-degree assault, kidnaping, arson, sexual assault, and a variety of other serious crimes. Once taken, a DNA sample may not be processed or placed in a database before the individual is arraigned (unless the individual consents). It is at this point that a judicial officer ensures that there is probable cause to detain the arrestee on a qualifying serious offense. If "all qualifying criminal charges are determined to be unsupported by probable cause . . . the DNA sample shall be immediately destroyed." DNA samples are also destroyed if "a criminal action begun against the individual . . . does not result in a conviction," "the conviction is finally reversed or vacated and no new trial is permitted," or "the individual is granted an unconditional pardon."
>
> The Act also limits the information added to a DNA database and how it may be used. Specifically, "[o]nly DNA records that directly relate to the identification of individuals shall be collected and stored." No purpose other than identification is permissible: "A person may not willfully test a DNA sample for information that does not relate to the identification of individuals as specified in this subtitle." Tests for familial matches are also prohibited. The officers involved in taking and analyzing respondent's DNA sample complied with the Act in all respects.

Based on *Marper*, if England and Wales adopted the Maryland law to replace the PACE system struck down there, would it conform to the European Convention? Conversely, what is your intuition about whether the US Supreme Court would find a system like PACE constitutional under the Fourth Amendment? Civil liberties groups in California have challenged that state's DNA collection program under both the US Constitution and that state's constitutional privacy protection. Both suits remained pending as of this writing in early 2016. *See Haskell v. Harris*, 745 F.3d 1269 (9th Cir. 2014) (en banc) (per curiam) (affirming denial of preliminary injunction and remanding for further proceedings); *People v. Buza*, 342 P.3d 415 (Cal. 2015) (granting review).

---

## CALIFORNIA CONSTITUTION

### ARTICLE I, SECTION 1

All people are by nature free and independent and have inalienable rights. Among these are enjoying and defending life and liberty, acquiring, possessing, and protecting property, and pursuing and obtaining safety, happiness, and privacy.

---

## Focus

### State Constitutional Privacy

The specific reference to "privacy" as an "inalienable right" in the California Constitution was added by a voter initiative in 1972. Since that time, the California Supreme Court has determined that, like most European constitutions, Article I protects a positive liberty and may apply at times to private actors as well as the state. *See, e.g., Hill v. Nat'l Collegiate Athletic Assn.*, 865 P.2d 633, 644 (Cal. 1994) (holding that the intention of voters adopting the initiative was to create a constitutional right of action "against private as well as government entities"). The challenge to DNA testing in California that was mentioned in the previous note relies partly on this provision.

Later decisions have established a three-part test: "The party claiming a violation of the constitutional right of privacy established in article I, section 1 of the California Constitution must establish (1) a legally protected privacy interest, (2) a reasonable expectation of privacy under the circumstances, and (3) a serious invasion of the privacy interest." *Int'l Fed'n of Prof'l & Technical Engineers, Local 21, AFL–CIO v. Superior Court*, 165 P.3d 488, 499 (Cal. 2007). While this test is demanding, there is a significant amount of litigation challenging both public and private information-handling under the constitutional provision.

Nine other states also have specific references to privacy in their constitutions (Alaska, Arizona, Florida, Hawaii, Illinois, Louisiana, Montana, South Carolina, and Washington), although none has extended them to cover private actors as California has done. Many privacy claims brought under these state constitutional provisions are decided in tandem with parallel provisions in the US Constitution.

Other states that do not specifically name privacy in their constitutions have sometimes found that other provisions of their state constitutions exceed the protection of the US Constitution. As noted earlier [see Section B, above], in *Tattered Cover, Inc. v. City of Thornton*, 44 P.3d 1044 (Colo. 2002), the Colorado Supreme Court found that its state constitution barred a search warrant for books purchased by a criminal defendant. New Jersey, meanwhile, has persistently interpreted the third party doctrine narrowly under its state constitution. So, for example, the New Jersey Supreme Court has found that records held by telephone companies and ISPs are presumptively private under the state constitution. *State v. Reid*, 945 A.2d 26 (N.J. 2008); *see also State v. Hunt*, 450 A.2d 952 (N.J. 1982) (rejecting the third party doctrine under the state constitution).

Thus, when evaluating constitutional privacy, it is important not to forget state constitutions—particularly in California, where private entities may find themselves engaged in constitutional litigation unlike any they would encounter elsewhere in the US.

---

## CHAPTER 2

# TORT LAW

From the very beginning of the 20th century until at least the 1960s, torts were the principal law governing the handling of information by private parties. Tort law focuses only on certain aspects of privacy (and, until recently, it virtually ignored information security). But today torts remain fundamental to understanding modern data privacy and security law for two principal reasons. First, even though their importance has declined, tort remedies remain a potential source of liability for every entity that handles personal information. Second, and for our purposes perhaps even more significant, the evolution of tort law, along with the simultaneous development of Fourth Amendment jurisprudence [see Chapter 1], first grappled with many issues that continue to challenge privacy law today. These include questions about the division between public and private spheres, the balance between privacy and free expression, the definition of privacy harms, the duties owed by people and organizations that use personal data, and the law's response to new technology.

## A. FOUNDATIONS

This casebook includes few long excerpts from legal scholarship, but one particular law review article towers over all of data privacy law. In 1890, two prominent young Boston attorneys penned an essay in the *Harvard Law Review* arguing that existing principles of common law provided a remedy for invasions of privacy. One of the authors, Louis Brandeis, went on to be among the greatest Supreme Court justices of the 20th century and wrote numerous landmark opinions. But this article, coauthored with his friend Samuel D. Warren, remains one of his most influential works. According to one study, it is the second-most-cited law review article of all time (behind only R.H. Coase's *The Problem of Social Cost*). *See* Fred R. Shapiro and Michelle Pearse, *The Most-Cited Law Review Articles of All Time*, 110 MICH. L. REV. 1483, 1489 (2012).

The essay is exceptionally well-organized. Almost every paragraph can be boiled down to one clear proposition. As you read, try summarizing each paragraph in one simple phrase. Also consider the reasons for this essay's outsized influence on subsequent development of privacy law. Why were they so influential? And what would Warren and Brandeis think of modern privacy and data protection law?

## Samuel D. Warren and Louis D. Brandeis, *The Right to Privacy*

4 Harv. L. Rev. 193 (1890)

That the individual shall have full protection in person and in property is a principle as old as the common law; but it has been found necessary from time to time to define anew the exact nature and extent of such protection. Political, social, and economic changes entail the recognition of new rights, and the common law, in its eternal youth, grows to meet the demands of society. Thus, in very early times, the law gave a remedy only for physical interference with life and property, for trespasses *vi et armis*. Then the "right to life" served only to protect the subject from battery in its various forms; liberty meant freedom from actual restraint; and the right to property secured to the individual his lands and his cattle. Later, there came a recognition of man's spiritual nature, of his feelings and his intellect. Gradually the scope of these legal rights broadened; and now the right to life has come to mean the right to enjoy life,—the right to be let alone; the right to liberty secures the exercise of extensive civil privileges; and the term "property" has grown to comprise every form of possession—intangible, as well as tangible.

Thus, with the recognition of the legal value of sensations, the protection against actual bodily injury was extended to prohibit mere attempts to do such injury; that is, the putting another in fear of such injury. From the action of battery grew that of assault. Much later there came a qualified protection of the individual against offensive noises and odors, against dust and smoke, and excessive vibration. The law of nuisance was developed. So regard for human emotions soon extended the scope of personal immunity beyond the body of the individual. His reputation, the standing among his fellow-men, was considered, and the law of slander and libel arose. Man's family relations became a part of the legal conception of his life, and the alienation of a wife's affections was held remediable. Similar to the expansion of the right to life was the growth of the legal conception of property. From corporeal property arose the incorporeal rights issuing out of it; and then there opened the wide realm of intangible property, in the products and processes of the mind, as works of literature and art, goodwill, trade secrets, and trademarks.

This development of the law was inevitable. The intense intellectual and emotional life, and the heightening of sensations which came with the advance of civilization, made it clear to men that only a part of the pain, pleasure, and profit of life lay in physical things. Thoughts, emotions, and sensations demanded legal recognition, and the beautiful capacity for growth which characterizes the common law enabled the judges to afford the requisite protection, without the interposition of the legislature.

Recent inventions and business methods call attention to the next step which must be taken for the protection of the person, and for securing to the individual what Judge Cooley calls the right "to be let alone." Instantaneous photographs and newspaper enterprise have invaded the sacred precincts of private and domestic life; and numerous mechanical devices threaten to make good the prediction that "what is whispered in the closet shall be proclaimed from the house-tops." For years there has been a feeling that the law must afford some remedy for the unauthorized circulation of portraits of private persons; and the evil of the invasion of privacy by the newspapers, long keenly felt, has been but recently discussed by an able writer. [T]he question whether our law will recognize and protect the right to privacy in this and in other respects must soon come before our courts for consideration.

Of the desirability—indeed of the necessity—of some such protection, there can, it is believed, be no doubt. The press is overstepping in every direction the obvious bounds of propriety and of decency. Gossip is no longer the resource of the idle and of the vicious, but has become a trade, which is pursued with industry as well as effrontery. To satisfy a prurient taste the details of sexual relations are spread broadcast in the columns of the daily papers. To occupy the indolent, column upon column is filled with idle gossip, which can only be procured by intrusion upon the domestic circle. The intensity and complexity of life, attendant upon advancing civilization, have rendered necessary some retreat from the world, and man, under the refining influence of culture, has become more sensitive to publicity, so that solitude and privacy have become more essential to the individual; but modern enterprise and invention have, through invasions upon his privacy, subjected him to mental pain and distress, far greater than could be inflicted by mere bodily injury. Nor is the harm wrought by such invasions confined to the suffering of those who may be made the subjects of journalistic or other enterprise. In this, as in other branches of commerce, the supply creates the demand. Each crop of unseemly gossip, thus harvested, becomes the seed of more, and, in direct proportion to its circulation, results in a lowering of social standards and of morality. Even gossip apparently harmless, when widely and persistently circulated, is potent for evil. It both belittles and perverts. It belittles by inverting the relative importance of things, thus dwarfing the thoughts and aspirations of a people. When personal gossip attains the dignity of print, and crowds the space available for matters of real interest to the community, what wonder that the ignorant and thoughtless mistake its relative importance. Easy of comprehension, appealing to that weak side of human nature which is never wholly cast down by the misfortunes and frailties of our neighbors, no one can be surprised that it usurps the place of interest in brains capable of other things. Triviality destroys at once robustness of thought and delicacy of feeling. No enthusiasm can flourish, no generous impulse can survive under its blighting influence.

It is our purpose to consider whether the existing law affords a principle which can properly be invoked to protect the privacy of the individual; and, if it does, what the nature and extent of such protection is.

Owing to the nature of the instruments by which privacy is invaded, the injury inflicted bears a superficial resemblance to the wrongs dealt with by the law of slander and of libel, while a legal remedy for such injury seems to involve the treatment of mere wounded feelings, as a substantive cause of action. The principle on which the law of defamation rests, covers, however, a radically-different class of effects from those for which attention is now asked. It deals only with damage to reputation, with the injury done to the individual in his external relations to the community, by lowering him in the estimation of his fellows.

It is not however necessary, in order to sustain the view that the common law recognizes and upholds a principle applicable to cases of invasion of privacy, to invoke the analogy, which is but superficial, to injuries sustained, either by an attack upon reputation or by what [Roman law] called a violation of honor; for the legal doctrines relating to infractions of what is ordinarily termed the common-law right to intellectual and artistic property are, it is believed, but instances and applications of a general right to privacy, which properly understood afford a remedy for the evils under consideration.

The common law secures to each individual the right of determining, ordinarily, to what extent his thoughts, sentiments, and emotions shall be communicated to others. The same protection is accorded to a casual letter or an entry in a diary and to the most valuable poem or essay, to a botch or daub and to a masterpiece. In every such case the individual is entitled to decide whether that which is his shall be given to the public. The right is lost only when the author himself communicates his production to the public,—in other words, publishes it. It is entirely independent of the copyright laws, and their extension into the domain of art. The aim of those statutes is to secure to the author, composer, or artist the entire profits arising from; but the common-law protection enables him to control absolutely the act of publication, and in the exercise of his own discretion, to decide whether there shall be any publication at all. The statutory right is of no value, *unless* there is a publication; the common-law right is lost *as soon as* there is a publication.

What is the nature, the basis, of this right to prevent the publication of manuscripts or works of art? It is stated to be the enforcement of a right of property; and no difficulty arises in accepting this view, so long as we have only to deal with the reproduction of literary and artistic compositions. They certainly possess many of the attributes of ordinary property: they are transferable; they have a value; and publication or reproduction is a use by which that value is realized. But where the value of the production is found not in the right to take the profits arising from publication, but in the peace of mind or the relief afforded by the ability to prevent any publication at all, it is difficult to regard the right as one of property, in the common acceptation of that term.

These considerations lead to the conclusion that the protection afforded to thoughts, sentiments, and emotions, expressed through the medium of writing or of the arts, so far as it consists in preventing publication, is merely an instance of the enforcement of the more general right of the individual to be let alone. It is like the right not to be assaulted or beaten, the right not to be imprisoned, the right not to be maliciously prosecuted, the right not to be defamed. In each of these rights, as indeed in all other rights recognized by the law, there inheres the quality of being owned or possessed—and (as that is the distinguishing attribute of property) there may be some propriety in speaking of those rights as property. But, obviously, they bear little resemblance to what is ordinarily comprehended under that term. The principle which protects personal writings and all other personal productions, not against theft and physical appropriation, but against publication in any form, is in reality not the principle of private property, but that of an inviolate personality.

If we are correct in this conclusion, the existing law affords a principle which may be invoked to protect the privacy of the individual from invasion either by the too enterprising press, the photographer, or the possessor of any other modern device for recording or reproducing scenes or sounds. For the protection afforded is not confined by the authorities to those cases where any particular medium or form of expression has been adopted, nor to products of the intellect. The same protection is afforded to emotions and sensations expressed in a musical composition or other work of art as to a literary composition; and words spoken, a pantomime acted, a sonata performed, is no less entitled to protection than if each had been reduced to writing. The circumstance that a thought or emotion has been recorded in a permanent form renders its identification easier, and hence may be important from the point of view of evidence, but it has no significance as a matter of substantive right. If, then, the decisions indicate a general right to privacy for thoughts, emotions, and sensations, these should receive the same protection, whether expressed in writing, or in conduct, in conversation, in attitudes, or in facial expression.

It should be stated that, in some instances where protection has been afforded against wrongful publication, the jurisdiction has been asserted, not on the ground of property, or at least not wholly on that ground, but upon the ground of an alleged breach of an implied contract or of a trust or confidence.

This process of implying a term in a contract, or of implying a trust (particularly where the contract is written, and where there is no established usage or custom), is nothing more nor less than a judicial declaration that public morality, private justice, and general convenience demand the recognition of such a rule, and that the publication under similar circumstances would be considered an intolerable abuse. So long as these circumstances happen to present a contract upon which such a term can be engrafted by the judicial mind, or to supply relations upon which a trust or confidence can be erected, there may be no objection to working out the desired protection through the doctrines of contract or of trust. But the court can hardly stop there. The narrower doctrine may have satisfied the demands of society at a time when the abuse to be guarded against could rarely have arisen without violating a contract or a special confidence; but now that modern devices afford abundant opportunities for the perpetration of such wrongs without any participation by the injured party, the protection granted by the law must be placed upon a broader foundation. While, for instance, the state of the photographic art was such that one's picture could seldom be taken without his consciously "sitting" for the purpose, the law of contract or of trust might afford the prudent man sufficient safeguards against the improper circulation of his portrait; but since the latest advances in photographic art have rendered it possible to take pictures surreptitiously, the doctrines of contract and of trust are inadequate to support the required protection, and the law of tort must be resorted to. The right of property in its widest sense, including all possession, including all rights and privileges, and hence embracing the right to an inviolate personality, affords alone that broad basis upon which the protection which the individual demands can be rested.

Thus, the courts, in searching for some principle upon which the publication of private letters could be enjoined, naturally came upon the ideas of a breach of confidence, and of an implied contract; but it required little consideration to discern that this doctrine could not afford all the protection required, since it would not support the court in granting a remedy against a stranger; and so the theory of property in the contents of letters was adopted.

A similar groping for the principle upon which a wrongful publication can be enjoined is found in the law of trade secrets. There, injunctions have generally been granted on the theory of a breach of contract, or of an abuse of confidence. It would, of course, rarely happen that any one would be in the possession of a secret unless confidence had been reposed in him. But can it be supposed that the court would hesitate to grant relief against one who had obtained his knowledge by an ordinary trespass,—for instance, by wrongfully looking into a book in which the secret was recorded, or by eavesdropping?

We must therefore conclude that the rights, so protected, whatever their exact nature, are not rights arising from contract or from special trust, but are rights as against the world; and, as above stated, the principle which has been applied to protect these rights is in reality not the principle of private property, unless that word be used in an extended and unusual sense. The principle which protects personal writings and any other productions of the intellect or of the emotions, is the right to privacy, and the law has no new principle to formulate when it extends this protection to the personal appearance, sayings, acts, and to personal relations, domestic or otherwise.

If the invasion of privacy constitutes a legal *injuria*, the elements for demanding redress exist, since already the value of mental suffering, caused by an act wrongful in itself, is recognized as a basis for compensation.

The right of one who has remained a private individual, to prevent his public portraiture, presents the simplest case for such extension; the right to protect one's self from pen portraiture, from a discussion by the press of one's private affairs, would be a more important and far-reaching one. If casual and unimportant statements in a letter, if handiwork, however inartistic and valueless, if possessions of all sorts are protected not only against reproduction, but against description and enumeration, how much more should the acts and sayings of a man in his social and domestic relations be guarded from ruthless publicity. If you may not reproduce a woman's face photographically without her consent, how much less should be tolerated the reproduction of her face, her form, and her actions, by graphic descriptions colored to suit a gross and depraved imagination.

It remains to consider what are the limitations of this right to privacy, and what remedies may be granted for the enforcement of the right. To determine in advance of experience the exact line at which the dignity and convenience of the individual must yield to the demands of the public welfare or of private justice would be a difficult task; but the more general rules are furnished by the legal analogies already developed in the law of slander and libel, and in the law of literary and artistic property.

**1. The right to privacy does not prohibit any publication of matter which is of public or general interest.**

In determining the scope of this rule, aid would be afforded by the analogy, in the law of libel and slander, of cases which deal with the qualified privilege of comment and criticism on matters of public and general interest. There are of course difficulties in applying such a rule; but they are inherent in the subject-matter, and are certainly no greater than those which exist in many other branches of the law,—for instance, in that large class of cases in which the reasonableness or unreasonableness of an act is made the test of liability.

In general, then, the matters of which the publication should be repressed may be described as those which concern the private life, habits, acts, and relations of an individual, and have no legitimate connection with his fitness for a public office which he seeks or for which he is suggested, or for any public or quasi-public position which he seeks or for which he is suggested, and have no legitimate relation to or bearing upon any act done by him in a public or quasi public capacity. The foregoing is not designed as a wholly accurate or exhaustive definition, since that which must ultimately in a vast number of cases become a question of individual judgment and opinion is incapable of such definition; but it is an attempt to indicate broadly the class of matters referred to. Some things all men alike are entitled to keep from popular curiosity, whether in public life or not, while others are only private because the persons concerned have not assumed a position which makes their doings legitimate matters of public investigation.

**2. The right to privacy does not prohibit the communication of any matter, though in its nature private, when the publication is made under circumstances which would render it a privileged communication according to the law of slander and libel.**

Under this rule, the right to privacy is not invaded by any publication made in a court of justice, in legislative bodies, or the committees of those bodies; in municipal assemblies, or the committees of such assemblies, or practically by any communication made in any other public body, municipal or parochial, or in any body quasi public, like the large voluntary associations formed for almost every purpose of benevolence, business, or other general interest; and (at least in many jurisdictions) reports of any such proceedings would in some measure be accorded a like privilege. Nor would the rule prohibit any publication made by one in the discharge of some public or private duty, whether legal or moral, or in conduct of one's own affairs, in matters where his own interest is concerned.

**3. The law would probably not grant any redress for the invasion of privacy by oral publication in the absence of special damage.**

The same reasons exist for distinguishing between oral and written publications of private matters, as is afforded in the law of defamation by the restricted liability for slander as compared with the liability for libel. The injury resulting from such oral communications would ordinarily be so trifling that the law might well, in the interest of free speech, disregard it altogether.

**4. The right to privacy ceases upon the publication of the facts by the individual, or with his consent.**

This is but another application of the rule which has become familiar in the law of literary and artistic property. The cases there decided establish also what should be deemed a publication,—the important principle in this connection being that a private communication or circulation for a restricted purpose is not a publication within the meaning of the law.

**5. The truth of the matter published does not afford a defence.**

Obviously this branch of the law should have no concern with the truth or falsehood of the matters published. It is not for injury to the individual's character that redress or prevention is sought, but for injury to the right of privacy. For the former, the law of slander and libel provides perhaps a sufficient safeguard. The latter implies the right not merely to prevent inaccurate portrayal of private life, but to prevent its being depicted at all.

**6. The absence of "malice" in the publisher does not afford a defence.**

Personal ill-will is not an ingredient of the offence, any more than in an ordinary case of trespass to person or to property. Viewed as a wrong to the individual, this rule is the same pervading the whole law of torts, by which one is held responsible for his intentional acts, even though they are committed with no sinister intent; and viewed as a wrong to society, it is the same principle adopted in a large category of statutory offences.

The remedies for an invasion of the right of privacy are also suggested by those administered in the law of defamation, and in the law of literary and artistic property, namely:—

1. An action of tort for damages in all cases. Even in the absence of special damages, substantial compensation could be allowed for injury to feelings as in the action of slander and libel.

2. An injunction, in perhaps a very limited class of cases.

It would doubtless be desirable that the privacy of the individual should receive the added protection of the criminal law, but for this, legislation would be required. Perhaps it would be deemed proper to bring the criminal liability for such publication within narrower limits; but that the community has an interest in preventing such invasions of privacy, sufficiently strong to justify the introduction of such a remedy, cannot be doubted. Still, the protection of society must come mainly through a recognition of the rights of the individual. Each man is responsible for his own acts and omissions only. If he condones what he reprobates, with a weapon at hand equal to his defence, he is responsible for the results. If he resists, public opinion will rally to his support. Has he then such a weapon? It is believed that the common law provides him with one, forged in the slow fire of the centuries, and to-day fitly tempered to his hand. The common law has always recognized a man's house as his castle, impregnable, often, even to its own officers engaged in the execution of its commands. Shall the courts thus close the front entrance to constituted authority, and open wide the back door to idle or prurient curiosity?

## NOTES

**1.** ***Technological and Social Change.*** At many points in their article, Warren and Brandeis sound very similar to modern observers who blame interlinked technological and social changes for an erosion of privacy. They point especially to the advent of "instantaneous photographs and newspaper enterprise [that] have invaded the sacred precincts of private and domestic life." When they wrote in the late 19th century, photographic technology had advanced so that pictures could be taken with fast, portable cameras, enabling snapshots in addition to the formal posed photographs that previously had required painstaking preparation and cumbersome equipment. Unlike photos of the past, snapshots could be taken without the cooperation of their subject. At the same time, journalism changed. More sensationalistic coverage in the "penny press" aimed at a mass readership, featuring many of those new photographs and a more muckraking tone than the sober newspapers of the past. Do you see similar comments made today about the internet and the rise of blogs and social media?

2. ***The Development of Common Law.*** Carefully read the portions of the article portraying privacy-related torts as a natural next step in the evolution of the common law. By framing their argument skillfully in this historical context, Warren and Brandeis manage to make recognition of privacy claims seem nearly inevitable. As they analyze previously existing claims of various types, they draw the conclusion that, all along, an underlying "right to be let alone" must have supported these claims at least in part. Are they right? Exactly what types of precedents do they rely on to show this progression?

3. ***The Value of "Gossip."*** Warren and Brandeis emphasize a dramatically worded and morally charged argument about the pernicious effect of gossip on its audience:

> Each crop of unseemly gossip, thus harvested, becomes the seed of more, and, in direct proportion to its circulation, results in a lowering of social standards and of morality. . . . Easy of comprehension, appealing to that weak side of human nature which is never wholly cast down by the misfortunes and frailties of our neighbors, no one can be surprised that it usurps the place of interest in brains capable of other things. Triviality destroys at once robustness of thought and delicacy of feeling. No enthusiasm can flourish, no generous impulse can survive under its blighting influence.

Needless to say, their warnings have not exactly proven influential 125 years later, in the era of *Us Weekly* and TMZ. Some commentators opine that Warren and Brandeis were wrong about the merits of gossip. Disclosures that some might call "gossip" can convey useful information and reinforce community values. C. Edwin Baker, an influential First Amendment scholar, argues:

> Formulating, debating, teaching, and changing the norms of social life may be the most important social function of gossip. . . . Additionally, gossip's democratic qualities should not be ignored. The ubiquity of the capacity to gossip and roughly equal distribution of this capacity make gossip an especially significant democratic tool of societal self-constitution.

C. Edwin Baker, *Autonomy and Informational Privacy, Or Gossip: The Central Meaning of the First Amendment*, in FREEDOM OF SPEECH 215, 261–62 (Ellen Frankel Paul et al., eds. 2004).

4. ***Privacy for the Elite?*** Many critics have noted that Warren and Brandeis were up-and-coming Harvard-trained attorneys who belonged to

the Brahmin elite of Boston society. Warren had married the daughter of Thomas Bayard, a prominent United States Senator who had recently served as the Secretary of State. Their social engagements were fodder for the Boston press. To what extent is the authors' real worry that a mass audience now had access to information and images related to members of the upper class? If that is their perspective, does it color their analysis?

5. ***Exceptions.*** How well do Warren and Brandeis define the exceptions to the tort they propose recognizing? One of their exceptions differentiates between oral and written invasions of privacy, based on a similar distinction between the law of libel and slander, which are essentially the written and oral forms of defamation. In modern defamation law, however, there is no longer much meaningful difference between the two. Should alleged invasions of privacy still be treated differently based on whether they are widely published rather than orally delivered to a smaller audience? Why or why not? Similarly, they expend quite a lot of effort discussing the different treatment of persons serving in "public or quasi-public" roles. They offer the straightforward example of a congressman, but as we will see repeatedly throughout this chapter and this book, such lines are not always so easily drawn. Before reading further, consider how you would shape a privacy tort to strike the balance Warren and Brandeis sought.

6. ***Brandeis Through the Years.*** Compare the logic and language here with Justice Brandeis' famous dissent in *Olmstead* [see Chapter 1], written almost 40 years later. How do they compare?

---

## Focus

### Development of the Privacy Torts

The common law right proposed by Warren and Brandeis gained general acceptance rather quickly—at least by the standards of common-law jurisprudential development—but the first milestone in the evolution of the tort was a rejection. In that case, a flour mill had used a woman's photograph in 25,000 posters advertising its wares. New York's highest court acknowledged the Warren and Brandeis article but dismissed the woman's suit:

> Mention of such a right is not to be found in Blackstone, Kent, or any other of the great commentators upon the law; nor, so far as the learning of counsel or the courts in this case have been able to discover, does its existence seem to have been asserted prior to about the year 1890, when it was presented with attractiveness, and no inconsiderable ability, in the *Harvard Law Review*. . . .
>
> The legislative body could very well interfere and arbitrarily provide that no one should be permitted for his own selfish purpose to use the picture or the name of another for advertising purposes without his consent. In such event no embarrassment would result to the general body of the law, for the rule would be applicable only to cases provided for by the statute. The courts, however, being without authority to legislate, are required to decide cases upon principle, and so are necessarily embarrassed by precedents created by an extreme, and therefore unjustifiable, application of an old principle.

*Id.* at 443 *Roberson v. Rochester Folding Box Co.*, 64 N.E. 442, 443 (N.Y. 1902). The decision was quite unpopular among the public, the press, and the Legislature, which soon took the court's invitation and passed a statute creating a private right of action for invasion of privacy. This law remains in force today. *See* N.Y. Civil Rights Law § 51.

The first clear judicial recognition of the tort came from the Georgia Supreme Court in *Pavesich v. New England Life Insurance Co.,* 50 S.E. 68 (Ga. 1905), another case involving the unauthorized use of a plaintiff's photograph in an advertisement. The *Pavesich* court acknowledged the novelty of treating the invasion of privacy as a distinct tort claim, it reviewed Warren and Brandeis and other cases, it critiqued *Roberson*, and it concluded:

> So thoroughly satisfied are we that the law recognizes, within proper limits, as a legal right, the right of privacy, and that the publication of one's picture without his consent by another as an advertisement, for the mere purpose of increasing the profits and gains of the advertiser, is an invasion of this right, that we venture to predict that the day will come that the American bar will marvel that a contrary view was ever entertained by judges of eminence and ability, just as in the present day we stand amazed that . . . Lord Hale, with perfect composure of manner and complete satisfaction of soul, imposed the death penalty for witchcraft upon ignorant and harmless women.

*Id.* at 80–81. In the following decades, courts considered hundreds of suits raising similar claims of invasion of privacy and allowed a cause of action in the large majority of them. The law was fluid, however, and arguably chaotic. Courts examined starkly different factual situations under many of the same principles of "invasion of privacy," whether they involved use of likenesses without permission as in *Roberson* and *Pavesich*, or peeping toms, or disclosures in the press of the sort Warren and Brandeis emphasized.

In the middle of the twentieth century, the great torts scholar William Prosser began cataloging and analyzing these privacy cases as part of his comprehensive treatise on torts. From that work, he published the second-most influential law review article ever written about privacy law, in which he organized the varied theories into four distinct privacy torts, each with their own elements:

> 1. Intrusion upon the plaintiff's seclusion or solitude, or into his private affairs.
>
> 2. Public disclosure of embarrassing private facts about the plaintiff.
>
> 3. Publicity which places the plaintiff in a false light in the public eye.
>
> 4. Appropriation, for the defendant's advantage, of the plaintiff's name or likeness.

William Prosser, *Privacy*, 48 CAL. L. REV. 383 (1960). Prosser then served as the reporter for the second *Restatement of Torts*, which adopted his four-part taxonomy in full. As two important modern privacy scholars summarize it, "Whereas Warren and Brandeis planted the germinal seed for tort privacy, Prosser systematized and organized the law, giving it an order and legitimacy that it had previously lacked." Neil M. Richards & Daniel J. Solove, *Prosser's Privacy Law: A Mixed Legacy*, 98 CAL. L. REV. 1887, 1888 (2010).

After they were codified in the *Restatement*, these four privacy torts became the dominant model. Almost all the states have adopted most or all of the four torts. Those jurisdictions that previously granted relief for invasions of privacy frequently reinterpreted past precedents to line up with the new quadripartite order. As we will see, courts have continued to develop the torts, and in many cases circumscribed them, but always along the paths first laid out by Prosser over 50 years ago.

---

## B. INTRUSION ON SECLUSION

### RESTATEMENT (SECOND) OF TORTS (1977)

### § 652B. INTRUSION UPON SECLUSION

One who intentionally intrudes, physically or otherwise, upon the solitude or seclusion of another or his private affairs or concerns, is subject to liability to the other for invasion of his privacy, if the intrusion would be highly offensive to a reasonable person.

### Plaxico v. Michael

735 So. 2d 1036 (Miss. 1999)

■ SMITH, JUSTICE, for the Court:

Glenn Michael and his wife were divorced. They had one female child who was about six (6) years old at the time of trial. The Chancellor gave custody of the child to Michael's wife in the Divorce Decree. Michael's former wife and child lived in a cabin that had been rented by Michael as the family home prior to their divorce. Plaxico moved into the cabin with Michael's former wife and his child sometime after the divorce.

Michael was later informed that his ex-wife was having a relationship with the Plaintiff, Rita Plaxico. Michael wanted to modify the child custody based on the fact that his former wife and Plaxico were romantically involved with each other.

On[e] night in June, 1993, Michael slipped up to a window in the cabin through which [he] witnessed Plaxico and his former wife having sexual relations. He left to retrieve a camera from his vehicle. After doing so, he returned and took three (3) photographs of Plaxico, who was sitting in bed naked. However, the bed covers covered her from the waist down.

Michael had the photographs developed and delivered the pictures to his attorney. He then, on November 16, 1993, filed for modification of child custody. Michael testified that he did not show the photographs to anyone other than his lawyer. His lawyer produced the photographs to Michael's former wife's attorney in response to discovery requests in the child custody matter pending between Michael and his former wife in which the Chancellor granted Michael the custody of his child. Plaxico became aware of the photographs through Michael's former wife's attorney, who represented both Plaxico and Mrs. Michael.

Plaxico subsequently filed suit for invasion of privacy. She claimed that Michael intentionally intruded upon her seclusion and solitude, and she suffered damages as a result of this tort. She further testified and acknowledged that she and Michael's former wife were lovers and had engaged in sexual relations. Plaxico's complaint and action were dismissed by the Circuit Court of Tippah County, Mississippi, and appealed to this Court.

The trial court's decision will be affirmed unless there is a " 'definite and firm conviction that the court below committed a clear error of judgment in the conclusion it reached upon weighing of relevant factors.' "

[A plaintiff] must meet a heavy burden of showing a substantial interference with his seclusion of a kind that " 'would be highly offensive to the ordinary, reasonable man, as the result of conduct to which the reasonable man would strongly object.' " [quoting Restatement (Second) of Torts, § 652B, cmt. d (1977)]. Further, the plaintiff must show some bad faith or utterly reckless prying to recover on an invasion of privacy cause of action. However, the general rule is that there is no requirement of publication or communication to a third party in cases of intrusion upon a plaintiff's seclusion or solitude.

In the present case, Plaxico did not prove each element of intentional intrusion upon solitude or seclusion of another. Plaxico was in a state of solitude or seclusion in the privacy of her bedroom where she had an expectation of privacy. However, we conclude that a reasonable person would not feel Michael's interference with Plaxico's seclusion was a substantial one that would rise to the level of gross offensiveness as required to prove the sub-tort of intentional intrusion upon seclusion or solitude.

No one would dispute that parents have a predominant and primary interest in the nurture and care of their children. In child custody matters the best interest of the child is the polestar consideration. Here, Michael became concerned about the welfare of his daughter, who was in the custody of his former wife. Michael's former wife subleased a cabin from him, and invited Plaxico to be her roommate. His concern was based on numerous rumors of an illicit lesbian sexual relationship between Plaxico and his former wife. Michael decided that it was not in the best interests of his daughter to allow her to remain in the custody of her mother, and he wanted to obtain custody of the child. It is of no consequence that the mother was having an affair with another woman. She could have been carrying on an illicit affair with a man in the home where the child was, and any father would feel that this too was inappropriate behavior to be carried on in the presence of the child. A modification would still be desired by the parent.

In the present case, Michael did want to file for modification of child custody. However, he had no proof that there actually was [a] lesbian sexual relationship which could be adversely affecting his minor child. In order to obtain such proof, he went to the cabin, peered through the window and took pictures of the two women engaged in sexual conduct. Three pictures were actually developed which were of Plaxico in a naked state from her waist up in her bed. Michael believed that he took these pictures for the sole purpose to protect his minor child. Although these actions were done without Plaxico's consent, this conduct is not highly offensive to the ordinary person which would cause the reasonable person to object. In fact, most reasonable people would feel Michael's actions were justified in order to protect the welfare of his minor child. Therefore, the elements necessary to establish the tort of intentional intrusion upon solitude or seclusion are not present.

Accordingly, we affirm the judgment of the Tippah County Circuit Court.

■ BANKS, JUSTICE, dissenting:

Upon the apparent theory that no reasonable person could believe that the ends do not justify the means[,] in this case the majority opinion improperly concludes that Michael's unreasonably intrusive conduct would not be highly offensive to a reasonable person. I disagree both with the premise and the conclusion. Accordingly, I respectfully dissent.

In my view, peeping into the bedroom window of another is a gross invasion of privacy which may subject one to liability for intentional intrusion upon the solitude or seclusion of that other. *See Candebat v. Flanagan*, 487 So.2d 207, 209–10 (Miss.1986); Restatement (Second) of Torts § 652B cmt. b, illus. 2 (1977) (invasion of privacy would occur if private investigator, seeking evidence for use in a lawsuit, looks into plaintiff's bedroom window with telescope for two weeks and takes intimate photographs).

The trial court found refuge in what it found to be a qualified privilege to see to the best interest of a child. Neither rumors concerning an ex-wife's lifestyle nor a parent's justifiable concern over the best of interests of his child, however, gave Michael license to spy on a person's bedroom, take photographs of her in a semi-nude state and have those photographs developed by third parties and delivered to his attorney thereby exposing them to others. While it is not my view that the publication to others is necessary for tort liability here, I make reference to it to demonstrate the highly offensive nature of the behavior here involved.

In another context, we have observed that "the end does not justify the means. . . . Our society is one of law, not expediency. This message must be repeated at every opportunity." I regret that today's majority here does not follow these worthy ideals.

■ MCRAE, JUSTICE, dissenting:

While the majority did not reach the issue, it impliedly affirms the lower court's finding that Michael had a qualified privilege to take the semi-nude photographs of Plaxico to obtain information helpful to him in his custody battle with his former wife. Ms. Plaxico, the paramour of Michael's ex-wife, however, was not a party to the custody proceedings. As the majority points out, it matters not whether Michael's former wife was involved in a lesbian or a heterosexual relationship. Michaels was not at liberty to peek in the women's bedroom window, an act that can only be characterized as voyeuristic. Nor was he at liberty to take photographs of Plaxico and share them with his attorney. At best, only pictures of his former wife could possibly be characterized as helpful to Michael's case. As to Plaxico, any privilege allowed Michael is misplaced. Accordingly, I dissent.

## Anderson v. Mergenhagen

642 S.E. 2d 105 (Ga. App. 2007)

■ BARNES, CHIEF JUDGE.

Maureen Anderson sued Paul Mergenhagen for stalking, invasion of privacy, and intentional infliction of emotional distress, seeking a restraining order, damages, and fees. For the reasons that follow, we reverse the grant of summary judgment to Mergenhagen on Anderson's invasion of privacy claim.

On appeal we review the trial court's grant of summary judgment de novo to determine whether the evidence, viewed in the light most favorable to the nonmoving party, demonstrates a genuine issue of material fact.

This dispute apparently arose from the campaign of an ex-wife (Karyn Anderson) and her new partner (appellee Mergenhagen) to harass an ex-husband's second wife (appellant Maureen Anderson). The animus between the parties to this suit has its origins in the collapse of Dick Anderson's marriage. After his divorce from his first wife, Karyn Anderson, Dick Anderson learned that he was not the father of the two children born to the couple. Mergenhagen was seeing Karyn Anderson at this time. After Karyn began harassing Dick Anderson's second wife, Maureen Anderson, by driving a car toward her on four occasions, Maureen swore out a warrant for her arrest, after which time Karyn stopped harassing her. Maureen alleges that it was around this time that Mergenhagen began following her.

Though the parties' accounts of their contacts diverge widely in their details, Anderson contends that from early spring 2003 to mid-2005, Mergenhagen followed her on many occasions with increasing frequency, taking pictures, making obscene gestures, and otherwise letting her know he was there. She details at least 15 such occasions, beginning in June 2003, when Mergenhagen followed her in his car, sometimes taking pictures through his windshield, other times pulling alongside her car and taking pictures from his open window. She testified that these events left her frightened, disturbed, distracted, nervous, upset, shaken, and scared. She called the police several times to report that Mergenhagen was following her, and she became frightened all of the time and particularly feared that she would have an accident because he often distracted her while she was driving.

For example, on one occasion in July 2003, Anderson pulled onto Steeplechase Drive to take her children to the community pool when Mergenhagen began following her and taking pictures. Anderson passed the pool entrance and fled down a side road, but Mergenhagen followed her, slowing at each driveway. Anderson turned her car around, and as she drove past Mergenhagen, he rolled down his window to take more pictures, and began laughing. Anderson yelled for him to stop stalking her, and went home shaken, scared, and angry because she "just wanted to go to the pool."

On another occasion in November 2003, Anderson was walking in her neighborhood with her two small children when Mergenhagen drove up alongside them, rolled down his window, and began taking pictures of her. She cut her walk short and took her children home because she was afraid of him. These incidents occurred approximately monthly from June 2003 to July 2004, and several times afterward.

By his own account, Mergenhagen followed Anderson at least four times and took more than 30 pictures of her car. He admits that at least two of these encounters occurred after Anderson sent Mergenhagen a cease-and-desist letter in December 2003. Additionally, the security guard at the entrance to the Andersons' subdivision gave undisputed testimony that Mergenhagen frequently lay in wait for Maureen's car outside the guard house, and that she was "visibly shaken and upset, almost to the point of tears," by one incident.

Anderson contends on appeal that the trial court erred when it granted Mergenhagen's motion for summary judgment on Anderson's invasion of privacy claim. We agree. As far back as 1905, our Supreme Court recognized a right to privacy.

> The right of privacy, or the right of the individual to be let alone, is a personal right, which is not without judicial recognition. It is the complement of the right to the immunity of one's person. The individual has always been entitled to be protected in the exclusive use and enjoyment of that which is his own. The common law regarded his person and property as inviolate, and he has the absolute right to be let alone. The principle is fundamental, and essential in organized society, that every one, in exercising a personal right and in the use of his property, shall respect the rights and properties of others.

*Pavesich v. New England Life. Ins. Co.,* 50 S.E. 68 (Ga. 1905). In 1966, our court adopted the analysis of the tort of "invasion of privacy" as accepted at that time by a number of legal scholars, who had divided that right into four categories.

With regard to the tort of intrusion upon seclusion or solitude, which is the claim made here, the [Georgia] Supreme Court has held that the "unreasonable intrusion" aspect involves a prying or intrusion, which would be offensive or objectionable to a reasonable person, into a person's private concerns. [Previously,] the Georgia Court of Appeals [had] held in several cases that, to state a claim under the "unreasonable intrusion" tort, the plaintiff must allege a physical intrusion which is analogous to a trespass.

The physical intrusion requirement arose for the first time in *Peacock v. Retail Credit Co.,* 302 F. Supp. 418, 422 (N.D. Ga. 1969), aff'd 429 F.2d 31 (5th Cir. 1970). In that case, the plaintiff claimed that the publication of a false credit report constituted the invasion of his privacy by placing him in a false light; by making an unwarranted intrusion into his private affairs; and by making an unwarranted public disclosure of embarrassing private facts about him. The district court reviewed eight Georgia cases, and all of them happened to involve physical intrusions of one sort or another, such as an intrusion into a residence, a hotel room, a hospital room, and a ship stateroom. Thus the district court concluded that the plaintiff had no privacy claim for intrusion into his private affairs because "the Georgia cases require that the intrusion must be physical, analogous to a trespass."

Subsequent Georgia cases have quoted *Peacock's* conclusion that "the intrusion must be physical, analogous to a trespass," but concurrent cases have recognized that this "physical" requirement can be met by showing that the defendant conducted surveillance on the plaintiff or otherwise monitored her activities. "Traditionally, watching or observing a person in a public place is not an intrusion upon one's privacy. However, Georgia courts have held that surveillance of an individual on public thoroughfares, where such surveillance aims to frighten or torment a person, is an unreasonable intrusion upon a person's privacy." *Summers v. Bailey*, 55 F.3d 1564, 1566 (11th Cir. 1995).

In cases holding that public surveillance did not establish a privacy violation, we have found that the surveillance was reasonable in light of the situation. For example, reasonable surveillance of a residence from a public road to investigate a husband's disability claim constituted no intrusion upon his wife's seclusion or solitude, or into her private affairs. *Ellenberg v. Pinkerton's,* 202 S.E.2d 701 (Ga. App. 1973). The surveillance of the husband at his house and on public roads also did not establish a privacy violation.

> Reasonable surveillance is recognized as a common method to obtain evidence to defend a lawsuit. It is only when such is conducted in a vicious or malicious manner not reasonably limited and designated to obtain information needed for the defense of a lawsuit or deliberately calculated to frighten or torment the plaintiff, that the courts will not countenance it.

*Id.* at 701. Additionally, no privacy violation was established by a father's "watching, eavesdropping, and spying" of his children's mother to determine her fitness for custody. *Bodrey v. Cape*, 172 S.E.2d 643 (Ga. App. 1969). On the other hand, when a private investigator investigated a resident who was mistaken for another woman who had filed a workers' compensation claim, we held that "a genuine issue of material fact remains as to whether the investigators' conduct constituted an unreasonable intrusion into Smith's seclusion and private affairs." *Assn. Svcs. v. Smith*, 549 S.E.2d 454 (Ga. App. 2001).

In this case, Anderson alleges that her privacy was violated when Mergenhagen followed her repeatedly in the car and took numerous photographs of her and her car. While the *Restatement (Second) of Torts* suggests that a driver may have no cause of action for mere observation or even for having her photograph taken, a relatively harmless activity can become tortious with repetition, as when, for example, telephone calls "are repeated with such persistence and frequency as to amount to a course of hounding the plaintiff," and becoming "a substantial burden to his existence." Restatement (Second) of Torts, § 652B, cmts. d, c (1977). Similarly, repeatedly following a woman, who was pregnant for part of that time and was frequently alone or with her small children, photographing her at least 40 times, repeatedly causing her to become frightened and upset, to flee to her home, and to call the police seeking help, creates a jury question as to whether the defendant's actions amounted to "a course of hounding the plaintiff" that intruded upon her privacy.

We must therefore conclude that the trial court erred when it granted summary judgment to Mergenhagen on this claim. Georgia law does not require physical intrusion to establish a claim of invasion of privacy.

## NOTES

1. ***Beyond Physical Intrusion.*** Peering in windows, as happened in *Plaxico*, may be the paradigmatic scenario for potential intrusion liability, but the *Mergenhagen* court emphasizes that the concept is broader. How much broader? Would the plaintiff need to prove "vicious or malicious" behavior? Or is that simply all that was required to deny summary judgment on the facts of the case and leave the question to a jury? The degree of seclusion required for the tort raises a "privacy in public" problem that also comes up throughout privacy law, including everywhere from Fourth Amendment cases like *United States v. Jones* [see Chapter 1] to disputes about online privacy. Communications scholar Helen Nissenbaum argues that "privacy in public" should be based on "contextual integrity"—a determination about the social norms of appropriateness of certain information in a particular context and of distribution of that information. People discuss details of their finances with their bank but usually not with social acquaintances, and even before the law required it, banks generally kept that information private anyway. Helen Nissenbaum, PRIVACY IN CONTEXT (2011). How does this approach differ from a "reasonable expectations" test under the Fourth Amendment? Does it help identify what should be "private" under the intrusion tort? Perhaps the tort already incorporates some notion of "contextual integrity" by judging behavior based on its offensiveness.

2. ***Hounding.*** Where is the boundary between legitimate contact and tortiously intrusive "hounding?" The defendant's activities in *Mergenhagen* were enough to avoid summary judgment, but what about the following description of attempts by P & C, a debt collection agency, to contact the widower of a woman who owed $11,154.67 on a credit card when she died?

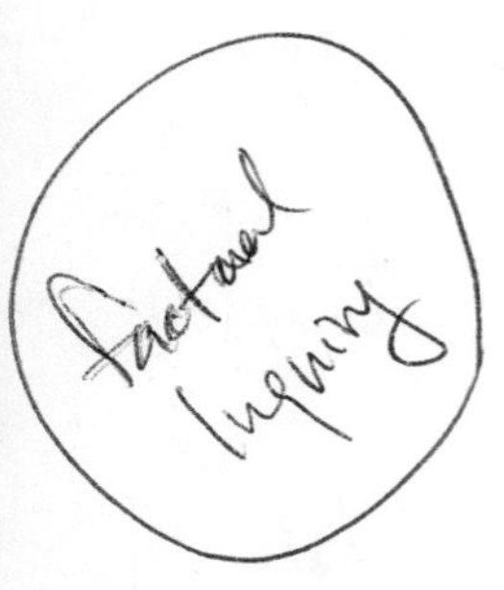

> In this case, the evidence of record indicates that P & C called Mr. Desmond at least fourteen times, eight times during the nine-day period from February 20, 2008 through February 29, 2008, and six times from March 3, 2008 through May 19, 2008. The record shows that P & C sent four letters to the Desmond residence. Those letters were dated February 21, 2008, May 13, 2008, June 16, 2008, and July 3, 2008, and were addressed to "the Estate of Jill C. Desmond." The record indicates that P & C left at least one or two messages on Mr. Desmond's answering machine. [In the remaining instances, P & C did not leave messages, but Mr. Desmond sometimes saw P & C's number on his caller ID.] In addition, a P & C account specialist, Ms. Lohr, spoke to Mr. Desmond on one occasion, after Mr. Desmond sent a cease and desist letter to P & C. Moreover, P & C continued to send letters to the Desmond estate after Mr. Desmond indicated, via letter twice and once via phone, that he wanted to be left alone. Although Mr. Desmond has admitted that Ms. Lohr was polite to him on the phone, did not make any threats to him, and agreed with him that he did not have to pay the outstanding debt, whether P & C's intrusion into Mr. Desmond's privacy, taken as a whole, was substantial or highly offensive to a reasonable person is a question of fact for the jury to decide.

*Desmond v. Phillips & Cohen Associates, Ltd.*, 724 F. Supp. 2d 562 (W.D. Pa. 2010). There are many such intrusion on seclusion cases brought against debt collection agencies, sometimes accompanying other consumer-related claims under state law or the federal Fair Credit Reporting Act [see Chapter 6]. Disputes concerning repeated telephone calls arise frequently. *See, e.g., Joseph v. J.J. Mac Intyre Cos.*, 238 F. Supp. 2d 1158 (N.D. Cal. 2002); *Donnell v. Lara*, 703 S.W. 2d 257 (Tex. App. 1985). The decisions in these cases are split, although many courts refuse summary judgment because the question is highly factual, as happened in *Mergenhagen* and *Desmond*.

Probably the most famous "hounding" case came about when consumer activist Ralph Nader emerged as a well-known critic of automobile safety in the 1960s. A private detective hired by General Motors engaged in a "campaign of intimidation against him" that included tapping his phone, keeping him under constant surveillance, and sending young women to proposition him in the hopes of luring him into a sex scandal. *See Nader v. General Motors Corp.*, 255 N.E. 2d 765 (N.Y. 1970). Nader sued, and the court held that he stated a claim for intrusion upon seclusion under District of Columbia law, in part because the "overzealous" nature of the investigation had the cumulative effect of invading his privacy. GM later settled the case for $425,000, the largest settlement of a privacy tort case at that time.

3. ***Stalking and Other Overlaps.*** Modern statutes against stalking often overlap with the intrusion tort. They also offer additional remedies,

often including an injunction against the stalking behavior and sometimes criminal liability. On the other hand, they are often much narrower than the tort. In *Anderson*, the plaintiff brought another claim under Georgia's stalking statute and sought a restraining order. The statute, OCGA § 16–5–90(a)(1), contained a stringent intent requirement. For "harassing and intimidating behavior" to qualify as unlawful stalking, it needed to be "a knowing and willful course of conduct directed at a specific person which causes emotional distress by placing such person in reasonable fear for such person's safety or the safety of a member of his or her immediate family, by establishing a pattern of harassing and intimidating behavior, and which serves no legitimate purpose." In *Anderson*, the district court determined after a bench trial that the statute was not satisfied. The appeals court, reviewing that decision under an abuse of discretion standard, did not overrule it. Why do you think this mens rea requirement is included in stalking law but not the intrusion tort? Plaintiffs often combine intrusion claims with other causes of action as well. We saw that *Desmond* alleged FCRA violations. Depending on the facts, other claims might, for example, fall under employment law, constitutional law, or other torts such as infliction of emotional distress, assault, or battery.

4. ***Offensiveness and Community Values.*** The "highly offensive" requirement necessarily depends on community values. Do you accept the *Plaxico* majority's contention that the result would be the same even if Michael's ex-wife were engaged in a relationship with a man instead of a woman? Note the 1969 Georgia case cited in *Mergenhagen*, finding no liability for "a father's 'watching, eavesdropping, and spying' of his children's mother to determine her fitness for custody." In that case, the ex-wife had a relationship with a man, not a woman (although the man in question was her former husband's father!). Might a court today, in the era of national same-sex marriage, or then, in a state with less conservative mores about extramarital sexual activity, come out differently than did the *Plaxico* court in Mississippi in 1999? On the other hand, this type of inconsistency also respects local values and it allows for them to change over time. How could a tort defined by what is "highly offensive to a reasonable person" ever be judged other than by consulting local mores?

5. ***Judge or Jury?*** The courts in *Plaxico* and *Mergenhagen* show different amounts of deference to the jury's role in determining liability under the intrusion tort. There are familiar drawbacks to each approach. You might be concerned that the *Plaxico* court imposed its own moral views on the case, rather than drawing on a broader cross-section of the community represented on a jury. You also might be concerned that too deferential an approach would allow frivolous suits to go to trial, or coerce defendants to settle. Some might argue that, if a case like *Desmond* [described above in Note 2] goes to a jury, then it might be impossible to win summary judgment in any intrusion cases. To what extent should intrusion be a jury issue? Is your answer different for different elements of the analysis?

6. ***Restatement Illustrations.*** Courts often use the bare-bones illustrations of the privacy torts from the *Restatement* to support their opinions, as seen in *Mergenhagen*. But these can be extremely pliable. In

*Plaxico*, Justice Banks points to an illustration from the *Restatement* to support his dissenting opinion. Does the majority opinion decline to adopt his reading of the intrusion tort, or does it distinguish the facts of *Plaxico* from those in the *Restatement* illustration?

7. ***Google Street View.*** Google sends cars equipped with cameras down public roads throughout the world to capture images for use in its Street View component of its Google Maps product. Google employs automated technology to blur faces and license plates and considers requests from individuals to further disguise images, even to the point of obscuring an entire house. Is Street View an invasion of privacy? There has been some public discussion of privacy objections to Street View in the United States, but little by way of legal challenge. In one case, a couple sued Google, alleging that images had been captured from their driveway located off an unpaved private road marked clearly with "No Trespassing" signs. A Pennsylvania federal court dismissed the intrusion on seclusion claim because, in order to show that Google's actions were "highly offensive," plaintiffs needed to prove they "could be expected to cause mental suffering, shame, or humiliation to a person of ordinary sensibilities." *Boring v. Google, Inc.*, 598 F. Supp. 2d 695, 700 (W.D. Pa. 2009) (internal quotation omitted). In Germany, by contrast, continuing high-profile court fights about the service eventually led the company to abandon Street View in that country.

8. ***Intrusion and Trespass.*** The same facts often will give rise to potential claims of both the intrusion upon seclusion and trespass torts. Where trespass theories are available, however, they usually will be preferable, especially because the prima facie case for trespass in most states assumes harm merely from the defendant's unauthorized presence without requiring any other showing. As one court explained, that showing usually will not be sufficient for intrusion liability. "Trespassing onto real property, without more, is simply not the form or magnitude of interference into a person's solitude or seclusion that would rise to the level of being highly offensive to a reasonable person, such as might be actionable under" trespass. *Whipps Land & Cattle Co., Inc. v. Level 3 Commc'ns, LLC*, 658 N.W.2d 258, 270 (Neb. 2003). Plaintiffs also pled both theories in the *Boring* case about Google Street View [see Note 7]. Although the district court dismissed both claims, an unpublished appeals court opinion reinstated the trespass claim while affirming dismissal of the intrusion claim. As the appeals court noted, "Of course, it may well be that, when it comes to proving damages from the alleged trespass, the Borings are left to collect one dollar and whatever sense of vindication that may bring, but that is for another day." *Boring v. Google Inc.*, 362 F. App'x 273, 281 (3d Cir. 2010).

9. ***Intrusion and the Third Party Doctrine.*** Just as in the Fourth Amendment context, a person's actions can undermine "seclusion" and thus waive privacy rights. As a result, the tort seldom applies to modern data processing or cloud computing, which typically are conducted with some measure of consent. A representative decision reached this conclusion back in 1995. The case challenged data mining by American Express, which analyzed its credit card customers' shopping patterns and then rented lists

of those with characteristics like "Rodeo Drive Chic" or "Value Oriented." The court rejected an intrusion on seclusion claim:

> The alleged wrongful actions involve the defendants' practice of renting lists that they have compiled from information contained in their own records. By using the American Express card, a cardholder is voluntarily, and necessarily, giving information to defendants that, if analyzed, will reveal a cardholder's spending habits and shopping preferences. We cannot hold that a defendant has committed an unauthorized intrusion by compiling the information voluntarily given to it and then renting its compilation.

*Dwyer v. American Express Co.*, 652 N.E.2d 1351, 1354 (Ill. App. Ct. 1995).

**10. *No Disclosure Necessary.*** The *Plaxico* court notes that intrusion liability does not depend on any further dissemination of information. Indeed, although Plaxico took pictures (and Mergenhagen at least pretended to), there need not even be any recording or gathering of personal information for intrusion liability to attach, if the requirements of solitude and offensiveness are satisfied.

---

## Focus

### Intrusion and the Media

Unlike the tort of publication of private facts [discussed in the next section], there is no element of the intrusion tort that specifically limits liability in matters of public concern. As a result, media defendants are more likely to be liable for intrusion than for disclosure. This tracks the general tendency of free expression doctrine to be more solicitous toward actual speech than toward other behavior, such as gathering information, that facilitates speech.

That said, as *Plaxico* demonstrates, the justification offered for allegedly intrusive behavior can make a big difference to the outcome. Some courts have considered the fact that an intrusion occurred as part of newsgathering when deciding whether it "would be highly offensive to a reasonable person." For example, one California Supreme Court case involved a film crew from a dramatic television documentary series that "rode along" with first responders in a rescue helicopter to the scene of a serious auto accident. *See Shulman v. Group W Productions, Inc.*, 955 P.2d 469 (Cal. 1998). The crew filmed the accident scene and recorded the use of the "jaws of life" to cut the plaintiffs free from the vehicle, the interactions of a nurse with one plaintiff, and the transport of that victim to the hospital by helicopter. The victims sued for intrusion on seclusion, among other claims. The court determined that a reasonable jury could decide the "offensiveness" prong of intrusion either way:

> In deciding . . . whether a reporter's alleged intrusion into private matters (i.e., physical space, conversation or data) is "offensive" and hence actionable as an invasion of privacy, courts must consider the extent to which the intrusion was, under the circumstances, justified by the legitimate motive of gathering the news. Information-collecting techniques that may be highly offensive when done for socially unprotected reasons—for purposes of harassment, blackmail or prurient curiosity, for example—may

> not be offensive to a reasonable person when employed by journalists in pursuit of a socially or politically important story.
>
> The mere fact the intruder was in pursuit of a "story" does not, however, generally justify an otherwise offensive intrusion; offensiveness depends as well on the particular method of investigation used. At one extreme, "'routine reporting techniques,' " such as asking questions of people with information (including those with confidential or restricted information) could rarely, if ever, be deemed an actionable intrusion. At the other extreme, violation of well-established legal areas of physical or sensory privacy—trespass into a home or tapping a personal telephone line, for example—could rarely, if ever, be justified by a reporter's need to get the story. Such acts would be deemed highly offensive even if the information sought was of weighty public concern; they would also be outside any protection the Constitution provides to newsgathering.
>
> Between these extremes lie difficult cases, many involving the use of photographic and electronic recording equipment. Equipment such as hidden cameras and miniature cordless and directional microphones are powerful investigative tools for newsgathering, but may also be used in ways that severely threaten personal privacy. California tort law provides no bright line on this question; each case must be taken on its facts.

*Id.* at 493–94.

Another important consideration is the degree of solitude allegedly invaded. In the classic case of *Dietmann v. Time, Inc.*, 449 F.2d 245 (9th Cir. 1971), for example, two employees of *Life Magazine* visited the home of the plaintiff, a journeyman plumber who offered unlicensed and rather unscientific healing services, which the court described as "simple quackery." The *Life* employees posed as patients and surreptitiously made audio recordings and took photographs with hidden equipment. The magazine later published an article, "Crackdown on Quackery," which discussed the encounter and the plaintiff's later arrest for practicing medicine without a license. The court, emphasizing that the invasion occurred in the plaintiff's den in his home, found an intrusion:

> Plaintiff's den was a sphere from which he could reasonably expect to exclude eavesdropping newsmen. He invited two of defendant's employees to the den. One who invites another to his home or office takes a risk that the visitor may not be what he seems, and that the visitor may repeat all he hears and observes when he leaves. But he does not and should not be required to take the risk that what is heard and seen will be transmitted by photograph or recording, or in our modern world, in full living color and hi-fi to the public at large or to any segment of it that the visitor may select. A different rule could have a most pernicious effect upon the dignity of man and it would surely lead to guarded conversations and conduct where candor is most valued, e.g., in the case of doctors and lawyers.

*Id.* at 249; *see also Sanders v. ABC*, 978 P.2d 67 (Cal. 1999) (finding liability of a reporter who got a job as a telephone psychic and videotaped recordings in the workplace). By contrast, in *Desnick v. ABC*, 44 F.3d 1345 (7th Cir. 1995), in an opinion by Judge Posner [the author of *Haynes*, in the next section], the court found no intrusion by reporters with hidden video cameras posing as patients at an ophthalmology clinic. *Desnick* distinguished *Dietmann* because the encounter occurred in an office not a home, and with a business advertising services for a fee as opposed to private noncommercial quackery. *See also Med. Lab. Mgmt. Consultants v. ABC, Inc.*, 306 F.3d 806 (9th Cir. 2002) (affirming summary judgment for journalists who secretly filmed a supposed business meeting at a commercial medical laboratory).

Paparazzi photographers, whose techniques often satisfy both the offensiveness and seclusion prong, have long been targets of the intrusion tort. For example, former first lady Jacqueline Kennedy Onassis won an injunction in a tort suit against the infamous early paparazzi photographer Ron Galella, who frequently took pictures of Onassis and her children. *Galella v. Onassis*, 487 F.2d 986 (2d Cir. 1973). In 1998, California went outside the parameters of the tort and passed the Anti-Paparazzi Act, Cal. Civ. Code § 1708.8, which included a number of provisions aimed at constraining the paparazzi. As subsequently amended, the statute creates a new ground for liability called "constructive invasion of privacy," which arises:

> when the defendant attempts to capture, in a manner that is offensive to a reasonable person, any type of visual image, sound recording, or other physical impression of the plaintiff engaging in a personal or familial activity under circumstances in which the plaintiff had a reasonable expectation of privacy, through the use of a visual or auditory enhancing device, regardless of whether there is a physical trespass, if this image, sound recording, or other physical impression could not have been achieved without a trespass unless the visual or auditory enhancing device was used.

*Id.* § 1708.8(b). Other provisions include enhanced damages and liability for publishing images or recordings with "actual knowledge" that they were obtained in violation of the Act. Note the multiple conditions for liability woven into this statute. Does it offer more protection than the intrusion tort? The constitutionality of the Anti-Paparazzi Act under the First Amendment remains the subject of some debate but has never been determined by a court. Does the statute offer sufficient protection to newsgathering? Whatever its doctrinal merits, the statute certainly has not prevented the significant growth of paparazzi activity since its 1998 enactment.

---

## C. DISCLOSURE OF PRIVATE FACTS

### Restatement (Second) of Torts (1977)

### § 652D. Publicity Given To Private Life

One who gives publicity to a matter concerning the private life of another is subject to liability to the other for invasion of his privacy, if the matter publicized is of a kind that (a) would be highly offensive to a reasonable person, and (b) is not of legitimate concern to the public.

### 1. "PUBLICITY"

The tort described in § 652D goes by several different names. This book generally calls it the "disclosure" tort. Others sometimes call it the "publicity" or "publication" tort, but those terms have particular narrower meanings, as the next case demonstrates.

## Bodah v. Lakeville Motor Express

663 N.W. 2d 550 (Minn. 2003)

■ ANDERSON, RUSSELL A., JUSTICE.

In this case, the court of appeals reversed the district court's order dismissing, on the pleadings, [a putative class action complaint by employees of Lakeville Motor Express (LME) against their employer]. On review, we consider an issue of first impression: whether allegations in the complaint constitute the requisite "publicity" under Minnesota law to support a claim for publication of private facts, an invasion of privacy tort. We adopt the definition of "publicity" from the Restatement (Second) of Torts § 652D cmt. a (1977). Further, we hold that the complaint does not allege the requisite "publicity" to support a claim for publication of private facts. We reverse.

On January 4, 2001, LME Safety Director William Lowell Frame (Frame) sent a facsimile transmission to the terminal managers of 16 freight terminals. The cover sheet was addressed to "Terminal Managers," not to named individuals, and stated that the purpose of the fax was to allow LME to "keep computer records for terminal accidents-injuries etc." The cover sheet requested that the terminal managers "[p]lease review [the] list for your terminals[;] add or delete accordingly." Attached to the cover sheet was a five-page list of the names and social security numbers of 204 LME employees.

The district court determined that the dissemination did not constitute "publicity" under a claim for publication of private facts and granted LME's motion to dismiss. The court of appeals reversed and remanded, holding that "[a]n actionable situation requires a level of publication that unreasonably exposes the appellant to significant risk of loss under all the circumstances," and concluding that the appropriate consideration includes the nature of the private fact and the harm to which the plaintiff is exposed as a result of the dissemination as well as the breadth of disclosure.

Under the Restatement, "[p]ublicity . . . means that the matter is made public, by communicating it to the public at large, or to so many persons that the matter must be regarded as substantially certain to become one of public knowledge."

[W]e choose not to embrace the court of appeals' approach to defining "publicity." The court of appeals' hybrid approach uses the Restatement's breadth of disclosure analysis but adds as an additional factor "the nature of private data and the damage." Using both factors, the court of appeals fashioned a narrow publicity requirement under the facts of this case: "where the dissemination was not for profit or with malicious intent, [the publicity requirement] ought to be whether [the dissemination] unreasonably exposed appellants to a significant risk that their social security numbers would be misused." We think this definition emasculates the distinction between public and private by suggesting that "publicity" can be established by "either widespread dissemination or improper use." (emphasis added).

Furthermore, by looking to the nature of the private data as part of the "publicity" element, the court blurs the distinction between the "publicity" element and the other elements of the tort of publication of private facts which require that the private data "not [be] of legitimate concern to the public" and that the publicity be "highly offensive." Finally, a lack of reasonableness is neither an element of the invasion of privacy tort of publication of private facts nor part of the publicity analysis. As such, the court of appeals' determination that "[a]n actionable situation requires a level of publication that unreasonably exposes the appellant to significant risk of loss under all the circumstances" inappropriately emphasizes the reasonableness of the defendant's actions.

We also reject the "special relationship" or "particular public" approach taken by some jurisdictions. These jurisdictions have concluded that certain situations—where there is a special relationship between the plaintiff and the public—warrant departure from the Restatement's stringent publicity requirement. *See, e.g., McSurely v. McClellan*, 753 F.2d 88, 112, 113 (D.C. Cir.1985) (holding that publication of private facts "may be satisfied by proof of disclosure to a very limited number of people when a special relationship exists between the plaintiff and the 'public' to whom the information has been disclosed," and concluding that the publicity element was satisfied where the wife's private papers discussing her premarital behavior were disclosed to her spouse); *Miller v. Motorola, Inc.*, 560 N.E.2d 900, 903 (Ill. App. 1990) ("Where a special relationship exists between the plaintiff and the 'public' to whom the information has been disclosed, the disclosure may be just as devastating to the person even though the disclosure was made to a limited number of people. . . . Plaintiff's allegation that her medical condition was disclosed to her fellow employees sufficiently satisfies the requirement that publicity be given to the private fact."); *Beaumont v. Brown*, 257 N.W.2d 522, 531 (Mich. 1977) (holding a disclosure made to a "particular public" with a special relationship to the plaintiff, such as co-workers, family, or neighbors, could be actionable), overruled in part on other grounds by *Bradley v. Saranac Cmt. Sch. Bd. of Educ.*, 565 N.W.2d 650, 658 (Mich. 1997).

We decide, instead, to adopt the Restatement definition of "publicity." We conclude, therefore, that "publicity" means that "the matter is made public, by communicating it to the public at large, or to so many persons that the matter must be regarded as substantially certain to become one of public knowledge." Restatement (Second) of Torts § 652D cmt. a (1977). In doing so, we have considered whether there are legitimate or compelling reasons of public policy that justify imposing liability for egregious but limited disclosures of private information. We conclude, nevertheless, that the Restatement's publicity requirement

best addresses the invasion of privacy cause of action—absent dissemination to the public at large, the claimant's "private persona" has not been violated.

Furthermore, we think the Restatement definition appropriately limits the publication of private facts cause of action. Though much has been written on the subject, we reflect on the concerns of Samuel Warren and Justice Louis Brandeis—"the evil of the invasion of privacy by the newspapers" and "whether our law will recognize and protect the right to privacy in this and in other respects"—and Warren's and Brandeis' recognition of limitations to this right. Samuel D. Warren & Louis D. Brandeis, *The Right to Privacy*, 4 HARV. L. REV. 193, 195, 196, 214–19 (1890). These concerns provided the foundation for all four invasion of privacy torts but resonate particularly with the tort of publication of private facts. William L. Prosser, *Privacy*, 48 CAL. L. REV. 383, 383–89 (1960) (tracing the evolution of the four invasion of privacy torts).

We understand the tort of publication of private facts to focus on a very narrow gap in tort law—to provide a remedy for the truthful but damaging dissemination of private facts, which is nonactionable under defamation rules. The *Restatement*'s definition of "publicity," which requires a broad reach, constrains the tort of publication of private facts.

We turn now to the application of the Restatement's publicity requirement to the instant facts. We conclude that respondents' claim that LME disseminated 204 employees' social security numbers to 16 terminal managers in six states does not constitute publication to the public or to so large a number of persons that the matter must be regarded as substantially certain to become public.

## NOTES

1. ***"General Public" and "Limited Public."*** The *Restatement* definition adopted in *Bodah* represents the majority position, but a significant minority of jurisdictions observe some form of the "particular public" threshold discussed and rejected in *Bodah*. One of leading decisions in this minority explains:

> Communication of embarrassing facts about an individual to a public not concerned with that individual and with whom the individual is not concerned obviously is not a "serious interference" with plaintiff's right to privacy, although it might be "unnecessary" or "unreasonable." An invasion of a plaintiff's right to privacy is important if it exposes private facts to a public whose knowledge of those facts would be embarrassing to the plaintiff. Such a public might be the general public, if the person were a public figure, or a particular public such as fellow employees, club members, church members, family, or neighbors, if the person were not a public figure.

*Beaumont v. Brown*, 257 N.W.2d 522, 530–31 (Mich. 1977). Or, as Robert Post argues, "We often care more about what those within our 'group' think of us than we do about our reputation among the strangers who comprise the general public." Robert C. Post, *The Social Foundations of Privacy: Community and Self in the Common Law Tort*, 55 MD. L. REV. 425, 438 (1996). On the other hand, as the *Bodah* court notes, Warren and Brandeis themselves emphasized broad dissemination and limited their proposed privacy tort in several respects to capture only those situations, including their suggestion that "[t]he injury resulting from . . . oral communications would ordinarily be so trifling that the law might well, in the interest of free speech, disregard it altogether."

2. ***Publicity in New Media.*** How should the *Restatement* publicity requirement, oriented as it is toward traditional mass media like newspapers and broadcasting, judge publicity in new media? An intermediate appellate court in Minnesota, bound by the *Bodah* precedent, considered a case where acquaintances of a clinic patient learned from her medical records that she "had a sexually transmitted disease and a new sex partner other than her husband." They posted the information on the social network MySpace, where it remained visible on an unrestricted page for 24–48 hours, although viewed by "a small number of people." The court held this was sufficient publicity:

> Unlike *Bodah*, where the private information went through a private medium to reach a finite, identifiable group of privately situated recipients, Yath's private information was posted on a public MySpace.com webpage for anyone to view. This Internet communication is materially similar in nature to a newspaper publication or a radio broadcast because upon release it is available to the public at large. That the Internet vastly enlarges both the amount of information publicly available and the number of sources offering information does not erode the reasoning leading us to hold that posting information on a publicly accessible webpage constitutes publicity. If a late-night radio broadcast aired for a few seconds and potentially heard by a few hundred (or by no one) constitutes publicity as a matter of law, a maliciously fashioned webpage posted for one or two days and potentially read by hundreds, thousands, millions (or by no one) also constitutes publicity as a matter of law.

*Yath v. Fairview Clinics, N.P.*, 767 N.W.2d 34, 43 (Minn. App. 2009). Is this a sensible extension of *Restatement* principles? Does the definition of publicity from the *Restatement* need to be reconsidered?

## 2. "PRIVATE MATTERS" AND "HIGHLY OFFENSIVE DISCLOSURES"

## Y.G. and L.G. v. Jewish Hospital of St. Louis

795 S.W.2d 488 (Mo. App. 1990)

■ JOSEPH J. SIMEONE, SENIOR JUDGE.

These proceedings involve the common law tort of an alleged invasion of the privacy of the plaintiffs-appellants, Y.G. and L.G., husband and wife. The trial court dismissed the petition of the plaintiffs. We reverse and remand for further proceedings.

The petition alleged that the wife, L.G., was five months pregnant, bearing triplets "conceived through a medical process known as in vitro fertilization at and under the auspices of [Jewish Hospital]." The hospital had planned to have a "social function" and a "meeting of [the] couples" presently and previously involved in its in vitro program to commemorate the fifth anniversary of the in vitro fertilization program at the hospital. Plaintiffs were invited to this "social gathering" and "meeting." The petition specifically alleged that the hospital "assured" them that no "publicity nor public exposure of persons attending" the function would occur. At the invitation of the Hospital, plaintiffs attended the "function." The plaintiffs alleged that at that "function" a "film and reporting news team of KSDK was present." Plaintiffs were twice requested to give an interview on television film but each time they refused, and made every "reasonable effort" to avoid being filmed or interviewed by the representatives of the electronic media.

[P]laintiffs had [previously] "told no one" about their attempt to procreate, other than Y.G.'s mother. The petition then alleged that "without permission," and after having been denied "express permission, waiver or privilege, KSDK filmed the function and showed it on their television program that evening . . . [that] L.G. [and Y.G.] were present at [the] Hospital's function, . . . and the newscast [although not mentioning their names] told [that they were] expecting triplets by reason of their participation in [the] Hospital's in vitro program."

The petition concluded that the "acts" of defendants [Jewish Hospital and KSDK–TV] constituted an invasion of plaintiffs' privacy. Plaintiffs' identification as parents of triplets conceived through the in vitro program was a private matter in which the public had no legitimate concern. The "acts of defendants damaged Plaintiffs by loss of their privacy, by embarrassment and by ridicule . . . by those who viewed" the news program of KSDK, and that the "acts of defendants were such to bring humiliation or shame to a person of ordinarily sensibilities." Plaintiffs prayed for actual and punitive damages. An affidavit by Y.G. was filed with the petition. The affidavit stated that after the televised broadcast, she received numerous calls, and embarrassing questions and in addition was chastised by her church. The husband's affidavit stated he was ridiculed at work.

The elements of an action for publication of a private matter are (1) publication or "publicity," (2) absent any waiver or privilege, (3) of private matters in which the public has no legitimate concern, (4) so as to bring shame or humiliation to a person of ordinary sensibilities.

The defendants contend that the plaintiffs waived any right to privacy they had by attending the function. As to waiver by attending the function, we hold that there was no waiver. Plaintiffs were assured that the function would be private, they twice refused an interview, and by merely attending the function there was no express voluntary waiver of a known right.

KSDK's motion alleged that appellants waived their right to privacy by attending the party because they disclosed their in vitro program participation to the other attendees. Respondent cites *Gill v. Hearst Publishing Co.*, 253 P. 2d 441 (Cal. 1953), for the proposition that a person photographed while open to public view has no privacy cause of action upon publication of that photograph. The Gill court stated that the photograph of an amorous couple in a public park did not disclose anything which until then had been private but rather only extended knowledge of the particular incident to a somewhat larger public than had actually witnessed it at the time of occurrence. There are numerous cases holding that matters of public record or events taking place in a public location may be publicized without invasion of privacy.

The mere fact that an event takes place where others are present does not waive the right to privacy. Similarly, disclosing private facts to an individual, even a member of the press, is not "consent" to publication since a "selective disclosure" is "based on a judgment as to whether knowledge by that person would be felt to be objectionable."

In the case at bar, the allegations of the petition show that appellants were assured that the persons invited would include only other persons involved in the IVF program, and would not be open to the public or the media. By attending such a function, appellants clearly chose to disclose their participation to only the other in vitro couples. By so attending this limited gathering, they did not waive their right to keep their condition and the process of in vitro private, in respect to the general public.

Defendants contend that the television report would not and did not bring shame or humiliation to an ordinary person. We believe this to be a factual question which the jury should resolve, and which is not appropriate to determine upon a motion to dismiss or upon summary judgment.

Respondents place great emphasis on the fact that a large part of appellants' distress stemmed from their religious affiliations and argue that appellants are extra-sensitive. It is not clear whether a reasonable person would be insensitive [to] disclosure of his participation in the program. The implications of this participation, and the physical problems which exist with the couple's reproductive systems or that they are incapable of performing sexually, are matters that could embarrass a reasonable person, and such matters should be left for a factual determination.

■ CARL R. GAERTNER, PRESIDING JUDGE, dissenting.

[L]iability for publication of private matters is dependent not upon the subjective view of the individual, but rather upon the more objective standard of reasonableness. This objective standard, in my opinion, encompasses each of the elements under consideration: the reasonableness of plaintiffs' expectation of privacy, the reasonableness of defendants' awareness that publication would be highly offensive, the reasonableness of defendants' belief the matter is of legitimate concern to the public. Is it reasonable for plaintiffs to volunteer for participation in the In Vitro Fertilization Project, a matter of widespread, international publicity, without recognition of the likelihood of disclosure? Is it reasonable for plaintiffs to accept the invitation to attend the five-year celebration of the program without awareness that their participation would be made known to all those in attendance as well as all who observe them entering and leaving the gathering? Is it reasonable for plaintiffs to maintain an expectation of privacy when, after seeing the cameras and refusing to be interviewed, they remain in the midst of the group of approximately forty people who were all being filmed without objection rather than stepping to the side of the room until the camera was lowered? In my opinion, each question, viewed individually and certainly when considered collectively, requires a negative answer. I do not believe reasonable minds could avoid concluding that by their conduct plaintiffs waived any right of privacy they may have subjectively desired.

## NOTES

1. ***Elements of the Tort.*** Notice that the *Jewish Hospital* court organizes and states the elements of the disclosure tort rather differently than the Restatement does. That is because Missouri courts first adopted a tort for invasion of privacy in 1911, decades before Prosser's work. *See Munden v. Harris*, 134 S.W. 1076 (Mo. App. 1911). Minnesota, by contrast, did not adopt any of the privacy torts until decades after the Restatement and its courts generally adhere to the Restatement structure, as demonstrated in *Bodah*. *See Lake v. Wal-Mart Stores, Inc.*, 582 N.W.2d 231 (Minn. 1998) (first adopting privacy torts). While the Restatement has been broadly influential in the elaboration of all the privacy torts, many states have developed their own variations, so it can be important to know the particulars of state law.

2. ***Seclusion Redux.*** The disclosure tort requires that the information revealed was "private." In *Jewish Hospital*, the court discusses the famous *Gill* case holding that activity visible in public cannot meet this requirement. It also includes the following string cite of other cases so holding:

> *Machleder v. Diaz*, 801 F.2d 46, 59 (2nd Cir. 1986) (business man filmed outside his office building, on privately owned property, but no signs asking public to keep out); *Intern. Union v. Garner*, 601 F. Supp. 187 (M.D. Tenn. 1985) (no invasion of privacy right where police merely observed persons arriving at union meeting and reported identities to employer); *Jackson v. Playboy Enterprises, Inc.*, 574 F. Supp. 10, 13–14 (S.D. Ohio 1983) (plaintiff photographed on public street); *Neff v. Time, Inc.*, 406 F. Supp. 858,

861 (W.D. Pa. 1976) (plaintiff photographed at football game); *Jaubert v. Crowley Post-Signed, Inc.*, 375 So. 2d 1386, 1387 (La. 1979) (plaintiff photographed at residence from middle of street); *Cefalu v. Globe Newspaper Co.*, 391 N.E.2d 935, 939 (Mass. App. 1979) [photograph of people lined up at a government office to apply for unemployment benefits].

How does the *Jewish Hospital* majority distinguish all these cases? Compare this issue of "privacy in public" to the question of "seclusion" under the intrusion tort.

3. ***Reasonableness, Social Context, and Eggshell Plaintiffs.*** How should courts decide if a disclosure "would be highly offensive to a reasonable person," as the *Restatement* puts it? Is the dissent right that answers to the reasonableness inquiries can be made on a motion to dismiss or summary judgment, or is the majority correct to reserve those decisions for a jury? Relatedly, how should courts define the social context from which reasonableness is determined? Many parents might choose to announce proudly that their child was conceived through assisted reproductive technology like in vitro fertilization, while others might consider this information deeply private and stigmatizing. The passage of time also matters: IVF was still quite new and rare in 1988 when the social function in *Jewish Hospital* occurred, but a recent study estimated that more than five million births have now resulted from IVF procedures. Would this change the "offensiveness" ruling if the case occurred today? Finally, the disclosure may be particularly embarrassing or disruptive for a certain plaintiff—as with the plaintiffs in *Jewish Hospital*, whose use of assisted reproductive technology apparently was criticized by other adherents of their religion. Should they be handled like "eggshell plaintiffs" in traditional tort law, whose atypically significant damages fall on the defendant? Or do emotional harms like privacy infractions require a different approach?

4. ***Social Network Analysis.*** Lior Strahilevitz proposes drawing on social science research to improve the determination about whether information qualifies as "private" in tort cases. Long before social media platforms popularized the term, a large amount of empirical research studied individuals' "social networks" and the factors that shaped them. According to Strahilevitz, by looking at the structure of an individual's interpersonal connections and the nature of the information (particularly whether it is complex, salient, and interesting), a sociologist can make reasonably good predictions about how far that information will likely spread after an initial disclosure. This empirical measure could then help a court to evaluate the plaintiff's actions. Lior Jacob Strahilevitz, *A Social Networks Theory of Privacy*, 72 U. CHI. L. REV. 919 (2005). Would that approach be better than the ones employed by the majority and dissent in *Jewish Hospital*?

### 3. THE NEWSWORTHINESS TEST

The *Restatement*'s requirement that disclosed information "is not of legitimate concern to the public" has come to be called the "newsworthiness" test. This exception, descended from concerns about free speech voiced by Warren and Brandeis in their original article, can reduce the prospect of a clash between the First Amendment and the enforcement of tort liability, but the devil is in the details. In defining legitimate concerns, the *Restatement*'s comments distinguish "information to which the public is entitled" from "morbid and sensational prying into private lives for its own sake." Can courts make this judgment and maintain the neutrality demanded by the First Amendment? Consider how Judge Posner navigates that boundary in the following case.

## Haynes v. Alfred A. Knopf, Inc.

8 F.3d 1222 (7th Cir. 1993)

■ POSNER, CHIEF JUDGE.

Luther Haynes and his wife, Dorothy Haynes née Johnson, appeal from the dismissal on the defendants' motion for summary judgment of their suit against Nicholas Lemann, the author of a highly praised, best-selling book of social and political history called *The Promised Land: The Great Black Migration and How It Changed America* (1991), and Alfred A. Knopf, Inc., the book's publisher. The plaintiffs claim that the book libels Luther Haynes and invades both plaintiffs' right of privacy.

Between 1940 and 1970, five million blacks moved from impoverished rural areas in the South to the cities of the North in search of a better life. *The Promised Land* is a history of the migration. It is not history as a professional historian, a demographer, or a social scientist would write it. Lemann is none of these. He is a journalist and has written a journalistic history, in which the focus is on individuals whether powerful or representative. In the former group are the politicians who invented, executed, or exploited the "Great Society" programs. In the latter are a handful of the actual migrants. Foremost among these is Ruby Lee Daniels. Her story is the spine of the book. We are introduced to her on page 7; we take leave of her on page 346, within a few pages of the end of the text of the book.

When we meet her, it is the early 1940s and she is a young woman picking cotton on a plantation in Clarksdale, Mississippi. Glowing reports from an aunt who had moved to Chicago persuaded Ruby Daniels to move there in 1946. Luther Haynes, born in 1924 or 1925, a sharecropper from Mississippi, had moved to Chicago in an effort to effect a reconciliation with his wife. The effort had failed. When he met Ruby Daniels he had a well-paying job in an awning factory. They lived together, and had children. But then "Luther began to drink too much. When he drank he got mean, and he and Ruby would get into ferocious quarrels. He was still working, but he wasn't always bringing his paycheck home." Ruby got work as a maid. They moved to a poorer part of the city. The relationship went downhill. "It got to the point where [Luther] would go out on Friday evenings after picking up his paycheck, and Ruby would hope he wouldn't come home, because she knew he would be drunk. On the Friday evenings when he did come home—over the years Ruby developed a devastating imitation of Luther, and could re-create the scene quite vividly—he would walk into the apartment, put on a record and turn up the volume, and saunter into their bedroom, a bottle in one hand and a cigarette in the other, in the mood for love. On one such night, Ruby's last child, Kevin, was conceived. Kevin always had something wrong with him—he was very moody, he was scrawny, and he had a severe speech impediment. Ruby was never able to find out exactly what the problem was, but she blamed it on Luther; all that alcohol must have gotten into his sperm, she said."

Ruby was on public aid, but was cut off when social workers discovered she had a man in the house. She got a night job. Luther was supposed to stay with the children while she was at work, especially since they lived in a dangerous neighborhood; but often when she came home, at 3:00 a.m. or so, she would "find the older children awake, and when she would ask them if Luther had been there, the answer would be, 'No, ma'am.'" Ruby's last aid check, arriving providentially after she had been cut off, enabled the couple to buy a modest house on contract—it "was, by a wide margin, the best place she had ever lived." But "after only a few months, Luther ruined everything by going out and buying a brand-new 1961 Pontiac. It meant more to him than the house did, and when they couldn't make the house payment, he insisted on keeping the car" even though she hadn't enough money to buy shoes for the children. The family was kicked out of the house. They now moved frequently. They were reaching rock bottom. At this nadir, hope appeared in the ironic form of the Robert Taylor Homes, then a brand-new public housing project, now a notorious focus of drug addiction and gang violence. Ruby had had an application for public housing on file for many years, but the housing authority screened out unwed mothers. Told by a social worker that she could have an apartment in the Taylor Homes if she produced a marriage license, she and Luther (who was now divorced from his first wife) were married forthwith and promptly accepted as tenants.

Meanwhile Luther had lost his job in the awning factory "that he had had for a decade, and then bounced around a little. He lost jobs because of transportation problems, because of layoffs, because of a bout of serious illness, because of his drinking, because he had a minor criminal record (having been in jail for disorderly conduct following a fight with Ruby), and because creditors were after him." He resumed "his old habit of not returning from work on Fridays after he got his paycheck." One weekend he didn't come home at all. In a search of his things Ruby discovered evidence that Luther was having an affair with Dorothy Johnson, a former neighbor. "Luther was not being particularly careful; he saw in Dorothy, who was younger than Ruby, who had three children compared to Ruby's eight, who had a job while Ruby was on public aid, the promise of an escape from the ghetto, and he was entranced." The children discovered the affair. [One of Ruby's sons] tried to strangle Luther. In 1965 Luther moved out permanently, and eventually he and Ruby divorced.

After divorcing Ruby, Luther Haynes married Dorothy Johnson. He is still married to her, "owns a home on the far South Side of Chicago, and has worked for years as a parking-lot attendant; only recently have he and Ruby found that they can speak civilly to each other on the phone."

There is much more to the book than our paraphrase and excerpts—much about other migrants, about the travails of Ruby's children, about discrimination against blacks in both the North and the South, and about the politics of poverty programs in Washington and Chicago. But the excerpts we have quoted contain all the passages upon which the Hayneses' lawsuit is founded.

Even people who have nothing rationally to be ashamed of can be mortified by the publication of intimate details of their life. Most people in no wise deformed or disfigured would nevertheless be deeply upset if nude photographs of themselves were published in a newspaper or a book. They feel the same way about photographs of their sexual activities, however "normal," or about a narrative of those activities, or about having their medical records publicized. Although it is well known that every human being defecates, no adult human being in our society wants a newspaper to show a picture of him defecating. The desire for privacy illustrated by these examples is a mysterious but deep fact about human personality. It deserves and in our society receives legal protection.

But this is not the character of the depictions of the Hayneses in *The Promised Land*. Although the plaintiffs claim that the book depicts their "sex life" and "ridicules" Luther Haynes's lovemaking (the reference is to the passage we quoted in which the author refers to Ruby's "devastating imitation" of Luther's manner when he would come home Friday nights in an amorous mood), these characterizations are misleading. No sexual act is described in the book. No intimate details are revealed. Entering one's bedroom with a bottle in one hand and a cigarette in the other is not foreplay. Ruby's speculation that Kevin's problems may have been due to Luther's having been a heavy drinker is not the narration of a sexual act.

The branch of privacy law that the Hayneses invoke in their appeal is not concerned with, and is not a proper surrogate for legal doctrines that are concerned with, the accuracy of the private facts revealed. It is concerned with the propriety of stripping away the veil of privacy with which we cover the embarrassing, the shameful, the tabooed, truths about us. The revelations in the book are not about the intimate details of the Hayneses' life. They are about misconduct, in particular Luther's. (There is very little about Dorothy in the book, apart from the fact that she had had an affair with Luther while he was still married to Ruby and that they eventually became and have remained lawfully married.) The revelations are about his heavy drinking, his unstable employment, his adultery, his irresponsible and neglectful behavior toward his wife and children. So we must consider cases in which the right of privacy has been invoked as a shield against the revelation of previous misconduct.

Two early cases illustrate the range of judicial thinking. In *Melvin v. Reid*, 297 Pac. 91 (Cal. App. 1931), the plaintiff was a former prostitute, who had been prosecuted but acquitted of murder. She later had married and (she alleged) for seven years had lived a blameless respectable life in a community in which her lurid past was unknown—when all was revealed in a movie about the murder case which used her maiden name. The court held that these allegations stated a claim for invasion of privacy. The Hayneses' claim is similar although less dramatic. They have been a respectable married couple for two decades. Luther's alcohol problem is behind him. He has steady employment as a doorman. His wife is a nurse, and in 1990 he told Lemann that the couple's combined income was $60,000 a year. He is not in trouble with the domestic relations court. He is a deacon of his church. He has come a long way from sharecropping in Mississippi and public housing in Chicago and he and his wife want to bury their past just as Mrs. Melvin wanted to do and in *Melvin v. Reid* was held entitled to do. In Luther Haynes's own words, from his deposition, "I know I haven't been no angel, but since almost 30 years ago I have turned my life completely around. I stopped the drinking and all this bad habits and stuff like that, which I deny, some of [it] I didn't deny, because I have changed my life. It take me almost 30 years to change it and I am deeply in my church. I look good in the eyes of my church members and my community. Now, what is going to happen now when this public reads this garbage which I didn't tell Mr. Lemann to write? Then all this is going to go down the drain. And I worked like a son of a gun to build myself up in a good reputation and he has torn it down."

But with *Melvin v. Reid* compare *Sidis v. F–R Publishing Corp.*, 113 F.2d 806 (2d Cir. 1940), another old case but one more consonant with modern thinking about the proper balance between the right of privacy and the freedom of the press. A child prodigy had flamed out; he was now an eccentric recluse. The *New Yorker* ran a "where is he now" article about him. The article, entitled "April Fool," did not reveal any misconduct by Sidis but it depicted him in mocking tones as a comical failure, in much the same way that the report of Ruby's "devastating imitation" of the amorous Luther Haynes could be thought to have depicted him as a comical failure, albeit with sinister consequences absent from Sidis's case. The invasion of Sidis's privacy was palpable. But the publisher won. No intimate physical details of Sidis's life had been revealed; and on the other side was the undoubted newsworthiness of a child prodigy, as of a woman prosecuted for murder. Sidis, unlike Mrs. Melvin, was not permitted to bury his past.

Evolution along the divergent lines marked out by *Melvin* and *Sidis* continued until *Cox Broadcasting Corp. v. Cohn*, 420 U.S. 469 (1975), which may have consigned the entire *Melvin* line to the outer darkness. A Georgia statute forbade the publication of names of rape victims. A television station obtained the name of a woman who had been raped and murdered from the indictment of her assailants (a public document), and broadcast it in defiance of the statute. The woman's father brought a tort suit against the broadcaster, claiming that the broadcast had violated his right of privacy. The broadcaster argued that the name of the woman was a matter of public concern, but the Georgia supreme court held that the statute established the contrary, and affirmed a finding of liability. The U.S. Supreme Court reversed, holding that the statute violated the First Amendment. The Court declined to rule whether the publication of truthful information can ever be made the basis of a tort suit for invasion of privacy, but held that the First Amendment creates a privilege to publish matters contained in public records even if publication would offend the sensibilities of a reasonable person. Years later the Court extended the rule laid down in *Cox* to a case in which a newspaper published a rape victim's name (again in violation of a state statute) that it had obtained from a police report that was not a public document. *Florida Star v. B.J.F.*, 491 U.S. 524, 532 (1989). Again the Court was careful not to hold that states can never provide a tort remedy to a person about whom truthful, but intensely private, information of some interest to the public is published.

People who do not desire the limelight and do not deliberately choose a way of life or course of conduct calculated to thrust them into it nevertheless have no legal right to extinguish it if the experiences that have befallen them are newsworthy, even if they would prefer that those experiences be kept private. The possibility of an involuntary loss of privacy is recognized in the modern formulations of this branch of the privacy tort, which require not only that the private facts publicized be such as would make a reasonable person deeply offended by such publicity but also that they be facts in which the public has no legitimate interest.

The two criteria, offensiveness and newsworthiness, are related. An individual, and more pertinently perhaps the community, is most offended by the publication of intimate personal facts when the community has no interest in them beyond the voyeuristic thrill of penetrating the wall of privacy that surrounds a stranger. The reader of a book about the black migration to the North would have no legitimate interest in the details of Luther Haynes's sex life; but no such details are disclosed. Such a reader does have a legitimate interest in the aspects of Luther's conduct that the book reveals. For one of Lemann's major themes is the transposition virtually intact of a sharecropper morality characterized by a family structure "matriarchal and elastic" and by an "extremely unstable" marriage bond to the slums of the northern cities, and the interaction, largely random and sometimes perverse, of that morality with governmental programs to alleviate poverty. Public aid policies discouraged Ruby and Luther from living together; public housing policies precipitated a marriage doomed to fail. No detail in the book claimed to invade the Hayneses' privacy is not germane to the story that the author wanted to tell, a story not only of legitimate but of transcendent public interest.

The Hayneses question whether the linkage between the author's theme and their private life really is organic. They point out that many social histories do not mention individuals at all, let alone by name. That is true. But it would be absurd to suggest that cliometric or other aggregative, impersonal methods of doing social history are the only proper way to go about it and presumptuous to claim even that they are the best way. Lemann's methodology places the individual case history at center stage. If he cannot tell the story of Ruby Daniels without waivers from every person who she thinks did her wrong, he cannot write this book.

Well, argue the Hayneses, at least Lemann could have changed their names. But the use of pseudonyms would not have gotten Lemann and Knopf off the legal hook. The details of the Hayneses' lives recounted in the book would identify them unmistakably to anyone who has known the Hayneses well for a long time (members of their families, for example), or who knew them before they got married; and no more is required for liability either in defamation law or in privacy law. Lemann would have had to change some, perhaps many, of the details. But then he would no longer have been writing history. He would have been writing fiction.

*The Promised Land* does not afford the reader a titillating glimpse of tabooed activities. The tone is decorous and restrained. Painful though it is for the Hayneses to see a past they would rather forget brought into the public view, the public needs the information conveyed by the book, including the information about Luther and Dorothy Haynes, in order to evaluate the profound social and political questions that the book raises.

Ordinarily the evaluation and comparison of offensiveness and newsworthiness would be, like other questions of the application of a legal standard to the facts of a particular case, matters for a jury, not for a judge on a motion for summary judgment. But summary judgment is properly granted to a defendant when on the basis of the evidence obtained in pretrial discovery no reasonable jury could render a verdict for the plaintiff, and that is the situation here.

## NOTES

1. ***Involuntary Public Figures.*** Defamation law applies much stricter standards for liability when the alleged defamation concerns a "public figure" such as a politician or movie star. It also has generated a

doctrine about "involuntary public figures" whose connection to newsworthy events can turn them into public figures in discussions of those events. Cases involving the privacy torts often borrow much of this taxonomy. Luther Haynes, or the former child prodigy in the *Sidis* case discussed by the court, fall into the "involuntary public figure" category. So did Oliver Sipple, who was a bystander in a San Francisco crowd when a would-be assassin tried to shoot President Gerald Ford in 1975. Sipple, a former Marine, grabbed the gun and was hailed as a hero for saving the President. It turned out Sipple was also gay and basically out of the closet in San Francisco, where he marched in gay pride parades and worked on several political campaigns for gay activists including Harvey Milk. When newspaper coverage of his heroism mentioned this fact, however, he was "outed" to his parents and other family back in Michigan, causing severe ruptures in his relationships with many of them. When Sipple sued the newspapers under the disclosure tort, the court rejected his claim, holding both that his sexual orientation was not a private fact (because of his activities in San Francisco) and that it was newsworthy. Not only was the assassination attempt itself a major news event, the court held, but Sipple's sexual orientation was relevant both to "dispel the false impression that gays were timid, weak and unheroic figures" and also because some reports had speculated that the President might not have thanked Sipple promptly because of anti-gay bias. (It later turned out that President Ford did, in fact, send Sipple a note thanking him soon after the event.) The court distinguished this newsworthiness inquiry from the Restatement's concerns about "morbid and sensational prying into appellant's private life." *See Sipple v. Chronicle Publishing Co.*, 154 Cal. App. 3d 1040 (1984). Warren and Brandeis distinguished "public or quasi-public" activities from private ones; would they agree with the outcomes in *Haynes, Sidis*, and *Sipple*?

2. ***Deference to the Media.*** Rather than determining whether a disclosure was connected to an important matter and thereby distinguished from "morbid and sensational prying," many courts simply defer to the media. As one court concluded, "[W]hat is newsworthy is primarily a function of the publisher, not the courts." *Heath v. Playboy Enters., Inc.*, 732 F. Supp. 1145, 1149 (S.D. Fla. 1990). These courts often say that the judiciary ought not to dictate what counts as "public interest" in speech. On the other hand, Daniel Solove criticizes what he calls the "leave-it-to-the-press approach" as appealing to the lowest common denominator: while a sex tape sells better than a presidential speech, Solove suggests, that is not the key indicator. "What is of interest to most of society is not the same question as what is of legitimate public concern." Daniel J. Solove, *The Virtues of Knowing Less: Justifying Privacy Protections Against Disclosure*, 53 DUKE L.J. 967, 1003 (2003).

3. ***Newsworthiness Without Gatekeepers.*** In the increasingly disintermediated digital world, disclosure by an ordinary individual is just a tweet away. Does this mean courts should take on a larger role in determining newsworthiness because the institutional norms of traditional journalism have broken down? Or, on the other hand, should they be less

active because norms around communication are in flux and judicial intervention may be premature?

4. ***Newsworthiness as a Matter of Law.*** Note that Judge Posner acknowledges in *Haynes* that newsworthiness ordinarily would be a question for the jury. The appeals court affirmed summary judgment nevertheless because it found that no reasonable jury could rule for the plaintiffs. How could the facts in *Haynes* be changed hypothetically so that a jury would need to determine newsworthiness? What are the virtues and drawbacks of deciding newsworthiness on summary judgment?

5. ***An EU Comparison.*** Most European countries do not have privacy torts similar to the *Restatement*. Instead, an individual can allege a violation of his or her right to privacy under Article 8 of the European Convention on Human Rights, which extends to private as well as government behavior [see Chapter 1]. Under case law at the European Court of Human Rights, such a claim under Article 8 against a potentially newsworthy report must be balanced against the coequal right to free expression under Article 10. This balancing requires an intensive fact-specific analysis that considers whether the report is of general interest, whether the person is well known, how the reported information was obtained, and the consequences of publication. *See, e.g., Axel Springer AG v Germany (No.2)* ([2014] ECHR 745). After the Convention was incorporated into the law in England, a previously expansive understanding of newsworthiness under its limited privacy torts changed, as explained in one important English case:

> If the first hurdle can be overcome, by demonstrating a reasonable expectation of privacy, it is now clear that the court is required to carry out the next step of weighing the relevant competing Convention rights in the light of an "intense focus" upon the individual facts of the case. It was expressly recognised that no one Convention right takes automatic precedence over another. In the present context, for example, it has to be accepted that any rights of free expression, as protected by Article 10, must no longer be regarded as simply "trumping" any privacy rights that may be established on the part of the Claimant. Language of that kind is no longer used. Nor can it be said, without qualification, that there is a "public interest that the truth should out." *Fraser v Evans* [1969] 1 QB 349, 360F–G (C.A.) (Lord Denning, M.R.).
>
> This modern approach of applying an "intense focus" is thus obviously incompatible with making broad generalisations of the kind to which the media often resorted in the past such as, for example, "Public figures must expect to have less privacy" or "People in positions of responsibility must be seen as 'role models' and set us all an example of how to live upstanding lives." Sometimes factors of this kind may have a legitimate role to play when the "ultimate balancing exercise" comes to be carried out, but generalisations can never be determinative. In every case "it all depends" (i.e. upon what is revealed by the intense focus on the individual circumstances).

*Mosley v. News of the World*, [2008] EWHC 1777 (Q.B.), [10]–[12]. The case was brought by Max Mosley, who was the president of the organization that oversees Formula One auto racing and is also the son of a very famous (or more appropriately infamous) politician who founded a British fascist party in the 1930s. The younger Mosley had participated in a sadomasochistic orgy with five women, and a tabloid newspaper paid one of the women to take photographs and be interviewed about it for a sensational front-page story ("F1 BOSS HAD SICK NAZI ORGY WITH HOOKERS"). The court held that, despite the fact that Mosley was a public figure to some degree, there was insufficient justification for the intrusion on his private and consensual sexual activities. The court acknowledged that there might have been a public interest if the chief of Formula One racing were in fact mocking the Holocaust (presumably increased because of his family history, although the court did not say so). After examining the facts at length, however, the court found the tabloid's "Nazi" characterization was inaccurate. Without it, the court held, there was no countervailing public interest in the publication, and no reasonable journalist could conclude otherwise:

> It is not for the state or for the media to expose sexual conduct which does not involve any significant breach of the criminal law. That is so whether the motive for such intrusion is merely prurience or a moral crusade. It is not for journalists to undermine human rights, or for judges to refuse to enforce them, merely on grounds of taste or moral disapproval. Everyone is naturally entitled to espouse moral or religious beliefs to the effect that certain types of sexual behaviour are wrong or demeaning to those participating. That does not mean that they are entitled to hound those who practise them or to detract from their right to live life as they choose.

*Id.* at ¶ 127. Would Mosley have prevailed in a disclosure tort case in the US?

6. ***Is the Disclosure Tort Dead?*** Many scholars consider the conflict between free speech and the disclosure tort so serious that they think the tort should be retired—and some suggest that Supreme Court First Amendment cases like those cited in *Haynes* effectively have killed it already. For a sampling of the large literature criticizing the privacy torts, and especially the disclosure tort, on free speech grounds, see, e.g., C. Edwin Baker, *Autonomy and Informational Privacy, Or Gossip: The Central Meaning of the First Amendment*, in FREEDOM OF SPEECH 215, 261–62 (Ellen Frankel Paul et al., eds. 2004); Peter B. Edelman, *Free Press v. Privacy: Haunted by the Ghost of Justice Black*, 68 TEX. L. REV. 1195 (1990); Harry Kalven, Jr., *Privacy in Tort Law—Were Warren and Brandeis Wrong?*, 31 LAW & CONTEMP. PROBS., 326 (1966); Rodney A. Smolla, *Privacy and the First Amendment Right to Gather News*, 67 GEO. WASH. L. REV. 1097 (1999); Neil M. Richards, *The Puzzle of Brandeis, Privacy, and Speech*, 63 VAND. L.R. 1295 (2010); Eugene Volokh, *Freedom of Speech and Information Privacy: The Troubling Implications of a Right to Stop People from Speaking About You*, 52 STAN. L. REV. 1049 (2000); Diane L. Zimmermann, *Requiem for a*

*Heavyweight: A Farewell to Warren and Brandeis's Privacy Tort*, 68 CORNELL L. REV. 291 (1983).

---

## Practice

Newsworthy or Not?

Evaluate arguments about newsworthiness if a disclosure tort were alleged in the following cases. How much do your responses depend upon the test you apply? What other factors matter?

(a) *Shulman v. Group W Productions*, the intrusion case [see Section B above] involving the rescue helicopter.

(b) A reality television star who often bragged about his sex life publicly insisted that he had never had sex with his friend's wife, but a gossip-oriented web site publishes excerpts from a video showing him doing just that.

(c) A newspaper publishes an article revealing that the newly-elected president of the student body at local a community college had lived in a nearby homeless shelter as a child, a fact the student revealed to almost no one.

(d) Gary Gadfly is a blogger who writes about local government in a suburban town, with a particular focus on taxes and spending. Gadfly is not widely read, except by people heavily involved in local politics. He writes several entries discussing reimbursements the elected local school board approved for an evaluation of one child by a private psychologist to diagnose learning disabilities. Gadfly's posts express skepticism about the child's diagnosis and the cost of the evaluation, and he names the child's parents.

(e) Gadfly also writes an entry disclosing that a member of the school board is having an extramarital affair.

(f) After Gadfly wrote the posts in (d) and (e) above, a local newspaper discloses that Gadfly is having an extramarital affair.

---

# D. OTHER TORTS

## 1. APPROPRIATION AND PUBLICITY RIGHTS

### RESTATEMENT (SECOND) OF TORTS (1977)

### § 652C. PUBLICITY GIVEN TO PRIVATE LIFE

One who appropriates to his own use or benefit the name or likeness of another is subject to liability to the other for invasion of his privacy.

## Pavesich v. New England Life Ins. Co.

50 S.E. 68 (Ga. 1905)

■ COBB, J.

[Recall that *Pavesich* was the first case to recognize the right to privacy articulated by Warren and Brandeis. An insurance company used a photo of the plaintiff in a newspaper advertisement accompanied by the fabricated quote, "In my healthy and productive period of life I bought insurance in the New England Mutual Life Insurance Co., of Boston, Mass., and today my family is protected and I am drawing an annual dividend on my paid-up policies." The plaintiff did not give permission to use the photo, did not make the statement, and indeed had never purchased any insurance policy from the defendant.]

If one's picture may be used by another for advertising purposes, it may be reproduced and exhibited anywhere. If it may be used in a newspaper, it may be used on a poster or a placard. It may be posted upon the walls of private dwellings or upon the streets. It may ornament the bar of the saloon keeper or decorate the walls of a brothel. By becoming a member of society, neither man nor woman can be presumed to have consented to such uses of the impression of their faces and features upon paper or upon canvas.

What we have ruled cannot be in any sense construed as an abridgment of the liberty of speech and of the press as guarantied in the Constitution. There is in the publication of one's picture for advertising purposes not the slightest semblance of an expression of an idea, a thought, or an opinion, within the meaning of the constitutional provision which guaranties to a person the right to publish his sentiments on any subject. Such conduct is not embraced within the liberty to print, but is a serious invasion of one's right of privacy, and may in many cases, according to the circumstances of the publication and the uses to which it is put, cause damages to flow which are irreparable in their nature. The knowledge that one's features and form are being used for such a purpose, and displayed in such places as such advertisements are often liable to be found, brings not only the person of an extremely sensitive nature, but even the individual of ordinary sensibility, to a realization that his liberty has been taken away from him; and, as long as the advertiser uses him for these purposes, he cannot be otherwise than conscious of the fact that he is for the time being under the control of another, that he is no longer free, and that he is in reality a slave, without hope of freedom, held to service by a merciless master; and if a man of true instincts, or even of ordinary sensibilities, no one can be more conscious of his enthrallment than he is.

## CALIFORNIA CIVIL CODE

### § 3344

Any person who knowingly uses another's name, voice, signature, photograph, or likeness, in any manner, on or in products, merchandise, or goods, or for purposes of advertising or selling, or soliciting purchases of, products, merchandise, goods or services, without such person's prior consent, or, in the case of a minor, the prior consent of his parent or legal guardian, shall be liable for any damages sustained by the person or persons injured as a result thereof. In addition, in any action brought under this section, the person who violated the section shall be liable to the injured party or parties in an amount equal to the greater of seven hundred fifty dollars ($750) or the actual damages suffered by him or her as a result of the unauthorized use, and any profits from the unauthorized use that are attributable to the use and are not taken into account in computing the actual damages. In establishing such profits, the injured party or parties are required to present proof only of the gross revenue attributable to such use, and the person who violated this section is required to prove his or her deductible expenses. Punitive damages may also be awarded to the injured party or parties. The prevailing party in any action under this section shall also be entitled to attorney's fees and costs. . . .

(d) For purposes of this section, a use of a name, voice, signature, photograph, or likeness in connection with any news, public affairs, or sports broadcast or account, or any political campaign, shall not constitute a use for which consent is required under subdivision (a). . . .

(f) Nothing in this section shall apply to the owners or employees of any medium used for advertising, including, but not limited to, newspapers, magazines, radio and television networks and stations, cable television systems, billboards, and transit ads, by whom any advertisement or solicitation in violation of this section is published or disseminated, unless it is established that such owners or employees had knowledge of the unauthorized use of the person's name, voice, signature, photograph, or likeness as prohibited by this section.

(g) The remedies provided for in this section are cumulative and shall be in addition to any others provided for by law.

---

## Focus

### The Emergence of Publicity Rights

Early courts applying the privacy tort that the Restatement eventually identified as "appropriation" struggled to distinguish the dignitary interests in controlling one's own name or image from the pecuniary interests in exploiting the commercial value of that persona, especially for celebrities. A 1953 decision by Judge Jerome Frank, a celebrated appellate jurist, recognized the latter as a distinct right, based in property as much as in tort:

> This right might be called a 'right of publicity.' For it is common knowledge that many prominent persons (especially actors and ball-players), far from having their feelings bruised through public exposure of their likenesses, would feel sorely deprived if they no longer received money for authorizing advertisements, popularizing their countenances, displayed in newspapers, magazines, busses, trains and subways. This right of publicity would usually yield them no money unless it could be made the subject of an exclusive grant which barred any other advertiser from using their pictures.

*Haelan Laboratories, Inc. v. Topps Chewing Gum, Inc.*, 202 F.2d 866, 868 (2d Cir. 1953); *see also* Melville Nimmer, *The Right of Publicity*, 19 LAW & CONTEMP. PROBS. 203 (1954) (advancing similar but more comprehensive arguments for distinct publicity rights).

The majority of states now have statutes recognizing some entitlement to publicity rights that is closer to a form of intellectual property than a privacy right. Many of them are similar to the California statute excerpted above, but there are significant variations between states concerning the existence, scope, and duration of rights. In California and many other states the rights, unlike privacy tort rights, continue for a period after a person's death and can be inherited.

Many states also continue to recognize tort claims for both publicity rights and appropriation, often alongside distinct statutory rights, and sometimes they permit claims under trademark and unfair competition law as well. As a consequence, court decisions and scholarly examinations of publicity rights and privacy can become deeply confusing. Furthermore, this overlapping law often means that plaintiffs can bring multiple claims and prevail on whichever one survives on particular facts. Ordinary individuals can and do make claims under many publicity rights statutes, especially because many of them have favorable damages provisions. Conversely, even where publicity rights statutes exist, celebrities still make tort claims as well. For example, the famous singer Bette Midler included tort claims in her suit over a television commercial featuring the voice of her former backup singer, Ula Hedwig, imitating Midler's distinctive vocal style:

> California Civil Code section 3344 is of no aid to Midler. The statute affords damages to a person injured by another who uses the person's "name, voice, signature, photograph or likeness, in any manner." The defendants did not use Midler's name or anything else whose use is prohibited by the statute. The voice they used was Hedwig's, not hers. The term 'likeness' refers to a visual image not a vocal imitation. The statute, however, does not preclude Midler from pursuing any cause of action she may have at common law; the statute itself implies that such common law causes of action do exist because it says its remedies are merely "cumulative."

*Midler v. Ford Motor Co.*, 849 F.2d 460, 463 (9th Cir. 1988). The following opinion tried to sort out the distinctions between protecting privacy and publicity. The opinion also highlights the difference between commercial and personal harms.

---

## Joe Dickerson & Associates, LLC v. Dittmar

34 P.3d 995 (Colo. 2001)

■ JUSTICE BENDER delivered the Opinion of the Court.

### FACTS AND PROCEEDINGS BELOW

Defendants Joe Dickerson & Associates, LLC and Joe Dickerson were hired during a child custody dispute to investigate plaintiff Rosanne Marie (Brock) Dittmar. During the course of this investigation, Dickerson noticed inconsistencies in the way Dittmar came to possess certain bearer bonds. He reported the results of his investigation to authorities. Thereafter, Dittmar was charged with and convicted of felony theft of these bonds.

Dickerson publishes a newsletter called "The Dickerson Report," which is sent free of charge to law enforcement agencies, financial institutions, law firms, and others. This report contains articles about financial fraud investigations, tips for avoiding fraud, activities of private investigator boards, information about upcoming conferences, and the like. Dickerson ran a series of articles in the report under the heading "Fraud DuJour." This column included such articles as "Fraud DuJour—Wireless Cable Investments," "Fraud DuJour—Prime Bank Instruments," and the article at issue here, "Fraud DuJour—Five Cases, 100%+ Recovery."

In this article, Dickerson related the role his firm played in five cases in recovering 100%—and in one case more than 100%—of the value of stolen assets. Dittmar's case was discussed first. Dickerson's article detailed how Dittmar, who worked as a secretary at a brokerage firm, stole a customer's bearer bonds from her place of employment and cashed them for personal use. In addition, the article described Dickerson's investigation of Dittmar, the fact that the jury convicted Dittmar of theft, and how the court ordered her to pay restitution to the theft victim. This article appears on the front page of The Dickerson Report, mentions Dittmar by name, and includes her photograph.

Dittmar sued Dickerson on a number of tort theories including defamation, outrageous conduct, and invasion of privacy by appropriation of another's name or likeness. The trial court granted summary judgment for Dickerson on all claims. With respect to Dittmar's claim for invasion of privacy by appropriation of another's name or likeness, the only claim relevant to this appeal, the trial court noted that Colorado has not explicitly recognized this tort. The trial court granted Dickerson's motion for summary judgment because, even assuming the tort was cognizable under Colorado law, Dittmar "present[ed] no evidence that her name or likeness had any value." The trial court noted that, under the definition of the tort, appropriation requires more than mere publication of the plaintiff's name or likeness:

> The value of a plaintiff's name is not appropriated by mere mention of it, or by reference to it in connection with legitimate mention of his public activities; nor is the value of his likeness appropriated when it is published for purposes other than taking advantage of his reputation, prestige, or other value associated with him, for purposes of publicity.

Restatement (Second) of Torts § 652C, cmt. d (1977)).

The court of appeals agreed with the trial court that this tort requires the defendant to appropriate certain values associated with the plaintiff's name or likeness: "In order for liability to exist, the defendant must have appropriated to his or her own use or benefit the reputation, prestige, social or commercial standing, public interest or other values of the plaintiff's name or likeness." The court of appeals concluded, however, that the plaintiff raised issues of material fact regarding different aspects of the tort, namely the purpose of the publication and whether the use benefited Dickerson. These issues of fact, the court of appeals reasoned, precluded summary judgment in favor of Dickerson.

Dickerson petitioned this court for certiorari on whether the tort of invasion of privacy based on appropriation of another's name or likeness is cognizable under Colorado law; [and] if so, whether an appropriation claim requires evidence that the plaintiff's name has an exploitable value.

We agree with the court of appeals' recognition of this tort but we disagree that a plaintiff must provide evidence of the value of her name and likeness when she seeks only personal damages.

## ANALYSIS

### A. Overview of the Appropriation Tort

In 1890, an influential law review article outlined the contours of the tort of invasion of privacy. Samuel D. Warren & Louis D. Brandeis, *The Right To Privacy*, 4 HARV. L. REV. 193 (1890). Warren and Brandeis proposed that the right of privacy would protect a person's rights in their appearance, sayings, acts, and personal relations. To Warren and Brandeis, the right of privacy did not involve property so much as the "more general immunity of the person—the right to one's personality." In short, they desired to protect the individual's right "to be let alone."

Over the years, almost every state has recognized, either statutorily or by case law, that one way that an individual's privacy can be invaded is when a defendant appropriates a plaintiff's name or likeness for that defendant's own benefit. While the exact parameters of this tort vary from state to state, it has always been clear that a plaintiff could recover for personal injuries such as mental anguish and injured feelings resulting from an appropriation.

There has been a great deal of debate, however, over the ability of a plaintiff to recover for pecuniary loss resulting from an unauthorized commercial exploitation of her name or likeness. Courts initially had difficulty reconciling how a celebrity, well-known to the public, could recover under the misleading heading of "privacy." Such plaintiffs often sought damages for commercial injury that resulted when defendants used plaintiffs' identities in advertising.

Therefore, in the context of pecuniary damages, some courts and commentators have resorted by analogy to property law and have recognized a "right of publicity" which permits plaintiffs to recover for injury to the commercial value of their identities.

In a seminal law review article, William Prosser described invasion of privacy as a complex of four related torts: (1) unreasonable intrusion upon the seclusion of another; (2) publicity that places another in a false light before the public; (3) public disclosure of embarrassing private facts about another; and (4) appropriation of another's name or likeness. The first three of these four torts protect only personal interests. But, perhaps in response to the simmering legal debate about the scope of the protection afforded by the appropriation tort, Prosser defined the appropriation tort as protective of both personal and economic interests.

In doing so, Prosser emphasized the proprietary nature of the appropriation tort without removing it from the framework of privacy: "The interest protected is not so much a mental as a proprietary one, in the exclusive use of the plaintiff's name and likeness as an aspect of his identity."

Thus, Prosser's formulation of the appropriation tort subsumed the two types of injuries—personal and commercial—into one cause of action that existed under the misleading label of "privacy." The privacy label is misleading both because the interest protected (name and/or likeness) is not "private" in the same way as the interests protected by other areas of privacy law and because the appropriation tort often applies to protect well-known "public" persons. Despite these problems, Prosser's view of the appropriation tort was ultimately incorporated into the Second Restatement of Torts.

Prosser's emphasis on the property-like aspects of the tort has led to a great deal of confusion in the law of privacy. Some courts have partially rejected the Prosser formulation, choosing to distinguish claims for injury to personal feelings caused by an unauthorized use of a plaintiff's identity ("right of privacy") from claims seeking redress for pecuniary damages caused by an appropriation of the commercial value of the identity ("right of publicity"). [I]n those jurisdictions, the right of publicity is viewed as an independent doctrine distinct from the right of privacy. This view finds support in the Third Restatement of Unfair Competition, which recognizes that the right of publicity protects against commercial injury, while the right of privacy appropriation tort protects against personal injury.

Some jurisdictions attempt to follow Prosser's formulation of the tort and provide relief for both personal and commercial harm through a single common law or statutory cause of action. In other states, however, the parameters or even the existence of the appropriation tort remain undetermined. Such is the case in Colorado.

### B. Colorado's Recognition of the Appropriation Tort

A brief review of the development of the tort of invasion of privacy in Colorado demonstrates that recognition of the appropriation tort is a natural outgrowth of our earlier precedent.

We have recognized that invasion of privacy is a cognizable tort under Colorado law. [In *Rugg v. McCarty* (1970)], we relied both on a Colorado statute that protected a privacy right and the fact that a majority of jurisdictions had recognized the tort of invasion of privacy. We did not, however, "attempt to comprehensively define the right of privacy, nor to categorize the character of all invasions which may constitute a violation of such right."

Recently, we recognized the tort of invasion of privacy by unreasonable publicity given to another's private life. As in *Rugg,* we relied upon the fact that a majority of jurisdictions have recognized this tort.

Similarly, the tort of invasion of privacy by appropriation of a plaintiff's name or likeness has been recognized throughout most of the United States, either statutorily or through the common law. We now hold that Colorado recognizes the tort of invasion of privacy by appropriation of an individual's name or likeness.

### C. Elements of the Tort

Having recognized that the invasion of privacy by appropriation of name or likeness tort is recognized in Colorado, we now consider the elements of this tort.

The Second Restatement of Torts articulates the tort of appropriation of another's name or likeness, stating: "One who appropriates to his own use or benefit the name or likeness of another is subject to liability to the other for invasion of his privacy." The defendant, Dickerson, argues that summary judgment in his favor is appropriate because the plaintiff, Dittmar, has presented no evidence that her name and likeness had any value.

Comment c [to Restatement § 652C] implies that one element that a plaintiff must prove is that the plaintiff's identity has value, stating that "the defendant must have appropriated to his own use or benefit the reputation, prestige, social or commercial standing, public interest or other values of the plaintiff's name or likeness." Based on this and other comments to section 652C, some courts that follow the Restatement have explicitly required that one element of the tort is that the plaintiff's identity must have had pre-existing commercial value.

However, as discussed above, the Restatement takes a property-oriented approach to the law of appropriation, an approach not wholly embraced in all jurisdictions. In the context of damages intended to remedy a proprietary injury to the plaintiff's commercial interests, it may make sense to require a plaintiff to prove the value of her identity, either as part of her proof of damages or as an element of the tort. This does not necessarily mean that the value of the plaintiff's identity is relevant when the plaintiff seeks damages only for her mental anguish.

It appears illogical to require the plaintiff to prove that her identity has value in order for her to recover for her personal damages. The market value of the plaintiff's identity is unrelated to the question of whether she suffered mental anguish as a result of the alleged wrongful appropriation. A plaintiff whose identity had no commercial value might still experience mental anguish based on an unauthorized use of her name and likeness. Of the numerous cases that have considered the tort of invasion of privacy by appropriation of the plaintiff's name or likeness, few have suggested that there is any requirement that the plaintiff prove the value of her identity as a prerequisite to recovery for mental suffering. Rather, a more typical summary of the law is found in

*Motschenbacher v. R.J. Reynolds Tobacco Co.,* where the 9th Circuit attempted to reconcile the relationship between commercial damages, mental anguish damages, and the requirement of value, stating:

> It is true that the injury suffered from an appropriation of the attributes of one's identity may be "mental and subjective"—in the nature of humiliation, embarrassment and outrage. However, where the identity appropriated has a commercial value, the injury may be largely, or even wholly, of an economic or material nature.

Hence, we hold that the elements of an invasion of privacy by appropriation claim are: (1) the defendant used the plaintiff's name or likeness; (2) the use of the plaintiff's name or likeness was for the defendant's own purposes or benefit, commercially or otherwise; (3) the plaintiff suffered damages; and (4) the defendant caused the damages incurred.

Applying these elements in this case, we conclude that Dittmar, the plaintiff, alleged sufficient facts to satisfy each of the required elements. We do not require the plaintiff, who seeks only personal damages, to prove the value of her identity. Thus, her failure to do so is not fatal to her claim.

## NOTES

1. ***Newsworthiness.*** *Dickerson* raises questions of newsworthiness yet again. Remember that in *Haynes v. Alfred A. Knopf, Inc.*, 8 F.3d 1222 (7th Cir. 1993), the court relied upon the Restatement's requirement that the information "is not of legitimate concern to the public" to define a newsworthiness exception. The Restatement comments distinguish "information to which the public is entitled" from "morbid and sensational prying into private lives for its own sake." Into which of these categories does "The Dickerson Report" fall? How would the *Dickerson* court handle an article about Dittmar's conviction, accompanied by her photo, in a traditional newspaper like the Denver Post? Does it matter that the information pertained to an arrest and conviction? Does it matter that "The Dickerson Report" was intended to solicit business for Dickerson's firm?

2. ***Use or Benefit.*** The Restatement defines the appropriation tort based on the defendant's "use or benefit." Most publicity rights statutes, like California's, include some requirement that the plaintiff's persona was used for commercial purposes. Sometimes, as in *Pavesich*, one can clearly see that type of commercial benefit from a defendant's actions. Other cases, such as *Dickerson*, may move closer to the edge. But at least one court has indicated that circulating nude photos of another person among acquaintances without her consent might satisfy the "use or benefit" requirement of the appropriation tort. *See Lake v. Wal-Mart Stores, Inc.*, 582 N.W.2d 231 (Minn. 1998).

3. ***Varying Rationales.*** Scholars are divided about the purpose of publicity rights. Some view them as similar to more traditional intellectual property rights, offering an incentive for individuals to invest in their image to society's benefit. Roberta Kwall, for example, emphasizes the investment that entertainers and other public figures make in their public persona. In her view, courts see the tort as "fostering creativity, safeguarding the individual's enjoyment of the fruits of her labors, preventing consumer deception, and preventing unjust enrichment." Roberta Kwall, *The Right of Publicity vs. the First Amendment: A Property and Liability Rule Analysis*, 70 IND. L.J. 47, 54 (1994) (citations omitted). Others suggest that the interests of celebrities and private citizens are not so different after all. *See* Mark P. McKenna, *The Right of Publicity and Autonomous Self-Definition*, 67 U. PITT. L. REV. 225, 229 (2005) ("The things and people with which individuals choose to associate reflect their character and values . . . Importantly, this interest in autonomous self-definition is just as relevant for celebrities as it is for non-celebrities.").

4. ***Altered Images.*** Images that are altered or distorted can present more complex questions. Some states limit publicity rights and intrusion actions to situations where a defendant capitalized on the plaintiff's name or exact likeness. A case decided under New York's post-*Roberson* privacy statute illustrated this point. The plaintiff was "The Naked Cowboy," a well-known street performer in New York City's Times Square described by the court as "wearing only a white cowboy hat, cowboy boots, and underpants, and carrying a guitar strategically placed to give the illusion of nudity." An electronic billboard advertisement in Times Square depicted anthropomorphic M & M candies posing as New York tourist attractions such as the Statute of Liberty, including "a blue M & M dressed exactly like The Naked Cowboy, wearing only a white cowboy hat, cowboy boots, and underpants, and carrying a guitar." *Burck v. Mars, Inc.*, 571 F. Supp. 2d 446, 448 (S.D.N.Y. 2008). The court held that the man who appeared as the Naked Cowboy failed to state a claim because the statute applied to commercial use of a "name, portrait, picture or voice," N.Y. Civ. Rights Law § 51, and the M & M caricature of his signature outfit fell outside all these categories. In contrast, Vanna White, hostess of the long-running game show *Wheel of Fortune*, prevailed in a case decided under California law about a print advertisement depicting a futuristic robot that strongly resembled her, turning letters on a game show. One judge wrote a stinging opinion objecting that the decision conferred too strong a right of publicity, noting that "[o]verprotecting intellectual property is as harmful as underprotecting it. Creativity is impossible without a rich public domain." *White v. Samsung Electronics America, Inc.*, 989 F.2d 1512 (9th Cir. 1993) (Kozinski, J., dissenting from the order rejecting the suggestion for rehearing en banc); *see also* *Cardtoons, L.C. v. Major League Baseball Players Ass'n*, 95 F.3d 959 (10th Cir. 1996) (holding that parody trading cards with caricatures of active major league baseball players violated a state publicity rights statute—but the card producer's First Amendment right outweighed the players' right of publicity).

5. ***Release Forms.*** Liability depends on a lack of consent. For this reason, stock photography agencies require that their models sign extremely broad waivers irrevocably releasing all possible claims against future uses of their photos for any purpose, including permission to manipulate or alter them. This sweeping permission avoids thickets of rights clearance that would interfere with the use of the photos. The law uniformly enforces such waivers. But it can lead to some odd results. One actor who signed such a release found himself featured in public service advertisements throughout New York City, particularly in subways and buses. The ads warned of the dangers of diabetes and his photo was edited digitally so that he had crutches and an amputated leg. *See* Patrick McGeehan, *Imagine His Shock. His Leg Had Vanished*, N.Y. TIMES (Jan. 29, 2012) at A15. Another woman who had photos taken with her boyfriend and signed releases later found both of their pictures in ads for an online singles site. As she concluded, "Our faces might be conscripted for any purpose, to sell almost any product, in any medium, with any modification, for a duration described by my release as 'perpetuity.'" Reyhan Harmanci, *I Found My Boyfriend's Face on a Dating Website*, SLATE (March 29, 2012).

6. ***Appropriation in Social Media.*** Several class action lawsuits against social media platforms, especially Facebook, have objected to features that allow advertisers to promote users' activity in sponsored posts (as in, "Your friend Joe liked these pants at our store.") [see Chapter 8 for more about these suits]. The posts typically feature a user's name and profile picture. Do they raise issues of appropriation or publicity rights? What if information about the feature is included in the platform's terms of service? What if users can opt out of the feature? *See Fraley v. Facebook, Inc.*, 830 F. Supp. 2d 785 (N.D. Cal. 2011) (denying a motion to dismiss a right of publicity claim against Facebook's "sponsored stories" feature); William McGeveran, *Disclosure, Endorsement, and Identity in Social Marketing*, 2009 U. ILL. L. REV. 1105 (2009).

7. ***The Human Cannonball.*** Hugo Zacchini performed a human cannonball act at county fairs which lasted about 15 seconds. When a local news station filmed his full act without permission and broadcast it on its 11:00 news program, Zacchini sued for appropriation. The Ohio Supreme Court held the broadcast was protected from liability by the First Amendment. The US Supreme Court disagreed, emphasizing that the broadcast showed the entire act, thus undermining its commercial value. The Court distinguished appropriation or publicity rights cases (it used these two terms interchangeably) from other privacy torts because they served different purposes. In appropriation cases, the Court opined, "the State's interest is closely analogous to the goals of patent and copyright law, focusing on the right of the individual to reap the reward of his endeavors and having little to do with protecting feelings or reputation." *Zacchini v. Scripps-Howard Broad. Co.*, 433 U.S. 562, 573 (1977). Do you agree? On one hand, does it make sense for the law to offer more protection to commercially valuable persona rights? On the other, doesn't this suggest that there would often be *less* First Amendment protection for speech about public figures than about ordinary people?

## Practice

Applying the Appropriation Tort and Publicity Rights

What would be the arguments for and against liability under appropriation or publicity rights theories in each of the following scenarios? When does it matter what version of the law applies (privacy or publicity, tort or statute, California or New York)? What other facts might you need to know to determine your answer?

(a) Defendant sells t-shirts through an online web site decorated with a celebrity's image and a caption making fun of the celebrity.

(b) Ruby writes a memoir discussing her past marriage to Luther.

(c) A glossy magazine showcases recent fashion trends in a feature article that superimposes celebrities' faces on the models.

(d) Before an election, an organization opposing abortion mails a pamphlet to voters illustrated with a stock photo of a woman looking concerned; Ann, the woman appearing in the photo, supports abortion rights.

(e) A farmer creates an elaborate corn maze in the shape of pop singer Taylor Swift's face, and charges admission to the maze, which contains clues based on her songs. (This really happened.)

## 2. FALSE LIGHT

### RESTATEMENT (SECOND) OF TORTS (1977)

### § 652E. PUBLICITY PLACING PERSON IN FALSE LIGHT

One who gives publicity to a matter concerning another that places the other before the public in a false light is subject to liability to the other for invasion of his privacy, if

(a) the false light in which the other was placed would be highly offensive to a reasonable person, and

(b) the actor had knowledge of or acted in reckless disregard as to the falsity of the publicized matter and the false light in which the other would be placed.

## Welling v. Weinfeld

866 N.E.2d 1051 (Ohio 2007)

■ PFEIFER, J.

From neighborhood friction that spiraled into dueling litigation has emerged a significant question for this court: Does Ohio recognize the "false light" theory of the tort of invasion of privacy? Today we recognize that theory of recovery.

The plaintiff-appellee, Lauri Weinfeld, and defendants-appellants, Robert and Katherine Welling, are neighbors in Perry Township in Stark

County. Weinfeld owns and operates a party center next to her home, which hosts banquets, parties, and outdoor weddings. The Wellings live next to the party center. Weinfeld and the Wellings each alleged on a number of theories that the activities of the other interfered with their legitimate use of their own property. It is one of the Wellings' counterclaims, invasion of privacy, that is the focus of this case.

During the spring of 2000, someone threw a rock through a plate-glass window at Weinfeld's party center. Weinfeld suspected that the culprit was the Wellings' son, Robert. Weinfeld created handbills, printed on 8 ½-by-11-inch paper, offering a reward for information regarding the perpetrator. The handbill read:

$500.00
REWARD
for any information which leads to the
conviction of the person(s) responsible
for throwing a rock through the window
of Lakeside Center Banquet Hall
(also known as the "Party Center")
in the Dee Mar Allotment, in Perry
Township, on Monday, May 8th or
Tuesday, May 9th, 2000.
Any tips will be kept confidential.
Call the Perry Township Police
Department's Detective Bureau at
478–5121.
Reward will be paid in cash.

Weinfeld admitted that she had no proof that the Wellings were responsible for the damage. She further admitted that she distributed the handbills at two locations outside the neighborhood that were of special significance to the Wellings: at the Pepsi bottling plant where Robert Welling and his son worked and at the school the Welling children attended.

The Wellings allege that Weinfeld's distribution of the handbills spread wrongful publicity about them that unreasonably placed them in a false light before the public.

A jury entered a verdict in favor of the Wellings on Weinfeld's claims and further found that Weinfeld had invaded the Wellings' privacy. The jury interrogatory on the invasion-of-privacy claim did not delineate the facts upon which the jury based its verdict. The jury awarded the Wellings $5,412.38 in compensatory damages and $250,000 in punitive damages. Attorney fees were stipulated to be $10,000.

[Ohio recognizes the other three privacy torts identified in the *Restatement*, but not false light.] A majority of jurisdictions in the United States have recognized false-light invasion of privacy as a distinct, actionable tort. *See West v. Media Gen. Convergence, Inc.*, 53 S.W.3d 640, 644 (Tenn. 2001). However, the two most recent state supreme courts to address the issue, Tennessee and Colorado, have made divergent holdings. In *West,* the Tennessee Supreme Court recognized false-light invasion of privacy as a cause of action. In *Denver Publishing Co. v. Bueno* 54 P.3d 893 (Colo. 2002), however, the Colorado Supreme Court, in "a deliberate exercise of caution," ruled that false light "is too amorphous a tort for Colorado, and it risks inflicting an unacceptable chill on those in the media seeking to avoid liability." Those two cases mark well the boundaries of the opposing viewpoints on the issue.

*Bueno* points to the central concern of the cases and commentary against false light—that there is an unacceptable overlap between false light and defamation. *Bueno* describes the interest protected in a false-light claim as the "individual's peace of mind, *i.e.,* his or her interest in not being made to appear before the public in an objectionable false light or false position, or in other words, otherwise than as he is," while the action for defamation is to protect a person's interest in a good reputation.

While conceding the distinction of those interests, *Bueno* held that "recognition of the different interests protected rests primarily on parsing a too subtle distinction between an individual's personal sensibilities and his or her reputation in the community."

Ultimately, *Bueno* characterized potential false-light claims as encompassing "a decidedly narrow band of cases" and held that such plaintiffs would be protected by the existing remedies of defamation, appropriation, and intentional infliction of emotional distress

[The Colorado Supreme Court was also concerned] that a falselight tort would have negative implications on First Amendment principles. The court reasoned that the theory of false-light invasion of privacy fails the test of providing a clear identification of wrongful conduct: "The sole area in which it differs from defamation is an area fraught with ambiguity and subjectivity. Recognizing 'highly offensive' information, even framed within the context of what a reasonable person would find highly offensive, necessarily involves a subjective component."

*Bueno* concludes that the ambiguity and subjectivity surrounding false-light invasion of privacy would "invariably chill open and robust reporting." Other states rejecting false light as a theory of recovery have also pointed to First Amendment implications in their reasoning. *See, e.g., Lake v. Wal-Mart Stores, Inc.*, 582 N.W.2d 231, 235–236 (Minn. 1998); *Cain v. Hearst Corp.*, 878 S.W.2d 577, 579–580 (Tex. 1994); *Renwick v. News & Observer Publishing Co.*, 312 S.E.2d 405 (N.C. 1984).

In *West,* the Tennessee Supreme Court held that a cause of action for false-light invasion of privacy protects an important individual right complementary to other privacy rights and that there are adequate protections guaranteeing the First Amendment rights of potential defendants.

We agree with *West* that the viability of a false-light claim maintains the integrity of the right to privacy, complementing the other right-to-privacy torts. In Ohio, we have already recognized that a claim for invasion of privacy can arise when *true* private details of a person's life are publicized. The right to privacy naturally extends to the ability to control false statements made about oneself.

Without false light, the right to privacy is not whole, as it is not fully protected by defamation laws:

> Certainly situations may exist in which persons have had attributed to them certain qualities, characteristics, or beliefs that, while not injurious to their reputation, place those persons in an undesirable false light. However, in situations such as these, victims of invasion of privacy would be without recourse under defamation law. False light therefore provides a viable, and we believe necessary, action for relief apart from defamation.

*West,* 53 S.W.3d at 646.

Will a recognition of false-light invasion of privacy result in a parade of persons with hurt feelings clogging our courthouses? There is no indication that that scenario is the case in the states that already recognize false-light claims. The requirements imposed by the *Restatement* make a false-light claim difficult to prove.

First, the statement made must be untrue. Second, the information must be "publicized" [using the *Restatement* publicity standard for the disclosure tort rather than the standard for defamation, which requires only the communication of the information to any other person]. Another element of a successful false-light claim is that the misrepresentation made must be serious enough to be highly offensive to a reasonable person.

Like the court in *West,* we believe that the First Amendment concerns that some courts have raised in regard to false-light claims are overblown. False-light defendants enjoy protections at least as extensive as defamation defendants. *West* makes the standard of fault identical for defamation and false-light claims: a negligence standard in regard to statements made about private citizens and an actual-malice standard for statements made about public figures. We choose to follow the *Restatement* standard, requiring that the defendant "had knowledge of or acted in reckless disregard as to the falsity of the publicized matter and the false light in which the other would be placed," in cases of both private and public figures. In part, this heightened requirement is a recognition that a statement that is not defamatory is less apt to be a red flag for editors and checked for accuracy.

The world has changed since *Renwick,* one of the early decisions in which the court refused to recognize false-light claims due in part to First Amendment concerns. In *Renwick,* 312 S.E.2d 405 (1984), the court stated that the right to privacy had first been developed during the period of the excesses of yellow journalism and that formal training in journalism and ethics had ameliorated the concerns of the early leading legal lights as to the damage that could be done to individuals by the press. At the time of *Renwick* in 1984, Greener's law—"Never argue with a man who buys ink by the barrel"—still applied. Today, thanks to the accessibility of the Internet, the barriers to generating publicity are slight, and the ethical standards regarding the acceptability of certain discourse have been lowered. As the ability to do harm has grown, so must the law's ability to protect the innocent.

We therefore recognize the tort of false-light invasion of privacy and adopt Restatement of the Law 2d, Torts, Section 652E.

## NOTES

1. ***The Least Popular Privacy Tort.*** Although a majority of states recognize false light, in recent decades the tort has become much less universally accepted than the other *Restatement* privacy torts, as the *Welling* court acknowledges. It "remains the least-recognized and most controversial aspect of invasion of privacy." *Denver Publ'g Co. v. Bueno,* 54 P.3d 893, 897–98 (Colo. 2002). After *Welling* was decided, Florida rejected the tort in *Jews For Jesus, Inc. v. Rapp*, 997 So. 2d 1098 (Fla. 2008), joining the states of Colorado, Minnesota, Texas, and North Carolina listed in the *Welling* decision.

2. ***Scholarly Disagreement.*** Commentators are just as divided as courts in their opinions about the merits of the false light tort. Some favor the tort's existence. *See, e.g.*, Bryan R. Lasswell, *In Defense of False Light: Why False Light Must Remain a Viable Cause of Action*, 34 S. TEX. L. REV. 149 (1993); Nathan E. Ray, Note, *Let There Be False Light: Resisting the Growing Trend Against an Important Tort*, 84 MINN. L. REV. 713 (2000); Gary T. Schwartz, *Explaining and Justifying a Limited Tort of False Light Invasion of Privacy*, 41 CASE W. RES. L. REV. 885 (1990); Ray Yasser, *Warren Spahn's Legal Legacy: The Right to Be Free from False Praise*, 18 SETON HALL J. SPORTS & ENT. L. 49 (2008). Others oppose it. *See, e.g.*, Sandra Chance & Christina Locke, *When Even the Truth Isn't Good Enough: Judicial Inconsistency in False Light Cases Threatens Free Speech*, 9 FIRST AMEND. L. REV. 546 (2011); J. Clarke Kelso, *False Light Privacy: A Requiem*, 32 SANTA CLARA L. REV. 783 (1992); Diane Leenheer Zimmerman, *False Light Invasion of Privacy: The Light That Failed*, 64 N.Y.U. L. REV. 364 (1989); Harvey L. Zuckman, *Invasion of Privacy—Some Communicative Torts Whose Time Has Gone*, 47 WASH. & LEE L. REV. 253, 258 (1990).

3. ***Distinctions Between False Light and Defamation.*** In its opinion adopting the false light tort, the West Virginia Supreme Court offered this summary of the general distinctions between privacy and defamation:

> In defamation law only statements that are false are actionable[;] truth is, almost universally, a defense. In privacy law, other than in false light cases, the facts published are true; indeed it is the very truth of the facts that creates the claimed invasion of privacy. Secondly, in defamation cases the interest sought to be protected is the objective one of reputation, either economic, political, or personal, in the outside world. In privacy cases the interest affected is the subjective one of injury to [the] inner person. Thirdly, where the issue is truth or falsity, the marketplace of ideas furnishes a forum in which the battle can be fought. In privacy cases, resort to the marketplace simply accentuates the injury.

*Crump v. Beckley Newspapers, Inc.*, 320 S.E. 2d 70, 83 (W. Va. 1984) (internal quotations omitted). How does this comparison of privacy to defamation compare to the *Welling* court's narrower explanation of the distinctions between false light and defamation? Is it persuasive?

4. ***The Actual Malice Standard.*** The Supreme Court has held that one legal rule applicable to defamation also covers false light. In that case, the Hill family had been held hostage in their home by three escaped convicts. Naturally, there was news coverage of the dramatic incident. A writer later used the story as inspiration for a novel, *The Desperate Hours*, which significantly embellished the actual events; the novel was later made into both a play and a movie. Life Magazine wrote an article which the Hills claimed gave the false impression that the fictional play portrayed their experience accurately. The Hills sued under the New York privacy statute enacted after *Roberson* [see Section A above]. The Supreme Court held "that the constitutional protections for speech and press preclude the application of the New York statute to redress false reports of matters of public interest in the absence of proof that the defendant published the report with knowledge of its falsity or in reckless disregard of the truth." *Time, Inc. v. Hill*, 385 U.S. 374, 387–88 (1967). This is the same "actual malice" standard the Court had applied previously to defamation cases in *New York Times Co. v. Sullivan*, 376 U.S. 254 (1964). Thus, when speech concerns a matter of public interest, the plaintiff in a false light case will has the same heightened burden of proof to show "actual malice"—essentially, knowledge or recklessness—by the defendant.

5. ***False Statements and False Implications.*** The *Welling* court says that, under false light, "the statement made must be untrue." Is that quite right? In the case itself, what was the false statement made in the flyers distributed by Ms. Weinfeld? As expressed in the Restatement, the gravamen of the tort is that "the defendant places the [plaintiff] before the public in a false light." A perfectly true statement may, perhaps because of context or omissions, leave an inaccurate impression. So, by distributing the flyers at the locations she did, Weinfeld allegedly implied that the Wellings' son threw the rock at her window, placing the Welling family in a false light.

Some courts point to exactly this possibility as a justification for recognizing a separate false light tort distinct from defamation. *See, e.g.*, *Godbehere v. Phoenix Newspapers, Inc.*, 783 P.2d 781, 787 (Ariz. 1989). In most states, however, these types of inaccurate impressions can be addressed in a defamation case under the doctrine of "defamation by implication." *See Parnigoni v. St. Columba's Nursery Sch.*, 681 F. Supp. 2d 1, 19 (D.D.C. 2010) (holding that overlapping allegations of defamation by implication and false light both state a claim, but recovery will only be allowed for one of them); *Jews For Jesus, Inc. v. Rapp*, 997 So. 2d 1098, 1106 (Fla. 2008) ("Although proponents often argue that allowing recovery for these types of true statements justifies the necessity of false light, defamation already recognizes the concept that literally true statements can be defamatory where they create a false impression.").

6. ***Reputational Injury.*** In theory, false light could fill another gap in the defamation tort, which requires an injury to reputation for liability. But when does a statement cause no provable reputational damage, yet still rise to the level of offensiveness to justify compensation under false light? The Colorado Supreme Court identified two possible situations:

> The first involves cases where the defendant reveals intimate and personal, but false, details of plaintiff's private life, for example, portraying plaintiff as the victim of sexual harassment, or as being poverty-stricken, or as having a terminal illness or suffering from depression. These depictions are not necessarily defamatory, but are potentially highly offensive. The second category encompasses portrayals of the plaintiff in a *more positive* light than he deserves.

*Denver Publ'g Co. v. Bueno*, 54 P.3d 893, 902–03 (Colo. 2002) [citing cases and Gary T. Schwartz, *Explaining and Justifying a Limited Tort of False Light Invasion of Privacy*, 41 CASE W. RES. L. REV. 885 (1990)]. How likely are these scenarios? What is the precise nature of the harm caused by each one?

7. ***Does It Matter?*** Even while acknowledging that situations existed in theory where false light would provide relief when defamation did not, the *Bueno* court also said, "Remarkably few instances exist where the false light claim proceeded, but defamation failed. Those that did were on atypical facts or dubious legal grounds." *Denver Pub. Co. v. Bueno*, 54 P.3d 893, 902 (Colo. 2002). The Florida Supreme Court went further, concluding, "We are struck by the fact that our review of these decisions has revealed no case, nor has one been pointed out to us, in which a judgment based solely on a false light cause of action was upheld." *Jews For Jesus, Inc. v. Rapp*, 997 So. 2d 1098, 1113 (Fla. 2008); *see also Cain v. Hearst Corp.*, 878 S.W.2d 577, 579–580 (Tex. 1994) (finding no Texas case where false light was the only available legal theory that could be brought). If the situation that requires false light is so rare, is it worth recognizing the tort? Or does this suggest the converse, that little harm will come of doing so?

8. ***Changing Times, Again.*** Notice how the *Welling* court distinguishes the present day from the 1980s. Now that the internet has made it easier to disseminate allegedly false information, and

professionalized journalists no longer serve as gatekeepers, the court believes a false light tort has become more important. Don't these judges sound like Warren and Brandeis? And isn't that a strange observation in a case about paper handbills distributed in person?

## 3. MISCELLANEOUS TORTS IN PRIVACY CASES

A few other torts that often come up in privacy cases deserve mention. Plaintiffs typically want to plead in the alternative, raising every possible basis for liability. Thus, many complaints raising the Restatement torts include some of these claims as well.

**1. *Breach of Confidentiality.*** In some professions with special duties of confidentiality—medicine, banking, or law, for example—courts have recognized torts for breaches of that duty. [For an example, see Chapter 12]. In these cases, the heightened duty comes from the nature of the relationship between the plaintiff and the defendant. In the United Kingdom, which does not recognize common law privacy torts like the four classic ones in the Restatement, that duty of confidentiality has been expanded to a broader set of relationships instead. In one English case, for example, a famous married male actor had an affair with another man, who subsequently disclosed the relationship and showed some of the actor's letters to a tabloid newspaper. After the tabloid report created a scandal, the actor sued his former lover under a breach of confidence tort and won. The court held, "when people enter into a personal relationship of this nature, they do not do so for the purpose of it subsequently being published in *The Sun*, or any other newspaper. The information about the relationship is for the relationship and not for a wider purpose." *Barrymore v. News Group Newspapers Ltd.*, [1997] E.S.R. 600 (Ch.) (U.K.). Neil Richards and Daniel Solove argue that the comparatively narrow American breach of confidentiality tort misses an opportunity to protect important interests:

> The law of confidentiality in England also has attributes that the American privacy torts lack. In America, the prevailing belief is that people assume the risk of betrayal when they share secrets with each other. But in England, spouses, ex-spouses, friends, and nearly anyone else can be liable for divulging confidences. As one English court noted, "when people kiss and later one of them tells, that second person is almost certainly breaking a confidential arrangement." Confidentiality thus recognizes that nondisclosure expectations emerge not only from norms of individual dignity, but also from norms of relationships, trust, and reliance on promises. American privacy law has never fully embraced privacy within relationships; it typically views information exposed to others as no longer private. Although a tort remedying breach of confidence would emerge later on in American law, it developed slowly in comparison to the Warren and Brandeis privacy torts.

Neil M. Richards & Daniel J. Solove, *Privacy's Other Path: Recovering the Law of Confidentiality*, 96 GEO. L.J. 123, 126 (2007). Do you agree with their analysis?

2. ***Infliction of Emotional Distress.*** Privacy tort claims often are accompanied by claims for intentional or negligent infliction of emotional distress, known in some states as the tort of "outrage." Some states (including Florida) have refused to recognize this tort at all, and other states (including Texas and New York) deny recovery when another tort shares the same gravamen as the emotional distress claim. Even courts that allow the plaintiff to claim alternative theories ordinarily prevent the collection of duplicative damages. Because "outrageous" conduct is an element of several privacy torts, and the damages most often arise from emotional harm, the emotional distress claims often fall by the wayside as litigation progresses, but attorneys often plead them—either from an abundance of caution or because they make a complaint seem more imposing.

3. ***Defamation and Trespass.*** Whether or not a state recognizes false light claims, facts often give rise to both privacy and defamation claims. This is most obviously so where a communication mixes truthful but allegedly private information with falsehoods. Even when the false light tort is available, plaintiffs usually plead defamation (and that is often the more significant claim, with false light included as a backup). Similarly, as noted above, intrusion on seclusion claims frequently involve trespass.

4. ***Intellectual Property.*** Some privacy claims combine naturally with certain types of intellectual property. Appropriation claims often blend with rights of publicity and also with allegations of "false endorsement" under federal and state trademark law. In the all-too-common scenario of the private selfie being circulated by someone else online, the subject of the photo is also its creator. This situation allows plaintiffs to plead copyright claims, because doing so allows for enhanced damages and gives the person the right to demand the photo be taken down under the Digital Millennium Copyright Act, 17 U.S.C. § 512. Claims couched in terms of intellectual property also may navigate around the immunity enjoyed by some online intermediaries, discussed below [see Section E].

5. ***Statutory Claims.*** The privacy torts do not exist in isolation. In much of the rest of this book we will see statutes that grant private rights of action, sometimes on privacy grounds and sometimes for other reasons. Complaints brought under statutes such as the Electronic Communications Privacy Act [Chapter 5], the Fair Credit Reporting Act [Chapter 6], or the Video Privacy Protection Act [Chapter 14] may state additional prima facie claims under the privacy torts. In addition, cases in areas such as employment discrimination, police misconduct, or family law frequently include privacy tort claims, because the underlying conflicts can give rise to privacy injuries. Again, courts will forbid

duplicative damages, but plainitffs may be prudent to plead any that are colorable.

## E. LIMITS ON TORT LIABILITY

We have seen several internal doctrinal limitations contained in the torts themselves—the newsworthiness exception under disclosure or the commercial use requirement under many appropriation and publicity rights laws, for example. In addition, a number of other doctrines tend to further limit the application of privacy torts across the board. This section considers several of these.

### COMMUNICATIONS DECENCY ACT

47 U.S.C. § 230

**§ 230 Protection for Private Blocking and Screening of Offensive Material**

[The statute begind with extensive hortatory congressional findings in sections (a) and (b).]

(c) Protection for "Good Samaritan" blocking and screening of offensive material

(1) Treatment of publisher or speaker

No provider or user of an interactive computer service shall be treated as the publisher or speaker of any information provided by another information content provider.

(2) Civil liability

No provider or user of an interactive computer service shall be held liable on account of—

(A) any action voluntarily taken in good faith to restrict access to or availability of material that the provider or user considers to be obscene, lewd, lascivious, filthy, excessively violent, harassing, or otherwise objectionable, whether or not such material is constitutionally protected; or

(B) any action taken to enable or make available to information content providers or others the technical means to restrict access to material described in paragraph (1). . . .

(f) Definitions

. . . (2) Interactive computer service

The term "interactive computer service" means any information service, system, or access software provider that provides or enables computer access by multiple users to a computer server, including specifically a service or system that provides access to the Internet and such systems operated or services offered by libraries or educational institutions.

(3) Information content provider

The term "information content provider" means any person or entity that is responsible, in whole or in part, for the creation or development of information provided through the Internet or any other interactive computer service.

## S.C. v. Dirty World LLC

2012 WL 3335284 (W.D. Mo. 2012)

■ DEAN WHIPPLE, DISTRICT JUDGE.

Defendant Dirty World operates www.TheDirty.com (the "Website"), which was founded by Defendant [Nik] Richie. Richie is also the Website's editor-in-chief. Visitors to the Website may submit posts on any topic, and the posts vary in type and subject matter. Some posts are about the news, sports, and politics. Other posts offer gossip and commentary about both public and private individuals.

The Website does not require that a post be about any particular topic or individual. Instead, users are simply instructed to describe "what's happening. Remember to tell us Who, What, When, Where, Why." The submission process asks the user to enter a title for their submission, along with the applicable "City," "College," and "Category." The Category field has more than forty options, including "I HAVE NO IDEA," "Business," "News," "Spring Break," and "Would You?"

The "Would You?" category is more of an inquiry for Richie to state whether he would be romantically interested in the person submitted. Richie responds negatively to nearly all of these inquiries, allegedly "to express his view as to the absurdity and fallacy of today's perfection-seeking culture." Though Richie does not fact-check each submission, he generally reviews them so that he can eliminate posts that he deems to be "inappropriate" or "unduly offensive."

On January 24, 2011, a third party submitted the following post under the title "Nasty Church Girl:"

> Nik, I was living in Miami Beach for 4 months for work, and this nasty bitch [referring to the Plaintiff] who was my 'friend' started fcking [sic] my boyfriend in my bed and bringing her nasty ass horse teeth around my son trying to play house. This slut claims to be a sweet little church girl. She even works for the church! Fugly slut! Is this girl worth having sex with ___ I wouldn't think so! LEE'S SUMMIT SLUT!!

(hereinafter the "Church Girl Post"). The author of the post also submitted a photo of the Plaintiff. Richie published the post on the Website, and opined immediately below it that "Her gumlines [sic] as big as her teeth, that's amazing.–nik." Richie did not author, modify, or alter any portion of the Church Girl Post or its title. Instead, he published the post as submitted to the Website. Richie does not personally know and has not knowingly spoken to the author of the Church Girl Post. Richie also does not know the Plaintiff and had never heard of her prior to the Church Girl Post.

The Plaintiff filed this lawsuit on April 14, 2011. The remaining claims in her First Amended Complaint are for defamation through libel (Count I), public disclosure of private facts (Count II), false light invasion of privacy (Count III), and intentional infliction of emotional distress (Count IV). The Complaint alleges in part that the Church Girl Post, suggesting that Plaintiff "was unchaste, a 'slut,' and was 'fcking' [sic] the poster's boyfriend in her bed" is false and places the Plaintiff in a false light. The Plaintiff alleges that the post was especially harmful to her "as an active member and employee of the United Methodist denomination church." For each count, the Plaintiff requests $900,000 in compensatory damages, as well as punitive and other damages.

The pending Motion [for summary judgment] argues that the Defendants are entitled to [Communications Decency Act] immunity because they did not create or develop the Church Girl Post. *See* 47 U.S.C. § 230(c)(1). The Plaintiff argues in part that the CDA does not apply because "the site's owner and operator . . . encourages the offensive and defamatory material. . . ."

[CDA § 230] immunizes website operators from liability for content provided "by another information content provider." Consequently, websites are treated differently than newspapers, magazines or television and radio stations, all of which may be held liable for publishing obscene or defamatory material written or prepared by others.

Courts in this circuit and elsewhere have described CDA immunity as "broad" and "robust." As explained by one court, "*Congress granted most Internet services immunity* from liability for publishing false or defamatory material *so long as the information was provided by another party*" [emphasis supplied by court]. That said, a website will lose immunity if it is also "an information content provider," which is defined as "any person or entity that is *responsible, in whole or in part, for the creation or development* of information provided through the Internet or any other interactive computer service." 47 U.S.C. § 230(f)(3) [emphasis supplied by court].

In this case, it is undisputed that a third party authored and then submitted the Church Girl Post. The Defendants did not alter the post, and published it as submitted to the Website. Consequently, CDA immunity turns on whether the Defendants are "responsible, in whole or in part, for the creation or development of" the Church Girl Post. *See* 47 U.S.C. § 230(f)(3). The Plaintiff argues in part that Defendants are responsible because they "encourage development of what is offensive about the content through the tenor of the [W]ebsite and Richie's own actions in commenting on posts and interaction with his readers."

The Court first examines the meaning of "development" under the CDA. Though that term continues to evolve under case law, the Tenth Circuit recently stated that "[a] website helps to develop unlawful content, and thus falls within the exception to section 230, if it contributes materially to the alleged illegality of the conduct." *F.T.C. v. Accusearch Inc.*, 570 F.3d 1187, 1200 (10th Cir. 2009) (quoting *Fair Hous. Council v. Roommates.com, LLC,* 521 F.3d 1157, 1168 (9th Cir. 2008)). The Court finds that this meaning is in accordance with the existing case law, and adopts it for purposes of this Order.

Therefore, for example, a website may help develop unlawful content if it *requires* or *pays for* the submission of illegal information. A website may also materially contribute to the illegality of a post "such as by removing the word "not" from a user's message reading "[Name] did *not* steal the artwork" in order to transform an innocent message into a libelous one.

Applying this meaning, the Court finds that the Defendants did not materially contribute to the development of the Church Girl Post. Most importantly, it is undisputed that the Church Girl Post was unilaterally drafted and submitted by a third party. The Defendants have further established that (a) they did nothing to induce a post specifically directed at the Plaintiff; (b) Richie does not personally know and has never knowingly spoken to the author of the Church Girl Post; (c) Richie had never heard of the Plaintiff prior to commencement of this action; and (d) the Defendants did not add to or otherwise alter the substance of the post. In addition, the Website does not require the posting of actionable material, and it does not pay for such information. To the contrary, users of the Website may submit posts on any topic.

In sum, a third party unilaterally created and submitted the Church Girl Post without specific instructions or requests from the Defendants to do so. This is precisely the type of situation that warrants CDA immunity. *Doe v. MySpace, Inc.*, 528 F.3d 413, 419 (5th Cir.2008) ("[S]o long as a third party willingly provides the essential published content, the interactive service provider receives full immunity regardless of the specific editing or selection process.").

In light of the foregoing, the Plaintiff focuses more on the general structure and operation of the Website. She claims that because the Website does not publish all submissions, the Defendants develop the content by "hand select[ing] those juicy tidbits of trash that are titillating to the public." Case law, however, does not support this argument. The CDA protects the exercise of a publisher's traditional editorial functions—such as deciding *whether to publish*.

The Plaintiff also argues that Richie generally helps develop content "by his interaction with 'the Dirty Army' [the nickname for the site's fans] and in the creation and execution of categories like 'Would You?' where users submit content specifically to get Richie's views and expect an answer from him." This argument fails because the CDA focuses on the specific post at issue.

Finally, the Plaintiff argues that the Website encourages and "exists solely for people to post 'dirt' about their neighbors without regard for truth." This argument fails both legally and factually. As a matter of law, and even if true, merely encouraging defamatory posts is not sufficient to defeat CDA immunity. Factually, the Plaintiff has not presented any evidence that the Website is devoted to "dirt" about private citizens or is merely a portal for defamatory material. To the contrary, the Defendant has shown that the Website contains posts on a number of topics, including sports, politics, and other world events.

For all these reasons, the Court concludes that the Plaintiff's claims are barred because the Defendants are entitled to CDA immunity. That said—and to avoid any confusion—the Court disagrees with the Defendants' apparent belief that they are immune for any and all postings on their Website. Instead, the Court simply holds that the Defendants are entitled to immunity under the facts of this case. This holding does not necessarily mean that the Plaintiff is without recourse [because she can still sue the person who wrote the Church Girl Post].

## NOTES

1. ***Content Providers and Service Providers.*** Section 230 distinguishes between "information content providers" and "interactive service providers." The former provide the actual content which may lead to liability, while the latter are only conduits for that content and immunized from liability. When the Communications Decency Act passed as part of a comprehensive telecommunications statute in 1996, the World Wide Web was in its infancy. The distinction became crucial with the rise of the commercial internet, particularly user-generated content and social media. Massive intermediaries such as Facebook, YouTube, and Twitter did not yet exist, but they generally fall comfortably within the definition of interactive service providers. Their users may be the information content providers. Courts generally read the scope of the immunity for online forums broadly, consistent with the *S.C. v. Dirty World* decision. In 2013, a district court in another tort suit against TheDirty ruled the other way, but this decision was overturned on appeal. *See Jones v. Dirty World Entm't Recordings LLC*, 755 F.3d 398 (6th Cir. 2014).

2. ***The Meaning of "Development."*** The decision turns on the interpretation of the "development of information" under § 230(f)(3). If TheDirty *developed* the information, it is an information content provider and legally responsible for the content. The court cites reasoning from the earlier *Accusearch* and *Roommates.com* cases saying a web site develops content "if it contributes materially to the alleged illegality of the conduct." Eric Goldman, a strong supporter of broad § 230 immunity, criticizes *S.C.*

and another recent decision for their development of the "development" standard:

> It's disconcerting to see both courts parsing the meaning of the word 'development' as the immunity's linchpin. After the *Roommates.com* train wreck, it's clear that no one knows what the word 'development' means. While the . . . opinions both get to a decent place, the more often that courts play around with the meaning of the term 'development,' the more likely it is that we'll see goofy defense losses. Defendants, if you're fighting the *Roommates.com* battle, please try to get courts to focus on this standard from *Roommates.com*: 'The message to website operators is clear: If you don't encourage illegal content, or design your website to require users to input illegal content, you will be immune.'

Eric Goldman, *TheDirty Gets Its First 47 USC 230 Win*, TECHNOLOGY & MARKETING LAW BLOG (March 13, 2012), http://blog.ericgoldman.org/archives/2012/03/thedirty_gets_i.htm. Goldman notes that it can be very difficult to determine whether a web site contributes to alleged illegality at an early stage of litigation—but an immunity defense only works properly if it allows for early resolution. And, Goldman warns, many web sites, including YouTube, sometimes pay money for user-generated content.

3. ***Support for § 230.*** According to YouTube, users upload 100 hours of video to the site every minute. It would be impossible to vet all of this content to determine whether any of it might create liability under the privacy torts—especially because the site usually lacks any information about the people discussed or depicted in user-generated content. Indeed, in a letter opposing proposals to diminish immunity under § 230, a group of organizations and scholars emphasized the importance of § 230 to the development of online resources:

> Section 230 is the legal cornerstone of the Internet economy, enabling the unprecedented scope of lawful commerce and free expression that the Internet supports today.
>
> Section 230 is essential to eliminating the liability risk that would otherwise chill service providers from hosting third-party content. Without it, operators of services like content hosts, blogging platforms, social networks, and even search engines would risk liability every time they hosted or displayed content provided by others, including user-generated content. This would dramatically reduce opportunities for free expression online.

*Coalition Letter to Congress on Section 230*, Ctr. for Democracy and Technology et al. (July 31, 2013), https://cdt.org/insight/coalition-letter-to-congress-on-section-230/. These scholars and advocates argue that free online platforms like YouTube, Facebook, or Reddit could never have arisen without § 230.

4. ***Criticism of § 230.*** Critics of § 230 consider it overly broad and argue that it vitiates meaningful remedies for many victims of privacy invasions. Intermediary immunity leaves numerous plaintiffs who have

suffered significant harm without an identifiable defendant to sue. As Ann Bartow argues:

> ISPs, which are in the best position to control the distribution of harmful postings, have no incentive or obligation to do so. . . . By writing § 230 into law, Congress left . . . Internet harassment victims vulnerable and helpless, especially if they are not able independently to identify the sources of the abuse.

Ann Bartow, *Internet Defamation as Profit Center: The Monetization of Online Harassment*, 32 HARV. J. L. & GENDER 383, 417–18 (2009). The "revenge porn" phenomenon illustrates the problem. Angry or spurned individuals, often former partners, post intimate or embarrassing photographs online, frequently alongside the victims' contact information. A network of revenge porn sites actively seeks to saturate search engine results about the victim so that anyone looking for information about her will find the photos. It is notable that revenge porn sites victimize women in particular. In a comprehensive book about such online abuse, Danielle Keats Citron catalogues stories of women targeted for harassment—which she characterizes as a civil rights issue akin to hostile work environments of an earlier era—and discusses the way § 230 shields intermediaries from responsibility for it. *See* DANIELLE KEATS CITRON, HATE CRIMES IN CYBERSPACE (2014). Recognizing that § 230 also has value, Citron proposes a narrow amendment that would exclude "the very worst actors" from its immunity, including sites "that principally host cyber stalking or nonconsensual pornography." *Id.* at 177.

5. ***The Notice and Takedown Alternative.*** Section 230 explicitly removes intellectual property infringement from immunity. Instead, copyright law provides a "notice and takedown" regime under the Digital Millennium Copyright Act (DMCA). *See* 17 U.S.C. § 512. The DMCA offers a safe harbor from copyright liability if service providers create a mechanism for copyright holders to send them a takedown notice and they remove the material when they receive a notice. There are provisions for the original poster to send a "counter-notice" and certain other conditions as well. Many critics of § 230 have suggested that a similar regime for privacy invasions might offer better balance than the current blanket immunity. Section 230's supporters reply that the DMCA process has been abused with frivolous takedown notices and that privacy issues are more factually complex than copyright.

6. ***Other Exemptions from the Exemption.*** In addition to intellectual property infringement, § 230 does not provide immunity for violations of federal criminal law or of the Electronic Communications Privacy Act [see Chapter 5], which forbids certain forms of electronic eavesdropping. *State* criminal law that would penalize intermediaries *is* preempted by § 230. *See, e.g.*, *Backpage.com, LLC v. McKenna*, 881 F. Supp. 2d 1262 (W.D. Wash. 2012). A July 2013 letter to Congress signed by almost every state attorney general asked Congress to amend this language and exempt state criminal law from § 230 immunity as well, citing concerns about online advertisements for prostitution and especially child sex trafficking. Supporters of § 230 have objected that this change would expose

intermediaries to a patchwork of diverse laws, effectively forcing them to monitor all third-party content and vitiating the protection of § 230.

7. ***A Victim's Limited Options.*** When a person's privacy has been invaded by user-generated content and § 230 prevents a privacy tort lawsuit against the intermediary, what else can the person do? As the *S.C.* court notes in closing, a plaintiff can sue the person who posted the content. But frequently there are serious problems with this approach. Users are often anonymous, and they may be untraceable. A court could permit the plaintiff to name a "John Doe" defendant and then serve a subpoena on the intermediary to discover the defendant's identity or information such as an IP address that could lead to that identity. But this will require effort and expense, and the poster may have taken steps to maintain anonymity such as using an internet café or library. Even an original poster who can be located may well lack resources to pay any judgment. A wronged plaintiff might be satisfied by the vindication of a court ruling alone, but it will be difficult to hire an attorney to sue a judgment-proof defendant. Some plaintiffs avoid § 230 problems by recasting their complaints as intellectual property claims. For example, plaintiffs who hold the copyright in a photograph (or can obtain the copyright by transfer) may use the DMCA notice and takedown procedures [see Note 5]. Celebrities and others who can make plausible claims of trademark or publicity rights also may avoid § 230 based on the IP exemption. Finally, rather than pursuing legal remedies, some people simply ask that the intermediary remove the content voluntarily. (Indeed, TheDirty initially removed the Church Girl Post at S.C.'s request.) Some established platforms for user-generated content agree to such requests routinely—Twitter and Facebook, for example, have established policies that they will remove revenge porn—but the lack of legal consequences leaves it entirely to their discretion. Other sites pride themselves on their refusal to take down any posts. And of course, on the internet, even if one site takes a post down, others may cache or repost the same content.

8. ***"Dirty Politics."*** TheDirty might seem to provide the ultimate example of the type of gossip that Warren and Brandeis abhorred. And certainly much of the site is exactly that. Yet as the *S.C.* court notes several times, the site is not devoted solely to collecting "dirt" about private individuals. In perhaps the most famous example, the site's "Dirty Politics" page was the first to reveal that former Congressman Anthony Weiner had continued online sexual communications with women after the scandal that forced his resignation from the House of Representatives, fatally wounding his comeback campaign for New York City's mayoralty.

9. ***A Uniquely American Approach.*** No other nation extends protection to online intermediaries similar to § 230. In most other countries, intermediaries can be liable for content posted by users in a broad range of circumstances. So, for example, a recent ruling of the Court of Justice for the European Union ordered Google to honor a "right to be forgotten;" when a citizen of a European Union nation demonstrates a privacy interest in online material, even a newspaper article, Google can be required to remove that item from results for a search of the person's name. [See Chapter 4 for more

on this issue.] Intermediaries may respond to the differing legal requirements in other countries by delivering different content in different locations, either by changing the local domain (altering google.es in Spain but leaving google.com the same, for example) or by tracing the IP address of users and tailoring content based on the country of origin. Such requirements burden the intermediary—but, on the other hand, this response demonstrates that country-specific responses are technologically feasible, even if difficult or expensive to implement.

## Gawker Media v. Bollea

129 So. 3d 1196 (Fla. App. 2014)

■ BLACK, JUDGE.

Terry Bollea sought to enjoin Gawker Media, LLC, from publishing and otherwise distributing the written report about his extramarital affair that includes video excerpts from the sexual encounter. The circuit court granted Mr. Bollea's motion for temporary injunction, though it did not articulate the reasons for doing so. On appeal, Gawker Media challenges the circuit court's order. Because the temporary injunction is an unconstitutional prior restraint under the First Amendment, we reverse.

### I. Background

In 2006, Mr. Bollea engaged in extramarital sexual relations with a woman in her home. Allegedly without Mr. Bollea's consent or knowledge, the sexual encounter was videotaped. On or about October 4, 2012, Gawker Media posted a written report about the extramarital affair on its website, including excerpts of the videotaped sexual encounter ("Sex Tape"). Mr. Bollea maintains that he never consented to the Sex Tape's release or publication. Gawker Media maintains that it was not responsible for creating the Sex Tape and that it received a copy of the Sex Tape from an anonymous source for no compensation.

Mr. Bollea filed a motion for temporary injunction seeking to enjoin Gawker Media from publishing and otherwise distributing the video excerpts from the sexual encounter and complementary written report. Following a hearing, the circuit court issued an order on April 25, 2012, granting the motion for temporary injunction. The court did not make any findings at the hearing or in its written order to support its decision. On May 15, 2013, this court stayed the order granting the motion for temporary injunction pending the resolution of this appeal.

### II. Applicable Standards

The primary purpose of a temporary injunction is to preserve the status quo while the merits of the underlying dispute are litigated. In the context of the media, the status quo is to publish news promptly that editors decide to publish. A restraining order disturbs the status quo and impinges on the exercise of editorial discretion. A temporary injunction is an "extraordinary remedy" that should be granted sparingly and only after the moving party has alleged and proved facts entitling him to relief.

A temporary injunction aimed at speech, as it is here, is a classic example of prior restraint on speech triggering First Amendment concerns, and as such, it is prohibited in all but the most exceptional cases, *Near v. Minn. ex rel. Olson,* 283 U.S. 697 (1931). Since "prior restraints on speech and publication are the most serious and least tolerable infringement on First Amendment rights," the moving party bears the "heavy burden" of establishing that there are no less extreme measures available to mitigate the effects of the unrestrained publication and that the restraint will indeed effectively accomplish its purpose. *Neb. Press Ass'n v. Stuart,* 427 U.S. 539, 558–59, 562 (1976). Furthermore, where a direct prior restraint is imposed upon the reporting of news by the media, each passing day may constitute a separate and cognizable infringement of the First Amendment.

We generally review orders granting temporary injunctions for an abuse of discretion. However, we apply a de novo standard of review to the determination of whether a temporary injunction constitutes an unconstitutional prior restraint on free speech. And though an injunction order generally comes to this court clothed with a presumption of correctness, orders restraining protected speech must be considered presumptively invalid and will only be permitted if there are no less restrictive means available.

### III. First Amendment

It is not clear from the hearing transcript, and certainly not from the order, why the circuit court granted the motion for temporary injunction. Based upon the few interjections the court made during the hearing, it appears that the court believed Mr. Bollea's right to privacy was insurmountable and that publishing the content at issue was otherwise impermissible because it was founded upon illegal actions.

"[W]here matters of purely private significance are at issue, First Amendment protections are often less rigorous." *Snyder v. Phelps,* 562 U.S. 443 (2011) (citing *Hustler Magazine, Inc. v. Falwell,* 485 U.S. 46, 56 (1988)).

On the other hand, speech on matters of public concern is at the heart of the First Amendment's protection.

> Speech deals with matters of public concern when it can be fairly considered as relating to any matter of political, social, or other concern to the community, or when it is a subject of legitimate news interest; that is, a subject of general interest and of value and concern to the public. The arguably inappropriate or controversial character of a statement is irrelevant to the question whether it deals with a matter of public concern.

*Id.* at 1216 (citations omitted) (internal quotation marks omitted).

Mr. Bollea, better known by his ring name Hulk Hogan, enjoyed the spotlight as a professional wrestler, and he and his family were depicted in a reality television show detailing their personal lives. Mr. Bollea openly discussed an affair he had while married to Linda Bollea in his published autobiography and otherwise discussed his family, marriage, and sex life through various media outlets. Further, prior to the publication at issue in this appeal, there were numerous reports by various media outlets regarding the existence and dissemination of the Sex Tape, some including still shots therefrom. Despite Mr. Bollea's public persona, we do not suggest that every aspect of his private life is a subject of public concern. However, the mere fact that the publication contains arguably inappropriate and otherwise sexually explicit content does not remove it from the realm of legitimate public interest.

It is clear that as a result of the public controversy surrounding the affair and the Sex Tape, exacerbated in part by Mr. Bollea himself, the report and the related video excerpts address matters of public concern. *See Bartnicki v. Vopper,* 532 U.S. 514, 534 (2001) ("[P]rivacy concerns give way when balanced against the interest in publishing matters of public importance. . . . One of the costs associated with participation in public affairs is an attendant loss of privacy.").

In support of his contention that the report and video excerpts do not qualify as matters of public concern, Mr. Bollea relies on *Michaels v. Internet Entertainment Group, Inc.,* 5 F. Supp. 2d 823 (C.D. Cal. 1998) (*Michaels I*), in which the court enjoined the commercial distribution of an entire sex tape that infringed the plaintiffs' copyrights. However, the court in *Michaels I* found the use of the sex tape to be purely commercial in nature. Specifically, the copyrighted tape was sold via the internet to paying subscribers, and the internet company displayed short segments of the tape as a means of advertisement to increase the number of subscriptions. In contrast, Gawker Media has not attempted to sell the Sex Tape or any of the material creating the instant controversy, for that matter. Rather, Gawker Media reported on Mr. Bollea's extramarital affair and complementary thereto posted excerpts from the video.

The court in *Michaels I* pointed out that although "[t]he plaintiffs are entitled to an injunction against uses of their names or likenesses to sell the [sex tape,] [t]he injunction may not reach the use of their names or likenesses to report or comment on matters of public interest." In accord with this conclusion, the court held in the companion case that the publication of a news report and brief excerpts of the sex tape was not an invasion of privacy and was protected speech. Here, the written report and video excerpts are linked to a matter of public concern—Mr. Bollea's extramarital affair and the video evidence of such—as there was ongoing public discussion about the affair and the Sex Tape, including by Mr. Bollea himself. Therefore, Mr. Bollea failed to meet the heavy burden to overcome the presumption that the temporary injunction is invalid as an unconstitutional prior restraint under the First Amendment. As such, it was within Gawker Media's editorial discretion to publish the written report and video excerpts.

The circuit court's order granting Mr. Bollea's motion for temporary injunction is reversed because it acts as an unconstitutional prior restraint under the First Amendment.

## NOTES

1. ***The Doctrinal Obstacle Course.*** Reread Part II of the *Bollea* opinion and make a list of all the doctrinal obstacles to an appellate court upholding a prior restraint. There may not be any other situation in US law with as many roadblocks. Can you imagine a prior restraint that might be upheld under these circumstances? The classic hypothetical example involves troop movements in wartime, where it might be possible for the government to constrain publication to protect the safety of combat personnel and preserve the secrecy of military operations. Even there, mere speculation about the possible harmful effects of such disclosures probably would not suffice. The famous "Pentagon Papers" prior restraint case did involve military information, but a 6–3 majority of the Supreme Court apparently believed the government had failed to carry its burden of demonstrating direct or imminent harm from publication. Because each justice wrote separately, the resulting precedent is very fragmented, but the general theme of strong hostility to prior restraints pervaded many of the opinions. *See New York Times Co. v. United States*, 403 U.S. 713 (1971) (per curiam).

2. ***The Reasons for Special Treatment.*** Why are prior restraints even more disfavored than punishing speech after it has occurred? Many reasons have been offered. For one, a prior restraint prevents speech from ever reaching the marketplace of ideas, whereas a post hoc punishment does not deny the audience the opportunity to hear the speech. Prior restraints also venture near the core purpose of the First Amendment in avoiding censorship: advance government decisions about what speech will be permitted strongly resonate with the suspicion of government power and the orientation toward liberty that animates the Bill of Rights. Finally, there is a practical argument that imposing prior restraints will likely result in overly broad restrictions, as the Supreme Court explained in another frequently quoted case from the 1970s:

> Behind the distinction [between prior restraints and post hoc penalties for speech] is a theory deeply etched in our law: a free society prefers to punish the few who abuse rights of speech after they break the law than to throttle them and all others beforehand. It is always difficult to know in advance what an individual will say, and the line between legitimate and illegitimate speech is often so finely drawn that the risks of freewheeling censorship are formidable.

*Southeastern Promotions, Ltd. v. Conrad*, 420 U.S. 546, 559 (1975). Indeed, in the Pentagon Papers case itself, dire predictions about the bad consequences of publication generally were not borne out.

3. ***The Cat is Out of the Bag.*** Strong judicial disfavor toward prior restraints can put parties facing privacy harms in a difficult position, of course. It is nearly impossible to use a tort claim to prevent a disclosure before it occurs; an injured party can only get compensation for the resulting harm after the fact. For some types of privacy invasion, particularly those involving information a person wishes to keep secret, this will be a very unsatisfactory remedy. If you accept at face value the assertion by Hulk Hogan that he was embarrassed about the possible release of the Sex Tape, then he may have been in a similar position. Most likely there would be a large number of people viewing the tape as soon as Gawker posted it, and by the time any later remedy were imposed it would be "old news" and most of the privacy damage that was going to occur would already be done.

4. ***Public Figures by Choice.*** The *Bollea* opinion repeatedly notes that the plaintiff's sex life was a matter of public interest largely because of his own attention-seeking behavior. The court shows its disbelief most clearly in a footnote omitted from the excerpt above:

> We are hard-pressed to believe that Mr. Bollea truly desired the affair and Sex Tape to remain private or to otherwise be "swept under the rug." For example, in March 2012, Mr. Bollea called into TMZ Live, a celebrity and entertainment media outlet, and disclosed that he could not identify the woman in the Sex Tape because he had a number of "conquests" during the time it was filmed. Furthermore, in October 2012, Mr. Bollea appeared on *The Howard Stern Show* and professed that his good friend, Todd Alan Clem, known professionally as Bubba the Love Sponge, allowed Mr. Bollea to have sex with Mr. Clem's then-wife Heather Clem. Mr. Bollea was certainly not shy about disclosing the explicit details of another affair he had while married to Linda Bollea in his autobiography.

In this case, is Bollea merely reaping what he sowed? Or, to use a different cliché for the opposite view, is the court blaming the victim? Does talking about his sex life waive his privacy interest in people watching him have sex? Oliver Sipple, the gay man who thwarted President Ford's assassin [see Section C above], was not a public figure by choice in the same way as Bollea. Would he be able to enjoin publication of a newspaper story about his sexual orientation? In the end, does the fact that Bollea himself promoted public interest in his sex life make a difference to the outcome?

5. ***Further Developments.*** Bollea did not get the preliminary injunction he sought here, but as of early 2016 he had achieved considerable success in the overall litigation. After trial, the jury awarded Bollea $140 million, including $25 million in punitive damages. Gawker has vowed to appeal, and expressed concern that a sum that size would be financially ruinous for the small publication.

---

## Focus

Defining Harm in the Privacy Torts

One theme woven throughout this discussion of torts is the question of harm. How do invasions of privacy injure individuals? Which of those injuries should lead to legally cognizable claims?

Go through each of the torts and consider the nature of the injury. How do they differ? How do they overlap? In some instances, the torts protect individuals against profound personal embarrassment. In others, they are safeguarding an individual's reputation within the community, similar to the aim of defamation law. At still other times, torts appear to value an individual's ability to control personal information. And this list is not exhaustive. How would Warren and Brandeis view these different understandings of harm? Which ones do you consider important?

Danielle Keats Citron argues that Prosser's taxonomy imposed a particular vision of harm on the privacy torts that left them inflexible and unable to adapt to contemporary challenges such as the permanent availability of embarrassing information online through a Google search or the risk of identity theft caused by a data breach:

> Whereas Warren and Brandeis sought to protect an individual's right to be "let alone" from unwanted disclosure and intrusion, Prosser saw privacy tort law as protecting a person from emotional, reputational, and proprietary harm caused by specific activities. This narrowed the reach of the privacy torts from an approach that could adapt to changing circumstances to one that addressed four narrow types of privacy-invasive activities and their accompanying injuries. Importantly, it stopped courts from fleshing out the contours of the "right to be let alone" protected by tort privacy.
>
> Courts adopted Prosser's privacy taxonomy with such rigidity that privacy tort law is now locked into a "writ system." Courts recognize the four privacy torts but only those privacy torts. Legal forms naturally tend to shape our thinking, and Prosser's prestige and work on the Second Restatement of Torts additionally ensured the adoption of this constricted approach. At the same time, courts have narrowly construed the elements of the four privacy torts, further limiting their reach. This is surely due to the concern that privacy claimants could recover for trivialities given the ethereal nature of the alleged harm.

Danielle Keats Citron, *Mainstreaming Privacy Torts*, 98 CAL. L. REV. 1805, 1825–26 (2010).

As Citron notes, various doctrinal structures aim to prevent recovery for merely "ethereal" harms. For example, intrusions and disclosures must be "highly offensive." The mere collection of mundane personal data rarely clears this hurdle. In the same symposium, Neil Richards and Daniel Solove share Citron's view that Prosser's taxonomy has ossified the law and frozen in place a crude definition of harm that prevents expansion to encompass modern data practices:

> Courts often are dismissive of privacy harms because they lack a physical component. For example, courts have struggled to recognize harm from leaked or improperly disseminated data. Courts can readily understand the harm caused by the disclosure of a naked photograph of a person, but they struggle in locating a harm when non-embarrassing data is disclosed or leaked. A broader understanding of harm is needed in order for the privacy

> torts to apply to the extensive gathering, dissemination, and use of information by various businesses and organizations.

Neil M. Richards & Daniel J. Solove, *Prosser's Privacy Law: A Mixed Legacy*, 98 CAL. L. REV. 1887, 1922–23 (2010). Ryan Calo suggests that increased collection and processing of personal data allows firms to engage in "digital market manipulation," and the resulting harms justify privacy restrictions:

> A specific set of emerging technologies and techniques will empower corporations to discover and exploit the limits of each individual consumer's ability to pursue his or her own self-interest. Firms will increasingly be able to trigger irrationality or vulnerability in consumers—leading to actual and perceived harms that challenge the limits of consumer protection law, but which regulators can scarcely ignore.

Ryan Calo, *Digital Market Manipulation*, 82 GEO. WASH. L. REV. 995, 999 (2014). In contrast to these views, Jane Yakowitz Bambauer argues that the best understanding of harm for modern privacy law *does* come from Prosser's torts—specifically, the curbs on observation in the intrusion on seclusion tort. She thinks proposals based on broader visions of harm unduly restrict the flow of truthful and useful information and turn their back on the flexibility of common-law reasoning embodied in torts:

> Popular privacy proposals, though politically expedient, will undermine the public's interests in innovation and knowledge-production. In contrast, regulation targeting information flow at its source—at the point of observation—can be significantly expanded without running into conceptual pitfalls.

Jane Yakowitz Bambauer, *The New Intrusion*, 88 NOTRE DAME L. REV. 205, 209 (2012). There have been numerous proposals to reshape the privacy torts to deal with new technology and resulting changes in practices. Yet we shall see that torts are not the only privacy remedies that display ambivalence and imprecision about the nature of the underlying harm they address. What harms should the law address and how? Keep in mind these issues of defining harm, particularly nonphysical harm, as you study other aspects of privacy and data protection law.

---

# CHAPTER 3

# CONSUMER PROTECTION

Constitutional law and tort law once provided the most significant protection for privacy, but over the last few decades the center of gravity has shifted. While these judge-made doctrines remain in effect, and have great historical importance in the development of privacy law, typical practitioners today pay them little attention and focus instead on statutory and regulatory sources of privacy rules. Most of the rest of this casebook covers these more recent forms of law. We begin here and in the next chapter with the privacy regulations with the greatest scope, affecting organizations of all types. As explained in a moment, Chapter 3 considers consumer protection law. Chapter 4 will turn to a different set of laws that can be grouped together as "data protection" measures, which dominate in the rest of the world but also can be found in more narrowly applicable US law.

Consumer protection law safeguards expansively defined individual rights in the context of commercial transactions. While consumer protection law does not address privacy from government intrusion, it does provide a flexible and broad basis for policing the handling of personal data by businesses. This power is not inherently limited by the type of information, industry sector, or technological methods that may be involved. Such latitude distinguishes consumer protection law from many other forms of privacy law, especially in the US, which tend to cover only certain practices, or to protect only certain types of data. You will encounter many of those types of "sectoral" privacy rules in Part II, and especially in Part III. In contrast, all businesses, whatever they do, must consider whether consumer protection law restricts their information-handling practices.

Thus, in the United States consumer protection regulators generally have the most wide-ranging mandate to govern privacy and information security. At the national level, the Federal Trade Commission (FTC) is the most significant of these regulators. State attorneys general and other consumer protection agencies play a supporting role, and often an important one. These governmentally-imposed requirements are supplemented by self-regulatory consumer protection measures, most obviously the widespread adoption of privacy policies, but also certain industry guidelines that have a binding effect on participating businesses. Consumer protection laws sometimes give individual plaintiffs, or putative classes, an opportunity to bring lawsuits as well. While these private actions have had limited success overall, some have resulted in settlements.

This chapter begins with self-regulatory measures in Section A. Section B considers private lawsuits. The most significant part of the chapter is Section C, which is devoted to administrative regulators; Section C concentrates especially on the FTC's exercise of authority related to both privacy and security, and case law reaffirming that power. Finally, Section D adds state consumer protection regulators to the picture, particularly focusing on robust enforcement by the California Office of the Attorney General.

## A. PRIVACY POLICIES AND SELF-REGULATION

---

### Focus

Why Bother with A Privacy Policy?

Why do companies create privacy policies in the first place? There are many reasons, but three stand out.

1. ***Legal.*** The Federal Trade Commission encourages companies to have privacy policies. Some industry-specific statutes go further and require that companies formulate and disclose a privacy policy. For example, regulations under the Health Insurance Portability and Accountability Act (HIPAA) require many entities in the health care industry to do so [see Chapter 12], and the Gramm-Leach-Bliley Act imposes some of the same requirements on financial services businesses [see Chapter 13]. The broadest such requirement comes in a California statute, passed in 2003, known as the California Online Privacy Protection Act (CalOPPA):

> (a) An operator of a commercial Web site or online service that collects personally identifiable information through the Internet about individual consumers residing in California who use or visit its commercial Web site or online service shall conspicuously post its privacy policy on its Web site, or in the case of an operator of an online service, make that policy available in accordance with paragraph (5) of subdivision (b) of Section 22577 [which requires the online service use "a reasonably accessible means of making the privacy policy available for consumers of the online service"]. An operator shall be in violation of this subdivision only if the operator fails to post its policy within 30 days after being notified of noncompliance.
>
> (b) The privacy policy required by subdivision (a) shall do all of the following:
>
>> (1) Identify the categories of personally identifiable information that the operator collects through the Web site or online service about individual consumers who use or visit its commercial Web site or online service and the categories of third-party persons or entities with whom the operator may share that personally identifiable information.
>>
>> (2) If the operator maintains a process for an individual consumer who uses or visits its commercial Web site or online service to review and request changes to any of his or her personally identifiable information that is collected through the Web site or online service, provide a description of that process.
>>
>> (3) Describe the process by which the operator notifies consumers who use or visit its commercial Web site or online service of material

changes to the operator's privacy policy for that Web site or online service.

(4) Identify its effective date.

Under the statute, a web site may "conspicuously post" its privacy policy whenever a "functional hyperlink . . . is so displayed that a reasonable person would notice it."

CAL. BUS. & PROF. CODE §§ 22575–22579. Look at a few of your favorite sites on the internet and evaluate how they comply with these rules. In 2012, California Attorney General Kamala Harris sent notices to over 100 operators of mobile apps requiring them to comply with CalOPPA. Her office subsequently reached an agreement with the proprietors of most leading mobile platforms and app stores, and as a result they promised to maintain consistent locations for apps' privacy policies.

2. ***Internal Management.*** It is a cliché in the business world to say "if you don't measure it you can't manage it." Privacy policies spur companies to audit their information collection and handling practices to assess how they actually handle personal data in everyday operations and to make changes as needed. They also establish clear internal procedures that can serve as a basis for training employees and designing computer systems that reflect the organization's activities. And, if something goes wrong, having a clear policy helps to manage the aftermath of the problem, be it a data breach by a hacker or a lawsuit challenging company procedures. Corporate privacy counsel and chief privacy officers sometime refer to policies like these as "company law," because they establish consistent expectations across the business that function like legal requirements (and, of course, are designed to comply with formal law as well).

3. ***Customer Relations.*** Once it became standard practice to develop a privacy policy and to post a link to the policy on the bottom of a web site home page, any company that did not do so might seem out of step. It could appear to care less about consumers' privacy concerns than its competitors do. Crucially, marketing research suggests quite strongly that consumers feel comforted by the existence of a privacy policy, and believe that the presence of a policy indicates that the company handles personal information responsibly—regardless of what the policy says.

With these considerations in mind, read the example of a privacy policy excerpted below, and then two cases considering whether privacy policies create enforceable contracts with customers.

---

## Amazon.com Privacy Notice

Last updated March 3, 2014

Amazon.com knows that you care how information about you is used and shared, and we appreciate your trust that we will do so carefully and sensibly. This notice describes our privacy policy. **By visiting Amazon.com, you are accepting the practices described in this Privacy Notice.**

### What Personal Information About Customers Does Amazon.com Gather?

The information we learn from customers helps us personalize and continually improve your Amazon experience. Here are the types of information we gather. [More specific examples are listed at the end of the policy; this section includes hyperlinks to that section.]

- **Information You Give Us:** We receive and store any information you enter on our Web site or give us in any other way. You can choose not to provide certain information, but then you might not be able to take advantage of many of our features. We use the information that you provide for such purposes as responding to your requests, customizing future shopping for you, improving our stores, and communicating with you.
- **Automatic Information:** We receive and store certain types of information whenever you interact with us. For example, like many Web sites, we use "cookies," and we obtain certain types of information when your Web browser accesses Amazon.com or advertisements and other content served by or on behalf of Amazon.com on other Web sites.
- **Mobile:** When you download or use apps created by Amazon or our subsidiaries, we may receive information about your location and your mobile device, including a unique identifier for your device. We may use this information to provide you with location-based services, such as advertising, search results, and other personalized content. Most mobile devices allow you to turn off location services.
- **E-mail Communications:** To help us make e-mails more useful and interesting, we often receive a confirmation when you open e-mail from Amazon.com if your computer supports such capabilities. We also compare our customer list to lists received from other companies, in an effort to avoid sending unnecessary messages to our customers. If you do not want to receive e-mail or other mail from us, please adjust your Customer Communication Preferences.
- **Information from Other Sources:** We might receive information about you from other sources and add it to our account information.

**What About Cookies?**

- Cookies are unique identifiers that we transfer to your device to enable our systems to recognize your device and to provide features such as 1-Click purchasing, Recommended for You, personalized advertisements on other Web sites (e.g., Amazon Associates with content served by Amazon.com and Web sites using Checkout by Amazon payment service), and storage of items in your Shopping Cart between visits.
- The Help feature on most browsers will tell you how to prevent your browser from accepting new cookies, how to have the browser notify you when you receive a new cookie,

or how to disable cookies altogether. Additionally, you can disable or delete similar data used by browser add-ons, such as Flash cookies, by changing the add-on's settings or visiting the Web site of its manufacturer. Because cookies allow you to take advantage of some of Amazon.com's essential features, we recommend that you leave them turned on. For instance, if you block or otherwise reject our cookies, you will not be able to add items to your Shopping Cart, proceed to Checkout, or use any Amazon.com products and services that require you to Sign in.

**Does Amazon.com Share the Information It Receives?**

Information about our customers is an important part of our business, and we are not in the business of selling it to others. We share customer information only as described below and with subsidiaries Amazon.com, Inc. controls that either are subject to this Privacy Notice or follow practices at least as protective as those described in this Privacy Notice.

- **Affiliated Businesses We Do Not Control:** We work closely with affiliated businesses. In some cases, such as Marketplace sellers, these businesses operate stores at Amazon.com or sell offerings to you at Amazon.com. In other cases, we operate stores, provide services, or sell product lines jointly with these businesses. You can tell when a third party is involved in your transactions, and we share customer information related to those transactions with that third party.
- **Third-Party Service Providers:** We employ other companies and individuals to perform functions on our behalf. Examples include fulfilling orders, delivering packages, sending postal mail and e-mail, removing repetitive information from customer lists, analyzing data, providing marketing assistance, providing search results and links (including paid listings and links), processing credit card payments, and providing customer service. They have access to personal information needed to perform their functions, but may not use it for other purposes.
- **Promotional Offers:** Sometimes we send offers to selected groups of Amazon.com customers on behalf of other businesses. When we do this, we do not give that business your name and address. If you do not want to receive such offers, please adjust your Customer Communication Preferences.
- **Business Transfers:** As we continue to develop our business, we might sell or buy stores, subsidiaries, or business units. In such transactions, customer information

generally is one of the transferred business assets but remains subject to the promises made in any pre-existing Privacy Notice (unless, of course, the customer consents otherwise). Also, in the unlikely event that Amazon.com, Inc., or substantially all of its assets are acquired, customer information will of course be one of the transferred assets.

- **Protection of Amazon.com and Others:** We release account and other personal information when we believe release is appropriate to comply with the law; enforce or apply our Conditions of Use and other agreements; or protect the rights, property, or safety of Amazon.com, our users, or others. This includes exchanging information with other companies and organizations for fraud protection and credit risk reduction. Obviously, however, this does not include selling, renting, sharing, or otherwise disclosing personally identifiable information from customers for commercial purposes in violation of the commitments set forth in this Privacy Notice.
- **With Your Consent:** Other than as set out above, you will receive notice when information about you might go to third parties, and you will have an opportunity to choose not to share the information.

**How Secure Is Information About Me?**

- We work to protect the security of your information during transmission by using Secure Sockets Layer (SSL) software, which encrypts information you input.
- We reveal only the last four digits of your credit card numbers when confirming an order. Of course, we transmit the entire credit card number to the appropriate credit card company during order processing.
- It is important for you to protect against unauthorized access to your password and to your computer. Be sure to sign off when finished using a shared computer.

**What About Third-Party Advertisers and Links to Other Websites?**

Our site includes third-party advertising and links to other Web sites. For more information about third-party advertising at Amazon.com, including personalized or interest-based ads, please read our Interest-Based Ads policy.

**Are Children Allowed to Use Amazon.com?**

Amazon.com does not sell products for purchase by children. We sell children's products for purchase by adults. If you are under 18, you may use Amazon.com only with the involvement of a parent or guardian.

### Does Amazon.com Participate in the Safe Harbor Program?

Amazon.com is a participant in the Safe Harbor program developed by the U.S. Department of Commerce and (1) the European Union and (2) Switzerland, respectively. We have certified that we adhere to the Safe Harbor Privacy Principles agreed upon by the U.S. and (1) the E.U. and (2) Switzerland, respectively.

In compliance with the US-EU and US–Swiss Safe Harbor Principles, we endeavor to resolve all complaints about privacy and the collection or use of customer information.

Under the Safe Harbor program, any unresolved privacy complaints can be referred to an independent dispute resolution mechanism. We use the BBB EU Safe Harbor Program, which is operated by the Council of Better Business Bureaus. [This Safe Harbor section also includes hyperlinks for more information and contact information for questions and complaints.]

### Conditions of Use, Notices, and Revisions

If you choose to visit Amazon.com, your visit and any dispute over privacy is subject to this Notice and our Conditions of Use, including limitations on damages, resolution of disputes, and application of the law of the state of Washington. If you have any concern about privacy at Amazon.com, please contact us with a thorough description, and we will try to resolve it. Our business changes constantly, and our Privacy Notice and the Conditions of Use will change also. We may e-mail periodic reminders of our notices and conditions, but you should check our Web site frequently to see recent changes. Unless stated otherwise, our current Privacy Notice applies to all information that we have about you and your account. We stand behind the promises we make, however, and will never materially change our policies and practices to make them less protective of customer information collected in the past without the consent of affected customers.

### Examples of Information Collected

### Information You Give Us

You provide most such information when you search, buy, post, participate in a contest or questionnaire, or communicate with customer service. For example, you provide information when you search for a product; place an order through Amazon.com or one of our third-party sellers; provide information in Your Account (and you might have more than one if you have used more than one e-mail address when shopping with us) or Your Profile; communicate with us by phone, e-mail, or otherwise; complete a questionnaire or a contest entry form; use our services such as Amazon Instant Video; compile Wish Lists or other gift registries; participate in Discussion Boards or other community features; provide and rate Reviews; specify a Special Occasion Reminder; and employ Product Availability Alerts, such as Available to Order Notifications. As a result of those actions, you might supply us with such information as your name, address, and phone numbers; credit card information; people to whom purchases have been shipped, including addresses and phone number; people (with addresses and phone numbers) listed in 1-Click settings; e-mail addresses of your friends and other people; content of reviews and e-mails to us; personal description and photograph in Your Profile; and financial information, including Social Security and driver's license numbers.

### Automatic Information

Examples of the information we collect and analyze include the Internet protocol (IP) address used to connect your computer to the Internet; login; e-mail address; password; computer and connection information such as browser type, version, and time zone setting, browser plug-in types and versions, operating system, and platform; purchase history, which we sometimes aggregate with similar information from other customers to create features like Top Sellers; the full Uniform Resource Locator (URL) clickstream to, through, and from our Web site, including date and time; cookie number; products you viewed or searched for; and the phone number you used to call our 800 number. We may also use browser data such as cookies, Flash cookies (also known as Flash Local Shared Objects), or similar data on certain parts of our Web site for fraud prevention and other purposes. During some visits we may use software tools such as JavaScript to measure and collect session information, including page response times, download errors, length of visits to certain pages, page interaction information (such as scrolling, clicks, and mouse-overs), and methods used to browse away from the page. We may also collect technical information to help us identify your device for fraud prevention and diagnostic purposes.

### Mobile

Most mobile devices provide users with the ability to disable location services. Most likely, these controls are located in the device's settings menu. If you have questions about how to disable your device's location services, we recommend you contact your mobile service carrier or your device manufacturer.

### Information from Other Sources

Examples of information we receive from other sources include updated delivery and address information from our carriers or other third parties, which we use to correct our records and deliver your next purchase or communication more easily; account information, purchase or redemption information, and page-view information from some merchants with which we operate co-branded businesses or for which we provide technical, fulfillment, advertising, or other services; search term and search result information from some searches conducted through the Web search features offered by our subsidiary, Alexa Internet; search results and links, including paid listings (such as Sponsored Links); and credit history information from credit bureaus, which we use to help prevent and detect fraud and to offer certain credit or financial services to some customers.

**Co-branded and Joint Offerings**

Examples of businesses with which we offer joint or co-branded products and other offerings include Starbucks, OfficeMax, American Apparel, Verizon Wireless, Sprint, T-Mobile, AT&T, J&R Electronics, PacSun, Eddie Bauer and Northern Tool + Equipment.

**Information You Can Access**

Examples of information you can access easily at Amazon.com include up-to-date information regarding recent orders; personally identifiable information (including name, e-mail, password, communications and personalized advertising preferences, address book, and 1-Click settings); payment settings (including credit card information and promotional certificate and gift card balances); e-mail notification settings (including Product Availability Alerts, Delivers, Special Occasion Reminders, and newsletters); Recommendations (including Recommended for You and Improve Your Recommendations); shopping lists and gift registries (including Wish Lists and Baby and Wedding Registries); Seller accounts; and Your Profile (including your product Reviews, Recommendations, Listmania lists, Reminders, personal profile, and Wish List).

## In re Northwest Airlines Privacy Litigation

2004 WL 1278459 (D. Minn. 2004)

■ MAGNUSON, DISTRICT JUDGE.

Plaintiffs are customers of Defendant Northwest Airlines, Inc. ("Northwest"). After September 11, 2001, the National Aeronautical and Space Administration ("NASA") requested that Northwest provide NASA with certain passenger information in order to assist NASA in studying ways to increase airline security. Northwest supplied NASA with passenger name records ("PNRs"), which are electronic records of passenger information. PNRs contain information such as a passenger's name, flight number, credit card data, hotel reservation, car rental, and any traveling companions.

[The plaintiffs brought multiple class actions against Northwest and NASA subcontractors working on the security project, which were consolidated. The various claims included a claim of breach of contract.] The basis for most of Plaintiffs' claims is that Northwest's website contained a privacy policy that stated that Northwest would not share customers' information except as necessary to make customers' travel arrangements. Plaintiffs contend that Northwest's provision of PNRs to NASA violated Northwest's privacy policy, giving rise to the legal claims noted above. [Northwest moved to dismiss the complaint.]

Northwest contends that the privacy policy on Northwest's website does not, as a matter of law, constitute a unilateral contract, the breach of which entitles Plaintiffs to damages. Northwest also argues that, even if the privacy policy constituted a contract or express warranty, Plaintiffs' contract and warranty claims fail because Plaintiffs have failed to plead any contract damages. Plaintiffs rely on the following statement from Northwest's website as the basis for their contract and warranty claims:

> When you reserve or purchase travel services through Northwest Airlines nwa.com Reservations, we provide only the relevant information required by the car rental agency, hotel, or other involved third party to ensure the successful fulfillment of your travel arrangements.

Plaintiffs do not allege that they actually read this privacy statement prior to providing Northwest with their personal information, although they do generally allege that they "relied to their detriment" on this policy. The usual rule in contract cases is that general statements of policy are not contractual. In the employment context, the Minnesota Supreme Court has found that statements in an employee handbook as specific as "[a] person is not dismissed without cause, and it is customary to give a warning and an opportunity to 'make good' before final dismissal" did not create an employment contract that altered the presumed at-will employment relationship. *Cederstrand v. Lutheran Bhd.*, 117 N.W.2d 213, 215–16 (Minn. 1962). The court characterized the statement as a "general polic[y], not an offer of contractual character."

The privacy statement on Northwest's website did not constitute a unilateral contract. The language used vests discretion in Northwest to determine when the information is "relevant" and which "third parties" might need that information. Moreover, absent an allegation that Plaintiffs actually read the privacy policy, not merely the general allegation that Plaintiffs "relied on" the policy, Plaintiffs have failed to allege an essential element of a contract claim: that the alleged "offer" was accepted by Plaintiffs. Plaintiffs' contract and warranty claims fail as a matter of law.

Even if the privacy policy was sufficiently definite and Plaintiffs had alleged that they read the policy before giving their information to Northwest, it is likely that Plaintiffs' contract and warranty claims would fail as a matter of law. Defendants point out that Plaintiffs have failed to allege any contractual damages arising out of the alleged breach. As Defendants note, the damages Plaintiffs claim are damages arising out of the torts alleged in the Amended Complaint, not damages arising out of the alleged contract. Damages are an essential element of a breach of contract claim, and the failure to allege damages would be fatal to Plaintiffs' contract claims.

## In re Jetblue Airways Corp. Privacy Litigation

379 F. Supp. 2d 299, 316–18 (E.D.N.Y. 2005)

■ AMON, DISTRICT JUDGE.

[The next year, a different federal court faced similar arguments in a motion to dismiss a similar consolidated class action against JetBlue. The contract analysis follows.]

Plaintiffs allege that they made reservations to fly with JetBlue in reliance on express promises made by JetBlue in the company's privacy policy. The substance of the contract alleged is therefore a promise by JetBlue not to disclose passengers' personal information to third parties. Plaintiffs allege that JetBlue breached that promise, thereby causing injury.

An action for breach of contract under New York law requires proof of four elements: the existence of a contract, performance of the contract by one party, breach by the other party, and damages. JetBlue contends that plaintiffs have failed to plead facts sufficient to establish the existence of a contract or that they suffered damages.

With regard to the existence of a contract, plaintiffs contend that JetBlue undertook a "self-imposed contractual obligation by and between [itself] and the consumers with whom it transacted business" by publishing privacy policies on its website or otherwise disclosing such policies to its consumers.

JetBlue argues that failure to allege that plaintiffs read the privacy policy defeats any claim of reliance [necessary for the first element]. Although plaintiffs do not explicitly allege that the class members actually read or saw the privacy policy, they do allege that they and other class members relied on the representations and assurances contained in the privacy policy when choosing to purchase air transportation from JetBlue. Reliance presupposes familiarity with the policy. It may well be that some members of the class did not read the privacy policy and thus could not have relied on it, but the issue of who actually read and relied on the policy would be addressed more properly at the class certification stage. For purposes of this motion, the Court considers an allegation of reliance to encompass an allegation that some putative members of the class read or viewed the privacy policy. The Court recognizes that contrary authority exists on this point, but considers the holding in that case to rest on an overly narrow reading of the pleadings [citing *Northwest*]. Accordingly, failure to specifically allege that all plaintiffs and class members read the policy does not defeat the existence of a contract for purposes of this motion to dismiss.

JetBlue also argues that plaintiffs have failed to meet their pleading requirement with respect to damages, citing an absence of any facts in the Amended Complaint to support this element of the claim. Plaintiffs' sole allegation on the element of contract damages consists of the statement that JetBlue's breach of the company privacy policy injured plaintiffs and members of the class and that JetBlue is therefore liable for "actual damages in an amount to be determined at trial." At oral argument, when pressed to identify the "injuries" or damages referred to in the Amended Complaint, counsel for plaintiffs stated that the "contract damage could be the loss of privacy," acknowledging that loss of privacy "may" be a contract damage. The support for this proposition was counsel's proffer that he had never seen a case that indicates that loss of privacy cannot as a matter of law be a contract damage. In response to the Court's inquiry as to whether a further specification of damages could be set forth in a second amended complaint, counsel suggested only that perhaps it could be alleged or argued that plaintiffs were deprived of the "economic value" of their information. Despite being offered the opportunity to expand their claim for damages, plaintiffs failed to proffer any other element or form of damages that they would seek if given the opportunity to amend the complaint.

It is apparent based on the briefing and oral argument held in this case that the sparseness of the damages allegations is a direct result of plaintiffs' inability to plead or prove any actual contract damages. As plaintiffs' counsel concedes, the only damage that can be read into the present complaint is a loss of privacy. [It is a] well-settled principle that recovery in contract, unlike recovery in tort, allows only for economic losses flowing directly from the breach.

Plaintiffs allege that in a second amended complaint, they could assert as a contract damage the loss of the economic value of their information, but while that claim sounds in economic loss, the argument ignores the nature of the contract asserted. Plaintiffs may well have expected that in return for providing their personal information to JetBlue and paying the purchase price, they would obtain a ticket for air travel and the promise that their personal information would be safeguarded consistent with the terms of the privacy policy. They had no reason to expect that they would be compensated for the "value" of their personal information. In addition, there is absolutely no support for the proposition that the personal information of an individual JetBlue passenger had any value for which that passenger could have expected to be compensated. It strains credulity to believe that, had JetBlue not provided the PNR data en masse to Torch [a government subcontractor working on the airline security study], Torch would have gone to each individual JetBlue passenger and compensated him or her for access to his or her personal information. There is likewise no support for the proposition that an individual passenger's personal information has or had any compensable value in the economy at large.

Accordingly, plaintiffs having claimed no other form of damages apart from those discussed herein and having sought no other form of relief in connection with the breach of contract claim, JetBlue's motion to dismiss the claim is granted.

## NOTES

1. ***Dissecting a Privacy Policy.*** In order to understand how privacy policies work it is important to really dissect them. Answer the following questions based on the Amazon.com web site.

- What personal information does Amazon.com collect from users?
- What does Amazon.com do with the personal information it collects?
- Who else besides Amazon.com might have access to collected personal information?
- What benefits might a customer get from Amazon.com's collection and use of personal data?
- What steps can a user take to reduce or control the personal information collected or how it is used?
- If law enforcement officers asked Amazon.com for information about merchandise ordered by a suspected criminal, would the company provide the information?
- What would happen if Amazon.com went bankrupt? What if a company went bankrupt that provides services to Amazon.com, such as analyzing use of its web site for marketing purposes?
- Precisely what does Amazon.com do to protect personal information from hackers?

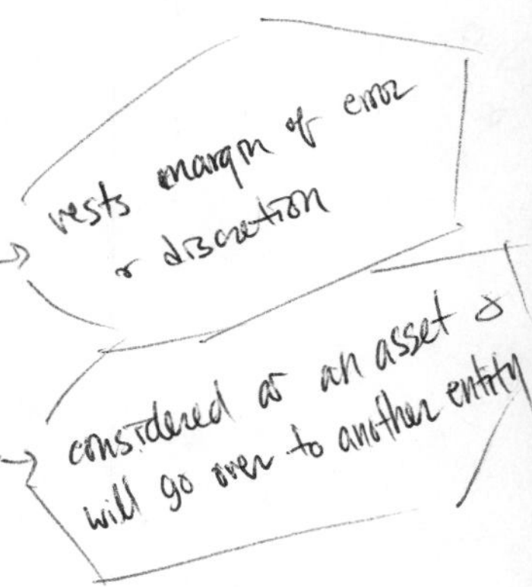


Also consider whether this version of the Amazon policy satisfies the requirements of the California law described above, *see* CAL. BUS. & PROF. CODE §§ 22575–22579.

2. ***Obstacles in Contract Doctrine.*** The courts in *Northwest Airlines* and *JetBlue* considered two different challenges against two different airline privacy policies, but both arose from essentially the same facts and both asserted claims for breach of contract. The two courts reach broadly similar conclusions about the futility of the contract claims—but not for entirely the same reasons. Clearly identify the precise doctrinal issue of contract law in each case. How are the two cases similar and different? These cases are representative of the contract analysis in other cases. What do they suggest about the viability of contract claims alleging privacy policy violations?

3. ***Unilateral Changes in Terms.*** Look back at the Amazon.com privacy policy and see what it says about future changes in its terms. Companies update privacy policies frequently, and most policies contain language warning that they may change. This is still another doctrinal obstacle to treating them like contracts. An agreement where one side explicitly reserves the right to make unilateral alterations in any of its terms probably does not represent a definite meeting of the minds necessary to form a contract. That said, the FTC typically expects companies to treat

personal information in accordance with the privacy policies in place when it was collected, so new policies apply only prospectively [see Section C, below]. What conditions, if any, does CalOPPA place on a company changing its privacy-related terms?

4. ***Gobbledygook and Plain English.*** How clear and easy to read do you find the Amazon.com privacy policy? In the early days of privacy policies, most used very dense and legalistic language. More recently there has been a move, especially among highly established companies and web sites, to make the policies more approachable and comprehensible. What are the incentives in each direction, encouraging either lawyerly gobbledygook or "plain English?"

5. ***Who Reads a Privacy Policy?*** Do you read privacy polices when you visit web sites? A study at Carnegie Mellon University calculated the amount of time it would take an average person to read all the privacy policies applicable to that person, accounting for variables such as reading level and the number of sites that collect personal information from an average person. The result? It would take 76 full working days a year! *See* Aleecia M. McDonald & Lorrie Faith Cranor, *The Costs of Reading Privacy Policies*, 4 I/S J. OF L. & POLICY 540 (2008). In light of this staggering number, isn't it quite rational for most people not to bother reading the policies?

6. ***Legal Self-Protection.*** Not surprisingly, much of a privacy policy's language aims to protect an organization from liability. Some provisions of the Amazon.com policy apparently respond to particular legal obligations. Statements about the Safe Harbor Program in this 2014 policy were keyed to an important mechanism for crossborder data transfers, now defunct [see Chapter 8]. The ban on use by minors seeks to avoid additional liability for compromising children's privacy (although many companies set the cutoff at age 13, as required by the Children's Online Privacy Protection Act (COPPA) [see Chapter 4], rather than Amazon.com's cut-off of age 18). Do you see other examples?

---

## Focus

### Industry Self-Regulation

In addition to developing their own privacy policies, businesses engage in other self-regulation efforts. The FTC and other authorities, both in the US and in other countries, often encourage companies to band together and develop their own standards and practices about privacy. Privacy advocates sometimes criticize these structures as fig leafs and argue that they are vague and self-serving and lack real enforcement. Even though they are usually less stringent than most legal requirements, however, companies that pledge to abide by such codes should be careful not to violate them, because doing so can cause public relations damage at a minimum and may raise concerns with the FTC [see Section 3.B].

1. ***Standards and Practices.*** Some industry sectors have voluntary rules that spell out responsible data handling practices. So, for example, a coalition of trade associations involved in online marketing, including the American Association of Advertising Agencies (AAAA), the Direct Marketing Association (DMA), and the

Interactive Advertising Bureau (IAB) developed a broad set of standards called *Self-Regulatory Principles for Online Behavioral Advertising. See* http://www.iab.net/public_policy/behavioral-advertisingprinciples.

2. ***Trustmarks.*** A number of independent third-party entities such as TrustE and BBBOnline issue "trustmarks" or "privacy seals" to certify a company's adherence to requirements set by the issuer. Companies that promise to obey the rules are allowed to display the trustmark on their web site and other materials. Critics argue that the requirements for certification are lax and that trustmark issuers have little incentive to police compliance, especially because their operations are funded by fees paid by monitored companies. In late 2014 these criticisms seemed to be borne out, at least in part, when TrustE settled with the FTC over charges that the organization did not conduct annual recertifications of companies as it had claimed. *See In re True Ultimate Standards Everywhere, Inc. (TRUSTe)* (consent order), FTC Docket No. C–4512 (March 12, 2015). Proponents argue that trustmarks, similar to labels like "organic" on food, can provide valuable information to consumers and that trustmark issuers also provide dispute resolution services that can help consumers address privacy-related complaints. Data protection regulators in the United Kingdom recently advanced proposals to encourage accredited privacy seals there, and they already exist in France and Germany as well.

3. ***Disclosure and Opt Out.*** A consortium of trade groups called the Digital Advertising Alliance has promoted the use of a small "Ad Choices" icon, depicted below, on the corner of web-based advertising. Clicking the icon redirects the user to a page that provides more information about marketing-related use of personal data and allows consumers to indicate that they do not want future data profiling by companies that participate in the initiative. *See* www.youradchoices.com. Critics point out that the icon has not exactly become universally known, and also object that the choices are not presented in an even-handed way. Proponents respond that "interest-based advertising" is convenient and informative for consumers and that it helps fund popular free online services. The companies themselves point out that they are voluntarily allowing consumers to opt out of receiving such targeted advertising without any legal requirement to do so. Efforts to develop broader consensus around a broader technologically-based opt-out known as "Do Not Track" appear to have stalled without reaching agreement [see Chapter 5].

4. ***Contracts.*** Companies often engage in private ordering about data handling practices through contracts [see Chapter 8]. So, for example, a company that shares personal data with service providers usually will do so pursuant to a data transfer agreement that establishes certain data protections. The contract would be legally enforceable in the event of a violation, but the requirements it contains would be generated entirely by the private organizations involved. A particularly elaborate and important version of such contractual self-regulation can be seen in credit card practices, where independently administered Payment Card Industry (PCI) rules create detailed data security obligations for vendors that accept credit card payments under contracts with the card issuers. [See Chapter 7 for more on PCI rules.]

5. ***Coregulation.*** Finally, government regulators may participate in ongoing cooperative efforts with affected parties to develop privacy rules. This model is sometimes known as "coregulation." A number of legislative proposals in the US concerning privacy, advanced by both the Obama Administration and members of Congress, embrace this model, but none have become law. More informally, many agencies urge companies to develop self-policing on certain issues—often threatening, ether explicitly or implicitly, that the government will intervene to write rules if businesses cannot develop satisfactory ones themselves. This was the

approach the FTC took in attempting to spur the development of "Do Not Track" rules by private stakeholders, an effort that has not borne fruit thus far [see Chapter 14]. In the Netherlands, the government relies on a form of "coregulation" known as the "Polder Model," named for the cooperatively developed dikes that protect the low-lying Dutch coast from flooding. The Dutch data protection regulator uses this model for privacy as well, negotiating with industry groups to develop their own codes of conduct for data handling, and then ratifying those as legally binding if they are acceptable. Unlike the US versions discussed above, however, in the Netherlands a government agency has the final say concerning the content of the rules. *See* Dennis D. Hirsch, *Going Dutch? Collaborative Dutch Privacy Regulation and the Lessons It Holds for U.S. Privacy Law*, 2013 MICH ST. L. REV. 83.

---

## B. CONSUMER LAWSUITS

According to statistics compiled by the law firm of Bryan Cave LLP, in 15 months from mid-2013 to mid-2014, plaintiffs filed 672 privacy class actions in federal court. DAVID ZETOONY ET AL., BRYAN CAVE LLP, 2015 DATA PRIVACY LITIGATION REPORT, *available at* http://www.bryancavedatamatters.com/category/miscellaneous/litigation/. (The count surely would be higher if it also included lawsuits in state court and those that did not seek class certification.) Many of those filings respond to data breaches and allege inadequate security measures by a company, although Bryan Cave found privacy lawsuits were filed six times more frequently than data breach suits. [For more information about data security suits, see Chapter 7.] Many complaints are brought under sectoral statutes that provide private rights of action, particularly the Telephone Consumer Privacy Act (TCPA) [see Chapter 14]. But others, discussed here, are brought under general-purpose state consumer protection laws—most of which, unlike their federal counterpart, give individual plaintiffs the right to sue for violations.

When brought in federal court, these suits can face difficulty demonstrating Article III standing—a task that could become more difficult depending on how the Supreme Court decides the case of *Spokeo, Inc. v. Robins*, which was still pending at the time of this writing in early 2016. Even in state court, where constitutional standing is not required, the consumer protection statutes themselves impose their own standing requirements. For the last several years, plaintiffs and defendants have been engaged in trench warfare over the scope of injury, and therefore standing, covered by these consumer protection laws. The two cases that follow are examples of that ongoing struggle.

### In re iPhone Application Litigation

2013 WL 6212591 (N.D. Cal. 2013)

■ LUCY H. KOH, UNITED STATES DISTRICT JUDGE.

Plaintiffs, on behalf of themselves and a putative class, bring this action against Apple, Inc. ("Apple") for alleged violations of California's

Consumers Legal Remedies Act ("CLRA") and California's Unfair Competition Law ("UCL"). Before the Court is Apple's Motion for Summary Judgment. Having considered the parties' submissions and oral arguments, the relevant law, and the record in this case, the Court GRANTS Apple's Motion for Summary Judgment.

## I. BACKGROUND

Plaintiffs filed their Third Amended Consolidated Complaint ("TAC") on behalf of four named Plaintiffs who assert two separate types of claims and seek to represent two separate classes of individuals.

### 1. Parties

Plaintiffs Anthony Chiu ("Chiu") and Cameron Dwyer ("Dwyer") assert "iDevice Claims."

Plaintiffs Isabella Capiro ("Isabella") and Alejandro Capiro ("Alejandro") assert "Geolocation Claims."

Defendant Apple is a California corporation that manufactures iPhones and other devices. Apple's iPhones generally consist of two components: the iPhone hardware and the mobile operating system firmware ("iOS"). Apple frequently updates iOS, and users can install new versions of iOS as they become available, without cost.

### 2. iDevice Claims

Plaintiffs allege that Apple attracts consumers to purchase iPhones and other "iDevices," partly by offering thousands of purportedly "free" Apps in Apple's proprietary "App Store." Plaintiffs further allege that Apple regulates the Apps that are available in the App Store. App developers can only create Apps using Apple-supplied software development kits, and Apps can only be distributed in the App Store upon Apple's approval. In addition, Apple controls what data Apps can and cannot transmit to third parties.

To users of the App Store, Apple represents in its Privacy Policy that it "takes precautions—including administrative, technical, and physical measures—to safeguard your personal information against loss, theft, and misuse, as well as against unauthorized access, disclosure, alteration, and destruction." Apple's Privacy Policy further claims that users' privacy is a priority to Apple.

According to Plaintiffs, however, Apple allegedly "designed the iOS environment to easily transmit" Plaintiffs' "personal information" to third parties that collect and analyze such data without user consent or detection. Apple allegedly failed to adequately disclose to Plaintiffs that the "free" Apps collected Plaintiffs' information and sent it to third parties without user consent or detection.

Plaintiffs claim that they relied upon Apple's representations about privacy and data collection in purchasing their iPhones. In light of Apple's statements about protecting users' privacy, Plaintiffs did not consent to the App developers transmitting Plaintiffs' information to third parties. Plaintiffs assert that as a result of Apple's misrepresentations regarding its privacy and data collection practices, Plaintiffs both overpaid for their iPhones and suffered diminishment to their iPhones' battery, bandwidth, and storage "resources."

### 3. Geolocation Claims

Plaintiffs further allege that for iPhone users "who ran iOS versions 4.1 and later from June 21, 2010, through April 27, 2011," Apple "collect[ed] and exchange[d] location information with Apple's servers" even when the "Location Services" setting on a user's iPhone was set to "off." The "location information" exchanged with Apple's servers appears to have consisted of lists of wifi hotspots and cell towers located in the general vicinity of the iPhone.

Apple's iPhone Software License Agreements ("SLAs") state that consumers can prevent Apple from collecting location information "by going to the Location Services setting . . . [and] turning off the global Location Services setting." Plaintiffs contend that Apple's representations regarding a user's ability to disable Location Services were false and misleading because Apple, prior to April 2011, continued to collect wifi hotspot and cell tower information from the iPhones, even after users, including Plaintiff Isabella Capiro, turned off the Location Services on their devices. Apple, for its part, attributes the iPhones' ability to continue to transmit wifi hotspot and cell tower data even when Location Services was turned off to a "software bug" that it resolved starting with iOS version 4.3.3.

Alejandro claims that he would have paid significantly less for the iPhones he purchased for himself and Isabella had he known that Apple continued to collect data about a user's locations even after the user turned the iPhone's Location Services off. Further, the Capiros contend that the exchange of location information with Apple's servers consumed their iPhones' resources.

## II. LEGAL STANDARD

Summary judgment is proper where the pleadings, discovery, and affidavits show that there is "no genuine dispute as to any material fact and [that] the movant is entitled to judgment as a matter of law." Fed. R. Civ. P. 56(a).

## III. DISCUSSION

Apple moves for summary judgment on the grounds that: (1) Plaintiffs lack Article III standing; (2) Plaintiffs lack standing under the UCL and the CLRA; and (3) Plaintiffs have failed to create a genuine issue of material fact concerning the substantive elements of Plaintiffs' UCL and CLRA claims. For the reasons discussed below, the Court concludes that Plaintiffs have failed to create a genuine issue of material fact concerning their standing under Article III or the CLRA and UCL to bring their claims and therefore that Apple is entitled to summary judgment in its favor. Because this conclusion disposes of the case, the Court will not address the substantive elements of Plaintiffs' claims.

### 1. Legal Standards

#### a. Article III Standing

To have Article III standing, a plaintiff must plead and prove that he or she has suffered sufficient injury to satisfy the "case or controversy" requirement of Article III of the United States Constitution. Therefore, for Article III standing, a plaintiff must establish: (1) injury-in-fact that is concrete and particularized, as well as actual or imminent; (2) that this injury is fairly traceable to the challenged action of the defendant; and (3) that this injury is redressable by a favorable ruling from the court.

The party invoking federal jurisdiction bears the burden of establishing these elements. [A]t summary judgment, a plaintiff may no longer rely on "mere allegations," but rather must set forth "specific facts" supporting standing.

#### b. Statutory Standing Under the CLRA and UCL

The CLRA and UCL also require Plaintiffs to demonstrate standing. To have standing under the CLRA, a plaintiff must allege that she relied on the defendant's alleged misrepresentations and that she suffered economic injury as a result.

Likewise, to establish standing under the UCL, a plaintiff must demonstrate that she suffered injury in fact and lost money or property as a result of the unfair competition. Interpreting this statutory language—which California voters added to the UCL in 2004 through the passage of Proposition 64—California courts have held that when the "unfair competition" underlying a plaintiff's UCL claim consists of a defendant's misrepresentation, a plaintiff must have actually relied on the misrepresentation, and suffered economic injury as a result of that reliance, in order to have standing to sue.

Here, the gravamen of Plaintiffs' claims is that Apple misrepresented its data collection and privacy practices, thereby luring Plaintiffs into spending more money for their iPhones than they would have had they known the true nature of the data being collected by Apple and the third party apps. Accordingly, to demonstrate standing under the UCL, Plaintiffs must set forth specific facts showing that they actually relied on Apple's misrepresentations and suffered economic injury as a result of that reliance.

While a plaintiff need not demonstrate that the defendant's misrepresentations were "the sole or even the predominant or decisive factor influencing his conduct," the misrepresentations must have "played a substantial part" in the plaintiff's decisionmaking.

### 2. Analysis

#### a. Injury

As explained above, to establish standing under either Article III or the CLRA and UCL, Plaintiffs must demonstrate that they have suffered a concrete injury in fact. Furthermore, to have standing under the CLRA and UCL, this injury must be economic in nature. Here, Plaintiffs identify two forms of economic harm. First, Plaintiffs claim that they overpaid for their iPhones. Second, Plaintiffs claim that the unauthorized transmission of data from their iPhones taxed the phones' resources by draining the battery and using up storage space and bandwidth.

Apple argues that Plaintiffs have conceded that they did not suffer *any* harm as a result of Apple's alleged misconduct. The Court is not convinced. Although Plaintiffs' depositions contain potentially damaging testimony in which Plaintiffs struggle to identify what harm they suffered, other portions of these same depositions support Plaintiffs' claims of harm.

While the apparent conflicts in Plaintiffs' deposition testimony may weaken the credibility of the evidence supporting Plaintiffs' claims of injury, the fact remains that there is evidence in the record supporting each side's position on injury. The Court finds that this conflicting evidence is sufficient to create a genuine issue of material fact regarding whether Plaintiffs have suffered injury in fact. Summary judgment is not warranted on this ground.

#### b. Causation/Actual Reliance

Adequately establishing injury in fact, however, is only part of the battle. To demonstrate standing, Plaintiffs must also show that this injury is causally linked to Apple's misrepresentations regarding data collection and privacy. As discussed above, for purposes of standing under the CLRA and UCL, a showing of causation requires a showing that Plaintiffs actually relied on Apple's alleged misrepresentations regarding data collection and privacy to their detriment. In addition, the Court finds, in the context of this case, that Plaintiffs must establish actual reliance on Apple's alleged misrepresentations to demonstrate causation for purposes of Article III standing. Plaintiffs' theory of this case is that they suffered harm, in the form of overpayment and reduced battery life, bandwidth, and storage, as a result of Apple's misrepresentations concerning its data collection and privacy policies. For the Plaintiffs' harm to be "fairly traceable" to Apple's misrepresentations, Plaintiffs must have seen the misrepresentations and taken some action based on what they saw—that is, Plaintiffs must have actually relied on the misrepresentations to have been harmed by them. Accordingly, the Court concludes that actual reliance is an essential element of standing in this case under Article III, as well as the CLRA and UCL.

Unfortunately for Plaintiffs, the Court also concludes that Plaintiffs have failed to establish a genuine issue of material fact concerning actual reliance. The reasons for this conclusion are set forth below.

***i. Apple's Alleged Misrepresentations***

Plaintiffs identify a number of alleged Apple misrepresentations regarding data collection and privacy, nearly all of which appear in either Apple's Privacy Policy, the iPhone SLA, or the App Store/iTunes Terms and Conditions. For instance, Plaintiffs identify the following alleged misrepresentations in Apple's Privacy Policy:

- "Your privacy is important to Apple. So we've developed a Privacy Policy that covers how we collect, use, disclose, transfer, and store your information."
- "To make sure your personal information is secure, we communicate our privacy and security guidelines to Apple employees and strictly enforce privacy safeguards within the company."
- "Apple takes precautions—including administrative, technical, and physical measures—to safeguard your personal information against loss, theft, and misuse as well as against unauthorized access, disclosure, alteration, and destruction."
- "Personal information is data that can be used to uniquely identify or contact a single person. . . . We also collect non-personal information—data in a form that does not permit direct association with any specific individual. . . . The following are some examples of non-personal information that we collect[:] . . . occupation, language, zip code, area code, unique device identifier, location, and the time zone where an Apple product is used. . . ."

Plaintiffs identify the following additional misrepresentations in the SLA:

- "You agree that Apple and its subsidiaries and agents may collect, maintain and process and use . . . information, including but not limited to information about your iPhone . . . as long as it is collected anonymously in a form that does not personally identify you, to improve our products or to provide services or technologies to you."
- "You may withdraw [consent to have location data collected] at any time by going to the Location Services setting on your iPhone and either turning off the global Location Services setting or turning off the individual location settings of each location-aware application on your iPhone."

- "The location data and queries collected by Apple are collected in a form that does not personally identify you and may be used by Apple and its partners and licensees to provide location-based products and services."

***ii. Absence of Evidence that Plaintiffs Relied on Any Alleged Misrepresentation***

**(a) iDevice Claims**

While the iDevice Plaintiffs identify numerous purported misrepresentations and argue that they relied on them in purchasing their iPhones, the evidentiary record is devoid of "specific facts" to support Plaintiffs' assertions. Critically, *none* of the Plaintiffs presents evidence that he or she even saw, let alone read and relied upon, the alleged misrepresentations contained in the Apple Privacy Policies, SLAs, or App Store Terms and Conditions, either prior to purchasing his or her iPhone, or at any time thereafter.

In their depositions, Plaintiffs either could not recall having read any of these policies (or any other Apple representation) in connection with obtaining their iPhones, or expressly disavowed having read any Apple policy, or anything else about the iPhone, prior to purchasing one.

Dwyer stated he did not read anything other than online reviews in connection with his purchase of the iPhone.

Chiu stated that he recalled having read some Apple agreement in connection with setting up his iTunes account, but he did not recall either the nature of the document or the content of what he read. Chiu did not recall reading anything in connection with purchasing his iPhone or with using the App store.

Alejandro Capiro stated that he did not read anything related to the iPhone prior to purchasing iPhones for himself and his children, either in deciding to buy the iPhones or at the Apple store when he went to purchase the iPhones.

Finally, Isabella Capiro did not purchase her phone, but she testified that she did not read anything about the iPhone in connection with deciding to ask for one from her father.

In declarations filed after Plaintiffs' depositions, and after this Court expressed concern about Plaintiffs' ability to demonstrate actual reliance at the February 28 Hearing, Plaintiffs attempt to retreat from their deposition testimony concerning reliance.

These declarations are flawed in multiple respects. To begin with, the Court notes that attempting to create a genuine issue of material fact by submitting an affidavit contradicting one's own prior deposition testimony is generally disfavored. More importantly, however, none of these declarations actually states that Plaintiffs read or relied on any particular Apple misrepresentation regarding privacy. Plaintiffs each allude to a vague "understanding" regarding Apple's privacy policies without providing any evidence whatsoever concerning the basis for this understanding. The declarations, with their unsupported references to an amorphous "understanding" about privacy, do not satisfy Plaintiffs' burden to show standing at summary judgment.

**(b) Geolocation Claims**

As with the iDevice Plaintiffs, the Court finds that the Geolocation Plaintiffs (Alejandro and Isabella Capiro) fail to set forth specific facts supporting their standing to pursue their claims. Alejandro conceded in his deposition testimony that he did not even realize that Location Services existed at the time he purchased his iPhone.

Isabella stated that in mid-March 2011—at a time when her iPhone was running a version of iOS containing the "bug" that allowed an iPhone to query wifi hotspot and cell tower information even when Location Services was turned off—she visited an Apple store to address problems she was having with her iPhone's battery, which was draining rapidly. Isabella further testified that an Apple store employee told her that she could preserve her iPhone's battery life by, among other things, turning Location Services off.

The problem with using this statement from the Apple store employee as a basis for establishing standing, however, is that Isabella cannot demonstrate that this statement was causally linked to any of the harms she claims to have suffered.

Accordingly, the Court finds that while Isabella identifies a specific Apple misrepresentation, Isabella cannot establish that she suffered any injury as a result of this misrepresentation.

***iii. Plaintiffs' Arguments in Support of Standing Are Not Persuasive***

Plaintiffs asserted additional arguments in support of standing. None of [these] arguments is persuasive.

First, Plaintiffs suggest that standing is established as long as a plaintiff "receives" a misrepresentation. The implication of this argument seems to be that a plaintiff can show standing as long as the defendant has disseminated the alleged misrepresentation to her in some fashion, regardless of whether the plaintiff ever actually sees, reads, or hears the defendant's statement. The Court questions how one can act in reliance on a statement one does not see, read, or hear. Moreover, this argument is foreclosed by case law interpreting the actual reliance requirements in the UCL and CLRA.

Second, Plaintiffs argue that the Court should infer reliance from the fact that Plaintiffs had iTunes accounts and therefore had to, at some point, agree to Apple's Terms and Conditions and Privacy Policy. Plaintiffs ask the Court to infer that Plaintiffs must have read and relied on misrepresentations contained in Apple's Privacy Policy at some point during the class period.

There are two problems with this theory. Most critically, it has no evidentiary support. No Plaintiff, in either a deposition or declaration, identified an Apple Privacy Policy as the source of his or her "understanding" regarding Apple's policies concerning privacy and data collection. Indeed, no Plaintiff states anywhere in the record that he or she ever saw or read or even heard of any version of Apple's Privacy Policy, either before or after July 2010.

What is more, the mere fact that Plaintiffs had to scroll through a screen and click on a box stating that they agreed with the Apple Privacy Policy in July 2010 does not establish, standing alone, that Plaintiffs actually read the alleged misrepresentations contained in that Privacy Policy, let alone that these misrepresentations subsequently formed the basis for Plaintiffs' "understanding" regarding Apple's privacy practices. Accordingly, the existence of Plaintiffs' iTunes accounts does not, *by itself,* demonstrate that Plaintiffs actually read and relied on any misrepresentations contained in the updated Privacy Policy from July 2010.

The Court acknowledges that, on a motion for summary judgment, the Court is required to draw all justifiable inferences in favor of the nonmoving party. Were Plaintiffs' "iTunes account/Privacy Policy" theory of actual reliance supported by *something* more than Plaintiffs' counsel's mere say so, the Court might conclude that it could justifiably infer that Plaintiffs relied on misrepresentations contained in the July 2010 updated Privacy Policy, even if no Plaintiff explicitly identified this Privacy Policy as the source of the alleged misrepresentations on which he or she actually relied. But here there is nothing more.

As Plaintiffs have failed to show that there is a genuine issue of material fact concerning whether any Plaintiff actually relied on any of Apple's alleged misrepresentations, the Court concludes that no Plaintiff has standing to pursue either the iDevice or Geolocation claims. The Court therefore GRANTS Apple's Motion for Summary Judgment in full.

## Tyler v. Michaels Stores, Inc.

984 N.E.2d 737 (Mass. 2013)

■ BOTSFORD, J.

In 2011, Melissa Tyler, a customer of Michaels Stores, Inc. (Michaels), filed an action on behalf of herself and a putative class of Michaels customers in the United States District Court for the District of Massachusetts. Tyler's complaint alleged that Michaels unlawfully writes customers' personal identification information on credit card transaction forms in violation of Mass. G.L. c. 93, § 105(a), when Michaels's employees request and record customers' zip codes in processing credit card transactions. A judge of the United States District Court for the District of Massachusetts certified the following questions to this court pursuant to S.J.C. Rule 1:03:

1. Under [G.L. c.] 93, [§ ] 105(a), may a [zip code] be 'personal identification information' because a [zip code] could be necessary to the credit card issuer to identify the card holder in order to complete the transaction?"

2. Under [G.L. c.] 93, [§ ] 105(a), may a plaintiff bring an action for this privacy right violation absent identity fraud?

3. Under [G.L. c.] 93, [§ ] 105(a), may the words 'credit card transaction form' refer equally to an electronic or a paper transaction form?

We answer "Yes" to the first question, but for different reasons than the judge set forth in the question itself. We also answer "Yes" to the second and third questions.

**Background**

Tyler's complaint alleges the following facts that we accept as true for the purposes of answering the certified questions. On several occasions during the past year, Tyler made purchases with a credit card at a Michaels retail store in Everett. During these transactions, a Michaels employee asked Tyler to provide her zip code. Tyler disclosed the number under the mistaken impression that she was required to do so in order to complete the credit card transaction, but in fact, the credit card issuer did not require Michaels to request zip codes. Michaels maintains a policy of writing customers' names, credit card numbers, and zip codes on electronic credit card transaction forms in connection with credit card purchases. Michaels used Tyler's name and zip code in conjunction with other commercially available databases to find her address and telephone number. Tyler subsequently received unsolicited and unwanted marketing material from Michaels.

Tyler filed her class action complaint against Michaels on May 23, 2011, claiming that Michaels's electronic recording of customer zip codes amounts to writing personal identification information on a credit card transaction form in violation of § 105(a) and therefore constitutes an unfair or deceptive act or practice as defined in G.L. c. 93A, § 2 [the Massachusetts unfair and deceptive practices statute]. The complaint also contains a claim for unjust enrichment and seeks a declaratory judgment that Michaels's collection of zip codes violates § 105(a). Michaels filed a motion to dismiss the complaint on July 22, 2011. On January 6, 2012, the District Court judge granted the motion. The judge concluded that (1) Tyler sufficiently alleged a violation of § 105(a) because zip codes constitute personal identification information, and Michaels's electronic credit card terminal may contain "credit card transaction form[s]" within the meaning of § 105 (a); but (2) the complaint failed to allege that Michaels's collection of zip codes caused Tyler an injury cognizable under G.L. c. 93A. The judge also concluded that the complaint failed to state a claim for unjust enrichment and that Tyler was not entitled to the declaratory relief she sought. At the invitation of the judge, on January 13, 2012, Tyler filed a motion to certify certain questions concerning the proper interpretation of § 105(a) to this court. The judge certified the three questions set forth supra.

**Discussion**

All three questions turn on the meaning and purpose of § 105(a), and G.L. c. 93, § 105 more generally. It is therefore useful to identify the purpose or purposes of these statutory provisions at the outset.

Section 105(a) provides:

> No person, firm, partnership, corporation or other business entity that accepts a credit card for a business transaction shall write, cause to be written or require that a credit card holder write personal identification information, not required by the credit card issuer, on the credit card transaction form. Personal identification information shall include, but shall not be limited to, a credit card holder's address or telephone number. The provisions of this section shall apply to all credit card transactions; provided, however, that the provisions of this section shall not be construed to prevent a person, firm, partnership, corporation or other business entity from requesting information . . . necessary for shipping, delivery or installation of purchased merchandise or services or for a warranty when such information is provided voluntarily by a credit card holder.

Section 105(d) states that "[a]ny violation of the provisions of this chapter shall be deemed to be an unfair and deceptive trade practice, as defined in section 2 of chapter 93A." Thus, a violation of § 105(a) is unlawful under G.L. c. 93A, § 2, and may be the basis for a claim under c. 93A, § 9.4.

The judge opined that the main purpose of § 105(a) is to prevent identity fraud and not, as Tyler contends, to protect consumer privacy. Michaels advances the same interpretation of the statute as the judge. We disagree for three reasons.

First, keeping in mind the rule that the actual words chosen by the Legislature are critical to the task of statutory interpretation, there is nothing in the actual language of § 105(a) to suggest that its purpose is confined to preventing identity fraud. Rather, by its inclusive terms § 105(a) reflects concern about, and an intent to limit, disclosure of personal information leading to the identification of a particular consumer generally.

Thus, § 105 (a) expressly "applies to all credit card transactions" and delineates a general prohibition. The statute also defines "[p]ersonal identification information" in a nonexclusive manner, stating that the term "shall include, but shall not be limited to, a credit card holder's address or telephone number." We discern nothing in these expansive and general terms that indicates or suggests that prevention of identity fraud was the single point of legislative focus.

Second, and contrary to the District Court judge, we find the title of § 105 to offer useful guidance. Section 105 was inserted in the General Laws by St. 1991, c. 414, § 1. The title of this act is "An Act relative to consumer privacy in commercial transactions." The significance of this title gains strength from the fact that in the text itself, the Legislature inserted a caption into the General Laws for this new legislation. Thus, St. 1991, c. 414, § 1, begins: "Chapter 93 of the General Laws is hereby amended by adding under the caption 'CONSUMER PRIVACY IN COMMERCIAL TRANSACTIONS,' the following two sections: [§§ 104 and 105]." Both title and caption thus expressly reference "consumer privacy in commercial transactions," reinforcing the view that the Legislature indeed was concerned, as Tyler suggests, about privacy issues in the realm of commercial dealings and in any event was not necessarily focused solely on preventing identity fraud.

The third reason for our disagreement relates to the legislative history of § 105. [T]his history strongly suggests that there were at least two privacy-related purposes underlying § 105: credit card identity fraud and consumer privacy. [The court conducted a lengthy analysis of the drafting history and documents that accompanied the legislation.]

These documents indicate that the proposed legislation had two distinct goals: for check transactions (now covered in § 105(b)), the goal or purpose was to prohibit recording of credit card information on checks to prevent misuse and credit card fraud; and for credit card transactions (now covered in § 105(a)), the purpose was to safeguard consumer privacy and more particularly to protect consumers using credit cards from becoming the recipients of unwanted commercial solicitations from merchants with access to their identifying information.

To summarize: based on the text, title and caption, and legislative history of § 105, we are persuaded that the principal purpose of § 105(a), in contrast to § 105(b), is to guard consumer privacy in credit card transactions, not to protect against credit card identity fraud. Against this backdrop, we now turn to the three certified questions.

**1. Meaning of "personal identification information."** The first certified question asks whether a zip code is "[p]ersonal identification information" under § 105(a). The statute defines "personal identification information" as including, but not limited to, "a credit card holder's address or telephone number." G.L. c. 93, § 105(a). As indicated previously, this definition is explicitly nonexhaustive. Although a cardholder's address and telephone number unquestionably constitute personal identification information, the definition leaves open the possibility that other information may also so qualify. Tyler contends that because a zip code is part of an address, and § 105(a) defines a cardholder's address as personal identification information, the zip code automatically qualifies as personal identification information as well.

Even if we agree with Michaels that this deductive reasoning fails, we still conclude that a zip code may well qualify as personal identification information under § 105(a). This is so because, according to (and accepting for present purposes) the allegations of the complaint, a consumer's zip code, when combined with the consumer's name, provides the merchant with enough information to identify through publicly available databases the consumer's address or telephone number, the very information § 105(a) expressly identifies as personal identification information. In other words, to conclude in those circumstances that zip codes are not "personal identification information" under the statute would render hollow the statute's explicit prohibition on the collection of customer addresses and telephone numbers, and undermine the statutory purpose of consumer protection.

2. **Requirements for bringing an action under § 105(a).** The second question asks whether a plaintiff may bring an action for a violation of § 105(a) absent identity fraud. We see no reason to read into the statute a requirement that one be the victim of identity fraud in order to assert a claim under that statute. It does not contain an express limitation to that effect, and as previously discussed, we interpret § 105(a) itself as being intended primarily to address invasion of consumer privacy by merchants, not identity fraud. The achievement of this purpose would be hindered rather than advanced by imposing a requirement that the plaintiff be a victim of identity fraud in order to raise a claim of statutory violation.

Accordingly, our direct answer to the second question is that a plaintiff may bring an action for a violation of § 105(a) without alleging a claim of identity fraud. We accept the judge's invitation to expand on this answer, however, and consider briefly the issue of what must be alleged in such an action with respect to injury or loss.

Because § 105(d) provides that a violation of § 105(a) "shall be deemed to be an unfair and deceptive trade practice," a consumer seeking to bring an action for a violation of this statute would do so pursuant to G.L. c. 93A, § 9(1), as Tyler has done in this case. A complaint under G.L. c. 93A, § 9(1) must allege that the plaintiff has been "injured" by the act or practice claimed to be unfair or deceptive and therefore unlawful under c. 93A, § 2.

[O]ur recent decisions generally establish the following. The invasion of a consumer's legal right (a right, for example, established by statute or regulation), without more, may be a violation of G.L. c. 93A, § 2, and even a per se violation of § 2, but the fact that there is such a violation does not necessarily mean the consumer has suffered an injury or a loss entitling her to at least nominal damages and attorney's fees; instead, the violation of the legal right that has created the unfair or deceptive act or practice must cause the consumer some kind of separate, identifiable harm arising from the violation itself.

Returning to § 105(a), there appear to be at least two types of injury or harm that might in theory be caused by a merchant's violation of the statute: the actual receipt by a consumer of unwanted marketing materials as a result of the merchant's unlawful collection of the consumer's personal identification information; and the merchant's sale of a customer's personal identification information or the data obtained from that information to a third party. When a merchant acquires personal identification information in violation of § 105 (a) and uses the information for its own business purposes, whether by sending the customer unwanted marketing materials or by selling the information for a profit, the merchant has caused the consumer an injury that is distinct from the statutory violation itself and cognizable under G.L. c. 93A, § 9.20.

**3. Meaning of "credit card transaction form."** The third question asks whether the term "credit card transaction form" in § 105(a) should be understood to refer equally to electronic and paper transaction forms.

Section 105(a) affirmatively declares that its provisions "shall apply to *all* credit card transactions" (emphasis supplied), and it contains no language expressly limiting a "credit card transaction form" to a paper form. Accordingly, as noted by the judge, the language of § 105(a) naturally appears to include all such transactions, whether they are processed manually or electronically. The reference to the verb "write" in § 105(a) does not foreclose such an interpretation because by definition, the verb encompasses inscriptions made by hand and by typing. Webster's Third New International Dictionary 2640–2641 (1993) (defining "write" to include "to form or produce [a legible character] in, upon, or by means of a suitable medium," "to produce [symbols or words] by machine," and "to form or produce letters, words, or sentences with a pen, pencil, or machine"). Based on the words chosen by the Legislature, therefore, we interpret "credit card transaction form" to apply to transactions involving both electronic and paper forms.

There are other reasons to reject a narrow interpretation of the statutory language advocated by Michaels. To construe § 105(a) as inapplicable to electronic credit card transactions would render the statute essentially obsolete in a world where paper credit card transactions are a rapidly vanishing event. Such a construction would thus fail to carry out the statutory purpose of protecting consumer privacy because it would allow merchants to avoid the statute's prohibition against collecting personal identification information simply by using electronic means to capture and reflect any electronic credit card transaction. Where possible, a statute should not be interpreted to render it ineffective.

## Conclusion

As to the first certified question, we respond that a zip code constitutes personal identification information for the purposes of G.L. c.

93, § 105(a). As to the second certified question, we respond that a plaintiff may bring an action for violation of G.L. c. 93, § 105(a), absent identity fraud. As to the third certified question, we respond that the term "credit card transaction form" in G.L. c. 93, § 105(a), refers equally to electronic and paper transaction forms.

## NOTES

1. ***Legal Bases for Suit.*** At the federal level, the FTC Act and similar consumer protection laws generally do not give individual consumers the right to sue, reserving enforcement for regulatory agencies like the FTC. Most equivalent state laws, by contrast, explicitly create private rights of action as well as allowing enforcement by an official such as the state's Attorney General. [See Section C for more on federal regulatory action and Section D for more on state regulatory actions.] Twelve states have enacted a model statute from the 1960s, the Uniform Deceptive Trade Practices Act, which includes a private right of action. Most other states have some analogue, and these are sometimes known collectively as "Baby FTC Acts." In addition to their general provisions banning "unfair or deceptive practices" or the equivalent, many of these consumer protection laws include more specific prohibitions, such as the Massachusetts statute in *Tyler* that forbids the collection of address information with credit card transactions. Many other statutes you will encounter throughout this book also create private rights of action. Notable examples at the federal level include the Electronic Communications Privacy Act (ECPA), 18 U.S.C. §§ 2510 et seq. [see Chapter 5]; the Fair Credit Reporting Act (FCRA), 15 U.S.C. §§ 1681–1681u [see Chapter 6]; the Telephone Consumer Protection Act (TCPA), 42 U.S.C. § 227 [see Chapter 14]; and the Video Privacy Protection Act (VPPA), 18 U.S.C. § 2710 [see Chapter 14]. Some narrower state statutes also offer plaintiffs opportunities to bring suit for particular offenses, from Illinois' Biometric Information Privacy Act ("BIPA"), 740 ILL. COMP. STAT. 14, to laws in multiple states prohibiting employers from requesting social media passwords from employees or job applicants, *see, e.g.*, MICH. COMP. LAWS §§ 37.271 et seq.; UTAH CODE §§ 34–48–101 et seq. Finally, if the facts permit it, torts and constitutional violations may also give rise to privacy litigation by individual plaintiffs or class actions. And these theories can, of course, be combined. Twitter, without admitting fault, settled a putative class action lawsuit in 2015 that had alleged claims for breach of contract, disclosure tort, intentional misrepresentation, negligent misrepresentation, negligence, misappropriation, violation of the California Online Privacy Protection Act, and violations of both the UCL and CLRA.

2. ***Constitutional and Statutory Standing.*** Be sure you comprehend the difference between the standing requirements under Article III and those under the California consumer protection statutes in *iPhone*. Do you understand the court's reasoning that the requirements to show causation should be analyzed the same way for both claims in this case? Can you think of situations where they would diverge?

3. ***Alleging Standing.*** It seems clear that counsel for the *iPhone* plaintiffs recognized the need to demonstrate injury to satisfy standing

requirements, and so relied on allegations of elevated prices for Apple devices and drained batteries. Note that the court here *accepts* the possibility that these alleged harms could be concrete injuries in fact, but rejects them as the basis for both constitutional and statutory standing anyway. What are they missing, according to the *iPhone* court? If you were plaintiffs planning to bring a similar case for consumer protection violations in the wake of this decision, do you think you could structure your complaint to avoid the same fate as these plaintiffs? How? What was the injury in *Tyler*? Would it satisfy the requirements of constitutional standing if brought in federal court? Can you think of a situation where a request for a zip code would not be an injury in fact? Consider the following footnote from *Tyler*, omitted from the excerpt above, speculating about a situation where a violation of § 105(a) would not cause actual injury:

> In the present case, for example, if Michaels obtained a customer's zip code, placed that information in a file (paper or electronic), and never used the information for any purpose thereafter, a consumer would not have a cause of action for damages under G.L. c. 93A, § 9, even though Michaels's request for and saving of the zip code information may have violated § 105(a) and thereby qualified as an unfair or deceptive act.

*Tyler v. Michaels Stores, Inc.*, 984 N.E.2d 737, 746 n. 17 (Mass. 2013). Thus, a violation of § 105(a) standing by itself does not itself create standing under consumer protection law. Why not?

**4. Spokeo *and Standing*.** As this book went to print, the Supreme Court was considering a case argued in late 2015 that raised some of the same issues as the *iPhone* and *Tyler* cases. It involves a "people finder" web site called Spokeo.com that aggregates dossiers of personal information and has promoted its services for employers to use when researching the background of applicants. [For more general discussion about privacy and employers' applicant screening, see Chapter 11.] The plaintiff alleged that Spokeo included inaccurate information in its profile of him, that he was searching for employment, that he had not yet found work, and that the inaccuracies caused "actual harm" to his employment prospects. The complaint claimed a willful violation of the Fair Credit Reporting Act (FCRA), 15 U.S.C. §§ 1681 et seq. FCRA imposes duties upon certain information aggregators—the plaintiff argued that Spokeo fell within its scope—to ensure the accuracy of the personal information they distribute. [For more about FCRA in general and regulatory enforcement against Spokeo in particular, see Chapter 6.] The district court found that the plaintiff lacked Article III standing because he could not demonstrate actual injury. The Ninth Circuit reversed in *Robins v. Spokeo, Inc.*, 742 F.3d 409 (9th Cir. 2014), holding that "the violation of a statutory right is usually a sufficient injury in fact to confer standing." The Supreme Court granted cert., 135 S. Ct. 1892 (2015), on the following question: "Whether Congress may confer Article III standing upon a plaintiff who suffers no concrete harm, and who therefore could not otherwise invoke the jurisdiction of a federal court, by authorizing a private right of action based on a bare violation of a federal statute." Depending on how it is decided, the case could have a considerable impact on future privacy cases of all types. At this writing, a decision was expected by the end of the Court's term in June 2016. Does *Tyler* grant standing based on "the violation of a statutory right" alone?

5. ***Concrete Harm.*** This question of "concrete" harm circles privacy cases of all types. Does the circulation of personal information itself injure an individual? Should the fact that the legislature defines a disclosure or use of data as an injury affect the analysis? Or is it necessary for the plaintiff to show that the mishandling of personal information in turn caused some additional negative consequence? Those later consequential harms certainly could include identity theft, interference with employment prospects, or blackmail. Would they include reputational harm? Embarrassment? The receipt of unwanted marketing pitches and junk mail, as in *Tyler*? A drained smart phone battery, as in *iPhone*? A feeling of lost control? A rule that leans strongly toward requiring consequential harms could make it impossible to prove certain kinds of injury—the plaintiff in *Spokeo* may be unlikely to have access to evidence about the reliance of individual employers on Spokeo's profiles to reject his application. A rule that learns too far in the other direction may allow plaintiffs to file nuisance lawsuits against companies seeking potentially huge aggregate statutory damages for very small infractions.

6. ***Zip Codes and Marketing.*** How was Michaels able to find Tyler's home address using only her name and zip code? Zip codes are a much stronger identifier than you might think; there are over 32,000 unique zip codes in the United States, each tying the consumer to a fairly small geographic area. From there, it's a simple statistical leap to connect the consumer's name to an address using publicly available information. In one study, nearly half of the US population could be uniquely identified by zip code, gender, and date of birth alone. *See* Latanya Sweeney, *Simple Demographics Often Identify People Uniquely* (Carnegie Mellon Univ., Data Privacy Working Paper No. 3, 2000). Thus, zip codes are often a key tool for marketers, especially those who target consumers through the mail.

7. ***An Invitation to Sue.*** The *Tyler* decision encouraged other class action plaintiffs to file suit against retailers for unlawful zip code collection. According to the Boston Globe, at least 25 such lawsuits seeking a total of over $100 million were filed soon after the ruling. "About a third have been settled and about a half dismissed, while the rest continue to wind their way through the courts." Jack Newsham, *The ZIP Code War: Mass. Retailers Ask, and Lawsuits Follow*, BOSTON GLOBE (Jan. 19, 2015), 2015 WLNR 1691701; *see, e.g.*, *Derby v. Jos. A. Bank Clothiers, Inc.*, No. CIV.A. 14–12347–FDS, 2014 WL 7361023, at *8 (D. Mass. Dec. 23, 2014) (denying a motion to dismiss a zip code collection suit brought under § 105(a)). Other jurisdictions have split on the question of whether zip code collection violates consumer protection statutes that bar requests for a cardholder's address as part of credit card transactions. *Compare Pineda v. Williams-Sonoma Stores, Inc.*, 246 P.3d 612 (2011) (finding zip code requests violate state's Song—Beverly Credit Card Act of 1971) *with Hancock v. Urban Outfitters, Inc.*, 32 F. Supp. 3d 26 (D.D.C. 2014) (reading District of Columbia statute more narrowly to require a precise street address).

**8. *Temporary Zip Code Storage.*** It may not always be the case that collecting zip code information violates the Massachusetts law. Judge Young, the same federal district judge who certified the questions in *Tyler*, later faced another § 105(a) case involving zip code collection and ruled for the defendant. In that case, a gas station required customers who wanted to "pay at the pump" with a credit card to enter a zip code into the machine—but the zip code was used only to check for fraudulent use of the card and was not stored more permanently. The court reasoned:

> It is uncontroverted in the record that a customer's zip code is only held in volatile memory and is never recorded or written in any accessible form, as is required by the explicit terms of Section 105. While it is by no means dispositive, the legislative history cited by the SJC in *Tyler* underscores the notion that it is only the recording of and future access to personal identification information that Section 105 is intended to combat.

*Diviacchi v. Speedway LLC*, No. CIV.A. 15–10655–WGY, 2015 WL 3648693, at *7 (D. Mass. June 12, 2015). Is this a good interpretation of the statute applied to these facts? Would the *Tyler* court agree with it?

**9. *The FACTA Truncation Requirement.*** Small prohibitions like the Massachusetts zip code rule are sprinkled through state consumer protection laws, and there are a few requirements of this nature in federal law too. For example, as part of the Fair and Accurate Credit Transactions Act in 2003, Congress included a provision stating that "no person that accepts credit cards or debit cards for the transaction of business shall print more than the last 5 digits of the card number or the expiration date upon any receipt provided to the cardholder at the point of the sale or transaction." 15 U.S.C. § 1681c(g)(1). The language was incorporated into the Fair Credit Reporting Act (FCRA) [see Chapter 6], and thereby allows private suits and provides statutory damages of between $100 and $1000, as FCRA does. *See* 15 U.S.C. § 1681n(a)(1)(A). Courts have found that consumers whose card numbers were not truncated had Article III standing, and have permitted class action suits raising this claim to proceed. *See, e.g.*, *Armes v. Sogro, Inc.*, 932 F. Supp. 2d 931 (E.D. Wis. 2013).

**10. *Privacy Injuries as Consumer Protection Injuries.*** Relying on consumer protection law as a vehicle to address privacy can complicate the question of harm. Statutes like California's CLRA and UCL are intended to address harm to individuals arising from commercial interactions. Plaintiffs who rely on these statutes must shoehorn their privacy allegations into a consumer injury framework. For defendants, the often open-ended definitions of unlawful activity in these statutes can leave them vulnerable to unpredictable allegations of privacy violations. On the other hand, the flexibility of these laws may allow for the incremental development of privacy law to the benefit of both consumers and companies, at least as compared to highly regulatory alternatives sometimes seen in the data protection model [see Chapter 4].

---

## Focus

Class Action Privacy Lawsuits

The damages for almost every individual privacy injury grounded in consumer protection law will be small—the statutory damages award under ch. 93A in Massachusetts, for example, is $25. However, privacy injuries often affect a very large number of consumers, and aggregating those small awards in class actions can add up to huge potential recoveries. One famous class action suit against ComScore, a firm offering data analytics for online marketing, alleged that the company installed software on users' computers that unlawfully tracked their activity and transmitted information about files on their computers. Reportedly, the class would have included some 10 million individuals nationwide, each of whom could claim entitlement to statutory damages of $10,000 for each violation of the Electronic Communications Privacy Act (ECPA), 18 U.S.C. §§ 2510 et seq. [see Chapter 5]. Through the magic of multiplication, the potential damage award facing ComScore exceeded a billion dollars. *See generally Harris v. ComScore, Inc.*, 292 F.R.D. 579, 590 (N.D. Ill. 2013) (granting motion for class certification on federal statutory claims).

By bringing a class action, plaintiffs hope to gain leverage that may encourage a defendant company to settle rather than fight the suit. If plaintiffs pass the first few hurdles—a motion to dismiss, and perhaps a class certification decision—companies often elect to settle. Defendants may believe they would ultimately prevail, but worry about high costs for discovery and other litigation expenses and the public relations problems from protracted litigation. Moreover, even if there is only a small chance of total victory for the plaintiff class, the potentially crippling damage award certainly influences the defendant's risk assessment. In the *Harris* case against ComScore, the parties settled for $14 million after the Seventh Circuit denied an appeal of the district court's decision certifying the class. That was a reasonable price to avoid the danger, however remote, of a billion-dollar award.

One putative class action challenged Facebook over a program called Beacon, launched in 2007, which disclosed information in users' Facebook news feeds about their otherwise unrelated activity on partners' web sites. Here is what happened next:

> Facebook denied liability and filed a motion to dismiss the plaintiffs' claims. Before the district court ruled on Facebook's motion, the parties elected to attempt settling their case through private mediation. The parties' initial settlement talks reached an impasse over whether Facebook should terminate the Beacon program permanently, but after two mediation sessions and several months of negotiations, Facebook and the plaintiffs arrived at a settlement agreement. In September of 2009, plaintiff Sean Lane submitted the parties' finalized settlement agreement to the district court for preliminary approval.
>
> The terms of the settlement agreement provided that Facebook would permanently terminate the Beacon program and pay a total of $9.5 million in exchange for a release of all the plaintiffs' class claims. Of the $9.5 million pay-out, approximately $3 million would be used to pay attorneys' fees, administrative costs, and incentive payments to the class representatives. Facebook would use the remaining $6.5 million or so in settlement funds to set up a new charity organization called the Digital Trust Foundation ('DTF'). The stated purpose of DTF would be to 'fund and sponsor programs designed to educate users, regulators[,] and enterprises regarding critical issues relating to protection of identity and

> personal information online through user control, and the protection of users from online threats.'

*Lane v. Facebook, Inc.*, 696 F.3d 811, 817 (9th Cir. 2012), cert. denied, 134 S. Ct. 8 (2013). The district court certified a settlement class and approved the settlement, effectively barring other private plaintiffs from suing over Beacon. The Ninth Circuit affirmed this ruling on appeal. Facebook promised to terminate the Beacon program (in fact, it had already done so on its own initiative because it was highly controversial), the lawyers made about $3 million, and the Digital Trust Foundation plans to distribute $6.5 million in grants by the end of 2015 and then disband. Why do you suppose Facebook chose to settle this class action litigation while, in cases excerpted earlier in this chapter, the airlines and Apple did not?

Not surprisingly, the combination of large potential damage awards with legally and technically complex cases has fueled the development of a small but growing privacy class action plaintiffs' bar. According to the Bryan Cave report mentioned at the outset of this Section, 240 law firms filed the 672 class action complaints studied there, but most of these firms filed just one of them. Four firms were behind 235 of the suits—over a third of all those filed. *See* DAVID ZETOONY ET AL., BRYAN CAVE LLP, 2015 DATA PRIVACY LITIGATION REPORT AT 10, *available at* http://www.bryancavedatamatters.com/category/miscellaneous/litigation/. In April 2015, the New York Times profiled Jay Edelson, a pioneer of privacy class actions and founder of the Chicago law firm Edelson LLC, calling him the technology industry's "bogeyman." Michael Rhodes, a lawyer who has defended clients in privacy suits brought by Edelson's firm, decried his strategy to the Times: "It's legal gotcha, and he tries to convince you that because there's a legal gotcha with a big number, then you should pay him instead of litigating. That's his business model." Conor Dougherty, *Jay Edelson, the Class-Action Lawyer Who May Be Tech's Least Friended Man*, N.Y. TIMES, BU1 (April 5, 2015). In a criticism familiar from other areas of law, adversaries argue that class action lawyers take large payouts and consumers receive relatively little compensation. Responding to another article discussing such objections, Edelson said that private law firms like his moved more quickly than government regulators to protect individual rights against large companies: "The reason a lot of companies don't like us is that [in] the world we're in now . . . you have these startups that move as quickly as possible and they don't have the resources to get lawyers and think about the law. They're focused on growing as fast as possible. What happens is they hit and then they try to sort out the problems. I think that's the wrong way to do it." Nicholas Carlson, *Meet The Most Feared And Loathed Law Firm In Silicon Valley*, BUSINESS INSIDER (June 23, 2011), http://www.businessinsider.com/meet-the-most-feared-and-loathed-law-firm-in-silicon-valley—2011—6.

Overall, it has become much more difficult to file and sustain class actions suits in the wake of Supreme Court decisions cutting back on them such as *Wal-Mart v. Dukes*, 564 U.S. 338 (2011) (tightening rules for class certification), and *AT&T Mobility LLC v. Concepcion*, 563 U.S. 333 (2011) (expanding enforcement of mandatory arbitration clauses). Developments in privacy law, particularly standing doctrine, have also increased the obstacles to private suits, including class actions. That said, privacy class action suits will remain a significant legal threat to companies for the foreseeable future, and an important consideration in any analysis of privacy liability risk.

---

## C. FTC ENFORCEMENT

### 1. THE SOURCE OF FTC AUTHORITY

### Federal Trade Commission Act, Section 5

15 U.S.C. § 45

(a) **Declaration of unlawfulness . . .**

(1) Unfair methods of competition in or affecting commerce, and unfair or deceptive acts or practices in or affecting commerce, are hereby declared unlawful.

(2) The Commission is hereby empowered and directed to prevent persons, partnerships, or corporations . . . from using unfair methods of competition in or affecting commerce and unfair or deceptive acts or practices in or affecting commerce [with enumerated exceptions of entities regulated by other agencies, such as banks and telecommunications companies].

. . .

(n) **Standard of proof; public policy considerations**

The Commission shall have no authority under this section . . . to declare unlawful an act or practice on the grounds that such act or practice is unfair unless the act or practice causes or is likely to cause substantial injury to consumers which is not reasonably avoidable by consumers themselves and not outweighed by countervailing benefits to consumers or to competition. In determining whether an act or practice is unfair, the Commission may consider established public policies as evidence to be considered with all other evidence. Such public policy considerations may not serve as a primary basis for such determination.

### Federal Trade Commission v. Accusearch, Inc.

570 F.3d 1187 (10th Cir. 2009)

■ HARTZ, CIRCUIT JUDGE

Abika.com is a website that has sold various personal data, including telephone records. The Federal Trade Commission (FTC) brought suit against the operator of the website, Accusearch Inc., and its president and owner, Jay Patel (collectively, Accusearch), to curtail Accusearch's sale of confidential information and to require it to disgorge its profits from the sale of information in telephone records. The FTC alleged that Accusearch's trade in telephone records (which are protected from disclosure under § 702 of the Telecommunications Act of 1996, 47 U.S.C. § 222 (2006)) constituted an unfair practice in violation of § 5(a) of the Federal Trade Commission Act (FTCA), 15 U.S.C. § 45(a) (2006). The district court granted the FTC summary judgment, and after further briefing entered an injunction restricting Accusearch's future trade in telephone records and other personal information.

On appeal Accusearch contends that the FTC's unfair-practice claim should have been dismissed because Accusearch broke no law and because the FTC had no authority to enforce the Telecommunications Act. We reject each of Accusearch's contentions and affirm. Conduct may constitute an unfair practice under § 5(a) of the FTCA even if it is not otherwise unlawful, and the FTC may pursue an unfair practice even if the practice is facilitated by violations of a law not administered by the FTC, such as the Telecommunications Act. The injunction was proper despite Accusearch's prior halt to its unfair practices and the possibility that the resumption of those practices would be criminally prosecuted.

## I. BACKGROUND

Although the parties characterize the Abika.com website differently, they do not dispute the essential aspects of its operation. Any person interested in Abika.com's services could access the website through a search engine or by typing its address into an Internet browser. A visitor to the website would first see its homepage, which displayed various categories of information that could be searched. The record contains one printout of the website from December 20, 2006, and one from November 27, 2007. The printouts show that some searches advertised on the homepage targeted information generally contained in government records, such as "court dockets," "sex offender records," and "Tax . . . Liens." Other search categories related to intimate personal information, such as "Romantic Preferences," "Personality traits," and "Rumors."

From February 2003 to January 2006 the Abika.com website advertised access to personal telephone records. The website stated that its customers could acquire "details of incoming or outgoing calls from any phone number, prepaid calling card or Internet Phone," and that "Phone searchers are available for every country of the world." Abika.com's customers could purchase both cellphone and landline records. The website specified that cellphone records would detail the numbers dialed from a particular cellphone and generally include the "date, time and duration of the calls" made. Landline records would include the same information, save for the specific time at which calls were made.

Acquisition of this information would almost inevitably require someone to violate the Telecommunications Act or to circumvent it by fraud or theft.

The FTC filed suit against Accusearch on May 1, 2006, roughly four months after Accusearch ceased to offer telephone records. The complaint alleged that telephone records are protected against disclosure by the Telecommunications Act and that trade in such records constitutes an unfair practice in violation of § 5(a) of the FTCA, 15 U.S.C. § 45(a). Accusearch responded with a motion to dismiss, contending that the complaint failed to state a claim because the Telecommunications Act applies only to telephone carriers and because selling confidential telephone records was not otherwise unlawful. The district court denied the motion and Accusearch filed an answer. After conducting discovery the parties each moved for summary judgment.

The court ruled that the FTC had established each element of its unfair-practice claim. After further briefing the district court entered an injunction restricting Accusearch's future trade in telephone records and other personal information. Accusearch was also ordered, among other things, to disgorge $199,692.71 in profits from the sale of telephone-record information.

## II. DISCUSSION

The FTCA prohibits "unfair or deceptive acts or practices in or affecting commerce," 15 U.S.C. § 45(a)(1), and vests the FTC with authority to prevent such practices by issuing cease-and-desist orders, *id.* § 45(b), by prescribing rules, *id.* § 57a(a)(1)(B), and by seeking injunctive relief in federal district court, *id.* § 53(b). To be "unfair," a practice must be one that "[1] causes or is likely to cause substantial injury to consumers [2] which is not reasonably avoidable by consumers themselves and [3] not outweighed by countervailing benefits to consumers or to competition." *Id.* § 45(n).

The FTC argued below that Accusearch's practice of offering consumer telephone records over the Internet satisfied all three requirements. First, the FTC contended that substantial injury was caused by the subversion of the Telecommunications Act; it argued that consumers whose telephone records were obtained through Abika.com suffered emotional harm (sometimes from being stalked or otherwise harassed) and often incurred substantial costs in changing telephone providers to prevent future privacy breaches. Second, the FTC contended that because Accusearch's researchers could override password encryption, consumers could not protect themselves by reasonable means but only by extreme measures such as ceasing telephonic communication altogether. Third, the FTC contended that the unconsented-to disclosure of telephone records provided no countervailing benefits to consumers.

On appeal Accusearch does not challenge this analysis of the unfair-practice elements. Its arguments relate only to the FTC's reliance on the Telecommunications Act. One argument is that the FTC could not rely on the Act because it applied solely to telecommunications carriers, not to Accusearch or its researchers; during the period at issue, contends Accusearch, there was "no law preventing a third-party from collecting telephone records."

We reject the argument. Its premise appears to be that a practice cannot be an unfair one unless it violates some law independent of the FTCA. But the FTCA imposes no such constraint. On the contrary, the

FTCA enables the FTC to take action against unfair practices that have not yet been contemplated by more specific laws.

To be sure, violations of law may be relevant to the unfairness analysis. *See* 15 U.S.C. § 45(n) ("In determining whether an act or practice is unfair, the Commission may consider established public policies as evidence to be considered with all other evidence. Such public policy considerations may not serve as a primary basis for such determination."). Here, for example, the FTC alleged that the substantial-injury element of an unfair practice was met partly by the subversion of consumer privacy protections afforded by the Telecommunications Act. But the existence of that injury turns on whether the Telecommunications Act was violated (by somebody), not on whether Accusearch could itself be held liable under the Telecommunications Act.

Accusearch also raises the related argument that the FTC had no authority to bring its claim because only the Federal Communications Commission may enforce the Telecommunications Act. This argument fundamentally misapprehends the nature of this lawsuit. The FTC brought suit under the Federal Trade Commission Act, seeking to enjoin an unfair practice affecting commerce. *See id.* § 45(a) (declaring unfair practices unlawful); *id.* at § 53(b) (giving the FTC authority to seek enjoinment of unfair practices in federal district court). As set out above, the Telecommunications Act was relevant to that claim. But the complaint does not allege that Accusearch violated that Act. In any event, the FTC may proceed against unfair practices even if those practices violate some other statute that the FTC lacks authority to administer. Indeed, condemnation of a practice in criminal or civil statutes may well mark that practice as "unfair." By the same token, a practice, such as Accusearch's, which either encourages such condemned conduct or encourages the use of fraud or theft to circumvent the statute, may likewise be considered "unfair."

The FTCA provides that "in proper cases the Commission may seek, and after proper proof, the court may issue, a permanent injunction." 15 U.S.C. § 53(b). Although Accusearch ceased dealing in telephone records before the FTC filed its complaint, the district court determined that prospective injunctive relief was appropriate to prevent Accusearch from engaging in similar unfair practices with respect to telephone records or the other information it provided. Accordingly, the injunction prohibits Accusearch from doing, among other things, the following:

> (1) Trading in "customer phone records" unless doing so would be "clearly permitted by any law, regulation, or lawful court order" and
>
> (2) Trading in other "consumer personal information without the express written permission of [the consumer], unless [the] consumer personal information was lawfully obtained from publically available information."

The injunction defines *consumer personal information* as "any individually identifiable information concerning a consumer."

A "court's power to grant injunctive relief survives the discontinuance of the illegal conduct." *United States v. W.T. Grant Co.*, 345 U.S. 629, 633 (1953). When, as in this case, a defendant has ceased offending conduct, the party seeking injunctive relief must demonstrate to the court "that there exists some cognizable danger of recurrent violation, something more than the mere possibility which serves to keep the case alive." *Id.* In assessing the likelihood of recurrence, a court may consider "all the circumstances," including the "bona fides of the expressed intent to comply, the effectiveness of the discontinuance and, in some cases, the character of the past violations." *Id.* We review the decision to grant a permanent injunction for abuse of discretion. The district court's discretion in this context is necessarily broad and a strong showing of abuse must be made to reverse it.

Accusearch has not persuaded us that the district court abused its discretion. True, Accusearch ceased offering telephone records before litigation commenced. But, as the district court noted, because Accusearch remained in the "information brokerage business" it had the capacity to "engag[e] in similar unfair acts or practices" in the future. In Accusearch's view it has proved the absence of any need for prospective relief by expressing a willingness to disgorge nearly $200,000 in ill-gotten profits. But a district court is best situated to judge the sincerity of a litigant's contrition and Accusearch has given us no ground to second-guess the district court's judgment.

Accusearch also argues that the injunction was improper because [the Telephone Records and Privacy Protection Act of 2006], enacted by Congress after this suit was filed, criminalizes the sale and receipt of confidential telephone records absent customer consent. Stressing that the government could prosecute under [this statute] if it resumed its trade in telephone records, Accusearch asserts that prospective injunctive relief would be redundant, and, as such, improper.

To be sure, injunctions against criminalized conduct have historically been disfavored. But in keeping with the characteristic flexibility of equitable remedies, they have never been absolutely prohibited. An injunction can have several advantages over the threat posed by a criminal statute. To begin with, it can encompass conduct not barred by the statute. Here, the injunction covers all "individually identifiable" consumer information, whereas the criminal statute covers only telephone records. Also, because an injunction can be drawn more precisely than a criminal statute, it can have a greater deterrent effect by removing any doubt in the mind of the enjoined party that particular conduct is forbidden. Furthermore, proving a violation of an injunction is generally less burdensome than proving a criminal violation. For example, to violate [the new statute] one must act "knowingly and intentionally." The injunction, on the other hand, imposes no scienter requirement and the law does not necessarily imply one. And a violation need not be proved to a jury beyond a reasonable doubt. The district court did not impose an inconsequential injunction. Thus, Accusearch's argument fails on its own terms.

In any event, Congress has power to provide for civil injunctive relief against activities which adversely affect interstate commerce, and that power extends to activities which are made criminal by state or federal law. In enacting the FTCA, Congress gave the FTC express authority to seek permanent injunctive relief in federal court to prevent violations of § 5(a).

Affirmed.

## NOTES

1. ***An Unusual Challenge to the FTC's Authority.*** The FTC has brought over 170 cases related to data privacy or security using its authority under Section 5 of the FTC Act, and the annual number of these cases is increasing steadily. Of these, so far only three have failed to settle at the complaint phase. *Accusearch* was the first. Two other companies have since challenged FTC authority over data security enforcement; one of these challenges is being adjudicated within the FTC, while the other has resulted in another appeals court opinion affirming FTC authority [see Section B.3 below]. In all other privacy-related cases the FTC has brought, it negotiated with the target of the complaint to reach a settlement, embodied in a consent decree that is binding on the defendant. In litigated consumer protection cases outside the realm of privacy and security, courts have granted the FTC considerable leeway in its enforcement powers. *Accusearch* largely followed the precedent in these cases, leaving the FTC rather sweeping authority to define the scope of "unfairness" and "deception" in its enabling statute.

2. ***Emergence of the FTC's Role.*** The FTC became the dominant federal agency overseeing privacy in part to fill a vacuum, because no other regulator had clear authority in the area. In the late 1990s and early 2000s there was something of a turf war in Washington between the FTC and other potential privacy watchdogs, particularly the Department of Commerce. In the last 10 years, as the FTC has devoted more resources to privacy and security—and especially as it has exercised its preexisting general enforcement powers—it has become the chief federal agency responsible for regulating in these areas. To be sure, other federal agencies have roles to play; in recent years Congress has conferred new privacy enforcement powers on the Consumer Financial Protection Board, the Department of Health and Human Services, and the Federal Communications Commission, to name a few. None of these bodies has the same scope of authority as the FTC enjoys under Section 5, however. In addition to its general power under the FTC Act, Congress has also assigned the FTC specific roles in enforcing provisions of other statutes [see "FOCUS: FTC Authority Beyond Section 5," below]. The FTC has stated that it would appreciate a specific congressional mandate explicitly empowering it to handle general consumer privacy issues, and perhaps some additional powers such as greater investigative power and

larger fines. There seems little likelihood of such legislation passing in the near future, however. For more on the history of the rise of FTC privacy and security enforcement, see Daniel J. Solove & Woodrow Hartzog, *The FTC and the New Common Law of Privacy*, 114 COLUM. L. REV. 583, 590–606 (2014).

3. ***Unfair vs. Deceptive.*** Section 5 empowers the FTC to regulate "unfair or deceptive acts or practices." Was the conduct in *Accusearch* determined to be unfair or deceptive? The FTC's power to find deception is significantly broader than its unfairness authority. Look again at Section 5(n) of the statute to see why. The FTC brings the majority of its privacy actions based on deception—though it has gradually increased the scope of its definition of deception. According to a count by the International Association of Privacy Professionals Westin Research Center at the beginning of 2015, of 132 FTC consent decrees in privacy and security, 117 included deception claims and 56 included unfairness claims. (The overlap results because the FTC includes both types of claims in some cases.) *See* IAPP FTC CASEBOOK at privacyassociation.org/resources/ftc-casebook. The rate of unfairness claims may be increasing, however, particularly in the area of data security.

4. ***Penalties.*** Section 5 does not, on its own, give the FTC the power to impose monetary penalties. Some other statutes that confer authority on the FTC to enforce privacy law include fines, but Section 5 focuses on equitable forms of relief. The FTC may pursue disgorgement of profits or restitution where the facts show clear financial harm—such as ordinary fraud cases brought under Section 5—but in most privacy cases, they do not. The FTC can secure monetary remedies for violations of consent decrees, however, which is another reason to pursue settlements with long-term consent decrees.

5. **Accusearch *and Section 230.*** In addition to its importance as an affirmation of the FTC's power over data privacy, *Accusearch* is also a significant case interpreting § 230 intermediary immunity [see Chapter 2]. The defendant argued that the search results it obtained were user-generated content and it was not the "speaker or publisher" of the information. In a portion of the opinion not reprinted above, the court described the functioning of the site as follows:

> Accusearch stresses on appeal that the search services offered on Abika.com were primarily services provided by third-party researchers, who were required by Accusearch to provide assurances that they would perform their work in accordance with applicable law. The researchers had no direct contact with Abika.com's customers. As Accusearch explains, "all information passed between [customer] and researcher went through Abika.com, as an intermediary." In placing a search order, a customer paid Accusearch an "administrative search fee," and selected the type of search desired, not a specific researcher or a search identified with a specific researcher. Accusearch would forward the search request to a researcher who could fulfill it. After completing a search, the researcher would send the results to

> Accusearch and bill Accusearch directly. Accusearch would then email the results to the customer and post them on the customer's Abika.com account. A customer could know that a third-party researcher was involved in a transaction only by reading boilerplate contained on the website and in Accusearch's email correspondence. And even then, the customer was not provided contact information for any researcher.

Based on these facts, the court rejected the immunity claim. It held that Accusearch was, in the words of the statute, "responsible, in whole or in part, for the creation or development of information," and therefore ineligible for the safe harbor:

> Accusearch attempts to portray itself as the provider of neutral tools, stressing that it merely provided "a forum in which people advertise and request" telephone records. But that phrasing mischaracterizes the record. As explained above, Accusearch solicited requests for confidential information protected by law, paid researchers to find it, knew that the researchers were likely to use improper methods, and charged customers who wished the information to be disclosed. Accusearch's actions were not "neutral" with respect to generating offensive content; on the contrary, its actions were intended to generate such content. Accusearch is not entitled to immunity under the CDA.

Does this ruling square with those discussed in Chapter 2?

## 2. GROWTH OF FTC PRIVACY REGULATION

# Prepared Testimony of FTC Chairman Jon Leibowitz Before US Senate Committee on Commerce, Science, and Transportation

(May 9, 2012)

### I. Introduction

Chairman Rockefeller, Ranking Member Hutchison, and members of the Committee, I am Jon Leibowitz, Chairman of the Federal Trade Commission ("FTC" or "Commission").

This is a critical juncture for consumer privacy, as the marketplace continues to rapidly evolve and new approaches to privacy protection are emerging in the United States and around the world. After careful consideration, the Commission recently released the final privacy report ("Final Report") [a comprehensive review of privacy issues based on staff work and consultation with stakeholders]. The Final Report sets forth best practices for businesses to guide current efforts to protect consumer privacy while ensuring that companies can continue to innovate. The Commission urges industry to use this guidance to improve privacy practices and accelerate the pace of self-regulation. Importantly, we have seen promising developments by industry toward a Do Not Track mechanism and we ask the Committee to continue to encourage industry to move towards full implementation. The Report also calls on Congress to consider enacting general privacy legislation. We reiterate today our call to Congress to enact legislation requiring companies to implement reasonable security measures and notify consumers in the event of certain security breaches, as well as targeted legislation that would provide consumers with access to information about them held by data brokers.

Privacy has been a key part of the Commission's consumer protection mission for more than 40 years. Throughout, the Commission's goal has remained constant: to protect consumers' personal information and ensure that they have the confidence to take advantage of the many benefits offered by the dynamic and ever-changing marketplace. To meet this objective, the Commission has undertaken substantial efforts to promote privacy in the private sector through law enforcement, education, and policy initiatives. For example, since 2001, the Commission has brought 36 data security cases; more than 100 spam and spyware cases; and 18 cases for violation of the Children's Online Privacy Protection Act ("COPPA"). The Commission has also brought highly publicized privacy cases against companies such as Google and Facebook and, most recently, Myspace. The Commission has distributed millions of copies of educational materials for consumers and businesses to address ongoing threats to security and privacy. And the FTC continues to examine the implications of new technologies and business practices on consumer privacy through ongoing policy initiatives, such as the Commission's Final Report.

## II. Final Privacy Report

The FTC recently released its Final Report, setting forth best practices for companies that collect and use consumer data. These best practices can assist companies as they develop and maintain processes and systems to operationalize privacy and data security practices within their businesses. To the extent these best practices exceed existing legal requirements, they are not intended to serve as a template for law enforcement or regulations under laws currently enforced by the FTC.

The Final Report supports the three key principles laid out in the preliminary staff report. Companies should adopt a "privacy by design" approach by building privacy protections into their everyday business practices. Such protections include providing reasonable security for consumer data, collecting only the data needed for a specific business purpose, retaining data only as long as necessary to fulfill that purpose, safely disposing of data no longer in use, and implementing reasonable procedures to promote data accuracy.

Companies also should provide simpler and more streamlined choices to consumers about their data practices. Companies do not need to provide choice before collecting and using consumers' data for practices that are consistent with the context of the transaction, the company's relationship with the consumer, or as required or specifically authorized by law. For all other data practices, consumers should have the ability to make informed and meaningful choices at a relevant time and context and in a uniform and comprehensive way.

Finally, companies should take steps to make their data practices more transparent to consumers. For instance, companies should improve their privacy disclosures and work toward standardizing them so that consumers, advocacy groups, regulators, and others can compare data practices and choices across companies, thus promoting competition among companies. Consumers should also have reasonable access to the data that companies maintain about them, particularly for non-consumer-facing entities such as data brokers. The extent of access should be proportional to the volume and sensitivity of the data and to its intended use.

In addition, the Final Report makes general and specific legislative recommendations. The Report supports the development of general privacy legislation to ensure basic privacy protections across all industry sectors, and can inform Congress, should it consider such privacy legislation. The Commission recommends that any such legislation be technologically neutral and sufficiently flexible to allow companies to continue to innovate. In addition, the Commission believes that any legislation should allow the Commission to seek civil penalties to deter statutory violations. Such legislation would provide businesses with the certainty they need to understand their obligations as well as the incentive to meet those obligations, while also assuring consumers that companies will respect their privacy. We believe this approach would foster an environment that allows businesses to innovate and consumers to embrace those innovations without risking their privacy. The Final Report also calls on Congress to enact legislation requiring companies to implement reasonable security measures and notify consumers in the event of certain security breaches, as well as targeted legislation for data brokers. We look forward to working with Congress and other stakeholders to craft this legislation.

### III. Other Policy Initiatives

In addition, the Commission holds public workshops and issues reports to examine the implications of new technologies and business practices on consumer privacy. [The testimony went on to describe a staff report about mobile applications for children, workshops to consult with experts and the public about privacy implications of facial recognition technology and about data collection by large operations such as internet service providers or social media platforms, and revisions to regulations under COPPA, see Chapter 4.]

### IV. Enforcement

In addition to its engagement on the policy front, enforcement remains a top priority for the agency. To date, the Commission has brought 36 data security cases; almost 80 cases against companies for improperly calling consumers on the Do Not Call registry; 86 cases against companies for violating the Fair Credit Reporting Act ("FCRA"); more than 100 spam and spyware cases; 18 COPPA cases; and numerous cases against companies for violating the FTC Act by making deceptive claims about the privacy and security protections they afford to consumer data. Where the FTC has authority to seek civil penalties, it has aggressively done so. It has obtained $60 million in civil penalties in Do Not Call cases; $21 million in civil penalties under the FCRA; $5.7 million under the CAN-SPAM Act; and $6.6 million under COPPA. Where the Commission does not have authority to seek civil penalties, as in the data security and spyware areas, it has sought such authority from Congress.

### V. Education

The FTC conducts outreach to businesses and consumers in the area of consumer privacy. The Commission's well-known OnGuard Online website educates consumers about many online threats to consumer privacy and security, including spam, spyware, phishing, peer-to-peer ("P2P") file sharing, and social networking. Furthermore, the FTC provides consumer education to help consumers better understand the privacy and security implications of new technologies. For example, last year the Commission issued a guide that provides consumers with information about mobile apps, including what apps are, the types of data they can collect and share, and why some apps collect geolocation information.

The Commission has also issued numerous education materials to help consumers protect themselves from identity theft and to deal with its consequences when it does occur. The FTC has distributed over 3.8 million copies of a victim recovery guide, *Take Charge: Fighting Back Against Identity Theft*, and has recorded over 3.5 million visits to the Web version. In addition, the FTC has developed education resources specifically for children, parents, and teachers to help children stay safe online.

Business education is also an important priority for the FTC. The Commission seeks to educate businesses by developing and distributing free guidance. For example, the Commission developed a widely-distributed guide to help small and medium-sized businesses implement appropriate data security for the personal information they collect and maintain. The Commission also creates business educational materials on specific topics—such as the privacy and security risks associated with peer-to-peer file-sharing programs and companies' obligations to protect consumer and employee information from these risks and how to properly secure and dispose of information on digital copiers. These publications, as well as other business education materials, are available through the FTC's Business Center website, which averages one million unique visitors each month. The Commission also hosts a Business Center blog, which frequently features consumer privacy and data security topics;

presently, approximately 3,500 attorneys and business executives subscribe to these email blog updates.

Another way the Commission seeks to educate businesses by publicizing its complaints and orders and issuing public closing and warning letters. For example, the Commission recently sent warning letters to the marketers of six mobile apps that provide background screening services. The letters state that some of the apps included criminal record histories, which bear on an individual's character and general reputation and are precisely the type of information that is typically used in employment and tenant screening. The FTC warned the apps marketers that, if they have reason to believe the background reports they provide are being used for employment screening, housing, credit, or other similar purposes, they must comply with the FCRA. [See Chapter 6.] The Commission made no determination as to whether the companies are violating the FCRA, but encouraged them to review their apps and their policies and procedures to ensure they comply with the Act.

## VI. Conclusion

These policy, enforcement, and education efforts demonstrate the Commission's continued commitment to protecting consumers' privacy and security—both online and offline. As noted above, the Commission encourages Congress to develop general privacy legislation and to adopt targeted legislation addressing data brokers. We appreciate the leadership of Chairman Rockefeller and this Committee on these issues and look forward to continuing to work with Congress, the Administration, industry and other critical stakeholders on these issues in the future.

## NOTES

1. ***The Final Report and Norm Entrepreneurship.*** The "Final Report" that Chairman Leibowitz highlighted was "final" in that it followed an earlier draft report, as well as multiple public workshops and a public comment period. Privacy lawyers viewed the eventual product as a significant signal from the FTC about its regulatory priorities and expectations. But the FTC also used the Report as a means of influencing debate about privacy law. By promoting concepts like "Privacy by Design" and "Do Not Track," the FTC hopes to encourage companies to think seriously about these approaches in their self-regulatory activities, and perhaps to promote subsequent law, either in Congress or in the FTC's own enforcement. This is a type of technique some scholars call "norm entrepreneurship," where actors like government agencies use their "bully pulpit" to promote the development of certain values among regulated entities, legislators, and the public. *See* Cass R. Sunstein, *Social Norms and Social Roles*, 96 COLUM. L. REV. 903 (1996). The FTC has relied on this power frequently and extensively. For example, in the late 1990s the FTC was a critical force in the successful effort to encourage companies to voluntarily

adopt and publicize privacy policies. This, in turn, codified their promises in ways that gave the FTC greater scope to enforce those obligations. *See* Steven Hetcher, *The FTC as Internet Privacy Norm Entrepreneur*, 53 VAND. L. REV. 2041 (2000).

2. ***Responsive Regulation and the FTC.*** The FTC's emphasis on norm entrepreneurship can be viewed through a prism of the technique administrative law scholars call "responsive regulation." Using this approach, an agency relies first on advice, exhortation, and industry cooperation, turning to penalties only when these methods fail. Responsive regulation is typically illustrated as a pyramid. Tactics of dialogue and persuasion lie at the broad base of the pyramid; agencies should use these first and most frequently. Such informal methods often spur regulated entities to improve their practices without any official action at all. At the next level up the pyramid, methods are more formal but still not directly punitive. A warning letter or a public rebuke may get the attention of a company's leadership. Even an announcement that a practice will be investigated can have the desired effect of fixing the problem. The classic pyramid then moves up through civil penalties to criminal ones. At the apex of the pyramid are "nuclear" weapons such as the revocation of a company's license to operate—although arguably the FTC lacks these strongest powers in privacy and security cases. For an introduction to these concepts, see IAN AYRES & JOHN BRAITHWAITE, RESPONSIVE REGULATION (1992). It is noteworthy that Chairman Leibowitz's testimony dwells at such length on the Final Report and its recommended (but voluntary) best practices, and on the FTC's education and guidance activities aimed at consumers and businesses, rather than on traditional adversarial enforcement. As you read on, consider why the FTC relies on these techniques so much. Is this a second-best alternative because the FTC lacks fining authority under Section 5? Is it an attempt to avoid backlash from regulated entities and possibly Congress? Is the FTC "captured" by industry or otherwise insufficiently vigilant? Or does responsive regulation offer, as some administrative law scholars believe, a more effective strategy than a focus on punitive regulation?

3. ***The FTC's Structure.*** Before going further, it is worth pointing out that the FTC is structured somewhat differently from many other executive agencies. It is an independent agency, led by five commissioners appointed to seven-year terms. No more than three of the commissioners may be from the same political party. The President selects the Chair, who essentially serves as the deciding fifth vote and, even more important, has power to set the FTC's agenda. Consequently, the White House can influence privacy law a great deal by choosing the FTC Chair. Civil servants do much of the policy and enforcement work, but major actions such as complaints must be approved by a majority of commissioners. *See* 15 U.S.C. § 41. There are three bureaus within the FTC; privacy issues fall under the Bureau of Consumer Protection, which also handles diverse matters such as fraud and false advertising. Within the Bureau of Consumer Protection, a separate Division of Privacy and Identity Protection (DPIP) was formed in 2006, and most of the FTC's privacy and security activity is centered there.

# In re Snapchat, Inc.

FTC Docket No. C–4501 (Dec. 23, 2014)

## COMPLAINT

The Federal Trade Commission, having reason to believe that Snapchat, Inc. ("respondent") has violated the provisions of the Federal Trade Commission Act, and it appearing to the Commission that this proceeding is in the public interest, alleges:

1. Respondent Snapchat, Inc. ("Snapchat"), the successor corporation to Toyopa Group LLC, is a Delaware corporation with its principal office or place of business at 63 Market Street, Venice, California 90291.

2. The acts and practices of respondent as alleged in this complaint have been in or affecting commerce, as "commerce" is defined in Section 4 of the Federal Trade Commission Act.

## RESPONDENT'S BUSINESS PRACTICES

3. Snapchat provides a mobile application that allows consumers to send and receive photo and video messages known as "snaps." Before sending a snap, the application requires the sender to designate a period of time that the recipient will be allowed to view the snap. Snapchat markets the application as an "ephemeral" messaging application, having claimed that once the timer expires, the snap "disappears forever."

4. Snapchat launched its mobile application on Apple Inc.'s iOS operating system in September 2011 and on Google Inc.'s Android operating system in October 2012. Snapchat added video messaging to the iOS version of its application in December 2012 and to the Android version of its application in February 2013.

5. Both the iTunes App Store and the Google Play store list Snapchat among the top 15 free applications. As of September 2013, users transmit more than 350 million snaps daily.

## SNAPCHAT'S "DISAPPEARING" MESSAGES (Counts 1 and 2)

6. Snapchat marketed its application as a service for sending "disappearing" photo and video messages, declaring that the message sender "control[s] how long your friends can view your message." Before sending a snap, the application requires the sender to designate a period of time—with the default set to a maximum of 10 seconds—that the recipient will be allowed to view the snap, as depicted below:

7. Since the application's launch on iOS until May 2013, and since the application's launch on Android until June 2013, Snapchat disseminated, or caused to be disseminated, to consumers the following statements on its product description page on the iTunes App Store and Google Play:

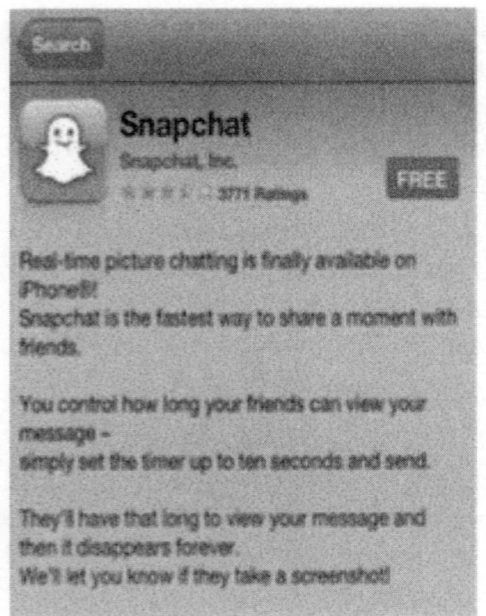


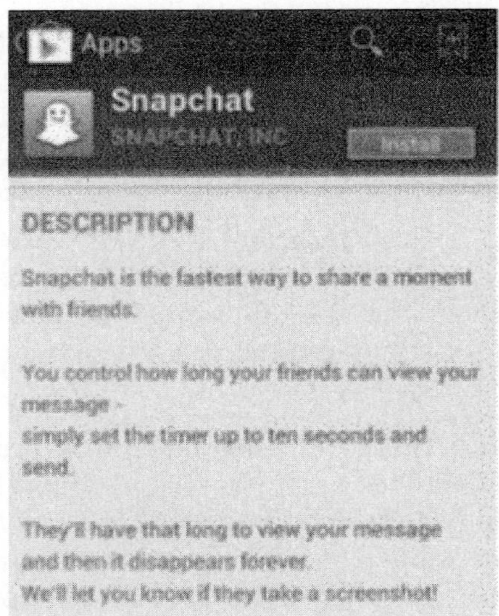


8. From October 2012 to October 2013, Snapchat disseminated, or caused to be disseminated, to consumers the following statement on the "FAQ" page on its website:

> [Q:] Is there any way to view an image after the time has expired?
>
> [A:] No, snaps disappear after the timer runs out. . . .

9. Despite these claims, several methods exist by which a recipient can use tools outside of the application to save both photo and video messages, allowing the recipient to access and view the photos or videos indefinitely.

10. For example, when a recipient receives a video message, the application stores the video file in a location outside of the application's "sandbox" (i.e., the application's private storage area on the device that other applications cannot access). Because the file is stored in this unrestricted area, until October 2013, a recipient could connect his or her mobile device to a computer and use simple file browsing tools to locate and save the video file. This method for saving video files sent through the application was widely publicized as early as December 2012. Snapchat did not mitigate this flaw until October 2013, when it began encrypting video files sent through the application.

11. Furthermore, third-party developers have built applications that can connect to Snapchat's application programming interface ("API"), thereby allowing recipients to log into the Snapchat service without using the official Snapchat application. Because the timer and related "deletion" functionality is dependent on the recipient's use of the official Snapchat application, recipients can instead simply use a third-party application to download and save both photo and video messages. As early as June 2012, a security researcher warned Snapchat that it would be "pretty easy to write a tool to download and save the images a user receives" due to the way the API functions. Indeed, beginning in spring 2013, third-party developers released several applications on the iTunes App Store and Google Play that recipients can use to save and view photo or video messages indefinitely. On Google Play alone, ten of these applications have been downloaded as many as 1.7 million times.

12. The file browsing tools and third-party applications described in paragraphs 10 and 11 are free or low cost and publicly available on the Internet. In order to download, install, and use these tools, a recipient need not make any modifications to the iOS or Android operating systems and would need little technical knowledge.

13. In addition to the methods described in paragraphs 10–12, a recipient can use the mobile device's screenshot capability to capture an image of a snap while it appears on the device screen.

14. Snapchat claimed that if a recipient took a screenshot of a snap, the sender would be notified. On its product description pages, as described in paragraph 7, Snapchat stated: "We'll let you know if [recipients] take a screenshot!" In addition, from October 2012 to February 2013, Snapchat disseminated, or caused to be disseminated, to consumers the following statement on the "FAQ" page on its website:

> [Q:] What if I take a screenshot?
>
> [A:] Screenshots can be captured if you're quick. The sender will be notified immediately.

15. However, recipients can easily circumvent Snapchat's screenshot detection mechanism. For example, on versions of iOS prior to iOS 7, the recipient need only double press the device's Home button in rapid succession to evade the detection mechanism and take a screenshot of any snap without the sender being notified. This method was widely publicized.

### Count 1

16. As described in Paragraphs 6, 7, and 8, Snapchat has represented, expressly or by implication, that when sending a message through its application, the message will disappear forever after the user-set time period expires.

17. In truth and in fact, as described in Paragraph 9–12, when sending a message through its application, the message may not disappear forever after the user-set time period expires. Therefore, the representation set forth in Paragraph 16 is false or misleading.

### Count 2

18. As described in Paragraphs 7 and 14, Snapchat has represented, expressly or by implication, that the sender will be notified if the recipient takes a screenshot of a snap.

19. In truth and in fact, as described in Paragraph 15, the sender may not be notified if the recipient takes a screenshot of a snap. Therefore, the representation set forth in Paragraph 18 is false or misleading.

## SNAPCHAT'S COLLECTION OF GEOLOCATION INFORMATION

### (Count 3)

20. From June 2011 to February 2013, Snapchat disseminated or caused to be disseminated to consumers the following statements in its privacy policy:

> We do not ask for, track, or access any location-specific information from your device at any time while you are using the Snapchat application.

21. In October 2012, Snapchat integrated an analytics tracking service in the Android version of its application that acted as its service provider. While the Android operating system provided notice to consumers that the application may access location information, Snapchat did not disclose that it would, in fact, access location information, and continued to represent that Snapchat did "not ask for, track, or access any location-specific information . . ."

22. Contrary to the representation in Snapchat's privacy policy, from October 2012 to February 2013, the Snapchat application on Android transmitted Wi-Fi-based and cell-based location information from users' mobile devices to its analytics tracking service provider.

### Count 3

23. As described in Paragraph 21, Snapchat has represented, expressly or by implication, that it does not collect users' location information.

24. In truth and in fact, as described in Paragraph 22, Snapchat did collect users' location information. Therefore, the representation set forth in Paragraph 23 is false or misleading.

## SNAPCHAT'S COLLECTION OF CONTACTS INFORMATION (Counts 4 and 5)

### Snapchat's Deceptive Find Friends User Interface

25. Snapchat provides its users with a feature to find friends on the service. During registration, the application prompts the user to "Enter your mobile number to find your friends on Snapchat!," implying—prior to September 2012—through its user interface that the mobile phone number was the only information Snapchat collected to find the user's friends, as depicted below:

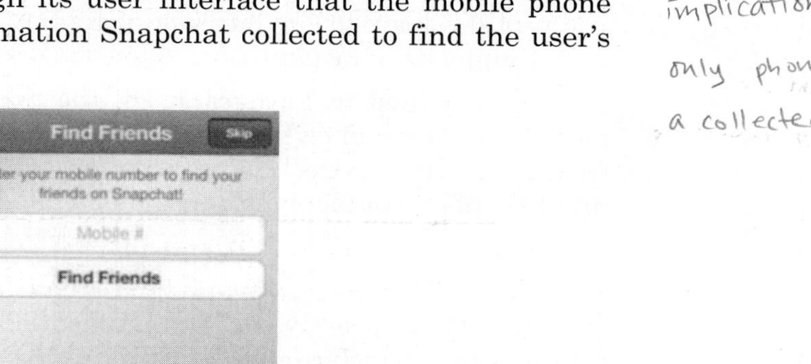


Users can also access this "Find Friends" feature at any time through the application's menu options.

26. However, when the user chooses to Find Friends, Snapchat collects not only the phone number a user enters, but also, without informing the user, the names and phone numbers of all the contacts in the user's mobile device address book.

27. Snapchat did not provide notice of, or receive user consent for, this collection until September 2012, at which time the iOS operating system was updated to provide a notification when an application accessed the user's address book.

### Count 4

28. As described in Paragraphs 25, through its user interface, Snapchat represented, expressly or by implication, that the only personal

information Snapchat collected when the user chose to Find Friends was the mobile number that the user entered.

29. In truth and in fact, as described in Paragraph 26, the mobile number that the user entered was not the only personal information that Snapchat collected. Snapchat also collected the names and phone numbers of all contacts in the user's mobile device address book. Therefore, the representation set forth in Paragraph 28 is false or misleading.

### Snapchat's Deceptive Privacy Policy Statement Regarding the Find Friends Feature

30. From June 2011 to February 2013, Snapchat disseminated or caused to be disseminated to consumers the following statements, or similar statements, in its privacy policy regarding its Find Friends feature:

> Optional to the user, we also collect an email, phone number, and facebook id for purpose of finding friends on the service. (Emphasis in original).

31. As explained in Paragraph 26, the Snapchat application collected more than email, phone number, and Facebook ID for purpose of finding friends on the service. The application collected the names and phone numbers of all contacts in the user's mobile device address book.

### Count 5

32. As described in Paragraph 30, Snapchat, through its privacy policy, represented, expressly or by implication, that the only personal information Snapchat collected from a user for the purpose of finding friends on the service was email, phone number, and Facebook ID.

33. In truth and in fact, as described in Paragraph 31, email, phone number, and Facebook ID was not the only personal information that Snapchat collected for the purpose of finding friends on the service. Snapchat collected the names and phone numbers of all contacts in the user's mobile device address book when the user chose to Find Friends. Therefore, the representation set forth in Paragraph 32 is false or misleading.

[The complaint also included a Count 6, concerning data security.]

45. The acts and practices of respondent as alleged in this complaint constitute deceptive acts or practices in or affecting commerce in violation of Section 5(a) of the Federal Trade Commission Act, 15 U.S.C. § 45(a).

THEREFORE, the Federal Trade Commission this twenty-third day of December, 2014, has issued this complaint against respondent.

## CONSENT ORDER

The Federal Trade Commission ("Commission") has conducted an investigation of certain acts and practices of Snapchat, Inc. ("Snapchat" or "proposed respondent"). Proposed respondent, having been represented by counsel, is willing to enter into an agreement containing a consent order resolving the allegations contained in the attached draft complaint. Therefore,

**IT IS HEREBY AGREED** by and between Snapchat, Inc., by its duly authorized officers, and counsel for the Federal Trade Commission that:

1. Proposed respondent Snapchat, Inc., the successor corporation to Toyopa Group LLC, is a Delaware corporation with its principal office or place of business at 63 Market Street, Venice, California 90291.

2. Proposed respondent neither admits nor denies any of the allegations in the draft complaint, except as specifically stated in this order. Only for purposes of this action, proposed respondent admits the facts necessary to establish jurisdiction.

3. Proposed respondent waives:

    A. any further procedural steps;

    B. the requirement that the Commission's decision contain a statement of findings of fact and conclusions of law; and

    C. all rights to seek judicial review or otherwise to challenge or contest the validity of the order entered pursuant to this agreement.

4. This agreement shall not become part of the public record of the proceeding unless and until it is accepted by the Commission. If this agreement is accepted by the Commission, it, together with the draft complaint, will be placed on the public record for a period of thirty (30) days and information about it publicly released. The Commission thereafter may either withdraw its acceptance of this agreement and so notify proposed respondent, in which event it will take such action as it may consider appropriate, or issue and serve its complaint (in such form as the circumstances may require) and decision in disposition of the proceeding.

5. This agreement is for settlement purposes only and does not constitute an admission by proposed respondent that the law has been violated as alleged in the draft complaint, or that the facts as alleged in the draft complaint, other than the jurisdictional facts, are true.

6. This agreement contemplates that, if it is accepted by the Commission, the Commission may, without further notice to proposed respondent, (1) issue its complaint corresponding in form and substance with the attached draft complaint and its decision containing the following order in disposition of the proceeding, and (2) make information about it public.

7. Proposed respondent has read the draft complaint and consent order. Proposed respondent understands that it may be liable for civil penalties in the amount provided by law and other appropriate relief for each violation of the order after it becomes final.

## DEFINITIONS

For purposes of this Order, the following definitions shall apply:

1. "Covered information" shall mean information from or about an individual consumer, including but not limited to (a) a first and last name; (b) a home or other physical address, including street name and name of city or town; (c) an email address or other online contact information, such as an instant messaging user identifier or a screen name; (d) a telephone number; (e) a persistent identifier, such as a customer number held in a "cookie," a static Internet Protocol ("IP") address, a mobile device ID, or processor serial number; (f) precise geo-location data of an individual or mobile device, including GPS-based, Wi-Fi-based, or cell-based location information; (g) an authentication credential, such as a username or password; or (h) any communications or content that is transmitted or stored through respondent's products or services.

2. "Computer" shall mean any desktop, laptop computer, tablet, handheld device, telephone, or other electronic product or device that has a platform on which to download, install, or run any software program, code, script, or other content and to play any digital audio, visual, or audiovisual content.

### I.

**IT IS ORDERED** that respondent and its officers, agents, representatives, and employees, directly or indirectly, shall not misrepresent in any manner, expressly or by implication, in or affecting commerce, the extent to which respondent or its products or services maintain and protect the privacy, security, or confidentiality of any covered information, including but not limited to: (1) the extent to which a message is deleted after being viewed by the recipient; (2) the extent to which respondent or its products or services are capable of detecting or notifying the sender when a recipient has captured a screenshot of, or otherwise saved, a message; (3) the categories of covered information collected; or (4) the steps taken to protect against misuse or unauthorized disclosure of covered information.

### II.

**IT IS FURTHER ORDERED** that respondent, in or affecting commerce, shall, no later than the date of service of this order, establish and implement, and thereafter maintain, a comprehensive privacy program that is reasonably designed to: (1) address privacy risks related to the development and management of new and existing products and services for consumers, and (2) protect the privacy and confidentiality of covered information, whether collected by respondent or input into, stored on, captured with, or accessed through a computer using respondent's products or services. Such program, the content and implementation of which must be fully documented in writing, shall contain privacy controls and procedures appropriate to respondent's size and complexity, the nature and scope of respondent's activities, and the sensitivity of the covered information, including:

A. the designation of an employee or employees to coordinate and be accountable for the privacy program;

B. the identification of reasonably foreseeable, material risks, both internal and external, that could result in the respondent's unauthorized collection, use, or disclosure of covered information, and assessment of the sufficiency of any safeguards in place to control these risks. At a minimum, this privacy risk assessment should include consideration of risks in each area of relevant operation, including, but not limited to: (1) employee training and management, including training on the requirements of this order; and (2) product design, development and research;

C. the design and implementation of reasonable privacy controls and procedures to address the risks identified through the privacy risk assessment, and regular testing or monitoring of the effectiveness of the privacy controls and procedures;

D. the development and use of reasonable steps to select and retain service providers capable of maintaining security practices consistent with this order, and requiring service providers by contract to implement and maintain appropriate safeguards;

E. the evaluation and adjustment of respondent's privacy program in light of the results of the testing and monitoring required by subpart C, any material changes to respondent's operations or business arrangements, or any other circumstances that respondent knows, or has reason to know, may have a material impact on the effectiveness of its privacy program.

## III.

**IT IS FURTHER ORDERED** that, in connection with its compliance with Part II of this order, respondent shall obtain initial and biennial assessments and reports ("Assessments") from a qualified, objective, independent third-party professional, who uses procedures and standards generally accepted in the profession. A person qualified to prepare such Assessments shall have a minimum of three (3) years of experience in the field of privacy and data protection. All persons selected to conduct such assessments and prepare such reports shall be approved by the Associate Director for Enforcement, Bureau of Consumer Protection, Federal Trade Commission. The reporting period for the Assessments shall cover: (1) the first one hundred eighty (180) days after service of the order for the initial Assessment; and (2) each two (2) year period thereafter for twenty (20) years after service of the order for the biennial Assessments. Each Assessment shall:

A. set forth the specific privacy controls that respondent has implemented and maintained during the reporting period;

B. explain how such privacy controls are appropriate to respondent's size and complexity, the nature and scope of respondent's activities, and the sensitivity of the covered information;

C. explain how the safeguards that have been implemented meet or exceed the protections required by Part II of this order; and

D. certify that the privacy controls are operating with sufficient effectiveness to provide reasonable assurance to protect the privacy of covered information and that the controls have so operated throughout the reporting period.

[The initial Assessment shall be provided to the FTC.] All subsequent biennial Assessments shall be retained by respondent until the order is terminated and provided to the Associate Director of Enforcement within ten (10) days of request.

IV.

**IT IS FURTHER ORDERED** that respondent shall maintain and upon request make available to the Federal Trade Commission for inspection and copying, unless respondent asserts a valid legal privilege, a print or electronic copy of:

A. for a period of five (5) years from the date of preparation or dissemination, whichever is later, statements disseminated to consumers that describe the extent to which respondent maintains and protects the privacy, security and confidentiality of any covered information, with all materials relied upon in making or disseminating such statements;

B. for a period of five (5) years from the date received, all consumer complaints directed at respondent, or forwarded to respondent by a third party, that relate to the conduct prohibited by this order and any responses to such complaints;

C. for a period of five (5) years from the date received, any documents, whether prepared by or on behalf of respondent that contradict, qualify, or call into question respondent's compliance with this order; and

D. for a period of five (5) years after the date of preparation of each Assessment required under Part III of this order, all materials relied upon to prepare the Assessment.

V.

**IT IS FURTHER ORDERED** that respondent shall deliver a copy of this order to all current and future subsidiaries, current and future principals, officers, directors, and managers, and to all current and future employees, agents, and representatives having responsibilities relating to the subject matter of this order.

VI.

**IT IS FURTHER ORDERED** that respondent shall notify the Commission at least thirty (30) days prior to any change in the corporation(s) that may affect compliance obligations arising under this order.

VII.

**IT IS FURTHER ORDERED** that respondent within ninety (90) days after the date of service of this order, shall file with the Commission a true and accurate report, in writing, setting forth in detail the manner and form of its compliance with this order.

VIII.

This order will terminate twenty (20) years from the date of its issuance, or twenty (20) years from the most recent date that the United States or the Commission files a complaint (with or without an accompanying consent decree) in federal court alleging any violation of the order, whichever comes later.

## NOTES

1. ***Consent Decrees as Law.*** The structure of this "case"—an FTC complaint followed by a consent decree—is not the ordinary law school case featuring a judicial opinion. It is typical for FTC enforcement in the privacy and security sphere, however. When announcing a consent decree, the FTC typically publishes the complaint it filed, or prepared to file, outlining the defendant's allegedly unfair or deceptive practices. As often occurs in private litigation, that complaint initiates settlement negotiations with the defendant. As noted above, almost every defendant against whom the FTC prepared a complaint concerning privacy or security has opted to settle rather than mount a challenge in administrative proceedings or court. The FTC and the defendant typically work out a consent order that includes changes in the defendant's practices, without the defendant conceding that those practices were unlawful. The orders are approved by a vote of the FTC's commissioners and published in the *Federal Register*. As more of these complaints and consent decrees have accumulated, privacy lawyers have taken to using them as guidance for how to comply with Section 5. *See* Daniel J. Solove & Woodrow Hartzog, *The FTC and the New Common Law of Privacy*, 114 COLUM. L. REV. 583 (2014). Does that make the complaints and consent decrees a form of "law" like statutes or judicial decisions?

2. ***Why Settle?*** Why do you suppose defendants settle almost all the time? Are the reasons similar to those encouraging class action settlements?

Surely a major incentive, as with any settlement, is the desire to avoid the expense and distraction of litigating a major dispute. Where the opposing party is a regulator, this incentive may be greater because the opponent has more power than an ordinary plaintiff. Defendants also have much more control over the outcome when they negotiate a consent decree; they can always refuse to accept terms they consider excessive, whereas a loss in an adjudication leaves them at the mercy of the FTC, the court, or both. Finally, it is vital to consider public relations. An ongoing public dispute probably causes much more damage to a company's reputation for respecting customer privacy than does a one-time announcement by the FTC—especially where the company does not even need to admit fault.

3. ***Broken Promises.*** The *Snapchat* complaint alleges deceptive practices rather than unfairness. This type of "broken promises" allegation—that a company said one thing and did another—has dominated FTC privacy enforcement actions since the mid-1990s. There are several reasons for this pattern. First, the allegation generally will be cleaner: by finding a statement and then alleging contradictory behavior, the FTC relies on a more straightforward factual argument. Perhaps more importantly, as discussed in *Accusearch*, the FTC's unfairness authority is limited by the requirement that it satisfy the three-part test under 15 U.S.C. § 45(n): that a practice "[1] causes or is likely to cause substantial injury to consumers [2] which is not reasonably avoidable by consumers themselves and [3] not outweighed by countervailing benefits to consumers or to competition." These additional elements of a successful action encourage the FTC to couch privacy and security claims in terms of deception rather than unfairness. That said, there is a trend toward more unfairness allegations, particularly in data security cases.

4. ***Indirect Promises.*** Early on, allegedly misleading claims identified by the FTC were usually embodied in formal statements found in privacy policies, terms of service, or the like. More recent cases include representations made in a larger variety of ways, such as the implications reasonably drawn from statements, or the suggestions made by the design of a user interface. Look through the *Snapchat* complaint and identify the exact representations the FTC says were deceptive. Which of these allegedly broken promises were contained in the company's privacy policies? Which were direct statements of any kind? Consider how the assertion of FTC authority over more indirect representations changes the advice you would give as an attorney counseling a client that wants to avoid an FTC complaint (which is to say, all clients).

5. ***Privacy by Design.*** The enforcement of indirect promises advances the FTC's promotion of "privacy by design" as a best practice in the Final Report, as discussed in Chairman Leibovitz's testimony above. The term "privacy by design" was first coined by Anne Cavoukian, the former privacy commissioner for the Canadian province of Ontario. Cavoukian urged companies under her jurisdiction to integrate considerations of privacy and security in the earliest phases of their planning for new products or services. If engineers and designers are thinking about these issues from the outset, they can avoid future problems and prevent the disruption that arises

when privacy or security features must be added belatedly into a design that has already been developed. In many organizations, privacy by design may require a significant culture change. In those that embrace it, attorneys and other privacy professionals may need to be consulted much earlier in the life span of a project. How do you think a "privacy by design" approach would have affected the development of Snapchat? If you were the lawyer urging greater attention to privacy in the design of Snapchat's interface, what objections would you anticipate receiving from colleagues with other functions at the company, such as programming or marketing?

6. ***Bad Guys, Big Guys, and Saving the Children.*** The FTC has limited resources, so it must select its cases carefully to maximize their impact. Several trends can be seen in these choices; *Snapchat* exemplifies all of them to some degree. As a threshold matter, like any regulator, the FTC prefers strong cases where its investigation uncovers compelling evidence. But among strong cases, the FTC clearly sets certain other priorities. First, larger companies whose practices affect more users get more scrutiny. In mid-2014, Snapchat reportedly had over 100 million monthly users, two-thirds of whom used the app daily. A list of other privacy consent decrees reads somewhat like a roll call of major American consumer-facing technology companies, including not only Snapchat, but names like Facebook, Google, Microsoft, and Sony. Second, the FTC understandably goes after more egregious cases with more serious harms. Snapchat was widely understood to be a "private" photo-sharing app, and news reports indicated it was being used widely to send photos with nudity, drug or alcohol use, and other sensitive depictions. Furthermore, the contradiction between the company's representations and publicly-available information to the contrary seemed particularly stark. As another example, the FTC's complaint in *Accusearch*, above, alleged that the phone records at issue must have been obtained by either fraud or theft. Where underlying data is particularly sensitive, the FTC is also more likely to act. In sum, more serious apparent violations draw greater regulatory scrutiny. Third and finally, the FTC is particularly concerned about children's privacy. Notice how Chairman Leibowitz repeatedly emphasized the FTC's enforcement activities under COPPA [see Chapter 4 for more on this law]. Minors may be more vulnerable to privacy invasions and suffer greater harms as a result—and in any event the political consensus about the need to protect kids is much stronger. Snapchat is widely used by young people, particularly teenagers. Surely the specter of teens "sexting" nude photos in the mistaken belief that they could not be recirculated made this a particularly compelling case from the FTC's viewpoint. These predictable points of emphasis—going after "big guys" and "bad guys" and protecting kids—indicate that some types of companies have a higher probability than others of being scrutinized by the FTC. When assessing risks for clients, wise privacy lawyers take these factors into consideration.

7. ***Consequences of a Consent Order.*** In lieu of direct monetary penalties, what consequences did Snapchat suffer due to its alleged violations of Section 5? Instead of financial remedies, much of the *Snapchat* consent decree is taken up with the requirement that the company establish

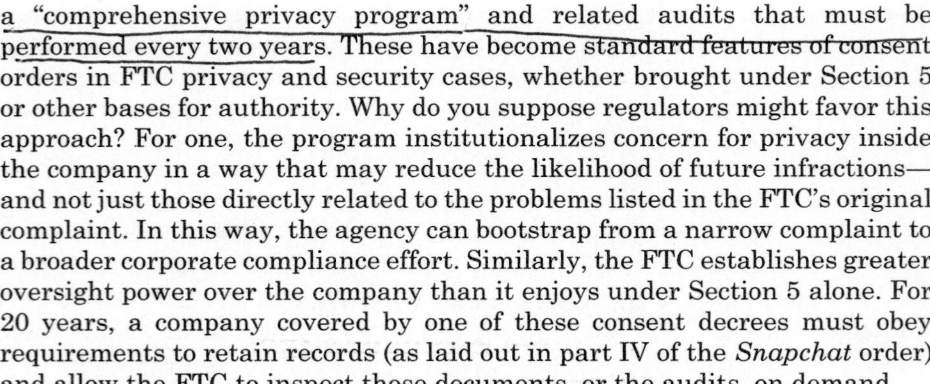

a "comprehensive privacy program" and related audits that must be performed every two years. These have become standard features of consent orders in FTC privacy and security cases, whether brought under Section 5 or other bases for authority. Why do you suppose regulators might favor this approach? For one, the program institutionalizes concern for privacy inside the company in a way that may reduce the likelihood of future infractions—and not just those directly related to the problems listed in the FTC's original complaint. In this way, the agency can bootstrap from a narrow complaint to a broader corporate compliance effort. Similarly, the FTC establishes greater oversight power over the company than it enjoys under Section 5 alone. For 20 years, a company covered by one of these consent decrees must obey requirements to retain records (as laid out in part IV of the *Snapchat* order) and allow the FTC to inspect those documents, or the audits, on demand.

Finally, the FTC can bring future complaints—or threaten to bring them—for violations *of the consent order* rather than underlying law. And those violations, unlike the original Section 5 infractions, do come with monetary penalties. In 2012, for example, the FTC went after Google for "broken promises" related to tracking users of the Safari browser. The year before, Google had entered into a consent decree with ongoing obligations, so the FTC framed its new complaint as a violation of the earlier order, not just of Section 5 itself. For this second offense, Google was obliged to pay a $22.5 million fine as well as taking corrective action. Less publicly, the FTC often warns companies operating under consent decrees, either publicly or privately, when they take actions that might violate the earlier order. As the *Snapchat* decree demonstrates, however, these orders are worded broadly enough to cover many types of violations. At times they might be activities that would not, in themselves, clearly violate Section 5. Thus, the FTC can use consent decrees to expand its supervisory authority over the companies that sign them.

8. ***Compliance Programs.*** As you can imagine, one indirect result of the FTC's regulatory technique has been to fuel explosive growth in the field of privacy professionals, including lawyers, technical experts, and compliance specialists. Someone has to manage all these comprehensive privacy programs and conduct all these periodic audits mandated by consent decrees. In addition, *other* companies have adopted some of the same self-regulatory techniques embodied in the consent decrees as insulation against potential liability later. Most privacy lawyers counsel clients that regulators respond more favorably to companies that undertake their own internal management of privacy risks before getting into trouble—because those companies can demonstrate that they are making efforts to protect privacy. The consent decrees give companies a road map of the kinds of practices the FTC might value. In this way, even the FTC's enforcement actions have become a form of norm entrepreneurship that influences behavior by companies which are not themselves targets.

## 3. GROWTH OF FTC SECURITY REGULATION

FTC regulation is just one of several sources of law governing information security. Others include private lawsuits based in negligence and other legal theories; state statutes explicitly directed at data security; sector-specific rules in industries such as health care and financial services; and self-regulatory measures backed by contractual agreements. [For more on data security law, see Chapter 7.] That said, data security is at the frontier of the FTC's consumer regulation model. This is an area where the agency has sought to expand its authority over "unfair" practices, and it is the subject of the most recent case reaffirming the agency's power over privacy law. For that reason, FTC data security regulation merits a first look in this chapter.

## In re Dave & Buster's Inc.

FTC Docket No. C–4291 (June 8, 2010)

### COMPLAINT

The Federal Trade Commission, having reason to believe that Dave and Buster's, Inc. ("Respondent") has violated the provisions of the Federal Trade Commission Act, and it appearing to the Commission that this proceeding is in the public interest, alleges:

1. Respondent Dave & Buster's, Inc. is a Missouri corporation with its principal office or place of business at 2481 Manana Drive, Dallas, Texas 75220.

2. The acts and practices of respondent as alleged in this complaint have been in or affecting commerce, as "commerce" is defined in Section 4 of the Federal Trade Commission Act.

3. Respondent owns and operates 53 restaurant/entertainment complexes in the United States under the names Dave & Buster's, Dave & Buster's Grand Sports Café, and Jillian's. Consumers pay for purchases at these stores with credit and debit cards (collectively, "payment cards"), or cash.

4. Respondent operates networks in each store ("in-store networks") as well as a corporate computer network (collectively, "networks"). These networks link corporate headquarters in the United States with each store, and, among other things, are used to process sales transactions.

5. In conducting its business, respondent routinely collects information from consumers to obtain authorization for payment card purchases. Among other things, it collects: the credit card account number, expiration date, and an electronic security code for payment card authorization (collectively, "personal information"). This information is particularly sensitive because it can be used to facilitate payment card fraud and other consumer harm.

6. To obtain payment card authorization, respondent collects personal information at its various in-store terminals, transfers the data to its in-store servers, and then transmits the data to a third-party credit card processing company.

7. In collecting and processing sensitive personal information, respondent engaged in a number of practices that, taken together, failed to provide reasonable and appropriate security for personal information on its networks. In particular, respondent:

(a) failed to employ sufficient measures to detect and prevent unauthorized access to computer networks or to conduct security investigations, such as by employing an intrusion detection system and monitoring system logs;

(b) failed to adequately restrict third-party access to its networks, such as by restricting connections to specified IP addresses or granting temporary, limited access;

(c) failed to monitor and filter outbound traffic from its networks to identify and block export of sensitive personal information without authorization;

(d) failed to use readily available security measures to limit access between in-store networks, such as by employing firewalls or isolating the payment card system from the rest of the corporate network; and

(e) failed to use readily available security measures to limit access to its computer networks through wireless access points on the networks.

8. Between April 30, 2007 and August 28, 2007 an intruder, exploiting some of the vulnerabilities set forth in Paragraph 7, connected to respondent's networks numerous times without authorization, installed unauthorized software, and intercepted personal information in transit from in-store networks to respondent's credit card processing company. After learning of the breach, respondent took steps to prevent further unauthorized access and to notify law enforcement and the credit card companies of affected consumers.

9. The breach compromised approximately 130,000 unique payment cards used by consumers in the United States. To date, issuing banks have collectively claimed several hundred thousand dollars in fraudulent charges on some of these implicated accounts.

10. As described in Paragraphs 7 through 9, respondent's failure to employ reasonable and appropriate security measures to protect personal information caused or is likely to cause substantial injury to consumers that is not offset by countervailing benefits to consumers or competition and is not reasonably avoidable by consumers. This practice was and is an unfair act or practice.

11. The acts and practices of respondent as alleged in this complaint constitute unfair acts or practices in or affecting commerce in violation of Section 5(a) of the Federal Trade Commission Act, 15 U.S.C § 45(a).

THEREFORE, the Federal Trade Commission this twentieth day of May, 2010, has issued this complaint against respondent.

## DECISION AND ORDER

The Federal Trade Commission having initiated an investigation of certain acts and practices of the Respondent named in the caption hereof, and the Respondent having been furnished thereafter with a copy of a draft Complaint that the Bureau of Consumer Protection proposed to present to the Commission for its consideration and which, if issued by the Commission, would charge the Respondent with violation of the Federal Trade Commission Act, 15 U.S.C. §§ 45 et seq.;

The Respondent, its attorney, and counsel for the Commission having thereafter executed an Agreement Containing Consent Order ("Consent Agreement"), an admission by the Respondent of all the jurisdictional facts set forth in the aforesaid draft Complaint, a statement that the signing of said Consent Agreement is for settlement purposes only and does not constitute an admission by Respondent that the law has been violated as alleged in such Complaint, or that the facts as alleged in such Complaint, other than jurisdictional facts, are true, and waivers and other provisions as required by the Commission's Rules; and

The Commission having thereafter considered the matter and having determined that it has reason to believe that the Respondent has violated the said Act, and that a Complaint should issue stating its charges in that respect, and having thereupon accepted the executed Consent Agreement and placed such Consent Agreement on the public record for a period of thirty (30) days for the receipt and consideration of public comments, the Commission hereby issues its Complaint, makes the following jurisdictional findings and enters the following Order:

## ORDER

### I.

**IT IS ORDERED** that respondent, in connection with the advertising, marketing, promotion, offering for sale, or sale of any product or service, in or affecting commerce, shall, no later than the date of service of this order, establish and implement, and thereafter maintain, a comprehensive information security program that is reasonably designed to protect the security, confidentiality, and integrity of personal information collected from or about consumers. Such program, the content and implementation of which must be fully documented in writing, shall contain administrative, technical, and physical safeguards appropriate to respondent's size and complexity, the nature and scope of respondent's activities, and the sensitivity of the personal information collected from or about consumers, including:

A. the designation of an employee or employees to coordinate and be accountable for the information security program;

B. the identification of material internal and external risks to the security, confidentiality, and integrity of personal information that could result in the unauthorized disclosure, misuse, loss, alteration, destruction, or other compromise of such information, and assessment of the sufficiency of any safeguards in place to control these risks. At a minimum, this risk assessment should include consideration of risks in each area of relevant operation, including, but not limited to: (1) employee training and management; (2) information systems, including network and software design, information processing, storage, transmission, and disposal; and (3) prevention, detection, and response to attacks, intrusions, or other systems failures;

C. the design and implementation of reasonable safeguards to control the risks identified through risk assessment and regular testing or monitoring of the effectiveness of the safeguards' key controls, systems, and procedures;

D. the development and use of reasonable steps to select and retain service providers capable of appropriately safeguarding personal information they receive from respondent, and requiring service providers by contract to implement and maintain appropriate safeguards; and

E. the evaluation and adjustment of respondent's information security program in light of the results of the testing and monitoring required by sub-Part C, any material changes to respondent's operations or business arrangements, or any other circumstances that respondent knows or has reason to know may have a material impact on the effectiveness of its information security program.

II.

**IT IS FURTHER ORDERED** that, in connection with its compliance with Part I of this order, respondent shall obtain initial and biennial assessments and reports ("Assessments") from a qualified, objective, independent third-party professional, who uses procedures and standards generally accepted in the profession. The reporting period for the Assessments shall cover: (1) the first one hundred and eighty (180) days after service of the order for the initial Assessment, and (2) each two (2) year period thereafter for ten (10) years after service of the order for the biennial Assessments. Each Assessment shall:

A. set forth the specific administrative, technical, and physical safeguards that respondent has implemented and maintained during the reporting period;

B. explain how such safeguards are appropriate to respondent's size and complexity, the nature and scope of respondent's activities, and the sensitivity of the personal information collected from or about consumers;

C. explain how the safeguards that have been implemented meet or exceed the protections required by the Part I of this order; and

D. certify that respondent's security program is operating with sufficient effectiveness to provide reasonable assurance that the security, confidentiality, and integrity of personal information is protected and has so operated throughout the reporting period.

[The initial Assessment shall be provided to the FTC.] All subsequent biennial Assessments shall be retained by respondent until the order is terminated and provided to the Associate Director of Enforcement within ten (10) days of request.

III.

**IT IS FURTHER ORDERED** that respondent shall maintain, and upon request make available to the Federal Trade Commission for inspection and copying:

A. for a period of five (5) years, a print or electronic copy of each document relating to compliance, including but not limited to documents, prepared by or on behalf of respondent, that contradict, qualify, or call into question respondent's compliance with this order; and

B. for a period of three (3) years after the date of preparation of each Assessment required under Part II of this order, all materials relied upon to prepare the Assessment, whether prepared by or on behalf of the respondent, including but not limited to all plans, reports, studies, reviews, audits, audit trails, policies, training materials, and assessments, and any other materials relating to respondent's compliance with Parts I and II of this order, for the compliance period covered by such Assessment.

IV.

**IT IS FURTHER ORDERED** that respondent shall deliver a copy of this order to all current and future principals, officers, directors, and managers at corporate headquarters, regional offices, and at each store having responsibilities relating to the subject matter of this order. Respondent shall deliver this order to such current personnel within thirty (30) days after service of this order, and to such future personnel within thirty (30) days after the person assumes such position or responsibilities.

V.

**IT IS FURTHER ORDERED** that respondent shall notify the Commission at least thirty (30) days prior to any change in the corporation that may affect compliance obligations arising under this order.

VI.

**IT IS FURTHER ORDERED** that respondent shall, within ninety (90) days after service of this order, and at such other times as the Federal Trade Commission may require, file with the Commission a report, in writing, setting forth in detail the manner and form in which it has complied with this order.

VII.

This order will terminate on May 20, 2030, or twenty (20) years from the most recent date that the United States or the Federal Trade Commission files a complaint (with or without an accompanying consent decree) in federal court alleging any violation of the order, whichever comes later.

## NOTES

1. ***Boilerplate Consent Decrees.*** Having read *In re Snapchat*, the language of the *Dave & Buster's* consent decree should be familiar. In fact, the FTC frequently repeats the precise terms of consent decrees from one company to the next. The language has been refined over time, but there is no particular reason to reinvent terms in every case. What changes do you identify between the June 2010 *Dave & Buster's* order and the *Snapchat* order from the end of 2014?

2. ***Deception and Unfairness.*** Note that the complaint against Dave & Buster's is brought under the FTC's unfairness authority rather than deception. Why do you suppose this is so? Since *Dave & Buster's*, a number of other FTC complaints have suggested that seriously inadequate security measures constitute unfair trade practices. This allegation presupposes a standard of care or best practices that companies should follow, in order to establish a baseline and show that the defendant company departed from it dramatically.

3. ***The Three-Part Test.*** Recall that the FTC must satisfy the three-part test from 15 U.S.C. § 45 in order to allege unfairness. How good of a case does the FTC have against Dave & Buster's under this test?

4. ***Security Professionals.*** There are more well-established credentials for data security professionals than for privacy professionals, and the FTC relies on them when defining the necessary background and experience for the persons who conduct audits under security consent decrees. A portion of the *Dave & Buster's* order omitted above lays out who should perform assessments: "a person qualified as a Certified Information System Security Professional (CISSP) or as a Certified Information Systems Auditor (CISA); a person holding Global Information Assurance Certification (GIAC) from the SysAdmin, Audit, Network, Security (SANS) Institute; or a similarly qualified person or organization approved by the Associate Director for Enforcement, Bureau of Consumer Protection, Federal Trade Commission." [For more on data security credentials, and data security law in general, see Chapter 7.]

## FTC v. Wyndham Worldwide Corp.

799 F.3d 236 (3d Cir. 2015)

■ AMBRO, CIRCUIT JUDGE.

The Federal Trade Commission Act prohibits "unfair or deceptive acts or practices in or affecting commerce." 15 U.S.C. § 45(a). In 2005 the Federal Trade Commission began bringing administrative actions under this provision against companies with allegedly deficient cybersecurity that failed to protect consumer data against hackers. The vast majority of these cases have ended in settlement.

On three occasions in 2008 and 2009 hackers successfully accessed Wyndham Worldwide Corporation's computer systems. In total, they stole personal and financial information for hundreds of thousands of consumers leading to over $10.6 million dollars in fraudulent charges. The FTC filed suit in federal District Court, alleging that Wyndham's conduct was an unfair practice and that its privacy policy was deceptive. The District Court denied Wyndham's motion to dismiss, and we granted interlocutory appeal on two issues: whether the FTC has authority to regulate cybersecurity under the unfairness prong of § 45(a); and, if so, whether Wyndham had fair notice its specific cybersecurity practices could fall short of that provision. We affirm the District Court.

### BACKGROUND

### A. Wyndham's Cybersecurity

Wyndham Worldwide is a hospitality company that franchises and manages hotels and sells timeshares through three subsidiaries. Wyndham licensed its brand name to approximately 90 independently owned hotels. Each Wyndham-branded hotel has a property management system that processes consumer information that includes names, home addresses, email addresses, telephone numbers, payment card account numbers, expiration dates, and security codes. Wyndham manages these systems and requires the hotels to purchase and configure them to its own specifications. It also operates a computer network in Phoenix, Arizona, that connects its data center with the property management systems of each of the Wyndham-branded hotels.

The FTC alleges that, at least since April 2008, Wyndham engaged in unfair cybersecurity practices that, "taken together, unreasonably and unnecessarily exposed consumers' personal data to unauthorized access and theft." This claim is fleshed out as follows.

1. The company allowed Wyndham-branded hotels to store payment card information in clear readable text.

2. Wyndham allowed the use of easily guessed passwords to access the property management systems. For example, to gain "remote access to at least one hotel's system," which was developed by Micros Systems, Inc., the user ID and password were both "micros."

3. Wyndham failed to use "readily available security measures"—such as firewalls—to "limit access between [the] hotels' property management systems, corporate network, and the Internet."

4. Wyndham allowed hotel property management systems to connect to its network without taking appropriate cybersecurity precautions. It did not ensure that the hotels implemented "adequate information security policies and procedures." Also, it knowingly allowed at least one hotel to connect to the Wyndham network with an out-of-date operating system that had not received a security update in over three years. It allowed hotel servers to connect to Wyndham's network even though "default user IDs and passwords were enabled which were easily available to hackers through simple Internet searches." And, because it failed to maintain an "adequate inventory [of] computers connected to [Wyndham's] network [to] manage the devices," it was unable to identify the source of at least one of the cybersecurity attacks.

5. Wyndham failed to "adequately restrict" the access of third-party vendors to its network and the servers of Wyndham-branded hotels. For example, it did not "restrict connections to specified IP addresses or grant temporary, limited access, as necessary."

6. It failed to employ "reasonable measures to detect and prevent unauthorized access" to its computer network or to "conduct security investigations."

7. It did not follow "proper incident response procedures." The hackers used similar methods in each attack, and yet Wyndham failed to monitor its network for malware used in the previous intrusions.

Although not before us on appeal, the complaint also raises a deception claim, alleging that since 2008 Wyndham has published a privacy policy on its website that overstates the company's cybersecurity.

### B. The Three Cybersecurity Attacks

As noted, on three occasions in 2008 and 2009 hackers accessed Wyndham's network and the property management systems of Wyndham-branded hotels. In April 2008, hackers first broke into the local network of a hotel in Phoenix, Arizona, which was connected to Wyndham's network and the Internet. They then used the brute-force method—repeatedly guessing users' login IDs and passwords—to access an administrator account on Wyndham's network. This enabled them to obtain consumer data on computers throughout the network. In total, the hackers obtained unencrypted information for over 500,000 accounts, which they sent to a domain in Russia.

In March 2009, hackers attacked again, this time by accessing Wyndham's network through an administrative account. The FTC claims that Wyndham was unaware of the attack for two months until consumers filed complaints about fraudulent charges. Wyndham then discovered "memory-scraping malware" used in the previous attack on more than thirty hotels' computer systems. The FTC asserts that, due to

Wyndham's "failure to monitor [the network] for the malware used in the previous attack, hackers had unauthorized access to [its] network for approximately two months." In this second attack, the hackers obtained unencrypted payment card information for approximately 50,000 consumers from the property management systems of 39 hotels.

Hackers in late 2009 breached Wyndham's cybersecurity a third time by accessing an administrator account on one of its networks. Because Wyndham "had still not adequately limited access between the Wyndham-branded hotels' property management systems, [Wyndham's network], and the Internet," the hackers had access to the property management servers of multiple hotels. Wyndham only learned of the intrusion in January 2010 when a credit card company received complaints from cardholders. In this third attack, hackers obtained payment card information for approximately 69,000 customers from the property management systems of 28 hotels.

The FTC alleges that, in total, the hackers obtained payment card information from over 619,000 consumers, which (as noted) resulted in at least $10.6 million in fraud loss. It further states that consumers suffered financial injury through "unreimbursed fraudulent charges, increased costs, and lost access to funds or credit," and that they "expended time and money resolving fraudulent charges and mitigating subsequent harm."

## FTC'S REGULATORY AUTHORITY UNDER § 45(a)

### A. Legal Background

The Federal Trade Commission Act of 1914 prohibited "unfair methods of competition in commerce." Congress "explicitly considered, and rejected, the notion that it reduce the ambiguity of the phrase 'unfair methods of competition' by enumerating the particular practices to which it was intended to apply." *FTC v. Sperry & Hutchinson Co.*, 405 U.S. 233, 239–40 (1972) (citing S. Rep. No. 63–597, at 13 (1914)). The takeaway is that Congress designed the term as a "flexible concept with evolving content," *FTC v. Bunte Bros.*, 312 U.S. 349, 353 (1941), and "intentionally left [its] development . . . to the Commission," *Atl. Ref. Co. v. FTC*, 381 U.S. 357, 367 (1965).

After several early cases limited "unfair methods of competition" to practices harming competitors and not consumers, Congress inserted an additional prohibition in § 45(a) against "unfair or deceptive acts or practices in or affecting commerce." Wheeler-Lea Act, Pub. L. No. 75–447, § 5, 52 Stat. 111, 111 (1938).

For the next few decades, the FTC interpreted the unfair-practices prong primarily through agency adjudication. But in 1964 it issued a "Statement of Basis and Purpose" for unfair or deceptive advertising and labeling of cigarettes, 29 Fed. Reg. 8324, 8355 (July 2, 1964), which explained that the following three factors governed unfairness determinations:

> (1) whether the practice, without necessarily having been previously considered unlawful, offends public policy as it has been established by statutes, the common law, or otherwise—whether, in other words, it is within at least the penumbra of some common-law, statutory or other established concept of unfairness; (2) whether it is immoral, unethical, oppressive, or unscrupulous; [and] (3) whether it causes substantial injury to consumers (or competitors or other businessmen).

*Id.* Almost a decade later, the Supreme Court implicitly approved these factors, apparently acknowledging their applicability to contexts other than cigarette advertising and labeling. *Sperry*, 405 U.S. at 244 n. 5. The Court also held that, under the policy statement, the FTC could deem a practice unfair based on the third prong—substantial consumer injury—without finding that at least one of the other two prongs was also satisfied.

During the 1970s, the FTC embarked on a controversial campaign to regulate children's advertising through the unfair-practices prong of § 45(a). At the request of Congress, the FTC issued a second policy statement in 1980 that clarified the three factors [hereinafter "1980 Policy Statement"]. It explained that public policy considerations are relevant in determining whether a particular practice causes substantial consumer injury. Next, it "abandoned" the "theory of immoral or unscrupulous conduct altogether" as an "independent" basis for an unfairness claim. And finally, the Commission explained that "unjustified consumer injury is the primary focus of the FTC Act" and that such an injury "by itself can be sufficient to warrant a finding of unfairness." This "does not mean that every consumer injury is legally 'unfair.' " Indeed,

> to justify a finding of unfairness the injury must satisfy three tests. [1] It must be substantial; [2] it must not be outweighed by any countervailing benefits to consumers or competition that the practice produces; and [3] it must be an injury that consumers themselves could not reasonably have avoided.

In 1994, Congress codified the 1980 Policy Statement at 15 U.S.C. § 45(n):

> The Commission shall have no authority under this section . . . to declare unlawful an act or practice on the grounds that such act or practice is unfair unless the act or practice causes or is likely to cause substantial injury to consumers which is not reasonably avoidable by consumers themselves and not outweighed by countervailing benefits to consumers or to competition. In determining whether an act or practice is unfair, the Commission may consider established public policies as evidence to be considered with all other evidence. Such public policy considerations may not serve as a primary basis for such determination.

Like the 1980 Policy Statement, § 45(n) requires substantial injury that is not reasonably avoidable by consumers and that is not outweighed by the benefits to consumers or competition. It also acknowledges the potential significance of public policy and does not expressly require that an unfair practice be immoral, unethical, unscrupulous, or oppressive.

**B. Plain Meaning of Unfairness**

Wyndham argues that the three requirements of 15 U.S.C. § 45(n) are necessary but insufficient conditions of an unfair practice and that the plain meaning of the word "unfair" imposes independent requirements that are not met here. Arguably, § 45(n) may not identify all of the requirements for an unfairness claim. (While the provision forbids the FTC from declaring an act unfair "unless" the act satisfies the three specified requirements, it does not answer whether these are the only requirements for a finding of unfairness.) Even if so, some of Wyndham's proposed requirements are unpersuasive, and the rest are satisfied by the allegations in the FTC's complaint.

First, citing *FTC v. R.F. Keppel & Brother, Inc.*, 291 U.S. 304 (1934), Wyndham argues that conduct is only unfair when it injures consumers "through unscrupulous or unethical behavior." But *Keppel* nowhere says that unfair conduct must be unscrupulous or unethical. Moreover, in *Sperry* the Supreme Court rejected the view that the FTC's 1964 policy statement required unfair conduct to be "unscrupulous" or "unethical." 405 U.S. at 244 n. 5. Wyndham points to no subsequent FTC policy statements, adjudications, judicial opinions, or statutes that would suggest any change since *Sperry*.

Next, citing one dictionary, Wyndham argues that a practice is only "unfair" if it is "not equitable" or is "marked by injustice, partiality, or deception." Whether these are requirements of an unfairness claim makes little difference here. A company does not act equitably when it publishes a privacy policy to attract customers who are concerned about data privacy, fails to make good on that promise by investing inadequate resources in cybersecurity, exposes its unsuspecting customers to substantial financial injury, and retains the profits of their business. We recognize this analysis of unfairness encompasses some facts relevant to the FTC's deceptive practices claim. But facts relevant to unfairness and deception claims frequently overlap.

unfair!

Continuing on, Wyndham asserts that a business "does not treat its customers in an 'unfair' manner when the business itself is victimized by criminals." It offers no reasoning or authority for this principle, and we can think of none ourselves. Although unfairness claims usually involve actual and completed harms, they may also be brought on the basis of likely rather than actual injury. And the FTC Act expressly contemplates the possibility that conduct can be unfair before actual injury occurs. 15 U.S.C. § 45(n) ("[An unfair act or practice] causes or is *likely to cause* substantial injury" (emphasis added)). More importantly, that a company's conduct was not the most proximate cause of an injury generally does not immunize liability from foreseeable harms. For good reason, Wyndham does not argue that the cybersecurity intrusions were unforeseeable. That would be particularly implausible as to the second and third attacks.

Finally, Wyndham posits a reductio ad absurdum, arguing that if the FTC's unfairness authority extends to Wyndham's conduct, then the FTC also has the authority to "regulate the locks on hotel room doors, to require every store in the land to post an armed guard at the door," and to sue supermarkets that are "sloppy about sweeping up banana peels." The argument is alarmist to say the least. And it invites the tart retort that, were Wyndham a supermarket, leaving so many banana peels all over the place that 619,000 customers fall hardly suggests it should be immune from liability under § 45(a).

We are therefore not persuaded by Wyndham's arguments that the alleged conduct falls outside the plain meaning of "unfair."

### C. Subsequent Congressional Action

Wyndham next argues that, even if cybersecurity were covered by § 45(a) as initially enacted, three legislative acts since the subsection was amended in 1938 have reshaped the provision's meaning to exclude cybersecurity. A recent amendment to the Fair Credit Reporting Act directed the FTC and other agencies to develop regulations for the proper disposal of consumer data. *See* Pub. L. No. 108–159, § 216(a), 117 Stat. 1952, 1985–86 (2003) (codified as amended at 15 U.S.C. § 1681w). The Gramm-Leach-Bliley Act required the FTC to establish standards for financial institutions to protect consumers' personal information. *See* Pub. L. No. 106–102, § 501(b), 113 Stat. 1338, 1436–37 (1999) (codified as amended at 15 U.S.C. § 6801(b)). And the Children's Online Privacy Protection Act ordered the FTC to promulgate regulations requiring children's websites, among other things, to provide notice of "what information is collected from children . . ., how the operator uses such information, and the operator's disclosure practices for such information." Pub. L. No. 105–277, § 1303, 112 Stat. 2681 (1998) (codified as amended at 15 U.S.C. § 6502). [Wyndham also pointed to a variety of cybersecurity bills that Congress has considered and not passed.]

We are not persuaded. The inference to congressional intent based on post-enactment legislative activity in [*FDA v. Brown and Williamson Tobacco Corp.*, 529 U.S. 120 (2000)] was far stronger. There, the Food and Drug Administration had repeatedly disclaimed regulatory authority over tobacco products for decades. During that period, Congress enacted six statutes regulating tobacco. The FDA later shifted its position, claiming authority over tobacco products. The Supreme Court held that Congress excluded tobacco-related products from the FDA's authority in enacting the [later] statutes. As tobacco products would necessarily be banned if subject to the FDA's regulatory authority, any interpretation to the contrary would contradict congressional intent to regulate rather than ban tobacco products outright. Wyndham does not argue that recent privacy laws contradict reading corporate cybersecurity into § 45(a). Instead, it merely asserts that Congress had no reason to enact them if the FTC could already regulate cybersecurity through that provision.

We disagree that Congress lacked reason to pass the recent legislation if the FTC already had regulatory authority over some cybersecurity issues. The Fair Credit Reporting Act requires (rather than authorizes) the FTC to issue regulations and expands the scope of the FTC's authority. The Gramm-Leach-Bliley Act similarly requires the FTC to promulgate regulations and relieves some of the burdensome § 45(n) requirements for declaring acts unfair. And the Children's Online Privacy Protection Act required the FTC to issue regulations and empowered it to do so under the procedures of the Administrative Procedure Act, rather than the more burdensome Magnuson-Moss procedures under which the FTC must usually issue regulations, 15 U.S.C. § 57a. Thus none of the recent privacy legislation was "inexplicable" if the FTC already had some authority to regulate corporate cybersecurity through § 45(a).

Next, Wyndham claims that the FTC's interpretation of § 45(a) is "inconsistent with its repeated efforts to obtain from Congress the very authority it purports to wield here." Yet again we disagree. In two of the statements cited by Wyndham, the FTC clearly said that some cybersecurity practices are "unfair" under the statute.

In the two other cited statements, given in 1998 and 2000, the FTC only acknowledged that it cannot require companies to adopt "fair information practice policies." These policies would protect consumers from far more than the kind of "substantial injury" typically covered by § 45(a). In addition to imposing some cybersecurity requirements, they would require companies to give notice about what data they collect from consumers, to permit those consumers to decide how the data is used, and to permit them to review and correct inaccuracies. Our conclusion is this: that the FTC later brought unfairness actions against companies whose inadequate cybersecurity resulted in consumer harm is not inconsistent with the agency's earlier position.

Having rejected Wyndham's arguments that its conduct cannot be unfair, we assume for the remainder of this opinion that it was.

## FAIR NOTICE

A conviction or punishment violates the Due Process Clause of our Constitution if the statute or regulation under which it is obtained fails to provide a person of ordinary intelligence fair notice of what is prohibited, or is so standardless that it authorizes or encourages seriously discriminatory enforcement. Wyndham claims that, notwithstanding whether its conduct was unfair under § 45(a), the FTC failed to give fair notice of the specific cybersecurity standards the company was required to follow.

### A. Legal Standard

The level of required notice for a person to be subject to liability varies by circumstance. In *Bouie v. City of Columbia*, the Supreme Court held that a "judicial construction of a criminal statute" violates due process if it is "unexpected and indefensible by reference to the law which had been expressed prior to the conduct in issue." 378 U.S. 347, 354 (1964).

The fair notice doctrine extends to civil cases, particularly where a penalty is imposed. Lesser degrees of specificity are allowed in civil cases because the consequences are smaller than in the criminal context. The standards are especially lax for civil statutes that regulate economic activities. For those statutes, a party lacks fair notice when the relevant standard is so vague as to be no rule or standard at all.

A different set of considerations is implicated when agencies are involved in statutory or regulatory interpretation. Broadly speaking, agencies interpret in at least three contexts. One is where an agency administers a statute without any special authority to create new rights or obligations. When disputes arise under this kind of agency interpretation, the courts give respect to the agency's view to the extent it is persuasive, but they retain the primary responsibility for construing the statute [citing *Skidmore v. Swift & Co.*, 323 U.S. 134 (1944)]. As such, the standard of notice afforded to litigants about the meaning of the statute is not dissimilar to the standard of notice for civil statutes generally because the court, not the agency, is the ultimate arbiter of the statute's meaning.

The second context is where an agency exercises its authority to fill gaps in a statutory scheme. There the agency is primarily responsible for interpreting the statute because the courts must defer to any reasonable construction it adopts. *See Chevron, U.S.A., Inc. v. NRDC*, 467 U.S. 837 (1984).

The third context is where an agency interprets the meaning of its own regulation. Here also courts typically must defer to the agency's reasonable interpretation. We and several of our sister circuits have stated that private parties are entitled to know with "ascertainable certainty" an agency's interpretation of its regulation.

A higher standard of fair notice applies in the second and third contexts than in the typical civil statutory interpretation case because agencies engage in interpretation differently than courts. In resolving ambiguity in statutes or regulations, courts generally adopt the best or most reasonable interpretation. But, as the agency is often free to adopt any reasonable construction, it may impose higher legal obligations than required by the best interpretation.

Furthermore, courts generally resolve statutory ambiguity by applying traditional methods of construction. Private parties can reliably predict the court's interpretation by applying the same methods. In contrast, an agency may also rely on technical expertise and political values. It is harder to predict how an agency will construe a statute or regulation at some unspecified point in the future, particularly when that interpretation will depend on the political views of the President in office at that time.

Wyndham argues it was entitled to "ascertainable certainty" of the FTC's interpretation of what specific cybersecurity practices are required by § 45(a). Yet it has contended repeatedly—no less than seven separate occasions in this case—that there is no FTC rule or adjudication about cybersecurity that merits deference here. The necessary implication, one that Wyndham itself has explicitly drawn, is that federal courts are to interpret § 45(a) in the first instance to decide whether Wyndham's conduct was unfair.

Wyndham's position is unmistakable: the FTC has not yet declared that cybersecurity practices can be unfair; there is no relevant FTC rule, adjudication or document that merits deference; and the FTC is asking the federal courts to interpret § 45(a) in the first instance to decide whether it prohibits the alleged conduct here. The implication of this position is similarly clear: if the federal courts are to decide whether Wyndham's conduct was unfair in the first instance under the statute without deferring to any FTC interpretation, then this case involves ordinary judicial interpretation of a civil statute, and the ascertainable certainty standard does not apply. The relevant question is not whether Wyndham had fair notice of the FTC's interpretation of the statute, but whether Wyndham had fair notice of what the statute itself requires.

If later proceedings in this case develop such that the proper resolution is to defer to an agency interpretation that gives rise to Wyndham's liability, we leave to that time a fuller exploration of the level of notice required. For now, however, it is enough to say that we accept Wyndham's forceful contention that we are interpreting the FTC Act (as the District Court did). As a necessary consequence, Wyndham is only entitled to notice of the meaning of the statute and not to the agency's interpretation of the statute.

### B. Did Wyndham Have Fair Notice of the Meaning of § 45(a)?

Having decided that Wyndham is entitled to notice of the meaning of the statute, we next consider whether the case should be dismissed based on fair notice principles. We do not read Wyndham's briefs as arguing the company lacked fair notice that cybersecurity practices can, as a general matter, form the basis of an unfair practice under § 45(a). Wyndham argues instead it lacked notice of what specific cybersecurity practices are necessary to avoid liability. We have little trouble rejecting this claim.

Subsection 45(n) asks whether "the act or practice causes or is likely to cause substantial injury to consumers which is not reasonably avoidable by consumers themselves and not outweighed by countervailing benefits to consumers or to competition." While far from precise, this standard informs parties that the relevant inquiry here is a cost-benefit analysis that considers a number of relevant factors, including the probability and expected size of reasonably unavoidable harms to consumers given a certain level of cybersecurity and the costs to consumers that would arise from investment in stronger cybersecurity. We acknowledge there will be borderline cases where it is unclear if a particular company's conduct falls below the requisite legal threshold. But under a due process analysis a company is not entitled to such precision as would eliminate all close calls. Fair notice is satisfied here as long as the company can reasonably foresee that a court could construe its conduct as falling within the meaning of the statute.

Wyndham's as-applied challenge falls well short given the allegations in the FTC's complaint. As the FTC points out in its brief, the complaint does not allege that Wyndham used weak firewalls, IP address restrictions, encryption software, and passwords. Rather, it alleges that Wyndham failed to use any firewall at critical network points, did not restrict specific IP addresses at all, did not use any encryption for certain customer files, and did not require some users to change their default or factory-setting passwords at all.

Wyndham's as-applied challenge is even weaker given it was hacked not one or two, but three, times. At least after the second attack, it should have been painfully clear to Wyndham that a court could find its conduct failed the cost-benefit analysis. That said, we leave for another day whether Wyndham's alleged cybersecurity practices do in fact fail, an issue the parties did not brief. We merely note that certainly after the second time Wyndham was hacked, it was on notice of the possibility that a court could find that its practices fail the cost-benefit analysis.

Several other considerations reinforce our conclusion that Wyndham's fair notice challenge fails. In 2007 the FTC issued a guidebook, *Protecting Personal Information: A Guide for Business*, which describes a "checklist" of practices that form a "sound data security plan." The guidebook does not state that any particular practice is required by § 45(a), but it does counsel against many of the specific practices alleged here.

As the agency responsible for administering the statute, the FTC's expert views about the characteristics of a "sound data security plan" could certainly have helped Wyndham determine in advance that its conduct might not survive the cost-benefit analysis.

Before the attacks, the FTC also filed complaints and entered into consent decrees in administrative cases raising unfairness claims based on inadequate corporate cybersecurity. The agency published these materials on its website and provided notice of proposed consent orders in the Federal Register. Wyndham responds that the complaints cannot satisfy fair notice principles because they are not "adjudications on the merits." But even where the "ascertainable certainty" standard applies to fair notice claims, courts regularly consider materials that are neither regulations nor "adjudications on the merits." That the FTC commissioners—who must vote on whether to issue a complaint—believe that alleged cybersecurity practices fail the cost-benefit analysis of § 45(n) certainly helps companies with similar practices apprehend the possibility that their cybersecurity could fail as well.

In sum, we have little trouble rejecting Wyndham's fair notice claim.

## CONCLUSION

The three requirements in § 45(n) may be necessary rather than sufficient conditions of an unfair practice, but we are not persuaded that any other requirements proposed by Wyndham pose a serious challenge to the FTC's claim here. Furthermore, Wyndham repeatedly argued there is no FTC interpretation of § 45(a) or (n) to which the federal courts must defer in this case, and, as a result, the courts must interpret the meaning of the statute as it applies to Wyndham's conduct in the first instance. Thus, Wyndham cannot argue it was entitled to know with ascertainable certainty the cybersecurity standards by which the FTC expected it to conform. Instead, the company can only claim that it lacked fair notice of the meaning of the statute itself—a theory it did not meaningfully raise and that we strongly suspect would be unpersuasive under the facts of this case.

We thus affirm the District Court's decision.

## NOTES

1. ***A Long Awaited Decision.*** Privacy lawyers waited on tenterhooks for many months for the Third Circuit's decision in *Wyndham*. Because FTC enforcement actions typically result in settlement, there have been relatively few judicial precedents in the area, making its outcome less predictable. Some observers believed the court might limit the FTC's authority, at least in data security cases if not more broadly in its exercise of Section 5 authority. The Chamber of Commerce and National Federation of Independent Businesses filed an amicus brief supporting Wyndham's position, as did the Washington Legal Foundation, a free market interest group. A number of privacy advocacy groups including Public Citizen, the Electronic Privacy Information Center, the Center for Democracy and Technology, and the Electronic Frontier Foundation lined up as amici on the other side. In the end, the court largely reaffirmed the FTC's power and the decision was considered a victory for the agency and privacy advocates. Nonetheless, in several places the court tied its reasoning quite closely to the facts of the case before it and the particular arguments raised by Wyndham. If you were a lawyer for the Chamber of Commerce, do you see any tidbits from this case that might be used in a future challenge to the FTC's authority? If you were mounting an argument in a different circuit court that the FTC did not provide enough guidance about data security, how would you structure your argument to try to avoid the outcome in *Wyndham*? We

probably have not heard the last of the dispute about the FTC's Section 5 power.

2. ***History of the Three-Part Test.*** The *Accusearch* decision earlier in this chapter discussed the three-part test for unfairness; the *Wyndham* court explains more about its lineage. As you see from this discussion, the FTC itself and the Supreme Court both played roles in developing the conditions for unfairness that Congress eventually codified as the three-part test of § 45(n) in 1994. Now that it is part of the statute, it is locked more firmly into place as a precondition for liability. That said, the *Wyndham* court does not apply its requirements with too much rigor, at least at this initial stage of the motion to dismiss.

3. ***Deferring to Nothing.*** The Third Circuit's reasoning boxed Wyndham into a bit of a corner. According to the court, the company had argued vociferously that there was not a shred of usable guidance from the FTC, so by that logic there was nothing issued by the agency that was entitled to judicial deference. The court was free to construe the statute—and Wyndham could not then claim a lack of ascertainable certainty in the contents of a law that is interpreted by ordinary judicial methods of statutory construction. Do you agree that a court's reading of a statute is more predictable than an agency's? In part what the *Wyndham* court means is that, at least in theory, a court has less latitude to choose its interpretation based on considerations of policy and politics. An administrative agency, the court says, may choose any reasonable interpretation of a statute, while a court must opt for the *most* reasonable one. Does this reflect your experience of studying judicial opinions and administrative determinations? In a related argumentative move that could perhaps be called sleight of hand, in the end the court actually does refer—if not defer—to FTC pronouncements to inform its interpretation. Conversely, the court here leaves the door open for revisiting the issue in *this* litigation, if "later proceedings in this case develop such that the proper resolution is to defer to an agency interpretation that gives rise to Wyndham's liability." Thus, perhaps the FTC is also boxed into a corner of its own: the conclusion that companies have sufficient notice about data security requirements depends on a finding that the FTC has not offered the sort of guidance that requires judicial deference—and if the FTC did so, then that conclusion about companies' adequate notice might not hold any longer. Does this opinion actually create further disincentives for the FTC to write more detailed rules?

4. ***Knowing What the FTC Thinks.*** Wyndham strongly objected that the lack of formal regulation and fully adjudicated adversarial proceedings made it impossible for companies to know what data security practices the FTC would consider unfair under Section 5. Where do practicing lawyers look for information about the FTC's expectations, both in data security and in other areas of privacy law? First of all, as noted previously, they read consent decrees. Within the privacy bar, the issuance of a new consent decree is big news and will be heavily scrutinized for clues about the FTC's direction. In addition, as discussed in the *Wyndham* decision, "soft law" of FTC advice and educational materials notifies companies about acceptable data handling techniques. Further indications

can come from other areas of law. In its *Accusearch* opinion, the Tenth Circuit emphasized that an underlying violation of a different federal statute helped justify a determination that a trade practice was unfair under Section 5. So in the realm of data security, even though Section 5 may not require the same rigorous security standards imposed by regulation on the health care or financial services industries, for example, the parameters laid down in those laws might assist companies to understand the gold standard for security and use that as a benchmark. Finally, as elaborated more fully in Chapter 7, an emerging set of professional best practices for data security has begun to shape both business culture and legal reasoning concerning acceptable data handling practices. This also helps define what counts as adequate security.

5. ***Defining Worst Practices.*** The court returns several times to the details of the truly horrible data security in Wyndham's systems. The company suffered three major security breaches, and persisted in poor security practices such as the failure to use firewalls or encryption in critical portions of the network or to change default "out of the box" passwords. For the most part, *Wyndham* (and *Dave & Buster's*) do not tell companies what best practices to use, they highlight "worst practices" to avoid. Does that provide guidance? Can a company with mediocre security assess its risk of liability using such "worst practices" examples? Should Wyndham have known, from reading the *Dave & Buster's* order, that its security was deficient under Section 5?

6. ***Why Doesn't the FTC Write Regulations?*** Wyndham argued that the FTC should be required to lay out its definitions of acceptable and unfair security practices in formal regulations. Why hasn't the FTC elected to do so? One big reason is that Congress has imposed much more burdensome procedural obstacles in the path of any regulations the FTC might promulgate. A federal consumer protection statute called the Magnuson-Moss Warranty Act, passed in 1975, formally gave the FTC rulemaking power, but combined it with so many conditions that the power became unusable. As privacy scholar Chris Hoofnagle explains it:

> Congress added procedure that had the effect of slowing down the FTC drastically. In addition to the requirements of the Administrative Procedures Act, Magnuson-Moss required the Agency to be more specific in detailing the reasons for proposing a rule; required it to provide more opportunities for public participation in the rulemaking, including informal hearings; required it to engage in more regulatory analysis, including economic analysis and considerations of the rule's effects on small business; and required it to engage in more fact-finding and justification, including stating the prevalence of an unwanted practice and the basis for considering it deceptive and/or unfair. Prior to the rule's enforcement, interested parties can challenge it substantively or procedurally for violating these requirements.

CHRIS JAY HOOFNAGLE, FEDERAL TRADE COMMISSION PRIVACY LAW AND POLICY (2016); *see also id.* at 101–102 ("The rule-making structure created by Congress in the Magnuson-Moss Act is considered a failure by the Commission and is unlikely to be used for privacy matters.").

Even though ordinary federal agency rulemaking is a complex and difficult process, it is a picnic next to FTC rulemaking, which takes many years and commonly produces a record of tens of thousands of pages even for comparatively narrow topics. Combine those obstacles with the inevitability that any general privacy or security regulation would surely be challenged in court on the basis of that voluminous record, and it begins to become clear why the FTC has not chosen to make privacy rules in this fashion. Congress has authorized (or sometimes ordered) the FTC to promulgate privacy regulations under the less byzantine procedures of the Administrative Procedures Act in certain circumstances, such as specific delegations in the Children's Online Privacy Protection Act (COPPA) (concerning online data about minors under age 13), 5 U.S.C. §§ 6501–6505 [see Chapter 4] and the Gramm-Leach-Bliley Act (concerning financial data), 15 U.S.C. §§ 6801–6809 [see Chapter 13], sometimes with deadlines. In those cases, the FTC has indeed written rules. While the FTC has urged Congress to repeal the Magnuson-Moss conditions on its privacy-related rulemaking authority under Section 5, Congress has declined this invitation. As a result, privacy compliance guidance to companies concerning unfair or deceptive trade practices has been less formal, as described in *Wyndham* and illustrated in consent decrees such as *In re Snapchat* and *In re Dave & Buster's*.

7. ***Be Careful What You Wish For?*** Suppose Wyndham had its druthers and the FTC did issue formal regulations specifying minimum security practices in detail. What would they look like? Would they be better for regulated entities like Wyndham? Might they be less desirable in certain respects? Moreover, note that even comparatively specific regulations like the HIPAA Security Rule [see Chapter 12] really are rather open-ended standards, not precise rules. Privacy and security regulations are unlike certain environmental regulations, which can stipulate exactly how many parts per million of a certain carcinogenic substance will be allowed, on the basis of scientific evidence about its human health effects. The assessments of risk and harm will vary by context. To say it another way: should Wyndham and its allies be careful what they wish for? Would they be satisfied if they got it? How does the status quo of Section 5 enforcement benefit them?

---

## Focus

### FTC Privacy Authority Beyond Section 5

The FTC's Section 5 power over unfair and deceptive trade practices is the cornerstone of its regulatory authority in privacy and security. And it is also the law with the broadest application to the most activities; almost any private organization involved in any facet of data collection or processing can be covered by Section 5. Several of the sources excerpted in this section (such as Chairman Leibowitz's congressional testimony and *FTC v. Wyndham Worldwide*) have also referred to other statutes giving the FTC additional powers. In general, these statutes apply to a somewhat narrower range of activities, but they give the FTC additional powers such as more latitude to write regulations (and sometimes even requirements that it develop regulations) and the ability to impose fines. There is more coverage of each of these statutes elsewhere in the book, but they are noted here to provide a more complete picture of the FTC's role in US privacy and data protection law.

1. ***The Children's Online Privacy Protection Act (COPPA),*** 5 U.S.C. §§ 6501–6505 [see Chapter 4]: In COPPA, Congress directed the FTC to write detailed regulations concerning online services like web sites and apps that are directed at children under the age of 13. The rules apply much more specific and demanding rules to online activity by children in that age group. The enhanced requirements include notice and disclosure mandates, mechanisms for parental approval, and rights of access, correction, and deletion that allow parents to inspect personal information collected about their children and withdraw their consent for subsequent processing, disclosure, or storage. The FTC regulates compliance and, unlike typical Section 5 cases, the agency has the power to impose fines for COPPA violations. Sometimes the FTC brings both Section 5 and COPPA claims against a defendant who might engage in unfair or deceptive practices in relation to children under 13 years old. COPPA is examined in the next chapter as a representative example of a US statute that relies more on a data protection rationale.

2. ***The Fair Credit Reporting Act (FCRA),*** 15 U.S.C. §§ 1681–1681u [see Chapter 6]: After Section 5, FCRA is the oldest source of FTC authority in this area; it was first enacted in 1970. FCRA applies to "credit reports," a definition that extends to many collections of personal data used for various purposes such as consumer screening and employment background checks. Data covered by FCRA must be used only for specified purposes, and there are provisions for notice to data subjects and correction of errors. A number of additional statutes passed in the last decade, including the Fair and Accurate Credit Transactions Act (FACTA) and the Dodd-Frank Act (passed in response to the recent financial crisis) expanded FCRA, increasing its significance for a variety of businesses. FCRA gives affected consumers a private right of action and also confers enforcement authority on numerous agencies, including the FTC. The pending *Spokeo v. Robins* Supreme Court case noted earlier was brought under FCRA.

3. ***The Gramm-Leach-Bliley Act,*** 15 U.S.C. §§ 6801–6809 [see Chapter 13]: Congress passed a broad financial deregulation bill in 1999, commonly referred to using the names of its congressional sponsors (or by the acronym "GLBA"), especially among privacy lawyers. Its many provisions included laws to increase privacy protection for personal consumer information held by banks and other financial institutions. Jurisdiction under the Act is complex. The FTC has a large enforcement role but so do numerous banking regulatory agencies, especially the Consumer Financial Protection Bureau. The main features of the Gramm-Leach-Bliley Act include requirements to send regular notices of privacy practices to consumers, a Safeguards Rule imposing enhanced data security duties, and provisions for customers to opt out of certain third-party data sharing.

---

## D. STATE CONSUMER PROTECTION REGULATORS

### California v. Comcast Cable Communications Management, LLC

Case No. 15786197 (Cal. Superior Ct, Alameda County, Sept. 17, 2015)

#### COMPLAINT

Plaintiff, the People of the State of California, by and through Kamala D. Harris, Attorney General of the State of California, and through the California Public Utilities Commission (collectively, "Plaintiff"), allege on information and belief:

5. At all relevant times, Defendants Comcast Cable, Comcast Phone, LLC, Comcast Phone of California LLC, and Comcast IP Phone II, LLC (collectively, "Defendants" or "Comcast") have transacted business in the County of Alameda and elsewhere within the State of California. The violations of law described herein occurred in the County of Alameda and elsewhere in the State of California.

#### DEFENDANTS' BUSINESS ACTS AND PRACTICES

#### Background

6. Comcast provides telephone services to residential subscribers in California through a product known as XFINITY Voice.

7. XFINITY Voice is a Voice over Internet Protocol (VoIP) service.

8. Comcast provided its residential XFINITY Voice telephone customers' directory listing information (i.e., name, address, phone number) directly to third party publishers of printed phone books until approximately 2012.

9. In July 2010, Comcast began publishing its directory listings online on Ecolisting.com. Beginning in November 2010, Comcast also licensed its directory listings for approximately one year to a nationwide directory assistance provider through Neustar, Inc. ("Neustar"). Currently, Comcast makes its XFINITY Voice telephone customers' listings available nationally for directory assistance through a vendor.

10. Once a directory listing appears in telephone directories (in print, on the Internet, or on disks) or in directory assistance, it may be sorted, packaged, repackaged and made available again in different formats by anyone.

11. For a monthly charge, non-published and non-listed directory service options are available to Comcast' s XFINITY Voice residential telephone subscribers who choose to not have their listings in online directories, phone books and directory assistance.

12. In California, Comcast charged $1.50 per month for non-published status and $1.25 per month for non-listed status.

### Disclosure of Non-Published/Non-Listed Numbers

14. In connection with a system-wide account number change in California that occurred in October and December 2009, a significant portion of those California customers who elected non-published status prior to December 2009 were mistakenly not flagged as "non-published" and thus were made available for publishing in July 2010 via Neustar.

17. Therefore, for varying periods of time between July 2010 to December 2012, and for many customers the entire period, approximately 75,000 Comcast residential subscribers in California who had paid Comcast the monthly fee for a non-published or non-listed phone number nevertheless had their subscriber listing information published on Ecolisting, and (in some cases) in phone books, and/or made available by a directory assistance provider.

### Customer Inquiries

18. Comcast has the capability to search its customer records databases for customer contacts related to non-published/non-listed numbers.

19. Comcast has issue codes that could identify trouble tickets related to the publication of non-published/non-listed numbers. From January 2010 through October 2012, Comcast opened approximately 350 trouble tickets bearing the problem code related to non-published/non-listed numbers. Of these 350 trouble tickets, approximately 75 trouble tickets were associated with customers who were affected by Comcast's erroneous publication of non-published/non-listed listings.

20. Prior to receiving two complaints in October 2012 about non-published listings being published in error, with one from a California customer and one from a customer in another state, Comcast did not determine the root cause of complaints dealing with the erroneous publication of nonpublished/non-listed listings.

### Remedial & Notification Efforts

21. On or around December 10, 2012, Comcast had the non-published/non-listed directory listings deleted from Ecolisting.

22. Comcast attempted to notify by mail all of the approximately 75,000 non-published/non-listed subscribers to inform them that Comcast had inadvertently published their listings.

23. The notification letter informed the approximately 54,000 customers who still subscribed to a Comcast service as of December 5, 2012 ("current customers") that Comcast had posted a credit to their account for the non-published/non-listed charges paid during the period these customers were published in error. The approximately 21,000 customers who had terminated service on or before December 5, 2012 ("former customers") were told in the letter to contact Comcast in order to receive a refund for the non-published/non-listed charges. The notification letter provided a toll-free hotline number for customers who had questions or required further assistance.

25. Comcast received approximately 11,000 calls from affected customers on the hotline: Approximately 200 of those customers raised safety concerns. Safety concerns included, but were not limited to, those from law enforcement personnel, judges, victims of crime, domestic violence victims, and the elderly. Other affected customers who contacted Comcast on the hotline also voiced concerns about an increase in telemarketing calls and a general concern for their loss of privacy.

### FIRST CAUSE OF ACTION: VIOLATION OF BUSINESS AND PROFESSIONS CODE, SECTION 17500 ET SEQ. (FALSE ADVERTISING) (Brought by the Attorney General on behalf of The People of the State of California)

27. Comcast has violated California Business and Professions Code section 17500 et seq. by making or disseminating false or misleading statements to the general public and to its subscribers, including but not limited to the following:

a. Comcast represented that it would not publish directory listing information relating to its residential subscribers who purchased unlisted service; and

b. Comcast represented that it took reasonable precautions to ensure that the directory information of those subscribers who purchased unlisted service would remain unlisted.

28. Comcast made these false representations in order to induce members of the general public to purchase Comcast services, and to induce its subscribers to continue to use and pay for Comcast services.

### SECOND CAUSE OF ACTION: VIOLATION OF BUSINESS AND PROFESSIONS CODE, SECTION 17200 ET SEQ. (UNFAIR BUSINESS PRACTICES) (Brought by the Attorney General on behalf of The People of the State of California)

30. Comcast has engaged in business acts or practices that were unlawful, unfair, deceptive, or misleading, and therefore violated Section 17200 of the California Unfair Competition. Comcast's acts or practices include, but are not limited to, the following:

a. Comcast violated Business and Professions Code section 17500 et seq., as alleged above in the First Cause of Action;

b. Comcast violated California Public Utilities Code section 2891.1, subdivision (a)[,] by selling or licensing residential subscribers' telephone numbers that were assigned as unlisted and unpublished, when those subscribers had not waived the protection provided by section 2891.1, subdivision (a);

c. Comcast violated the Cable Communications Policy Act of 1984, 47 U.S.C § 551(c)(1), by disclosing personally identifiable information concerning its subscribers without the prior written or electronic consent of such subscribers and by failing to take such actions as were necessary to prevent unauthorized access to personally identifiable information concerning its subscribers by a person other than the subscriber or cable operator; and

d. Comcast violated Code of Federal Regulations section 51.217, subdivision (c)(iv), by providing access to unlisted telephone numbers that its subscribers had asked it not to make available.

## THIRD CAUSE OF ACTION: VIOLATION OF PUBLIC UTILITIES CODE SECTIONS 451 AND 2891.1 (DISCLOSURE OF UNLISTED ORUNPUBLISHED PHONE NUMBERS)

**(Brought by the California Public Utilities Commission on behalf of The People of the State of California)**

32. Comcast violated California Public Utilities Code section 2891 by including the telephone numbers of subscribers assigned a non-listed or non-published telephone number in the lists of customers Comcast provided online, and licensed to directory publishers and directory assistance providers.

## PRAYER FOR RELIEF

WHEREFORE, Plaintiff prays for judgment as follows:

1. That under California Business and Professions Code sections 17203 and 17535, and Public Utilities Code sections 451 and 2891, Defendants, their successors, agents, employees, and all persons who act in concert with them be permanently enjoined from committing any unlawful, unfair or fraudulent acts of unfair competition and from making any false or misleading statements, as alleged in this complaint;

2. That under California Business and Professions Code sections 17206 and 17536, Defendants be ordered to pay $2,500 for each violation of California Business and Professions Code sections 17200 and 17500 as proved at trial;

3. That under Public Utilities Code section 2107 and other relevant law, Defendants be ordered to pay $1,000 for each violation of Public Utilities Code sections 2891.i and 451 as proved at trial;

4. That Plaintiff recover its costs of suit herein, including costs of investigation; and

5. For such other and further relief as the Court may deem just and proper.

## FINAL JUDGMENT AND PERMANENT INJUNCTION

[The parties,] without the taking of proof and without trial or adjudication of any fact or law, and without Comcast admitting any liability, and with all parties having waived their right to appeal, and the Court having considered the matter and good cause appearing:

**IT IS HEREBY ORDERED, ADJUDGED AND DECREED THAT:**

1. This Court has jurisdiction over the allegations and subject matter of the complaint filed in this action, and the parties to this action; venue is proper in this County; and this Court has jurisdiction to enter this Judgment.

3. Nothing in this Judgment alters the requirements of federal or state law to the extent they offer greater protection to consumers.

4. The following definitions shall apply for purposes of this Judgment:

a. The term "non-published" shall refer to both the "non-published" and "non-listed" features offered by Defendants to their XFINITY Voice telephone customers.

e. The term "XFINITY Voice" refers to the residential telephone service offered by Comcast via Voice-over-Internet-Protocol (VoIP) technology. This Judgment applies to such residential telephone service offered by Defendants via VoIP, regardless of the brand name utilized.

**INJUNCTION**

5. The injunctive provisions of this Judgment shall apply to Defendants as well as their subsidiaries; their successors and the assigns of all or substantially all of the assets of their businesses; and their directors, officers, employees, agents, independent contractors, partners, associates and representatives of each of them with respect to their provision of XFINITY Voice services in California.

6. Defendants are hereby permanently enjoined and restrained from directly or indirectly engaging in any of the following acts or practices in connection with offering to sell or selling any goods or services to consumers in California:

(A) Selling or licensing to third party directory publishers the Directory Listing Information, addresses combined with telephone numbers, or telephone numbers (in isolation) of residential customers who have purchased or selected the non-published feature of XFINITY Voice service;

(B) Publishing, selling, or allowing to be published on Ecolisting or any other Comcast-controlled directory listing site, the Directory Listing Information, addresses combined with telephone numbers, or telephone numbers (in isolation) of residential customers who have purchased or selected the non-published feature of XFINITY Voice service; and

(C) Misrepresenting in Comcast published materials the precautions that Defendants take to ensure the confidentiality of Directory Listing Information, addresses combined with telephone numbers, or telephone numbers (in isolation) of XFINITY Voice residential customers who have purchased or selected non-published service; and

7. Defendants shall develop, implement, and maintain a program designed to prevent further instances of improper disclosure of Directory Listing Information of residential customers who have purchased or selected the non-published feature, as set forth below. That program shall consist of the injunctive provisions set forth in the sub-parts to this Paragraph. Unless otherwise stated, the injunctive provisions set forth in the sub-parts to this Paragraph shall remain in effect for a period of three (3) years from the date of the Implementation Report.

(A) Comcast shall commission an annual third party audit of its Directory Listing Information Agent.

(B) Comcast will take the following steps to restrict its vendors' use of Directory Listing Information:

(i) Comcast shall maintain its current policy of including restrictive language in contracts with vendors that have access to Directory Listing Information.

(ii) Comcast shall request annual certifications from the following entities that they are using the Directory Listing Information of Comcast's customers consistent with the contractual restrictions discussed above in Paragraph 7(B)(i): (1) Comcast's current Directory Listing Agent; (2) the vendors Comcast uses to telemarket its products and services ("telemarketing vendors"); and (3) any directory assistance provider(s). Comcast shall also request that its telemarketing vendors include in their certifications that they are complying with "do not call' " limitations.

(iii) Within thirty (30) days of the date of entry of this Judgment and once more on the first anniversary of the date of the entry of Judgment, Comcast shall direct its then-current Directory Listing Information Agent, Neustar, Inc., to eliminate Directory Listing Information in Neustar's national database that matches the non-published Directory Listing Information of the approximately 35,000 affected customers who are at that time still Comcast customers.

(C) Comcast shall make available to its XFINITY Voice California residential customers a simplified and easily readable disclosure of the ways in which Comcast uses non-published numbers and other personal information. [The settlement included a model form for this purpose, and required Comcast to notify state authorities of any significant revisions it made to the form. The consent decree also included detailed provisions for the distribution of this form to Comcast customers, including timelines, recipients, and a requirement that it make the form available in other languages it uses for marketing: English, Chinese, Spanish, Hmong, Korean, and Russian.]

(D) Within three months from the date of entry of this Judgment, but no later than its service of the Implementation Report, Comcast shall adopt revised methods and procedures to address the process for handling customer inquiries and complaints about the publication of nonpublished listings. The methods and procedures shall require, at a minimum:

(i) the creation of a "trouble ticket" for all customer incoming calls where the customer care representative verifies that the customer is paying for a non-published feature on the customer's XFINITY Voice service and the customer claims that his/her number, name or address is being published;

(ii) root cause analysis for each of the trouble tickets;

(iii) review of all trouble tickets to detect patterns;

(iv) quarterly review of the first 25% of the resolved California trouble tickets within the quarter (but not less than 5 or the total if less than 5) to confirm for quality assurance purposes that the process outlined in the methods and procedures was properly followed; and

(v) ongoing training of all Comcast personnel whose primary job responsibilities are to address and resolve directory listings complaints.

**RESTITUTION**

8. Comcast shall pay a total of $7,909,400 in restitution, which monies will be paid out as follows:

(A) $7,477,400 to the 74,774 California consumers who selected or paid for nonpublished Comcast XFINITY Voice service but whose Directory Listing Information was published on the Internet, in phone books, or through directory assistance ("Affected Customers"). Subject to Paragraph 8(B), Affected Customers who currently receive any Comcast service shall receive their restitution award as a one hundred dollar ($100) bill credit. Affected Customers who no longer receive any Comcast service shall receive their restitution award as a one hundred dollar ($100) check.

(B) $432,000 in additional restitution to consumers eligible to receive restitution pursuant to Paragraph 8(A) and who identified personal safety concerns to Comcast as of August 2014.

11. Any portion of the $7,909,400 not paid out to consumers within 12 months after the date of entry of this Judgment will be transferred to the State Controller's Office in accordance with California's Unclaimed Property Law, so that it may be claimed by the Affected Customers.

## OTHER MONETARY PROVISIONS

13. Within 30 days of the date of entry of this Judgment, Defendants shall pay twenty five million dollars ($25,000,000) in total penalties and related monies.

## COMPLIANCE

15. For a period of three (3) years from the date of the Implementation Report, Defendants shall prepare periodic reports regarding their compliance with the terms of this Judgment.

### NOTES

1. ***$33 million!*** Comcast certainly paid a large financial price in this case, especially considering this was a settlement agreement it accepted voluntarily. The $25 million civil penalty is probably the most eye-catching component of the award. Adding the expense of internal monitoring and restitution administration probably pushes the total cost to Comcast over $35 million. As with the class action cases considered above, the aggregation of numerous small statutory damages awards added up here. The state alleged that 75,000 customers were affected, and sought $2,500 per violation under consumer protection law and another $1,000 per violation under public utilities law (which is a specialized form of consumer protection regulation). If each of the 75,000 customers gave rise to a $3,500 fine, the total would reach $262.5 million—an order of magnitude larger than the $25 million penalty the state collected in the settlement.

2. ***Aggravating Factors.*** Besides the simple mathematics, there are other possible reasons Comcast may have paid such a hefty price. For one, the nature of its consumer protection offense was comparatively egregious: for several years it continued to charge customers for a service it simply did not deliver. (Indeed, Comcast then turned around and received compensation for licensing those customers' personal information, so in a sense it got paid twice.) The complaint also emphasizes that Comcast had the means to discover the problem by analyzing reports from customers but failed to do so for several years. If the complaint is accurate, it is not clear what sort of defense Comcast could have mounted had the case proceeded. Furthermore, as a telephone and cable company, Comcast is more heavily regulated than other businesses. The involvement of the Pubic Utilities Commission and the additional violations and penalties under that body of regulation turned up the heat. The mere fact that Comcast is sometimes dependent on state regulators concerning other aspects of its operations, such as securing franchises and rate-setting, also may have reduced its realistic leverage in settlement negotiations. All of this is speculation, of course—Comcast said

little about the settlement and by its terms admits no wrongdoing. But it is important for privacy lawyers who are analyzing risk to consider these types of factors when determining their own company's possible legal exposure by comparison.

3. ***Defining Consumer Protection Violations through Other Law.*** Recall that the *Accusearch* court validated the FTC's technique of using violations of another statute as a mechanism to define unfair conduct. California regulators do the same here. The false statements alleged under Count One and the violations of public utilities law alleged under Count Three supported the claim of unfair business practices in Count Two. The complaint also invokes the federal Cable Communications Policy Act and federal telecommunications regulations [see Chapter 14] as further support for its allegations against Comcast under state consumer protection law.

4. ***Regulators and Private Parties.*** Do you think plaintiffs could bring a class action against Comcast under the same legal theories as the Attorney General and Public Utilities Commission used here? What obstacles would they face?

# CHAPTER 4

# DATA PROTECTION

The consumer protection model discussed in Chapter 3 emerged in response to a vacuum. Because there was concern about privacy and no law covered it specifically, private plaintiffs and regulators like the FTC adapted preexisting law to address it.

In contrast, other legal rules about data handling were specifically designed from the outset to protect individual privacy or data security. This book groups many of those together as representative of a "data protection" model, distinct from consumer protection measures. Not every data protection law is identical, but they tend to share several interrelated features. First, they originate from a more sweeping conception of individual rights over data, regardless of the nature of the transaction involved. So, where the FTC analyzes privacy problems as possible flaws in the character of a commercial relationship between a company and an individual, in a data protection model, privacy rights originate in the individual's inherent control over personal information, sometimes classified as a human right.

Second, and related, the two systems also start from converse assumptions about which data practices are permissible. The consumer protection model is permissive while data protection law is restrictive. One way to think about this difference is that the two regimes have opposite default rules. In consumer protection law, collection and processing usually are allowed unless they are banned; in data protection law, collection and processing are banned unless they are allowed.

Third, many data protection laws derive their protections from one or more codes of "fair information practices" that trace their lineage back to the 1970s. As a result, most data protection laws provide people with certain affirmative rights, usually including rights of access to personal data an organization holds about them and rights to have that data modified or deleted under certain circumstances.

Finally, because data protection laws are rights-based and require parties handling personal information to do so under specific legal justifications, they tend to be detailed and rule-based. This, too, differs from the more standard-based shape of consumer protection regulation, with its reliance on concepts of reasonableness from tort law or on the expectations emerging from FTC enforcement and guidance.

All of these characteristics of data protection regimes ultimately derive from the fundamental principle that people have rights to control the flow of information about themselves. This view tends to result in law that places more demands on organizations that handle personal data, at least on paper. That said, what really matters is the enforcement of the rules, and we will see throughout the book that different regulators range from more to less strict and more to less adversarial within both consumer protection and data protection models, regardless of the letter of the law.

The bulk of this chapter considers the most evident generally applicable data protection regime, which is found in the European Union (EU) [Section A]. All 28 EU member states, which govern a combined population of over 500 million people, have omnibus data protection laws modeled on the EU's Data Protection Directive, 95/46/EC (1995). A brand new overhaul of that law, known as the General Data Protection Regulation (GDPR), was enacted in early 2016 and will come into effect in 2018. There are many differences between the approach to data practices in the EU and the US. Indeed, they extend even to nomenclature: in most European nations, regulation of the handling of personal information is called "data protection law." To a European, "privacy" is a broader and more amorphous concept; data protection is a fundamental rule set for handling personal data in a way that protects the rights of the individual. Students of American law will find it useful to study the EU regime as a comparison with the US consumer protection model.

More importantly, however, the requirements of EU data protection law increasingly apply to US companies. Any US organization with European customers, donors, users, or employees could find itself subject to EU data protection regulation—as Google learned in one case excerpted below. Moreover, the European-style data protection model has proven influential in many other countries as varied as, for example, Argentina, Canada, and Israel. Thus, well-informed privacy lawyers must be conversant with the EU approach. Section A introduces both the content and the enforcement of the Data Protection Directive, and then explains how the GDPR is expected to change it.

While the European version may be the most prominent and most complete realization of a data protection model, there are also data protection laws in the US. These tend to be narrower in scope, covering only certain industry sectors or certain practices. The Children's Online Privacy Protection Act (COPPA) and its regulatory scheme [Section B] shares many features with the European data protection model—but also stands apart from it in important ways. Understanding COPPA will allow you to evaluate numerous other statutes and regulations that make up a large proportion of the rest of this book.

# A. EUROPEAN UNION DATA PROTECTION LAW

## 1. THE EU DATA PROTECTION DIRECTIVE

### OECD Guidelines on the Protection of Privacy and Transborder Flows of Personal Data

(1980)

1. For the purposes of these Guidelines:

a) "data controller" means a party who, according to domestic law, is competent to decide about the contents and use of personal data regardless of whether or not such data are collected, stored, processed or disseminated by that party or by an agent on its behalf;

b) "personal data" means any information relating to an identified or identifiable individual (data subject). . . .

**Collection Limitation Principle**

7. There should be limits to the collection of personal data and any such data should be obtained by lawful and fair means and, where appropriate, with the knowledge or consent of the data subject.

**Data Quality Principle**

8. Personal data should be relevant to the purposes for which they are to be used, and, to the extent necessary for those purposes, should be accurate, complete, and kept up-to-date.

**Purpose Specification Principle**

9. The purposes for which personal data are collected should be specified not later than at the time of data collection and the subsequent use limited to the fulfillment of those purposes or such others as are not incompatible with those purposes and as are specified on each occasion of change of purpose.

**Use Limitation Principle**

10. Personal data should not be disclosed, made available or otherwise used for purposes other than those specified in accordance with Paragraph 9 except:

a) with the consent of the data subject; or

b) by the authority of law.

**Security Safeguards Principle**

11. Personal data should be protected by reasonable security safeguards against such risks as loss or unauthorised access, destruction, use, modification or disclosure of data.

### Openness Principle

12. There should be a general policy of openness about developments, practices, and policies with respect to personal data. Means should be readily available of establishing the existence and nature of personal data, and the main purposes of their use, as well as the identity and usual residence of the data controller.

### Individual Participation Principle

13. An individual should have the right:

a) to obtain from a data controller, or otherwise, confirmation of whether or not the data controller has data relating to him;

b) to have communicated to him, data relating to him within a reasonable time;

- at a charge, if any, that is not excessive;
- in a reasonable manner; and
- in a form that is readily intelligible to him;

c) to be given reasons if a request made under subparagraphs (a) and (b) is denied, and to be able to challenge such denial; and

d) to challenge data relating to him and, if the challenge is successful to have the data erased, rectified, completed or amended.

### Accountability Principle

14. A data controller should be accountable for complying with measures which give effect to the principles stated above.

## NOTES

1. ***The OECD.*** The Organization for Economic Cooperation and Development (OECD) is a 36-nation organization originally founded in 1961. Its members are scattered around the globe, including not only the US and many European nations, but also, for example, Japan, Mexico, Australia, and Israel. The OECD's policy recommendations are nonbinding, but often have significant influence. As you read about the Data Protection Directive and the GDPR below, see where you detect inspiration from the Privacy Guidelines; they clearly shaped the approach to data protection in many countries over the last few decades.

2. ***Fair Information Practices.*** The elements of the OECD Privacy Guidelines, in turn, borrowed from several earlier articulations of privacy principles. In particular, consider the influence of the Code of Fair Information Practices released in 1973 by the US Department of Health, Education, and Welfare (HEW) (later reorganized into several departments including the Department of Health and Human Services):

> 1. There must be no personal data record-keeping systems whose very existence is secret.

2. There must be a way for a person to find out what information about the person is in a record and how it is used.

3. There must be a way for a person to prevent information about the person that was obtained for one purpose from being used or made available for other purposes without the person's consent.

4. There must be a way for a person to correct or amend a record of identifiable information about the person.

5. Any organization creating, maintaining, using, or disseminating records of identifiable personal data must assure the reliability of the data for their intended use and must take precautions to prevent misuses of the data.

How do the OECD Guidelines and this Code produced by HEW resemble one another and how do they differ? Collectively, the ideas articulated in both statements are widely known among privacy lawyers as the "FIPs" (or sometimes "FIPPs"). There have been additional varied articulations of the FIPs over the years, but throughout this evolution the different statements have maintained similar themes and core principles. *See generally* Robert Gellman, *Fair Information Practices: A Basic History* (2015), available at http://ssrn.com/abstract=2415020. For example, the work of privacy law scholar Alan Westin in the late 1960s and early 1970s was highly influential in conceptualizing this model. *See, e.g.,* ALAN F. WESTIN, PRIVACY AND FREEDOM (1967).

The FIPs are often seen as the most fundamental expression of robust privacy and data protection law. Of course, their high level of generality still leaves them open to interpretation in many specific situations. Does the US consumer protection model for privacy protection [see Chapter 3] embody the FIPs? What about the European Union's two key provisions concerning data protection—the first more akin to a constitution, the second to a statute—which are excerpted next?

## Charter of Fundamental Rights of the European Union

Articles 7 and 8

### Article 7: Respect for private and family life

Everyone has the right to respect for his or her private and family life, home, and communications.

### Article 8: Protection of personal data

1. Everyone has the right to the protection of personal data concerning him or her.

2. Such data must be processed fairly for specified purposes and on the basis of the consent of the person concerned or some other legitimate basis laid down by law. Everyone has the right of access to data which

has been collected concerning him or her, and the right to have it rectified.

3. Compliance with these rules shall be subject to control by an independent authority.

## European Union Data Protection Directive

Directive 95/46/EC (1995)

### Article 1: Object of the Directive

1. In accordance with this Directive, Member States shall protect the fundamental rights and freedoms of natural persons, and in particular their right to privacy with respect to the processing of personal data.

2. Member States shall neither restrict nor prohibit the free flow of personal data between Member States for reasons connected with the protection afforded under paragraph 1.

### Article 2: Definitions

For the purposes of this Directive:

(a) "personal data" shall mean any information relating to an identified or identifiable natural person ('data subject'); an identifiable person is one who can be identified, directly or indirectly, in particular by reference to an identification number or to one or more factors specific to his physical, physiological, mental, economic, cultural or social identity;

(b) "processing of personal data" ("processing") shall mean any operation or set of operations which is performed upon personal data, whether or not by automatic means, such as collection, recording, organization, storage, adaptation or alteration, retrieval, consultation, use, disclosure by transmission, dissemination or otherwise making available, alignment or combination, blocking, erasure or destruction;

(c) "personal data filing system" ("filing system") shall mean any structured set of personal data which are accessible according to specific criteria, whether centralized, decentralized or dispersed on a functional or geographical basis;

(d) "controller" shall mean the natural or legal person, public authority, agency or any other body which alone or jointly with others determines the purposes and means of the processing of personal data;

(e) "processor" shall mean a natural or legal person, public authority, agency or any other body which processes personal data on behalf of the controller;

(f) "third party" shall mean any natural or legal person, public authority, agency or any other body other than the data subject, the controller, the processor, and the persons who, under the direct authority of the controller or the processor, are authorized to process the data;

(g) "recipient" shall mean a natural or legal person, public authority, agency or any other body to whom data are disclosed, whether a third party or not;

(h) "the data subject's consent" shall mean any freely given specific and informed indication of his wishes by which the data subject signifies his agreement to personal data relating to him being processed.

**Article 3: Scope**

1. This Directive shall apply to the processing of personal data wholly or partly by automatic means, and to the processing otherwise than by automatic means of personal data which form part of a filing system or are intended to form part of a filing system.

2. This Directive shall not apply to the processing of personal data:

- in the course of an activity which falls outside the scope of Community law, and in any case to processing operations concerning public security, defence, State security (including the economic well-being of the State when the processing operation relates to State security matters), and the activities of the State in areas of criminal law,
- by a natural person in the course of a purely personal or household activity.

**Article 4: National Law Applicable**

1. Each Member State shall apply the national provisions it adopts pursuant to this Directive to the processing of personal data where:

(a) the processing is carried out in the context of the activities of an establishment of the controller on the territory of the Member State; when the same controller is established on the territory of several Member States, he must take the necessary measures to ensure that each of these establishments complies with the obligations laid down by the national law applicable;

(b) the controller is not established on the Member State's territory, but in a place where its national law applies by virtue of international public law;

(c) the controller is not established on Community territory and, for purposes of processing personal data makes use of equipment, automated or otherwise, situated on the territory of the said Member State, unless such equipment is used only for purposes of transit through the territory of the Community.

2. In the circumstances referred to in paragraph 1(c), the controller must designate a representative established in the territory of that

Member State, without prejudice to legal actions which could be initiated against the controller himself.

**Article 6 [Principles Relating to Data Quality]**

1. Member States shall provide that personal data must be:

(a) processed fairly and lawfully;

(b) collected for specified, explicit, and legitimate purposes and not further processed in a way incompatible with those purposes. Further processing of data for historical, statistical or scientific purposes shall not be considered as incompatible provided that Member States provide appropriate safeguards;

(c) adequate, relevant, and not excessive in relation to the purposes for which they are collected and/or further processed;

(d) accurate and, where necessary, kept up to date; every reasonable step must be taken to ensure that data which are inaccurate or incomplete, having regard to the purposes for which they were collected or for which they are further processed, are erased or rectified;

(e) kept in a form which permits identification of data subjects for no longer than is necessary for the purposes for which the data were collected or for which they are further processed. Member States shall lay down appropriate safeguards for personal data stored for longer periods for historical, statistical or scientific use.

2. It shall be for the controller to ensure that paragraph 1 is complied with.

. . .

**Article 7 [Criteria for Making Data Processing Legitimate]**

Member States shall provide that personal data may be processed only if:

(a) the data subject has unambiguously given his consent; or

(b) processing is necessary for the performance of a contract to which the data subject is party or in order to take steps at the request of the data subject prior to entering into a contract; or

(c) processing is necessary for compliance with a legal obligation to which the controller is subject; or

(d) processing is necessary in order to protect the vital interests of the data subject; or

(e) processing is necessary for the performance of a task carried out in the public interest or in the exercise of official authority vested in the controller or in a third party to whom the data are disclosed; or

(f) processing is necessary for the purposes of the legitimate interests pursued by the controller or by the third party or parties to whom the data are disclosed, except where such interests are overridden by the interests for fundamental rights and freedoms of the data subject.

### Article 8 [Processing of Special Categories of Data]

1. Member States shall prohibit the processing of personal data revealing racial or ethnic origin, political opinions, religious or philosophical beliefs, trade-union membership, and the processing of data concerning health or sex life.

2. Paragraph 1 shall not apply where:

(a) the data subject has given his explicit consent to the processing of those data, except where the laws of the Member State provide that the prohibition referred to in paragraph 1 may not be lifted by the data subject's giving his consent; or

(b) processing is necessary for the purposes of carrying out the obligations and specific rights of the controller in the field of employment law in so far as it is authorized by national law providing for adequate safeguards; or

(c) processing is necessary to protect the vital interests of the data subject or of another person where the data subject is physically or legally incapable of giving his consent; or

(d) processing is carried out in the course of its legitimate activities with appropriate guarantees by a foundation, association or any other non-profit-seeking body with a political, philosophical, religious or trade-union aim and on condition that the processing relates solely to the members of the body or to persons who have regular contact with it in connection with its purposes and that the data are not disclosed to a third party without the consent of the data subjects; or

(e) the processing relates to data which are manifestly made public by the data subject or is necessary for the establishment, exercise or defence of legal claims.

### Article 9: Processing of Personal Data and Freedom of Expression

Member States shall provide for exemptions or derogations for the processing of personal data carried out solely for journalistic purposes or the purpose of artistic or literary expression only if they are necessary to reconcile the right to privacy with the rules governing freedom of expression.

### Article 10 [Information to be Provided to the Data Subject]

Member States shall provide that the controller or his representative must provide a data subject from whom data relating to himself are collected with at least the following information, except where he already has it:

(a) the identity of the controller and of his representative, if any;

(b) the purposes of the processing for which the data are intended;

(c) any further information such as

- the recipients or categories of recipients of the data,
- whether replies to the questions are obligatory or voluntary, as well as the possible consequences of failure to reply,
- the existence of the right of access to and the right to rectify the data concerning him in so far as such further information is necessary, having regard to the specific circumstances in which the data are collected, to guarantee fair processing in respect of the data subject.

. . .

**Article 12: Right of Access**

Member States shall guarantee every data subject the right to obtain from the controller:

(a) without constraint at reasonable intervals and without excessive delay or expense:

- confirmation as to whether or not data relating to him are being processed and information at least as to the purposes of the processing, the categories of data concerned, and the recipients or categories of recipients to whom the data are disclosed,
- communication to him in an intelligible form of the data undergoing processing and of any available information as to their source,
- knowledge of the logic involved in any automatic processing of data concerning him at least in the case of the automated decisions referred to in Article 15 (1);

(b) as appropriate the rectification, erasure or blocking of data the processing of which does not comply with the provisions of this Directive, in particular because of the incomplete or inaccurate nature of the data;

(c) notification to third parties to whom the data have been disclosed of any rectification, erasure or blocking carried out in compliance with (b), unless this proves impossible or involves a disproportionate effort.

## Article 13: Exemptions and Restrictions

1. Member States may adopt legislative measures to restrict the scope of the obligations and rights provided for in Articles 6 (1), 10, 11 (1), 12, and 21 when such a restriction constitutes a necessary measure to safeguard:

(a) national security;

(b) defence;

(c) public security;

(d) the prevention, investigation, detection, and prosecution of criminal offences, or of breaches of ethics for regulated professions;

(e) an important economic or financial interest of a Member State or of the European Union, including monetary, budgetary, and taxation matters;

(f) a monitoring, inspection or regulatory function connected, even occasionally, with the exercise of official authority in cases referred to in (c), (d) and (e);

(g) the protection of the data subject or of the rights and freedoms of others.

## Article 14: The Data Subject's Right to Object

Member States shall grant the data subject the right:

(a) at least in the cases referred to in Article 7 (e) and (f), to object at any time on compelling legitimate grounds relating to his particular situation to the processing of data relating to him, save where otherwise provided by national legislation. Where there is a justified objection, the processing instigated by the controller may no longer involve those data;

(b) to object, on request and free of charge, to the processing of personal data relating to him which the controller anticipates being processed for the purposes of direct marketing, or to be informed before personal data are disclosed for the first time to third parties or used on their behalf for the purposes of direct marketing, and to be expressly offered the right to object free of charge to such disclosures or uses.

Member States shall take the necessary measures to ensure that data subjects are aware of the existence of the right referred to in the first subparagraph of (b).

. . .

## Article 17: Security of Processing

1. Member States shall provide that the controller must implement appropriate technical and organizational measures to protect personal data against accidental or unlawful destruction or accidental loss,

alteration, unauthorized disclosure or access, in particular where the processing involves the transmission of data over a network, and against all other unlawful forms of processing. Having regard to the state of the art and the cost of their implementation, such measures shall ensure a level of security appropriate to the risks represented by the processing and the nature of the data to be protected.

2. The Member States shall provide that the controller must, where processing is carried out on his behalf, choose a processor providing sufficient guarantees in respect of the technical security measures and organizational measures governing the processing to be carried out, and must ensure compliance with those measures.

3. The carrying out of processing by way of a processor must be governed by a contract or legal act binding the processor to the controller and stipulating in particular that:

- the processor shall act only on instructions from the controller,
- the obligations set out in paragraph 1, as defined by the law of the Member State in which the processor is established, shall also be incumbent on the processor.

4. For the purposes of keeping proof, the parts of the contract or the legal act relating to data protection and the requirements relating to the measures referred to in paragraph 1 shall be in writing or in another equivalent form.

. . .

### Article 25 [Transfer Of Personal Data To Third Countries]

1. The Member States shall provide that the transfer to a third country of personal data which are undergoing processing or are intended for processing after transfer may take place only if, without prejudice to compliance with the national provisions adopted pursuant to the other provisions of this Directive, the third country in question ensures an adequate level of protection.

## NOTES

1. ***Understanding the European Union.*** The European Union is a multinational partnership of primarily economic origin; all of its members agree to various free-trade and open-border provisions, and many (but not all) share the euro as a common currency. All members of the EU must ratify the European Convention on Human Rights [see Chapter 1], thus becoming bound by the privacy protections in that Convention's Article 8 and by decisions of the European Court of Human Rights enforcing it. Moreover, after the Treaty of Lisbon became effective in 2009, the EU's Charter of Fundamental Rights (usually referred to simply as "the Charter"), excerpted above, became binding on all member states. The Charter's provisions generally echo the Convention, but its data protection language is somewhat more specific.

The legal relationship between the European Union and its member nations is complicated; explaining it fully would require a book of its own. The most important point for the study of privacy law is the nature of the Data Protection Directive. Countries within the EU are expected to implement its directives by enacting national statutes consistent with their requirements. There is room for countries to adapt its legislation to fit their own conditions, but some elements of the Data Protection Directive are mandatory. Enforcement first occurs in each member state through a national regulator and through its own national courts. Disputes can be referred to the Court of Justice of the European Union (CJEU) (not to be confused with the European Court of Human Rights), which may order a member state to bring its national laws into compliance with a directive. For these reasons, the Data Protection Directive is very important, because most EU countries have enacted laws closely mirroring its terms, and they are subject to judgments in the CJEU if they are found to move too far outside its bounds. (As described below, the new GDPR will have a somewhat different relationship with the law of member states.)

2. ***The Dual Purposes of the Directive.*** The Data Protection Directive has two distinct goals, named in Article 1. On one hand, the Directive aims to standardize law across all member states so that data controllers do not face a patchwork of regulation within the unified EU market and so that they can move data freely between member states. Alongside this goal, the Directive also seeks to guarantee the same baselines of human rights throughout the EU.

3. ***Opposite Default Rules.*** Now that you have read the Data Protection Directive, consider again the comments that opened this chapter about the difference between consumer protection law and data protection law. How does the Directive compare to the privacy and security rules imposed by the FTC [see Chapter 3]? Notice the legitimizing criteria in Article 7, and the additional requirements under Article 8 for processing sensitive personal data. How do these rules compare to US consumer protection law? How does Article 14 compare to the handling of direct marketing in US consumer protection law?

4. ***Data Protection Regulators.*** Article 28 of the Directive requires every EU country to establish a data protection authority (or "DPA") to oversee and enforce the provisions of its conforming statute. Most industrialized or developing nations outside Europe (including countries as far flung as Canada, Argentina, New Zealand, and South Korea) also have dedicated data protection regulators. Of course, the regulatory approaches of these agencies may vary widely. Germany and Spain are generally considered more stringent regulators than the UK or Ireland, for example. Most DPAs also promulgate guidance documents and work with industry to develop best practices—sometimes performing a role very similar to the FTC. In addition, Article 29 of the Directive establishes a body at the European Commission composed of the DPAs from all member states and central EU data protection officials. The "Article 29 Working Party," as it has become known, issues opinions which, while nonbinding, often guide individual DPAs and attempt to harmonize standards and enforcement throughout the

EU. The GDPR will take this harmonization effort further by allowing the DPA in a company's primary location to take the lead in regulating its data practices, and creating a new European Data Protection Board to moderate disagreements among national DPAs about enforcement.

5. ***Crossborder Transfers.*** Note that Article 25 prohibits the transfer of any personal data to countries that do not have an "adequate level of protection" for privacy of that data. While it has never been formally determined, consensus opinion assumes that the United States does not meet this standard. A recent decision by the CJEU invalidated the US-EU Safe Harbor Agreement, which had been the primary justification for transfers of data from the US to the EU for the preceding 15 years [see Chapter 8]. As a result, the issue of crossborder transfers is currently in turmoil.

6. ***Registration Requirements.*** Several Articles not excerpted above require that, with some exemptions, data controllers must notify the data protection authority before conducting any automated processing of personal data [see Chapter 6]. In most countries this has resulted in a registration system where data controllers fill out forms, often online. The GDPR will eliminate many of these obligations.

---

## Practice

### Working with the Directive

What provisions of the EU Data Protection Directive might permit the following activities? (More than one provision may apply.)

(a) Amazon.com collecting purchase data in order to make customized recommendations?

(b) Facebook displaying status updates of its members?

(c) A hospital maintaining former patients' medical records in an electronic database for potential follow-up if they are readmitted?

(d) A small factory keeping employee records in a locked filing cabinet in the office?

(e) The contact list in your smart phone?

(f) A national police force maintaining records of persons reported for suspicious behavior?

---

## 2. DATA PROTECTION ENFORCEMENT IN EUROPE

As noted above, Article 28 of the Directive requires the establishment of a data protection authority (DPA) in each EU member state. In some countries these regulators may have duties beyond data protection—in the UK, for example, the Information Commissioner's Office also handles freedom of information law. But none of the DPAs has additional duties on the scale of the FTC (which also works on consumer fraud, antitrust, and advertising issues), not to mention the numerous other responsibilities of the health, financial, or educational agencies that enforce US privacy law in their respective spheres. Not only are DPAs generally focused on data protection, but their power crosses boundaries much more than in US privacy law. EU data protection laws apply to the public and private sectors, to individuals and organizations, across all industries, and for all types of data practices; the DPAs enforce the law in all these settings. The following excerpts offer examples of three different national DPAs engaging in three different types of enforcement.

## Ryneš v. Úšrad pro Ochranu Osobních Údajů

Court of Justice of the European Union (Fourth Chamber) (2014)

1. This request for a preliminary ruling concerns the interpretation of Article 3(2) of Directive 95/46/EC of the European Parliament and of the Council of 24 October 1995 on the protection of individuals with regard to the processing of personal data and on the free movement of such data.

2. The request has been made in proceedings between Mr. Ryneš and the Úšrad pro ochranu osobních údajů ([Czech] Office for Personal Data Protection; "the Office"), concerning a decision by which the Office found that Mr. Ryneš had committed a number of offences in relation to the protection of personal data.

**The dispute in the main proceedings and the question referred for a preliminary ruling**

13. During the period from 5 October 2007 to 11 April 2008, Mr. Ryneš installed and used a camera system located under the eaves of his family home. The camera was installed in a fixed position and could not turn; it recorded the entrance to his home, the public footpath, and the entrance to the house opposite. The system allowed only a visual recording, which was stored on recording equipment in the form of a continuous loop, that is to say, on a hard disk drive. As soon as it reached full capacity, the device would record over the existing recording, erasing the old material. No monitor was installed on the recording equipment, so the images could not be studied in real time. Only Mr. Ryneš had direct access to the system and the data.

14. The Nejvyšsšsí správní soud (Supreme Administrative Court, Czech Republic; or "the referring court") notes that Mr. Ryneš's only reason for operating the camera was to protect the property, health, and life of his family and himself. Indeed, both Mr. Ryneš and his family had for several years been subjected to attacks by persons unknown whom it had not been possible to identify. Furthermore, the windows of the family home had been broken on several occasions between 2005 and 2007.

15. On the night of 6 to 7 October 2007, a further attack took place. One of the windows of Mr. Ryneš's home was broken by a shot from a catapult. The video surveillance system at issue made it possible to

identify two suspects. The recording was handed over to the police and relied on in the course of the subsequent criminal proceedings.

16. By decision of 4 August 2008, following a request from one of the suspects for confirmation that Mr. Ryneš's surveillance system was lawful, the Office found that Mr. Ryneš had infringed [the Czech Republic's conforming data protection statute under the Directive], since:

- as a data controller, he had used a camera system to collect, without their consent, the personal data of persons moving along the street or entering the house opposite;
- he had not informed those persons of the processing of that personal data, the extent and purpose of that processing, by whom and by what means the personal data would be processed, or who would have access to the personal data; and
- as a data controller, Mr. Ryneš had not fulfilled the obligation to report that processing to the Office.

17. Mr. Ryneš brought an action challenging that decision, which the Mšestský soud v Praze (Prague City Court) dismissed by judgment of 25 April 2012. Mr. Ryneš brought an appeal on a point of law against that judgment before the referring court.

18. [The referring court] decided to stay proceedings and refer the following question to the Court of Justice for a preliminary ruling:

> Can the operation of a camera system installed on a family home for the purposes of the protection of the property, health, and life of the owners of the home be classified as the processing of personal data "by a natural person in the course of a purely personal or household activity" for the purposes of Article 3(2) of Directive 95/46 . . ., even though such a system also monitors a public space?

**Consideration of the question referred**

20. It should be noted that, under Article 3(1) of Directive 95/46, the directive is to apply to "the processing of personal data wholly or partly by automatic means, and to the processing otherwise than by automatic means of personal data which form part of a filing system or are intended to form part of a filing system."

21. The term "personal data" as used in that provision covers, according to the definition under Article 2(a) of Directive 95/46, "any information relating to an identified or identifiable natural person," an identifiable person being "one who can be identified, directly or indirectly, in particular by reference . . . to one or more factors specific to his physical . . . identity."

22. Accordingly, the image of a person recorded by a camera constitutes personal data within the meaning of Article 2(a) of Directive 95/46 inasmuch as it makes it possible to identify the person concerned.

23. As regards the "processing of personal data," it should be noted that Article 2(b) of Directive 95/46 defines this as "any operation or set of operations which is performed upon personal data, . . . such as collection, recording, . . . [or] storage."

24. As can be seen, in particular, from recitals 15 and 16 to Directive 95/46, video surveillance falls, in principle, within the scope of that directive in so far as it constitutes automatic processing.

25. Surveillance in the form of a video recording of persons, as in the case before the referring court, which is stored on a continuous recording device—the hard disk drive—constitutes, pursuant to Article 3(1) of Directive 95/46, the automatic processing of personal data.

26. The referring court is uncertain whether such processing should nevertheless, in circumstances such as those of the case before it, escape the application of Directive 95/46 in so far as it is carried out "in the course of a purely personal or household activity" for the purposes of the second indent of Article 3(2) of the directive.

27. As is clear from Article 1 of that directive and recital 10 thereto, Directive 95/46 is intended to ensure a high level of protection of the fundamental rights and freedoms of natural persons, in particular their right to privacy, with respect to the processing of personal data.

28. In that connection, it should be noted that, according to settled case-law, the protection of the fundamental right to private life guaranteed under Article 7 of the Charter of Fundamental Rights of the European Union ("the Charter") requires that derogations and limitations in relation to the protection of personal data must apply only in so far as is strictly necessary.

29. Since the provisions of Directive 95/46, in so far as they govern the processing of personal data liable to infringe fundamental freedoms, in particular the right to privacy, must necessarily be interpreted in the light of the fundamental rights set out in the Charter, the exception provided for in the second indent of Article 3(2) of that directive must be narrowly construed.

30. The fact that Article 3(2) of Directive 95/46 falls to be narrowly construed has its basis also in the very wording of that provision, under which the directive does not cover the processing of data where the activity in the course of which that processing is carried out is a "purely" personal or household activity, that is to say, not simply a personal or household activity.

31. In the light of the foregoing considerations, it must be held that the processing of personal data comes within the exception provided for in the second indent of Article 3(2) of Directive 95/46 only where it is carried out in the purely personal or household setting of the person processing the data.

32. Accordingly, so far as natural persons are concerned, correspondence and the keeping of address books constitute, in the light of recital 12 to Directive 95/46, a "purely personal or household activity" even if they incidentally concern or may concern the private life of other persons.

33. To the extent that video surveillance such as that at issue in the main proceedings covers, even partially, a public space and is accordingly directed outwards from the private setting of the person processing the data in that manner, it cannot be regarded as an activity which is a purely "personal or household" activity for the purposes of the second indent of Article 3(2) of Directive 95/46.

34. At the same time, the application of Directive 95/46 makes it possible, where appropriate, to take into account—in accordance, in particular, with Articles 7(f), 11(2), and 13(1)(d) and (g) of that directive—legitimate interests pursued by the controller, such as the protection of the property, health, and life of his family and himself, as in the case in the main proceedings.

35. Consequently, the answer to the question referred is that the second indent of Article 3(2) of Directive 95/46 must be interpreted as meaning that the operation of a camera system, as a result of which a video recording of people is stored on a continuous recording device such as a hard disk drive, installed by an individual on his family home for the purposes of protecting the property, health, and life of the home owners, but which also monitors a public space, does not amount to the processing of data in the course of a purely personal or household activity, for the purposes of that provision.

## Think W3, Ltd. Monetary Penalty Notice

Information Commissioner's office (2014) (United Kingdom)

### Statutory framework

Think W3 Limited ("TW3") is the data controller, as defined in section 1(1) of the Data Protection Act 1998 (the "Act"), in respect of the processing of personal data carried out by TW3 and is referred to in this notice as the "data controller". Section 4(4) of the Act provides that it is the duty of a data controller to comply with the data protection principles in relation to all personal data in respect of which he is the data controller.

Under sections 55A and 55B of the Act the Commissioner may, in certain circumstances, where there has there been a serious contravention of section 4(4) of the Act, serve a monetary penalty notice on a data controller requiring the data controller to pay a monetary penalty of an amount determined by the Commissioner and specified in the notice but not exceeding £500,000 [about $750,000][:]

(1) The Commissioner may serve a data controller with a monetary penalty notice if the Commissioner is satisfied that—

(a) there has been a serious contravention of section 4(4) of the Act by the data controller,

(b) the contravention was of a kind likely to cause substantial damage or substantial distress, and

(c) subsection (2) or (3) applies.

(2) This subsection applies if the contravention was deliberate.

(3) This subsection applies if the data controller—

(a) knew or ought to have known—

(i) that there was a risk that the contravention would occur, and

(ii) that such a contravention would be of a kind likely to cause substantial damage or substantial distress, but

(b) failed to take reasonable steps to prevent the contravention.

**Background**

TW3 is the data controller in respect of the personal data collected from customers of its wholly owned subsidiary and trading brand, Essential Travel Ltd ("ETL"). ETL acts as a booking agent for airport car parking, travel insurance, and other travel-related services that are made available online.

In early 2006 the data controller internally developed a car parking system for ETL to maintain car park rates and availability. The system was for internal purposes only and was installed on the same web server which contained ETL's main e-commerce application used to store customer personal data. In order to facilitate homeworking this system could be accessed via a login page on a non-customer facing website which was publicly available over the internet.

Unfortunately the website login page coding was not secure as it contained a coding error in the authentication scripts of the administrative interface. The data controller conducted functionality tests when the system was implemented but did not carry out security checks and reviews on the system and website coding at the time of implementation, or subsequently. The login page for the website was therefore vulnerable since the system was implemented in early 2006.

The data controller did not subject the web server to appropriate penetration tests or internal vulnerability scans and checks which took place on other servers on the basis that the website and web server were not external facing. However the website (and therefore associated system and web server) could still be discovered and accessed over the internet by anyone with sufficient technical knowledge.

On 21 December 2012 an attacker targeted the website and associated system. The coding error on the website login page enabled the attacker to bypass the authentication process for logging into the system using Structured Query Language injection, and log in to the website's administrative interface.

Having exploited this vulnerability the attacker then proceeded to upload malicious web shells onto the connected web server which gave the attacker administrative access to all of the data held on the web server. These allowed the attacker to access and modify files within ETL's virtual network, including data within the e-commerce application which contained ETL's customer database and files used to process payment cards.

Evidence obtained as a result of the data controller's own internal investigation suggests that the attacker then created a custom file that would query the customer database to extract and decrypt stored cardholder data (both active and expired cards) using the decryption key which was not stored securely on the web server. The attacker targeted credit and debit card primary account numbers, expiry dates, CVV values, and account user names and surnames. Fortunately CVV values were not stored on the database. However following successful extraction of the available data the attacker then extracted other customer details relating to each card, specifically: customer name, address, postcode, mobile and home phone numbers, and email address.

The attacker extracted a total of 1,163,996 credit and debit card records, of which 430,599 were identified as current and 733,397 as expired. Cardholder data had not been deleted from the server since 2006.

The data controller discovered the breach in security on 24 December 2012 during a routine server check which revealed a notification from the antivirus software installed on the server. This resulted in the data controller taking prompt remedial action to lock down the relevant website, systems, and web server in order to prevent any further disclosure of data.

**Grounds on which the Commissioner proposes to serve a monetary penalty notice**

The relevant provision of the Act is the Seventh Data Protection Principle which provides:

> Appropriate technical and organisational measures shall be taken against unauthorised or unlawful processing of personal data and against accidental loss or destruction of, or damage to, personal data.

Paragraph 9 at Part II of Schedule 1 to the Act provides that:

> Having regard to the state of technological development and the cost of implementing any measures, the measures must ensure a level of security appropriate to—
>
> (a) the harm that might result from such unauthorised or unlawful processing or accidental loss, destruction or damage as are mentioned in the seventh principle, and
>
> (b) the nature of the data to be protected.

The Commissioner is satisfied that there has been a serious contravention of the Seventh Data Protection Principle.

In particular, the data controller failed to take appropriate technical measures against the unauthorised or unlawful processing of personal data by failing to:

- Properly understand the extent to which the web server could be accessed via the internet. This led to the data controller deliberately excluding the web server from penetration and vulnerability tests which were carried out on "external-facing" servers,
- Properly test/check/review the security of the coding of the website at the time of, and following, the website's implementation in 2006,
- Implement a suitable intrusion detection system for the website and server,
- Implement suitable file-integrity monitoring software,
- Implement a suitable encryption key-management process,
- Implement a suitable security policy addressing technical security issues,
- Patch software when updates were available,
- Update anti-virus software properly on some desktop systems,
- Fully comply with the requirements of the Payment Card Industry-Data Security Standard.

The contravention is serious because the measures taken by the data controller did not ensure a level of security appropriate to the harm that might result from such unauthorised or unlawful processing, and the nature and volume of the date to be protected.

The Commissioner is satisfied that the contravention is of a kind likely to cause substantial damage or substantial distress.

Active payment card data was obtained. Whilst CVV values were not obtained, and there has been no evidence/confirmation of fraud having taken place as a result of this incident, the personal data that was obtained was clearly of interest to the attacker given the targeted nature of the attack, and could be used for fraudulent transactions/purposes. It is reasonable to assume therefore that it is likely that the attacker would use this information in a manner that would cause substantial damage to the data subjects either in the short or long term.

The data subjects would also be likely to suffer from substantial distress if they were to be informed that their personal data had been accessed by an unauthorised third party and could have been further disclosed even though, so far as the Commissioner is aware, there has been no evidence of fraudulent transactions being conducted as a result of this incident. The knowledge of this access alone is likely to cause substantial distress.

The Commissioner is satisfied that section 55A(3) of the Act applies in that the data controller knew or ought to have known that there was a risk that the contravention would occur, and that such a contravention would be of a kind likely to cause substantial damage or substantial distress, but failed to take reasonable steps to prevent the contravention.

**Aggravating features the Commissioner has taken into account in determining the amount of a monetary penalty**

*Impact on the data controller*

- Data controller is a limited company [the UK equivalent of a corporation] so liability to pay a monetary penalty will not fall on any individual.
- Data controller has access to sufficient financial resources to pay a monetary penalty up to the maximum without causing undue financial hardship.

**Mitigating features the Commissioner has taken into account in determining the amount of the monetary penalty**

*Nature of the contravention*

- The data controller's systems were subjected to a criminal attack.
- No previous similar security breach that the Commissioner is aware of.

*Effect of the contravention*

- No evidence or confirmation has been received that the personal data has been used for fraudulent transactions.

*Behavioural issues*

- Voluntarily reported to Commissioner's office
- The data controller has been co-operative with the Commissioner's office.
- The data controller promptly locked down the website and associated systems when the breach was discovered and

escalated the matter quickly despite the timing of the incident.

*Impact on the data controller*

- Significant impact on reputation of data controller as a result of this security breach.

**Other considerations**

The Commissioner's underlying objective in imposing a monetary penalty notice is to promote compliance with the Act and this is an opportunity to reinforce the need for data controllers to ensure that appropriate and effective security measures are applied to personal data stored on their information technology systems.

**Amount of the monetary penalty**

The Commissioner considers that the contravention of the seventh data protection principle is very serious and that the imposition of a monetary penalty is appropriate. Further that a monetary penalty in the sum of £150,000 [about $225,000] is reasonable and proportionate given the particular facts of the case and the underlying objective in imposing the penalty. In reaching this decision, the Commissioner considered other cases of a similar nature in which a monetary penalty had been imposed, and the facts and aggravating and mitigating features referred to above.

## Case Study: Swan Leisure

2011 Annual Report, Office of the Data Protection Commissioner (Ireland)

In October 2010 I received a complaint from an individual in relation to a leisure centre, Swan Leisure in Rathmines, refusing him and his child entry to its swimming pool because he declined to complete its Guest Registration Form. The complainant provided a copy of the Guest Registration Form. The first page of the form requested details such as the individual's name, address, date of birth, email, and mobile phone number. The second page consisted of a list of medical-related questions such as the person's family medical history of heart disease, respiratory disease, and diabetes, the extent to which they may be overweight, and details of their lifestyle. The complainant refused to complete the registration form because he considered it to be too intrusive as it required him to divulge sensitive, personal medical information. He said that he should be able to take his child for a swim without having to provide sensitive personal information.

Section 2(1)(c) of the Data Protection Acts, 1988 and 2003 provides that data "shall be adequate, relevant, and not excessive" in relation to the purpose for which it is kept. My Office informed Swan Leisure that we considered its practice of requesting the aforementioned information to be excessive. In addition we pointed out that medical data is deemed to be sensitive personal data and its processing is subject to additional safeguards under the Acts. We asked the leisure centre to outline to us the basis on which medical data was sought and how the processing of that information complied with its obligations under the Acts.

In its reasoning for asking guests who attend the facility to provide their name and contact information, Swan Leisure referred to its Child Protection Policy. It indicated that in order to safeguard children attending its facilities it was imperative that it take a record of everyone that came onto the premises. It was not clear to us how having the name and address of every person attending the facility was relevant to child protection. In relation to the medical screening forms, the leisure centre informed us that the reason for requesting guests' medical data was to help prevent injuries or medical issues arising from the use of its facilities. It also referred to advice given by the American College of Sports Medicine (1976) stating that anyone who has risk factors for heart disease (a family history of heart disease, a history of smoking, high blood pressure or high blood fat levels) should be given a full medical examination before exercising in a health club. The leisure centre informed us that it was collecting medical information under Section 2(B)1 of the Acts which, among other things, allows the processing of sensitive personal data where the processing is necessary to prevent injury or other damage to the health of the data subject or another person.

Having reviewed its response, we told Swan Leisure that its policy of recording the name, contact details, and medical information of all of its patrons was unacceptable. We acknowledged the importance of protecting children and safeguarding the health and well-being of patrons during the use of the leisure facilities. However, we informed it that from a data protection perspective, the systematic recording of patrons' information was a disproportionate response to the aims it sought to further, i.e. health promotion and the protection of children. We further informed the leisure centre that the request for such information could not be justified by reference to the policy guidelines and academic commentary it had cited.

In its response, the Centre referred to the Institute of Leisure and Amenity Management (ILAM) facility standards. Following further communications with my Office, the leisure centre subsequently confirmed that in order for it to meet both ILAM's guidelines and the Data Protection Guidelines it had changed its policy so that it now offers a guest register form. However, the completion of this form is no longer a condition of entry to the leisure centre and the right of patrons not to provide the personal information requested is respected. In relation to the forms already completed prior to the introduction of this change, it informed us that guests would be given the option to have their data deleted at any point during or after their time with the centre. As a result of this complaint, members of the public may now use the swimming pool at the leisure centre on an anonymous basis and that is as it should be.

## NOTES

1. ***Different Forms of Enforcement.*** The three proceedings excerpted above involved three different forms of enforcement in three different EU countries. In *Ryneš*, the complaint grew out of criminal proceedings in the Czech Republic using footage from the disputed home CCTV camera as evidence. After the national DPA ruled the camera unlawful, Ryneš appealed to national courts, which referred the question to EU courts. In *Think W3*, a company that had suffered a security breach reported it to the UK data protection authority, the Information Commissioner's Office (ICO). The breach was big news in the UK because of its size and the severity of the theft. The ICO imposed a fine, which is somewhat unusual under British data protection law but not unheard of. Finally, the DPA in the Republic of Ireland responded to a consumer complaint and worked out a satisfactory resolution by reaching an agreement with the data controller about changes in its practices. All of these modes of enforcement can be found in most EU countries. Note, however, the central role of the DPA in all types of disputes, whether they began in court, from self-reporting, or out of a consumer complaint.

2. ***Writing Style.*** The rhetorical style of many European legal documents can take some getting used to for American lawyers. Some of this comes from the realities of EU documents, which must be capable of translation into numerous languages, so can sometimes read as stilted. But it also stems from the different views of the role of the judge in common law systems and civil law systems. Civil law judges are technicians. Most EU member states (although not the UK or Ireland) use civil law in their own courts. EU courts theoretically use a mixture, but judges do tend to gravitate toward reasoning that reflects their legal training. In most civil law countries, judges join the judiciary at the beginning of their legal careers and work their way up to higher positions, like other civil servants. This is quite different from judges in common law cultures such as the UK, the US, and many other former parts of the British Empire around the world, where judges often are distinguished former litigators. Broadly speaking, US readers tend to consider EU and civil law opinions a bit dry, narrow, and technocratic; readers from a civil law tradition can find US and common law opinions flowery, abstract, and arbitrary. Meanwhile, European regulatory documents like *Think W3* and *Swan Leisure* often are more *informal* than their US analogues. To an American, they may feel more like interoffice memos than official legal determinations. Reading non-US legal documents is a skill worth learning in an increasingly international economy. It also helps an American lawyer to perceive that there are many alternative ways to present legal rulings, and that there is nothing magical or inevitable about the form of the judicial or administrative rulings we spend so much time reading and analyzing in the US, both in law school and in practice.

3. ***EU Courts.*** The EU's judicial structure is complex. Further confusing matters, the Treaty of Lisbon made many significant changes to the judiciary when it was ratified in 2009, even extending to the names of various institutions. The overall judicial system of the EU is now known as the Court of Justice of the European Union (CJEU), and the highest court

within the CJEU is the Court of Justice. There are 28 judges on the Court of Justice, who sit in "chambers" of three or five justices for more routine cases or in a "Grand Chamber" of 15 judges for more significant cases. The Court's interpretations of EU law, such as the Data Protection Directive, are binding on member states.

4. ***A Textual Approach.*** Notice how closely all these rulings, judicial and regulatory, stick to statutory language. The EU Charter, the Data Protection Directive, and national data protection law all provide quite specific parameters for the enforcement of data protection rights. In part, as noted at the beginning of the chapter, this is a result of a structure where data practices must be justified under law in every case. It also stems in part, once again, from differences between common law and civil law traditions. In general, civil law prioritizes constitutional or statutory text over judicial interpretation, and typically recognizes only rights that can be traced to such authoritative textual sources. In comparison, the FTC relies on fluid consumer protection standards of deception and unfairness—some would call them vague. What are the advantages and disadvantages of each approach to privacy and data protection law?

5. ***Before and After* Ryneš.** Prior to the CJEU decision in *Ryneš* there had been different interpretations of the "personal or household activity" exemption in different EU countries; the UK and Ireland would have allowed the use of a CCTV camera to monitor the home while Austria, Belgium, and Spain would not. The CJEU made it clear that the exemption did not apply to allow the camera, because that provision needed to be interpreted narrowly. Yet there are other potential arguments that the camera at the Ryneš home was lawful under the Directive. Can you identify them? When the case returned to the Czech courts, they ruled in Ryneš' favor. Although the "personal or household" exemption was inapplicable, meaning the DPA had authority over the CCTV camera, the court balanced protection of property, home, and life against the data protection rights of passersby. Because the camera could not be an effective means of protection without viewing part of a public area, and especially in light of previous attacks against Ryneš, a crusading journalist, the court decided the camera was lawful.

6. ***The US-EU Comparison.*** Consider each of the three data protection decisions excerpted above. How do you think each would be resolved under US law? By what legal mechanism—courts, the FTC, some other regulator?

## 3. FRONTIERS IN EU DATA PROTECTION LAW

The next several years will be a period of great upheaval in EU data protection law. Europe-wide courts have issued several recent blockbuster decisions that disrupted the law further. One of these, excerpted below, established the "right to be forgotten" as a feature of the current Data Protection Directive. Around the same time, the European Court of Human Rights invalidated a different EU directive concerning data retention [see Chapter 1]. Most recently of all, the Court of Justice of the European Union overturned the European Commission's agreement with the US concerning transatlantic data transfers [see Chapter 8]. All of this activity is sure to change EU data protection law significantly. On top of these developments, the upcoming transition to the General Data Protection Regulation is sure to be eventful, as data processors assess their new obligations and prepare, while at the same time continuing to comply with the Directive, which remains the applicable law until the GDPR takes effect in 2018.

## Google Spain SL v. AEPD

Court of Justice of the European Union, 2014 E.C.R.

1. This request for a preliminary ruling concerns the interpretation of Article 2(b) and (d), Article 4(1)(a) and (c), Article 12(b), and subparagraph (a) of the first paragraph of Article 14 of [Directive 95/46, also known as the Data Protection Directive] and of Article 8 of the Charter of Fundamental Rights of the European Union ("the Charter").

2. The request has been made in proceedings between, on the one hand, Google Spain SL ("Google Spain") and Google Inc. and, on the other, the Agencia Española de Protección de Datos (Spanish Data Protection Agency; "the AEPD") and Mr. Costeja González concerning a decision by the AEPD upholding the complaint lodged by Mr. Costeja González against those two companies and ordering Google Inc. to adopt the measures necessary to withdraw personal data relating to Mr. Costeja González from its index and to prevent access to the data in the future.

13. Directive 95/46 was transposed into Spanish Law by Organic Law No 15/1999 of 13 December 1999 on the protection of personal data.

**The dispute in the main proceedings and the questions referred for a preliminary ruling**

14. On 5 March 2010, Mr. Costeja González, a Spanish national resident in Spain, lodged with the AEPD a complaint against La Vanguardia Ediciones SL, which publishes a daily newspaper with a large circulation, in particular in Catalonia (Spain) ("La Vanguardia"), and against Google Spain and Google Inc. The complaint was based on the fact that, when an internet user entered Mr. Costeja González's name in the search engine of the Google group ("Google Search"), he would obtain links to two pages of La Vanguardia's newspaper, of 19 January and 9 March 1998 respectively, on which an announcement mentioning Mr. Costeja González's name appeared for a real-estate auction connected with attachment proceedings for the recovery of social security debts.

15. By that complaint, Mr. Costeja González requested, first, that La Vanguardia be required either to remove or alter those pages so that

the personal data relating to him no longer appeared or to use certain tools made available by search engines in order to protect the data. Second, he requested that Google Spain or Google Inc. be required to remove or conceal the personal data relating to him so that they ceased to be included in the search results and no longer appeared in the links to La Vanguardia. Mr. Costeja González stated in this context that the attachment proceedings concerning him had been fully resolved for a number of years and that reference to them was now entirely irrelevant.

16. By decision of 30 July 2010, the AEPD rejected the complaint in so far as it related to La Vanguardia, taking the view that the publication by it of the information in question was legally justified as it took place upon order of the Ministry of Labour and Social Affairs and was intended to give maximum publicity to the auction in order to secure as many bidders as possible.

17. On the other hand, the complaint was upheld in so far as it was directed against Google Spain and Google Inc. The AEPD considered in this regard that operators of search engines are subject to data protection legislation given that they carry out data processing for which they are responsible and act as intermediaries in the information society. The AEPD took the view that it has the power to require the withdrawal of data and the prohibition of access to certain data by the operators of search engines when it considers that the locating and dissemination of the data are liable to compromise the fundamental right to data protection and the dignity of persons in the broad sense, and this would also encompass the mere wish of the person concerned that such data not be known to third parties. The AEPD considered that that obligation may be owed directly by operators of search engines, without it being necessary to erase the data or information from the website where they appear, including when retention of the information on that site is justified by a statutory provision.

18. Google Spain and Google Inc. brought separate actions against that decision before the Audiencia Nacional ([Spanish] National High Court).

19. That court states in the order for reference that the actions raise the question of what obligations are owed by operators of search engines to protect personal data of persons concerned who do not wish that certain information, which is published on third parties' websites and contains personal data relating to them that enable that information to be linked to them, be located, indexed, and made available to internet users indefinitely. The answer to that question depends on the way in which Directive 95/46 must be interpreted in the context of these technologies, which appeared after the directive's publication. [The Spanish court's questions, numbered 1–3 and subdivided into sub-parts, are reviewed below—but not in the order they are numbered.]

## Consideration of the questions referred

### Question 2(a) and (b), concerning the material scope of Directive 95/46

21. By Question 2(a) and (b), the referring court asks, in essence, whether Article 2(b) of Directive 95/46 is to be interpreted as meaning that the activity of a search engine as a provider of content which consists in finding information published or placed on the internet by third parties, indexing it automatically, storing it temporarily and, finally, making it available to internet users according to a particular order of preference must be classified as "processing of personal data" within the meaning of that provision when that information contains personal data. If the answer is in the affirmative, the referring court seeks to ascertain furthermore whether Article 2(d) of Directive 95/46 is to be interpreted as meaning that the operator of a search engine must be regarded as the "controller" in respect of that processing of the personal data, within the meaning of that provision.

22. According to Google Spain and Google Inc., the activity of search engines cannot be regarded as processing of the data which appear on third parties' web pages displayed in the list of search results, given that search engines process all the information available on the internet without effecting a selection between personal data and other information. Furthermore, even if that activity must be classified as 'data processing', the operator of a search engine cannot be regarded as a 'controller' in respect of that processing since it has no knowledge of those data and does not exercise control over the data.

23. On the other hand, Mr. Costeja González, the Spanish, Italian, Austrian and Polish Governments, and the European Commission consider that that activity quite clearly involves 'data processing' within the meaning of Directive 95/46, which is distinct from the data processing by the publishers of websites and pursues different objectives from such processing. [They argue that] the operator of a search engine is the "controller" in respect of the data processing carried out by it since it is the operator that determines the purposes and means of that processing.

24. In the Greek Government's submission, the activity in question constitutes such "processing," but inasmuch as search engines serve merely as intermediaries, the undertakings which operate them cannot be regarded as "controllers," except where they store data in an "intermediate memory" or "cache memory" for a period which exceeds that which is technically necessary.

25. Article 2(b) of Directive 95/46 defines "processing of personal data" as "any operation or set of operations which is performed upon personal data, whether or not by automatic means, such as collection, recording, organisation, storage, adaptation or alteration, retrieval, consultation, use, disclosure by transmission, dissemination or otherwise

making available, alignment or combination, blocking, erasure, or destruction."

26. As regards in particular the internet, the Court has already had occasion to state that the operation of loading personal data on an internet page must be considered to be such 'processing' within the meaning of Article 2(b) of Directive 95/46 (see Case C–101/01 *Lindqvist* EU:C:2003:596, paragraph 25).

27. It is not contested that the data found, indexed, and stored by search engines and made available to their users include information relating to identified or identifiable natural persons and thus "personal data" within the meaning of Article 2(a) of that directive.

28. Therefore, it must be found that, in exploring the internet automatically, constantly and systematically in search of the information which is published there, the operator of a search engine "collects" such data which it subsequently "retrieves," "records," and "organizes" within the framework of its indexing programmes, "stores" on its servers and, as the case may be, "discloses" and "makes available" to its users in the form of lists of search results. As those operations are referred to expressly and unconditionally in Article 2(b) of Directive 95/46, they must be classified as "processing" within the meaning of that provision, regardless of the fact that the operator of the search engine also carries out the same operations in respect of other types of information and does not distinguish between the latter and the personal data.

29. Nor is the foregoing finding affected by the fact that those data have already been published on the internet and are not altered by the search engine.

32. As to the question whether the operator of a search engine must be regarded as the "controller" in respect of the processing of personal data that is carried out by that engine in the context of an activity such as that at issue in the main proceedings, it should be recalled that Article 2(d) of Directive 95/46 defines "controller" as "the natural or legal person, public authority, agency or any other body which alone or jointly with others determines the purposes and means of the processing of personal data."

33. It is the search engine operator which determines the purposes and means of that activity and thus of the processing of personal data that it itself carries out within the framework of that activity and which must, consequently, be regarded as the "controller" in respect of that processing pursuant to Article 2(d).

34. Furthermore, it would be contrary not only to the clear wording of that provision but also to its objective—which is to ensure, through a broad definition of the concept of "controller," effective and complete protection of data subjects—to exclude the operator of a search engine from that definition on the ground that it does not exercise control over the personal data published on the web pages of third parties.

35. In this connection, it should be pointed out that the processing of personal data carried out in the context of the activity of a search engine can be distinguished from and is additional to that carried out by publishers of websites, consisting in loading those data on an internet page.

36. Moreover, it is undisputed that that activity of search engines plays a decisive role in the overall dissemination of those data in that it renders the latter accessible to any internet user making a search on the basis of the data subject's name, including to internet users who otherwise would not have found the web page on which those data are published.

37. Also, the organisation and aggregation of information published on the internet that are effected by search engines with the aim of facilitating their users' access to that information may, when users carry out their search on the basis of an individual's name, result in them obtaining through the list of results a structured overview of the information relating to that individual that can be found on the internet enabling them to establish a more or less detailed profile of the data subject.

38. Inasmuch as the activity of a search engine is therefore liable to affect significantly, and additionally compared with that of the publishers of websites, the fundamental rights to privacy and to the protection of personal data, the operator of the search engine as the person determining the purposes and means of that activity must ensure, within the framework of its responsibilities, powers, and capabilities, that the activity meets the requirements of Directive 95/46 in order that the guarantees laid down by the directive may have full effect and that effective and complete protection of data subjects, in particular of their right to privacy, may actually be achieved.

39. Finally, the fact that publishers of websites have the option of indicating to operators of search engines, by means in particular of exclusion protocols such as 'robot.txt' or codes such as 'noindex' or 'noarchive', that they wish specific information published on their site to be wholly or partially excluded from the search engines' automatic indexes does not mean that, if publishers of websites do not so indicate, the operator of a search engine is released from its responsibility for the processing of personal data that it carries out in the context of the engine's activity.

40. That fact does not alter the position that the purposes and means of that processing are determined by the operator of the search engine. Furthermore, even if that option for publishers of websites were to mean that they determine the means of that processing jointly with that operator, this finding would not remove any of the latter's responsibility as Article 2(d) of Directive 95/46 expressly provides that that determination may be made "alone or jointly with others."

41. It follows from all the foregoing considerations that the answer to Question 2(a) and (b) is that Article 2(b) and (d) of Directive 95/46 are to be interpreted as meaning that, first, the activity of a search engine consisting in finding information published or placed on the internet by third parties, indexing it automatically, storing it temporarily and, finally, making it available to internet users according to a particular order of preference must be classified as "processing of personal data" within the meaning of Article 2(b) when that information contains personal data and, second, the operator of the search engine must be regarded as the "controller" in respect of that processing, within the meaning of Article 2(d).

**Question 1(a) to (d), concerning the territorial scope of Directive 95/46**

42. By Question 1(a) to (d), the referring court seeks to establish whether it is possible to apply the national legislation transposing Directive 95/46 in circumstances such as those at issue in the main proceedings.

43. In this respect, the referring court has established the following facts:

- Google Search is offered worldwide through the website "www.google.com." In numerous States, a local version adapted to the national language exists. The version of Google Search in Spanish is offered through the website "www.google.es," which has been registered since 16 September 2003. Google Search is one of the most used search engines in Spain.
- Google Search is operated by Google Inc., which is the parent company of the Google Group and has its seat in the United States.
- Google Search indexes websites throughout the world, including websites located in Spain. The information indexed by its "web crawlers" or robots, that is to say, computer programmes used to locate and sweep up the content of web pages methodically and automatically, is stored temporarily on servers whose State of location is unknown, that being kept secret for reasons of competition.
- Google Search does not merely give access to content hosted on the indexed websites, but takes advantage of that activity and includes, in return for payment, advertising associated with the internet users' search terms, for undertakings which wish to use that tool in order to offer their goods or services to the internet users.
- The Google group has recourse to its subsidiary Google Spain for promoting the sale of advertising space generated on the website "www.google.com." Google Spain, which was

established on 3 September 2003 and possesses separate legal personality, has its seat in Madrid (Spain). Its activities are targeted essentially at undertakings based in Spain, acting as a commercial agent for the Google group in that Member State.

- Google Inc. designated Google Spain as the controller, in Spain, in respect of two filing systems registered by Google Inc. with the AEPD; those filing systems were intended to contain the personal data of the customers who had concluded contracts for advertising services with Google Inc.

49. It is not disputed that Google Spain engages in the effective and real exercise of activity through stable arrangements in Spain. As it moreover has separate legal personality, it constitutes a subsidiary of Google Inc. on Spanish territory and, therefore, an "establishment" within the meaning of Article 4(1)(a) of Directive 95/46.

50. In order to satisfy the criterion laid down in that provision, it is also necessary that the processing of personal data by the controller be "carried out in the context of the activities" of an establishment of the controller on the territory of a Member State.

51. Google Spain and Google Inc. dispute that this is the case since the processing of personal data at issue in the main proceedings is carried out exclusively by Google Inc., which operates Google Search without any intervention on the part of Google Spain; the latter's activity is limited to providing support to the Google group's advertising activity which is separate from its search engine service.

52. Nevertheless, as the Spanish Government and the Commission in particular have pointed out, Article 4(1)(a) of Directive 95/46 does not require the processing of personal data in question to be carried out "by" the establishment concerned itself, but only that it be carried out "in the context of the activities" of the establishment.

53. Furthermore, in the light of the objective of Directive 95/46 of ensuring effective and complete protection of the fundamental rights and freedoms of natural persons, and in particular their right to privacy, with respect to the processing of personal data, those words cannot be interpreted restrictively.

57. As has been stated in paragraphs 26 to 28 of the present judgment, the very display of personal data on a search results page constitutes processing of such data. Since that display of results is accompanied, on the same page, by the display of advertising linked to the search terms, it is clear that the processing of personal data in question is carried out in the context of the commercial and advertising activity of the controller's establishment on the territory of a Member State, in this instance Spanish territory.

58. That being so, it cannot be accepted that the processing of personal data carried out for the purposes of the operation of the search engine should escape the obligations and guarantees laid down by Directive 95/46, which would compromise the directive's effectiveness and the effective and complete protection of the fundamental rights and freedoms of natural persons which the directive seeks to ensure, in particular their right to privacy, with respect to the processing of personal data, a right to which the directive accords special importance.

**Question 2(c) and (d), concerning the extent of the responsibility of the operator of a search engine under Directive 95/46**

62. By Question 2(c) and (d), the referring court asks, in essence, whether Article 12(b) and subparagraph (a) of the first paragraph of Article 14 of Directive 95/46 are to be interpreted as meaning that, in order to comply with the rights laid down in those provisions, the operator of a search engine is obliged to remove from the list of results displayed following a search made on the basis of a person's name links to web pages, published by third parties and containing information relating to that person, also in a case where that name or information is not erased beforehand or simultaneously from those web pages, and even, as the case may be, when its publication in itself on those pages is lawful.

63. Google Spain and Google Inc. submit that, by virtue of the principle of proportionality, any request seeking the removal of information must be addressed to the publisher of the website concerned, because it is he who takes the responsibility for making the information public, who is in a position to appraise the lawfulness of that publication and who has available to him the most effective and least restrictive means of making the information inaccessible. Furthermore, to require the operator of a search engine to withdraw information published on the internet from its indexes would take insufficient account of the fundamental rights of publishers of websites, of other internet users and of that operator itself.

64. According to the Austrian Government, a national supervisory authority may order such an operator to erase information published by third parties from its filing systems only if the data in question have been found previously to be unlawful or incorrect or if the data subject has made a successful objection to the publisher of the website on which that information was published.

65. Mr. Costeja González, the Spanish, Italian, and Polish Governments, and the Commission submit that the national authority may directly order the operator of a search engine to withdraw from its indexes and intermediate memory information containing personal data that has been published by third parties, without having to approach beforehand or simultaneously the publisher of the web page on which that information appears. Furthermore, according to Mr. Costeja González, the Spanish and Italian Governments, and the Commission, the fact that the information has been published lawfully and that it still

appears on the original web page has no effect on the obligations of that operator under Directive 95/46. On the other hand, according to the Polish Government that fact is such as to release the operator from its obligations.

[The Court then reviewed relevant provisions of the Charter and the Directive.]

80. It must be pointed out at the outset that, as has been found in paragraphs 36 to 38 of the present judgment, processing of personal data, such as that at issue in the main proceedings, carried out by the operator of a search engine is liable to affect significantly the fundamental rights to privacy and to the protection of personal data when the search by means of that engine is carried out on the basis of an individual's name, since that processing enables any internet user to obtain through the list of results a structured overview of the information relating to that individual that can be found on the internet—information which potentially concerns a vast number of aspects of his private life and which, without the search engine, could not have been interconnected or could have been only with great difficulty—and thereby to establish a more or less detailed profile of him. Furthermore, the effect of the interference with those rights of the data subject is heightened on account of the important role played by the internet and search engines in modern society, which render the information contained in such a list of results ubiquitous.

81. In the light of the potential seriousness of that interference, it is clear that it cannot be justified by merely the economic interest which the operator of such an engine has in that processing. However, inasmuch as the removal of links from the list of results could, depending on the information at issue, have effects upon the legitimate interest of internet users potentially interested in having access to that information, in situations such as that at issue in the main proceedings a fair balance should be sought in particular between that interest and the data subject's fundamental rights under Articles 7 and 8 of the Charter. Whilst it is true that the data subject's rights protected by those articles also override, as a general rule, that interest of internet users, that balance may however depend, in specific cases, on the nature of the information in question and its sensitivity for the data subject's private life and on the interest of the public in having that information, an interest which may vary, in particular, according to the role played by the data subject in public life.

82. Following the appraisal of the conditions for the application of Article 12(b) and subparagraph (a) of the first paragraph of Article 14 of Directive 95/46 which is to be carried out when a request such as that at issue in the main proceedings is lodged with it, the supervisory authority or judicial authority may order the operator of the search engine to remove from the list of results displayed following a search made on the basis of a person's name links to web pages published by third parties

containing information relating to that person, without an order to that effect presupposing the previous or simultaneous removal of that name and information—of the publisher's own accord or following an order of one of those authorities—from the web page on which they were published.

83. As has been established in paragraphs 35 to 38 of the present judgment, inasmuch as the data processing carried out in the context of the activity of a search engine can be distinguished from and is additional to that carried out by publishers of websites and affects the data subject's fundamental rights additionally, the operator of the search engine as the controller in respect of that processing must ensure, within the framework of its responsibilities, powers, and capabilities, that that processing meets the requirements of Directive 95/46, in order that the guarantees laid down by the directive may have full effect.

84. Given the ease with which information published on a website can be replicated on other sites and the fact that the persons responsible for its publication are not always subject to European Union legislation, effective and complete protection of data users could not be achieved if the latter had to obtain first or in parallel the erasure of the information relating to them from the publishers of websites.

85. Furthermore, the processing by the publisher of a web page consisting in the publication of information relating to an individual may, in some circumstances, be carried out "solely for journalistic purposes" and thus benefit, by virtue of Article 9 of Directive 95/46, from derogations from the requirements laid down by the directive, whereas that does not appear to be so in the case of the processing carried out by the operator of a search engine. It cannot therefore be ruled out that in certain circumstances the data subject is capable of exercising the rights referred to in Article 12(b) and subparagraph (a) of the first paragraph of Article 14 of Directive 95/46 against that operator but not against the publisher of the web page.

86. Finally, it must be stated that not only does the ground, under Article 7 of Directive 95/46, justifying the publication of a piece of personal data on a website not necessarily coincide with that which is applicable to the activity of search engines, but also, even where that is the case, the outcome of the weighing of the interests at issue to be carried out under Article 7(f) and subparagraph (a) of the first paragraph of Article 14 of the directive may differ according to whether the processing carried out by the operator of a search engine or that carried out by the publisher of the web page is at issue, given that, first, the legitimate interests justifying the processing may be different and, second, the consequences of the processing for the data subject, and in particular for his private life, are not necessarily the same.

87. Indeed, since the inclusion in the list of results, displayed following a search made on the basis of a person's name, of a web page and of the information contained on it relating to that person makes

access to that information appreciably easier for any internet user making a search in respect of the person concerned and may play a decisive role in the dissemination of that information, it is liable to constitute a more significant interference with the data subject's fundamental right to privacy than the publication on the web page.

88. In the light of all the foregoing considerations, the answer to Question 2(c) and (d) is that Article 12(b) and subparagraph (a) of the first paragraph of Article 14 of Directive 95/46 are to be interpreted as meaning that, in order to comply with the rights laid down in those provisions and in so far as the conditions laid down by those provisions are in fact satisfied, the operator of a search engine is obliged to remove from the list of results displayed following a search made on the basis of a person's name links to web pages, published by third parties and containing information relating to that person, also in a case where that name or information is not erased beforehand or simultaneously from those web pages, and even, as the case may be, when its publication in itself on those pages is lawful.

**Question 3, concerning the scope of the data subject's rights guaranteed by Directive 95/46**

89. By Question 3, the referring court asks, in essence, whether Article 12(b) and subparagraph (a) of the first paragraph of Article 14 of Directive 95/46 are to be interpreted as enabling the data subject to require the operator of a search engine to remove from the list of results displayed following a search made on the basis of his name links to web pages published lawfully by third parties and containing true information relating to him, on the ground that that information may be prejudicial to him or that he wishes it to be "forgotten" after a certain time.

90. Google Spain, Google Inc., the Greek, Austrian, and Polish Governments and the Commission consider that this question should be answered in the negative. Google Spain, Google Inc., the Polish Government and the Commission submit in this regard that Article 12(b) and subparagraph (a) of the first paragraph of Article 14 of Directive 95/46 confer rights upon data subjects only if the processing in question is incompatible with the directive or on compelling legitimate grounds relating to their particular situation, and not merely because they consider that that processing may be prejudicial to them or they wish that the data being processed sink into oblivion. The Greek and Austrian Governments submit that the data subject must approach the publisher of the website concerned.

91. According to Mr. Costeja González and the Spanish and Italian Governments, the data subject may oppose the indexing by a search engine of personal data relating to him where their dissemination through the search engine is prejudicial to him and his fundamental rights to the protection of those data and to privacy—which encompass the "right to be forgotten"—override the legitimate interests of the

operator of the search engine and the general interest in freedom of information.

92. As regards Article 12(b) of Directive 95/46, the application of which is subject to the condition that the processing of personal data be incompatible with the directive, it should be recalled that, as has been noted in paragraph 72 of the present judgment, such incompatibility may result not only from the fact that such data are inaccurate but, in particular, also from the fact that they are inadequate, irrelevant or excessive in relation to the purposes of the processing, that they are not kept up to date, or that they are kept for longer than is necessary unless they are required to be kept for historical, statistical or scientific purposes.

93. It follows from those requirements, laid down in Article 6(1)(c) to (e) of Directive 95/46, that even initially lawful processing of accurate data may, in the course of time, become incompatible with the directive where those data are no longer necessary in the light of the purposes for which they were collected or processed. That is so in particular where they appear to be inadequate, irrelevant or no longer relevant, or excessive in relation to those purposes and in the light of the time that has elapsed.

94. Therefore, if it is found, following a request by the data subject pursuant to Article 12(b) of Directive 95/46, that the inclusion in the list of results displayed following a search made on the basis of his name of the links to web pages published lawfully by third parties and containing true information relating to him personally is, at this point in time, incompatible with Article 6(1)(c) to (e) of the directive because that information appears, having regard to all the circumstances of the case, to be inadequate, irrelevant or no longer relevant, or excessive in relation to the purposes of the processing at issue carried out by the operator of the search engine, the information and links concerned in the list of results must be erased.

95. It must be pointed out that in each case the processing of personal data must be authorised under Article 7 for the entire period during which it is carried out.

96. In the light of the foregoing, when appraising such requests made in order to oppose processing such as that at issue in the main proceedings, it should in particular be examined whether the data subject has a right that the information relating to him personally should, at this point in time, no longer be linked to his name by a list of results displayed following a search made on the basis of his name. In this connection, it must be pointed out that it is not necessary in order to find such a right that the inclusion of the information in question in the list of results causes prejudice to the data subject.

97. As the data subject may, in the light of his fundamental rights under Articles 7 and 8 of the Charter, request that the information in

question no longer be made available to the general public by its inclusion in such a list of results, it should be held, as follows in particular from paragraph 81 of the present judgment, that those rights override, as a rule, not only the economic interest of the operator of the search engine but also the interest of the general public in finding that information upon a search relating to the data subject's name. However, that would not be the case if it appeared, for particular reasons, such as the role played by the data subject in public life, that the interference with his fundamental rights is justified by the preponderant interest of the general public in having, on account of inclusion in the list of results, access to the information in question.

98. As regards a situation such as that at issue in the main proceedings, which concerns the display, in the list of results that the internet user obtains by making a search by means of Google Search on the basis of the data subject's name, of links to pages of the on-line archives of a daily newspaper that contain announcements mentioning the data subject's name and relating to a real-estate auction connected with attachment proceedings for the recovery of social security debts, it should be held that, having regard to the sensitivity for the data subject's private life of the information contained in those announcements and to the fact that its initial publication had taken place 16 years earlier, the data subject establishes a right that that information should no longer be linked to his name by means of such a list. Accordingly, since in the case in point there do not appear to be particular reasons substantiating a preponderant interest of the public in having, in the context of such a search, access to that information, a matter which is, however, for the referring court to establish, the data subject may, by virtue of Article 12(b) and subparagraph (a) of the first paragraph of Article 14 of Directive 95/46, require those links to be removed from the list of results.

99. It follows from the foregoing considerations that the answer to Question 3 is that Article 12(b) and subparagraph (a) of the first paragraph of Article 14 of Directive 95/46 are to be interpreted as meaning that, when appraising the conditions for the application of those provisions, it should inter alia be examined whether the data subject has a right that the information in question relating to him personally should, at this point in time, no longer be linked to his name by a list of results displayed following a search made on the basis of his name, without it being necessary in order to find such a right that the inclusion of the information in question in that list causes prejudice to the data subject. As the data subject may, in the light of his fundamental rights under Articles 7 and 8 of the Charter, request that the information in question no longer be made available to the general public on account of its inclusion in such a list of results, those rights override, as a rule, not only the economic interest of the operator of the search engine but also the interest of the general public in having access to that information upon a search relating to the data subject's name. However, that would

not be the case if it appeared, for particular reasons, such as the role played by the data subject in public life, that the interference with his fundamental rights is justified by the preponderant interest of the general public in having, on account of its inclusion in the list of results, access to the information in question.

## NOTES

1. ***An Unexpected Ruling.*** The breadth of the *Google Spain* decision greatly surprised most observers. There had been a general concept of such a deletion right in the law of several continental countries—"le droit a l'oubli" in French or "derecho al olvidado" in Spanish, translated more literally as a "right to oblivion," but better known in English as the "right to be forgotten." At the time of *Google Spain*, a debate about adding such a right to the explicit text of the GDPR had become a major point of controversy. Thus it was unexpected for the Court to find that the right existed under EU law *already*. Moreover, procedures at the CJEU typically include the issuance of a preliminary opinion by a staff member called the advocate general, whose views usually prove very influential with the Court. Not this time, however: the advocate general had recommended a ruling largely favorable to Google, but the Court reached a different conclusion.

2. ***Parsing Definitions.*** The Court's answer to Questions 2(a) and 2(b) turns on technical statutory interpretation, but it is crucial to the decision and important for understanding the breadth of the Directive more generally. Note how close the decision stays to the language of the Directive. The Court emphasizes that "processing" is defined broadly, encompassing a host of activities. It considers irrelevant the fact that much of the data Google processes cannot be understood as personal data, because the rest of it can, including the information about Costeja González. In paragraph 28, the Court lists numerous verbs that qualify as forms of processing, many of which can be said to apply to a search engine. Then in paragraph 32, the Court finds Google is a "data controller," quoting language from the Directive which defines that term to include anyone who "determines the purposes and means of the processing of personal data." All of these interpretations are links in the logical chain that leads to the Court's ultimate result.

3. ***Territoriality.*** The Court's response to Question 1, about territoriality and enforcement, received less attention than the recognition of the right to be forgotten, but it has the potential to be even more significant. Google Spain SL is a small operation with about 75 employees. Google Inc. argued that the activities of this Madrid office—primarily selling advertising—were not connected to the data processing at issue in the case, which was the operation of the search engine itself. The Court, reading the "in the context of" language from Article 4 broadly, rejected this argument. Does that mean that any presence of a company in an EU country might make its global operations subject to the Data Protection Directive, at least when personal data from people in the EU is concerned? If not, what are the limits after *Google Spain*?

4. ***Google's Response.*** After the *Google Spain* decision, Google announced that it would evaluate requests for deletion of links from EU citizens on a case-by-case basis. The company maintains a page where it reports statistics about such requests and anonymized examples of those it has granted and rejected. As of April 2016, Google had received over 420,000 requests, concerning links to almost 1.5 million individual URLs. *See* http://www.google.com/transparencyreport/removals/europeprivacy/. When Google decides to eliminate a search result, it only affects searches for the requesting party's name, and Google informs the webmaster of the delinked URL. The Article 29 Working Party, (which you will recall is composed of data protection regulators from both EU institutions and member states' DPAs) has since issued an advisory opinion scolding Google for deleting links only for searches made through its European top-level domains (such as google.co.uk in the UK or google.es in Spain) and not those made on the main google.com site. According to the regulators, this practice circumvents the right to be forgotten and fails to provide sufficient protection to EU citizens. Google has responded that the ruling does not extend to domains outside Europe. Based on the analysis of territoriality questions in the *Google Spain* decision, who has the better argument on this point? Other critics have suggested instead that Google did too much in response to the ruling, not too little; these commenters object that Google should have required citizens seeking deletion to get rulings from their national DPA rather than conferring the decisionmaking power on itself. If you represented Google, what advice would you give the company about handling its legal obligations in the wake of this ruling? In addition to complying with EU-imposed obligations, what other legal and practical considerations might be important to Google in deciding how to respond?

5. ***Speech and Privacy.*** Could a rule like the right to be forgotten be recognized in the US? Removing links posted by a private company restricts that company's choices of what content to highlight and it also interferes with the public's ability to find certain information. Such legal requirements may violate current interpretations of the First Amendment. Note, however, that there are speech-related exceptions in EU law, as the *Google Spain* decision recognized: Article 9 of the Data Protection Directive states, "Member States shall provide for exemptions or derogations for the processing of personal data carried out solely for journalistic purposes or the purpose of artistic or literary expression only if they are necessary to reconcile the right to privacy with the rules governing freedom of expression." Costeja González did not succeed in his effort to require the removal of the underlying newspaper story from the internet, because the Spanish courts found the announcement of the real estate auction had been made in accordance with legal requirements about publicizing such sales. Indeed, a person paging through the online edition of La Vanguardia today may still read about the past financial troubles Costeja González experienced. Does that go far enough to satisfy the US conception of free speech? Does the speech queston turn on the characterization of Google's search results as a form of expression?

6. ***California's Internet Eraser Statute.*** Although there have been no cases like *Google Spain* in the US, one state has taken a step towards the right to be forgotten through legislation. California's "Internet Eraser" statute, CAL. BUS. & PROF. CODE § 22581, took effect in 2015. The law allows minors to obtain removal of content they posted on an operator's website, online service, or mobile application. It also requires that operators provide notice of the right to remove such content, and instructions on how to do so. There are significant exceptions, however, including: if the operator is legally obligated to maintain the content; if a third party posted the content; if the content was posted anonymously; if the minor didn't follow instructions for removal; or if the minor received compensation or other consideration for providing the content. Further, in order for the statute to apply, the operator must actually own the website, rather than merely manage or host it. In what ways does the California statute embody the right to be forgotten as illustrated in *Google Spain*? Based on what you've learned in this chapter, does the Internet Eraser law more closely reflect the data protection model or the consumer protection model?

7. ***Intermediary Liability.*** Aside from First Amendment considerations, *Google Spain* also underscores the EU's dramatic difference from American law in its treatment of the search engine as an online intermediary. In the US, provisions like Section 230 [see Chapter 2] often absolve platforms from liability when they aggregate third-party content. Clearly the EU does not share the same level of concern about making intermediaries responsible for user-generated material. Indeed, the *Google Spain* court emphasized that Google "makes access to that information appreciably easier for any internet user making a search in respect of the person concerned and may play a decisive role in the dissemination of that information." Which view of an intermediary's responsibility makes more sense?

8. ***The "Black Box" of Search Algorithms.*** How does Google decide the ranking of search results anyhow? We don't really know, because the company carefully guards its search algorithms as trade secrets. Separate from the question of what information should be disclosed, as in *Google Spain*, some critics argue that the content of highly influential internal sorting mechanisms like search engines, credit ratings, or employee scoring tools should be regulated more heavily to ensure fairness. *See* FRANK PASQUALE, THE BLACK BOX SOCIETY: THE SECRET ALGORITHMS THAT CONTROL MONEY AND INFORMATION (2015). Note that Article 15 the EU Data Protection Directive sets limits on automated decisionmaking. How does the government interest in regulating *public disclosure* of personal data compare to the government interest in regulating *private analysis* of personal data?

---

## Focus

### The General Data Protection Regulation (GDPR)

The adoption of the EU General Data Protection Regulation (GDPR) became official in mid-2016, and the new law will take effect in 2018 after a two-year transition period. Under EU law, regulations such as the GDPR automatically apply in all EU countries, without the need for each one to enact conforming legislation as they do under a directive. Because the GDPR is built on the same fundamental principles as the Data Protection Directive, many of the latter's key features will remain in place. Some of the more significant changes under the GDPR include the following:

1. ***Territoriality.*** The GDPR purports to apply not only to organizations with establishments in the EU, but to any data controller or data processor that offers goods or services in the EU in connection with its data processing activities.

2. ***Consent.*** Consent of the data subject will remain a legitimizing condition for data processing, but the GDPR defines consent more restrictively and in more detail than the Directive. Not only must consent be "unambiguous," it must be secured separately from agreement to other terms of service, and consent cannot be a condition for using a service unless the data processing is necessary to deliver the service. While this definition will not always require an affirmative opt-in, it is more demanding than existing EU law. Data subjects may always revoke consent later. By default, parents must give consent on behalf of children under the age of 16 for data processing by "information society" services, although individual nations may establish rules that reduce the age as low as 13.

3. ***Legitimate Interests.*** As under the Directive, an organization may rely on its "legitimate interests" to justify data processing, but the language of this provision gives greater weight to a data subject's individual interests, which must be balanced against the organization's.

4. ***Data Portability.*** The GDPR imposes a new requirement that, where technologically feasible, individuals have a right to receive their personal data in a format that allows them to move to a competing service.

5. ***Right of Erasure.*** A form of the right to be forgotten is included explicitly in the text of the GDPR.

6. ***Transparency.*** The GDPR specifies certain disclosures that must be made to data subjects, including the purposes of data collection, contact information for the data processor, and retention periods for personal data.

7. ***Security Breach Notification.*** For the first time, the GDPR establishes EU-wide standards for notifying regulators and affected individuals in the event of a data security breach [see Chapter 7 for US requirements of this type]. Data protection authorities must be told of incidents "without undue delay," usually no more than 72 hours after discovery. Other provisions require notice to data subjects based on risk of harm to their interests.

8. ***Internal Organizational Requirements.*** The GDPR imposes several new responsibilities on organizations that collect or process personal data. Larger ones must designate "Data Protection Officers (DPOs)" responsible for privacy and security. The GDPR also instructs data controllers to embrace "privacy by design" in planning new offerings, including a rule that default settings limit disclosure of data. Organizations engaging in "high risk" processing activities must complete "Data Privacy Impact Assessments (DPIAs)."

9. ***Enforcement.*** Existing national DPAs remain the primary regulators under the GDPR. Early proposals included "one-stop shopping" provisions under which organizations would be regulated only by the DPA in the country where their "main establishment" is located. This provision was amended, so that now this "lead DPA" will have primary responsibility, but will consult with other DPAs in countries where the organiation's data processing has an impact. Disputes between national DPAs over enforcement can be referred to a new European Data Protection Board (EDPB) for resolution. This new body will replace the Article 29 Working Party.

**10.** Penalties. The GDPR authorizes fines of up to €20 million or four percent of a company's worldwide revenue, whichever is greater. These are potentially enormous sums: Apple, for example, which had global revenue of $53.4 billion in 2015, could be fined over two billion dollars. It remains to be seen how large fines will actually be when the GDPR comes into effect.

---

## Focus

The Data Protection Model Around the World

Most nations outside the US that have adopted significant privacy laws have gravitated toward comprehensive data protection statutes similar to the EU model. Possible reasons for this difference with the US approach include, among many: the influence of international documents like the OECD Guidelines; other countries' greater receptiveness to framing national rights in terms of international human rights and as positive liberties [see Chapter 1]; a government's desire to be found to offer an "adequate level of protection" under Article 25 of the EU Directive in order to facilitate trade; greater comfort with more rule-oriented and bureaucratic enforcement mechanisms than in the US, which often approaches commercial regulation with a comparatively laissez-faire attitude and relies more on civil lawsuits to fill gaps; and different domestic political climates in various countries.

That said, laws around the world certainly are not monolithic. Even those that the EU has found to offer an "adequate level of protection" do not all operate in the same way, although they do share characteristics of the data protection model exemplified by the EU. A few examples follow of countries with data protection laws.

> ***Argentina*** has a comprehensive data protection statute, the Personal Data Protection Law ("PDPL"), and has been deemed an "adequate" jurisdiction by the EU. Argentina observed a version of the right to be forgotten before the *Google Spain* decision, under which individual data subjects can sue for access to their personal information held by data collectors and require correction or deletion of those records. The PDPL recognizes fewer exceptions than EU law, and generally requires consent of the data subject for collection and processing of data. Although the country has comparatively strict written rules, enforcement by the Argentinian DPA generally is based on auditing and compliance assistance rather than penalties.

> ***Canada*** enacted the Personal Information Protection and Electronic Documents Act (PIPEDA) in 2000. The statute governs only private commercial enterprises. There are additional privacy statutes for some industry areas, primarily in the financial services sector, as well as provincial privacy laws. Privacy laws in the provinces of Alberta, British Columbia and Québec have been found substantially equivalent to PIPEDA, which means that provincial law replaces PIPEDA for most data controllers in those places. Amendments to the statute in 2015 created an exemption for sharing stored personal data in connection with certain business transactions such as mergers or acquisitions and another partial exemption for collecting business contact information. It also created nationwide security breach notification rules for the first time in Canada [see Chapter 7 for more about US breach notification laws]. PIPEDA is centered around 10 privacy principles: accountability; disclosure of purposes; consent; limiting collection; limiting use, disclosure, and retention; accuracy; data security; transparency; access rights; and the ability of individuals to bring complaints. The EU has found Canada an

"adequate protection" jurisdiction in relation to commercial enterprises (that is, those covered by PIPEDA and its provincial equivalents). A different federal law, the Privacy Act, concerns privacy in Canadian federal government institutions.

***Israel*** has a long list of sector-specific data protection laws, including separate statutes for health information, financial data, and genetic information. It also has a general statute that regulates "databases," defined to include most compendiums of personal data held in a computerized format. Individuals whose information is held in such databases have rights of access and correction, and database operators have obligations concerning downstream disclosure of the information they hold. Israel has been deemed to have "adequate" protection to receive EU data transfers.

***South Africa*** enacted a new Protection of Personal Information Act (POPIA) in 2013, but its implementation has been very slow. The statute calls for a one-year transition period to the new law to begin some time after the appointment of a DPA, but as of this writing in early 2016, no DPA has been named.As drafted, the POPIA's terms borrow extensively from UK law and the Data Protection Directive. Personal data may only be collected on the basis of certain legitimizing conditions and sensitive data is subject to additional requirements.

***South Korea*** has not been determined officially to offer an "adequate level of protection" under EU law, but its Personal Information Protection Act (PIPA) limits collection of personal data to a list of six legitimizing conditions similar to those in the EU Data Protection Directive. Consent of the data subject is one of these conditions, but is defined somewhat narrowly. Conditions for collection of sensitive data are stricter.

In other nations, the law requires notice about the collection of data and the purposes for which it will be used, but does not necessarily limit these practices to certain defined legitimate purposes. In most such systems, there are stricter rules for sensitive data and sometimes narrower laws applicable to certain industry areas, technologies, or collection methods. Does that describe a data protection regime, a more American-style consumer protection model, or something in between?

***Australia*** has multiple privacy laws. The most important is the federal Privacy Act, under which data practices are governed by 13 "Australian Privacy Principles." Many of the principles require notice but do not create a closed list of legitimate conditions. Personal data may be used only for the purpose for which it was collected or for related secondary purposes. There are increased requirements for sensitive data, and a number of narrower statutes aimed at certain industries or technologies at both the federal and state level. Employee records are broadly exempt from Australia's Privacy Act.

***Japan*** just amended its national data protection law to broaden its coverage; the new rules became effective at the beginning of 2016. The law previously applied only to businesses that held personal data of over 5,000 individuals, but that limit has been removed. Under Japanese law, a business must provide notice of the data collected and its purpose, and must use data only for the stated purpose, but there are few outright bans other than deceptive practices. Collection of sensitive data requires consent.

***Mexico*** revised its law in 2015 and the full impact of the changes is not yet clear. The country's Data Protection Law ("DPL"), first enacted in 2010, is largely standards-based, requiring that data handling adhere to statutorily defined principles such as lawfulness, notice, purpose limitation, and proportionality. The law requires specific notice to data subjects when their personal information is collected, but if they do not opt out in response to notice, their consent can be implied. Despite a law that is less specific than some others, however, the Mexican DPA has been an aggressive enforcer, imposing significant fines in a noticeable number of cases.

---

## B. THE CHILDREN'S ONLINE PRIVACY PROTECTION ACT

In 1998, just as the commercial internet began to transform the way we communicate, Congress passed the Children's Online Privacy Protection Act, 15 U.S.C. §§ 6501 et seq., which established demanding requirements for the handling of personal data in the relatively narrow circumstances of: (a) online data collection (b) from children under the age of 13. The statute directed the FTC to write regulations putting the law into effect. The resulting Children's Online Privacy Protection Rule (or "COPPA Rule") is excerpted directly below.

COPPA departs from the consumer protection model found in much other US law [see Chapter 3]. In many ways it resembles data protection rules like those in the EU. As you read about COPPA, think about the ways it does and does not follow that lead. It certainly is not the only statute in US privacy law to share some features with the data protection model; others are found throughout this book, a few of which are noted at the end of this chapter.

It might seem that the narrow scope of COPPA means it would be of little concern to most organizations. And to be sure, its coverage is not nearly as sweeping as the EU's data protection regime. That said, you will notice that online data collectors of all sorts may end up running afoul of COPPA, whether or not they aim specifically at children. For that reason, privacy lawyers advising any enterprise with an online presence must consider the prospect of COPPA liability and then help their clients design an interface that reduces that risk. The responsibilities that can be triggered are extensive, including securing verifiable parental consent for data collection in advance, providing parents with access to their children's personal information, and allowing them to delete that data.

### Children's Online Privacy Protection Rule

16 C.F.R. Part 312

#### § 312.1 Scope of regulations in this part.

This part implements the Children's Online Privacy Protection Act of 1998, which prohibits unfair or deceptive acts or practices in connection with the collection, use, and/or disclosure of personal information from and about children on the Internet.

**§ 312.2 Definitions.**

*Child* means an individual under the age of 13.

*Collects* or *collection* means the gathering of any personal information from a child by any means, including but not limited to:

(1) Requesting, prompting, or encouraging a child to submit personal information online;

(2) Enabling a child to make personal information publicly available in identifiable form. An operator shall not be considered to have collected personal information under this paragraph if it takes reasonable measures to delete all or virtually all personal information from a child's postings before they are made public and also to delete such information from its records; or

(3) Passive tracking of a child online.

*Commission* means the Federal Trade Commission.

*Delete* means to remove personal information such that it is not maintained in retrievable form and cannot be retrieved in the normal course of business.

*Disclose* or *disclosure* means, with respect to personal information:

(1) The release of personal information collected by an operator from a child in identifiable form for any purpose, except where an operator provides such information to a person who provides support for the internal operations of the Web site or online service; and

(2) Making personal information collected by an operator from a child publicly available in identifiable form by any means, including but not limited to a public posting through the Internet, or through a personal home page or screen posted on a Web site or online service; a pen pal service; an electronic mail service; a message board; or a chat room.

. . .

*Obtaining verifiable consent* means making any reasonable effort (taking into consideration available technology) to ensure that before personal information is collected from a child, a parent of the child:

(1) Receives notice of the operator's personal information collection, use, and disclosure practices; and

(2) Authorizes any collection, use, and/or disclosure of the personal information.

*Online contact information* means an email address or any other substantially similar identifier that permits direct contact with a person online, including but not limited to, an instant messaging user identifier, a voice over internet protocol (VOIP) identifier, or a video chat user identifier.

*Operator* means any person who operates a Web site located on the Internet or an online service and who collects or maintains personal information from or about the users of or visitors to such Web site or online service, or on whose behalf such information is collected or maintained, or offers products or services for sale through that Web site or online service [involving interstate commerce or commerce between the US and a foreign nation]. This definition does not include any nonprofit entity that would otherwise be exempt from coverage under Section 5 of the Federal Trade Commission Act (15 U.S.C. 45). Personal information is *collected or maintained on behalf of an operator* when:

(1) It is collected or maintained by an agent or service provider of the operator; or

(2) The operator benefits by allowing another person to collect personal information directly from users of such Web site or online service.

. . .

*Personal information* means individually identifiable information about an individual collected online, including:

(1) A first and last name;

(2) A home or other physical address including street name and name of a city or town;

(3) Online contact information as defined in this section;

(4) A screen or user name where it functions in the same manner as online contact information, as defined in this section;

(5) A telephone number;

(6) A Social Security number;

(7) A persistent identifier that can be used to recognize a user over time and across different Web sites or online services. Such persistent identifier includes, but is not limited to, a customer number held in a cookie, an Internet Protocol (IP) address, a processor or device serial number, or unique device identifier;

(8) A photograph, video, or audio file where such file contains a child's image or voice;

(9) Geolocation information sufficient to identify street name and name of a city or town; or

(10) Information concerning the child or the parents of that child that the operator collects online from the child and combines with an identifier described in this definition.

*Release of personal information* means the sharing, selling, renting, or transfer of personal information to any third party.

. . .

*Web site or online service directed to children* means a commercial Web site or online service, or portion thereof, that is targeted to children.

(1) In determining whether a Web site or online service, or a portion thereof, is directed to children, the Commission will consider its subject matter, visual content, use of animated characters or child-oriented activities and incentives, music or other audio content, age of models, presence of child celebrities or celebrities who appeal to children, language or other characteristics of the Web site or online service, as well as whether advertising promoting or appearing on the Web site or online service is directed to children. The Commission will also consider competent and reliable empirical evidence regarding audience composition, and evidence regarding the intended audience.

(2) A Web site or online service shall be deemed directed to children when it has actual knowledge that it is collecting personal information directly from users of another Web site or online service directed to children.

(3) A Web site or online service that is directed to children under the criteria set forth in paragraph (1) of this definition, but that does not target children as its primary audience, shall not be deemed directed to children if it:

(i) Does not collect personal information from any visitor prior to collecting age information; and

(ii) Prevents the collection, use, or disclosure of personal information from visitors who identify themselves as under age 13 without first complying with the notice and parental consent provisions of this part. . . .

**§ 312.3 Regulation of unfair or deceptive acts or practices in connection with the collection, use, and/or disclosure of personal information from and about children on the Internet.**

*General requirements.* It shall be unlawful for any operator of a website or online service directed to children, or any operator that has actual knowledge that it is collecting or maintaining personal information from a child, to collect personal information from a child in a manner that violates the regulations prescribed under this part. Generally, under this part, an operator must:

(a) Provide notice on the website or online service of what information it collects from children, how it uses such information, and its disclosure practices for such information (§ 312.4(b));

(b) Obtain verifiable parental consent prior to any collection, use, and/or disclosure of personal information from children (§ 312.5);

(c) Provide a reasonable means for a parent to review the personal information collected from a child and to refuse to permit its further use or maintenance (§ 312.6);

(d) Not condition a child's participation in a game, the offering of a prize, or another activity on the child disclosing more personal information than is reasonably necessary to participate in such activity (§ 312.7); and

(e) Establish and maintain reasonable procedures to protect the confidentiality, security, and integrity of personal information collected from children (§ 312.8).

**§ 312.4 Notice.**

(a) *General principles of notice.* All notices under §§ 312.3(a) and 312.5 must be clearly and understandably written, be complete, and must contain no unrelated, confusing, or contradictory materials.

[The remainder of § 312.4 sets out very detailed requirements for the placement and content of privacy notices required on the operator's web site or service, and also detailed requirements for the content and transmission methods of notice sent to parents pursuant to § 312.5.]

**§ 312.5 Parental consent.**

(a) *General requirements.*

(1) An operator is required to obtain verifiable parental consent before any collection, use, or disclosure of personal information from children, including consent to any material change in the collection, use, or disclosure practices to which the parent has previously consented.

(2) An operator must give the parent the option to consent to the collection and use of the child's personal information without consenting to disclosure of his or her personal information to third parties.

(b) *Methods for verifiable parental consent.*

(1) An operator must make reasonable efforts to obtain verifiable parental consent, taking into consideration available technology. Any method to obtain verifiable parental consent must be reasonably calculated, in light of available technology, to ensure that the person providing consent is the child's parent.

(2) Existing methods to obtain verifiable parental consent that satisfy the requirements of this paragraph include:

(i) Providing a consent form to be signed by the parent and returned to the operator by postal mail, facsimile, or electronic scan;

(ii) Requiring a parent, in connection with a monetary transaction, to use a credit card, debit card, or other online payment system that provides notification of each discrete transaction to the primary account holder;

(iii) Having a parent call a toll-free telephone number staffed by trained personnel;

(iv) Having a parent connect to trained personnel via video-conference;

(v) Verifying a parent's identity by checking a form of government-issued identification against databases of such information, where the parent's identification is deleted by the operator from its records promptly after such verification is complete; or

(vi) *Provided that,* an operator that does not "disclose" (as defined by § 312.2) children's personal information, may use an email coupled with additional steps to provide assurances that the person providing the consent is the parent. Such additional steps include: Sending a confirmatory email to the parent following receipt of consent, or obtaining a postal address or telephone number from the parent and confirming the parent's consent by letter or telephone call. An operator that uses this method must provide notice that the parent can revoke any consent given in response to the earlier email. . . .

(c) *Exceptions to prior parental consent.* Verifiable parental consent is required prior to any collection, use, or disclosure of personal information from a child *except* as set forth in this paragraph:

(1) Where the sole purpose of collecting the name or online contact information of the parent or child is to provide notice and obtain parental consent under § 312.4(c)(1). If the operator has not obtained parental consent after a reasonable time from the date of the information collection, the operator must delete such information from its records;

(2) Where the purpose of collecting a parent's online contact information is to provide voluntary notice to, and subsequently update the parent about, the child's participation in a Web site or online service that does not otherwise collect, use, or disclose children's personal information. In such cases, the parent's online contact information may not be used or disclosed for any other purpose . . . ;

(3) Where the sole purpose of collecting online contact information from a child is to respond directly on a one-time basis to a specific request from the child, and where such information is not used to re-contact the child or for any other

purpose, is not disclosed, and is deleted by the operator from its records promptly after responding to the child's request;

(4) Where the purpose of collecting a child's and a parent's online contact information is to respond directly more than once to the child's specific request, and where such information is not used for any other purpose, disclosed, or combined with any other information collected from the child. In such cases, the operator must make reasonable efforts, taking into consideration available technology, to ensure that the parent receives notice as described in § 312.4(c)(3). An operator will not be deemed to have made reasonable efforts to ensure that a parent receives notice where the notice to the parent was unable to be delivered;

(5) Where the purpose of collecting a child's and a parent's name and online contact information, is to protect the safety of a child, and where such information is not used or disclosed for any purpose unrelated to the child's safety . . . ;

(6) Where the purpose of collecting a child's name and online contact information is to:

(i) Protect the security or integrity of its Web site or online service;

(ii) Take precautions against liability;

(iii) Respond to judicial process; or

(iv) To the extent permitted under other provisions of law, to provide information to law enforcement agencies or for an investigation on a matter related to public safety; and where such information is not be used for any other purpose;

[The Rule also exempts certain collection of persistent identifiers (such as device ID numbers) for purely operational purposes.] . . .

### § 312.6 Right of parent to review personal information provided by a child.

(a) Upon request of a parent whose child has provided personal information to a Web site or online service, the operator of that Web site or online service is required to provide to that parent the following:

(1) A description of the specific types or categories of personal information collected from children by the operator, such as name, address, telephone number, email address, hobbies, and extracurricular activities;

(2) The opportunity at any time to refuse to permit the operator's further use or future online collection of personal

information from that child, and to direct the operator to delete the child's personal information; and

(3) Notwithstanding any other provision of law, a means of reviewing any personal information collected from the child. The means employed by the operator to carry out this provision must:

(i) Ensure that the requestor is a parent of that child, taking into account available technology; and

(ii) Not be unduly burdensome to the parent.

(b) Neither an operator nor the operator's agent shall be held liable under any Federal or State law for any disclosure made in good faith and following reasonable procedures in responding to a request for disclosure of personal information under this section.

(c) Subject to the limitations set forth in § 312.7, an operator may terminate any service provided to a child whose parent has refused, under paragraph (a)(2) of this section, to permit the operator's further use or collection of personal information from his or her child or has directed the operator to delete the child's personal information.

**§ 312.7 Prohibition against conditioning a child's participation on collection of personal information.**

An operator is prohibited from conditioning a child's participation in a game, the offering of a prize, or another activity on the child's disclosing more personal information than is reasonably necessary to participate in such activity.

. . .

**§ 312.10 Data retention and deletion requirements.**

An operator of a Web site or online service shall retain personal information collected online from a child for only as long as is reasonably necessary to fulfill the purpose for which the information was collected. The operator must delete such information using reasonable measures to protect against unauthorized access to, or use of, the information in connection with its deletion.

## NOTES

1. ***Consumer Protection or Data Protection?*** In what ways does COPPA resemble a consumer protection regime like others overseen by the FTC [see Chapter 3]? In what ways does it resemble a data protection structure similar to those seen in the EU [see Section A, above]? If you had to classify COPPA and its regulations as either a consumer protection or a data protection model, which would you choose?

2. ***A Different Rulemaking Structure.*** The FTC issued detailed regulations interpreting COPPA in 2000, two years after the statute passed. A decade later, the FTC launched a two-year notice-and-comment rulemaking process to revise the COPPA regulations, which were finalized

in 2012 and came into effect in 2013. The Rule excerpted above incorporates those changes. In general, the 2013 amendments extended COPPA's reach. These included a broader definition of personal information, greater responsibilities for third parties such as advertisers that may collect children's data on a web site, and more specific requirements about data retention and data destruction. The countervailing shift to make compliance easier was a revision to the methods of parental consent, although these are still complex. Congress allowed the FTC to promulgate regulations under COPPA using the ordinary procedures of the Administrative Procedure Act, rather than the more burdensome rulemaking procedures required under Section 5 [see Chapter 3]. Does the COPPA Rule reflect the type of regulations the FTC or another agency might issue under an omnibus privacy law? If so, is the specificity it contains better, worse, or a mixed bag compared to the regime under Section 5?

3. ***Who Is an Operator?*** One matter clarified by the 2013 amendment of the regulations was the question of who qualifies as an "operator" under COPPA. The revised Rule defines "operator" broadly to include an entity that does not itself "operate" functions on a web site, but delegates that activity to others. As a result, proprietors may be held responsible for COPPA violations committed through the data collection activities of third parties such as advertising networks or providers of widgets, plug-ins, and other such hosted services. This interpretation grew out of enforcement actions the FTC had already taken under the original Rule against email and message board providers that were distinct from the primary operator of a web site. In guidance, the FTC has emphasized that the definition of "operator" is meant to be pragmatic, and to apply only to the entities that truly control or benefit from challenged data practices. Nevertheless, the revised Rule caused some discomfort among companies that protested they lacked the capacity to monitor the legal propriety of data collection by independent advertisers and providers.

4. ***"Verifiable Parental Consent."*** Unless a specific exception applies, COPPA requires an operator to obtain "verifiable parental consent" *before* collecting personal information from children under the age of 13. How? First, the Rule sets out extremely specific requirements for the "notice" that must be provided to parents. *See* 16 C.F.R. § 312.4. Second, unlike other "notice and choice" models that assume a user who is dissatisfied with the data practices described in the notice will opt out by simply going elsewhere, COPPA generally requires some manifestation of *affirmative* parental opt-in. *See id.* § 312.5. Review those measures and see if you can explain them in plain English. The final listed mechanism for parental consent is usually referred to as the "email plus" method. Parents can send (or reply to) an email consenting to data collection from their children, but then the operator must take "additional steps"—most often by sending a followup "confirmatory email" several days later. Note, however, that email plus is available only to operators that do not "disclose" children's information, which the Rule defines to include providing any opportunity for children to disclose their own data publicly (such as through a social media function).In your view, how effective are these methods of securing verifiable parental

consent? Are they convenient for parents? If you were a 12-year-old determined to use a site without getting a parent's permission, do you think you could do so under these rules? How much of a burden do the consent mechanisms in § 312.5 place on operators? On parents? Can you think of any better methods?

5. ***Consent with Exceptions.*** COPPA's default rule requires advance parental consent in all circumstances except those specified in § 312.5(c). Does this sound more like a consumer protection model or a data protection model?

6. ***Access and Deletion.*** Under § 312.6(a), parents can review personal information about their children held by an operator, can revoke their consent, and can require the deletion of previously collected data. These types of rights resemble those under the EU Directive, and generally are not available under consumer protection regimes.

7. ***Enforcement.*** The FTC enforces COPPA violations in the same manner that it exercises its Section 5 powers. And, as is usual with the FTC's exercise of its ordinary consumer protection authority [see Chapter 3], FTC enforcement of COPPA ends in immediate settlements. Indeed, no defendant has ever challenged an FTC complaint brought under COPPA. There are also important dissimilarities between FTC authority under COPPA and Section 5, however. The difference in rulemaking authority, already discussed above, is a huge one. Another key distinction is illustrated in the cases that follow: the FTC can impose financial penalties under COPPA that are not allowed under Section 5.

## United States v. Yelp, Inc.

Case No. 3:14–CV–04163 (N.D. Cal. Sept. 17, 2014)

### COMPLAINT

Plaintiff, the United States of America, acting upon notification and authorization to the Attorney General by the Federal Trade Commission ("FTC" or "Commission"), for its Complaint alleges that:

1. Plaintiff brings this action under Section 5(a)(1), 5(m)(1)(A), 13(b), 16(a), and 19 of the Federal Trade Commission Act ("FTC Act"), 15 U.S.C. §§ 45(a)(1), 45(m)(1)(A), 53(b), 56(a), and 57b, and Sections 1303(c) and 1306(d) of the Children's Online Privacy Protection Act of 1998 ("COPPA"), 15 U.S.C. §§ 6502(c) and 6505(d), to obtain monetary civil penalties, a permanent injunction, and other equitable relief for Defendant's violations of the Commission's Children's Online Privacy Protection Rule ("Rule" or "COPPA Rule"), 16 C.F.R. Part 312.

### THE CHILDREN'S ONLINE PRIVACY PROTECTION ACT RULE

5. Congress enacted COPPA in 1998 to protect the safety and privacy of children online by prohibiting the unauthorized or unnecessary collection of children's personal information online by operators of Internet websites and online services. COPPA directed the Commission

to promulgate a rule implementing COPPA. The Commission promulgated the Children's Online Privacy Protection Rule, 16 C.F.R. Part 312, on November 3, 1999. The Rule went into effect on April 21, 2000.

## DEFENDANT'S BUSINESS PRACTICES

8. Since 2004, Yelp has provided a free service that aims "to connect people with great local businesses" and purports to be the "leading local guide for real word-of-mouth on everything from boutiques and mechanics to restaurants and dentists." Yelp allows users to read and create reviews of local businesses, and connect with other users online and at local events. Businesses may advertise with Yelp, communicate with users publicly and privately, and create special deals for Yelp users.

9. In 2008, Yelp launched its first mobile application for Apple, Inc.'s iOS operating system. Since then, Yelp has released mobile applications for Google, Inc.'s Android operating system, and for Microsoft Corporation's Windows Phone operating system, Blackberry, Ltd.'s Blackberry operating system, and Palm, Inc.'s webOS operating system.

10. Consumers can register for and access Yelp's service through an Internet website (www.yelp.com), a mobile Internet website (m.yelp.com), and mobile applications for the iOS and Android operating systems ("Yelp App").

11. Users of Yelp's service are able to post content on Yelp, including photos of themselves and profiles with detailed information about themselves. Globally, Yelp had an average monthly total of approximately 102 million unique visitors over the first quarter of 2013.

12. The Yelp App offers some of the same user functions as the website and mobile site, including the ability to upload photos, and, on some devices, post reviews. In addition, Yelp App users can "check in," indicating their presence at businesses, and write "Tips" and "Comments" about businesses. Since January 1, 2011, the Yelp App has been downloaded more than 25 million times.

## DEFENDANT'S BUSINESS PRACTICES REGARDING COLLECTION OF INFORMATION FROM CHILDREN UNDER THE AGE OF 13

13. For purposes of Paragraphs 13 through 29 herein, the terms "child," "collects," "collection," "disclosure," "Internet," "operator," "parent," "personal information," "verifiable consent," and "website or online service directed to children," are defined as those terms are defined in Section 312.2 of the COPPA Rule, 16 C.F.R. § 312.2.

14. The Rule applies to any operator of a commercial website or online service that has actual knowledge that it collects, uses, and/or discloses personal information from children. Among other things, the Rule requires website operators to meet specific requirements prior to

collecting online, using, or disclosing personal information from children, including but not limited to:

(a) posting a privacy policy on its website or online service providing clear, understandable, and complete notice of its information practices, including what information the website operator collects from children online, how it uses such information, its disclosure practices for such information, and other specific disclosures set forth in the Rule;

(b) providing clear, understandable, and complete notice of its information practices, including specific disclosures, directly to parents when required by the Rule; and

(c) obtaining verifiable parental consent prior to collecting, using, and/or disclosing personal information from children.

15. In 2009, Defendant introduced a registration feature in the Yelp App, allowing users to register for new accounts through the application. Previously, users could only register through the website, where Defendant had a screening mechanism to prohibit users under the age of 13 from registering. However, Defendant failed to implement a functional age-screen mechanism in the new in-app registration feature. As a result, the Yelp App accepted registrations from users who input dates of birth indicating they were under the age of 13. Over a year later, as part of a mobile certification process, Defendant hired a third party who performed a privacy review of the Yelp App. The July 2010 results of the third-party test erroneously noted that the iOS application prohibited registrations from users under the age of 13. In fact, both the iOS and Android versions of the Yelp App accepted these registrations; indeed, an iOS user registered with an age under 13 the very same day as the test. Defendant did not test the age-restriction aspect of the registration feature of the iOS version of the Yelp App again, and never tested it in the Android version. From April 2009 to April 2013, both the iOS and Android versions of the Yelp App accepted registrations from users who inputted any date of birth, including dates of birth indicating that the user was under the age of 13.

16. Users who initiated registration through the Yelp App by providing a first name, last name, email address, and ZIP code and, possibly, any date of birth and gender, were then required to confirm their email addresses to complete their registration. All users who completed registration, including those who provided birthdates indicating that they were under 13, were granted full access to the Yelp service through the Yelp App and the Yelp website. For example, they could add information to their personal profiles, including photos, their current city, hometown, and any other information they chose to provide in free-form text fields. They could also "check-in" at local businesses, and post "Tips" and "Comments" about such businesses.

17. Yelp also collected certain information automatically from the phones of Yelp App users. Specifically, Yelp collected users' Mobile Device IDs, or unique identifiers assigned to devices, in order to obtain metrics about its mobile user base. In addition, in order to provide location-based services such as local search results, Yelp collected the precise locations of users' phones based on Global Positioning Systems contained in the phones of those users who chose to allow Yelp to use their location.

18. As set forth in Paragraphs 15 through 17, Defendant collected personal information, including but not limited to full names and email addresses, from several thousand individuals who input birthdates indicating that they were between the ages of 9 and 13. A portion of these users completed the registration process and thus were able to post reviews and provide other information through Yelp's service.

19. Because Defendant collected information from users who provided birthdates indicating that they were under 13, Yelp is deemed to have had "actual knowledge" under the COPPA Rule that it was collecting information from several thousand children under 13, in violation of the COPPA Rule.

## DEFENDANT'S VIOLATION OF THE COPPA RULE

21. In numerous instances, in connection with operating the Yelp App, Defendant collected, used, and/or disclosed, with actual knowledge, personal information online from children under the age of 13.

22. Defendant is an "operator" as defined by the COPPA Rule, 16 C.F.R. § 312.2.

23. Through the means described in Paragraphs 15 through 20 above, Defendant violated:

(a) Section 312.4(b) of the Rule, which requires an operator to provide sufficient notice on its website or online services of the information it collects online from children, how it uses such information, and its disclosure practices for such information, among other required content;

(b) Section 312.4(c) of the Rule, which requires an operator to provide direct notice to parents of the information Defendant collects online from children, how it uses such information, and its disclosure practices for such information, among other required content; and

(c) Section 312.5(a)(1) of the Rule, which requires an operator to obtain verifiable parental consent before any collection, use, and/or disclosure of personal information from children.

## United States v. Artist Arena, LLC

Case No. 112–CV–07386 (S.D.N.Y. Oct. 4, 2012)

### COMPLAINT

Plaintiff, the United States of America, acting upon notification and authorization to the Attorney General by the Federal Trade Commission ("FTC" or "Commission"), for its Complaint alleges:

### DEFENDANT

6. Defendant Artist Arena LLC ("Artist Arena") is a New York limited liability company with its principal place of business a1 853 Broadway, 3rd Floor, New York, NY 10003. At all times material to this Complaint, acting alone or in concert with others, Artist Arena operated recording artists' fan club and newsletter subscription websites on the Internet.

### DEFENDANT'S BUSINESS ACTIVITIES

8. Since at least 2009, Defendant has operated various recording artist websites through which users are able to register for paid fan clubs and subscribe to free online newsletters after submitting certain items of personal information online. Registered fan club members can create online profiles, and are able to interact publicly online by, for example, posting comments to members' walls and sending and accepting friend requests. Newsletter subscribers receive an electronic newsletter about a particular recording artist.

9. Defendant's websites, www.RihannaNow.com, www.DemiLovato FanClub.net, www.BieberFever.com. and www.SelenaGomez.com, have attracted a significant number of children under age 13. Defendant offered a newsletter subscription on RihannaNow.com, fan clubs on DemiLovatoFanClub.net and BieberFever.com, and both fan club and newsletter services on SelenaGomez.com.

#### RihannaNow.com Online Newsletter

10. Defendant automatically registered a user for Rihanna's online newsletter when he or she entered a first and last name, email address, cell phone number, country of residence, and birth date.

11. Between November 18, 2010 and August 17, 2011, Defendant knowingly registered 8,940 newsletter subscribers who indicated they were under the age of 13.

12. Defendant failed to meet the Rule's direct notice and parental consent requirements. Defendant did not: (1) provide parents with a direct notice of its information practices: and (2) obtain verifiable parental consent prior to collecting, using, or disclosing children's personal information in connection with RihannaNow.com.

#### DemiLovatoFanClub.net Fan Club

13. Prior to the launch of DemiLovatoFanClub.net, Defendant maintained a webpage on Demi Lovato's official website, DemiLovato.com, to solicit registrations for its future fan club. Defendant

required a user who expressed interest in the fan club to provide an email address, first name, and birth date. Regardless of the birth date entered, Defendant provided a check box for the user to certify he or she had read and agreed to the terms of the user agreement, and was over age 13. The web page also stated "[i]f you are under 13 and live in the US . . . your parent or legal guardian may complete this registration on your behalf." Defendant did not collect a parent's email address.

14. Once DemiLovatoFanClub.net launched, Defendant required a user to enter a birth date to register for the online fan club. If the birth date indicated the user was under age 13, Defendant requested the child's email address, street address including city and state, first name, gender, t-shirt size, parent's first and last name, parent's email address, credit card information, and billing address. (After 14 months of operation, Artist Arena stopped requiring a child to enter his or her email address and first name.) The registration page told the child to "be sure to get your parent's OK and enter [your parent's] First and Last name" and "be sure to get your parent's OK—as the confirmation email will be sent [to you] at [your parent's] address.

15. After collecting from the child the personal information described in Paragraph 14 above, Defendant sent to the child, at the parent's email address, a confirmation message containing fan club log-in instructions. This confirmation email did not provide parents with proper notice of Defendant's information collection and use practices, or seek their consent to such practices.

16. Through DemiLovatoFanClub.net, Defendant knowingly registered 634 children between April 15, 2009 and August 2, 2011. Defendant collected and maintained personal information from an additional 4,586 children who started, but did not complete, their fan club registrations.

17. Defendant failed to meet the Rule's direct notice and parental consent requirements. Defendant did not: (1) provide parents with a direct notice of its information practices; and (2) obtain verifiable parental consent prior to collecting, using, or disclosing children's personal information in connection with DemiLovatoFanClub.net.

**BieberFever.com Fan Club**

18. Defendant required a user seeking to join Justin Bieber's online fan club to add a membership to his or her shopping cart on BieberFever.com, and to enter an email address, user name, password, country, and birth date. If the birth date indicated the user was under age 13, Defendant required the child to enter a parent's name and email address. Upon entry of this information, the child immediately received an on-screen notice that the registration was "successful" and that he or she was "logged in." The notice also directed the child to ask the child's parent "to check his or her email and click on the link provided" to become a fan club member.

19. At the same time the child received the on-screen notice that his or her registration was successful, Defendant sent an email to the parent's email address. The email stated that: (1) Artist Arena needed the parent's consent to "complete" the child's registration; (2) the parent could provide consent by clicking on a link in the email message; and (3) the parent did not need to take any action if he or she did not consent to the child's fan club registration. lf the parent clicked the link contained in the email, Defendant led the parent to a BieberFever.com webpage that stated. "Thank you for validating this child. The child you are validating can now log in to the fan club site. You may also continue any order that may be in progress."

20. At this point, the child could return to his or her shopping cart to "Checkout." The child next received a pop-up box that told the child to "Grab a parent with a credit card," and then click "CONTINUE." Clicking "CONTINUE" took the child or parent to another pop-up box that explained why Defendant collected credit card information: "to verify parental consent for your child to join BieberFever.com and have access to all its features" and "to process your membership fee." The child or parent then arrived at the Checkout page, where he or she would enter delivery, billing, and credit card information to complete the child's registration.

21. One month after the website launched, Defendant ceased emailing the parent after collecting the information described in Paragraph 18 above. Instead, once the child completed the registration fields, he or she immediately returned to the shopping cart to input the information as described in Paragraph 20 above. Defendant then sent the child a confirmation email.

22. Through BieberFever.com, Defendant registered 4,943 children between June 2010 and August 2, 2011. In addition, Defendant collected and maintained personal information from 21,507 children who started but did not complete their fan club registrations.

23. Defendant failed to meet the Rule's direct notice and parental consent requirements. Defendant did not: (1) provide parents with a direct notice of its information practices; and (2) obtain verifiable parental consent prior to collecting, using, or disclosing children's personal information. Defendant's emails to parents and pop-up boxes failed to: (1) clearly and completely disclose that it had *already* collected personal information from their children; and (2) state that Defendant retained children's personal information even when parents did not respond to Defendant's email notification or complete the registration process. Finally, Defendant's pop-up boxes failed to inform parents of their rights to have their children's personal information deleted and to refuse to permit further collection or use of their children's information.

### SelenaGomez.com Online Newsletter

24. Defendant required a user to enter an email address, user name, password, birth date, country, parent's name, and parent's email address to subscribe to the Selena Gomez online newsletter. Defendant in some instances also required a child to provide his or her first name, last name, city, state, and postal code information. The child then received an on-screen notice that stated, "Registration successful. You are now logged in."

25. Upon receiving this on-screen notice that his or her registration was successful. the child was able to edit his or her online profile, and add any text to a large signature block at the bottom of the profile page. (The website indicated that the text the child entered to the signature block would be "publicly displayed at the end of [his or her] comments.") In addition, a child who had not already been required to provide his or her full name, city, state, and zip code could add it to his or her account.

26. At the same time that a child could access his or her Selena Gomez account, Defendant sent an email to the parent's email address stating that it needed the parent's consent to "complete" the child's newsletler registration. The email directed the parent to provide consent by clicking on a link in the email message, and falsely stated that if "you DO NOT want to approve your child's signup, you do not need to do anything else: simply do not click on the above link." Despite this assertion, as described in Paragraphs 24 and 25 above, Defendant had already registered the child and allowed the child to complete his or her profile without any action by the parent.

[The complaint went on to describe sign-up for the SelenaGomez.com fan club, which was generally similar to the BieberFever.com process described above.]

34. In connection with its operation of RihannaNow.com, DemiLovatoFanClub.net, BieberFever.com, and SelenaGomez.com, Defendant collected, used, and/or disclosed personal information from approximately 101,363 children in violation of the Children's Online Privacy Protection Rule.

### VIOLATIONS OF THE CHILDREN'S ONLINE PRIVACY PROTECTION RULE

36. Defendant is an "operator" as defined by the Rule, 16 C.F.R. § 312.2.

37. Defendant violated:

(a) Section 312.4(c) of the Rule, which requires an operator to provide direct notice to parents of what information it collects from children, how it uses such information, and its disclosure practices for such information, among other required content; and

(b) Section 312.5(a)(1) of the Rule, which requires an operator to obtain verifiable parental consent prior to its collection, use, and/or disclosure of personal information from children.

## VIOLATIONS OF THE FTC ACT

41. Section 5(a) of the FTC Act, 15 U.S.C. § 45(a), prohibits "unfair or deceptive acts or practices in or affecting commerce."

42. Misrepresentations or deceptive omissions of material fact constitute deceptive acts or practices prohibited by Section 5(a) of the FTC Act.

43. Through statements made in emails sent to parents from SelenaGomez.com and BieberFever.com, as referenced in Paragraphs 19, 26, and 28 above, Defendant has represented, directly or indirectly, expressly or by implication, that: (1) it would not collect personal information online from children without prior parental consent; and (2) as to the Selena Gomez online newsletter, it would not activate a child's registration for the newsletter absent a parent's express consent.

44. In truth and in fact: (1) on SelenaGomez.com and BieberFever.com, Defendant collected personal information online from children without prior parental consent; and (2) on SelenaGomez.com, Defendant activated a child's registration for the newsletter absent a parent's express consent.

45. Therefore, Defendant's representations as set forth in Paragraph 43 of this Complaint are false and misleading, and constitute deceptive acts or practices in violation of Section 5(a) of the FTC Act.

## NOTES

1. ***Settlements.*** Predictably, both Yelp and Artist Arena settled these complaints; federal courts entered consent decrees ordering them to remedy their COPPA compliance failures and to delete all data they had collected from children under the age of 13. Yelp also agreed, as part of its consent decree, to monitor and keep records of its compliance with COPPA for 10 years after the order. The *Artist Arena* order included an interesting "consumer education remedy," requiring that the Defendant

> in connection with its operation of any website or online service directed to children, and any website or online service through which Defendant, with actual knowledge, collects, uses, and/or discloses personal information from children, shall place a clear and conspicuous notice: (1) within the privacy policy required to be posted by Section 312.4(b) of the Rule; (2) within the direct notice required to be sent to parents by Section 312.4(c) of the Rule; and (3) at each location on the website or online service where personal information is collected, which states as follows in bold typeface:
>
> > NOTICE: Visit www.OnGuardOnline.gov for tips from the Federal Trade Commission on protecting kids' privacy online.

Finally, unlike most consumer protection settlements reached by the FTC, COPPA settlements frequently include civil monetary penalties; Yelp paid $450,000 and Artist Arena paid one million dollars. Neither defendant admitted fault.

2. ***Epic Fails.*** You might be tempted to smack your forehead as you read these complaints. The legal compliance failures at these two companies were entirely avoidable. Yelp implemented an effective age screening mechanism on its web site, but did not apply that understanding to its mobile app. Worse, the app collected age information but then gathered additional data from users under the age of 13 without parental consent anyway, making itself responsible for "actual knowledge" of children using the app. It appears that the third-party auditor who examined the company's iPhone app did a poor job. The systems at Artist Arena also seem flawed. How did the firm manage to create processes apparently intended to comply with COPPA on four different sites, all of them different, yet all of them allegedly violating COPPA in different ways? If you were asked to develop a sensible model for COPPA compliance across Artist Arena's web sites—one that would avoid future COPPA violations but allow a seamless and appealing experience for young music fans—what would you recommend?

3. ***The* Sony BMG *Precedent.*** In 2008, four years before *Artist Arena*, the FTC reached a consent decree with the music industry behemoth Sony BMG for exactly the same types of violations. According to the complaint in *United States v. Sony BMG Music Entertainment*, Sony hosted 196 web sites for musicians signed to its label that collected personal data without parental consent from at least 30,000 children. The remedy will sound familiar: a one million dollar fine and a requirement that Sony's artist web sites contain links to FTC educational materials about children's privacy. Does the existence of a consent decree for the same behavior makes the compliance failures at Artist Arena more troubling?

4. ***"Directed to Children."*** Both Yelp and Artist Arena had actual knowledge of users under the age of 13. What if they did not? The FTC warns that the question of whether a web site or online service is "directed to children" requires fact-specific analysis. Paragraph (1) of the relevant definition in the COPPA Rule includes numerous considerations such as the inclusion of "child-oriented activities and incentives" and the "presence of . . . celebrities who appeal to children." 16 C.F.R. § 312.2 An FTC consent decree against a game app provider called TinyCo, which was announced the same day as the one in *Yelp*, illustrates the application of this rule. The complaint described the animation, language, and themes of TinyCo's games to demonstrate how they met the requirement. For example, according to the complaint, "Tiny Zoo" was "a game in which users collect, feed, and breed animated animals to build a zoo. The description of the game in Apple's App Store stated, 'Build the BEST zoo and raise ADORABLE animals in Tiny Zoo Friends! Come back everyday to discover EXCITING new animal friends!' " *United States v. TinyCo, Inc.*, Case No. 3:14–cv–04164 (N.D. Cal. Sept. 17, 2014) (Complaint). The determination that a site is directed to children triggers all the requirements of COPPA, and the lack of direct knowledge about the age of a particular user will not absolve the operator of liability.

Look back at the considerations identified in the Rule and then at the facts of *Yelp* and *Artist Arena.* If their operators did not have actual knowledge of users under the age of 13, would they still be deemed "directed to children" under the COPPA Rule?

5. ***Age Screening.*** The 2013 changes to the Rule added an escape clause for some web sites and online services to avoid being classified as "directed to children" when they serve a broader audience. Under paragraph (3) of the definition, a site or service that "does not target children as its primary audience"—again, a fact-specific judgment—may screen for age by requesting date of birth and identifying those whose responses indicate they are under the age of 13. In that case, the operator will only be required to obey COPPA with respect to a user below that age. This last step is where Yelp went wrong: the app asked about age, but then failed to use the information it learned in order to comply with COPPA. In guidance materials accompanying the rule, the FTC set detailed criteria for age screening. For example, the age screening request cannot indicate that a person will be unable to use the site or service if under the age of 13, and it must use cookies or similar devices to prevent a child from simply re-entering a new date of birth after being rejected. Perhaps perversely, the age screening rule may encourage some web sites and online services to request an otherwise unnecessary date of birth—which is often regarded as one of the more sensitive data points about an individual, because it is used frequently as an identifier in financial and health care settings.

6. ***To Screen or Not to Screen?*** You surely know from personal experience that most web sites do not request your date of birth before you can use them. It would be rather intrusive and inconvenient if they did. COPPA creates no affirmative obligation to screen. So why would an operator do so? Screening helps avoid situations where a site or service gains actual knowledge of a user's age later on—perhaps through a comment in a monitored online forum, for example—and then fails to obey COPPA with respect to that user. While not quite a safe harbor, screening can help avoid such accidental COPPA compliance failures. (Of course, for this strategy to work the operator must then, unlike Yelp, follow through on differential treatment for younger users.) The need for every web site or online service to make this decision—to screen or not to screen—makes COPPA a privacy law that organizations of all types must consider, including general-purpose providers who do not consider themselves oriented toward children. Would Yelp have been better off if it never asked for the date of birth?

7. ***Disclosure.*** The capacious definition of "disclosure" in the COPPA Rule plays a part in both *Yelp* and *Artist Arena.* In addition to disclosures that the data collector might make to additional parties, such as subcontractors or marketing partners, COPPA also regulates disclosures made *by the child* when using the site or service. Yelp gathered unique device identification and geolocation data for its own purposes, such as tailored search results. But the FTC complaint devoted at least as much attention to the ability of children under the age of 13 to "add information to their personal profiles, including photos, their current city, hometown, and any other information they chose to provide in free-form text fields." Unlike

adults, who are often considered to have waived privacy interests when they volunteer information, privacy law does not necessarily consider young children capable of making that decision without parental input.

8. ***COPPA and the Life Cycle of Data.*** Part Two of this book will examine the life cycle of data as it is handled by an organization. The cycle begins with data collection, moves to the processing and use of that information, then to its storage and attendant security considerations, and finally to any subsequent disclosure or transfer of the data. Many data privacy rules focus on one or perhaps two of these phases. When the FTC exercises its consumer protection powers under Section 5, for example, it emphasizes collection and security. But the COPPA Rule targets all four phases of the life cycle. 16 C.F.R. § 312.3 is framed as a regulation of "collection, use, and/or disclosure," and indeed reaches all of these. The statute sharply restricts collection of children's data and usually requires parental consent as a condition for doing so. It ensures that this data is used only for limited purposes and broadly prohibits many types of disclosure that are standard for other types of data. And although the title of § 312.3 does not refer to storage, its language requires that parents have access to data when it is in storage and that operators establish "reasonable procedures to protect the confidentiality, security, and integrity of personal information collected from children." The FTC enforces these COPPA obligations together, just as it does in ordinary consumer protection cases. So, for example, it filed a complaint against a social platform called RockYou that allowed users to play games and make slideshows from photos. Not only did RockYou collect information without parental consent from users when the company had actual knowledge they were under the age of 13, but it also used inadequate encryption and other protection measures when it stored that data, and suffered a hacking attack that compromised personal information from 32 million users, including children. The FTC addressed both violations, and the resulting consent decree imposed a duty to implement and audit security measures for 20 years as well as imposing a $250,000 civil penalty. *See United States v. RockYou, Inc.*, Case No. 12–cv–01487 (N.D. Cal. Mar. 27, 2012) (Complaint and Consent Order).

---

## Focus

Other US Data Protection Laws

Even though it is a sectoral US statute with relatively narrow applicability, COPPA resembles a full data protection regime like the EU's model in multiple respects. It certainly is not the only US regulatory structure like this. Other US statutes covered elsewhere in the book that are partially or entirely data protection statutes include:

***The Fair Credit Reporting Act (FCRA),*** 15 U.S.C. §§ 1681–1681u [see Chapter 6]: Like COPPA, this statute applies to certain narrowly defined information based on its characteristics—in that case, the intended use of the information for assessment of creditworthiness, employment screening, or certain similar determinations. Where it applies, however, FCRA establishes affirmative obligations that limit the lawful uses of "credit reports" to a closed set of purposes, confers rights of access and correction on data subjects, and confines downstream distribution of personal information.

***The Privacy Act,*** 5 U.S.C. §§ 551 et seq. [see Chapter 10]: Personal information collected and held by the federal government is subject to a series of limitations derived straight from the Fair Information Practices that also influenced the OECD Guidelines and, ultimately, the EU Data Protection Directive. Information collected for one purpose can only be used for other purposes if a government agency applies specific statutory exceptions and follows explicit procedural safeguards. Citizens have access to information about themselves as well as limited correction rights.

***The Health Insurance Portability and Accountability Act (HIPAA),*** Pub. L. 104–191 [see Chapter 12]: The privacy provisions passed by Congress in HIPAA were fairly broad guidelines, but the statute directed the US Department of Health and Human Services to issue more detailed regulations, and that agency took the task to heart, *see* 45 C.F.R. Parts 160, 162, and 164. Almost certainly the most elaborate data privacy provisions in US law, the HIPAA Privacy Rule, HIPAA Security Rule, and associated regulations spell out a complex set of instructions for data practices within large portions of the healthcare industry, especially insurers and providers such as doctors and hospitals. Under HIPAA, data may be collected or used only for certain identified purposes and no others. The regulations also impose obligations to give patients access to their medical records and a right to challenge their accuracy.

***The Family Education Rights and Privacy Act (FERPA),*** 20 U.S.C. § 1232g [see Chapter 15]: Like the other statutes here, FERPA has a narrow scope of coverage: "educational records" held by an elementary or secondary school or a college or university. Also like the other statutes, within that ambit, FERPA functions as a data protection regime. Schools may collect data for certain predefined purposes and may not circulate or release information from educational records without being able to point to an exemption that covers the situation.

## PART 2

# THE LIFE CYCLE OF DATA

Lawmakers and regulators developing privacy and data protection law tend to assess data practices based on the type of information involved, the particular technology used, or the industry sector that would be subject to legal restrictions. None of these organizing principles fully captures the perspective of privacy lawyers helping organizations comply with the law. They usually think about data practices in connection with the flows of data through the organizations they advise, the internal policies in place at each step, and the organization's needs. Thus, Part Two of this book follows the "life cycle of data" and some of the legal issues that arise in each of its phases.

Each chapter in Part Two considers a different phase: data collection [Chapter 5], processing and use of data [Chapter 6], storage of data and accompanying security issues [Chapter 7], and finally downstream disclosures or transfers of personal data outside the organization [Chapter 8]. Obviously, the real-life flow of data in any organization is not so linear and one-directional. A company might collect data from a customer, store it immediately, process it for marketing purposes later before storing it again, disclose it to a partner organization that conducts more processing to collect the customer's payment, then use it once more by referring to it when the customer returns. All the while employees may continue to use the continuously stored data internally as well, and perhaps disclose it again for other purposes like third party marketing assistance. The company might periodically collect more data from that same customer, which would then flow into the organization and start the life cycle all over again. The stylized division of the life cycle into four phases merely helps capture considerations at each phase, without suggesting that data flows necessarily follow this simplified schematic.

Each chapter in Part Two begins with a description of some of the business and organizational realities that influence data practices at that phase. Each then considers a case study that highlights a real world challenge in privacy and data protection law: internet cookies for collection, "Big Data" for processing, payment security for storage, and social media for disclosure. Finally, each chapter then turns to particular legal rules that are especially important at that phase. Much privacy and data protection law, especially in the US, applies only in certain sector-specific contexts, and Part Three will review many of these. By contrast, the law discussed in Part Two is more generally pertinent. Most of the legal rules in this Part should be of concern to a large variety of organizations, regardless of the industry they fall within or the precise type of personal data they collect.

## CHAPTER 5

# COLLECTION

In *Alice in Wonderland*, the King of Hearts offers sound advice to the White Rabbit: " 'Begin at the beginning,' the King said gravely, 'and go on till you come to the end: then stop.' " The life cycle of data begins, naturally, when an organization first collects personal data from or about an individual. By definition, uncollected information remains private and never raises any issues of privacy and data protection law. Perhaps for this reason—and perhaps because collection frequently will be the only phase of the life cycle that is visible to an individual data subject—much discussion and regulation about privacy focuses on this initial interaction.

This book considers the collection phase in the life cycle of data at numerous other points. Those include, to name just some of the major laws covering collection:

- Government searches of people or property for law enforcement or program administration [see Chapter 1], for national security purposes [see Chapter 9], in government workplaces [see Chapter 11], or in public schools [see Chapter 15].
- The intrusion on seclusion tort [see Chapter 2].
- Data collection notices and privacy policies governed by consumer protection law [Chapter 3], health privacy law such as HIPAA [see Chapter 12], and financial services regulation [see Chapter 13].
- Limits on data collection in the Children's Online Privacy Protection Act and in European data protection law [see Chapter 4].

The reasons for data collection vary as widely as the entities collecting it. Government may engage in data collection as part of its efforts to investigate criminal activity or protect national security. In the private sector, some personal information is simply necessary for the services being provided. A vendor may need a mailing address to deliver a requested product or credit card information to process payment. Doctors collect medical information to treat their patients, phone companies know the numbers their customers dial in order to connect their calls, and banks find out about financial transactions when they clear checks. In other cases, personal data may not be strictly necessary to complete an interaction, but it improves services, allows customization, or increases convenience. Over time, Google figures out whether your searches for "turkey" seek information about the food or the nation, and prioritizes results accordingly. Location tracking on a smart phone allows apps to tailor search results or driving directions. Educational software in schools can track performance on math problems and provide additional explanations in areas where the student is struggling. Sometimes the benefits to a data subject are less direct, but data can help organizations improve their offerings to everyone. Many web site analytics tools gather individual information about users' experiences to improve the site (although often this information is not associated with other personal data). Other forms of customer relations management help marketers analyze their customer base and make better business decisions. And of course, personal information enables targeted advertisements that rely on a customer's demographic features and past preferences.

Data collection may be either active or passive. Active data collection happens when a data subject provides requested personal information, for instance by filling out a form. Passive data collection may raise more issues, in both consumer protection and data protection frameworks, because individuals are not even aware that they have provided personal data to anyone. New technology presents particular challenges arising from passive data collection. Organizations simply accumulate personal information in the ordinary course of business: they may end up collecting an IP address (the unique ID of an internet connection, which can reveal location, organizations like companies and schools that host the connection, and sometimes identity); a referer (a mechanism that tells a web site the URL of the previous site you visited and sometimes other information); various mobile phone identification numbers; images of people captured on surveillance cameras; and even biometrics like voice prints or DNA.

This chapter begins with a case study [Section A] of an early passive collection technique, the internet cookie, and several attempts to regulate its functioning, especially in Europe. The balance of the chapter [Section B] considers the Electronic Communications Privacy Act, a very important US privacy statute that governs the collection of information through all forms of digital technology.

## A. CASE STUDY: COOKIES

---

### Focus

Explaining Internet Cookies

As the use of the World-Wide Web became more widespread around the beginning of the 21st century, some of the earliest concerns about internet privacy centered on a tiny feature called the cookie. The simplified discussion here will help you understand what cookies are, how they work, and what privacy issues they raise. While cookies no longer represent the technological cutting edge of privacy issues, they are a good case study of the legal response to data collection technology, because regulators attempted to respond to them with mixed results.

Cookies helped solve an early problem in the mechanics of the web: the maintenance of "state," or a web site's ability to retain information about user activity. So, for example, suppose Elizabeth visits a grocery shopping web site where she puts a box of Oreos in her virtual shopping cart on one page, adds a gallon of milk on another page, and then moves on to look at several other products. Obviously, it is important that the Oreos and milk remain in her cart when she decides to purchase them at the end of her visit. But in standard web browsing, each movement between pages actually involves sending a new request to the server that runs the web site, mixed in with the requests of everyone else using that site at the same time. How can the grocery site "remember" that Elizabeth is the customer who set aside the Oreos and milk for possible purchase on the separate pages she viewed previously?

A cookie is a text file that a server (the computer running the web site) places on a client (the computer of the person who visits the site). Cookies became a standard method for offering the familiar functionality of a shopping cart online. In one implementation, when Elizabeth clicked a button to place Oreos in her cart, the site would place a cookie on her computer with a code identifying the Oreos, and then send another cookie when she selected the milk. When she navigates to the checkout, the server would consult all the cookies it had placed on her hard drive to see which items should be shown. Alternatively, the server could place a single cookie with a unique code at the beginning of Elizabeth's shopping trip, and keep information on its own computers matching that ID with the Oreos and milk. When Elizabeth reaches the checkout, the server would check this cookie to figure out who Elizabeth was, and then compare that ID to the data held on the "server side" indicating the products she had chosen earlier. Whether the cookie itself identifies Elizabeth or her products, it fulfills the same function of keeping track of which user took which prior actions.

There are many other routine situations where state must be maintained during browsing, and cookies often provide the simplest and best way to do so. The same techniques can customize information for a particular user. Thus, the grocery site might show Elizabeth the brand of milk she ordered last time, or a sports site might default to showing information about the favorite teams Elizabeth identified on another occasion. Today, these preferences are often contained in a user profile held by the web site, which a person accesses by logging in to the site. Even there, however, cookies play a significant role—they allow the site to remember that Elizabeth has logged in, and which profile is hers, throughout her time on the site navigating between various pages. Servers often send cookies after a person logs in successfully, and then check the cookie whenever there is a need to authenticate that login. So, for example, if Elizabethhad an account with the grocery site, she might log in to gain access to her user profile, which may contain personal information such as her credit card number or contact information. Each time the grocery site intended to use or disclose this information, the server could consult the cookie to make sure this user was in fact Elizabeth and that Elizabeth had indeed logged in at the start of the browsing session.

Not all cookies operate in the same way. Some cookies, called "session cookies," expire at the end of a browsing session. They effectively contain self-destruct mechanisms. Others, called "persistent cookies," remain on a user's computer indefinitely and can be checked again whenever a user returns to the site. Another important distinction separates "first party cookies" from "third party cookies." A first party cookie is "set," or placed, by the primary web site with whom the user interacts. So, when the grocery site sets a cookie indicating that Elizabeth put Oreos in her cart, this is a first party cookie. The other type of cookie is a third party cookie, which is placed by someone else associated with the site. Third party cookies that are also persistent, which some people call "tracking cookies," have received the most attention. Where do these cookies originate and what do they do? How do they differ from the cookies used for maintaining state as described above?

A single web site often displays data drawn from a large variety of sources. When Elizabeth visits most news web sites, the advertisements she sees (and perhaps some other content as well) do not actually come directly from the news site's servers. Usually they do not come from the advertiser's servers either. In the vast majority of cases, both the advertiser and the news site have entered into an arrangement with a digital marketing firm. Some of these are specialized internet advertising companies with names like AdRoll or Criteo; others are digital portions of more traditional advertising agencies like J. Walter Thompson; still others are subsidiaries of familiar technology giants such as DoubleClick, which began as an independent firm but is now owned by Google. The digital marketing firm acts as an intermediary. It makes deals with advertisers to promote their products or services, and with web sites to place ads on their pages. Thus, when Elizabeth visits the Washington Post web site, her computer loads the news stories from the Post while simultaneously loading advertisements from digital marketing firms. If such a firm had a contract with Nabisco, it might insert a banner ad for Oreos onto the page. And each page may receive content from many different sources; a newspaper site like the Post might routinely receive content from two dozen different places, all loaded more or less simultaneously. (Browser plug-ins such as Ghostery, which identifies and optionally blocks cookies and other tracking mechanisms, illustrate this point emphatically by disclosing to the user all the content sources on every page.)

As an example, assume that DoubleClick has a contract to place Oreo ads for Nabisco. It will then agree with web sites like washingtonpost.com to place ads on their pages (and, obviously, pay to do so). When Elizabeth visits the Washington Post site, DoubleClick will transmit an Oreo ad to appear as a banner on the web page she views, and also place a cookie on her computer. This typically will be a persistent cookie, which DoubleClick can consult each time Elizabeth returns to the Washington Post site. But here is where two issues of concern to privacy advocates arise. First, suppose DoubleClick also has a contract to place ads on the we bsites of the New York Times, Politico, and the Onion. When Elizabeth visits those sites, DoubleClick can consult the same cookie it placed earlier when she was on the Washington Post page. The firm effectively monitors Elizabeth across multiple sites. If Elizabeth has already seen the Oreo ad and did not click it, DoubleClick's computerized ad placement system might note this and place an ad for Fig Newtons instead, or for a client other than Nabisco. More importantly, DoubleClick's cookie can also collect and store data about Elizabeth's movement through both of these sites, and indeed through all the sites with which it cooperates. This practice, often called behavioral tracking, allows a digital marketing firm to gather a lot of information about people, in the hopes of improving the effectiveness of the advertisements it places—and in turn generating higher prices for such ads at web sites like the Washington Post, and higher fees for intermediaries like DoubleClick.

The actual structure of the market is enormously more complicated, and includes the wrinkle that most fees for most ads are based on "clickthrough" rates: how often users actually click and open the pages that are advertised. In reality there may also be additional layers of intermediaries such as ad exchanges, which use technology to conduct nearly instantaneous auctions between digital marketers for ad space. These complexities are important, but they go beyond what is needed to understand the privacy issues here.

The combination of the two features just described—access to the cookie at multiple sites and recording of user activity at all of them—gave rise to controversy about "tracking cookies." By using tracking cookies, digital marketers can target ads much more effectively and tailor them to individual characteristics. Firms like DoubleClick can display ads for guitars to Woody and for ski equipment to Margot, selecting sales pitches based on each person's shopping history and predicted preferences. These firms can also engage in "retargeting," a practice in which advertisers show ads for a bicycle Elizabeth previously looked at online, or perhaps put in a vendor's shopping cart, but did not purchase. Thus, when she visits the grocery site or the Washington Post, she may see the ad for the bicycle again. The fact that internet users generally are unaware of these practices and have never heard of companies like DoubleClick increased discomfort.

Today, there are reasons cookies may be getting less effective as tracking mechanisms. First, users can delete cookies manually, and many do, although it is unclear just how many exercise this type of control. Two surveys in 2013, one commissioned by Microsoft and the other by the Pew Research Center Internet and American Life Project, both found that just under two-thirds of respondents claimed to do so. Other studies have found much lower numbers. People may overstate their actual propensity to delete cookies, but many of these studies are older and the habit of managing cookies may have grown over time. Perhaps more significant, today all major internet browsers offer settings that will "clear cookies" routinely, either after every session or after set periods of time, and some browsers refuse certain cookies by default. The increased focus on cookie privacy in the design (and marketing) of browsers surely has increased the rate of rejecting or deleting cookies, particularly those set by third parties.

Furthermore, as users connect to the internet on an increasing number and variety of devices, cookies tied to a single machine do not provide advertisers with as much information as they once did. In a speech to the online advertising industry, the head of the FTC's Bureau of Consumer Protection explained the landscape this way:

> [I]t is far from clear that consumers even know that they are being "tracked" when they visit internet sites. Some consumers still don't know what cookies are. But we are so beyond cookies at this point, and online tracking is only becoming more invisible as technology advances in the marketing world.
>
> Companies are creating single, universal identifiers to track consumers across multiple devices and connect their offline, email, and digital interactions. Companies hope to follow consumers across all their connected devices, including smartphones, tablets, personal computers, connected TVs, and even smartwatches and other wearables. This enhanced tracking is often invisible to users.
>
> In addition, companies are expanding their use of techniques such as device fingerprinting—which was originally developed to thwart illegal copying and fraud—to uniquely identify a broad range of internet-connected devices and build profiles about the people who use them. These profiles are often supplemented with data obtained from various third-party offline sources, making them even more detailed and personalized. Even those consumers who know about tracking and want to avoid it can't do so effectively.

Jessica Rich, Dir., FTC Bureau of Consumer Prot., Speech at AdExchanger Industry Preview 2015, *Beyond Cookies: Privacy Lessons for Online Advertising* (January 21, 2015).

That said, law takes a little while to catch up to changing technology and marketing practices. Cookies are the tracking technology that has received the most regulatory attention, even though they are no longer the cutting edge. You will learn important principles about data collection—and the reactions of privacy regulators—by understanding cookies.

The first three excerpts below represent three layers of requirements and advice relevant to the handling of cookies under European Union law. The first is a directive promulgated by the EU itself. The second is the regulation adopted in the United Kingdom to comply with these EU requirements. The third contains the less formal guidance provide by the UK's data protection authority. We will then look at an attempt in the US to respond to cookies and other tracking technology with a self-regulatory structure. As you read, ask yourself how the principles established in regulation of cookies might transform in response to innovations in consumer tracking. How flexible are these rules? How effective are they? How do the consumer proitetion and data protection model differ in their responses?

---

## The European Union E-Privacy Directive

EU Directive 2002/58/EC (as amended by EU Directive 2009/136/EC)

### Article 5. Confidentiality of the communications

1. Member States shall ensure the confidentiality of communications and the related traffic data by means of a public communications network and publicly available electronic communications services, through national legislation. In particular, they shall prohibit listening, tapping, storage or other kinds of interception or surveillance of communications and the related traffic data by persons other than users, without the consent of the users concerned, except when legally authorised to do so. This paragraph shall not prevent technical storage which is necessary for the conveyance of a communication without prejudice to the principle of confidentiality.

2. Paragraph 1 shall not affect any legally authorised recording of communications and the related traffic data when carried out in the course of lawful business practice for the purpose of providing evidence of a commercial transaction or of any other business communication.

3. Member States shall ensure that the storing of information, or the gaining of access to information already stored, in the terminal equipment of a subscriber or user is only allowed on condition that the subscriber or user concerned has given his or her consent, having been provided with clear and comprehensive information, in accordance with [the EU Data Protection Directive of 1995], inter alia, about the purposes of the processing. This shall not prevent any technical storage or access for the sole purpose of carrying out the transmission of a communication over an electronic communications network, or as strictly necessary in order for the provider of an information society service explicitly requested by the subscriber or user to provide the service.

## The UK Privacy and Electronic Communications (EC Directive) Regulations 2003

2003 No. 2426 (as amended 2011)

### 4. Relationship Between These Regulations and the Data Protection Act 1998

Nothing in these Regulations shall relieve a person of his obligations under the Data Protection Act 1998 in relation to the processing of personal data. . . .

### 6. Confidentiality of Communications

(1) Subject to paragraph (4), a person shall not store or gain access to information stored, in the terminal equipment of a subscriber or user unless the requirements of paragraph (2) are met.

(2) The requirements are that the subscriber or user of that terminal equipment—

(a) is provided with clear and comprehensive information about the purposes of the storage of, or access to, that information; and

(b) has given his or her consent.

(3) Where an electronic communications network is used by the same person to store or access information in the terminal equipment of a subscriber or user on more than one occasion, it is sufficient for the purposes of this regulation that the requirements of paragraph (2) are met in respect of the initial use.

(3A) For the purposes of paragraph (2), consent may be signified by a subscriber who amends or sets controls on the internet browser which the subscriber uses or by using another application or programme to signify consent.

(4) Paragraph (1) shall not apply to the technical storage of, or access to, information—

(a) for the sole purpose of carrying out the transmission of a communication over an electronic communications network; or

(b) where such storage or access is strictly necessary for the provision of an information society service requested by the subscriber or user.

## Guidance on the Rules on Use of Cookies and Similar Technologies

UK Information Commissioner's Office (2012)

Since 2003 anyone using cookies has been required to provide clear information about those cookies. In May 2011 the existing rules [in the UK] were amended. Under the revised Regulations the requirement is not just to provide clear information about the cookies but also to obtain consent from users or subscribers to store a cookie on their device.

### Practical advice for those wishing to comply

The Information Commissioner wants to provide as much flexibility as possible for organisations to design solutions that meet their business needs and provide users with the choices they require.

It is not enough simply to continue to comply with the 2003 requirement to tell users about cookies and allow them to opt out. The law has changed and whatever solution an organisation implements has to do more than comply with the previous requirements in this area.

### First steps

If you have not started work on complying with these rules it is important to do so now. First steps should be to:

1. Check what type of cookies and similar technologies you use and how you use them.
2. Assess how intrusive your use of cookies is.
3. Where you need consent—decide what solution to obtain consent will be best in your circumstances.

### 1. Check what type of cookies you use and how you use them

You should already know what cookies you are using but it would be sensible to recheck that at this point. This might have to be a comprehensive audit of your website or it could be as simple as checking what data files are placed on user terminals and why.

You should analyse which cookies are strictly necessary and might not need consent. You might also use this as an opportunity to 'clean up' your web pages and stop using any cookies that are unnecessary or which have been superseded as your site has evolved.

### 2. Assess how intrusive your use of these cookies is

Although the law makes no distinction between different types of cookie it is intended to add to the level of protection afforded to the privacy of internet users. Therefore it follows that the more intrusive your use of cookies is, the more priority you will need to give to considering changing how you use it.

It might be useful to think of this in terms of a sliding scale, with privacy neutral cookies at one end of the scale and more intrusive uses of the technology at the other. You can then focus your efforts on achieving compliance appropriately providing more information and offering more detailed choices at the intrusive end of the scale.

The Information Commissioner recognises that "how intrusive" an activity [is] will depend to an extent on the view taken by the user so it can be difficult to judge. This difficulty, however, should not be a barrier to making a sensible judgement about which of your activities might cause users concern and which will not.

### 3. Decide what solution to obtain consent will be best in your circumstances

Once you know what you do, how you do it and for what purpose, you need to think about the best method for gaining consent. The more privacy intrusive your activity, the more you will need to do to get meaningful consent.

### Conducting a cookies audit

An audit of cookies could involve the following steps and considerations:

- Identify which cookies are operating on or through your website
- Confirm the purpose(s) of each of these cookies
- Confirm whether you link cookies to other information held about users—such as usernames
- Identify what data each cookie holds
- Confirm the type of cookie—session or persistent
- If it is a persistent cookie how long is its lifespan?
- Is it a first or third party cookie? If it is a third party cookie who is setting it?
- Double check that your privacy policy provides accurate and clear information about each cookie

### Providing information about cookies

The Regulations are not prescriptive about the sort of information that should be provided, but the text should be sufficiently full and intelligible to allow individuals to clearly understand the potential consequences of allowing the cookies should they wish to do so.

### Getting consent in practice

Which method will be appropriate to get consent for cookies will depend in the first instance on what the cookies you use are doing and to some extent on the relationship you have with users.

When considering how to provide information about cookies and how to obtain consent it may be helpful to look at the methods most websites already use to draw users' attention to information or choices they want to highlight.

Many websites make use of different techniques to highlight things they want users to see, such as promotions, special offers, or customer satisfaction surveys. Websites also commonly obtain agreement or consent from individuals in other contexts, such as verification of minimum age requirements, changes in terms and conditions and to double check whether customers definitely want to proceed with a purchase. Providing users with information and obtaining their agreement is not a new feature of the internet. The approach you take for cookies can build on these existing mechanisms.

***Pop ups and similar techniques***

Pop-ups or similar techniques such as message bars or header bars might initially seem an easy option to achieve compliance—you are asking someone directly if they agree to you putting something on their computer and if they click yes, you have their consent—but it's also one which might well spoil the experience of using a website if not implemented carefully.

However, you might still consider gaining consent in this way if you think it will make the position absolutely clear for you and your users. Many websites routinely and regularly use pop ups or 'splash pages' to make users aware of changes to the site or to ask for user feedback. Similar techniques could, if designed well enough, be a useful way of highlighting the use of cookies and obtaining consent.

***Terms and conditions***

It is not uncommon for consent to be gained online using the terms of use or terms and conditions to which the user agrees when they register or sign up. Where users open an online account or sign in to use the services you offer, they will be giving their consent to allow you to operate the account and offer the service. There is no reason why consent for the cookies cannot be gained in the same way.

However, it is important to note that changing the terms of use alone to include consent for cookies would not be good enough even if the user had previously consented to the overarching terms. Consent has to be specific and informed. To satisfy the rules on cookies, you have to make users aware of the changes and specifically that the changes refer to your use of cookies. You then need to gain a positive indication that users understand and agree to the changes. This is most commonly obtained by asking the user to tick a box to indicate that they consent to the new terms.

The key point is that you should be upfront with your users about how your website operates. You must gain consent by giving the user specific information about what they are agreeing to and providing them with a way to show their acceptance. Any attempt to gain consent that relies on users' ignorance about what they are agreeing to is unlikely to be compliant.

***Settings-led consent***

Some cookies are deployed when a user makes a choice about how the site works for them. In these cases, consent could be gained as part of the process by which the user confirms what they want to do or how they want the site to work.

For example, some websites "remember" which version a user wants to access such as a version of a site in a particular language. If this feature is enabled by the storage of a cookie, then you could explain this to the user and that it will mean you won't ask them every time they visit the site. You can explain to them that by allowing you to remember their choice they are giving you consent to set the cookie. Agreement for the cookie could therefore be seamlessly integrated with the choice the user is already making.

***Feature-led consent***

Some objects are stored when a user chooses to use a particular feature of the site such as watching a video clip or when the site remembers what they have done on previous visits in order to personalise the content the user is served. In these cases, presuming that the user is taking some action to tell the webpage what they want to happen—either opening a link, clicking a button or agreeing to the functionality being "switched on"—then you can ask for their consent to set a cookie at this point. Provided you make it clear to the user that by choosing to take a particular action then certain things will happen you may interpret this as their consent. The more complex or intrusive the activity the more information you will have to provide.

**Functional and analytical uses**

You will often collect information about how people access and use your site. This work is often done "in the background" and not at the request of the user. A first party analytic cookie might not appear to be as intrusive as others that might track a user across multiple sites but you still need consent. You should consider how you currently explain your policies to users and make that information more prominent. You must also think about giving people more details about what you do so that users can make an informed choice about what they will allow.

Where a user logs into a website, or chooses to download a particular service that uses cookies, it should be relatively straightforward to put in place a mechanism to obtain consent for analytical and functional cookies at the point the user logs in. Clear information about the activities of these cookies can be provided and the user can be prompted to make a specific and informed choice before logging on to signify their agreement.

It is likely to be more difficult to obtain consent for this type of cookie where you do not have any direct relationship with a user—for example where users just visit a site to browse. In this case websites should ensure the information they provide to users about cookies in this area is absolutely clear and is highlighted in a prominent place (not just included through a general privacy policy link). As far as possible measures should be put in place to highlight the use of cookies and to try to obtain agreement to set these cookies.

If the information collected about website use is passed to a third party you should make this absolutely clear to the user. You should review what this third party does with the information about your website visitors. You may be able to alter the settings of your account to limit the sharing of your visitor information. Similarly, any options the user has should be prominently displayed and not hidden away.

---

## Practice

### Managing Cookies in Europe

Suppose your client is a US-based online retailer that plans to open a site oriented toward customers in the UK. The domain name will end in ".co.uk," prices and payments will be rendered in pounds sterling, and shipping will originate in a warehouse in England. (It can be difficult to determine exactly what counts as a site covered by EU law [see Chapter 4], but these facts clearly bring your client under UK jurisdiction.) What questions would you ask, and what advice would you offer, to develop policies so that the new site's use of cookies complies with UK law?

Keep in mind the cautionary note in Section 4 of the UK regulations. Requirements originating from the EU's E-Privacy Directive are layered on top of foundational EU data protection law [see Chapter 4] and do not replace obligations stemming from this law. How does that affect your questions and advice?

---

## Focus

### The "Do Not Track" Initiative

Tracking cookies also garnered criticism in the US. Under the consumer protection model, however, they are not necessarily unlawful unless a specific provision of law departs from the general default rule that allows collection. Some plaintiffs tried to bring civil suits raising arguments under privacy torts or contract law, but these failed for many of the reasons seen in Chapters 2 and 3—the harm is not sufficient, privacy policies are not enforceable contracts and, moreover, most companies did not claim to eschew tracking in the first place. Other early lawsuits invoked the Electronic Communications Privacy Act which, as the next Section explains, does not cover tracking cookies either. Finally, the FTC did not interpret the use of tracking cookies or other behavioral targeting as unfair or deceptive trade practices in themselves. But FTC staff publicly and privately encouraged industry to work with privacy advocates and other stakeholders to develop "rules of the road" to govern these practices. The industry established the "Ad Choices" program and other self-regulatory initiatives [see Chapter 3], but these did not achieve buy-in from other constituencies.

At first, many interests—including some representatives of the FTC, industry, privacy and internet activists, and the technologists who help develop the protocols of the internet through organizations such as the World-Wide Web Consortium ("W3C")—coalesced around the concept of a technological "Do Not Track" mechanism. This idea had a long pedigree. "Do Not Track" borrowed from the highly popular and successful "Do Not Call" list, which forbids telemarketers from calling numbers that have been placed on a federal government "opt out" list by their owners [see Chapter 14]. In part, Do Not Track also looked back to a much earlier W3C project from the late 1990s and early 2000s called the Platform for Privacy Preferences ("P3P"). The idea behind P3P was that users could select the level of privacy they wanted through browsers or plug-ins, which would then scan uniform machine-readable privacy policies at web sites and warn consumers about sites that violated their stated preferences. W3C working groups developed the standardized computer language for sites to encode privacy policies and communicate with users' browsers; the problem was that almost no web sites expressed their privacy policies in the special P3P language, which in turn made it pointless for users to set preferences.

With a push from the FTC—backed by an implicit threat to enforce more actively in the space if parties did not agree—a new W3C working group began efforts to create a Do Not Track standard. The technology was not really problematic: expressing a simple binary choice is much easier than conveying the complex ideas communicated through P3P. A wrinkle arose because the simplest way for a user to register and maintain a global Do Not Track preference would be—ironically—to embody it in a persistent cookie. But users had been trained by years of previous privacy education that the best step they could take to avoid online tracking was to *delete* their cookies, as increasing numbers have done. This technical difficulty was solved, however, by instead using the headers a computer sends when communicating with a web site.

The truly intractable problem was essentially a policy dispute. It concerned the default rule: should a browser be set to Do Not Track "out of the box," or should that require an affirmative step by the user? Because experience suggests that the overwhelming majority of users leave these initial settings intact, this became the crucial decision. [For another debate about whether a default should be to opt out or opt in, involving financial privacy, see Chapter 13.] The working group broke down into competing factions, one aligned primarily with industry and the other with privacy advocates. Complicating the picture further, several browser providers, led by Microsoft, unilaterally decided to "turn on" Do Not Track by default in their products, to the outrage of industry representatives in the working group. Eventually, many companies and industry organizations left the working group, so the W3C's eventual Do Not Track standard provides an option that few data collectors have adopted. Most web sites ignore "Do Not Track" signals, and do not claim to obey them in their privacy policies or public statements—thus preventing deceptive trade practices actions by the FTC. Users, meanwhile, have moved on to other technological solutions, such as ad blocking plug-ins, and web sites now use a broader range of tracking mechanisms beyond cookies. Despite good intentions and hard work, Do Not Track appears destined, like P3P before it, to be a voluntary self-regulatory response to online tracking that no one uses.

---

## B. THE ELECTRONIC COMMUNICATIONS PRIVACY ACT

Soon after the Supreme Court ruled in *Olmstead v. United States*, 277 U.S. 438 (1928), that wiretaps without warrants did not violate the Fourth Amendment [see Chapter 1], Congress passed legislation that barred at least some early forms of electronic eavesdropping. The original Wiretap Act was passed as Section 605 of the Communications Act of 1934, a comprehensive telecommunications law that also created the Federal Communications Commission and transformed regulation of both telephone and radio. Ever since, there has been a federal statute concerning wiretapping, which has undergone two significant overhauls. First, after *Katz v. United States*, 389 U.S. 347 (1967), Congress rewrote and expanded the statute considerably. This version is often referred to as "Title III" based on its numbering when it was included in a much broader omnibus crime bill. Title III went beyond regulation of government wiretapping; it made private individuals' interception of telephone calls a crime and established a private right of action for individuals to bring civil suits against either government or private defendants for violations of the statute. But its scope was limited mostly to recordings of intercepted telephone calls, the classic wiretapping scenario. In 1986, as networked computer technology came into more widespread use—but before the mainstreaming of internet use with the advent of the World Wide Web in the mid-1990s—Congress again changed and enlarged the statute, passing the Electronic Communications Privacy Act (ECPA), which remains in force today.

ECPA contains three distinct sets of rules, each contained in a different title of the legislation, but relying on some common definitions and other principles. The first two titles of ECPA govern the acquisition of communications by both government and private actors, and they contemplate enforcement through a range of warrant requirements, criminal penalties, and civil suits. The Wiretap Act (Title I of ECPA) prohibits unauthorized interceptions of communications while they are in transit, replacing the older Title III. The Stored Communications Act (Title II of ECPA) concerns unauthorized access to communications after they have been stored. We will consider each of these in turn below. Title III, the Pen Register Act, is more narrow and will be covered briefly.

Fair warning before we begin: ECPA is a dense statute. Furthermore, because most of it was drafted before certain technological developments, it can be fiendishly difficult to apply to contemporary factual situations. But it is the most broadly applicable statute governing data collection in the US, so we must dig in.

### 1. THE WIRETAP ACT

## Electronic Communications Privacy Act, Title I

18 U.S.C. §§ 2510 et seq.

### § 2510 Definitions

(1) "wire communication" means any aural transfer made in whole or in part through the use of facilities for the transmission of communications by the aid of wire, cable, or other like connection between the point of origin and the point of reception (including the use of such connection in a switching station) furnished or operated by any person engaged in providing or operating such facilities for the transmission of interstate or foreign communications or communications affecting interstate or foreign commerce;

(2) "oral communication" means any oral communication uttered by a person exhibiting an expectation that such communication is not subject to interception under circumstances justifying such expectation, but such term does not include any electronic communication; . . .

(4) "intercept" means the aural or other acquisition of the contents of any wire, electronic, or oral communication through the use of any electronic, mechanical, or other device[;] . . .

(8) "contents", when used with respect to any wire, oral, or electronic communication, includes any information concerning the substance, purport, or meaning of that communication; . . .

(11) "aggrieved person" means a person who was a party to any intercepted wire, oral, or electronic communication or a person against whom the interception was directed;

(12) "electronic communication" means any transfer of signs, signals, writing, images, sounds, data, or intelligence of any nature transmitted in whole or in part by a wire, radio, electromagnetic, photoelectronic or photooptical system that affects interstate or foreign commerce, but does not include—

> (A) any wire or oral communication; . . .
>
> (C) any communication from a tracking device [defined elsewhere as "an electronic or mechanical device which permits the tracking of the movement of a person or object."] . . .

(13) "user" means any person or entity who—

> (A) uses an electronic communication service; and
>
> (B) is duly authorized by the provider of such service to engage in such use;

(14) "electronic communications system" means any wire, radio, electromagnetic, photooptical or photoelectronic facilities for the transmission of wire or electronic communications, and any computer facilities or related electronic equipment for the electronic storage of such communications;

(15) "electronic communication service" means any service which provides to users thereof the ability to send or receive wire or electronic communications; . . .

(17) "electronic storage" means—

> (A) any temporary, intermediate storage of a wire or electronic communication incidental to the electronic transmission thereof; and
>
> (B) any storage of such communication by an electronic communication service for purposes of backup protection of such communication;

(18) "aural transfer" means a transfer containing the human voice at any point between and including the point of origin and the point of reception; . . .

### § 2511 Interception and disclosure of wire, oral, or electronic communications prohibited

(1) Except as otherwise specifically provided in this chapter any person who—

(a) intentionally intercepts, endeavors to intercept, or procures any other person to intercept or endeavor to intercept, any wire, oral, or electronic communication; . . .

(c) intentionally discloses, or endeavors to disclose, to any other person the contents of any wire, oral, or electronic communication, knowing or having reason to know that the information was obtained through the interception of a wire, oral, or electronic communication in violation of this subsection;

shall be punished as provided in subsection (4) . . .

(2)

(a)

(i) It shall not be unlawful under this chapter for an operator of a switchboard, or an officer, employee, or agent of a provider of wire or electronic communication service, whose facilities are used in the transmission of a wire or electronic communication, to intercept, disclose, or use that communication in the normal course of his employment while engaged in any activity which is a necessary incident to the rendition of his service or to the protection of the rights or property of the provider of that service, except that a provider of wire communication service to the public shall not utilize service observing or random monitoring except for mechanical or service quality control checks. . . .

(c) It shall not be unlawful under this chapter for a person acting under color of law to intercept a wire, oral, or electronic communication, where such person is a party to the communication or one of the parties to the communication has given prior consent to such interception.

(d) It shall not be unlawful under this chapter for a person not acting under color of law to intercept a wire, oral, or electronic communication where such person is a party to the communication or where one of the parties to the communication has given prior consent to such interception unless such communication is intercepted for the purpose of committing any criminal or tortious act in violation of the Constitution or laws of the United States or of any State. . . .

(g) It shall not be unlawful under this chapter or [the Stored Communications Act] for any person

(i) to intercept or access an electronic communication made through an electronic communication system that is configured so that such electronic communication is readily accessible to the general public . . .

(4)

(a) . . . [W]hoever violates subsection (1) of this section shall be fined under this title or imprisoned not more than five years, or both. . . .

**§ 2515 Prohibition of use as evidence of intercepted wire or oral communications**

Whenever any wire or oral communication has been intercepted, no part of the contents of such communication and no evidence derived therefrom may be received in evidence in any trial, hearing, or other proceeding in or before any court, grand jury, department, officer, agency, regulatory body, legislative committee, or other authority of the United States, a State, or a political subdivision thereof if the disclosure of that information would be in violation of this chapter. . . .

**§ 2518 Procedure for interception of wire, oral, or electronic communications**

(1) Each application for an order authorizing or approving the interception of a wire, oral, or electronic communication under this chapter shall be made in writing upon oath or affirmation to a judge of competent jurisdiction and shall state the applicant's authority to make such application. . . .

(3) Upon such application the judge may enter an ex parte order, as requested or as modified, authorizing or approving interception of wire, oral, or electronic communications within the territorial jurisdiction of the court in which the judge is sitting (and outside that jurisdiction but within the United States in the case of a mobile interception device authorized by a Federal court within such jurisdiction), if the judge determines on the basis of the facts submitted by the applicant that—

(a) there is probable cause for belief that an individual is committing, has committed, or is about to commit a particular offense enumerated in section 2516 of this chapter [a lengthy list of crimes, mostly felonies];

(b) there is probable cause for belief that particular communications concerning that offense will be obtained through such interception;

(c) normal investigative procedures have been tried and have failed or reasonably appear to be unlikely to succeed if tried or to be too dangerous;

(d) . . . there is probable cause for belief that the facilities from which, or the place where, the wire, oral, or electronic communications are to be intercepted are being used, or are about to be used, in connection with the commission of such offense, or are leased to, listed in the name of, or commonly used by such person. . . .

(5) No order entered under this section may authorize or approve the interception of any wire, oral, or electronic communication for any period longer than is necessary to achieve the objective of the authorization, nor in any event longer than thirty days. . . . Extensions of an order may be granted, but only upon application for an extension made in accordance with subsection (1) of this section and the court making the findings required by subsection (3) of this section. The period of extension shall be no longer than the authorizing judge deems necessary to achieve the purposes for which it was granted and in no event for longer than thirty days. Every order and extension thereof shall contain a provision that the authorization to intercept shall be executed as soon as practicable, shall be conducted in such a way as to minimize the interception of communications not otherwise subject to interception under this chapter, and must terminate upon attainment of the authorized objective, or in any event in thirty days.

**§ 2520 Recovery of civil damages authorized**

(a) In General.—Except as provided in section 2511 (2)(a)(ii), any person whose wire, oral, or electronic communication is intercepted, disclosed, or intentionally used in violation of this chapter may in a civil action recover from the person or entity, other than the United States, which engaged in that violation such relief as may be appropriate.

(b) Relief.—In an action under this section, appropriate relief includes—

(1) such preliminary and other equitable or declaratory relief as may be appropriate;

(2) damages under subsection (c) and punitive damages in appropriate cases; and

(3) a reasonable attorney's fee and other litigation costs reasonably incurred.

(c) Computation of Damages.—. . .

(2) . . . [T]he court may assess as damages whichever is the greater of—

(A) the sum of the actual damages suffered by the plaintiff and any profits made by the violator as a result of the violation; or

(B) statutory damages of whichever is the greater of $100 a day for each day of violation or $10,000.

(d) Defense.—A good faith reliance on—

(1) a court warrant or order, a grand jury subpoena, a legislative authorization, or a statutory authorization; . . . [or]

(3) a good faith determination that [provider exceptions] permitted the conduct complained of;

is a complete defense against any civil or criminal action brought under this chapter or any other law.

(e) Limitation.—A civil action under this section may not be commenced later than two years after the date upon which the claimant first has a reasonable opportunity to discover the violation. . . .

## NOTES

1. ***Three Types of Communication.*** Be sure you can explain clearly the difference between a wire communication, an oral communication, and an electronic communication. Come up with one or two everyday examples of interception of each type of communication. When do the distinctions between the three types matter under the Wiretap Act?

2. ***Keeping Pace with Technological Development.*** As already noted, one challenge of interpreting ECPA is applying its 1980s terminology and assumptions to 21st century communications technology. Congress has intervened at times to address particularly egregious difficulties presented by new technology. For example, earlier versions of the statutory language did not apply to conversations intercepted from a cordless phone—that is, a phone handset that is not connected to its base unit with a physical wire. At one time cordless phones were innovative, but now they are so universal that the very name has nearly gone out of use, because almost all home phones are cordless (though many people do still have traditional wired phones in their offices). In 1994, Congress slightly amended the statute to clarify that cordless phone calls are wire communications, transmitted by wire "in whole *or in part*." It is likewise now clear that calls on satellite phones, cellular phones, and voice-over-internet protocol (VoIP) services such as Vonage also qualify as wire communications. But it has been difficult to adapt ECPA to the evolution of the telephone from a simple instrument attached to a wire toward a variety of connection types more akin to networked minicomputers. Under ECPA's definitions, how would you classify SMS text messages carried on telephone networks? What about voice text messages? Videoconferencing communications such as Skype? For recent assessments of the ways ECPA has fallen out of step with technology, and some proposals to fix it, see, e.g., Bruce E. Boyden, *Can a Computer Intercept Your Email?*, 34 CARDOZO L. REV. 669 (2012); Susan Freiwald & Sylvain Métille, *Reforming Surveillance Law: The Swiss Model*, 28 BERKELEY TECH. L.J. 1261 (2013); Orin S. Kerr, *The Next Generation Communications Privacy Act*, 162 U. PA. L. REV. 373 (2014).

3. ***More than a Warrant?*** Some portions of the Wiretap Act concerning law enforcement, particularly § 2518, require a showing of probable cause to secure a warrant before engaging in wiretapping. But that just restates the Fourth Amendment requirement, which the government must satisfy anyhow under the Supreme Court's decision in *Katz v. United States*, 389 U.S. 347 (1967) [see Chapter 1]. So why did Congress write a separate statute? A hint: what *else* does the Wiretap Act require of law

enforcement to get judicial approval for wiretapping? Note that, in addition to those excerpted above, another provision of the statute limits applications for wiretapping orders to certain specified crimes and requires that they be approved by particular officials in the Justice Deprtment or state law enforcement agencies. *See* 18 U.S.C. § 2516.

4. ***Cookies.*** A number of early lawsuits challenged the use of tracking cookies as a violation of the Wiretap Act. These claims did not succeed; look at the language of the statute and figure out why not.

## In re Pharmatrak, Inc. Privacy Litigation

329 F.3d 9 (1st Cir. 2003)

■ LYNCH, CIRCUIT JUDGE.

This case raises important questions about the scope of privacy protection afforded internet users under the Electronic Communications Privacy Act of 1986 (ECPA), 18 U.S.C. §§ 2511, 2520 (2000).

In sum, pharmaceutical companies invited users to visit their websites to learn about their drugs and to obtain rebates. An enterprising company, Pharmatrak, sold a service, called "NETcompare," to these pharmaceutical companies. That service accessed information about the internet users and collected certain information meant to permit the pharmaceutical companies to do intra-industry comparisons of website traffic and usage. Most of the pharmaceutical companies were emphatic that they did not want personal or identifying data about their web site users to be collected. In connection with their contracting to use NETcompare, they sought and received assurances from Pharmatrak that such data collection would not occur. As it turned out, some such personal and identifying data was found, using easily customized search programs, on Pharmatrak's computers. Plaintiffs, on behalf of the purported class of internet users whose data Pharmatrak collected, sued both Pharmatrak and the pharmaceutical companies asserting, inter alia, that they intercepted electronic communications without consent, in violation of the ECPA.

The district court entered summary judgment for defendants on the basis that Pharmatrak's activities fell within an exception to the statute where one party consents to an interception. The court found the client pharmaceutical companies had consented by contracting with Pharmatrak and so this protected Pharmatrak. The plaintiffs dismissed all ECPA claims as to the pharmaceutical companies. This appeal concerns only the claim that Pharmatrak violated Title I of the ECPA.

We hold that the district court incorrectly interpreted the "consent" exception to the ECPA; we also hold that Pharmatrak "intercepted" the communication under the statute. We reverse and remand for further proceedings. This does not mean that plaintiffs' case will prevail: there remain issues which should be addressed on remand, particularly as to whether defendant's conduct was intentional within the meaning of the ECPA.

## I.

Pharmatrak provided its NETcompare service to pharmaceutical companies including American Home Products, Pharmacia, SmithKline Beecham, Pfizer, and Novartis from approximately June 1998 to November 2000. The pharmaceutical clients terminated their contracts with Pharmatrak shortly after this lawsuit was filed in August 2000. As a result, Pharmatrak was forced to cease its operations by December 1, 2000.

NETcompare was marketed as a tool that would allow a company to compare traffic on and usage of different parts of its website with the same information from its competitors' websites. The key advantage of NETcompare over off-the-shelf software was its capacity to allow each client to compare its performance with that of other clients from the same industry.

NETcompare was designed to record the webpages a user viewed at clients' websites; how long the user spent on each webpage; the visitor's path through the site (including her points of entry and exit); the visitor's IP address; and, for later versions, the webpage the user viewed immediately before arriving at the client's site (i.e., the "referrer URL"). This information-gathering was not visible to users of the pharmaceutical clients' websites. According to Wes Sonnenreich, former Chief Technology Officer of Pharmatrak, and Timothy W. Macinta, former Managing Director for Technology of Pharmatrak, NETcompare was not designed to collect any personal information whatsoever.

NETcompare operated as follows. A pharmaceutical client installed NETcompare by adding five to ten lines of HTML code to each webpage it wished to track and configuring the pages to interface with Pharmatrak's technology. When a user visited the website of a Pharmatrak client, Pharmatrak's HTML code instructed the user's computer to contact Pharmatrak's web server and retrieve from it a tiny, invisible graphic image known as a "clear GIF" (or a "web bug"). The purpose of the clear GIF was to cause the user's computer to communicate directly with Pharmatrak's web server. When the user's computer requested the clear GIF, Pharmatrak's web servers responded by either placing or accessing a "persistent cookie" on the user's computer. On a user's first visit to a webpage monitored by NETcompare, Pharmatrak's servers would plant a cookie on the user's computer. If the user had already visited a NETcompare webpage, then Pharmatrak's servers would access the information on the existing cookie.

Each Pharmatrak cookie contained a unique alphanumeric identifier that allowed Pharmatrak to track a user as she navigated through a client's site and to identify a repeat user each time she visited clients' sites. If a person visited www.pfizer.com in June 2000 and www.

pharmacia.com in July 2000, for example, then the persistent cookie on her computer would indicate to Pharmatrak that the same computer had been used to visit both sites.5 [The cookie expired after 90 days.] As NETcompare tracked a user through a website, it used JavaScript and a JavaApplet to record information such as the URLs the user visited. This data was recorded on the access logs of Pharmatrak's web servers.

Pharmatrak sent monthly reports to its clients juxtaposing the data collected by NETcompare about all pharmaceutical clients. These reports covered topics such as the most heavily used parts of a particular site; which site was receiving the most hits in particular areas such as investor or media relations; and the most important links to a site.

The monthly reports did not contain any personally identifiable information about users. The only information provided by Pharmatrak to clients about their users and traffic was contained in the reports (and executive summaries thereof). Slides from a Pharmatrak marketing presentation did say the company would break data out into categories and provide "user profiles." In practice, the aggregate demographic information in the reports was limited to the percentages of users from different countries; the percentages of users with different domain extensions (i.e., the percentages of users originating from for-profit, government, academic, or other not-for-profit organizations); and the percentages of first-time versus repeat users. An example of a NETcompare "user profile" is: "The average Novartis visitor is a first-time visitor from the U.S., visiting from a .com domain."

While it was marketing NETcompare to prospective pharmaceutical clients, Pharmatrak repeatedly told them that NETcompare did not collect personally identifiable information. It said its technology could not collect personal information, and specifically provided that the information it gathered could not be used to identify particular users by name. In their affidavits and depositions, executives of Pharmatrak clients consistently said that they believed NETcompare did not collect personal information, and that they did not learn otherwise until the onset of litigation. Some, if not all, pharmaceutical clients explicitly conditioned their purchase of NETcompare on Pharmatrak's guarantees that it would not collect users' personal information. For example, Pharmacia's April 2000 contract with Pharmatrak provided that NETcompare would not collect personally identifiable information from users. Michael Sonnenreich, Chief Executive Officer of Pharmatrak, stated unequivocally at his deposition that none of his company's clients consented to the collection of personally identifiable information.

Pharmatrak nevertheless collected some personal information on a small number of users. Pharmatrak distributed approximately 18.7 million persistent cookies through NETcompare. The number of unique cookies provides a rough estimate of the number of users Pharmatrak monitored. Plaintiffs' expert was able to develop individual profiles for just 232 users.

The following personal information was found on Pharmatrak servers: names, addresses, telephone numbers, email addresses, dates of birth, genders, insurance statuses, education levels, occupations, medical conditions, medications, and reasons for visiting the particular website. Pharmatrak also occasionally recorded the subject, sender, and date of the web-based email message a user was reading immediately prior to visiting the website of a Pharmatrak client. Most of the individual profiles assembled by plaintiffs' expert contain some but not all of this information.

The personal information in 197 of the 232 user profiles was recorded due to an interaction between NETcompare and computer code written by one pharmaceutical client, Pharmacia, for one of its webpages. Starting on or before August 18, 2000 and ending sometime between December 2, 2000 and February 6, 2001, the client Pharmacia used the "get" method to transmit information from a rebate form on its Detrol website; the webpage was subsequently modified to use the "post" method of transmission. This was the source of the personal information collected by Pharmatrak from users of the Detrol website. [Detrol is a bladder control medication.]

Web servers use two methods to transmit information entered into online forms: the get method and the post method. The get method is generally used for short forms such as the "Search" box at Yahoo! and other online search engines. The post method is normally used for longer forms and forms soliciting private information. When a server uses the get method, the information entered into the online form becomes appended to the next URL. For example, if a user enters "respiratory problems" into the query box at a search engine, and the search engine transmits this information using the get method, then the words "respiratory" and "problems" will be appended to the query string at the end of the URL of the webpage showing the search results. By contrast, if a website transmits information via the post method, then that information does not appear in the URL. Since NETcompare was designed to record the full URLs of the webpages a user viewed immediately before and during a visit to a client's site, Pharmatrak recorded personal information transmitted using the get method.

There is no evidence Pharmatrak instructed its clients not to use the get method. The detailed installation instructions Pharmatrak provided to pharmaceutical clients ignore entirely the issue of the different transmission methods.

In addition to the problem at the Detrol website, there was also another instance in which a pharmaceutical client used the get method to transmit personal information entered into an online form. The other personal information on Pharmatrak's servers was recorded as a result of software errors. These errors were a bug in a popular email program (reported in May 2001 and subsequently fixed) and an aberrant web browser.

II.

On June 28, 2001, plaintiffs filed an amended consolidated class action complaint13 against Pharmatrak; its parent company, Glocal Communications, Ltd.; and five pharmaceutical companies. Plaintiffs alleged nine counts including violation of Title I of the ECPA, 18 U.S.C. §§ 2510 et seq.; violation of Title II of the ECPA, 18 U.S.C. 2701 et seq.; violation of the Computer Fraud and Abuse Act, 18 U.S.C. § 1030; violation of Mass. Gen. Laws ch. 272, § 99 (2000); violation of Mass. Gen. Laws ch. 93A (2001); invasion of privacy; trespass to chattels and conversion; and unjust enrichment.

The plaintiffs employed computer scientist C. Matthew Curtin and his company, Interhack, to analyze Pharmatrak's servers between December 17, 2001 and January 18, 2002. In about an hour, Curtin wrote three custom computer programs, including "getneedle.pl," to extract and organize personal information on Pharmatrak's web server access logs, which he "colloquially termed 'haystacks.' " Curtin then cross-referenced the information he extracted with other sources such as internet telephone books. Plaintiffs also conducted the Rule 30(b)(6) depositions.

After discovery was completed, Pharmatrak, Glocal, and other defendants renewed their motions for summary judgment; plaintiffs opposed these motions and moved for summary judgment against Pharmatrak and Glocal on the claim based on Title I of the ECPA.

Following a hearing on the motions, the district court issued a memorandum and order on August 13, 2002 denying plaintiffs' motion for summary judgment and granting in part defendants' summary judgment motions. The court held that the claim against Pharmatrak under Title I of the ECPA was precluded because "the Pharmaceutical Defendants consented to the placement of code for Pharmatrak's NETcompare service on their websites." The court granted summary judgment to all defendants on all federal law causes of action; it then declined to retain jurisdiction over the state law causes of action and dismissed them without prejudice.

III.

## B. Elements of the ECPA Cause of Action

ECPA amended the Federal Wiretap Act by extending to data and electronic transmissions the same protection already afforded to oral and wire communications. The paramount objective of the Wiretap Act is to protect effectively the privacy of communications.

The post-ECPA Wiretap Act provides a private right of action against one who "intentionally intercepts, endeavors to intercept, or procures any other person to intercept or endeavor to intercept, any wire, oral, or electronic communication." 18 U.S.C. § 2511(1)(a); see 18 U.S.C. § 2520. The Wiretap Act defines "intercept" as "the aural or other acquisition of the contents of any wire, electronic, or oral communication through the use of any electronic, mechanical, or other device." Id.

§ 2510(4). Thus, plaintiffs must show five elements to make their claim under Title I of the ECPA: that a defendant (1) intentionally (2) intercepted, endeavored to intercept or procured another person to intercept or endeavor to intercept (3) the contents of (4) an electronic communication (5) using a device. This showing is subject to certain statutory exceptions, such as consent.

In its trial and appellate court briefs, Pharmatrak sought summary judgment on only one element of § 2511(1)(a), interception, as well as on the statutory consent exception. We address these issues below. Pharmatrak has not contested whether it used a device or obtained the contents of an electronic communication. This is appropriate. The ECPA adopts a broad, functional definition of an electronic communication. This definition includes "any transfer of signs, signals, writing, images, sounds, data, or intelligence of any nature transmitted in whole or in part by a wire, radio, electromagnetic, photoelectric, or photooptical system that affects interstate or foreign commerce," with certain exceptions unrelated to this case. 18 U.S.C. § 2510(12). Transmissions of completed online forms, such as the one at Pharmacia's Detrol website, to the pharmaceutical defendants constitute electronic communications. See *United States v. Steiger*, 318 F.3d 1039, 1047 (11th Cir. 2003); *Konop v. Hawaiian Airlines, Inc.*, 302 F.3d 868, 876 (9th Cir. 2002).

The ECPA also says that " 'contents,' when used with respect to any wire, oral, or electronic communication, includes any information concerning the substance, purport, or meaning of that communication." 18 U.S.C. § 2510(8). This definition encompasses personally identifiable information such as a party's name, date of birth, and medical condition. Finally, it is clear that Pharmatrak relied on devices such as its web servers to capture information from users.

### C. Consent Exception

There is a pertinent statutory exception to § 2511(1)(a) "where one of the parties to the communication has given prior consent to such interception unless such communication is intercepted for the purpose of committing any criminal or tortious act. . . ." 18 U.S.C. § 2511(2)(d). Plaintiffs, of course, bear the burden of establishing a violation of the ECPA. Our case law is unclear as to who has the burden of showing the statutory exception for consent. We think, at least for the consent exception under the ECPA in civil cases, that it makes more sense to place the burden of showing consent on the party seeking the benefit of the exception, and so hold. That party is more likely to have evidence pertinent to the issue of consent. Plaintiffs do not allege that Pharmatrak acted with a criminal or tortious purpose. Therefore, the question under the exception is limited to whether the pharmaceutical defendants gave consent to the interception. Because the district court disposed of the case on the grounds that Pharmatrak's conduct fell within the consent exception, we start there.

The district court adopted Pharmatrak's argument that the only relevant inquiry is whether the pharmaceutical companies consented to use Pharmatrak's NETcompare service, regardless of how the service eventually operated. In doing so, the district court did not apply this circuit's general standards for consent under the Wiretap Act and the ECPA set forth in [*Griggs-Ryan v. Smith*, 904 F.2d 112 (1st Cir.1990)]. It also misread two district court opinions on which it purported to rely: *Chance v. Avenue A, Inc.*, 165 F. Supp. 2d 1153 (W.D. Wash. 2001), and *In re DoubleClick Inc. Privacy Litigation*, 154 F. Supp. 2d 497 (S.D.N.Y. 2001).

This court addressed the issue of consent under the Wiretap Act in *Griggs-Ryan*. A party may consent to the interception of only part of a communication or to the interception of only a subset of its communications. "Thus, 'a reviewing court must inquire into the dimensions of the consent and then ascertain whether the interception exceeded those boundaries.'" *Gilday v. Dubois*, 124 F.3d 277, 297 (1st Cir.1997) (quoting *Griggs-Ryan*, 904 F.2d at 119). Consent may be explicit or implied, but it must be actual consent rather than constructive consent. Pharmatrak argues that it had implied consent from the pharmaceutical companies.

Consent should not casually be inferred. Without actual notice, consent can only be implied when the surrounding circumstances convincingly show that the party knew about and consented to the interception [citing cases].

The district court made an error of law, urged on it by Pharmatrak, as to what constitutes consent. It did not apply the standards of this circuit. Moreover, DoubleClick and Avenue A do not set up a rule, contrary to the district court's reading of them, that a consent to interception can be inferred from the mere purchase of a service, regardless of circumstances. If these cases did so hold, they would be contrary to the rule of this circuit established in *Griggs-Ryan*. DoubleClick and Avenue A, rather, were concerned with situations in which the defendant companies' clients purchased their services for the precise purpose of creating individual user profiles in order to target those users for particular advertisements. This very purpose was announced by DoubleClick and Avenue A publicly, as well as being self-evident. These decisions found it would be unreasonable to infer that the clients had not consented merely because they might not understand precisely how the user demographics were collected. The facts in our case are the mirror image of those in DoubleClick and Avenue A: the pharmaceutical clients insisted there be no collection of personal data and the circumstances permit no reasonable inference that they did consent.

On the undisputed facts, the client pharmaceutical companies did not give the requisite consent. The pharmaceutical clients sought and received assurances from Pharmatrak that its NETcompare service did not and could not collect personally identifiable information. Far from consenting to the collection of personally identifiable information, the pharmaceutical clients explicitly conditioned their purchase of NETcompare on the fact that it would not collect such information.

The interpretation urged by Pharmatrak would, we think, lead to results inconsistent with the statutory intent. It would undercut efforts by one party to a contract to require that the privacy interests of those who electronically communicate with it be protected by the other party to the contract. It also would lead to irrational results. Suppose Pharmatrak, for example, had intentionally designed its software, contrary to its representations and its clients' expectations, to redirect all possible personal information to Pharmatrak servers, which collected and mined the data. Under the district court's approach, Pharmatrak would nevertheless be insulated against liability under the ECPA on the theory that the pharmaceutical companies had "consented" by simply buying Pharmatrak's product. Or suppose an internet service provider received a parent's consent solely to monitor a child's internet usage for attempts to access sexually explicit sites—but the ISP installed code that monitored, recorded and cataloged all internet usage by parent and child alike. Under the theory we have rejected, the ISP would not be liable under the ECPA.

Nor did the users consent. On the undisputed facts, it is clear that the internet user did not consent to Pharmatrak's accessing his or her communication with the pharmaceutical companies. The pharmaceutical companies' websites gave no indication that use meant consent to collection of personal information by a third party. Rather, Pharmatrak's involvement was meant to be invisible to the user, and it was. Deficient notice will almost always defeat a claim of implied consent. Pharmatrak makes a frivolous argument that the internet users visiting client Pharmacia's webpage for rebates on Detrol thereby consented to Pharmatrak's intercepting their personal information. On that theory, every online communication would provide consent to interception by a third party.

### D. Interception Requirement

The parties briefed to the district court the question of whether Pharmatrak had "intercepted" electronic communications. If this question could be resolved in Pharmatrak's favor, that would provide a ground for affirmance of the summary judgment. It cannot be answered in favor of Pharmatrak.

The ECPA prohibits only "interceptions" of electronic communications. "Intercept" is defined as "the aural or other acquisition of the contents of any wire, electronic, or oral communication through the use of any electronic, mechanical, or other device." Id. § 2510(4).

Before enactment of the ECPA, some courts had narrowed the Wiretap Act's definition of interception to include only acquisitions of a communication contemporaneous with transmission. *See, e.g.*, *Steve Jackson Games, Inc. v. U.S. Secret Serv.*, 36 F.3d 457, 460–61 (5th Cir. 1994) (applying pre-ECPA interpretation to post-ECPA case). There was a resulting debate about whether the ECPA should be similarly restricted. The debate is well described in *Konop*, 302 F.3d at 876–79 & n. 6. Other circuits have invoked the contemporaneous, or "real-time," requirement to exclude acquisitions apparently made a substantial amount of time after material was put into electronic storage. *Steiger*, 318 F.3d at 1048–50 (pornographic images gradually collected on hard drive); *Konop*, 302 F.3d at 872–73 (static website content available on an ongoing basis); *Steve Jackson Games*, 36 F.3d at 458 (accumulation of unread emails). These circuits have distinguished between materials acquired in transit, which are interceptions, and those acquired from storage, which purportedly are not.

We share the concern of the Ninth and Eleventh Circuits about the judicial interpretation of a statute written prior to the widespread usage of the internet and the World Wide Web in a case involving purported interceptions of online communications. In particular, the storage-transit dichotomy adopted by earlier courts may be less than apt to address current problems. As one court recently observed, "[T]echnology has, to some extent, overtaken language. Traveling the internet, electronic communications are often—perhaps constantly—both 'in transit' and 'in storage' simultaneously, a linguistic but not a technological paradox." *United States v. Councilman*, 245 F.Supp.2d 319, 321 (D. Mass. 2003).

The facts here do not require us to enter the debate over the existence of a real-time requirement. The acquisition by Pharmatrak was contemporaneous with the transmission by the internet users to the pharmaceutical companies. Both Curtin, the plaintiffs' expert, and Wes Sonnenreich, Pharmatrak's former CTO, observed that users communicated simultaneously with the pharmaceutical client's web server and with Pharmatrak's web server. After the user's personal information was transmitted using the get method, both the pharmaceutical client's server and Pharmatrak's server contributed content for the succeeding webpage; as both Curtin and Wes Sonnenreich acknowledged, Pharmatrak's content (the clear GIF that enabled the interception) sometimes arrived before the content delivered by the pharmaceutical clients. Even those courts that narrowly read "interception" would find that Pharmatrak's acquisition was an interception.

Pharmatrak argues that there was no interception because "there were always two separate communications: one between the Web user and the Pharmaceutical Client, and the other between the Web user and Pharmatrak." This argument fails for two reasons. First, as a matter of law, even the circuits adopting a narrow reading of the Wiretap Act merely require that the acquisition occur at the same time as the transmission; they do not require that the acquisition somehow constitute the same communication as the transmission. Second, Pharmatrak acquired the same URL query string (sometimes containing personal information) exchanged as part of the communication between the pharmaceutical client and the user. Separate, but simultaneous and identical, communications satisfy even the strictest real-time requirement.

## E. Intent Requirement

At oral argument this court questioned the parties about whether the "intent" requirement under § 2511(a)(1) had been met. We remand this issue because it was not squarely addressed by both parties before the district court.

Still, we wish to avoid uncertainty about the legal standard for intent under the ECPA on remand, and so we address that point. Congress amended 18 U.S.C. § 2511 in 1986 to change the state of mind requirement from "willful" to "intentional". Since "intentional" itself may have different glosses put on it, we refer to the legislative history, which states:

> As used in the Electronic Communications Privacy Act, the term "intentional" is narrower than the dictionary definition of "intentional." "Intentional" means more than that one voluntarily engaged in conduct or caused a result. Such conduct or the causing of the result must have been the person's conscious objective. An "intentional" state of mind means that one's state of mind is intentional as to one's conduct or the result of one's conduct if such conduct or result is one's conscious objective. The intentional state of mind is applicable only to conduct and results. Since one has no control over the existence of circumstances, one cannot "intend" them.

S. Rep. No. 99–541, at 23 (1986), reprinted in 1986 U.S.C.C.A.N. 3555, 3577. Congress made clear that the purpose of the amendment was to underscore that inadvertent interceptions are not a basis for criminal or civil liability under the ECPA. An act is not intentional if it is the product of inadvertence or mistake. There is also authority suggesting that liability for intentionally engaging in prohibited conduct does not turn on an assessment of the merit of a party's motive. That is not to say motive is entirely irrelevant in assessing intent. An interception may be more likely to be intentional when it serves a party's self-interest to engage in such conduct.

## F. Conclusion

We reverse and remand for further proceedings consistent with this opinion.

# In re Zynga Privacy Litigation

750 F.3d 1098 (9th Cir. 2014)

■ IKUTA, CIRCUIT JUDGE:

The plaintiffs in these cases appeal the district court's dismissal with prejudice of their claims for violations of the Wiretap Act and the Stored Communications Act, two chapters within the Electronic Communications Privacy Act of 1986 (ECPA). The plaintiffs allege that Facebook, Inc., a social networking company, and Zynga Game Network, Inc., a social gaming company, disclosed confidential user information to third parties. We have consolidated these cases for this opinion and conclude that the plaintiffs in both cases have failed to state a claim because they did not allege that either Facebook or Zynga disclosed the "contents" of a communication, a necessary element of their ECPA claims. We therefore affirm the district court.

## I

Facebook operates Facebook.com, a social networking website. Zynga is an independent online game company that designs, develops, and provides social gaming applications that are accessible to users of Facebook. To understand the claims at issue, some background on Facebook and internet communication is necessary.

### A

Upon registration, Facebook assigns each user a unique Facebook User ID. The User ID is a string of numbers, but a user can modify the ID to be the user's actual name or invented screen name. Facebook considers the IDs to be personally identifiable information.

To generate revenue, Facebook sells advertising to third parties who want to market their products to Facebook users. Facebook helps advertisers target their advertising to a specific demographic group by providing them with users' demographic information. For example, a purveyor of spring training baseball memorabilia can choose to display its ads to males between the ages of 18 and 49 who like baseball and live in Phoenix, Arizona, on the theory that the members of that particular demographic group will be more likely to click on the ad and view the offer. Nevertheless, Facebook's privacy policy states that it will not reveal a user's specific identity and that only anonymous information is provided to advertisers.

In addition to its social networking and advertising services, Facebook offers a platform service that allows developers to design applications that run on the Facebook webpage. Zynga is one such developer. It offers free social gaming applications through Facebook's platform that are used by millions of Facebook users. Until November 30, 2010, Zynga's privacy policy stated that it did "not sell or rent your 'Personally Identifiable Information' to any third party."

## B

A brief review of how computers communicate on the internet is helpful to understand what happens when a Facebook user clicks on a link or icon. The hypertext transfer protocol, or HTTP, is the language of data transfer on the internet and facilitates the exchange of information between computers. The protocol governs how communications occur between "clients" and "servers." A "client" is often a software application, such as a web browser, that sends requests to connect with a server. A server responds to the requests by, for instance, providing a "resource," which is the requested information or content. Uniform Resource Locators, or URLs, both identify a resource and describe its location or address. And so when users enter URL addresses into their web browser using the "http" web address format, or click on hyperlinks, they are actually telling their web browsers (the client) which resources to request and where to find them.

The basic unit of HTTP communication is the message, which can be either a request from a client to a server or a response from a server to a client. A request message has several components, including a request line, the resource identified by the request, and request header fields. A request header known as the "referer" provides the address of the webpage from which the request was sent.

During the period at issue in this case, when a user clicked on an ad or icon that appeared on a Facebook webpage, the web browser sent an HTTP request to access the resource identified by the link. The HTTP request included a referer header that provided both the user's Facebook ID and the address of the Facebook webpage the user was viewing when the user clicked the link. Accordingly, if the Facebook user clicked on an ad, the web browser would send the referer header information to the third party advertiser.

To play a Zynga game through Facebook, a registered Facebook user would log into the user's Facebook account and then click on the Zynga game icon within the Facebook interface. Like the HTTP request to view an ad on Facebook, the HTTP request to launch a Zynga game contained a referer header that displayed the user's Facebook ID and the address of the Facebook webpage the user was viewing before clicking on the game icon. In response to the user's HTTP request, the Zynga server would load the game in an inline frame on the Facebook website. The inline frame allows a user to view one webpage embedded within another; consequently, a user who is playing a Zynga game is viewing both the Facebook page from which the user launched the game and, within that page, the Zynga game.

According to the relevant complaint, Zynga programmed its gaming applications to collect the information contained in the referer header, and then transmit this information to advertisers and other third parties. As a result, both Facebook and Zynga allegedly disclosed the information provided in the referer headers (i.e., the user's Facebook IDs and the address of the Facebook webpage the user was viewing when the user clicked the link) to third parties.

[The district court dismissed the complaints for failure to state a claim, and the plaintiffs appealed.]

II

We review de novo the district court's dismissal for failure to state a claim. To survive a motion to dismiss, a complaint must contain sufficient factual matter, accepted as true, to state a claim to relief that is plausible on its face.

As relevant here, the amended Wiretap Act provides that (with certain exceptions), "a person or entity" (1) "providing an electronic communication service to the public" (2) "shall not intentionally divulge the contents of any communication (other than one to such person or entity, or an agent thereof)" (3) "while in transmission on that service" (4) "to any person or entity other than an addressee or intended recipient of such communication or an agent of such addressee or intended recipient." 18 U.S.C. § 2511(3)(a). The "contents" of a communication are defined as "any information concerning the substance, purport, or meaning of that communication." Id. § 2510(8). Even if a disclosure is otherwise prohibited by § 2511(3)(a), an electronic communications service provider can reveal the contents of communications transmitted on its service "with the lawful consent of the originator or any addressee or intended recipient of such communication." Id. § 2511(3)(b)(ii). [The court also reviewed parallel provisions of the Stored Communications Act, which include reliance on the same definition of "contents."]

III

On appeal, the plaintiffs argue that the district court erred in holding that Facebook, Zynga, and the third parties were the intended recipients of the referer headers containing the user's Facebook IDs and the URLs. According to the plaintiffs, because their complaints allege that Facebook and Zynga had privacy policies which precluded them from providing personally identifiable information to third parties, the exceptions in §§ 2511(3) and 2702(b) for intended recipients are inapplicable. Facebook and Zynga, in turn, raise a number of arguments as to why we should affirm the district court. Because the plaintiffs' complaints suffer from a common defect—they fail to allege that either Facebook or Zynga divulged the contents of a communication to a third party—we focus our analysis on this single ground. In doing so, we express no opinion on the other elements of an ECPA claim.

A

Because the plaintiffs alleged that Facebook and Zynga violated ECPA by disclosing the HTTP referer information to third parties, we must determine whether such information is the "contents" of a communication.

To answer this question, we first must determine Congress's intended meaning of the word "contents." In ascertaining the plain meaning of the statute, the court must look to the particular statutory language at issue, as well as the language and design of the statute as a whole. We start with the plain language of the statutes. [T]he word "contents" is defined as "any information concerning the substance, purport, or meaning of [a] communication." Because the words "substance, purport, or meaning" are not further defined, we consider the ordinary meaning of these terms, including their dictionary definition. A dictionary in wide circulation during the relevant time frame provides the following definitions: (1) 'substance' means "the characteristic and essential part," Webster's Third New International Dictionary 2279 (1981); (2) "purport" means the "meaning conveyed, professed or implied," *id.* at 1847; and (3) "meaning" refers to "the thing one intends to convey . . . by language," *id.* at 1399. These definitions indicate that Congress intended the word "contents" to mean a person's intended message to another (i.e., the "essential part" of the communication, the "meaning conveyed," and the "thing one intends to convey").

The language and design of the statute as a whole sheds further light on the meaning of "contents" by indicating that "contents" does not include "record" information. Specifically, the Stored Communications Act provides that a covered service provider "may divulge a record or other information pertaining to a . . . customer" but may not divulge "the contents of communications." 18 U.S.C. §§ 2702(c), 2703(c)(1). Customer record information (which can be disclosed under certain circumstances) includes the "name," "address," and "subscriber number or identity" of a subscriber or customer. Id. § 2702(c)(2). Accordingly, we conclude that "contents" does not include such record information.

This conclusion is confirmed by ECPA's amendments to the Wiretap Act enacted in 1968. Before ECPA, the Wiretap Act defined "contents" as including "the identity of the parties to such communication or the existence, substance, purport, or meaning of that communication." When it enacted ECPA, Congress amended the definition of "contents" to eliminate the words "identity of the parties to such communication," indicating its intent to exclude such record information from its definition of "contents."

Accordingly, we hold that under ECPA, the term "contents" refers to the intended message conveyed by the communication, and does not include record information regarding the characteristics of the message that is generated in the course of the communication.

### B

The referer header information that Facebook and Zynga transmitted to third parties included the user's Facebook ID and the address of the webpage from which the user's HTTP request to view another webpage was sent. This information does not meet the definition of "contents," because these pieces of information are not the "substance, purport, or meaning" of a communication. A Facebook ID identifies a Facebook user and so functions as a "name" or a "subscriber number or identity." Similarly, the webpage address identifies the location of a webpage a user is viewing on the internet, and therefore functions like an "address." Congress excluded this sort of record information from the definition of "contents."

The plaintiffs argue that the referer header discloses content information, because when the referer header provides the advertiser with a Facebook ID (which, at the election of the user, may have been changed to a user name) along with the address of the Facebook page the user was previously viewing, an enterprising advertiser could uncover the user's profile page and any personal information made available to the public on that page. But the statutes at issue in these cases do not preclude the disclosure of personally identifiable information; indeed, they expressly allow it. There is no language in ECPA equating "contents" with personally identifiable information. Thus, an allegation that Facebook and Zynga disclosed personally identifiable information is not equivalent to an allegation that they disclosed the contents of a communication.

The plaintiffs also argue that record information can become content if the record is the subject of a communication, as in an email message saying "here's my Facebook ID number," or "you have to check out this website." Such was the case in *In re Pharmatrak*, where the First Circuit recognized an ECPA violation when an entity intercepted the content of the sign-up information customers provided to pharmaceutical websites and provided this information to third parties. Because the users had communicated with the website by entering their personal medical information into a form provided by a website, the First Circuit correctly concluded that the defendant was disclosing the contents of a communication. But the complaints here do not plausibly allege that Facebook and Zynga divulged a user's communications to a website; rather, they allege that Facebook and Zynga divulged identification and address information contained in a referer header automatically generated by the web browser. Unlike the information disclosed in *Pharmatrak*, the information allegedly disclosed by Facebook and Zynga is record information about a user's communication, not the communication itself. ECPA does not apply to such disclosures.

Finally, the plaintiffs rely on cases analyzing when disclosure of a URL may provide the contents of a communication, rather than record information, for purposes of Fourth Amendment protections.

This argument fails. As a threshold matter, our task in interpreting ECPA is to discern Congress's intent, and our Fourth Amendment jurisprudence is largely irrelevant to this enterprise of statutory interpretation. But even assuming that Congress considered the body of law regarding persons' reasonable expectation of privacy under the Fourth Amendment in making the statutory distinction between content and record information at issue in ECPA, we disagree with the plaintiffs' claims. Under the Fourth Amendment, courts have long distinguished between the contents of a communication (in which a person may have a reasonable expectation of privacy) and record information about those communications (in which a person does not have a reasonable expectation of privacy). Thus the warrantless installation of pen registers, which capture only the telephone numbers that are dialed and not the calls themselves, does not violate the Fourth Amendment. Courts have made a similar distinction between the outside of an envelope and its contents in mail cases. And we have allowed the warrantless collection of email and IP addresses under the same reasoning because email and IP addresses constitute addressing information and do not necessarily reveal any more about the underlying contents of communication than do phone numbers.

Nor does dicta about URL information being "content" under some circumstances help the plaintiffs. Under some circumstances, a user's request to a search engine for specific information could constitute a communication such that divulging a URL containing that search term to a third party could amount to disclosure of the contents of a communication. But the referer header information at issue here includes only basic identification and address information, not a search term or similar communication made by the user, and therefore does not constitute the contents of a communication.

## NOTES

1. **Pharmatrak *on Remand.*** Can you guess what the district court did on remand of the *Pharmatrak* case? You probably guessed correctly: it granted summary judgment to defendants based on the intent requirement. *In re Pharmatrak, Inc. Privacy Litig.*, 292 F. Supp. 2d 263 (D. Mass. 2003). Identify the facts and law in the appellate opinion that supported this result. Why did the appeals court write such an involved opinion when the same eventual outcome, summary judgment for defendants, seems to have been preordained?

2. ***Swapping Rationales?*** Could the decision in *Pharmatrak* have rested on the basis for the holding in *Zynga*, that the data in question was not the contents of a communication for ECPA purposes? Could the *Zynga* court have found that the consent exception applied to the situation before it?

3. ***Consent.*** As you can imagine, the consent requirement is a significant limitation on potential liability under the Wiretap Act, especially because only *one* party to the communication needs to consent. In other words, ECPA does not forbid you from recording your own telephone conversations, even without telling the other person with whom you are speaking. This is one reason most cases involving web sites collecting data from customers are nonstarters under the Wiretap Act, including the *Avenue A* and *DoubleClick* cases discussed by the *Pharmatrak* court: the owner of the web site is one of the parties to the communication. As *Pharmatrak*

demonstrates, however, if *neither* party to the conversation consented, then ECPA may apply. Furthermore, 12 states have their own versions of ECPA which require that *both* parties to a communication consent. This is why the recorded message at the beginning of a customer service telephone call almost always informs you that "your call may be monitored and recorded for quality assurance and training purposes." By staying on the line after this notification, you have manifested sufficient implied consent to what might otherwise be an interception under these states' electronic eavesdropping statutes. Finally, note that the consent exception does not apply if a "communication is intercepted for the purpose of committing any criminal or tortious act." *See* 18 U.S.C. § 2511(2)(d).

4. ***"Contents" of a Communication.*** As the *Zynga* decision makes clear, not every piece of data serves as the "contents" of a communication covered by ECPA. What are other examples of data that can be intercepted without implicating the Wiretap Act? In litigation over the iPhone's transmission of a person's geolocation data to third-party apps [see Chapter 3], that court decided that location data is not a communication. *See In re iPhone Application Litig.*, 844 F. Supp. 2d 1040 (N.D. Cal. 2012). In that vein, look at 18 U.S.C. § 2510(12)(C): it specifically excludes any "tracking device" from ECPA's coverage, presumably including the use of a GPS tracker found to violate the Fourth Amendment in *United States v. Jones*, 132 S. Ct. 945 (2012) [see Chapter 1]. *Zynga* suggests, however, that sometimes information similar to a referer might contain the contents of a communication. The opinion gives the example of a search engine query embedded in a referer. It also distinguishes *Pharmatrak* as involving a communication. Under this logic, it counts as a communication to tell a search engine or a pharmaceutical company web site, "I want to know about diabetes drugs," but not to tell them "I am user 65432, whom you know, from previous interactions, has an interest in diabetes" or "I am at the dialysis center right now." Can you explain that outcome?

5. ***"Interception."*** It is difficult to apply ECPA's concept of interception to email, which is constantly and nearly instantaneously being copied and recopied in its movement across the internet to a final destination. The *Pharmatrak* court refers unsympathetically to case law about the *timing* of an interception covered by the Wiretap Act. Most courts hold that electronic eavesdropping must copy data while it is still "in transit" in order for it to qualify as "interception." Otherwise, any liability arises under the considerably less stringent Stored Communications Act, not the Wiretap Act. While everyone could agree that eavesdroppers routinely intercepted telephone conversations while they were in progress, digital communications like email are another matter:

> [T]here is only a narrow window during which an E-mail interception may occur—the seconds or mili-seconds before which a newly composed message is saved to any temporary location following a send command. Therefore, unless some type of automatic routing software is used (for example, a duplicate of all of an employee's messages are automatically sent to the employee's

> boss), interception of E-mail within the prohibition of [the Wiretap Act] is virtually impossible.

*United States v. Steiger*, 318 F.3d 1039, 1050 (11th Cir. 2003) (quoting Jarrod J. White, *E-Mail@Work.com: Employer Monitoring of Employee E-Mail*, 48 ALA. L. REV. 1079, 1083 (1997)). This is not to say that online interception never occurs. In *Pharmatrak*, the web bug routed data to NETCompare at the same moment that it went to the pharmaceutical web sites. In *O'Brien v. O'Brien*, 899 So. 2d 1133 (Fla. App. 2005), a wife installed spyware on a home computer to monitor her unfaithful husband; the program "secretly took snapshots of what appeared on the computer screen, and the frequency of these snapshots allowed Spector to capture and record all chat conversations, instant messages, e-mails sent and received, and the websites visited by the user of the computer." The court held this an interception under Florida's version of ECPA, which the court interpreted by reference to the federal law.

Another interpretive difficulty arises because the internet functions on a "store and forward" architecture: emails and other communications are broken into smaller packets which are routed through multiple computers on their journey to a final destination, where they are reassembled into the full message. Nodes on the network may hold the packets if they cannot be transmitted immediately, and in any event may store backups briefly. One controversial appellate decision held that accessing messages while stored in this way was not an interception. An en banc court reversed the panel, "holding that an e-mail message does not cease to be an 'electronic communication' during the momentary intervals, intrinsic to the communication process, at which the message resides in transient electronic storage." *United States v. Councilman*, 418 F.3d 67, 79 (1st Cir. 2005) (en banc).

6. ***Borrowing from the Fourth Amendment.*** The *Zynga* court rejects the plaintiffs' reliance on Fourth Amendment cases which have found a reasonable expectation of privacy in referers and other URLs. Is the court correct as a general proposition that the reasonable expectations test is not relevant to statutory interpretation? Would it be appropriate to graft Fourth Amendment reasoning onto any parts of ECPA? If so, which ones?

7. ***Contents and Envelopes.*** The *Zynga* court emphasizes a distinction between the internal "contents" of a message and the outside "envelope" or "addressing" information, sometimes referred to as "metadata." As the court notes, Title III of ECPA provides much less protection for pen register information than does Title I for contents. But this same difference also arises constantly under the Fourth Amendment and in other areas of privacy law. The categorization, manipulable though it can be, often turns out to be vitally important to the outcome in a privacy case. *See generally* Orin S. Kerr, *Internet Surveillance Law After the USA Patriot Act: The Big Brother that Isn't*, 97 NW. U. L. REV. 607 (2003); Matthew J. Tokson, *The Content/Envelope Distinction in Internet Law*, 50 WM. & MARY L. REV. 2105 (2009).

2. STORED COMMUNICATIONS ACT

## Electronic Communications Privacy Act, Title II

18 U.S.C. §§ 2701 et seq.

### § 2701 Unlawful access to stored communications

(a) Offense.—Except as provided in subsection (c) of this section whoever—

(1) intentionally accesses without authorization a facility through which an electronic communication service is provided; or

(2) intentionally exceeds an authorization to access that facility;

and thereby obtains, alters, or prevents authorized access to a wire or electronic communication while it is in electronic storage in such system shall be punished as provided in subsection (b) of this section.

(b) Punishment.—The punishment for an offense under subsection (a) of this section is—

(1) if the offense is committed for purposes of commercial advantage, malicious destruction or damage, or private commercial gain, or in furtherance of any criminal or tortious act in violation of the Constitution or laws of the United States or any State—

(A) a fine under this title or imprisonment for not more than 5 years, or both, in the case of a first offense under this subparagraph; and

(B) a fine under this title or imprisonment for not more than 10 years, or both, for any subsequent offense under this subparagraph; and

(2) in any other case—

(A) a fine under this title or imprisonment for not more than 1 year or both, in the case of a first offense under this paragraph; and

(B) a fine under this title or imprisonment for not more than 5 years, or both, in the case of an offense under this subparagraph that occurs after a conviction of another offense under this section.

(c) Exceptions.—Subsection (a) of this section does not apply with respect to conduct authorized—

(1) by the person or entity providing a wire or electronic communications service; [or]

(2) by a user of that service with respect to a communication of or intended for that user . . . .

### § 2702 Voluntary disclosure of customer communications or records

(a) Prohibitions.—Except as provided in subsection (b) or (c)—

(1) a person or entity providing an electronic communication service to the public shall not knowingly divulge to any person or entity the contents of a communication while in electronic storage by that service; and . . .

(3) a provider of remote computing service [defined in § 2711] or electronic communication service to the public shall not knowingly divulge a record or other information pertaining to a subscriber to or customer of such service (not including the contents of communications covered by paragraph (1) . . .) to any governmental entity.

(b) Exceptions for Disclosure of Communications.—A provider described in subsection (a) may divulge the contents of a communication—

(1) to an addressee or intended recipient of such communication or an agent of such addressee or intended recipient;

(2) as otherwise authorized in [§ 2703 or certain sections of the Wiretap Act];

(3) with the lawful consent of the originator or an addressee or intended recipient of such communication, . . . ;

(4) to a person employed or authorized or whose facilities are used to forward such communication to its destination;

(5) as may be necessarily incident to the rendition of the service or to the protection of the rights or property of the provider of that service; . . .

(8) to a governmental entity, if the provider, in good faith, believes that an emergency involving danger of death or serious physical injury to any person requires disclosure without delay of communications relating to the emergency.

(c) Exceptions for Disclosure of Customer Records.—A provider described in subsection (a) may divulge a record or other information pertaining to a subscriber to or customer of such service (not including the contents of communications covered by subsection (a)(1) . . .)—

(1) as otherwise authorized in section 2703;

(2) with the lawful consent of the customer or subscriber;

(3) as may be necessarily incident to the rendition of the service or to the protection of the rights or property of the provider of that service;

(4) to a governmental entity, if the provider, in good faith, believes that an emergency involving danger of death or serious physical injury to any person requires disclosure without delay of information relating to the emergency;

(6) to any person other than a governmental entity.

. . .

**§ 2703 Required disclosure of customer communications or records**

(a) Contents of Wire or Electronic Communications in Electronic Storage.—A governmental entity may require the disclosure by a provider of electronic communication service of the contents of a wire or electronic communication, that is in electronic storage in an electronic communications system for one hundred and eighty days or less, only pursuant to a warrant issued using the procedures described in the Federal Rules of Criminal Procedure (or, in the case of a State court, issued using State warrant procedures) by a court of competent jurisdiction. A governmental entity may require the disclosure by a provider of electronic communications services of the contents of a wire or electronic communication that has been in electronic storage in an electronic communications system for more than one hundred and eighty days by the means available under subsection (b) of this section.

(b) Contents of Wire or Electronic Communications in a Remote Computing Service.—

(1) A governmental entity may require a provider of remote computing service to disclose the contents of any wire or electronic communication to which this paragraph is made applicable by paragraph (2) of this subsection—

(A) without required notice to the subscriber or customer, if the governmental entity obtains a warrant issued using the procedures described in the Federal Rules of Criminal Procedure (or, in the case of a State court, issued using State warrant procedures) by a court of competent jurisdiction; or

(B) with prior notice from the governmental entity to the subscriber or customer if the governmental entity—

(i) uses an administrative subpoena authorized by a Federal or State statute or a Federal or State grand jury or trial subpoena; or

(ii) obtains a court order for such disclosure under subsection (d) of this section;

except that delayed notice may be given pursuant to section 2705 of this title.

(2) Paragraph (1) is applicable with respect to any wire or electronic communication that is held or maintained on that service—

(A) on behalf of, and received by means of electronic transmission from . . . a subscriber or customer of such remote computing service; and

(B) solely for the purpose of providing storage or computer processing services to such subscriber or customer, if the provider is not authorized to access the contents of any such communications for purposes of providing any services other than storage or computer processing.

(c) Records Concerning Electronic Communication Service or Remote Computing Service.—

(1) A governmental entity may require a provider of electronic communication service or remote computing service to disclose a record or other information pertaining to a subscriber to or customer of such service (not including the contents of communications) only when the governmental entity—

(A) obtains a warrant issued using the procedures described in the Federal Rules of Criminal Procedure (or, in the case of a State court, issued using State warrant procedures) by a court of competent jurisdiction;

(B) obtains a court order for such disclosure under subsection (d) of this section;

(C) has the consent of the subscriber or customer to such disclosure; [or] . . .

(E) seeks information under paragraph (2).

(2) A provider of electronic communication service or remote computing service shall disclose to a governmental entity the—

(A) name;

(B) address;

(C) local and long distance telephone connection records, or records of session times and durations;

(D) length of service (including start date) and types of service utilized;

(E) telephone or instrument number or other subscriber number or identity, including any temporarily assigned network address; and

(F) means and source of payment for such service (including any credit card or bank account number),

of a subscriber to or customer of such service when the governmental entity uses an administrative subpoena authorized by a Federal or State statute or a Federal or State grand jury or trial subpoena or any means available under paragraph (1).

(3) A governmental entity receiving records or information under this subsection is not required to provide notice to a subscriber or customer.

(d) Requirements for Court Order.—A court order for disclosure under subsection (b) or (c) may be issued by any court that is a court of competent jurisdiction and shall issue only if the governmental entity offers specific and articulable facts showing that there are reasonable grounds to believe that the contents of a wire or electronic communication, or the records or other information sought, are relevant and material to an ongoing criminal investigation. In the case of a State governmental authority, such a court order shall not issue if prohibited by the law of such State. A court issuing an order pursuant to this section, on a motion made promptly by the service provider, may quash or modify such order, if the information or records requested are unusually voluminous in nature or compliance with such order otherwise would cause an undue burden on such provider.

. . .

(f) Requirement To Preserve Evidence.—

(1) In general.—A provider of wire or electronic communication services or a remote computing service, upon the request of a governmental entity, shall take all necessary steps to preserve records and other evidence in its possession pending the issuance of a court order or other process.

(2) Period of retention.—Records referred to in paragraph (1) shall be retained for a period of 90 days, which shall be extended for an additional 90-day period upon a renewed request by the governmental entity. . . .

### § 2705 Delayed notice

(a) Delay of Notification.—

(1) A governmental entity acting under section 2703 (b) of this title may—

(A) where a court order is sought, include in the application a request, which the court shall grant, for an order delaying the notification required under section 2703 (b) of this title for a period not to exceed ninety days, if the court determines that there is reason to believe that notification of the existence of the court order may have an adverse result described in paragraph (2) of this subsection . . .

(B) where an administrative subpoena . . . is obtained, delay the notification required under section 2703 (b) of this title for a period not to exceed ninety days upon the execution of a written certification of a supervisory official that there is reason to believe that notification of the existence of the subpoena may have an adverse result described in paragraph (2) of this subsection.

(2) An adverse result for the purposes of paragraph (1) of this subsection is—

(A) endangering the life or physical safety of an individual;

(B) flight from prosecution;

(C) destruction of or tampering with evidence;

(D) intimidation of potential witnesses; or

(E) otherwise seriously jeopardizing an investigation or unduly delaying a trial. . . .

(4) Extensions of the delay of notification provided in section 2703 of up to ninety days each may be granted by the court upon application, or by certification by a governmental entity, but only in accordance with subsection (b) of this section.

### § 2707 Civil action

(a) Cause of Action.—Except as provided in section 2703(e), any provider of electronic communication service, subscriber, or other person aggrieved by any violation of this chapter in which the conduct constituting the violation is engaged in with a knowing or intentional state of mind may, in a civil action, recover from the person or entity, other than the United States, which engaged in that violation such relief as may be appropriate.

(b) Relief.—In a civil action under this section, appropriate relief includes—

(1) such preliminary and other equitable or declaratory relief as may be appropriate;

(2) damages under subsection (c); and

(3) a reasonable attorney's fee and other litigation costs reasonably incurred.

(c) Damages.—The court may assess as damages in a civil action under this section the sum of the actual damages suffered by the plaintiff and any profits made by the violator as a result of the violation, but in no case shall a person entitled to recover receive less than the sum of $1,000. If the violation is willful or intentional, the court may assess punitive damages. In the case of a successful action to enforce liability under this section, the court may assess the costs of the action, together with reasonable attorney fees determined by the court.

### § 2711 Definitions for chapter

As used in this chapter—

(1) the terms defined in section 2510 of this title have, respectively, the definitions given such terms in that section;

(2) the term "remote computing service" means the provision to the public of computer storage or processing services by means of an electronic communications system[.] . . .

## NOTES

1. ***Comparing Titles I and II.*** Identify the most significant differences between the Wiretap Act and the Stored Communications Act. In particular, how does each limit law enforcement access to communications? What are the penalties for violations of each?

2. ***The 180-Day Rule.*** In § 2703(a), note the distinction between emails up to 180 days old and those older than 180 days. How are the two categories treated differently? Why do you suppose Congress drew this distinction when it enacted ECPA in 1986? A proposal backed by civil liberties organizations and technology companies would impose the "180 days or less" requirements on all stored communications regardless of their age. A bill doing so passed the Senate Judiciary Committee unanimously in 2013, but then stalled because of concerns stated by law enforcement. It has since been reintroduced but has come no closer to passage. Meanwhile, California and a few other states have made this change in their own "baby ECPA" statutes, and other states are considering bills to do so.

3. ***Warrants and Orders.*** Work your way through the tangled requirements of § 2703 to figure out why the 180-day rule is so important. What exactly is the standard for law enforcement access to stored communications that are three months old? Nine months old?

4. ***Exclusionary Rule.*** ECPA's exclusionary rule applies only to certain types of communications and certain types of eavesdropping. Can you figure out which ones? The Wiretap Act imposes an exclusionary rule on wire or oral communications gathered by law enforcement in violation of the statute. There is no exclusionary rule applicable to evidence gathered in violation of the SCA. What, then, are the disincentives for law enforcement to violate the SCA in an investigation?

5. ***Notice.*** Make sure you understand when law enforcement must provide notice to the target of an investigation that it is seeking access to that person's stored communications through an intermediary. It appears from § 2703 that any access triggered by less than a search warrant entails notice, but § 2705 complicates that picture. How? What if federal investigators secure a traditional warrant when one is not required—must they provide notice?

6. ***Pen Registers.*** Title III of ECPA, the Pen Register Act, applies only to law enforcement, not to private actors. This statute requires the government to secure a court order—but not a full search warrant—before gaining access to certain forms of communications "metadata." Pen registers may also be called "dialed number recorders" or "trap and trace devices." In the context of telephone communications, pen registers record the numbers dialed and durations of calls, but not contents of communications. The standards for obtaining a court order are fairly modest: the "court shall enter an ex parte order authorizing the installation and use of a pen register or trap and trace device anywhere within the United States, if the court finds that the attorney for the Government has certified to the court that the information likely to be obtained by such installation and use is relevant to an ongoing criminal investigation." 18 U.S.C. § 3123(a)(1). How do these

requirements compare to the Wiretap Act and the Stored Communications Act? Similar considerations have arisen in the controversy over extensive surveillance by the National Security Agency, which gathered vast quantities of telephone metadata, but not content [seeChapter 9].

## United States v. Warshak

631 F.3d 266 (6th Cir. 2010)

■ BOGGS, CIRCUIT JUDGE.

Berkeley Premium Nutraceuticals, Inc., was an incredibly profitable company that served as the distributor of Enzyte, an herbal supplement purported to enhance male sexual performance. In this appeal, defendants Steven Warshak ("Warshak"), Harriet Warshak ("Harriet"), and TCI Media, Inc. ("TCI"), challenge their convictions stemming from a massive scheme to defraud Berkeley's customers.

### The Search & Seizure of Warshak's Emails

Warshak argues that the government's warrantless, ex parte seizure of approximately 27,000 of his private emails constituted a violation of the Fourth Amendment's prohibition on unreasonable searches and seizures. The government counters that, even if government agents violated the Fourth Amendment in obtaining the emails, they relied in good faith on the Stored Communications Act ("SCA"), 18 U.S.C. §§ 2701 et seq., a statute that allows the government to obtain certain electronic communications without procuring a warrant. The government also argues that any hypothetical Fourth Amendment violation was harmless. We find that the government did violate Warshak's Fourth Amendment rights by compelling his Internet Service Provider ("ISP") to turn over the contents of his emails. However, we agree that agents relied on the SCA in good faith, and therefore hold that reversal is unwarranted.

#### 1. *The Stored Communications Act*

The [SCA] permits a "governmental entity" to compel a service provider to disclose the contents of [electronic] communications in certain circumstances. As this court explained in *Warshak II* [a previous opinion in the long-running Warshak prosecution]:

> Three relevant definitions bear on the meaning of the compelled-disclosure provisions of the Act. "[E]lectronic communication service[s]" permit "users . . . to send or receive wire or electronic communications," § 2510(15), a definition that covers basic e-mail services. "[E]lectronic storage" is "any temporary, intermediate storage of a wire or electronic communication . . . and . . . any storage of such communication by an electronic communication service for purposes of backup protection of such communication." 18 U.S.C. § 2510(17). "[R]emote computing service[s]" provide "computer storage or

processing services" to customers, id. § 2711(2), and are designed for longer-term storage.

The compelled-disclosure provisions give different levels of privacy protection based on whether the e-mail is held with an electronic communication service or a remote computing service and based on how long the e-mail has been in electronic storage. The government may obtain the contents of e-mails that are "in electronic storage" with an electronic communication service for 180 days or less "only pursuant to a warrant." 18 U.S.C. § 2703(a). The government has three options for obtaining communications stored with a remote computing service and communications that have been in electronic storage with an electronic service provider for more than 180 days: (1) obtain a warrant; (2) use an administrative subpoena; or (3) obtain a court order under § 2703(d). Id. § 2703(a), (b).

### 2. *Factual Background*

Email was a critical form of communication among Berkeley personnel. As a consequence, Warshak had a number of email accounts with various ISPs, including an account with NuVox Communications. In October 2004, the government formally requested that NuVox prospectively preserve the contents of any emails to or from Warshak's email account. The request was made pursuant to 18 U.S.C. § 2703(f) and it instructed NuVox to preserve all future messages. NuVox acceded to the government's request and began preserving copies of Warshak's incoming and outgoing emails—copies that would not have existed absent the prospective preservation request. Per the government's instructions, Warshak was not informed that his messages were being archived.

In January 2005, the government obtained a subpoena under § 2703(b) and compelled NuVox to turn over the emails that it had begun preserving the previous year. In May 2005, the government served NuVox with an ex parte court order under § 2703(d) that required NuVox to surrender any additional email messages in Warshak's account. In all, the government compelled NuVox to reveal the contents of approximately 27,000 emails. Warshak did not receive notice of either the subpoena or the order until May 2006.

### 3. *The Fourth Amendment*

The fundamental purpose of the Fourth Amendment is to safeguard the privacy and security of individuals against arbitrary invasions by government officials.

Not all government actions are invasive enough to implicate the Fourth Amendment. The Fourth Amendment's protections hinge on the occurrence of a "search," a legal term of art whose history is riddled with complexity. A "search" occurs when the government infringes upon "an expectation of privacy that society is prepared to consider reasonable."

This standard breaks down into two discrete inquiries: first, has the target of the investigation manifested a subjective expectation of privacy in the object of the challenged search? Second, is society willing to recognize that expectation as reasonable?

Turning first to the subjective component of the test, we find that Warshak plainly manifested an expectation that his emails would be shielded from outside scrutiny. As he notes in his brief, his "entire business and personal life was contained within the . . . emails seized." Given the often sensitive and sometimes damning substance of his emails, we think it highly unlikely that Warshak expected them to be made public, for people seldom unfurl their dirty laundry in plain view. Therefore, we conclude that Warshak had a subjective expectation of privacy in the contents of his emails.

The next question is whether society is prepared to recognize that expectation as reasonable. This question is one of grave import and enduring consequence, given the prominent role that email has assumed in modern communication. Cf. *Katz v. United States*, 389 U.S. 347, 352 (1967) (suggesting that the Constitution must be read to account for "the vital role that the public telephone has come to play in private communication"). Since the advent of email, the telephone call and the letter have waned in importance, and an explosion of Internet-based communication has taken place. People are now able to send sensitive and intimate information, instantaneously, to friends, family, and colleagues half a world away. Lovers exchange sweet nothings, and businessmen swap ambitious plans, all with the click of a mouse button. Commerce has also taken hold in email. Online purchases are often documented in email accounts, and email is frequently used to remind patients and clients of imminent appointments. In short, "account" is an apt word for the conglomeration of stored messages that comprises an email account, as it provides an account of its owner's life. By obtaining access to someone's email, government agents gain the ability to peer deeply into his activities. Much hinges, therefore, on whether the government is permitted to request that a commercial ISP turn over the contents of a subscriber's emails without triggering the machinery of the Fourth Amendment.

In confronting this question, we take note of two bedrock principles. First, the very fact that information is being passed through a communications network is a paramount Fourth Amendment consideration. Second, the Fourth Amendment must keep pace with the inexorable march of technological progress, or its guarantees will wither and perish. *See Kyllo v. United States*, 533 U.S. 27, 34 (2001) (noting that evolving technology must not be permitted to "erode the privacy guaranteed by the Fourth Amendment"); *see also* Orin S. Kerr, *Applying the Fourth Amendment to the Internet: A General Approach*, 62 STAN. L. REV. 1005, 1007 (2010) (arguing that "the differences between the facts of physical space and the facts of the Internet require courts to identify new Fourth Amendment distinctions to maintain the function of Fourth Amendment rules in an online environment").

With those principles in mind, we begin our analysis by considering the manner in which the Fourth Amendment protects traditional forms of communication. In *Katz*, the Supreme Court was asked to determine how the Fourth Amendment applied in the context of the telephone. There, government agents had affixed an electronic listening device to the exterior of a public phone booth, and had used the device to intercept and record several phone conversations. The Supreme Court held that this constituted a search under the Fourth Amendment, notwithstanding the fact that the telephone company had the capacity to monitor and record the calls. In the eyes of the Court, the caller was "surely entitled to assume that the words he utter[ed] into the mouthpiece w[ould] not be broadcast to the world." *Katz*, 389 U.S. at 352. The Court's holding in *Katz* has since come to stand for the broad proposition that, in many contexts, the government infringes a reasonable expectation of privacy when it surreptitiously intercepts a telephone call through electronic means.

Letters receive similar protection. While a letter is in the mail, the police may not intercept it and examine its contents unless they first obtain a warrant based on probable cause. This is true despite the fact that sealed letters are handed over to perhaps dozens of mail carriers, any one of whom could tear open the thin paper envelopes that separate the private words from the world outside. Put another way, trusting a letter to an intermediary does not necessarily defeat a reasonable expectation that the letter will remain private.

Given the fundamental similarities between email and traditional forms of communication, it would defy common sense to afford emails lesser Fourth Amendment protection. *See* Patricia L. Bellia & Susan Freiwald, *Fourth Amendment Protection for Stored E-Mail*, 2008 U. CHI. LEGAL F. 121, 135 (2008) (recognizing the need to "eliminate the strangely disparate treatment of mailed and telephonic communications on the one hand and electronic communications on the other"); *City of Ontario v. Quon*, 560 U.S. 746 (2010) (implying that "a search of [an individual's] personal e-mail account" would be just as intrusive as "a wiretap on his home phone line"); *United States v. Forrester*, 512 F.3d 500, 511 (9th Cir. 2008) (holding that "[t]he privacy interests in [mail and email] are identical"). Email is the technological scion of tangible mail, and it plays an indispensable part in the Information Age. Over the last decade, email has become "so pervasive that some persons may consider [it] to be [an] essential means or necessary instrument[ ] for self-expression, even self-identification." [citing *Quon*] It follows that email requires strong protection under the Fourth Amendment; otherwise, the Fourth Amendment would prove an ineffective guardian of private communication, an essential purpose it has long been recognized to serve.

As some forms of communication begin to diminish, the Fourth Amendment must recognize and protect nascent ones that arise.

If we accept that an email is analogous to a letter or a phone call, it is manifest that agents of the government cannot compel a commercial ISP to turn over the contents of an email without triggering the Fourth Amendment. An ISP is the intermediary that makes email communication possible. Emails must pass through an ISP's servers to reach their intended recipient. Thus, the ISP is the functional equivalent of a post office or a telephone company. As we have discussed above, the police may not storm the post office and intercept a letter, and they are likewise forbidden from using the phone system to make a clandestine recording of a telephone call—unless they get a warrant, that is. It only stands to reason that, if government agents compel an ISP to surrender the contents of a subscriber's emails, those agents have thereby conducted a Fourth Amendment search, which necessitates compliance with the warrant requirement absent some exception.

[The government argued] that NuVox contractually reserved the right to access Warshak's emails for certain purposes. While we acknowledge that a subscriber agreement might, in some cases, be sweeping enough to defeat a reasonable expectation of privacy in the contents of an email account, we doubt that will be the case in most situations, and it is certainly not the case here.

As an initial matter, it must be observed that the mere ability of a third-party intermediary to access the contents of a communication cannot be sufficient to extinguish a reasonable expectation of privacy. In *Katz*, the Supreme Court found it reasonable to expect privacy during a telephone call despite the ability of an operator to listen in. Similarly, the ability of a rogue mail handler to rip open a letter does not make it unreasonable to assume that sealed mail will remain private on its journey across the country. Therefore, the threat or possibility of access is not decisive when it comes to the reasonableness of an expectation of privacy.

Our conclusion finds additional support in the application of Fourth Amendment doctrine to rented space. Hotel guests, for example, have a reasonable expectation of privacy in their rooms. This is so even though maids routinely enter hotel rooms to replace the towels and tidy the furniture. Similarly, tenants have a legitimate expectation of privacy in their apartments. That expectation persists, regardless of the incursions of handymen to fix leaky faucets. Consequently, we are convinced that some degree of routine access is hardly dispositive with respect to the privacy question.

Again, however, we are unwilling to hold that a subscriber agreement will never be broad enough to snuff out a reasonable expectation of privacy. If the ISP expresses an intention to "audit, inspect, and monitor" its subscriber's emails, that might be enough to render an expectation of privacy unreasonable. But where, as here, there is no such statement, the ISP's control over the emails and ability to access them under certain limited circumstances will not be enough to overcome an expectation of privacy.

We recognize that our conclusion may be attacked in light of the Supreme Court's decision in *United States v. Miller*, 425 U.S. 435 (1976). In *Miller*, the Supreme Court held that a bank depositor does not have a reasonable expectation of privacy in the contents of bank records, checks, and deposit slips. The Court noted, "The depositor takes the risk, in revealing his affairs to another, that the information will be conveyed by that person to the Government."

But *Miller* is distinguishable. First, *Miller* involved simple business records, as opposed to the potentially unlimited variety of "confidential communications" at issue here. Second, the bank depositor in *Miller* conveyed information to the bank so that the bank could put the information to use "in the ordinary course of business." By contrast, Warshak received his emails through NuVox. NuVox was an intermediary, not the intended recipient of the emails. Thus, *Miller* is not controlling.

Accordingly, we hold that a subscriber enjoys a reasonable expectation of privacy in the contents of emails that are stored with, or sent or received through, a commercial ISP. The government may not compel a commercial ISP to turn over the contents of a subscriber's emails without first obtaining a warrant based on probable cause. Therefore, because they did not obtain a warrant, the government agents violated the Fourth Amendment when they obtained the contents of Warshak's emails. Moreover, to the extent that the SCA purports to permit the government to obtain such emails warrantlessly, the SCA is unconstitutional.

### 4. *Good-Faith Reliance*

Even though the government's search of Warshak's emails violated the Fourth Amendment, the emails are not subject to the exclusionary remedy if the officers relied in good faith on the SCA to obtain them.

Naturally, Warshak argues that the provisions of the SCA at issue in this case were plainly unconstitutional. He argues that any reasonable law enforcement officer would have understood that a warrant based on probable cause would be required to compel the production of private emails.

However, we disagree that the SCA is so conspicuously unconstitutional as to preclude good-faith reliance. As we noted in *Warshak II*, "[t]he Stored Communications Act has been in existence since 1986 and to our knowledge has not been the subject of any successful Fourth Amendment challenges, in any context, whether to § 2703(d) or to any other provision." Furthermore, given the complicated thicket of issues that we were required to navigate when passing on the constitutionality of the SCA, it was not plain or obvious that the SCA was unconstitutional, and it was therefore reasonable for the government to rely upon the SCA in seeking to obtain the contents of Warshak's emails.

■ KEITH, CIRCUIT JUDGE, concurring.

Although I concur in the result the majority reaches, I write separately to provide clarification concerning whether Warshak's emails, obtained in violation of the Fourth Amendment, should have been excluded from trial under the exclusionary rule.

Here, we are presented with a unique situation. As the majority notes, because the government requested a secret subpoena to confiscate Warshak's personal emails without his knowledge pursuant to § 2703(b) and (d) of the Stored Communications Act ("SCA"), there is no need to exclude the evidence. Therefore, the majority rightfully affirms the district court's refusal to suppress Warshak's emails. With this I agree.

However, there is a further wrongdoing that troubles me today. Specifically, the government's request that NuVox preserve Warshak's stored and future email communications without Warshak's knowledge and without a warrant pursuant to § 2703(f). Under § 2703(f), "[a] provider of wire or electronic communication services or a remote computing service, upon the request of a governmental entity, shall take all necessary steps to preserve records and other evidence *in its possession* pending the issuance of a court order or other process." 18 U.S.C. § 2703(f) (emphasis added). This subsection was added to the SCA in 1996 in an effort to supplement law enforcement resources and security. While added in a completely different context from the creation of the statute, it is worthwhile to review the purpose of the statute as a whole when considering the meaning of this subsection.

Section 2703, as part of the Electronic Communications Privacy Act ("ECPA"), was enacted in 1986 as part of Congress's effort to maintain a fair balance between the privacy expectations of American citizens and the legitimate needs of law enforcement agencies. Moreover, the advent of the ECPA was precipitated by concerns about advancements in technology and the desire to protect personal and business information which individuals can no longer "lock away" with ease. The plain language of § 2703(f) permits only the preservation of emails in the service provider's possession at the time of the request, not the preservation of future emails. Moreover, the Department of Justice, along with some theorists, emphasize that these requests have no prospective effect. I find this statutory interpretation persuasive.

Following NuVox's policy, the provider would have destroyed Warshak's old emails but for the government's request that they maintain all current and prospective emails for almost a year without Warshak's knowledge. In practice, the government used the statute as a means to monitor Warshak after the investigation started without his knowledge and without a warrant. Such a practice is no more than back-door wiretapping. I doubt that such actions, if contested directly in court, would withstand the muster of the Fourth Amendment. To interpret § 2703(f) as having both a retroactive and prospective effect would be contrary to the purpose of the statute as a whole.

While it was not the issue in today's decision, a policy whereby the government requests emails prospectively without a warrant deeply concerns me. [However], the majority was correct in holding that the evidence falls within the good faith exception to the exclusionary rule.

## NOTES

1. ***Can Officers Still Rely on the SCA?*** At the end of the last paragraph in the excerpt of the *Warshak* majority opinion, the court inserted this footnote: "Of course, after today's decision, the good-faith calculus has changed, and a reasonable officer may no longer assume that the Constitution permits warrantless searches of private emails." The *Warshak* court allowed the use of the evidence in the case before it, but prospectively invalidated the compelled disclosure provisions of the Stored Communications Act within the states of the Sixth Circuit: Michigan, Ohio, Kentucky, and Tennessee. As this footnote suggests, its future effect on law enforcement practices in other states has been less direct, but still significant. With *Warshak* on the books, even as merely persuasive authority, it became more possible that a later court might reject a defense of good-faith reliance on the SCA and exclude evidence as a result. How true is this for officers outside the Sixth Circuit? If you were advising law enforcement authorities outside the Sixth Circuit after this ruling, what would you recommend they do the next time they want to secure emails like Warshak's? Does it matter that, at the time of the decision, some departments already elected to secure warrants for similar stored communications to avoid any doubt about the future admissibility of the evidence?

2. ***The Influence of* Warshak *on Other Courts.*** As of this writing in early 2016, no other federal court of appeals has joined the Sixth Circuit in holding these provisions of the SCA unconstitutional because they violate the Fourth Amendment—but none has rejected *Warshak* outright either. Moreover, the logic of the case does seem likely to have influenced the Supreme Court's concurring justices in *United States v. Jones* [see Chapter 1].

3. ***Content and Records.*** *Warshak* is a case about obtaining communication content under § 2701 of the SCA. How might the analysis change if Warshak had challenged the government's acquisition of his *records* under § 2703?

4. ***Stricter State Rules.*** Aside from federal court decisions, a number of jurisdictions have created rules requiring warrants for access to all stored emails. California, Maine, Texas, and Utah have all amended their statutory electronic surveillance law to impose this requirement. Many other states are considering bills to do the same. These provisions do not constrain federal law enforcement activities, but they do align the statutory rules for state officials with the warrant requirement articulated in *Warshak*. A number of

states have also imposed warrant requirements for access to ISP records. New Jersey's Supreme Court did so through an interpretation of the state's constitution. *See State v. Reid*, 954 A.2d 503 (N.J. 2008). There are also statutes to that effect in Minnesota, MINN. STAT. 325M.02, and Nevada, NRS 205.498.

**5. *Voluntary (Non)compliance.*** Many communications service providers have taken the position that they will not respond to law enforcement inquiries inconsistent with *Warshak*, whether or not they occur within the geographical boundaries of the Sixth Circuit. Facebook was one of the first large internet intermediaries to do so; its *Guidelines for Law Enforcement* explain the company's position on responses to requests for user information:

> We disclose account records solely in accordance with our terms of service and applicable law, including the federal Stored Communications Act ("SCA"), 18 U.S.C. Sections 2701–2712. Under US law:
>
> - A valid subpoena issued in connection with an official criminal investigation is required to compel the disclosure of basic subscriber records (defined in 18 U.S.C. Section 2703(c)(2)), which may include: name, length of service, credit card information, email address(es), and a recent login/logout IP address(es), if available.
> - A court order issued under 18 U.S.C. Section 2703(d) is required to compel the disclosure of certain records or other information pertaining to the account, not including contents of communications, which may include message headers and IP addresses, in addition to the basic subscriber records identified above.
> - A search warrant issued under the procedures described in the Federal Rules of Criminal Procedure or equivalent state warrant procedures upon a showing of probable cause is required to compel the disclosure of the stored contents of any account, which may include messages, photos, videos, wall posts, and location information.

Facebook's requirement of a warrant for content was a somewhat atypical position at first, but has become much more common. The Electronic Frontier Foundation (EFF), a well-known advocacy group, publishes annual reports evaluating the policies of communications companies such as wireless carriers, messaging apps, and social networking platforms when they receive law enforcement requests for user information. By the time EFF included the category in its 2013 report, out of the 18 large intermediaries it analyzed, 11 required a probable-cause warrant for stored content. The 2015 report assessed 24 companies, and only one did not follow the *Warshak* rule. (The outlier was WhatsApp—strangely, since the company is now owned by Facebook.) In other words, whether or not law enforcement authorities want to seek a traditional Fourth Amendment warrant, many of the communications intermediaries who hold that information demand they do so.

---

## Practice

Applying ECPA

Which of the following scenarios might violate the Electronic Communications Privacy Act? If you think a scenario might violate ECPA, cite the provision and identify the elements that would need to be proven. What elements would a plaintiff have to prove? What penalties could be imposed in each situation if a violation were found?

(a) Mr. Rynes installed a security camera at his front door that captured silent video of his front door, portions of the public sidewalk in front of his house, and portions of the neighbor's back yard [see Chapter 4 for this case].

(b) Miranda Priestly barked some orders at her secretary, Andy Sachs, on her iPhone, and then dropped the phone into her handbag. Miranda did not realize that the phone bumped something in her bag and redialed Andy. Andy answered and said "hello," and then waited, assuming Miranda was distracted and would soon bark more orders. Instead, Andy overheard a long conversation full of informative office gossip between Miranda and her colleague Nigel. Andy believed that Miranda was preparing to fire her friend Emily for illegally discriminatory reasons, and began taking notes about what she said and used her laptop to make an audio recording of some of it.

(c) Betty suspected her husband Don was cheating on her. She guessed the passcode on his iPhone and read all of his text messages for the last year. (She was right.)

(d) Mickey Doyle was a confederate of gang boss Nucky Thompson. Mickey "wore a wire" when he met with Nucky to discuss their criminal plans. The concealed microphone transmitted their conversation to a van parked outside where federal agents recorded it.

(e) Officer Krupke approached CloudLocker, a provider of "cloud computing" services, and requested access to word processing documents stored in the account of David Riley, who is under investigation for gang activity. He made the same request of ZipMail, a cloud provider of email services. Krupke also asked both services to provide access to future content from Riley's account. Riley has used both services for a year. Finally, Krupke asked V-Swift, a wireless carrier, for records of all calls made by Riley for the past year and all future calls.

---

## CHAPTER 6

# PROCESSING AND USE

So, an organization has collected personal data. Now what? The next phase of the life cycle of data involves the processing and use of that data to do something with it. This stage covers two interrelated activities: the processing of data to generate new information or insights, and the organization's use of data, in either its raw or processed form.

Processing is the further manipulation of data after it becomes available. Computerized databases are beneficial not only because they can store vast quantities of data, but also because they can perform further operations that yield additional insights. A medical researcher can correlate numerous different pieces of information about a patient to determine what factors contribute to disease. A vendor can run algorithms to help determine what products are most likely to interest a customer, and tailor advertising or the design of an online shopping interface accordingly. (So, for example, Amazon.com recommends products you may like based not only on your own past browsing and purchasing history but also on a comparison of your history with that of its other customers.) Political campaigns analyzing a voter's likely preferences refer not only to individual voting history, but considerations as diverse as neighborhood, marital status, the kind of car owned, and even the supermarket where the person shops. (Campaigns can then use this information to direct particular messages to different voters, so one house may receive direct mail about education issues while the house next door gets a flyer about tax policy.) Businesses process data to evaluate individuals before taking on risks in offering employment, insurance, or credit, again drawing on multiple data sources and utilizing increasingly sophisticated analytical tools. (Thus, credit card companies have found that people who buy floor protector pads to put under their chairs and avoid scratching the floor are also likely to pay their bills on time.) Law enforcement and national security authorities can process data to discern patterns of behavior that identify potentially illegal activity.

Increasingly, companies known collectively as data brokers perform these functions of processing data and adapting it for new uses. The largest data brokers, including companies such as Acxiom and Datalogix, hold at least some data pertaining to most US households. This information is collected from numerous varied sources: everything from public records, to purchasing data provided by stores or credit card companies, to employment information. Data brokers will provide profile information about individuals at a client's request—to perform a background check on a prospective employee for example. Most data brokers also repackage this data by classifying individuals in a dizzying array of demographic categories, often with evocative names such as "Rural and Barely Making It," "Cosmopolitan Strivers," or "McMansions and Minivans." The brokers then allow clients interested in targeting small niches of the market to use these lists, for a significant fee.

Even without any such additional processing, stores of raw data collected for one reason may be repurposed for new applications. A factory that collects data about its machinery in order to monitor safety may discover that the very same data can help to analyze individual workers' productivity. A vendor that obtains an email address to send a receipt to a customer may want to send future offers to that customer as well.

The tradeoffs involved in data processing and use are extremely complex. What are the benefits and risks?

Many privacy advocates argue that the very act of slicing and dicing personal information in this manner is invasive and dehumanizing, so that it infringes on individual autonomy. They also point to collateral harm arising from the uses themselves. Data can segment the market in ways that give advantages to certain consumers over others; some might receive discounts and others might be denied services on the basis of their assumed proclivities arising from data analysis. They could even be offered different prices for the same item. Critics condemn such uses as "digital redlining," comparing them to racially discriminatory housing practices. Inaccuracies in underlying data are inevitable, and can spread through continued processing and distribution. Moreover, all these processes happen largely out of public view, and many organizations are wary of disclosing their practices, fearing not only that the public will object but also that competitors may thereby gain access to the trade secrets embedded in their algorithms.

Notwithstanding these concerns, increased processing and use of personal data is inevitable and offers enormous value to society. Many of the insights that result unquestionably improve the world—consider again the medical researcher using massive data processing for an epidemiological study. Data processing also creates significant economic welfare, not only increasing companies' profits but also reducing prices for everyone. The provision of insurance or credit inherently reflects complex judgments about risk that are dependent on information. Literally for centuries, society has accepted that insurers use actuarial calculations to underwrite policies and that lenders charge different interest rates based on perceived creditworthiness. Reducing the amount of information available to make these determinations certainly will increase the price of those services for everyone. In many settings, digitized data processing is simply an improvement in the technological methods of accomplishing those same tasks. Data processing also radically increases convenience. Although targeted marketing has its skeptics, many believe that it works because the selected customers are more likely to be interested in the product for sale. A customer who receives tailored information that cuts through the overwhelming clutter of the modern digital marketplace may receive a benefit from that matching as well. Overall, the use of data improves the quality and efficiency of innumerable transactions in modern life.

Ideally, privacy law seeks to maximize these benefits and reduce risks of harm, of course. When it comes to governing data processing and use, this balance is not always so easy to achieve.

In addition to the rules covered in this chapter, areas of law covered elsewhere in this book center on this phase in the life cycle of data. Pause for a moment and think for yourself of the topics you have already covered that fall into this category. A few prominent examples might include:

- The appropriation tort, which turns on an alleged tortfeasor's "use or benefit" from the appropriated likeness [see Chapter 2].
- Provisions in a privacy policy specifying the uses of data [see Chapter 3].
- Requirements of the EU Data Protection Directive limiting the legitimate purposes for which data may be used [see Chapter 4].
- Restrictions on federal government databases in the Privacy Act, including rules about data matching [see Chapter 10].
- Distinctions between permitted and forbidden uses of data in US regimes regulating health information [see Chapter 12], financial information [see Chapter 13], or data about students [see Chapter 15].
- The Genetic Information Nondiscrimination Act, which outlaws basing certain insurance and employment decision on genetic data rather than attempting to stop the collection of such data [see Chapter 12].

Some scholars have argued that the law should focus more on this phase in the life cycle of data, worrying less about the initial collection of information and instead seeking to ensure that it is not used for socially injurious purposes. As you read this chapter, consider whether you agree that this such a shift in emphasis would be wise.

Section A of this chapter looks at the advent of "Big Data," one of the most dramatic changes to affect the processing phase. Section B examines perhaps the most widely applicable privacy statute to govern processing and use, as opposed to other phases of the life cycle of data: the Fair Credit Reporting Act. Finally, Section C considers the different approach taken to regulation of data processing in the European Union.

## A. CASE STUDY: BIG DATA

### *Big Data: Seizing Opportunities, Preserving Values*

The White House Big Data and
Privacy Working Group (2014)

For purposes of this study, the review group focused on data that is so large in volume, so diverse in variety or moving with such velocity, that traditional modes of data capture and analysis are insufficient—characteristics colloquially referred to as the "3 Vs." The declining cost of collection, storage, and processing of data, combined with new sources of data like sensors, cameras, geospatial and other observational technologies, means that we live in a world of near-ubiquitous data collection. The volume of data collected and processed is unprecedented. This explosion of data—from web-enabled appliances, wearable technology, and advanced sensors to monitor everything from vital signs to energy use to a jogger's running speed—will drive demand for high-performance computing and push the capabilities of even the most sophisticated data management technologies.

Used well, big data analysis can boost economic productivity, drive improved consumer and government services, thwart terrorists, and save lives.

Big data technology holds tremendous promise for better managing demand across electricity grids, improving energy efficiency, boosting agricultural productivity in the developing world, and projecting the spread of infectious diseases, among other applications.

**Finding the Needle in the Haystack**

Computational capabilities now make "finding a needle in a haystack" not only possible, but practical. In the past, searching large datasets required both rationally organized data and a specific research question, relying on choosing the right query to return the correct result. Big data analytics enable data scientists to amass lots of data, including unstructured data, and find anomalies or patterns. A key privacy challenge in this model of discovery is that in order to find the needle, you have to have a haystack. To obtain certain insights, you need a certain quantity of data.

For example, a genetic researcher at the Broad Institute found that having a large number of genetic datasets makes the critical difference in identifying the meaningful genetic variant for a disease. In this research, a genetic variant related to schizophrenia was not detectable when analyzed in 3,500 cases, and was only weakly identifiable using 10,000 cases, but was suddenly statistically significant with 35,000 cases. As the researcher observed, "There is an inflection point at which everything changes." The need for vast quantities of data—particularly personally sensitive data like genetic data—is a significant challenge for researchers for a variety of reasons, but notably because of privacy laws that limit access to data.

### The Benefits and Consequences of Perfect Personalization

The fusion of many different kinds of data, processed in real time, has the power to deliver exactly the right message, product, or service to consumers before they even ask. Small bits of data can be brought together to create a clear picture of a person to predict preferences or behaviors. These detailed personal profiles and personalized experiences are effective in the consumer marketplace and can deliver products and offers to precise segments of the population—like a professional accountant with a passion for knitting, or a home chef with a penchant for horror films.

Unfortunately, "perfect personalization" also leaves room for subtle and not-so-subtle forms of discrimination in pricing, services, and opportunities. For example, one study found web searches involving black-identifying names (e.g., "Jermaine") were more likely to display ads with the word "arrest" in them than searches with white-identifying names (e.g., "Geoffrey"). This research was not able determine exactly why a racially biased result occurred, recognizing that ad display is algorithmically generated based on a number of variables and decision processes. But it's clear that outcomes like these, by serving up different kinds of information to different groups, have the potential to cause real harm to individuals, whether they are pursuing a job, purchasing a home, or simply searching for information.

### Toward a Policy Framework for Big Data: Big Data and Privacy

Together, these trends may require us to look closely at the notice and consent framework that has been a central pillar of how privacy practices have been organized for more than four decades. In a technological context of structural over-collection, in which re-identification is becoming more powerful than de-identification, focusing on controlling the collection and retention of personal data, while important, may no longer be sufficient to protect personal privacy. In the words of the President's Council of Advisors for Science & Technology, "The notice and consent [model] is defeated by exactly the positive benefits that big data enables: new, non-obvious, unexpectedly powerful uses of data."

Putting greater emphasis on a responsible use framework has many potential advantages. It shifts the responsibility from the individual, who is not well equipped to understand or contest consent notices as they are currently structured in the marketplace, to the entities that collect, maintain, and use data. Focusing on responsible use also holds data collectors and users accountable for how they manage the data and any harms it causes, rather than narrowly defining their responsibility to whether they properly obtained consent at the time of collection.

Focusing more attention on responsible use does not mean ignoring the context of collection. Part of using data responsibly could mean respecting the circumstances of its original collection. There could, in effect, be a "no surprises" rule, as articulated in the "respect for context" principle in the Consumer Privacy Bill of Rights [proposed by the Obama Administration]. Data collected in a consumer context could not suddenly be used in an employment one. Technological developments support this shift toward a focus on use. Advanced data-tagging schemes can encode details about the context of collection and uses of the data already granted by the user, so that information about permissive uses travels along with the data wherever it goes. If well developed and brought widely into use, such a data-tagging scheme would not solve all the dilemmas posed by big data, but it could help address several important challenges.

Perhaps most important of all, a shift to focus on responsible uses in the big data context allows us to put our attention more squarely on the hard questions we must reckon with: how to balance the socially beneficial uses of big data with the harms to privacy and other values that can result in a world where more data is inevitably collected about more things. Should there be an agreed-upon taxonomy that distinguishes information that you do not collect or use under any circumstances, information that you can collect or use without obtaining consent, and information that you collect and use only with consent? How should this taxonomy be different for a medical researcher trying to cure cancer and a marketer targeting ads for consumer products?

As President Obama said upon the release of the Consumer Privacy Bill of Rights, "Even though we live in a world in which we share personal information more freely than in the past, we must reject the conclusion that privacy is an outmoded value." Privacy, the President said, "has been at the heart of our democracy from its inception, and we need it now more than ever." This is even truer in a world powered by big data.

## Paul Ohm, *The Underwhelming Benefits of Big Data*

161 U. Pa. L. Rev. Online 339 (2013)

Whether applied to crises in medicine, in climate, in food safety, or in some other arena, Big Data techniques will lead to significant, new, life-enhancing (even life-saving) benefits that we would be ill advised to electively forego. . . . To argue against Big Data is to argue against science.

But some Big Data projects will also lead to bad outcomes, like invasions of privacy and hard-to-detect invidious discrimination. Big Data techniques can help governments spy on their citizens and criminals prey on their victims. As we worry about these negative consequences, and particularly as we consider whether we might forego or shape some forms of Big Data so as to limit their negative effects, we must weigh the associated costs and benefits. In doing so, we should scrutinize carefully claims that the benefits of Big Data outweigh the costs to individuals and society.

First, we should separate benefits built upon data sets that are full of information about people from those built upon data that has almost nothing to do with personal information, and thus almost nothing to do with personal privacy. Big Data techniques can unlock mysteries of manufacturing, climate change, financial markets, and cybersecurity without delving into data at the individual level. We should be mindful, however, that sometimes data that seems not to involve individuals will often reveal individual information through inference.

Second, we should recognize that many of the benefits we care most deeply about, including most medical research, originate in research institutions with an established track record of respecting personal privacy. Particularly as more medical research is conducted by profit-driven companies—whether large corporations or small startups—we should worry about forcing the public to accept new risks to privacy with little countervailing benefit and none of the controls.

Third, we should distinguish between research that benefits the public and that which serves only narrow and private gain. This is not to say that only non-profit or public institutions can benefit the public good through Big Data, but it does mean that we should expect research produced by private institutions and built upon the private secrets of users to give something back to the public in exchange, perhaps in the form of new therapies or drugs. And in demanding meaningful returns for the public good, we should not confuse for science the kinds of daily trivia—blurbs and tweets and infographics—that ricochet around the web and die shortly thereafter.

## Omer Tene & Jules Polonetsky, *Big Data for All: Privacy and User Control in the Age of Analytics*

11 NW. J. TECH & INTELL. PROP. 239 (2013)

[T]o solve the big data privacy quandary, individuals must be offered meaningful rights to access their data in a usable, machine-readable format. This, in turn, will unleash a wave of innovation for user-side applications and services based on access to PII, a process we refer to as the "featurization" of big data. Featurization will allow individuals to declare their own policies, preferences and terms of engagement, and do it in ways that can be automated both for them and for the companies they engage. Where individual access to data is impracticable, data are likely to be de-identified to an extent sufficient to diminish privacy concerns. Where access is possible, organizations must provide it with robust mechanisms for user authentication and through secure channels to prevent leakage. This implies the development of user-centric or federated identity management schemes, which include single sign-on capability and at the same time do not become vehicles for universal surveillance. To minimize concerns of untoward data usage, organizations should disclose the logic underlying their decision-making processes to the extent possible without compromising their trade secrets or intellectual property rights.

Big data may facilitate predictive analysis with stark implications for individuals susceptible to disease, crime, or other socially stigmatizing characteristics or behaviors. To be sure, predictive analysis can be used for societally beneficial goals, such as planning disaster recovery in an earthquake prone area based on individuals' evacuation paths and purchase needs. Yet it can easily cross the "creepiness" threshold.

Consider a recent story in the New York Times, which uncovered that the retailing giant, Target Inc., assigns a "pregnancy prediction score" to customers based on their purchase habits. According to the Times, Target employed statisticians to sift back through historical buying records of women who had signed up for baby registries. The statisticians discovered latent patterns, such as women's preference for unscented lotion around the beginning of their second trimester or a tendency to buy supplements like calcium, magnesium and zinc within the first 20 weeks of a pregnancy. They were able to determine a set of products that, when grouped together, allowed Target to accurately predict a customer's pregnancy and due date. In one case, the Times reported that a father of a teenage girl stormed into a Target store to complain that his daughter received coupons and advertisements for baby products. A few days later, he called the store manager to apologize, admitting that, "There's been some activities in my house I haven't been completely aware of. She's due in August."

Predictive analysis is particularly problematic when based on sensitive categories of data, such as health, race, or sexuality. It is one thing to recommend for a customer books, music or movies she might be interested in based on her previous purchases; it is quite another thing to identify when she is pregnant before her closest family knows.

[We argue for] the development of a legal model where the benefits of data for organizations and researchers are shared with individuals. If organizations provide individuals with access to their data in usable formats, creative powers will be unleashed to provide users with applications and features building on their data for new innovative uses. In addition, transparency with respect to the logic underlying organizations' data processing will deter unethical, sensitive data use and allay concerns about inaccurate inferences.

---

## Practice

<u>Privacy in a World of Big Data</u>

Assume you work on the staff of a US senator. Your boss has skimmed the Obama Administration's report on Big Data excerpted above, and has spoken with many technology executives from your home state about the exciting, promising, and economically valuable "paradigm shift" that it represents. But the senator is concerned about the implications as well, saying to you: "I don't want to get into a situation like in that movie *Minority Report,* where we're guessing what you're going to do before you even do it. That is creepy, and un-American."

You are assigned to propose legislative action that could be taken to respond. The senator is particularly interested in the White House suggestion that "greater emphasis on a responsible use framework has many potential advantages." What does that mean in this context? How could it be put into practice? Would it work? Would it be politically controversial and, if so, who would object and why? What steps do you propose for the senator?

---

## B. THE FAIR CREDIT REPORTING ACT

As suggested in the previous section, traditionally most US privacy laws have focused on the collection phase of the life cycle of data, and sometimes on disclosure. Recently, storage and security have become a more common area of attention. Of the four phases in the life cycle, processing and use receive the least attention in general-purpose US privacy law. The Fair Credit Reporting Act, however, is a notable exception. Its core definitions are centered on the anticipated use of personal data for decisionmaking.

## The Fair Credit Reporting Act

15 U.S.C. §§ 1681 et seq.

### § 1681a. Definitions; rules of construction [§ 603]

(a) Definitions and rules of construction set forth in this section are applicable for the purposes of this subchapter.

(b) The term "person" means any individual, partnership, corporation, trust, estate, cooperative, association, government or governmental subdivision or agency, or other entity.

(c) The term "consumer" means an individual.

(d) Consumer report.

(1) In general.

The term "consumer report" means any written, oral, or other communication of any information by a consumer reporting agency bearing on a consumer's credit worthiness, credit standing, credit capacity, character, general reputation, personal characteristics, or mode of living which is used or expected to be used or collected in whole or in part for the purpose of serving as a factor in establishing the consumer's eligibility for—

(A) credit or insurance to be used primarily for personal, family, or household purposes;

(B) employment purposes; or

(C) any other purpose authorized under section 1681b of this title. . . .

(e) The term "investigative consumer report" means a consumer report or portion thereof in which information on a consumer's character, general reputation, personal characteristics, or mode of living is obtained through personal interviews with neighbors, friends, or associates of the consumer reported on or with others with whom he is acquainted or who may have knowledge concerning any such items of information. However, such information shall not include specific factual information on a consumer's credit record obtained directly from a creditor of the consumer or from a consumer reporting agency when such information was obtained directly from a creditor of the consumer or from the consumer.

(f) The term "consumer reporting agency" means any person which, for monetary fees, dues, or on a cooperative nonprofit basis, regularly engages in whole or in part in the practice of assembling or evaluating consumer credit information or other information on consumers for the purpose of furnishing consumer reports to third parties, and which uses any means or facility of interstate commerce for the purpose of preparing or furnishing consumer reports.

(g) The term "file", when used in connection with information on any consumer, means all of the information on that consumer recorded and retained by a consumer reporting agency regardless of how the information is stored.

**§ 1681b. Permissible purposes of consumer reports [§ 604]**

(a) In general

Subject to subsection (c) of this section, any consumer reporting agency may furnish a consumer report under the following circumstances and no other:

(1) In response to the order of a court having jurisdiction to issue such an order, or a subpoena issued in connection with proceedings before a Federal grand jury.

(2) In accordance with the written instructions of the consumer to whom it relates.

(3) To a person which it has reason to believe—

(A) intends to use the information in connection with a credit transaction involving the consumer on whom the information is to be furnished and involving the extension of credit to, or review or collection of an account of, the consumer; or

(B) intends to use the information for employment purposes; or

(C) intends to use the information in connection with the underwriting of insurance involving the consumer; or

(D) intends to use the information in connection with a determination of the consumer's eligibility for a license or other benefit granted by a governmental instrumentality required by law to consider an applicant's financial responsibility or status; or

(E) intends to use the information, as a potential investor or servicer, or current insurer, in connection with a valuation of, or an assessment of the credit or prepayment risks associated with, an existing credit obligation; or

(F) otherwise has a legitimate business need for the information—

(i) in connection with a business transaction that is initiated by the consumer; or

(ii) to review an account to determine whether the consumer continues to meet the terms of the account. . . .

[Other more narrow purposes listed here and below include investigation or enforcement of child support obligations, provisions related to government liquidation of insolvent financial institutions, and employment-related uses by national security agencies.]

(b) Conditions for furnishing and using consumer reports for employment purposes

[This subsection specifies additional requirements imposed on both consumer reporting agencies and their clients concerning use of a consumer report for employment purposes under § 1681b(a)(3)(B). For more information about these provisions, see Chapter 11.] . . .

**§ 1681e. Compliance procedures. [§ 607]**

(a) Identity and purposes of credit users

Every consumer reporting agency shall maintain reasonable procedures designed to avoid violations of section 1681c [which generally forbids the inclusion in credit reports of certain outdated financial information such as bankruptcies or liens] and to limit the furnishing of consumer reports to the purposes listed under section 1681b of this title. These procedures shall require that prospective users of the information identify themselves, certify the purposes for which the information is sought, and certify that the information will be used for no other purpose. Every consumer reporting agency shall make a reasonable effort to verify the identity of a new prospective user and the uses certified by such prospective user prior to furnishing such user a consumer report. No consumer reporting agency may furnish a consumer report to any person if it has reasonable grounds for believing that the consumer report will not be used for a purpose listed in section 1681b of this title.

(b) Accuracy of report

Whenever a consumer reporting agency prepares a consumer report it shall follow reasonable procedures to assure maximum possible accuracy of the information concerning the individual about whom the report relates. . . .

(d) Notice to users and furnishers of information

> (1) Notice requirement.—A consumer reporting agency shall provide to any person—
>
> > (A) who regularly and in the ordinary course of business furnishes information to the agency with respect to any consumer; or
> >
> > (B) to whom a consumer report is provided by the agency;
>
> a notice of such person's responsibilities under this subchapter.

---

## Focus

### Enforcement of FCRA

FCRA has a rather complex enforcement structure. First, the statute authorizes consumers affected by violations to bring private lawsuits. *See* 15 U.S.C. § 1681o ("Any person who is negligent in failing to comply with any requirement imposed under this subchapter with respect to any consumer is liable to that consumer. . . ."). Suits alleging negligent violations may secure actual damages, costs, and reasonable attorney's fees. *Id.* In addition, if a court finds willful noncompliance, it may award (1) statutory damages of between $100 and $1000 in place of actual damages, and (2) punitive damages. *Id.* at § 1681n.

Congress has empowered federal regulators to enforce FCRA as well, but the boundaries between those regulators can be confusing. Until recently, the FTC was the primary agency enforcing FCRA, although many other parts of the federal government also had authority, from the Federal Reserve Bank to the Farm Credit Administration. In many instances these agencies brought actions for violations; occasionally more than one had a plausible claim to jurisdiction over a particular situation.

In 2010, Congress further complicated this landscape by passing the statute that created the Consumer Financial Protection Bureau (CFPB). That law transferred much of the existing authority over FCRA to the CFPB, but maintained a role for at least ten other federal offices and agencies, the FTC prominent among them. The CFPB now has the primary power to write regulations under FCRA, and has already created or revised some of those rules. Both the CFPB and the FTC continue to bring actions against alleged violations. In recent years, one of the CFPB's priorities has been cracking down on violations by furnishers of data—that is, companies that provide data about their customers' credit activities to credit reporting agencies

(CRAs). For example, in 2014 the CFPB entered into a consent decree with DriveTime Automotive Group, a network of "buy here pay here" car dealers and an affiliated finance company. The CFPB alleged that DriveTime reported inaccurate information to CRAs, lacked required policies to govern its data furnishing, failed to take adequate precautions to ensure accuracy, and did not properly investigate complaints about errors or correct them, all as required by FCRA. As part of the settlement, in addition to promising to take corrective action and develop a compliance program to avoid future violations, DriveTime agreed to pay an $8 million civil penalty.

State consumer protection regulators such as attorneys general may also bring enforcement actions under FCRA, which they often combine with exercises of their powers under state law. At the same time, FCRA also preempts the enforcement of many provisions of state law, both common law and statutory, when they are inconsistent with the statute. The interpretation of FCRA's preemption provisions can be quite convoluted, and federal courts struggle with it on a regular basis.

---

## In re Spokeo

FTC Matter/File Number 1023163 (June 12, 2012)

## COMPLAINT

### The Fair Credit Reporting Act

7. The FCRA was enacted in 1970, became effective on April 25, 1971, and has been in force since that date.

8. Section 621 of the FCRA, 15 U.S.C. § 1681s, authorizes the Commission to use all of its functions and powers under the FTC Act to enforce compliance with the FCRA by all persons subject thereto except to the extent that enforcement specifically is committed to some other governmental agency, irrespective of whether the person is engaged in commerce or meets any other jurisdictional tests set forth by the FTC Act.

### Violations of the Fair Credit Reporting Act

9. [Respondent] Spokeo assembles consumer information from "hundreds of online and offline sources," such as social networking sites, data brokers, and other sources to create consumer profiles, which Defendant promotes as "coherent people profiles" and "powerful intelligence." These consumer profiles identify specific individuals and display such information as the individual's physical address, phone number, marital status, age range, or email address. Spokeo profiles are further organized by descriptive headers denoting, among other things, a person's hobbies, ethnicity, religion, or participation on social networking sites, and may contain photos or other information, such as economic health graphics, that Spokeo attributes to a particular individual. Among other things, Spokeo sells the profiles through paid subscriptions, which provide a set number of searches based on

subscription level, as well as through Application Program Interfaces ("API") that provide customized and/or higher volume access.

10. Since at least 2008, Spokeo has provided its consumer profiles to businesses, including entities operating in the human resources ("HR"), background screening, and recruiting industries, to serve as a factor in deciding whether to interview a job candidate or whether to hire a candidate after a job interview.

a. Spokeo entered into API user agreements with, and provided high volume access to, paying business customers, including entities operating in the human resources, background screening, and recruiting industries.

b. In its marketing and advertising, the company has promoted the use of its profiles as a factor in deciding whether to interview a job candidate or whether to hire a candidate after a job interview. Spokeo purchased thousands of online advertising keywords including terms targeting employment background checks, applicant screening, and recruiting. Spokeo ran online advertisements with taglines to attract recruiters and encourage HR professionals to use Spokeo to obtain information about job candidates' online activities.

c. Spokeo has affirmatively targeted companies operating in the human resources, background screening, and recruiting industries. It created a portion of its website intended specifically for recruiters, which was available through a dedicated click tab labeled "recruiters" that was prominently displayed at the top of the Spokeo home page. Recruiters were encouraged to "Explore Beyond the Resume." In addition, Defendant promoted the Spokeo.com/HR URL to recruiters in the media and in marketing to third parties, and offered special subscription plans for its HR customers.

11. In 2010, Spokeo changed its website Terms of Service to state that it was not a consumer reporting agency and that consumers may not use the company's website or information for FCRA-covered purposes. However, Spokeo failed to revoke access to or otherwise ensure that existing users, including subscribers who may have joined Spokeo through its Spokeo.com/HR page, or those who had previously purchased access to profiles through API user agreements, did not use the Company's website or information for FCRA-covered purposes.

12. The consumer profiles Spokeo provides to third parties are "consumer reports" as defined in section 603(d) of the FCRA, 15 U.S.C. § 1681a(d). Spokeo profiles are consumer reports because they bear on a consumer's character, general reputation, personal characteristics, or mode of living and/or other attributes listed in section 603(d), and are "used or expected to be used . . . in whole or in part" as a factor in

determining the consumer's eligibility for employment or other purposes specified in section 604.

13. In providing "consumer reports" Spokeo is now and has been a "consumer reporting agency" ("CRA") as that term is defined in section 603(f) of the FCRA, 15 U.S.C. § 1681a(f). Spokeo regularly assembles "information on consumers" into consumer reports that it provides to third parties in interstate commerce, including companies in the human resources, background screening, and recruiting industries. Defendant is in the business of furnishing consumer reports to third parties that are "used or expected to be used" for "employment purposes."

14. Section 607(a) of the FCRA, 15 U.S.C. § 1681e(a), requires CRAs to maintain reasonable procedures to limit the furnishing of consumer reports to the purposes specified in section 604, 15 U.S.C. § 1681b. These procedures require that the CRA, prior to furnishing a user with a consumer report, require the prospective users of the information to identify themselves to the CRA, certify the purpose for which the information is sought, and certify that the information will be used for no other purpose. The CRA must make a reasonable effort to verify the identity of each new prospective user and the uses certified prior to furnishing such user a consumer report. In addition, section 607(a) prohibits any CRA from furnishing a consumer report to any person it has reasonable grounds to believe will not use the consumer report for a permissible purpose. Spokeo has failed to maintain any procedures required by section 607(a).

15. Section 607(b) of the FCRA, 15 U.S.C. § 1681e(b), requires all consumer reporting agencies to follow reasonable procedures to assure maximum possible accuracy of consumer report information. Spokeo has failed to follow any reasonable procedures to assure maximum possible accuracy of the information in reports that it prepared as required by section 607(b).

16. Section 607(d) of the FCRA, 15 U.S.C. § 1681e(d), requires CRAs to provide a "Notice to Users of Consumer Reports: Obligations of Users Under the FCRA" ("User Notice") to any person to whom a consumer report is provided by the CRA. As required by section 607(d), the Commission has prescribed the content of the User Notice through a model notice. The User Notice provides users of consumer reports with important information regarding their obligations under the FCRA, including the obligation of the user to provide a notice to consumers who are the subject of an adverse action (e.g., denial of employment) based in whole or in part on information contained in the consumer report. Spokeo has failed to provide the section 607(d) User Notice to those who purchase consumer reports.

17. Section 604 of the FCRA, 15 U.S.C. § 1681b, prohibits CRAs from furnishing consumer reports to persons who the consumer reporting agency does not have reason to believe have a "permissible purpose." Section 604(b), 15 U.S.C. § 1681b(b), includes employment purposes as a

permissible purpose but prescribes certain conditions for furnishing and using consumer reports for employment purposes. Spokeo regularly furnishes consumer reports to third parties without procedures to inquire into the purpose for which the user is buying the report. Spokeo has violated Section 604, 15 U.S.C. § 1681b, in furnishing consumer reports to persons that it did not have a reason to believe had a permissible purpose to obtain a consumer report.

**This Court's Power to Grant Relief**

39. Section 621(a)(2)(A) of the FCRA, 15 U.S.C. § 1681s(a)(2)(A), authorizes the Court to award monetary civil penalties in the event of a knowing violation of the FCRA, which constitutes a pattern or practice. Spokeo's violations of the FCRA, as alleged in this Complaint, have been knowing and have constituted a pattern or practice of violations. [Under federal civil penalty statutes,] the Court is authorized to award a penalty of not more than $2,500 per violation for violations occurring before February 10, 2009, and $3,500 per violation for violations occurring on or after that date.

40. Each instance in which Spokeo has failed to comply with the FCRA constitutes a separate violation of the FCRA for the purpose of assessing monetary civil penalties under section 621 of the FCRA, 15 U.S.C. § 1681s. Plaintiff seeks monetary civil penalties for every separate violation of the FCRA.

41. Under the FCRA and the FTC Act, this Court is authorized to issue a permanent injunction prohibiting Defendant from violating the FTC Act and the FCRA.

## NOTES

1. ***The* Spokeo *Settlement.*** As typically happens with FTC privacy actions [see Chapter 3], Spokeo and the FTC settled this case. They negotiated a stipulated consent decree entered by the court under which: (a) Spokeo paid a civil penalty of $800,000; (b) the court enjoined the company (and related entities) from all the violations alleged in the FTC's complaint; and (c) Spokeo undertook a 20-year program of compliance monitoring, recordkeeping, and reporting to the FTC. Spokeo did not admit legal wrongdoing under the settlement. One important difference between this resolution and many the FTC has reached in other privacy cases was the monetary penalty, which was available under FCRA and would not have been obtainable under the agency's more usual jurisdiction through Section 5 of the FTC Act.

2. ***Sock Puppetry.*** The FTC also alleged, and Spokeo settled, claims that the company violated Section 5 of the FTC Act by publishing phony endorsements of its services. According to the complaint:

> Defendant directed its employees to draft comments endorsing Spokeo to be posted on news and technology websites. These comments were reviewed and edited by Spokeo managers and then

> posted using account names, provided by Spokeo, that would give the readers of these comments the impression they had been submitted by independent, ordinary consumers or business users of Spokeo.

It seems uncontroversial that, if true, this paragraph alleged a deceptive trade practice unrelated to privacy. Do you think this enforcement action would have been brought by itself under Section 5 even if FCRA had not also been applicable? How do you think the addition of these allegations to the FCRA case might have affected its outcome?

3. ***Private Lawsuits and Standing.*** Before the FTC action was complete, a putative class of plaintiffs also sued Spokeo under FCRA's private right of action. One of these cases went all the way to the Supreme Court, where it was argued in November 2015 (and was not decided in time for inclusion in this book). The case there turned on the type of individual harm necessary to establish constitutional standing. The named plaintiff in that case was unemployed, and alleged that his Spokeo profile inaccurately stated that he had a graduate degree and much greater wealth than he did. According to this argument, employers could rely on these errors to determine the plaintiff was overqualified for jobs and exclude him from consideration, but Spokeo and its clients did not receive his consent or provide him notice of adverse actions as FCRA requires. Spokeo responded that these allegations failed to allege concrete harm, because they did not show that the failure to get a job was a result of any misstatements by Spokeo. Fundamentally, the parties differed about the nature of the injury. The plaintiff maintained that the inaccuracy itself was an injury and that Congress had created the private right of action to help individuals police their own consumer reporting information. Spokeo suggested that injury did not occur until and unless the violations of FCRA actually resulted in a demonstrable loss of a benefit such as employment opportunities. The Ninth Circuit sided with the plaintiff and found standing, *Robins v. Spokeo, Inc.*, 742 F.3d 409 (9th Cir. 2014), and the Supreme Court granted cert. to decide the standing question, 135 S. Ct. 1892 (2015).

4. ***The Importance of Definitions.*** The core of the case really is the determination by Spokeo (and its lawyers) that it was not a credit reporting agency in the first place. It is hard to overstate the importance of this kind of threshold definition under many privacy statutes. There are only certain websites directed at minors under COPPA [see Chapter 4] or certain "covered entities" under HIPAA [see Chapter 12]. Do you agree with the FTC that Spokeo was wrong, and that it actually was a CRA? Is Spokeo's contrary interpretation defensible? Why do you suppose the company reached it? Which actions of Spokeo most undermined its claims in the eyes of the FTC? Given that the company did end up facing liability that imposed a fine and 20 years of monitoring, do you think Spokeo miscalculated regulatory risk, or was it just unlucky?

5. ***The Path to Compliance.*** Spokeo remains in business today. Go back through the complaint and identify the violations of FCRA that are now forbidden in the permanent injunction against the company. Suppose you are Spokeo's attorney, advising the company on its compliance with the

consent decree in the future. Separate those requirements that will be fairly easy for Spokeo to satisfy after the settlement from those that will be more costly or difficult. How many of each do you find? What do you think will be the most significant impact on Spokeo's practices going forward? What advice would you give the company about changes in its practices?

**6. *Section Numbers in FCRA.*** In case you were wondering, experts often refer to sections of FCRA based on their original numbering in the Act, from § 601 to § 629. In Title 15 of the United States Code, however, the numbering of FCRA starts with hortatory Congressional findings in § 1691, and then proceeds through substantive sections listed alphabetically from § 1691a through § 1691x. You may see one or both numbering schemes cited interchangeably in cases and regulatory filings. The statutory excerpt above provides the original bill numbering in brackets at the end of the section titles.

## Bakker v. McKinnon

152 F.3d 1007 (8th Cir. 1998)

■ MCMILLIAN, CIRCUIT JUDGE.

Laura J. McKinnon, an attorney, appeals from a final judgment entered in the United States District Court for the Western District of Arkansas, following a bench trial, finding that she had intentionally and willfully violated the Fair Credit Reporting Act ("FCRA" or "the Act"), 15 U.S.C. §§ 1681 et seq. The district court awarded to each appellee, Dr. Johnny L. Bakker and his two daughters, Teresa Bakker and Carrie Ann Bakker, $500 in compensatory damages and $5,000 in punitive damages. For reversal, appellant contends that the district court erred in finding that she violated the FCRA and in awarding an unreasonable amount for punitive damages.

For the reasons given herein, we affirm the judgment of the district court.

In September 1996 appellees Dr. Johnny L. Bakker, who is a dentist, and his adult daughters, Teresa Bakker and Carrie Ann Bakker, filed this lawsuit alleging that appellant had requested several consumer credit reports about them from a local credit bureau in violation of the FCRA. Appellant represents several women patients of Dr. Bakker who claimed that Dr. Bakker had committed dental malpractice by improperly touching them during the course of dental treatments. Appellant filed lawsuits in state court on behalf of these women against Dr. Bakker.

The district court found that appellant and her associates had engaged in numerous acts which, in the district court's view, "grossly crossed the line in respect to what is proper in conducting litigation." Basically, the district court concluded that appellant and her associates had requested the credit reports as part of the litigation process to force a settlement. The district court noted that a speaker at a meeting of the

Arkansas Trial Lawyer's Association (of which appellant was a member of the board of governors and a former president) had recommended that consumer credit reports be routinely obtained against defendants or prospective defendants.

Appellant admitted that she (or, more precisely, someone in her office) obtained the credit reports, but she argued that (1) she obtained them for a commercial or a professional purpose and, thus, the credit reports were not consumer credit reports within the meaning of the FCRA, 15 U.S.C. §§ 1681a(d), 1681b, or (2) in the alternative, assuming the credit reports were consumer reports within the meaning of the FCRA, she had a legitimate business need for requesting them [citing predecessor to current § 1681b(3)(F)].

The underlying facts are not substantially disputed. Whether the credit reports were consumer reports and, if so, whether the business need exception applies are questions of statutory interpretation of the FCRA. The district court found that appellant had engaged in numerous acts, which in its view, grossly crossed the line in respect to what is proper in conducting litigation; during the litigation against Dr. Bakker, appellant had attempted to "dig up as much dirt" as possible about appellees without regard to its relevance; appellant had threatened to destroy and ruin Dr. Bakker's dental practice through litigation and publicity; and appellant had improperly accused Dr. Bakker of being a child molester. The district court found that appellant's reason for obtaining the credit reports was a blatant attempt to coerce a settlement from Dr. Bakker's insurance carrier.

When appellant obtained the credit reports in September 1995 and April 1996, 15 U.S.C. § 1681b(3) provided in part that

> any consumer reporting agency may furnish a consumer report under the following circumstances and no other:
>
> (3) To a person which it has reason to believe—
>
> > (E) otherwise has a legitimate business need for the information in connection with a business transaction involving the consumer.

In 1996 § 1681b was amended and the "business need" exception was renumbered as § 1681b(a)(3)(F). That subsection now provides that a party may obtain a report if it "otherwise has a legitimate business need for the information—(i) in connection with a business transaction that is initiated by the consumer; or (ii) to review an account to determine whether the consumer continues to meet the terms of the account." Consumer Credit Reform Act of 1996, Pub. L. No. 104–208, § 2403 (1996). Because the 1996 amendment does not apply here (its effective date was 365 days after September 30, 1996), our statutory analysis does not consider it.

Appellant testified that she obtained the credit report on Dr. Bakker seeking information concerning his ability to satisfy a judgment if the parties settled the underlying litigation. She admitted that the first credit report did not contain any such information. Yet, she subsequently obtained a second credit report on Dr. Bakker and his two daughters. Her explanation for obtaining credit reports on Dr. Bakker's daughters was to see if Dr. Bakker was transferring assets to his daughters. Appellant gave no explanation why she thought the later reports might provide helpful information even though the earlier report had not done so.

Appellant argues that, because she obtained the credit reports in connection with the underlying litigation against Dr. Bakker, they were obtained for a commercial or professional use and not in connection with a consumer transaction. Thus, she contends that the credit reports are not consumer reports covered by the FCRA. The district court rejected this argument, holding that appellant's alleged purpose did not alter the fact that the credit reports in question were consumer reports within the meaning of the Act. The definition of "consumer reports" under the Act is limited to information that is "used or expected to be used or collected" in connection with a "business transaction" involving one of the "consumer purposes" set out in the statute, that is, eligibility for personal credit or insurance, employment purposes, and licensing.

We hold that, regardless of appellant's intended use of the credit reports, these reports are consumer reports within the meaning of the FCRA because the information contained therein was collected for a consumer purpose. Under the FCRA whether a credit report is a consumer report does not depend solely upon the ultimate use to which the information contained therein is put, but instead, it is governed by the purpose for which the information was originally collected in whole or in part by the consumer reporting agency.

Furthermore, appellant's contract with the Credit Bureau of Fayetteville/Springdale indicated that the reports were subject to the Act and that she agreed that she would only request the information when she intended to use the information in relation to consumer purposes identical to those set out in the Act.

Next, appellant contends that she had a legitimate business need for the credit reports. Appellees, of course, argue that appellant failed to articulate a legitimate business need within the Act's exception. We hold that appellant cannot be said to have a legitimate business need within the meaning of the Act unless and until she can prove or establish that she and appellees were involved in a business transaction involving a consumer. In order to be entitled to the business need exception, the business transaction must relate to a consumer relationship between the party requesting the report and the subject of the report regarding credit, insurance eligibility, employment, or licensing. Appellant admits that she and appellees were not involved in any consumer transaction involving the extension of credit, insurance, employment, or licensing. Thus, no consumer relationship existed between appellant, the party requesting the reports, and appellees, the subjects of the reports, and the business need exception did not apply.

Finally, we consider appellant's argument that the punitive damages award was unreasonable. Obtaining a credit report under false pretenses creates civil liability under the FCRA. Where civil liability exists because of a willful failure to comply with the requirements of the Act, the consumer may recover (1) any actual damages sustained by the consumer as a result of the failure; (2) such punitive damages as the court may allow; and (3) in the case of any successful action to enforce liability under this section, the costs of the action together with reasonable attorney's fees as determined by the court. 15 U.S.C. § 1681n(a).

Therefore, the question becomes whether the evidence showed that appellant's and her associates' conduct in obtaining the reports was willfully done. To show willful noncompliance with the FCRA, the plaintiff must show that the defendant knowingly and intentionally committed an act in conscious disregard for the rights of others, but need not show malice or evil motive.

Here, the district court found that at the very early stages of the underlying litigation, appellant and her associates set out upon a course of conduct, which willfully violated both the spirit and the letter of the Fair Credit Reporting Act. That conduct was obviously a blatant attempt to extract a settlement from Dr. Bakker's insurance carrier, without regard to whether such conduct was fair or a clear violation of Rule 4.4 of the Arkansas Rules of Professional Conduct.

The district court further found that appellant intentionally and egregiously threatened Dr. Bakker with loss of his profession, both by the destruction of his name and by forfeiture or suspension of his dental license. Appellant's conduct included allegations that Dr. Bakker and his wife had been involved in child molestation matters, allegations that could have had a devastating effect upon their lives even if false. Finally, the district court found that appellant's multiple requests for credit reports on Dr. Bakker and his daughters were designed and intended to carry on the "vendetta" that appellant's law firm pursued against appellees.

While it is true that appellees were not able to produce any actual out-of-pocket expenses or costs incurred as a result of appellant's willful conduct, appellees testified about how they felt when appellant obtained their credit reports and violated their privacy, thereby causing them some emotional distress. We hold that the district court did not abuse its discretion in awarding appellees actual and punitive damages.

Accordingly, the judgment of the district court is affirmed.

## NOTES

**1.** ***The Business Need Amendment.*** The *Bakker* court explains that the definition of "business need" was amended in 1996. What changed under this amendment? Did this change make the statute more stringent or less? Would this case have come out differently if it were decided under the new version of the statute?

2. ***The Central Role of Purpose.*** As explained in both *In re Spokeo* and *Bakker*, a consumer report is defined primarily by the purposes for which it is expected to be used. When it is one of the purposes listed in the statute, "a consumer reporting agency may furnish a consumer report under [those] circumstances and no other." 15 U.S.C. § 1681b(a). This is closer to the EU's data protection default rule, under which the law sets out a list of permissible justifications for data processing and forbids others, than to the usual American consumer protection concept. It is also different from many other data protection statutes, which define their scope based on the subject matter of the underlying data—medical data, educational records, information about children, etc.—rather than on the ways that data is expected to be used. What are the consequences of structuring the statute in this way?

3. ***Notice to Recipients.*** The *Bakker* Court emphasized that the defendant received the standard notice required under FCRA when a credit reporting agency provides a credit report to a customer. This is the type of notice that Spokeo got in trouble for failing to provide to its users. What do you view as the function of this notice requirement in the statute? How does it function in this case? It is not the same as the notice given to job applicants when they have not been hired based on information in a credit report, is it? The CFPB recently issued a new model notice form for CRAs to use.

4. ***Individual Harm Under FCRA.*** Articulate the harm Dr. Bakker and his daughters suffered for which they received damages. Recall that the Supreme Court is considering an argument that the named plaintiff in the private case against Spokeo did not plead the type of harm necessary for constitutional standing [see Chapter 3]. Do the Bakkers have a better argument for injury? Also note the damages awarded in *Bakker*. The punitive damages are ten times higher than the actual damages found by the court. Is that an appropriate multiplier? Is this really just about judicial distaste for McKinnon's litigation behavior, or do you think a violation in another context might trigger a similar punitive damages award?

5. ***Private Lawsuits and Regulatory Design.*** Should a private right of action exist alongside regulatory authority? After all, as a result of the *In re Spokeo* settlement, the FTC secured a monetary penalty, a court order to stop misbehavior, and a 20-year monitoring regime. Yet Spokeo also faces a consumer lawsuit. What is the benefit of allowing individuals such as the *Bakker* plaintiffs to sue as well? Many other federal privacy laws, including Section Five of the FTC Act as well as HIPAA [see Chapter 12] and the Gramm-Leach-Bliley Act [see Chapter 13], rely only on regulatory enforcement, not on private lawsuits. Other statutes have private claims paired with criminal enforcement, such as the Electronic Communications Privacy Act [see Chapter 5], and a few, such as the Video Privacy Protection Act, even rely mostly on civil actions alone [see Chapter 14]. What are the pros and cons of including both civil regulatory authority and a private right of action? Why do you suppose Congress chose to do so in FCRA?

6. ***Class Actions and FCRA.*** Not surprisingly, many private FCRA lawsuits are putative class actions. While a total award of $16,500 might be meaningful to the Bakkers—and could be a consequential disincentive to an individual trial lawyer like the defendant in that case—it is not a very significant sum for typical federal litigation. Multiply that number by a class of potentially thousands of consumers, however, and the calculus changes quickly. Plaintiff class actions for failure to abide by FCRA's complex requirements are common and can produce significant settlements.

7. ***FCRA Claims as a Sideshow.*** Another common type of private FCRA claim is an accompaniment to a broader dispute between parties who are already adverse. The claim in *Bakker* appears to be just such a "sideshow" claim, playing a role in the much larger fight between Dr. Bakker and the defendants' clients over their allegations of his sexual misconduct. In other typical cases, FCRA claims arise from preexisting employment disputes or debt collection matters.

8. ***FACTA and the Affiliate Marketing Rule.*** Congress amended FCRA substantially in 2003 by passing the Fair and Accurate Credit Transactions Act (FACTA), Pub. L. No. 108–159 (2003), which added an array of additional provisions to the statute that are relevant to privacy and data protection law. Most significantly, this is the law that permits consumers access to an annual credit report from each of the major credit reporting agencies free of charge (and, thus, it is responsible for those extremely irritating television advertisements urging you to take advantage of this service). In part, the free credit report provision is aimed at helping consumers recognize and address identity theft. FACTA also instructed agencies to develop regulations concerning certain uses of shared data for marketing; the result was the Affiliate Marketing Rule, 12 C.F.R. Part 41, Subpart C, which became effective in 2008. Basically, the Rule requires that a company give a consumer "clear and conspicuous" notice before marketing to the consumer using credit information that the company has received from an affiliate (that is, from another company under the same ownership or control). The requirement is subject to multiple enumerated exceptions. An illustration on the Rule helps clarify its scope:

> A consumer has a homeowner's insurance policy with an insurance company. The insurance company furnishes eligibility information about the consumer to its affiliated depository institution. Based on that eligibility information, the depository institution wants to make a solicitation to the consumer about its home equity loan products. The depository institution does not have a pre-existing business relationship with the consumer and none of the other exceptions apply. The depository institution is prohibited from using eligibility information received from its insurance affiliate to make solicitations to the consumer about its home equity loan products unless the consumer is given a notice and opportunity to opt out and the consumer does not opt out.

12 CFR § 41.21(a)(iii)(2). The Gramm-Leach-Bliley Act also imposes notice and opt-out requirements on financial institutions for certain marketing

uses of customer data [see Chapter 13], which may sometimes overlap with these requirements.

**9.** ***The FACTA Disposal Rule.*** While most of FCRA and FACTA focus on the use phase of the life cycle of data, another regulation issued under FACTA called the "Disposal Rule," 16 C.F.R. Part 682, is more concerned with security [see Chapter 7 for more on data security rules generally]. The Disposal Rule, promulgated cooperatively by multiple agencies, requires that those in possession of a consumer report in any format, paper or electronic, must "properly dispose of such information by taking reasonable measures to protect against unauthorized access to or use of the information in connection with its disposal." 16 C.F.R. § 682.3(a). The Disposal Rule then goes on to specify certain "illustrative" examples of acceptable disposal methods, including "burning, pulverizing, or shredding of papers" and "the destruction or erasure of electronic media containing consumer information so that the information cannot practicably be read or reconstructed." *Id.* § 682.3(b). Additional portions of FACTA apply to a narrower set of financial institutions, particularly its Red Flags Rule concerning identity theft [see Chapter 13]. This contrasts with the wide ambit of most FCRA requirements—including the Disposal Rule—which bind everyone who uses credit reports for any reason.

## C. EU PROCESSING REGULATIONS

The European Union has a different approach to the regulation of data processing. As explained in the EU Data Protection Directive, which has been incorporated into the national legislation of every EU member state, the automated processing of information, rather than its collection, is the core activity that defines a "data controller" subject to the law. Most EU countries also require data controllers to register their processing activities in advance with the national data protection authority, although the GDPR will eliminate most such rule when it comes into effect. [See Chapter 4 for more information about EU data protection law.]

Because data may be collected only on the basis of a particular purpose for which it will be used, that reason for processing or use becomes central to the regime. The first excerpt below comes from an opinion issued by the Article 29 Working Party, an EU-level advisory body on data protection; it concludes that the purpose articulated at the time of collection is the only one that may be used to justify later processing focused on individual rather than aggregate data. While this opinion is not binding, it is influential. The rise of Big Data was one of the motivations for the issuance of the Opinion, and it includes specific conclusions relevant to the questions about Big Data posed earlier in this chapter.

Furthermore, under Article 15 of the Data Protection Directive:

> Member States shall grant the right to every person not to be subject to a decision which produces legal effects concerning him

> or significantly affects him and which is based solely on automated processing of data intended to evaluate certain personal aspects relating to him, such as his performance at work, creditworthiness, reliability, [or] conduct.

The second excerpt below comes from regulatory guidance about this prohibition, issued by the UK's data protection authority. How does this rule compare to the requirements of FCRA?

## Opinion on Purpose Limitation

Article 29 Working Party Opinion 03/2013 (April 2, 2013)

Purpose limitation protects data subjects by setting limits on how data controllers are able to use their data while also offering some degree of flexibility for data controllers. The concept of purpose limitation has two main building blocks: personal data must be collected for "specified, explicit and legitimate" purposes (purpose specification) and not be "further processed in a way incompatible" with those purposes (compatible use).

Further processing for a different purpose does not necessarily mean that it is incompatible: compatibility needs to be assessed on a case-by-case basis. A substantive compatibility assessment requires an assessment of all relevant circumstances. In particular, account should be taken of the following key factors:

- the relationship between the purposes for which the personal data have been collected and the purposes of further processing;
- the context in which the personal data have been collected and the reasonable expectations of the data subjects as to their further use;
- the nature of the personal data and the impact of the further processing on the data subjects;
- the safeguards adopted by the controller to ensure fair processing and to prevent any undue impact on the data subjects.

### First building block: purpose specification

*Collection for "specified, explicit and legitimate" purposes*

Article 6(1)(b) of the Directive requires that personal data should only be collected for "specified, explicit and legitimate" purposes. Data are collected for certain aims; these aims are the "raison d'être" of the processing operations. As a prerequisite for other data quality requirements, purpose specification will determine the relevant data to be collected, retention periods, and all other key aspects of how personal data will be processed for the chosen purpose/s.

First, any purpose must be **specified**, that is, sufficiently defined to enable the implementation of any necessary data protection safeguards, and to delimit the scope of the processing operation.

Second, to be **explicit**, the purpose must be sufficiently unambiguous and clearly expressed. Comparing the notion of "explicit purpose" with the notion of "hidden purpose" may help to understand the scope of this requirement.

Third, purposes must also be **legitimate**. This notion goes beyond the requirement to have a legal ground for the processing under Article 7 of the Directive and also extends to other areas of law. Purpose specification under Article 6 and the requirement to have a legal ground under Article 7 are thus two separate and cumulative requirements.

The use of the term 'legitimate' in Article 6 provides a link to Article 7 but also to broader legal principles of applicable law, such as non-discrimination. The notion of legitimacy must also be interpreted within the context of the processing, which determines the "reasonable expectations" of the data subject.

*Pre-requisite for other data quality requirements*

When applying data protection law, it must first be ensured that the purpose is specific, explicit and legitimate. This is a prerequisite for other data quality requirements, including adequacy, relevance and proportionality (Article 6(1)(c)), accuracy and completeness (Article 6(1)(d)) and requirements regarding the duration of retention (Article 6(1)(e)).

In cases where different purposes exist from the beginning and different kinds of data are collected and processed simultaneously for these different purposes, the data quality requirements must be complied with separately for each purpose.

### Second building block: compatible use

Article 6(1)(b) of the Directive also introduces the notions of "further processing" and "incompatible" use and requires that further processing must not be incompatible with the purposes for which personal data were collected.

*The concept of "functional separation"*

When it comes to the safeguards to be adopted, the notion of functional separation may be of particular relevance. This means that data used for statistical purposes or other research purposes should not be available to "support measures or decisions" that are taken with regard to the individual data subjects concerned (unless specifically authorized by the individuals concerned). To comply with this requirement, controllers need to guarantee the security of the data, and take all other necessary technical and organisational measures to ensure functional separation.

[F]ull or partial anonymisation, in particular, can be relevant to the safe use or sharing of data within organisations, particularly large ones with diverse functions. When full anonymisation and use of aggregated data (at a sufficiently high level of aggregation) are not possible, data will often at least need to be partially anonymised (e.g. pseudo-anonymised, key-coded, and stripped of direct identifiers) and additional safeguards may also be required.

[The Opinion considered questions related to Big Data in a separate appendix or "annex" at the end of the document, excerpted here:]

In order to identify what safeguards are necessary, it may be helpful to make a distinction between two different scenarios. In the first one, the organisations processing the data want to detect trends and correlations in the information. In the second one, the organisations are interested in individuals.

In the first scenario, the concept of *functional separation* is likely to play a key role, and the extent to which this may be achieved could be an important factor in deciding whether further use of the data for (marketing or other) research can be considered compatible. In these cases, data controllers need to guarantee the confidentiality and security of the data, and take all necessary technical and organisational measures to ensure functional separation.

The second potential scenario is when an organisation specifically wants to analyse or predict the personal preferences, behaviour and attitudes of individual customers, which will subsequently inform "measures or decisions" that are taken with regard to those customers.

In these cases, free, specific, informed and unambiguous "opt-in" consent would almost always be required, otherwise further use cannot be considered compatible. Importantly, such consent should be required, for example, for tracking and profiling for purposes of direct marketing, behavioural advertisement, data-brokering, location-based advertising or tracking-based digital market research.

## THE GUIDE TO DATA PROTECTION

Information Commissioner's Office
(UK) (Last Updated 2015)

### Automated Decision Taking

*When do the rights arise (what is an automated decision)?*

The rights in respect of automated decisions only arise if two requirements are met. First, the decision has to be taken using personal data processed solely by automatic means.

> Example: An individual applies for a personal loan online. The website uses algorithms and auto credit searching to provide an immediate yes/no decision on the application.

Example: A factory worker's pay is linked to his productivity, which is monitored automatically. The decision about how much pay the worker receives for each shift he works is made automatically by reference to the data collected about his productivity.

So the rights explained here do not apply to any decision involving human intervention. Many decisions that are commonly regarded as "automated" actually involve human intervention.

Example: An employee is issued with a warning about late attendance at work. The warning was issued because the employer's automated clocking-in system flagged the fact that the employee had been late on a defined number of occasions. However, although the warning was issued on the basis of the data collected by the automated system, the decision to issue it was taken by the employer's HR manager following a review of that data. So the decision was not taken by automated means.

The second requirement is that the decision has to have a significant effect on the individual concerned.

Example: In the above example on monitoring the productivity of a factory worker, it is obvious that a decision about how much pay he is entitled to will have a significant effect on him.

So these rights do not apply to decisions that only affect the individual to a trivial or negligible extent.

Example: An individual enters an online "personality quiz." She answers questions about herself on a website, which uses her responses to automatically generate a personality profile for her. The individual's data is not retained and the profile is not sent to anyone else. The automated decisions on which the personality profile is based do not have a significant effect on the individual.

*Are all automated decisions subject to these rights?*

No. Some decisions are called "exempt decisions" because the rights do not apply, even though they are taken using solely automated means and do significantly affect the individual concerned.

Exempt decisions:

are authorised or required by legislation; OR

are taken in preparation for, or in relation to, a contract with the individual concerned

AND

are to give the individual something they have asked for; OR

are where steps have been taken to safeguard the legitimate interests of the individual, such as allowing them to appeal the decision.

*What rights do individuals have?*

The Act gives individuals three rights in relation to automated decision taking.

The first is the right to prevent such a decision being taken. You must not take an automated decision if an individual has given notice in writing asking you not to.

The second right applies where no such notice has been given. An organisation that takes an automated decision must inform the individual concerned that it has done this. It must do so as soon as is practicable in the circumstances.

The third right relates to the options available to an individual on receiving this information. If an individual is unhappy that an automated decision has been taken, they have 21 days to ask you to reconsider the decision or to take a new decision on a different basis. In most cases, both these options are likely to involve a review of the automated decision.

> Example: An individual complains to a credit provider because his online application for credit was declined automatically. The application was declined because the information provided by the individual did not match pre-defined acceptance criteria applied by the automated system. The credit provider undertakes manual underwriting checks to review the original decision.

If a court is satisfied that you have failed to comply with these rights, it may order you to do so.

## NOTES

1. ***Purpose Specification in the US.*** Purpose specification is often a central feature of data protection regimes, and not just in Europe. US data protection laws within certain sectors include purpose specification requirements that resemble those in generally applicable European law. For example, under the HIPAA Privacy Rule [see Chapter 12], medical providers must announce the purposes for which information will later be used, and typically they cannot process the data in other ways. Thus, a doctor's office might have a patient sign a consent form indicating that medical information may be used for diagnosis, treatment, insurance claims, and payment collection. If medical research is not included in this initial list, personally identifiable data from that patient generally cannot be used for research without securing a new consent.

2. ***Functional Separation.*** The concept of "functional separation" is widespread in statistical research. Once personal information is aggregated into larger data sets, it is used only for analytical purposes to draw insights from the entire data set, and not to go back and re-examine personally identifiable data points or apply the information to individuals. Yet the separation is not always as neat and clear as it might seem. Suppose a hospital processed a large set of deidentified patient data and determined

that people with naturally blond hair were considerably more likely to contract a particular serious contagious disease often transmitted in hospitals. Surely the hospital should now take extra precautions to protect blond patients, and perhaps begin asking patients whether they dye their hair as part of intake. In other words, the conclusions reached in statistical analysis will affect individuals, just not so directly.

3. ***Assumptions About Automated Decisionmaking*** The ICO's guidance suggests that highly consequential decisionmaking processes that are also fully automated would be relatively unusual. But as demonstrated in the Big Data case study at the outset of this chapter, algorithmic processing has an increasing role in all organization. In particular, individual data profiles are used for everything from marketing to employment pre-screening to evaluating credit applications. Does the rise of Big Data call the ICO's characterization into question? Consider also the underlying assumptions here about the problems with automated decisionmaking. What are its dangers? Mightn't automated decisions be more accurate and less biased than those reached entirely by humans? Should automated decisions be subject to different legal restrictions than those reviewed by humans in a totally cursory fashion?

4. ***Allowable Automated Decisionmaking.*** UK data protection law does not ban all automated decisionmaking. The exceptions allow automated processing, for example, to give people "something they have asked for" pursuant to a contract with them. What specific examples can you think of that might be permitted on this basis? What about the exception when "steps have been taken to safeguard the legitimate interests of the individual?" Isn't that potentially a very broad exception?

5. ***Scholarship on Automated Processing.*** Privacy scholars have been paying a great deal of attention recently to the use of personal data in automated decisionmaking. In general, they warn that the combination of large quantities of data, highly sophisticated processing methods, and lack of transparency about methods and results may lead to mistreatment of individuals. Large organizations and governments are especially likely to have voluminous personal information, the capacity to process it, and the influence to make important decisions. In response, they argue for safeguards that would rebalance those scales in favor of the individual. *See, e.g.*, FRANK PASQUALE, THE BLACK BOX SOCIETY: THE SECRET ALGORITHMS THAT CONTROL MONEY AND INFORMATION (2015); DANIEL J. SOLOVE, THE DIGITAL PERSON: TECHNOLOGY AND PRIVACY IN THE INFORMATION AGE (2004); Ryan Calo, *Digital Market Manipulation*, 82 GEO. WASH. L. REV. 995–1051 (2014); Danielle Keats Citron & Frank Pasquale, *The Scored Society: Due Process for Automated Predictions*, 89 WASH. L. REV. 1 (2014). How does FCRA work as a model for the sort of "digital due process" that might address such threats? How well does the EU Data Protection Directive work?

---

## Practice

Data Processing for Marketing

You are a lawyer for a retailer, T.C. Pritchard, that sells large household appliances such as stoves and washing machines in both the US and the UK. The company allows some selected customers to buy appliances on deferred payment plans ("Buy now and pay nothing for six months!"), based on evaluation of their credit history. T.C. Pritchard has contracted with a market research firm called InSiteSmart to improve identification of potential customers. These are some of the marketing firm's recommendations from its rather glossy report:

> We analyzed your customer information from the last three years and combined it with information obtained from reputable data brokers. We found your customers disproportionately tend to be in the "Frugal Planners" segment. You should structure future advertising accordingly. We also suggest you automatically run credit checks for the Frugal Planners segment and send them personalized marketing messages extending them preapproval of deferred payment plans and offering more protective warranty plans to insure their purchases. At the same time, a smaller but still sizable segment of your customers are in the "Pay for Quality" segment; we can set up a program that automatically excludes them from discount coupons because they willingly pay the higher price.
>
> Your data also tells you when an appliance bought by a past customer is likely nearing the end of its useful life span. You should set up a schedule to offer discounts to customers for new purchases about a year before their old appliances are likely to "conk out" (an average of 8–14 years after purchase, depending on variables such as the type of appliance, the brand, and the price paid—all of which you can calculate from information that's in your database already).
>
> Finally, as you know, T.C. Pritchard sends customer satisfaction surveys to every purchaser approximately a month after the purchase. In the past this has primarily been a marketing gimmick—a way of showing customers you truly care about them—but at times it has also identified problematic patterns of deficient service that you were able to fix. We suggest you analyze that data and combine it with data broker information to look for patterns of highly satisfied past customers who also spend on big-ticket items, and extend them all pre-approval for deferred payment as well.

What legal concerns do you have about these marketing ideas (based primarily on the law studied in this chapter)? How can you help T.C. Pritchard move forward with them but remain compliant with US and UK law? How, if at all, will strategies in the US and the UK differ?

---

## CHAPTER 7

# STORAGE AND SECURITY

The comedian Stephen Wright once observed, "You can't have everything. Where would you put it?" He made this wisecrack before the advent of enormously cheap digital storage, however. Today many organizations find that, once they have collected personal information, it is not very difficult or expensive to keep it indefinitely. If use and processing of data for important purposes are ongoing, this may be a reasonable approach. Most often, that will apply to continuous relationships. A bank's account holders, a social network's registered users, a store's loyalty-card customers, and a doctor's patients would all be quite irritated if they had to re-register every time they returned to the same service provider. Sometimes data must be retained under legal or other mandates—records needed in connection with taxes, insurance, billing disputes, or financial regulatory compliance, to name a few, may contain personal data. And credit bureaus, government agencies, and marketing firms all retain data precisely because they are creating dossiers about individuals over time.

Sometimes, however, data ends up in storage out of inertia, or based on the fuzzy idea that future unpredicted utility may emerge some day. Sensible data destruction policies often will require more effort than perpetual data retention. This habit increases the risk and the potential seriousness of data breaches, which can be one of the most damaging forms of privacy invasion, from the perspective of both companies and individuals.

Thus storage, and its attendant security, are important stages in the life cycle of data. Some experts insist that security is a concept distinct from privacy that should be conceptualized separately. To be sure, there are notable differences between this stage of the life cycle and others, chiefly the central role of information technology in protecting stored data. But there is no doubt that security problems cause privacy problems, or that both concern the harms that can come from improper or unwise handling of personal data. Moreover, in practice most businesses and lawyers evaluate and manage risks to security as part of their overall approach to privacy issues, integrated into the life cycle of data.

The scale and importance of the problem are undeniable. The Privacy Rights Clearinghouse, a consumer advocacy organization, keeps a running tally of publicly known security breaches. As of early 2016 this list included 4,790 data breaches since 2005, affecting an estimated 896,258,345 records. *See* www.privacyrights.org/data-breach. Because some security incidents are not made public, the actual numbers must be even higher. Not only are security failures common, but the harm that can result is among the most concrete and widely accepted in privacy law. As seen throughout this book, there is broad societal debate about the significance of harms from things like government surveillance or corporate data mining. But no one disputes that it is a serious problem when hackers steal personal information to commit identity theft or fraud. As a result, at least under US law, liability arising from security problems can be more serious than other privacy liability. Quantifiable damages may be more likely, especially when security lapses lead to financial swindles like counterfeit credit cards or unauthorized withdrawals.

As in other phases of the life cycle we have seen, many different aspects of privacy and data protection law govern storage. Those covered elsewhere in the book include:

- General consumer protection regulation related to bad security, such as enforcement actions by the FTC or state agencies against security deficiencies as unfair or deceptive trade practices [see Chapter 3].
- Responsibilty for safe storage under the EU Data Protection Directive [see Chapter 4].
- Heightened security requirements for medical information, particularly the HIPAA Security Rule [see Chapter 12].
- Special protection for stored financial information, including the Safeguards Rule [see Chapter 13].

Storage and security come up tangentially in many other areas of privacy law as well. Even in constitutional law, cases such as *Whalen v. Roe*, 429 U.S. 589 (1977) [see Chapter 1], can be interpreted as evaluations of the security of databases and protections against their misuse.

This chapter considers data storage and security in the context of the life cycle of data. Unlike the sectoral security laws covered in Part Three of the book, those discussed in this chapter apply broadly across many industries and types of data. This chapter should help you understand the practical effect of security provisions in all of privacy law. It begins with a case study in Section A, focused on the particularly important self-regulatory structure around security for the credit and debit cards used throughout our consumer economy. Section B then considers the emerging importance of private lawsuits as a source of liability for security shortcomings. Section C turns the focus to preventing and managing data security risks; it examines both self-regulatory and legal best practices in data security and the complex thicket of state laws requiring that organizations notify individuals who are affected by a security breach, whether caused by hacking or by mistake. Finally, Section D examines laws that attempt to address malicious hacking directly, particularly the Computer Fraud and Abuse Act.

## A. CASE STUDY: DATA SECURITY IN THE PAYMENT CARD INDUSTRY

### Focus

The Payment Card Industry

When the cashier instructs you to swipe your credit or debit card at the store, you may not think much about the complicated series of financial transactions that occurs invisibly and almost instantaneously as a result. Most of the time they proceed without incident, and then they are followed by a series of money transfers that culminate when you pay your credit card bill the next month. All these interactions increase the vulnerability of the data, however. And when a security compromise does cause fraud or theft, it is important to figure out who ends up holding the bag and paying the associated costs. A self-regulatory structure that is probably the most elaborate in privacy and data protection law arose to address these difficult issues.

To understand this self-regulatory construction, you must first understand the basics of our payment card system. Visa and MasterCard are really networks of financial institutions, which include both giant banks like Citibank or Capital One and small credit unions or community banks. Acting as "issuer banks," these institutions individually approve card applications, manage consumers' accounts, authorize transaction requests, and bill the cardholder. When Capital One advertises its cards on television ("What's In Your Wallet?"), it is promoting its services as an issuer bank to consumers. Financial institutions—sometimes the same ones that operate as issuer banks—also function as "acquirer banks," entering into contracts with merchants to process their credit card transactions. Finally, both issuer and acquirer banks may have contracts with credit card companies, and many use subcontractors known as payment processors to perform tasks necessary to complete transactions. (American Express and Discover are more integrated networks than Visa and MasterCard, because they themselves usually play the issuer and acquirer roles rather than contracting with separate banks, but there still may be multiple entities involved in processing their transactions.)

A simplified example illustrates how these different functions operate in a typical credit card sale. Suppose Estella buys a soccer ball at Sports Warehouse, a bricks-and-mortar vendor, and pays with a Visa credit card. Despite the logo on her credit card, Visa itself has no direct relationship with either Estella or Sports Warehouse. Rather, Sports Warehouse has a contract with ABC Bank to act as its acquirer bank. When Estella swipes her card at the cashier's terminal, Sports Warehouse transmits the information from the card to ABC Bank as part of an authorization request. ABC Bank determines that Neighborhood Bank issued Estella's card to her, or more likely forwards the request to a payment processor to make that determination. Either ABC Bank or the processor then forwards the authorization request to Neighborhood Bank. Upon receipt, Neighborhood Bank will determine whether the transaction should be approved. It might reject the request if, for example, Estella has reached her credit limit or failed to pay recent bills. It also might decline authorization if the card has been frozen or deactivated because it was reported stolen or if unusual account activity indicated possible fraud.

Whatever the determination, Neighborhood Bank sends it back through ABC Bank to Sports Warehouse, which then completes or declines the sale accordingly. All of these interactions are automated and happen almost instantaneously. Afterwards, Neighborhood Bank will transfer funds to ABC Bank to be credited to

Sports Warehouse's account. Neighborhood Bank will then add the charge to Estella's monthly bill. Depending on the organization of the network, additional entities such as payment processors may again participate as go-betweens in transmitting information or in "settlement"—the actual moving of the money. All of these numerous institutions will use, and to some extent retain, data from Estella's credit card: Sports Warehouse, ABC Bank, Neighborhood Bank, and their subcontractors.

Suppose the soccer ball purchase is made by a thief using Estella's stolen credit card, or a counterfeiter who has manufactured a fake card using her information. If Estella notices the fraudulent transaction on her bill, she almost surely will not need to pay for the soccer ball. The Federal Reserve Bank has promulgated a rule known as Regulation Z, 12 C.F.R. § 205.11, under the Truth in Lending Act, 15 U.S.C. § 1601, which limits consumer liability for unauthorized credit card transactions to $50. As a matter of law, under the Electronic Fund Transfer Act, 15 U.S.C. §§ 1693 et seq., debit card liability could be somewhat higher. In practice, however, issuer banks do not charge cardholders anything for fraudulent transactions using either credit or debit cards, because they want to maintain good customer relations in a competitive market. Under federal law, Estella has two years to dispute a charge on her card (although most banks try to resolve such disputes within six months).

In addition to identity theft or similar criminal activity, Estella might also dispute a charge for other reasons. Perhaps she says that Sports Warehouse charged her more than the agreed price, or that its product was defective. She may claim that she was waiting for delivery of a product that never arrived or that it was damaged when she received it. In all these situations, Neighborhood Bank would investigate her claim and likely send a "chargeback" to ABC Bank for the amount of the purchase. If ABC Bank complies, it will likely then take the chargeback from Sports Warehouse's account, along with an administrative fee. Disagreements may arise at any point in this sequence, but other than the heavily regulated consumer relationship between Neighborhood Bank and Estella, most of the rules for handling these situations are based on contracts between the parties.

Obviously, given the complexity of this system, fraud is a serious problem for the payment card industry. Efforts to curb fraud took on greater urgency as the volume of transactions involving credit or debit cards mushroomed throughout the 1990s and early 2000s. In particular, the growth of e-commerce meant that more vendors were accepting card numbers for payment without the presentation of a physical card, and many who set up shop online did not have the capacity or expertise to safeguard sensitive customer data with sufficient care. Along with these changes, sophisticated criminal operations developed the ability to coordinate fraud on a large scale, doing everything from stealing personal information out of databases to forging cards to managing small armies of fraudulent purchasers who obtained gift cards or merchandise that was easy to resell such as consumer electronics.

In response, credit card companies like Visa began establishing more specific security standards to prevent breaches and fraud and also reassure consumers about the safety of using their cards. Eventually, Visa and MasterCard joined together to issue the Payment Card Industry Data Security Standard ("PCI DSS") in 2004. By 2006, the other major credit card companies had joined them, and an independent organization was established to oversee and update various PCI standards applicable to different entities in the payment card system. There have been several revisions of the most important standard, the PCI DSS; at this writing the latest release was the PCI DSS 3.1 in April 2015.

A requirement of compliance with PCI standards is incorporated into the web of contracts that connect the various institutions authorizing transactions and transferring funds to cover them. So, in the example above, Visa's contracts allowing

Neighborhood Bank to issue Visa cards and allowing ABC Bank to process merchants' Visa card transactions would both impose conditions requiring that the banks adhere to the most recent PCI rules. As banks, these institutions probably already have relatively strong data security, because of heavier regulation on the financial services industry generally and in particular because of requirements like the Safeguards Rule, 16 C.F.R § 314.4, issued under the Gramm-Leach-Bliley Act, 15 U.S.C. §§ 6801 et seq. [see Chapter 13]. The more significant duty imposed in contracts with companies like Visa is the requirement that these banks police other entities, particularly merchants and processors.

Larger merchants must conduct quarterly and annual audits and tests on their security systems, and many of these must be performed by certified security professionals, all as specified in PCI standards. Businesses that conduct a smaller volume of payment card transactions may certify themselves by answering an online self-assessment questionnaire. Acquirer and issuer banks also have particular ongoing monitoring responsibilities. These security checkups do not immunize an organization from penalties if the business is later found to be noncompliant with PCI standards; they merely aim to prevent such situations from occurring in the first place.

PCI standards are completely self-regulatory, not overseen by any government entity. Indeed, in 2007, California Gov. Arnold Schwarzenegger vetoed a bill that would have codified payment card security rules, because, he said, "the marketplace has already assigned responsibilities and liabilities that provide for the protection of consumers." Even though the California bill mimicked the requirements of the PCI DSS, Schwarzenegger worried that legislation might conflict with later updates and thus make the self-regulatory standard less nimble in response to changed circumstances. In the years since, this concern has become the conventional wisdom about direct government regulation of payment card security.

Enforcement mechanisms are not built into the PCI standards themselves, but are handled in individual contracts. Typically, the credit card companies' contracts with issuer banks and acquirer banks hold them responsible for ensuring compliance. Those banks may be forced to absorb losses from fraud, and also may be required to pay fines to the credit card companies if they are handling noncompliant transactions. Acquirer banks, in turn, have contracts with merchants or processors that may impose compliance obligations on them—and pass along costs and penalties to them if they are noncompliant. Any of these contracts might also include additional potential penalties, such as restricting the ability to handle future transactions. Issuing banks can impose duties on the processors with whom they have agreements, but they are not likely to have direct contractual relationships with merchants. (In the example above, Neighborhood Bank interacted with Sports Warehouse only through ABC Bank.) As noted below, this can lead to litigation when something goes wrong. In the end, any entity that processes, stores, or transmits payment card data is expected to comply with PCI rules.

The PCI rules are not the only self-regulatory data security regime in the payment card industry. For example, another completely distinct technical standard is called EMV. (The name derives from the initials of Europay, MasterCard, and Visa, which are the companies that started it; EMV is now managed independently and includes many more companies.) EMV governs the addition of embedded microchips to credit and debit cards instead of (or alongside) the magnetic stripes that have been issued most widely in the US. These newer cards can be used in concert with a personal identification number; such "chip and PIN" transactions are significantly more secure than those that rely on the magnetic stripe and a signature. The chip and PIN setup is deployed widely in Europe, where it was mandated by some governments, but it has been slow to spread in the US because of the costs involved.

In October 2015, a number of credit card companies implemented so-called "liability shifts" related to EMV. In cases where this shift has occurred, when merchants have not updated their equipment to accept EMV-compliant cards but issuer banks have implemented the technology in the cards they provide to consumers, then the merchant, rather than the issuer, will be responsible for fraudulent charges. The rule is intended to encourage updating terminals to include EMV-compliant chip readers. As with PCI standards, these rules are derived from private agreements without government involvement, but they certainly have a strong regulatory effect on the parties involved.

The PCI standards are expressed in levels of increasing specificity. The first excerpt below specifies the requirements of PCI DSS in very basic terms. The second excerpt below provides more guidance concerning the third requirement, the protection of stored data, as an example of the types of security standards included in PCI rules. The full PCI DSS document, available at https://www.pcisecuritystandards.org/, lays out each of these general best practices in even greater detail, including specific technological means to meet the requirements.

---

## PCI Security Standards Council, PCI DSS Quick Reference Guide: Understanding the Payment Card Industry

Data Security Standard version 3.1 (2015)

### The PCI Data Security Standard

PCI DSS is the global data security standard adopted by the payment card brands for all entities that process, store or transmit cardholder data and/or sensitive authentication data. It consists of steps that mirror security best practices.

### Build and Maintain a Secure Network and Systems

1. Install and maintain a firewall configuration to protect cardholder data

2. Do not use vendor-supplied defaults for system passwords and other security parameters

### Protect Cardholder Data

3. Protect stored cardholder data

4. Encrypt transmission of cardholder data across open, public networks

### Maintain a Vulnerability Management Program

5. Protect all systems against malware and regularly update anti-virus software or programs

6. Develop and maintain secure systems and applications

### Implement Strong Access Control Measures

7. Restrict access to cardholder data by business need to know

8. Identify and authenticate access to system components

9. Restrict physical access to cardholder data

**Regularly Monitor and Test Networks**

10. Track and monitor all access to network resources and cardholder data

11. Regularly test security systems and processes

**Maintain an Information Security Policy**

12. Maintain a policy that addresses information security for all personnel

* * *

**Protect Cardholder Data**

Cardholder data refers to any information printed, processed, transmitted or stored in any form on a payment card. Entities accepting payment cards are expected to protect cardholder data and to prevent its unauthorized use—whether the data is printed or stored locally, or transmitted over an internal or public network to a remote server or service provider.

**Requirement 3: Protect stored cardholder data**

Cardholder data should not be stored unless it's necessary to meet the needs of the business. Sensitive data on the magnetic stripe or chip must never be stored after authorization. If your organization stores [the primary account number, or "PAN"], it is crucial to render it unreadable (see 3.4, and table below[,] for guidelines).

**3.1** Limit cardholder data storage and retention time to that which is required for business, legal, and/or regulatory purposes, as documented in your data retention policy. Purge unnecessary stored data at least quarterly.

**3.2** Do not store sensitive authentication data after authorization (even if it is encrypted). See table below. Render all sensitive authentication data unrecoverable upon completion of the authorization process. Issuers and related entities may store sensitive authentication data if there is a business justification, and the data is stored securely.

**3.3** Mask PAN when displayed (the first six and last four digits are the maximum number of digits you may display), so that only authorized people with a legitimate business need can see the full PAN. This does not supersede stricter requirements that may be in place for displays of cardholder data, such as on a point-of-sale receipt.

**3.4** Render PAN unreadable anywhere it is stored—including on portable digital media, backup media, in logs, and data received from or stored by wireless networks. Technology solutions for this requirement may include strong one-way hash functions of the entire PAN, truncation, index tokens with securely stored pads, or strong cryptography.

**3.5** Document and implement procedures to protect any keys used for encryption of cardholder data from disclosure and misuse.

**3.6** Fully document and implement key management processes and procedures for cryptographic keys used for encryption of cardholder data.

**3.7** Ensure that related security policies and operational procedures are documented, in use, and known to all affected parties.

**Guidelines for Cardholder Data Elements**

| | Data Element | Storage Permitted | Render Stored Data Unreadable per Requirement 3.4 |
|---|---|---|---|
| Cardholder Data | Primary Account Number (PAN) | Yes | Yes |
| | Cardholder Name | Yes | No |
| | Service Code | Yes | No |
| | Expiration Date | Yes | No |
| Sensitive Authentication Data[1] | Full Track Data[2] | No | Cannot store per Requirement 3.2 |
| | CAV2/CVC2/CVV2/CID[3] | No | Cannot store per Requirement 3.2 |
| | PIN/PIN Block[4] | No | Cannot store per Requirement 3.2 |

[1] Sensitive authentication data must not be stored after authorization (even if encrypted)
[2] Full track data from the magnetic stripe, equivalent data on the chip, or elsewhere.
[3] The three- or four-digit value printed on the front or back of a payment card
[4] Personal Identification Number entered by cardholder during a transaction, and/or encrypted PIN block present within the transaction message

## NOTES

1. ***Nongovernmental "Law."*** As you can imagine, for many businesses, compliance with PCI rules can be as imperative as any formal legal obligation. In what ways do these requirements resemble legal obligations? What are the benefits and shortcomings of relying on contract-based self-regulation for a system like payment card security?

2. ***The Role of Law in Private Standards.*** Despite the independent nature of the PCI rules, inescapably they do rely on the existence of surrounding law. First of all, the parties all depend on the legal enforcement of their contracts. Without that, their agreements would have no teeth. In addition, the rules are shaped by consumer protection laws such as Regulation Z. How might the PCI rules look different if individuals, not banks, absorbed the costs of fraud? Furthermore, the data security rules imposed on most banks by general financial regulatory statutes such as the Gramm-Leach-Bliley Act [see Chapter 13] influence the content of the PCI rules. Because banks are already subject to stringent requirements, they may be more willing to accept the demands of PCI rules. Of course, banks

also have an interest in seeing that other entities in the payment card system have good security.

**3.** ***The Professionalization of Data Security.*** One consequence of specific security rules like the PCI DSS, and especially those that require periodic auditing, is the rise of a professional class of IT-oriented experts in data security—and more work for lawyers well versed in these issues. Someone needs to create all those systems and conduct all those audits. Section C of this chapter discusses the best practices for data security that emerge as a result.

## B. CIVIL SUITS

### Paul v. Providence Health System

273 P.3d 106 (Or. 2012)

■ BALMER, J.

The issue in this case is whether a healthcare provider can be liable in damages when the provider's negligence permitted the theft of its patients' personal information, but the information was never used or viewed by the thief or any other person. Plaintiffs claimed economic and noneconomic damages for financial injury and emotional distress that they allegedly suffered when, through defendant's alleged negligence, computer disks and tapes containing personal information from an estimated 365,000 patients (including plaintiffs) were stolen from the car of one of defendant's employees. We conclude that, in the absence of allegations that the stolen information was used in any way or even was viewed by a third party, plaintiffs have not suffered an injury that would provide a basis for a negligence claim or an action under the [Oregon Unlawful Trade Practices Act (UTPA)]. We therefore affirm, although our analysis differs in some respects from that of the Court of Appeals.

We take the facts from plaintiffs' third amended complaint. When reviewing a trial court order granting a motion to dismiss, we accept as true all well-pleaded facts in the complaint. The named plaintiffs were patients of defendant, a nonprofit corporation that provides health care. An employee of defendant left computer disks and tapes containing records of 365,000 patients in a car; the disks and tapes were subsequently stolen on or about December 30–31, 2005. The records included names, addresses, phone numbers, Social Security numbers, and patient care information. Defendant notified all individuals whose information was contained on the disks and tapes and advised them to take precautions to protect themselves against identify theft.

Plaintiffs filed this class action on behalf of themselves and other individuals whose records had been stolen. Plaintiffs asserted common law negligence and negligence *per se* claims, alleging that defendant's conduct had caused them financial injury in the form of past and future costs of credit monitoring, maintaining fraud alerts, and notifying various government agencies regarding the theft, as well as possible future costs related to identity theft. Plaintiffs did not allege any intentional conduct by defendant. Nor did plaintiffs allege that any unauthorized person ever had accessed any of the information contained on the disks and tapes, or that any plaintiff had suffered any actual financial loss, credit impairment, or identity theft. In addition to their negligence claims, plaintiffs alleged that defendant had violated the UTPA by representing that patient data would be kept confidential when defendant knew that such data was inadequately safeguarded.

Defendant filed a motion to dismiss plaintiffs' complaint for failure to state ultimate facts sufficient to constitute a claim for relief. The trial court granted defendant's motion, holding that the damages plaintiffs alleged were not compensable under *Lowe v. Philip Morris USA, Inc.*, 142 P.3d 1079 (Or. App. 2006), 183 P.3d 181 (Or. 2008), because plaintiffs' claimed damages—although reflecting, in part, expenses that plaintiffs actually had incurred—were premised on the *risk* of future injury, rather than actual present harm.

Plaintiffs appealed, and the Court of Appeals affirmed. That court began by analyzing whether plaintiffs had stated a negligence claim for economic damages. To recover damages for purely economic harm, liability must be predicated on some duty of the negligent actor to the injured party beyond the common law duty to exercise reasonable care to prevent foreseeable harm. The Court of Appeals held that plaintiffs had failed to identify a "heightened duty of care to protect against economic harm arising out of the relationship between themselves as patients and defendant as a health care provider." The court rejected plaintiffs' argument that state and federal statutes protecting the confidentiality of medical records established an independent standard of care that defendant had violated, reasoning that those statutes did not create a special relationship between the parties that would give rise to a heightened duty owed to plaintiffs. Because plaintiffs failed to identify a special relationship between the parties, the court concluded that plaintiffs could not, under this court's opinion in *Lowe,* recover for the expenses of monitoring a future potential harm.

We begin with plaintiffs' claim for common law negligence. As we recently stated in *Lowe*, "Not all negligently inflicted harms give rise to a negligence claim." Rather, to recover in negligence, a plaintiff must suffer harm "to an interest of a kind that the law protects against negligent invasion." Plaintiffs, in their third amended complaint, describe their injury as follows:

> Plaintiffs and class members suffered *economic damages* in the form of past out-of-pocket expenses *for credit monitoring services,* credit injury, long distance and time loss from employment to address these issues. In addition, plaintiffs and class members have suffered *non-economic damages* in the past and will do so in the future in the form of *impairment of access*

> *to credit* inherent in placing and maintaining fraud alerts, *as well as worry and emotional distress* associated with the initial disclosure and the risk of any future subsequent identity theft.

(Emphasis added.) Thus, plaintiffs allege that defendant's negligence created the *risk* of future identify theft, and they seek economic damages for the past and future expense of credit monitoring services and related expenditures made to address the risk of identity theft. Although plaintiffs allege that an unknown person stole digital records containing plaintiffs' information from defendant's employee's car, they do not allege that the thief or any third person actually *used* plaintiffs' information in any way that caused financial harm to them. They allege no actual "identity theft," as that term is used in Oregon statutes, nor do they allege that defendant's actions caused them actual financial injury, apart from the expenses that they incurred in the form of credit monitoring that they initiated.

Under the economic loss doctrine, "[O]ne ordinarily is not liable for negligently causing a stranger's purely economic loss without injuring his person or property." Damages for purely economic losses, however, are available when a defendant has a duty to guard against the economic loss that occurred. A duty to protect against economic loss can arise "from a defendant's particular status or relationships, or from legislation, beyond the generalized standards that the common law of negligence imposes on persons at large."

We need not resolve the dispute between the parties as to whether common law tort principles or statutes concerning the protection of patient information provide a basis for plaintiffs' claims for economic damages. Assuming, without deciding, that defendant owed a duty to protect plaintiffs against economic losses, we nevertheless conclude, for the reasons that follow, that plaintiffs' allegations here are insufficient because plaintiffs do not allege actual, present injury caused by defendant's conduct.

To the extent that plaintiffs seek damages for *future* harm to their credit or financial well-being, *Lowe* forecloses such a claim because " 'the threat of future harm, by itself, is insufficient as an allegation of damage in the context of a negligence claim,' " Plaintiffs argue, however, that they should be able to recover as economic damages the past and present expenses (such as the cost of credit monitoring) that they have incurred to protect themselves from the *risk* of future economic harm. Defendant and *amici* respond that, in *Lowe,* this court stated that it was unwilling to "overul[e] Oregon's well-established negligence requirements" to require a defendant whose conduct increased the plaintiffs' risk of cancer to pay for medical monitoring, and argue that to require defendant here to pay for credit monitoring because of the increased *risk* of a purely *economic* future harm would require an even greater departure from existing case law. We agree.

As this court stated in *Lowe*, "the fact that a defendant's negligence poses a threat of future physical harm is not sufficient, standing alone, to constitute an actionable injury." We then quoted Prosser and Keeton's comment that, as the law of negligence developed, " 'it retained the rule that proof of damage was an essential part of the plaintiff's case' " and that " '[n]ominal damages, to vindicate a technical right, cannot be recovered in a negligence action, where no actual loss has occurred.' " In *Lowe*, we applied that rule in rejecting a claim for medical monitoring expenses when the plaintiff had suffered no present physical harm.

Although plaintiffs are correct that this case is factually distinguishable from *Lowe* because of the relationship between plaintiffs and defendant here, they are incorrect in arguing that *Lowe* stands for the proposition that, had there been such a relationship in that case, this court would have permitted recovery for monitoring expenses, notwithstanding the absence of some present harm to plaintiffs. As we said in *Lowe*, "Under a long line of this court's cases, the present economic harm that defendants' actions allegedly have caused—the cost of medical monitoring—is not sufficient to give rise to a negligence claim." That rule applies whether or not there is a "relationship" between the plaintiff and the defendant. It follows, in our view, that the cost of credit monitoring that results, not from any "present economic harm" (to borrow the phrase from *Lowe*) to plaintiffs, but rather from the *risk* of possible future harm, also is insufficient to state a negligence claim.

That conclusion is similar to those reached by other courts that have considered claims for credit monitoring damages in the absence of present identity theft or other harm. In *Pisciotta v. Old Nat. Bancorp*, 499 F.3d 629 (7th Cir. 2007), the court rejected negligence claims for credit monitoring by a bank's customers whose personal information had been accessed by a computer "hacker." The court noted that Indiana cases had rejected medical monitoring damages based on "exposure to a future potential harm" and had required instead "an actual exposure-related illness or disease." It concluded that a similar distinction between "exposure" to future harm and actual harm should apply in the credit monitoring context. The court also observed that even states that had allowed damages in medical monitoring negligence cases "have expressed doubt that credit monitoring also should be compensable." Every court that has addressed damage claims for credit monitoring following the theft of computer records containing personal information—but no wrongful use of that information—has reached a similar conclusion.

In contrast to those cases are several decisions that have allowed at least some damage claims when stolen personal information actually has been used to perpetrate identify theft, causing individuals present financial injury. *Anderson v. Hannaford Bros. Co.*, 659 F.3d 151 (1st Cir. 2011), is illustrative. There, the First Circuit, applying Maine law, permitted certain claims by credit card holders against the defendant, a processor of credit card payments whose system had been hacked by third parties. The court distinguished the cases cited above (and many similar decisions) because those cases—like plaintiffs' case here—alleged no actual use of any of the plaintiffs' personal information:

> Unlike the cases cited by [the defendant], this case does not involve inadvertently misplaced or lost data which has not been accessed or misused by third parties. Here, there was actual misuse, and it was apparently global in reach. The thieves appeared to have expertise in accomplishing their theft and to be sophisticated in how to take advantage of the stolen numbers. The data was used to run up thousands of improper charges across the globe to the customers' accounts. The card owners were not merely exposed to a hypothetical risk, but to a real risk of misuse.

Here, plaintiffs have alleged no actual identity theft or financial harm, other than credit monitoring and similar mitigation costs. Plaintiffs have not offered a cogent basis "for overruling Oregon's well-established negligence requirements," which require the allegation of such present injury.

[The court briefly affirmed dismissal of the UTPA claims as well, holding that the statute requires an "ascertainable loss of money or property" and that the analysis above demonstrates that this requirement had not been satisfied.]

## Resnick v. AvMed, Inc.

693 F.3d 1317 (11th Cir. 2012)

■ WILSON, CIRCUIT JUDGE:

[Plaintiffs in a putative class action complaint, which alleges claims under Florida state law against AvMed, Inc., appeal the district court's dismissal of their complaint for failure to state a claim.] We conclude that the Complaint sufficiently alleges the causation element of negligence, negligence per se, breach of contract, breach of implied contract, breach of the implied covenant of good faith and fair dealing, and breach of fiduciary duty. The Complaint similarly alleges facts sufficient to withstand a motion to dismiss on the restitution/unjust enrichment claim. However, the Complaint fails to allege entitlement to relief under Florida law for the claims of negligence per se and breach of the implied covenant of good faith and fair dealing. We therefore reverse in part, affirm in part, and remand the case to the district court for further proceedings.

### I

We state the facts as alleged in the Complaint, accept them as true, and construe them in the light most favorable to Plaintiffs. AvMed, Inc. is a Florida corporation that delivers health care services through health plans and government-sponsored managed-care plans. AvMed has a corporate office in Gainesville, Florida, and in December 2009, two laptop computers were stolen from that office. Those laptops contained AvMed customers' sensitive information, which included protected health information, Social Security numbers, names, addresses, and phone numbers. AvMed did not take care to secure these laptops, so when they were stolen the information was readily accessible. The laptops were sold to an individual with a history of dealing in stolen property. The unencrypted laptops contained the sensitive information of approximately 1.2 million current and former AvMed members.

The laptops contained personal information of Juana Curry and William Moore ["Plaintiffs"]. Plaintiffs are careful in guarding their sensitive information and had never been victims of identity theft before the laptops were stolen. Curry guards physical documents that contain her sensitive information and avoids storing or sharing her sensitive information digitally. Similarly, Moore guards physical documents that contain his sensitive information and is careful in the digital transmission of this information.

Notwithstanding their care, Plaintiffs have both become victims of identity theft. Curry's sensitive information was used by an unknown third party in October 2010—ten months after the laptop theft. Bank of America accounts were opened in Curry's name, credit cards were activated, and the cards were used to make unauthorized purchases. Curry's home address was also changed with the U.S. Postal Service. Moore's sensitive information was used by an unknown third party in February 2011—fourteen months after the laptop theft. At that time, an account was opened in Moore's name with E*Trade Financial, and in April 2011, Moore was notified that the account had been overdrawn.

## II

In November 2010, five named plaintiffs seeking to represent the class of individuals whose information was stored on the unsecured laptops filed this case in Florida state court. AvMed removed the case to federal court pursuant to the Class Action Fairness Act of 2005, 28 U.S.C. § 1332(d) and filed a motion to dismiss for failure to state a claim. *See* Fed.R.Civ.P. 12(b)(6). The district court granted [a motion to dismiss] without prejudice on the ground that the plaintiffs failed to state a cognizable injury. Specifically, the district court reasoned that the plaintiffs sought to "predicate recovery upon a mere specter of injury: a heightened likelihood of identity theft."

Plaintiffs [filed an amended complaint (the "Complaint" at issue here) seeking] to represent the class of AvMed customers whose sensitive information was stored on the stolen laptops and a subclass of individuals whose identities have been stolen since the laptop theft. Plaintiffs brought seven counts against AvMed under Florida law. Plaintiffs allege that AvMed was negligent in protecting their sensitive information and [was] negligent per se when it violated section 395.3025 of the Florida Statutes, which protects medical information. Plaintiffs also allege that

AvMed breached its contract with Plaintiffs, and alternatively that AvMed breached its implied contract with Plaintiffs. In the alternative to the breach of contract claim, Plaintiffs also allege a claim for restitution/unjust enrichment. Finally, Plaintiffs allege that AvMed breached the implied covenant of good faith and fair dealing, and that AvMed breached the fiduciary duty it owed to Plaintiffs.

AvMed filed a motion to dismiss the Complaint for failure to state a claim, and the district court granted the motion, stating only that "[a]mong its other deficiencies, [the Complaint] again fails to allege any cognizable injury." Plaintiffs appeal.

## III

Litigants must show that their claim presents the court with a case or controversy under the Constitution and meets the irreducible constitutional minimum of standing.

At the pleading stage, general factual allegations of injury resulting from the defendant's conduct may suffice" to establish standing.

Plaintiffs allege that they have become victims of identity theft and have suffered monetary damages as a result. This constitutes an injury in fact under the law.

## IV

We review a district court's dismissal of a complaint for failure to state a claim upon which relief may be granted de novo.

## V

AvMed contends that the Complaint fails to allege a cognizable injury under Florida law and that the Complaint fails to allege facts sufficient to establish causation under the federal pleading standards. We address each argument in turn.

Plaintiffs brought seven counts against AvMed, all under Florida law. Of the seven causes of action alleged, Florida law requires a plaintiff to show that the defendant's challenged action caused the plaintiff's harm in six of them: negligence, negligence per se, breach of fiduciary duty, breach of contract, breach of contract implied in fact, and breach of the implied covenant of good faith and fair dealing.

In discussing causation, Plaintiffs allege that "AvMed's data breach caused [Plaintiffs'] identity theft," that the facts Plaintiffs allege have "sufficiently shown that the data breach caused [the] identity theft," and that "but for AvMed's data breach, [Plaintiffs'] identit[ies] would not have been stolen." Although at this stage in the proceedings we accept plaintiffs' allegations as true, we are not bound to extend the same assumption of truth to plaintiffs' conclusions of law. These claims state merely that AvMed was the cause of the identity theft—a conclusion we are not bound to accept as true.

We now consider the well-pleaded factual allegations relating to causation to determine whether they plausibly suggest an entitlement to relief. The complaint alleges that, prior to the data breach, neither Curry nor Moore had ever had their identities stolen or their sensitive information "compromised in any way." It further alleges that "Curry took substantial precautions to protect herself from identity theft," including not transmitting sensitive information over the Internet or any unsecured source; not storing her sensitive information on a computer or media device; storing sensitive information in a "safe and secure physical location;" and destroying "documents she receives in the mail that may contain any of her sensitive information, or that contain any information that could otherwise be used to steal her identity, such as credit card offers." [Moore made similar allegations.] Plaintiffs became victims of identity theft for the first time in their lives ten and fourteen months after the laptops containing their sensitive information were stolen. Curry's sensitive information was used to open a Bank of America account and change her address with the United States Post Office, and Moore's sensitive information was used to open an E*Trade Financial account in his name.

Taken as true, these factual allegations are consistent with Plaintiffs' conclusion that AvMed's failure to secure Plaintiffs' information caused them to become victims of identity theft. After thorough consideration, we conclude that the allegations are sufficient to cross the line from merely possible to plausible [citing *Ashcroft v. Iqbal*, 556 U.S. 662, 681 (2009); *Bell Atlantic Corp. v. Twombly*, 550 U.S. 544, 570 (2007)].

Generally, to prove that a data breach caused identity theft, the pleadings must include allegations of a nexus between the two instances beyond allegations of time and sequence. In an unpublished opinion on summary judgment, the Ninth Circuit found that a plaintiff sufficiently showed a causal relationship where "(1) [plaintiff] gave [the defendant] his personal information; (2) the identity fraud incidents began *six weeks* after the hard drives containing [defendant's] customers' personal information were stolen; and (3) [plaintiff had] previously not suffered any such incidents of identity theft." *Stollenwerk v. Tri-West Health Care Alliance*, 254 Fed. Appx. 664, 667 (9th Cir. 2007) (emphasis added). There, the court stated that these three facts, in conjunction with the inference a jury could make that the type of information stolen was the same type of information needed to open the fraudulent accounts, were sufficient to defeat a motion for summary judgment brought on the basis of a failure to establish causation.

Plaintiffs in the present case have pled facts indicating causation similar to those pled in *Stollenwerk*, but the inferential leap they ask us to make from the initial data breach to the stolen identities includes a time span more than six times greater than the one in *Stollenwerk*. Rather than a six-week gap between the initial data breach and the identity theft, Plaintiffs here allege gaps of ten and fourteen months between the two events. As the *Stollenwerk* court stated, a mere temporal connection is not sufficient; Plaintiffs' pleadings must indicate a logical connection between the two incidents. Here, Plaintiffs allege a nexus between the two events that includes more than a coincidence of time and sequence: they allege that the sensitive information on the stolen laptop was the same sensitive information used to steal Plaintiffs' identity. Plaintiffs explicitly make this connection when they allege that Curry's identity was stolen by changing her address and that Moore's identity was stolen by opening an E*Trade Financial account in his name because in both of those allegations, Plaintiffs state that the identity thief used Plaintiffs' sensitive information. We understand Plaintiffs to make a similar allegation regarding the bank accounts opened in Curry's name even though they do not plead precisely that Curry's sensitive information was used to open the Bank of America account. The Complaint states that Curry's sensitive information was on the unencrypted stolen laptop, that her identity was stolen, and that the stolen identity was used to open unauthorized accounts. Considering the Complaint as a whole and applying common sense to our understanding of this allegation, we find that Plaintiffs allege that the same sensitive information that was stored on the stolen laptops was used to open the Bank of America account. Thus, Plaintiffs' allegations that the data breach caused their identities to be stolen move from the realm of the possible into the plausible. Had Plaintiffs alleged fewer facts, we doubt whether the Complaint could have survived a motion to dismiss. However, Plaintiffs have sufficiently alleged a nexus between the data theft and the identity theft and therefore meet the federal pleading standards for their allegations on the counts of negligence, negligence per se, breach of fiduciary duty, breach of contract, breach of implied contract, and breach of the implied covenant of good faith and fair dealing.

Plaintiffs' unjust enrichment claim does not have a causation element, so we analyze the sufficiency of the Complaint on that claim separately. In the Complaint, Plaintiffs allege that AvMed cannot equitably retain their monthly insurance premiums—part of which were intended to pay for the administrative costs of data security—because AvMed did not properly secure Plaintiffs' data, as evinced from the fact that the stolen laptop containing sensitive information was unencrypted. AvMed argues that the district court correctly dismissed the Complaint because Plaintiffs' alleged injuries are not cognizable under the law and because Plaintiffs paid AvMed not for data security but for health insurance.

To establish a cause of action for unjust enrichment/restitution, a Plaintiff must show that (1) the plaintiff has conferred a benefit on the defendant; (2) the defendant has knowledge of the benefit; (3) the defendant has accepted or retained the benefit conferred; and (4) the circumstances are such that it would be inequitable for the defendant to retain the benefit without paying fair value for it.

Plaintiffs allege that they conferred a monetary benefit on AvMed in the form of monthly premiums, that AvMed "appreciates or has knowledge of such benefit," that AvMed uses the premiums to "pay for the administrative costs of data management and security," and that AvMed "should not be permitted to retain the money belonging to Plaintiffs . . . because [AvMed] failed to implement the data management and security measures that are mandated by industry standards." Plaintiffs also allege that AvMed either failed to implement or inadequately implemented policies to secure sensitive information, as can be seen from the data breach. Accepting these allegations as true, we find that Plaintiffs alleged sufficient facts to allow this claim to survive a motion to dismiss.

### VI

AvMed argues that we can affirm the district court because the Complaint fails to allege an entitlement to relief under Florida law on each count. On review, we find that two of the pled causes of action do not allow Plaintiffs to recover under Florida law. We address only the two claims that fail: negligence per se, and breach of the covenant of good faith and fair dealing.

### A

Plaintiffs allege that AvMed was negligent per se when it violated section 395.3025 of the Florida Statutes by disclosing "Plaintiffs' health information without authorization."

Florida Statute section 395.3025(4) states that "[p]atient records are confidential and must not be disclosed without the consent of the patient." This statute is contained in a chapter regulating the licensure, development, establishment, and minimum standard enforcement of hospitals, ambulatory surgical centers, and mobile surgical facilities. Because AvMed is an integrated managed-care organization and not a hospital, ambulatory surgical center, or mobile surgical facility, AvMed is not subject to this statute. Section 395.3025 does not purport to regulate AvMed's behavior, and so AvMed's failure to comply with the statute cannot serve as a basis for a negligence per se claim.

### B

While every contract contains an implied covenant of good faith and fair dealing under Florida law, a breach of this covenant—standing alone—does not create an independent cause of action. A claimant asserting a cause of action for breach of the implied covenant must allege "a failure or refusal to discharge contractual responsibilities, prompted not by an honest mistake, bad judgment or negligence; but, rather by a conscious and deliberate act, which unfairly frustrates the agreed common purpose and disappoints the reasonable expectations of the other party." *Tiara Condo. Ass' n, Inc. v. Marsh & McLennan Cos., Inc.*, 607 F.3d 742, 747 (11th Cir. 2010) (applying Florida law).

Plaintiffs here allege that AvMed breached the express provision of the service contract, which required AvMed "to ensure the 'confidentiality of information about members' medical health condition being maintained by the Plan and the right to approve or refuse the release of member specific information including medical records, by AvMed, except when the release is required by law.' " However, Plaintiffs do not allege that AvMed's failures to secure their data resulted from a conscious and deliberate act, which unfairly frustrates the agreed common purpose as required under Florida law.

**VII**

In this digital age, our personal information is increasingly becoming susceptible to attack. People with nefarious interests are taking advantage of the plethora of opportunities to gain access to our private information and use it in ways that cause real harm. Even though the perpetrators of these crimes often remain unidentified and the victims are left to clean up the damage caused by these identity thieves, cases brought by these victims are subject to the same pleading standards as are plaintiffs in all civil suits. Here, Plaintiffs have pled a cognizable injury and have pled sufficient facts to allow for a plausible inference that AvMed's failures in securing their data resulted in their identities being stolen. They have shown a sufficient nexus between the data breach and the identity theft beyond allegations of time and sequence. However, the Complaint fails to sufficiently allege an entitlement to relief under Florida law on the allegations of negligence per se and breach of the implied covenant of good faith and fair dealing. We therefore affirm in part, reverse in part, and remand to the district court for further proceedings.

■ PRYOR, CIRCUIT JUDGE, dissenting.

I agree with the majority opinion that Curry and Moore have standing to sue, but Curry and Moore's complaint should be dismissed for failure to state a claim. Their complaint fails to allege a plausible basis for finding that AvMed caused them to suffer identity theft, and their claim of unjust enrichment fails as a matter of law.

The parties do not dispute that laptops containing the sensitive information of Curry and Moore was stolen from AvMed, but Curry and Moore's second amended complaint fails to plead enough facts to allow a factfinder to draw a reasonable inference that the sensitive information identity thieves used to open the fraudulent accounts in the plaintiffs' names was obtained from AvMed. In an attempt to bridge this gap, Curry and Moore allege that they have both been very careful to protect their sensitive information. But the manner in which Curry and Moore care for the sensitive information they receive from third parties tells us nothing about how the third parties care for that sensitive information before or after they send it to Curry and Moore.

The complaint fails to allege a plausible basis for inferring that the unknown identity thieves obtained the sensitive information of Curry and Moore from AvMed. The complaint, for example, does not allege that only AvMed possessed the sensitive information used to open the fraudulent accounts. The complaint does not even allege what sensitive information was used to open financial accounts in the plaintiffs' names. The complaint alleges, for example, that the sensitive information stolen from AvMed included health and medical information, but the complaint fails to allege that this kind of information was used to open financial accounts in the plaintiffs' names.

The complaint also fails to state a claim of unjust enrichment under Florida law. Florida courts have held that a plaintiff cannot pursue a quasi-contract claim for unjust enrichment if an express contract exists concerning the same subject matter. The parties do not dispute that they entered into an enforceable contract; they dispute whether the contract has been breached. In that circumstance, a claim of unjust enrichment cannot be maintained.

I respectfully dissent.

## Lone Star National Bank, N.A. v. Heartland Payment Systems

729 F.3d 421 (5th Cir. 2013)

■ EMILIO M. GARZA, CIRCUIT JUDGE.

This case arises out of a group of hackers' breach of Heartland Payment Systems, Inc.'s ("Heartland's") data systems, compromising confidential information belonging to customers of the plaintiff banks (together, the "Issuer Banks"). The district court dismissed the Issuer Banks' claims. The Issuer Banks appeal only the dismissal of their negligence claim. We REVERSE and REMAND for proceedings consistent with this opinion.

### I

The Issuer Banks have contracts with Visa and MasterCard that allow them to issue payment cards, including both credit and debit cards, to their customers. When a customer uses one of these cards at a merchant, the card information is first sent to a bank with whom the merchant contracts, known as the "acquirer bank." The acquirer bank then sends the information to a processor, such as Heartland, and the processor sends the information to the issuer bank that issued the card. The approval or disapproval of use of the card is then transmitted back to the merchant through this chain.

Heartland contracted with [acquirer banks belonging to the Visa and MasterCard networks] to process their transactions. These contracts required Heartland to comply with the Visa and MasterCard regulations, which contain mechanisms for Visa and MasterCard network members to recoup losses in the event of a data breach.

Such a data breach occurred when hackers infiltrated Heartland's data systems and stole payment card information. As a result, the Issuer Banks allege they incurred costs associated with replacing the compromised cards and reimbursing customers for fraudulent charges. Lacking a written contract with Heartland, the Issuer Banks asserted various claims, including negligence and contract claims as third party beneficiaries of Heartland's contracts with other entities.

As to the negligence claim, the parties disputed whether Texas or New Jersey law governs. They agreed the economic loss doctrine under Texas law would bar the Issuer Banks' negligence claim, but disputed the applicability of the economic loss doctrine under New Jersey law. The district court dismissed all the Issuer Banks' claims, holding that even under New Jersey law, the economic loss doctrine would bar the Issuer Banks' negligence claim. The district court reasoned that by entering into the web of contractual relationships established by Visa and MasterCard, the Issuer Banks contracted for the specific remedies afforded by the Visa and MasterCard regulations and thus could not bring common law tort claims against another participant in the same web.

The Issuer Banks timely appealed the district court's dismissal of their negligence claim against Heartland.

## II

We review motions to dismiss under Federal Rule of Civil Procedure 12(b)(6) de novo, accepting all well-pleaded facts as true and viewing those facts in the light most favorable to the plaintiff.

The Issuer Banks assert that under New Jersey law, the economic loss doctrine does not bar their negligence claim. We agree. The economic loss doctrine generally limits a plaintiff seeking to recover purely economic losses, such as lost profits, to contractual remedies. The New Jersey Supreme Court explained:

> Generally speaking, tort principles, such as negligence, are better suited for resolving claims involving unanticipated physical injury, particularly those arising out of an accident. Contract principles, on the other hand, are generally more appropriate for determining claims for consequential damage that the parties have, or could have, addressed in their agreement.

*Spring Motors Distribs., Inc. v. Ford Motor Co.*, 489 A.2d 660, 672 (N.J. 1985). The Court reasoned that "[a]s between commercial parties, . . . the allocation of risks in accordance with their agreement better serves the public interest than an allocation achieved as a matter of policy without reference to that agreement." *Id.* at 671.

Nevertheless, [in *People Express Airlines, Inc. v. Consolidated Rail Corp.*, 495 A.2d 107 (N.J. 1985)], the Court held the economic loss doctrine does not bar tort recovery in every case where the plaintiff suffers economic harm without any attendant physical harm. There, a fire at a railroad freight yard resulted in the evacuation of an adjacent terminal at Newark International Airport. Employees of the plaintiff, an airline based in the evacuated terminal, could not return to the terminal for twelve hours, causing the plaintiff to suffer economic losses as a result of canceled flights and lost reservations. The plaintiff sued the railroad defendant for negligence, among other causes of action. After a survey of the economic loss doctrine and its exceptions, the Court articulated how the doctrine operates in New Jersey:

> We hold therefore that a defendant owes a duty of care to take reasonable measures to avoid the risk of causing economic damages, aside from physical injury, to particular plaintiffs or plaintiffs comprising an identifiable class with respect to whom defendant knows or has reason to know are likely to suffer such damages from its conduct. . . .
>
> We stress that an identifiable class of plaintiffs is not simply a foreseeable class of plaintiffs. . . . An identifiable class of plaintiffs must be particularly foreseeable in terms of the type of persons or entities comprising the class, the certainty or predictability of their presence, the approximate numbers of those in the class, as well as the type of economic expectations disrupted.
>
> We recognize that some cases will present circumstances that defy the categorization here devised to circumscribe a defendant's orbit of duty, limit otherwise boundless liability and define an identifiable class of plaintiffs that may recover. In these cases, the courts will be required to draw upon notions of fairness, common sense and morality to fix the line limiting liability as a matter of public policy, rather than an uncritical application of the principle of particular foreseeability.

*Id.* at 116. Accordingly, under New Jersey law, the economic loss doctrine does not bar tort recovery where the defendant causes an identifiable class of plaintiffs to which it owes a duty of care to suffer economic loss that does not result in boundless liability.

Turning to the case sub judice, we hold the economic loss doctrine under New Jersey law does not preclude the Issuer Banks' negligence claim against Heartland at the motion to dismiss stage. First, the Issuer Banks constitute an "identifiable class" as contemplated by *People Express*. Heartland had reason to foresee the Issuer Banks would be the entities to suffer economic losses were Heartland negligent. The identities, nature, and number of the victims are easily foreseeable, as the Issuer Banks are the very entities to which Heartland sends payment card information. Furthermore, Heartland would not be exposed to "boundless liability," but rather to the reasonable amount of loss from a limited number of entities. Accordingly, even absent physical harm, Heartland may owe the Issuer Banks a duty of care and may be liable for their purely economic losses.

Second, viewing the pleadings in the light most favorable to the Issuer Banks, in the absence of a tort remedy, the Issuer Banks would be left with no remedy for Heartland's alleged negligence, defying "notions of fairness, common sense and morality." *People Express*, 495 A.2d at 116. [I]t is not clear whether Heartland's contracts with the Acquirer Banks, which require Heartland to comply with Visa and MasterCard rules and regulations, provide the Issuer Banks with compensation mechanisms for losses that may be caused by Heartland's negligence. Though Visa and MasterCard investigated Heartland's data breach and directed its members to avoid using Heartland's services for a period of time, it is not clear that Heartland can take part in the dispute-resolution mechanisms solely by virtue of agreeing with the Acquirer Banks to be bound by the regulations.

Further, it is unclear whether Heartland has contracts with Visa and MasterCard, let alone what the contents of such contracts may be. Though the district court permitted some discovery on the existence of these contracts at the motion to dismiss stage, the results were inconclusive and thus do not aid our inquiry. This uncertainty in the record leaves open the issue of the Issuer Banks' bargaining power with respect to Heartland's participation in the Visa and MasterCard networks. While it seems the Issuer Banks' remedies vis-à-vis the Acquiring Banks under the regulations are clear because both the Issuer Banks and the Acquirer Banks are members of the Visa and MasterCard networks, any contractual remedies the Issuer Banks have to recoup losses caused by Heartland are not evident. As such, it is not clear that the allocation of risk could have been the subject of negotiations between the Issuer Banks and Heartland by way of contracts with Visa and MasterCard.

Mindful that "[t]he New Jersey Supreme Court has long been a leader in expanding tort liability," *Hakimoglu v. Trump Taj Mahal Assocs.*, 70 F.3d 291, 295 (3d Cir.1995) (Becker, J., dissenting), and in light of the lack of a developed record illuminating any contractual remedies available to the Issuer Banks, we hold, under the alleged facts of this case, the economic loss doctrine does not bar the Issuer Banks' negligence claim at this stage of the litigation.

[Reversed and remanded.]

## NOTES

1. ***Data Breaches and the* Restatement *Torts.*** Work through each of the four Prosser privacy torts [see Chapter 2] and explain why none of

them provides consumers relief for data breaches like those in *Paul* or *Resnick*.

2. ***The Lost Laptop and the Hacker.*** The "lost laptop" is a very common scenario in data breach cases. (If you remember nothing else from this course, by the end at least you should learn that it is very foolish to leave computer equipment in your car.) Employees often possess large quantities of personal data on laptops or thumb drives (or, as in *Paul*, older storage media like tapes and disks). When that hardware gets lost or stolen, there is always the risk that the data it contains will be misused. The court in *Paul* distinguishes between cases of disappearing equipment and those, like the *Hannaford* decision it describes, involving a malicious hacker who steals information from a database. *Resnick* blurs that line because the complaint alleges not only that laptops were stolen, but that they fell into the hands of identity thieves. Moreover, evidence that a hacker stole data still may not be sufficient to plead harm according to some courts. The Seventh Circuit's *Pisciotta* decision, described in *Paul*, involved a hacking incident. Because there was no indication that the stolen data had then been used to commit identity theft or other fraud, the court there found the potential injury to be too speculative. Other judges, like the dissenter in *Resnick*, are skeptical of inferences necessary to attribute later identity theft to any particular mishandling of data. There may be a trend toward courts being more willing to accept plaintiffs' allegations of harm, although it is difficult to say for certain. The trend may simply indicate that security breaches are becoming larger and more serious and identity theft more common. How would you advise consumer plaintiffs to plead their claims in light of these precedents?

3. ***Mitigated Harm.*** It has become commonplace for companies to offer free credit monitoring to those affected by a data breach. Doing so helps placate potentially angry customers, of course. And in some circumstances it might be required by laws such as the California statute discussed in Section C below. Some credit monitoring services offer steep discounts on these bulk orders—after all, they get many new customers, some of whom may later continue the service at their own expense. There is another sensible reason to offer monitoring, however: it further undermines any subsequent argument that monitoring expenses establish compensable injury, because they have already been paid for. Even when identity theft occurs, individual victims are sometimes shielded from direct harm. As noted above, federal law greatly limits liability for payment card account holders and most issuer banks do not expect customers to pay anything in cases of fraud. Sometimes identity theft involves phony accounts, as in *Resnick*, or even loans. But in many of these scenarios, the liability may not end up with the consumer either. If a plaintiff has suffered identity theft but receives free credit monitoring and owes no money based on fraud, has there been cognizable harm under tort law? What about under contract and related theories like unjust enrichment?

4. ***Settlements.*** As often occurs in class action litigation, AvMed settled soon after losing the appellate decision, for an estimated total of about $3 million. The settlement provided reimbursement to customers whose data was lost on the unencrypted laptops and who had paid insurance premiums

to the company; each of them was entitled to $10 for each year of premiums paid, for up to 3 years. It also gave $750,000 to the plaintiffs' attorneys. Finally, under the settlement AvMed was required to improve its security practices, including enhanced employee training, improved physical security at its facilities, and encryption and GPS tracking on its laptops. Heartland had settled with some acquirer banks before the Eleventh Circuit ruling and settled with the remaining ones after it; the estimated total payments to institutions within the Visa, MasterCard, and American Express networks exceeded $100 million.

5. ***Tort and Contract.*** Do you understand why the plaintiff issuers in *Lone Star Bank* relied on a negligence tort theory rather than contract for recovery? The consumer plaintiffs in *Resnick*, meanwhile, include both tort-related and contract-related claims in their complaint, yet the court handles their analysis in largely the same way. Can you explain that? What are the advantages of pleading both types of claims in *Resnick*?

6. ***Business to Business Breach Litigation.*** While consumer class action suits may garner more attention, the *Lone Star* decision and the settlement that followed it suggest that the most significant liability after a security breach can arise from suits by other businesses. That was also true after a breach at Target Corporation, where hackers infiltrated the payment card system and stole personal data of approximately 110 million customers—including payment card information for 40 million people—making it one of the largest US data breaches ever. A blizzard of lawsuits followed, including both consumer class action complaints and actions brought by issuer banks. These were largely removed to federal court and consolidated by the Judicial Panel on Multidistrict Litigation in federal district court in Minnesota, where Target is headquartered. Target filed motions to dismiss, but these were denied. Target then settled the consumer action for $10 million, plus about another $6 million in attorney's fees. Negotiations with banks took much longer, and many plaintiff financial institutions drove a hard bargain. Settlements that have been reached with Visa-affiliated banks alone will cost Target an estimated $67 million. By some estimates the total cost of the breach to Target will exceed $250 million; projected liability to issuer banks dwarfs payments to consumers.

7. ***Regulatory Enforcement.*** Remember that when companies experience security breaches they may face regulatory enforcement as well as private lawsuits. For example, in a footnote omitted from the above excerpt, the *Paul* opinion notes:

> Shortly after the incident, the defendant settled with the [Oregon] Attorney General under the UTPA. The defendant agreed to contract with a credit monitoring company to provide two years of credit monitoring and restoration services to any patient who requested it, to reimburse any patient for any financial loss resulting from the misuse of credit or identity theft, and to establish a website and toll-free call center to assist patients with questions related to the theft. Under the agreement, the defendant also paid the Attorney General more than $95,000. The defendant

estimated the cost of the credit monitoring and other services that it agreed to provide at approximately $7 million.

The U.S. Department of Health and Human Services investigated AvMed after its breach, but reportedly found no actionable security deficiencies and did not pursue an enforcement action. The FTC likewise launched a major investigation of the Heartland breach, but also closed the case without taking any action publicly. Lawyers for a company that has experienced a security incident can expect to respond on two fronts, to both consumers (probably starting in litigation) and to regulators (typically starting in behind-the-scenes investigation).

---

## C. BEST PRACTICES AND STATE LAW

### 1. DATA SECURITY MANAGEMENT

The PCI standards discussed above in Section A are just one example of sectoral best practices for data security, in that instance applicable to the specific requirements of payment card systems. As noted earlier, legal regulation establishes data security requirements in other settings such as the health care and financial services industries. For organizations outside of these specialized areas, data security obligations are not as well defined by regulation, private or public. Through its consent decrees, the Federal Trade Commission has begun to identify certain data security arrangements as presumptively unacceptable as a matter of law, but these are relatively egregious shortcomings, and they are defined in the negative rather than establishing affirmative best practices. [See Chapter 3.]

Notwithstanding the legal void at the national level, professional best practices have begun to coalesce among data security experts. A bewildering alphabet soup of certifications now exists for specialists who claim knowledge about data security: employees working in IT and related fields might be Information Systems Security Engineering Professionals (ISSEP/CISSP), Global Industrial Cyber Security Professionals (GICSP), Certified Secure Software Lifecycle Professionals (CSSLP), or Certified Information Security Managers (CISM), among many others. Each of these programs trains its students in certain technical and organizational methods, creating a professional understanding of security requirements that has developed "on the ground." As an example, the excerpt below provides guidance from the International Association of Privacy Professionals (IAPP), the best-known certification organization for privacy compliance, about dealing with security incidents. It is followed by an excerpt from an especially detailed state law establishing security standards, in Massachusetts.

## Peter P. Swire & Kenesa Ahmad, Incident Management and Data Breach Notification

FROM INTL. ASS'N OF PRIVACY PROFESSIONALS, FOUNDATIONS OF INFORMATION PRIVACY AND DATA PROTECTION 104–111 (2012)

Despite the strongest software tools, the best employee and awareness training programs, the most well developed contingency plan and the best communicated and rehearsed business continuance procedures, data breaches can—and inevitably will—occur. It simply isn't possible to prevent them completely. Thus organizations need to be prepared for incident management and data breach notification.

The life cycle of incident management can be thought of as a four-step process. [Each step is discussed below.]

### 1. Discovery of an Incident

The methods employed by rogue employees, hackers and exploit artists are often revealed in basic behaviors that can be detected and observed by a discriminating information security professional or software. These behaviors include multiple failed system login attempts; use of long-idle or dormant access accounts; unexplained changes in access permissions; activity during nonbusiness hours; use of unauthorized new accounts, files or applications; and gaps in system logs.

It is important to keep in mind that while system failures and malicious attacks are typical causes of data breaches, two of the most common sources of data breaches are third-party mistakes and employee negligence. For example, in the healthcare industry in 2011, 49 percent of organizations experienced data incidents caused by a lost or stolen computing device, 46 percent experienced a data breach due to a third-party error, and 41 percent experienced a breach caused by an unintentional employee action. Therefore, security personnel must stress to employees the importance of reporting errors, as they are likely the main method of detecting non-IT-related breaches. Contractual obligations requiring third-party vendors to notify the organization of any incident that involves the organization's data are also an important means of discovering incidents. Without such reporting obligations, many errors, such as lost paper records or break-ins to the premises of third-party partners, may occur without the organization's knowledge.

### 2. Containment and Analysis

Once discovered, the next step is containment and analysis. Immediate response to incidents is especially important if that compromise causes a systemwide failure, leads to a breach that triggers legal notification obligations or poses a risk of harm to individuals.

Containment involves stopping the unauthorized practice, recovering the records, shutting down the system that was breached, revoking access or correcting any weakness in physical security. It may also involve notifying the police if criminal activity or theft was involved.

In cases of e-mail errors, certain services may offer recall functions that can delete any e-mails sent before they are read. To contain data breaches where a laptop or smartphone is lost, some devices have remote wipe technology.

Some initial analysis will need to be performed to determine which systems and networks were impacted. It is a priority to limit use of a network or system that has been compromised until forensic experts can analyze the system fully and verify its condition. Most people do not know that even logging into a system can destroy important evidence.

After initial containment, an in-depth, complete analysis and documentation of the incident is required. In IT-related incidents, computer forensics can offer the necessary details to troubleshoot a security breach. These details can be used in negotiations with other affected parties or in litigation that may result.

The aim of forensics is to prevent further damage resulting from the incident, thus limiting the potential liabilities and minimizing potential damage. The results should indicate how the system was exploited and what was compromised, which can help IT formulate a plan for remedying the exploit.

Where a data breach was caused by inadvertent employee error or accidental loss of storage media, computer forensics can also help determine the scope of any data that may have been impacted by the error or data loss.

For incidents involving paper records or third parties, containment may be more difficult. It may be hard to recover paper documents that have been lost. Other than conducting a search for the paper records, and trying to establish their path, it may be impossible to contain the breach.

When an incident takes place at a third-party partner's site, there may be resistance to the organization's efforts to perform analysis or investigation of the third party's systems and employees. Contractual arrangements need to be in place, delineating each party's obligations in response to a breach, including containment, investigation and analysis.

The analysis of an incident will need to determine what type of information was affected (e.g., personally identifiable information, intellectual property, trade secrets, etc.), the number of people who were impacted, and the groups that were impacted (employees, customers, out-of-state residents). This analysis will inform the organization's notification obligations.

### 3. Notification

Beginning with Senate Bill 1386 in California in 2003, notification following a data breach became a legal requirement. This requirement spread throughout the United States (at the time of writing, 46 states and the District of Columbia have breach notification laws) and to many parts of the world.

Factors that vary based on the laws include:

- The trigger for notification
- Whom to notify
- Timing of notification
- Contents of notices
- Methods of providing notification

**Trigger for Notification**

In some jurisdictions, organizations are legally required to notify affected individuals only if there is some degree of harm to the individual, while in other jurisdictions all data breaches must be notified. Types of harm that may result from a breach include risks to personal safety, identity theft, financial loss, loss of business or employment opportunities, and humiliation or embarrassment.

Notification may be limited to circumstances where the harm is serious or significant. The level of risk posed by harm depends on factors such as the type and amount of personal information involved, extent and cause of the breach (i.e., was it malicious or inadvertent), who was affected by the breach and any foreseeable harm. Even if not legally obliged to provide notification, an organization may wish to notify affected individuals as a best practice where there is a high degree of risk to them and they may be able to take steps to protect themselves.

In many cases, personal information that is protected by means like encryption, such that it cannot be read, [does not require notification] due to the remote possibility of harm.

**Whom to Notify**

Whom to notify is a key issue that must be determined. Possible recipients of a breach report include:

- Regulators
- Law enforcement
- Affected individuals
- Insurers
- Any relevant service providers (e.g., call center support or insurance providers)
- The media
- Any other stakeholders (e.g., shareholders or employees)

**When to Notify**

The desire for expedient notification to allow individuals to mitigate any risk of harm may need to be balanced against legal requirements and the need to fully understand the scope of the breach to avoid overnotification (e.g., where fewer individuals were affected then originally believed). The timing of notification varies by law and may range from 24 hours to "in the most expedient time possible" to "within a reasonable amount of time." Some laws provide that organizations may delay notification when law enforcement is investigating the breach, or when the delay is necessary to restore the reasonable integrity of the information systems.

**What to Include in Notification**

The content of notifications will vary depending on who is being notified. Regulators may want greater information about the cause and scope of the breach, while it may be more important for individuals to learn about steps they can take to protect themselves from fallout.

What should be included in the notification may be dictated by law, but may include:

- The nature of the incident in general terms
- Type of personal information breached
- Any assistance the organization is offering the individual (e.g., credit monitoring, replacing credit or debit cards, identity theft insurance, etc.)
- Any steps the individual can take to protect himself
- A point of contact within the organization form whom the individual can seek more information about the breach

**How to Notify**

Depending on the availability of contact information and the number of affected individuals, methods of notification may include direct mail, telephone, e-mail, facsimile and publication of notice in a general-circulation newspaper or on the organization's website. Although not currently addressed under the laws, some organizations consider alternative methods of notification, such as through social networking sites or via text messages, where these are the ordinary methods used to communicate with the affected individuals. The general rule is that the organization in the direct relationship with the individual is the one that provides notification. Thus, if a breach occurs at an organization's service provider, the organization notifies individuals, but the service provider should be under contractual obligation to notify the organization.

### 4. Eradication and Prevention

The final step of the incident management is investigating the root cause of the breach, with the view to taking steps to remediate any gaps discovered in security, processes or training. A breach should be examined to determine if there are systemic problems that need to be addressed or whether it was an isolated incident. Maintaining the internal report of all breaches allows the organization to monitor for patterns that would underlie systemic issues.

When regulators have been involved in the aftermath of a breach, they have demanded that organizations take certain steps to prevent breaches in the future. For example these might include:

- Implementing a comprehensive information security program reasonably designed to protect the security, confidentiality and integrity of personal information. Program elements may include appointing staff to be accountable for the program, conducting risk assessments and implementing employee training.
- Implementing administrative, technical and physical safeguards that are proportionate to the organization's size and complexity, nature and scope of the organization's activities and sensitivity of the personal information held.
- Implementing encryption or using higher encryption standards.
- Updating privacy notices and retention schedules.
- Implementing additional security measures, such as monitoring software, adding firewalls and changing passwords.

Complete documentation of incidents should be maintained to share with any regulators, as well as to defend against class action lawsuits that may arise as a result of the data breach. Documentation may include details on the cause and scope of the incident, date the incident was discovered and how it was discovered, who was notified and what they were notified of, and the steps the organization has taken to mitigate any harm.

Given the employee negligence or error is one of the leading causes of data breaches, employees need to be trained on how to protect data and what to do in the event of the breach. The organization must instill a culture of privacy, having every employee recognize his or her role in achieving a secure environment. Training should include basic awareness training for frontline employees and more detailed privacy instruction for those with access to personally identifiable information. Refresher training can take place following a breach event, using real-world examples of what has occurred either within organization or at other similarly situated organizations. Continual privacy education and verbal and written reminders can help keep privacy in the forefront of employees' minds. Any time the incident response protocol is changed, employees should be provided an update. The organizational culture must also foster an atmosphere where employees feel protected if they report a suspected or actual data breach; employees will underreport if they feel their job is in jeopardy due to their mistake.

As the end of the incident life cycle is reached, the organization should be better positioned to discover and respond to any subsequent events and proceed through the life cycle with greater familiarity in the future. A detailed incident response plan should be developed that specifies how the enterprise will address an incident the moment it has detected. This plan should include staff reporting obligations to escalate any instances of actual or possible incidents to management, the privacy office or any other designated official.

## Standards for the Protection of Personal Information of Residents of the Commonwealth

201 C.M.R. 17.00 (Mass. 2015)

. . .

### 17.02. Definitions

The following words as used herein shall, unless the context requires otherwise, have the following meanings:

**Breach of security**, the unauthorized acquisition or unauthorized use of unencrypted data or, encrypted electronic data and the confidential process or key that is capable of compromising the security, confidentiality, or integrity of personal information, maintained by a person or agency that creates a substantial risk of identity theft or fraud against a resident of the commonwealth. A good faith but unauthorized acquisition of personal information by a person or agency, or employee or agent thereof, for the lawful purposes of such person or agency, is not a breach of security unless the personal information is used in an unauthorized manner or subject to further unauthorized disclosure. . . .

**Encrypted**, the transformation of data into a form in which meaning cannot be assigned without the use of a confidential process or key.

**Owns or licenses**, receives, stores, maintains, processes, or otherwise has access to personal information in connection with the provision of goods or services or in connection with employment. . . .

**Personal information**, a Massachusetts resident's first name and last name or first initial and last name in combination with any one or more of the following data elements that relate to such resident: (a) Social Security number; (b) driver's license number or state-issued identification card number; or (c) financial account number, or credit or debit card number, with or without any required security code, access code, personal identification number or password, that would permit access to a resident's financial account; provided, however, that "Personal information" shall not include information that is lawfully obtained from publicly available information, or from federal, state or local government records lawfully made available to the general public.

**Record or Records**, any material upon which written, drawn, spoken, visual, or electromagnetic information or images are recorded or preserved, regardless of physical form or characteristics. . . .

## 17.03. Duty to Protect and Standards for Protecting Personal Information

(1) Every person that owns or licenses personal information about a resident of the Commonwealth shall develop, implement, and maintain a comprehensive information security program that is written in one or more readily accessible parts and contains administrative, technical, and physical safeguards that are appropriate to (a) the size, scope and type of business of the person obligated to safeguard the personal information under such comprehensive information security program; (b) the amount of resources available to such person; (c) the amount of stored data; and (d) the need for security and confidentiality of both consumer and employee information. The safeguards contained in such program must be consistent with the safeguards for protection of personal information and information of a similar character set forth in any state or federal regulations by which the person who owns or licenses such information may be regulated.

(2) Without limiting the generality of the foregoing, every comprehensive information security program shall include, but shall not be limited to:

(a) Designating one or more employees to maintain the comprehensive information security program;

(b) Identifying and assessing reasonably foreseeable internal and external risks to the security, confidentiality, and/or integrity of any electronic, paper or other records containing personal information, and evaluating and improving, where necessary, the effectiveness of the current safeguards for limiting such risks, including but not limited to:

1. ongoing employee (including temporary and contract employee) training;

2. employee compliance with policies and procedures; and

3. means for detecting and preventing security system failures.

(c) Developing security policies for employees relating to the storage, access and transportation of records containing personal information outside of business premises.

(d) Imposing disciplinary measures for violations of the comprehensive information security program rules.

(e) Preventing terminated employees from accessing records containing personal information.

(f) Oversee[ing] service providers, by:

1. Taking reasonable steps to select and retain third-party service providers that are capable of maintaining appropriate security measures to protect such personal

information consistent with these regulations and any applicable federal regulations; and

2. Requiring such third-party service providers by contract to implement and maintain such appropriate security measures for personal information.

(g) Reasonable restrictions upon physical access to records containing personal information, and storage of such records and data in locked facilities, storage areas or containers.

(h) Regular monitoring to ensure that the comprehensive information security program is operating in a manner reasonably calculated to prevent unauthorized access to or unauthorized use of personal information; and upgrading information safeguards as necessary to limit risks.

(i) Reviewing the scope of the security measures at least annually or whenever there is a material change in business practices that may reasonably implicate the security or integrity of records containing personal information.

(j) Documenting responsive actions taken in connection with any incident involving a breach of security, and mandatory post-incident review of events and actions taken, if any, to make changes in business practices relating to protection of personal information.

### 17.04. Computer System Security Requirements

Every person that owns or licenses personal information about a resident of the Commonwealth and electronically stores or transmits such information shall include in its written, comprehensive information security program the establishment and maintenance of a security system covering its computers, including any wireless system, that, at a minimum, and to the extent technically feasible, shall have the following elements:

(1) Secure user authentication protocols including:

(a) control of user IDs and other identifiers;

(b) a reasonably secure method of assigning and selecting passwords, or use of unique identifier technologies, such as biometrics or token devices;

(c) control of data security passwords to ensure that such passwords are kept in a location and/or format that does not compromise the security of the data they protect;

(d) restricting access to active users and active user accounts only; and

(e) blocking access to user identification after multiple unsuccessful attempts to gain access or the limitation placed on access for the particular system;

(2) Secure access control measures that:

(a) restrict access to records and files containing personal information to those who need such information to perform their job duties; and

(b) assign unique identifications plus passwords, which are not vendor supplied default passwords, to each person with computer access, that are reasonably designed to maintain the integrity of the security of the access controls;

(3) Encryption of all transmitted records and files containing personal information that will travel across public networks, and encryption of all data containing personal information to be transmitted wirelessly.

(4) Reasonable monitoring of systems, for unauthorized use of or access to personal information;

(5) Encryption of all personal information stored on laptops or other portable devices;

(6) For files containing personal information on a system that is connected to the Internet, there must be reasonably up-to-date firewall protection and operating system security patches, reasonably designed to maintain the integrity of the personal information.

(7) Reasonably up-to-date versions of system security agent software which must include malware protection and reasonably up-to-date patches and virus definitions and is set to receive the most current security updates on a regular basis.

(8) Education and training of employees on the proper use of the computer security system and the importance of personal information security.

## NOTES

1. ***Security Policies Compared.*** How does the guidance from Swire and Ahmad of the IAPP compare to the legal rules laid down in Massachusetts? Would an organization following the IAPP's advice thereby comply with the Massachusetts regulations? How do both sets of rules compare to the PCI standards excerpted earlier in this chapter, and to others you have studied thus far?

2. ***Technical Protection and "Company Law."*** There are plenty of best practices about technical implementations, particularly among the alphabet soup certifications. These recommend hardware, software, network configurations, protocols, and other IT specifications to reduce and manage security risk. As the IAPP guidance acknowledges, however, even if all of these instructions concerning technical safeguards are followed perfectly, data breaches may still occur, particularly because human activities can cause breaches regardless of technology. In that event, it will be an

organization's policy that helps manage the resulting incident and its risks. (Remember the lost laptop!) The Massachusetts regulations avoid detailed technological requirements, as do most other security rules, including FTC guidance [see Chapter 3] and the HIPAA Security Rule [see Chapter 12]. These recommendations and rules all promote the development of internal policies tailored to an organization's circumstances, including its resources, its threat assessment, and its tolerance of risk. Privacy professionals, often lawyers, must develop this internal "company law," and then educate employees about it and enforce it. This is a common role for attorneys in large organizations performing compliance functions of all sorts, including those required under privacy and security law.

3. ***A Risk-Based Approach.*** Informal guidance about compliance with 201 CMR 17.00 on the web site of the Massachusetts Office of Consumer Affairs and Business Regulation clarifies that the rule does not impose one-size-fits-all requirements:

> The regulation adopts a risk-based approach to information security. A risk-based approach is one that is designed to be flexible while directing businesses to establish a written security program that takes into account the particular business's size, scope of business, amount of resources and the need for security. For example, if you only have employee data with a small number of employees, you should lock your files in a storage cabinet and lock the door to that room. You should permit access to only those who require it for official duties. Conversely, if you have both employee and customer data containing personal information, then your security approach would be more stringent. If you have a large volume of customer data containing personal information, then your approach would be even more stringent.

Other government regulations, notably including the HIPAA Security Rule [Chapter 12], also adopt similar risk-based formulations. What are the advantages and disadvantages of rules calibrated in this fashion?

4. ***Massachusetts as an Outlier.*** The Massachusetts Legislature passed a statute, M.G.L. c. 93H, directing a state executive agency to promulgate the regulations excerpted above. Most states have not issued such detailed regulations for data security. California has a statutory provision, but it is extremely general: "A business that owns, licenses, or maintains personal information about a California resident shall implement and maintain reasonable security procedures and practices appropriate to the nature of the information, to protect the personal information from unauthorized access, destruction, use, modification, or disclosure." Cal. Civ. Code § 1798.81.5(b). Why have most states shied away from specifying security standards?

5. ***Employees as the Linchpin.*** The IAPP and the Massachusetts regulation both stress the central role of front-line employees in the everyday maintenance of good security. Note how Massachusetts requires a plan to include ongoing training of employees and monitoring of their adherence to an organization's policy. Many compliance-oriented professionals working on

privacy and security issues identify training as one of their most important functions in the organization. A written policy without training to support it may be worse than no policy at all from a standpoint of liability risk: the organization will have acknowledged the need for internal security practices but will not have taken the steps necessary to make them happen. Both regulators in enforcement actions and juries in lawsuits may look unkindly on such a failure.

6. ***PII, Again.*** How broad is the Massachusetts regulation's definition of "personal information"? How does it compare with other treatments of PII you have encountered in the course? Is the definition used here an appropriate one?

7. ***Scope and Enforcement of Massachusetts Regulations.*** The scope of the Massachusetts regulations' coverage is quite broad. According to 201 C.M.R. 17.01(2), its requirements "apply to all persons that own or license personal information about a resident of the Commonwealth." Then 201 C.M.R. 17.02 defines almost any nongovernmental entity as a person, and the curious phrase "own or license" includes a person who "receives, stores, maintains, processes, or otherwise has access to personal information in connection with the provision of goods or services or in connection with employment." There is no territorial limitation, so the regulation applies to companies and other organizations outside the state, provided they store personal information about Massachusetts residents. And the list of activities covered is capacious enough to apply to countless organizations. The statute that authorized the regulations in Massachusetts gave the attorney general authority to enforce against violations, using the state's general consumer protection statute. *See* M.G.L. c. 93H(5). Since the regulations came into effect in 2010, almost all enforcement actions have aimed at Massachusetts entities, particularly those handling health care information. In 2014, however, the state's attorney general reached a settlement with a Rhode Island hospital that lost unencrypted backup tapes in violation of the regulations. The hospital agreed to pay $150,000 and undertook significant remedial action. If you were counseling a company in a state like Rhode Island that shares a border with Massachusetts, how would you assess the risk of liability under 201 C.M.R. 17.00? What about a national company based in California that has customers in every state?

## 2. BREACH NOTIFICATION STATUTES

As of early 2016, all but three states (Alabama, New Mexico, and South Dakota) had enacted laws requiring organizations to disclose security breaches in many circumstances. Typically for privacy law, California was the first state to pass such legislation, in 2003. That law's requirements, excerpted below, remain a national model. But as the passage above from the IAPP explains, the differences between various states' laws can be significant. There are also distinct nationwide breach notification standards as part of sectoral regulations governing areas such as health care and financial services. Proposals for a uniform national data breach notification standard stall in Congress every year, despite support from prominent members of both parties, including President Obama. (Why would you suspect these proposals fail?)

Excerpts of the breach notification statutes in California, Michigan, and North Carolina follow. They share many features. All three states allow for delay of requests during law enforcement investigations or internal investigation and remediation efforts, provided the notice follows soon after those conditions have passed. All of them require third-party processors or others in possession of data to notify the primary "owner" of the data, who in turn provides any required notice to affected individuals. Like most other state statutes, these three require notice to the state government (usually the state attorney general) of breaches above a certain size. Most states allow "substitute" notice in place of individual written notice for very large breaches; a company must notify major media, put an announcement on its web site, and send email messages where contact information is available. The threshold for substitute notice in these three states, like many others, requires a showing that individualized notice would cost over $250,000 or require sending it to over 500,000 people in the state.

As you look at the excerpts of breach statutes below, consider how they are similar and different. The "Practice" exercise after the statutory excerpts will help you in that task.

## Cal. Civ. Code § 1798.82

(a) A person or business that conducts business in California, and that owns or licenses computerized data that includes personal information, shall disclose a breach of the security of the system following discovery or notification of the breach in the security of the data to a resident of California whose unencrypted personal information was, or is reasonably believed to have been, acquired by an unauthorized person. The disclosure shall be made in the most expedient time possible and without unreasonable delay. . . .

. . .

(d) A person or business that is required to issue a security breach notification pursuant to this section shall meet all of the following requirements:

> (1) The security breach notification shall be written in plain language.
>
> (2) The security breach notification shall include, at a minimum, the following information:
>
> > (A) The name and contact information of the reporting person or business subject to this section.
> >
> > (B) A list of the types of personal information that were or are reasonably believed to have been the subject of a breach.

(C) If the information is possible to determine at the time the notice is provided, then any of the following: (i) the date of the breach, (ii) the estimated date of the breach, or (iii) the date range within which the breach occurred. The notification shall also include the date of the notice.

(D) Whether notification was delayed as a result of a law enforcement investigation, if that information is possible to determine at the time the notice is provided.

(E) A general description of the breach incident, if that information is possible to determine at the time the notice is provided.

(F) The toll-free telephone numbers and addresses of the major credit reporting agencies if the breach exposed a social security number or a driver's license or California identification card number.

(G) If the person or business providing the notification was the source of the breach, an offer to provide appropriate identity theft prevention and mitigation services, if any, shall be provided at no cost to the affected person for not less than 12 months, along with all information necessary to take advantage of the offer to any person whose information was or may have been breached if the breach exposed or may have exposed [an individual's first name or first initial and last name in combination with a social security number, driver's license number, or California identification card number, when either of these elements is not encrypted.]

. . .

(g) For purposes of this section, "breach of the security of the system" means unauthorized acquisition of computerized data that compromises the security, confidentiality, or integrity of personal information maintained by the person or business. . . .

. . .

["Personal information" is defined in essentially the same way as the Massachusetts regulation excerpted above.] . . .

## Mich. Comp. Laws §§ 445.63, 445.72

**§ 445.63. Definitions.**

As used in this act:

. . .

(b) "Breach of the security of a database" or "security breach" means the unauthorized access and acquisition of data that compromises the security or confidentiality of personal information maintained by a person or agency as part of a database of personal information regarding multiple individuals. . . .

. . .

(g) "Encrypted" means transformation of data through the use of an algorithmic process into a form in which there is a low probability of assigning meaning without use of a confidential process or key, or securing information by another method that renders the data elements unreadable or unusable.

. . .

(r) "Personal information" means the first name or first initial and last name linked to 1 or more of the following data elements of a resident of this state:

(i) Social security number.

(ii) Driver license number or state personal identification card number.

(iii) Demand deposit or other financial account number, or credit card or debit card number, in combination with any required security code, access code, or password that would permit access to any of the resident's financial accounts.

. . .

**§ 445.72. Notice of security breach; requirements.**

(1) Unless the person or agency determines that the security breach has not or is not likely to cause substantial loss or injury to, or result in identity theft with respect to, 1 or more residents of this state, a person or agency that owns or licenses data that are included in a database that discovers a security breach . . . shall provide a notice of the security breach to each resident of this state who meets 1 or more of the following:

(a) That resident's unencrypted and unredacted personal information was accessed and acquired by an unauthorized person.

(b) That resident's personal information was accessed and acquired in encrypted form by a person with unauthorized access to the encryption key.

. . .

(3) In determining whether a security breach is not likely to cause substantial loss or injury to, or result in identity theft with respect to, 1 or more residents of this state . . . a person or agency shall act with the care an ordinarily prudent person or agency in like position would exercise under similar circumstances.

(4) A person or agency shall provide any notice required under this section without unreasonable delay. . . .

. . .

(6) A notice under this section shall do all of the following:

(a) . . . [B]e written in a clear and conspicuous manner and contain the content required under subdivisions (c) to (g).

(c) Describe the security breach in general terms.

(d) Describe the type of personal information that is the subject of the unauthorized access or use.

(e) If applicable, generally describe what the agency or person providing the notice has done to protect data from further security breaches.

(f) Include a telephone number where a notice recipient may obtain assistance or additional information.

(g) Remind notice recipients of the need to remain vigilant for incidents of fraud and identity theft.

. . .

(13) Subject to subsection (14), a person that knowingly fails to provide any notice of a security breach required under this section may be ordered to pay a civil fine of not more than $250.00 for each failure to provide notice. The attorney general or a prosecuting attorney may bring an action to recover a civil fine under this section.

(14) The aggregate liability of a person for civil fines under subsection (13) for multiple violations of subsection (13) that arise from the same security breach shall not exceed $750,000.00.

(15) Subsections (12) and (13) do not affect the availability of any civil remedy for a violation of state or federal law.

. . .

## N.C. Gen. Stat. §§ 75–61, 75–65

**§ 75–61. Definitions.**

The following definitions apply in this Article:

(1) “Business”.—A sole proprietorship, partnership, corporation, association, or other group, however organized and whether or not organized to operate at a profit. . . . Business shall not include any government or governmental subdivision or agency.

. . .

(8) “Encryption”.—The use of an algorithmic process to transform data into a form in which the data is rendered unreadable or unusable without use of a confidential process or key.

. . .

(10) “Personal information”.—A person’s first name or first initial and last name in combination with [the following list incorporated by reference from another statute: social security or employer taxpayer

identification numbers; drivers license, State identification card, or passport numbers; checking account numbers; savings account numbers; credit card numbers; debit card numbers, personal identification (PIN) code; electronic identification numbers; electronic mail names or addresses, Internet account numbers, or Internet identification names; digital signatures; any other numbers or information that can be used to access a person's financial resources; biometric data; fingerprints; passwords; parent's legal surname prior to marriage.]

. . .

(12) "Records".—Any material on which written, drawn, spoken, visual, or electromagnetic information is recorded or preserved, regardless of physical form or characteristics.

. . .

(14) "Security breach".—An incident of unauthorized access to and acquisition of unencrypted and unredacted records or data containing personal information where illegal use of the personal information has occurred or is reasonably likely to occur or that creates a material risk of harm to a consumer. Any incident of unauthorized access to and acquisition of encrypted records or data containing personal information along with the confidential process or key shall constitute a security breach.

**§ 75–65. Protection from security breaches.**

(a) Any business that owns or licenses personal information of residents of North Carolina or any business that conducts business in North Carolina that owns or licenses personal information in any form (whether computerized, paper, or otherwise) shall provide notice to the affected person that there has been a security breach following discovery or notification of the breach. The disclosure notification shall be made without unreasonable delay, consistent with the legitimate needs of law enforcement . . . . For the purposes of this section, personal information shall not include electronic identification numbers, electronic mail names or addresses, Internet account numbers, Internet identification names, parent's legal surname prior to marriage, or a password unless this information would permit access to a person's financial account or resources.

. . .

(d) The notice shall be clear and conspicuous. The notice shall include all of the following:

(1) A description of the incident in general terms.

(2) A description of the type of personal information that was subject to the unauthorized access and acquisition.

(3) A description of the general acts of the business to protect the personal information from further unauthorized access.

(4) A telephone number for the business that the person may call for further information and assistance, if one exists.

(5) Advice that directs the person to remain vigilant by reviewing account statements and monitoring free credit reports.

(6) The toll-free numbers and addresses for the major consumer reporting agencies.

(7) The toll-free numbers, addresses, and Web site addresses for the Federal Trade Commission and the North Carolina Attorney General's Office, along with a statement that the individual can obtain information from these sources about preventing identity theft.

. . .

(g) Any waiver of the provisions of this Article is contrary to public policy and is void and unenforceable.

. . .

(i) A violation of this section is a violation of G.S. 75–1.1 [the state's unfair and deceptive trade practices statute]. No private right of action may be brought by an individual for a violation of this section unless such individual is injured as a result of the violation.

---

## Practice

### Security Incident Response

You work as counsel to brooding millionaire philanthropist Bruce Wayne and the multinational conglomerate Wayne Enterprises, which he owns in full. Advise Wayne and the company's managers about handling each of the incidents listed below. What questions do you ask? How great is the potential for liability in each situation? Is notice required under the law of California, Michigan, or North Carolina?. If so, can and should your client write a single notice message to satisfy its obligations in all three states? Use the guidance from the IAPP and the law you have read in this chapter to help plot your course.

(a) Russian hackers appear to have copied a significant number of names and social security numbers from a database of customer information that was protected by encryption and sophisticated technical safeguards.

(b) An executive for Wayne Enterprises' insurance investigations division was mugged and his briefcase stolen. The briefcase contained printed files with the names, birth dates, photographs, and fingerprints of approximately 500 policyholders whose disability claims were being reviewed.

(c) After a department moved to a new office building across the street from Wayne Enterprises' headquarters, its staff could not find a small backup computer drive containing names and checking account numbers of 35,000 customers who pay for services through direct debit from their accounts.

(d) An unknown hacker appears to have accessed the server containing matched email addresses and passwords used by teachers logging in to their accounts with the nonprofit Wayne Educational Foundation.

---

## D. HACKING LAWS

---

### Focus

"Cybersecurity"

One of the most serious threats to modern businesses is unauthorized access to stored data—and the resulting theft of personal information or intellectual property by online intruders. This criminal activity is commonly called "hacking," although that term can be confusing and controversial because it also refers to perfectly ethical computer programming activities (for example, problem-solving programming events called hackathons). A number of recent high-profile data intrusions, including breaches at Home Depot, Target, and Sony, have highlighted the vulnerability of corporate data security systems. The public sector is also vulnerable: in June 2015 the United States Office of Personnel Management was the target of a devastating hacking incident that affected 22.1 million people, nearly seven percent of the US population. A number of these cyberattacks have been attributed to hackers acting in conjunction with foreign governments, notably China and North Korea, although these nations deny any responsibility. Other intrusions are the work of sophisticated organized crime groups, particularly those based in Russia, Ukraine, and other eastern European countries.

In response, some have called for international regulation of cybersecurity, such as through a formal international treaty for "cyber disarmament." Some security officials in the US, including NSA Director Admiral Michael Rogers, have expressed skepticism that a comprehensive global accord would be effective, especially against non-state actors. There have been some smaller-scale agreements between individual groups of national governments. In 2015, President Obama and Chinese President Xi Jinping announced an agreement that neither country's government will sponsor computer-assisted theft of privately-owned intellectual property, including trade secrets, in the other's country. The "Group of 20" of major world economies later issued a communiqué calling for similar commitments by its members. More elaborate and binding restrictions—including limits on hacking government networks—remain unrealized, at least for now.

Without any comprehensive international protections, US businesses must rely on domestic legislation to prevent and respond to online hacking attacks. These protections are limited, however. For example, there is currently no independent federal private right of action for trade secret theft, and some critics oppose such a measure because they are concerned about potential anticompetitive abuse. Attackers may be criminally prosecuted under the Computer Fraud and Abuse Act [see below], the Economic Espionage Act, or identity theft statutes, and businesses may have civil remedies available under those statutes. They may also pursue claims under state law. Even if they do find a basis to sue, often it will be difficult to identify and subpoena a defendant. Talented hackers can cover their tracks fairly effectively online.

President Obama signed the Cybersecurity Information Sharing Act (CISA) as part of a 2,000-page omnibus spending bill at the end of 2015. The statute immunizes companies from liability for sharing personal information with the federal government that reflects on cybersecurity threats, even if such sharing would violate the company's privacy policy. Proponents argue that clear legal permission will encourage companies to reveal information that will help government and business assess vulnerabilities and respond quickly and effectively. Critics of the measure fear that CISA will open a "back door" for surveillance, because it also confers immunity for sharing information of a "specific threat" beyond cybersecurity matters, and gives additional federal intelligence and law enforcement agencies access to some of the information.

---

## The Computer Fraud and Abuse Act

18 U.S.C. § 1030

### § 1030. Fraud and related activity in connection with computers

(a) Whoever—

(1) having knowingly accessed a computer without authorization or exceeding authorized access, and by means of such conduct having obtained information that has been determined by the United States Government pursuant to an Executive order or statute to require protection against unauthorized disclosure for reasons of national defense or foreign relations, . . . with reason to believe that such information so obtained could be used to the injury of the United States, or to the advantage of any foreign nation[,] willfully communicates, delivers, [or] transmits . . . the same to any person not entitled to receive it . . . [;]

(2) intentionally accesses a computer without authorization or exceeds authorized access, and thereby obtains—

(A) information contained in a financial record of a financial institution, or of a [credit card] issuer[,] . . . or contained in a file of a consumer reporting agency on a consumer, as such terms are defined in the Fair Credit Reporting Act (15 U.S.C. §§ 1681 et seq.);

(B) information from any department or agency of the United States; or

(C) information from any protected computer;

. . .

(4) knowingly and with intent to defraud, accesses a protected computer without authorization, or exceeds authorized access, and by means of such conduct furthers the intended fraud and obtains anything of value, unless the object of the fraud and the thing obtained consists only of the use of the computer and the value of such use is not more than $5,000 in any 1-year period;

(5)

(A) knowingly causes the transmission of a program, information, code, or command, and as a result of such conduct, intentionally causes damage without authorization, to a protected computer;

(B) intentionally accesses a protected computer without authorization, and as a result of such conduct, recklessly causes damage; or

(C) intentionally accesses a protected computer without authorization, and as a result of such conduct, causes damage and loss.

(6) knowingly and with intent to defraud traffics in any password or similar information through which a computer may be accessed without authorization, if—

(A) such trafficking affects interstate or foreign commerce; or

(B) such computer is used by or for the Government of the United States[.]

(7) with intent to extort from any person any money or other thing of value, transmits in interstate or foreign commerce any communication containing any—

(A) threat to cause damage to a protected computer;

(B) threat to obtain information from a protected computer without authorization or in excess of authorization or to impair the confidentiality of information obtained from a protected computer without authorization or by exceeding authorized access; or

(C) demand or request for money or other thing of value in relation to damage to a protected computer, where such damage was caused to facilitate the extortion;

shall be punished [according to a complex penalty structure elsewhere in the statute].

(b) Whoever conspires to commit or attempts to commit an offense under subsection (a) of this section shall be punished [according to a complex penalty structure elsewhere in the statute].

. . .

(e) As used in this section—

(1) the term "computer" means an electronic, magnetic, optical, electrochemical, or other high speed data processing device performing logical, arithmetic, or storage functions, and includes any data storage facility or communications facility directly related to or operating in conjunction with such device, but such term does not include an automated typewriter or typesetter, a portable hand held calculator, or other similar device;

(2) the term "protected computer" means a computer—

(A) exclusively for the use of a financial institution or the United States Government, or, in the case of a computer not exclusively for such use, used by or for a financial institution or the United States Government and the conduct constituting the offense affects that use by or for the financial institution or the Government; or

(B) which is used in or affecting interstate or foreign commerce or communication, including a computer located outside the United States that is used in a manner that affects interstate or foreign commerce or communication of the United States; . . .

(6) the term "exceeds authorized access" means to access a computer with authorization and to use such access to obtain or alter information in the computer that the accesser is not entitled so to obtain or alter; . . .

(8) the term "damage" means any impairment to the integrity or availability of data, a program, a system, or information; . . .

(11) the term "loss" means any reasonable cost to any victim, including the cost of responding to an offense, conducting a damage assessment, and restoring the data, program, system, or information to its condition prior to the offense, and any revenue lost, cost incurred, or other consequential damages incurred because of interruption of service[.] . . .

(f) This section does not prohibit any lawfully authorized investigative, protective, or intelligence activity of a law enforcement agency of the United States, a State, or a political subdivision of a State, or of an intelligence agency of the United States.

(g) Any person who suffers damage or loss by reason of a violation of this section may maintain a civil action against the violator to obtain compensatory damages and injunctive relief or other equitable relief. A civil action for a violation of this section may be brought only if the conduct involves 1 of the factors set forth in [the following subclauses (incorporated from elsewhere in the section):]

[(I) loss to 1 or more persons during any 1-year period . . . aggregating at least $5,000 in value;]

[(II) the modification or impairment, or potential modification or impairment, of the medical examination, diagnosis, treatment, or care of 1 or more individuals;]

[(III) physical injury to any person;]

[(IV) a threat to public health or safety;]

[(V) damage affecting a computer used by or for an entity of the United States Government in furtherance of the administration of justice, national defense, or national security.]

Damages for a violation involving only conduct described in [subclause I] are limited to economic damages. No action may be brought under this subsection unless such action is begun within 2 years of the date of the act complained of or the date of the discovery of the damage. No action may be brought under this subsection for the negligent design or manufacture of computer hardware, computer software, or firmware.

## International Airport Centers, LLC v. Citrin

440 F.3d 418 (7th Cir. 2006)

■ POSNER, CIRCUIT JUDGE.

This appeal from the dismissal of the plaintiffs' suit for failure to state a claim mainly requires us to interpret the word "transmission" in a key provision of the Computer Fraud and Abuse Act, 18 U.S.C. § 1030. The complaint alleges the following facts, which for purposes of deciding the appeal we must take as true. The defendant, Citrin, was employed by the plaintiffs—affiliated companies engaged in the real estate business that we'll treat as one to simplify the opinion, and call "IAC"—to identify properties that IAC might want to acquire, and to assist in any ensuing acquisition. IAC lent Citrin a laptop to use to record data that he collected in the course of his work in identifying potential acquisition targets.

Citrin decided to quit IAC and go into business for himself, in breach of his employment contract. Before returning the laptop to IAC, he deleted all the data in it—not only the data that he had collected but also data that would have revealed to IAC improper conduct in which he had engaged before he decided to quit. Citrin loaded into the laptop a secure-erasure program, designed, by writing over the deleted files, to prevent their recovery. IAC had no copies of the files that Citrin erased.

The provision of the Computer Fraud and Abuse Act on which IAC relies provides that whoever "knowingly causes the transmission of a program, information, code, or command, and as a result of such conduct, intentionally causes damage without authorization, to a protected computer [a defined term that includes the laptop that Citrin used]," violates the Act. 18 U.S.C. § 1030(a)(5)(A). Citrin argues that merely erasing a file from a computer is not a "transmission." Pressing a delete or erase key in fact transmits a command, but it might be stretching the statute too far (especially since it provides criminal as well as civil sanctions for its violation) to consider any typing on a computer keyboard to be a form of "transmission" just because it transmits a command to the computer.

There is more here, however: the transmission of the secure-erasure program to the computer. We do not know whether the program was downloaded from the Internet or copied from a floppy disk (or the equivalent of a floppy disk, such as a CD) inserted into a disk drive that was either inside the computer or attached to it by a wire. Oddly, the complaint doesn't say; maybe IAC doesn't know—maybe all it knows is that when it got the computer back, the files in it had been erased. But we don't see what difference the precise mode of transmission can make.

In either the Internet download or the disk insertion, a program intended to cause damage (not to the physical computer, of course, but to its files—but "damage" includes "any impairment to the integrity or availability of data, a program, a system, or information," 18 U.S.C. § 1030(e)(8)) is transmitted to the computer electronically. The only difference, so far as the mechanics of transmission are concerned, is that the disk is inserted manually before the program on it is transmitted electronically to the computer. The difference vanishes if the disk drive into which the disk is inserted is an external drive, connected to the computer by a wire, just as the computer is connected to the Internet by a telephone cable or a broadband cable or wirelessly.

There is the following contextual difference between the two modes of transmission, however: transmission via disk requires that the malefactor have physical access to the computer. By using the Internet, Citrin might have erased the laptop's files from afar by transmitting a virus. Such long-distance attacks can be more difficult to detect and thus to deter or punish than ones that can have been made only by someone with physical access, usually an employee. The inside attack, however, while easier to detect[,] may also be easier to accomplish. Congress was concerned with both types of attack: attacks by virus and worm writers, on the one hand, which come mainly from the outside, and attacks by disgruntled programmers who decide to trash the employer's data system on the way out (or threaten to do so in order to extort payments), on the other. If the statute is to reach the disgruntled programmer, which Congress intended by providing that whoever "*intentionally* accesses a protected computer without authorization, and as a result of such conduct, recklessly causes damage" violates the Act, 18 U.S.C. § 1030(a)(5)(B) (emphasis added), it can't make any difference that the destructive program comes on a physical medium, such as a floppy disk or CD.

Citrin violated that subsection too. For his authorization to access the laptop terminated when, having already engaged in misconduct and decided to quit IAC in violation of his employment contract, he resolved to destroy files that incriminated himself and other files that were also the property of his employer, in violation of the duty of loyalty that agency law imposes on an employee.

Muddying the picture some, the Computer Fraud and Abuse Act distinguishes between "without authorization" and "exceeding authorized access," 18 U.S.C. §§ 1030(a)(1), (2), (4), and, while making both punishable, defines the latter as "access[ing] a computer with authorization and . . . us[ing] such access to obtain or alter information in the computer that the accesser is not entitled so to obtain or alter." § 1030(e)(6). That might seem the more apt description of what Citrin did.

The difference between "without authorization" and "exceeding authorized access" is paper thin, but not quite invisible. In *EF Cultural*

*Travel BV v. Explorica, Inc.*, 274 F.3d 577, 583–84 (1st Cir. 2001), for example, the former employee of a travel agent, in violation of his confidentiality agreement with his former employer, used confidential information that he had obtained as an employee to create a program that enabled his new travel company to obtain information from his former employer's website that he could not have obtained as efficiently without the use of that confidential information. The website was open to the public, so he was authorized to use it, but he exceeded his authorization by using confidential information to obtain better access than other members of the public.

Our case is different. Citrin's breach of his duty of loyalty terminated his agency relationship and with it his authority to access the laptop, because the only basis of his authority had been that relationship. Unless otherwise agreed, the authority of the agent terminates if, without knowledge of the principal, he acquires adverse interests or if he is otherwise guilty of a serious breach of loyalty to the principal.

The judgment is reversed with directions to reinstate the suit, including the supplemental claims that the judge dismissed because he was dismissing IAC's federal claim.

## United States v. Nosal

676 F.3d 854 (9th Cir. 2012) (En Banc)

■ KOZINSKI, CHIEF JUDGE.

Computers have become an indispensable part of our daily lives. We use them for work; we use them for play. Sometimes we use them for play at work. Many employers have adopted policies prohibiting the use of work computers for nonbusiness purposes. Does an employee who violates such a policy commit a federal crime? How about someone who violates the terms of service of a social networking website? This depends on how broadly we read the Computer Fraud and Abuse Act (CFAA), 18 U.S.C. § 1030.

### FACTS

David Nosal used to work for Korn/Ferry, an executive search firm. Shortly after he left the company, he convinced some of his former colleagues who were still working for Korn/Ferry to help him start a competing business. The employees used their log-in credentials to download source lists, names and contact information from a confidential database on the company's computer, and then transferred that information to Nosal. The employees were authorized to access the database, but Korn/Ferry had a policy that forbade disclosing confidential information. [The opening screen of the database also warned: "This product is intended to be used by Korn/Ferry employees for work on Korn/Ferry business only."] The government indicted Nosal on twenty counts, including trade secret theft, mail fraud, conspiracy and violations of the CFAA. The CFAA counts charged Nosal with violations of 18 U.S.C. § 1030(a)(4), for aiding and abetting the Korn/Ferry employees in "exceed[ing their] authorized access" with intent to defraud.

Nosal filed a motion to dismiss the CFAA counts, arguing that the statute targets only hackers, not individuals who access a computer with authorization but then misuse information they obtain by means of such access. The district court initially rejected Nosal's argument, holding that when a person accesses a computer "knowingly and with the intent to defraud . . . [it] renders the access unauthorized or in excess of authorization." Shortly afterwards, however, we decided *LVRC Holdings LLC v. Brekka*, 581 F.3d 1127 (9th Cir. 2009), which construed narrowly the phrases "without authorization" and "exceeds authorized access" in the CFAA. Nosal filed a motion for reconsideration and a second motion to dismiss. [The district court then dismissed the CFAA counts, and the government appealed.] We review de novo.

**DISCUSSION**

The CFAA defines "exceeds authorized access" as "to access a computer with authorization and to use such access to obtain or alter information in the computer that the accesser is not entitled so to obtain or alter." 18 U.S.C. § 1030(e)(6). This language can be read either of two ways: First, as Nosal suggests and the district court held, it could refer to someone who's authorized to access only certain data or files but accesses unauthorized data or files—what is colloquially known as "hacking." For example, assume an employee is permitted to access only product information on the company's computer but accesses customer data: He would "exceed [ ] authorized access" if he looks at the customer lists. Second, as the government proposes, the language could refer to someone who has unrestricted physical access to a computer, but is limited in the use to which he can put the information. For example, an employee may be authorized to access customer lists in order to do his job but not to send them to a competitor.

The government argues that the statutory text can support only the latter interpretation of "exceeds authorized access." In its opening brief, it focuses on the word "entitled" in the phrase an "accesser is not entitled so to obtain or alter." Pointing to one dictionary definition of "entitle" as "to furnish with a right," the government argues that Korn/Ferry's computer use policy gives employees certain rights, and when the employees violated that policy, they "exceed[ed] authorized access." But "entitled" in the statutory text refers to how an accesser "obtain[s] or alter[s]" the information, whereas the computer use policy uses "entitled" to limit how the information is used after it is obtained. This is a poor fit with the statutory language. An equally or more sensible reading of "entitled" is as a synonym for "authorized." So read, "exceeds authorized access" would refer to data or files on a computer that one is not authorized to access.

In its reply brief and at oral argument, the government focuses on the word "so" in the same phrase. The government reads "so" to mean "in that manner," which it claims must refer to use restrictions. In the government's view, reading the definition narrowly would render "so" superfluous.

The government's interpretation would transform the CFAA from an anti-hacking statute into an expansive misappropriation statute. This places a great deal of weight on a two-letter word that is essentially a conjunction. If Congress meant to expand the scope of criminal liability to everyone who uses a computer in violation of computer use restrictions—which may well include everyone who uses a computer—we would expect it to use language better suited to that purpose. Under the presumption that Congress acts interstitially, we construe a statute as displacing a substantial portion of the common law only where Congress has clearly indicated its intent to do so.

In any event, the government's "so" argument doesn't work because the word has meaning even if it doesn't refer to use restrictions. Suppose an employer keeps certain information in a separate database that can be viewed on a computer screen, but not copied or downloaded. If an employee circumvents the security measures, copies the information to a thumb drive and walks out of the building with it in his pocket, he would then have obtained access to information in the computer that he is not "entitled so to obtain." Or, let's say an employee is given full access to the information, provided he logs in with his username and password. In an effort to cover his tracks, he uses another employee's login to copy information from the database. Once again, this would be an employee who is authorized to access the information but does so in a manner he was not authorized "so to obtain." Of course, this all assumes that "so" must have a substantive meaning to make sense of the statute. But Congress could just as well have included "so" as a connector or for emphasis.

The government fails to acknowledge that its own construction of "exceeds authorized access" suffers from the same flaw of superfluity by rendering an entire element of subsection 1030(a)(4) meaningless. Subsection 1030(a)(4) requires a person to (1) knowingly and (2) with intent to defraud (3) access a protected computer (4) without authorization or exceeding authorized access (5) in order to further the intended fraud. *See* 18 U.S.C. § 1030(a)(4). Using a computer to defraud the company necessarily contravenes company policy. Therefore, if someone accesses a computer with intent to defraud—satisfying elements (2) and (3)—he would invariably satisfy (4) under the government's definition.

While the CFAA is susceptible to the government's broad interpretation, we find Nosal's narrower one more plausible. Congress enacted the CFAA in 1984 primarily to address the growing problem of computer hacking. The government agrees that the CFAA was concerned with hacking, which is why it also prohibits accessing a computer "without authorization." According to the government, that prohibition applies to hackers, so the "exceeds authorized access" prohibition must apply to people who are authorized to use the computer, but do so for an unauthorized purpose. But it is possible to read both prohibitions as applying to hackers: "[W]ithout authorization" would apply to outside hackers (individuals who have no authorized access to the computer at all) and "exceeds authorized access" would apply to inside hackers (individuals whose initial access to a computer is authorized but who access unauthorized information or files). This is a perfectly plausible construction of the statutory language that maintains the CFAA's focus on hacking rather than turning it into a sweeping Internet-policing mandate.

The government's construction of the statute would expand its scope far beyond computer hacking to criminalize any unauthorized use of information obtained from a computer. This would make criminals of large groups of people who would have little reason to suspect they are committing a federal crime. While ignorance of the law is no excuse, we can properly be skeptical as to whether Congress, in 1984, meant to criminalize conduct beyond that which is inherently wrongful, such as breaking into a computer.

Minds have wandered since the beginning of time and the computer gives employees new ways to procrastinate, by g-chatting with friends, playing games, shopping or watching sports highlights. Such activities are routinely prohibited by many computer-use policies, although employees are seldom disciplined for occasional use of work computers for personal purposes. Nevertheless, under the broad interpretation of the CFAA, such minor dalliances would become federal crimes.

Basing criminal liability on violations of private computer use polices can transform whole categories of otherwise innocuous behavior into federal crimes simply because a computer is involved. Employees who call family members from their work phones will become criminals if they send an email instead. Employees can sneak in the sports section of the New York Times to read at work, but they'd better not visit ESPN.com. And sudoku enthusiasts should stick to the printed puzzles, because visiting www.dailysudoku.com from their work computers might give them more than enough time to hone their sudoku skills behind bars.

The effect this broad construction of the CFAA has on workplace conduct pales by comparison with its effect on everyone else who uses a computer, smart-phone, iPad, Kindle, Nook, X-box, Blu-Ray player or any other Internet-enabled device. The Internet is a means for communicating via computers: Whenever we access a web page, commence a download, post a message on somebody's Facebook wall, shop on Amazon, bid on eBay, publish a blog, rate a movie on IMDb, read www.NYT.com, watch YouTube and do the thousands of other things we routinely do online, we are using one computer to send commands to other computers at remote locations. Our access to those remote computers is governed by a series of private agreements and policies that most people are only dimly aware of and virtually no one reads or understands.

The government assures us that, whatever the scope of the CFAA, it won't prosecute minor violations. But we shouldn't have to live at the mercy of our local prosecutor. And it's not clear we can trust the government when a tempting target comes along. Take the case of the mom who posed as a 17-year-old boy and cyber-bullied her daughter's classmate. The Justice Department prosecuted her under 18 U.S.C. § 1030(a)(2)(C) for violating MySpace's terms of service, which prohibited lying about identifying information, including age. *See United States v. Drew*, 259 F.R.D. 449 (C.D. Cal. 2009). Lying on social media websites is common: People shave years off their age, add inches to their height and drop pounds from their weight. The difference between puffery and prosecution may depend on whether you happen to be someone an AUSA has reason to go after.

We remain unpersuaded by the decisions of our sister circuits that interpret the CFAA broadly to cover violations of corporate computer use restrictions or violations of a duty of loyalty. *See United States v. Rodriguez*, 628 F.3d 1258 (11th Cir. 2010); *United States v. John*, 597 F.3d 263 (5th Cir. 2010); *Int'l Airport Ctrs., LLC v. Citrin*, 440 F.3d 418 (7th Cir. 2006). These courts looked only at the culpable behavior of the defendants before them, and failed to consider the effect on millions of ordinary citizens caused by the statute's unitary definition of "exceeds authorized access." They therefore failed to apply the long-standing principle that we must construe ambiguous criminal statutes narrowly so as to avoid "making criminal law in Congress's stead." *United States v. Santos*, 553 U.S. 507, 514 (2008).

We therefore respectfully decline to follow our sister circuits and urge them to reconsider instead. For our part, we continue to follow in the path blazed by *Brekka*, 581 F.3d 1127, and the growing number of [district] courts that have reached the same conclusion. These courts recognize that the plain language of the CFAA "target[s] the unauthorized procurement or alteration of information, not its misuse or misappropriation." *Shamrock Foods Co. v. Gast*, 535 F. Supp. 2d 962, 965 (D. Ariz. 2008).

**CONCLUSION**

We need not decide today whether Congress could base criminal liability on violations of a company or website's computer use restrictions. Instead, we hold that the phrase "exceeds authorized access" in the CFAA does not extend to violations of use restrictions. If Congress wants to incorporate misappropriation liability into the CFAA, it must speak more clearly.

The rule of lenity not only ensures that citizens will have fair notice of the criminal laws, but also that Congress will have fair notice of what conduct its laws criminalize. We construe criminal statutes narrowly so that Congress will not unintentionally turn ordinary citizens into criminals. Because of the seriousness of criminal penalties, and because criminal punishment usually represents the moral condemnation of the community, legislatures and not courts should define criminal activity.

This narrower interpretation is also a more sensible reading of the text and legislative history of a statute whose general purpose is to punish hacking—the circumvention of technological access barriers—not misappropriation of trade secrets—a subject Congress has dealt with elsewhere. Therefore, we hold that "exceeds authorized access" in the CFAA is limited to violations of restrictions on access to information, and not restrictions on its use.

Because Nosal's accomplices had permission to access the company database and obtain the information contained within, the government's charges fail to meet the element of "without authorization, or exceeds authorized access" under 18 U.S.C. § 1030(a)(4). Accordingly, we affirm the judgment of the district court dismissing [the CFAA charges] for failure to state an offense. The government may, of course, prosecute Nosal on the remaining counts of the indictment.

■ SILVERMAN, CIRCUIT JUDGE, with whom TALLMAN, CIRCUIT JUDGE concurs, dissenting:

This case has nothing to do with playing sudoku, checking email, fibbing on dating sites, or any of the other activities that the majority rightly values. It has everything to do with stealing an employer's valuable information to set up a competing business with the purloined data, siphoned away from the victim, knowing such access and use were prohibited in the defendants' employment contracts. The indictment here charged that Nosal and his co-conspirators knowingly exceeded the access to a protected company computer they were given by an executive search firm that employed them; that they did so with the intent to defraud; and further, that they stole the victim's valuable proprietary information by means of that fraudulent conduct in order to profit from using it. In ridiculing scenarios not remotely presented by this case, the majority does a good job of knocking down straw men—far-fetched hypotheticals involving neither theft nor intentional fraudulent conduct, but innocuous violations of office policy.

The majority also takes a plainly written statute and parses it in a hyper-complicated way that distorts the obvious intent of Congress. No other circuit that has considered this statute finds the problems that the majority does.

18 U.S.C. § 1030(a)(4) is quite clear. It states, in relevant part:

(a) Whoever—

(4) knowingly and with intent to defraud, accesses a protected computer without authorization, or exceeds authorized access, and by means of such conduct furthers the intended fraud and obtains anything of value . . .

shall be punished. . . .

Thus, it is perfectly clear that a person with both the requisite mens rea and the specific intent to defraud—but only such persons—can violate this subsection in one of two ways: first, by accessing a computer without authorization, or second, by exceeding authorized access. 18 U.S.C. § 1030(e)(6) defines "exceeds authorized access" as "to access a computer with authorization and to use such access to obtain or alter information in the computer that the accesser is not entitled so to obtain or alter."

"[T]he definition of the term 'exceeds authorized access' from § 1030(e)(6) implies that an employee can violate employer-placed limits on accessing information stored on the computer and still have authorization to access that computer. The plain language of the statute therefore indicates that 'authorization' depends on actions taken by the employer." *LVRC Holdings LLC v. Brekka*, 581 F.3d 1127, 1135 (9th Cir. 2009). In *Brekka*, we explained that a person "exceeds authorized access" when that person has permission to access a computer but accesses information on the computer that the person is not entitled to access. In that case, an employee allegedly emailed an employer's proprietary documents to his personal computer to use in a competing business. We held that one does not exceed authorized access simply by breaching a state law duty of loyalty to an employer and that, because the employee did not breach a contract with his employer, he could not be liable under the Computer Fraud and Abuse Act.

This is not an esoteric concept. A bank teller is entitled to access a bank's money for legitimate banking purposes, but not to take the bank's money for himself. A new car buyer may be entitled to take a vehicle around the block on a test drive. But the buyer would not be entitled—he would "exceed his authority"—to take the vehicle to Mexico on a drug run. A person of ordinary intelligence understands that he may be totally prohibited from doing something altogether, or authorized to do something but prohibited from going beyond what is authorized. The statute contemplates both means of committing the theft.

The majority holds that a person "exceeds authorized access" only when that person has permission to access a computer generally, but is completely prohibited from accessing a different portion of the computer (or different information on the computer). The majority's interpretation conflicts with the plain language of the statute. Furthermore, none of the circuits that have analyzed the meaning of "exceeds authorized access" as used in the Computer Fraud and Abuse Act read the statute the way the majority does. Both the Fifth and Eleventh Circuits have explicitly held that employees who knowingly violate clear company computer restrictions agreements "exceed authorized access" under the CFAA.

In *United States v. John*, 597 F.3d 263, 271–73 (5th Cir. 2010), the Fifth Circuit held that an employee of Citigroup exceeded her authorized access in violation of § 1030(a)(2) when she accessed confidential customer information in violation of her employer's computer use restrictions and used that information to commit fraud. At the very least, when an employee "knows that the purpose for which she is accessing information in a computer is both in violation of an employer's policies and is part of[a criminally fraudulent] scheme, it would be 'proper' to conclude that such conduct 'exceeds authorized access.' "*Id.* at 273.

Similarly, the Eleventh Circuit held in *United States v. Rodriguez*, 628 F.3d 1258, 1263 (11th Cir. 2010), that an employee of the Social Security Administration exceeded his authorized access under § 1030(a)(2) when he obtained personal information about former girlfriends and potential paramours and used that information to send the women flowers or to show up at their homes. The court rejected Rodriguez's argument that unlike the defendant in *John*, his use was "not criminal." The court held: "The problem with Rodriguez's argument is that his use of information is irrelevant if he obtained the information without authorization or as a result of exceeding authorized access." *Id.; see also EF Cultural Travel BV v. Explorica, Inc.*, 274 F.3d 577, 583–84 (1st Cir. 2001) (holding that an employee likely exceeded his authorized access when he used that access to disclose information in violation of a confidentiality agreement).

In *United States v. Teague*, 646 F.3d 1119, 1121–22 (8th Cir. 2011), the court upheld a conviction under § 1030(a)(2) where an employee of a government contractor used his privileged access to a government database to obtain President Obama's private student loan records.

The majority's opinion is driven out of a well meaning but ultimately misguided concern that if employment agreements or internet terms of service violations could subject someone to criminal liability, all internet users will suddenly become criminals overnight. I fail to see how anyone can seriously conclude that reading ESPN.com in contravention of office policy could come within the ambit of 18 U.S.C. § 1030(a)(4), a statute explicitly requiring an intent to defraud, the obtaining of something of value by means of that fraud, while doing so "knowingly." And even if an imaginative judge can conjure up far-fetched hypotheticals producing federal prison terms for accessing word puzzles, jokes, and sports scores while at work, well, . . . that is what an as-applied challenge is for. Meantime, back to this case, 18 U.S.C. § 1030(a)(4) clearly is aimed at, and limited to, knowing and intentional fraud. Because the indictment adequately states the elements of a valid crime, the district court erred in dismissing the charges.

I respectfully dissent.

## NOTES

1. ***Lacking Authorization and Exceeding Authorization.*** Apply the reasoning of *Citrin* to the facts of *Nosal*. Under Judge Posner's logic in *Citrin*, did Mr. Nosal access the Korn/Ferry computers lacking any authorization, or did he exceed authorized access to the database? How about his confederates? Now apply the reasoning of *Nosal* to the facts of *Citrin*. Would Judge Kozinski find that Mr. Citrin exceeded his authorized access to the IAC computer? Is the difference between these two concepts "paper thin" as *Citrin* suggests? Would the statute work better if it did not make the distinction?

2. ***The Varieties of Fraud and Abuse.*** Look with care at the different subsections of the CFAA implicated in *Citrin* and *Nosal*. In *Citrin*, the plaintiffs invoked the "damage" provisions of § 1030(a)(5). *Nosal* involved the "fraud" provisions of § 1030(a)(4). The CFAA also contains "theft" provisions in § 1030(a)(2). At least for criminal prosecutions, one important difference between all of these subsections arises from the penalties available for the various offenses. The baseline maximum imprisonment term for the "fraud" offenses starts at five years; the term for the "theft" provisions starts at one year (although it can go up to five years based on aggravating factors and possibly 10 years for a repeat CFAA offense). *See* § 1030(c). How else do these all differ? As *Citrin* discussed, there are also three different subclauses of the "damage" provisions. How are these distinguishable from one another? Which one of them does the *Citrin* court hold was adequately pleaded in that case? As you examine this language, consider why it may have been important that the defendant in that case was found to lack authorization altogether rather than merely exceeding his authorization.

3. **Nosal *on Remand.*** The en banc *Nosal* court affirmed the district court's dismissal of five CFAA counts against the defendant, but noted in closing that he could still be prosecuted on other counts in the indictment. He was convicted at a subsequent trial where his alleged co-conspirators testified against him. Perhaps surprisingly, three of the six counts for which he was convicted were CFAA offenses. The dismissed CFAA charges considered in the en banc appeal involved Nosal's co-conspirators using their passwords while employed at Korn/Ferry to download information for Nosal's competing venture. The charges that were not dismissed involved one co-conspirator who was still at Korn/Ferry sharing her password with the others, who had already left the company to work for Nosal. These now-departed employees used the still-employed conspirator's password to gain access to the Korn/Ferry database and download additional information for the use of Nosal's venture. On remand, Nosal moved that the district court dismiss the remaining CFAA charges on the basis of the Ninth Circuit's en banc opinion, but his motion was denied. Was that the correct decision? Nosal's conviction is now on appeal to the Ninth Circuit again; oral arguments were heard in 2015 but there had been no decision yet by the time of this writing in early 2016. (In addition to the CFAA arguments, Nosal's

appeal also challenges the other basis for his conviction under the Economic Espionage Act, 18 U.S.C. § 1832, and a related conspiracy count.)

4. ***Criminal Prosecutions and Civil Suits.*** Like ECPA [see Chapter 5], the CFAA is a criminal statute that allows a private right of action for wronged individuals. Remember that, despite the shared legal standards, the burden of proof will differ in civil and criminal cases, requiring only a preponderance of the evidence in the former and proof beyond a reasonable doubt in the latter. In *Nosal*, a criminal case, Judge Kozinski emphasizes that the rule of lenity demands narrow interpretations of criminal statutes for a variety of reasons related to due process, fair notice, and separation of powers. In *Citrin*, a civil case, Judge Posner also notes that "stretching the statute too far" would be problematic because it is a criminal law. Note also that civil suits are available only in a defined subset of cases. *See* 18 U.S.C. § 1030(g). What is the justification for the statute's selection of the particular cases where a civil suit is permitted? What are the benefits and drawbacks of drafting a statute that defines criminal offenses and civil liability simultaneously? By the way, Korn/Ferry did pursue civil suits against Nosal and the other former employees involved in that case.

5. ***CFAA as Privacy Protection.*** Prevention and punishment of hacking is a data security measure, of course. It can also be seen in part as a form of data privacy protection, because often (although not always), the data compromised by hackers will include personal information. A number of recent high-profile intrusions that led to disclosures that invaded privacy would probably fall within the scope of the CFAA if the perpetrators could be caught: the 2014 theft of photos of Jennifer Lawrence and other celebrities, many of them nude, by hackers exploiting shortcomings in the security of Apple's iCloud storage system; the copying of names and other information of users of the online site Ashley Madison, which offered matchmaking for adulterous spouses; and the compromise of personnel records and employee emails stored by Sony Pictures. All of these files were later released publicly by the hackers. In other cases, CFAA prosecutions based on privacy invasions have succeeded. For example, a college student who hacked into Republican vice presidential candidate Sarah Palin's email account during the 2008 campaign was convicted under 18 U.S.C. § 1030(a)(2)(C) and imprisoned. And, while *Citrin* and *Nosal* did not involve personal information, the *Nosal* dissent notes other cases involving employees exceeding authorization that did. In *United States v. Teague*, 646 F.3d 1119 (8th Cir. 2011), the defendant exceeded authorized access by looking up the President's student loan records. *United States v. Rodriguez*, 628 F.3d 1258 (11th Cir. 2010), concerned an employee of the Social Security Administration who repeatedly accessed information about ex-girlfriends and women in whom he was interested, to creepy effect:

> Dana Fennell, a professor of sociology from Mississippi, testified that she met Rodriguez at a Unitarian Universalist church study group when she was visiting her parents in Florida. After Fennell returned to her home in Mississippi, she received flowers from Rodriguez on Valentine's Day even though she had not given Rodriguez her address. Rodriguez later arrived at Fennell's

> doorstep unannounced, and Fennell was surprised and frightened by his presence. On another occasion, Rodriguez mentioned Fennell's father's birthday to Fennell even though she had never mentioned her father to Rodriguez. Rodriguez later called Fennell to wish her a happy "half-birthday" although she did not recall telling Rodriguez her date of birth. Rodriguez accessed Fennell's personal information on Administration databases 65 times, and he accessed the personal information of Fennell's mother and father multiple times.
>
> Jessica Fox also met Rodriguez at the church study group. Fox testified that she received a letter from Rodriguez at her home address and was shocked because she had not given Rodriguez her address, she ordinarily receives all her mail at a post office box, and her middle initial was on the envelope although she had not used it since grade school. Rodriguez accessed Fox's personal information 45 times.

*Id.* at 1261. If Rodriguez were not prosecuted criminally, could these women bring a CFAA civil suit against him?

6. ***From Hacking to Trade Secrets.*** In *Nosal*, Judge Kozinski repeatedly states that the CFAA was enacted as a measure to prevent computer hacking. Many of its provisions clearly indicate that intent, as does much of the legislative history. Over time, however, the use of the CFAA has evolved and a large proportion of current litigation under the law—both criminal and civil—now involves the misappropriation of confidential business information or trade secrets, as seen in both *Citrin* and *Nosal*. It is not inherently problematic for the purposes of a statute to evolve from the original intended uses to new ones. Some critics object that this particular expansion of the CFAA indirectly creates a federal civil private right of action for trade secret misappropriation in factual situations like *Citrin* and *Nosal*, even though there is not an omnibus federal trade secret law. Using the CFAA, a plaintiff can establish subject-matter jurisdiction in federal court and also avoid many of the limitations built into traditional state trade secret doctrine such as the requirement that information be valuable *because of* its secrecy. *See, e.g.*, Kyle W. Brenton, *Trade Secret Law and the Computer Fraud and Abuse Act: Two Problems and Two Solutions*, 2009 U. ILL. J.L. TECH. & POL'Y 429.

---

## Focus

### Prosecutorial Discretion and CFAA Reform Proposals

The *Nosal* majority opinion repeatedly suggests that a broad construction of the CFAA's "authorization" provisions could give prosecutors too much discretion to bring cases in situations where they want to convict a person for other reasons but use CFAA charges instead. The dissent criticizes its reliance on "far-fetched hypotheticals." But there certainly are examples where federal prosecutors used CFAA charges to go after persons who may have been in their sights notwithstanding any hacking allegations. In response to these concerns, critics have proposed changes to the CFAA that might return it to its original narrower focus on computer security against hacking, but also might reduce its usefulness as protection against unfair competitive practices and theft of confidential data, as alleged in both *Citrin* and *Nosal*.

In his *Nosal* opinion, Judge Kozinski invokes the example of Lori Drew, a mother who participated in bullying of her daughter's classmate on MySpace. He does not mention that the 13-year-old neighbor they bullied, Megan Meier, committed suicide in direct response to the hoax. The story garnered massive attention. Prosecutors determined there was no charge they could bring under state law, but a U.S. Attorney in California prosecuted her under the CFAA for violating the social network's terms of service. The district court eventually dismissed the case against Drew, over the government's objections. *See United States v. Drew*, 259 F.R.D. 449 (C.D. Cal. 2009). In another sensational case, federal prosecutors charged a New York City police officer, Gilberto Valle, with conspiracy to commit kidnapping based on many exchanges in fetish-related internet chat rooms where he discussed in detail his desires to kidnap, rape, and murder women and then eat their bodies. New York tabloids dubbed him "the cannibal cop" and covered his case extensively; it was also the subject of an HBO documentary and—inevitably—the inspiration for an episode of *Law and Order*. A jury convicted Valle of conspiracy to kidnap, but the district court overturned the conviction after trial because it found the evidence only demonstrated horrific fantasies and not the requisite intent to act on them. However, Valle was also convicted on one other count, under the CFAA, which arose from a single occasion when he looked up information about a woman in a law enforcement database without any investigative purpose. The district court upheld this conviction. On appeal, the Second Circuit found the "exceeds authorization" language capable of multiple readings, and concluded, "Where, as here, ordinary tools of legislative construction fail to establish that the Government's position is unambiguously correct, we are required by the rule of lenity to adopt the interpretation that favors the defendant." *United States v. Valle*, 807 F.3d 508, 526 (2d Cir. 2015) A dissenting judge would have affirmed the conviction. *Id.* at 537 (Straub, J., dissenting).

Both Drew and Valle were unsympathetic defendants in the extreme, but prosecutors faced difficulty convicting them under any other theories. If their violations of the CFAA were minor or tenuous, was it an abuse of prosecutorial discretion to charge them? On the other hand, Al Capone was eventually convicted of income tax evasion over his ill-gotten gains, not murder, extortion, or even bootlegging. Are prosecutors using the CFAA creatively in a similar manner?

Another CFAA case where prosecutors have been criticized involved Aaron Swartz, a talented young computer programmer who, as a teenager, helped develop the code for the RSS feed, Creative Commons, and Reddit. Swartz also became a political activist who founded the group Demand Progress, which campaigns for internet causes such as net neutrality and more liberal intellectual property rules. He was indicted after he used an account he had obtained from MIT to connect a laptop to the university's network and download millions of academic journal articles from the JSTOR database, in violation of its terms of service. It is not clear why he did so, but authorities believed he planned to make the articles available on the internet to people who did not pay for subscriptions to JSTOR. The criminal charges against Swartz could have carried sentences of 35 years or more. Federal prosecutors proposed a plea bargain under which Swartz would plead guilty and serve six months in prison, but he rejected the offer. A few months later, with trial approaching, Swartz committed suicide. Swartz had suffered from depression in the past, but his family and many supporters blamed an overzealous prosecution for his death, saying Swartz had no malicious intent and that the culture of MIT viewed victimless hacking as a harmless prank at most.

One reform proposal was introduced in Congress as "Aaron's Law" in honor of Swartz by Rep. Zoe Lofgren (D–CA), Sen. Ron Wyden (D–OR), and Sen. Rand Paul (R–KY). H.R. 1918, 114th Cong. (2015); S. 1030, 114th Cong. (2015). It would state that violations of purely contractual prohibitions such as terms of service or employment handbooks cannot form the basis for liability under the CFAA; the bills would also reduce some of the penalties under the CFAA. The Electronic Frontier Foundation has also proposed excluding certain circumvention techniques from liability, such as changing IP addresses, that the group says can be used to protect privacy and conduct research on computer security. Orin Kerr, a law professor who has written extensively about internet crime and the CFAA, has proposed a significant rewrite which would eliminate the "exceeding authorized access" language and redefine "access without authorization" as "to circumvent technological access barriers to a computer or data without the express or implied permission of the owner or operator of the computer." More broadly, Kerr has argued that "authorization" in statutes like the CFAA ought to be reconceptualized to follow norms about online behavior—just as, he suggests, norms influence our legal understanding of trespass in physical space:

> The process of identifying norms is mostly intuitive when courts interpret physical trespass crimes. Think of a chimney. Everyone knows that you don't have permission to enter someone else's house through its chimney. The rule isn't written down. Instead, we know from common experience that chimneys are there to let smoke out rather than let people in. The norms of physical space tell us that entering through a chimney is unauthorized. The same approach should be used to interpret computer trespass laws. Courts should begin by identifying the norms of the virtual space; turn to the permitted means of access online; and then address the context of permitted access.

*See* Orin S. Kerr, *Norms of Computer Trespass*, 116 COLUM. L. REV. ___ (forthcoming 2016). Does the CFAA need a significant revision? If so, which of these ideas seems most promising to you?

---

# CHAPTER 8

# DISCLOSURES AND TRANSFERS

The last phase of the life cycle of data is the release of information to other parties. Disclosures or transfers of personal data raise some of the most complicated questions in privacy law. The other life cycle phases—collection, processing, and storage—center primarily on a two-party relationship between the data subject and the organization handling personal data. When that organization turns around and shares personal information with other parties, new issues arise.

There are many sound reasons for "downstream" releases of personal data. Data processors routinely use subcontractors of various kinds for functions such as data entry, marketing, customer service management, analysis of traffic patterns on a web site, or the fulfillment and shipping of product orders. The rise of cloud computing means third parties may simply be warehousing data for an organization that previously might have stored its own. Law enforcement or national security agencies may request disclosure to aid their investigations, or require it with warrants and other court orders. Affiliated organizations may share data to improve their marketing or to coordinate their activities. And of course, sometimes personal information is released to the general public or to some portion of it: journalists, for example, gather newsworthy information in order to publish it. The case study in Section A, below, concerns a new arena for such public disclosure: social media platforms.

That said, oftentimes subsequent disclosure is the thing people actually fear when they express privacy concerns. They may be content when a business with which they interact collects and stores data about them in order to use it for various purposes, if they find the relationship personally beneficial. Security might raise qualms for some users—but this largely amounts to anxiety over possible unauthorized disclosures to unexpected parties. The most important issue for these users will be the notion that personal information is "out there," being viewed, used, and stored by others with whom they have no direct relationship and in whom they have no trust. There is a reason many privacy policies make sweeping promises like, "We never sell or trade your information to any other party for their own use." If this statement is accurate, it can reassure customers about their most salient doubts concerning data handling. (If it is not true, of course, it can lead to a public relations disaster and the risk of liability under consumer protection law [see Chapter 3].)

Given this high level of concern, it is not surprising that a great deal of privacy law centers on the regulation of disclosures. Some of the many examples covered elsewhere in this book include:

- The tort for publication of private facts (sometimes called the "disclosure" tort) [see Chapter 2].
- The Fair Credit Reporting Act's restrictions on permissible recipients of certain credit information [see Chapter 6].
- The privacy exemptions to the Freedom of Information Act, which protect personal information in the government's possession that would otherwise be divulged in documents requested by members of the public [see Chapter 10].
- Requirements in HIPAA that covered entities, such as hospitals and insurers, must enter into written contracts with business associates specifying conditions for data handling before transferring protected health information to them [see Chapter 12].
- Provisions of the Gramm-Leach-Bliley Act that control whether certain financial information may be shared with unaffiliated companies [see Chapter 13].

This chapter begins in Section A with a case study about the legal response to the rise of social media, using Facebook as the example. Section B considers another relatively new problem of disclosure: the massive flow of personal data across national borders. The European Union, in particular, has extended its conception of individual data protection rights to the transfer of data outside the EU after it was collected from people in EU nations, which presents serious complications for US firms doing business in Europe. Section C looks at one of the most frequent sources of legal obligations applied to disclosures: contracts between those who provide the information and those who receive it. Finally, Section D reviews some of the tangled First Amendment jurisprudence that attempts to balance privacy interests against the constitutional protection for speech that may apply to disclosures of personal information.

## A. CASE STUDY: FACEBOOK

It can be easy to forget that social media is such a recent phenomenon, given how much it now permeates most Americans' daily lives. Friendster, the prototypical social network, was founded in 2002; the much more successful MySpace started in 2003, and Facebook—initially the upstart challenger—in 2004. Barely more than a decade later, Facebook claims an average of over one billion daily active users. Individuals' posts, comments, likes, and other actions on social media platforms typically disclose personal information, about either themselves or others. Such a novel form of disclosure does not fit well with previous regulatory models, which generally assumed the only realistic means for releasing information to the broad public went through centralized conduits that were actively overseen by gatekeepers, such as professional journalists. The arrival of the internet, and especially of social media platforms like Facebook, upended this assumption. Resulting disclosures have generated persistent privacy-related controversy. Many critics focus on Facebook in particular. The following excerpts present just a few of the many legal challenges to the ways Facebook has disseminated personal information. They rely on foundational privacy rules discussed in Part I of this book: a civil suit based on state publicity rights and unfair trade practices law in California [see Chapters 2 and 3]; an FTC action to enforce consumer protection regulation [see Chapter 3]; and a European data protection authority's audit [see Chapter 4]. The new context required creative thinking about these older sources of law. Thus, actions against Facebook have begun to reshape our understanding of privacy law in the disclosure phase of the life cycle of data.

## Fraley v. Facebook, Inc.

830 F. Supp. 2d 785 (N.D. Cal. 2011)

■ LUCY H. KOH, DISTRICT JUDGE.

Facebook, Inc. ("Facebook") owns and operates Facebook.com, a social networking site with over 600 million members worldwide and over 153 million members in the United States. While members join Facebook.com for free, Facebook generates its revenue through the sale of advertising targeted at its users. At issue here is one of Facebook's advertising practices in particular, "Sponsored Stories," which appear on a member's Facebook page, and which typically consist of another member's name, profile picture, and an assertion that the person "likes" the advertiser, coupled with the advertiser's logo. Sponsored Stories are generated when a member interacts with the Facebook website or affiliated sites in certain ways, such as by clicking on the "Like" button on a company's Facebook page.

In this putative class action, Plaintiffs, on behalf of themselves and all others similarly situated, allege that Facebook's Sponsored Stories violate California's Right of Publicity Statute, Civil Code § 3344; California's Unfair Competition Law, Business and Professions Code §§ 17200, et seq. ("UCL"); and the common law doctrine of unjust enrichment. Plaintiffs allege that Facebook unlawfully misappropriated Plaintiffs' names, photographs, likenesses, and identities for use in paid advertisements without obtaining Plaintiffs' consent. [Defendant filed a motion to dismiss based on multiple theories.] [T]he Court GRANTS in part and DENIES in part Defendant's motion to dismiss.

### BACKGROUND

Unless otherwise noted, the following allegations are taken from the Complaint and judicially noticeable documents and are presumed to be true for purposes of ruling on Defendant's motion to dismiss. Facebook is a free, web-based social networking site with over 153 million members in the United States. To join Facebook, a user must provide his or her name, age, gender, and a valid e-mail address, and agree to Facebook's terms of service. Once registered, a member receives a "Profile" page, may upload a "profile photo" representing him or herself, and may establish connections with other members by approving them as Facebook "Friends." In addition, Facebook allows members to share information with their Friends in a variety of ways: members may "Post" by adding text, images, videos, and hyperlinks to their own profile page, "Check-in" by announcing their geographical location within the feature "Places," and "Like" content by clicking on a thumbs-up button that appears next to certain items on the Internet, both within Facebook.com and on external sites. Whenever members take one of these actions, Facebook generates a "Story," which then appears on their Friends' "News Feed."

Facebook earns revenue primarily through the sale of targeted advertising that appears on members' Facebook pages. Plaintiffs challenge one of Facebook's advertising services in particular, known as "Sponsored Stories," which Facebook launched on January 25, 2011, and which was enabled for all members by default. A Sponsored Story is a form of paid advertisement that appears on a member's Facebook page and that generally consists of another Friend's name, profile picture, and an assertion that the person "likes" the advertiser. A Sponsored Story may be generated whenever a member utilizes the Post, Like, or Check-in features, or uses an application or plays a game that integrates with the Facebook website, and the content relates to an advertiser in some way determined by Facebook. For example, Plaintiff Angel Fraley, who registered as a member with the name Angel Frolicker, alleges that she visited Rosetta Stone's Facebook profile page and clicked the "Like" button in order to access a free software demonstration. Subsequently, her Facebook user name and profile picture, which bears her likeness, appeared on her Friends' Facebook pages in a "Sponsored Story" advertisement consisting of the Rosetta Stone logo and the sentence, "Angel Frolicker likes Rosetta Stone." [Other named plaintiffs pleaded similar facts about clicking on a "Like" button and then being featured in a "Sponsored Story."] Plaintiffs allege that they were unaware at the time they clicked those "Like" buttons that their actions would be interpreted and publicized by Facebook as an endorsement of those advertisers, products, services, or brands. Plaintiffs further allege that members are often enticed to click on a "Like" button simply to receive discounts on products, support social causes, or to see a humorous image.

Unlike ordinary "Stories" that appear in a member's News Feed, Sponsored Stories are offset along with other advertisements paid by Facebook advertisers. The [complaint] quotes Facebook CEO Mark Zuckerberg explaining that "[n]othing influences people more than a recommendation from a trusted friend" and that "[a] trusted referral is the Holy Grail of advertising." According to Facebook, members are twice as likely to remember seeing a Sponsored Story advertisement compared to an ordinary advertisement without a Friend's endorsement and three times as likely to purchase the advertised service or product. Plaintiffs therefore assert that the value of a Sponsored Story advertisement is at least twice the value of a standard Facebook.com advertisement, and that Facebook presumably profits from selling this added value to advertisers.

Plaintiffs assert that Sponsored Stories constitute "a new form of advertising which drafted millions of [Facebook members] as unpaid and unknowing spokespersons for various products," for which they are entitled to compensation under California law. Although Facebook's Statement of Rights and Responsibilities provides that members may alter their privacy settings to "limit how your name and [Facebook] profile picture may be associated with commercial, sponsored, or related content (such as a brand you like) served or enhanced by us," members are unable to opt out of the Sponsored Stories service altogether. Furthermore, although the Statement of Rights and Responsibilities provides that "[y]ou give us permission to use your name and [Facebook] profile picture in connection with [commercial, sponsored, or related] content, subject to the limits you place," Plaintiffs all registered for a Facebook account prior to January 25, 2011. Therefore, they could not have known about Sponsored Stories at the time they agreed to Facebook's Terms of Use, nor did Facebook ask them to review or re-affirm the Terms of Use upon introduction of the Sponsored Story advertising feature.

Plaintiffs bring this putative class action on behalf of all persons in the United States who were registered members of Facebook.com as of January 24, 2011, and whose names, photographs, likenesses, or identities associated with their account were used by Facebook in a "Sponsored Story" advertisement. Plaintiffs seek declaratory and injunctive relief, as well as damages and other equitable relief.

## DISCUSSION

[The court first found that the Plaintiffs had pleaded injury sufficient for constitutional standing to sue. It then rejected Facebook's argument that the suit was barred by the safe harbor from liability for online intermediaries under Section 230 [see Chapter 2], because Facebook's participation in the development of Sponsored Stories meant it was not simply a conduit for user-generated content.]

### Individual Causes of Action

Defendant moves to dismiss all three causes of action for failure to state a claim upon which relief can be granted, pursuant to Federal Rule of Civil Procedure 12(b)(6).

Plaintiffs assert three causes of action: (1) commercial misappropriation under California Civil Code § 3344; (2) unlawful, unfair, and fraudulent business practices in violation of the California UCL; and (3) unjust enrichment. Both Plaintiffs' § 3344 and UCL claims appear to present novel issues of state law for which there is no binding authority. Where the state's highest court has not decided an issue, the task of the federal courts is to predict how the state high court would resolve it. In answering that question, this court looks for "guidance" to decisions by intermediate appellate courts of the state and by courts in other jurisdictions.

### 1. Misappropriation Under California Civil Code § 3344

California has long recognized a right to protect one's name and likeness against appropriation by others for their advantage. California law provides two vehicles for asserting such a right: a common law cause of action for commercial misappropriation, and a statutory remedy for commercial misappropriation under California Civil Code § 3344. To state a common law cause of action for misappropriation, a plaintiff must plead sufficient facts to establish "(1) the defendant's use of the plaintiff's identity; (2) the appropriation of plaintiff's name or likeness to defendant's advantage, commercially or otherwise; (3) lack of consent; and (4) resulting injury." To state a statutory cause of action under § 3344, a plaintiff must plead all the elements of the common law action and must also prove (5) "a knowing use by the defendant," and (6) "a direct connection between the alleged use and the commercial purpose."

The statute further provides that a party in violation of § 3344 "shall be liable to the injured party or parties in an amount equal to the greater of [$750] or the actual damages suffered by him or her as a result of the unauthorized use," and shall disgorge "any profits from the unauthorized use that are attributable to the use and are not taken into account in computing the actual damages."

Defendant moves to dismiss on grounds that (1) Facebook's actions fall within § 3344(d)'s "newsworthy" exception for which consent is not required; (2) in any event, Plaintiffs consented to the use of their names, photographs, and likenesses; and (3) Plaintiffs fail to allege sufficient injury under § 3344(a). Notably, Defendant does not at this juncture dispute that it knowingly used Plaintiffs' identity, or that the use of Plaintiffs' names or likenesses was to Defendant's advantage.

#### a. Newsworthiness

Under California law, the "newsworthiness" exception under § 3344(d) tracks the constitutional right to freedom of speech under the First Amendment. A statutory cause of action for commercial appropriation therefore will not lie for the publication of matters in the public interest, which rests on the right of the public to know and the freedom of the press to tell it.

Defendant's argument is twofold. Facebook argues that its republication of members' names or profile images next to statements about pages or content they "Like" or other actions they have taken is newsworthy because (1) Plaintiffs are "public figures" to their friends, and (2) "expressions of consumer opinion" are generally newsworthy. Plaintiffs deny that they are public figures and dispute whether their act of clicking on a "Like" button—which they may do simply out of curiosity rather than affinity—may be accurately characterized as "expressions of consumer opinion."

The Court agrees with Defendant that Plaintiff "cannot have it both ways"—Plaintiffs cannot assert economic injury under the theory that they are "celebrities" to their Facebook Friends, while at the same time denying that they are "public figures" to those same friends for newsworthy purposes.

Nonetheless, the Court is not convinced that Defendant gains much from its own argument. [E]ven newsworthy actions may be subjects of § 3344 liability when published for commercial rather than journalistic purposes. Thus, even if the underlying actions taken by Plaintiffs are newsworthy, Plaintiffs assert that Facebook's commercial use of those actions in Sponsored Stories removes them from the scope of § 3344(d)'s newsworthy privilege. The Court agrees.

**b. Consent**

Defendant next argues that even if consent was required, Plaintiffs gave the necessary consent by registering for and using the Facebook website under its Terms of Use, which informs members that "[y]ou can use your privacy settings to limit how your name and profile picture may be associated with commercial, sponsored, or related content (such as a brand you like) served or enhanced by us. You give us permission to use your name and [Facebook] profile picture in connection with that content, subject to the limits you place." According to Facebook, "Sponsored Stories are only delivered to your confirmed friends and respect the privacy settings you configure for News Feed." Members may also prevent a specific story from being republished as a Sponsored Story by clicking the "X" displayed in the upper right side of a story and choosing the appropriate option when prompted. Thus, although members may not opt out of the Sponsored Stories feature wholesale, they exercise control over whether to take actions that can become Sponsored Stories, whether individual actions may be republished as Sponsored Stories, and the precise audience to whom their Sponsored Stories are shown.

Plaintiffs here contend that they never consented in any form to the use of their names or likenesses in Sponsored Stories, noting that Sponsored Stories were not even a feature of Facebook at the time they became registered members, and alleging that Plaintiffs were never asked to review or renew their Terms of Use subsequent to Facebook's introduction of the Sponsored Stories feature, which operates on an opt-out basis. [T]he Court determines that whether Facebook's Statement of Rights and Responsibilities, Privacy Policy, or Help Center pages unambiguously give Defendant the right to use Plaintiffs' names, images, and likenesses in the form of Sponsored Story advertisements for

Facebook's commercial gain remains a disputed question of fact and is not proper grounds for dismissal at this time.

#### c. Injury

Here, Plaintiffs allege not that they suffered mental anguish as a result of Defendant's actions, but rather that they suffered economic injury because they were not compensated for Facebook's commercial use of their names and likenesses in targeted advertisements to their Facebook Friends. Defendant does not deny that Plaintiffs may assert economic injury, but insists that, because they are not celebrities, they must demonstrate some preexisting commercial value to their names and likenesses, such as allegations that they "previously received remuneration for the use of their name or likeness, or that they have ever sought to obtain such remuneration."

First, the Court finds nothing in the text of the statute or in case law that supports Defendant's interpretation of § 3344 as requiring a plaintiff pleading economic injury to provide proof of *preexisting* commercial value and efforts to capitalize on such value in order to survive a motion to dismiss. Indeed, in cases involving celebrity plaintiffs, the mere allegation that the plaintiff was not compensated has been deemed sufficient to satisfy the injury prong.

Nor does the Court find any reason to impose a higher pleading standard on non-celebrities than on celebrities. California courts have clearly held that the statutory right of publicity exists for celebrity and non-celebrity plaintiffs alike. Thus, courts have long recognized that a person's name, likeness, or other attribute of identity can have commercial value, even if the individual is relatively obscure.

Admittedly, previous non-celebrity plaintiffs have typically been models, entertainers, or other professionals who have cultivated some commercially exploitable value through their own endeavors. Nevertheless, the Court finds nothing requiring that a plaintiff's commercially exploitable value be a result of his own talents or efforts in order to state a claim for damages under § 3344. In a society dominated by reality television shows, YouTube, Twitter, and online social networking sites, the distinction between a "celebrity" and a "non-celebrity" seems to be an increasingly arbitrary one.

Moreover, even if non-celebrities are subject to a heightened pleading standard under § 3344, the Court finds that Plaintiffs' allegations satisfy the requirements for pleading a claim of economic injury under § 3344. While traditionally, advertisers had little incentive to exploit a non-celebrity's likeness because such endorsement would carry little weight in the economy at large, Plaintiffs' allegations suggest that advertisers' ability to conduct targeted marketing has now made friend endorsements "a valuable marketing tool," just as celebrity endorsements have always been so considered. Given that the protection of name and likeness from unwarranted intrusion or exploitation is the heart of the law of privacy, the Court finds Plaintiffs' arguments sufficiently compelling to withstand dismissal.

Of course, at summary judgment or at trial, Plaintiffs may not simply demand $750 in statutory damages in reliance on a bare allegation that their commercial endorsement has provable value, but rather must prove actual damages like any other plaintiff whose name has commercial value. At this stage, however, the Court finds their allegations of provable commercial value sufficient to survive a motion to dismiss and accordingly denies Defendant's 12(b)(6) motion with respect to the § 3344 claim.

### 2. Violation of Unfair Competition Law ("UCL")

Plaintiffs also allege that Defendant's actions violate California's UCL, which does not prohibit specific activities but instead broadly proscribes "any unfair competition, which means "any unlawful, unfair or fraudulent business act or practice." Plaintiffs assert that Defendant's conduct violates all three prongs of the UCL. Defendant contends that Plaintiffs lack [statutory] standing to assert a UCL claim and that, even if they have standing, their claim fails on its merits.

#### a. Standing

Only those who have both suffered injury in fact and lost money or property as a result of the alleged unfair competition may bring suit under the UCL. Cal. Bus. & Prof. Code § 17204

Plaintiffs contend they assert sufficient facts to meet both requirements for standing under § 17204. The Court agrees that they have asserted an injury in fact under § 17204, which is defined as either "a distinct and palpable injury suffered as a result of the defendant's actions," or "an invasion of a legally protected interest which is (a) concrete and particularized; and (b) actual or imminent, not conjectural or hypothetical."

The more difficult question is whether Plaintiffs have adequately alleged loss of money or property caused by unfair competition. Defendant argues that Plaintiffs are unable to allege loss of money or property because "Facebook is, and always has been, a free service," and because " 'personal information does not constitute property for purposes of a UCL claim" [quoting *In re Facebook Privacy Litig.*, 791 F. Supp. 2d 705, 714 (N.D. Cal. 2011)]. It is undisputed that Plaintiffs did not pay for Facebook's services, and several courts have held that the unauthorized release of "personal information" does not constitute a loss of money or property for purposes of establishing standing under the UCL. *See, e.g., Id.* at 714–15 (finding no loss of money or property where alleged injury consisted of unlawfully sharing plaintiffs' "personally identifiable information" with third-party advertisers who then sent plaintiffs targeted advertising); *Ruiz v. Gap, Inc.*, 540 F. Supp. 2d 1121, 1127 (N.D. Cal. 2008) (finding no loss of money or property where job applicant alleged that employer negligently permitted laptops containing his unencrypted personal information to be stolen); *In re iPhone Application Litig.*, 2011 WL 4403963 (N.D. Cal. Sept. 20, 2011) (finding no loss of money or property where plaintiffs, users of mobile devices, alleged that defendants violated their privacy rights by allowing third-party application developers to collect and make use of their personal information for commercial purposes, without user consent or knowledge); *Thompson v. Home Depot, Inc.*, No. 07–cv–1058–IEG, 2007 WL 2746603 (S.D. Cal. Sept. 18, 2007) (finding no loss of money or property where plaintiff alleged that defendant required customers to provide their personal information as a condition to performing a credit card transaction and used such information for marketing purposes); *cf. In re JetBlue Airways Corp. Privacy Litig.*, 379 F. Supp. 2d 299, 327 (E.D.N.Y. 2005) (holding that airline's disclosure of passengers' personal information to third-party data mining company in violation of airline's privacy policy did not amount to a compensable economic loss); *In re DoubleClick Inc. Privacy Litig.*, 154 F. Supp. 2d 497, 525 (S.D.N.Y. 2001) (holding that website visitors did not suffer a cognizable economic loss from the collection of their data for purposes of stating a claim under the Computer Fraud and Abuse Act).

Nevertheless, the Court finds the reasoning in this line of cases inapplicable to Plaintiffs' misappropriation claim, which, as previously discussed, is of an entirely different nature than a privacy tort claim. Plaintiffs here do not assert that their personal information has inherent economic value and that the mere disclosure of such data constitutes a loss of money or property. Rather, Plaintiffs insist they have sustained economic loss resulting from Facebook's failure to compensate them for their valuable endorsement of third-party products and services to their Facebook Friends, and that under § 3344, they have an expectation interest in a minimum statutory damages award of $750.

To the extent Plaintiffs allege they have a right to be paid for their endorsements and can establish how much these endorsements are worth, the Court finds that they have alleged a loss of money or property sufficient to state a claim under the UCL. Under the UCL, the concept of restoration or restitution is not limited only to the return of money or property that was once in the possession of that person. Instead, restitution is broad enough to allow a plaintiff to recover money or property in which he or she has a vested interest. For example, a plaintiff has a vested interest in unpaid wages and therefore may state a restitution claim under the UCL to recover such lost money or property. Though Plaintiffs are not models or celebrities per se, the Court agrees that they have a vested interest in their own right of publicity, which Plaintiffs allege Defendant has unlawfully appropriated without their consent.

However, to the extent Plaintiffs rely on the $750 minimum statutory damages award under § 3344, the California Supreme Court has recently made clear that a mere "expectation interest" in a statutory damage award is not a "vested interest" for purposes of stating a claim for restitution under the UCL. *See Pineda v. Bank of America*, 241 P.3d 870 (Cal. 2010). Plaintiffs may have suffered loss of money or property in the form of unpaid compensation for the use of their names, photographs, and likenesses in Sponsored Stories, and therefore have adequately alleged standing to bring a UCL claim, but the $750 minimum statutory damage award provided for under § 3344 is not a vested interest to which they have a restitution claim under the UCL.

For the reasons stated above, Defendant's motion to dismiss Plaintiffs' UCL claim for lack of standing is denied.

**b. Unlawful**

An unlawful business practice proscribed by the UCL "includes anything that can properly be called a business practice and that at the same time is forbidden by law." *Farmers Ins. Exch. v. Superior Court*, 826 P.2d 730 (Cal. 1992). By borrowing violations of other laws, the UCL deems those violations independently actionable under the UCL. Facebook's alleged commercial misappropriation of Plaintiffs' names and likenesses without their consent can properly be characterized as a business practice. Plaintiffs' properly pled § 3344 claim may therefore serve as the predicate unlawful business practice under the UCL. Accordingly, the Court denies Defendant's motion to dismiss for failure to allege unlawful conduct.

**c. Unfair**

Plaintiffs have stated a claim for unfair conduct under the UCL. To the extent Plaintiffs have alleged that Defendant's conduct is unlawful under § 3344, Plaintiffs have also successfully alleged that Defendant's practice is contrary to a statutorily declared public policy of preventing the nonconsensual appropriation of an individual's name, photograph, or likeness for commercial gain. Presently, the Court has no basis for finding that Defendant's conduct has any utility, much less that its utility outweighs the gravity of the alleged harm to Plaintiffs. The Court therefore denies Defendant's motion to dismiss for failure to allege unfair conduct.

**d. Fraudulent**

Plaintiffs allege that their false belief of control over the use of their names, photographs, and likenesses led them to join Facebook and to engage with Facebook in ways that rendered them unwitting commercial spokespersons without compensation, in violation of their statutory right of publicity. Alternatively, Plaintiffs argue that to the extent Facebook modified its Terms of Use at a later time to truthfully represent a member's inability to meaningfully opt out of Sponsored Stories, Facebook acted fraudulently by knowingly and intentionally failing to seek and acquire members' informed consent regarding changes to the Terms of Use. Plaintiffs have properly alleged fraudulent conduct, and Defendant's motion to dismiss for failure to do so is therefore denied.

For all the reasons stated above, the Court finds that Plaintiffs have adequately alleged unlawful, unfair, and fraudulent conduct under the UCL, and accordingly denies Defendant's motion to dismiss this claim.

### 3. Unjust Enrichment

Notwithstanding earlier cases suggesting the existence of a separate, stand-alone cause of action for unjust enrichment, the California Court of Appeals has recently clarified that "[u]njust enrichment is not a cause of action, just a restitution claim." *Hill v. Roll Int'l Corp.*,128 Cal. Rptr. 3d 109 (Ct. App. 2011).

Because Plaintiffs have already properly pleaded restitution in their demand for relief under § 3344 and the UCL, and because they cannot cure through amendment the fact that unjust enrichment is not an independent cause of action under California law, the Court finds no need to grant Plaintiffs leave to amend their third cause of action. The Court therefore grants Defendant's motion to dismiss Plaintiffs' third cause of action for unjust enrichment with prejudice.

## NOTES

1. ***Who's Newsworthy on Facebook?*** Look again at the court's reasoning about the newsworthiness of the plaintiffs' online activities, at least to their friends. This analysis grapples with one of the most novel features of social media disclosures. Before social media, it was difficult to target disclosures about a person narrowly within his or her circle of acquaintances. Now it is easy. The law is only beginning to respond to the ways this disrupts doctrine built on assumptions made by Warren and Brandeis about the distinction between matters of public interest and private affairs [see Chapter 2]. For purposes of standing, the *Fraley* court finds that the plaintiffs' identities have monetary value, because their micro-celebrity among friends increases the value of ads that highlight their apparent endorsements. If so, Facebook responds, then those disclosures must be newsworthy and exempt from § 3344. The court cuts through this knot by pointing out that even disclosures about celebrities may not be newsworthy if they are entirely commercial. That may resolve the conundrum satisfactorily in this case. Accepting the premise that each of us is newsworthy in disclosures to our friends may complicate future cases, however. Surely the *Fraley* opinion is correct when it observes, "In a society dominated by reality television shows, YouTube, Twitter, and online social networking sites, the distinction between a 'celebrity' and a 'non-celebrity' seems to be an increasingly arbitrary one."

2. ***Disclosure and the Disclosure Tort.*** The plaintiffs' objection to Sponsored Stories centers on a disclosure of their activity—divulging to friends that a user has clicked on a "Like" button affiliated with an advertiser. Yet they do not plead their claim about this allegedly problematic disclosure under the disclosure tort, opting instead for a publicity rights theory much closer to the appropriation tort [see Chapter 2]. Why do they make this choice? Does this suggest the disclosure tort is always ill-suited to

protect privacy in social media? Or are there situations where it might work better? Do Facebook posts satisfy the elements of publicity and of not being of legitimate public interest? While the life cycle of data may be a useful organizing concept, it certainly does not automatically tell a lawyer which legal theories might apply to a situation: disclosures may not be governed by the diosclosure tort.

3. ***Privacy and Property.*** In *Fraley*, conceptualizing control over the disclosure of private information through publicity rights or appropriation allows these plaintiffs to claim economic damage. Compare the *Fraley* plaintiffs to a hypothetical class of plaintiffs who might claim that Facebook disclosed highly embarrassing photos of them on the open internet with insufficient warning. This fact pattern resembles the one in *Fraley* in some ways, but without the advertising component. Can these plaintiffs claim a property harm?

4. ***Subsequent History of* Fraley.** This decision was rendered in December 2011. In May 2012, the parties reached a settlement, shortly before the court was to hear arguments concerning class certification. Another district court judge refused to approve an initial version of the settlement agreement for several reasons, including an expression of concern that it did not offer financial compensation to plaintiff class members. Perhaps this was a bit ironic in a suit supposedly based on the financial interests of the class members. As explained by Judge Seeborg, who rejected the first settlement:

> Plaintiffs offer the argument, in which Facebook vigorously joins, that any settlement calling for cash payments to class members is simply not practicable in this case, given the size of the class. For example, even paying each class member the modest sum of $10, might require a settlement fund of $1 billion (assuming a class size of 100 million), apart from administration costs.

*Fraley v. Facebook, Inc.*, No. C 11–1726 RS, 2012 WL 5838198, at *2 (N.D. Cal. Aug. 17, 2012). The parties revised their agreement and eventually a settlement was approved under which Facebook placed $20 million in a fund. So few users filed claims for payments that there was money left over after paying those claims, attorney's fees, and administrative costs; the balance was distributed to privacy advocacy groups as part of a program established under the settlement.

5. ***Other Facebook Class Actions.*** The *Fraley* litigation over Sponsored Stories has not been the only privacy class action against Facebook by any means. Another prominent example was an earlier case brought over Facebook's short-lived Beacon feature, a sort of predecessor to Sponsored Stories under which some activities in external sites were turned into Facebook stories and disclosed on Friends' News Feeds—even without the user clicking a Like button or taking any other action evidently related to Facebook. Actions that could end up in the News Feed under Beacon included rating movies on video rental web sites, reading stories on news sites, and making purchases on e-commerce sites. In 2008, a class of plaintiffs filed suit challenging Beacon and relying on quite different legal

theories than those at issue in *Fraley*. In addition to consumer protection law, the complaint alleged violations of the Electronic Communications Privacy Act [see Chapter 5], the Computer Fraud and Abuse Act and its California state law analogue [see Chapter 7], and the Video Privacy Protection Act [see Chapter 14]. Before even filing a motion to dismiss, Facebook reached a $9.5 million settlement which was eventually approved; like the *Fraley* settlement, it included cy pres awards to nonprofit privacy advocacy groups. *See Lane v. Facebook, Inc.*, 696 F.3d 811 (9th Cir. 2012). Could the plaintiffs in this Facebook Beacon case have relied on the same legal theories asserted in *Fraley*? Why or why not?

## In re Facebook

FTC Docket No. C–4365 (Aug. 10, 2012)

### COMPLAINT

The Federal Trade Commission, having reason to believe that Facebook, Inc., a corporation ("Respondent") has violated the Federal Trade Commission Act ("FTC Act"), and it appearing to the Commission that this proceeding is in the public interest, alleges:

1. Respondent Facebook, Inc. ("Facebook"), is a Delaware corporation with its principal office or place of business at 1601 Willow Road, Menlo Park, California 94025.

2. The acts and practices of Respondent as alleged in this complaint have been in or affecting commerce, as "commerce" is defined in Section 4 of the FTC Act.

### FACEBOOK'S BUSINESS PRACTICES

3. Since at least 2004, Facebook has operated www.facebook.com, a social networking website. Users of the site create online profiles, which contain content about them such as their name, interest groups they join, the names of other users who are their "friends" on the site, photos albums and videos they upload, and messages and comments they post or receive from their friends. Users also may add content to other users' profiles by sharing photos, sending messages, or posting comments. As of March 2012, Facebook had approximately 900 million users.

4. Since approximately May 2007, Facebook has operated the Facebook Platform ("Platform"), a set of tools and programming interfaces that enables third parties to develop, run, and operate software applications, such as games, that users can interact with online ("Platform Applications").

5. Facebook obtains revenue by placing third-party advertisements on its site and by selling Facebook Credits, a virtual currency that it offers on its website and through retail outlets. In 2009, the company had revenues of approximately $777.2 million.

## FACEBOOK'S COLLECTION AND STORAGE OF USER INFORMATION

6. Facebook has collected extensive "profile information" about its users, including, but not limited to:

a. mandatory information that a user must submit to register with the site, including Name, Gender, Email Address, and Birthday;

b. optional information that a user may submit, such as:

i. Profile Picture;

ii. Hometown;

iii. Interested in (i.e., whether a user is interested in men or women);

iv. Looking for (i.e., whether a user is looking for friendship, dating, a relationship, or networking);

v. Relationships (e.g., marital or other relationship status and the names of family members);

vi. Political and Religious Views;

vii. Likes and Interests (e.g., activities, interests, music, books, or movies that a user likes); and

viii. Education and Work (e.g., the name of a user's high school, college, graduate school, and employer); and

c. other information that is based on a user's activities on the site over time, such as:

i. A Friend List (i.e., a list of users with whom a user has become "Friends" on the site);

ii. Pages (e.g., any web page on Facebook's web site, belonging to an organization, brand, interest group, celebrity, or other entity, that a user has clicked an online button to "fan" or "like");

iii. Photos and Videos, including any that a user has uploaded or been "tagged in" (i.e., identified by a user such that his or her name is displayed when a user "hovers" over the likeness); and

iv. Messages that a user posts and comments made in response to other users' content.

7. Each user's profile information becomes part of the user's online profile and can be accessible to others, as described below.

8. Facebook has stored users' profile information on a computer network that it controls. It has assigned to each user a User Identification Number ("User ID"), a persistent, unique number that Platform Applications and others can use to obtain certain profile information from Facebook.

9. Facebook has designed its Platform such that Platform Applications can access user profile information in two main instances. First, Platform Applications that a user authorizes can access the user's profile information. Second, if a user's "Friend" authorizes a Platform Application, that application can access certain of the user's profile information, even if the user has not authorized that Application. For example, if a user authorizes a Platform Application that provides reminders about Friends' birthdays, that application could access, among other things, the birthdays of the user's Friends, even if these Friends never authorized the application.

## FACEBOOK'S DECEPTIVE PRIVACY SETTINGS

## (Count 1)

12. Although the precise language has changed over time, Facebook's Central Privacy Page and Profile Privacy Page [and Privacy Settings] have, in many instances, stated that the Profile Privacy Settings allow users to "control who can see" their profile information, by specifying who can access it, e.g., "Only Friends" or "Friends of Friends."

14. None of [Facebook's various privacy notices] have disclosed that a user's choice to restrict profile information to "Only Friends" or "Friends of Friends" would be ineffective as to certain third parties. Despite this fact, in many instances, Facebook has made profile information that a user chose to restrict to "Only Friends" or "Friends of Friends" accessible to any Platform Applications that the user's Friends have used (hereinafter "Friends' Apps"). Information shared with such Friends' Apps has included, among other things, a user's birthday, hometown, activities, interests, status updates, marital status, education (e.g., schools attended), place of employment, photos, and videos.

16. [Many of the links Facebook provided to these policies] failed to disclose that a user's choices made through Profile Privacy Settings have been ineffective against Friends' Apps. For example, the language alongside the Applications link has stated, "[c]ontrol what information is available to applications ***you use*** on Facebook." (Emphasis added). Thus, users who did not themselves use applications would have had no reason to click on this link, and would have concluded that their choices to restrict profile information through their Profile Privacy Settings were complete and effective.

## Count 1

17. Facebook has represented, expressly or by implication, that, through their Profile Privacy Settings, users can restrict access to their profile information to specific groups, such as "Only Friends" or "Friends of Friends."

18. In truth and in fact, in many instances, users could not restrict access to their profile information to specific groups, such as "Only Friends" or "Friends of Friends" through their Profile Privacy Settings. Instead, such information could be accessed by Platform Applications

that their Friends used. Therefore, the representation set forth in Paragraph 17 constitutes a false or misleading representation.

## FACEBOOK'S UNFAIR AND DECEPTIVE DECEMBER 2009 PRIVACY CHANGES

### (Count 2 and Count 3)

19. On approximately November 19, 2009, Facebook changed its privacy policy to designate certain user information as "publicly available" ("PAI"). On approximately December 8, 2009, Facebook began implementing the changes referenced in its new policy ("the December Privacy Changes") to make public in new ways certain information that users previously had provided.

20. Before December 8, 2009, users could, and did, use their Friends' App Settings to restrict Platform Applications' access to their PAI. For example, as of November 2009, approximately 586,241 users had used these settings to "block" Platform Applications that their Friends used from accessing any of their profile information, including their Name, Profile Picture, Gender, Friend List, Pages, and Networks. Following the December Privacy Changes, Facebook users no longer could restrict access to their PAI through these Friends' App Settings, and all prior user choices to do so were overridden.

21. Before December 8, 2009, users could, and did, use their Profile Privacy Settings to limit access to their Friend List. Following the December Privacy Changes, Facebook users could no longer restrict access to their Friend List through their Profile Privacy Settings, and all prior user choices to do so were overridden, making a user's Friend List accessible to other users. Although Facebook reinstated these settings shortly thereafter, they were not restored to the Profile Privacy Settings and instead were effectively hidden.

22. Before December 8, 2009, users could, and did, use their Search Privacy Settings to restrict access to their Profile Picture and Pages from other Facebook users who found them by searching for them on Facebook. For example, as of June 2009, approximately 2.5 million users who had set their Search Privacy Settings to "Everyone," still hid their Profile Picture. Following the December Privacy Changes, Facebook users could no longer restrict the visibility of their Profile Picture and Pages through these settings, and all prior user choices to do so were overridden.

23. To implement the December Privacy Changes, Facebook required each user to click through a multi-page notice, known as the Privacy Wizard, which was composed of:

a. an introductory page, which announced:

> We're making some changes to give you more control of your information and help you stay connected. We've simplified the Privacy page and added the ability to set privacy on everything you share, from status updates to photos.

> At the same time, we're helping everyone find and connect with each other by keeping some information—like your name and current city—publicly available. The next step will guide you through choosing your privacy settings.

b. privacy update pages, which required each user to choose, via a series of radio buttons, between new privacy settings that Facebook "recommended" and the user's "Old Settings," for ten types of profile information, and which stated:

> Facebook's new, simplified privacy settings give you more control over the information you share. We've recommended settings below, but you can choose to apply your old settings to any of the fields.

c. a confirmation page, which summarized the user's updated Privacy Settings.

24. The Privacy Wizard did not disclose adequately that users no longer could restrict access to their newly-designated PAI via their Profile Privacy Settings, Friends' App Settings, or Search Privacy Settings, or that their existing choices to restrict access to such information via these settings would be overridden. For example, the Wizard did not disclose that a user's existing choice to share his or her Friend List with "Only Friends" would be overridden, and that this information would be made accessible to the public.

25. The information that Facebook failed to disclose as described in Paragraph 24 was material to Facebook users.

26. Facebook's designation of PAI caused harm to users, including, but not limited to, threats to their health and safety, and unauthorized revelation of their affiliations. Among other things:

a. certain users were subject to the risk of unwelcome contacts from persons who may have been able to infer their locale, based on the locales of their Friends (e.g., their Friends' Current City information) and of the organizations reflected in their Pages;

b. each user's Pages became visible to anyone who viewed the user's profile, thereby exposing potentially controversial political views or other sensitive information to third parties—such as prospective employers, government organizations, or business competitors—who sought to obtain personal information about the user;

c. each user's Friend List became visible to anyone who viewed the user's profile, thereby exposing potentially sensitive affiliations, that could, in turn, reveal a user's political views, sexual orientation, or business relationships, to third parties—such as prospective employers, government organizations, or business competitors—who sought to obtain personal information about the user; and

d. each user's Profile Photo became visible to anyone who viewed the user's profile, thereby revealing potentially embarrassing or political images to third parties whose access users previously had restricted.

**Count 2**

27. As described in Paragraph 23, Facebook has represented, expressly, or by implication, that its December Privacy Changes provided users with "more control" over their information, including by allowing them to preserve their "Old Settings," to protect the privacy of their profile information.

28. As described in Paragraph 24–26, Facebook failed to disclose, or failed to disclose adequately, that, following the December Privacy Changes, users could no longer restrict access to their Name, Profile Picture, Gender, Friend List, Pages, or Networks by using privacy settings previously available to them. Facebook also failed to disclose, or failed to disclose adequately, that the December Privacy Changes overrode existing user privacy settings that restricted access to a user's Name, Profile Picture, Gender, Friend List, Pages, or Networks. These facts would be material to consumers. Therefore, Facebook's failure to adequately disclose these facts, in light of the representation made, constitutes a deceptive act or practice.

**Count 3**

29. As described in Paragraphs 19–26, by designating certain user profile information publicly available that previously had been subject to privacy settings, Facebook materially changed its promises that users could keep such information private. Facebook retroactively applied these changes to personal information that it had previously collected from users, without their informed consent, in a manner that has caused or has been likely to cause substantial injury to consumers, was not outweighed by countervailing benefits to consumers or to competition, and was not reasonably avoidable by consumers. This practice constitutes an unfair act or practice.

## SCOPE OF PLATFORM APPLICATIONS' ACCESS TO FACEBOOK USERS' INFORMATION

**(Count 4)**

30. Facebook has disseminated or caused to be disseminated numerous statements to users stating that Platform Applications they use will access only the profile information these applications need to operate.

31. Contrary to the[se] statements, in many instances, a Platform Application could access profile information that was unrelated to the Application's purpose or unnecessary to its operation. For example, a Platform Application with a narrow purpose, such as a quiz regarding a television show, in many instances could access a user's Relationship

Status, as well as the URL for every photo and video that the user had uploaded to Facebook's web site, despite the lack of relevance of this information to the Application.

**Count 4**

32. As set forth in Paragraph 30, Facebook has represented, expressly or by implication, that it has provided each Platform Application access only to such user profile information as the Application has needed to operate.

33. In truth and in fact, as described in Paragraph 31, from approximately May 2007 until July 2010, in many instances, Facebook has provided Platform Applications unrestricted access to user profile information that such Applications have not needed to operate. Therefore, the representation set forth in Paragraph 32 constitutes a false or misleading representation.

THEREFORE, the Federal Trade Commission this twenty-seventh day of July, 2012, has issued this complaint against Respondent.

By the Commission, Commissioner Rosch dissenting and Commissioner Ohlhausen not participating.

## Report of Audit: Facebook Ireland, Ltd.

Office of the Data Protection Commissioner [Ireland] (2011)

[In the following excerpt, responses by Facebook-Ireland are indicated in *italics*, which is how they were identified in the original audit report.]

This is a report of an audit of Facebook-Ireland (FB-I) carried out by the Office of the Data Protection Commissioner of Ireland in the period October–December 2011. It builds on work carried out by other regulators, notably the Canadian Privacy Commissioner, the US Federal Trade Commission and the Nordic and German Data Protection Authorities.

The audit was conducted with the full cooperation of FB-I. It found a positive approach and commitment on the part of FB-I to respecting the privacy rights of its users. Arising from the audit, FB-I has already committed to either implement, or to consider positively, further specific "best practice" improvements recommended by the audit team.

In examining FB-I's practices and policies, it was necessary to examine its responsibilities in two distinct areas. The first is the extent to which it provides users with appropriate controls over the sharing of their information with other users and information on the use of such controls—including in relation to specific features such as "tagging." Various recommendations have been made for "best practice" improvements in this area.

The second main area where we examined FB-I's practices and policies related to the extent to which FB-I uses personal data of users to target advertising to them. FB-I provides a service that is free to the user. Its business model is based on charging advertisers to deliver advertisements which are targeted on the specific interests disclosed by users. This basic "deal" is acknowledged by the user when s/he signs up to FB-I and agrees to the Statement of Rights and Responsibilities and the related Data Use Policy.

**Privacy Policy/Data Use Policy**

Facebook by its very nature is a complex and multifaceted online experience that has enjoyed remarkable success by virtue of the number of members and active users in a very short period. It is seen as an essential part of the routine of at least 800 million users who log on every month. Any assessment of the privacy policy and consent must have due regard to these realities. However, the role of this Office is to assess matters from a purely data protection perspective.

[T]he operation of the privacy controls available to users within Facebook are complex. This is despite efforts by Facebook to simplify the settings in order to make them more easily understandable and usable. [T]here are a multitude of different controls that must be accessed by the user to express their preference in relation to the use of their personal data. In addition to the controls available from the privacy settings, there are separate and distinct controls for Apps, for Ads and for Security. In order to fully understand the use of their information and the options available to them a user must read the full Privacy Policy, the Statement of Rights and Responsibilities, the advertising policy, information on the use of social plugins, information on Facebook Credits etc. It is clearly impractical to expect the average user, never mind, a thirteen year old joining the site for the first time to digest and understand this information and make informed choices. The difficulty in this area is further exacerbated by the fact that the choices which a person should make when joining or thereafter once they have begun to understand the social nature of Facebook are not in any real way presented to them in a manner in which they can fully understand and exercise real choice.

The problem of effective choice and control of a user is made more problematic by the default settings which Facebook has chosen for the user. Many of the default settings for adults (though not for minors) are set at what might be considered the most liberal possible. Facebook in this respect is obviously entitled to assert that social networking by its very nature is social and there is no point joining that experience if the person does not wish to interact with others. This is accepted but the combination of liberal default settings and the lack of a uniform method to present privacy choices to users is not reflecting the appropriate balance in this space. *FB-I indicated that it believes it has made great improvements in providing users better control over their privacy settings by moving most of the settings inline. This means that users with every new post or comment or upload can see the audience with whom they are sharing at the precise moment that information is most relevant and choose precisely the audience they want rather than having to refer back to a setting page.*

A specific example outlined above related to the upload of a profile photo when joining. At no point in that process is it clarified to the user that by uploading their photo it will be by default publicly searchable until they change the setting and that furthermore their profile photo once uploaded will be used in a range of scenarios including advertising purposes to their friends with varying levels of control. FB-I could legitimately say in response that it would be abundantly clear to a user from using the site that their profile photo would be used in this way but it clearly would not be in any way clear to a new user.

However, the concern of this Office is not focused on specific issues such as these but rather the bigger picture around appropriately informing, in a meaningful way, a new or current user and then providing easy to use and accessible tools to users. In this respect it is notable that if a user or new user does not add a certain number of friends or provided certain details in the sign-up process that they are constantly reminded to do so on their profile page or upon log-in. There are no such reminders or prompts about the desirability of selecting privacy settings that the user is comfortable with or adjusting them over time in light of their experience or where they are in their lives at a particular time.

From the privacy perspective therefore it would be a far better position for users if there were no default settings upon sign-up. A user then would be asked via a process what their broad preferences are with settings that reflect such broad preferences and a consequent ability for the user to refine those settings all of which should be available from one place. This Office has no difficulty with FB-I expressing its position as to what it believes a person should select to gain the greatest experience from the site but we do not accept that the current approach is reflecting the appropriate balance for Facebook users. By extension it is clearly the case that the process also needs to be adjusted for current users to take account of this approach. This Office therefore recommends that FB-I undertake a thorough re-evaluation of the process by which it empowers its users both new and current to make meaningful choices about how they control the use of their personal information. This Office does not wish to be prescriptive at this point as to the eventual route chosen but expects FB-I to take full account of the suggestions outlined above. This is clearly an issue which will form part of an ongoing engagement with FB-I and which will be thoroughly reviewed in July 2012.

### Disclosures to Third Parties

A standard feature of audits conducted by this Office involve an examination of the procedures in place for handling requests from third parties to access personal data held by the audited entity.

FB-I receives a large number of requests from law enforcement authorities throughout the Europe and Middle Eastern Region (EMEA). It was therefore necessary to examine its approach to the handling of these requests throughout the audit. A detailed interview was held with the Facebook Law Enforcement Team based in Dublin and subsequently with the Facebook Chief Security Officer. At the outset it can be recognised that Facebook and FB-I sit in an almost unique position given the vast number of users and the justified and specific concern to ensure that Facebook is a safe place for minors aged over 13 to interact with their friends. There are well-documented cases where internet platforms, including Facebook, have been used by individuals for criminal and other inappropriate purposes. FB-I indicates that it places a high priority on addressing such behaviour and as a consequence has a large focus on identifying and dealing with any such activity.

Under [the Irish data protection statute, which tracks the EU Data Protection Directive], FB-I is enabled to provide personal data following a lawful request if it is satisfied that to not do so could prejudice the prevention, detection or investigation of an offence. Additionally, a data controller is enabled to provide personal data if it is required urgently to prevent injury or other damage to the health of a person or serious loss of or damage to property. These would appear to be the most relevant considerations for FB-I when responding to lawful requests.

In order to assess whether FB-I was appropriately applying this criteria, five random recent requests received from law enforcement authorities were examined. These requests were received from the UK, Italy, Belgium, Germany and Ireland. In all cases, the requests received cited a relevant legal basis underpinning the request and in the case of the UK, all such requests are now coming from designated single points of contact (SPOC). The advantage of this approach is that it minimises the risk of inappropriate requests for data as all such requests must be gated through designated expert staff in each UK Police force. It was clarified that the legal basis cited in each request is examined for compatibility with applicable law and if any doubt arises further advice is sought from in-house or external legal counsel. Two of the cases related to missing children and therefore regardless of the legal basis that was cited FB-I could also have relied upon Section 8(e) of the Acts which allows for disclosure, inter alia, where the life of a person may be at risk. It was also confirmed that all requests are either made to a dedicated fax machine or via email with all responses issuing by encrypted email.

FB-I has emphasised that it does not respond to law enforcement requests which are broad in nature or seek data on more than one user. One of the sample law enforcement requests examined was refused on this basis. FB-I has emphasised that "*should the law enforcement agency require content information from FB-I, we will require that we be served with a legally compelling request under Irish law. The Gardaí (Irish Police) will be required to produce a search warrant or similar coercive document. Non-Irish search warrants will only be respected by FB-I if they are enforceable as a matter of Irish law. This will require that any such orders be domesticated by way of application to the Department of Justice pursuant to the Criminal Justice (Mutual Assistance) Act 2008*." The non-provision of content data was confirmed by examination of the sample requests examined.

This Office recommends a continuation and extension of the SPOC arrangement with law enforcement authorities. As the requests are made to FB-I it is important that any such forms etc. developed for this purpose make clear that the responsible entity is FB-I. At present any requests for user data under the control of FB-I are returned if they are not correctly addressed. The SPOC arrangement should be further strengthened by a requirement for all such requests to be signed-off on or validated by a designated officer of a senior rank and for this to be recordable in the request. It is not a sufficient safeguard for the requests to issue from a designated email box as such a box can be used by multiple users. We also recommended that the standard form be further strengthened by requiring all requesting entities to fully complete the section as to why the requested user data is sought so as to ensure that FB-I when responding can form a good faith belief that such provision of data is necessary as required by its privacy policy. FB-I should also re-examine its privacy policy to ensure that the current information provided is consistent with its actual approach in this area.

FB-I in response has indicated that it is implementing the above actions.

### Tagging

The ability to apply tags is not limited to pictures or indeed friends. A tag can be placed on any object and a name attributed to it. For instance a picture of the Eiffel Tower can be tagged with "Eiffel Tower" or indeed any other tag a user wishes to put on it. The tags themselves as they have no separate logic attaching to them are not associated with a particular user. If however a member tags a picture or a comment, post etc[.] with a tag identifying a friend, an association with the friend is made and they are sent a notification of the tag with an ability to remove it. In fact as tags generate an automatic notification to a friend they are used by many members as an automated means to notify a friend of something via the tag even if the content is completely unrelated to that person.

For those members who do not wish to be tagged at all, it is the case that at present there is no ability for them to express their preferences. However, a user can stop another individual user from tagging him or her by blocking that individual user. While preventing the tagging of yourself would mean that you would be less likely to become aware of a picture, post or comment in which you are referenced, there does not appear to be a compelling case as to why a member cannot decide to prevent tagging of them once they fully understand the potential loss of control and prior notification that comes with it.

*FB-I's response: Tagging is core activity on Facebook and has been positively received by Facebook users, especially as Facebook develops tagging in new ways in order to give users more means for connecting, sharing, and communicating. In contrast, there is generally no easy way for people to learn when someone has commented about them on the internet, uploaded a photo that includes them or created other content that includes descriptions of them. And even when people do become aware of such content, there is often no way for them to learn the identity of the author or request that content be modified, corrected or deleted. Facebook users have much greater protections. They always receive notifications when they have been tagged and they have always had the ability to un-tag themselves. Tagging enables users to get immediately informed when their friends mention them in a post or a photo. It gives them more control since they can react positively, express their discomfort and ask for the removal of the content if they wish or simply respond to an assertion in which they're mentioned. As tagging has expanded, Facebook has been sensitive to those users who may want more control over the process and further added the ability for users to preapprove tags before they appear on their Timelines (formerly, profiles). Thus, Facebook ensures 1) notice of all tags to users; 2) the ability to require prior notice of all tags; 3) the ability to un-tag; and 4) the ability to simply block it from appearing on the user's own Timeline. Facebook firmly believes that it has struck the right balance in terms of product development and user control. Based on this Office's recommendation, FB-I will examine the broader implications of this recommendation and will engage further on this issue in the July 2012 review.*

## NOTES

1. ***Harm.*** Identify the precise privacy harms the FTC alleged in its complaint against Facebook. Would these particular harms, as opposed to those discussed in *Fraley*, be actionable if individual consumers sued Facebook? The whole point of participating in a social networking site is to disclose information about oneself to others. How much control should the law give a user over the exact audience that receives those disclosures? Is a social media intermediary like Facebook required to provide any particular level of control to the user? Should it be? Does it matter whether personal information was originally posted by the user (as with profile data) or was uploaded by others (as with many tagged photos)? Are there meaningful differences between information shared with third-party apps and advertisers, with friends, and with the general public? How clearly can you articulate these accounts of harm?

2. ***Unfairness and Deception.*** Does the FTC's *Facebook* complaint allege primarily unfair practices or deceptive practices? Point to the specific parts of the complaint that support your answer to this question. Consider

how that may influence choices of Facebook and other social media platforms going forward.

**3. *The* Facebook *Consent Decree*.** As usually occurs after FTC privacy complaints [see Chapter 3], Facebook settled with the Commission and entered into a typical consent decree with a 20-year term. Facebook did not admit wrongdoing and paid no monetary penalty. The consent decree obliges Facebook to establish a "comprehensive privacy program," to conduct biennial audits of its privacy performance, and to make certain records available to the FTC on request. What sets it apart from some other consent decrees is a set of specific requirements when Facebook changes the mechanisms for disclosure of users' personal information:

> Prior to any sharing of a user's nonpublic user information by Respondent with any third party, which materially exceeds the restrictions imposed by a user's privacy setting(s), [Facebook] shall:
>
> > A. clearly and prominently disclose to the user, separate and apart from any "privacy policy," "data use policy," "statement of rights and responsibilities" page, or other similar document: (1) the categories of nonpublic user information that will be disclosed to such third parties, (2) the identity or specific categories of such third parties, and (3) that such sharing exceeds the restrictions imposed by the privacy setting(s) in effect for the user; and
> >
> > B. obtain the user's affirmative express consent.

The consent decree also specifies at length how Facebook must "clearly and prominently" display notification about changes in its disclosure policy:

> A. in textual communications (e.g., printed publications or words displayed on the screen of a computer or mobile device), the required disclosures are of a type, size, and location sufficiently noticeable for an ordinary consumer to read and comprehend them, in print that contrasts highly with the background on which they appear;
>
> B. in communications disseminated orally or through audible means (e.g., radio or streaming audio), the required disclosures are delivered in a volume and cadence sufficient for an ordinary consumer to hear and comprehend them;
>
> C. in communications disseminated through video means (e.g., television or streaming video), the required disclosures are in writing in a form consistent with subpart (A) of this definition and shall appear on the screen for a duration sufficient for an ordinary consumer to read and comprehend them, and in the same language as the predominant language that is used in the communication; and
>
> D. in all instances, the required disclosures: (1) are presented in an understandable language and syntax; and (2) include nothing contrary to, inconsistent with, or in mitigation of any statement

contained within the disclosure or within any document linked to or referenced therein.

Does the consent decree change the legal obligations Facebook had already? If so, how?

4. ***Other Counts in the FTC Complaint.*** In addition to the FTC's disclosure-related claims excerpted above, the complaint included additional allegations that Facebook engaged in deceptive business practices. Count 5 asserted that, despite assurances that Facebook did not reveal personally identifying information to advertisers, it sometimes disclosed the Facebook IDs of users, potentially allowing those advertisers to identify users and learn about some of their personal attributes. Count 6 concerned allegedly misleading statements about the care with which Facebook reviewed the practices of "verified apps." Count 7 alleged that, even if a user deleted a Facebook account, certain content such as photos remained accessible if users typed in a direct URL where the content had previously been posted. Count 8 alleged that Facebook claimed in its public statements to comply with the terms of the US-EU Safe Harbor Agreement [see Section B, below], but that, in fact, it did not. Where does each of these alleged shortcomings fall in the life cycle of data?

5. ***ODPC Audit Recommendations.*** The ODPC made recommendations for "best practices" in 14 areas overall; only portions of three of them are excerpted above as examples. In July 2012, Facebook-Ireland submitted a 74-page report to the ODPC outlining the company's response to the audit's recommendations, and in September 2012, the ODPC pronounced itself generally satisfied with the changes the company had made. That said, the ODPC report also made it clear that the case was not closed in any real sense: "Ongoing engagement with the company will be necessary as it continues to bring forward new innovations. The value of such engagement to identify and deal with any data protection concerns prior to launch is fully accepted by FB-I." The reports by both the regulator and Facebook strike an extremely cooperative tone throughout, and ODPC is quick to point out the degree of communication between them, stating at one point, "A continuous assessment of FB-I's compliance with the recommendations made during the initial audit took place throughout 2012. Daily emails, phone calls, and videoconferences were utilized to ensure that FB-I was clear on the changes to be made to comply with the recommendations." This is a dramatic example of a European regulator embracing the kind of collaborative regulatory style also seen at the FTC and many other US privacy enforcement agencies [see Chapter 3].

6. ***Other International Regulatory Actions.*** The Irish authorities have a particularly important role to play in overseeing Facebook because the company has based its operations outside of North America in Dublin. Users in all countries besides the US and Canada actually enter into terms of service agreements with FB-I, not with the parent company Facebook, Inc., based in California. That said, many other regulatory agencies have examined Facebook in particular and social media in general. The Article 29 Working Party, an EU-wide organization of data protection authorities from all the member states [see Chapter 4], issued an opinion about the

application of the EU Data Protection Directive to a social network service ("SNS"), and made a sweeping recommendation about disclosures of information:

> An important element of the privacy settings is the access to personal data published in a profile. If there are no restrictions to such access, third parties may link all kinds of intimate details regarding the users, either as a member of the SNS or via search engines. However, only a minority of users signing up to a service will make any changes to default settings. Therefore, SNS should offer privacy-friendly default settings which allow users to freely and specifically consent to any access to their profile's content that is beyond their self-selected contacts in order to reduce the risk of unlawful processing by third parties. Decisions to extend access may not be implicit, for example with an "opt-out" provided by the controller of the SNS.

Are the Irish recommendations consistent with this reasoning? Canada also completed a large-scale investigation of Facebook in 2010 and issued its own series of changes for Facebook to adopt. In early 2016, as many as six European DPAs besides the Irish ODPC were investigating a range of concerns about Facebook including the aggregation of data from different services and the use of "Like" buttons on other sites to engage in behavioral tracking. Is all this intensive (and at times contradictory) regulatory scrutiny of a single company excessive? Or is that the price Facebook pays for its global success?

7. ***Facebook and Privacy "Spillovers."*** How much do differences between the dynamics of Facebook and those of real-world social interactions affect the types of privacy concerns raised in *Facebook*? James Grimmelmann documented numerous ways the structure of online social networks could create unique privacy issues, including what he describes as "spillovers."

> If Hamlet and Gertrude are contacts, then when Gertrude accepts Claudius's contact request, she may compromise Hamlet's privacy from Claudius. Relying on network structure to limit profile visibility often means relying on the discretion of your contacts and their contacts. But as Clay Shirky observes, " '[F]riend of a friend of a friend' is pronounced 'stranger.' "
>
> There's an important underlying dynamic that makes these spillover problems more likely. A social network site in motion tends to grow. We've seen the various reasons that people add contacts. One of them is disproportionately important: it's hard to say no to a contact request. Because of explicit representation, there's no way to finesse requests from people you'd rather not invite; rather than embarrass both them and yourself with a visible rejection, it's easier just to click on "Confirm." The same goes for removing contacts; "I don't like you as much as I used to" is a hard message to send, so we don't. And so the networks grow.

> This leads not only to large, dense social networks, but also to ones in which the social meaning of being a contact is ambiguous. Facebook "friends" include not only people we'd call "friends" offline, but also those we'd call "acquaintances." Contact links are a mixture of what sociologists would call "strong ties" and "weak ties." Weak ties are essential for networking (whether it be finding a job or a spouse); social network sites usefully amplify our limited ability to manage weak ties. The price we pay for that networking, however, is that we must delegate some of our privacy decisions to people with whom we don't have close relationships. Those are precisely the people who are less likely to understand or respect our individual privacy preferences.

James Grimmelmann, *Saving Facebook*, 94 IOWA L. REV. 1137 (2009) (licensed under the Creative Commons Attribution 3.0 United States license, http://creativecommons.org/licenses/by/3.0/us/). How do you navigate the privacy challenges presented by undifferentiated, dense social networks in your own life? Should the law hold Facebook responsible for mitigating the effects of the privacy spillovers Grimmelmann describes? Has the passage of time since he wrote in 2009 changed the nature or severity of these problems? Do you think it will do so in the future?

8. ***Compliance and Counseling.*** If you were consulted by a competing social media platform about activities similar to those investigated by the FTC and ODPC, what would you advise your client to do to avoid running afoul of US and European regulators? Class action lawsuits like *Fraley*? To what extent can you provide bright-line rules about your client's future conduct?

## B. INTERNATIONAL DATA TRANSFERS

### EU DATA PROTECTION DIRECTIVE

Directive 95/46/EC

#### Article 25. Principles [of Data Transfer]

1. The Member States shall provide that the transfer to a third country of personal data which are undergoing processing or are intended for processing after transfer may take place only if, without prejudice to compliance with the national provisions adopted pursuant to the other provisions of this Directive, the third country in question ensures an adequate level of protection.

2. The adequacy of the level of protection afforded by a third country shall be assessed in the light of all the circumstances surrounding a data transfer operation or set of data transfer operations; particular consideration shall be given to the nature of the data, the purpose and duration of the proposed processing operation or operations, the country of origin and country of final destination, the rules of law, both general and sectoral, in force in the third country in question and the professional rules and security measures which are complied within that country.

3. The Member States and the Commission shall inform each other of cases where they consider that a third country does not ensure an adequate level of protection within the meaning of paragraph 2.

4. Where the Commission finds . . . that a third country does not ensure an adequate level of protection within the meaning of paragraph 2 of this Article, Member States shall take the measures necessary to prevent any transfer of data of the same type to the third country in question.

5. At the appropriate time, the Commission shall enter into negotiations with a view to remedying the situation resulting from the finding made pursuant to paragraph 4.

6. The Commission may find, in accordance with the procedure referred to in Article 31 (2), that a third country ensures an adequate level of protection within the meaning of paragraph 2 of this Article, by reason of its domestic law or of the international commitments it has entered into, particularly upon conclusion of the negotiations referred to in paragraph 5, for the protection of the private lives and basic freedoms and rights of individuals.

Member States shall take the measures necessary to comply with the Commission's decision.

---

## Focus

### EU Law and Cross-Border Data Transfers

Data crossing national boundaries puts pressure on regulatory systems that protect data differentlyfrom one another. Article 25 of the EU Data Protection Directive, which was completed in 1995, prohibited the transfer of personal data from the EU to countries that did not provide what the EU regarded as "an adequate level of protection" for the data. At the time, many viewed this provision as a safeguard against European data collectors evading the new law by simply outsourcing their data processing activities to third parties offshore. It quickly became apparent, however, that stringent regulation of cross-border data transfers would inhibit international commercial activity.

The European Commission has been sparing in using its authority under Article 25(6) to officially declare other countries' laws adequate; to date it has found adequacy in only 11 jurisdictions, half of them tiny European microstates with populations under 100,000. (The complete list: Andorra, Argentina, Canada (for businesses only), the Faroe Islands, Guernsey, Israel, the Isle of Man, Jersey, New Zealand, Switzerland, and Uruguay.) The process for deeming adequacy has been criticized as complex and overly politicized. *See* Christopher Wolf, *Delusions of Adequacy? Examining the Case for Finding the United States Adequate for Cross-Border EU–U.S. Data Transfers*, 43 WASH. U. J.L. & POL'Y 227. Presuming that the US consumer protection model for privacy law would never be considered "adequate" under European standards, an American-based company with activities in Europe could be unable to move personal data about its employees or customers to the company's US headquarters. The potential negative consequences of this rule for international commerce were significant.

While EU data protection authorities abstained from immediate enforcement of the crossborder data transfer limits, European and American diplomats worked for several years, in sometimes contentious negotiations, to hammer out a trade pact that would allow transatlantic data flows to continue. The result was the "US-EU Safe Harbor Agreement," approved in 2000. The European Commission, something like the executive branch of the European Union, formally adopted the Safe Harbor in its Commission Decision 2000/520/EC, relying on its power under Article 25(6). In 2015, the decision by the Court of Justice for the European Union in *Schrems v. Commissioner*, excerpted below, effectively invalidated the Safe Harbor. As you read these materials, consider where that judicial decision leaves companies that have relied on the Safe Harbor to transfer data to the US lawfully.

As explained further in *Schrems*, the Safe Harbor Agreement allowed US companies to certify annually that they would observe certain general data protection principles. These requirements were less detailed and less demanding than those imposed by the Data Protection Directive itself. Certification was accomplished by registering online with the US Department of Commerce. Companies that certified their adherence to the Safe Harbor principles were permitted to receive transferred data from the EU about EU persons. Enforcement of Safe Harbor requirements was left to the machinery of consumer protection regulation at the heart of US privacy law [see Chapter 3]. Especially in recent years, US companies that claimed to be Safe Harbor participants, but had failed to self-certify or to renew their certifications, became targets of FTC "broken promises" actions for deceptive trade practices. (As noted just above, Facebook was one of these.) All the Safe Harbor complaints ended with typical consent decrees. There was no examination of companies' substantive data handling activities to determine whether their practices actually fulfilled baseline requirements of the Safe Harbor—and those requirements were sufficiently vague that it would have been difficult to tell anyhow.

The Safe Harbor was never the only alternative for organizations that wanted to process EU personal data outside the EU. European data protection regulators have promulgated model clauses that can be inserted into contracts authorizing the transfer of data from the EU to other countries. In order to comply, the clauses must be used verbatim, which can lead to inflexibility and somewhat awkward drafting at times. Still, contract clauses are a frequent means of controlling data handling practices by third parties in many other contexts [see Section C, below]. The model clauses have worked well for some companies.

"Binding Corporate Rules" ("BCRs") are another basis for legitimate data transfers out of the EU. To secure a BCR, a multinational firm develops a code of conduct for itself and its affiliated companies around the world. The company submits the proposed internal rules to one DPA in the EU (usually in a country where it has a particularly significant presence), and that regulator then consults with other DPAs. The resulting rounds of followup questions and negotiations can take several years. The process also involves a significant amount of internal work to analyze data flows and then develop rules that will be workable for the company but robust enough to satisfy the DPA that they offer an adequate level of protection for EU persons' personal data. All of that requires resources. Because of the substantial time, expense, and difficulty required to gain approval for BCRs, they have been adopted only by the largest corporations. As of early 2016, there were 82 companies with approved BCRs, although more are in the process of securing them. Despite these disadvantages, once a company has a final BCR in place, it can transfer data within its corporate structure throughout the world—whereas the Safe Harbor only covered transfers between EU countries and the US. A large global enterprise might find it especially difficult to monitor innumerable bilateral contracts that would need to incorporate the EU's model clauses every time they were revised or rebid, and thus might opt for a BCR. Under the Directive, a company with a BCR is something like a country of its own, with adequate data protection. The primary regulation of privacy within that institution becomes the codes of conduct supporting its BCR—internally developed, specifically approved by a regulator, and tailored to the company's needs.

Model contract clauses and BCRs do not seem like good options for many, perhaps most, US companies. As a result, the Safe Harbor was by far the most widely used mechanism for lawful transfers of personal data from the EU to the US. In recent years, approximately 4,500 US institutions certified that they adhered to the Safe Harbor principles. The Safe Harbor Agreement has always been somewhat controversial, however, especially among many privacy advocates and some members of the European Parliament, and increasingly so in recent years. As the European Union continued its ongoing work to craft a comprehensive revision of its data protection law [see Chapter 4], critics of the Safe Harbor Agreement sought to eliminate it, or at least strengthen its requirements considerably, in the new General Data Protection Regulation. In response, US government figures argued that US privacy law is more robust than many Europeans believe—and at the same time, the number of Safe Harbor enforcement actions by US regulators increased noticeably, surely no coincidence.

This growing dissatisfaction came to a dramatic culmination in *Schrems*, below, when the Court of Justice of the European Union invalidated the European Commission's opinion approving the Safe Harbor Agreement. As discussed below, diplomats are developing a new "EU-US Privacy Shield" initiative in an attempt to replace the Safe Harbor, but its details are not fully developed as of this writing in early 2016, and most observers believe it will face a renewed legal challenge in the EU. As you read, consider what options the *Schrems* ruling leaves for those diplomats, and for businesses transferring data.

---

## Schrems v. Data Protection Commissioner

Case C–362/14, Curia, Court of Justice (Oct. 6, 2015)

1. This request for a preliminary ruling relates to the interpretation, in the light of Articles 7, 8 and 47 of the Charter of Fundamental Rights of the European Union ("the Charter"), of Articles 25(6) and 28 of Directive 95/46/EC [the Data Protection Directive] and, in essence, to the validity of Commission Decision 2000/520/EC on the adequacy of the protection provided by the safe harbour privacy principles and related ["]frequently asked questions["] issued by the US Department of Commerce.

2. The request has been made in proceedings [in Irish courts] between Mr. Schrems and the [Republic of Ireland's] Data Protection Commissioner ("the Commissioner") concerning the latter's refusal to investigate a complaint made by Mr. Schrems regarding the fact that Facebook Ireland Ltd ("Facebook Ireland") transfers the personal data of its users to the United States of America and keeps it on servers located in that country.

**The dispute in the main proceedings and the questions referred for a preliminary ruling**

26. Mr. Schrems, an Austrian national residing in Austria, has been a user of the Facebook social network ("Facebook") since 2008.

27. Any person residing in the European Union who wishes to use Facebook is required to conclude, at the time of his registration, a contract with Facebook Ireland, a subsidiary of Facebook Inc. which is itself established in the United States. Some or all of the personal data of Facebook Ireland's users who reside in the European Union is transferred to servers belonging to Facebook Inc. that are located in the United States, where it undergoes processing.

28. On 25 June 2013 Mr. Schrems made a complaint to the Commissioner by which he in essence asked the latter to exercise his statutory powers by prohibiting Facebook Ireland from transferring his personal data to the United States. He contended in his complaint that the law and practice in force in that country did not ensure adequate protection of the personal data held in its territory against the surveillance activities that were engaged in there by the public authorities. Mr. Schrems referred in this regard to the revelations made by Edward Snowden concerning the activities of the United States intelligence services, in particular those of the National Security Agency ("the NSA").

29. Since the Commissioner took the view that he was not required to investigate the matters raised by Mr. Schrems in the complaint, he rejected it as unfounded. The Commissioner considered that there was no evidence that Mr. Schrems' personal data had been accessed by the NSA. He added that the allegations raised by Mr. Schrems in his complaint could not be profitably put forward since any question of the adequacy of data protection in the United States had to be determined in accordance with Decision 2000/520[,] and the Commission had found in that decision that the United States ensured an adequate level of protection.

30. Mr. Schrems brought an action before the [Irish] High Court [the court of first instance for important cases] challenging the decision at issue in the main proceedings. After considering the evidence adduced by the parties to the main proceedings, the High Court found that the electronic surveillance and interception of personal data transferred from the European Union to the United States serve necessary and indispensable objectives in the public interest. However, it added that the revelations made by Edward Snowden had demonstrated a "significant over-reach" on the part of the NSA and other federal agencies.

31. According to the High Court, [EU] citizens have no effective right to be heard [in challenges to NSA surveillance]. Oversight of the intelligence services' actions is carried out within the framework of an *ex*

*parte* and secret procedure. Once the personal data has been transferred to the United States, it is capable of being accessed by the NSA and other federal agencies, such as the Federal Bureau of Investigation (FBI), in the course of the indiscriminate surveillance and interception carried out by them on a large scale.

32. The High Court stated that Irish law precludes the transfer of personal data outside national territory save where the third country ensures an adequate level of protection for privacy and fundamental rights and freedoms. The importance of the rights to privacy and to inviolability of the dwelling, which are guaranteed by the Irish Constitution, requires that any interference with those rights be proportionate and in accordance with the law.

33. Thus, according to the High Court, if the main proceedings were to be disposed of on the basis of Irish law alone, it would then have to be found that, given the existence of a serious doubt as to whether the United States ensures an adequate level of protection of personal data, the Commissioner should have proceeded to investigate the matters raised by Mr. Schrems in his complaint and that the Commissioner was wrong in rejecting the complaint.

34. However, the High Court considers that this case concerns the implementation of EU law and that the legality of the decision at issue in the main proceedings must therefore be assessed in the light of EU law.

35. The High Court further observes that in his action Mr. Schrems in reality raises the legality of the safe harbour regime which was established by Decision 2000/520 and gives rise to the decision at issue in the main proceedings. Thus, even though Mr. Schrems has not formally contested the validity of either Directive 95/46 or Decision 2000/520, the question is raised, according to the High Court, as to whether the [Irish Data Protection] Commissioner was bound by the [European] Commission's finding in Decision 2000/520 that the United States ensures an adequate level of protection or whether Article 8 of the Charter authorised the Commissioner to break free, if appropriate, from such a finding.

**Consideration of the questions referred**

[The Court acknowledged that the European Commission, by adopting Decision 2000/520, had acted under Article 25(6) to determine that the US had an "adequate level of protection" for data processing by companies within the Safe Harbor program. Because this decision had the force of EU law, it was "binding on all the Member States," and national DPAs could not "adopt measures contrary to that decision, such as acts intended to determine with binding effect that the third country covered by it does not ensure an adequate level of protection." However, the Court continued, individuals such as Schrems remain free to challenge the decision. When, as Schrems did, individuals "contest[ ] the compatibility of that decision with the protection of the privacy and of the fundamental rights and freedoms of individuals, it is incumbent upon the national supervisory authority to examine the claim with all due diligence."]

***The validity of Decision 2000/520***

67. Mr. Schrems contends in the main proceedings that United States law and practice do not ensure an adequate level of protection within the meaning of Article 25 of Directive 95/46. Mr. Schrems expresses doubts, which the referring court indeed seems essentially to share, concerning the validity of Decision 2000/520. In such circumstances, it should be examined whether that decision complies with the requirements stemming from Directive 95/46 read in the light of the Charter.

***The requirements stemming from Article 25(6) of Directive 95/46***

68. Article 25(1) of Directive 95/46 prohibits transfers of personal data to a third country not ensuring an adequate level of protection.

70. It is true that neither Article 25(2) of Directive 95/46 nor any other provision of the directive contains a definition of the concept of an adequate level of protection.

71. However, first, as is apparent from the very wording of Article 25(6) of Directive 95/46, that provision requires that a third country "ensures" an adequate level of protection by reason of its domestic law or its international commitments. Secondly, according to the same provision, the adequacy of the protection ensured by the third country is assessed "for the protection of the private lives and basic freedoms and rights of individuals."

72. Thus, Article 25(6) of Directive 95/46 implements the express obligation laid down in Article 8(1) of the Charter to protect personal data and is intended to ensure that the high level of that protection continues where personal data is transferred to a third country.

73. The word "adequate" in Article 25(6) of Directive 95/46 admittedly signifies that a third country cannot be required to ensure a level of protection identical to that guaranteed in the EU legal order. However, the term "adequate level of protection" must be understood as requiring the third country in fact to ensure, by reason of its domestic law or its international commitments, a level of protection of fundamental rights and freedoms that is essentially equivalent to that guaranteed within the European Union by virtue of Directive 95/46 read in the light of the Charter. If there were no such requirement, the objective referred to in the previous paragraph of the present judgment would be disregarded. Furthermore, the high level of protection guaranteed by Directive 95/46 read in the light of the Charter could easily be circumvented by transfers of personal data from the European Union to third countries for the purpose of being processed in those countries.

75. Accordingly, when examining the level of protection afforded by a third country, the Commission is obliged to assess the content of the applicable rules in that country resulting from its domestic law or international commitments and the practice designed to ensure compliance with those rules, since it must, under Article 25(2) of Directive 95/46, take account of all the circumstances surrounding a transfer of personal data to a third country.

76. Also, in the light of the fact that the level of protection ensured by a third country is liable to change, it is incumbent upon the Commission, after it has adopted a decision pursuant to Article 25(6) of Directive 95/46, to check periodically whether the finding relating to the adequacy of the level of protection ensured by the third country in question is still factually and legally justified. Such a check is required, in any event, when evidence gives rise to a doubt in that regard.

***Article 1 of Decision 2000/520***

80. An organisation adheres to the safe harbour principles on the basis of a system of self-certification.

81. Whilst recourse by a third country to a system of self-certification is not in itself contrary to the requirement laid down in Article 25(6) of Directive 95/46 that the third country concerned must ensure an adequate level of protection "by reason of its domestic law or . . . international commitments," the reliability of such a system, in the light of that requirement, is founded essentially on the establishment of effective detection and supervision mechanisms enabling any infringements of the rules ensuring the protection of fundamental rights, in particular the right to respect for private life and the right to protection of personal data, to be identified and punished in practice.

82. In the present instance, the safe harbour principles are "intended for use solely by US organisations receiving personal data from the European Union for the purpose of qualifying for the safe harbour and the presumption of 'adequacy' it creates." Those principles are therefore applicable solely to self-certified United States organisations receiving personal data from the European Union, and United States public authorities are not required to comply with them.

84. In addition, the applicability of the safe harbour principles may be limited, in particular, "to the extent necessary to meet national security, public interest, or law enforcement requirements" and "by statute, government regulation, or case-law that create conflicting obligations or explicit authorisations."

85. In this connection, Decision 2000/520 states, "[c]learly, where US law imposes a conflicting obligation, US organisations whether in the safe harbour or not must comply with the law."

86. Thus, Decision 2000/520 lays down that "national security, public interest, or law enforcement requirements" have primacy over the safe harbour principles, primacy pursuant to which self-certified United

States organisations receiving personal data from the European Union are bound to disregard those principles without limitation where they conflict with those requirements and therefore prove incompatible with them.

87. Decision 2000/520 thus enables interference, founded on national security and public interest requirements or on domestic legislation of the United States, with the fundamental rights of the persons whose personal data is or could be transferred from the European Union to the United States. To establish the existence of an interference with the fundamental right to respect for private life, it does not matter whether the information in question relating to private life is sensitive or whether the persons concerned have suffered any adverse consequences on account of that interference.

89. Nor does Decision 2000/520 refer to the existence of effective legal protection against interference of that kind. [P]rocedures before the Federal Trade Commission—the powers of which are limited to commercial disputes—and the private dispute resolution mechanisms concern compliance by [private organisations in the US] with the safe harbour principles and cannot be applied in disputes relating to the legality of interference with fundamental rights that results from measures originating from the State.

91. As regards the level of protection of fundamental rights and freedoms that is guaranteed within the European Union, EU legislation involving interference with the fundamental rights guaranteed by Articles 7 and 8 of the Charter must, according to the Court's settled case-law, lay down clear and precise rules governing the scope and application of a measure and imposing minimum safeguards, so that the persons whose personal data is concerned have sufficient guarantees enabling their data to be effectively protected against the risk of abuse and against any unlawful access and use of that data. The need for such safeguards is all the greater where personal data is subjected to automatic processing and where there is a significant risk of unlawful access to that data.

92. Furthermore and above all, protection of the fundamental right to respect for private life at EU level requires derogations and limitations in relation to the protection of personal data to apply only in so far as is strictly necessary.

94. [L]egislation permitting the public authorities to have access on a generalised basis to the content of electronic communications must be regarded as compromising the essence of the fundamental right to respect for private life, as guaranteed by Article 7 of the Charter.

95. Likewise, legislation not providing for any possibility for an individual to pursue legal remedies in order to have access to personal data relating to him, or to obtain the rectification or erasure of such data,

does not respect the essence of the fundamental right to effective judicial protection, as enshrined in Article 47 of the Charter.

98. Consequently, without there being any need to examine the content of the safe harbour principles, it is to be concluded that Article 1 of Decision 2000/520 fails to comply with the requirements laid down in Article 25(6) of Directive 95/46, read in the light of the Charter, and that it is accordingly invalid.

***Article 3 of Decision 2000/520***

100. [T]he first subparagraph of Article 3(1) of Decision 2000/520 lays down specific rules regarding the powers available to the national supervisory authorities in the light of a Commission finding relating to an adequate level of protection, within the meaning of Article 25 of Directive 95/46.

102. The first subparagraph of Article 3(1) of Decision 2000/520 must be understood as denying the national supervisory authorities the powers which they derive from Article 28 of Directive 95/46, where a person, in bringing a claim under that provision, puts forward matters that may call into question whether a Commission decision that has found, on the basis of Article 25(6) of the directive, that a third country ensures an adequate level of protection is compatible with the protection of the privacy and of the fundamental rights and freedoms of individuals.

103. The implementing power granted by the EU legislature to the Commission in Article 25(6) of Directive 95/46 does not confer upon it competence to restrict the national supervisory authorities' powers referred to in the previous paragraph.

104. That being so, it must be held that, in adopting Article 3 of Decision 2000/520, the Commission exceeded the power which is conferred upon it in Article 25(6) of Directive 95/46, read in the light of the Charter, and that Article 3 of the decision is therefore invalid.

105. As Articles 1 and 3 of Decision 2000/520 are inseparable from Articles 2 and 4 of that decision and the annexes thereto, their invalidity affects the validity of the decision in its entirety.

106. Having regard to all the foregoing considerations, it is to be concluded that Decision 2000/520 is invalid.

## NOTES

1. ***Procedural Posture.*** Be sure you understand where this case came from. Schrems filed a complaint with Ireland's ODPC about transatlantic data transfers by Facebook-Ireland, but the ODPC determined that national DPAs were bound to accept the Safe Harbor Agreement. (This can be compared in some ways—but not all—to a situation where US federal law preempts state law.) Schrems appealed that decision to an Irish court, which made some comments sympathetic to his claims but also suggested that the ODPC might be correct that it was required to defer to the European

Commission's adoption of the Safe Harbor Agreement. The Irish court then referred that specific question to EU courts.

2. ***Reasoning.*** There are actually two key determinations in *Schrems*. The first concerns the power and responsibilities of a national DPA and the judicial recourse available to a citizen. The CJEU agrees that the ODPC was bound by the European Commission's Safe Harbor decision, but also finds that this obligation does not eliminate a DPA's obligation to investigate citizen complaints. The Data Protection Directive requires DPAs to act on complaints and, at the end of its opinion, the court says that the Commission lacks any authority to say otherwise. The second decision comes when the CJEU—which, unlike Irish regulators or courts, *does* have the power to strike down Commission actions—invalidates the Commission's decision. (American readers can compare this decision to a US court's invalidation of agency regulations for exceeding the authority Congress granted to the agency in the underlying statute, although once again the resemblance is not complete.) The CJEU rests this second decision largely on the primacy of data protection rights guaranteed by the EU Charter. Even without considering the substance of the Safe Harbor Principles, the court says, it is clear that they constrain only private entities, not the US government. This alone is enough to prevent an effective "adequacy" determination. In paragraphs 75 and 76, the court also derives from the text of the Directive the requirements that adequacy determinations account for all the circumstances and remain open for reevaluation as those circumstances change. According to the CJEU, the Commission's one-time adoption of the Safe Harbor Agreement, and failure to revisit it, violated those provisions.

3. ***Remand.*** Having found the European Commission's decision invalid, the CJEU had answered the Irish High Court's questions. That sends the case back to the Irish courts for further proceedings. The ODPC has already announced that it will investigate Schrems' complaint in light of the CJEU ruling.

4. ***Impact.*** The disruptions caused by the ruling have not yet played out fully as of this writing in early 2016. Negotiators unveiled a new "EU-US Privacy Shield" arrangement, but details were still being worked out. As part of the deal, the US Director of National Intelligence formally pledged that American intelligence would gather EU persons' data only in certain pre-defined circumstances. As another precursor to an agreement, Congress passed and President Obama signed the Judicial Redress Act, P.L. 114–126 (2016), which in some circumstances allows EU citizens to bring claims in US courts alleging that the federal government's handling of their personal data violated the Privacy Act [see Chapter 10]. Despite all this activity, some observers believe the logic of *Schrems* makes it difficult to imagine the CJEU accepting any new agreement that gives the US government as much scope to gather EU persons' data as the Privacy Shield appears to allow. Schrems himself, and many other privacy advocates, have assailed the direction of the Privacy Shield negotations as a mere retread of the Safe Harbor. Meanwhile, some European data protection regulators are already preparing to penalize companies for data transfers that violate the Directive. How would you

advise a US company that wanted to transfer personal data from the EU to the US in the face of this uncertainty?

5. ***Territoriality and Transfers.*** The recent ruling in *Google Spain SL v. AEPD*, 2014 E.C.R. 317 [Chapter 4] read the territorial scope of the Data Protection Directive broadly. How does *Google Spain* interact with *Schrems*? Under *Google Spain*, surely activities of many companies would already be covered by EU law directly because of their activities in Europe. Does that mean transatlantic transfers matter only for data processors with minimal presence in the EU?

6. ***Leaving the Adequacy Question Open.*** Another impediment to replacing the Safe Harbor Agreement arises from the *Schrems* court's conclusion that adequacy determinations must be revisited periodically. A transfer mechanism constantly subject to revocation by EU authorities does not do very much to give assurance to companies as they transfer data across borders. The *Schrems* court also said that adequacy should be checked whenever facts arise calling it into question. If that is the rule, then if a development like the Snowden revelations occurred during the term of an agreement, the Commission would be obliged to reevaluate and possibly revoke the adequacy determination at that time, rather than waiting for the deal to expire. For that matter, some observers—including federal and state DPAs in Germany—have suggested that the obligation to reevaluate that was articulated in *Schrems* logically must apply to model contract clauses and even BCRs as well. In that case, companies may find they are better off trying to come into decent compliance with EU law rather than depending on a potentially unreliable transfer mechanism.

## C. DISCLOSURES GOVERNED BY CONTRACT

Agreements accompanying the transfer of information are woven throughout the law: contracts related to employee handling of trade secrets, nondisclosure agreements signed before businesses can discuss an acquisition, confidential settlements in litigation, duties of confidentiality undertaken by lawyers and doctors, and the list goes on. Lawyers drafting such agreements for daily use by companies must keep numerous considerations and contingencies in mind. The following excerpts consider one of the most important types of contract in privacy and data protection law: agreements between an organization and the third party vendors that will store their data, process it, or provide subcontracted services using it.

### Governing Information With Vendors—Contracting with Service Providers from Leslie T. Thornton & Edward R. McNicholas

5 Successful Partnering Between Inside and Outside Counsel § 82.17 (2015)

Companies that use third-party service providers for data related services must rely on effective contracting practices to control how the company's data is used, accessed, and protected because the company generally retains its legal obligation to comply with privacy and data security laws even though it has outsourced related activities to a cloud provider or other third-party vendor.

In-house counsel should appreciate that transferring data to a third-party vendor necessarily requires that the company relinquish some degree of control over the fate of its data unless it is willing to pay extra for more customized treatment. Vendors vary widely in this rapidly evolving area, and not all companies are as reputable or advanced as others. Some are likely to have hired employees without conducting sufficient background checks, inadvertently giving access to persons who could perpetuate a breach.

Many third parties attempt to force a "one-size-fits-all" approach to privacy and security through the provision of standard terms and conditions of service that frequently provide only a general outline of the services provided, limit warranties and indemnities, and shift the risks to customers. It would be a serious mistake to simply accept these contracts as offered. Companies must ensure that their contracts with providers accomplish the following important goals. First, your company should, to the extent possible, retain control over, and access to, its information. Vendors should identify where data will be stored and transferred. If necessary, companies should contractually limit vendor activities to certain geographic locations in order to control and minimize regulatory exposure arising from cross border information flows. Companies should also require that vendors (i) provide authorized employees of the company access to data both during the ordinary course of business and for purposes of discovery during the course of litigation, investigations or other similar circumstances; (ii) implement and adhere to your company's existing data-retention and back-up policies; (iii) establish protocols that will be used to return the company's data upon the dissolution of the vendor relationship or transfer it to a new vendor; and (iv) provide for the access and preservation of your company's data in the event of the vendor's bankruptcy or termination of its operations.

Second, your company should contract for required service levels and obtain confirmation that vendors will provide a continuity of service during outages, and comply with applicable laws and industry best practices. It is also important that the contract's terms do not shift obligations by holding companies contractually accountable for future, undefined amendments to the provider's internal policies or to the terms and conditions of the service contract.

As noted above, companies that rely on third-party vendors retain legal responsibility for how the company's data are used, disclosed and safeguarded. As a result, contracts must constrain the vendor's ability to access, use or disclose data in any way other than expressly provided for by the contract. For example, a company could require a confidentiality clause that limits data access to authorized personnel for authorized purposes and sets forth encryption and other information security requirements. The contract should also require that the vendor implement and adhere to sufficient data security measures that satisfy your company's legal obligations. Importantly, vendors must be obligated to monitor and provide notice of possible data breaches. The obligations of each party when responding to a data breach should be clearly set out to the vendor, including obligations to obtain insurance coverage for such incidents.

Vendors should not be given blanket consent to intercept or disclose corporate data in response to government requests, legal process, or other third-party requests. The agreement should protect a company's privileges and ensure that the company is made aware of any third-party requests. Finally, it is very important that the vendor contract does not agree to disclaimers or limitations on the vendor's liability that would undermine your company's ability to pursue recoveries following data incidents or the failure to comply with data privacy requirements.

## David Katz, Contracting in a World of Data Breaches and Insecurity: Managing Third-Party Vendor Engagements

LexisNexis Corporate Law Advisory (May 2, 2013)

The ultimate goal of a functioning [third party vendor management] program is to appropriately identify and mitigate the risk of exposure that exists as a result of the engagement of a third-party vendor that may receive or access the organization's data. This exposure could be as broad as a full-blown data breach requiring mass notifications or as limited as any other unauthorized access or disclosure of the organization's data

### The Case for Vendor Management

As organizations begin to examine and weigh the risks associated with a failure to fully identify and appropriately vet either new or existing vendors that may be receiving or accessing confidential corporate data, customer or employee data that is Personally Identifiable Information (PII), one can imagine the steady increase in the anxiety level among privacy, information assurance, risk management and legal professionals leading the organization. Given the legal and regulatory environment which currently exists for organizations that may have suffered a data breach, it is critical that the flow of and access to data be closely scrutinized prior to the release of, or granting access to, the organization's data. Even more critical is that the appropriate due diligence measures are established by clear policies, specific and detailed standards, and that these policies and standards are enforced. Finally, insistence on adherence to these policies and standards along with a robust program of review and oversight must be clearly communicated from the top down. To the extent that companies fail to conduct their own due diligence and make a careful record of that process, they operate in an environment which could potentially expose the organization.

## What is Vendor Management?

Vendor management is a multi-functional process involving elements of IT, Information Assurance, Legal, Compliance, Risk Management and the Internal Business Owner. In short, these parties are working in concert in an attempt to identify and mitigate the potential risks created by engaging a third-party vendor that may have access to or receive data from the organization. As the risk landscape and regulatory environment continue to evolve, these elements must work in unison to create a process that is properly calibrated to the organization to credibly, methodically and defensibly identify and determine an acceptable level of risk to the organization. Only through mutual cooperation and alignment of these individual business units can this process properly function.

## What Are the Risks?

The risks of failure to establish an appropriately scoped program are potential loss of ownership rights to the organization's data, lack of data security, lack of data privacy protections and controls, loss of data backup and recovery, inappropriate or incomplete incident response, failure to notify of data loss or data breach, brand erosion or collapse, loss of shareholder confidence, increased regulatory scrutiny or action and potential class action litigation.

## The Legal Perspective to Protecting Data: Key Contractual Components

This list is not exhaustive and the contractual language needs to be specifically tailored after a comprehensive risk assessment. The purpose of providing these elements is solely to identify the core elements that should be a starting point as part of the negotiations with the third-party vendor.

**1) Qualified Counsel & Clear Definitions.** The organization must engage qualified counsel to draft the appropriate provisions specific to the transaction. These elements can be included as part of the original agreement or as part of an addendum or amendment to an existing agreement. The key elements of the essential contractual provisions should focus on providing a clear definition of personal information.

**2) Vendor Compliance.** The organization should, at a minimum, require the third-party vendor to represent and warrant compliance with all applicable federal, state and local laws, rules and regulations that pertain to the possession or use of personal information. The language should require the third-party vendor to comply with the organization's privacy and information assurance policies and the organization's notice of privacy practices.

**3) Security Programs.** The third-party vendor should be required to maintain to the extent feasible its own privacy and information security program, and conduct regular risk assessments of its security and information assurance practices. There should be a very clear requirement that the third-party vendor provide notification of a privacy or information assurance event and require the third-party vendor to take immediate steps to the extent possible to immediately address the event.

**4) Audits.** The organization should insist on audit rights and insist on the right to hire third parties if necessary to conduct the audits.

**5) Safeguards.** Organizations should require by contract that their vendors warrant they are capable of maintaining appropriate safeguards for the organization's data.

**6) Indemnification.** Third-party vendors should be capable of providing broad based indemnification for their failure to comply with applicable privacy laws, for loss of the organization's data, for negligence, gross negligence or bad faith, or any security breach involving the organization's data.

**7) Confidentiality.** Finally, the organization should require a confidentiality provision ensuring adequate protection of the organization's data. There should be specific provisions to address protection, destruction and return upon conclusion of the agreement.

## NOTES

1. ***An Ounce of Prevention***. Third party vendor management programs require a great deal of effort, thought, and time to manage properly. Many privacy lawyers spend a large portion of their day overseeing such agreements precisely because of their importance and complexity. As the famous aphorism by Benjamin Franklin reminds us, "An ounce of prevention is worth a pound of cure." By establishing policies and systems in advance, organizations can reduce the likelihood of later problems that might carry the risk of legal liability (and other forms of harm, such as reputational injury). Those efforts include management of internal policies through assessment of practices, employee training, and internal compliance audits. But as increasing amounts of personal data leave the direct control of the organization, contractual arrangements are an integral part of the task as well.

2. ***Statutory Contracting Requirements.*** In certain areas of the law, contracts covering the transfer of data are required by law. For example, the Health Insurance Portability and Accountability Act (HIPAA) mandates that entities covered by the law, including most medical providers and health insurers, must enter into "business associate agreements" with any entity to which they transfer most types of records about patients [see Chapter 12]. Federal regulations promulgated under HIPAA also specify numerous terms that must be included in such agreements, including listing methods the third-party business associate will use to secure the information, prohibiting unauthorized further disclosure, and identifying protocols to follow if a data breach occurs. What are the advantages and disadvantages of such regulatory requirements? Why are such rules imposed on certain industries

like health care in the US and not more broadly on all third-party vendor relationships?

3. ***Non-Disclosure Agreements.*** Another contract companies often enter into when they reveal information to other parties is the non-disclosure agreement (NDA). As the name suggests, an NDA prevents one party from revealing key information about the other party—including trade secrets, proprietary information, or performance statistics. It is often used when companies are contemplating entering into some business transaction—for example a joint venture, an asset sale, or a merger. Company A may need to learn more about the operations of Company Z before agreeing to such a deal, but Company Z needs to protect certain types of information from wider disclosure—and also from misuse by Company A if the potential deal does not come to fruition. An NDA may limit the people within Company A who may have access to information, and prohibit those people from disclosing it further or using it for other purposes. Sometimes such an NDA may even require that information is viewed only by third parties (like lawyers and investment bankers) who are advising Company A about the transaction. Large entities also enter into NDAs with individuals. Visitors to a factory may be required to sign NDAs to prevent them from revealing information about what they see. Employees of a firm, as well as its consultants and even job applicants, may be asked to sign confidentiality agreements of this type as a condition of continuing to interact with the company. Often the information covered by an NDA may include personal information about customers, employees, or other individuals, but NDAs cover much more than privacy protection. Non-disclosure agreements can be unilateral, where only one party is prevented from disclosing information about the other, or bilateral, where the prohibition applies to both parties.

4. ***Contracting with Cloud Service Providers.*** Modern technology, particularly the "software as service" model of cloud computing, has increased the need for third party vendor contracts for entities of all sizes, from Fortune 500 companies to small businesses to nonprofit groups. Personal data that once would have been stored in the organization's file cabinets, and more recently on its own computer servers, now gets sent to cloud storage providers. Major technology companies such as Amazon, Google, and Microsoft, as well as specialist providers such as Dropbox, Rackspace, and Box, all compete to provide this service. Just as individuals' use of cloud storage complicates constitutional provisions such as the third party doctrine [see Chapter 1], this technological shift has disrupted preexisting legal rules in other areas. Many data flows that once would have stopped at the "storage" phase in the life cycle now proceed to the "disclosure" phase, as the entity that originally collected data transfers it to a new entity that provides storage. Can contracts address all the risks created by these extra data flows? Does consumer protection law need to intervene as well? *See* Daniel J. Solove & Woodrow Hartzog, *The FTC and Privacy and Security Duties for the Cloud*, 13 BNA PRIVACY & SECURITY LAW REPORT 577 (2014).

## D. SPEECH PROTECTIONS FOR DISCLOSURES

Disclosures of private information are instances of speech, and consequently they may be protected by the First Amendment. We have seen this tension before, most obviously in the privacy torts [see Chapter 2]. Challenges to all sorts of privacy statutes and regulations rely on the argument that they violate the First Amendment. As the cases excerpted here demonstrate, courts struggle with analysis of this theory.

### 1. MATTERS OF PUBLIC CONCERN AND THE FIRST AMENDMENT

## Cohen v. Cowles Media Co.

501 U.S. 663 (1991)

■ JUSTICE WHITE delivered the opinion of the Court.

The question before us is whether the First Amendment prohibits a plaintiff from recovering damages, under state promissory estoppel law, for a newspaper's breach of a promise of confidentiality given to the plaintiff in exchange for information. We hold that it does not.

During the closing days of the 1982 Minnesota gubernatorial race, Dan Cohen, an active Republican associated with Wheelock Whitney's Independent-Republican gubernatorial campaign, approached reporters from the St. Paul Pioneer Press Dispatch (Pioneer Press) and the Minneapolis Star and Tribune (Star Tribune) and offered to provide documents relating to a candidate in the upcoming election. Cohen made clear to the reporters that he would provide the information only if he was given a promise of confidentiality. Reporters from both papers promised to keep Cohen's identity anonymous, and Cohen turned over copies of two public court records concerning Marlene Johnson, the Democratic-Farmer-Labor candidate for Lieutenant Governor. The first record indicated that Johnson had been charged in 1969 with three counts of unlawful assembly, and the second that she had been convicted in 1970 of petit theft. Both newspapers interviewed Johnson for her explanation, and one reporter tracked down the person who had found the records for Cohen. As it turned out, the unlawful assembly charges arose out of Johnson's participation in a protest of an alleged failure to hire minority workers on municipal construction projects, and the charges were eventually dismissed. The petit theft conviction was for leaving a store without paying for $6.00 worth of sewing materials. The incident apparently occurred at a time during which Johnson was emotionally distraught, and the conviction was later vacated.

After consultation and debate, the editorial staffs of the two newspapers independently decided to publish Cohen's name as part of their stories concerning Johnson. In their stories, both papers identified Cohen as the source of the court records, indicated his connection to the Whitney campaign, and included denials by Whitney campaign officials of any role in the matter. The same day the stories appeared, Cohen was fired by his employer.

Cohen sued respondents, the publishers of the Pioneer Press and Star Tribune, in Minnesota state court, alleging fraudulent misrepresentation and breach of contract. The trial court rejected respondents' argument that the First Amendment barred Cohen's lawsuit. A jury returned a verdict in Cohen's favor. [On appeal, the Minnesota Court of Appeals reversed the fraud verdict. The Minnesota Supreme Court found that the only claim available was based on promissory estoppel, and that "enforcement of the promise of confidentiality under a promissory estoppel theory would violate defendants' First Amendment rights."]

Respondents rely on the proposition that, "if a newspaper lawfully obtains truthful information about a matter of public significance, then state officials may not constitutionally punish publication of the information, absent a need to further a state interest of the highest order. *Smith v. Daily Mail Publishing Co.*, 443 U.S. 97, 103 (1979). That proposition is unexceptionable, and it has been applied in various cases that have found insufficient the asserted state interests in preventing publication of truthful, lawfully obtained information.

This case[,] however, is not controlled by this line of cases but rather by the equally well-established line of decisions holding that generally applicable laws do not offend the First Amendment simply because their enforcement against the press has incidental effects on its ability to gather and report the news. As the cases relied on by respondents recognize, the truthful information sought to be published must have been lawfully acquired. The press may not with impunity break and enter an office or dwelling to gather news. Neither does the First Amendment relieve a newspaper reporter of the obligation shared by all citizens to respond to a grand jury subpoena and answer questions relevant to a criminal investigation, even though the reporter might be required to reveal a confidential source. *Branzburg v. Hayes*, 408 U.S. 665 (1972). The press, like others interested in publishing, may not publish copyrighted material without obeying the copyright laws. *See Zacchini v. Scripps-Howard Broadcasting Co.*, 433 U.S. 562, 576–579 (1977). Similarly, the media must obey the National Labor Relations Act, *Associated Press v. NLRB*, 301 U.S. 103 (1937), and the Fair Labor Standards Act, *Oklahoma Press Publishing Co. v. Walling*, 327 U.S. 186, 192–193 (1946); may not restrain trade in violation of the antitrust laws, *Associated Press v. United States*, 326 U.S. 1 (1945); *Citizen Publishing Co. v. United States*, 394 U.S. 131, 139 (1969); and must pay nondiscriminatory taxes. *Murdock v. Pennsylvania*, 319 U.S. 105, 112 (1943); *Minneapolis Star and Tribune Co. v. Minnesota Commissioner of Revenue*, 460 U.S. 575, 581–583 (1983). It is therefore beyond dispute that "[t]he publisher of a newspaper has no special immunity from the application of general laws. He has no special privilege to invade the rights and liberties of others." *Associated Press v. NLRB*, 301 U.S. at 132–133. Accordingly, enforcement of such general laws against the press is not subject to stricter scrutiny than would be applied to enforcement against other persons or organizations.

There can be little doubt that the Minnesota doctrine of promissory estoppel is a law of general applicability. It does not target or single out the press. Rather, insofar as we are advised, the doctrine is generally applicable to the daily transactions of all the citizens of Minnesota. The First Amendment does not forbid its application to the press.

Justice Blackmun suggests [in his dissent] that applying Minnesota promissory estoppel doctrine in this case will "punish" Respondents for publishing truthful information that was lawfully obtained. This is not strictly accurate, because compensatory damages are not a form of punishment, as were the criminal sanctions at issue in *Smith*. In any event, as indicated above, the characterization of the payment makes no difference for First Amendment purposes when the law being applied is a general law, and does not single out the press. Moreover, Justice Blackmun's reliance on cases like [*Daily Mail*] is misplaced. In those cases, the State itself defined the content of publications that would trigger liability. Here, by contrast, Minnesota law simply requires those making promises to keep them. The parties themselves, as in this case, determine the scope of their legal obligations, and any restrictions which may be placed on the publication of truthful information are self-imposed.

Also, it is not at all clear that Respondents obtained Cohen's name "lawfully" in this case, at least for purposes of publishing it. Unlike the situation in [*Florida Star v. B.J.F.*, 491 U.S. 524, 532 (1989)], where the rape victim's name was obtained through lawful access to a police report, respondents obtained Cohen's name only by making a promise which they did not honor. The dissenting opinions suggest that the press should not be subject to any law, including copyright law for example, which in any fashion or to any degree limits or restricts the press' right to report truthful information. The First Amendment does not grant the press such limitless protection.

Nor is Cohen attempting to use a promissory estoppel cause of action to avoid the strict requirements for establishing a libel or defamation claim. Thus, this is not a case like *Hustler Magazine, Inc. v. Falwell*, 485 U.S. 46 (1988), where we held that the constitutional libel standards apply to a claim alleging that the publication of a parody was a state law tort of intentional infliction of emotional distress.

Respondents and amici argue that permitting Cohen to maintain a cause of action for promissory estoppel will inhibit truthful reporting because news organizations will have legal incentives not to disclose a confidential source's identity even when that person's identity is itself newsworthy. Justice Souter makes a similar argument [in his dissent]. But if this is the case, it is no more than the incidental, and constitutionally insignificant, consequence of applying to the press a generally applicable law that requires those who make certain kinds of promises to keep them. Accordingly, the judgment of the Minnesota Supreme Court is reversed, and the case is remanded for further proceedings not inconsistent with this opinion.

■ JUSTICE BLACKMUN, with whom JUSTICE MARSHALL and JUSTICE SOUTER join, dissenting.

I do not read the decision of the Supreme Court of Minnesota to create any exception to or immunity from the laws of that State for members of the press. In my view, the court's decision is premised not on the identity of the speaker, but on the speech itself.

Contrary to the majority, I regard our decision in *Hustler Magazine, Inc. v. Falwell* to be precisely on point. There, we found that the use of a claim of intentional infliction of emotional distress to impose liability for the publication of a satirical critique violated the First Amendment. There was no doubt that Virginia's tort of intentional infliction of emotional distress was "a law of general applicability" unrelated to the suppression of speech. Nonetheless, a unanimous Court found that, when used to penalize the expression of opinion, the law was subject to the strictures of the First Amendment. In applying that principle, we concluded that [the "actual malice" standard applied to the case].

As in *Hustler*, the operation of Minnesota's doctrine of promissory estoppel in this case cannot be said to have a merely "incidental" burden on speech; the publication of important political speech is the claimed violation. Thus, as in *Hustler*, the law may not be enforced to punish the expression of truthful information or opinion. In the instant case, it is undisputed that the publication at issue was true.

To the extent that truthful speech may ever be sanctioned consistent with the First Amendment, it must be in furtherance of a state interest "of the highest order." Because the Minnesota Supreme Court's opinion makes clear that the State's interest in enforcing its promissory estoppel doctrine in this case was far from compelling, I would affirm that court's decision.

I respectfully dissent.

■ JUSTICE SOUTER, with whom JUSTICE MARSHALL, JUSTICE BLACKMUN and JUSTICE O'CONNOR join, dissenting.

I agree with Justice Blackmun that this case does not fall within the line of authority holding the press to laws of general applicability where commercial activities and relationships, not the content of publication, are at issue. Even such general laws as do entail effects on the content of speech, like the one in question, may of course be found constitutional, but only, as Justice Harlan observed, "when [such effects] have been justified by subordinating valid governmental interests, a prerequisite to constitutionality which has necessarily involved a weighing of the governmental interest involved." *Konigsberg v. State Bar of California*,

366 U.S. 36, 51 (1961). Because I do not believe the fact of general applicability to be dispositive, I find it necessary to articulate, measure, and compare the competing interests involved in any given case to determine the legitimacy of burdening constitutional interests, and such has been the Court's recent practice in publication cases. *See Hustler Magazine, Inc. v. Falwell*, 485 U.S. 46 (1988); *Zacchini v. Scripps-Howard Broadcasting Co.*, 433 U.S. 562 (1977).

Nor can I accept the majority's position that we may dispense with balancing because the burden on publication is in a sense "self-imposed" by the newspaper's voluntary promise of confidentiality. This suggests both the possibility of waiver, the requirements for which have not been met here, as well as a conception of First Amendment rights as those of the speaker alone, with a value that may be measured without reference to the importance of the information to public discourse. But freedom of the press is ultimately founded on the value of enhancing such discourse for the sake of a citizenry better informed, and thus more prudently self-governed.

The importance of this public interest is integral to the balance that should be struck in this case. There can be no doubt that the fact of Cohen's identity expanded the universe of information relevant to the choice faced by Minnesota voters in that State's 1982 gubernatorial election, the publication of which was thus of the sort quintessentially subject to strict First Amendment protection. The propriety of his leak to respondents could be taken to reflect on his character, which in turn could be taken to reflect on the character of the candidate who had retained him as an adviser. An election could turn on just such a factor; if it should, I am ready to assume that it would be to the greater public good, at least over the long run.

This is not to say that the breach of such a promise of confidentiality could never give rise to liability. One can conceive of situations in which the injured party is a private individual, whose identity is of less public concern than that of the petitioner; liability there might not be constitutionally prohibited. Nor do I mean to imply that the circumstances of acquisition are irrelevant to the balance, although they may go only to what balances against, and not to diminish, the First Amendment value of any particular piece of information.

Because I believe the State's interest in enforcing a newspaper's promise of confidentiality insufficient to outweigh the interest in unfettered publication of the information revealed in this case, I respectfully dissent.

## Bartnicki v. Vopper

532 U.S. 514 (2001)

■ JUSTICE STEVENS delivered the opinion of the Court.

These cases raise an important question concerning what degree of protection, if any, the First Amendment provides to speech that discloses the contents of an illegally intercepted communication. That question is both novel and narrow. Despite the fact that federal law has prohibited such disclosures since 1934, this is the first time that we have confronted such an issue.

The suit at hand involves the repeated intentional disclosure of an illegally intercepted cellular telephone conversation about a public issue. The persons who made the disclosures did not participate in the interception, but they did know—or at least had reason to know—that the interception was unlawful. Accordingly, these cases present a conflict between interests of the highest order—on the one hand, the interest in the full and free dissemination of information concerning public issues, and, on the other hand, the interest in individual privacy and, more specifically, in fostering private speech. The Framers of the First Amendment surely did not foresee the advances in science that produced the conversation, the interception, or the conflict that gave rise to this action. It is therefore not surprising that Circuit judges, as well as the Members of this Court, have come to differing conclusions about the First Amendment's application to this issue. Nevertheless, having considered the interests at stake, we are firmly convinced that the disclosures made by respondents in this suit are protected by the First Amendment.

### I

During 1992 and most of 1993, the Pennsylvania State Education Association, a union representing the teachers at the Wyoming Valley West High School, engaged in collective-bargaining negotiations with the school board. Petitioner Kane, then the president of the local union, testified that the negotiations were "contentious" and received "a lot of media attention." In May 1993, petitioner Bartnicki, who was acting as the union's "chief negotiator," used the cellular phone in her car to call Kane and engage in a lengthy conversation about the status of the negotiations. An unidentified person intercepted and recorded that call.

In their conversation, Kane and Bartnicki discussed the timing of a proposed strike, difficulties created by public comment on the negotiations, and the need for a dramatic response to the board's intransigence. At one point, Kane said: "If they're not gonna move for three percent, we're gonna have to go to their, their homes. . . . To blow off their front porches, we'll have to do some work on some of those guys. (PAUSES). Really, uh, really and truthfully because this is, you know, this is bad news. (UNDECIPHERABLE)."

In the early fall of 1993, the parties accepted a nonbinding arbitration proposal that was generally favorable to the teachers. In connection with news reports about the settlement, respondent Vopper, a radio commentator who had been critical of the union in the past, played a tape of the intercepted conversation on his public affairs talk show. Another station also broadcast the tape, and local newspapers published its contents. After filing suit against Vopper and other representatives of the media, Bartnicki and Kane (hereinafter petitioners) learned through discovery that Vopper had obtained the tape from respondent Jack Yocum, the head of a local taxpayers' organization that had opposed the union's demands throughout the negotiations. Yocum, who was added as a defendant, testified that he had found the tape in his mailbox shortly after the interception and recognized the voices of Bartnicki and Kane. Yocum played the tape for some members of the school board, and later delivered the tape itself to Vopper.

## II

In their amended complaint, petitioners alleged that their telephone conversation had been surreptitiously intercepted by an unknown person using an electronic device, that Yocum had obtained a tape of that conversation, and that he intentionally disclosed it to Vopper, as well as other individuals and media representatives. Thereafter, Vopper and other members of the media repeatedly published the contents of that conversation. The amended complaint alleged that each of the defendants "knew or had reason to know" that the recording of the private telephone conversation had been obtained by means of an illegal interception. Relying on both federal and Pennsylvania statutory provisions, petitioners sought actual damages, statutory damages, punitive damages, and attorney's fees and costs.

[The district court denied cross-motions for summary judgment, including a motion by defendants that their disclosures were protected by the First Amendment, but allowed an interlocutory appeal.] All three members of the [appeals court] panel agreed with petitioners and the Government that the federal and Pennsylvania wiretapping statutes are "content-neutral" and therefore subject to "intermediate scrutiny." Applying that standard, the majority concluded that the statutes were invalid because they deterred significantly more speech than necessary to protect the privacy interests at stake. The court remanded the case with instructions to enter summary judgment for respondents. In dissent, Senior Judge Pollak expressed the view that the prohibition against disclosures was necessary in order to remove the incentive for illegal interceptions and to preclude compounding the harm caused by such interceptions through wider dissemination. In so doing, he agreed with the majority opinion in a similar case decided by the Court of Appeals for the District of Columbia, *Boehner v. McDermott*, 191 F.3d 463 (D.C. Cir. 1999). We granted certiorari to resolve the conflict.

### III

One of the stated purposes of [the Wiretap Act, part of the Electronic Communications Privacy Act] [see Chapter 5] was "to protect effectively the privacy of wire and oral communications." In addition to authorizing and regulating electronic surveillance for law enforcement purposes, [the statute] also regulated private conduct. One part of those regulations, § 2511(1), defined five offenses punishable by a fine of not more than $10,000, by imprisonment for not more than five years, or by both. The provision most directly at issue in this suit applied to any person who "willfully discloses, or endeavors to disclose, to any other person the contents of any wire or oral communication, knowing or having reason to know that the information was obtained through the interception of a wire or oral communication in violation of this subsection."

### IV

The constitutional question before us concerns the validity of the statutes as applied to the specific facts of these cases. Because of the procedural posture of these cases, it is appropriate to make certain important assumptions about those facts. We accept petitioners' submission that the interception was intentional, and therefore unlawful, and that, at a minimum, respondents "had reason to know" that it was unlawful. Accordingly, the disclosure of the contents of the intercepted conversation by Yocum to school board members and to representatives of the media, as well as the subsequent disclosures by the media defendants to the public, violated the federal and state statutes. Under the provisions of the federal statute, as well as its Pennsylvania analogue, petitioners are thus entitled to recover damages from each of the respondents. The only question is whether the application of these statutes in such circumstances violates the First Amendment.

In answering that question, we accept respondents' submission on three factual matters that serve to distinguish most of the cases that have arisen under § 2511. First, respondents played no part in the illegal interception. Rather, they found out about the interception only after it occurred, and in fact never learned the identity of the person or persons who made the interception. Second, their access to the information on the tapes was obtained lawfully, even though the information itself was intercepted unlawfully by someone else. Third, the subject matter of the conversation was a matter of public concern. If the statements about the labor negotiations had been made in a public arena—during a bargaining session, for example—they would have been newsworthy. This would also be true if a third party had inadvertently overheard Bartnicki making the same statements to Kane when the two thought they were alone.

### V

We agree with petitioners that § 2511(1)(c), as well as its Pennsylvania analog[ue], is in fact a content-neutral law of general applicability. In determining whether a regulation is content based or content neutral, we look to the purpose behind the regulation; typically, government regulation of expressive activity is content neutral so long as it is justified without reference to the content of the regulated speech.

The statute does not distinguish based on the content of the intercepted conversations, nor is it justified by reference to the content of those conversations. Rather, the communications at issue are singled out by virtue of the fact that they were illegally intercepted—by virtue of the source, rather than the subject matter.

On the other hand, the naked prohibition against disclosures is fairly characterized as a regulation of pure speech. Unlike the prohibition against the "use" of the contents of an illegal interception in § 2511(1)(d), subsection (c) is not a regulation of conduct. It is true that the delivery of a tape recording might be regarded as conduct, but given that the purpose of such a delivery is to provide the recipient with the text of recorded statements, it is like the delivery of a handbill or a pamphlet, and as such, it is the kind of "speech" that the First Amendment protects.

### VI

As a general matter, "state action to punish the publication of truthful information seldom can satisfy constitutional standards." *Smith v. Daily Mail Publishing Co.*, 443 U.S. 97, 102 (1979). More specifically, this Court has repeatedly held that "if a newspaper lawfully obtains truthful information about a matter of public significance then state officials may not constitutionally punish publication of the information, absent a need . . . of the highest order." *Id.* at 103.

Accordingly, in *New York Times Co. v. United States*, 403 U.S. 713 (1971) (per curiam), the Court upheld the right of the press to publish information of great public concern obtained from documents stolen by a third party.

[*Daily Mail* and *New York Times*] raised, but did not resolve, the question "whether, in cases where information has been acquired unlawfully by a newspaper or by a source, government may ever punish not only the unlawful acquisition, but the ensuing publication as well." The question here, however, is a narrower version of that still-open question. Simply put, the issue here is this: Where the punished publisher of information has obtained the information in question in a manner lawful in itself but from a source who has obtained it unlawfully, may the government punish the ensuing publication of that information based on the defect in a chain?

The Government identifies two interests served by the statute—first, the interest in removing an incentive for parties to intercept private conversations, and second, the interest in minimizing the harm to persons whose conversations have been illegally intercepted.

Although this suit demonstrates that there may be an occasional situation in which an anonymous scanner will risk criminal prosecution by passing on information without any expectation of financial reward or public praise, surely this is the exceptional case. The justification for any such novel burden on expression must be far stronger than mere speculation about serious harms. Accordingly, the Government's first suggested justification for applying § 2511(1)(c) to an otherwise innocent disclosure of public information is plainly insufficient.

The Government's second argument, however, is considerably stronger. Privacy of communication is an important interest and Title III's restrictions are intended to protect that interest, thereby encouraging the uninhibited exchange of ideas and information among private parties. Moreover, the fear of public disclosure of private conversations might well have a chilling effect on private speech.

We need not decide whether that interest is strong enough to justify the application of § 2511(c) to disclosures of trade secrets or domestic gossip or other information of purely private concern. In other words, the outcome of these cases does not turn on whether § 2511(1)(c) may be enforced with respect to most violations of the statute without offending the First Amendment. The enforcement of that provision in these cases, however, implicates the core purposes of the First Amendment because it imposes sanctions on the publication of truthful information of public concern.

In these cases, privacy concerns give way when balanced against the interest in publishing matters of public importance. As Warren and Brandeis stated in their classic law review article: "The right of privacy does not prohibit any publication of matter which is of public or general interest." *The Right to Privacy*, 4 HARV. L. REV. 193, 214 (1890). One of the costs associated with participation in public affairs is an attendant loss of privacy.

Our opinion in *New York Times Co. v. Sullivan*, 376 U.S. 254 (1964), reviewed many of the decisions that settled the "general proposition that freedom of expression upon public questions is secured by the First Amendment." Those cases all relied on our "profound national commitment to the principle that debate on public issues should be uninhibited, robust, and wide-open." It was the overriding importance of that commitment that supported our holding that neither factual error nor defamatory content, nor a combination of the two, sufficed to remove the First Amendment shield from criticism of official conduct.

We think it clear that parallel reasoning requires the conclusion that a stranger's illegal conduct does not suffice to remove the First Amendment shield from speech about a matter of public concern. The months of negotiations over the proper level of compensation for teachers at the Wyoming Valley West High School were unquestionably a matter of public concern, and respondents were clearly engaged in debate about that concern.

■ JUSTICE BREYER, with whom JUSTICE O'CONNOR joins, concurring.

I join the Court's opinion. I agree with its narrow holding limited to the special circumstances present here: (1) the radio broadcasters acted lawfully (up to the time of final public disclosure); and (2) the information publicized involved a matter of unusual public concern, namely, a threat of potential physical harm to others. I write separately to explain why, in my view, the Court's holding does not imply a significantly broader constitutional immunity for the media.

I would ask whether the statutes strike a reasonable balance between their speech-restricting and speech-enhancing consequences. Or do they instead impose restrictions on speech that are disproportionate when measured against their corresponding privacy and speech-related benefits, taking into account the kind, the importance, and the extent of these benefits, as well as the need for the restrictions in order to secure those benefits? What this Court has called "strict scrutiny"—with its strong presumption against constitutionality—is normally out of place where, as here, important competing constitutional interests are implicated.

Nonetheless, looked at more specifically, the statutes, as applied in these circumstances, do not reasonably reconcile the competing constitutional objectives. Rather, they disproportionately interfere with media freedom. For one thing, the broadcasters here engaged in no unlawful activity other than the ultimate publication of the information another had previously obtained. They neither encouraged nor participated directly or indirectly in the interception.

For another thing, the speakers had little or no legitimate interest in maintaining the privacy of the particular conversation. That conversation involved a suggestion about "blow[ing] off . . . front porches" and "do[ing] some work on some of those guys," thereby raising a significant concern for the safety of others.

Further, the speakers themselves, the president of a teacher's union and the union's chief negotiator, were "limited public figures," for they voluntarily engaged in a public controversy. They thereby subjected themselves to somewhat greater public scrutiny and had a lesser interest in privacy than an individual engaged in purely private affairs.

This is not to say that the Constitution requires anyone, including public figures, to give up entirely the right to private communication, i.e., communication free from telephone taps or interceptions. But the subject matter of the conversation at issue here is far removed from that in situations where the media publicizes truly private matters.

Thus, in finding a constitutional privilege to publish unlawfully intercepted conversations of the kind here at issue, the Court does not create a "public interest" exception that swallows up the statutes' privacy-protecting general rule. Rather, it finds constitutional protection for publication of intercepted information of a special kind. Here, the speakers' legitimate privacy expectations are unusually low, and the public interest in defeating those expectations is unusually high. Given these circumstances, along with the lawful nature of respondents' behavior, the statutes' enforcement would disproportionately harm media freedom.

I emphasize the particular circumstances before us because, in my view, the Constitution permits legislatures to respond flexibly to the challenges future technology may pose to the individual's interest in basic personal privacy. Clandestine and pervasive invasions of privacy, unlike the simple theft of documents from a bedroom, are genuine possibilities as a result of continuously advancing technologies. Eavesdropping on ordinary cellular phone conversations in the street (which many callers seem to tolerate) is a very different matter from eavesdropping on encrypted cellular phone conversations or those carried on in the bedroom. But the technologies that allow the former may come to permit the latter. And statutes that may seem less important in the former context may turn out to have greater importance in the latter. Legislatures also may decide to revisit statutes such as those before us, creating better tailored provisions designed to encourage, for example, more effective privacy-protecting technologies.

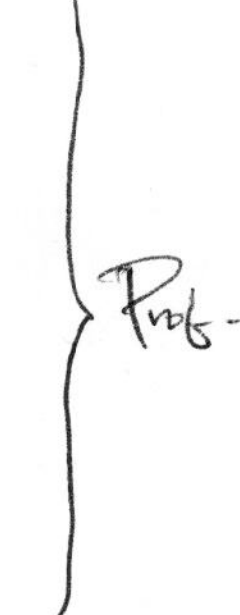

For these reasons, we should avoid adopting overly broad or rigid constitutional rules, which would unnecessarily restrict legislative flexibility. I consequently agree with the Court's holding that the statutes as applied here violate the Constitution, but I would not extend that holding beyond these present circumstances.

■ CHIEF JUSTICE REHNQUIST, with whom JUSTICE SCALIA and JUSTICE THOMAS join, dissenting.

Technology now permits millions of important and confidential conversations to occur through a vast system of electronic networks. These advances, however, raise significant privacy concerns. We are placed in the uncomfortable position of not knowing who might have access to our personal and business e-mails, our medical and financial records, or our cordless and cellular telephone conversations. In an attempt to prevent some of the most egregious violations of privacy, the United States, the District of Columbia, and 40 States have enacted laws prohibiting the intentional interception and knowing disclosure of electronic communications. The Court holds that all of these statutes violate the First Amendment insofar as the illegally intercepted conversation touches upon a matter of "public concern," an amorphous concept that the Court does not even attempt to define. But the Court's decision diminishes, rather than enhances, the purposes of the First Amendment, thereby chilling the speech of the millions of Americans who rely upon electronic technology to communicate each day.

The antidisclosure provision is based solely upon the manner in which the conversation was acquired, not the subject matter of the conversation or the viewpoints of the speakers. The same information, if obtained lawfully, could be published with impunity. As the concerns motivating strict scrutiny are absent, these content-neutral restrictions upon speech need pass only intermediate scrutiny.

These [nondisclosure] laws are content neutral; they only regulate information that was illegally obtained; they do not restrict republication of what is already in the public domain; they impose no special burdens upon the media; they have a scienter requirement to provide fair warning; and they promote the privacy and free speech of those using cellular telephones. It is hard to imagine a more narrowly tailored prohibition of the disclosure of illegally intercepted communications, and it distorts our precedents to review these statutes under the often fatal standard of strict scrutiny. These laws therefore should be upheld if they further a substantial governmental interest unrelated to the suppression of free speech, and they do.

Were there no prohibition on disclosure, an unlawful eavesdropper who wanted to disclose the conversation could anonymously launder the interception through a third party and thereby avoid detection. Indeed, demand for illegally obtained private information would only increase if it could be disclosed without repercussion. The law against interceptions, which the Court agrees is valid, would be utterly ineffectual without these antidisclosure provisions.

At base, the Court's decision to hold these statutes unconstitutional rests upon nothing more than the bald substitution of its own prognostications in place of the reasoned judgment of 41 legislative bodies and the United States Congress.

Although the Court recognizes and even extols the virtues of this right to privacy, these are "mere words," W. Shakespeare, *Troilus and Cressida*, act v, sc. 3, overridden by the Court's newfound right to publish unlawfully acquired information of "public concern." The Court concludes that the private conversation between Gloria Bartnicki and Anthony Kane is somehow a "debate. . . . worthy of constitutional protection." The point, however, is that Bartnicki and Kane had no intention of contributing to a public "debate" at all, and it is perverse to hold that another's unlawful interception and knowing disclosure of their conversation is speech worthy of constitutional protection. The Constitution should not protect the involuntary broadcast of personal conversations. Even where the communications involve public figures or concern public matters, the conversations are nonetheless private and worthy of protection. Although public persons may have forgone the right to live their lives screened from public scrutiny in some areas, it does not and should not follow that they also have abandoned their right to have a private conversation without fear of it being intentionally intercepted and knowingly disclosed.

Surely "the interest in individual privacy," at its narrowest, must embrace the right to be free from surreptitious eavesdropping on, and involuntary broadcast of, our cellular telephone conversations. The Court subordinates that right, not to the claims of those who themselves wish to speak, but to the claims of those who wish to publish the intercepted conversations of others. Congress' effort to balance the above claim to privacy against a marginal claim to speak freely is thereby set at naught.

## NOTES

1. ***Two Cases Passing in the Night?*** Characterized broadly, *Cohen* concerns enforcement of a nondisclosure *promise* protecting personal information and *Bartnicki* concerns enforcement of a nondisclosure *statute* protecting personal information. Shouldn't the same rule apply to both? The *Cohen* majority finds the contract doctrine of promissory estoppel to be a law that does not target speech (even though in that particular case it does), and considers *Daily Mail* and its progeny irrelevant. The *Bartnicki* majority decides just the opposite and applies the *Daily Mail* rule requiring a government interest of "the highest order." In each case, dissenters criticize the approach taken. Can the *Cohen* and *Bartnicki* decisions be reconciled? Is it simply a matter of how widely or narrowly one frames the characterization of the law at issue (such as the difference between "promissory estoppel law" and "this promise")? Is the important difference that the journalists' broken promise in *Cohen* implicated them in the unlawfulness, whereas in *Bartnicki* the defendants were innocent recipients of information who were not involved in its interception? Does that matter, and should it?

2. ***Nondisclosure Contracts.*** Today, *Cohen* is often cited for the proposition that a voluntary contractual promise not to reveal information is enforceable. The contracts discussed above in Section C presumably would all be covered by this rule. Surely, much of the argument in favor of enforcement of the contract in *Cohen* rests on the fact that the journalists voluntarily made the commitment not to reveal information. Does Justice Souter raise a good point in his dissent in that case, when he objects that even if this rule protects would-be speakers, it can shortchange the First Amendment interests of society in hearing the speech? When might that argument apply to other nondisclosure contracts? To other privacy rules?

3. ***Matters of Public Concern.*** The *Bartnicki* majority and (especially) Justice Breyer's concurrence both emphasize that the dispute over a new teachers' contract was a matter of intense civic interest and debate. An exemption for information of public concern has long been embedded in the structure of tort law, and particularly in the "newsworthiness" exception to the disclosure tort [see Chapter 2]. The Court's citation of Warren and Brandeis' 1890 article demonstrates its awareness of this connection. The tort cases demonstrate, however, that it is not always easy to decide when something qualifies as a matter of public concern. Nor have judges been unanimous in drawing that line under ECPA. In *Bartnicki*, Chief Justice Rehnquist's dissent scoffs at the idea that an intentionally private conversation can be automatically absorbed into the public sphere. Justice Breyer suggests that the union leader's comment about blowing off front porches represented "a matter of unusual public concern, namely, a threat of potential physical harm to others." Is that really the reason this conversation was of public interest? Would Justice Breyer

decide the case differently if it involved union leaders discussing strategy without using such language? The case that created the circuit split resolved in *Bartnicki* also demonstrates inconsistent judicial views. *See Boehner v. McDermott*, 191 F.3d 463 (D.C. Cir. 1999). *Boehner* involved a civil suit under the Wiretap Act by a Republican congressman (John Boehner, who later became Speaker of the House) against a Democratic congressman. Political activists using a radio scanner intercepted a cell phone signal and recorded a conference call in which members of the Republican leadership of the House of Representatives discussed their response to ethics charges against then-Speaker Newt Gingrich. The activists met with a Democratic congressman and gave him the tape, he gave it to the press, and its contents were published. The three-judge panel of the D.C. Circuit produced three different opinions about this convoluted situation, although two judges voted to allow Boehner to sue his Democratic colleague. Is the truly important point in *Bartnicki* that the intercepted conversation was between union leaders who were "limited public figures" when discussing the dispute? If the public interest rationale is so powerful, why wouldn't it apply in *Boehner*? Or in *Cohen* to a gubernatorial election campaign in its closing days?

4. ***The Pentagon Papers and Public Concern.*** The *Bartnicki* majority also cites *New York Times Co. v. United States*, 403 U.S. 713 (1971) (per curiam), better known as the "Pentagon Papers" case. In this landmark decision, the Supreme Court found the First Amendment protected the publication of a classified Defense Department study about the Vietnam War. Daniel Ellsberg, an employee of a defense contractor, had unlawfully copied the voluminous report and provided it to the Times and the Washington Post. (The parallels are inescapable between Ellsberg's situation and the more recent case of Edward Snowden, also an employee of a contractor who provided classified documents to newspapers [see Chapter 9].) The government argued there would be dire national security consequences if the Pentagon Papers were published, yet the justices in that case all voted to prohibit an injunction. Is some information sufficiently vital to public debate that it would be unconstitutional to prevent its disclosure? What if the television series *House of Cards* were more realistic than it seems, and a newspaper came into possession of stolen documents revealing that the President had committed murder? A rule that allowed that publication to be enjoined merely because of impropriety in obtaining the proof would be untenable, wouldn't it? Yet, once that concession is made, doesn't that leave only the question of how to draw the lines defining a matter of sufficiently crucial public concern to overcome unlawful activity by a source? This reasoning also returns us to Justice Souter's point in his *Cohen* dissent that the public right to hear information might be a distinct First Amendment concern. Would that also add weight to the disclosure side of the scale here? Is it problematic to take the position that a party who obtained the information might be punished, even prosecuted criminally, but the newspaper would not?

5. ***Generally Applicable Law.*** The *Cohen* majority relies on a series of cases where the press received no exemption from "generally applicable laws" that did not target speech in particular. Courts will scrutinize those

laws to ensure that they are not speech penalties in disguise, however. Thus, the press must pay a general "nondiscriminatory" tax—but not, as explained in one of the cases cited by *Cohen*, a tax on ink and newsprint paper payable only by those who spend over $100,000 a year on them, because that imposed unique tax burdens on a few large newspapers without any justification for singling them out. *See Minneapolis Star and Tribune Co. v. Minn. Comm'r of Revenue*, 460 U.S. 575 (1983). Yet didn't that case (which, incidentally, involved the same newspaper as *Cohen*) require the Court to explore the application of a facially neutral tax law? So why doesn't the *Cohen* majority similarly explore the case-specific impact of facially neutral promissory estoppel law, as the two dissents do? Of course, numerous *statutes* exempt the press from general laws that might otherwise apply—for example, many states have "press shield" laws that frequently protect journalists from subpoenas to reveal their sources. Is that a better way to safeguard the press than using First Amendment jurisprudence?

6. ***Reporters as Ostriches.*** The *Bartnicki* majority and concurrence emphasize that the radio station in that case did not participate in the illegal interception of the plaintiffs' conversation, even though the Court also accepts that the station knew or should have known it was recorded illegally. Isn't that line also difficult to draw? In 1998, a few years before *Bartnicki*, the Cincinnati Enquirer withdrew a story accusing Chiquita International executives of extensive bribery and fraud and paid the company a $10 million settlement. It turned out an Enquirer reporter had received voice mail login codes from a former employee, and himself accessed and recorded executives' recorded messages to support the story. Presumably that access was unlawful under the Stored Communications Act [see Chapter 5]. Would it be allowed under *Bartnicki*? Should it be different if the ex-employee accessed the messages (presumably without authorization, thus also violating the Stored Communications Act) and gave them to the reporter? What if the ex-employee told the reporter in advance that he intended to copy the messages? What if the reporter replied, "Okay"? What if the reporter stood over the former employee's shoulder as he accessed the voice mails and said nothing? Can journalists stick their heads in the sand (the so-called "ostrich defense") when sources or tipsters violate privacy and other laws? If you say no, what happens if the information obtained concerns the previous *House of Cards* example of a murderous President?

7. ***Speech Rights, Not Press Rights.*** The facts in these cases involve the traditional established media. But the decisions apply to all exercises of First Amendment free expression rights by anyone, including private individuals. Now that the internet and social media give individuals much more access to mechanisms for their speech to be heard, we can expect more cases falling outside traditional media institutions. The distinctions in these cases may become even more difficult to draw. Does *Bartnicki* cover anyone who sends a tweet using information of public interest that was obtained illegally by someone else?

8. ***Privacy's Value.*** The opinions in both *Cohen* and *Bartnicki* devote some ink to extolling the importance of privacy. But neither decision really considers the weight of those interests with care. The doctrinal analysis

concentrates almost entirely on the speech side of the balance, and the extent to which the law impinged on speech rights or targeted particular speech. Should the degree of the privacy intrusion play a greater role in the evaluation? Should it matter whether the story exposes highly intimate information or relatively benign personal data?

## 2. PERSONAL DATA AND THE FIRST AMENDMENT

### Trans Union Corp. v. FTC

245 F.3d 809 (D.C. Cir. 2001)

■ TATEL, CIRCUIT JUDGE.

Petitioner, a consumer reporting agency, sells lists of names and addresses to target marketers—companies and organizations that contact consumers with offers of products and services. The Federal Trade Commission determined that these lists were "consumer reports" under the Fair Credit Reporting Act and thus could no longer be sold for target marketing purposes. Challenging this determination, petitioner argues that the Commission's decision is unsupported by substantial evidence and that the Act itself is unconstitutional. Because we find both arguments without merit, we deny the petition for review.

Petitioner Trans Union sells two types of products. First, as a credit reporting agency, it compiles credit reports about individual consumers from credit information it collects from banks, credit card companies, and other lenders. It then sells these credit reports to lenders, employers, and insurance companies. Trans Union receives credit information from lenders in the form of "tradelines." A tradeline typically includes a customer's name, address, date of birth, telephone number, Social Security number, account type, opening date of account, credit limit, account status, and payment history. Trans Union receives 1.4 to 1.6 billion records per month. The company's credit database contains information on 190 million adults.

Trans Union's second set of products—those at issue in this case—are known as target marketing products. These consist of lists of names and addresses of individuals who meet specific criteria such as possession of an auto loan, a department store credit card, or two or more mortgages. Marketers purchase these lists, then contact the individuals by mail or telephone to offer them goods and services. To create its target marketing lists, Trans Union maintains a database known as MasterFile, a subset of its consumer credit database. MasterFile consists of information about every consumer in the company's credit database who has (A) at least two tradelines with activity during the previous six months, or (B) one tradeline with activity during the previous six months plus an address confirmed by an outside source. The company compiles target marketing lists by extracting from MasterFile the names and addresses of individuals with characteristics chosen by list purchasers. For example, a department store might buy a list of all individuals in a particular area code who have both a mortgage and a credit card with a $10,000 limit. Although target marketing lists contain only names and addresses, purchasers know that every person on a list has the characteristics they requested because Trans Union uses those characteristics as criteria for culling individual files from its database. Purchasers also know that every individual on a target marketing list satisfies the criteria for inclusion in MasterFile.

The Fair Credit Reporting Act of 1970 ("FCRA"), 15 U.S.C. §§ 1681, 1681a–1681u, regulates consumer reporting agencies like Trans Union, imposing various obligations to protect the privacy and accuracy of credit information. The Federal Trade Commission, acting pursuant to its authority to enforce the FCRA, determined that Trans Union's target marketing lists were "consumer reports" subject to the Act's limitations. [The FTC then found that the sale of the lists violated FCRA and ordered Trans Union to stop. After lengthy regulatory proceedings and a previous appeal to the D.C. Circuit, that decision was reaffirmed and Trans Union again petitioned for review.]

[The court rejected Trans Union's argument that the FTC's determination was not supported by substantial evidence as a matter of administrative law. It also rejected a constitutional argument that FCRA was unconstitutionally vague in violation of the Due Process Clause. The court then turned to Trans Union's First Amendment argument.]

Banning the sale of target marketing lists, the company says, amounts to a restriction on its speech subject to strict scrutiny. Trans Union misunderstands our standard of review. In *Dun & Bradstreet, Inc. v. Greenmoss Builders, Inc.*, 472 U.S. 749 (1985), the Supreme Court held that a consumer reporting agency's credit report warranted reduced constitutional protection because it concerned "no public issue." "The protection to be accorded a particular credit report," the Court explained, "depends on whether the report's 'content, form, and context' indicate that it concerns a public matter." Like the credit report in *Dun & Bradstreet*, which the Supreme Court found "was speech solely in the interest of the speaker and its specific business audience," the information about individual consumers and their credit performance communicated by Trans Union target marketing lists is solely of interest to the company and its business customers and relates to no matter of public concern. Trans Union target marketing lists thus warrant "reduced constitutional protection."

We turn then to the specifics of Trans Union's First Amendment argument. The company first claims that neither the FCRA nor the Commission's Order advances a substantial government interest. The "Congressional findings and statement of purpose" at the beginning of the FCRA state: "There is a need to insure that consumer reporting agencies exercise their grave responsibilities with . . . respect for the consumer's right to privacy." 15 U.S.C. § 1681 (a)(4). Contrary to the company's assertions, we have no doubt that this interest—protecting the privacy of consumer credit information—is substantial.

Trans Union next argues that Congress should have chosen a "less burdensome alternative," i.e., allowing consumer reporting agencies to sell credit information as long as they notify consumers and give them the ability to "opt out." Because the FCRA is not subject to strict First Amendment scrutiny, however, Congress had no obligation to choose the least restrictive means of accomplishing its goal.

Finally, Trans Union argues that the FCRA is underinclusive because it applies only to consumer reporting agencies and not to other companies that sell consumer information. But given consumer reporting agencies' unique "access to a broad range of continually-updated, detailed information about millions of consumers' personal credit histories" [quoting FTC opinion below], we think it not at all inappropriate for Congress to have singled out consumer reporting agencies for regulation. As we explained in *Blount v. SEC*, "a regulation is not fatally underinclusive simply because an alternative regulation, which would restrict more speech or the speech of more people, could be more effective." 61 F.3d 938, 946 (D.C. Cir. 1995) . To survive a First Amendment underinclusiveness challenge, therefore, "neither a perfect nor even the best available fit between means and ends is required." *Id.* The FCRA easily satisfies this standard.

## Sorrell v. IMS Health Inc.

131 S. Ct. 2653 (2011)

■ JUSTICE KENNEDY delivered the opinion of the Court.

Vermont law restricts the sale, disclosure, and use of pharmacy records that reveal the prescribing practices of individual doctors. Vt. Stat. Ann., Tit. 18, § 4631. Subject to certain exceptions, the information may not be sold, disclosed by pharmacies for marketing purposes, or used for marketing by pharmaceutical manufacturers. Vermont argues that its prohibitions safeguard medical privacy and diminish the likelihood that marketing will lead to prescription decisions not in the best interests of patients or the State. It can be assumed that these interests are significant. Speech in aid of pharmaceutical marketing, however, is a form of expression protected by the Free Speech Clause of the First Amendment. As a consequence, Vermont's statute must be subjected to heightened judicial scrutiny. The law cannot satisfy that standard.

### I

### A

Pharmaceutical manufacturers promote their drugs to doctors through a process called "detailing." This often involves a scheduled visit to a doctor's office to persuade the doctor to prescribe a particular pharmaceutical. Detailers bring drug samples as well as medical studies that explain the "details" and potential advantages of various prescription drugs. Interested physicians listen, ask questions, and receive followup data. Salespersons can be more effective when they know the background and purchasing preferences of their clientele, and pharmaceutical salespersons are no exception. Knowledge of a physician's prescription practices—called "prescriber-identifying information"—enables a detailer better to ascertain which doctors are likely to be interested in a particular drug and how best to present a particular sales message.

Pharmacies, as a matter of business routine and federal law, receive prescriber-identifying information when processing prescriptions. *See* 21 U.S.C. § 353(b); *see also* Vt. Bd. of Pharmacy Admin. Rule 9.1 (2009); Rule 9.2. Many pharmacies sell this information to "data miners," firms that analyze prescriber-identifying information and produce reports on prescriber behavior. Data miners lease these reports to pharmaceutical manufacturers subject to nondisclosure agreements. Detailers, who represent the manufacturers, then use the reports to refine their marketing tactics and increase sales.

In 2007, Vermont enacted the Prescription Confidentiality Law. The measure is also referred to as Act 80. It has several components. The central provision of the present case is § 4631(d). [That provision prohibits pharmacies, insurers, and similar entities from selling, disclosing, or using information identifying prescribers for marketing purposes without their consent.]

The Act's prohibitions on sale, disclosure, and use are subject to a list of exceptions. For example, prescriber-identifying information may be disseminated or used for "health care research"; to enforce "compliance" with health insurance formularies, or preferred drug lists; for "care management educational communications provided to" patients on such matters as "treatment options"; for law enforcement operations; and for purposes "otherwise provided by law." [The same statute also funded so-called "counterdetailing" programs to educate doctors about less expensive generic alternatives to branded pharmaceuticals.]

Act 80 was accompanied by legislative findings. Vermont found, for example, that the "goals of marketing programs are often in conflict with the goals of the state" and that the "marketplace for ideas on medicine safety and effectiveness is frequently one-sided in that brand-name companies invest in expensive pharmaceutical marketing campaigns to doctors." The legislature further found that detailing increases the cost of health care and health insurance; encourages hasty and excessive reliance on brand-name drugs, before the profession has observed their effectiveness as compared with older and less expensive generic alternatives; and fosters disruptive and repeated marketing visits tantamount to harassment.

[Health care data aggregators sued for injunctive relief against the Vermont law, arguing that it violated the First Amendment.]

## II

On its face, Vermont's law enacts content-and speaker-based restrictions on the sale, disclosure, and use of prescriber-identifying information. The statute disfavors marketing, that is, speech with a particular content. More than that, the statute disfavors specific speakers, namely pharmaceutical manufacturers. As a result of these content-and speaker-based rules, detailers cannot obtain prescriber-identifying information, even though the information may be purchased or acquired by other speakers with diverse purposes and viewpoints. Detailers are likewise barred from using the information for marketing, even though the information may be used by a wide range of other speakers. For example, it appears that Vermont could supply academic organizations with prescriber-identifying information to use in countering the messages of brand-name pharmaceutical manufacturers and in promoting the prescription of generic drugs. But § 4631(d) leaves detailers no means of purchasing, acquiring, or using prescriber-identifying information. The law on its face burdens disfavored speech by disfavored speakers.

Any doubt that § 4631(d) imposes an aimed, content-based burden on detailers is dispelled by the record and by formal legislative findings. Formal legislative findings accompanying § 4631(d) confirm that the law's express purpose and practical effect are to diminish the effectiveness of marketing by manufacturers of brand-name drugs. The Vermont Legislature explained that detailers, in particular those who promote brand-name drugs, convey messages that "are often in conflict with the goals of the state."

Act 80 is designed to impose a specific, content-based burden on protected expression. It follows that heightened judicial scrutiny is warranted.

This Court has held that the creation and dissemination of information are speech within the meaning of the First Amendment [citing *Bartnicki v. Vopper*, 532 U.S. 514, 527 (2001) ("[I]f the acts of 'disclosing' and 'publishing' information do not constitute speech, it is hard to imagine what does fall within that category, as distinct from the category of expressive conduct.")]. Facts, after all, are the beginning point for much of the speech that is most essential to advance human knowledge and to conduct human affairs. There is thus a strong argument that prescriber-identifying information is speech for First Amendment purposes.

In the ordinary case it is all but dispositive to conclude that a law is content-based and, in practice, viewpoint-discriminatory. The State argues that a different analysis applies here because, assuming § 4631(d) burdens speech at all, it at most burdens only commercial speech. As in previous cases, however, the outcome is the same whether a special commercial speech inquiry or a stricter form of judicial scrutiny is applied.

Under a commercial speech inquiry, it is the State's burden to justify its content-based law as consistent with the First Amendment. To sustain the targeted, content-based burden § 4631(d) imposes on protected expression, the State must show at least that the statute directly advances a substantial governmental interest and that the measure is drawn to achieve that interest. *See Central Hudson Gas & Elec. Corp. v. Pub. Serv. Comm'n*, 447 U.S. 557, 566 (1980). There must be a fit between the legislature's ends and the means chosen to accomplish those ends. As in other contexts, these standards ensure not only that the State's interests are proportional to the resulting burdens placed on speech but also that the law does not seek to suppress a disfavored message.

The State's asserted justifications for § 4631(d) come under two general headings. First, the State contends that its law is necessary to protect medical privacy, including physician confidentiality, avoidance of harassment, and the integrity of the doctor-patient relationship. Second, the State argues that § 4631(d) is integral to the achievement of policy objectives—namely, improved public health and reduced healthcare costs. Neither justification withstands scrutiny.

Perhaps the State could have addressed physician confidentiality through a more coherent policy. For instance, the State might have advanced its asserted privacy interest by allowing the information's sale or disclosure in only a few narrow and well-justified circumstances. *See, e.g.*, Health Insurance Portability and Accountability Act of 1996, 42 U.S.C. § 1320d–2; 45 CFR pts. 160 and 164 (2010). A statute of that type would present quite a different case than the one presented here. But the State did not enact a statute with that purpose or design. Instead, Vermont made prescriber-identifying information available to an almost limitless audience. The explicit structure of the statute allows the information to be studied and used by all but a narrow class of disfavored speakers. Given the information's widespread availability and many permissible uses, the State's asserted interest in physician confidentiality does not justify the burden that § 4631(d) places on protected expression.

The capacity of technology to find and publish personal information, including records required by the government, presents serious and unresolved issues with respect to personal privacy and the dignity it seeks to secure. In considering how to protect those interests, however, the State cannot engage in content-based discrimination to advance its own side of a debate.

If Vermont's statute provided that prescriber-identifying information could not be sold or disclosed except in narrow circumstances then the State might have a stronger position. Here, however, the State gives possessors of the information broad discretion and wide latitude in disclosing the information, while at the same time restricting the information's use by some speakers and for some purposes, even while the State itself can use the information to counter the speech it seeks to suppress. Privacy is a concept too integral to the person and a right too essential to freedom to allow its manipulation to support just those ideas the government prefers.

The judgment of the Court of Appeals is affirmed.

■ JUSTICE BREYER, with whom JUSTICE GINSBURG and JUSTICE KAGAN join, dissenting.

The Vermont statute before us adversely affects expression in one, and only one, way. It deprives pharmaceutical and data-mining companies of data, collected pursuant to the government's regulatory mandate, that could help pharmaceutical companies create better sales messages. In my view, this effect on expression is inextricably related to a lawful governmental effort to regulate a commercial enterprise. The First Amendment does not require courts to apply a special "heightened" standard of review when reviewing such an effort. And, in any event, the statute meets the First Amendment standard this Court has previously applied when the government seeks to regulate commercial speech. For any or all of these reasons, the Court should uphold the statute as constitutional.

In this case I would ask whether Vermont's regulatory provisions work harm to First Amendment interests that is disproportionate to their furtherance of legitimate regulatory objectives. And in doing so, I would give significant weight to legitimate commercial regulatory objectives. The far stricter, specially "heightened" First Amendment standards that the majority would apply to this instance of commercial regulation are out of place here.

Because many, perhaps most, activities of human beings living together in communities take place through speech, and because speech-related risks and offsetting justifications differ depending upon context, this Court has distinguished for First Amendment purposes among different contexts in which speech takes place. Thus, the First Amendment imposes tight constraints upon government efforts to restrict, e.g., "core" political speech, while imposing looser constraints when the government seeks to restrict, e.g., commercial speech, the speech of its own employees, or the regulation-related speech of a firm subject to a traditional regulatory program.

To apply a strict First Amendment standard virtually as a matter of course when a court reviews ordinary economic regulatory programs (even if that program has a modest impact upon a firm's ability to shape a commercial message) would work at cross-purposes with this more basic constitutional approach. Since ordinary regulatory programs can affect speech, particularly commercial speech, in myriad ways, to apply a "heightened" First Amendment standard of review whenever such a program burdens speech would transfer from legislatures to judges the primary power to weigh ends and to choose means, threatening to distort or undermine legitimate legislative objectives.

Regulators will often find it necessary to create tailored restrictions on the use of information subject to their regulatory jurisdiction. A car dealership that obtains credit scores for customers who want car loans can be prohibited from using credit data to search for new customers. *See* 15 U.S.C. § 1681b; *cf. Trans Union Corp. v. FTC*, 245 F.3d 809 (D.C. Cir. 2001). Medical specialists who obtain medical records for their existing patients cannot purchase those records in order to identify new patients. *See* 45 CFR § 164.508(a)(3) (2010). Or, speaking hypothetically, a public utilities commission that directs local gas distributors to gather usage information for individual customers might permit the distributors to share the data with researchers (trying to lower energy costs) but forbid sales of the data to appliance manufacturers seeking to sell gas stoves.

The ease with which one can point to actual or hypothetical examples with potentially adverse speech-related effects at least roughly comparable to those at issue here indicates the danger of applying a "heightened" or "intermediate" standard of First Amendment review where typical regulatory actions affect commercial speech (say, by withholding information that a commercial speaker might use to shape the content of a message).

Nothing in Vermont's statute undermines the ability of persons opposing the State's policies to speak their mind or to pursue a different set of policy objectives through the democratic process. Whether Vermont's regulatory statute "targets" drug companies (as opposed to affecting them unintentionally) must be beside the First Amendment point.

I believe that the statute before us satisfies the "intermediate" standards this Court has applied to restrictions on commercial speech. A fortiori it satisfies less demanding standards that are more appropriately applied in this kind of commercial regulatory case—a case where the government seeks typical regulatory ends (lower drug prices, more balanced sales messages) through the use of ordinary regulatory means (limiting the commercial use of data gathered pursuant to a regulatory mandate). The speech-related consequences here are indirect, incidental, and entirely commercial.

The Court reaches its conclusion through the use of important First Amendment categories—"content-based," "speaker-based," and "neutral"—but without taking full account of the regulatory context, the nature of the speech effects, the values these First Amendment categories seek to promote, and prior precedent. At best the Court opens a Pandora's Box of First Amendment challenges to many ordinary regulatory practices that may only incidentally affect a commercial message. At worst, it reawakens *Lochner*'s pre-New Deal threat of substituting judicial for democratic decisionmaking where ordinary economic regulation is at issue. *See Central Hudson*, 447 U.S., at 589, 100 S.Ct. 2343 (Rehnquist, J., dissenting).

Regardless, whether we apply an ordinary commercial speech standard or a less demanding standard, I believe Vermont's law is consistent with the First Amendment. And with respect, I dissent.

## NOTES

1. ***Passing in the Night Again?*** In *Trans Union*, the court emphasizes that a commercial credit report, used for marketing, is entitled to "reduced constitutional protection." But how is the raw data about doctors' prescribing practices in *Sorrell* any different? The majority there emphasizes that the challenged law singled out a particular type of company and a particular type of data, making its requirements "content-and speaker-based restrictions." Yet doesn't FCRA target certain information about creditworthiness and certain institutions that qualify as credit reporting agencies? *Trans Union* is older and it is a decision from the court of appeals, not the Supreme Court. Is it still good law after *Sorrell*? The *Sorrell* dissent cites *Trans Union* as the kind of case that could be threatened by the "Pandora's Box of First Amendment challenges" opened by the majority. Is it?

2. ***Is* Sorrell *a Privacy Case?*** A different interpretation of *Sorrell* limits its impact on privacy law by suggesting that physician confidentiality was never the Vermont Legislature's true goal, so that Act 80 was not really a privacy law at all. Under this reading, lawmakers used privacy as a flimsy excuse when the true objective was influencing doctors to prescribe cheaper generics rather than branded drugs. There is some support in the majority opinion for this understanding of *Sorrell*. The Court repeatedly emphasizes statements about the cost of pharmaceuticals in the Act and its legislative history; it notes the legislation's support for "counterdetailing" to present a message in opposition to the detailers' promotional efforts; and, perhaps most of all, it cites privacy restrictions under HIPAA [see Chapter 12] as an example of the type of law that might have represented "a more coherent policy" for privacy protection, adding, "A statute of that type would present quite a different case than the one presented here."

3. ***Gathering Data and Disclosing Data.*** Ordinarily, judicial scrutiny of speech restrictions is more significant when the rules constrain disclosure of information than when they limit information gathering. *Bartnicki*, above, is just one such example; another is the difference in treatment of the media under the torts of intrusion on seclusion and disclosure [see Chapter 2]. This pair of cases could be seen as disturbing that general pattern. In *Trans Union*, the plaintiff certainly wanted to communicate information to its clients—Jane Smith has a mortgage, Jose Diaz pays his bills on time, and so forth. The court upheld a rule forbidding it from doing so. On the other hand, Act 80 in *Sorrell* prevented the plaintiff from obtaining certain information in the first place—Dr. Smith prescribes lots of generic drugs, Dr. Diaz puts more patients on Paxil than on Prozac, and so forth. Are these cases backwards?

4. ***Blanket Rules and Narrow Exceptions.*** Suppose Act 80 simply forbade pharmacies from selling prescription information to anyone at all. Would the *Sorrell* case have come out differently? If so, doesn't that suggest that its logic encourages the government to enact *broader* speech restrictions? Would pharmacies have a basis to challenge that rule?

5. ***Speech as a Metaphor.*** In what ways can the disclosures of personal data reviewed in these cases be understood as speech? Modern First Amendment jurisprudence reaches many actions that connect to self-expression even if they seem far from the direct communication of actual words, such as burning a flag or a cross, *see Texas v. Johnson*, 491 U.S. 397 (1989); *R.A.V. v. City of St. Paul, Minn.*, 505 U.S. 377 (1992), or contributing money to a political campaign, *see Citizens United v. Fed. Election Com'n*, 558 U.S. 310 (2010). At the same time, some things that are clearly speech in the ordinary sense—Oliver Wendell Holmes' famous example of shouting "Fire!" in a crowded movie theater—are unprotected. How close to speech is the communication of raw personal data?

6. ***Scholarly Debate.*** Judges are not the only ones who find these distinctions challenging. There is a lively ongoing scholarly debate concerning the extent to which First Amendment principles limit regulation of the disclosure of raw personal data, such as the rules considered in *Trans Union* and *Sorrell*. One of the best-known examples of the argument that First Amendment principles forbid many privacy laws is a 2000 essay by Eugene Volokh, which he begins as follows:

> Privacy is a popular word, and government attempts to "protect our privacy" are easy to endorse. Government attempts to let us "control information about ourselves" sound equally good: Who wouldn't want extra control? And what fair-minded person could oppose requirements of "fair information practices"?
>
> The difficulty is that the right to information privacy—my right to control your communication of personally identifiable information about me—is a right to have the government stop you from speaking about me. We already have a code of "fair information practices," and it is the First Amendment, which generally bars the government from controlling the communication of information (either by direct regulation or through the authorization of private lawsuits), whether the communication is "fair" or not. While privacy protection secured by contract is constitutionally sound, broader information privacy rules are not easily defensible under existing free speech law.
>
> Of course, the Supreme Court and even lower courts can create new First Amendment exceptions or broaden existing ones; and if the courts did this for information privacy speech restrictions, I can't say that I'd be terribly upset about the new exception for its own sake. Speech restrictions aimed at protecting individual privacy just don't get my blood boiling. Maybe they should, but they don't. Perhaps this is because, from a selfish perspective, I'd like the ability to stop others from talking about me, and while I wouldn't

> like their stopping *me* from talking about *them,* the trade-off might be worth it.
>
> Nonetheless, I'm deeply worried about the possible downstream effects of any such new exception. Most of the justifications given for information privacy speech restraints are directly applicable to other speech controls that have already been proposed. If these justifications are accepted in the attractive case of information privacy speech restrictions, such a decision will be a powerful precedent for those other restraints and for still more that might be proposed in the future.

Eugene Volokh, *Freedom of Speech and Information Privacy: The Troubling Implications of a Right to Stop People From Speaking About You*, 52 STAN. L. REV. 1049, 1050–51 (2000). More recently, Jane Bambauer has taken a somewhat different tack, arguing that data, including personal data, does and should receive First Amendment protection because it is the raw material for analysis that creates new knowledge:

> Expanded knowledge is an end goal of American speech rights, and accurate information, along with other, more subjective expressions, provides the fuel. [I]f a court is uncertain whether a regulation targets "speech," it should analyze the regulation purposively rather than simply considering the regulation in the abstract. [T]hese principles suggest that state action will trigger the First Amendment any time it purposefully interferes with the creation of knowledge.
>
> [F]or all practical purposes, and in every context relevant to the current debates in information law, data is speech. Privacy regulations are rarely incidental burdens to knowledge. Instead, they are deliberately designed to disrupt knowledge creation. These disruptions in knowledge creation might sometimes, or even frequently, be justified in order to protect compelling societal interests—for instance, living without constant surveillance. Although the First Amendment creates a barrier to the enforcement of new and existing information laws, that barrier is not insurmountable. It simply requires, as it should, a lively inquiry into whether the harms caused by the collection of information are probable enough, and serious enough, to outweigh the right to learn things.

Jane Bambauer, *Is Data Speech?, 66 STAN. L. REV.* 57, 63–64 (2014). Neil Richards responds that conferring strong First Amendment protection on commercial data flows is inconsistent with free speech doctrine and interferes with important governmental regulation of privacy and other values:

> The First Amendment has never been interpreted as an absolute protection for all uses of words, much less for automated and mechanized data flows or the sale of information as a commodity. American lawyers are perhaps the group most protective of free speech in the history of the world. But even in the United States,

> virtually all strong, speech-protective interpretations of the First Amendment carve out large chunks of the ways we use words or information from heightened First Amendment protection. They do this so the First Amendment can do its job—protecting political and artistic expression—without swallowing the rest of the law. And the system works.
>
> From this perspective, we can see why asking whether the data is "speech" is the wrong question. Commercial data flows are certainly within the outermost bounds of the First Amendment, but so, too, are sexual harassment, criminal and antitrust contracting, threats, and securities disclosures. But putting data flows in this category merely means that the government can regulate them if it acts rationally to further a legitimate government purpose. Something more is needed to show that regulation of commercial data flows is suspect like regulation of traditional categories of expression, like political speech or protest, commentary on matters of public concern, artistic expression, or (less important) advertising to consumers that proposes a commercial transaction
>
> We must not be sidetracked by misleading First Amendment arguments, because the costs of not regulating the trade in commercial data are significant. As we enter the Information Age, where the trade in information is a multibillion-dollar industry, government should be able to regulate the huge flows of personal information as well as uses to which this information can be put. Moreover, if our lives become digital, but if data is speech, regulation of many kinds of social problems will become impossible.

NEIL RICHARDS, INTELLECTUAL PRIVACY: RETHINKING CIVIL LIBERTIES IN THE DIGITAL AGE 86–87, 90 (2015).

# PART 3

# SECTOR-SPECIFIC REGULATION

Parts One and Two of this book examined broadly applicable privacy and data protection law that will be essential for any attorney to consider when evaluating data handling practices. Unlike countries with comprehensive data protection regimes, however, US law in this area is highly fragmented. Policymakers establish different law for different situations, depending on variables such as the industry sector, the type of information, the technology involved, and the interests that might weigh against maximizing privacy. The resulting hodgepodge is overseen by more than a dozen different federal regulatory authorities as well as state attorneys general, courts, and private self-regulatory institutions.

There are advantages and disadvantages to this approach. The problems include the potential for confusion—even among organizations that are earnestly trying to comply with the law—as well as some inefficient duplication of effort by government agencies and the possibility that troubling practices may slip through the cracks between the different laws. On the other hand, rules can be tailored to particular circumstances. Specialized regulators with strong relationships and expertise within an industry sector can oversee compliance. Whatever the tradeoffs, it is the law we have in the US and it is not going away, so privacy attorneys must grapple with the many disparate provisions of this sectoral system.

Each chapter in Part Three focuses on one of these sectors. It begins by returning to privacy issues unique to the government: the law applicable to national security investigations [Chapter 9] and the tension between requirements for privacy and freedom of information that must be balanced in the management of ordinary government databases [Chapter 10]. The following chapter considers privacy restrictions on employers in both private and public sector workplaces [Chapter 11]. The subsequent three chapters turn to industries that are subject to additional layers of comparatively strict US privacy law: health care [Chapter 12], financial services [Chapter 13], and marketing and communications [Chapter 14]. Finally, the book closes by considering privacy in a context important to most readers of this book: educational institutions, both public and private, from kindergartens to universities [Chapter 15].

If you follow this book from the beginning through Part Three, you will see the layered nature of privacy and data protection law: older sources of privacy restrictions like torts continue to play a role, but they have been joined by broadly applicable consumer protection and data protection law, general rules governing certain stages of the life cycle of data, and sector-specific regulation. Privacy and data protection attorneys must keep all of these layers in mind if they are to master this complex area of law.

# CHAPTER 9

# NATIONAL SECURITY

At the very beginning of this book, we saw that courts conceptualize privacy restrictions differently in national security cases than in others. The second most important dicta in the concurrences from *Katz v. United States*, 389 U.S. 347 (1967) [Chapter 1]—after the "reasonable expectation of privacy" test—involved a disagreement about the role of the Fourth Amendment's warrant requirement in national security investigations. In his concurrence, Justice White opined, "We should not require the warrant procedure and the magistrate's judgment if the President of the United States or his chief legal officer, the Attorney General, has considered the requirements of national security and authorized electronic surveillance as reasonable." Justice Douglas disagreed with characteristic vigor, calling White's view "a wholly unwarranted green light for the Executive Branch to resort to electronic eavesdropping without a warrant." He argued that, because the President and Attorney General are responsible for protecting national security, "they are not detached, disinterested, and neutral as a court or magistrate must be."

Almost 50 years later, one can find both of these viewpoints expressed, along with many others, in a raging debate over the balance between the protection of privacy and national security. This is one of the most contentious areas in privacy law. And, while cases after *Katz* offered some more clarity about the Fourth Amendment's role, and Congress has passed multiple bills concerning eavesdropping for foreign intelligence or counterterrorism purposes, this topic still generates considerable uncertainty as well as vigorous disagreement.

This chapter first considers foundations of privacy-related national security law [Section A], including two major Supreme Court cases and the Foreign Intelligence Surveillance Act (FISA). It then moves to the debate unleashed when Edward Snowden disclosed that the National Security Agency (NSA) was procuring large quantities of information about Americans' telephone calls under the authority of FISA, and the judicial and congressional response to that revelation [Section B]. The end of Section B also takes note of several other controversies in this especially unsettled area of privacy law.

## A. FOUNDATIONS

### 1. THE *KEITH* CASE

The only other case in which the Supreme Court has confronted the Fourth Amendment issues deferred in *Katz* came just a few years later. In a prosecution of left-wing radicals calling themselves the "White

Panther Party" for the 1968 bombing of a Central Intelligence Agency recruiting office in Michigan, it emerged that the government had engaged in warrantless wiretapping as part of the investigation. Judge Damon Keith, the district court judge presiding over the case, rejected prosecutors' argument that the Fourth Amendment was inapplicable because the case involved national security. The government filed for a writ of mandamus, and the case is commonly known by the name of Judge Keith, the official against whom the writ was sought. The case then wound its way to the Supreme Court. As you read, compare the analysis and rhetoric in *Keith* with contemporary discussion of the balance between national security and privacy rights.

## United States v. United States District Court [The "Keith" Case]

407 U.S. 297 (1972)

■ MR. JUSTICE POWELL delivered the opinion of the Court.

The issue before us is an important one for the people of our country and their Government. It involves the delicate question of the President's power, acting through the Attorney General, to authorize electronic surveillance in internal security matters without prior judicial approval. Successive Presidents for more than one-quarter of a century have authorized such surveillance in varying degrees, without guidance from the Congress or a definitive decision of this Court. This case brings the issue here for the first time. Its resolution is a matter of national concern, requiring sensitivity both to the Government's right to protect itself from unlawful subversion and attack and to the citizen's right to be secure in his privacy against unreasonable Government intrusion.

This case arises from a criminal proceeding in the United States District Court for the Eastern District of Michigan, in which the United States charged three defendants with conspiracy to destroy Government property. One of the defendants, Plamondon, was charged with the dynamite bombing of an office of the Central Intelligence Agency in Ann Arbor, Michigan.

During pretrial proceedings, the defendants moved to compel the United States to disclose certain electronic surveillance information and to conduct a hearing to determine whether this information "tainted" the evidence on which the indictment was based or which the Government intended to offer at trial. In response, the Government filed an affidavit of the Attorney General, acknowledging that its agents had overheard conversations in which Plamondon had participated. The affidavit also stated that the Attorney General approved the wiretaps "to gather intelligence information deemed necessary to protect the nation from attempts of domestic organizations to attack and subvert the existing structure of the Government." The logs of the surveillance were filed in a sealed exhibit for in camera inspection by the District Court.

On the basis of the Attorney General's affidavit and the sealed exhibit, the Government asserted that the surveillance was lawful, though conducted without prior judicial approval, as a reasonable exercise of the President's power (exercised through the Attorney General) to protect the national security. The District Court held that the surveillance violated the Fourth Amendment, and ordered the Government to make full disclosure to Plamondon of his overheard conversations.

The Government then filed in the Court of Appeals for the Sixth Circuit a petition for a writ of mandamus to set aside the District Court order. That court held that the surveillance was unlawful and that the District Court had properly required disclosure of the overheard conversations. We granted certiorari.

**I**

Title III of the Omnibus Crime Control and Safe Streets Act, 18 U.S.C. §§ 2510–2520, authorizes the use of electronic surveillance for classes of crimes carefully specified in 18 U.S.C. § 2516. The Act represents a comprehensive attempt by Congress to promote more effective control of crime while protecting the privacy of individual thought and expression. Much of Title III was drawn to meet the constitutional requirements for electronic surveillance enunciated by this Court in *Berger v. New York*, 388 U.S. 41 (1967), and *Katz v. United States*, 389 U.S. 347 (1967).

Together with the elaborate surveillance requirements in Title III, there is the following proviso, 18 U.S.C. § 2511(3):

> Nothing contained in this chapter or in section 605 of the Communications Act of 1934 shall limit the constitutional power of the President to take such measures as he deems necessary to protect the Nation against actual or potential attack or other hostile acts of a foreign power, to obtain foreign intelligence information deemed essential to the security of the United States, or to protect national security information against foreign intelligence activities. *Nor shall anything contained in this chapter be deemed to limit the constitutional power of the President to take such measures as he deems necessary to protect the United States against the overthrow of the Government by force or other unlawful means, or against any other clear and present danger to the structure or existence of the Government.* The contents of any wire or oral communication intercepted by authority of the President in the exercise of the foregoing powers may be received in evidence in any trial hearing, or other proceeding only where such interception was reasonable, and shall not be otherwise used or disclosed except as is necessary to implement that power.' [Emphasis supplied in opinion.]

The Government relies on § 2511(3). It argues that "in excepting national security surveillances from the Act's warrant requirement Congress recognized the President's authority to conduct such surveillances without prior judicial approval." The section thus is viewed as a recognition or affirmance of a constitutional authority in the President to conduct warrantless domestic security surveillance such as that involved in this case.

We think the language of § 2511(3), as well as the legislative history of the statute, refutes this interpretation. The relevant language is that:

> Nothing contained in this chapter. . . . shall limit the constitutional power of the President to take such measures as he deems necessary to protect . . .

against the dangers specified. At most, this is an implicit recognition that the President does have certain powers in the specified areas. Few would doubt this, as the section refers—among other things—to protection "against actual or potential attack or other hostile acts of a foreign power." But so far as the use of the President's electronic surveillance power is concerned, the language is essentially neutral.

Section 2511(3) certainly confers no power, as the language is wholly inappropriate for such a purpose. It merely provides that the Act shall not be interpreted to limit or disturb such power as the President may have under the Constitution. In short, Congress simply left presidential powers where it found them. [The Court then reviewed statutory structure and legislative history to support this interpretation of § 2511(3).]

If we could accept the Government's characterization of § 2511(3) as a congressionally prescribed exception to the general requirement of a warrant, it would be necessary to consider the question of whether the surveillance in this case came within the exception and, if so, whether the statutory exception was itself constitutionally valid. But viewing § 2511(3) as a congressional disclaimer and expression of neutrality, we hold that the statute is not the measure of the executive authority asserted in this case. Rather, we must look to the constitutional powers of the President.

## II

It is important at the outset to emphasize the limited nature of the question before the Court. This case raises no constitutional challenge to electronic surveillance as specifically authorized by Title III of the Omnibus Crime Control and Safe Streets Act of 1968. Nor is there any question or doubt as to the necessity of obtaining a warrant in the surveillance of crimes unrelated to the national security interest. Further, the instant case requires no judgment on the scope of the President's surveillance power with respect to the activities of foreign powers, within or without this country. The Attorney General's affidavit in this case states that the surveillances were "deemed necessary to protect the nation from attempts of *domestic organizations* to attack and subvert the existing structure of Government" [emphasis supplied in opinion]. There is no evidence of any involvement, directly or indirectly, of a foreign power.

Our present inquiry, though important, is therefore a narrow one. It addresses a question left open by *Katz*:

> Whether safeguards other than prior authorization by a magistrate would satisfy the Fourth Amendment in a situation involving the national security. . . .

The determination of this question requires the essential Fourth Amendment inquiry into the "reasonableness" of the search and seizure in question, and the way in which that "reasonableness" derives content and meaning through reference to the warrant clause.

We begin the inquiry by noting that the President of the United States has the fundamental duty, under Art. II, s 1, of the Constitution, to "preserve, protect and defend the Constitution of the United States." Implicit in that duty is the power to protect our Government against those who would subvert or overthrow it by unlawful means. In the discharge of this duty, the President—through the Attorney General—may find it necessary to employ electronic surveillance to obtain intelligence information on the plans of those who plot unlawful acts against the Government. The use of such surveillance in internal security cases has been sanctioned more or less continuously by various Presidents and Attorneys General since July 1946. Herbert Brownell, Attorney General under President Eisenhower, urged the use of electronic surveillance both in internal and international security matters on the grounds that those acting against the Government

> turn to the telephone to carry on their intrigue. The success of their plans frequently rests upon piecing together shreds of information received from many sources and many nests. The participants in the conspiracy are often dispersed and stationed in various strategic positions in government and industry throughout the country.

Though the Government and respondents debate their seriousness and magnitude, threats and acts of sabotage against the Government exist in sufficient number to justify investigative powers with respect to them. The covertness and complexity of potential unlawful conduct against the Government and the necessary dependency of many conspirators upon the telephone make electronic surveillance an effective investigatory instrument in certain circumstances. The marked acceleration in technological developments and sophistication in their use have resulted in new techniques for the planning, commission, and concealment of criminal activities. It would be contrary to the public interest for Government to deny to itself the prudent and lawful employment of those very techniques which are employed against the Government and its law-abiding citizens.

There is, understandably, a deep-seated uneasiness and apprehension that this capability will be used to intrude upon cherished privacy of law-abiding citizens. We look to the Bill of Rights to safeguard this privacy. Though physical entry of the home is the chief evil against which the wording of the Fourth Amendment is directed, its broader spirit now shields private speech from unreasonable surveillance. Our decision in *Katz* refused to lock the Fourth Amendment into instances of actual physical trespass. That decision implicitly recognized that the broad and unsuspected governmental incursions into conversational privacy which electronic surveillance entails necessitate the application of Fourth Amendment safeguards.

National security cases, moreover, often reflect a convergence of First and Fourth Amendment values not present in cases of "ordinary" crime. Though the investigative duty of the executive may be stronger in such cases, so also is there greater jeopardy to constitutionally protected speech. History abundantly documents the tendency of Government—however benevolent and benign its motives—to view with suspicion those who most fervently dispute its policies. Fourth Amendment protections become the more necessary when the targets of official surveillance may be those suspected of unorthodoxy in their political beliefs. The danger to political dissent is acute where the Government attempts to act under so vague a concept as the power to protect "domestic security." Given the difficulty of defining the domestic security interest, the danger of abuse in acting to protect that interest becomes apparent.

### III

As the Fourth Amendment is not absolute in its terms, our task is to examine and balance the basic values at stake in this case: the duty of Government to protect the domestic security, and the potential danger posed by unreasonable surveillance to individual privacy and free expression. If the legitimate need of Government to safeguard domestic security requires the use of electronic surveillance, the question is whether the needs of citizens for privacy and the free expression may not be better protected by requiring a warrant before such surveillance is undertaken. We must also ask whether a warrant requirement would unduly frustrate the efforts of Government to protect itself from acts of subversion and overthrow directed against it.

Inherent in the concept of a warrant is its issuance by a "neutral and detached magistrate." The further requirement of "probable cause" instructs the magistrate that baseless searches shall not proceed.

The Fourth Amendment does not contemplate the executive officers of Government as neutral and disinterested magistrates. Their duty and responsibility are to enforce the laws, to investigate, and to prosecute. But those charged with this investigative and prosecutorial duty should not be the sole judges of when to utilize constitutionally sensitive means in pursuing their tasks. The historical judgment, which the Fourth Amendment accepts, is that unreviewed executive discretion may yield too readily to pressures to obtain incriminating evidence and overlook potential invasions of privacy and protected speech.

It may well be that, in the instant case, the Government's surveillance of Plamondon's conversations was a reasonable one which readily would have gained prior judicial approval. But this Court "has never sustained a search upon the sole ground that officers reasonably expected to find evidence of a particular crime and voluntarily confined their activities to the least intrusive means consistent with that end" [quoting *Katz*].

It is true that there have been some exceptions to the warrant requirement. But those exceptions are few in number and carefully delineated; in general, they serve the legitimate needs of law enforcement officers to protect their own well-being and preserve evidence from destruction. Even while carving out those exceptions, the Court has reaffirmed the principle that the police must, whenever practicable, obtain advance judicial approval of searches and seizures through the warrant procedure.

The Government argues that the special circumstances applicable to domestic security surveillances necessitate a further exception to the warrant requirement. It is urged that the requirement of prior judicial review would obstruct the President in the discharge of his constitutional duty to protect domestic security. We are told further that these surveillances are directed primarily to the collecting and maintaining of intelligence with respect to subversive forces, and are not an attempt to gather evidence for specific criminal prosecutions. It is said that this type of surveillance should not be subject to traditional warrant requirements which were established to govern investigation of criminal activity, not ongoing intelligence gathering.

The Government further insists that courts "as a practical matter would have neither the knowledge nor the techniques necessary to determine whether there was probable cause to believe that surveillance was necessary to protect national security." These security problems, the Government contends, involve "a large number of complex and subtle factors" beyond the competence of courts to evaluate.

As a final reason for exemption from a warrant requirement, the Government believes that disclosure to a magistrate of all or even a significant portion of the information involved in domestic security surveillances "would create serious potential dangers to the national security and to the lives of informants and agents. . . . Secrecy is the essential ingredient in intelligence gathering; requiring prior judicial authorization would create a greater danger of leaks . . . because in addition to the judge, you have the clerk, the stenographer and some other officer like a law assistant or bailiff who may be apprised of the nature of the surveillance."

These contentions in behalf of a complete exemption from the warrant requirement, when urged on behalf of the President and the national security in its domestic implications, merit the most careful consideration. We certainly do not reject them lightly, especially at a time of worldwide ferment and when civil disorders in this country are more prevalent than in the less turbulent periods of our history. There is, no doubt, pragmatic force to the Government's position.

But we do not think a case has been made for the requested departure from Fourth Amendment standards. The circumstances described do not justify complete exemption of domestic security surveillance from prior judicial scrutiny. Official surveillance, whether its purpose be criminal investigation or ongoing intelligence gathering, risks infringement of constitutionally protected privacy of speech. Security surveillances are especially sensitive because of the inherent vagueness of the domestic security concept, the necessarily broad and continuing nature of intelligence gathering, and the temptation to utilize such surveillances to oversee political dissent. We recognize, as we have before, the constitutional basis of the President's domestic security role, but we think it must be exercised in a manner compatible with the Fourth Amendment. In this case we hold that this requires an appropriate prior warrant procedure.

We cannot accept the Government's argument that internal security matters are too subtle and complex for judicial evaluation. Courts regularly deal with the most difficult issues of our society. There is no reason to believe that federal judges will be insensitive to or uncomprehending of the issues involved in domestic security cases. Certainly courts can recognize that domestic security surveillance involves different considerations from the surveillance of "ordinary crime." If the threat is too subtle or complex for our senior law enforcement officers to convey its significance to a court, one may question whether there is probable cause for surveillance.

Nor do we believe prior judicial approval will fracture the secrecy essential to official intelligence gathering. The investigation of criminal activity has long involved imparting sensitive information to judicial officers who have respected the confidentialities involved. Moreover, a warrant application involves no public or adversary proceedings: it is an ex parte request before a magistrate or judge. Whatever security dangers clerical and secretarial personnel may pose can be minimized by proper administrative measures, possibly to the point of allowing the Government itself to provide the necessary clerical assistance.

Thus, we conclude that the Government's concerns do not justify departure in this case from the customary Fourth Amendment requirement of judicial approval prior to initiation of a search or surveillance. Although some added burden will be imposed upon the

Attorney General, this inconvenience is justified in a free society to protect constitutional values. By no means of least importance will be the reassurance of the public generally that indiscriminate wiretapping and bugging of law-abiding citizens cannot occur.

### IV

We emphasize, before concluding this opinion, the scope of our decision. As stated at the outset, this case involves only the domestic aspects of national security. We have not addressed, and express no opinion as to, the issues which may be involved with respect to activities of foreign powers or their agents. Nor does our decision rest on the language of § 2511(3) or any other section of Title III of the Omnibus Crime Control and Safe Streets Act of 1968. That Act does not attempt to define or delineate the powers of the President to meet domestic threats to the national security.

Moreover, we do not hold that the same type of standards and procedures prescribed by Title III are necessarily applicable to this case. We recognize that domestic security surveillance may involve different policy and practical considerations from the surveillance of "ordinary crime." The gathering of security intelligence is often long range and involves the interrelation of various sources and types of information. The exact targets of such surveillance may be more difficult to identify than in surveillance operations against many types of crime specified in Title III. Often, too, the emphasis of domestic intelligence gathering is on the prevention of unlawful activity or the enhancement of the Government's preparedness for some possible future crisis or emergency. Thus, the focus of domestic surveillance may be less precise than that directed against more conventional types of crime.

Given those potential distinctions between Title III criminal surveillances and those involving the domestic security, Congress may wish to consider protective standards for the latter which differ from those already prescribed for specified crimes in Title III. Different standards may be compatible with the Fourth Amendment if they are reasonable both in relation to the legitimate need of Government for intelligence information and the protected rights of our citizens.

We do not attempt to detail the precise standards for domestic security warrants any more than our decision in *Katz* sought to set the refined requirements for the specified criminal surveillances which now constitute Title III. We do hold, however, that prior judicial approval is required for the type of domestic security surveillance involved in this case and that such approval may be made in accordance with such reasonable standards as the Congress may prescribe.

■ MR. JUSTICE DOUGLAS, concurring.

While I join in the opinion of the Court, I add these words in support of it.

This is an important phase in the campaign of the police and intelligence agencies to obtain exemptions from the Warrant Clause of the Fourth Amendment. For, due to the clandestine nature of electronic eavesdropping, the need is acute for placing on the Government the heavy burden to show that exigencies of the situation make its course imperative.

If the Warrant Clause were held inapplicable here, then the federal intelligence machine would literally enjoy unchecked discretion.

[W]e are currently in the throes of another national seizure of paranoia, resembling the hysteria which surrounded the Alien and Sedition Acts, the Palmer Raids, and the McCarthy era. Those who register dissent or who petition their governments for redress are subjected to scrutiny by grand juries, by the FBI, or even by the military. Their associates are interrogated. Their homes are bugged and their telephones are wiretapped. They are befriended by secret government informers. Their patriotism and loyalty are questioned.

When the Executive attempts to excuse these tactics as essential to its defense against internal subversion, we are obliged to remind it, without apology[,] of this Court's long commitment to the preservation of the Bill of Rights from the corrosive environment of precisely such expedients.

The Warrant Clause has stood as a barrier against intrusions by officialdom into the privacies of life. But if that barrier were lowered now to permit suspected subversives' most intimate conversations to be pillaged then why could not their abodes or mail be secretly searched by the same authority? To defeat so terrifying a claim of inherent power we need only stand by the enduring values served by the Fourth Amendment.

## NOTES

1. ***The Scope of* Keith.** More than once, the *Keith* majority characterized the opinion as narrow in scope. Work out exactly what types of cases are covered and not covered by the opinion's holding. Precisely what questions were left for another day? Perhaps it would be helpful to consider this footnote, omitted from the above excerpt of the majority opinion:

> Section 2511(3) refers to "the constitutional power of the President" in two types of situations: (i) where necessary to protect against attack, other hostile acts or intelligence activities of a "foreign power;" or (ii) where necessary to protect against the overthrow of the Government or other clear and present danger to the structure or existence of the Government. Although both of the specified situations are sometimes referred to as "national security" threats, the term "national security" is used only in the first sentence of § 2511(3) with respect to the activities of foreign powers. This case involves only the second sentence of § 2511(3), with the threat emanating—according to the Attorney General's affidavit—from

> "domestic organizations." Although we attempt no precise definition, we use the term "domestic organization" in this opinion to mean a group or organization (whether formally or informally constituted) composed of citizens of the United States and which has no significant connection with a foreign power, its agents or agencies. No doubt there are cases where it will be difficult to distinguish between "domestic" and "foreign" unlawful activities directed against the Government of the United States where there is collaboration in varying degrees between domestic groups or organizations and agents or agencies of foreign powers. But this is not such a case.

Some readers of *Keith* describe its holding as establishing a "trichotomy" for the Fourth Amendment, with ordinary crime on one side, "foreign" national security surveillance on the other, and "domestic" security cases like Plamondon's in the middle. On this reading, the middle category is subject to the warrant requirement, but not necessarily to every detail of Fourth Amendment doctrine that governs "ordinary crime" situations. Do you agree with this interpretation?

2. ***Kicking the Can.*** A narrow decision often leaves unanswered questions. How much was resolved by *Keith* and how much was deferred, again, for another day? Articulate the precise legal questions that remain open after *Keith*.

3. ***Defining "Domestic" Terrorism.*** The Court acknowledged in *Keith*, and particularly in the footnote reprinted in Note 1 above, that it may be difficult to tell the difference between "domestic" and "foreign" national security cases. Those words seem particularly salient today. Sometimes, the division is fairly obvious: the bombing of a federal building in Oklahoma City by right-wing extremist Timothy McVeigh had no evident connection to foreign sources of any kind, and so resembles the bombing allegedly committed by Plamondon and his left-wing co-conspirators. But what about the 2015 mass shooting in San Bernardino, California, committed by an American-born husband and Pakistani-born wife who appear to have been influenced by foreign Islamic terrorist organizations, but may not have received their direct support? Moreover, how can this line be drawn *during* an investigation—the time when a warrant would need to be sought—if intelligence officials may not yet know whether a developing conspiracy in the US has ties to foreign sources of support? Must the Court even try to draw this line between domestic and foreign threats? Could it be abandoned?

4. ***Threats, Technology, and Rhetoric.*** How did Justice Powell's majority opinion describe contemporary threats to national security in 1972? How did it describe the role of technology in amplifying those threats? Go through the opinion to find examples of rhetoric used in these descriptions. How does it compare to the equivalent language in Justice Douglas' concurrence? In what ways does it resemble statements heard in today's debates over national security and privacy?

5. ***The Import of Title III.*** The statutory provision that the majority opinion referred to as § 2511(3) was part of the Wiretap Act, or "Title III." It

would be revised many years later with enactment of the Electronic Communications Privacy Act [see Chapter 5]. Can you explain the interaction of the Fourth Amendment and the Wiretap Act? The Court also suggested that Congress could and perhaps should intervene to establish specific procedures for "domestic security" scenarios like the case before it. Congress has not taken up this invitation to develop a separate set of rules for the "domestic security" category in the *Keith* trichotomy.

6. ***Unanimous Result.*** No justices dissented from the holding in *Keith*. Chief Justice Burger concurred in the result alone but joined no opinion. Justice White wrote a concurrence arguing that the case should have been decided on a statutory basis by parsing the § 2511(3) exception discussed by the majority. Justice Rehnquist recused himself; he had joined the Court only six months before, and previously worked as a high-ranking official in the Nixon Administration Justice Department. The remaining six justices (including Justice Douglas, who also wrote separately) joined the majority opinion.

### 2. REGULATION OF FOREIGN INTELLIGENCE SURVEILLANCE

The *Keith* decision explicitly invited Congress to establish procedures for national security surveillance. In the years that followed, multiple congressional investigations, particularly a special Senate panel known as the "Church Committee," revealed extensive warrantless surveillance programs managed by the Nixon Administration, many aimed at domestic organizations. The most famous of these was called "COINTELPRO" (for "Counter-Intelligence Program") and it involved the FBI spying on—and at times disrupting the activities of—varied US political organizations, including Communist parties, the Ku Klux Klan, the Black Panthers, and groups opposed to the Vietnam War.

In 1978, Congress passed the Foreign Intelligence Surveillance Act ("FISA"), 50 U.S.C. §§ 1801 et seq., in part to respond to these controversial practices. Notwithstanding the concerns about domestic security raised by *Keith* and COINTELPRO, FISA focused on the *foreign* security portion of the *Keith* trichotomy: counterespionage targeting "agents of a foreign power." Congress endeavored to strike a balance between privacy concerns and the need for timely and often secretive intelligence activities. The statute has been amended many times, especially since the September 11, 2001 terrorist attacks. In particular, the Uniting and Strenghtning America by Providing Appropriate Tools Required to Intercept and Obstruct Terrorism Act, better known as the USA PATRIOT Act (or "Patriot Act"), P.L. 107–56 (2001), which passed immediately after those attacks, expanded several portions of FISA.

FISA is a complex statute. Its core provisions allow intelligence and law enforcement investigators to conduct foreign surveillance by securing an order from the Foreign Intelligence Surveillance Court (FISC), a special court established by FISA. The FISC is composed of 11 sitting federal district judges from around the country, who undertake their

FISC duties alongside their normal docket. As with traditional search warrant applications, the proceedings are ex parte. The standard for FISC orders is less demanding than the ordinary requirement of probable cause under the Fourth Amendment, but it is designed to provide some check on the government, and particularly to prevent the government from evading Fourth Amendment restrictions on spying aimed at US persons by invoking tenuous allegations of links to foreign sources . The portion of FISA excerpted below authorizes electronic surveillance under certain circumstances. FISA also includes:

- provisions concerning physical searches that are generally similar to the electronic surveillance rules;
- a newer section enacted in 2008 (and discussed below in *Clapper v. Amnesty International*) imposing less stringent requirements on surveillance of non-US persons reasonably believed to be located outside the US; and
- a broadened authorization of access to business records and tangible things, which became the linchpin of the NSA's collection of communications metadata [see Section B below].

Many other sources of legal authority besides FISA affect the power of the federal government to gather information for intelligence purposes. One of these, Executive Order 12333 (often referred to as "Twelve Triple Three"), formally permits intelligence-related agencies (including the CIA, FBI, and NSA) to collect and archive personal information in a variety of situations—which include retaining information about US persons that is collected "incidentally" during otherwise foreign-directed surveillance. A short excerpt of E.O. 12333 is included further below.

## Foreign Intelligence Surveillance Act

50 U.S.C. §§ 1801 et seq.

### § 1801. Definitions.

As used in this subchapter:

(a) "Foreign power" means—

(1) a foreign government or any component thereof, whether or not recognized by the United States;

(2) a faction of a foreign nation or nations, not substantially composed of United States persons;

(3) an entity that is openly acknowledged by a foreign government or governments to be directed and controlled by such foreign government or governments;

(4) a group engaged in international terrorism or activities in preparation therefor;

(5) a foreign-based political organization, not substantially composed of United States persons;

(6) an entity that is directed and controlled by a foreign government or governments; or

(7) an entity not substantially composed of United States persons that is engaged in the international proliferation of weapons of mass destruction.

(b) "Agent of a foreign power" means—

(1) any person other than a United States person, who—

(A) acts in the United States as an officer or employee of a foreign power, or as a member of a foreign power as defined in subsection (a)(4) of this section, irrespective of whether the person is inside the United States;

(B) acts for or on behalf of a foreign power which engages in clandestine intelligence activities in the United States contrary to the interests of the United States . . . ;

(C) engages in international terrorism or activities in preparation therefor[ ];

(2) any person who—

(A) knowingly engages in clandestine intelligence gathering activities for or on behalf of a foreign power, which activities involve or may involve a violation of the criminal statutes of the United States;

(B) pursuant to the direction of an intelligence service or network of a foreign power, knowingly engages in any other clandestine intelligence activities for or on behalf of such foreign power, which activities involve or are about to involve a violation of the criminal statutes of the United States;

(C) knowingly engages in sabotage or international terrorism, or activities that are in preparation therefor, for or on behalf of a foreign power;

(D) knowingly enters the United States under a false or fraudulent identity for or on behalf of a foreign power or, while in the United States, knowingly assumes a false or fraudulent identity for or on behalf of a foreign power; or

(E) knowingly aids or abets any person in the conduct of activities described in subparagraph (A), (B), or (C) or knowingly conspires with any person to engage in activities described in subparagraph (A), (B), or (C).

(c) "International terrorism" means activities that—

(1) involve violent acts or acts dangerous to human life that are a violation of the criminal laws of the United States or of any

State, or that would be a criminal violation if committed within the jurisdiction of the United States or any State;

(2) appear to be intended—

(A) to intimidate or coerce a civilian population;

(B) to influence the policy of a government by intimidation or coercion; or

(C) to affect the conduct of a government by assassination or kidnapping; and

(3) occur totally outside the United States, or transcend national boundaries in terms of the means by which they are accomplished, the persons they appear intended to coerce or intimidate, or the locale in which their perpetrators operate or seek asylum.

. . .

(f) "Electronic surveillance" means—

(1) the acquisition by an electronic, mechanical, or other surveillance device of the contents of any wire or radio communication sent by or intended to be received by a particular, known United States person who is in the United States, if the contents are acquired by intentionally targeting that United States person, under circumstances in which a person has a reasonable expectation of privacy and a warrant would be required for law enforcement purposes;

(2) the acquisition by an electronic, mechanical, or other surveillance device of the contents of any wire communication to or from a person in the United States, without the consent of any party thereto, if such acquisition occurs in the United States . . . ;

(3) the intentional acquisition by an electronic, mechanical, or other surveillance device of the contents of any radio communication, under circumstances in which a person has a reasonable expectation of privacy and a warrant would be required for law enforcement purposes, and if both the sender and all intended recipients are located within the United States; or

(4) the installation or use of an electronic, mechanical, or other surveillance device in the United States for monitoring to acquire information, other than from a wire or radio communication, under circumstances in which a person has a reasonable expectation of privacy and a warrant would be required for law enforcement purposes.

. . .

(h) "Minimization procedures", with respect to electronic surveillance, means—

(1) specific procedures, which shall be adopted by the Attorney General, that are reasonably designed in light of the purpose and technique of the particular surveillance, to minimize the acquisition and retention, and prohibit the dissemination, of nonpublicly available information concerning unconsenting United States persons consistent with the need of the United States to obtain, produce, and disseminate foreign intelligence information;

(2) procedures that require that nonpublicly available information, which is not foreign intelligence information, as defined in subsection (e)(1) of this section, shall not be disseminated in a manner that identifies any United States person, without such person's consent, unless such person's identity is necessary to understand foreign intelligence information or assess its importance;

(3) notwithstanding paragraphs (1) and (2), procedures that allow for the retention and dissemination of information that is evidence of a crime which has been, is being, or is about to be committed and that is to be retained or disseminated for law enforcement purposes; . . .

(i) "United States person" means a citizen of the United States, an alien lawfully admitted for permanent residence . . ., an unincorporated association a substantial number of members of which are citizens of the United States or aliens lawfully admitted for permanent residence, or a corporation which is incorporated in the United States, but does not include a corporation or an association which is a foreign power, as defined in subsection (a)(1), (2), or (3) of this section. . . .

**§ 1802. Electronic surveillance authorization without court order. . . .**

(a)

(1) Notwithstanding any other law, the President, through the Attorney General, may authorize electronic surveillance without a court order under this subchapter to acquire foreign intelligence information for periods of up to one year if the Attorney General certifies in writing under oath that—

(A) the electronic surveillance is solely directed at—

(i) the acquisition of the contents of communications transmitted by means of communications used exclusively between or among foreign powers . . . or

(ii) the acquisition of technical intelligence, other than the spoken communications of individuals, from property or premises under the open and exclusive control of a foreign power . . . ;

(B) there is no substantial likelihood that the surveillance will acquire the contents of any communication to which a United States person is a party; and

(C) the proposed minimization procedures with respect to such surveillance meet the definition of minimization procedures under section 1801(h) of this title [and are reported to House and Senate Intelligence Committees].

[§ 1803 establishes the FISC and an accompanying appeals court, the FIS Court of Review (or "FISCR").]

**§ 1804. Application for court orders.**

(a) Submission by Federal officer; approval of Attorney General; contents

Each application for an order approving electronic surveillance under this subchapter shall be made by a Federal officer in writing upon oath or affirmation to a judge [on the FISC]. Each application shall require the approval of the Attorney General based upon his finding that it satisfies the criteria and requirements of such application as set forth in this subchapter. It shall include—

(1) the identity of the Federal officer making the application;

(2) the identity, if known, or a description of the specific target of the electronic surveillance;

(3) a statement of the facts and circumstances relied upon by the applicant to justify his belief that—

(A) the target of the electronic surveillance is a foreign power or an agent of a foreign power; and

(B) each of the facilities or places at which the electronic surveillance is directed is being used, or is about to be used, by a foreign power or an agent of a foreign power;

(4) a statement of the proposed minimization procedures;

(5) a description of the nature of the information sought and the type of communications or activities to be subjected to the surveillance;

(6) a certification or certifications by [certain executive branch officials]—

(A) that the certifying official deems the information sought to be foreign intelligence information;

(B) that a significant purpose of the surveillance is to obtain foreign intelligence information;

(C) that such information cannot reasonably be obtained by normal investigative techniques;

(D) that designates the type of foreign intelligence information being sought according to the categories described in section 1801(e) of this title; and

(E) including a statement of the basis for the certification that—

(i) the information sought is the type of foreign intelligence information designated; and

(ii) such information cannot reasonably be obtained by normal investigative techniques;

(7) a summary statement of the means by which the surveillance will be effected and a statement whether physical entry is required to effect the surveillance;

(8) a statement of the facts concerning all previous applications that have been made to any judge under this subchapter involving any of the persons, facilities, or places specified in the application, and the action taken on each previous application; and

(9) a statement of the period of time for which the electronic surveillance is required to be maintained . . . .

## Executive Order 12333

United States Intelligence Activities

. . .

### Part 2: Conduct of Intelligence Activities

2.1 *Need.* Accurate and timely information about the capabilities, intentions and activities of foreign powers, organizations, or persons and their agents is essential to informed decisionmaking in the areas of national defense and foreign relations. Collection of such information is a priority objective and will be pursued in a vigorous, innovative and responsible manner that is consistent with the Constitution and applicable law and respectful of the principles upon which the United States was founded.

2.2 *Purpose.* This Order is intended to enhance human and technical collection techniques, especially those undertaken abroad, and the acquisition of significant foreign intelligence, as well as the detection and countering of international terrorist activities and espionage conducted by foreign powers. Set forth below are certain general principles that, in addition to and consistent with applicable laws, are intended to achieve the proper balance between the acquisition of essential information and protection of individual interests. Nothing in this Order shall be construed to apply to or interfere with any authorized civil or criminal law enforcement responsibility of any department or agency.

2.3 *Collection of Information*. Agencies within the Intelligence Community are authorized to collect, retain or disseminate information concerning United States persons only in accordance with procedures established by the head of the agency concerned and approved by the Attorney General. . . . Those procedures shall permit collection, retention and dissemination of the following types of information:

(a) Information that is publicly available or collected with the consent of the person concerned;

(b) Information constituting foreign intelligence or counterintelligence, including such information concerning corporations or other commercial organizations. . . . ;

(c) Information obtained in the course of a lawful foreign intelligence, counterintelligence, international narcotics or international terrorism investigation;

(d) Information needed to protect the safety of any persons or organizations, including those who are targets, victims or hostages of international terrorist organizations;

(e) Information needed to protect foreign intelligence or counterintelligence sources or methods from unauthorized disclosure. . . . ;

(f) Information concerning persons who are reasonably believed to be potential sources or contacts for the purpose of determining their suitability or credibility;

. . .

(i) Incidentally obtained information that may indicate involvement in activities that may violate federal, state, local or foreign laws; and

(j) Information necessary for administrative purposes.

2.4 *Collection Techniques*. Agencies within the Intelligence Community shall use the least intrusive collection techniques feasible within the United States or directed against United States persons abroad. Agencies are not authorized to use such techniques as electronic surveillance, unconsented physical search, mail surveillance, physical surveillance, or monitoring devices unless they are in accordance with procedures established by the head of the agency concerned and approved by the Attorney General. Such procedures shall protect constitutional and other legal rights and limit use of such information to lawful governmental purposes. . . .

## 3. SECTION 702 AND STANDING

### Clapper v. Amnesty International

133 S. Ct. 1138 (2013)

■ JUSTICE ALITO delivered the opinion of the Court.

Section 702 of the Foreign Intelligence Surveillance Act of 1978 ["FISA"], 50 U.S.C. § 1881a, allows the Attorney General and the Director of National Intelligence to acquire foreign intelligence information by jointly authorizing the surveillance of individuals who are not "United States persons" [as defined by § 1801(i)] and are reasonably believed to be located outside the United States. Before doing so, the Attorney General and the Director of National Intelligence normally must obtain the Foreign Intelligence Surveillance Court's approval. Respondents are United States persons whose work, they allege, requires them to engage in sensitive international communications with individuals who they believe are likely targets of surveillance under § 1881a. Respondents seek a declaration that § 1881a is unconstitutional, as well as an injunction against § 1881a-authorized surveillance. The question before us is whether respondents have Article III standing to seek this prospective relief.

Respondents assert that they can establish injury in fact because there is an objectively reasonable likelihood that their communications will be acquired under § 1881a at some point in the future. But respondents' theory of future injury is too speculative to satisfy the well-established requirement that threatened injury must be "certainly impending." And even if respondents could demonstrate that the threatened injury is certainly impending, they still would not be able to establish that this injury is fairly traceable to § 1881a. As an alternative argument, respondents contend that they are suffering present injury because the risk of § 1881a-authorized surveillance already has forced them to take costly and burdensome measures to protect the confidentiality of their international communications. But respondents cannot manufacture standing by choosing to make expenditures based on hypothetical future harm that is not certainly impending. We therefore hold that respondents lack Article III standing.

#### I

#### A

When Congress enacted the FISA Amendments Act of 2008 (FISA Amendments Act) it left much of FISA intact, but it established a new and independent source of intelligence collection authority, beyond that granted in traditional FISA. As relevant here, § 702 of FISA, 50 U.S.C. § 1881a, which was enacted as part of the FISA Amendments Act, supplements pre-existing FISA authority by creating a new framework under which the Government may seek the FISC's authorization of certain foreign intelligence surveillance targeting the communications of non-U.S. persons located abroad. Unlike traditional FISA surveillance, § 1881a does not require the Government to demonstrate probable cause that the target of the electronic surveillance is a foreign power or agent of a foreign power. And, unlike traditional FISA, § 1881a does not require the Government to specify the nature and location of each of the particular facilities or places at which the electronic surveillance will occur.

The present case involves a constitutional challenge to § 1881a. Surveillance under § 1881a is subject to statutory conditions, judicial authorization, congressional supervision, and compliance with the Fourth Amendment. Section 1881a provides that, upon the issuance of an order from the Foreign Intelligence Surveillance Court, "the Attorney General and the Director of National Intelligence may authorize jointly, for a period of up to 1 year . . . the targeting of persons reasonably believed to be located outside the United States to acquire foreign intelligence information." Surveillance under § 1881a may not be intentionally targeted at any person known to be in the United States or any U.S. person reasonably believed to be located abroad. Additionally, acquisitions under § 1881a must comport with the Fourth Amendment. Moreover, surveillance under § 1881a is subject to congressional oversight and several types of Executive Branch review.

Section 1881a mandates that the Government obtain the Foreign Intelligence Surveillance Court's approval of "targeting" procedures, "minimization" procedures, and a governmental certification regarding proposed surveillance. Among other things, the Government's certification must attest that (1) procedures are in place "that have been approved, have been submitted for approval, or will be submitted with the certification for approval by the [FISC] that are reasonably designed" to ensure that an acquisition is "limited to targeting persons reasonably believed to be located outside" the United States; (2) minimization procedures adequately restrict the acquisition, retention, and dissemination of nonpublic information about unconsenting U.S. persons, as appropriate; (3) guidelines have been adopted to ensure compliance with targeting limits and the Fourth Amendment; and (4) the procedures and guidelines referred to above comport with the Fourth Amendment.

The Foreign Intelligence Surveillance Court's role includes determining whether the Government's certification contains the required elements. Additionally, the Court assesses whether the targeting procedures are "reasonably designed" (1) to "ensure that an acquisition . . . is limited to targeting persons reasonably believed to be located outside the United States" and (2) to "prevent the intentional acquisition of any communication as to which the sender and all intended recipients are known . . . to be located in the United States." The Court analyzes whether the minimization procedures "meet the definition of minimization procedures under section 1801(h) . . ., as appropriate." The Court also assesses whether the targeting and minimization procedures are consistent with the statute and the Fourth Amendment.

### B

Respondents are attorneys and human rights, labor, legal, and media organizations whose work allegedly requires them to engage in sensitive and sometimes privileged telephone and e-mail communications with colleagues, clients, sources, and other individuals located abroad. Respondents believe that some of the people with whom they exchange foreign intelligence information are likely targets of surveillance under § 1881a. Specifically, respondents claim that they communicate by telephone and e-mail with people the Government "believes or believed to be associated with terrorist organizations," "people located in geographic areas that are a special focus" of the Government's counterterrorism or diplomatic efforts, and activists who oppose governments that are supported by the United States Government.

Respondents claim that § 1881a compromises their ability to locate witnesses, cultivate sources, obtain information, and communicate confidential information to their clients. Respondents also assert that they "have ceased engaging" in certain telephone and e-mail conversations. According to respondents, the threat of surveillance will compel them to travel abroad in order to have in-person conversations. In addition, respondents declare that they have undertaken "costly and burdensome measures" to protect the confidentiality of sensitive communications.

### C

On the day when the FISA Amendments Act was enacted, respondents filed this action seeking (1) a declaration that § 1881a, on its face, violates the Fourth Amendment, the First Amendment, Article III, and separation-of-powers principles and (2) a permanent injunction against the use of § 1881a. Respondents assert what they characterize as two separate theories of Article III standing. First, they claim that there is an objectively reasonable likelihood that their communications will be acquired under § 1881a at some point in the future, thus causing them injury. Second, respondents maintain that the risk of surveillance under § 1881a is so substantial that they have been forced to take costly and burdensome measures to protect the confidentiality of their international communications; in their view, the costs they have incurred constitute present injury that is fairly traceable to § 1881a.

After both parties moved for summary judgment, the District Court held that respondents do not have standing. On appeal, however, a panel of the Second Circuit reversed. The panel agreed with respondents' argument that they have standing due to the objectively reasonable likelihood that their communications will be intercepted at some time in the future. In addition, the panel held that respondents have established that they are suffering "present injuries in fact—economic and professional harms—stemming from a reasonable fear of future harmful government conduct." The Second Circuit denied rehearing en banc by an equally divided vote.

Because of the importance of the issue and the novel view of standing adopted by the Court of Appeals, we granted certiorari and we now reverse.

## II

Article III of the Constitution limits federal courts' jurisdiction to certain "Cases" and "Controversies." As we have explained, no principle is more fundamental to the judiciary's proper role in our system of government than the constitutional limitation of federal-court jurisdiction to actual cases or controversies. One element of the case-or-controversy requirement is that plaintiffs must establish that they have standing to sue.

The law of Article III standing, which is built on separation-of-powers principles, serves to prevent the judicial process from being used to usurp the powers of the political branches. In keeping with the purpose of this doctrine, our standing inquiry has been especially rigorous when reaching the merits of the dispute would force us to decide whether an action taken by one of the other two branches of the Federal Government was unconstitutional. Relaxation of standing requirements is directly related to the expansion of judicial power.

To establish Article III standing, an injury must be concrete, particularized, and actual or imminent; fairly traceable to the challenged action; and redressable by a favorable ruling. Although imminence is concededly a somewhat elastic concept, it cannot be stretched beyond its purpose, which is to ensure that the alleged injury is not too speculative for Article III purposes—that the injury is certainly impending. Thus, we have repeatedly reiterated that threatened injury must be certainly impending to constitute injury in fact and that "allegations of possible future injury" are not sufficient.

## III

### A

Respondents assert that they can establish injury in fact that is fairly traceable to § 1881a because there is an objectively reasonable likelihood that their communications with their foreign contacts will be intercepted under § 1881a at some point in the future. This argument fails. [R]espondents' argument rests on their highly speculative fear that: (1) the Government will decide to target the communications of non-U.S. persons with whom they communicate; (2) in doing so, the Government will choose to invoke its authority under § 1881a rather than utilizing another method of surveillance; (3) the Article III judges who serve on the Foreign Intelligence Surveillance Court will conclude that the

Government's proposed surveillance procedures satisfy § 1881a's many safeguards and are consistent with the Fourth Amendment; (4) the Government will succeed in intercepting the communications of respondents' contacts; and (5) respondents will be parties to the particular communications that the Government intercepts. [R]espondents' theory of standing, which relies on a highly attenuated chain of possibilities, does not satisfy the requirement that threatened injury must be certainly impending. Moreover, even if respondents could demonstrate injury in fact, the second link in the above-described chain of contingencies—which amounts to mere speculation about whether surveillance would be under § 1881a or some other authority—shows that respondents cannot satisfy the requirement that any injury in fact must be fairly traceable to § 1881a.

### B

Respondents' alternative argument—namely, that they can establish standing based on the measures that they have undertaken to avoid § 1881a-authorized surveillance—fares no better. Respondents assert that they are suffering ongoing injuries that are fairly traceable to § 1881a because the risk of surveillance under § 1881a requires them to take costly and burdensome measures to protect the confidentiality of their communications. Respondents claim, for instance, that the threat of surveillance sometimes compels them to avoid certain e-mail and phone conversations, to "talk in generalities rather than specifics," or to travel so that they can have in-person conversations.

The Second Circuit's analysis improperly allowed respondents to establish standing by asserting that they suffer present costs and burdens that are based on a fear of surveillance, so long as that fear is not "fanciful, paranoid, or otherwise unreasonable." This improperly waters down the fundamental requirements of Article III. Respondents' contention that they have standing because they incurred certain costs as a reasonable reaction to a risk of harm is unavailing—because the harm respondents seek to avoid is not certainly impending. In other words, respondents cannot manufacture standing merely by inflicting harm on themselves based on their fears of hypothetical future harm that is not certainly impending. Any ongoing injuries that respondents are suffering are not fairly traceable to § 1881a.

### IV

Respondents also suggest that they should be held to have standing because otherwise the constitutionality of § 1881a could not be challenged. It would be wrong, they maintain, to "insulate the government's surveillance activities from meaningful judicial review." Respondents' suggestion is both legally and factually incorrect. First, "[t]he assumption that if respondents have no standing to sue, no one would have standing, is not a reason to find standing." *Valley Forge Christian Coll. v. Americans United for Separation of Church & State*, Inc., 454 U.S. 464, 489 (1982).

Second, our holding today by no means insulates § 1881a from judicial review. As described above, Congress created a comprehensive scheme in which the Foreign Intelligence Surveillance Court evaluates the Government's certifications, targeting procedures, and minimization procedures—including assessing whether the targeting and minimization procedures comport with the Fourth Amendment. Any dissatisfaction that respondents may have about the Foreign Intelligence Surveillance Court's rulings—or the congressional delineation of that court's role—is irrelevant to our standing analysis.

Additionally, if the Government intends to use or disclose information obtained or derived from a § 1881a acquisition in judicial or administrative proceedings, it must provide advance notice of its intent, and the affected person may challenge the lawfulness of the acquisition. Thus, if the Government were to prosecute one of respondent-attorney's foreign clients using § 1881a-authorized surveillance, the Government would be required to make a disclosure. In such a situation, unlike in the present case, it would at least be clear that the Government had acquired the foreign client's communications using § 1881a-authorized surveillance.

Finally, any electronic communications service provider that the Government directs to assist in § 1881a surveillance may challenge the lawfulness of that directive before the FISC. Indeed, at the behest of a service provider, the Foreign Intelligence Surveillance Court of Review previously analyzed the constitutionality of electronic surveillance directives issued pursuant to a now-expired set of FISA amendments.

We hold that respondents lack Article III standing because they cannot demonstrate that the future injury they purportedly fear is certainly impending and because they cannot manufacture standing by incurring costs in anticipation of non-imminent harm. We therefore reverse the judgment of the Second Circuit and remand the case for further proceedings consistent with this opinion.

■ JUSTICE BREYER, with whom JUSTICE GINSBURG, JUSTICE SOTOMAYOR, and JUSTICE KAGAN join, dissenting.

The plaintiffs' standing depends upon the likelihood that the Government, acting under the authority of 50 U.S.C. § 1881a, will harm them by intercepting at least some of their private, foreign, telephone, or e-mail conversations. In my view, this harm is not "speculative." Indeed it is as likely to take place as are most future events that commonsense inference and ordinary knowledge of human nature tell us will happen. This Court has often found the occurrence of similar future events sufficiently certain to support standing. I dissent from the Court's contrary conclusion.

Several considerations, based upon the record along with commonsense inferences, convince me that there is a very high likelihood that Government, acting under the authority of § 1881a, will intercept at least some of the communications just described. First, the plaintiffs have engaged, and continue to engage, in electronic communications of a kind that the 2008 amendment, but not the prior Act, authorizes the Government to intercept. These communications include discussions with family members of those detained at Guantanamo, friends and acquaintances of those persons, and investigators, experts and others with knowledge of circumstances related to terrorist activities. These persons are foreigners located outside the United States. They are not "foreign power[s]" or "agent[s] of . . . foreign power [s]." And the plaintiffs state that they exchange with these persons "foreign intelligence information," defined to include information that "relates to" "international terrorism" and "the national defense or the security of the United States."

Second, the plaintiffs have a strong motive to engage in, and the Government has a strong motive to listen to, conversations of the kind described.

We need only assume that the Government is doing its job (to find out about, and combat, terrorism) in order to conclude that there is a high probability that the Government will intercept at least some electronic communication to which at least some of the plaintiffs are parties. The majority is wrong when it describes the harm threatened plaintiffs as "speculative."

The majority more plausibly says that the plaintiffs have failed to show that the threatened harm is "certainly impending." But, as the majority appears to concede, certainty is not, and never has been, the touchstone of standing. The future is inherently uncertain. Yet federal courts frequently entertain actions for injunctions and for declaratory relief aimed at preventing future activities that are reasonably likely or highly likely, but not absolutely certain, to take place. And that degree of certainty is all that is needed to support standing here.

How could the law be otherwise? Suppose that a federal court faced a claim by homeowners that (allegedly) unlawful dam-building practices created a high risk that their homes would be flooded. Would the court deny them standing on the ground that the risk of flood was only 60, rather than 90, percent?

Would federal courts deny standing to a plaintiff in a diversity action who claims an anticipatory breach of contract where the future breach depends on probabilities? The defendant, say, has threatened to load wheat onto a ship bound for India despite a promise to send the wheat to the United States. No one can know for certain that this will happen. Perhaps the defendant will change his mind; perhaps the ship will turn and head for the United States. Yet, despite the uncertainty, the Constitution does not prohibit a federal court from hearing such a claim.

In sum, as the Court concedes, the word "certainly" in the phrase "certainly impending" does not refer to absolute certainty. As our case law demonstrates, what the Constitution requires is something more akin to "reasonable probability" or "high probability." The use of some such standard is all that is necessary here to ensure the actual concrete injury that the Constitution demands.

While I express no view on the merits of the plaintiffs' constitutional claims, I do believe that at least some of the plaintiffs have standing to make those claims. I dissent, with respect, from the majority's contrary conclusion.

## NOTES

1. ***Section 702.*** The statutory provision that the Court refers to as "section 1181a" (for its numbering in the United States Code) is more commonly referred to as "section 702," for its numbering in the FISA Amendments Act of 2008, which inserted the new provision into the law. It is one of the most controversial provisions of FISA, because it does not require any individualized evaluation of suspicion related to particular targets of the surveillance. Any collection of communications by US persons would be incidental to the targeting of a foreign person. The government maintains that minimization procedures reduce the likelihood that such surveillance would invade the privacy of US persons, but critics are not persuaded. Go back through the Court's explanation of Section 702's requirements. Is this arrangement consistent with *Keith*? What are the arguments on each side of that question?

2. ***Certainty and Standing.*** As Justice Breyer suggests, many federal court cases present at least some degree of uncertainty, yet no one doubts the existence of standing. Do the majority and dissent disagree about the standard to be applied for determining standing, about how much speculation the plaintiffs rely upon, or both? Who do you think has the more persuasive arguments about the standard? Who characterizes the degree of uncertainty in the plaintiffs' claims more accurately?

3. ***Reasons for Standing Doctrine.*** Why does the Constitution demand that federal courts must find standing before adjudicating a case? Clearly articulate the separation of powers principle at stake. Who benefits from a stricter standing requirement? A more relaxed one?

4. ***Defining Privacy Harms.*** We have seen repeatedly how the definition of harm can be troublesome in privacy cases. Frequently, the subject of surveillance will not be aware of it—that is often the whole point. In their effort to establish standing, the plaintiffs point to consequential harms such as the need to take special precautions when speaking with certain people in order to avoid potential surveillance. Are these really the reasons they oppose NSA surveillance?

5. ***The Reviewability of National Security Surveillance.*** At the end of the majority opinion, Justice Alito addresses the plaintiffs' argument that they should have standing because there could be no judicial review of national security surveillance otherwise. The Court concludes that this outcome might be acceptable—"the assumption that if respondents have no standing to sue, no one would have standing, is not a reason to find

standing." Are some government actions essentially unreviewable by courts? Moreover, the Court maintains that there are, in fact, situations when NSA surveillance would be reviewable. What scenarios does the *Clapper* opinion present? Can you think of others? Search warrants in ordinary criminal cases are issued secretly; is there similar concern about their reviewability?

---

## Practice

National Security Surveillance

Based on the excerpts above, determine what is required to conduct each of the following propsed surveillance activities lawfully:

1. A wiretap on the phone in the apartment shared by five University of Michigan graduate students, one of whomis a Yemeni national who holds a valid student visa and has newly been identified as visiting an Al Qaeda training camp in Afghanistan.
2. A listening device placed in the office of a small Washington, DC nonprofit organization believed to be a front group funneling money to the Boko Haram terrorist organization based in Nigeria.
3. Interception of email and telephone communications to and from the office of a small international communist party organization in London, with chapters around the world including the US.
4. A wiretap on the cell phone of a Russian businessman visiting Dallas to conduct negotiations with a US petroleum services company, whom the FBI believes is also secretly working for a Russian intelligence agency.
5. A wiretap on the cell phone of the president of a right-wing extremist organization in Idaho who is suspected of planning an armed assault on a federal forest ranger station there

---

## B. THE COMMUNICATIONS METADATA CONTROVERSY

In June 2013, the British newspaper The Guardian published a bombshell front-page story. Journalists had obtained a classified opinion issued by the FISC; it ordered the US telephone company Verizon to provide the NSA with essentially all records of its customers' calls on a "daily ongoing basis." Other newspapers including the New York Times, the Washington Post, and Der Speigel in Germany soon published numerous follow-up articles with additional revelations about NSA surveillance activities. It quickly became evident that the NSA was collecting metadata—information such as the phone numbers dialed and the length of calls—about most telephone calls in the United States.

The journalists based their stories on a huge trove of classified information copied and supplied to them by Edward Snowden, a former employee of an NSA contractor. Snowden left the US before the first story appeared and is now living in Russia, which granted him temporary asylum; the federal government has indicted him for violations of the

Espionage Act and theft of government property. Estimates of the number of documents he took range from tens of thousands to millions.

The federal government confirmed the authenticity of the Verizon order and some other documents referred to in the news reports, and over time released others voluntarily. When defending the program, law enforcement and intelligence officials repeatedly invoked the same image: the search for communications between terrorist suspects was like the search for a needle in a haystack. In order to find the needle, investigators needed the haystack—the bulk telephony metadata—even though they were interested only in the needle. They also argued vociferously that the collection of metadata was authorized by FISA and approved by the FISC. Specifically, they said, a provision added to FISA by Section 215 of the USA PATRIOT Act (and generally known as "Section 215") allowed the FBI to petition the FISC for access to business records relevant to a terrorism investigation; the FBI was then permitted to share this data with the NSA. Critics were just as vehement that the program exceeded the scope of FISA and violated the First and Fourth Amendments. Within days of the first revelations, several advocacy organizations had filed lawsuits, and by the end of 2013 there were two district court decisions, both excerpted below along with a later appellate decision in one of the cases. As explained further below, Congress has since changed the rules for the collection of metadata, so these opinions are already historical documents in some sense—but they typify the sharply differing responses to counterterrorism measures and their privacy impact.

## Klayman v. Obama

957 F. Supp. 2d 1 (D.D.C. 2013)

■ RICHARD J. LEON, UNITED STATES DISTRICT JUDGE.

On June 6, 2013, plaintiffs brought the first of two related lawsuits challenging the constitutionality and statutory authorization of certain intelligence-gathering practices by the United States government relating to the wholesale collection of the phone record metadata of all U.S. citizens. These related cases are two of several lawsuits arising from public revelations over the past six months that the federal government, through the National Security Agency ("NSA"), and with the participation of certain telecommunications and internet companies, has conducted surveillance and intelligence-gathering programs that collect certain data about the telephone and internet activity of American citizens within the United States.

Before the Court are plaintiffs' two Motions for Preliminary Injunction, one in each case.

[T]he Court concludes that plaintiffs have standing to challenge the constitutionality of the Government's bulk collection and querying of phone record metadata, that they have demonstrated a substantial likelihood of success on the merits of their Fourth Amendment claim, and that they will suffer irreparable harm absent preliminary injunctive relief.

## BACKGROUND

On June 5, 2013, the British newspaper The Guardian reported the first of several "leaks" of classified material from Edward Snowden, a former NSA contract employee, which have revealed—and continue to reveal—multiple US government intelligence collection and surveillance programs. That initial media report disclosed a FISC order dated April 25, 2013 ["April 25, 2013 Secondary Order"], compelling Verizon Business Network Services to produce to the NSA on "an ongoing daily basis . . . all call detail records or 'telephony metadata' created by Verizon for communications (i) between the United States and abroad; or (ii) wholly within the United States, including local telephone calls." According to the news article, this order "show[ed] . . . that under the Obama administration the communication records of millions of US citizens are being collected indiscriminately and in bulk—regardless of whether they are suspected of any wrongdoing." In response to this disclosure, the Government confirmed the authenticity of the April 25, 2013 FISC Order, and, in this litigation and in certain public statements, acknowledged the existence of a "program" under which "the FBI obtains orders from the FISC pursuant to Section 215 [of the USA PATRIOT Act] directing certain telecommunications service providers to produce to the NSA on a daily basis electronic copies of 'call detail records.'" Follow-on media reports revealed other Government surveillance programs, including the Government's collection of internet data pursuant to a program called "PRISM."

Soon after the first public revelations in the news media, plaintiffs filed their complaints in these two cases.

### I. Statutory Background

### FISA and Section 215 of the USA PATRIOT Act (50 U.S.C. § 1861)

In 1978, Congress enacted the Foreign Intelligence Surveillance Act, 50 U.S.C. §§ 1801 et seq. ("FISA"), to authorize and regulate certain governmental electronic surveillance of communications for foreign intelligence purposes.

In addition to authorizing wiretaps, §§ 1801–1812, FISA was subsequently amended to add provisions enabling the Government to obtain ex parte orders authorizing physical searches, §§ 1821–1829, as well as pen registers and trap-and-trace devices, §§ 1841–1846. In 1998, Congress added a "business records" provision to FISA. Under that provision, the FBI was permitted to apply for an ex parte order authorizing specified entities, such as common carriers, to release to the FBI copies of business records upon a showing in the FBI's application that "there are specific and articulable facts giving reason to believe that the person to whom the records pertain is a foreign power or an agent of a foreign power." 50 U.S.C. § 1862(b)(2)(B).

Following the September 11, 2001 terrorist attacks, Congress passed the USA PATRIOT Act, which made changes to FISA and several other laws. Section 215 of the PATRIOT Act replaced FISA's business-records provision with a more expansive "tangible things" provision. Codified at 50 U.S.C. § 1861, it authorizes the FBI to apply "for an order requiring the production of any tangible things (including books, records, papers, documents, and other items) for an investigation to obtain foreign intelligence information not concerning a United States person or to protect against international terrorism or clandestine intelligence activities." § 1861(a)(1). While this provision originally required that the FBI's application "shall specify that the records concerned are sought for" such an investigation, Congress amended the statute in 2006 to provide that the FBI's application must include "a statement of facts showing that there are reasonable grounds to believe that the tangible things sought are relevant to an authorized investigation . . . to obtain foreign intelligence information not concerning a United States person or to protect against international terrorism or clandestine intelligence activities." § 1861(b)(2)(A).

Section 1861 also imposes other requirements on the FBI when seeking to use this authority. For example, the investigation pursuant to which the request is made must be authorized and conducted under guidelines approved by the Attorney General under Executive Order No. 12,333 (or a successor thereto). If the FISC judge finds that the FBI's application meets these requirements, he "shall enter an ex parte order as requested, or as modified, approving the release of tangible things" (hereinafter, "production order"). § 1861(c)(1).

Under Section 1861's "use" provision, information that the FBI acquires through such a production order "concerning any [US] person may be used and disclosed by Federal officers and employees without the consent of the [US] person only in accordance with the minimization procedures adopted" by the Attorney General and approved by the FISC. § 1861(h). Meanwhile, recipients of Section 1861 production orders are obligated not to disclose the existence of the orders, with limited exceptions.

**Judicial Review by the FISC**

While the recipient of a production order must keep it secret, Section 1861 does provide the recipient—but only the recipient—a right of judicial review of the order before the FISC pursuant to specific procedures. Prior to 2006, recipients of Section 1861 production orders had no express right to judicial review of those orders, but Congress added such a provision when it reauthorized the PATRIOT Act that year.

Under Section 1861, "[a] person receiving a production order may challenge the legality of that order by filing a petition" [with the petition review pool of FISC judges]. The FISC review pool judge considering the petition may grant the petition "only if the judge finds that [the] order does not meet the requirements of [Section 1861] or is otherwise unlawful." § 1861(f)(2)(B). Once the FISC review pool judge rules on the petition, either the Government or the recipient of the production order may seek an en banc hearing before the full FISC, § 1803(a)(2)(A), or may appeal the decision by filing a petition for review with the FISC Court of Review, § 1861(f)(3). Finally, after the FISC Court of Review renders a written decision, either the Government or the recipient of the production order may then appeal this decision to the Supreme Court on petition for writ of certiorari. §§ 1861(f)(3), 1803(b). A production order "not explicitly modified or set aside consistent with [Section 1861(f)] shall remain in full effect." § 1861(f)(2)(D).

Consistent with other confidentiality provisions of FISA, Section 1861 provides that "[a]ll petitions under this subsection shall be filed under seal," § 1861(f)(5), and the "record of proceedings . . . shall be maintained under security measures established by the Chief Justice of the United States, in consultation with the Attorney General and the Director of National Intelligence," § 1861(f)(4).

## II. Collection of Bulk Telephony Metadata Pursuant to Section 1861

In broad overview, the Government has developed a "counterterrorism program" under Section 1861 in which it collect[s], compiles, retains, and analyzes certain telephone records, which it characterizes as "business records" created by certain telecommunications companies (the "Bulk Telephony Metadata Program"). The records collected under this program consist of "metadata," such as information about what phone numbers were used to make and receive calls, when the calls took place, and how long the calls lasted. According to the representations made by the Government, the metadata records collected under the program do not include any information about the content of those calls, or the names, addresses, or financial information of any party to the calls. Through targeted computerized searches of those metadata records, the NSA tries to discern connections between terrorist organizations and previously unknown terrorist operatives located in the United States.

The Government has conducted the Bulk Telephony Metadata Program for more than seven years. Beginning in May 2006 and continuing through the present, the FBI has obtained production orders from the FISC under Section 1861 directing certain telecommunications companies to produce, on an ongoing daily basis, these telephony metadata records, which the companies create and maintain as part of their business of providing telecommunications services to customers. The NSA then consolidates the metadata records provided by different telecommunications companies into one database, and under the FISC's orders, the NSA may retain the records for up to five years. According to

Government officials, this aggregation of records into a single database creates "an historical repository that permits retrospective analysis," enabling NSA analysts to draw connections, across telecommunications service providers, between numbers reasonably suspected to be associated with terrorist activity and with other, unknown numbers.

The FISC orders governing the Bulk Telephony Metadata Program specifically provide that the metadata records may be accessed only for counterterrorism purposes (and technical database maintenance). Specifically, NSA intelligence analysts, without seeking the approval of a judicial officer, may access the records to obtain foreign intelligence information only through "queries" of the records performed using "identifiers," such as telephone numbers, associated with terrorist activity. An "identifier" (i.e., selection term, or search term) used to start a query of the database is called a "seed," and "seeds" must be approved by one of twenty-two designated officials in the NSA's Homeland Security Analysis Center or other parts of the NSA's Signals Intelligence Directorate. Such approval may be given only upon a determination by one of those designated officials that there exist facts giving rise to a "reasonable, articulable suspicion" ("RAS") that the selection term to be queried is associated with one or more of the specified foreign terrorist organizations approved for targeting by the FISC. In 2012, for example, fewer than 300 unique identifiers met this RAS standard and were used as "seeds" to query the metadata, but "the number of unique identifiers has varied over the years."

When an NSA intelligence analyst runs a query using a "seed," the minimization procedures provide that query results are limited to records of communications within three "hops" from the seed. The query results thus will include only identifiers and their associated metadata having a direct contact with the seed (the first "hop"), identifiers and associated metadata having a direct contact with first "hop" identifiers (the second "hop"), and identifiers and associated metadata having a direct contact with second "hop" identifiers (the third "hop"). In plain English, this means that if a search starts with telephone number (123) 456–7890 as the "seed," the first hop will include all the phone numbers that (123) 456–7890 has called or received calls from in the last five years (say, 100 numbers), the second hop will include all the phone numbers that each of those 100 numbers has called or received calls from in the last five years (say, 100 numbers for each one of the 100 "first hop" numbers, or 10,000 total), and the third hop will include all the phone numbers that each of those 10,000 numbers has called or received calls from in the last five years (say, 100 numbers for each one of the 10,000 "second hop" numbers, or 1,000,000 total).

Once a query is conducted and it returns a universe of responsive records (i.e., a universe limited to records of communications within three hops from the seed), trained NSA analysts may then perform new searches and otherwise perform intelligence analysis within that universe of data without using RAS-approved search terms. According to the Government, following the "chains of communication"—which, for chains that cross different communications networks, is only possible if the metadata is aggregated—allows the analyst to discover information that may not be readily ascertainable through other, targeted intelligence-gathering techniques. For example, the query might reveal that a seed telephone number has been in contact with a previously unknown U.S. telephone number—i.e., on the first hop. And from there, "contact-chaining" out to the second and third hops to examine the contacts made by that telephone number may reveal a contact with other telephone numbers already known to the Government to be associated with a foreign terrorist organization.

Since the program began in May 2006, the FISC has repeatedly approved applications under Section 1861 and issued orders directing telecommunications service providers to produce records in connection with the Bulk Telephony Metadata Program. Through October 2013, fifteen different FISC judges have issued thirty-five orders authorizing the program. Under those orders, the Government must periodically seek renewal of the authority to collect telephony records (typically every ninety days). The Government has nonetheless acknowledged, as it must, that failures to comply with the minimization procedures set forth in the orders have occurred. For instance, in January 2009, the Government reported to the FISC that the NSA had improperly used an "alert list" of identifiers to search the bulk telephony metadata, which was composed of identifiers that had not been approved under the RAS standard. After reviewing the Government's reports on its noncompliance, Judge Reggie Walton of the FISC concluded that the NSA had engaged in "systematic noncompliance" with FISC-ordered minimization procedures over the preceding three years, since the inception of the Bulk Telephony Metadata Program, and had also repeatedly made misrepresentations and inaccurate statements about the program to the FISC judges. As a consequence, Judge Walton concluded that he had no confidence that the Government was doing its utmost to comply with the court's orders, and ordered the NSA to seek FISC approval on a case-by-case basis before conducting any further queries of the bulk telephony metadata collected pursuant to Section 1861 orders. This approval procedure remained in place from March 2009 to September 2009.

Notwithstanding this six-month "sanction" imposed by Judge Walton, the Government apparently has had further compliance problems relating to its collection programs in subsequent years. In October 2011, the Presiding Judge of the FISC, Judge John Bates, found that the Government had misrepresented the scope of its targeting of certain internet communications pursuant to 50 U.S.C. § 1881a (a different collection program than the Bulk Telephony Metadata Program at issue here). Both Judge Walton's and Judge Bates's opinions were only recently declassified by the Government in response to the Congressional and public reaction to the Snowden leaks.

## ANALYSIS

[The court found that the text and structure of FISA impliedly denied the judicial review that is ordinarily available under the Administrative Procedure Act, thus preempting the plaintiffs' claims that the NSA program exceeded the authority granted by Section 215. The court then proceeded to the constitutional challenges, first finding that it did have jurisdiction to entertain these claims. It then turned to the plaintiffs' likelihood of success on the merits of the constitutional claims, the primary factor for deciding the preliminary injunction motion.]

### Constitutional Claims

In addressing plaintiffs' likelihood of success on the merits of their constitutional claims, I will focus on their Fourth Amendment arguments, which I find to be the most likely to succeed. First, however, I must address plaintiffs' standing to challenge the various aspects of the Bulk Telephony Metadata Program.

**Plaintiffs Have Standing to Challenge Bulk Telephony Metadata Collection and Analysis.**

The NSA's Bulk Telephony Metadata Program involves two potential searches: (1) the bulk collection of metadata and (2) the analysis of that data through the NSA's querying process. For the following reasons, I have concluded that the plaintiffs have standing to challenge both. First, as to the collection, the Supreme Court decided *Clapper* just months before the June 2013 news reports revealed the existence and scope of certain NSA surveillance activities. Thus, whereas the plaintiffs in *Clapper* could only speculate as to whether they would be surveilled at all, plaintiffs in this case can point to strong evidence that, as Verizon customers, their telephony metadata has been collected for the last seven years (and stored for the last five) and will continue to be collected barring judicial or legislative intervention. In addition, the Government has declassified and authenticated an April 25, 2013 FISC Order signed by Judge Vinson, which confirms that the NSA has indeed collected telephony metadata from Verizon.

Likewise, I find that plaintiffs also have standing to challenge the NSA's querying procedures.

The Government describes the advantages of bulk collection in such a way as to convince me that plaintiffs' metadata—indeed everyone's metadata—is analyzed, manually or automatically, whenever the Government runs a query using as the "seed" a phone number or identifier associated with a phone for which the NSA has not collected metadata (e.g., phones operating through foreign phone companies).

Querying a foreign phone number is like entering a library and trying to find every book that cites *Battle Cry of Freedom* as a source. It might be referenced in a thousand books. It might be in just ten. It could be in zero. The only way to know is to check every book. At the end of a very long month, you are left with the "hop one" results (those books that cite *Battle Cry of Freedom*), but to get there, you had to open every book in the library.

Accordingly, plaintiffs meet the standing requirements set forth in *Clapper*, as they can demonstrate that the NSA has collected and analyzed their telephony metadata and will continue to operate the program consistent with FISC opinions and orders. Whether doing so violates plaintiffs' Fourth Amendment rights is, of course, a separate question and the subject of the next section, which addresses the merits of their claims.

**Plaintiffs Are Likely to Succeed on the Merits of Their Fourth Amendment Claim.**

The threshold issue that I must address [to analyze the Fourth Amendment question] is whether plaintiffs have a reasonable expectation of privacy that is violated when the Government indiscriminately collects their telephony metadata along with the metadata of hundreds of millions of other citizens without any particularized suspicion of wrongdoing, retains all of that metadata for five years, and then queries, analyzes, and investigates that data without prior judicial approval of the investigative targets. If they do—and a Fourth Amendment search has thus occurred—then the next step of the analysis will be to determine whether such a search is "reasonable."

**The Collection and Analysis of Telephony Metadata Constitutes a Search.**

The analysis of this threshold issue of the expectation of privacy must start with the Supreme Court's landmark opinion in *Smith v. Maryland*, 442 U.S. 735 (1979), which the FISC has said "squarely control[s]" when it comes to "[t]he production of telephone service provider metadata" [citing FISC Order of Aug. 29, 2013]. In *Smith*, police were investigating a robbery victim's reports that she had received threatening and obscene phone calls from someone claiming to be the robber. Without obtaining a warrant or court order, police installed a pen register, which revealed that a telephone in Smith's home had been used to call the victim on one occasion. The Supreme Court held that Smith had no reasonable expectation of privacy in the numbers dialed from his phone because he voluntarily transmitted them to his phone company, and because it is generally known that phone companies keep such information in their business records. The main thrust of the Government's argument here is that under *Smith*, no one has an expectation of privacy, let alone a reasonable one, in the telephony metadata that telecom companies hold as business records; therefore, the Bulk Telephony Metadata Program is not a search. I disagree.

The question before me is not the same question that the Supreme Court confronted in *Smith*. To say the least, "whether the installation and use of a pen register constitutes a 'search' within the meaning of the Fourth Amendment,"—under the circumstances addressed and contemplated in that case—is a far cry from the issue in this case.

Indeed, the question in this case can more properly be styled as follows: When do present-day circumstances—the evolutions in the Government's surveillance capabilities, citizens' phone habits, and the relationship between the NSA and telecom companies—become so thoroughly unlike those considered by the Supreme Court thirty-four years ago that a precedent like *Smith* simply does not apply? The answer, unfortunately for the Government, is now.

In *United States v. Jones*, 132 S. Ct. 945 (2012), five justices found that law enforcement's use of a GPS device to track a vehicle's movements for nearly a month violated Jones's reasonable expectation of privacy [see Chapter 1]. Significantly, the justices did so without questioning the validity of the Court's earlier decision in *United States v. Knotts*, 460 U.S. 276 (1983), that use of a tracking beeper does not constitute a search because "[a] person travelling in an automobile on public thoroughfares has no reasonable expectation of privacy in his movements from one place to another." Instead, they emphasized the many significant ways in which the short-range, short-term tracking device used in *Knotts* differed from the constant month-long surveillance achieved with the GPS device attached to Jones's car.

Just as the Court in *Knotts* did not address the kind of surveillance used to track *Jones*, the Court in *Smith* was not confronted with the NSA's Bulk Telephony Metadata Program. Nor could the Court in 1979 have ever imagined how the citizens of 2013 would interact with their phones. I am convinced that the surveillance program now before me is so different from a simple pen register that *Smith* is of little value in assessing whether the Bulk Telephony Metadata Program constitutes a Fourth Amendment search. To the contrary, for the following reasons, I believe that bulk telephony metadata collection and analysis almost certainly does violate a reasonable expectation of privacy.

First, the pen register in *Smith* was operational for only a matter of [13] days, and there is no indication from the Court's opinion that it expected the Government to retain those limited phone records once the case was over. This short-term, forward-looking (as opposed to historical), and highly-limited data collection is what the Supreme Court was assessing in *Smith*. The NSA telephony metadata program, on the other hand, involves the creation and maintenance of a historical database containing five years worth of data. And I might add, there is the very real prospect that the program will go on for as long as America is combatting terrorism, which realistically could be forever!

Second, the relationship between the police and the phone company in *Smith* is nothing compared to the relationship that has apparently evolved over the last seven years between the Government and telecom companies. In *Smith*, the Court considered a one-time, targeted request for data regarding an individual suspect in a criminal investigation, which in no way resembles the daily, all-encompassing, indiscriminate dump of phone metadata that the NSA now receives as part of its Bulk Telephony Metadata Program. It's one thing to say that people expect phone companies to occasionally provide information to law enforcement; it is quite another to suggest that our citizens expect all phone companies to operate what is effectively a joint intelligence-gathering operation with the Government.

Third, the almost-Orwellian technology that enables the Government to store and analyze the phone metadata of every telephone user in the United States is unlike anything that could have been conceived in 1979. The notion that the Government could collect similar data on hundreds of millions of people and retain that data for a five-year period, updating it with new data every day in perpetuity, was at best, in 1979, the stuff of science fiction. By comparison, the Government has at its disposal today the most advanced twenty-first century tools, allowing it to "store such records and efficiently mine them for information years into the future." *Jones*, 132 S. Ct. at 956 (Sotomayor, J., concurring). And these technologies are "cheap in comparison to conventional surveillance techniques and, by design, proceed[ ] surreptitiously," thereby "evad[ing] the ordinary checks that constrain abusive law enforcement practices: limited police . . . resources and community hostility." *Id.*

Finally, and most importantly, not only is the Government's ability to collect, store, and analyze phone data greater now than it was in 1979, but the nature and quantity of the information contained in people's telephony metadata is much greater, as well. The number of mobile subscribers in 2013 is more than 3,000 times greater than the 91,600 subscriber connections in 1984, and more than triple the 97,035,925 subscribers in June 2000. It is now safe to assume that the vast majority of people reading this opinion have at least one cell phone within arm's reach (in addition to other mobile devices). In fact, some undoubtedly will be reading this opinion on their cellphones. Count the phones at the bus stop, in a restaurant, or around the table at a work meeting or any given occasion. Thirty-four years ago, none of those phones would have been there. Thirty-four years ago, city streets were lined with pay phones. Thirty-four years ago, when people wanted to send "text messages," they wrote letters and attached postage stamps.

Admittedly, what metadata *is* has not changed over time. As in *Smith*, the types of information at issue in this case are relatively limited: phone numbers dialed, date, time, and the like. But the ubiquity of phones has dramatically altered the quantity of information that is now available and, more importantly, what that information can tell the Government about people's lives. Put simply, people in 2013 have an entirely different relationship with phones than they did thirty-four years ago. As a result, people make calls and send text messages now that they would not (really, could not) have made or sent back when *Smith* was decided This rapid and monumental shift towards a cell phone-centric culture means that the metadata from each person's phone "reflects a wealth of detail about her familial, political, professional, religious, and sexual associations," *Jones*, 132 S.Ct. at 955 (Sotomayor, J., concurring), that could not have been gleaned from a data collection in 1979. Records that once would have revealed a few scattered tiles of information about a person now reveal an entire mosaic—a vibrant and constantly updating picture of the person's life. Whereas some may assume that these cultural changes will force people to "reconcile themselves" to an "inevitable" "diminution of privacy that new technology entails," *Jones*, 132 S. Ct. at 962 (Alito, J., concurring), I think it is more likely that these trends have resulted in a greater expectation of privacy and a recognition that society views

In sum, the *Smith* pen register and the ongoing NSA Bulk Telephony Metadata Program have so many significant distinctions between them that I cannot possibly navigate these uncharted Fourth Amendment waters using as my North Star a case that predates the rise of cell phones. As I said at the outset, the question before me is not whether *Smith* answers the question of whether people can have a reasonable expectation of privacy in telephony metadata under all circumstances. Rather, the question that I will ultimately have to answer when I reach the merits of this case someday is whether people have a reasonable expectation of privacy that is violated when the Government, without any basis whatsoever to suspect them of any wrongdoing, collects and stores for five years their telephony metadata for purposes of subjecting it to high-tech querying and analysis without any case-by-case judicial approval. For the many reasons set forth above, it is significantly likely that on that day, I will answer that question in plaintiffs' favor.

**There Is a Significant Likelihood Plaintiffs Will Succeed in Showing that the Searches Are Unreasonable.**

Having found that a search occurred in this case, I next must examine the totality of the circumstances to determine whether [the] search is reasonable within the meaning of the Fourth Amendment. As a general matter, warrantless searches are per se unreasonable under the Fourth Amendment.

The Supreme Court has recognized only a few specifically established and well-delineated exceptions to that general rule, including one that applies when "special needs," beyond the normal need for law enforcement, make the warrant and probable-cause requirement impracticable. Even where the government claims "special needs," as it does in this case, a warrantless search is generally unreasonable unless based on some quantum of individualized suspicion. Still, a suspicionless search may be reasonable where the privacy interests implicated by the search are minimal, and where an important governmental interest furthered by the intrusion would be placed in jeopardy by a requirement of individualized suspicion.

For reasons I have already discussed at length, I find that plaintiffs have a very significant expectation of privacy in an aggregated collection of their telephony metadata covering the last five years, and the NSA's Bulk Telephony Metadata Program significantly intrudes on that expectation. Whether the program violates the Fourth Amendment will therefore turn on the nature and immediacy of the government's concerns and the efficacy of the [search] in meeting them. The Government asserts that the Bulk Telephony Metadata Program serves the "programmatic purpose" of "identifying unknown terrorist operatives and preventing terrorist attacks"—an interest that everyone, including this Court, agrees is of the highest order of magnitude. A closer examination of the record, however, reveals that the Government's interest is a bit more nuanced—it is not merely to investigate potential terrorists, but rather, to do so faster than other investigative methods might allow.

Yet, turning to the efficacy prong, the Government does not cite a single instance in which analysis of the NSA's bulk metadata collection actually stopped an imminent attack, or otherwise aided the Government in achieving any objective that was time-sensitive in nature. In fact, none of the three "recent episodes" cited by the Government that supposedly "illustrate the role that telephony metadata analysis can play in preventing and protecting against terrorist attack" involved any apparent urgency. In the first example, the FBI learned of a terrorist plot still "in its early stages" and investigated that plot before turning to the metadata "to ensure that all potential connections were identified." In the second example, it appears that the metadata analysis was used only after the terrorist was arrested "to establish [his] foreign ties and put them in context with his U.S. based planning efforts." And in the third, the metadata analysis "revealed a previously unknown number for [a] co-conspirator . . . and corroborated his connection to [the target of the investigation] as well as to other U.S.-based extremists." Again, there is no indication that these revelations were immediately useful or that they prevented an impending attack. Given the limited record before me at this point in the litigation—most notably, the utter lack of evidence that a terrorist attack has ever been prevented because searching the NSA database was faster than other investigative tactics—I have serious doubts about the efficacy of the metadata collection program as a means of conducting time-sensitive investigations in cases involving imminent threats of terrorism. Thus, plaintiffs have a substantial likelihood of showing that their privacy interests outweigh the Government's interest in collecting and analyzing bulk telephony metadata and therefore the NSA's bulk collection program is indeed an unreasonable search under the Fourth Amendment.

## CONCLUSION

This case is yet the latest chapter in the Judiciary's continuing challenge to balance the national security interests of the United States with the individual liberties of our citizens. The Government, in its understandable zeal to protect our homeland, has crafted a counterterrorism program with respect to telephone metadata that strikes the balance based in large part on a thirty-four year old Supreme Court precedent, the relevance of which has been eclipsed by technological advances and a cell phone-centric lifestyle heretofore inconceivable. In the months ahead, other Article III courts, no doubt, will wrestle to find the proper balance consistent with our constitutional system. But in the meantime, for all the above reasons, I will grant [plaintiffs'] requests for an injunction.

However, in light of the significant national security interests at stake in this case and the novelty of the constitutional issues, I will stay my order pending appeal. In doing so, I hereby give the Government fair notice that should my ruling be upheld, this order will go into effect forthwith. Accordingly, I fully expect that during the appellate process, which will consume at least the next six months, the Government will take whatever steps necessary to prepare itself to comply with this order when, and if, it is upheld. Suffice it to say, requesting further time to comply with this order months from now will not be well received and could result in collateral sanctions.

# ACLU v. Clapper

959 F. Supp. 2d 724 (S.D.N.Y. 2013)

■ WILLIAM H. PAULEY III, DISTRICT JUDGE:

The September 11th terrorist attacks revealed, in the starkest terms, just how dangerous and interconnected the world is. While Americans depended on technology for the conveniences of modernity, al-Qaeda plotted in a seventh-century milieu to use that technology against us. It was a bold jujitsu. And it succeeded because conventional intelligence gathering could not detect diffuse filaments connecting al-Qaeda.

The Government learned from its mistake and adapted to confront a new enemy: a terror network capable of orchestrating attacks across the world. It launched a number of counter-measures, including a bulk telephony metadata collection program—a wide net that could find and isolate gossamer contacts among suspected terrorists in an ocean of seemingly disconnected data.

This blunt tool only works because it collects everything. Such a program, if unchecked, imperils the civil liberties of every citizen. Each time someone in the United States makes or receives a telephone call, the telecommunications provider makes a record of when, and to what telephone number the call was placed, and how long it lasted. The NSA collects that telephony metadata. If plumbed, such data can reveal a rich profile of every individual as well as a comprehensive record of people's associations with one another.

The natural tension between protecting the nation and preserving civil liberty is squarely presented by the Government's bulk telephony metadata collection program. Edward Snowden's unauthorized disclosure of Foreign Intelligence Surveillance Court ("FISC") orders has provoked a public debate and this litigation. While robust discussions are underway across the nation, in Congress, and at the White House, the question for this Court is whether the Government's bulk telephony metadata program is lawful. This Court finds it is. But the question of whether that program should be conducted is for the other two coordinate branches of Government to decide.

[The ACLU brought this lawsuit] challenging the legality of the NSA's telephony metadata collection program. The ACLU moves for a preliminary injunction and the Government moves to dismiss the complaint. For the reasons that follow, this Court grants the Government's motion to dismiss and denies the ACLU's motion for a preliminary injunction.

## BACKGROUND

While the FISC is composed of Article III judges, it operates unlike any other Article III court. Proceedings in Article III courts are public. And the public enjoys a general right to inspect and copy public records and documents, including judicial records and documents.

But FISC proceedings are secret. Congress created a secret court that operates in a secret environment to provide judicial oversight of secret Government activities. While the notion of secret proceedings may seem antithetical to democracy, the Founding Fathers recognized the need for the Government to keep secrets. See U.S. Const. Art. I § 5, cl. 3. ("Each House shall keep a Journal of its Proceedings, and from time to time publish the same, excepting such Parts as may in their Judgment require Secrecy.")

Congress has long appreciated the Executive's paramount need to keep matters of national security secret. FISC is an exception to the presumption of openness and transparency—in matters of national security, the Government must be able to keep its means and methods secret from its enemies.

In 1998, Congress amended FISA to allow for orders directing common carriers, public accommodation facilities, storage facilities, and vehicle rental facilities to provide business records to the Government. These amendments required the Government to make a showing of "specific and articulable facts giving reason to believe that the person to whom the records pertain is a foreign power or an agent of a foreign power."

After the September 11th attacks, Congress expanded the Government's authority to obtain additional records. *See* USA PATRIOT Act of 2001, Pub. L. 107–56, § 215 (codified as amended at 50 U.S.C. § 1861) ("section 215"). Section 215 allows the Government to obtain an order "requiring the production of any tangible things (including books, records, papers, documents, and other items)," eliminating the restrictions on the types of businesses that can be served with such orders and the requirement that the target be a foreign power or their agent. The Government invoked this authority to collect virtually all call detail records or "telephony metadata."

Bulk telephony metadata collection under FISA is subject to extensive oversight by all three branches of government. It is monitored by the Department of Justice, the intelligence Community, the FISC, and Congress. To collect bulk telephony metadata, the Executive must first seek judicial approval from the FISC. Then, on a semi-annual basis, it must provide reports to the Permanent Select Committee on Intelligence of the House of Representatives, the Select Committee on Intelligence of the Senate, and the Committees on the Judiciary of the House of Representatives and the Senate. Those reports must include: (1) a summary of significant legal interpretations of section 215 involving matters before the FISC; and (2) copies of all decisions, orders, or opinions of the FISC that include significant construction or interpretation of section 215.

Since the initiation of the program, a number of compliance and implementation issues were discovered and self-reported by the Government to the FISC and Congress. The NSA addressed these problems. For example, in 2011, FISC Judge Bates engaged in a protracted iterative process with the Government—that included numerous written submissions, meetings between court staff and the Justice Department, and a hearing—over the Government's application for reauthorization of another FISA collection program. That led to a complete review of that program's collection and querying methods.

In August 2013, FISC Judge Eagan noted, "[t]he Court is aware that in prior years there have been incidents of non-compliance with respect to the NSA's handling of produced information. Through oversight by this Court over a period of months, those issues were resolved" [citing Aug. 29, 2013 FISC order]. And Congress repeatedly reauthorized the statute.

In recognition of the broad intelligence gathering capability Congress granted to the Executive Branch, section 215 included a sunset provision terminating that authority at the end of 2005. But the war on terror did not end. Congress has renewed section 215 seven times. In 2006, Congress amended section 215 to require the Government to provide "a statement of facts showing that there are reasonable grounds to believe that the tangible things sought are relevant to an authorized investigation."

[The court described the NSA's telephony metadata collection programs, including the FISC's "Secondary Order" concerning Verizon that was the first document from Snowden's cache to be disclosed in the press.]

[The ACLU and related organizations] filed this lawsuit on June 11, 2013, less than a week after the unauthorized disclosure of the Secondary Order. The Plaintiffs seek a declaratory judgment that the NSA's metadata collection exceeds the authority granted by section 215 and violates the First and Fourth Amendments, and it also seeks a permanent injunction enjoining the Government from continuing the collection.

The Government moves to dismiss the complaint under Federal Rules of Civil Procedure 12(b)(1) and 12(b)(6) for lack of standing and failure to state a claim. The ACLU moves under Rule 65 for a preliminary injunction.

## DISCUSSION

### I. Standing

Relying on the Supreme Court's decision in *Clapper v. Amnesty International*, 133 S. Ct. 1138, the Government contends that none of these alleged injuries are "concrete, particularized, and actual or imminent." [The ACLU entities among the plaintiffs were customers of Verizon, and the Snowden documents revealed that the NSA collected bulk telephony metadata from Verizon.]

Here, there is no dispute the Government collected telephony metadata related to the ACLU's telephone calls. Thus, the standing requirement is satisfied.

### II. Statutory Claim

[The court held that the statutory claim was precluded, the same conclusion reached by *Klayman* on this point. Unlike the *Klayman* court, however, this court went on to analyze the merits of the statutory claim as an alternative basis for its holding.]

To obtain a section 215 order, the Government must show (1) "reasonable grounds to believe that the tangible things sought are relevant to an authorized investigation" and (2) that the item sought must be able to be "obtained with a subpoena duces tecum . . . in aid of a grand jury investigation or with any other [court] order . . . directing the production of records or tangible things." 50 U.S.C. § 1861(b, c). The Government can obtain telephony metadata with grand jury subpoenas and other court orders.

A grand jury subpoena permits the Government to obtain tangible things unless "there is no reasonable possibility that the category of materials the Government seeks will produce information relevant to the general subject of the grand jury's investigation." *United States v. R. Enters., Inc.*, 498 U.S. 292, 301 (1991). The ACLU argues that the category at issue—all telephony metadata—is too broad and contains too much irrelevant information. That argument has no traction here. Because without all the data points, the Government cannot be certain it connected the pertinent ones. As FISC Judge Eagan noted, the collection of virtually all telephony metadata is "necessary" to permit the NSA, not the FBI, to do the algorithmic data analysis that allow the NSA to determine "connections between known and unknown international terrorist operatives." [citing partially redacted FISC opinion]

"Relevance" has a broad legal meaning. The Federal Rules of Civil Procedure allow parties to obtain discovery "regarding any nonprivileged matter that is relevant to any party's claim or defense." Fed. R. Civ. P. 26(b)(1). This Rule has been construed broadly to encompass any matter that bears on, or that reasonably could lead to other matter that could bear on, any issue that is or may be in the case. Tangible items are "relevant" under section 215 if they bear on or could reasonably lead to other matter that could bear on the investigation.

Under section 215, the Government's burden is not substantial. The Government need only provide "a statement of facts showing that there are reasonable grounds to believe that the tangible things sought are relevant." 50 U.S.C. § 1861(b)(2)(A).

The concept of relevance in the context of an investigation does not require the Government to parse out irrelevant documents at the start of its investigation. Rather, it allows that Government to get a category of materials if the category is relevant. Defining the reasonableness of a subpoena based on the volume of information to be produced would require the Government to determine wrongdoing before issuing a subpoena—but that determination is the primary purpose for a subpoena. And in the context of a counterterrorism investigation, that after-the-attack determination would be too late.

Here, there is no way for the Government to know which particle of telephony metadata will lead to useful counterterrorism information. When that is the case, courts routinely authorize large-scale collections of information, even if most of it will not directly bear on the investigation. *See In re Subpoena Duces Tecum*, 228 F.3d 341, 350–51 (4th Cir. 2000) (authorizing collection of 15,000 patient files); *In re Grand Jury Proceedings: Subpoenas Duces Tecum*, 827 F.2d 301 (8th Cir. 1987) (authorizing collection of all wire transactions over $1,000 for a 14-month period at a particular Western Union office).

Any individual call record alone is unlikely to lead to matter that may pertain to a terrorism investigation. But aggregated telephony metadata is relevant because it allows the querying technique to be comprehensive. And NSA's warehousing of that data allows a query to be instantaneous. This new ability to query aggregated telephony metadata significantly increases the NSA's capability to detect the faintest patterns left behind by individuals affiliated with foreign terrorist organizations. Armed with all the metadata, NSA can draw connections it might otherwise never be able to find.

The collection is broad, but the scope of counterterrorism investigations is unprecedented. National security investigations are fundamentally different from criminal investigations. They are prospective—focused on preventing attacks—as opposed to the retrospective investigation of crimes. National security investigations span long periods of time and multiple geographic regions. Congress was clearly aware of the need for breadth and provided the Government with the tools to interdict terrorist threats.

## III. Constitutional Claims

### A. Fourth Amendment

In *Smith v. Maryland*, 442 U.S. 735 (1979), the Supreme Court held individuals have no "legitimate expectation of privacy" regarding the telephone numbers they dial because they knowingly give that information to telephone companies when they dial a number. Smith's bedrock holding is that an individual has no legitimate expectation of privacy in information provided to third parties.

The privacy concerns at stake in *Smith* were far more individualized than those raised by the ACLU. *Smith* involved the investigation of a single crime and the collection of telephone call detail records collected by the telephone company at its central office, examined by the police, and related to the target of their investigation, a person identified previously by law enforcement. Nevertheless, the Supreme Court found there was no legitimate privacy expectation because "[t]elephone users . . . typically know that they must convey numerical information to the telephone company; that the telephone company has facilities for recording this information; and that the telephone company does in fact record this information for a variety of legitimate business purposes."

The ACLU argues that analysis of bulk telephony metadata allows the creation of a rich mosaic: it can "reveal a person's religion, political associations, use of a telephone-sex hotline, contemplation of suicide, addiction to gambling or drugs, experience with rape, grappling with sexuality, or support for particular political causes." Decl. of Edward Felten, Professor of Computer Science and Public Affairs, Princeton University, ¶ 42. But that is at least three inflections from the Government's bulk telephony metadata collection. First, without additional legal justification—subject to rigorous minimization procedures—the NSA cannot even query the telephony metadata database. Second, when it makes a query, it only learns the telephony metadata of the telephone numbers within three "hops" of the "seed." Third, without resort to additional techniques, the Government does not know who any of the telephone numbers belong to. In other words, all the Government sees is that telephone number A called telephone number B. It does not know who subscribes to telephone numbers A or B. Further, the Government repudiates any notion that it conducts the type of data mining the ACLU warns about in its parade of horribles.

The ACLU also argues that "[t]here are a number of ways in which the Government could perform three-hop analysis without first building its own database of every American's call records." That has no traction. At bottom, it is little more than an assertion that less intrusive means to collect and analyze telephony metadata could be employed. But, the Supreme Court has repeatedly refused to declare that only the "least intrusive" search practicable can be reasonable under the Fourth Amendment. *City of Ontario v. Quon*, 560 U.S. 746 (2010). That judicial Monday-morning quarterbacking "could raise insuperable barriers to the exercise of virtually all search-and-seizure powers" because judges engaging in after-the-fact evaluations of government conduct "can almost always imagine some alternative means by which the objectives might have been accomplished." *Quon*, 130 S.Ct. at 2632.

The ACLU's reliance on the concurring opinions in *United States v. Jones*, 132 S. Ct. 945 (2012) [see Chapter 1], is misplaced. In two separate concurring opinions, five justices appeared to be grappling with how the Fourth Amendment applies to technological advances.

But the Supreme Court did not overrule *Smith*. And the Supreme Court has instructed lower courts not to predict whether it would overrule a precedent even if its reasoning has been supplanted by later cases. Clear precedent applies because *Smith* held that a subscriber has no legitimate expectation of privacy in telephony metadata created by third parties. Inferior courts are bound by that precedent.

Telephones have far more versatility now than when *Smith* was decided, but this case only concerns their use as telephones. The fact that there are more calls placed does not undermine the Supreme Court's finding that a person has no subjective expectation of privacy in telephony metadata. Because *Smith* controls, the NSA's bulk telephony metadata collection program does not violate the Fourth Amendment.

### B. First Amendment

The ACLU alleges that "[t]he fact that the government is collecting this information is likely to have a chilling effect on people who would otherwise contact Plaintiffs." Significant impairments of First Amendment rights must withstand exacting scrutiny. The Government contends, however, that "surveillance consistent with Fourth Amendment protections . . . does not violate First Amendment rights, even though it may be directed at communicative or associative activities." The Government's argument is well-supported. And this consideration is built in to any section 215 application. *See* 50 U.S.C. § 1861 (requiring that the investigation not be conducted "solely upon the basis of activities protected by the [F]irst [A]mendment").

Any alleged chilling effect here arises from the ACLU's speculative fear that the Government will review telephony metadata related to the

ACLU's telephone calls. Fear that telephony metadata relating to the ACLU will be queried or reviewed or further investigated relies on a highly attenuated chain of possibilities. "[S]uch a fear is insufficient to create standing" [quoting *Clapper*]. Neither can it establish a violation of an individual's First Amendment rights.

## CONCLUSION

The right to be free from searches and seizures is fundamental, but not absolute. As Justice Jackson famously observed: "the Bill of Rights is not a suicide-pact." *Terminiello v. City of Chicago*, 337 U.S. 1 (1949). Whether the Fourth Amendment protects bulk telephony metadata is ultimately a question of reasonableness. Every day, people voluntarily surrender personal and seemingly-private information to transnational corporations, which exploit that data for profit. Few think twice about it, even though it is far more intrusive than bulk telephony metadata collection.

There is no evidence that the Government has used any of the bulk telephony metadata it collected for any purpose other than investigating and disrupting terrorist attacks. While there have been unintentional violations of guidelines, those appear to stem from human error and the incredibly complex computer programs that support this vital tool. And once detected, those violations were self-reported and stopped. The bulk telephony metadata collection program is subject to executive and congressional oversight, as well as continual monitoring by a dedicated group of judges who serve on the Foreign Intelligence Surveillance Court.

No doubt, the bulk telephony metadata collection program vacuums up information about virtually every telephone call to, from, or within the United States. That is by design, as it allows the NSA to detect relationships so attenuated and ephemeral they would otherwise escape notice. As the September 11th attacks demonstrate, the cost of missing such a thread can be horrific.

"Liberty and security can be reconciled; and in our system they are reconciled within the framework of the law." *Boumediene v. Bush*, 553 U.S. 723, 798 (2008). The success of one helps protect the other. The choice between liberty and security is a false one, as nothing is more apt to imperil civil liberties than the success of a terrorist attack on American soil.

For all of these reasons, the NSA's bulk telephony metadata collection program is lawful. Accordingly, the Government's motion to dismiss the complaint is granted and the ACLU's motion for a preliminary injunction is denied.

## ACLU v. Clapper

785 F.3d 787 (2d Cir. 2015)

This appeal concerns the legality of the bulk telephone metadata collection program (the "telephone metadata program"), under which the National Security Agency ("NSA") collects in bulk "on an ongoing daily basis" the metadata associated with telephone calls made by and to Americans, and aggregates those metadata into a repository or data bank that can later be queried. Appellants challenge the program on statutory and constitutional grounds. Because we find that the program exceeds the scope of what Congress has authorized, we vacate the decision below dismissing the complaint without reaching appellants' constitutional arguments. We affirm the district court's denial of appellants' request for a preliminary injunction.

[After reviewing the factual and statutory background at length, the Second Circuit agreed with the lower court (and *Klayman*) that the plaintiffs had standing, but differed from the district court (and *Klayman*) by finding that judicial review of the program's fidelity to FISA was *not* precluded. It then turned to an analysis of the statutory arguments.]

Although appellants vigorously argue that the telephone metadata program violates their rights under the Fourth Amendment to the Constitution, and therefore cannot be authorized by either the Executive or the Legislative Branch of government, or by both acting together, their initial argument is that the program simply has not been authorized by the legislation on which the government relies for the issuance of the orders to service providers to collect and turn over the metadata at issue. We naturally turn first to that argument.

Section 215 clearly sweeps broadly in an effort to provide the government with essential tools to investigate and forestall acts of terrorism. The statute permits the government to apply for "an order requiring the production of *any tangible things* . . . for an investigation . . . to protect against international terrorism or clandestine intelligence activities." 50 U.S.C. § 1861(a)(1) (emphasis added). A § 215 order may require the production of anything that "can be obtained with a subpoena duces tecum issued by a court of the United States in aid of a grand jury investigation" or any other court order. *Id.* § 1861(c)(2)(D).

While the *types* of "tangible things" subject to such an order would appear essentially unlimited, such "things" may only be produced upon a specified factual showing by the government. To obtain a § 215 order, the government must provide the FISC with "a statement of facts showing that there are reasonable grounds to believe that the tangible things sought are relevant to an authorized investigation (other than a threat assessment) conducted [under guidelines approved by the Attorney General]." *Id.* § 1861(b)(2)(A). The basic requirements for metadata collection under § 215, then, are simply that the records be *relevant* to an *authorized investigation* (other than a threat assessment).

For all the complexity of the statutory framework, the parties' respective positions are relatively simple and straightforward. The government emphasizes that "relevance" is an extremely generous standard, particularly in the context of the grand jury investigations to which the statute analogizes orders under § 215. Appellants argue that relevance is not an unlimited concept, and that the government's own use (or non-use) of the records obtained demonstrates that most of the records sought are not relevant to any particular investigation; the government does not seek the records, as is usual in a grand jury investigation, so as to review them in search of evidence bearing on a particular subject, but rather seeks the records to create a vast data bank, to be kept in reserve and queried if and when some particular set of records might be relevant to a particular investigation.

Thus, the government takes the position that the metadata collected—a vast amount of which does not contain directly "relevant" information, as the government concedes—are nevertheless "relevant" because they may allow the NSA, at some unknown time in the future, utilizing its ability to sift through the trove of irrelevant data it has collected up to that point, to identify information that *is* relevant. We agree with appellants that such an expansive concept of "relevance" is unprecedented and unwarranted.

The sheer volume of information sought is staggering; while search warrants and subpoenas for business records may encompass large volumes of paper documents or electronic data, the most expansive of such evidentiary demands are dwarfed by the volume of records obtained pursuant to the orders in question here.

Moreover, the distinction is not merely one of quantity—however vast the quantitative difference—but also of quality. Search warrants and document subpoenas typically seek the records of a particular individual or corporation under investigation, and cover particular time periods when the events under investigation occurred. The orders at issue here contain no such limits. The metadata concerning *every* telephone call made or received in the United States using the services of the recipient service provider are demanded, for an indefinite period extending into the future. The records demanded are not those of suspects under investigation, or of people or businesses that have contact with such subjects, or of people or businesses that have contact with others who are in contact with the subjects—they extend to every record that exists, and indeed to records that do not *yet* exist, as they impose a continuing obligation on the recipient of the subpoena to provide such records on an ongoing basis as they are created. The government can point to no grand jury subpoena that is remotely comparable to the real-time data collection undertaken under this program.

To the extent that § 215 was intended to give the government, as Senator Kyl proposed, the "same kinds of techniques to fight terrorists" that it has available to fight ordinary crimes such as "money laundering or drug dealing," 152 Cong. Rec. S1607 (daily ed. Mar. 2, 2006) (statement of Sen. Kyl), the analogy is not helpful to the government's position here. The techniques traditionally used to combat such ordinary crimes have not included the collection, via grand jury subpoena, of a vast trove of records of metadata concerning the financial transactions or telephone calls of ordinary Americans to be held in reserve in a data bank, to be searched if and when at some hypothetical future time the records might become relevant to a criminal investigation.

The government's emphasis on the potential breadth of the term "relevant," moreover, ignores other portions of the text of § 215. "Relevance" does not exist in the abstract; something is "relevant" or not in relation to a particular subject. Thus, an item relevant to a grand jury investigation may not be relevant at trial. In keeping with this usage, § 215 does not permit an investigative demand for any information relevant to fighting the war on terror, or anything relevant to whatever the government might want to know. It permits demands for documents "relevant to an authorized *investigation*." The government has not attempted to identify to what particular "authorized investigation" the bulk metadata of virtually all Americans' phone calls are relevant. Throughout its briefing, the government refers to the records collected under the telephone metadata program as relevant to "counterterrorism investigations," without identifying any specific investigations to which such bulk collection is relevant.

The government's approach essentially reads the "authorized investigation" language out of the statute. Indeed, the government's information-gathering under the telephone metadata program is inconsistent with the very concept of an "investigation." To "investigate" something, according to the Oxford English Dictionary, is "[t]o search or inquire into; to examine (a matter) systematically or in detail; to make an inquiry or examination into." Section 215's language thus contemplates the specificity of a particular investigation—not the general counterterrorism intelligence efforts of the United States government.

The government's approach also reads out of the statute another important textual limitation on its power under § 215. Section 215 permits an order to produce records to issue when the government shows that the records are "relevant to an authorized investigation (*other than a threat assessment*)." 50 U.S.C. § 1861(b)(2)(A) (emphasis added). The legislative history tells us little or nothing about the meaning of "threat assessment." The Attorney General's Guidelines for Domestic FBI Operations, however, tell us somewhat more. The Guidelines divide the category of "investigations and intelligence gathering" into three subclasses: assessments, predicated investigations (both preliminary and full), and enterprise investigations. Assessments are distinguished from investigations in that they may be initiated without any factual predication.

In limiting the use of § 215 to "investigations" rather than "threat assessments," then, Congress clearly meant to *prevent* § 215 orders from being issued where the FBI, without any particular, defined information that would permit the initiation of even a preliminary investigation, sought to conduct an inquiry in order to identify a potential threat in advance. The telephone metadata program, however, and the orders sought in furtherance of it, are even more remote from a concrete investigation than the threat assessments that—however important they undoubtedly are in maintaining an alertness to possible threats to national security—Congress found not to warrant the use of § 215 orders. After all, when conducting a threat assessment, FBI agents must have both a reason to conduct the inquiry and an articulable connection between the particular inquiry being made and the information being sought. The telephone metadata program, by contrast, seeks to compile data in advance of the need to conduct any inquiry (or even to examine the data), and is based on no evidence of any current connection between the data being sought and any existing inquiry.

We conclude that to allow the government to collect phone records only because they may become relevant to a possible authorized investigation in the future fails even the permissive "relevance" test. Such a monumental shift in our approach to combating terrorism requires a clearer signal from Congress than a recycling of oft-used language long held in similar contexts to mean something far narrower. The language of § 215 is decidedly too ordinary for what the government would have us believe is such an extraordinary departure from any accepted understanding of the term "relevant to an authorized investigation."

[Finally, the court took up the constitutional claims, stressing their weightiness and difficulty. Having resolved the case on statutory grounds, the court declined to reach those constitutional questions. It also remanded without reversing the district court's refusal to enter a preliminary injunction. The court noted the imminent expiration of Section 215 in its current form and ongoing congressional debate about revising it. As a result, "the statutory issues on which we rest our decision could become moot (at least as far as the future of the telephone metadata program is concerned), and the constitutional issues appellants continue to press radically altered, by events that will occur in a short time frame."]

## NOTES

1. ***Slow Courts and Fast Events.*** The two diametrically opposing district court opinions excerpted above were released within a couple of weeks of one another in December 2013, less than seven months after the

first Snowden disclosure. At the time, most observers assumed the issue would remain on a fast track, with expedited review in the courts of appeals and potentially Supreme Court resolution by 2015. (The end of the *Klayman* opinion echoed this assumption.) Instead, the circuit courts moved very deliberately, while debate intensified in Congress and in the public arena. The Second Circuit opinion excerpted above came in May 2015, almost a year and a half after the district court decisions. By then, Section 215 was due to expire just a few weeks later. Thus, the decision had limited direct importance in other courts—although it certainly influenced Congress in its revision of Section 215.As explained below, Congress passed the USA Freedom Act in June 2015, renewing Setion 215 while significantly changing its language, as explained below. The D.C. Circuit waited even longer to dispose of the appeal from the *Klayman* decision, issuing a fragmented ruling in August 2015 that vacated and remanded for more factual findings about standing. As of this writing in early 2016, the remanded *ACLU* and *Klayman* litigation, as well as a parallel case in the Ninth Circuit, continue to inch forward. What are the advantages of rapid resolution and of more deliberate consideration? Did the appeals courts do the right thing by slowing the pace of the litigation?

2. ***Factual Differences.*** As soon as the *Klayman* and *ACLU* opinions began their recitations of the facts, they telegraphed their different views of the outcome: *Klayman* started its factual narrative with the reports in The Guardian, quoting its characterization that "the communication records of millions of US citizens are being collected indiscriminately and in bulk." The first sentence of the *ACLU* opinion reads, "The September 11th terrorist attacks revealed, in the starkest terms, just how dangerous and interconnected the world is." Where else do you see differences in the factual frames used by these opinions? Do the two judges disagree about the underlying facts, or only in their interpretation of those facts and the narrative into which they fit?

3. ***The Statutory Argument.*** The *ACLU* district and appeals courts reached totally different conclusions about the interpretation of the statutory language (an issue *Klayman* did not reach). Who has the better argument about the scope of "relevance" in the statute? How would you expect these two viewpoints to influence future interpretations of national security statutes?

4. ***The Fourth Amendment Argument.*** The two district courts completely disagreed about the Fourth Amendment issues (which the Second Circuit—and for that matter, the D.C. Circuit—did not reach). Pinpoint the differences in the legal analysis of the two opinions. Clearly, the nature and role of the third party doctrine is central to each. Which court has a more persuasive argument about the correct bearing of *Smith v. Maryland* on the bulk telephony metadata collection program? Are there other important differences between the two courts in their analysis of the Fourth Amendment? Where do the two district courts *agree* about the law? Overall, which view would you support?

5. ***A Revolution in Standing?*** All three opinions do agree about one thing: these plaintiffs had standing to challenge the NSA's bulk telephony

metadata program. The Supreme Court decided *Clapper* in February 2013, about four months *before* The Guardian published the first Do the standing rulings in these cases mean that challenges to Section 702 like the one in *Clapper* would now be permissible?

6. ***Does Metadata Matter?*** The distinction between "content" of communications (data) and mere "addressing" information (metadata) is a familiar one, visible in the structure of ECPA, for example [see Chapter 5]. How sound is the intuition that individuals have a lower expectation of privacy—and a less strong desire for it—in metadata compared to the contents of communications themselves? How invasive can metadata be? The district court opinions diverge sharply on this point; find the place in each opinion that discussed the issue and compare their reasoning. One colorful demonstration of the power of metadata was a clever essay by Duke University sociologist Kieran Healy, who analyzed actual membership lists for social clubs associated with anti-British sympathies at the time of the American Revolution. He wrote in the voice of an imaginary agent of the "Royal Security Agency" using rudimentary techniques of social network analysis:

> Rest assured that we only collected *metadata* on these people, and no actual conversations were recorded or meetings transcribed. All I know is whether someone was a member of an organization or not. Surely this is but a small encroachment on the freedom of the Crown's subjects. I have been asked, on the basis of this poor information, to present some names for our field agents in the Colonies to work with.

After walking through fairly simple mathematical processes, Healy presented a detailed map of connections between the members:

> The analytical engine has arranged everyone neatly, picking out clusters of individuals and also showing both peripheral individuals and—more intriguingly—people who seem to bridge various groups in ways that might perhaps be relevant to national security. Look at that person right in the middle there. Zoom in if you wish. He seems to bridge several groups in an unusual (though perhaps not unique) way. His name is Paul Revere.
>
> Once again, I remind you that I know nothing of Mr. Revere, or his conversations, or his habits or beliefs, his writings (if he has any) or his personal life. All I know is this bit of metadata, based on membership in some organizations. And yet my analytical engine, on the basis of absolutely the most elementary of operations in Social Networke Analysis, seems to have picked him out of our 254 names as being of unusual interest.

Kieran Healy, *Using Metadata to Find Paul Revere*, SLATE (June 10, 2013). It seems plausible that the NSA's analysis of telephone networks, charting out three hops from a seed number that is suspected of being used in terrorist activity, would likewise identify certain persons of interest, especially since the techniques would be more sophisticated than the basic ones Healy described. But does this speak in favor of allowing such analysis or restricting it? Revere, after all, *was* a sensible person for the British to investigate if they were looking for Sons of Liberty eager to overthrow their government. The determination depends on the balance between the program's effectiveness and its invasiveness. On one hand, consider the responses of the *ACLU* district court to an affidavit by well-known Princeton University computer scientist Edward Felten, who argued that network analysis of metadata created a "mosaic" of revealing insights about individuals. The court suggested, in contrast, that the NSA would never even learn the identity of most ordinary people whose numbers were swept up by querying the hops from a seed. And it found no evidence of "the type of data mining the ACLU warns about in its parade of horribles." Meanwhile, the *Klayman* district court described the same analysis by Felten as an example of "almost-Orwellian technology" and quoted *Jones* to embrace the mosaic theory. That court also expressed strong skepticism that network analysis was ever useful in urgent situations, and suggested that, if its value came as a supporting investigative technique, it would be possible for investigators to satisfy a standard closer to traditional probable cause. So: how private should metadata be?

7. ***Oversight.*** The government strenuously argued in all of these cases that the bulk telephony metadata program was heavily supervised by all three branches of government. Congress enacted Section 215 and reauthorized it multiple times. High-ranking officials in the Justice Department and the intelligence community wrote restrictive guidelines and had to approve certain key operational aspects of the program such as minimization procedures and the selection of seed numbers. And, of course, the Article III judges on the FISC signed off on the program repeatedly. There were compliance lapses—which the opinions excerpted above portrayed very differently—but in any event those shortcomings were addressed eventually by both judicial and executive branch officials. Critics see all these mechanisms as sorely lacking. They argue that members of Congress received limited information under burdensome restrictions: they could only view information in secure locations for limited times, they could not consult staff, and sometimes members who were not on the intelligence committees received little or no detail at all. The executive branch, according to these critics, cannot be trusted to limit itself. And in their view the FISC, with its secret ex parte hearings and sealed opinions, did not have the independence that judges typically exercise in search warrant situations. Again, consider who has the better argument: was the program subject to adequate oversight or not?

8. ***Partisanship and the NSA.*** Note that Judge Pauley, who ruled for the NSA, was appointed by Democratic President Bill Clinton, while Judge Leon, who ruled against the NSA, was appointed by Republican President George W. Bush. It is a reminder, if any more were needed, that the partisan leanings of an appointing president may not help determine the outcome in politically salient cases. Besides, the politics of NSA surveillance have not broken down on party lines in other branches either. Both Presidents Bush and Obama authorized extensive NSA surveillance despite their differing party affiliations. And in Congress, the most active skeptics

of the intelligence community also have come from both parties (such as Senator Ron Wyden, a liberal Democrat, and Senator Rand Paul, a conservative Republican), as have its prominent congressional defenders (including Democratic Senator Dianne Feinstein and Republican Senator Marco Rubio). Why do you think views about the NSA's activities match imperfectly with partisan labels?

---

## Focus

### The USA Freedom Act

By June 2015, a number of factors had combined to force congressional action on changes to FISA: continuing debate and a shift in public opinion about NSA surveillance, the Second Circuit's *ACLU* opinion the month before, and most of all the expiration of Section 215 and a number of other FISA provisions under sunset clauses. Skeptics of surveillance programs, unable to defeat them outright, have frequently inserted these expiration provisions, hoping to achieve better results when the law needs to be reauthorized a few years later. To some degree, this strategy worked with the enactment of the USA Freedom Act, P.L. 114–23 (2015). The new law passed by a healthy bipartisan margin and President Obama signed it immediately. It reauthorized Section 215 and other expiring FISA rules, but also made notable changes, including these:

1. ***Who Holds the Haystack.*** Rather than allowing the government to collect and store bulk telephony metadata itself, the statute requires telecommunications companies to retain the metadata, and permits the FISC to order production of narrower categories in response to particular queries. The Attorney General retains the authority to require production of records without a FISC order if he or she determines that an emergency requires it, but in that case must notify the FISC immediately and secure the order approving of the production within seven days. In either case, the bulk records are held by the telephone companies, not the government.

2. ***The "Specific Selection Term."*** Applications to FISC to make those queries of the telephone company metadata must identify a "specific selection term" and be based on a "reasonable, articulable suspicion that the specific selection term is associated with a foreign power or an agent of a foreign power engaged in international terrorism or activities in preparation for such terrorism." For call records, the "specific selection term"—equivalent to the seed under the prior program—must "specifically identify an individual, account, or personal device." For other records, the definition is broader, but it still excludes queries for all the records held by a particular provider or for all records within a "broad geographic region" such as a zip code. These changes aim to prevent "dragnet" searches. As before, a FISC order may authorize examination of records within two hops of the specific selection term.

3. ***Expiration.*** All orders authorizing ongoing production of call records must be reevaluated by the FISC after 180 days.

4. ***FISC Amicus Curiae.*** The FISC is directed to identify individuals who can serve as amicus curiae in otherwise ex parte proceedings and allow them, at the FISC's discretion, to present positions the government might not, including "legal arguments that advance protection of individual privacy and civil liberties."

5. ***Partial Declassification of FISC Orders.*** The Director of National Intelligence (DNI) is to review all opinions from FISC or the FIS Court of Review to determine if they "include[ ] a significant construction or interpretation of any

provision of law." If so, the DNI is to endeavor to declassify them so that they are "publicly available to the greatest extent practicable, subject to permissible redactions."

6. ***Expanded Oversight.*** The law requires additional reports to Congress and audits by inspectors general.

7. ***Section 702 Limitations.*** If information obtained under the authority of Section 702 (the provision discussed in the Supreme Court's *Clapper* opinion, above) is later determined to have been obtained unlawfully (such as without required minimization procedures), it may be excluded from further use under some circumstances, although there are significant exceptions.

The USA Freedom Act delayed its effective date by six months, in order to give the telecommunications companies and intelligence agencies an opportunity to prepare. The NSA continued bulk telephony metadata collection until late November 2015, at which time the new system kicked in and remains in use.

Just because the USA Freedom Act has been signed into law does not mean the debate about bulk telephony metadata collection is over, however. In the 2016 election campaign, candidates on both sides raised NSA surveillance as an issue. And under the new law, Section 215 sunsets all over again in December 2019.

---

## Practice

### Designing Section 215

Suppose you were a staff member in the US Senate as the USA Freedom Act was being developed. Assume that the intelligence community needs at least some access to "business records" (however broadly defined) for use in national security investigations (however broadly defined). How would you propose redesigning Section 215? Consider all the provisions that ended up in the new law, and also think about whether you would have added any other changes. Given all of the weighty security and privacy interests, does the USA Freedom Act strike a good balance?

---

## Focus

### Other National Security Controversies

Of all the controversies surrounding privacy and national security in the last 15 years, bulk telephony metadata collection has received the most attention from the courts, the news media, and Congress. But it is far from the only contentious issue. Here are four others.

1. ***PRISM.*** Some of the earliest Snowden leaks concerned a program sometimes referred to as "PRISM," which intercepted the content of internet communications by non-US persons. As demonstrated by the Supreme Court's *Clapper* decision, the creation of new authority to conduct these interceptions under Section 702 generated considerable criticism. Privacy advocates argue that content of messages from a huge number of Americans has also been intercepted by this means. One examination of leaked documents by the Washington Post suggested that almost half of the intercepted messages came from US persons and some 90% were not from the intended target of the investigation. *See* Barton Gellman et al., *In NSA-Intercepted Data, Those Not Targeted Far Outnumber the Foreigners Who Are*, WASH. POST (July 5, 2014). This argument about collecting data on US persons through surveillance outside the US was made by the *Clapper* plaintiffs, and is now

being raised anew in lower courts by plaintiffs who hope to demonstrate standing. The intelligence community and its supporters respond that the program is aimed at the least protected portion of the *Keith* trichotomy: communications by non-US persons outside the US. They also say that algorithmic minimization procedures help ensure that the focus of the investigation remains on non-US targets.

2. ***National Security Letters.*** National security letters are a special form of administrative subpoena. They were first authorized in 1978 in the Right to Financial Privacy Act, 12 U.S.C. §§ 3401 et seq. [see Chapter 13]. The scope and reach of national security letters gradually grew through several other federal statutes, and then the USA PATRIOT Act expanded them dramatically. While they can only be used to obtain metadata rather than content, national security letters still might extend to various types of financial, telephone, and email records. There is no judicial authorization required, by the FISC or any other court. The most controversial feature of the national security letter has been the accompanying "gag order," which at one time permanently prohibited a recipient from discussing it with anyone. After the USA PATRIOT Act, it was not even clear that a recipient of a national security letter could consult a lawyer about it.

One recipient who operated a small internet service provider, now identified as Nicholas Merrill, challenged his national security letter in long-running litigation, which yielded two decisions finding the exercise of this power inconsistent with the First and Fourth Amendments. *See John Doe, Inc. v. Mukasey*, 549 F.3d 861 (2d Cir. 2008), as modified (Mar. 26, 2009); *Doe v. Ashcroft*, 334 F. Supp. 2d 471 (S.D.N.Y. 2004). Congress modified the rules for national security letters in the USA PATRIOT Improvement and Reauthorization Act, P.L. 109–177 and P.L. 109–178 (2006) to make judicial review available, clarify that recipients may consult attorneys, and provide for eventual dissolution of gag orders. Despite these changes, lawsuits have multiplied, and another district court has since found multiple constitutional violations in a challenge to a national security letter. *See In re Nat'l Sec. Letter*, 930 F. Supp. 2d 1064 (N.D. Cal. 2013). The USA Freedom Act made additional changes to the national security letter statutes in 2015, most notably requiring them, like Section 215 orders, to be aimed at a "specific selection term." In addition, the 2015 statute further modified the nondisclosure requirements, mandating that gag orders be justified by the specific facts of the case, and allowing companies to release certain aggregate statistics about their receipt of national security letters.

3. ***Watch Lists.*** Since the September 11, 2001 attacks, there has been dramatic growth in the use of watch lists by federal authorities. A multi-agency Terrorist Screening Center, housed in the FBI, maintains the Terrorist Screening Database (TSDB), which does not contain classified information. The National Counterterrorism Center keeps a larger database, known as TIDE (for "Terrorist Identities Datamart Environment"), which does contain classified information. There is no dispute that certain individuals with demonstrable ties to terrorism should be monitored. The disagreement arises in two main areas: the criteria for placing names on the list, and for taking them off.

There have been numerous instances of errors in watch lists, which often come to light when people are barred from boarding an aircraft (because the "no-fly list" is derived from the TSDB). Those stopped at airports because of such mistakes have included Senator Ted Kennedy, the actor David Nelson (who portrayed the older son in the 1950s television series *The Adventures of Ozzie and Harriet*), and a number of minors, at least one of them an 18-month old baby. Moreover, some activists claim that loose standards for adding names to the list allow for profiling, and particularly for discrimination against Muslims and those of Middle Eastern origin. The Associated Press reported in 2013 that the TSDB contained 700,000 names, and that the number of names proposed for inclusion on the list approached half a million in fiscal year 2013. When errors do occur, it can be difficult and time-consuming to correct them. In response, starting in 2007, the Department of Homeland Security began offering a Traveler Redress Inquiry Program (TRIP) enabling people who have experienced problems at airport security screenings to request review of their apparent designation on watch lists. A district court has since found this redress inadequate and a violation of both the plaintiffs' constitutional rights to procedural due process and the Administrative Procedure Act. *Latif v. Holder*, 28 F. Supp. 3d 1134 (D. Or. 2014), appeal dismissed (Dec. 31, 2014). If watch lists are accepted as an effective method for monitoring legitimate terrorist threats, it is not entirely clear what types of procedures should be put in place to make them more accurate, focused, and unbiased—without revealing the methodologies used to identify possible targets, which might enable countermeasures to avoid detection. Do you have ideas?

**4.** ***Encryption.*** Federal intelligence and law enforcement authorities have long expressed concern that encryption in consumer communications technology could thwart their ability to conduct electronic surveillance that has become quite routine—even when they have a warrant. Throughout the 1990s, the federal government used relaxed import rules and other inducements to promote the use of encryption with "key escrow"—decrypting code given to the government that would allow it access to encrypted data. The campaign was controversial, including among technology companies, and most of it was unsuccessful. In 1994, however, Congress did pass the Communications Assistance for Law Enforcement Act (CALEA), 47 U.S.C. §§ 1001 et seq., which mandated that telecommunications network equipment be designed to permit wiretapping.

The old disagreements about encryption revived in the last several years as the security of consumer electronics improved dramatically. In 2014, for example, Apple started enabling encryption by default in its iPhones, and introduced complementary security features such as an "auto-wipe" option that will erase the phone's memory after the entry of ten incorrect numeric passcodes. (This mechanism helps prevent "brute force" attacks, where a hacker would use a powerful computer to attempt every possible combination until it found the right one.) The government argued, as in the past, that it needed access to information for its investigations, while its opponents defended strong encryption as protection from snooping, hacking, and repressive foreign governments.

In early 2016, this ongoing dispute surged into the headlines when Apple challenged a court order that the company help the government circumvent encryption on an iPhone used by Syed Farook, one of the assailants in the San Bernardino terrorist attack of December 2015. The order, issued under the authority of the 1789 All Writs Act, would require Apple to develop new firmware allowing the FBI to bypass the auto-wipe feature on Farook's phone. Apple—supported by privacy advocates and other technology companies such as Facebook, Microsoft, and even arch-rival Samsung—argued that such a "back door" to its security features would create vulnerabilities in all customers' phones. The FBI responded that these dangers were exaggerated, and proposed that the code could be kept secure, could remain in Apple's possession, and could even be destroyed after its use. A more significant slippery slope is legal rather than technological: the All Writs Act was not designed to work as a general search warrant statute, and it does not contain the types of safeguards built into FISA or the Wiretap Act [see Section 5]. Apple also raised the argument that compulsion to create the computer code necessary for backdoor software would run afoul of the First Amendment. Finally, the power would not necessarily be limited to national security investigations like the Farook case; Apple is litigating a similar All Writs Act case involving the iPhone of an alleged drug dealer in New York federal court, where an initial opinion favored the company. In response, the government emphasizes that the searches it seeks to conduct would be under strict judicial supervision in accordance with the Fourth Amendment—after all, it has a court order in the Farook case, for example. While some have called on Congress to write legislation, it is not clear what it would include or whether there would be political consensus about it. As this book was completed in early 2016, the immediate dispute over Farook's phone ended because the FBI eventually cracked its security without Apple's assistance—but the broader legal battles over encryption and the All Writs Act continue.

---

## CHAPTER 10

# GOVERNMENT DATA COLLECTION

The federal government, like any other large organization, collects personal data from citizens for many purposes, from birth certificates to probate records. It relies on data about individual citizens in its roles as an employer (e.g. over 4 million federal workers including 1.5 million uniformed military), a health insurer (e.g. Medicare), a landlord (e.g. public housing), and a statistical clearinghouse (e.g. the census)—to name just a few. State and local governments likewise collect and use significant quantities of individual personal information.

Just as law enforcement access to personal data takes on a special complexion, any government database about citizens may raise special privacy concerns. At times these concerns implicate constitutional restrictions [see Chapter 1]. But even below the level of a possible constitutional violation, statutes and regulations impose additional limits on governmental collection, use, and storage of personally identifiable information. In addition, there are complex rules concerning the disclosure of that information—sometimes requiring it as a government transparency measure, and other times protecting privacy by requiring that information remain undisclosed.

In most countries with comprehensive regimes, including all those in the European Union, the same data protection rules applicable to the private sector also cover the government [see Chapter 4]. In the US, in the absence of an omnibus law, there are highly technical statutes and regulations tailored to privacy in government databases. Section A of this chapter covers the most important and comprehensive federal statute in this area: the Privacy Act, passed in 1974. Section B then explores the complex tension between rules to protect the privacy of personal data held by the government and those that require disclosure of public records. There can be powerful public interest arguments on all sides of this balance between administrative efficiency, government transparency, societal interests, and personal privacy.

## A. THE PRIVACY ACT

### The Privacy Act

5 U.S.C. § 552a

### § 552a. Records maintained on individuals

(a) Definitions.—For purposes of this section—. . .

(2) the term "individual" means a citizen of the United States or an alien lawfully admitted for permanent residence;

(3) the term "maintain" includes maintain, collect, use, or disseminate;

(4) the term "record" means any item, collection, or grouping of information about an individual that is maintained by an agency, including, but not limited to, his education, financial transactions, medical history, and criminal or employment history and that contains his name, or the identifying number, symbol, or other identifying particular assigned to the individual, such as a finger or voice print or a photograph;

(5) the term "system of records" means a group of any records under the control of any agency from which information is retrieved by the name of the individual or by some identifying number, symbol, or other identifying particular assigned to the individual;

(6) the term "statistical record" means a record in a system of records maintained for statistical research or reporting purposes only and not used in whole or in part in making any determination about an identifiable individual . . . ;

(7) the term "routine use" means, with respect to the disclosure of a record, the use of such record for a purpose which is compatible with the purpose for which it was collected . . .

(b) Conditions of Disclosure.—No agency shall disclose any record which is contained in a system of records by any means of communication to any person, or to another agency, except pursuant to a written request by, or with the prior written consent of, the individual to whom the record pertains, unless disclosure of the record would be—

(1) to those officers and employees of the agency which maintains the record who have a need for the record in the performance of their duties;

(2) required under section 552 of this title [the Freedom of Information Act];

(3) for a routine use as defined in subsection (a)(7) of this section and described [in a notice published by the agency in the *Federal Register* that identifies "each routine use of the records

contained in the system, including the categories of users and the purpose of such use"];

(4) to the Bureau of the Census for purposes of planning or carrying out a census or survey . . . ;

(5) to a recipient who has provided the agency with advance adequate written assurance that the record will be used solely as a statistical research or reporting record, and the record is to be transferred in a form that is not individually identifiable;

(6) to the National Archives and Records Administration as a record which has sufficient historical or other value to warrant its continued preservation by the United States Government, or for evaluation by the Archivist of the United States or the designee of the Archivist to determine whether the record has such value;

(7) to another agency or to an instrumentality of any governmental jurisdiction within or under the control of the United States for a civil or criminal law enforcement activity if the activity is authorized by law, and if the head of the agency or instrumentality has made a written request to the agency which maintains the record specifying the particular portion desired and the law enforcement activity for which the record is sought;

(8) to a person pursuant to a showing of compelling circumstances affecting the health or safety of an individual if upon such disclosure notification is transmitted to the last known address of such individual;

(9) to either House of Congress, or, to the extent of matter within its jurisdiction, any committee or subcommittee thereof . . . ;

(10) to the Comptroller General, or any of his authorized representatives, in the course of the performance of the duties of the Government Accountability Office;

(11) pursuant to the order of a court of competent jurisdiction; or

(12) to a consumer reporting agency in accordance with [provisions concerning collection of taxes and other debts to the government].

. . .

(d) Access to Records.—Each agency that maintains a system of records shall—

(1) upon request by any individual to gain access to his record or to any information pertaining to him which is contained in the system, permit him . . . to review the record and have a copy made of all or any portion thereof . . . ;

(2) permit the individual to request amendment of a record pertaining to him . . .

(3) permit the individual who disagrees with the refusal of the agency to amend his record to request a review of such refusal . . .

. . .

(g)

(1) Civil Remedies.—Whenever any agency

(A) makes a determination under subsection (d)(3) of this section not to amend an individual's record in accordance with his request, or fails to make such review in conformity with that subsection;

(B) refuses to comply with an individual request under subsection (d)(1) of this section;

(C) fails to maintain any record concerning any individual with such accuracy, relevance, timeliness, and completeness as is necessary to assure fairness in any determination relating to the qualifications, character, rights, or opportunities of, or benefits to the individual that may be made on the basis of such record, and consequently a determination is made which is adverse to the individual; or

(D) fails to comply with any other provision of this section, or any rule promulgated thereunder, in such a way as to have an adverse effect on an individual,

the individual may bring a civil action against the agency, and the district courts of the United States shall have jurisdiction in the matters under the provisions of this subsection.

(2)

(A) In any suit brought under the provisions of subsection (g)(1)(A) of this section, the court may order the agency to amend the individual's record in accordance with his request or in such other way as the court may direct. In such a case the court shall determine the matter de novo.

(B) The court may assess against the United States reasonable attorney fees and other litigation costs reasonably incurred in any case under this paragraph in which the complainant has substantially prevailed.

(3)

(A) In any suit brought under the provisions of subsection (g)(1)(B) of this section, the court may enjoin the agency from withholding the records and order the production to the complainant of any agency records improperly withheld from him. . . .

(B) The court may assess against the United States reasonable attorney fees and other litigation costs reasonably incurred in any case under this paragraph in which the complainant has substantially prevailed.

(4) In any suit brought under the provisions of subsection (g)(1)(C) or (D) of this section in which the court determines that the agency acted in a manner which was intentional or willful, the United States shall be liable to the individual in an amount equal to the sum of—

(A) actual damages sustained by the individual as a result of the refusal or failure, but in no case shall a person entitled to recovery receive less than the sum of $1,000; and

(B) the costs of the action together with reasonable attorney fees as determined by the court.

## Bechhoefer v. Drug Enforcement Administration

209 F.3d 57 (2d Cir. 2000)

■ JOSÉ A. CABRANES, CIRCUIT JUDGE:

This appeal requires us to clarify the definition of a "record" under the Privacy Act of 1974, 5 U.S.C. § 552a. Plaintiff Arthur S. Bechhoefer appeals from a judgment of the United States District Court for the Western District of New York granting summary judgment to the United States Drug Enforcement Administration ("DEA") and two DEA agents, Robert Nearing and Jeffrey Gelina, and dismissing Bechhoefer's claims under the Privacy Act and the First Amendment. On appeal, Bechhoefer challenges only the dismissal of his Privacy Act claim, contending that the District Court erred in holding that a letter he wrote to defendants was not a "record" within the meaning of the Privacy Act. We agree and therefore vacate the judgment of the District Court.

### I

The following facts are drawn from the record on appeal and, unless otherwise noted, are undisputed. Bechhoefer was a long-time resident of Yates County, New York, and an active member of two groups concerned with land use in the Keuka Lake area. During the summer of 1993, apparently in connection with his membership in these groups, Bechhoefer received a report of drug trafficking in the area. The report implicated several prominent people in Yates County, including at least one member of the Yates County Sheriff's Department.

On July 15, 1993, Bechhoefer called the Rochester office of the DEA and spoke with defendant Gelina about the report. In response, Gelina asked Bechhoefer to send him a letter detailing the information Bechhoefer had learned, including the names of those allegedly involved in drug trafficking and the names of Bechhoefer's own sources. According to Bechhoefer, he agreed to send the letter only after Gelina provided specific assurances that the letter would remain confidential. In an affidavit submitted to the District Court, however, Gelina avers that he told Bechhoefer he would try—but could not guarantee—to keep the letter confidential.

Bechhoefer sent Gelina a three-page letter dated July 17, 1993, naming several people suspected of involvement in drug trafficking and listing others who could provide information. The letter was written on stationery with Bechhoefer's full name, address, and voice/fax telephone number at the top, and was plainly labeled "CONFIDENTIAL." In the first paragraph of the letter, Bechhoefer identified himself as follows:

> I am a private businessman, running an investment advisory service. I also am an officer of the Bluff Point Association, a citizen watchdog group that has uncovered instances of malfeasance or outright misuse of public funds in the Town of Jerusalem and surrounding areas around Keuka Lake. Because our organization is known for its courageous stand against corruption, we receive reports on various issues, including in this case some serious problems on drug trafficking.

At the end of the letter, Bechhoefer cautioned that "[t]his is a very serious situation. Those of us who have been receiving information are probably in danger. The Sheriff's Department cannot be trusted to provide any security, nor can its members be considered reliable."

After receiving Bechhoefer's letter, Gelina and defendant Nearing tried to meet with Bechhoefer and to contact Bechhoefer's alleged sources. However, for reasons that are disputed, no meeting between the agents and Bechhoefer ever occurred, and the agents failed to reach Bechhoefer's sources. Based on the lack of corroboration of Bechhoefer's allegations, the agents declined to open a formal investigation.

Around this time, Michael J. Christensen, an investigator with the Yates County Sheriff's Department who was named in Bechhoefer's letter—albeit not directly implicated in the alleged drug trafficking—learned about the letter. On August 5, 1993, he apparently called Gelina and Nearing and, after confirming that they had received a letter from Bechhoefer, requested that they send it to him. In response to this request, and at the direction of the DEA Resident Agent In Charge, Nearing faxed a copy of Bechhoefer's letter to Christensen.

As a result of these events, Bechhoefer was charged in two separate criminal actions by the Yates County District Attorney. In addition, Bechhoefer was sued, apparently for defamation, in three state court actions. Bechhoefer was acquitted by a jury on one set of the criminal charges, and the other set eventually was dropped; Bechhoefer's brief on appeal indicates that the civil actions all have been dismissed as well.

In July 1995, Bechhoefer filed a complaint in the District Court [which] alleged that the DEA violated § 552a(b) of the Privacy Act by disclosing Bechhoefer's letter without his consent. [It also included First Amendment claims, but the plaintiff did not appeal dismissal of those claims. The parties filed cross-motions for summary judgment.]

The District Court ruled that Bechhoefer's Privacy Act claim was without merit because the letter in question is not a "record" within the meaning of the Privacy Act. Judgment was entered and this appeal followed.

## II

Congress enacted the Privacy Act to provide certain safeguards for an individual against an invasion of personal privacy, by requiring governmental agencies to maintain accurate records and providing individuals with more control over the gathering, dissemination, and accuracy of agency information about themselves. Subject to certain enumerated exceptions, § 552a(b) of the Privacy Act provides that

> [n]o agency shall disclose any record which is contained in a system of records by any means of communication to any person, or to another agency, except pursuant to a written request by, or with the prior written consent of, the individual to whom the record pertains.

5 U.S.C. § 552a(b); *see id.* § 552a(g)(1)(D) (creating a private right of action for violations of the Privacy Act). By its terms, to establish a violation of this provision, a plaintiff must first establish that the information in question is a "record" within the meaning of the Act.

The Privacy Act defines a "record" as "any item, collection, or grouping of information about an individual that is maintained by an agency, *including, but not limited to*, his education, financial transactions, medical history, and criminal or employment history and that contains his name . . . or other identifying particular." 5 U.S.C. § 552a(a)(4) (emphasis added). Neither party disputes that Bechhoefer's letter is an "item" or that the letter contains his name (and the names of several others). Thus, the critical question is whether Bechhoefer's letter is "about an individual" within the meaning of § 552a(a)(4).

Neither the Supreme Court nor this Court has ever articulated a test for determining whether an item qualifies as a "record" under § 552a(a)(4). Several other courts of appeals have done so, however, resulting in three different tests for whether an item is a "record" within the meaning of the Privacy Act: The Ninth and Eleventh Circuits have held that for an item to qualify as a "record" it "must reflect some quality or characteristic of the individual involved," *Boyd v. Secretary of the Navy*, 709 F.2d 684, 686 (11th Cir. 1983); *accord Unt v. Aerospace Corp.*, 765 F.2d 1440, 1449 (9th Cir. 1985); the D.C. Circuit has held that an item must contain "information that actually describes the individual in some way," *Tobey v. NLRB*, 40 F.3d 469, 472 (D.C. Cir. 1994); and the

Third Circuit has held, most liberally, that the "statutory definition of a record . . . [has] a broad meaning encompassing *any* information about an individual that is linked to that individual through an identifying particular," [citing *Quinn v. Stone*, 978 F.2d 126, 131 (3d Cir. 1992)] (emphasis in original).

For several reasons, we adopt a test much like the Third Circuit's test for what qualifies as a record under the Privacy Act. First and foremost, the Third Circuit's test is most consistent with the broad terms of the statutory definition. As quoted above, § 552a(a)(4) defines a "record" as "*any item*, collection, or grouping of information about an individual." 5 U.S.C. § 552a(a)(4) (emphasis added). Contrary to the test adopted by the Ninth and Eleventh Circuits, nothing in the Act suggests that information must reflect a "quality or characteristic" of an individual in order to qualify for protection. And while the test adopted by the D.C. Circuit in *Tobey* is not *necessarily* inconsistent with the terms of the statute, the *Tobey* test can, and has, been read to require something more than "any information" about an individual. Thus, in our view, the *Tobey* test also strains the statutory language of § 552a(a)(4).

Second, only the Third Circuit's test is consistent with the Supreme Court's decision in [*U.S. Dep't of Def. v. Fed. Labor Relations Auth.*, 510 U.S. 487 (1994) (hereafter "*FLRA*")]. In that case, the Supreme Court held that the information at issue—federal civil service employees' home addresses—qualified for protection under the Privacy Act, even though such information did not "actually describe" any individual [quoting the D.C. Circuit's *Tobey* test], or reflect some individual's "quality or characteristic" [quoting the 11th Circuit's *Boyd* test]. As the [*FLRA*] Court stated, without further elaboration or discussion, "The employee addresses are 'records' covered by the broad terms of the Privacy Act." To be sure, the principal issue in *FLRA* concerned construction of the Freedom of Information Act ("FOIA"), 5 U.S.C. § 552, and the Court did not closely analyze the statutory definition of "record" in the Privacy Act. Nevertheless, the Court's conclusion was a necessary part of its ultimate holding—and therefore does not constitute dictum. Accordingly, any test of what constitutes a "record" under the Privacy Act must encompass the information at issue in *FLRA*—and only the Third Circuit's test does so.

Finally, the Third Circuit's test is supported by the legislative history of the Privacy Act and by the relevant guidelines issued by the Office of Management and Budget ("OMB")—the entity assigned with chief responsibility for formulating guidelines on federal agency implementation of, and for overseeing federal agency compliance with, the Privacy Act. Both the legislative history and the OMB Guidelines emphasize that "a record can include as little as one descriptive item about an individual." Moreover, the OMB Guidelines themselves define "record" to mean "any item of information about an individual that includes an individual identifier."

In some respects, the legislative history of the Privacy Act supports a more limited reading of § 552(a)(4) than the one adopted by the Third Circuit. These references imply that Congress may have intended to limit the protections of the Act to information that somehow is private or personal. Nevertheless, the legislative history makes plain that Congress intended "personal information" itself to have a broad meaning, encompassing

> *all* information that describes, locates or indexes *anything* about an individual including his education, financial transactions, medical history, criminal, or employment record, or that affords a basis for inferring personal characteristics, such as finger and voice prints, photographs, or things done by or to such individual; and the record of his presence, registration, or membership in an organization or activity, or admission to an institution.

S. 3418, 93d Cong., § 301(3) (1974) (emphasis added). Moreover, when read in light of the broad language of the Act and the Supreme Court's decision in *FLRA*, nothing in the statute's legislative history supports the more limited tests adopted by the D.C., Ninth, and Eleventh Circuits.

We therefore hold that "record" under the Privacy Act has a broad meaning encompassing, at the very least, any personal information about an individual that is linked to that individual through an identifying particular. Applying this test to the facts of the instant case, we conclude that the District Court erred in holding that Bechhoefer's letter is not a "record" within the meaning of the Privacy Act. The letter contains both Bechhoefer's name and several pieces of "personal information" about him, including his address, his voice/fax telephone number, his employment, and his membership in the Bluff Point Association. If, as the Supreme Court held in *FLRA*, an employee's name and address are alone sufficient to qualify as a record under the Privacy Act, the information contained in the letter about Bechhoefer surely qualifies for the Act's protection.

## NOTES

1. ***The Privacy Act and the FIPs.*** The Privacy Act was passed in 1974. The year before, a major federal government study had examined then-emerging concerns about large government databases containing personal information. The capacity and scope of these databases were dramatic new developments, made possible by advances in digital technology during the 1960s and early 1970s. The 1973 report was promulgated by the Department of Health, Education, and Welfare ("HEW") (which was later split into two separate departments, for Health and Human Services and for Education). The "HEW Report" is famous among privacy lawyers as one of the first expressions of standards that have become known as the "Fair Information Practice Principles" ("FIPs" or, sometimes, "FIPPs"). These same concepts were later reflected in the OECD Guidelines and other foundational texts of

data protection law [see Chapter 4]. In this first articulation by HEW, the FIPs were:

- There must be no personal data record-keeping system whose very existence is secret.
- There must be a way for an individual to find out what information about him is in a record and how it is used.
- There must be a way for an individual to prevent information about him that was obtained for one purpose from being used or made available for other purposes without his consent.
- There must be a way for an individual to correct or amend a record of identifiable information about him.
- Any organization creating, maintaining, using, or disseminating records of identifiable personal data must assure the reliability of the data for their intended use and must take precaution to prevent misuse of the data.

The Privacy Act responded directly to the HEW Report. It attempted to enforce the FIPs in three primary ways: by limiting the uses the government could make of personal data, by giving individuals a right to inspect records about themselves and correct inaccurate information, and by creating elaborate internal procedures for the handling of personal information by government agencies. How well do you think the Privacy Act satisfied the HEW Report's goals?

2. ***Administration of the Privacy Act.*** The Office of Management and Budget (OMB), which coordinates administrative activities throughout the Executive Branch, issues detailed guidance for agencies about compliance with the Privacy Act. Courts generally view this guidance as a highly authoritative interpretation of the statute. Note how the *Bechhoefer* court places the OMB Guidelines virtually on a par with the statutory text itself.

3. ***Statutory Interpretation.*** Go back and dissect the three grounds for the *Bechhoefer* court's construction of the statutory definition of a "record" in the Privacy Act. Which arguments are the most important? The court says it considered the text "first and foremost." It acknowledges that "the test adopted by the D.C. Circuit in *Tobey* is not *necessarily* inconsistent with the terms of the statute," but finds that the *Tobey* test leads to narrow interpretations of the definition that are at odds with its broad framing ("*any* records"). Is that a textual argument? Consider what *Tobey* said about the text of § 552a(a)(4):

> From this definition at least two requirements emerge. First, in order to qualify as a record, information must be "about" an individual. Second, in addition to being "about" an individual, the information must contain the individual's name or other identifying particular. The second requirement leads to an obvious conclusion about the first: the fact that information contains an

> individual's name does not mean that the information is "about" the individual. If it did, the first requirement would be surplusage. A fundamental principle of statutory construction mandates that we read statutes so as to render all of their provisions meaningful. It is readily evident, therefore, that the information must both be "about" an individual and include his name or other identifying particular.

*Tobey v. N.L.R.B.*, 40 F.3d 469, 471 (D.C. Cir. 1994). In *Tobey*, an agency used its case management database to retrieve files about all the cases handled by individual field examiners in order to assess these employees' efficiency. Although each file did contain the initials of the field examiner who handled it, the court found that the case files were "about" the cases, not the field examiners, so they were not "records" as defined by the Act. Which circuit's test is better supported by the statutory text? Which one do you think is a better interpretation overall?

**4. *A "System of Records."*** The DEA also argued that the *Bechhoefer* court should affirm the district court's summary judgment ruling on an alternative ground: even if the letter were a "record" under the Privacy Act, it was not "contained in a system of records" as also required by the statute. The court of appeals declined to reach this argument, but on remand the district court accepted it and again granted summary judgment to the DEA. The plaintiff appealed once more, and this time the Second Circuit sided with the federal government and affirmed summary judgment:

> It is only when the document becomes incorporated into a record-keeping system under the agency's control that the Act's prescriptions apply. And as for documents like Bechhoefer's letter, which the agency regards as irrelevant to its mission and therefore never incorporates into its record-keeping system, but which are forwarded to another agency, discarded, or left in an employee's desk drawer, such documents never become part of the agency's system of records.

*Bechhoefer v. DOJ*, 312 F.3d 563, 566 (2d Cir. 2002). The majority of courts read the "system of records" limitation strictly, requiring not only that a record is included in some database that could contain personal information, but also that, in practice, the agency uses names or other individual identifiers to retrieve those records. *See, e.g., Henke v. United States Dep't of Commerce*, 83 F.3d 1453, 1459–61 (D.C. Cir. 1996); *but see Williams v. Dep't of Veterans Affairs*, 104 F.3d 670, 675 (4th Cir. 1997) ("This close textual reading by courts . . . appears to focus on the trees at the expense of the forest."). Do you see that requirement reflected in the text of § 552a(a)(5)? A policy argument about protecting agencies from overly broad Privacy Act claims supports this reading:

> The threshold issue in any claim alleging denial of access under the Privacy Act is whether the records sought by the plaintiff are maintained in a "system of records" retrievable by an "identifying particular assigned to" the plaintiff. This qualifying language in the statute reflects a statutory compromise between affording

> individuals access to those records relating directly to them and protecting federal agencies from the burdensome task of searching through agency records for mere mention of an individual's name.

*Bettersworth v. FDIC*, 248 F.3d 386, 391 (5th Cir. 2001). Many of the Privacy Act's key provisions—including the disclosure limitations central to *Bechhoefer* and individuals' rights of access to all records about them—turn on threshold definitional requirements that an item be a "record" and part of a "system of records." That said, some courts have found other claims under the Act, such as those concerning the inaccuracy of a record, do not require that the record be part of a system. This interpretation makes sense, they reason, because allegedly inaccurate records have already been identified by the plaintiff and the agency, so there is no need to avoid the danger of a "fishing expedition." *McCready v. Nicholson*, 465 F.3d 1, 11 (D.C. Cir. 2006).

5. ***The Privacy Act and PII.*** The preliminary definitional wrangling seen in *Bechhoefer* is common in Privacy Act cases. It is really just another instance of a familiar problem in privacy law of determining what counts as personally identifiable information (PII) covered within the scope of a legal rule. The three tests for defining a "record" all take different positions on the amount of identifiability needed to qualify for protection.

6. ***Data About Foreigners.*** What is the effect of § 552a(a)(2)? By its terms, the Privacy Act applies only to citizens or lawful permanent residents, not to most foreign nationals. Thus, for example, some databases connected with immigration or customs may be outside the scope of the law. In early 2016, however, Congress passed and President Obama signed the Judicial Redress Act, P.L. 114–126 (2016). This brand new law allows the Attorney General to designate countries with whom the US has a data transfer agreement, provided those countries cooperate and share information in US criminal invesatigations. A citizen of a designated country could then bring Privacy Act suits under those agreements, at least for certain types of violations. The statute was a direct response to an EU court ruling effectively prohibiting many transfers of EU personal data to the US without greater safeguards against the government, and particularly the NSA, gaining access to it [see Chapter 8].

7. ***Consent and Waivers.*** An individual may, of course, consent to an agency disclosure of personal data to a third party. But the OMB Guidelines require that such a waiver must be knowing and specific, and close in time

to the disclosure. Over time, a procedure developed of requiring signed waiver forms for most such disclosures, including when they benefit the data subject. So, for example, an attorney counseling a client in a tax or immigration matter, or a congressional office advocating on behalf of a constituent for veterans' benefits, often requires that the individual fill out and sign a waiver form granting permission to communicate directly with the federal government about the individual's case.

8. ***The 12 Exceptions.*** The Privacy Act departs from the standard American default rule about disclosures. Similar to a data protection regime, federal agencies can disclose covered records only with consent or under one of the twelve specific conditions listed in § 552a(b). This makes that list of

authorized disclosures supremely important. Review that list of exceptions. Which ones do you think agencies rely upon the most?

**9.** ***Routine Use.*** On its face, the "routine use" exception in § 552a(b)(3) is extremely broad. As one scholar has objected, "Federal agencies have cited this exemption to justify virtually any disclosure of information without the individual's permission." Paul M. Schwartz, *Privacy and Participation: Personal Information and Public Sector Regulation in the United States*, 80 IOWA L. REV. 553, 585 (1995). The statute defines routine uses as those "compatible with the purpose for which [data] was collected." Some courts have read this rule strictly. *See, e.g., Britt v. Naval Investigative Serv.*, 886 F.2d 544, 547–50 (3d Cir. 1989); *Swenson v. USPS*, 890 F.2d 1075 (9th Cir. 1989). However, a court's remedial power under 5 U.S.C. § 552a(g) is limited; typically that power will be confined to the particular case before it, and the court will not have any means to order more generally that an agency change its reliance upon the routine use exception. The Privacy Act also requires an agency to publish specific notice in the *Federal Register* identifying a routine use in order to qualify for the exception. Some courts have also considered, in addition to the constructive notice of *Federal Register* publication, whether an agency provided *actual* notice to the individual at the time data was collected. *See, e.g., USPS v. Nat'l Ass'n of Letter Carriers*, 9 F.3d 138 (D.C. Cir. 1993); *Covert v. Harrington*, 876 F.2d 751 (9th Cir. 1989). That last point explains the fine-print "Privacy Act notices" found at the bottom of many federal government forms collecting personal data.

**10.** ***Constitutional Restrictions on Data Collection?*** In *Whalen v. Roe*, 429 U.S. 589 (1977), the Supreme Court held open the possibility that certain excessive collection of personal data could violate constitutional rights of substantive due process. [See Chapter 1.] The recognition of the constitutional argument is far from universal, however, and some courts have concluded that there is no constitutional right to control government data collection.

---

## Focus

### Computer Matching and the Privacy Act

In 1988, Congress amended the Privacy Act by enacting the Computer Matching and Privacy Protection Act. *See* 5 U.S.C. §§ 552(a)(8)–(13), (e)(12), (o), (p), (q), (r) and (u). The statute regulates computer matching, the automated comparison of two different data sets in order to gather more information about an individual. In particular, matching programs can identify similarities and discrepancies between information in two separate databases. These patterns help identify persons who may not be eligible for certain government benefits. (An example of just such a program is discussed in the next case, *FAA v. Cooper.*) The computer matching provisions added to the Privacy Act apply not only to data sharing between federal agencies, but also sharing between federal agencies and outside entities such as state or local government. OMB has issued extremely detailed guidelines for compliance with the Privacy Act's computer matching requirements.

Prior to the 1988 amendments, there was little restriction on computer matching, as it was considered a routine use of data. The amendment imposed new procedural requirements on the practice. For example, agencies must report matching programs to the OMB and Congress and must establish internal Data Protection Boards to oversee matching activity. Agencies that share data for computer matching also must enter into written agreements specifying numerous details about the parameters of any matching program, including its purpose, the precise data elements to be matched, the number of records involved, and the start and end dates of the program.

The 1988 amendments originally prohibited agencies from taking adverse actions (such as terminating benefits) until subjects were given thirty days notice and the findings were independently verified. However, agencies quickly found this impractical. Congress passed an additional amendment in 1990 to remove the thirty-day time limit and allow an agency to waive the independent verification requirement when it has a high degree of confidence in the accuracy of data.

The computer matching rules face criticism from both directions. Some see its exhaustive requirements as a significant bureaucratic burden that slows down efforts to verify the eligibility of applicants for government benefits and the performance of other administrative tasks. At the same time, others object that all those procedures do not really provide any substantive safeguards against improper matching.

---

## FAA v. Cooper

132 S. Ct. 1441 (2012)

■ JUSTICE ALITO delivered the opinion of the Court.

The Privacy Act of 1974, codified in part at 5 U.S.C. § 552a, contains a comprehensive and detailed set of requirements for the management of confidential records held by Executive Branch agencies. If an agency fails to comply with those requirements "in such a way as to have an adverse effect on an individual," the Act authorizes the individual to bring a civil action against the agency. § 552a(g)(1)(D). For violations found to be "intentional or willful," the United States is liable for "actual damages." § 552a(g)(4)(A). In this case, we must decide whether the term "actual damages," as used in the Privacy Act, includes damages for mental or emotional distress. We hold that it does not.

### I

The Federal Aviation Administration (FAA) requires pilots to obtain a pilot certificate and medical certificate as a precondition for operating an aircraft. Pilots must periodically renew their medical certificates to ensure compliance with FAA medical standards. When applying for renewal, pilots must disclose any illnesses, disabilities, or surgeries they have had, and they must identify any medications they are taking.

Respondent Stanmore Cooper has been a private pilot since 1964. In 1985, he was diagnosed with a human immunodeficiency virus (HIV) infection and began taking antiretroviral medication. At that time, the FAA did not issue medical certificates to persons with respondent's condition. Knowing that he would not qualify for renewal of his medical certificate, respondent initially grounded himself and chose not to apply. In 1994, however, he applied for and received a medical certificate, but he did so without disclosing his HIV status or his medication. He renewed his certificate in 1998, 2000, 2002, and 2004, each time intentionally withholding information about his condition.

When respondent's health deteriorated in 1995, he applied for long-term disability benefits under Title II of the Social Security Act, 42 U.S.C. §§ 401 et seq. To substantiate his claim, he disclosed his HIV status to the Social Security Administration (SSA), which awarded him benefits for the year from August 1995 to August 1996.

In 2002, the Department of Transportation (DOT), the FAA's parent agency, launched a joint criminal investigation with the SSA, known as "Operation Safe Pilot," to identify medically unfit individuals who had obtained FAA certifications to fly. The DOT gave the SSA a list of names and other identifying information of 45,000 licensed pilots in northern California. The SSA then compared the list with its own records of benefit recipients and compiled a spreadsheet, which it gave to the DOT.

The spreadsheet revealed that respondent had a current medical certificate but had also received disability benefits. After reviewing respondent's FAA medical file and his SSA disability file, FAA flight surgeons determined in 2005 that the FAA would not have issued a medical certificate to respondent had it known his true medical condition.

When investigators confronted respondent with what had been discovered, he admitted that he had intentionally withheld from the FAA information about his HIV status and other relevant medical information. Because of these fraudulent omissions, the FAA revoked respondent's pilot certificate, and he was indicted on three counts of making false statements to a Government agency, in violation of 18 U.S.C. § 1001. Respondent ultimately pleaded guilty to one count of making and delivering a false official writing. He was sentenced to two years of probation and fined $1,000. [Respondent eventually applied for recertification as a pilot, which the FAA granted based on changes in its rules concerning HIV.]

Claiming that the FAA, DOT, and SSA (hereinafter Government) violated the Privacy Act by sharing his records with one another, respondent filed suit in the United States District Court for the Northern District of California. He alleged that the unlawful disclosure to the DOT of his confidential medical information, including his HIV status, had caused him "humiliation, embarrassment, mental anguish, fear of social ostracism, and other severe emotional distress." Notably, he did not allege any pecuniary or economic loss.

The District Court granted summary judgment against respondent. The court concluded that the Government had violated the Privacy Act and that there was a triable issue of fact as to whether the violation was intentional or willful. But the court held that respondent could not recover damages because he alleged only mental and emotional harm, not economic loss.

The United States Court of Appeals for the Ninth Circuit reversed and remanded. The court acknowledged that the term "actual damages" is a " 'chameleon' "in that "its meaning changes with the specific statute in which it is found." But the court nevertheless held that, as used in the Privacy Act, the term includes damages for mental and emotional distress.

The Government petitioned for rehearing or rehearing en banc, but a divided court denied the petition. The Government then petitioned for certiorari, and we granted review.

## II

Because respondent seeks to recover monetary compensation from the Government for mental and emotional harm, we must decide whether the civil remedies provision of the Privacy Act waives the Government's sovereign immunity with respect to such a recovery.

### A

We have said on many occasions that a waiver of sovereign immunity must be "unequivocally expressed" in statutory text. Legislative history cannot supply a waiver that is not clearly evident from the language of the statute. Any ambiguities in the statutory language are to be construed in favor of immunity so that the Government's consent to be sued is never enlarged beyond what a fair reading of the text requires. Ambiguity exists if there is a plausible interpretation of the statute that would not authorize money damages against the Government.

The question that confronts us here is not whether Congress has consented to be sued for damages under the Privacy Act. That much is clear from the statute, which expressly authorizes recovery from the Government for "actual damages." Rather, the question at issue concerns the scope of that waiver. For the same reason that we refuse to enforce a waiver that is not unambiguously expressed in the statute, we also construe any ambiguities in the scope of a waiver in favor of the sovereign.

### B

Because Congress did not define "actual damages," respondent urges us to rely on the ordinary meaning of the word "actual" as it is defined in standard general-purpose dictionaries. But as the Court of Appeals explained, "actual damages" is a legal term of art, and it is a "cardinal rule of statutory construction" that, when Congress employs a term of art, it presumably knows and adopts the cluster of ideas that were attached to each borrowed word in the body of learning from which it was taken.

Even as a legal term, however, the meaning of "actual damages" is far from clear. [A]s the Court of Appeals accurately observed, the precise meaning of the term changes with the specific statute in which it is found.

Because the term "actual damages" has this chameleon-like quality, we cannot rely on any all-purpose definition but must consider the particular context in which the term appears.

### C

Because the Act serves interests similar to those protected by defamation and privacy torts, there is good reason to infer that Congress relied upon those torts in drafting the Act.

In *Doe v. Chao*, 540 U.S. 614 (2004), we held that the Privacy Act's remedial provision authorizes plaintiffs to recover a guaranteed minimum award of $1,000 for violations of the Act, but only if they prove at least some "actual damages." Although we did not address the meaning of "actual damages," we observed that the provision "parallels" the remedial scheme for the common-law torts of libel per quod and slander, under which plaintiffs can recover "general damages," but only if they prove "special harm" (also known as "special damages"). "General damages," on the other hand, cover "loss of reputation, shame, mortification, injury to the feelings and the like and need not be alleged in detail and require no proof."

This parallel between the Privacy Act and the common-law torts of libel per quod and slander suggests the possibility that Congress intended the term "actual damages" in the Act to mean special damages. The basic idea is that Privacy Act victims, like victims of libel per quod or slander, are barred from any recovery unless they can first show actual—that is, pecuniary or material—harm. Upon showing some pecuniary harm, no matter how slight, they can recover the statutory minimum of $1,000, presumably for any unproven harm. That Congress would choose to use the term "actual damages" instead of "special damages" was not without precedent. The terms had occasionally been used interchangeably.

### D

We do not claim that the contrary reading of the statute accepted by the Court of Appeals and advanced now by respondent is inconceivable. But because the Privacy Act waives the Federal Government's sovereign immunity, the question we must answer is whether it is plausible to read the statute, as the Government does, to authorize only damages for economic loss. When waiving the Government's sovereign immunity, Congress must speak unequivocally. Here, we conclude that it did not. As a consequence, we adopt an interpretation of "actual damages" limited to proven pecuniary or economic harm. To do otherwise would expand the scope of Congress' sovereign immunity waiver beyond what the statutory text clearly requires.

■ JUSTICE SOTOMAYOR, with whom JUSTICE GINSBURG and JUSTICE BREYER join, dissenting.

Congress enacted the Privacy Act of 1974 for the stated purpose of safeguarding individual privacy against Government invasion. To that end, the Act provides a civil remedy entitling individuals adversely affected by certain agency misconduct to recover "actual damages" sustained as a result of the unlawful action.

Today the Court holds that "actual damages" is limited to pecuniary loss. Consequently, individuals can no longer recover what our precedents and common sense understand to be the primary, and often only, damages sustained as a result of an invasion of privacy, namely mental or emotional distress. That result is at odds with the text, structure, and drafting history of the Act. And it cripples the Act's core purpose of redressing and deterring violations of privacy interests. I respectfully dissent.

The majority concludes that "actual damages" in the civil-remedies provision of the Privacy Act allows recovery for pecuniary loss alone. But it concedes that its interpretation is not compelled by the plain text of the statute or otherwise required by any other traditional tool of statutory interpretation. And it candidly acknowledges that a contrary reading is not "inconceivable." Yet because it considers its reading of "actual damages" to be "plausible," the majority contends that the canon of sovereign immunity requires adoption of an interpretation most favorable to the Government.

The canon simply cannot bear the weight the majority ascribes it. The sovereign immunity canon is just that—a canon of construction. It is a tool for interpreting the law, and we have never held that it displaces the other traditional tools of statutory construction. Here, traditional tools of statutory construction—the statute's text, structure, drafting history, and purpose—provide a clear answer: The term "actual damages" permits recovery for all injuries established by competent evidence in the record, whether pecuniary or nonpecuniary, and so encompasses damages for mental and emotional distress. There is no need to seek refuge in a canon of construction, much less one that has been used so haphazardly in the Court's history.

After today, no matter how debilitating and substantial the resulting mental anguish, an individual harmed by a federal agency's intentional or willful violation of the Privacy Act will be left without a remedy unless he or she is able to prove pecuniary harm. That is not the result Congress intended when it enacted an Act with the express purpose of safeguarding individual privacy against Government invasion. And it is not a result remotely suggested by anything in the text, structure, or history of the Act. For those reasons, I respectfully dissent.

[Justice KAGAN took no part in the consideration or decision of this case.]

## NOTES

1. ***Sovereign Immunity.*** You may have learned about sovereign immunity in other classes. Absent a statutory waiver, federal and state governments are immune from suit by individuals because of their role as sovereigns. As explained by the majority, sovereign immunity is interpreted through a so-called "clear statement rule"—a presumption that Congress would only waive the federal government's immunity from suit through explicit statutory text. Of course, Congress has enacted numerous such waivers of federal sovereign immunity, such as the Federal Tort Claims Act for tort claims and the Tucker Act for contract claims. The *Cooper* Court accepts that Congress also waived sovereign immunity in the Privacy Act, but the dispute concerns the scope of that waiver. More fundamentally, the disagreement between the majority and the dissent centers on the strength of the clear statement rule. To the majority, any ambiguity whatsoever counts against a waiver, while the dissent considers this canon of construction much less determinative of the outcome.

2. ***Libel per Quod?*** As so often occurs in privacy law, this debate partly turns on a characterization of the nature of the harm caused by invasions of privacy. Is the Court's use of libel per quod and slander the correct parallel for the harms addressed by the Privacy Act? The *Cooper* Court explains in an omitted footnote:

> Libel per quod and slander (as opposed to libel and slander per se) apply to a communication that is not defamatory on its face but that is defamatory when coupled with some other extrinsic fact.

Is that what Privacy Act violations are like? If not, what would be better analogues?

3. ***Privacy Act Claims After* Cooper.** Does *Cooper* sound the death knell for private rights of action under the Privacy Act? Certainly, as the dissent indicates, many plaintiffs will be foreclosed from winning damages awards under § 552a(g)(4)(A). Can you think of how changes in the facts of *Cooper* might allow a plaintiff like this one to secure damages? Can other Privacy Act claims still be brought after this decision? What are the practical obstacles to bringing such claims?

4. ***A Sequel to* Doe v. Chao.** In many ways, *Cooper* is the sequel to an earlier Supreme Court case concerning damages under the Privacy Act, *Doe v. Chao*, 540 U.S. 614 (2004). As mentioned in *Cooper*, the Court there found that a plaintiff needed to prove some form of actual damages in order to be entitled to the sum of $1,000 in statutory damages provided by § 552a(g)(4)(A). But the Court stopped short of specifying what counted as "actual" damages; on the record before it, there was no proof of any kind of damages. The majority even commented in a footnote, "We do not suggest that out-of-pocket expenses are necessary for recovery of the $1,000 minimum; only that they suffice to qualify under any view of actual damages." *Id.* at 1212 n.12. That left an open question to be settled in *Cooper*. Notably, there is no mention of sovereign immunity anywhere in the *Doe* opinion.

5. ***Damages and Standing.*** In many other parts of this book, we encounter cases where an inability to allege or to prove harm from a privacy violation prevents a plaintiff from demonstrating constitutional standing to sue. *See, e.g., Clapper v. Amnesty Int'l USA*, 133 S. Ct. 1138 (2013) (plaintiffs lack standing to challenge foreign intelliegence surveillance because they cannot prove that they were subjected to such surveillance) [see Chapter 9]. How is *Cooper* similar to those situations and how is it different? Are there any important distinctions between a suit being foreclosed on standing grounds and on statutory interpretation grounds?

6. ***State Analogues to the Privacy Act.*** In contrast to the broader provisions in the federal Privacy Act, states generally have enacted only patchwork provisions regulating state government collection and use of personal data. *See* Paul M. Schwartz, *Privacy and Participation: Personal Information and Public Sector Regulation in the United States*, 80 IOWA L. REV. 553, 604–613 (1995). A few states have more detailed statutory schemes, although even these are not generally as comprehensive as federal law. Under California's Information Practices Act of 1977, for example, an agency may collect data only when it is "relevant and necessary to accomplish a purpose of the agency required or authorized by the California Constitution or statute or mandated by the federal government." Cal. Civ. Code § 1798.14. The California law also provides an individual with rights to inquire and be notified about government use of personal data, § 1798.32, and allows an individual to inspect and amend that data, § 1798.34. According to its text, this law's provisions should be "liberally construed so as to protect the rights of privacy arising under this chapter or under the Federal or State Constitution." § 1798.63. The Minnesota Government Data Practices Act requires state agencies to provide a specified notice to individuals when their personal data is collected stating the purpose and intended use of the requested data; whether the individual may refuse to supply the requested data; any known consequence arising from supplying or refusing to supply data; and the identity of other persons or entities authorized by state or federal law to receive the data. This law also gives individuals the right to inspect personal data agencies hold about them. *See* Minn. Stat. Ann. § 13.04. Around 14 states have some kind of law requiring proper disposal of government records containing personal data when they are no longer needed. These rules may include specific methods to make electronic data undecipherable and require shredding or burning of paper documents, and may impose obligations on third party vendors that dispose of government records. *See, e.g.*, Mass. Gen. Laws. Ch. 93I, § 2; Mich. Comp. Laws § 445.72a.

7. ***Extra Protection for Special Data.*** Beyond the Privacy Act, special categories of government-held personal data enjoy additional protection. For example, there are robust statutory bans on disclosing personal data that had been provided to the Census. *See* 13 U.S.C. §§ 9, 214. The Interneal Revenue Code also establishes strong confidentiality rules for tax return information. *See* 26 U.S.C.§ 6103. Another statute, the Driver's Privacy Protection Act, 18 U.S.C. §§ 2721 et seq., creates federal privacy rules for state records, namely driver's licenses information, enforceable with

a private right of action. Does it make sense to give these particular categories of personal information additional protection? Why or why not?

---

## Practice

Privacy Act Compliance

The district court in *Cooper* found that the government had violated the Privacy Act. The federal government prevailed only because of the plaintiff's inability to prove damages. But of course it would have been better to avoid the litigation entirely. The government needed to expend resources to argue the case all the way up to the Supreme Court. And, with somewhat different facts, Cooper might have had standing: for example, what if he were a professional pilot who lost his license, and therefore his livelihood, because of the alleged Privacy Act violation?

Imagine that it is 2002, and you are an OMB attorney responsible for helping federal agencies comply with the Privacy Act. The agencies considering implementation of Operation Safe Pilot have presented their plans for your approval. What advice would you offer them about methods they could use to achieve their goals consistent with the Privacy Act, and more likely avoid litigation like *Cooper*?

---

## Focus

The E-Government Act and Privacy Impact Assessments

In 2002, Congress passed the E-Government Act, which was primarily focused on promoting federal agencies' use of modern information technology, with an aim toward increasing both efficiency and public access to government resources. The statute gave OMB additional authority to coordinate IT policy for the federal government and created an organizational structure for chief information officers within agencies. Several of its provisions focused on privacy. For example, the law ordered OMB to issue additional rules concerning data privacy and security, and mandated that federal government web sites have privacy policies.

Section 208 of the E-Government Act requires federal agencies to conduct a "Privacy Impact Assessment" ("PIA") whenever they develop, procure, or modify information technology systems that handle personal information. These assessments resemble information privacy audits conducted in the private sector, examining all the stages of the life cycle of data. [See Part II of this book.] PIAs must consider variables such as the type of personal data collected or stored, its purposes and intended uses, how it will be shared or disclosed, the retention period for the data, and information security. The need for agencies to document consideration of all these factors in the procurement process has encouraged government IT contractors to promote their products' privacy features as a selling point and increased consciousness of privacy in the development of IT within the government. But critics say it can also inject cumbersome bureaucratic steps into that development process.

---

## B. GOVERNMENT DISCLOSURE RULES

As noted at the outset of the chapter, there is significant tension between the need to protect private information in the government's hands and the opposing desire for transparency of government operations. That dichotomy is represented well within the person of Louis Brandeis. On one hand, he is a legendary protector of privacy from government intrusion as the author of the landmark dissent in *Olmstead v. United States*, 277 U.S. 438 (1928) [see Chapter 1] and the coauthor of the most famous article ever to expound privacy interests, *The Right to Privacy*, 4 HARV. L. REV. 193 (1890) [see Chapter 2]. At the same time, however, perhaps the single most frequently used quotation of Brandeis captures his observation about the salutary effects of disclosure requirements: "Publicity is justly commended as a remedy for social and industrial diseases. Sunlight is said to be the best of disinfectants; electric light the most efficient policeman." LOUIS BRANDEIS, OTHER PEOPLE'S MONEY—AND HOW BANKERS USE IT 92 (1914). This section examines law that attempts to strike the complex balance between the privacy dangers of disclosure and the social benefits of sunlight.

1. FREEDOM OF INFORMATION ACT

## Freedom of Information Act

5 U.S.C. § 552

### § 552. Public information; agency rules, opinions, orders, records, and proceedings

(a) . . .

(3)

(A) . . . [E]ach agency, upon any request for records which (i) reasonably describes such records and (ii) is made in accordance with published rules stating the time, place, fees (if any), and procedures to be followed, shall make the records promptly available to any person.

(B) In making any record available to a person under this paragraph, an agency shall provide the record in any form or format requested by the person if the record is readily reproducible by the agency in that form or format. Each agency shall make reasonable efforts to maintain its records in forms or formats that are reproducible for purposes of this section.

(C) In responding under this paragraph to a request for records, an agency shall make reasonable efforts to search for the records in electronic form or format, except when such efforts would significantly interfere with the operation of the agency's automated information system.

(D) For purposes of this paragraph, the term "search" means to review, manually or by automated means, agency records for the purpose of locating those records which are responsive to a request. . . .

(4)

. . .

(B) On complaint, the district court . . . has jurisdiction to enjoin the agency from withholding agency records and to order the production of any agency records improperly withheld from the complainant. In such a case the court shall determine the matter de novo, and may examine the contents of such agency records in camera to determine whether such records or any part thereof shall be withheld under any of the exemptions set forth in subsection (b) of this section, and the burden is on the agency to sustain its action.

. . .

(E)

(i) The court may assess against the United States reasonable attorney fees and other litigation costs reasonably incurred in any case under this section in which the complainant has substantially prevailed.

(ii) For purposes of this subparagraph, a complainant has substantially prevailed if the complainant has obtained relief through either—

(I) a judicial order, or an enforceable written agreement or consent decree; or

(II) a voluntary or unilateral change in position by the agency, if the complainant's claim is not insubstantial.

(b) This section does not apply to matters that are—

(1)

(A) specifically authorized under criteria established by an Executive order to be kept secret in the interest of national defense or foreign policy and

(B) are in fact properly classified pursuant to such Executive order;

(2) related solely to the internal personnel rules and practices of an agency;

(3) specifically exempted from disclosure by statute . . .

(4) trade secrets and commercial or financial information obtained from a person and privileged or confidential;

(5) inter-agency or intra-agency memorandums or letters which would not be available by law to a party other than an agency in litigation with the agency;

(6) personnel and medical files and similar files the disclosure of which would constitute a clearly unwarranted invasion of personal privacy;

(7) records or information compiled for law enforcement purposes, but only to the extent that the production of such law enforcement records or information (A) could reasonably be expected to interfere with enforcement proceedings, (B) would deprive a person of a right to a fair trial or an impartial adjudication, (C) could reasonably be expected to constitute an unwarranted invasion of personal privacy, (D) could reasonably be expected to disclose the identity of a confidential source . . . , (E) would disclose techniques and procedures for law enforcement investigations or prosecutions . . . , or (F) could reasonably be expected to endanger the life or physical safety of any individual;

(8) contained in or related to examination, operating, or condition reports prepared by, on behalf of, or for the use of an agency responsible for the regulation or supervision of financial institutions; or

(9) geological and geophysical information and data, including maps, concerning wells.

Any reasonably segregable portion of a record shall be provided to any person requesting such record after deletion of the portions which are exempt under this subsection. . . .

---

## Focus

### Making a FOIA Request

To access information under FOIA, one must submit a written request to the agency holding the information. Any person, regardless of US citizenship, may make a FOIA request. Each agency has its own office responsible for responding to such requests. There is no mandatory method or form for submitting a request, although it must include the requester's name and contact information. The request must also describe the information sought in as much detail as possible and the desired format for receiving it. Most agencies now have systems for submitting requests on a web site or through email or fax.

After receiving a request, an agency typically sends a letter acknowledging receipt and providing a tracking number for it. The agency then searches through its records and determines what information can and should be sent to the individual under the terms of FOIA. The agency may redact portions of records that are protected from disclosure by one of the exemptions. As seen in the statute, these exemptions include trade secrets, privileged communications, information on supervision of financial institutions, and classified national security information. When the agency relies on an exemption to withhold or redact records, it will notify the requester of the exemption applied. FOIA does not require agencies to collect new records, conduct research, or analyze data in responding to a request.

The time it takes for an agency to respond to a request varies widely depending on the agency and the nature of the request. The initial acknowledgment must be sent within 20 days by statute, and sometimes the request is completely processed within that time. In practice, agencies often take longer, and because most agencies have large backlogs of requests, the wait to receive actual records in response to a request may stretch for months or even years. An individual may receive an expedited response for various reasons, depending on the agency. All agencies offer an expedited response if delay would threaten someone's life or physical safety or would substantially impair someone's due process rights.

Agencies may impose fees for a request in certain circumstances. Usually an agency charges the requester if a response requires over two hours of search time or over 100 pages of duplication. Note that a requester may still be required to pay the fees even if the search does not result in the production of releasable records. Individuals can stipulate in their requests a maximum amount they are willing to pay, and agencies will also notify individuals if the search will likely cost more than $25, allowing the request to be modified to reduce the charges. The government may issue a fee waiver if a requester proves that disclosure of the information requested is in the public interest in order to improve understanding of government operations and not primarily in the commercial interest of the individual.

---

## U.S. Dep't of Justice v. Reporters Comm. For Freedom of Press

489 U.S. 749 (1989)

■ JUSTICE STEVENS delivered the opinion of the Court.

The Federal Bureau of Investigation (FBI) has accumulated and maintains criminal identification records, sometimes referred to as "rap sheets," on over 24 million persons. The question presented by this case is whether the disclosure of the contents of such a file to a third party "could reasonably be expected to constitute an unwarranted invasion of personal privacy" within the meaning of the Freedom of Information Act (FOIA), 5 U.S.C. § 552(b)(7)(C).

### I

In 1924 Congress appropriated funds to enable the Department of Justice (Department) to establish a program to collect and preserve fingerprints and other criminal identification records. That statute authorized the Department to exchange such information with "officials of States, cities and other institutions." Six years later Congress created the FBI's identification division, and gave it responsibility for "acquiring, collecting, classifying, and preserving criminal identification and other crime records and the exchanging of said criminal identification records with the duly authorized officials of governmental agencies, of States, cities, and penal institutions." Rap sheets compiled pursuant to such authority contain certain descriptive information, such as date of birth and physical characteristics, as well as a history of arrests, charges, convictions, and incarcerations of the subject. Normally a rap sheet is preserved until its subject attains age 80. Because of the volume of rap sheets, they are sometimes incorrect or incomplete and sometimes contain information about other persons with similar names.

The local, state, and federal law enforcement agencies throughout the Nation that exchange rap-sheet data with the FBI do so on a voluntary basis. The principal use of the information is to assist in the detection and prosecution of offenders; it is also used by courts and corrections officials in connection with sentencing and parole decisions. As a matter of executive policy, the Department has generally treated rap sheets as confidential and, with certain exceptions, has restricted their use to governmental purposes. Consistent with the Department's basic policy of treating these records as confidential, Congress in 1957 amended the basic statute to provide that the FBI's exchange of rap-sheet information with any other agency is subject to cancellation "if dissemination is made outside the receiving departments or related agencies."

As a matter of Department policy, the FBI has made two exceptions to its general practice of prohibiting unofficial access to rap sheets. First, it allows the subject of a rap sheet to obtain a copy; and second, it occasionally allows rap sheets to be used in the preparation of press releases and publicity designed to assist in the apprehension of wanted persons or fugitives. [Congress also enacted several narrow exceptions, all adopted after FOIA, for example allowing some access to rap sheets within financial services and nuclear power industries for certain defined purposes.]

Although much rap-sheet information is a matter of public record, the availability and dissemination of the actual rap sheet to the public is limited. Arrests, indictments, convictions, and sentences are public events that are usually documented in court records. In addition, if a person's entire criminal history transpired in a single jurisdiction, all of the contents of his or her rap sheet may be available upon request in that jurisdiction. That possibility, however, is present in only three States. All of the other 47 States place substantial restrictions on the availability of criminal-history summaries even though individual events in those summaries are matters of public record.

## II

The statute known as the FOIA is actually a part of the Administrative Procedure Act (APA). Section 3 of the APA as enacted in 1946 gave agencies broad discretion concerning the publication of governmental records. In 1966 Congress amended that section to implement a general philosophy of full agency disclosure. If an agency improperly withholds any documents, the district court has jurisdiction to order their production. Unlike the review of other agency action that must be upheld if supported by substantial evidence and not arbitrary or capricious, the FOIA expressly places the burden "on the agency to sustain its action" and directs the district courts to "determine the matter de novo."

Congress exempted nine categories of documents from the FOIA's broad disclosure requirements. Three of those exemptions are arguably relevant to this case. Exemption 3 applies to documents that are specifically exempted from disclosure by another statute. § 552(b)(3). Exemption 6 protects "personnel and medical files and similar files the disclosure of which would constitute a clearly unwarranted invasion of personal privacy." § 552(b)(6). Exemption 7(C) excludes records or information compiled for law enforcement purposes, "but only to the extent that the production of such [materials] . . . could reasonably be expected to constitute an unwarranted invasion of personal privacy." § 552(b)(7)(C).

Exemption 7(C)'s privacy language is broader than the comparable language in Exemption 6 in two respects. First, whereas Exemption 6 requires that the invasion of privacy be "clearly unwarranted," the adverb "clearly" is omitted from Exemption 7(C). This omission is the product of a 1974 amendment adopted in response to concerns expressed by the President. Second, whereas Exemption 6 refers to disclosures that "would constitute" an invasion of privacy, Exemption 7(C) encompasses any disclosure that "could reasonably be expected to constitute" such an invasion. This difference is also the product of a specific amendment. Thus, the standard for evaluating a threatened invasion of privacy interests resulting from the disclosure of records compiled for law enforcement purposes is somewhat broader than the standard applicable to personnel, medical, and similar files.

## III

This case arises out of requests made by a CBS news correspondent and the Reporters Committee for Freedom of the Press (respondents) for information concerning the criminal records of four members of the Medico family. The Pennsylvania Crime Commission had identified the family's company, Medico Industries, as a legitimate business dominated by organized crime figures. Moreover, the company allegedly had obtained a number of defense contracts as a result of an improper arrangement with a corrupt Congressman.

The FOIA requests sought disclosure of any arrests, indictments, acquittals, convictions, and sentences of any of the four Medicos. Although the FBI originally denied the requests, it provided the requested data concerning three of the Medicos after their deaths. In their complaint in the District Court, respondents sought the rap sheet for the fourth, Charles Medico (Medico), insofar as it contained "matters of public record."

## IV

Exemption 7(C) requires us to balance the privacy interest in maintaining, as the Government puts it, the "practical obscurity" of the rap sheets against the public interest in their release.

The preliminary question is whether Medico's interest in the nondisclosure of any rap sheet the FBI might have on him is the sort of "personal privacy" interest that Congress intended Exemption 7(C) to protect. Because events summarized in a rap sheet have been previously disclosed to the public, respondents contend that Medico's privacy interest in avoiding disclosure of a federal compilation of these events approaches zero. We reject respondents' cramped notion of personal privacy.

To begin with, both the common law and the literal understandings of privacy encompass the individual's control of information concerning his or her person. In an organized society, there are few facts that are not at one time or another divulged to another. Thus the extent of the protection accorded a privacy right at common law rested in part on the degree of dissemination of the allegedly private fact and the extent to which the passage of time rendered it private. According to Webster's initial definition, information may be classified as "private" if it is "intended for or restricted to the use of a particular person or group or class of persons: not freely available to the public." Recognition of this attribute of a privacy interest supports the distinction, in terms of personal privacy, between scattered disclosure of the bits of information contained in a rap sheet and revelation of the rap sheet as a whole. The very fact that federal funds have been spent to prepare, index, and maintain these criminal-history files demonstrates that the individual items of information in the summaries would not otherwise be "freely available" either to the officials who have access to the underlying files or to the general public. Indeed, if the summaries were "freely available," there would be no reason to invoke the FOIA to obtain access to the information they contain. Granted, in many contexts the fact that information is not freely available is no reason to exempt that information from a statute generally requiring its dissemination. But the issue here is whether the compilation of otherwise hard-to-obtain information alters the privacy interest implicated by disclosure of that information. Plainly there is a vast difference between the public records that might be found after a diligent search of courthouse files, county archives, and local police stations throughout the country and a computerized summary located in a single clearinghouse of information.

This conclusion is supported by the web of federal statutory and regulatory provisions that limits the disclosure of rap-sheet information. That is, Congress has authorized rap-sheet dissemination to banks, local licensing officials, the securities industry, the nuclear-power industry, and other law enforcement agencies. Further, the FBI has permitted such disclosure to the subject of the rap sheet and, more generally, to assist in the apprehension of wanted persons or fugitives. Finally, the FBI's exchange of rap-sheet information "is subject to cancellation if dissemination is made outside the receiving departments or related agencies." This careful and limited pattern of authorized rap-sheet disclosure fits the dictionary definition of privacy as involving a restriction of information "to the use of a particular person or group or class of persons." Moreover, although perhaps not specific enough to constitute a statutory exemption under FOIA Exemption 3, these statutes and regulations, taken as a whole, evidence a congressional intent to protect the privacy of rap-sheet subjects, and a concomitant recognition of the power of compilations to affect personal privacy that outstrips the combined power of the bits of information contained within.

Also supporting our conclusion that a strong privacy interest inheres in the nondisclosure of compiled computerized information is the Privacy Act of 1974, 5 U.S.C. § 552a. The Privacy Act was passed largely out of concern over "the impact of computer data banks on individual privacy." The Privacy Act provides generally that "[n]o agency shall disclose any record which is contained in a system of records . . . except pursuant to a written request by, or with the prior written consent of, the individual to whom the record pertains." 5 U.S.C. § 552a(b). Although the Privacy Act contains a variety of exceptions to this rule, including an exemption for information required to be disclosed under the FOIA, Congress' basic policy concern regarding the implications of computerized data banks for personal privacy is certainly relevant in our consideration of the privacy interest affected by dissemination of rap sheets from the FBI computer.

Given this level of federal concern over centralized data bases, the fact that most States deny the general public access to their criminal-history summaries should not be surprising. State policies, of course, do not determine the meaning of a federal statute, but they provide evidence that the law enforcement profession generally assumes—as has the Department of Justice—that individual subjects have a significant privacy interest in their criminal histories. It is reasonable to presume that Congress legislated with an understanding of this professional point of view.

In sum, the fact that "an event is not wholly 'private' does not mean that an individual has no interest in limiting disclosure or dissemination of the information." Rehnquist, *Is an Expanded Right of Privacy Consistent with Fair and Effective Law Enforcement?*, Nelson Timothy Stephens Lectures, University of Kansas Law School, pt. 1, p. 13 (Sept. 26–27, 1974). The privacy interest in a rap sheet is substantial. The substantial character of that interest is affected by the fact that in today's society the computer can accumulate and store information that would otherwise have surely been forgotten long before a person attains age 80, when the FBI's rap sheets are discarded.

## V

Exemption 7(C), by its terms, permits an agency to withhold a document only when revelation "could reasonably be expected to constitute an unwarranted invasion of personal privacy." We must next address what factors might warrant an invasion of the interest described in Part IV, *supra*.

Our previous decisions establish that whether an invasion of privacy is warranted cannot turn on the purposes for which the request for information is made.

Thus whether disclosure of a private document under Exemption 7(C) is warranted must turn on the nature of the requested document and its relationship to the basic purpose of the Freedom of Information Act to open agency action to the light of public scrutiny.

In our leading case on the FOIA, we declared that the Act was designed to create a broad right of access to "official information." *EPA v. Mink*, 410 U.S. 73, 80 (1973). In his dissent in that case, Justice Douglas characterized the philosophy of the statute by quoting this comment by Henry Steele Commager:

> The generation that made the nation thought secrecy in government one of the instruments of Old World tyranny and committed itself to the principle that a democracy cannot function unless the people are permitted to know *what their government is up to.*

*Id.* at 105 (quoting from *The New York Review of Books*, Oct. 5, 1972, p. 7) (emphasis added).

This basic policy of full agency disclosure unless information is exempted under clearly delineated statutory language indeed focuses on the citizens' right to be informed about "what their government is up to." Official information that sheds light on an agency's performance of its statutory duties falls squarely within that statutory purpose. That purpose, however, is not fostered by disclosure of information about private citizens that is accumulated in various governmental files but that reveals little or nothing about an agency's own conduct. In this case—and presumably in the typical case in which one private citizen is seeking information about another—the requester does not intend to discover anything about the conduct of the agency that has possession of the requested records. Indeed, response to this request would not shed any light on the conduct of any Government agency or official.

Respondents argue that there is a two-fold public interest in learning about Medico's past arrests or convictions: He allegedly had improper dealings with a corrupt Congressman, and he is an officer of a corporation with defense contracts. But if Medico has, in fact, been arrested or convicted of certain crimes, that information would neither aggravate nor mitigate his allegedly improper relationship with the Congressman; more specifically, it would tell us nothing directly about the character of the Congressman's behavior. Nor would it tell us anything about the conduct of the Department of Defense (DOD) in awarding one or more contracts to the Medico Company. Arguably a FOIA request to the DOD for records relating to those contracts, or for documents describing the agency's procedures, if any, for determining whether officers of a prospective contractor have criminal records, would constitute an appropriate request for "official information." Conceivably Medico's rap sheet would provide details to include in a news story, but, in itself, this is not the kind of public interest for which Congress enacted the FOIA. In other words, although there is undoubtedly some public interest in anyone's criminal history, especially if the history is in some way related to the subject's dealing with a public official or agency, the FOIA's central purpose is to ensure that the Government's activities be opened to the sharp eye of public scrutiny, not that information about private citizens that happens to be in the warehouse of the Government be so disclosed. Thus, it should come as no surprise that in none of our cases construing the FOIA have we found it appropriate to order a Government agency to honor a FOIA request for information about a particular private citizen.

## VI

Both the general requirement that a court "shall determine the matter de novo" and the specific reference to an "unwarranted" invasion of privacy in Exemption 7(C) indicate that a court must balance the public interest in disclosure against the interest Congress intended the Exemption to protect. Although both sides agree that such a balance must be undertaken, how such a balance should be done is in dispute. The Court of Appeals majority expressed concern about assigning federal judges the task of striking a proper case-by-case, or ad hoc, balance between individual privacy interests and the public interest in the disclosure of criminal-history information without providing those judges standards to assist in performing that task. Our cases provide support for the proposition that categorical decisions may be appropriate and individual circumstances disregarded when a case fits into a genus in which the balance characteristically tips in one direction.

The privacy interest in maintaining the practical obscurity of rap-sheet information will always be high. When the subject of such a rap sheet is a private citizen and when the information is in the Government's control as a compilation, rather than as a record of "what the Government is up to," the privacy interest protected by Exemption 7(C) is in fact at its apex while the FOIA-based public interest in disclosure is at its nadir. Such a disparity on the scales of justice holds for a class of cases without regard to individual circumstances; the standard virtues of bright-line rules are thus present, and the difficulties attendant to ad hoc adjudication may be avoided. Accordingly, we hold as a categorical matter that a third party's request for law enforcement records or information about a private citizen can reasonably be expected to invade that citizen's privacy, and that when the request seeks no "official information" about a Government agency, but merely records that the Government happens to be storing, the invasion of privacy is "unwarranted." The judgment of the Court of Appeals is reversed.

■ JUSTICE BLACKMUN, with whom JUSTICE BRENNAN joins, concurring in the judgment.

I concur in the result the Court reaches in this case, but I cannot follow the route the Court takes to reach that result. In other words, the Court's use of "categorical balancing" under Exemption 7(C), I think, is not basically sound. Such a bright-line rule obviously has its appeal, but I wonder whether it would not run aground on occasion, such as in a situation where a rap sheet discloses a congressional candidate's conviction of tax fraud five years before. Surely, the FBI's disclosure of that information could not "reasonably be expected" to constitute an invasion of personal privacy, much less an unwarranted invasion, inasmuch as the candidate relinquished any interest in preventing the dissemination of this information when he chose to run for Congress.

I would not adopt the Court's bright-line approach but would leave the door open for the disclosure of rap-sheet information in some circumstances. Nonetheless, even a more flexible balancing approach would still require reversing the Court of Appeals in this case. I, therefore, concur in the judgment, but do not join the Court's opinion.

## Forest Guardians v. FEMA

410 F.3d 1214 (10th Cir. 2005)

■ BALDOCK, CIRCUIT JUDGE.

Plaintiff Forest Guardians brought this action under the Freedom of Information Act (FOIA), 5 U.S.C. § 552, seeking to compel Defendant Federal Emergency Management Agency (FEMA) to produce electronic mapping files that identify the location of structures insured under FEMA's National Flood Insurance Program (NFIP). The NFIP is a federally subsidized program that provides flood insurance to property owners located in flood plain areas with the participation of private insurance companies. FEMA administers the NFIP and is responsible for, among other things, providing and updating flood maps. The district court granted FEMA's cross-motion for summary judgment concluding that Plaintiff's FOIA request was exempt from disclosure under FOIA's Exemption 6, § 552(b)(6), which excludes "personnel and medical files and similar files the disclosure of which would constitute a clearly unwarranted invasion of personal privacy." Plaintiff appeals, arguing the district court erred in concluding Exemption 6 applied. According to Plaintiff, the substantial public interest in the information it requested from FEMA far outweighs any de minimis privacy interest that may exist. We have jurisdiction, review the district court's FOIA determination de novo, and affirm.

### I.

Plaintiff is a non-profit organization devoted to promoting environmental conservation. The organization is currently studying the loss of endangered species in flood plain areas. Plaintiff posits the NFIP encourages excessive development in flood plain areas. Specifically, according to Plaintiff, "the issuance of flood insurance policies under the NFIP facilitates development that results in significant harm to New Mexico's natural resources."

Plaintiff filed a FOIA request with FEMA in January 2001 ("2001 FOIA request"). In the 2001 FOIA request, Plaintiff sought to obtain information regarding FEMA's "efforts to comply with numerous federal environment laws while allowing local communities to participate in the [NFIP]." Plaintiff requested the "[n]ames and addresses of all insurance policy-holders who obtain flood insurance via FEMA's [NFIP]." Plaintiff limited its request "to New Mexico residents who have property within the 100-year floodplains of the Rio Grande and San Juan river." FEMA partially granted Plaintiff's FOIA request. The agency explained it would not disclose policyholders' names because such a disclosure would "clearly invade the privacy of an individual" under Exemption 6.

In the alternative, however, FEMA provided Plaintiff with sixteen "Geographic Information System (GIS) maps of the 27 communities that have a flood hazard designated by FEMA where the flooding source is the San Juan, Animas, or Rio Grande Rivers." In describing the information contained in the GIS maps, FEMA specifically noted:

> On these GIS maps, FEMA has displayed Digitized Q3 Data showing the designated Special Flood Hazard Area (SFHA) and geocoded flood insurance policy data. The geocoded flood policy information shows the general location of structures relative to the floodplain and whether the structure insured was constructed before or after the community participated in the NFIP. These maps show the entire communities not just the floodplains located within them.

Thereafter, Plaintiff filed a second FOIA request with FEMA, which is the subject of this appeal, on April 23, 2002 ("2002 FOIA request"). In the 2002 FOIA request, Plaintiff sought:

> electronic GIS files . . . for the 27 communities that have a flood hazard designated by FEMA where the flooding source is the San Juan, Animas, or Rio Grande Rivers, showing all of the geocoded flood insurance policy data (with names and addresses removed). . . . We are essentially requesting that your agency provide the electronic data equivalent to what we received in printed form from FEMA in response to our original January 29, 2001 FOIA [request].

FEMA denied Plaintiff's second request under Exemption 6. FEMA first indicated it had already provided Plaintiff the information in printed form. Second, FEMA claimed the electronic GIS files contained "personal identifying information" and, even with the names and addresses redacted, could be used to determine the "addresses of policyholders based on the GIS point locations with a reasonable level of confidence." In particular, disclosure of the electronic files could lead to the discovery of (1) an individual's name, address, and ownership interest in property, (2) the level of flood risk to property, and (3) the type of insurance and financing on property. Plaintiff sued FEMA after the agency denied its 2002 FOIA request, seeking to compel disclosure of the electronic GIS files.

## II.

FOIA facilitates public access to Government documents. A strong presumption exists in favor of disclosure under FOIA and the Government bears the burden of justifying the withholding of any requested documents. Public access to Government information is not, however, all-encompassing. Access is permitted only to information that sheds light upon the government's performance of its duties.

FOIA contains nine exemptions which, if applicable, preclude disclosure of certain types of information. 5 U.S.C. § 552(b). Exemption 6 prohibits the disclosure of information in "personnel and medical files and similar files the disclosure of which would constitute a clearly unwarranted invasion of personal privacy." 5 U.S.C. § 552(b)(6). "Similar files" under Exemption 6 has a "broad, rather than a narrow, meaning" and encompasses all information that "applies to a particular individual." *United States Department of State v. Washington Post Co.*, 456 U.S. 595, 600–02 (1982).

We apply a balancing test to determine whether disclosure would constitute a clearly unwarranted invasion of personal privacy under Exemption 6. If there is an important public interest in the disclosure of information and the invasion of privacy is not substantial, the private interest in protecting the disclosure must yield to the superior public interest. If, however, the public interest in the information is "virtually nonexistent" or "negligible," then even a "very slight privacy interest would suffice to outweigh the relevant public interest" [quoting *U.S. Dep't of Def. v. Fed. Labor Relations Auth.*, 510 U.S. 487, 497, 500 (1994) (hereafter "*FLRA*").]

The public interest to be weighed in Exemption 6's balancing test is the extent to which disclosure would serve the core purpose of FOIA. The purposes for which the request for information is made has no bearing on whether information must be disclosed under FOIA. Rather, the relevant inquiry is whether the requested information directly relates to and would facilitate the primary purpose of FOIA, which is to let citizens know "what their government is up to." [quoting *DOJ v. Reporters Comm.*, 489 U.S. 749, 773 (1989)].

The type of privacy interests Congress intended to protect under Exemption 6 encompass the individual's control of information concerning his or her person. Such private information includes, for example, an individual's name and home address. The privacy interest in an individual's home address becomes even more substantial when that information would be coupled with personal financial information.

## III.

In this case, the electronic GIS files are exempt from disclosure under Exemption 6. We first conclude the electronic GIS files are "similar files" under FOIA. The files reveal specific geographic point locations for NFIP insured structures. Such information, coupled with property records, can lead to, among other things, the names and addresses of individual property owners and thus applies to particular individuals.

As similar files, we next determine whether disclosure of the electronic GIS files would constitute a clearly unwarranted invasion of personal privacy under Exemption 6's balancing test. We hold that it would. The privacy interest at stake in this case, even if de minimus, outweighs the nonexistent public interest. The relevant public interest in the information Plaintiff requested from FEMA is negligible, at best, because FEMA already provided Plaintiff with the information.

We see little difference between the information contained in the hard-copy GIS maps Plaintiff already possesses and the information Plaintiff seeks in the electronic GIS files. Indeed, Plaintiff explicitly stated in its 2002 FOIA request that "we are essentially requesting that your agency provide electronic data *equivalent to what we received in printed form* from FEMA in response to [the 2001 FOIA Request]." Because the information Plaintiff now seeks is merely cumulative of the information FEMA already provided, no public interest exists in the disclosure of the electronic GIS files. Requiring FEMA to disclose the files would not, by any stretch of the imagination, facilitate Plaintiff's understanding of "what the government is up to." Plaintiff already knows what FEMA "is up to" by virtue of the GIS maps in its possession.

Against the nonexistent FOIA-related public interest in disclosure of the electronic GIS files, we next weigh the relevant privacy interest at stake in this case. Because a very slight privacy interest would suffice, we need not be exact in our quantification. Suffice it to say, some privacy interest exists in the electronic GIS files. The GIS files contain the specific geographic location of NFIP insured structures. Disclosure of the specific location of NFIP insured structures could easily lead to the discovery of an individual's name and home address because knowing the square and lot numbers of a parcel of land is only a step from being able to identify from state records the name of the individual property owner. Indeed, Plaintiff concedes the information it seeks "could be manipulated to derive the addresses of policyholders and potential policyholders." We have recognized a privacy interest in personal identifying information, such as names and addresses, under Exemption 6. Plaintiff's argument that such personal information is not "private" because the information is widely available to the public and easily accessible is foreclosed by Supreme Court precedent. "An individual's interest in controlling the dissemination of information regarding personal matters does not dissolve simply because that information may be available to the public in some form." *FLRA*, 510 U.S. at 500.

Moreover, disclosure of the electronic GIS files would not only reveal names and addresses, but could also reveal information regarding an individual's ownership of property, flood risks to property, an individual's decision to purchase federally subsidized flood insurance through the NFIP, and the manner in which property was purchased. Disclosing such personal information along with the other information Plaintiff seeks, such as particular "flood insurance policy data," would constitute an invasion of personal privacy. NFIP policyholders have a privacy interest—the extent of which we need not quantify today—in their decision to purchase federally subsidized flood insurance and other information concerning their properties. As the district court aptly noted, "the disclosure of information which will essentially lead to the revelation of flood policy holder's names and addresses, coupled with their status as participants in the federally subsidized program, represents a palpable threat to those person's privacy."

Furthermore, disclosure of the electronic GIS files and the concomitant disclosure of personal information, could subject individuals to unwanted contacts or solicitation by private insurance companies. Given the commercial interests involved in the NFIP and the large-scale participation by the private insurance industry, a palpable threat exists that disclosing information that could reveal names, home addresses, and other personal insurance policy information could lead to an influx of unwanted and unsolicited mail, if not more. As the Supreme Court has stated, "[m]any people simply do not want to be disturbed at home," *FLRA*, 510 U.S. at 501, and "[w]e are reluctant to disparage the privacy of the home, which is accorded special consideration in our Constitution, laws, and traditions." *Id.*

## IV.

The privacy interest in the electronic GIS files, even if minimal, clearly outweighs the nonexistent public interest in the files. Disclosing the files would thus constitute a "clearly unwarranted invasion of personal privacy" under FOIA's Exemption 6. The district court's order is therefore affirmed.

## NOTES

1. ***Rules and Standards.*** The disagreement between the majority and concurrence in *Reporters Committee* turned on a familiar dispute about the structure of legal analysis: the difference between rules and standards. The majority decided that a categorical rule could be applied to rap sheets, and the concurrence believed that the analysis must be a case-specific application of the "reasonably to be expected" standard. What are the arguments favoring each approach? Who had the better argument?

2. ***The Public Default.*** Both *Reporters Committee* and *Forest Guardians* characterized FOIA as making government documents public by default and imposing the burden on a government agency to justify withholding data. That said, note that agencies themselves are the initial arbiters of whether a document should be provided under the statute. What do you suppose their tendencies might be when faced with such requests? How might they compare with the tendencies of parties responding to discovery requests in civil litigation?

3. ***Legislative and Judicial Branches.*** FOIA applies only to executive branch agencies—and not, for example, to Congress, the federal judiciary, or parts of the Executive Office of the President. Some narrower "sunlight" requirements apply to members of Congress, such as financial disclosure rules. *See, e.g.*, 5 U.S.C. App. 4 § 102(a) (requiring members of Congress to disclose outside income to the public). As discussed later in this chapter, judicial records are covered to some degree by common law and constitutional presumptions of open access. But these parts of the federal government are also exempt from other features of FOIA, like its administrative requirements and enforcement mechanisms. Are there principled reasons for this difference, or is it simply a matter of Congress singling out the executive branch for obligations it does not impose on itself?

4. ***The Open Data Movement.*** A robust "open data" movement seeks to use publicly maintained data to promote social welfare by aggregating, processing, and using it in new and often unexpected ways. A community of computer coders and data analysts participates in "civic hacking" to develop new information tools using this data, from GIS-enabled mapping of crime patterns to apps that combine government weather and transportation information to track and predict flight delays. President Obama promulgated an executive order, "Making Open and Machine Readable the New Default for Government Information," which directed OMB to develop policies to make data as widely available as possible in order to "fuel entrepreneurship, innovation, and scientific discovery." Executive Order 13642, 78 Fed. Reg. 28111 (May 14, 2013). A federal web site, data.gov, provides access to thousands of data sets. Dozens of US states, counties, and municipalities also provide online public access to open government databases. Federal open data policy makes exceptions for privacy, personal information, and national security concerns. All that said, open data enthusiasts sometimes find that government agencies resist their efforts to "liberate" data. Although these activists wish to use information on behalf of the public good, are they working to find out "what the government is up to?" Thus, are their requests for data covered by the "core purposes" of FOIA?

5. ***Obscurity.*** The *Reporters Committee* Court acknowledged that the information contained in rap sheets was already public, and described the main privacy interest at stake as "practical obscurity." By this logic, the fact that information might be available publicly somewhere does not necessarily eliminate the privacy interest in making it more difficult to locate. In FOIA cases, the concept of practical obscurity has remained important. Most computer security researchers, on the other hand, only use the phrase "security by obscurity" mockingly, because they assume that supposedly

buried information can be ferreted out relatively easily. *See* Paul Ohm, *Broken Promises of Privacy: Responding to the Surprising Failure of Anonymization*, 57 UCLA. L. REV. 1701, 1724 (2010) (arguing that an "adversary" likely has the capacity to recognize private information even if it had been obscured through deidentification). Is the interest in obscurity under FOIA different in an environment where accessible online tools make information more widely available? According to Omer Tene,

> Before the advent of search engines, we enjoyed a degree of "practical obscurity," protecting our privacy interest in issues such as litigation, asset ownership, past employment, and political opinion. Although such information has always been in the public sphere, it was protected de facto from all but skilled investigators or highly motivated researchers, due to the practical difficulty and costs involved in uncovering and compiling the data. Today such information has become available instantly and free of charge through search engines such as Google.

Omer Tene, *What Google Knows: Privacy and Internet Search Engines*, 2008 UTAH L. REV. 1433, 1440 (2008); *see also* Woodrow Hartzog & Frederic D. Stutzman, *The Case for Online Obscurity*, 101 CAL. L. REV. 1 (2013). Does this make Medico's rap sheet less private? The lines between things that are secret, private, obscure, and public defy easy definition, but they allow a more sophisticated analysis than a simple "private or not" dichotomy.

6. ***Accept No Substitutes?*** What if FEMA had not already provided the printed maps in response to Forest Guardians' 2001 FOIA request? Would that have changed the court's analysis or conclusion? Note that FOIA instructs agencies to "provide the record in any form or format requested by the person if the record is readily reproducible by the agency in that form or format." 5 U.S.C. § 552(a)(3)(B). As a comparison, consider the rules for producing electronic documents in discovery, which allow objections to the production of "electronically stored information" when it is too burdensome, but otherwise assume that the responding party "must produce documents as they are kept in the usual course of business or must organize and label them to correspond to the categories in the request." FED. R. CIV. P. 34 (b)(2)(E)(i).

7. ***The* FLRA *Case.*** The decisions in both *Bechhoefer* and *Forest Guardians* referred to the Supreme Court opinion in *U.S. Dep't of Def. v. Fed. Labor Relations Auth.* ("*FLRA*"). That case arose because the Federal Labor Relations Authority had directed all federal agencies to provide labor unions with the home addresses of union-represented agency employees and the federal agencies refused, under the Federal Service Labor-Management Relations Act. The Supreme Court ultimately held that the Privacy Act barred the disclosure and nothing in FOIA or the labor statute required it. The case has become important for its interpretation of the Privacy Act, Exemption 6 of FOIA, and the interaction between them. The *FLRA* Court reiterated the determination in *Reporters Committee* that the only relevant consideration of public benefit in the balancing analysis under Exemption 6 of FOIA was the interest in public scrutiny of government activity. When that interest was minimal, the Court said, any invasion of privacy tips the

balance against disclosure under Exemption 6. As you have seen, courts have continued to apply these considerations in subsequent cases like *Forest Guardians*. The *FLRA* Court found little relevant public interest in the employees' home addresses; the fact that another statute sought to promote collective bargaining interests did not matter, the Court said, unless that law explicitly amended the default rules in the Privacy Act and FOIA, under which the data was private unless FOIA required release.

## 2. CONSTITUTIONAL SUNSHINE RULES

### Press-Enterprise Co. v. Superior Court (Press-Enterprise II)

478 U.S. 1 (1986)

■ CHIEF JUSTICE BURGER delivered the opinion of the Court.

We granted certiorari to decide whether petitioner has a First Amendment right of access to the transcript of a preliminary hearing growing out of a criminal prosecution.

I

On December 23, 1981, the State of California filed a complaint in the Riverside County Municipal Court, charging Robert Diaz with 12 counts of murder and seeking the death penalty. The complaint alleged that Diaz, a nurse, murdered 12 patients by administering massive doses of the heart drug lidocaine. The preliminary hearing on the complaint commenced on July 6, 1982. Diaz moved to exclude the public from the proceedings under Cal. Penal Code Ann. § 868, which requires such proceedings to be open unless "exclusion of the public is necessary in order to protect the defendant's right to a fair and impartial trial." The Magistrate granted the unopposed motion, finding that closure was necessary because the case had attracted national publicity and "only one side may get reported in the media."

The preliminary hearing continued for 41 days. Most of the testimony and the evidence presented by the State was medical and scientific; the remainder consisted of testimony by personnel who worked with Diaz on the shifts when the 12 patients died. Diaz did not introduce any evidence, but his counsel subjected most of the witnesses to vigorous cross-examination. Diaz was held to answer on all charges. At the conclusion of the hearing, petitioner Press-Enterprise Company asked that the transcript of the proceedings be released. The Magistrate refused and sealed the record. [The Press-Enterprise Company challenged this ruling, lost in lower California state courts, and appealed to the California Supreme Court.]

The California Supreme Court [held] that there is no general First Amendment right of access to preliminary hearings. The court reasoned that the right of access to criminal proceedings recognized in *Press-Enterprise Co. v. Superior Court*, 464 U.S. 501 (1984) (*Press-Enterprise*

*I*), and *Globe Newspaper Co. v. Superior Court*, 457 U.S. 596 (1982), extended only to actual criminal trials. Furthermore, the reasons that had been asserted for closing the proceedings in *Press-Enterprise I* and *Globe*—the interests of witnesses and other third parties—were not the same as the right asserted in this case—the defendant's right to a fair and impartial trial by a jury uninfluenced by news accounts.

We granted certiorari. We reverse. [The Court disposed of jurisdictional issues in Part II.]

### III

It is important to identify precisely what the California Supreme Court decided:

> [W]e conclude that the magistrate shall close the preliminary hearing upon finding a reasonable likelihood of substantial prejudice which would impinge upon the right to a fair trial. Penal code section 868 makes clear that the primary right is the right to a fair trial and that the public's right of access must give way when there is conflict.

It is difficult to disagree in the abstract with that court's analysis balancing the defendant's right to a fair trial against the public right of access. It is also important to remember that these interests are not necessarily inconsistent. Plainly, the defendant has a right to a fair trial but, as we have repeatedly recognized, one of the important means of assuring a fair trial is that the process be open to neutral observers.

The California Supreme Court concluded that the First Amendment was not implicated because the proceeding was not a criminal trial, but a preliminary hearing. However, the First Amendment question cannot be resolved solely on the label we give the event, i.e., "trial" or otherwise, particularly where the preliminary hearing functions much like a full-scale trial.

In cases dealing with the claim of a First Amendment right of access to criminal proceedings, our decisions have emphasized two complementary considerations. First, because, a "tradition of accessibility implies the favorable judgment of experiences" *Globe Newspaper*, 457 U.S., at 605, we have considered whether the place and process have historically been open to the press and general public.

In *Press-Enterprise I*, for example, we observed that "since the development of trial by jury, the process of selection of jurors has presumptively been a public process with exceptions only for good cause shown." 464 U.S. at 505. In [*Richmond Newspapers v. Virginia*, 448 U.S. 555 (1980)], we reviewed some of the early history of England's open trials from the day when a trial was much like a "town meeting." Plainly the modern trial with jurors open to interrogation for possible bias is a far cry from the "town meeting trial" of ancient English practice. Yet even our modern procedural protections have their origin in the ancient common-law principle which provided, not for closed proceedings, but rather for rules of conduct for those who attend trials.

Second, in this setting the Court has traditionally considered whether public access plays a significant positive role in the functioning of the particular process in question. *Globe Newspaper*, 457 U.S. at 606. Although many governmental processes operate best under public scrutiny, it takes little imagination to recognize that there are some kinds of government operations that would be totally frustrated if conducted openly. A classic example is that the proper functioning of our grand jury system depends upon the secrecy of grand jury proceedings. Other proceedings plainly require public access. In *Press-Enterprise I*, we summarized the holdings of prior cases, noting that openness in criminal trials, including the selection of jurors, "enhances both the basic fairness of the criminal trial and the appearance of fairness so essential to public confidence in the system." 464 U.S. at 501.

These considerations of experience and logic are, of course, related, for history and experience shape the functioning of governmental processes. If the particular proceeding in question passes these tests of experience and logic, a qualified First Amendment right of public access attaches. But even when a right of access attaches, it is not absolute. While open criminal proceedings give assurances of fairness to both the public and the accused, there are some limited circumstances in which the right of the accused to a fair trial might be undermined by publicity. In such cases, the trial court must determine whether the situation is such that the rights of the accused override the qualified First Amendment right of access. In *Press-Enterprise I* we stated:

> [T]he presumption may be overcome only by an overriding interest based on findings that closure is essential to preserve higher values and is narrowly tailored to serve that interest. The interest is to be articulated along with findings specific enough that a reviewing court can determine whether the closure order was properly entered.

464 U.S. at 510.

### IV

### A

The considerations that led the Court to apply the First Amendment right of access to criminal trials in *Richmond Newspapers* and *Globe* and the selection of jurors in *Press-Enterprise I* lead us to conclude that the right of access applies to preliminary hearings as conducted in California.

First, there has been a tradition of accessibility to preliminary hearings of the type conducted in California. Although grand jury proceedings have traditionally been closed to the public and the accused, preliminary hearings conducted before neutral and detached magistrates have been open to the public. Long ago in the celebrated trial of Aaron Burr for treason, for example, with Chief Justice Marshall sitting as trial judge, the probable-cause hearing was held in the Hall of the House of Delegates in Virginia, the courtroom being too small to accommodate the crush of interested citizens. From Burr until the present day, the near uniform practice of state and federal courts has been to conduct preliminary hearings in open court. Open preliminary hearings, therefore, have been accorded "the favorable judgment of experience."

The second question is whether public access to preliminary hearings as they are conducted in California plays a particularly significant positive role in the actual functioning of the process. We have already determined in *Richmond Newspapers, Globe*, and *Press-Enterprise I* that public access to criminal trials and the selection of jurors is essential to the proper functioning of the criminal justice system. California preliminary hearings are sufficiently like a trial to justify the same conclusion.

We therefore conclude that the qualified First Amendment right of access to criminal proceedings applies to preliminary hearings as they are conducted in California.

### B

Since a qualified First Amendment right of access attaches to preliminary hearings in California under Cal. Penal Code Ann. §§ 858 et seq., the proceedings cannot be closed unless specific, on the record findings are made demonstrating that closure is essential to preserve higher values and is narrowly tailored to serve that interest.

[R]isk of prejudice does not automatically justify refusing public access to hearings on every motion to suppress. Through voir dire, cumbersome as it is in some circumstances, a court can identify those jurors whose prior knowledge of the case would disable them from rendering an impartial verdict. And even if closure were justified for the hearings on a motion to suppress, closure of an entire 41-day proceeding would rarely be warranted. The First Amendment right of access cannot be overcome by the conclusory assertion that publicity might deprive the defendant of that right. And any limitation must be "narrowly tailored to serve that interest." *Press-Enterprise I*, 464 U.S. at 510.

The standard applied by the California Supreme Court failed to consider the First Amendment right of access to criminal proceedings. Accordingly, the judgment of the California Supreme Court is reversed.

[A dissent by Justice Stevens, joined in part by Justice Rehnquist, is omitted.]

## In re Boston Herald, Inc.

321 F.3d 174 (2003)

■ LYNCH, CIRCUIT JUDGE.

John J. Connolly, Jr., the defendant in a highly publicized criminal trial, applied under the Criminal Justice Act (CJA), 18 U.S.C. § 3006A (2000), for government funding for a portion of his attorneys' fees and legal expenses. Connolly had informed the court that he was already in debt to the counsel he had previously retained, and could no longer afford to pay his legal bills. He submitted financial affidavits and an additional document summarizing his total legal debt. The court granted him CJA assistance and, in response to his motions, placed the documents he had submitted under seal. After Connolly's conviction, the Boston Herald, one of Boston's two major daily newspapers, sought to intervene in the case and to unseal these financial documents, arguing that it had a right of access to them under both the First Amendment and the common law. Connolly opposed. A magistrate judge allowed the intervention but denied the motion to unseal, and the district court affirmed. The Herald then filed both an interlocutory appeal and a petition for a writ of mandamus with this court.

No federal court of appeals, to our knowledge, has considered whether there is a right of access to the narrow category of documents at issue here: those submitted by a criminal defendant to show financial eligibility for CJA funds. We conclude that there is no right of access to this category of documents under either the First Amendment or the common law. Even if there were a common law presumption of access, there was no abuse of discretion in denying access here. We affirm the district court and deny mandamus.

**I.**

Connolly is a former FBI agent who was accused of impropriety in his relationships with informants, including alleged organized crime figures such as James "Whitey" Bulger and Stephen Flemmi. Connolly's prosecution and trial garnered extensive media coverage and public interest nationwide, especially in the Boston area, where he had been employed by the FBI.

The magistrate judge granted Connolly's motions to seal three documents that he had submitted to demonstrate his CJA eligibility. The orders to seal these documents were issued without written findings; there was no objection to them at that time. Two of the three sealed documents are an original and an amended version of Connolly's completed CJA Form 23 (the "CJA forms"), a standard "financial affidavit" signed under penalty of perjury. [Form 23] requires comprehensive financial data, including employment income of the defendant and his or her spouse; all other income, cash, and property; identification of the defendant's dependents; and all obligations, debts, and monthly bills. The third document, submitted in response to a question from the magistrate judge, states the total of Connolly's outstanding legal fees from the date of his indictment, December 22, 1999, through February 28, 2002. The magistrate judge's written order appointing Connolly's lawyer under the CJA has always remained public.

## II.

### First Amendment Right of Access

The Supreme Court recognized a qualified First Amendment right of access to certain judicial proceedings and documents in *Richmond Newspapers, Inc. v. Virginia*, 448 U.S. 555 (1980). We examine two "complementary considerations" to determine if a constitutional right of access applies to particular documents such as Connolly's CJA forms and the summary statement of the legal fees he owed for prior representation. *Press-Enterprise Co. v. Superior Court (Press-Enterprise II)*, 478 U.S. 1, 8 (1986). First, we look at whether materials like these three documents have been open to the public in the past, "because a tradition of accessibility implies the favorable judgment of experience." *Press-Enterprise II*, 478 U.S. at 8. Second, we ask "whether public access plays a significant positive role in the functioning of the particular process in question." *Id.* If our inquiry into these considerations were to yield affirmative answers, the right could be overcome only by an "overriding interest." *Id.* We review constitutional access claims de novo.

Some courts have treated these considerations as a two-prong test, with a pair of elements that must both be satisfied. Connolly, not surprisingly, urges us to adopt this approach as well. We are unpersuaded that this is the correct reading of the "complementary considerations" of *Press-Enterprise II*. Because we find that neither of the standards is met here, however, we need not decide the question today.

1. CASE LAW APPLYING FIRST AMENDMENT STANDARDS

The full scope of the constitutional right of access is not settled in the law. Courts have evaluated individual cases when they arose and have determined whether each fell within the category of judicial activities to which the right applies. This process of case-by-case classification, based on the limited Supreme Court precedents, has produced a list of proceedings and records that are covered by a First Amendment right of access and a list of those where no such right attaches.

Supreme Court precedent clearly extends the First Amendment right to cover access to criminal trials, *Richmond Newspapers*, 448 U.S. at 580, including the voir dire of potential jurors, *Press-Enterprise I*, 464 U.S. at 509–10, and trial-like preliminary hearings in criminal cases, *Press-Enterprise II*, 478 U.S. at 10.

Beyond these few Supreme Court cases, lower courts have extended the right to various types of documents. This court has found the right applicable to legal memoranda filed with the court by parties in criminal cases and to records of completed criminal cases that ended without conviction.

Courts have also held that no right of access applies to some other types of proceedings and documents. The paradigmatic example is the grand jury, whose proceedings are conducted in secret. The secrecy of the grand jury is so important that this court and others have found no right of access attaches to distinct hearings and documents because they could reveal secret grand jury information. Courts have also rejected claims based on First Amendment rights of access to other types of documents, at least in certain circumstances. These have included discovery materials, withdrawn plea agreements, affidavits supporting search warrants, and presentence reports.

Two courts of appeals have considered the First Amendment right of access to documents concerning the CJA. In both cases, however, the documents at issue related to CJA payments to attorneys, which raise few privacy issues, rather than to the CJA eligibility documents filed by defendants. The results these courts reached were not entirely consistent. The Tenth Circuit found no First Amendment right of access to the vouchers or backup materials that attorneys submit to receive payment under the CJA. In a case concerned with access to the "barebones data" found in attorneys' CJA vouchers but not the more detailed backup materials, the Second Circuit found a constitutional right of access.

As these cases demonstrate, the First Amendment does not grant the press or the public an automatic constitutional right of access to every document connected to judicial activity. Rather, courts must apply the *Press-Enterprise II* standards to a particular class of documents or proceedings and determine whether the right attaches to that class.

2. TRADITION

One response to the "tradition" inquiry would point to the relatively recent vintage of the CJA, first enacted in 1964, and conclude that there has not been enough time for a longstanding practice of across-the-board disclosure to develop under the statute. Tradition is not meant, we think, to be construed so narrowly; we look also to analogous proceedings and documents of the same type or kind.

The analogies must be solid ones, however, which serve as reasonable proxies for the "favorable judgment of experience" concerning access to the actual documents in question. The Herald strays too far from the particular nature of the CJA eligibility documents when it proposes two supposedly analogous traditions of openness, namely access to criminal trials and access to information about the expenditure of public funds.

The asserted "criminal trial" tradition is too broad an analogy. As seen from examples such as grand jury materials and presentence reports, the mere connection of a document with a criminal case does not itself link the document to a tradition of public access.

The CJA eligibility documents are peripheral to Connolly's trial when compared to those processes where a tradition of access has triggered the First Amendment right, such as the selection of a jury or the legal memoranda submitted about the merits of the case. To conclude otherwise would create a right of access to everything remotely associated with criminal trials, and would be contrary to precedent employing more finely honed classifications.

The Herald also suggests that there is an "expenditure of public funds" tradition of access. This comparison collapses on examination as well. The premise is itself overbroad. Prosecutors, for instance, do not traditionally publish detailed information explaining their use of government resources, much less break it down on a case-by-case basis. The CJA itself contemplates ex parte non-adversarial proceedings for certain determinations involving expenditures for indigent defense, despite the resulting expenditure of public funds.

Connolly offers a better analogy when he cites to government benefits programs administered by the executive branch, where the strong tradition is one of confidentiality rather than disclosure. See, e.g., 42 U.S.C. § 302(a)(7) (2000) (establishing safeguards to prevent public disclosure of information about Social Security recipients). We would think it the exception, not the rule, to require applicants for benefits programs to disclose private financial data about themselves and their immediate family to the public.

The "judgment of experience" does not support a constitutional right of access to CJA eligibility materials.

3. POSITIVE FUNCTIONAL ROLE

The other consideration under *Press-Enterprise II* is whether access to CJA eligibility documents "plays a particularly significant positive role in the actual functioning of the process." Here, the process in question is one of determining eligibility for CJA assistance. Not only does public access to a defendant's financial documentation in support of a CJA application fall short of this standard, more likely it would play a negative role.

First, CJA eligibility determinations, if they are judicial at all, lie far from the core of judicial power or the merits of the criminal case. Unlike trials themselves, access to the defendant's CJA financial statements does not provide an "outlet for community concern, hostility, and emotion" concerning a crime. *Richmond Newspapers*, 448 U.S. at 571. And, unlike other decisions that may "impose official and practical consequences upon members of society at large," *id.* at 597 (Brennan, J., concurring), CJA eligibility determinations never do so.

A remaining functional advantage which the Herald advances is the oft-cited need for the public to have the full understanding necessary to serve as an effective check on the system. In isolation, the "full understanding" rationale proves too much—under it, even grand jury proceedings would be public.

The fact that an application was filed and an attorney appointed are public matters which are entered on the docket of a case. The general reason for Connolly's financial need, rational on its face, was articulated in the order appointing his attorney, also a public document. The amounts of money paid to Connolly's attorney will presumably be made public in due course under the [CJA rules]. The only significant aspects of Connolly's CJA application that were not made public are the details of his family's assets, liabilities, and financial obligations.

Public access to a defendant's financial information would not usually facilitate greater accuracy in decisionmaking. The standards for granting CJA assistance are flexible and give the benefit of the doubt to a defendant who applies for aid. The type of information on the forms is not typically in the public domain and so the public is not well-positioned to challenge accuracy. If the judge has doubts about the accuracy of the financial information submitted, the data may be investigated or more information provided by defendants, court officers, or prosecutors. If the data is inaccurate, the court may rescind the appointment and order the defendant to repay any funds spent. Since a defendant's financial condition is usually investigated in the process of preparing a presentence report, the court is aware that, in the event of a conviction, there will be an independent examination of a defendant's financial status at that time. In addition, there are possible criminal consequences for a defendant who knowingly files false information; CJA Form 23 indicates clearly that it is signed and submitted under penalty of perjury.

On the other hand, the disclosure of a defendant's sensitive personal financial information, which has no bearing on the merits of the criminal trial, could well undermine the judicial process in other ways. In itself, the invasion of privacy inherent in disclosing this data is of concern. This concern is magnified by the crucial role of the CJA as a vehicle to effectuate Sixth Amendment rights for defendants who cannot afford legal representation.

A constitutionally-based right of access to otherwise private personal financial data of one's own and one's family imposes a high price on the exercise of one's constitutional right to obtain counsel if in financial need. Our system of justice cherishes the principle that defendants are not to be avoidably discriminated against because of their indigency. But a strict disclosure requirement could well discourage eligible defendants from availing themselves of their right to counsel by forcing them to choose between privacy and CJA assistance—a choice that other defendants do not face. The specter of disclosure also might lead defendants (or other sources called upon by the court) to withhold information. Public disclosure of such information may put them at risk of harm to their property or their families if the information is misused by their enemies. There is a prospect of unbalancing the scales in a criminal prosecution if the information in CJA application materials could assist the prosecution, thus raising the specter of claims of denial of Fifth Amendment rights. Such effects tend to disrupt, not enhance, the functioning of the process.

On balance, then, disclosure would not play "a particularly significant positive role in the actual functioning of the process" of determining CJA eligibility. *Press-Enterprise II*, 478 U.S. at 11. Rather, disclosure is likely to play a negative role. Nor do the lessons of tradition support the wisdom of public access. The First Amendment does not grant a right of access, over the defendant's objection, to financial documents submitted to demonstrate the defendant's eligibility for CJA funds. The current CJA framework, in which these materials are typically disclosed unless the court decides that the documents should be sealed, is constitutional.

**Common Law Presumption of Access**

In addition to any constitutional right, there is also a presumption of public access to "judicial records" under the common law. *Nixon v. Warner Communications, Inc.*, 435 U.S. 589 (1978). The Herald argues that this presumption invalidates the sealing of Connolly's CJA eligibility documents. Assuming that any common law right has not been displaced by the statute, we hold that the presumption is not applicable to these types of documents, and that if it were, the magistrate judge still correctly exercised his discretion in finding it overcome by countervailing interests.

The common law presumption is limited to "judicial records." We do not think that CJA eligibility documents qualify as such. Rather, they are administrative paperwork generated as part of a ministerial process ancillary to the trial. While the review of these documents is conducted by a district judge or magistrate judge, that role could have been assigned to another institution.

Even assuming that CJA eligibility documents were covered by a common law presumption of access, we would still affirm the magistrate judge's decision to maintain the sealing of Connolly's CJA application materials. The standard for our review is abuse of discretion. The magistrate judge's short but clear order balanced the public interest in the information against privacy interests, and his conclusion was not an abuse of discretion.

Personal financial information, such as one's income or bank account balance, is universally presumed to be private, not public. The magistrate judge sensibly concluded that Connolly's strong interest in the privacy of his and his family's personal financial information outweighs any common law presumption in these circumstances.

Recognition of the importance of financial privacy is also enshrined in public policy. The Freedom of Information Act, applicable only to executive branch materials, exempts personal and confidential financial information from disclosure. *See* 5 U.S.C. § 552(b)(4) (2000). Congress recently singled out financial information for special privacy protection when it approved an overhaul of the nation's banking regulations. *See* Gramm-Leach-Bliley Act of 1999 (GLB Act), Pub. L. No. 106–102, §§ 501–

510 (1999) (codified at 15 U.S.C. §§ 6801–6809 (2000)). States are also considering greater protection for financial privacy.

Finally, the invasiveness of the disclosure sought here is further intensified because the information pertains not only to Connolly, but also to his wife and children.

Thus, even if a common law presumption applied to Connolly's CJA forms and statement of prior legal fees, we would still affirm the magistrate judge's decision.

The petition for a writ of mandamus is denied and the decision of the district court is affirmed.

■ LIPEZ, CIRCUIT JUDGE, dissenting.

This disposition of the Boston Herald's claims is tantamount to a ruling that CJA eligibility forms, which contain only personal financial information, may be shielded from public disclosure without balancing the public interest in a particular applicant's eligibility information against the degree of intrusion into the applicant's privacy. Because I conclude that a qualified right of public access attaches to CJA eligibility information under both the common law and the First Amendment, I cannot agree with the majority's decision to uphold the magistrate judge's summary dismissal of the Boston Herald's claims.

## I.

### A. The Judicial Character of the Documents

The critical role that judges play in the eligibility determination, coupled with the significance of the financial documents themselves to that determination, counsel strongly in favor of classifying the eligibility forms as judicial documents. The majority suggests, however, that the CJA eligibility forms fall outside the category of judicial documents by virtue of their "administrative" character, characterizing the documents as "administrative paperwork generated as part of a ministerial process ancillary to trial." Yet we have recognized that courts act at the apex of their Article III power whenever they conduct proceedings that determine the substantive rights of litigants.

Courts may act pursuant to their Article III authority in proceedings antecedent to a criminal trial even when they address matters that are peripheral to the merits of the underlying dispute. The Supreme Court acknowledged as much in *Press-Enterprise I*, ruling that a qualified right of public access attached to the transcript of the voir dire examination of potential jurors in a criminal trial.

The presumption of access is based on the need for federal courts, although independent—indeed, particularly because they are independent—to have a measure of accountability and for the public to have confidence in the administration of justice. Although courts have a number of internal checks, such as appellate review by multi-judge tribunals, professional and public monitoring is an essential feature of democratic control. Monitoring both provides judges with critical views of their work and deters arbitrary judicial behavior. Without monitoring, moreover, the public could have no confidence in the conscientiousness, reasonableness, or honesty of judicial proceedings. [A]ny rule that purports to confine the Article III imprimatur to documents that directly inform the adjudication of the underlying case or controversy is unduly narrow.

### B. The Presumption of Public Access Under the Common Law

The determination that particular documents are "judicial" documents ipso facto establishes a presumptive right of public access under the common law. However, not all presumptions of access are created equal:

> We believe that the weight to be given the presumption of access must be governed by the role of the material at issue in the exercise of Article III judicial power and the resultant value of such information to those monitoring the federal courts. Generally, the information will fall somewhere on a continuum from matters that directly affect an adjudication to matters that come within a court's purview solely to insure their irrelevance.

*United States v. Amodeo*, 71 F.3d 1044, 1049 (2d Cir. 1995).

Here, the CJA Form 23 information unmistakably falls on the "strong presumption" end of the Article III continuum. While the judge conducting the eligibility inquiry has the discretion to consider other factors, such as the nature of the proceeding for which the defendant seeks appointed counsel, the applicant's financial status is, for obvious reasons, of the utmost importance to the court. In many cases, the financial documents may be the only evidence submitted in the eligibility proceeding, a consideration that significantly strengthens the common law presumption of access: Judicial records are presumptively subject to public inspection.

### C. The Public Right of Access Under the First Amendment

It is true that there is no long "tradition of accessibility" to CJA forms. However, that is because the CJA itself is, in terms of "tradition," a fairly recent development, having been enacted in 1964. This lack of tradition for criminal proceedings of recent origin places intervenors like the Boston Herald in the awkward position of analogizing the documents or proceedings at issue to materials or proceedings with traditions of accessibility. Such analogies can be useful but not decisive. They are inevitably assailable on grounds that the comparison is imperfect, or that application of the tradition would prove too much. In the end there is no sound reason to exclude criminal proceedings of recent origin from the reach of the First Amendment simply because they cannot match the lineage of proceedings that have long been part of the criminal process.

As I read the precedents, the Supreme Court did not intend the logic prong to limit the reach of the First Amendment only to those judicial processes that would realize efficiency and accuracy gains in the "sunshine" of public access. On the contrary, *Richmond Newspapers* and its progeny suggest that the benefits accruing to society from a right of public access to judicial documents and proceedings are assumed prima facie under the logic prong. Accordingly, as the language of *Press Enterprise II* suggests, satisfaction of the logic prong turns on the narrower question of whether public disclosure would defeat the purpose of the specific judicial process at issue.

Nonetheless, the majority posits that the CJA appointment process is uniquely susceptible to privacy-based frustration, reasoning that prospective CJA applicants will be deterred from seeking court-appointed counsel by the prospect that their financial affidavits will be publicly disclosed. However, indigent criminal defendants facing hefty fines, long incarceration, or both are unlikely to forego the opportunity to seek court-appointed counsel out of concern for the confidentiality of their financial information. In the absence of any discernible court or government interest in the confidentiality of CJA eligibility information, the majority's holding that an intrusion into the defendant's privacy, without more, "totally frustrates" a judicial proceeding, *see Press-Enterprise II*, 478 U.S. at 8, expands unjustifiably the range of judicial documents and procedures integral to the criminal process but shielded from First Amendment scrutiny.

The CJA eligibility forms at issue bear every hallmark of judicial documents: (1) the eligibility proceeding potentially occurs within an adversarial setting, (2) the judge plays a critical role in the outcome, (3) the court relies heavily on the financial affidavits to reach its decision, and (4) the outcome of the proceeding is a substantive determination of the applicant's Sixth Amendment right to counsel. These considerations alone suffice to establish a common law presumption of access to the eligibility forms. Because CJA financial affidavits do not fall within the narrow category of judicial documents whose disclosure would frustrate the corresponding criminal judicial process, a First Amendment right of access attaches to these documents as well.

## NOTES

1. ***An Access Right in the First Amendment.*** In other contexts, courts reject the notion that free expression interests create any entitlement of access to information. So, for example, while the disclosure tort contains a capacious "newsworthiness" exception, there is no comparable lenience for free expression in the torts of trespass or intrusion on seclusion [see Chapter 2]. Similarly, the Supreme Court held in *Bartnicki v. Vopper*, 532 U.S. 514 (2001), that the Electronic Communications Privacy Act could not forbid publication of information that is in the public interest, but it specifically limited this holding to the disclosures of communications by people who had no role in gaining unlawful access to it [see Chapter 8]. In other words, free expression norms typically protect the right to communicate information, not

a right to get the information in the first place. Why is the First Amendment right of access to judicial records different?

2. ***A Strong Presumption.*** The presumption of access is usually articulated in strong terms, even though it is a qualified presumption. The *Boston Herald* majority and dissent divide in large part on the question of exactly how strong the presumption should be. Which opinion has the better of that argument?

3. ***Privacy as a Competing Value.*** The California provision at issue in *Press-Enterprise II* closed a preliminary hearing when doing so protected the right to a fair trial, not individual privacy rights. The *Boston Herald* majority discussed not only the privacy interests of Connolly and his family, but also the possibility that disclosure of CJA information would impede access to counsel for criminal defendants. Is privacy a less important value than these others? Would the majority still have come out the same way without the argument about right to counsel?

4. ***The Tradition Prong.*** The "tradition" prong of the *Press-Enterprise II* test is one of many places where legal doctrine attempts to define privacy in modern settings by analogizing those situations to more familiar past ones. Think, for example, of how courts and policymakers have compared expectations about the privacy of email messages with expectations related to telephone calls or postal letters. There are both benefits and dangers in deciding privacy questions on the basis of tradition. What are they? Who has the better analogy in *Boston Herald*?

5. ***The Function Prong.*** When *Press-Enterprise II* asks "whether public access plays a significant positive role in the functioning of the particular process in question," it does not define how significant that positive role must be. Moreover, the Supreme Court decisions in this line of cases generally assume that, all else equal, transparency of criminally-related proceedings is beneficial. Thus, isn't a court really instructed to ask whether public access would have a *negative* role in the functioning of a particular process, so that the general presumption of access should be displaced? (Though again, it may be difficult to define *how* negative that role must be to justify a denial of access.) The *Boston Herald* majority answers by balancing possible benefits and problems of making CJA applications public. The dissent instead asks the "narrower question of whether public disclosure would defeat the purpose of the specific judicial process at issue." Which of these is the correct framing? Finally, both *Press-Enterprise II* and *Boston Herald* take it for granted that there cannot be public access to the proceedings of the grand jury, and that this is central to the "function" prong in the test. But why? What are the features of the grand jury that make public disclosure so antithetical to its operation? Is it because a suspect has not yet been indicted? Or does the acceptance of the secret grand jury really arise from its long tradition, not from function after all?

6. ***Access in Civil Cases.*** In both *Press-Enterprise II* and *Boston Herald*, the underlying proceedings at issue were criminal prosecutions, not civil cases. All the Supreme Court cases concerning the First Amendment access right also involved criminal cases. Lower courts have applied the same

type of presumption to trials in civil cases as well. Although courts do not always extend access to ancillary proceedings and documents as readily in civil cases as in criminal ones, the definite trend is toward increasing access in civil as well as criminal litigation. For example, a federal appellate court ruled that a new procedure in Delaware courts under which parties could agree to confidential arbitration with a Chancery Court judge was equivalent to a civil trial and therefore the First Amendment required public access. *Delaware Coal. for Open Gov't v. Strine*, 733 F.3d 510 (3d Cir. 2013); *see, e.g., Grove Fresh Distribs., Inc. v. Everfresh Juice Co.*, 24 F.3d 893, 897 (7th Cir. 1994) ("[T]hough its original inception was in the realm of criminal proceedings, the right of access has since been extended to civil proceedings because the contribution of publicity is just as important there"). There usually will not be access, however, to civil discovery documents that are not made part of the record. *See Seattle Times Co. v. Rhinehart*, 467 U.S. 20 (1984).

7. ***Judicial Documents.*** Are judicial clerks' bench memos judicial documents? Memos exchanged between judges? Early drafts of opinions? Are there reasons these documents might not be covered by a presumption of public access in a criminal trial?

8. ***Cameras in the Courtroom.*** The Supreme Court has never found that the First Amendment right of access extends to the use of photography during court proceedings. Indeed, there are no cameras allowed at oral arguments of the US Supreme Court, and there is minimal camera coverage in any federal court proceedings, criminal or civil. In 1981, however, the Supreme Court held that the Constitution does not prohibit a state from allowing cameras in its courts. *Chandler v. Florida*, 449 U.S. 560 (1981). Every state supreme court now admits cameras to its arguments under some conditions. Rules in lower state courts range from very liberally allowing cameras in all types of public proceedings to quite constrained or almost nonexistent permission. States continue to struggle with the exact parameters for allowing the use of cameras in courtrooms.

## CHAPTER 11

# EMPLOYMENT AND PRIVACY

According to a widely cited estimate by management consultant Jessica Pryce-Jones, the average employed American spends some 90,000 hours at work over a lifetime. That's a lot of time. And Forrester Research estimates that people entering the workforce today will hold between 12 and 15 jobs in their lifetime. That's a lot of job searches. As a result of it all, private organizations accumulate significant amounts of personal data about prospective and current employees. Some of the resulting information is inherently sensitive, concerning everything from health to financial status. When most of us think of people we don't want learning our private information, current and future bosses are typically high on the list.

In the EU, comprehensive data protection law covers employers in the same fashion as other data processors, and regulators tend to be particularly strict in cases involving workplace information. For example, most European regulators apply consent standards especially rigorously in employment-related cases, requiring very explicit affirmative agreement or even finding valid consent unobtainable, because of what they view as the inherent power differential in the employment relationship. In addition, employee privacy is an important issue for European labor institutions such as works councils (employee representative bodies at individual workplaces, which are quite powerful in some European nations).

In the US, however, there is no single law, even a sectoral statute, that governs the privacy of employee data across the board. Instead, American employers must be mindful of a wide range of privacy laws, including torts [see Chapter 2], the Electronic Communications Privacy Act [see Chapter 5], the Fair Credit Reporting Act [see Chapter 6], and health-related privacy laws like the

Genetic Information Nondiscrimination Act (GINA) [see Chapter 12]. They also must attend to state law and to the interaction of privacy issues with the law of contracts, labor relations, and employment discrimination. Finally, employers in the public sector must layer Fourth Amendment and other constitutional protections [see Chapter 1] on top of these concerns. Increasingly, human resources professionals must build robust expertise in privacy law as well as in traditional employment law in order to avoid compliance risks. This chapter can serve only as an introduction; for excellent comprehensive coverage of the issues, see, e.g., MATTHEW W. FINKIN, PRIVACY IN EMPLOYMENT LAW (4th ed. 2013 & Supp. 2015).

This chapter groups the disparate privacy considerations relevant to all employers under two general headings, one related to the screening of job applicants and employees [Section A] and the other related to monitoring employees on the job [Section B]. The chapter closes by examining the additional legal rules applicable to government employers [Section C].

As you read, identify the legitimate interests organizations have in to collecting, processing, and storing personal information about job applicants and employees. At the same time, consider why policymakers often find privacy interests in the workplace particularly compelling.

## A. SCREENING APPLICANTS AND EMPLOYEES

Naturally, employers want to hire the best possible workers, and personal data can help predict whether a prospective employee will be a good one: not only well-trained, competent and experienced, but also possessing desirable personal attributes that might include punctuality, honesty, or creativity. Each new hire generates significant costs for recruitment, training, and startup. No one wants to waste that investment by making a poor choice. Similar data-gathering about current employees may identify those who should receive raises and promotions, and could help investigate potential wrongdoing. Workers' mistakes can create legal liability for an employer and harm the bottom line in many other ways. Those risks can be grave: an organization whose employees work with children or the elderly, for example, must take special care to prevent their abuse. An organization vulnerable to theft must pay very close attention to security. And employees calculating electrical load capacity or driving trucks have special responsibility for others' lives and safety. The digital revolution means that employers now have much more information available for screening and evaluation. But they must tread carefully when using these resources to avoid violations of either privacy law or employment law.

---

### Focus

Discrimination Law and Privacy

Employment discrimination law indirectly protects privacy because it strongly discourages inquiries about certain aspects of job applicants' personal information. Most federal and state statutes do not contain explicit prohibitions on inquiries about protected classifications such as sex, race, or religion. But many employers recognize that asking those questions opens them up to a potential inference of discrimination if the applicant does not get the job and pursues legal action. Similarly, inquiring whether women have children is ill-advised because of the potential for liability under the Pregnancy Discrimination Act. A number of states have enacted additional statutes restricting the use of particular sensitive information in employment decisions, such as HIV status, and the same compliance considerations arise under these laws as well.

A few legal regimes go further in explicitly prohibiting inquiries about certain personal information. The National Labor Relations Act directly forbids questions about labor union membership or views. Regulatory guidance from the Equal

Employment Opportunities Commission about compliance with the Americans with Disabilities Act ("ADA") indicates that asking whether an individual can perform major life activities such as standing or walking may violate the ADA.

Even apparent bans on data collection may be contingent on proof of underlying discrimination, however, as demonstrated in the following excerpt from *Delta Air Lines. v. New York State Div. of Human Rights*, 689 N.E.2d 898 (N.Y. 1997):

> After Pan Am's bankruptcy declaration in the summer of 1991, it entered into an Asset Purchase Agreement with Delta, by which Delta acquired a substantial portion of Pan Am's assets. Delta also agreed to hire approximately 6,000 Pan Am employees, predicated on specific criteria. These included seniority, language proficiency, personal interviews, and satisfaction of the least restrictive of the Delta or Pan Am small-to-medium weight standards referenced in Delta's height/weight charts. [The court rejected a wide range of discrimination complaints by former Pan Am employees who were not hired, including claims based on race and national origin, marital status, age, sex, and disability (weight).]
>
> Lastly, appellants challenge Delta's preemployment inquiries and medical examinations. They specifically argue that Delta unlawfully asked preemployment questions regarding age, disabilities and physical impairments, family relations, marital status, roommates, and prior treatment for drug or alcohol abuse. We agree with the Appellate Division that the record does not support the contention that the interview inquiries by Delta's representatives contributed to the eventual decision not to hire them. Merely establishing that a particular question was asked, even one that might be viewed as objectionable out of context or in the abstract, is insufficient, without some causal consequence or relevant relationship, to establish a claim for discrimination under the New York Human Rights Law in these circumstances.
>
> The State Executive Law declares unlawful the making of "any inquiry in connection with prospective employment, which expresses directly or indirectly, any limitation, specification or discrimination as to age, race, creed, color or national origin, sex, or disability or marital status, or any intent to make any such limitation." The interview inquiries here are not actionable or sustainable because appellants fail to produce any evidence or suggest any inference that the subject inquiries reflected a "limitation, specification or discrimination."
>
> As to Delta's preemployment physical examinations, suffice it to say that these routine examinations did not affect discriminatory hiring practices but were necessary, in part, to comply with FAA regulations.

Despite the outcome in this case, it is often prudent for a cautious employer to avoid certain kinds of questions in job applications, job interviews, and ongoing employee reviews—if only to eliminate potential "bad facts" in any subsequent dispute. Even if the question is innocent, it may appear less so in the context of a discrimination lawsuit. Although Delta prevailed here, it may be difficult to know in advance how subsequent litigation of this kind will turn out. For this reason, most human resources professionals advise employers to avoid any inquiries into areas within the scope of antidiscrimination law. It is standard practice in many workplaces to formulate a list of vetted interview questions with demonstrable relevance to the job and ask each applicant every question on the list and no others. This can help refute any later allegation of bias.

While antidiscrimination law may discourage collection of certain personal data, it also creates powerful incentives *against* employee privacy in other ways. Can you anticipate what those might be? Consider, for example, the employer's responsibility to prevent a hostile work environment under sex discrimination law. An employer who might face liability if workers are circulating offensive jokes through the company's email or instant messaging system might want to monitor all employee communications to reduce that risk.

---

## Employee Polygraph Protection Act ("EPPA")

29 U.S.C. §§ 2001 et seq.

### § 2001. Definitions.

As used in this chapter:

. . .

(3) Lie detector

The term "lie detector" includes a polygraph, deceptograph, voice stress analyzer, psychological stress evaluator, or any other similar device (whether mechanical or electrical) that is used, or the results of which are used, for the purpose of rendering a diagnostic opinion regarding the honesty or dishonesty of an individual.

(4) Polygraph

The term "polygraph" means an instrument that—

(A) records continuously, visually, permanently, and simultaneously changes in cardiovascular, respiratory, and electrodermal patterns as minimum instrumentation standards; and

(B) is used, or the results of which are used, for the purpose of rendering a diagnostic opinion regarding the honesty or dishonesty of an individual.

### § 2002. Prohibitions on lie detector use.

Except as provided in sections 2006 and 2007 of this title, it shall be unlawful for any employer engaged in or affecting commerce or in the production of goods for commerce—

(1) directly or indirectly, to require, request, suggest, or cause any employee or prospective employee to take or submit to any lie detector test;

(2) to use, accept, refer to, or inquire concerning the results of any lie detector test of any employee or prospective employee;

(3) to discharge, discipline, discriminate against in any manner, or deny employment or promotion to, or threaten to take any such action against—

(A) any employee or prospective employee who refuses, declines, or fails to take or submit to any lie detector test, or

(B) any employee or prospective employee on the basis of the results of any lie detector test; or

(4) [to retaliate against an employee or prospective employee for exercising rights under the statute.]

. . .

## Harmon v. CB Squared Services, Inc.

624 F. Supp. 2d 459 (E.D. Va. 2009)

■ HENRY E. HUDSON, DISTRICT JUDGE.

This case involves an alleged violation of the Employee Polygraph Protection Act ("EPPA"), 29 U.S.C. §§ 2001 et seq., by Defendant CB Squared Services Incorporated ("CB Squared"). Plaintiff Ollie Leon Harmon, a former employee of CB Squared, contends that Defendant wrongfully asked him to take a polygraph examination and unlawfully terminated him based on the test's results. For the reasons detailed herein, Plaintiff's Motion for Partial Summary Judgment will be granted and Defendant's Motion for Summary Judgment will be denied.

### I

Defendant CB Squared provides automotive maintenance services at several "Jiffy Lube" franchises that it owns and operates in and around the Commonwealth of Virginia. Plaintiff Harmon first entered Defendant's employ in the summer of 2007, when he was hired as a service technician at the company's Garrisonville, Virginia location. By December of 2007, Plaintiff had been promoted to a managerial position at another CB Squared facility in Virginia and soon thereafter was serving as Defendant's general "Customer Relations Manager" with responsibility for a number of Defendant's service centers throughout Virginia.

Plaintiff's career with CB Squared progressed steadily until early October of 2008, when Plaintiff informed several CB Squared executives that an individual identified only as "Chris" had offered Plaintiff a job with "STC," a competing Jiffy Lube franchisee. Concerned that STC had violated the Jiffy Lube franchise agreement, Mike Day, the President of CB Squared, contacted STC to investigate Plaintiff's allegations. After a representative of STC assured Day that no one from the company had approached Harmon, Day sought to "corroborate [Plaintiff's] claims" of misconduct by an STC employee. Accordingly, Day "asked Plaintiff if he would voluntarily submit to a polygraph test"—a request to which Plaintiff apparently agreed.

On October 14, 2008, CB Squared's "Operations Manager," Jason Russ, informed Plaintiff that the polygraph test would be given in Richmond, Virginia the next day. Accompanied by Russ, Plaintiff traveled to Richmond on October 15 where the polygraph examination was administered. Other than written directions to the polygraph test site, CB Squared provided Plaintiff with no documents or other information in advance of the examination. Rather, on the day of the exam, the polygraph examiner provided Plaintiff with a two-page "Polygraph Consent Form" detailing the examination procedures and a two-page "Polygraph Standards of Practice" form explaining Plaintiff's rights under Virginia law. Both of these documents were signed only by Plaintiff and the polygraph examiner, who was not a CB Squared employee.

Following the test, Day and several other CB Squared executives met with Plaintiff on October 16, 2008 and informed him that the results of his polygraph examination revealed "deception." After Plaintiff refused to divulge further information regarding STC's alleged solicitation, CB Squared demoted Plaintiff and reassigned him to a new store location. CB Squared contends that Plaintiff's performance on his polygraph test had no bearing on his reassignment and represents that Plaintiff instead was reassigned due to the company's concerns regarding his "disloyalty, lack of candor, and poor judgment." Dissatisfied with his demotion, Plaintiff provided CB Squared with his "two week notice" of resignation on October 16, 2009 and contends that he was terminated by CB Squared that same day. CB Squared denies terminating Plaintiff, arguing instead that it merely accepted his voluntary resignation.

Plaintiff subsequently instituted the present action, alleging three separate violations of the EPPA by CB Squared. Specifically, Count I contends that Defendant violated Section 2002(1) of the EPPA by requesting and/or suggesting on October 14, 2008 that Plaintiff take a polygraph examination. Count II further alleges that CB Squared violated Section 2002(2) of the EPPA when it used, accepted, and referred to the results of Plaintiff's polygraph test at the meeting between CB Squared executives and Harmon on October 16, 2009. Finally, Count III charges that Defendant CB Squared violated Section 2002(3) of the EPPA by terminating his employment on October 16, 2009 on the basis of the polygraph test's results.

Contending that there are no genuine issues of material fact and that he is entitled to judgment as a matter of law on Counts I and II, Plaintiff Harmon subsequently filed his Motion for Partial Summary Judgment. Defendant opposes Plaintiff's Motion on several grounds. Defendant CB Squared has also filed its own Motion for Summary Judgment on all counts.

## II

The Court may grant either party's motion for summary judgment only "if the pleadings, depositions, answers to interrogatories, and admissions on file, together with the affidavits . . . show that there is no genuine issue as to any material fact and that [the moving party] is entitled to a judgment as a matter of law." Fed. R. Civ. P. 56(c).

### III

Defendant asks the Court to grant summary judgment in its favor because Plaintiff may have provided misleading information on the employment application he submitted upon joining CB Squared in 2007. On the application, completed on June 29, 2007, Plaintiff represented that he had not been convicted previously of any felony and acknowledged that the company could terminate him for answering falsely. Apparently, Plaintiff had felony weapons charges pending in the District of Columbia at the time. Defendant now argues that because Plaintiff was "about to be convicted of a felony weapons charge" at the time he completed the application, his answer was false and thus "any claim Plaintiff may have against his employer should be barred by the unlawful pretext Plaintiff gave when seeking employment with Defendant."

As an initial matter, the record does not demonstrate conclusively that Plaintiff actually made any false statements on his employment application. When asked "Have you ever been convicted of a felony?", Defendant responded "No." Plaintiff's deposition testimony indicates that he was not convicted of the felony at issue until some point *after* completing the employment application and joining CB Squared in mid-2007. At the very least, whether Plaintiff's statement was in fact false when he completed the employment application remains a genuine issue of material fact that precludes summary judgment based on this issue at this stage.

Even if Plaintiff's alleged falsehood gave CB Squared cause to terminate him, Defendant has not explained why Plaintiff's misstatements would excuse it from all liability under the EPPA's several provisions that prohibit employer conduct.

In the present case, Plaintiff alleges that Defendant violated the EPPA not only by terminating him but also by requesting that he submit to a polygraph and by discussing the test's results with him on October 16th. Plaintiff's statement—assuming it was, in fact, false and gave Defendant cause to terminate him—did not also give CB Squared license to disregard the clear provisions of the EPPA by asking Harmon to take a polygraph and by referring to and discussing the test's results with him at the October 16th meeting. Accordingly, Plaintiff's alleged misstatement on his employment application provides no basis for granting Defendant CB Squared's Motion.

Defendant CB Squared also seeks summary judgment on the issue of punitive damages, cursorily arguing in a single paragraph: "under any rational analysis, punitive damages are not appropriate" because Defendant's alleged violation of the EPPA does "not rise to the level of malicious or reckless violations of the law." The Court is unaware of—[and] Defendant has failed to cite—any authority holding (or even suggesting) that punitive damages are not available under the EPPA.

## IV

Counts I and II of Plaintiff's Complaint charge Defendant CB Squared with violating the EPPA by causing Plaintiff to take a polygraph exam on October 15, 2008 and by using, accepting, and referring to the results of the examination at the October 16 meeting. Both parties now seek summary judgment on Counts I and II, each contending that the absence of any genuine issues of material fact demonstrate that it is entitled to judgment as a matter of law on both counts.

### A

Defendant CB Squared first argues that Harmon's Motion for Partial Summary Judgment on Counts I and II should be denied—and its own Motion for Summary Judgment granted—because Plaintiff's claims are outside the scope of the EPPA. Because STC, not Plaintiff, was the ostensible target of Defendant's investigation, CB Squared urges the Court to "construe the terms of the EPPA narrowly and hold that Plaintiff's claim was not one [Congress] intended to fall within its parameters."

Defendant's characterization of the EPPA misconstrues the statute's boundaries. In broad, clear language qualified only by the narrow exceptions detailed in Sections 2006 and 2007, Section 2002 of the EPPA forbids an employer to:

> (1) directly or indirectly, require, request, suggest, or cause *any employee* or prospective employee to take or submit to any lie detector test; [or]
>
> (2) to use, accept, refer to, or inquire concerning the results of any lie detector test *of any employee* or prospective employee. . . .

29 U.S.C. § 2002(1)–(2) (emphasis added). Nothing in the statute's language expressly imposes—or even suggests—a further requirement that an employee first show that he is the target of an employer's investigation to invoke the protections of the EPPA. Moreover, Congress's repeated use of the phrase "any employee" throughout Section 2002 evinces its intent that the EPPA's protections apply broadly in the workplace. The EPPA is thus fully applicable in the case at hand.

Defendant further argues that it is entitled to summary judgment on Counts I and II because the polygraph test results allegedly played no role in Harmon's demotion, reassignment, and potential constructive discharge. An employer's liability for unlawfully discharging an employee under Section 2002(3) of the EPPA is not a condition precedent for establishing a violation of the EPPA's other sections. Rather, each subsection of Section 2002 stands on its own and constitutes an independent basis for asserting the liability of an employer under the EPPA. Thus, even if the results of Plaintiff's polygraph results played no role in Defendant's decision to demote and reassign him (something that is far from clear at this stage), Plaintiff may still maintain separate and independent claims against CB Squared for other violations of Section 2002 of the EPPA.

**B**

Defendant CB Squared also contends that Harmon's Motion for Partial Summary Judgment must be denied because the EPPA's narrow "ongoing investigation exception" allowed the polygraph examination in this case. This "limited" exemption allows polygraphs if "the test is administered in connection with an ongoing investigation involving economic loss or injury to the employer's business, such as theft, embezzlement, misappropriation, or an act of unlawful industrial espionage or sabotage." 29 U.S.C. § 2006(d). Harmon responds that the ongoing investigation exception does not apply in this case because Defendant was investigating only a potential violation of the Jiffy Lube franchise agreement by STC, not an economic loss or injury that had already occurred.

Assuming, without deciding, that CB Squared was investigating a qualifying economic loss or injury to its business, Plaintiff's uncontroverted evidence nonetheless establishes that Defendant cannot rely on the ongoing investigation exemption to avoid liability as a matter of law in this case. To invoke the exemption, the employer must execute a detailed statement and provide it to the examinee-employee at least 48 hours before administration of the examination. This statement must, at a minimum, "set forth with particularity the specific incident or activity being investigated and the basis for testing particular employees." 29 U.S.C. § 2006(d)(4)(A); *see also* 29 C.F.R. § 801.12(g)(3) (explaining detail required in statement). The statement must further identify the specific economic loss or injury to the employer's business and describe the basis of the employer's reasonable suspicion that the examinee-employee was involved in the incident in question. Additionally, the statement provided to the examinee must be signed by the employer or some representative of the employer—other than the polygrapher—with authority to bind the employer legally.

Plaintiff's uncontradicted evidence establishes that Defendant CB Squared cannot rely on the ongoing investigation exemption to justify this polygraph exam. According to Plaintiff, the only document provided to him in advance of the October 15 polygraph examination was a map and written directions to the testing site in Richmond, Virginia. On the day of the examination, the polygrapher provided Plaintiff with just two additional documents. The first, a "Polygraph Consent Form", explained the nature of the examination, that the test results may be disclosed, and certain of Plaintiff's legal rights. The second, a "Polygraph Standards of Practice" form, explained his legal rights under Virginia law.

That these three documents were not provided to Plaintiff 48 hours in advance of his polygraph test would, by itself, be sufficient to deny Defendant refuge in the EPPA's ongoing investigation exemption. Scrutiny of the documents themselves, however, reveals that they fail to satisfy many of the exemption's numerous and strict requirements. Nowhere, for example, do the documents mention the incident being investigated or CB Squared's basis for suspecting Plaintiff's involvement. Nor is there any indication that the documents are signed by an employee of Defendant, much less an employee with the authority to legally bind CB Squared. In fact, Plaintiff's unrebutted evidence suggests that the polygraph examiner himself signed the documents in direct contravention of the ongoing investigation exemption's requirements.

The Court thus need not reach the issue of whether STC's alleged solicitation of Harmon constituted an economic loss or injury to CB Squared sufficient to invoke the EPPA's ongoing investigation exemption. Plaintiff's unrebutted evidence reveals that Defendant seems to have made no attempt to comply with the numerous, detailed requirements of the exemption as detailed Section 2006(d). CB Squared therefore cannot invoke the exemption to avoid liability under the EPPA and thereby defeat Plaintiff's Motion for Partial Summary Judgment on Counts I and II.

### C

Plaintiff contends that he is entitled to partial summary judgment on the issue of Defendant's liability on Counts I and II. The Court will consider each count in turn.

In Count I, Plaintiff alleges a violation of Section 2002(1) of the EPPA, which forbids any employer "directly or indirectly, to require, request, suggest, or cause any employee to take or submit to any lie detector test". 29 U.S.C. § 2002(1). Plaintiff's evidence indicates that CB Squared's President, Mike Day, "asked [him] to take a polygraph test in order to ascertain the veracity of [his] claim" that someone from STC had solicited him. Though Defendant now argues that [Plaintiff] "voluntarily agreed to undergo a polygraph test" to aid CB Squared's investigation, Day's own affidavit states: "I asked Plaintiff if he would voluntarily submit to a polygraph test." And when asked during his deposition whether he had "asked [Harmon] to take a polygraph test", Day responded: "Yes."

The coverage of the EPPA is broad—an employer violates Section 2002(1) by merely suggesting, even indirectly, that an employee submit to a polygraph. Whether the Court construes Day's own characterization of his communication to Harmon as a direct request or merely an indirect suggestion, it still contravenes the plain language of Section 2002(1). That Harmon may have "voluntarily" agreed to Day's request that he take a polygraph examination is immaterial—the statute does not require that an employee refuse the examination as a precondition to bringing suit. Both parties' evidence thus demonstrates the absence of any genuine issue of material fact as to whether Day requested—or at least indirectly suggested—that Plaintiff submit to a polygraph. Because such a request is sufficient to render Defendant liable under Section

2002(1), Plaintiff Harmon is entitled to judgment as a matter of law on Count I.

Count II charges CB Squared with a violation of Section 2002(2) of the EPPA, which provides that it is unlawful for an employer such as CB Squared "to use, accept, refer to, or inquire concerning the results of any lie detector test of any employee." 29 U.S.C. § 2002(2). The Fourth Circuit has construed the phrase "refer to", as it is used in the EPPA, to mean "to direct attention to or allude." *Worden v. SunTrust Banks, Inc.*, 549 F.3d 334, 347 n. 11 (4th Cir. 2008).

Plaintiff's evidence indicates that Day referenced the results of Plaintiff's test in violation of Section 2002(2) at the October 16th meeting when Day informed Plaintiff that he had failed the polygraph exam at issue because his results revealed "deception." Defendant's own evidence only confirms Plaintiff's account: Day, Defendant's President, states in an affidavit that he "met with Plaintiff and informed him of the results of his polygraph test." Defendant's evidence further reveals that several other CB Squared employees were also present at the October 16th meeting and that they discussed the Plaintiff's test results amongst themselves. It is undisputed, then, that CB Squared [employees] at least alluded to—and in fact, openly discussed—the results of Plaintiff's polygraph in violation of Section 2002(2).

Plaintiff also alleges in Count II that CB Squared violated Section 2002(2) by accepting the results of his polygraph exam. The Fourth Circuit has interpreted the term "accept," as it is employed in Section 2002(2), to mean "something other than mere unsolicited receipt." *Worden*, 549 F.3d at 346. Accepting polygraph results in violation of Section 2002(2) thus seems to require some sort of affirmative act or involvement by the employer.

It is undisputed here that CB Squared took an active role in procuring the polygraph at issue. Indeed, both parties' evidence indicates that CB Squared not only suggested that Plaintiff take the test but also arranged to have the test administered and had another employee accompany Plaintiff to the testing site. Since CB Squared's employees subsequently received, considered, and discussed the test's results, it is clear that Defendant actively accepted them in violation of Section 2002(2).

Because both parties' evidence demonstrates conclusively that CB Squared both accepted and referred to the results of Plaintiff's polygraph examination, no genuine issue of material fact remains as to whether CB Squared violated Section 2002(2) of the EPPA. Accordingly, Plaintiff is likewise entitled to judgment as a matter of law on the issue of CB Squared's liability under Count II.

## V

Count III of Plaintiff's Complaint charges CB Squared with violating the EPPA by improperly terminating him based on the results of his polygraph examination. Section 2002(3) of the EPPA broadly prohibits employers from discharging, disciplining, discriminating against, or otherwise denying employment or promotion to employees on the basis of polygraph results. Though Plaintiff concedes that outstanding issues of material fact preclude summary judgment on this issue, Defendant contends that Plaintiff's voluntary resignation following the October 16, 2009 meeting entitles it to summary judgment on Count III.

Plaintiff's decision to resign at the October 16th meeting is best analyzed as a potential "constructive discharge" under the EPPA.

To recover for improper termination under the EPPA, Plaintiff must, of course, also show that he was discharged (constructively or otherwise) "on the basis of" his polygraph examination. Even if Plaintiff was constructively discharged, Defendant CB Squared contends, the company is entitled to summary judgment because its decision to reassign and demote Plaintiff "was made independent of the polygraph test."

Plaintiff, however, has presented considerable evidence which could support a conclusion by the trier of fact that his polygraph test was at least a factor in his demotion. Plaintiff took the polygraph examination on October 15, 2008 and Day, Defendant's President, confronted Plaintiff with the test's results at a meeting the very next day. At the conclusion of that same meeting, after discussing the results of the test with Plaintiff, Defendant's executives collectively made the decision to demote him. Such evidence, if proven, would tend to rebut Defendant's bald assertion that Plaintiff's demotion was unrelated to his polygraph results.

[The Court also found that there was a genuine dispute of material fact about whether the Defendant's demotion and reassignment of the Plaintiff qualified as constructive discharge under federal law.]

### VI

The Court thus concludes that Plaintiff Harmon has demonstrated that no genuine issues of material fact remain and that he is entitled to judgment as a matter of law on Counts I and II of his Complaint. Because genuine issues of material fact remain regarding Plaintiff's termination, Defendant CB Squared's Motion for Summary Judgment on Count III must be denied. Accordingly, this case will proceed to trial on the limited issues of CB Squared's liability under the EPPA for its alleged wrongful termination of Harmon and any resulting damages suffered by Plaintiff.

## NOTES

1. ***Polygraphs and Their Accuracy.*** The polygraph machine measures physiological responses such as breathing, heart rate, and skin reactivity as questions are being asked, in an attempt to determine when the responses are dishonest. The question of whether these measures accurately reveal lying is very controversial. A comprehensive study by the National

Academies of Sciences (NAS) in 2002 determined that the polygraph's ability to detect lies was significantly better than chance, but also that it often indicated people were lying when they were actually telling the truth. The NAS also found that many earlier studies fell short of scientific standards. A number of polygraph critics publish information instructing people in methods that they say "beat" the test. According to them, simple tactics such as biting one's tongue during initial control questions can throw off the results and forestall detection. Supporters of the technology admit it is not perfect, but argue that it has an accuracy rate over 80%, and much higher than that when inconclusive results are disregarded (as is often standard practice). In conjunction with other investigative techniques, they say, polygraphs can be a useful tool.

2. ***Narrow Law.*** The EPPA is an excellent example of a narrowly-drawn privacy statute that is extremely strict but covers only a very specific technology in a particular context. Why do you suppose the use of polygraphs by employers attracted the attention of Congress? What other examples of such "rifle-shot" laws have you encountered in the course? What are the advantages and disadvantages of regulating specific privacy issues with narrow stand-alone laws?

3. ***Narrow Exemptions.*** There are just six exemptions to the EPPA listed in § 2006, which can be divided into two groups of three. The first group of exemptions makes the statute inapplicable to all federal, state, or local government employers, as well as to employees of contractors, consultants, and experts working with specified federal agencies that have sensitive missions (the intelligence agencies, the Defense Department, the FBI, and the Energy Department's "atomic energy defense activities" are named). The other group of three exemptions moves further away from direct government involvement; these are defined more precisely and they come with numerous added conditions. Two of them apply to employees in specified sensitive private-sector roles: certain workers for security companies, utilities, and public transportation providers, and those with direct access to controlled substances. The final allowance is the "ongoing investigation" exemption described in *Holden*. As discussed in the opinion, there are even more procedural requirements attached to this exception, such as the 48 hours written notice and the statement identifying the basis for the employer's reasonable suspicion of the employee. All three private-sector exemptions in this latter group must also comply with still more procedural requirements laid out in § 2007, including a lengthy list of examinee rights, qualifications for the person administering the test, protocols for its administration, and a requirement that the polygraph result may not be the sole basis for adverse employment action.

4. ***Increasing Government Reliance.*** The EPPA essentially eliminated routine use of polygraph tests in private sector employment screening. But its broad and nearly unconditional exemptions for government employees and contractors have facilitated significant *growth* in their routine use in the public sector. In 2010, for example, Congress mandated polygraph testing of all applicants to US Customs and Border Protection, the largest federal law enforcement agency. *See* Anti-Border

Corruption Act, P.L. 111–376 (2010). Polygraph testing has been a central feature of several high-profile espionage investigations, it is used extensively by the NSA to test its own employees, and it has taken on a significant role in investigations to assign security clearances at all major federal intelligence and law enforcement agencies. Numerous police departments and other state and local government agencies also rely on polygraphs. These governmental tests are not subject to the procedural restrictions applicable to, for example, the "ongoing investigations" exception in the EPPA. If it is good enough for rooting out spies and granting top secret clearance, why should employers be so constrained from using polygraphs in their internal investigations? Or, conversely, if polygraphs are sufficiently problematic to nearly ban them in the private sector, should they be removed from their central role in government hiring for sensitive positions?

5. ***Criminal Records.*** A side note in this case concerned the effect of Holden's answers to questions about his criminal record, which had been requested on his initial job application. Most courts would agree with *Holden* that a question directed at convictions does not require an applicant to divulge arrests or indictments. But the overall law concerning the use of criminal records in employment decisions is complex and at times can seem contradictory. Criminal background checks may seem like sensible protective measures, but because racial minorities are convicted of crimes disproportionately, it may be found discriminatory to observe a blanket rule denying employment to anyone with a criminal conviction (and even more so if such a policy affects anyone with merely a past arrest). Rather, it is safer to tailor such rules to job duties: checking for the driving records of those who will operate vehicles, or barring people with fraud convictions from finance jobs. On the other hand, numerous federal and state laws *require* criminal records checks for people in certain sensitive positions, even at private businesses, such as health care or child care workers and utility employees. And on the third hand, if there were one: multiple cities and states have recently adopted "Ban the Box" laws, which vary widely but typically prohibit most private employers from asking about criminal records, at least on initial job applications. As if all that were not enough, as discussed immediately below, the Fair Credit Reporting Act [see Chapter 6] also covers criminal background checks (and other data within the definition of a "credit report") obtained from another entity for purposes of employment screening.

## Fair Credit Reporting Act ("FCRA")

15 U.S.C. § 1681

. . .

### (b) Conditions for furnishing and using consumer reports for employment purposes

(1) Certification from user. A consumer reporting agency may furnish a consumer report for employment purposes only if—

(A) the person who obtains such report from the agency certifies to the agency that—

(i) the person has complied with paragraph (2) with respect to the consumer report, and the person will comply with paragraph (3) with respect to the consumer report if paragraph (3) becomes applicable; and

(ii) information from the consumer report will not be used in violation of any applicable Federal or State equal employment opportunity law or regulation; and

(B) the consumer reporting agency provides with the report, or has previously provided, a summary of the consumer's rights under this subchapter, as prescribed by the [Consumer Financial Protection Bureau].

(2) Disclosure to consumer

(A) In general. Except as provided in subparagraph (B), a person may not procure a consumer report, or cause a consumer report to be procured, for employment purposes with respect to any consumer, unless—

(i) a clear and conspicuous disclosure has been made in writing to the consumer at any time before the report is procured or caused to be procured, in a document that consists solely of the disclosure, that a consumer report may be obtained for employment purposes; and

(ii) the consumer has authorized in writing (which authorization may be made on the document referred to in clause (i)) the procurement of the report by that person. . . . (3) Conditions on use for adverse actions

(A) In general. Except as provided in subparagraph (B), in using a consumer report for employment purposes, before taking any adverse action based in whole or in part on the report, the person intending to take such adverse action shall provide to the consumer to whom the report relates—

(i) a copy of the report; and

(ii) a description in writing of the rights of the consumer under this subchapter, as prescribed by the [CFPB].

. . .

# Singleton v. Domino's Pizza LLC

2012 WL 245965 (D. Md. Jan. 25, 2012)

■ DEBORAH K. CHASANOW, DISTRICT JUDGE.

Presently pending and ready for resolution in this action arising under the Fair Credit Reporting Act ("FCRA") is the motion to dismiss filed by Defendant Domino's Pizza, LLC ("Domino's" or "the company"). For the reasons that follow, the company's motion will be denied.

## I. Background

### A. Factual Background

Plaintiffs Adrian Singleton and Justin D'Heilly allege the following facts in their first amended class action complaint and documents appended thereto. Domino's conducts background checks on all of its job applicants as part of a "standard screening process." In addition, it conducts background checks on existing employees "from time-to-time" during their employment. Domino's does not perform these background checks in-house; rather, it relies on two external consumer reporting agencies ("CRAs") to run the background checks and report the results directly to the company.

Before requesting that these firms perform background checks, Domino's requires its employees to complete a "Background Investigation Information and Consent" form ("BIIC form"). The BIIC form is included as "page 5" in the company's application packet. The first two paragraphs on the form state, in relevant part:

> I understand that you intend to make an independent investigation of my background which may include references, character, past employment, education, credit and consumer information, driving history, criminal or police records, or insurance claims records . . . for the purpose of confirming the information contained on my application and/or obtaining other information that may be material to my qualifications for employment (a background investigation).
>
> CONSENT. I hereby authorize you, as part of the application process, and from time to time during my employment, to the extent permitted by applicable law, to conduct a Background Investigation. . . . I authorize the release of such information to you.

The BIIC form also contains the following paragraph, which precedes the employee's signature authorizing Domino's to perform the background check:

> I release, without reservation, you and any person or entity which provides information pursuant to this authorization, from any and all liabilities, claims or causes of action in regards to the information obtained from any and all of the above reference sources used. I acknowledge that this is a standalone consumer

> notification informing me that a report will be requested and that the information obtained shall be used solely for the purpose of evaluating me for employment, promotion, reassignment, or retention as an employee.

In December 2008, D'Heilly applied to work as a delivery driver in one of the company's Minnesota stores. Prior to beginning work, he completed the "standard" application packet, which included the BIIC form. D'Heilly worked for Domino's without incident through August 2009. In September 2009, however, the store stopped scheduling him for work, and D'Heilly's employment was terminated the following month. At that time, D'Heilly's general manager advised him that he could no longer work as a delivery driver "because something had come up on a background check relating to his motor vehicle history." D'Heilly received no additional information regarding his termination, and Domino's never provided him with a copy of the background check. [D'Heilly later learned, after contacting the local police department on his own initiative, that his driving record listed two speeding tickets.]

Singleton, like D'Heilly, applied to work as a delivery driver at one of the company's Maryland stores during the spring of 2009. He, too, completed the "standard" application packet, including the BIIC form. Singleton then began work. Several weeks into his employment, and just following the July 4, 2009, holiday, Singleton learned that a "potential issue" had arisen with his employment application and that he had not been scheduled to work any additional hours. In an attempt to resolve the unspecified issue, Singleton submitted a second employment application, but he did not receive any work.

Instead, several days later, Singleton received a letter dated July 9, 2009, from Domino's entitled "FCRA Letter 2." The letter stated, in relevant part:

> As part of our employment selection process, we require that a consumer report be obtained before employment commences to any applicant being considered for the position for which you applied. You previously should have received a copy of your consumer report. . . . This is to advise you that our offer of employment is being withdrawn and your application for employment is being denied. In evaluating your application, the consumer reporting agency listed below provided us with . . . information which, in whole or in part, influenced our employment decision. Under the Fair Credit Reporting Act, you are entitled to disclosure of the information contained in your consumer report by contacting the consumer reporting agency directly, within sixty (60) days of this letter. You also have the right to dispute the completeness or accuracy of the report.

Contrary to the assertion in the letter, Singleton had not previously received a copy of the referenced report, and Domino's never provided him with this information.

### B. Procedural Background

The amended complaint alleges that Domino's systematically and willfully violated the FCRA in three ways: (1) by failing to provide employees with copies of their background investigations prior to taking adverse action against them, in violation of 15 U.S.C. § 1681b(b)(3)(A); (2) by using a BIIC form that did not comply with the disclosure requirements set forth in 15 U.S.C. § 1681b(b)(2)(A)(i); and (3) by using a BIIC form that did not comply with the authorization requirements set forth in 15 U.S.C. § 1681b(b)(2)(A)(ii). On September 26, 2011, Domino's moved to dismiss the amended complaint for failure to state a claim. Plaintiffs have opposed this motion in its entirety.

## II. Standard of Review

The purpose of a motion to dismiss pursuant to Rule 12(b)(6) is to test the sufficiency of the complaint. That showing must consist of more than "a formulaic recitation of the elements of a cause of action" or "naked assertion[s] devoid of further factual enhancement." *Ashcroft v. Iqbal*, 556 U.S. 662 (2009).

At this stage, the court must consider all well-pleaded allegations in a complaint as true and must construe all factual allegations in the light most favorable to the plaintiff.

## III. Analysis

Domino's initially asserts, as to all counts, that Plaintiffs have failed to allege adequately that Domino's willfully violated the FCRA, a requirement to recover statutory damages under the FCRA. To the extent that this argument is unavailing, Domino's further contends that counts two and three, which address the adequacy of the BIIC form, must be dismissed because: (1) they are time-barred; (2) the BIIC form complies with the FCRA's disclosure and authorization requirements; and (3) even if the BIIC form violates those requirements, Plaintiffs cannot "establish willful misconduct" because the company's interpretation of the FCRA's requirements was "not objectively unreasonable." Each of these arguments will be addressed in turn.

### A. The Amended Complaint Sufficiently Alleges Willfulness

The FCRA permits a plaintiff to recover damages when a defendant acted either negligently or willfully in violating the statute's requirements. In the absence of negligent or willful misconduct, however, a plaintiff may not recover at all. As a result, courts have routinely granted motions to dismiss where a plaintiff alleges neither that the defendant's negligence caused the plaintiff actual damages, nor that the defendant acted willfully. In the present case, Plaintiffs do not allege actual injury; rather, they contend that Domino's willfully violated the FCRA and seek only statutory damages. Domino's contends that Plaintiffs' allegations of willfulness are insufficient to survive a motion to dismiss.

In the wake of *Twombly* and *Iqbal*, a mere assertion of willful noncompliance with the FCRA will not, on its own, satisfy Rule 8(a). Thus, to avoid dismissal, plaintiffs asserting that a defendant willfully failed to comply with the FCRA must set forth specific allegations to demonstrate willfulness.

A defendant acts willfully under the FCRA by either knowingly or recklessly disregarding its statutory duty. Relying upon this definition, courts have found assertions that a defendant repeatedly violated the FCRA sufficient to allege reckless—and, therefore, willful—misconduct. In addition, assertions that a defendant was aware of the FCRA, but failed to comply with its requirements, are sufficient to support an allegation of willfulness and to avoid dismissal.

With regard to count one, Plaintiffs contend that Domino's engaged in a practice of violating the FCRA by systematically failing to provide employees with copies of background checks prior to taking adverse action against them. To support this assertion, Plaintiffs emphasize that neither Singleton nor D'Heilly received such copies prior to their termination. Additionally, Plaintiffs assert that Domino's was aware—through its "general counsel's office and outside employment counsel"—that the FCRA requires employers to provide employees with copies of background checks before taking adverse action against them. According to the complaint, Domino's disregarded the FCRA by "typically" failing to provide employees with copies of their background checks.

Plaintiffs set forth nearly identical allegations with regard to counts two and three. Specifically, they assert that Domino's repeatedly violated the FCRA by obtaining consumer reports for its employees, such as Singleton and D'Heilly, without providing the prerequisite disclosure and authorization information in a "stand-alone document." Additionally, Plaintiffs suggest that Domino's, again through its in-house and outside counsel, knew about these requirements, an assertion supported by the company's request that employees certify the BIIC form as a "stand-alone consumer notification." Yet despite the company's knowledge of the FCRA's disclosure and authorization requirements, Plaintiffs allege that the BIIC form did not actually qualify as a "standalone document" because it was part of the company's employment application and contained a liability release. [T]hese allegations are sufficient to support Plaintiffs' contention that Domino's willfully violated the FCRA.

On a motion to dismiss, plaintiffs need only provide allegations sufficient to demonstrate entitlement to relief; they need not prove their case at such an early stage in the proceedings.

### B. The Statute of Limitations Does Not Bar Counts Two and Three

The company's remaining arguments focus on dismissal of counts two and three, which address the adequacy of the BIIC form in light of the FCRA's disclosure and authorization requirements. To begin,

Domino's contends that these claims must be dismissed as time-barred because Plaintiffs did not file suit within two years of the time they completed the BIIC form.

The FCRA statute of limitations provides that a plaintiff must file suit "not later than the earlier of—(1) 2 years after the date of discovery by the plaintiff of the violation that is the basis for such liability; or (2) 5 years after the date on which the violation that is the basis for such liability occurs." 15 U.S.C. § 1681p. The parties agree that the two-year limitations period applies in this case. Domino's contends that because counts two and three stem from deficiencies within the BIIC form itself, Plaintiffs were on notice regarding these claims when they completed that form, a time the parties agree is outside the limitations period. While persuasive at first blush, this argument ultimately fails because it misconstrues the plain language of § 1681b(b)(2).

The company's limitations argument assumes that the violations in counts two and three occurred when Plaintiffs completed the purportedly deficient BIIC form. This assumption, however, neglects to consider that the violation was not complete until Domino's—through its external CRAs—actually obtained Plaintiffs' consumer reports. [U]ntil these background checks were performed, no violation of § 1681b(b)(2) had occurred. *See* 15 U.S.C. § 1681b(b)(2)(A)(i) (explaining that the employer may provide the requisite disclosures "at any time before the report is procured").

As a result, Plaintiffs could not have discovered the violations underlying counts two and three until they learned that the background checks had taken place. Here, the complaint indicates that Singleton and D'Heilly did not discover this information until after July 1, 2009, and September 2, 2009, respectively, time periods within the statute of limitations. Accordingly, contrary to the company's contention, counts two and three are timely.

### C. Domino's Has Not Shown that, as a Matter of Law, the BIIC Form Complies with the FCRA's Disclosure and Authorization Requirements

Domino's next contends that counts two and three fail to state a claim for relief because the BIIC form complies with the FCRA's disclosure and authorization requirements. Relying upon the statute's plain language and guidance from the Federal Trade Commission ("FTC"), Plaintiffs disagree, alleging that the form is deficient because (1) it is included within the company's application packet, and (2) it contains a liability release. Although the parties devote substantial portions of their argument to the former issue, it need not be addressed in resolving this motion because the latter is dispositive. That is, inclusion of the liability release in the BIIC form precludes Domino's from asserting that, as a matter of law, the BIIC form satisfies the FCRA's requirements.

The parties have not identified, and the court is not aware of, any case law addressing whether an employer may lawfully include a liability release "in the document consist[ing] solely of the disclosure" that informs an employee about procurement of a consumer report for employment purposes. 15 U.S.C. § 1681b (b)(2)(A)(i). Therefore, it is appropriate to start the analysis of § 1681b(b)(2) from the beginning—with an examination of the statute's plain text. In interpreting the plain language of a statute, courts give the terms their ordinary, contemporary, and common meaning, absent an indication Congress intended them to bear some different import.

Here, dictionary definitions of the word "solely" indicate that a document disclosing that an employer planned to obtain a consumer report would not "consist[ ] solely of the disclosure" if the document also contained a liability release.

Domino's makes only one argument in an effort to avoid the statute's plain language. According to the company, inclusion of such a release in the disclosure document must be permissible because "the statute itself provides that a consumer authorization may be made on the disclosure document." This contention, however, ignores the significance of congressional silence on an issue where Congress has otherwise spoken. Indeed, when mandating that an employer use a document that "consists solely of the disclosure," Congress expressly permitted employers to include language authorizing the employer to procure the consumer report. 15 U.S.C. § 1681b(b)(2)(A)(ii). Had Congress intended for employers to include additional information in these documents, it could easily have included language to that effect in the statute. It did not do so, however, and its silence is controlling.

In addition to the statutory text, FTC interpretations of § 1681b(b)(2) suggest that inclusion of a liability release in a disclosure form violates the FCRA. In 1998, in response to company inquiries, the FTC issued two opinion letters addressing § 1681b(b)(2)'s "consists solely" language. The first letter explicitly states that "inclusion of . . . a waiver [of one's FCRA rights] in a disclosure form will violate" § 1681b(b)(2) because the form will not "consist 'solely' of the disclosure." The reasoning employed in the second letter supports this conclusion, stating that the FCRA prohibits disclosure forms "encumbered by any other information . . . [in order] to prevent consumers from being distracted by other information side-by-side with the disclosure."

Ultimately, both the statutory text and FTC advisory opinions indicate that an employer violates the FCRA by including a liability release in a disclosure document. Because the BIIC form contains such a release, Domino's has not shown, as a matter of law, that the form complies with the FCRA. Its attempt to have counts two and three dismissed on this ground must, therefore, fail.

### D. Domino's Is Not Entitled to Dismissal of Counts Two and Three on the Ground that Its Interpretation of the FCRA "Was Not Objectively Unreasonable"

In its final argument, Domino's maintains that, even if the BIIC form did violate the FCRA, its interpretation of the statute's disclosure and authorization requirements "was, at a minimum, not objectively unreasonable."

The Supreme Court has held that a defendant does not willfully violate the FCRA "unless the [challenged] action is not only a violation under a reasonable reading of the statute's terms, but shows that the company ran a risk of violating the law substantially greater than the risk associated with a reading that was merely careless." *Safeco Ins. Co. v. Burr*, 551 U.S. 47, 69 (2007). That is, unless the defendant's interpretation of the statute is objectively unreasonable, a plaintiff will be unable to show that the defendant willfully violated the FCRA. Domino's clings to this language, asserting that its inclusion of the liability release in the BIIC form resulted from a reasonable reading of § 1681b(b)(2). The company's reliance on *Safeco*, however, is misplaced for two reasons.

First, the procedural posture of the *Safeco* case differed in a critical manner from the present action. The Supreme Court in *Safeco* was operating under a summary judgment standard of review. In this case, however, a motion to dismiss is pending, and discovery has not yet begun. On similar facts, numerous courts have declined to examine the reasonableness of a defendant's statutory interpretation when ruling on motions to dismiss.

Second, even if it were appropriate to reach this issue on a 12(b)(6) motion, Domino's would not prevail. Unlike in *Safeco*, where the FCRA provision at issue was "less-than-pellucid," 551 U.S. at 70, the text at issue here appears to have a plain and clearly ascertainable meaning.

## IV. Conclusion

For the foregoing reasons, the company's motion to dismiss the amended class action complaint will be denied.

### NOTES

1. ***Settlement.*** After this January 2012 decision, Domino's filed an answer and the parties commenced written discovery, providing each other their initial disclosures and propounding interrogatories and requests for production. In August, however, they requested a stay from the court to allow them to confer on a possible settlement. Negotiations, including formal mediation, extended until the following March. Eventually they agreed to a $2.5 million settlement, including substantial attorney's fees. The district court certified the class for purposes of approving the settlement. *See Singleton v. Domino's Pizza, LLC*, 976 F. Supp. 2d 665 (D. Md. 2013).

2. ***The Rise of FCRA Class Actions.*** The *Singleton* case was one of a number of FCRA class actions against employers over the last several years that suddenly began to focus significant attention on a previously sleepy area of privacy compliance. There has been a cluster of settlements in such cases for similar dollar amounts since 2012. A few class actions brought against credit reporting agencies themselves—rather than the employers who allegedly procured or used credit reports incorrectly—have settled for amounts six or seven times larger. As with certain other privacy laws based on the consumer protection model, modest statutory damages become quite large when multiplied by the number of violations involved in a class action against a large company. [For more discussion of this phenomenon, see Chapter 3.] Numerous other brand-name companies have since been hit with similar FCRA class action complaints, including Chipotle Mexican Grill and the online car service Uber.

3. ***Waiting for* Spokeo.** As of this writing in early 2016, the Supreme Court has not yet ruled in the pending case of *Spokeo, Inc. v. Robins* [see Chapters 3 and 6]. This important case, argued in 2015, involved a FCRA class action against an online service that sold background reports of job-seekers to prospective employers; the plaintiffs alleged that it qualified as a credit reporting agency and committed willful violations of FCRA. The unemployed plaintiff in that case could point to multiple inaccuracies in Spokeo's report about him, but had not demonstrated that any particular employer had declined to interview him or to hire him on the basis of those errors. Spokeo argued that the plaintiff lacked Article III standing as a result. Depending on its breadth, the opinion in the case could have a significant impact on standing in many privacy cases. If the Court agrees with Spokeo's position, would plaintiffs like those in *Singleton* lack standing as a result?

4. ***Hypertechnical?*** Employers (and their lawyers) have objected strenuously to the rise of FCRA class actions bringing claims for what they see as minor violations of § 1681b. As one employment defense firm sums it up, "These lawsuits can be frustrating for employers because typically they allege hyper-technical non-compliance with the FCRA (e.g., supposed defects in the employer's pre-employment forms and template notices). That is, the lawsuits appear to be lawyer-contrived cash grabs because no job applicant or employee possibly could have suffered any real harm." Rod Fliegel et al., Littler Mendelson, P.C., *The Swelling Tide of Fair Credit Reporting Act (FCRA) Class Actions: Practical Risk-Mitigating Measures for Employers* (August 2014), available at http://www.littler.com/files/press/pdf/WP_Fair_Credit_Reporting_Act_8–1–14.pdf. Would the *Singleton* plaintiffs have acted differently depending on whether the liability waiver was on the same page of the application packet as the BIIC form or a different page? If your answer is no, does that mean they have suffered no "real harm," as Fliegel says? How much of these employers' objection is to the mode of enforcement—that is, would they be less upset if the same violations were the subject of enforcement by a regulator like the CFPB rather than private class actions? Or are these actually substantive disagreements with the content of § 1681b? Why does the statute provide so much detail about the required format and

method of notifying employees? Should it do so? If it should not, is there any better way to protect employees' privacy and employment rights while sparing employers from "hypertechnical" compliance obligations?

5. ***Regulatory Guidance.*** The *Singleton* court relied on regulatory guidance from the FTC about the meaning of § 1681b. (Note that the primary rulemaking authority over this provision, like most of the rest of FCRA, has since shifted to the CFPB [see Chapters 6 and 13].) In an omitted portion of the opinion, Domino's objected that the court should not rely on mere advisory opinions, citing the Supreme Court's *Safeco* opinion. The district court responded that *Safeco* instructed courts not to be bound by advisory opinions as "authoritative guidance," but that they could still be helpful and persuasive sources. Besides, the court noted, the statutory text was clear. If the court had found the text more ambiguous, should it still have relied on the guidance? But does it make sense to say that a court should rely on agency guidance only when the statute is unambiguous—in which case, presumably, it isn't really necessary anyway?

6. ***Procedures for Mail and Online Applications.*** Portions of § 1681b omitted from the excerpt above provide specific alternative procedures to be used when a job-seeker has applied for employment at arm's length, such as by mail or through a web site. These procedures are available both for the notice and consent before procurement of the consumer report, *see* § 1681b(2), and for notice prior to adverse action, *see* § 1681b(3). The statute clearly indicates, however, that the alternative methods cannot be used when the employer has more direct interaction with the applicant or employee—such as Domino's had with the two named plaintiffs in *Singleton*.

7. ***Ensuring Compliance.*** In light of the increased prospect of class action lawsuits and costly settlements, what advice would you give to an employer client who wants to secure FCRA-covered background reports about job applicants? Figure out how to phrase your recommendations in terms understandable to a businessperson who is not a lawyer.

---

## Focus

### Drug and Alcohol Testing

In most states, it is legally permissible to require applicants and at-will employees to undergo routine random drug testing. But that one-sentence summary conceals a welter of considerations that significantly limit the conditions for testing.

State law on drug and alcohol testing varies widely. Statutes and regulations in many states govern the conduct of the tests and the operation of testing labs; forbid imposing the costs of drug tests on the employees who take them; mandate certain forms of notice or written policies; or require that employers who compel testing must make addiction assistance programs available for employees who fail the test. A few states strictly limit random or routine drug testing, allowing it only based on reasonable suspicion or a similar standard, or for safety-sensitive positions. *See, e.g.,* Conn. Gen. Stat. Ann. §§ 31–51t et seq.; Me. Rev. Stat. Ann. tit. 26, §§ 681 et seq.; Minn. Stat. §§ 181.950 et seq.; *see also Imme v. Fed. Express Corp.*, 193 F. Supp. 2d 519 (D. Conn. 2002) (finding an exception to the Connecticut drug testing statute applied, because the employee's behavior at the time gave rise to reasonable suspicion that he was under influence of drugs and, as a ramp handler at a warehouse facility, he might have caused safety risk to other employees if so). Many states forbid penalizing employees for off-duty use of alcohol or tobacco products, complicating any testing for alcohol abuse (as opposed to the use of illegal drugs) on the job.

Discrimination law can also have an effect: while the Americans with Disabilities Act explicitly offers no protection for current use of illegal drugs, alcoholism may be considered a disability if it does not interfere directly with job functions. And government employers face further restrictions to drug testing under the Fourth Amendment [see Section C].

Most US workers are at-will employees, meaning they can be fired at any time without their employer demonstrating cause (and at the same time, they have the option to quit the job as well). Other complications arise when workers are not at-will employees. Collective bargaining agreements covering unionized employees typically spell out detailed conditions and procedures related to any drug testing and resulting penalties; naturally, employers need to follow these negotiated requirements. Similarly, organizations that use employment contracts may face liability for breach if they require drug or alcohol tests, or act on their results, depending on the terms of the contracts.

Alongside these limits on drug and alcohol testing, some federal and state laws *require* testing in certain professions, such as for holders of commercial drivers' licenses. Another federal law mandates that recipients of many federal contracts and grants institute drug abuse prevention programs in the workplace, *see* Drug-Free Workplace Act, 41 U.S.C. §§ 701 et seq., which may encourage those employers to engage in testing.

In sum, while drug and alcohol testing of employees may be desirable in many cases and mandatory in a few, employers must proceed very cautiously to avoid breaking the law. It will often be possible for an employee to bring a private suit against an employer for requiring the test or for conducting it incorrectly, and regulators can also impose penalties. It may be wise to outsource testing to a well-established specialist who can assist with the difficult legal compliance challenges.

---

## B. MONITORING EMPLOYEES

---

### Focus

"Bring Your Own Device" Policies

Just a few years ago, organizations issued laptops, pagers, and cell phones to employees to help them stay connected with hardware that was owned by the company and restricted to professional uses. This often made them easier to monitor—the bookkeepers can examine the bills on a company-owned cell phone, for example—and also increased the legal justification for reviewing everything contained in a machine that is, after all, company property. Today, these arrangements are becoming increasingly archaic. In their place, "bring your own device" (BYOD) programs have become widespread. These allow employees to use their own personal devices for work, from receiving emails to accessing calendars and contacts.

Among employees, there is often widespread support for BYOD programs because of their convenience: no one wants to carry two phones, each referring to separate cloud-stored data. BYOD initiatives also facilitate remote work, for either telecommuting or business travel. And using the same familiar technology at home and work can increase efficiency further. Employers also benefit financially: employees are more likely to upgrade to the latest technology before companies do, and most BYOD programs require them to bear the cost of purchasing and maintaining the devices themselves. Besides, blanket resistance to allowing work activity on personal devices creates the risk that employees will do it anyway—with no safeguards in place to protect the employer or its data.

But BYOD programs also expose companies to risks. By allowing employees' personal devices to have access to potentially sensitive company data, employers give up some control over how that data will be stored and shared. This can increase vulnerability to hacks or theft. For comparison, consider how the carelessness of an employee resulted in the theft of 365,000 patient records from the employee's car in *Paul v. Providence Health System* [see Chapter 7.] These risks are especially nettlesome in certain industries where sector-specific laws impose special data security duties, such as health care [see Chapter 12] and financial services [see Chapter 13], making BYOD policies less common there. Trade secrets must be safeguarded vigilantly to protect their continued secrecy, and thus their legal status. Additionally, BYOD programs complicate discovery obligations when litigation arises, because measures like litigation holds (pauses on the destruction of data to avoid culpability for spoliation) and global data searches (to respond to requests efficiently) can be rendered ineffective. Those complications grow when it comes to former employees.

Thus, it is critically important that companies implementing a BYOD program develop acceptable-use policies clearly outlining company control of devices and data. These can also be backed by technological design that maximizes the storage of work-related communications and data under the employer's control—either on the organization's own servers or in its own secure cloud storage—rather than locally on employee-owned hardware or scattered through various personal email and other cloud-based accounts.

When drafting a BYOD policy, the first step is often establishing which devices are permitted under a BYOD program, including whether employees are limited to devices that meet minimum security requirements. At the same time, the employer should decide what institutional data resources will be available on personal devices, perhaps restricting access to especially sensitive data or to data that might trigger breach notification obligations [see Chapter 7]. Next, a BYOD policy should lay out what constitutes appropriate use and how devices will be monitored to ensure compliance. This oversight might include software or GPS tracking that can itself create privacy issues, so must be undertaken with care. Most importantly, policies should include robust security protection such as passwords, encryption, and restrictions on cloud storage. Policies and practices may even allow a company to remotely lock, erase, and wipe data if the device is lost or stolen, or upon employee termination—although this can press the boundaries between personal and business content. The final key component in a strong BYOD policy is to obtain written employee consent to all of it.

There are many tradeoffs between corporate control of all digital tools and liberal allowance for employees to access company resources using any gizmo they choose. In many settings, the first is no longer practical but the second is still unwise. A careful BYOD policy will balance risks and benefits. It will aim to respect employee privacy, safeguard the privacy of customers and other subjects of the organization's data, and protect the employer's interests.

---

## Hernandez v. Hillsides, Inc.

211 P.3d 1063 (Cal. 2009)

■ BAXTER, J. [for a unanimous court]

Defendants Hillsides, Inc., and Hillsides Children Center, Inc. (Hillsides) operated a private nonprofit residential facility for neglected and abused children, including the victims of sexual abuse. Plaintiffs Abigail Hernandez (Hernandez) and Maria-Jose Lopez (Lopez) were employed by Hillsides. They shared an enclosed office and performed clerical work during daytime business hours. Defendant John M. Hitchcock (Hitchcock), the director of the facility, learned that late at night, after plaintiffs had left the premises, an unknown person had repeatedly used a computer in plaintiffs' office to access the Internet and view pornographic Web sites. Such use conflicted with company policy and with Hillsides' aim of providing a safe haven for the children.

Concerned that the culprit might be a staff member who worked with the children, and without notifying plaintiffs, Hitchcock set up a hidden camera in their office. The camera could be made operable from a remote location, at any time of day or night, to permit either live viewing or videotaping of activities around the targeted workstation. It is undisputed that the camera was not operated for either of these purposes during business hours, and, as a consequence, that plaintiffs' activities in the office were not viewed or recorded by means of the surveillance system. Hitchcock did not expect or intend to catch plaintiffs on tape.

Nonetheless, after discovering the hidden camera in their office, plaintiffs filed this tort action alleging, among other things, that defendants intruded into a protected place, interest, or matter, and violated their right to privacy under both the common law and the state Constitution. The trial court granted defendants' motion for summary judgment and dismissed the case. The Court of Appeal reversed, finding triable issues that plaintiffs had suffered (1) an intrusion into a protected zone of privacy that (2) was so unjustified and offensive as to constitute a privacy violation.

We agree with defendants that the trial court properly granted their motion for summary judgment. However, we reach this conclusion for reasons more varied and nuanced than those offered by defendants.

### FACTS

In September 2003, plaintiffs Hernandez and Lopez filed this suit against defendants Hillsides and Hitchcock over the use of video surveillance equipment in plaintiffs' office. The complaint set forth three related causes of action in tort, and sought compensatory and punitive damages. The first cause of action alleged an invasion of privacy, alluding to principles and authorities under both the common law and the state Constitution. The other two claims alleged intentional and negligent infliction of emotional distress.

Beginning in 2001, plaintiffs shared an office in the administrative building at Hillsides. Each woman had her own desk and computer workstation. The office had three windows on exterior walls. Blinds on the windows could be opened and closed. The office also had a door that could be closed and locked. A "doggie" door near the bottom of the office door was missing its flap, creating a small, low opening into the office. Several people, besides plaintiffs, had keys to their office: five administrators, including Hitchcock, and all of the program directors [who were similar to security guards]. Hernandez estimated that there were five program directors. Hitchcock counted eight of them.

According to plaintiffs, they occasionally used their office to change or adjust their clothing. Hernandez replaced her work clothes with athletic wear before leaving Hillsides to exercise at the end of the day. Two or three times, Lopez raised her shirt to show Hernandez her postpregnancy figure. Both women stated in their declarations that the blinds were drawn and the door was closed when this activity occurred. Hernandez also recalled the door being locked when she changed clothes.

On or before August 22, 2002, Hillsides circulated an "E-Mail, Voicemail and Computer Systems Policy." This document stated that it was intended to prevent employees from using Hillsides' electronic communications systems in a manner that defamed, harassed, or harmed others, or that subjected the company to "significant legal exposure." Illegal and inappropriate activity was prohibited, such as accessing sexually offensive Web sites or displaying, downloading, or distributing sexually explicit material. The policy further contemplated the use of electronic "[p]ersonal passwords." However, it warned employees that they had "no reasonable expectation of privacy in any . . . use of Company computers, network and system." Along the same lines, the policy advised that all data created, transmitted, downloaded, or stored on the system was Hillsides' property, and that the company could "monitor and record employee activity on its computers, network . . . and e-mail systems," including "e-mail messages[,] . . . files stored or transmitted [,] and . . . web sites accessed."

In order to ensure compliance with Hillsides' computer policy and restrictions, [Tom] Foster, the computer specialist, could retrieve and print a list of all Internet Web sites accessed from every computer on the premises. The network server that recorded and stored such information could pinpoint exactly when and where such Web access had occurred. In July 2002, Foster determined that numerous pornographic Web sites had been viewed in the late-night and early-morning hours from at least two different computers. One of them was located in the computer laboratory, or classroom. The other one sat on the desk Lopez used in the office she shared with Hernandez.

The evidence indicated that Lopez's computer could have been accessed after hours by someone other than her, because she did not always log off before going home at night. Hitchcock explained in his deposition that employees were expected to turn off their computers when leaving work at the end of the day, that a personal password was required to log onto the computer again after it had been turned off, and that this policy was communicated orally to employees when their computers were first assigned.

Given the odd hours at which such activity had occurred, Hitchcock surmised that the perpetrator was a program director or other staff person who had unfettered access to Hillsides in the middle of the night.

In light of these circumstances, Hitchcock decided to use video equipment Hillsides already had in its possession to record the perpetrator in the act of using the computers at night.

He did not inform plaintiffs of this decision. He reasoned that the more people who knew and "gossiped" about the plan, the greater the chance the culprit would hear about it and never be identified or stopped.

Hence, at some point during the first week of October 2002, Hitchcock and Foster installed video recording equipment in plaintiffs' office and in a storage room nearby. First, in plaintiffs' office, they positioned a camera on the top shelf of a bookcase, among some plants, where it apparently was obscured from view. They also tucked a motion detector into the lap of a stuffed animal or toy sitting on a lower shelf of the same bookcase. Second, these devices connected [wirelessly] to a television that Hitchcock and Foster moved into the storage room. A videocassette recorder was built into the unit. The television had a 19-inch monitor on which images could be viewed. [These machines remained turned on and powered all the time, but the wireless receptors needed to be connected to the television and recorder for them to display or record any images. The system apparently did not record sound.]

Hitchcock rarely activated the camera and motion detector in plaintiffs' office, and never did so while they were there. His deposition testimony addressed these circumstances as follows: On three occasions, Hitchcock connected the wireless receptors to the television in the storage room after plaintiffs left work for the day, and then disconnected the receptors the next morning, before plaintiffs returned to work. In short, the camera and motion detector were always disabled during the workday, such that "there was no picture showing" and "no recording going on" while plaintiffs were in their office. Hitchcock further stated that between installation of the equipment in early October 2002, and his decision to remove it three weeks later, no one was videotaped or caught using the computer in plaintiffs' office. He assumed that the culprit had learned about the camera and stopped engaging in unauthorized activity.

Meanwhile, about 4:30 p.m. on Friday, October 25, 2002, plaintiffs discovered the video equipment in their office. A red light on the motion detector flashed at the time. The cord attached to the camera was plugged into the wall and was hot to the touch.

Shocked by the discovery, plaintiffs immediately reported it to two supervisors.

A short time later, Hitchcock called Hernandez in her office. He apologized for installing the camera, and said the surveillance was not aimed at plaintiffs, but at an intruder who had used Lopez's computer to access inappropriate Web sites. Hernandez expressed concern that she was videotaped while changing her clothes or that "personal stuff" in her office was somehow disturbed. Hitchcock replied by assuring Hernandez that "the only time we activated that camera and the video recorder was after you left at night and [we] deactivated the two devices before you came to work in the morning. [A]t no time did [we] ever capture [you] or [Lopez] on the tape."

During [a later] meeting, Lopez asked to see the surveillance videotape. Hitchcock agreed. According to the depositions of both plaintiffs, there was not much to see. No one appeared on the tape except for Hitchcock, who was briefly seen setting up the camera and moving around inside plaintiffs' office.

[The district court granted summary judgment to defendants, and the appellate court reversed.]

## DISCUSSION

### A. Summary Judgment Rules

A grant of summary judgment is proper where it appears no triable issues of material fact exist, and judgment is warranted as a matter of law.

### B. General Privacy Principles

Defendants (joined by their amici curiae) argue here, as below, that they did nothing wrong in attempting to videotape a nighttime intruder using the computer in plaintiffs' office, because no private information about plaintiffs was obtained. Defendants insist that plaintiffs, not being the intended targets of the surveillance plan, were never viewed or recorded, and thereby suffered no serious or actionable intrusion into their private domain. Plaintiffs disagree and urge us to adopt the Court of Appeal's approach in the present case. They insist that defendants were able to view and record plaintiffs at will, without their knowledge or consent, and unjustifiably deprived them of the privacy they reasonably expected to have while working behind closed doors in their shared office.

A privacy violation based on the common law tort of intrusion has two elements. First, the defendant must intentionally intrude into a place, conversation, or matter as to which the plaintiff has a reasonable expectation of privacy. Second, the intrusion must occur in a manner highly offensive to a reasonable person. These limitations on the right to privacy are not insignificant. Nonetheless, the cause of action recognizes a measure of personal control over the individual's autonomy, dignity, and serenity. The gravamen is the mental anguish sustained when both conditions of liability exist.

As to the first element of the common law tort, the defendant must have penetrated some zone of physical or sensory privacy . . . or obtained unwanted access to data by electronic or other covert means, in violation of the law or social norms. In either instance, the expectation of privacy must be objectively reasonable. In *Sanders v. American Broadcasting Companies*, 978 P.2d 67 (Cal. 1999), a leading case on workplace privacy that we discuss further below, this court linked the reasonableness of privacy expectations to such factors as (1) the identity of the intruder, (2) the extent to which other persons had access to the subject place, and could see or hear the plaintiff, and (3) the means by which the intrusion occurred.

The second common law element essentially involves a "policy" determination as to whether the alleged intrusion is "highly offensive" under the particular circumstances. Relevant factors include the degree and setting of the intrusion, and the intruder's motives and objectives.

The right to privacy in the California Constitution sets standards similar to the common law tort of intrusion.

### C. Intrusion Upon Reasonable Privacy Expectations

For reasons we now explain, we cannot conclude as a matter of law that the Court of Appeal erred in finding a prima facie case on the threshold question whether defendants' video surveillance measures intruded upon plaintiffs' reasonable expectations of privacy. Plaintiffs plausibly maintain that defendants cannot prevail on this element of the cause of action simply because they "never intended to view or record" plaintiffs, or because defendants did not "capture [plaintiffs'] images at all."

Our analysis starts from the premise that, while privacy expectations may be significantly diminished in the workplace, they are not lacking altogether. In *Sanders*, a reporter working undercover for a national broadcasting company obtained employment alongside the plaintiff as a telepsychic, giving "readings" to customers over the phone. The reporter then secretly videotaped and recorded interactions with the plaintiff and other psychics using a small camera hidden in her hat and a microphone attached to her brassiere. The taping occurred in a large room containing 100 cubicles that were open on one side and on top, and from which coworkers could be seen and heard nearby. Visitors could not enter this area without permission from the front desk. Ultimately, the plaintiff sued the reporter and the broadcasting company for violating his privacy after one of his secretly taped conversations aired on television.

This court emphasized [in *Sanders*] that privacy expectations can be reasonable even if they are not absolute. "[P]rivacy, for purposes of the intrusion tort, is not a binary, all-or-nothing characteristic. There are degrees and nuances to societal recognition of our expectations of privacy: the fact that the privacy one expects in a given setting is not complete or absolute does not render the expectation unreasonable as a matter of law."

In adopting this refined approach, *Sanders* highlighted various factors which, either singly or in combination, affect societal expectations of privacy. One factor was the identity of the intruder. We noted that the plaintiff in that case, and other employees, were deliberately misled into believing that the defendant reporter was a colleague, and had no reason to suspect she worked undercover to secretly tape their interactions for use in a national television program.

Also relevant in *Sanders* was the nature of the intrusion, meaning both the extent to which the subject interaction could be "seen and overheard" and the "means of intrusion."

Consistent with *Sanders*, which asks whether the employee could be "overheard or observed" by others when the tortious act allegedly occurred, courts have examined the physical layout of the area intruded upon, its relationship to the workplace as a whole, and the nature of the activities commonly performed in such places. At one end of the spectrum are settings in which work or business is conducted in an open and accessible space, within the sight and hearing not only of coworkers and supervisors, but also of customers, visitors, and the general public.

At the other end of the spectrum are areas in the workplace subject to restricted access and limited view, and reserved exclusively for performing bodily functions or other inherently personal acts [citing cases involving locker rooms and dressing rooms].

The present scenario falls between these extremes.

Plaintiffs plausibly claim that Hillsides provided an enclosed office with a door that could be shut and locked, and window blinds that could be drawn, to allow the occupants to obtain some measure of refuge, to focus on their work, and to escape visual and aural interruptions from other sources, including their employer. Such a protective setting generates legitimate expectations that not all activities performed behind closed doors would be clerical and work related. As suggested by the evidence here, employees who share an office, and who have four walls that shield them from outside view (albeit, with a broken "doggie" flap on the door), may perform grooming or hygiene activities, or conduct personal conversations, during the workday. Privacy is not wholly lacking because the occupants of an office can see one another, or because colleagues, supervisors, visitors, and security and maintenance personnel have varying degrees of access.

Regarding another relevant factor in *Sanders*, the "means of intrusion," employees who retreat into a shared or solo office, and who perform work and personal activities in relative seclusion there, would not reasonably expect to be the subject of televised spying and secret filming by their employer. As noted, in assessing social norms in this regard, we may look at both the "common law" and "statutory enactment."

Courts have acknowledged the intrusive effect for tort purposes of hidden cameras and video recorders in settings that otherwise seem private. It has been said that the "unblinking lens" can be more penetrating than the naked eye with respect to "duration, proximity, focus, and vantage point." *Cowles v. State* 23 P.3d 1168, 1182 (Alaska 2001) (Fabe, J., dissenting).

Not surprisingly, we discern a similar legislative policy against covert monitoring and recording that intrudes—or threatens to intrude—upon visual privacy. Some statutes criminalize the use of camcorders, motion picture cameras, or photographic cameras to violate reasonable expectations of privacy in specified areas in which persons commonly undress or perform other intimate acts [citing examples such as statutes aimed at covert locker room photography or at paparazzi].

As emphasized by defendants, the evidence shows that Hitchcock never viewed or recorded plaintiffs inside their office. He also did not intend or attempt to do so, and took steps to avoid capturing them on camera and videotape. While such factors bear on the offensiveness of the challenged conduct, as discussed below, we reject the defense suggestion that they preclude us from finding the requisite intrusion in the first place.

In particular, Hitchcock hid the video equipment in plaintiffs' office from view in an apparent attempt to prevent anyone from discovering, avoiding, or dismantling it. He used a camera and motion detector small enough to tuck inside and around decorative items perched on different bookshelves, both high and low. Plaintiffs presumably would have been caught in the camera's sights if they had returned to work after hours, or if Hitchcock had been mistaken about them having left the office when he activated the system.

In a related vein, plaintiffs cannot plausibly be found to have received warning that they would be subjected to the risk of such surveillance, or to have agreed to it in advance. We have said that notice of and consent to an impending intrusion can inhibit reasonable expectations of privacy. Here, however, the evidence shows that no one at Hillsides told plaintiffs that someone had used Lopez's computer to access pornographic Web sites. Nor were they told that Hitchcock planned to install surveillance equipment inside their office to catch the perpetrator on television and videotape.

Moreover, nothing in Hillsides' written computer policy mentioned or even alluded to the latter scenario. As noted earlier, the version in effect at the relevant time made clear that any monitoring and recording of employee activity, and any resulting diminution in reasonable privacy expectations, were limited to "use of Company computers" in the form of "e-mail" messages, electronic "files," and "web site" data. Foster performed this administrative function when he used the network server to produce the list of pornographic Web sites accessed in Lopez's office, and showed such computer-generated data to Hitchcock. There is no evidence that employees like plaintiffs had any indication that Hillsides would take the next drastic step and use cameras and recording devices to view and videotape employees sitting at their desks and computer workstations, or moving around their offices within camera range.

In sum, the undisputed evidence seems clearly to support the first of two basic elements we have identified as necessary to establish a violation of privacy as alleged in plaintiffs' complaint. Plaintiffs had no reasonable expectation that their employer would intrude so tangibly into their semi-private office.

### D. Offensiveness/Seriousness of the Privacy Intrusion

Plaintiffs must show more than an intrusion upon reasonable privacy expectations. Actionable invasions of privacy also must be "highly offensive" to a reasonable person and sufficiently serious and unwarranted as to constitute an "egregious breach of the social norms." Defendants claim that, in finding a triable issue in this regard, the Court of Appeal focused too narrowly on the mere presence of a functioning camera in plaintiffs' office during the workday, and on the inchoate risk that someone would sneak into the locked storage room and activate the monitoring and recording devices. Defendants imply that under a broader view of the relevant circumstances, no reasonable jury could find in plaintiffs' favor and impose liability on this evidentiary record. We agree.

For guidance, we note that this court has previously characterized the "offensiveness" element as an indispensible part of the privacy analysis. It reflects the reality that no community could function if every intrusion into the realm of private action" gave rise to a viable claim. Hence, no cause of action will lie for accidental, misguided, or excusable acts of overstepping upon legitimate privacy rights In light of such pragmatic policy concerns, a court determining whether this requirement has been met as a matter of law examines all of the surrounding circumstances, including the "degree and setting" of the intrusion and "the intruder's 'motives and objectives." Courts also may be asked to decide whether the plaintiff, in attempting to defeat a claim of competing interests, has shown that the defendant could have minimized the privacy intrusion through other reasonably available, less intrusive means.

1. ***Degree and Setting of Intrusion.*** This set of factors logically encompasses the place, time, and scope of defendants' video surveillance efforts. In this case, they weigh heavily against a finding that the intrusion upon plaintiffs' privacy interests was highly offensive or sufficiently serious to warrant liability.

In context, defendants took a measured approach in choosing the location to videotape the person who was misusing the computer system.

Defendants' surveillance efforts were largely confined to the area in which the unauthorized computer activity had occurred. Once the camera was placed in plaintiffs' office, it was aimed towards Lopez's desk and computer workstation. There is no evidence that Hitchcock intended or attempted to include Hernandez's desk in camera range. We can reasonably infer he avoided doing so because no improper computer use had been detected there.

Defendants' actual surveillance activities also were quite limited in scope. On the one hand, the camera and motion detector in plaintiffs' office were always plugged into the electrical circuit and capable of operating the entire time they were in place. On the other hand, Hitchcock took the critical step of connecting the wireless receptors and activating the system only three times. At most, he was responsible for monitoring and recording inside of plaintiffs' office an average of only once a week for three weeks. Such measures were hardly excessive or egregious.

Moreover, on each of these three occasions, Hitchcock connected the wireless devices and allowed the system to remotely monitor and record events inside plaintiffs' office only after their shifts ended, and after they normally left Hillsides' property. He never activated the system during regular business hours when plaintiffs were scheduled to work. The evidence shows they were not secretly viewed or taped while engaged in personal or clerical activities.

On the latter point, we agree with defendants that their successful effort to avoid capturing plaintiffs on camera is inconsistent with an egregious breach of social norms. For example, in a case closely on point, one court has held that even where an employer placed a camera in an area reserved for the most personal functions at work, such that heightened privacy expectations applied, the lack of any viewing or recording defeated the employee's invasion of privacy claim. *See Meche v. Wal-Mart Stores, Inc.* 692 So.2d 544, 547 (La. Ct. App. 1997) (camera concealed in ceiling of restroom to prevent theft).

2. ***Defendants' motives, justifications, and related issues.*** The undisputed evidence is that defendants installed video surveillance equipment in plaintiffs' office, and activated it three times after they left work, in order to confirm a strong suspicion—triggered by publicized

network tracking measures—that an unknown staff person was engaged in unauthorized and inappropriate computer use at night.

Such use of Hillsides' computer equipment by an employee violated written workplace policies circulated both before and after the challenged surveillance activities occurred. As those policies warned, and case law confirms, the offending conduct posed a risk that the perpetrator might expose Hillsides to legal liability from various quarters. At the very least, parties on both sides confirmed that accessing pornography on company computers was inconsistent with Hillsides' goal to provide a wholesome environment for the abused children in its care, and to avoid any exposure that might aggravate their vulnerable state.

We also note that Hitchcock's repeated assurances that he installed the surveillance equipment solely to serve the foregoing purposes and not to invade plaintiffs' privacy are corroborated by his actions afterwards. When confronted by plaintiffs about the camera in their office, he explained its presence, and tried to assuage their concerns about being suspected of wrongdoing and secretly videotaped. To this end, he showed them the actual surveillance tape on demand and without delay. Against this backdrop, a reasonable jury could find it difficult to conclude that defendants' conduct was utterly unjustified and highly offensive.

Plaintiffs insist triable issues exist as to whether defendants could have employed means less offensive than installing the camera in their office and connecting it to the monitor and recorder nearby. Examples include better enforcement of Hillsides' log-off/password-protection policy, installation of software filtering programs, closer nighttime monitoring of the camera outside the administration building, increased security patrols at night, and receipt of plaintiffs' informed consent to video surveillance.

Contrary to what plaintiffs imply, it appears defendants are not required to prove that there were no less intrusive means of accomplishing the legitimate objectives we have identified above in order to defeat the instant privacy claim. In the past, we have specifically declined to impose on a private organization, acting in a situation involving decreased expectations of privacy, the burden of justifying its conduct as the "least offensive alternative" possible under the circumstances.

The argument lacks merit in any event. First, the alternatives that plaintiffs propose would not necessarily have achieved at least one of defendants' aims—determining whether a program director was accessing pornographic Web sites in plaintiffs' office. Rather, it is the same suspect group of program directors on whom plaintiffs would have had defendants more heavily rely to monitor exterior cameras and perform office patrols. Obtaining plaintiffs' consent also might have risked disclosing the surveillance plan to other employees, including the program directors.

Second, privacy concerns are alleviated because the intrusion was limited and no information about plaintiffs was accessed, gathered, or disclosed. The video equipment was rarely activated and then only at night, when plaintiffs were gone. There was no covert surveillance of them behind closed doors.

## CONCLUSION

We appreciate plaintiffs' dismay over the discovery of video equipment—small, blinking, and hot to the touch—that their employer had hidden among their personal effects in an office that was reasonably secluded from public access and view. Nothing we say here is meant to encourage such surveillance measures, particularly in the absence of adequate notice to persons within camera range that their actions may be viewed and taped.

Nevertheless, considering all the relevant circumstances, plaintiffs have not established, and cannot reasonably expect to establish, that the particular conduct of defendants that is challenged in this case was highly offensive and constituted an egregious violation of prevailing social norms.

We therefore reverse the judgment of the Court of Appeal.

## Deal v. Spears

980 F.2d 1153 (8th Cir. 1992)

■ BOWMAN, CIRCUIT JUDGE.

This civil action is based on Title III of the Omnibus Crime Control and Safe Streets Act of 1968, 18 U.S.C. §§ 2510 et seq. [the Wiretap Act] [see Chapter 5].

Newell and Juanita Spears have owned and operated the White Oak Package Store near Camden, Arkansas, for about twenty years. The Spearses live in a mobile home adjacent to the store. The telephone in the store has an extension in the home, and is the only phone line into either location. The same phone line thus is used for both the residential and the business phones.

Sibbie Deal was an employee at the store from December 1988 until she was fired in August 1990. The store was burglarized in April 1990 and approximately $16,000 was stolen. The Spearses believed that it was an inside job and suspected that Deal was involved. Hoping to catch the suspect in an unguarded admission, Newell Spears purchased and installed a recording device on the extension phone in the mobile home. When turned on, the machine would automatically record all conversations made or received on either phone, with no indication to the parties using the phone that their conversation was being recorded. Before purchasing the recorder, Newell Spears told a sheriff's department investigator that he was considering this surreptitious monitoring and the investigator told Spears that he did not "see anything wrong with that."

Calls were taped from June 27, 1990, through August 13, 1990. During that period, Sibbie Deal, who was married to Mike Deal at the time, was having an extramarital affair with Calvin Lucas, then married to Pam Lucas. Deal and Lucas spoke on the telephone at the store frequently and for long periods of time while Deal was at work. (Lucas was on 100% disability so he was at home all day.) Based on the trial testimony, the District Court concluded that much of the conversation between the two was "sexually provocative." Deal also made or received numerous other personal telephone calls during her workday. Even before Newell Spears purchased the recorder, Deal was asked by her employers to cut down on her use of the phone for personal calls, and the Spearses told her they might resort to monitoring calls or installing a pay phone in order to curtail the abuse.

Newell Spears listened to virtually all twenty-two hours of the tapes he recorded, regardless of the nature of the calls or the content of the conversations, and Juanita Spears listened to some of them. Although there was nothing in the record to indicate that they learned anything about the burglary, they did learn, among other things, that Deal sold Lucas a keg of beer at cost, in violation of store policy. On August 13, 1990, when Deal came in to work the evening shift, Newell Spears played a few seconds of the incriminating tape for Deal and then fired her. Deal and Lucas filed this action on August 29, 1990, and the tapes and recorder were seized by a United States deputy marshal pursuant to court order on September 3, 1990.

Mike Deal testified that Juanita Spears told him about the tapes, and that she divulged the general nature of the tapes to him. Pam Lucas testified that Juanita Spears intimated the contents of the tapes to her. Juanita testified that she discussed the tapes and the nature of them, but only in general terms.

The Spearses challenge the court's finding of liability. They admit the taping but contend that the facts here bring their actions under two statutory exceptions to civil liability. Further, Juanita Spears alleges that she did not disclose information learned from the tapes, thus the statutory damages assessed against her on that ground were improper. For their part Deal and Lucas challenge the court's failure to award them punitive damages as permitted by statute.

The elements of a violation of the wire and electronic communications interception provisions (Title III) of the Omnibus Crime Control and Safe Streets Act of 1968 are set forth in the section that makes such interceptions a criminal offense. Under the relevant provisions of the statute, criminal liability attaches and a federal civil cause of action arises when a person intentionally intercepts a wire or electronic communication or intentionally discloses the contents of the interception. The successful civil plaintiff may recover actual damages plus any profits made by the violator. If statutory damages will result in a larger recovery than actual damages, the violator must pay the plaintiff "the greater of $100 a day for each day of violation or $10,000." Further, punitive damages, attorney fees, and "other litigation costs reasonably incurred" are allowed.

The Spearses first claim they are exempt from civil liability because Sibbie Deal consented to the interception of calls that she made from and received at the store. Under the statute, it is not unlawful "to intercept a wire, oral, or electronic communication . . . where one of the parties to the communication has given prior consent to such interception," and thus no civil liability is incurred. The Spearses contend that Deal's consent may be implied because Newell Spears had mentioned that he might be forced to monitor calls or restrict telephone privileges if abuse of the store's telephone for personal calls continued. They further argue that the extension in their home gave actual notice to Deal that her calls could be overheard, and that this notice resulted in her implied consent to interception. We find these arguments unpersuasive.

There is no evidence of express consent here. Although constructive consent is inadequate, actual consent may be implied from the circumstances.

We do not believe that Deal's consent may be implied from the circumstances relied upon in the Spearses' arguments. The Spearses did not inform Deal that they were monitoring the phone, but only told her they might do so in order to cut down on personal calls. Moreover, it seems clear that the couple anticipated Deal would not suspect that they were intercepting her calls, since they hoped to catch her making an admission about the burglary, an outcome they would not expect if she knew her calls were being recorded. As for listening in via the extension, Deal testified that she knew when someone picked up the extension in the residence while she was on the store phone, as there was an audible "click" on the line.

Given these circumstances, we hold as a matter of law that the Spearses have failed to show Deal's consent to the interception and recording of her conversations.

The Spearses also argue that they are immune from liability under what has become known as an exemption for business use of a telephone extension. The exception is actually a restrictive definition. Under Title III, a party becomes criminally and civilly liable when he or she "intercepts" wire communications. " '[I]ntercept' means the aural or other acquisition of the contents of any wire, electronic, or oral communication through the use of any electronic, mechanical, or other device[.]" Such a device is "any device or apparatus which can be used to intercept a wire, oral, or electronic communication" except when that device is a

> telephone . . . instrument, equipment or facility, or any component thereof, (i) furnished to the subscriber or user by a

> provider of wire or electronic communication service in the ordinary course of its business and being used by the subscriber or user in the ordinary course of its business or furnished by such subscriber or user for connection to the facilities of such service and used in the ordinary course of its business[.]

Thus there are two essential elements that must be proved before this becomes a viable defense: the intercepting equipment must be furnished to the user by the phone company or connected to the phone line, and it must be used in the ordinary course of business. The Spearses argue that the extension in their residence, to which the recorder was connected, meets the equipment requirement, and the listening-in was done in the ordinary course of business. We disagree.

The calls would not have been heard or otherwise acquired—that is, intercepted—at all but for the recording device, as the Spearses did not spend twenty-two hours listening in on the residential extension. When turned on, the recorder was activated automatically by the lifting of the handset of either phone, even though it was connected only to the extension phone. Further, Deal ordinarily would know (by the "click" on the line) when the residential extension was picked up while she was using the store phone; thus her calls likely would not have been intercepted if the recorder had not been in place.

It seems far more plausible to us that the recording device, and not the extension phone, is the instrument used to intercept the call. We do not believe the recording device falls within the statutory exemption. The recorder was purchased by Newell Spears at Radio Shack, not provided by the telephone company. Further, it was connected to the extension phone, which was itself the instrument connected to the phone line. There was no evidence that the recorder could have operated independently of the telephone.

We hold that the recording device, and not the extension phone, intercepted the calls. But even if the extension phone intercepted the calls, we do not agree that the interception was in the ordinary course of business.

We do not quarrel with the contention that the Spearses had a legitimate business reason for listening in: they suspected Deal's involvement in a burglary of the store and hoped she would incriminate herself in a conversation on the phone. Moreover, Deal was abusing her privileges by using the phone for numerous personal calls even, by her own admission, when there were customers in the store. The Spearses might legitimately have monitored Deal's calls to the extent necessary to determine that the calls were personal and made or received in violation of store policy.

But the Spearses recorded twenty-two hours of calls, and Newell Spears listened to all of them without regard to their relation to his business interests. Granted, Deal might have mentioned the burglary at any time during the conversations, but we do not believe that the Spearses' suspicions justified the extent of the intrusion. We conclude that the scope of the interception in this case takes us well beyond the boundaries of the ordinary course of business.

For the reasons we have indicated, the Spearses cannot avail themselves of the telephone extension/business use exemption of Title III.

Juanita Spears also contends that she did not communicate the information on the tapes, and thus she is not liable for disclosure under the statute. Liability attaches when a party "intentionally discloses . . . to any other person the contents of any wire, oral, or electronic communication, knowing or having reason to know that the information was obtained" through an interception illegal under Title III. The statutory definition of "contents," a term of art under Title III, brings Juanita's alleged disclosures within the purview of the statute; she need not play the tapes or repeat conversations to be liable. " '[C]ontents', when used with respect to any wire, oral, or electronic communication, includes any information concerning the substance, purport, or meaning of that communication[.]"

Finally, Deal and Lucas cross-appeal the District Court's failure to award punitive damages. Punitive damages are unwarranted under Title III unless Deal and Lucas can prove "a wanton, reckless or malicious violation." It is difficult to conceive of a case less appropriate for punitive damages than this one.

The Spearses had lost $16,000 by theft in what must have been a serious blow to their business, and installed the recorder in hopes that they would be able to recover their loss, or at least catch the thief. They suspected an inside job and naturally they were anxious to find out whether the burglar was one of their employees. Further, despite warnings about abuse of the phone, the Spearses were paying a salary to an employee for the hours she spent on personal calls, including (as it turned out) her conversations with her lover. She sometimes carried on these conversations in the presence of the store's customers and apparently not infrequently used salacious language. The Spearses were not taping to get "dirt" on Lucas and Deal, but believed their business interests justified the recording. Moreover, before installing the recorder, Newell Spears inquired of a law enforcement officer and was told that the officer saw nothing wrong with Spears tapping his own phone. While the Spearses' reliance on the officer's statement does not absolve them of liability, it clearly demonstrates that the taping was neither wanton nor reckless.

The judgment of the District Court is affirmed in all respects.

## Arias v. Mutual Central Alarm Service, Inc.

202 F.3d 553 (2d Cir. 2000)

■ KATZMANN, CIRCUIT JUDGE:

Lourdes Rachel Arias and Louis J. Albero seek civil damages under Title III [the Wiretap Act] [see Chapter 5], claiming that their former employer, Mutual Central Alarm Service, Inc. ("Mutual"), and certain of its officers unlawfully intercepted private and privileged telephone conversations by recording such conversations with a Dictaphone 9102 machine attached to Mutual's telephone system. [The district court granted summary judgment to defendants and plaintiffs appealed.] Plaintiffs contend on appeal that defendants' blanket recording of all incoming and outgoing telephone calls from Mutual's offices is not in the ordinary course of business and therefore in violation of Title III. We disagree and therefore affirm the judgment below.

### BACKGROUND

Mutual is a provider of central station alarm services, that is, it monitors the burglar and fire alarms of its customers and notifies the police, the fire department and/or other emergency services when it receives a signal that an alarm has been activated. In 1990, when Mutual began conducting business at its offices in New York City, it purchased a Dictaphone 9102 machine to comply with the industry-wide practice of monitoring and recording all telephone calls to and from the central station. Not only is the recording of all telephone conversations to which central station employees are parties routine among central station alarm companies, but such recording is recommended or even mandated by various standard-setting and regulatory bodies in the industry.

When the Dictaphone machine was initially installed in Mutual's offices at the end of 1990 or the beginning of 1991, it was directly connected to each of the telephones used by Mutual's employees at that time. In early 1994, following a renovation of Mutual's premises and in light of increases in the number of Mutual's employees, the Dictaphone machine was connected to Mutual's telephone system via the telephone lines used by Mutual, rather than attached to each of Mutual's telephones. The telephone lines entering Mutual's premises are connected to a demarcation or "demarc" junction box, which is owned by the telephone company. The demarc junction box, which indicates the boundary between equipment owned and maintained by the telephone company and that owned and maintained by Mutual, is further connected to a second junction box, which is in turn connected to the Dictaphone machine. The Dictaphone machine records all incoming and outgoing telephone calls on 30 sequentially numbered tapes, each of which records for approximately 24 hours. At the end of the thirtieth tape, recording continues over the first numbered tape.

Plaintiffs Albero and Arias were both employees of Mutual. Albero was hired in August 1990 as a bookkeeper and office manager shortly after Mutual was formed, and Arias was hired in September 1993 as an administrative assistant. While the record below is somewhat ambiguous regarding when the 24-hour recording of all telephone lines at Mutual began, plaintiffs allege that their private and personal telephone conversations were recorded by defendants from at least February 1994 onwards. Around December 1993 or January 1994, plaintiffs allege that they and other employees of Mutual began hearing "beeps" during their telephone conversations, and complained about this matter to their employers. Arias and Albero allege that defendant Norman Rubin, formerly the Chairman of the Board of Directors, Secretary and Treasurer of Mutual, assured Mutual's employees that their telephone conversations were not being recorded, and that Mutual's employees subsequently stopped hearing the "beeps" during their telephone calls.

There is no dispute that all of Mutual's telephone lines were being continually monitored and recorded, and that defendants listened to a number of plaintiffs' telephone conversations.

[Both plaintiffs stopped working for Mutual in 1995.] Albero and Arias initiated separate actions against defendants in November 1996, alleging that defendants intentionally intercepted, used and disclosed their private and personal telephone conversations. The district court consolidated these two actions for pretrial purposes, given the considerable factual and legal overlap between them. [It granted summary judgment for the defendants, and the plaintiffs appealed.]

## DISCUSSION

We review the district court's decision to grant summary judgment de novo. Viewing the evidence in the light most favorable to plaintiffs, the non-moving party, this Court's task is to determine whether there are any genuine issues of material fact sufficient to preclude summary judgment.

[An] interception is not actionable under Title III if the "aural or other acquisition" of the contents of plaintiffs' telephone conversations occurred (i) through the use of a telephone instrument; (ii) either furnished by the telephone service provider in the ordinary course of business or furnished by Mutual for connection to its telephone facilities; and (iii) used by Mutual in the ordinary course of its business. As the district court explicitly noted in its opinion below, plaintiffs have made a number of critical concessions enabling us to streamline the above analysis. [W]hile defendants acknowledge that the Dictaphone machine was not provided by the telephone company, plaintiffs conceded that the Dictaphone machine was furnished by Mutual for connection to the facilities of its telephone service. Plaintiffs do not dispute that they have made these concessions below, and have renewed them before this Court.

Thus, the sole remaining issue on appeal is whether the blanket recording of plaintiffs' conversations was in the ordinary course of business. Plaintiffs and amicus American Civil Liberties Union

Foundation argue that the surreptitious, 24-hour recording of all telephone conversations, regardless of the personal, private and privileged nature of some of the conversations, is not in the ordinary course of business. The argument, in effect, hinges on the allegedly surreptitious nature of the recording. Plaintiffs contend that even if 24-hour recording is supported by a purportedly legitimate business purpose, defendants must nevertheless provide plaintiffs with notice if such blanket recording is to fall within the ordinary course of business exception. We disagree.

As the district court recognized, there are genuine issues of material fact regarding whether plaintiffs had consented to the recording of their telephone conversations. Plaintiffs and defendants vigorously disagree whether Mutual's employees generally, and Albero in particular, could be said to have consented to the Dictaphone machine's recording of their telephone conversations. However, Title III has a separate exception permitting a person to intercept communications where "such person is a party to the communication or where one of the parties to the communication has given prior consent to such interception," unless the interception is for criminal or tortious purposes. 18 U.S.C. § 2511(2)(d). Given the existence of this distinct consent exception, we hold that it is a misreading of Title III to import wholesale a consent requirement into the ordinary course of business analysis at issue here. Rather, as the District of Columbia Circuit has stated, "if covert monitoring is to take place it must itself be justified by a valid business purpose, or, perhaps, at least must be shown to be undertaken normally." *Berry v. Funk*, 146 F.3d 1003, 1009 (D.C. Cir. 1998) (quoting *Sanders*, 38 F.3d at 741). In the matter before us, we do not need to articulate a precise rule in order to resolve this issue, because both of these elements, which comport with the common understanding of "ordinary course of business," are amply satisfied.

[In a footnote here, the court elaborated, "Thus, if consent to the recording had in fact been given, then the consent exception would apply and there would be no need to conduct the ordinary course of business analysis at all, and a fortiori no need to consider whether the kind of allegedly covert recording at issue here could ever be in the ordinary course of business. However, we note that although the consent exception is statutorily distinct, in certain situations both the consent and the ordinary course of business exceptions may apply, if, for example, notice of monitoring is customary in the industry."]

Legitimate business reasons support the continual recording of all incoming and outgoing telephone calls at Mutual. Central station alarm companies are the repositories of extremely sensitive security information, including information that could facilitate access to their customers' premises. Further, because such companies are contracted to contact promptly the various authorities and emergency services, accurate recording of such calls may assist the company, its customers and the police and fire departments. Complete records of calls made to and from central stations therefore are important tools for their operators to ensure that their personnel are not divulging sensitive customer information, that events are reported quickly to emergency services, that customer claims regarding events are verifiable, and that the police and other authorities may rely on these records in conducting any investigations. Not only is the 24-hour scope of the recording justified, but the alleged lack of notice is justified as well in this context. Whether notice is required depends on the nature of the asserted business justification, and here, where the recording is at least in part intended to deter criminal activity, the absence of notice may more effectively further this interest.

Finally, there is no dispute that the recording in question is standard practice within the central station alarm industry, is recommended by Mutual's underwriters and the relevant trade association, and may be required by the authorities in certain instances. There is no evidence in the record to indicate whether recording employees' telephone calls with notice of such recording is common in the industry, and plaintiffs have advanced no facts or arguments that suggest that notice is customary or required.

Therefore, we affirm the district court's holding with respect to the ordinary course of business issue, such that the grant of summary judgment was proper.

## NOTES

1. ***What Not to Do.*** If you were counseling Mr. and Mrs. Spears about how they could monitor Deal's telephone conversations for information about the burglary but avoid liability, what would you have recommended? (You should be able to do a better job than the sheriff's investigator they asked.) Similarly, if Hitchcock, the director of Hillsides, had consulted you in advance about his surveillance plan, how would you have advised him to proceed differently? (Even though Hillsides won, the litigation must have been costly and burdensome and it would have been far preferable to avoid it.) Formulate your recommendations before reading the remainder of the notes, and then see if you anticipated all the issues that arise.

2. ***It Depends.*** This small sample of three cases illustrates a fundamental point about all workplace monitoring: there is no single answer about what to do. It all depends—on the industry, the employees and their expectations, the purpose for the monitoring, the way it is conducted, the equipment used and how it works, the degree of transparency, and many other factors.

3. ***Legitimate Purpose.*** One of the most significant considerations is the underlying justification for monitoring, in light of all the circumstances. How would the *Hernandez* case have played out if the facility were not a home for abused children with high likelihood of sexual trauma? Or if the offending computer use were unauthorized online shopping or Facebook

surfing instead of viewing pornography? Similarly, note how much the *Arias* court relies on standard practices in the central alarm industry, and consider if the case would be the same if the monitoring occurred in the office of a shoe company. Even a sympathetic purpose—such as the Spearses' desire to catch the thief—may not be enough to protect employers from liability, but it can help justify the steps taken.

4. ***Minimization.*** Minimization is very important in law enforcement and intelligence surveillance [see Chapters 1, 5, and 9]. Employers are well advised to minimize the impact of their surveillance as well. Tailoring the amount of monitoring and recording to match the purpose for which it is undertaken can reduce the risk of liability. This may have been the fatal mistake by the defendants in *Deal*, who recorded and listened to 22 hours of telephone conversations, many of them "sexually provocative," when they were only investigating theft and personal use of the phone. The court dryly concludes, "[W]e do not believe that the Spearses' suspicions justified the extent of the intrusion." Conversely, the *Hernandez* court repeatedly commended Hitchcock for filming only for limited periods at the exact times and locations where the prohibited activity had already occurred—even aiming the camera at Lopez's desk and not Hernandez's.

5. ***Policies, Notice, and Consent.*** Many employers formulate consistent policies about surveillance that put employees on notice about the possibility of surveillance. Among the advantages to this approach, it reduces the likelihood that monitoring will be found offensive later. It may also let employers rely on the consent exception under ECPA, which is somewhat safer than the business use exception discussed in *Deal* and *Arias* because it depends less on the exact technical mechanisms used in interception. How did each of the employers in these three cases handle notice and consent, and why? Should they have approached notice to their employees differently?

6. ***Disclosure and Use.*** Employee monitoring falls most obviously within the "collection" phase in the life cycle of data, but legal dangers may be equally acute in the other phases. Mrs. Spears made a big mistake in this regard when she divulged the contents of the intercepted conversations to the spouses of Deal and Lucas. Indeed, it is worth wondering whether that litigation ever would have been brought absent the subsequent gossip. Surveillance may capture information that an employer would prefer *not* to have on record, potentially available in civil discovery or vulnerable to misuse. (Imagine a scenario where a large corporation recorded all of Deal's phone calls, and a fellow employee heard them and started the gossip.) On the other hand, later disclosure and use may be advantageous and permitted. There is a public interest exception to ECPA disclosure liability under *Bartnicki v. Vopper* [see Chapter 8]. What if the Spearses had heard information relevant to the burglary investigation—could they have divulged that information? To whom? How?

7. ***Drama.*** Often tort and ECPA claims are brought in highly emotional situations that may be driven by other grievances. [See Chapters 2 and 5 for other examples.] Thus, for example, the stakes might be raised in a suit for wrongful discharge or discrimination by the addition of privacy claims. The personal repercussions in *Deal* seem likely to have driven that

lawsuit (which was brought by Lucas as well as Deal). The *Arias* case arises from a convoluted soap opera backdrop. At the time of the recordings, Albero was secretly having an affair with Arias, but he originally had been hired because he was married to the granddaughter of company founder Rubin. Arias had already left the company under highly acrimonious and contested circumstances, and was threatening a lawsuit which may or may not have been meritorious. As the district court opinion explained, Rubin instructed Albero to call Arias and "find out what she was looking for." His report back made Rubin suspicious that he was in fact helping Arias.

> So Rubin asked another employee to locate the telephone call between Albero and Arias on the Dictaphone tape. The tape revealed that Albero began the conversation by telling Arias that the call was being taped, which fed Rubin's concern that Albero was not a loyal employee. So Rubin decided to investigate further.
>
> The further investigation revealed a number of conversations between Albero and Arias on four other Dictaphone tapes. These revealed that Albero, who still was married to Rubin's granddaughter although engaged in divorce or separation negotiations, "had a social and sexual relationship with Arias that went back 1½ years" and that Albero told Arias on one occasion that "he was on Arias' side in her controversy with Mutual." Rubin nevertheless did not then fire Albero because his granddaughter feared that such action would have an adverse impact on her financial settlement with Albero.

*Arias v. Mut. Cent. Alarm Servs., Inc.*, 182 F.R.D. 407, 411 (S.D.N.Y. 1998). Does this information change your view of the case? Does it help explain why the plaintiffs may have sued? As a privacy lawyer, it is crucial to help clients slow down and use good judgment in heated situations like these to avoid making their potential legal problems worse.

8. ***Effectiveness.*** One more important consideration for privacy lawyers giving advice to employers about monitoring is quite practical: how well does it work? Surveillance did not enable either Hillsides or the Spearses' business to find their culprits. To be sure, sometimes monitoring can be highly effective in investigating wrongdoing. Knowledge of potential monitoring may deter bad behavior by employees and others, and it can be useful for other reasons like quality control. But in addition to ensuring that the justifications for monitoring are legitimate, and the methods tailored to those purposes, smart privacy lawyers should also ask if the whole exercise is worth the trouble and risk. If that question cannot be answered with a strong affirmative, then perhaps it would be better not to engage in the monitoring.

9. ***The Stored Communications Act.*** In addition to the Wiretap Act discussed in *Deal* and *Arias*, ECPA also includes the Stored Communications Act ("SCA"), 18 U.S.C. §§ 2701 et seq. [see Chapter 5], which imposes limits on access to voicemails, emails, instant messages, and text messages when they are no longer "in transit" and have been stored. There are two primary

exemptions from liability other than those related to law enforcement, and both are important to employers:

> (c) Exceptions.—[The key liability provision] does not apply with respect to conduct authorized—
>
> > (1) by the person or entity providing a wire or electronic communications service;
> >
> > (2) by a user of that service with respect to a communication of or intended for that user . . .

These exceptions provide quite a lot of scope for employee monitoring. The first seems to allow employers who provide services such as voicemail and email to their employees to search those communications—and, unlike the Wiretap Act, this provision does not say it is limited to the "ordinary course of business." As one federal appeals court interpreted this language, in a case concerning a search by Nationwide Insurance of a former employee's emails on its system:

> [W]e read § 2701(c) literally to except from Title II's protection all searches by communications service providers. Thus, we hold that, because Fraser's e-mail was stored on Nationwide's system (which Nationwide administered), its search of that e-mail falls within § 2701(c)'s exception to [the SCA].

*Fraser v. Nationwide Mut. Ins. Co.*, 352 F.3d 107, 115 (3d Cir. 2003). Does this help explain why BYOD policies must be formulated carefully, as noted above? The second exception is similar to the Wiretap Act: a user—the employee—may consent to the employer gaining access to stored messages to or from that user.

**10. *Torts.*** As you should have gathered by now, the sources of law relevant to employee privacy are diffuse and numerous. Torts are a particularly slippery one. In addition to the intrusion claims seen in *Hernandez*, employers might be subject to suits under the disclosure tort, defamation, false light, or infliction of emotional distress. Common scenarios range from pre-employment investigations to on-the-job monitoring to even post-employment activities—such as statements in reference letters that allegedly reveal sensitive information or present inaccuracies. Recall, however, that there are many obstacles to tort recovery, especially in stand-alone suits but even as additional claims [see Chapter 2]. Could the plaintiffs in *Deal* and *Arias* have brought tort claims alongside their ECPA ones? Conversely, why do you suppose the *Hernandez* plaintiffs did not rely on ECPA [see Chapter 5 for inspiration]?

---

## Focus

### Social Media Monitoring

If you went to college recently, a routine part of career counseling at your school probably consisted of warnings to be careful about your image online, particularly in social media. Various surveys show dramatically different percentages of employers responding that they examine current or potential employees' online presence, but some register proportions as high as two-thirds of respondents or more. Whatever the exact number, it is clearly commonplace to "google" job applicants and employees. Online snooping carries enough legal risk that employers should tread cautiously, however. Before you read on, pause for a moment and see if you can think of some of the disparate sources of potential liability arising from online research about applicants and employees.

One of them, discussed above, is the possible impact on any subsequent employment discrimination suit. Suppose an employer scrupulously avoided questions in applications, interviews, and employee evaluations that might reveal disability or pregnancy, but then someone involved in the hiring or review process looked at an applicant's Facebook page and discovered the same information. If a dispute arose later accusing the employer of discriminatory behavior, this fact surely would emerge in discovery, and all the care taken in formal processes would be for naught.

Compliance with labor law also counsels caution. The National Labor Relations Board (NLRB) has been very active in defining "protected activity" in the context of social media. The concern arises because platforms like Facebook and Twitter have in many ways become the new water cooler, where employees can gripe about the boss and exchange workplace gossip. Under traditional labor law, employers may not punish or restrict "concerted activity" by employees—whether or not they are already unionized—including conversation about workplace grievances. The NLRB has tried to draw boundaries that allow discipline for inappropriate comments, disparagement, or unauthorized public statements online, but protect concerted activity by employees discussing terms and conditions of employment with one another.

These restrictions concern the unlawful use of information that was publicly available. When online information is not posted publicly, privacy restrictions are more significant. As of this writing in early 2016, nine states have enacted legislation forbidding employers from requiring that applicants or employees provide them with access to password-protected social media or other online content. Similar bills have been proposed in over a dozen other states. Claims under torts such as intrusion on seclusion are also possible if a reasonable person would find the examination objectionable. And using any form of subterfuge, such as phony Facebook profiles, to investigate applicants or employees is very unwise. In addition to potential liability, the public relations impact of such behavior could be very negative. When Hewlett-Packard engaged in such "pretexting" to find the source of leaks to the press, it unleashed a torrent of criticism and even congressional hearings.

Finally, ECPA [see Chapter 5] may also create complications for employers examining non-public online postings. State "baby ECPAs" may sometimes have different and more stringent requirements which must be observed as well. As usual with ECPA, however, the result depends on fine details about the exact means used to access an employee's communications. In one frequently cited case, an executive at Hawaiian Airlines examined a web site maintained by Robert Konop, a pilot who was critical of management. Konop restricted access to the site by requiring login credentials, which he provided only to certain rank-and-file workers, not to managers, on the condition that they not share their passwords. Two pilots nonetheless provided their passwords to a company vice president, who accessed the site. Because the communication was no longer "in transit," the court decided it was not "intercepted" under the Wiretap Act. In response to a Stored Communications Act claim, the airline argued it qualified for the consent exemption because the pilots who shared their passwords were "users" of the site and they authorized the airline's access—essentially a variation of the third party doctrine. On the facts of that case, the Ninth Circuit found that it was not clear that the pilots had ever visited the site themselves, so might not be "users" under the statute; it reversed summary judgment for the airline and remanded. *Konop v. Hawaiian Airlines, Inc.*, 302 F.3d 868 (9th Cir. 2002). (Incidentally, the *Konop* court also reversed the district court's dismissal of multiple claims under labor law related to the use of the web site for concerted activity.)

In sum, wise employers use caution when monitoring the social media presence of job applicants or workers. They should develop clear and legally compliant policies about social media use that are made clear to employees. While access to publicly-available content generally will be permissible by law, careless use of that content can lead to problems. And efforts to gain access to non-public information are riskier and ordinarily should not be attempted.

---

## Practice

Employee Monitoring

You are a lawyer who has been consulted by the president of Nationwide Fulfillment Solutions (NFS), a warehouse company that ships products and processes returns on behalf of online retailers without their own "back office" to do so. The computer systems of NFS clients forward new customer orders to the NFS computer network, which routes each one to the facility closest to the recipient. NFS keeps inventory from its clients in each facility. Employees working in assembly-line fashion pull the purchased items from the shelves, pack them, print out address labels, and ship them.

NFS has received an anonymous complaint through its process for reporting misconduct that a "bunch of the guys" in its warehouse in Maryland are "constantly cracking racist and sexist jokes and like to forward each other cartoons and dirty jokes on email." At the same time, the president has noticed that the same facility has a spike in "shrinkage"—the euphemism for lost inventory, some of which may be attributable to errors or damage, but some of which is surely theft. The president is likely to replace the manager of the facility in question, but also wants to investigate these issues and set up employee monitoring to prevent them in the future.

What questions do you ask? What recommendations do you make?

---

## C. PUBLIC SECTOR EMPLOYERS

Some of the legal rules presented in this chapter so far apply both to the public sector and to private employers, including, for example, ECPA. Others, such as the Employee Polygraph Protection Act, largely exempt the government. Constitutional privacy rules are the converse; they apply uniquely to government employers as state actors. This section considers the employment privacy implications of both due process privacy protection derived from *Whalen v. Roe* and the restrictions of the Fourth Amendment [see Chapter 1 for more general discussion of both].

# NASA v. Nelson

562 U.S. 134 (2011)

■ ALITO, J., delivered the opinion of the Court.

In two cases decided more than 30 years ago, this Court referred broadly to a constitutional privacy "interest in avoiding disclosure of personal matters." *Whalen v. Roe*, 429 U.S. 589, 599–600 (1977); *Nixon v. Administrator of General Services*, 433 U.S. 425, 457 (1977). Respondents in this case, federal contract employees at a Government laboratory, claim that two parts of a standard employment background investigation violate their rights under *Whalen* and *Nixon*. Respondents challenge a section of a form questionnaire that asks employees about treatment or counseling for recent illegal-drug use. They also object to certain open-ended questions on a form sent to employees' designated references.

We assume, without deciding, that the Constitution protects a privacy right of the sort mentioned in *Whalen* and *Nixon*. We hold, however, that the challenged portions of the Government's background check do not violate this right in the present case. The Government's interests as employer and proprietor in managing its internal operations, combined with the protections against public dissemination provided by the Privacy Act of 1974 [see Chapter 10], satisfy any "interest in avoiding disclosure" that may "arguably ha[ve] its roots in the Constitution" [quoting *Whalen*].

## I

### A

The National Aeronautics and Space Administration (NASA) is an independent federal agency charged with planning and conducting the Government's "space activities." NASA's workforce numbers in the tens of thousands of employees. While many of these workers are federal civil servants, a substantial majority are employed directly by Government contractors. Contract employees play an important role in NASA's mission, and their duties are functionally equivalent to those performed by civil servants.

One NASA facility, the Jet Propulsion Laboratory (JPL) in Pasadena, California, is staffed exclusively by contract employees. NASA owns JPL, but the California Institute of Technology (Cal Tech) operates the facility under a Government contract. JPL is the lead NASA center for deep-space robotics and communications. Most of this country's unmanned space missions—from the Explorer 1 satellite in 1958 to the Mars Rovers of today—have been developed and run by JPL. JPL scientists contribute to NASA earth-observation and technology-development projects. Many JPL employees also engage in pure scientific research on topics like "the star formation history of the universe" and "the fundamental properties of quantum fluids."

Twenty-eight JPL employees are respondents here. Many of them have worked at the lab for decades, and none has ever been the subject of a Government background investigation. At the time when respondents were hired, background checks were standard only for federal civil servants. In some instances, individual contracts required background checks for the employees of federal contractors, but no blanket policy was in place.

The Government has recently taken steps to eliminate this two-track approach to background investigations. In 2004, a recommendation by the 9/11 Commission prompted the President to order new, uniform identification standards for federal employees, including "contractor employees" [under a Homeland Security Presidential Directive known as "HSPD–12"]. The Department of Commerce implemented this directive by mandating that contract employees with long-term access to federal facilities complete a standard background check, typically the National Agency Check with Inquiries (NACI).

An October 2007 deadline was set for completion of these investigations. In January 2007, NASA modified its contract with Cal Tech to reflect the new background-check requirement. JPL management informed employees that anyone failing to complete the NACI process by October 2007 would be denied access to JPL and would face termination by Cal Tech.

## B

The NACI process has long been the standard background investigation for prospective civil servants. The process begins when the applicant or employee fills out a form questionnaire. Employees who work in "non-sensitive" positions (as all respondents here do) complete Standard Form 85 (SF–85). [More detailed forms are required for "public-trust and national-security positions."]

Most of the questions on SF–85 seek basic biographical information: name, address, prior residences, education, employment history, and personal and professional references. The form also asks about citizenship, selective-service registration, and military service. The last question asks whether the employee has "used, possessed, supplied, or manufactured illegal drugs" in the last year. If the answer is yes, the employee must provide details, including information about "any treatment or counseling received." A "truthful response," the form notes, cannot be used as evidence against the employee in a criminal proceeding. The employee must certify that all responses on the form are true and must sign a release authorizing the Government to obtain personal information from schools, employers, and others during its investigation.

Once a completed SF–85 is on file, the "agency check" and "inquiries" begin. The Government runs the information provided by the employee through FBI and other federal-agency databases. It also sends out form questionnaires to the former employers, schools, landlords, and references listed on SF–85. The particular form at issue in this case—the Investigative Request for Personal Information, Form 42—goes to the employee's former landlords and references. [Other forms, not at issue in the case, go to former employers, educational institutions, record repositories, and law enforcement agencies.]

Form 42 is a two-page document that takes about five minutes to complete. It explains to the reference that "[y]our name has been provided by" a particular employee or applicant to help the Government determine that person's "suitability for employment or a security clearance." After several preliminary questions about the extent of the reference's associations with the employee, the form asks if the reference has "any reason to question" the employee's "honesty or trustworthiness." It also asks if the reference knows of any "adverse information" concerning the employee's "violations of the law," "financial integrity," "abuse of alcohol and/or drugs," "mental or emotional stability," "general behavior or conduct," or "other matters." If "yes" is checked for any of these categories, the form calls for an explanation in the space below. That space is also available for providing "additional information" ("derogatory" or "favorable") that may bear on "suitability for government employment or a security clearance."

All responses to SF–85 and Form 42 are subject to the protections of the Privacy Act. The Act authorizes the Government to keep records pertaining to an individual only when they are "relevant and necessary" to an end "required to be accomplished" by law. Individuals are permitted to access their records and request amendments to them. Subject to certain exceptions, the Government may not disclose records pertaining to an individual without that individual's written consent.

### C

About two months before the October 2007 deadline for completing the NACI, respondents brought this suit, claiming, as relevant here, that the background-check process violates a constitutional right to informational privacy. The District Court denied respondents' motion for a preliminary injunction, but the Ninth Circuit granted an injunction pending appeal and later reversed the District Court's order. The court held that portions of both SF–85 and Form 42 are likely unconstitutional and should be preliminarily enjoined.

Turning first to SF–85, the Court of Appeals noted respondents' concession "that most of the questions" on the form are "unproblematic" and do not "implicate the constitutional right to informational privacy." But the court determined that the "group of questions concerning illegal drugs" required closer scrutiny. Applying Circuit precedent, the court upheld SF–85's inquiries into recent involvement with drugs as "necessary to further the government's legitimate interest" in combating illegal-drug use. The court went on to hold, however, that the portion of the form requiring disclosure of drug "treatment or counseling" furthered no legitimate interest and was thus likely to be held unconstitutional.

Form 42, in the Court of Appeals' estimation, was even "more problematic." The form's "open-ended and highly private" questions, the court concluded, were not "narrowly tailored" to meet the Government's interests in verifying contractors' identities and "ensuring the security of the JPL." As a result, the court held, these "open-ended" questions, like the drug-treatment question on SF–85, likely violate respondents' informational-privacy rights.

Over the dissents of five judges, the Ninth Circuit denied rehearing en banc. We granted certiorari.

### II

As noted, respondents contend that portions of SF–85 and Form 42 violate their "right to informational privacy." This Court considered a similar claim in *Whalen,* which concerned New York's practice of collecting "the names and addresses of all persons" prescribed dangerous drugs with both "legitimate and illegitimate uses." The patients who brought suit in *Whalen* argued that New York's statute "threaten[ed] to impair" both their "nondisclosure" interests and their interests in making healthcare decisions independently. The Court, however, upheld the statute as a "reasonable exercise of New York's broad police powers."

*Whalen* acknowledged that the disclosure of "private information" to the State was an "unpleasant invasion of privacy," but the Court pointed out that the New York statute contained "security provisions" that protected against "public disclosure" of patients' information. This sort of "statutory or regulatory duty to avoid unwarranted disclosures" of "accumulated private data" was sufficient, in the Court's view, to protect a privacy interest that "arguably ha[d] its roots in the Constitution." The Court thus concluded that the statute did not violate "any right or liberty protected by the Fourteenth Amendment."

### III

As was our approach in *Whalen,* we will assume for present purposes that the Government's challenged inquiries implicate a privacy interest of constitutional significance. We hold, however, that, whatever the scope of this interest, it does not prevent the Government from asking reasonable questions of the sort included on SF–85 and Form 42 in an employment background investigation that is subject to the Privacy Act's safeguards against public disclosure.

### A

#### 1

As an initial matter, judicial review of the Government's challenged inquiries must take into account the context in which they arise. When the Government asks respondents and their references to fill out SF–85 and Form 42, it does not exercise its sovereign power "to regulate or license." Rather, the Government conducts the challenged background checks in its capacity "as proprietor" and manager of its "internal operation." Time and again our cases have recognized that the Government has a much freer hand in dealing "with citizen employees than it does when it brings its sovereign power to bear on citizens at large." This distinction is grounded on the "common-sense realization" that if every "employment decision became a constitutional matter," the Government could not function.

An assessment of the constitutionality of the challenged portions of SF–85 and Form 42 must account for this distinction. The questions challenged by respondents are part of a standard employment background check of the sort used by millions of private employers. See Brief for Consumer Data Indus. Assn. et al. as *Amici Curiae* 2 (hereinafter CDIA Brief) ("[M]ore than 88% of U.S. companies . . . perform background checks on their employees"). The Government itself has been conducting employment investigations since the earliest days of the Republic. Since 1871, the President has enjoyed statutory authority to "ascertain the fitness of applicants" for the civil service "as to age, health, character, knowledge and ability for the employment sought." Standard background investigations similar to those at issue here became mandatory for all candidates for the federal civil service in 1953.

As this long history suggests, the Government has an interest in conducting basic employment background checks. Reasonable investigations of applicants and employees aid the Government in ensuring the security of its facilities and in employing a competent, reliable workforce. Courts must keep those interests in mind when asked to go line-by-line through the Government's employment forms and to scrutinize the choice and wording of the questions they contain.

Respondents argue that, because they are contract employees and not civil servants, the Government's broad authority in managing its affairs should apply with diminished force. But the Government's interest as "proprietor" in managing its operations does not turn on such formalities. The record shows that, as a practical matter, there are no relevant distinctions between the duties performed by NASA's civil-service workforce and its contractor workforce.

### 2

With these interests in view, we conclude that the challenged portions of both SF–85 and Form 42 consist of reasonable, employment-related inquiries that further the Government's interests in managing its internal operations. As to SF–85, the only part of the form challenged here is its request for information about "any treatment or counseling received" for illegal-drug use within the previous year. The "treatment or counseling" question, however, must be considered in context. It is a follow-up to SF–85's inquiry into whether the employee has "used, possessed, supplied, or manufactured illegal drugs" during the past year.

The Government has good reason to ask employees about their recent illegal-drug use. Like any employer, the Government is entitled to have its projects staffed by reliable, law-abiding persons who will efficiently and effectively discharge their duties. Questions about illegal-drug use are a useful way of figuring out which persons have these characteristics.

In context, the follow-up question on "treatment or counseling" for recent illegal-drug use is also a reasonable, employment-related inquiry. The Government, recognizing that illegal-drug use is both a criminal and a medical issue, seeks to separate out those illegal-drug users who are taking steps to address and overcome their problems. The Government thus uses responses to the "treatment or counseling" question as a mitigating factor in determining whether to grant contract employees long-term access to federal facilities.

We reject the argument that the Government, when it requests job-related personal information in an employment background check, has a constitutional burden to demonstrate that its questions are "necessary" or the least restrictive means of furthering its interests. So exacting a standard runs directly contrary to *Whalen*. The patients in *Whalen,* much like respondents here, argued that New York's statute was unconstitutional because the State could not "demonstrate the necessity" of its program. The Court quickly rejected that argument, concluding that New York's collection of patients' prescription information could "not be held unconstitutional simply because" a court viewed it as "unnecessary, in whole or in part."

That analysis applies with even greater force where the Government acts, not as a regulator, but as the manager of its internal affairs.

**3**

[The "open-ended inquiries" on Form 42], like the drug-treatment question on SF–85, are reasonably aimed at identifying capable employees who will faithfully conduct the Government's business. Asking an applicant's designated references broad, open-ended questions about job suitability is an appropriate tool for separating strong candidates from weak ones. It would be a truly daunting task to catalog all the reasons why a person might not be suitable for a particular job, and references do not have all day to answer a laundry list of specific questions. Form 42 takes just five minutes to complete.

The reasonableness of such open-ended questions is illustrated by their pervasiveness in the public and private sectors. Form 42 alone is sent out by the Government over 1.8 million times annually. In addition, the use of open-ended questions in employment background checks appears to be equally commonplace in the private sector. The use of similar open-ended questions by the Government is reasonable and furthers its interests in managing its operations.

### B

#### 1

Not only are SF–85 and Form 42 reasonable in light of the Government interests at stake, they are also subject to substantial protections against disclosure to the public. Both *Whalen* and *Nixon* recognized that government "accumulation" of "personal information" for "public purposes" may pose a threat to privacy. But both decisions also stated that a "statutory or regulatory duty to avoid unwarranted disclosures" generally allays these privacy concerns.

Respondents in this case, like the patients in *Whalen* and former President Nixon, attack only the Government's *collection* of information on SF–85 and Form 42. And here, no less than in *Whalen* and *Nixon*, the information collected is shielded by statute from "unwarranted disclosur[e]." The Privacy Act, which covers all information collected during the background-check process, allows the Government to maintain records "about an individual" only to the extent the records are "relevant and necessary to accomplish" a purpose authorized by law. The Act requires written consent before the Government may disclose records pertaining to any individual. And the Act imposes criminal liability for willful violations of its nondisclosure obligations. These requirements give forceful recognition to a Government employee's interest in maintaining the confidentiality of sensitive information in his personnel files. Like the protections against disclosure in *Whalen* and *Nixon*, they "evidence a proper concern" for individual privacy.

#### 2

Notwithstanding these safeguards, respondents argue that statutory exceptions to the Privacy Act's disclosure bar leave its protections too porous to supply a meaningful check against "unwarranted disclosures." Respondents point in particular to what they describe as a "broad" exception for "routine use[s]," defined as uses that are "compatible with the purpose for which the record was collected."

Respondents' reliance on these exceptions rests on an incorrect reading of both our precedents and the terms of the Privacy Act. As to our cases, the Court in *Whalen* and *Nixon* referred approvingly to statutory or regulatory protections against "*unwarranted* disclosures" and "*undue* dissemination" of personal information collected by the Government. Neither case suggested that an ironclad disclosure bar is needed to satisfy privacy interests that may be "root[ed] in the Constitution." The mere fact that the Privacy Act's nondisclosure requirement is subject to exceptions does not show that the statute provides insufficient protection against public disclosure.

Nor does the substance of the "routine use" exception relied on by respondents create any undue risk of public dissemination. None of the authorized "routine use[s]" of respondents' background-check information allows for release to the public. Rather, the established "routine use[s]" consist of limited, reasonable steps designed to complete the background-check process in an efficient and orderly manner. The remote possibility of public disclosure created by these narrow "routine use[s]" does not undermine the Privacy Act's substantial protections.

Citing past violations of the Privacy Act, respondents note that it is possible that their personal information could be disclosed as a result of a similar breach. But data breaches are a possibility any time the Government stores information. As the Court recognized in *Whalen,* the mere possibility that security measures will fail provides no "proper ground" for a broad-based attack on government information-collection practices.

In light of the protection provided by the Privacy Act's nondisclosure requirement, and because the challenged portions of the forms consist of reasonable inquiries in an employment background check, we conclude that the Government's inquiries do not violate a constitutional right to informational privacy.

■ JUSTICE SCALIA, with whom JUSTICE THOMAS joins, concurring in the judgment.

I agree with the Court, of course, that background checks of employees of government contractors do not offend the Constitution. But rather than reach this conclusion on the basis of the never-explained assumption that the Constitution requires courts to "balance" the Government's interests in data collection against its contractor employees' interest in privacy, I reach it on simpler grounds. Like many other desirable things not included in the Constitution, "informational privacy" seems like a good idea—wherefore the People have enacted laws at the federal level and in the states restricting the government's collection and use of information. But it is up to the People to enact those laws, to shape them, and, when they think it appropriate, to repeal them. A federal constitutional right to "informational privacy" does not exist.

This case is easily resolved on the simple ground that the Due Process Clause does not "guarante[e] certain (unspecified) liberties"; rather, it "merely guarantees certain procedures as a prerequisite to deprivation of liberty." Respondents make no claim that the State has deprived them of liberty without the requisite procedures, and their due process claim therefore must fail.

## Biby v. Board of Regents of the University of Nebraska at Lincoln

419 F.3d 845 (8th Cir. 2005)

■ MURPHY, CIRCUIT JUDGE.

After his employment as a technology transfer coordinator at the University of Nebraska at Lincoln was terminated, Gerald Biby sued its Board of Regents and several university officials. The district court awarded summary judgment to the defendants on all claims. [On appeal, Biby] claims that his constitutional rights were violated by the search of his office computer. We affirm.

Biby worked at the university's Industrial Agricultural Products Center (IAPC), which seeks to increase industrial and other nonfood uses of agricultural commodities. As a technology transfer coordinator for IAPC, Biby worked with private sector companies to identify research and marketing opportunities for new technologies.

While he was employed at the IAPC, Biby worked with [other employees] to develop horticultural applications for polylactic acid (PLA). Bill Brown, owner of Corn Card International, expressed an interest in using PLA to manufacture biodegradable plastic phone cards. Biby [and the others] modified the technology to suit that purpose and called it Soft Touch II. In March 1997 they offered the invention to the university, and a provisional patent application was subsequently filed.

In July 1997 the university entered into a licensing agreement or TLA with Corn Card. The TLA identified the university as the owner of the Soft Touch II technology and gave Corn Card the exclusive right to develop, market, and sell printable plastic phone cards incorporating the technology in the United States, Mexico, and Canada. Biby reports that he worked diligently with Brown to market the project successfully. In 1998 Brown began discussions with Gemplus, a card manufacturer interested in marketing cards using Soft Touch II technology in Europe. Brown and Gemplus hoped that the university would allow an assignment to Gemplus of Corn Card's rights under the TLA and that the marketing territory could be expanded worldwide. [The university, however, was reluctant to approve an assignment because of a potentially conflicting agreement with Cargill, Inc.]

In February 1999 Corn Card threatened to take legal action against the university if it did not approve the Gemplus assignment, alleging that it would be in breach of the TLA. Associate Vice Chancellor [Donald] Helmuth directed IAPC to give him all the information it had regarding Corn Card, and on March 5 it furnished him 975 pages of documents. Helmuth and Darrell Nelson, dean and director of the agricultural research division at the university, instructed Biby several times in early 1999 not to contact Corn Card directly and told him that any communication with Corn Card must go through legal counsel. Biby reports that his relationship with Helmuth and Nelson became strained, and he acknowledges that he openly accused them of lying about the Corn Card and Gemplus project and of breaching the TLA.

In compliance with the terms of the TLA, the dispute between Corn Card and the university was submitted to arbitration. On May 19, 1999 the parties executed a document called Terms of Reference in which they agreed to provide each other all relevant nonprivileged documents by June 10. Helmuth told Biby in a telephone conversation on June 2 that the university needed to go through his computer files to make sure that it had all of the documents it was required to turn over. Helmuth added that pursuant to university policy Biby would have to sign a consent to search form and that a member of the university police department would need to witness the signing. Biby said that he would be uncomfortable having a police officer involved and asked Helmuth to fax him a copy of the university policy establishing this procedure. Helmuth faxed Biby a memo from Ken Cauble, who was the chief of the university police department, and a copy of the university policy on technology and networks. The memo from Chief Cauble stated that the "internal policy on the use of Consent to Search forms is that the rights of the individual can only be waived to a commissioned member" of the university police department. The university computer policy which Helmuth also faxed has a section on privacy. That section states that the university will only search files if a legitimate reason exists, such as needed repair or maintenance of equipment, investigation of improper or illegal use of resources, and "response to a public records request, administrative or judicial order or request for discovery in the course of litigation." Consent to search forms are not mentioned, but the policy explicitly states that its terms are applicable to e-mail.

When the university attempted to review Biby's paper and computer files on June 3, he videotaped the encounter. The first person to arrive at his office was an operations analyst, Micha Uher, who intended to go through his paper files. Biby said that he did not want any files leaving his office because he was concerned that their integrity would be compromised. He claimed that [the University] was making IAPC the scapegoat in the dispute with Corn Card and said he would not participate in the destruction of evidence. Biby informed Uher that the 975 pages which IAPC had turned over to Helmuth had not included his personal notes and records or anything about Gemplus. He told Uher that he had not tried to withhold material, but that he was never asked for anything on Gemplus.

Computer specialist Anthony Spulak then arrived at Biby's office with a plainclothes officer. Spulak intended to search Biby's computer files after the officer first went over the consent form with him, but Biby refused to sign the consent form. He referred to the computer policy Helmuth had faxed and said that he assumed the search related to an investigation of improper or illegal use since there was no repair or maintenance issue. He said that he had been threatened, intimidated, and coerced by university officials and reiterated his concern about the integrity of his documents being compromised. Spulak replied that he would not conduct a search without the signed consent, and he and the others departed.

That afternoon Biby met with Associate Vice Chancellor Helmuth, Dean Nelson, and Director Hanna. Nelson gave Biby a letter he had prepared which directed Biby "to provide immediate access to all business, licensing, tech transfer and research files, records, or communications relating to Corn Card International, whether in paper or electronic form, to University Operations Analysis and computer specialist personnel" so the university could turn over all documents for the arbitration. Biby said he understood that the university needed the files, and the others told him that the necessary files were those dealing with Corn Card, Gemplus, and Cargill. They also told him there had been a misunderstanding that morning because Uher was only to go through the paper files with Biby and to copy documents rather than remove them. They assured him that the computer specialist would not delete or alter files, but that he would need Biby to answer questions about his filing process and indicate which files might be relevant. Biby agreed to be present the following morning so that Uher and Spulak could collect paper and computer files.

Biby videotaped the first part of the file collection process on June 4. Uher arrived first, and Biby handed him paper files that had not been included in the 975 pages turned over in March. Biby told him these documents related to Gemplus or Cargill or were his personal notes, and Uher made copies of them. After Spulak arrived with a uniformed officer from the university police department, he told Biby that Richard Wood, vice president and general counsel for the university, had decided signed consent was not necessary to search his computer because the university owned it. Spulak also said he had been instructed to search through all files, to copy those related to the dispute, and to close any personal or irrelevant files. Biby asked Spulak and the officer if they thought these instructions were consistent with Dean Nelson's letter from the previous day. They both looked at Nelson's letter and replied that they thought the instructions were consistent. Biby then told Spulak, "You can start wherever you want."

Spulak said he wanted to start with the Lotus Notes e-mail files, and Biby logged in to allow him access. Spulak conducted a key word search using terms related to the Corn Card dispute. Spulak reports that he immediately closed any file that appeared not to relate to the dispute but e-mailed himself all of the files which appeared to be related to the arbitration so that he could deliver them to Helmuth. Before Spulak was able to review the e-mail files Biby had retained on the Pegasus system, Biby complained that he was feeling ill. Spulak says that he offered to return at another time to complete the search but that Biby indicated that he could forward all of the e-mail files to his own account. Spulak says he later reviewed the e-mail and forwarded to Helmuth those files which appeared to be related to Corn Card.

The dispute between the university and Corn Card was settled in August or September 1999. In September Dean Nelson placed Biby on paid administrative leave, alleging that Biby had misrepresented himself in his dealings with Corn Card and Gemplus as having authority to obligate the university contractually and that he had disobeyed the order not to contact Corn Card directly. The dean met with Biby in October, and he was terminated on November 12, 1999.

Biby sued the Board of Regents and several university officers in their official and individual capacities on June 2, 2003.

Biby's appeal concerns his claims under 42 U.S.C. § 1983 for violation of privacy guaranteed by the Fourth and Fourteenth Amendments and denial of due process guaranteed by the Fifth and Fourteenth Amendments.

Biby's Fourth Amendment allegations are that he had a constitutionally protected privacy interest in his work computer, that the university's reasons for searching his computer were illegitimate, and that the scope of the search was unreasonable. He relies on the Supreme Court's decision in *O'Connor v. Ortega*, 480 U.S. 709 (1987), which held in part:

> [P]ublic employer intrusions on the constitutionally protected privacy interests of government employees for noninvestigatory, work-related purposes, as well as for investigations of work-related misconduct, should be judged by the standard of reasonableness under all the circumstances. Under this reasonableness standard, both the inception and the scope of the intrusion must be reasonable.

Biby denies that he consented to the search and claims that he was coerced into permitting it and that he only gave in when it became obvious he had no other choice.

Appellees respond that Biby did not have a reasonable expectation of privacy in his computer files because the university computer policy allows for searches when there is a discovery request in litigation. They contend that the university had legitimate reasons to search the computer files, the search was reasonable in scope, and Biby gave his consent to the search.

In *O'Connor*, the Supreme Court listed several factors which are relevant in determining whether an employee's expectation of privacy in the workplace is reasonable, and one such factor is the existence of a workplace privacy policy. In both versions of the university computer policy in the record here, the computer user is informed not to expect privacy if the university has a legitimate reason to conduct a search. The user is specifically told that computer files, including e-mail, can be searched when the university is responding to a discovery request in the course of litigation. Although Biby contends that the university's true motivation for the search was to find a reason to fire him and to tamper with evidence, the record discloses that the search was conducted within the discovery period for the arbitration, that it used key words related to the arbitration, and that Biby was told in advance that a search was necessary to locate documents related to the arbitration. A search of a government employee's office is justified under *O'Connor* "when there are reasonable grounds for suspecting that [it] is necessary for a noninvestigatory work-related purpose." Moreover, an official might reasonably have concluded from Biby's statements and conduct that he had consented to the search. In these circumstances we cannot conclude that it would have been clear to a reasonable official that his efforts to obtain the discovery materials were unlawful.

Biby complains that the key word search was unreasonably broad and that it yielded many personal or confidential files unrelated to the Corn Card project. He suggests that the search would have been reasonable if he had been allowed to sit down with the computer specialist conducting the search and review the files with him. A search is permissible in scope when "the measures adopted are reasonably related to the objectives of the search and not excessively intrusive" [quoting *O'Connor*]. The record shows that the university needed to search broadly to ascertain that it had gathered all discoverable documents, and Biby was neither a party to the TLA nor a lawyer. Moreover, Biby has not contended that any term used was unrelated to the Corn Card project.

Biby has not shown that he had a reasonable expectation of privacy in his computer files, and even if he had met that threshold requirement of *O'Connor*, he has failed to show that the search of his computer was unreasonable in inception or scope. We conclude that the district court did not err in granting summary judgment on his Fourth Amendment claim.

■ BYE, CIRCUIT JUDGE, concurring.

To the extent the majority opinion can be read to disavow Gerald Biby's expectation of privacy in his computer, I disagree. The University's privacy policy created an expectation the contents of his computer are to a certain degree private. The policy specifically states "a user can expect the files and data he or she generates to be private information." In addition to the policy, the fact his computer was password protected and located in his private office is further evidence of the heightened expectation of privacy. He also regularly used his computer for personal use, his e-mail for personal correspondence, and he kept highly confidential proprietary information in his computer. Moreover, the University acted as if he had an expectation of privacy in his computer by requiring him to consent to a search. Based upon these facts, I submit Biby had an expectation of privacy in his office computer. Nevertheless, because the University's need to gather information relevant to a pending arbitration outweighed Biby's privacy interests, I would find the search of the computer reasonable, and not in violation of the Fourth Amendment.

## NOTES

1. ***The* Whalen *Standard.*** What exactly is the standard by which the *NASA v. Nelson* Court decided the background checks did not violate the Constitution? The majority was only able to assume the right existed without deciding the question because, whatever the standard, the facts in this case would not violate such a right. Does that mean the NACI background check is clearly allowable by *any* standard? How, then, did the court of appeals reach a contrary conclusion in *Nelson*? Articulate changes in the facts that might have brought this case closer to the boundary of constitutionality in the majority's view. Does that help you identify the standard? Justice Scalia would have resolved the case by finding that the due process right discussed in *Whalen* does not exist. Would that be a better approach?

2. ***The Fourth Amendment Standard.*** The *O'Connor v. Ortega* decision cited in *Biby* is the leading case concerning employees' Fourth Amendment rights to be free of unreasonable searches and seizures. In some ways, the test in *O'Connor* is structured like some familiar Fourth Amendment doctrines. First, an employee's expectations of privacy in the area searched must be reasonable, based on a number of fact-related considerations. Then, the "inception" and "scope" conditions essentially mean that the government must have a legitimate reason to conduct the search and must tailor the search to that reason. This is very similar to the rule in public schools [see Chapter 15]. Fourth Amendment doctrine is much more lenient toward the government in these "proprietary" roles than in law enforcement cases. Look back at *Nelson*, a case that was not decided under the Fourth Amendment. How does the Fourth Amendment analysis influence that case nevertheless?

3. ***Expectations, Again.*** Did Biby have a reasonable expectation of privacy in the contents of his computer? The concurrence thinks so. Could the university have done anything else to reduce doubt on this point? If the facility in *Hernandez* had been a public institution subject to the Fourth Amendment, would Hernandez and Lopez have a reasonable expectation of privacy in their office? How did those considerations play out in that case, based in tort? Although reasonable expectations reasoning may originate in Fourth Amendment case law, it is not confined there.

4. ***Notice and Consent, Again.*** How good of a job did the employers in *Nelson* and *Biby* do in giving their employees notice of the screening and monitoring activities they were planning to undertake? How could they have done better? Did they get consent from their employees?

5. ***Minimization, Again.*** Why did Spulak, who searched Biby's computer files, immediately close those that appeared to be personal or irrelevant to the investigation? Did the Fourth Amendment require him to do so?

6. ***Government Acting Like a Business.*** The University of Nebraska is a public institution, and some of its functions are clearly governmental. Biby's work in the IAPC, while oriented toward the public goal of increasing markets for agriculture products important to the Nebraska economy, also had many features more like a private business,

however. He was negotiating with companies and developing products that would earn revenue for his employer through licensing agreements. Conversely, the Jet Propulsion Laboratory in *Nelson* is considered a private entity even though its employees are performing NASA's core functions. Does that seem intuitive—that thr JPL is private and the IAPC public? That said, on both occasions when Spulak came to search Biby's computer, he was accompanied not by private corporate security guards but by sworn officers of the university's police department, one of them in uniform. Should that be enough to require that the Fourth Amendment apply? The doctrine concerning the definition of a state actor is extremely complicated, and its results are not always self-evident.

7. ***Rocket Scientists.*** The *Nelson* case deals with background checks for—literally—rocket scientists. How relevant are the challenged background questions to the work conducted by the employees at the Jet Propulsion Laboratory? Should the questions be tailored to the nature of the employees' work, or just to defensible interests of an employer? Justice Alito evaluates the reasonableness of the questions by comparing them to background checks conducted in the private sector. Is that the correct approach?

8. ***Just Because I'm Paranoid . . .*** Like a number of the cases seen earlier in this chapter, the factual situation in *Biby* is an emotionally fraught dispute that arose after the employee was terminated. Again, because of the underlying conflicts and the charged atmosphere it can create, an employer must take care to proceed very carefully and in accordance with strict procedure. How well did the University do in that regard? Biby's relationship with his superiors and the University appears to have been deteriorating for some time. The court portrays him as defensive, emotional, rather dramatic, and perhaps even paranoid about the search of his computer and paper files. That said, the University did fire him, apparently based at least in part on evidence that emerged from the investigation into the Corn Card dispute. Even if the primary reason for the searches was to ensure that all relevant documents had been turned over for arbitration purposes, doesn't it seem that the University might also have been looking for reasons to terminate Biby? So how paranoid was he?

9. ***Public Sector Drug Testing.*** The 1980s "War on Drugs" produced a wave of litigation concerning drug testing requirements in public employment. Unlike the private sector drug testing discussed above [see Section A], government employers must also consider Fourth Amendment limits. In a pair of 1989 cases, the Supreme Court approved drug testing programs for railroad employees involved in accidents and safety breaches, *Skinner v. Railway Labor Executives' Ass'n*, 489 U.S. 602 (1989), and for customs agents applying for positions where they would carry firearms or have responsibility for drug interdiction, *Natl. Treasury Employees' Union v. Von Raab*, 489 U.S. 656 (1989). But the Court later overturned a Georgia statute that would have required drug testing of all candidates for public office. *Chandler v. Miller*, 520 U.S. 305 (1997). On the basis of these precedents, lower courts have generally allowed testing of government employees in situations with particular justifications related to safety or law

enforcement, but not in others. This can lead to some conflicting case law, such as in cases concerning public school teachers. *Compare Knox County Educ. Ass'n v. Knox County Bd. of Educ.*, 158 F.3d 361 (6th Cir. 1998) (approving testing) *with Am. Fed. of Teachers v. Kanawha Bd. of Educ.*, 592 F. Supp. 2d 883 (S.D. W. Va. 2009) (rejecting testing); *Bangert v. Hodel*, 705 F. Supp. 643 (D.D.C. 1989) (same). Overall, however, the doctrine has limited the use of routine, random, and suspicionless drug testing in government workplaces, but it has become routine for employees in certain roles.

# CHAPTER 12

# MEDICAL INFORMATION

Most of us would consider information about health conditions to be among the most personal and private types of data about an individual. It is unsurprising, then, that US law has long imposed more privacy-related obligations on the health care industry and related medical institutions than perhaps on any other portion of the private sector. Obligations of medical privacy trace their roots to foundations in the common law and in ethical rules, but now—like most privacy law—they are embodied primarily in complex statutes and regulations. This chapter will begin by examining older foundational medical privacy law, which remains in force today, particularly evidentiary privileges concerning medical information [Section A] and tort law [Section B]. Then it will turn to the more recent regulatory structures, and particularly to rules generated by the Health Insurance Portability and Accountability Act, better known by its acronym as HIPAA [Section C]. The chapter closes with an examination of genetic information and its special status in privacy and data protection law [Section D].

Before we go on, pause for a moment and consider what law you have studied already that may bear on privacy of health information. Writing before the HIPAA regulations became effective, one court summarized the principal sources of law that were already then in force concerning physicians' duties to preserve patients' confidences:

> In the absence of express legislation, courts have found the basis for a right of action for wrongful disclosure in four main sources: (1) state physician licensing statutes, (2) evidentiary rules and privileged communication statutes which prohibit a physician from testifying in judicial proceedings, (3) common law principles of trust, and (4) the Hippocratic Oath and principles of medical ethics which proscribe the revelation of patient confidences.

*McCormick v. England*, 494 S.E.2d 431, 435–36 (S.C. Ct. App. 1997). In addition to these, the law has long regulated the handling of medical information through all the foundational sources from Part One of this book, including constitutional law, tort law, consumer protection law, and data protection law.

Not only does medical privacy law come from many sources, it pursues multiple aims. Of course, we want to protect individuals' interests in the confidentiality of information about their medical conditions. Ask yourself why health information, in particular, enjoys this special status as intuitively private. At the same time, policymakers often articulate another reason for strong rules: the need to inspire confidence in patients, or subjects of medical research, in order to ensure that they provide full and accurate information. This second objective is important to society as well as to individuals. Patients will not receive the best clinical care if they are not fully honest with health care practitioners about highly personal areas, potentially including topics such as parentage, genetic information, addiction, mental illness, and sexually transmitted diseases. Nor will efforts to understand and cure diseases succeed if a cross-section of society does not voluntarily allow the use of medical information and even biological samples in research. At the same time, there is also a collective interest in gathering information that will help prevent the spread of communicable diseases. In other words, privacy rules must simultaneously try to *prevent* some collection and disclosure of information in order to *encourage* other disclosures. As you proceed through this chapter, keep in mind these multiple (and at times inconsistent) goals of most health privacy law.

## A. EVIDENTIARY PRIVILEGES

### Dierickx v. Cottage Hospital Corp.

393 N.W. 2d 564 (Mich. App. 1986)

■ PER CURIAM.

This is a medical malpractice suit arising from the birth of plaintiff Deanna Dierickx at defendant Cottage Hospital on May 20, 1980. Deanna's parents, Barbara and George Dierickx, have alleged other injuries to themselves for which they seek damages. Plaintiffs have alleged that Deanna has failed to develop normally and has suffered central nervous system damage, including cerebral palsy, psychomotor retardation, severe mental retardation, and seizure disorder as a proximate result of defendants' negligence and malpractice.

On June 22, 1981, plaintiffs had a second daughter, Katie, a normal, healthy child. On October 3, 1983, during discovery in this case, the Dierickxes had a third child, Kimberly.

At her April 2, 1984, deposition, plaintiff Barbara Dierickx testified that Kimberly began exhibiting neurological abnormalities and problems with vision shortly after birth. She further testified that Kimberly had been hospitalized on at least six different occasions in the first six months of her life in an effort by the Dierickxes to determine the etiology of her medical problems. Defendants obtained certain medical records concerning Kimberly through an error of the copy service. These records indicate that Deanna's condition is shared by Kimberly and that the treating physicians suspect a genetic disorder.

In an effort to fully explore a genetic causation defense theory, defendants moved to compel the production of the medical records of Katie and Kimberly. After a hearing on August 14, 1984, the trial court denied the motion, ruling that the physician-patient privilege was personal to these children and had not been waived. Defendants then moved to compel Katie and Kimberly to submit to a physical examination. After a hearing on August 31, 1984, the trial court denied the motion, apparently ruling that the physician-patient privilege shielded the children from this type of discovery.

The physician-patient privilege is set out in M.C.L. § 600.2157; M.S.A. § 27A.2157, which provides in relevant part:

> No person duly authorized to practice medicine or surgery shall be allowed to disclose any information which he may have acquired in attending any patient in his professional character, and which information was necessary to enable him to prescribe for such patient as a physician, or to do any act for him as a surgeon: Provided, however, That in case such patient shall bring an action against any defendant to recover for any personal injuries, or for any malpractice, if such plaintiff shall produce any physician as a witness in his own behalf, who has treated him for such injury, or for any disease or condition, with reference to which such malpractice is alleged, he shall be deemed to have waived the privilege hereinbefore provided for, as to any or all other physicians, who may have treated him for such injuries, disease or condition. . . .

The purpose of the physician-patient privilege is to enable persons to secure medical aid without betrayal of confidence.

Defendants seek production of the medical records of Katie and Kimberly which would include information acquired by a physician in attending a patient in a professional capacity and necessary to enable that physician to prescribe for the patient. Thus, the requested medical records come within the express terms of the statutory privilege. Being privileged documents, they are not subject to discovery. However, defendants attempt to bring this case within the statute's waiver provision, e.g., a malpractice action brought by a plaintiff-patient. Defendants argue that by bringing this action plaintiffs have placed the physical condition of the family at issue, thereby waiving their right to assert the physician-patient privilege on behalf of family members. We disagree.

The right to assert the physician-patient privilege is personal to the patient. Although Katie and Kimberly are related to plaintiffs, they are not parties to this action. The existence of a genetic defect may be an issue in this litigation, but Katie and Kimberly (or their representatives) have not placed the health of Katie and Kimberly in controversy. Thus, they have not waived the privilege.

Further, plaintiffs have not implicitly waived the statutory privilege as to Katie and Kimberly by bringing this lawsuit. A true waiver is an intentional, voluntary act and cannot arise by implication.

A guardian may legally act for his mentally incompetent ward, a minor, and may obtain access to the ward's medical records by executing a waiver without violating the statutory privilege. By analogy, a parent holds the right to assert the physician-patient privilege on behalf of his or her minor child. Thus, plaintiff Barbara Dierickx may properly assert the statutory privilege on behalf of Katie and Kimberly, while waiving the privilege as to Deanna.

Defendants also contend that the physician-patient privilege is not absolute where it is asserted solely to gain strategic advantage and to conceal evidence likely to establish the truth. The physician-patient privilege has been characterized as "an absolute bar" which prohibits a physician from disclosing even the names of patients who are not involved in litigation. We conclude that the force of the statutory privilege outweighs defendants' concern over plaintiffs' use of it to gain a strategic advantage.

In short, although the requested medical records may be relevant to defendants' theory of a genetically transmitted defect, the records are privileged and not subject to discovery.

Defendants next claim that the trial court erred by denying the request to compel a physical examination of Katie and Kimberly.

GCR 1963, 311.1 governs a request to compel a physical examination and provides:

> In an action in which the mental or physical condition or the blood relationship of a party, or of an agent or a person in the custody or under the legal control of a party, is in controversy, the court in which the action is pending may order the party to submit to a physical or mental or blood examination by a physician or to produce for such examination his agent or the person in his custody or legal control. The order may be made only for good cause shown and upon notice to the person to be examined and to all parties and shall specify the time, place, manner, conditions, and scope of the examination, the person or persons by whom it is to be made, and shall provide that the attorney for the person to be examined may be present at the examination.

This Court reviews a trial court's denial of a request for an order requiring a physical examination for an abuse of discretion.

Although the physician-patient privilege is not controlling, contrary to the trial court's ruling, we agree with the trial court that defendants are not entitled to an order compelling the physical examination of Katie and Kimberly. This result is warranted by the language of the court rule. The physical condition, the mental condition, and the blood relationship of Katie and Kimberly are not "in controversy" in this lawsuit. Instead, the health of Deanna and her parents is "in controversy."

Additional support for this view is found in F. R. Civ. P. 35, the comparable provision of federal civil procedure on which GCR 1963, 311 is modeled. The notes of the advisory committee on the 1970 amendment to F. R. Civ. P. 35(a) state that "[t]he amendment will settle beyond doubt that a parent or guardian suing to recover for injuries to a minor may be ordered to produce the minor for examination." The drafters of the rule did not contemplate a situation in which the examination of a minor nonparty sibling would be requested. Thus, we affirm the trial court's decision even though it was reached for the wrong reason.

## NOTES

1. ***Statutory Creation.*** Note that the court looks to a state statute as the basis for the privilege. Unlike some other ethical or tort duties related to medical information, the physician-patient evidentiary privilege did not exist at common law. Legislatures in many states have recognized some form of a physician-patient privilege in their laws of evidence. But they incorporate different details and exceptions, creating a patchwork of varied requirements across the country. For example, Louisiana law limits waiver of the privilege to testimony during trial or discovery of privileged communications, *see* LA CODE OF EVID. Ann. art. 510(E), while Texas has no such limitation, *see* TEX. R. EVID. 509. *See generally* 45 AM. JUR. PROOF OF FACTS 2D 595 (1986; Supp. 2016).

2. ***Structure of the Privilege.*** Like other privileges you may have studied in an evidence class—including the attorney-client privilege—a physician-related privilege imposes duties on the person being asked to disclose information, at the behest of the subject of that information. Doctors treating Katie and Kimberly Dierickx were not merely permitted to refuse to testify about their medical care (or to produce their records, which amounts to the same thing). They were *forbidden* from doing so, and the court refused to compel such production, because of the privilege. Patients may voluntarily waive that privilege, removing the obligation on their doctors and clearing the way for a subpoena to compel production of testimony or records. But such waivers are not implied lightly. Usually, a plaintiff in a civil action will be found to have waived the privilege concerning the matters placed in controversy by that lawsuit. The defendants are entitled to Deanna's medical records because, unlike her sisters, she waived her privilege (or her parents did so on her behalf) by filing suit.

3. ***Policy Arguments.*** What policy arguments might each side in the *Dierickx* case advance? What negative societal consequences could result from the court upholding the privilege? From finding it waived?

4. ***Medical Information Privileges in Federal Court.*** Despite such rules in many states, there actually is no general physician-patient privilege in federal courts. The committees that drafted the Federal Rules of Evidence included such a privilege in proposed language, but Congress deleted it before the Rules were approved in 1975. Although the Rules give federal courts general power to recognize additional privileges, judges have repeatedly rejected invitations to use that authority to establish a physician-

patient privilege. *See, e.g., United States v. Bek*, 493 F.3d 790, 801–02 (7th Cir. 2007) ("[W]e can find no circuit authority in support of a physician-patient privilege . . . and we can find no reason to create one now."); *United States v. Moore*, 970 F.2d 48, 50 (5th Cir. 1992) ("[T]here is no doctor-patient privilege under federal law."). Under Federal Rule of Evidence 501, state law concerning privileges applies to civil cases otherwise governed by state law. Generally, this means that state privileges will exist in cases where federal jurisdiction is based on diversity of citizenship, but not in criminal cases or in civil cases brought under federal question jurisdiction. There is, however, a federal *psychotherapist*-patient privilege in all cases, recognized by the Supreme Court in *Jaffee v. Redmond*, 518 U.S. 1 (1996). And, as noted in *Dierickx* (and explored further in the next note), the Federal Rules of Civil Procedure limit compelled physical examinations in litigation.

5. ***Rule 35 and Physical Exams.*** While the Federal Rules of Evidence do not contain special protection for medical information, the Federal Rules of Civil Procedure do. Rule 35 allows litigants to compel medical examinations of parties (but only parties) in civil litigation. Unlike any other discovery method, Rule 35 examinations require judicial permission based on a demonstration of good cause. Under Rule 35(a):

> **(1) In General.** The court where the action is pending may order a party whose mental or physical condition—including blood group—is in controversy to submit to a physical or mental examination by a suitably licensed or certified examiner. The court has the same authority to order a party to produce for examination a person who is in its custody or under its legal control.
>
> **(2) Motion and Notice; Contents of the Order.** The order:
>
> > (A) may be made only on motion for good cause and on notice to all parties and the person to be examined; and
> >
> > (B) must specify the time, place, manner, conditions, and scope of the examination, as well as the person or persons who will perform it.

These requirements under Rule 35—the limitation to parties, the degree of judicial oversight, and the need to demonstrate compelling reasons to take the exam—make it the most stringent discovery rule. As the Supreme Court has explained, these burdens

> are not met by mere conclusory allegations of the pleadings—nor by mere relevance to the case—but require an affirmative showing by the movant that each condition as to which the examination is sought is really and genuinely in controversy and that good cause exists for ordering each particular examination. Obviously, what may be good cause for one type of examination may not be so for another. The ability of the movant to obtain the desired information by other means is also relevant.
>
> Rule 35, therefore, requires discriminating application by the trial judge, who must decide, as an initial matter in every case, whether the party requesting a mental or physical examination or

> examinations has adequately demonstrated the existence of the Rule's requirements of 'in controversy' and 'good cause.'

*Schlagenhauf v. Holder*, 379 U.S. 104, 118–19 (1964).

6. ***Genetics and Family Information.*** What is the defendants' argument that an examination of Kimberly and access to Kimberly's records would be relevant to their case? The *Dierickx* case demonstrates how genetic information presents additional privacy challenges. Disclosing information about one family member's genetic makeup often can invade the privacy of other family members. We will examine genetic privacy issues in more detail at the end of this chapter [see Section D].

7. ***Ethical Requirements.*** Even if there is no privilege or a court finds it inapplicable, medical professionals still have independent ethical obligations to maintain patients' confidences. This understanding dates back to ancient times. The famous Oath of Hippocrates, written around 400 B.C., includes this promise:

> Whatever, in connection with my professional practice, or not in connection with it, I see or hear, in the life of men, which ought not to be spoken of abroad, I will not divulge, as reckoning that all such should be kept secret.

This same requirement is embodied in modern professional codes of ethics and in the law of many states. The American Medical Association's Code of Medical Ethics frames this responsibility, while also including exceptions:

> The information disclosed to a physician by a patient should be held in confidence. The patient should feel free to make a full disclosure of information to the physician in order that the physician may most effectively provide needed services. The patient should be able to make this disclosure with the knowledge that the physician will respect the confidential nature of the communication. The physician should not reveal confidential information without the express consent of the patient, subject to certain exceptions which are ethically justified because of overriding considerations.
>
> When a patient threatens to inflict serious physical harm to another person or to him or herself and there is a reasonable probability that the patient may carry out the threat, the physician should take reasonable precautions for the protection of the intended victim, which may include notification of law enforcement authorities.
>
> When the disclosure of confidential information is required by law or court order, physicians generally should notify the patient. Physicians should disclose the minimal information required by law, advocate for the protection of confidential information and, if appropriate, seek a change in the law.

Am. Med. Ass'n, Code of Medical Ethics, Opinion 5.05 (rev'd 2007). Note that, even when presented with a subpoena compelling testimony or the production of records, the AMA's ethics code requires physicians to take a number of steps to safeguard medical information to the maximum extent possible.

## B. TORTS REDUX

### Humphers v. First Interstate Bank of Oregon

696 P.2d 527 (Or. 1985)

■ LINDE, JUSTICE.

We are called upon to decide whether plaintiff [Ramona Humphers] has stated a claim for damages in alleging that her former physician revealed her identity to a daughter whom she had given up for adoption.

In 1959, according to the complaint, plaintiff, then known as Ramona Elwess or by her maiden name, Ramona Jean Peek, gave birth to a daughter in St. Charles Medical Center in Bend, Oregon. She was unmarried at the time, and her physician, Dr. Harry E. Mackey, registered her in the hospital as "Mrs. Jean Smith." The next day, Ramona consented to the child's adoption. The hospital's medical records concerning the birth were sealed and marked to show that they were not public. Ramona subsequently remarried and raised a family. Only Ramona's mother and husband and Dr. Mackey knew about the daughter she had given up for adoption.

Twenty-one years later the daughter, now known as Dawn Kastning, wished to establish contact with her biological mother. Unable to gain access to the confidential court file of her adoption (though apparently able to locate the attending physician), Dawn sought out Dr. Mackey, and he agreed to assist in her quest. Dr. Mackey gave Dawn a letter which stated that he had registered Ramona Jean Peek at the hospital, that although he could not locate his medical records, he remembered administering diethylstilbestrol to her, and that the possible consequences of this medication made it important for Dawn to find her biological mother. The latter statements were untrue and made only to help Dawn to breach the confidentiality of the records concerning her birth and adoption. In 1982, hospital personnel, relying on Dr. Mackey's letter, allowed Dawn to make copies of plaintiff's medical records, which enabled her to locate plaintiff, now Ramona Humphers.

Ramona Humphers was not pleased. The unexpected development upset her and caused her emotional distress, worry, sleeplessness, humiliation, embarrassment, and inability to function normally. She sought damages from the estate of Dr. Mackey, who had died, by this action against defendant as the personal representative. After alleging the facts recounted above, her complaint pleads for relief on five different theories: First, that Dr. Mackey incurred liability for "outrageous conduct"; second, that his disclosure of a professional secret fell short of the care, skill and diligence employed by other physicians in the community and commanded by statute; third, that his disclosure wrongfully breached a confidential or privileged relationship; fourth, that his disclosure of confidential information was an "invasion of privacy" in the form of an "unauthorized intrusion upon plaintiff's seclusion, solitude, and private affairs;" and fifth, that his disclosures to Dawn Kastning breached a contractual obligation of secrecy. The circuit court granted defendant's motion to dismiss the complaint on the grounds that the facts fell short of each theory of relief and ordered entry of judgment for defendant. On appeal, the Court of Appeals affirmed the dismissal of the first, second, and fifth counts but reversed on the third, breach of a confidential relationship, and the fourth, invasion of privacy. We allowed review. We hold that if plaintiff has a claim, it arose from a breach by Dr. Mackey of a professional duty to keep plaintiff's secret rather than from a violation of plaintiff's privacy.

A physician's liability for disclosing confidential information about a patient is not a new problem. In common law jurisdictions it has been more discussed than litigated throughout much of this century. The decisions do not always rest on a single theory.

Sometimes, defendant may have promised confidentiality expressly or by factual implication, in this case perhaps implied by registering a patient in the hospital under an assumed name. A contract claim may be adequate where the breach of confidence causes financial loss, and it may gain a longer period of limitations; but contract law may deny damages for psychic or emotional injury not within the contemplation of the contracting parties, though perhaps this is no barrier when emotional security is the very object of the promised confidentiality. A contract claim is unavailable if the defendant physician was engaged by someone other than the plaintiff, and it would be an awkward fiction at best if age, mental condition, or other circumstances prevent the patient from contracting; yet such a claim might be available to someone less interested than the patient, for instance her husband.

Malpractice claims, based on negligence or statute, in contrast, may offer a plaintiff professional standards of conduct independent of the defendant's assent. Finally, actions for intentional infliction of severe emotional distress fail when the defendant had no such intention or when a defendant was not reckless or did not behave in a manner that a factfinder could find to transcend "the farthest reaches of socially tolerable behavior." Among these diverse precedents, we need only consider the counts of breach of confidential relationship and invasion of privacy on which the Court of Appeals allowed plaintiff to proceed. Plaintiff did not pursue her other theories in her response to the petition for review and we express no view whether the dismissal of those counts was correct.

## PRIVACY

Although claims of a breach of privacy and of wrongful disclosure of confidential information may seem very similar in a case like the present, which involves the disclosure of an intimate personal secret, the two claims depend on different premises and cover different ground.

For our immediate purpose, the most important distinction is that only one who holds information in confidence can be charged with a breach of confidence. If an act qualifies as a tortious invasion of privacy, it theoretically could be committed by anyone. In the present case, Dr. Mackey's professional role is relevant to a claim that he breached a duty of confidentiality, but he could be charged with an invasion of plaintiff's privacy only if anyone else who told Dawn Kastning the facts of her birth without a special privilege to do so would be liable in tort for invading the privacy of her mother.

A daughter's interest in her personal identity here confronts a mother's interest in guarding her own present identity by concealing their joint past. But recognition of an interest or value deserving protection states only half a case. Tort liability depends on the defendant's wrong as well as on the plaintiff's interest, or "right," unless some rule imposes strict liability. One's preferred seclusion or anonymity may be lost in many ways; the question remains who is legally bound to protect those interests at the risk of liability.

[The court reviewed the Restatement privacy torts covered in Chapter 2. It quickly found appropriation inapplicable and held that there was no "publicity" as required for liability under the disclosure tort.]

The Court of Appeals concluded that the complaint alleges a case of tortious intrusion upon plaintiff's seclusion, not by physical means such as uninvited entry, wiretapping, photography, or the like, but in the sense of an offensive prying into personal matters that plaintiff reasonably has sought to keep private. We do not believe that the theory fits this case.

Doubtless plaintiff's interest qualifies as a "privacy" interest. That does not require the judgment of a court or a jury; it is established by the statutes that close adoption records to inspection without a court order. The statutes are designed to protect privacy interests of the natural parents, the adoptive parents, or the child. But as already stated, to identify an interest deserving protection does not suffice to collect damages from anyone who causes injury to that interest. Dr. Mackey helped Dawn Kastning find her biological mother, but we are not prepared to assume that Ms. Kastning became liable for invasion of privacy in seeking her out. Nor, we think, would anyone who knew the facts without an obligation of secrecy commit a tort simply by telling them to Ms. Kastning.

Dr. Mackey himself did not approach plaintiff or pry into any personal facts that he did not know; indeed, if he had written or spoken to his former patient to tell her that her daughter was eager to find her, it would be hard to describe such a communication alone as an invasion of privacy. The point of the claim against Dr. Mackey is not that he pried into a confidence but that he failed to keep one. If Dr. Mackey incurred liability for that, it must result from an obligation of confidentiality beyond any general duty of people at large not to invade one another's privacy. We therefore turn to plaintiff's claim that Dr. Mackey was liable for a breach of confidence, the third count of the complaint.

## BREACH OF CONFIDENCE

It takes less judicial innovation to recognize this claim than the Court of Appeals thought. A number of decisions have held that unauthorized and unprivileged disclosure of confidential information obtained in a confidential relationship can give rise to tort damages.

It requires more than custom to impose legal restraints on "the right to speak, write, or print freely on any subject whatever." Or. Const., Art. I, § 8. Tort liability, of course, may be a remedy for "injury to person, property, or reputation," Or. Const., Art. I, § 10, even by speech. But a legal duty not to speak, unless voluntarily assumed in entering the relationship, will not be imposed by courts or jurors in the name of custom or reasonable expectations. Tort liability is the consequence of a nonconsensual duty of silence, not its source.

In the case of the medical profession, courts in fact have found sources of a nonconsensual duty of confidentiality. Some have thought such a duty toward the patient implicit in the patient's statutory privilege to exclude the doctor's testimony in litigation, enacted in this state. More directly in point are legal duties imposed as a condition of engaging in the professional practice of medicine or other occupations.

This strikes us as the right approach to a claim of liability outside obligations undertaken expressly or implied in fact in entering a contractual relationship. The contours of the asserted duty of confidentiality are determined by a legal source external to the tort claim itself. A plaintiff asserting a breach of such a nonconsensual duty must identify its source and terms. If the tort claim asserts violation of a statute or regulation, the rule must validly apply to the facts, whether or not it actually is applied by those responsible for enforcement.

Because the duty of confidentiality is determined by standards outside the tort claim for its breach, so are the defenses of privilege or justification. Physicians, like members of many ordinarily confidential professions and occupations, also may be legally obliged to report medical information to others for the protection of the patient, of other individuals, or of the public. See, e.g., ORS 418.750 (physician's duty to report child abuse); ORS 433.003, 434.020 (duty to report certain diseases). Even without such a legal obligation, there may be a privilege to disclose information for the safety of individuals or important to the public in matters of public interest. A physician or other member of a regulated occupation is not to be held to a noncontractual duty of secrecy in a tort action when disclosure would not be a breach or would be privileged in direct enforcement of the underlying duty.

A physician's duty to keep medical and related information about a patient in confidence is beyond question. It is imposed by statute. ORS 677.190(5) provides for disqualifying or otherwise disciplining a physician for "wilfully or negligently divulging a professional secret."

It is less obvious whether Dr. Mackey violated ORS 677.190(5) when he told Dawn Kastning what he knew of her birth. She was not, after all, a stranger to that proceeding. If Ms. Kastning needed information about her natural mother for medical reasons, as Dr. Mackey pretended, the State Board of Medical Examiners likely would find the disclosure privileged against a charge under ORS 677.190(5); but the statement is alleged to have been a pretext designed to give her access to the hospital records. If only ORS 677.190(5) were involved, we do not know how the Board would judge a physician who assists at the birth of a child and decades later reveals to that person his or her parentage. But as already noted, other statutes specifically mandate the secrecy of adoption records. ORS 7.211 provides that court records in adoption cases may not be inspected or disclosed except upon court order, and ORS 432.420 requires a court order before sealed adoption records may be opened by the state registrar. Given these clear legal constraints, there is no privilege to disregard the professional duty imposed by ORS 677.190(5) solely in order to satisfy the curiosity of the person who was given up for adoption.

For these reasons, we agree with the Court of Appeals that plaintiff may proceed under her claim of breach of confidentiality in a confidential relationship. The decision of the Court of Appeals is reversed with respect to plaintiff's claim of invasion of privacy and affirmed with respect to her claim of breach of confidence in a confidential relationship, and the case is remanded to the circuit court for further proceedings on that claim.

## NOTES

1. ***Confidentiality vs. Other Legal Theories.*** Summarize the reasons the court rejects the plaintiff's traditional privacy tort claims in *Humphers* but denies the motion to dismiss her claim for breach of confidentiality. Do you agree with the analysis? Of course, on some facts, medical professionals could be liable under the other theories too. You may recall disclosure tort cases brought against health care institutions, such as *Yath v. Fairview Clinics* and *Y.G. v. Jewish Hospital* [see Chapter 2]. Do those cases undermine the justification for adopting a separate theory like confidentiality?

2. ***Malpractice as an Alternative.*** The Oregon Supreme Court did not rule on the applicability of medical malpractice because the plaintiff had dropped this claim. The intermediate appellate court had considered and rejected it, however, on the following basis:

> An action for medical malpractice will only lie for activities in which the defendant was involved in the practice of medicine. The issue, therefore, is whether Mackey's action in revealing plaintiff's name and giving the letter to Dawn over 20 years after he had terminated his treatment constitutes the practice of medicine. We hold that it does not.
>
> Nothing that Mackey did in 1980 had or could have had any medical effect on plaintiff's condition. In fact, the condition for which Mackey had treated plaintiff (pregnancy) had not been in existence for 20 years. The mere fact that Mackey utilized his medical records to enable him to take the action in 1980 does not make the action the practice of medicine.

*Humphers v. First Interstate Bank of Oregon*, 684 P.2d 581, 584 (Or. App. 1984). How do you think the Oregon Supreme Court would have ruled on this point?

3. ***Spread of the Breach of Confidentiality.*** The law in a majority of states now recognizes some tort duty of confidentiality requiring that doctors not disclose information about their patients. Like the ethical and evidentiary rules, the exact details of the various torts differ from one state to the next and they all have significant exceptions.

4. ***Connection with Other Laws.*** Note how heavily the *Humphers* analysis of the confidentiality tort depends on surrounding state laws, such as those concerning physician licensing or adoption records. Does this reliance of the breach of confidentiality tort upon other legal duties represent a strength of the tort, or a weakness?

5. ***Breach of Confidentiality as an Alternative to Privacy Torts.*** Instead of developing a common law right of privacy along the lines of the *Restatement* torts, the English legal system has expanded its breach of confidentiality tort far beyond the boundaries recognized in the United States [see Chapter 2]. The Humphers court emphasizes the central role of professional duty in the distinctive claim for breach of confidentiality. Is that a necessary component? Neil Richards and Daniel Solove have argued that a tort like the British version of breach of confidence, which extends to many nonprofessional relationships, would fill gaps left by the Restatement torts. Neil M. Richards & Daniel J. Solove, *Privacy's Other Path: Recovering the Law of Confidentiality*, 96 GEO. L.J. 123, 126 (2007). What are the advantages and disadvantages to the English approach? What would Justice Linde, the author of *Humphers*, think of this argument?

6. ***Adoption and Privacy.*** Adoption records provide an excellent example of the impact of changing social attitudes on privacy rules. Until the 1980s and 1990s, most adoptions in the United States were "closed adoptions" like the one in *Humphers*, where the adopted child has no access to information about biological parents, and usually the biological parents do not know specific information about the adoptive family. Today, almost all domestic adoptions in the U.S. are "open adoptions"—which, as the name suggests, are just the reverse. Typically the biological and adoptive parents meet before a baby is born; often the biological mother selects the adoptive

family. In many cases, there are arrangements for continued contact as the child grows up, sometimes including correspondence or periodic visits. While older adoption records usually remain sealed based upon the expectations of biological parents who agreed to closed adoptions, states have become much more willing to unseal those records in particular cases. Some 31 states have also established "mutual consent registries," where biological parents and adopted children can sign up to indicate their consent for disclosure of records and possibly contact. Critics, including some adoptees, have argued that these measures are still too restrictive. They maintain that they are entitled to information, both to discover potentially important family medical history and to satisfy the emotional yearning some adopted children have to learn about their origins. It can be difficult to reconcile these attitudes with the commitments made to biological parents in earlier eras. Whose interests should prevail in these situations? In a state that had already liberalized statutes about adoption records, might the facts in *Humphers* then fail to state a claim for breach confidentiality?

## Tarasoff v. Regents of the University of California

551 P.2d 334 (Cal. 1976)

■ TOBRINER, JUSTICE.

On October 27, 1969, Prosenjit Poddar killed Tatiana Tarasoff. Plaintiffs, Tatiana's parents, allege that two months earlier Poddar confided his intention to kill Tatiana to Dr. Lawrence Moore, a psychologist employed by the Cowell Memorial Hospital at the University of California at Berkeley. They allege that on Moore's request, the campus police briefly detained Poddar, but released him when he appeared rational. They further claim that Dr. Harvey Powelson, Moore's superior, then directed that no further action be taken to detain Poddar. No one warned plaintiffs of Tatiana's peril.

Plaintiffs' complaints predicate liability on defendants' failure to warn plaintiffs of the impending danger. Defendants, in turn, assert that they owed no duty of reasonable care to Tatiana.

We shall explain that defendant therapists cannot escape liability merely because Tatiana herself was not their patient. When a therapist determines, or pursuant to the standards of his profession should determine, that his patient presents a serious danger of violence to another, he incurs an obligation to use reasonable care to protect the intended victim against such danger. The discharge of this duty may require the therapist to take one or more of various steps, depending upon the nature of the case. Thus it may call for him to warn the intended victim or others likely to apprise the victim of the danger, to notify the police, or to take whatever other steps are reasonably necessary under the circumstances.

In the case at bar, plaintiffs admit that defendant therapists notified the police, but argue on appeal that the therapists failed to exercise reasonable care to protect Tatiana in that they did not confine Poddar and did not warn Tatiana or others likely to apprise her of the danger.

[The trial court dismissed the complaint for failure to state a claim. According to the allegations in the complaint,] on August 20, 1969, Poddar was a voluntary outpatient receiving therapy at Cowell Memorial Hospital. Poddar informed Moore, his therapist, that he was going to kill an unnamed girl, readily identifiable as Tatiana, when she returned home from spending the summer in Brazil. Moore, with the concurrence of Dr. Gold, who had initially examined Poddar, and Dr. Yandell, [a]ssistant to the director of the department of psychiatry, decided that Poddar should be committed for observation in a mental hospital. Moore orally notified Officers Atkinson and Teel of the campus police that he would request commitment. He then sent a letter to Police Chief William Beall requesting the assistance of the police department in securing Poddar's confinement.

Officers Atkinson, Brownrigg, and Halleran took Poddar into custody, but, satisfied that Poddar was rational, released him on his promise to stay away from Tatiana. Powelson, director of the department of psychiatry at Cowell Memorial Hospital, then asked the police to return Moore's letter, directed that all copies of the letter and notes that Moore had taken as therapist be destroyed, and "ordered no action to place Prosenjit Poddar in 72-hour treatment and evaluation facility."

The [complaint] can be amended to allege that Tatiana's death proximately resulted from defendants' negligent failure to warn Tatiana or others likely to apprise her of her danger. Plaintiffs contend that as amended, such allegations of negligence and proximate causation, with resulting damages, establish a cause of action. Defendants, however, contend that in the circumstances of the present case they owed no duty of care to Tatiana or her parents and that, in the absence of such duty, they were free to act in careless disregard of Tatiana's life and safety.

As a general principle, a defendant owes a duty of care to all persons who are foreseeably endangered by his conduct, with respect to all risks which make the conduct unreasonably dangerous. As we shall explain, however, when the avoidance of foreseeable harm requires a defendant to control the conduct of another person, or to warn of such conduct, the common law has traditionally imposed liability only if the defendant bears some special relationship to the dangerous person or to the potential victim. Since the relationship between a therapist and his patient satisfies this requirement, we need not here decide whether foreseeability alone is sufficient to create a duty to exercise reasonabl[e] care to protect a potential victim of another's conduct.

Although plaintiffs' pleadings assert no special relation between Tatiana and defendant therapists, they establish as between Poddar and defendant therapists the special relation that arises between a patient and his doctor or psychotherapist. Such a relationship may support affirmative duties for the benefit of third persons. Thus, for example, a hospital must exercise reasonable care to control the behavior of a patient which may endanger other persons. A doctor must also warn a patient if the patient's condition or medication renders certain conduct, such as driving a car, dangerous to others.

Decisions of other jurisdictions hold that the single relationship of a doctor to his patient is sufficient to support the duty to exercise reasonable care to protect others against dangers emanating from the patient's illness. The courts hold that a doctor is liable to persons infected by his patient if he negligently fails to diagnose a contagious disease or, having diagnosed the illness, fails to warn members of the patient's family.

There now seems to be sufficient authority to support the conclusion that by entering into a doctor-patient relationship the therapist becomes sufficiently involved to assume some responsibility for the safety, not only of the patient himself, but also of any third person whom the doctor knows to be threatened by the patient.

Defendants contend, however, that imposition of a duty to exercise reasonable care to protect third persons is unworkable because therapists cannot accurately predict whether or not a patient will resort to violence. In support of this argument amicus representing the American Psychiatric Association and other professional societies cites numerous articles which indicate that therapists, in the present state of the art, are unable reliably to predict violent acts; their forecasts, amicus claims, tend consistently to overpredict violence, and indeed are more often wrong than right. Since predictions of violence are often erroneous, amicus concludes, the courts should not render rulings that predicate the liability of therapists upon the validity of such predictions.

The role of the psychiatrist, who is indeed a practitioner of medicine, and that of the psychologist who performs an allied function, are like that of the physician who must conform to the standards of the profession and who must often make diagnoses and predictions based upon such evaluations. Thus the judgment of the therapist in diagnosing emotional disorders and in predicting whether a patient presents a serious danger of violence is comparable to the judgment which doctors and professionals must regularly render under accepted rules of responsibility.

We recognize the difficulty that a therapist encounters in attempting to forecast whether a patient presents a serious danger of violence. Obviously we do not require that the therapist, in making that determination, render a perfect performance; the therapist need only exercise that reasonable degree of skill, knowledge, and care ordinarily possessed and exercised by members of that professional specialty under similar circumstances. Within the broad range of reasonable practice and treatment in which professional opinion and judgment may differ, the therapist is free to exercise his or her own best judgment without liability; proof, aided by hindsight, that he or she judged wrongly is insufficient to establish negligence.

In the instant case, however, the pleadings do not raise any question as to failure of defendant therapists to predict that Poddar presented a serious danger of violence. On the contrary, the present complaints allege that defendant therapists did in fact predict that Poddar would kill, but were negligent in failing to warn.

The risk that unnecessary warnings may be given is a reasonable price to pay for the lives of possible victims that may be saved. We would hesitate to hold that the therapist who is aware that his patient expects to attempt to assassinate the President of the United States would not be obligated to warn the authorities because the therapist cannot predict with accuracy that his patient will commit the crime.

We recognize the public interest in supporting effective treatment of mental illness and in protecting the rights of patients to privacy, and the consequent public importance of safeguarding the confidential character of psychotherapeutic communication. Against this interest, however, we must weigh the public interest in safety from violent assault. The Legislature has undertaken the difficult task of balancing the countervailing concerns. In Evidence Code section 1014, it established a broad rule of privilege to protect confidential communications between patient and psychotherapist. In Evidence Code section 1024, the Legislature created a specific and limited exception to the psychotherapist-patient privilege: "There is no privilege . . . if the psychotherapist has reasonable cause to believe that the patient is in such mental or emotional condition as to be dangerous to himself or to the person or property of another and that disclosure of the communication is necessary to prevent the threatened danger."

We realize that the open and confidential character of psychotherapeutic dialogue encourages patients to express threats of violence, few of which are ever executed. Certainly a therapist should not be encouraged routinely to reveal such threats; such disclosures could seriously disrupt the patient's relationship with his therapist and with the persons threatened. To the contrary, the therapist's obligations to his patient require that he not disclose a confidence unless such disclosure is necessary to avert danger to others, and even then that he do so discreetly, and in a fashion that would preserve the privacy of his patient to the fullest extent compatible with the prevention of the threatened danger.

The revelation of a communication under the above circumstances is not a breach of trust or a violation of professional ethics; as stated in the Principles of Medical Ethics of the American Medical Association (1957), section 9: 'A physician may not reveal the confidence entrusted to him in the course of medical attendance . . . *unless he is required to do so by law or unless it becomes necessary in order to protect the welfare of the individual or of the community*." [Emphasis added by court.] We conclude that the public policy favoring protection of the confidential character of patient-psychotherapist communications must yield to the extent to which disclosure is essential to avert danger to others. The protective privilege ends where the public peril begins.

Our current crowded and computerized society compels the interdependence of its members. In this risk-infested society we can hardly tolerate the further exposure to danger that would result from a concealed knowledge of the therapist that his patient was lethal. If the exercise of reasonable care to protect the threatened victim requires the therapist to warn the endangered party or those who can reasonably be expected to notify him, we see no sufficient societal interest that would protect and justify concealment. The containment of such risks lies in the public interest For the foregoing reasons, we find that plaintiffs' complaints can be amended to state a cause of action against defendants Moore, Powelson, Gold, and Yandell and against the Regents as their employer, for breach of a duty to exercise reasonable care to protect Tatiana.

■ MOSK, JUSTICE (concurring and dissenting).

I concur in the result in this instance only because the complaints allege that defendant therapists did in fact predict that Poddar would kill and were therefore negligent in failing to warn of that danger. Thus the issue here is very narrow: we are not concerned with whether the therapists, pursuant to the standards of their profession, "should have" predicted potential violence; they allegedly did so in actuality. Under these limited circumstances I agree that a cause of action can be stated.

Whether plaintiffs can ultimately prevail is problematical at best. As the complaints admit, the therapists did notify the police that Poddar was planning to kill a girl identifiable as Tatiana. While I doubt that more should be required, this issue may be raised in defense and its determination is a question of fact.

I cannot concur, however, in the majority's rule that a therapist may be held liable for failing to predict his patient's tendency to violence if other practitioners, pursuant to the "standards of the profession," would have done so. The question is, what standards? Defendants and a responsible amicus curiae, supported by an impressive body of literature, demonstrate that psychiatric predictions of violence are inherently unreliable.

I would restructure the rule designed by the majority to eliminate all reference to conformity to standards of the profession in predicting violence. If a psychiatrist does in fact predict violence, then a duty to warn arises. The majority's expansion of that rule will take us from the world of reality into the wonderland of clairvoyance.

■ CLARK, JUSTICE (dissenting).

Overwhelming policy considerations weigh against imposing a duty on psychotherapists to warn a potential victim against harm. While offering virtually no benefit to society, such a duty will frustrate psychiatric treatment, invade fundamental patient rights and increase violence.

The importance of psychiatric treatment and its need for confidentiality have been recognized by this court. It is clearly recognized that the very practice of psychiatry vitally depends upon the reputation in the community that the psychiatrist will not tell.

Given the importance of confidentiality to the practice of psychiatry, it becomes clear the duty to warn imposed by the majority will cripple the use and effectiveness of psychiatry. Many people, potentially violent—yet susceptible to treatment—will be deterred from seeking it; those seeking it will be inhibited from making revelations necessary to effective treatment; and, forcing the psychiatrist to violate the patient's trust will destroy the interpersonal relationship by which treatment is effected.

By imposing a duty to warn, the majority contributes to the danger to society of violence by the mentally ill and greatly increases the risk of civil commitment—the total deprivation of liberty—of those who should not be confined. The impairment of treatment and risk of improper commitment resulting from the new duty to warn will not be limited to a few patients but will extend to a large number of the mentally ill. Although under existing psychiatric procedures only a relatively few receiving treatment will ever present a risk of violence, the number making threats is huge, and it is the latter group—not just the former—whose treatment will be impaired and whose risk of commitment will be increased.

Both the legal and psychiatric communities recognize that the process of determining potential violence in a patient is far from exact, being fraught with complexity and uncertainty.

This predictive uncertainty means that the number of disclosures will necessarily be large. As noted above, psychiatric patients are encouraged to discuss all thoughts of violence, and they often express such thoughts. However, unlike this court, the psychiatrist does not enjoy the benefit of overwhelming hindsight in seeing which few, if any, of his patients will ultimately become violent. Now, confronted by the majority's new duty, the psychiatrist must instantaneously calculate potential violence from each patient on each visit. The difficulties researchers have encountered in accurately predicting violence will be heightened for the practicing psychiatrist dealing for brief periods in his office with heretofore nonviolent patients. And, given the decision not to warn or commit must always be made at the psychiatrist's civil peril, one can expect most doubts will be resolved in favor of the psychiatrist protecting himself.

We should accept legislative and medical judgment, relying upon effective treatment rather than on indiscriminate warning.

The judgment should be affirmed.

## NOTES

1. ***The Spread of the* Tarasoff *Rule.*** A majority of states now recognize something like the *Tarasoff* rule. A number of courts have applied the duty in situations, unlike *Tarasoff*, where the defendant therapist claimed not to have reached any conclusive determination that the patient posed a potential threat. *See, e.g.*, *McIntosh v. Milano*, 403 A.2d 500, 508 (N.J. Super. 1979) ("It may be true that there cannot be a 100% [a]ccurate prediction of dangerousness in all cases. . . . Where reasonable men might differ and a fact issue exists, the therapist is only held to the standard for a therapist in the particular field in the particular community."). Since countless violent people still seek therapy, does the widespread adoption of the rule suggest that the dissent's dire predictions were unwarranted? In a footnote, the dissent noted one opinion survey in which "five of every seven people interviewed said they would be less likely to make full disclosure to a psychiatrist in the absence of assurance of confidentiality."

2. ***Disclosing Limits on Confidentiality.*** Should a therapist inform a client about the limitations on confidentiality? If so, should the notice be given at the beginning of the counseling relationship, or just whenever a patient begins to veer into topics that may require disclosure? If you were advising a therapist about the best policy, what would you recommend? What concerns do you think the therapist might have about your advice? How do attorneys handle disclosures to their clients about the boundaries of confidentiality?

3. ***Communicable Disease Reporting.*** As *Tarasoff* notes, there are numerous requirements for medical professionals to disclose otherwise confidential health information. For many decades, state laws have required physicians to report information about communicable diseases—sometimes to a government body like the health department, sometimes to family members or others potentially exposed to the disease, and sometimes to both. For example, at least 33 states have laws requiring that sexual partners of persons diagnosed with HIV receive notifications. These laws were particularly controversial because there has been so much social stigma associated with AIDS and because so many people infected with HIV are gay men, many of whom may consider their sexual orientation private. How do reporting requirements for communicable diseases resemble the *Tarasoff* rule and how are they different?

4. ***Child Abuse Reporting.*** Almost all states also require that professionals report indications of child abuse to the authorities. These "mandatory reporter" rules often apply not only to medical and psychological professionals, but also to others who may interact with children in their official capacity, such as teachers, day care workers, social workers, or law enforcement officers. These rules usually require a report when, in his or her official capacity, an individual suspects or has reason to believe a child has been abused or neglected; the applicability of the law may also depend on whether the mandatory reporter knows a child is in a condition that would

reasonably result in harm to the child. Failure to report in some states may result in criminal punishment ranging from misdemeanor to felony charges. How do these reporting requirements resemble the *Tarasoff* rule and how are they different?

5. ***Controlled Substance Prescriptions.*** Still another requirement for reporting and tracking medical information arises when health care providers authorize the use of controlled substances that otherwise might be classified as illegal drugs. This was the data collection at the heart of the Supreme Court's 1977 decision in *Whalen v. Roe*, 429 U.S. 589 (1977) [see Chapter 1], which involved prescriptions opiates and other highly regulated Schedule II drugs. A more recent development is the rise of medical marijuana laws that allow the use of cannabis to treat pain and certain chronic medical conditions. Roughly half the states have enacted some form of these laws; almost all of them require a patient registry or identification cards for authorized patients and approval of a medical professional.

6. ***Disincentives for Treatment.*** The majority in *Whalen v. Roe* considered and rejected an argument that a legal reporting requirement for the prescription of controlled substances would inhibit the use of potentially valuable therapies:

> Unquestionably, some individuals' concern for their own privacy may lead them to avoid or to postpone needed medical attention. Nevertheless, disclosures of private medical information to doctors, to hospital personnel, to insurance companies, and to public health agencies are often an essential part of modern medical practice even when the disclosure may reflect unfavorably on the character of the patient. Requiring such disclosures to representatives of the State having responsibility for the health of the community, does not automatically amount to an impermissible invasion of privacy.

429 U.S. 589, 602–03 (1977). How does this rationale compare to *Tarasoff*? Can patient inhibitions on their own ever be strong enough to justify constitutional or tort privacy protection?

7. ***Disclosures with Discretion.*** The majority decision emphasizes that, even when a therapist must reveal information about a possible danger, the disclosure must be made "discreetly, and in a fashion that would preserve the privacy of his patient to the fullest extent compatible with the prevention of the threatened danger."If you were counseling a therapist about the appropriate way to fulfill *Tarasoff* obligations if they ever arose, specifically what would you advise?

8. ***Reconciling* Humphers *and* Tarasoff.** Are *Humphers* and *Tarasoff* inconsistent with each other? Is a psychiatrist caught between two conflicting duties of care under these two cases?

## C. HEALTH PRIVACY STATUTES AND REGULATIONS

### 1. THE HIPAA PRIVACY RULE

Even people who know very little about privacy law may have a passing familiarity with "HIPAA"—the Health Insurance Portability and Accountability Act of 1996. Congress passed this broad-based law primarily to enact health insurance reforms, but instead it has become widely known because it created the most comprehensive federal privacy requirements in the US. The legislation sought to encourage the development of electronic health records, which have been demonstrated to reduce both health care costs and the risk of medical errors, but advocates noted this shift would also intensify privacy concerns. An amendment to the bill instructed the Department of Health and Human Services (HHS) to develop regulations for privacy of electronic health records if Congress failed to enact its own privacy law by a deadline three years later. The objective was to spur Congress to action, but—unsurprisingly to those who have observed Congress in the two decades since then—this tactic failed and no legislation passed before the deadline.

Consequently, HHS developed regulations, generally known as the HIPAA Privacy Rule and the HIPAA Security Rule. *See* 45 C.F.R. Parts 160, 162, and 164. As the material below explains in greater detail, HIPAA restrictions apply only to "covered entities," essentially (1) health care providers (such as doctors and hospitals) who use electronic transmissions in certain circumstances; (2) health insurers, and (3) health care clearinghouses. The regulations were supplemented later with the enactment of the 2009 Health Information Technology for Economic and Clinical Health Act (HITECH Act), which added additional privacy and security requirements and increased responsibilities for "business associates" of covered entities—separate organizations that perform functions for the covered entities that require access to protected data. The first excerpt that follows contains just about the entirety of the instructions Congress issued to HHS in HIPAA. The resulting regulations take up well over 100 pages in very small print; the second excerpt contains one of its less convoluted provisions, just so you have a sample of the regulations. It is followed by a judicial decision considering a challenge to that portion of the regulations. Finally, you will read from an informal summary of the entire Privacy Rule provided by HHS.

## Health Insurance Portability and Accountability Act

Public Law 104–191 (104th Cong. 1996)

### Sec. 264. Recommendations With Respect to Privacy of Certain Health Information.

(a) In General.—Not later than the date that is 12 months after the date of the enactment of this Act, the Secretary of Health and Human Services shall submit to the Committee on Labor and Human Resources and the Committee on Finance of the Senate and the Committee on Commerce and the Committee on Ways and Means of the House of Representatives detailed recommendations on standards with respect to the privacy of individually identifiable health information.

(b) Subjects for Recommendations.—The recommendations under subsection (a) shall address at least the following:

(1) The rights that an individual who is a subject of individually identifiable health information should have.

(2) The procedures that should be established for the exercise of such rights.

(3) The uses and disclosures of such information that should be authorized or required.

(c) Regulations.—

(1) In General.—If legislation governing standards with respect to the privacy of individually identifiable health information . . . is not enacted by the date that is 36 months after the date of the enactment of this Act, the Secretary of Health and Human Services shall promulgate final regulations containing such standards not later than the date that is 42 months after the date of the enactment of this Act. Such regulations shall address at least the subjects described in subsection (b).

(2) Preemption.—A regulation promulgated under paragraph (1) shall not supercede a contrary provision of State law, if the provision of State law imposes requirements, standards, or implementation specifications that are more stringent than the requirements, standards, or implementation specifications imposed under the regulation.

(d) Consultation.—In carrying out this section, the Secretary of Health and Human Services shall consult with—

(1) the National Committee on Vital and Health Statistics established under section 306(k) of the Public Health Service Act (42 U.S.C. 242k(k)); and

(2) the Attorney General.

# HIPAA Privacy Rule

45 C.F.R. Part 164

## SUBPART E—PRIVACY OF INDIVIDUALLY IDENTIFIABLE HEALTH INFORMATION

### § 164.506 Uses and disclosures to carry out treatment, payment, or health care operations.

(a) **Standard: Permitted uses and disclosures.** Except with respect to uses or disclosures that require an authorization under § 164.508(a)(2) through (4) or that are prohibited under § 164.502(a)(5)(i), a covered entity may use or disclose protected health information for treatment, payment, or health care operations as set forth in paragraph (c) of this section, provided that such use or disclosure is consistent with other applicable requirements of this subpart.

**(b) Standard: Consent for uses and disclosures permitted.**

(1) A covered entity may obtain consent of the individual to use or disclose protected health information to carry out treatment, payment, or health care operations.

(2) Consent, under paragraph (b) of this section, shall not be effective to permit a use or disclosure of protected health information when an authorization, under § 164.508, is required or when another condition must be met for such use or disclosure to be permissible under this subpart.

**(c) Implementation specifications: Treatment, payment, or health care operations.**

(1) A covered entity may use or disclose protected health information for its own treatment, payment, or health care operations. [These terms are defined elsewhere in the Rule.]

(2) A covered entity may disclose protected health information for treatment activities of a health care provider.

(3) A covered entity may disclose protected health information to another covered entity or a health care provider for the payment activities of the entity that receives the information.

(4) A covered entity may disclose protected health information to another covered entity for health care operations activities of the entity that receives the information, if each entity either has or had a relationship with the individual who is the subject of the protected health information being requested, the protected health information pertains to such relationship, and the disclosure is:

> (i) For a purpose listed in paragraph (1) or (2) of the definition of health care operations [which are found in § 164.501 and are:]
>
> ["Conducting quality assessment and improvement activities, including outcomes evaluation and development of clinical guidelines, provided that the obtaining of generalizable

knowledge is not the primary purpose of any studies resulting from such activities; patient safety activities (as defined in 42 C.F.R. § 3.20); population-based activities relating to improving health or reducing health care costs, protocol development, case management and care coordination, contacting of health care providers and patients with information about treatment alternatives; and related functions that do not include treatment;" and]

["Reviewing the competence or qualifications of health care professionals, evaluating practitioner and provider performance, health plan performance, conducting training programs in which students, trainees, or practitioners in areas of health care learn under supervision to practice or improve their skills as health care providers, training of non-health care professionals, accreditation, certification, licensing, or credentialing activities;"]

or

(ii) For the purpose of health care fraud and abuse detection or compliance.

(5) A covered entity that participates in an organized health care arrangement may disclose protected health information about an individual to other participants in the organized health care arrangement for any health care operations activities of the organized health care arrangement.

## Citizens for Health v. Leavitt

428 F.3d 167 (3d Cir. 2005)

■ RENDELL, CIRCUIT JUDGE.

Appellant Citizens for Health, along with nine other national and state associations and nine individuals (collectively "Citizens"), brought this action against the Secretary of the United States Department of Health and Human Services ("HHS" or "Agency") challenging a rule promulgated by the Agency pursuant to the administrative simplification provisions of the Health Insurance Portability and Accountability Act of 1996 ("HIPAA"). Citizens allege that the "Privacy Rule"—officially titled "Standards for Privacy of Individually Identifiable Health Information"—is invalid because it unlawfully authorizes health plans, health care clearinghouses, and certain health care providers to use and disclose personal health information for so-called "routine uses" without patient consent. The relevant part of the specific offending provision of the Privacy Rule reads:

(a) Standard: Permitted uses and disclosures. Except with respect to uses or disclosures that require an authorization under § 164.508(a)(2) [relating to psychotherapy notes] and (3)

> [relating to marketing], a covered entity *may use* or disclose protected health information for treatment, payment, or health care operations . . . provided that such use or disclosure is consistent with other applicable requirements of this subpart.
>
> (b) Standard: Consent for uses and disclosures permitted. (1) A covered entity *may* obtain consent of the individual to use or disclose protected health information to carry out treatment, payment, or health care operations.
>
> (2) Consent, under paragraph (b) of this section, shall not be effective to permit a use or disclosure of protected health information when an authorization, under § 164.508, is required or when another condition must be met for such use or disclosure to be permissible under this subpart.

45 C.F.R. § 164.506 [emphasis added by court].

Citizens challenge subsection (a) as authorizing disclosures that, they contend, violate individual privacy rights.

The District Court granted summary judgment to the Secretary on all of Citizens' claims. Because we reason to the same conclusions reached by the District Court, albeit under a slightly different analysis, we will affirm.

## Background

The objectionable provision is only one aspect of a complex set of regulations that is the last in a series of attempts by HHS to strike a balance between two competing objectives of HIPAA—improving the efficiency and effectiveness of the national health care system and preserving individual privacy in personal health information.

### A. HIPAA

HIPAA was passed by Congress in August 1996 to address a number of issues regarding the national health care and health insurance system. The statutory provisions relevant to the issues in this case are found in Subtitle F of Title II. Aimed at "administrative simplification," HIPAA Sections 261 through 264 provide for "the establishment of standards and requirements for the electronic transmission of certain health information." More specifically, these provisions direct the Secretary to adopt uniform national standards for the secure electronic exchange of health information.

Section 264 prescribes the process by which standards regarding the privacy of individually identifiable health information were to be adopted. This process contemplated that, within a year of HIPAA's enactment, the Secretary would submit detailed recommendations on such privacy standards, including individual rights concerning individually identifiable health information, procedures for exercising such rights, and the "uses and disclosures of such information that should be authorized or required," to Congress. If Congress did not enact further legislation within three years of HIPAA's enactment, the Secretary was directed to promulgate final regulations implementing the standards within 42 months of HIPAA's enactment. The Act specified that any regulation promulgated pursuant to the authority of Section 264 would provide a federal baseline for privacy protection, but that such regulations would "not supersede a contrary provision of State law, if the provision of State law imposes requirements, standards, or implementation specifications that are more stringent than the requirements, standards, or implementation specifications imposed under the regulation."

## B. The Privacy Rule

Because Congress did not enact privacy legislation by its self-imposed three-year deadline, the Secretary promulgated the privacy standards contemplated in Section 264 through an administrative rulemaking process. During this process, the Rule went through four iterations: the Proposed Original Rule, the Original Rule, the Proposed Amended Rule, and the Amended Rule. The Original Rule *required* covered entities to seek individual consent before using or disclosing protected health information for routine uses. Before the Original Rule could take effect, however, the Secretary was inundated with unsolicited criticism, principally from health care insurers and providers, warning that the Original Rule's mandatory consent provisions would significantly impact the ability of the health care industry to operate efficiently. He responded by reopening the rulemaking process. The final result was the Amended Rule—the currently effective, codified version of the Privacy Rule, which is the subject of Citizens' challenge here.

The Amended Rule retains most of the Original Rule's privacy protections. It prohibits "covered entities"—defined as health plans, health care clearinghouses, and health care providers who transmit any health information in electronic form in connection with a transaction covered by the regulations—from using or disclosing an individual's "protected health information"—defined as individually identifiable health information maintained in or transmitted in any form or media including electronic media—except as otherwise provided by the Rule. Covered entities must seek authorization from individuals before using or disclosing information unless a specific exception applies. Uses and disclosures that the Amended Rule allows must be limited to the "minimum necessary" to accomplish the intended purpose.

The Amended Rule departs from the Original Rule in one crucial respect. Where the Original Rule required covered entities to seek individual consent to use or disclose health information in all but the narrowest of circumstances, the Amended Rule allows such uses and disclosures without patient consent for "treatment, payment, and health care operations"—so-called "routine uses." "Health care operations," the broadest category under the routine use exception, refers to a range of management functions of covered entities, including quality assessment, practitioner evaluation, student training programs, insurance rating, auditing services, and business planning and development. The Rule allows individuals the right to request restrictions on uses and disclosures of protected health information and to enter into agreements with covered entities regarding such restrictions, but does not require covered entities to abide by such requests or to agree to any restriction. The Rule also permits, but does not require, covered entities to design and implement a consent process for routine uses and disclosures.

Importantly, the Rule contains detailed preemption provisions, which are consistent with HIPAA. These provisions establish that the Rule is intended as a "federal floor" for privacy protection, allowing state law to control where a "provision of State law relates to the privacy of individually identifiable health information and is *more stringent* than a standard, requirement, or implementation specification adopted under [the Privacy Rule]." 45 C.F.R. § 160.203 [emphasis added by court].

## Discussion

On appeal, Citizens reassert the claims they made before the District Court, that the Secretary, by promulgating the Privacy Rule, (1) unlawfully infringed Citizens' fundamental rights to privacy in personal health information under due process principles of the Fifth Amendment of the United States Constitution; (2) unlawfully infringed Citizens' rights to communicate privately with their medical practitioners under the First Amendment of the Constitution; (3) contravened Congress's intent in enacting HIPAA by eliminating Citizens' reasonable expectations of medical privacy; and (4) violated the [Administrative Procedure Act (APA)] by arbitrarily and capriciously reversing a settled course of behavior and adopting a policy that he had previously rejected.

### A. Fifth Amendment Substantive Due Process Claim

We begin our analysis with the premise that the right to medical privacy asserted by Citizens is legally cognizable under the Due Process Clause of the Fifth Amendment, although, as Citizens themselves concede, its "boundaries . . . have not been exhaustively delineated." Whatever those boundaries may be, it is undisputed that a violation of a citizen's right to medical privacy rises to the level of a *constitutional* claim only when that violation can properly be ascribed to the government. The Constitution protects against *state* interference with fundamental rights. It only applies to restrict private behavior in limited circumstances. Because such circumstances are not present in this case, and because the "violations" of the right to medical privacy that Citizens have asserted, if they amount to violations of that right at all, occurred at the hands of private entities, the protections of the Due Process Clause of the Fifth Amendment are not implicated in this case. We will accordingly affirm the District Court's finding that the Secretary did not violate Citizens' constitutional rights when he promulgated the Amended Rule.

By way of analogy, assume that Congress were to pass legislation permitting private cinema operators, at their discretion, to search all moviegoers for any reason, without any showing of probable cause or reasonable suspicion. Although the Fourth Amendment would preclude the federal government from conducting such a search, private cinema operators are not bound by the Fourth Amendment, and absent any other law prohibiting it, private cinema operators were already "permitted" to conduct such a search before the new legislation took effect. To the extent that this new legislation changes the legal landscape at all, then, it only codifies a power that cinema operators had already. The codification does not transform the private exercise of the codified power into "state action." Similarly, although the codification itself is clearly government action, it seems insufficient to endow a moviegoer's challenge to a search by a cinema operator with constitutional significance given that the codification has neither enhanced nor diminished the individual moviegoer's rights.

### B. First Amendment Claim

Citizens' First Amendment claim is that the Amended Rule infringes individuals' right to confidential communications with health care practitioners, *i.e.*, a right to refrain from public speech regarding private personal health information. Citizens argue that the effect of the Amended Rule is to chill speech between individuals and their health care practitioners because the possibility of nonconsensual disclosures makes individuals less likely to participate fully in diagnosis and treatment and more likely to be evasive and withhold important information. Further, because the Rule applies to "health information . . . whether oral or recorded in any form or medium," Citizens argue that the Rule is a content-based regulation reviewable under strict scrutiny.

Citizens' First Amendment claim fails on the same grounds as their Fifth Amendment claim: the potential "chilling" of patients' rights to free speech derives not from any action of the government, but from the independent decisions of private parties with respect to the use and disclosure of individual health information. We will therefore affirm the District Court's grant of summary judgment to the Secretary on Citizens' First Amendment claim.

### C. Claims Alleging Violations of HIPAA

In claims based on HIPAA's statutory language, Citizens argue (1) that the Secretary exceeded the regulatory authority delegated by HIPAA because the Act only authorizes the Secretary to promulgate regulations that *enhance* privacy and (2) that the Amended Rule impermissibly retroactively rescinded individual rights created by the Original Rule and disturbed Citizens' "settled expectations" in the privacy of their health information. However, Citizens' argument that the controlling policy underlying HIPAA is medical privacy and that the Amended Rule wholly sacrifices this interest to covered entities' interests in efficiency and flexibility ignores the Act's stated goals of "simplify[ing] the administration of health insurance," and "improv[ing] the efficiency and effectiveness of the health care system." As the District Court aptly explained, HIPAA requires the Secretary to "balance privacy protection and the efficiency of the health care system—not simply to enhance privacy." We thus conclude that Citizens' first HIPAA claim lacks merit.

We also agree with the District Court's finding that the Amended Rule does not retroactively eliminate rights that Citizens enjoyed under the Original Rule or under various laws or standards of practice that existed before the Amended Rule went into effect. Because the Original Rule was amended before its compliance date, covered entities were never under a legal obligation to comply with the Original Rule's consent requirement. Citizens, therefore, never enjoyed any rights under the Original Rule at all. Nor does the Amended Rule retroactively eliminate Citizens' reasonable expectations based on state law, standards of medical ethics and established standards of practice because the Amended Rule does not disturb any preexisting, "more stringent" state law privacy rights. Accordingly, we reject Citizens' second HIPPA claim as well, and will affirm the grant of summary judgment to the Secretary on these claims.

### D. APA Claims

Lastly, Citizens challenge the rulemaking process under the APA.

Citizens argue that the Secretary acted arbitrarily and capriciously in promulgating the Amended Rule by improperly reversing a "settled course of behavior" established in the Original Rule and adopting a policy that he had previously rejected. When an agency rejects a "settled course of behavior," however, it need only supply a "reasoned analysis" for the change to overcome any presumption that the settled rule best carries out the policies committed to the agency by Congress. Such an analysis requires the agency to examine the relevant data and articulate a satisfactory explanation for its action including a rational connection between the facts found and the choice made.

Here, the Secretary examined the relevant data and gave adequate consideration to the large volume of public comments that HHS received during the rulemaking process. The Secretary considered other alternatives and explained why they were unworkable. The Secretary also considered Congress's dual goals in devising the privacy standards, *i.e.,* protecting the confidentiality of personal health information and improving the efficiency and effectiveness of the national health care system.

In sum, the Secretary's decision to respond to the unintended negative effects and administrative burdens of the Original Rule by rescinding the consent requirement for routine uses and implementing more stringent notice requirements was explained in a detailed analysis that rationally connected the decision to the facts. Normally, an agency rule would be arbitrary and capricious if the agency has relied on factors which Congress has not intended it to consider, entirely failed to consider an important aspect of the problem, offered an explanation for its decision that runs counter to the evidence before the agency, or is so implausible that it could not be ascribed to a difference in view or the product of agency expertise. The Secretary has not failed in any of these respects, and, hence, we agree with the District Court's analysis and conclusion that the Secretary's decision was reasonable given the findings and that the Secretary did not act arbitrarily and capriciously in violation of the APA. Accordingly, we will affirm the grant of summary judgment to the Secretary on these claims.

## Summary of the HIPAA Privacy Rule

Office of Civil Rights, U.S. Dept. of Health and Human Services (May 2003)

### Covered Entities

The Privacy Rule, as well as all the Administrative Simplification rules, apply to health plans, health care clearinghouses, and to any health care provider who transmits health information in electronic form in connection with transactions for which the Secretary of HHS has adopted standards under HIPAA (the "covered entities").

***Health Plans.*** Individual and group plans that provide or pay the cost of medical care are covered entities. Health plans include health, dental, vision, and prescription drug insurers, health maintenance organizations ("HMOs"), Medicare, Medicaid, Medicare+Choice and Medicare supplement insurers, and long-term care insurers (excluding nursing home fixed-indemnity policies). Health plans also include employer-sponsored group health plans, government and church-sponsored health plans, and multi-employer health plans. There are exceptions—a group health plan with less than 50 participants that is administered solely by the employer that established and maintains the plan is not a covered entity. Two types of government-funded programs are not health plans: (1) those whose principal purpose is not providing or paying the cost of health care, such as the food stamps program; and (2) those programs whose principal activity is directly providing health care, such as a community health center, or the making of grants to fund the direct provision of health care. Certain types of insurance entities are also not health plans, including entities providing only workers' compensation, automobile insurance, and property and casualty insurance.

***Health Care Providers.*** Every health care provider, regardless of size, who electronically transmits health information in connection with certain transactions, is a covered entity. These transactions include claims, benefit eligibility inquiries, referral authorization requests, or other transactions for which HHS has established standards. Using electronic technology, such as email, does not mean a health care provider is a covered entity; the transmission must be in connection with a standard transaction. The Privacy Rule covers a health care provider whether it electronically transmits these transactions directly or uses a billing service or other third party to do so on its behalf. Health care providers include all "providers of services" (e.g., institutional providers such as hospitals) and "providers of medical or health services" (e.g., non-institutional providers such as physicians, dentists and other practitioners) as defined by Medicare, and any other person or organization that furnishes, bills, or is paid for health care.

***Health Care Clearinghouses.*** Health care clearinghouses are entities that process nonstandard information they receive from another entity into a standard (i.e., standard format or data content), or vice versa. Health care clearinghouses include billing services, repricing companies, community health management information systems, and value-added networks and switches if these entities perform clearinghouse functions.

**What Information Is Protected?**

***Protected Health Information.*** The Privacy Rule protects all *"individually identifiable health information"* held or transmitted by a covered entity or its business associate, in any form or media, whether electronic, paper, or oral. The Privacy Rule calls this information *"protected health information (PHI)."*

*"Individually identifiable health information"* is information, including demographic data, that relates to:

- the individual's past, present or future physical or mental health or condition,
- the provision of health care to the individual, or
- the past, present, or future payment for the provision of health care to the individual,

and that identifies the individual or for which there is a reasonable basis to believe can be used to identify the individual. Individually identifiable health information includes many common identifiers (e.g., name, address, birth date, Social Security Number).

***De-Identified Health Information.*** There are no restrictions on the use or disclosure of de-identified health information. De-identified health information neither identifies nor provides a reasonable basis to identify an individual. There are two ways to de-identify information; either: 1) a formal determination by a qualified statistician; or 2) the removal of specified identifiers of the individual and of the individual's relatives, household members, and employers is required, and is adequate only if the covered entity has no actual knowledge that the remaining information could be used to identify the individual.

**General Principle for Use or Disclosure**

***Required Disclosures.*** A covered entity must disclose protected health information in only two situations: (a) to individuals (or their personal representatives) specifically when the [illegible] access to, or an accounting of disclosures of, their protected he[illegible]n; and (b) to HHS when it is undertaking a compliance i[illegible] review or enforcement action.

**Limiting Uses and Disclosures to the Mi**[illegible]**ary**

***Minimum Necessary.*** A central aspect [illegible] Rule is the principle of "minimum necessary" use and d[illegible]vered entity must make reasonable efforts to use, disc[illegible]est only the minimum amount of protected health inform[illegible]o accomplish the intended purpose of the use, disclosure, [illegible]overed entity must develop and implement policies and p[illegible]asonably limit uses and disclosures to the minimum nec[illegible] the minimum necessary standard applies to a use or dis[illegible]red entity may not use, disclose, or request the entire m[illegible]or a particular purpose, unless it can specifically justify t[illegible]d as the amount reasonably needed for the purpose.

***Access and Uses.*** For internal uses[illegible]ity must develop and implement policies and procedures [illegible]ccess and uses of protected health information based on t[illegible]s of the members of their workforce. These policies and [illegible]must identify the persons, or classes of persons, in the [illegible]ho need access to protected health information to carry o[illegible]s, the categories of protected health information to wh[illegible] needed, and any conditions under which they need the i[illegible] do their jobs.

***Disclosures and Requests for D***[illegible]overed entities must establish and implement policies and procedu[illegible]hich may be standard protocols) for routine, recurring disclosures, or requests for disclosures, that limits the protected health information disclosed to that which is the minimum amount reasonably necessary to achieve the purpose of the disclosure. Individual review of each disclosure is not required. For non-routine, non-recurring disclosures, or requests for disclosures that it makes, covered entities must develop criteria designed to limit disclosures to the information reasonably necessary to accomplish the purpose of the disclosure and review each of these requests individually in accordance with the established criteria.

***Reasonable Reliance.*** If another covered entity makes a request for protected health information, a covered entity may rely, if reasonable under the circumstances, on the request as complying with this minimum necessary standard. Similarly, a covered entity may rely upon requests as being the minimum necessary protected health information from: (a) a public official, (b) a professional (such as an attorney or accountant) who is the covered entity's business associate, seeking the information to provide services to or for the covered entity; or (c) a researcher who provides the documentation or representation required by the Privacy Rule for research.

## NOTES

1. ***A Complex Rule.*** It is remarkable how little Congress said about the content of the HIPAA rules, and how elaborate those regulations became. They are a veritable spaghetti of intertwining cross-references and definitions—making them very difficult indeed to excerpt for a casebook. The comparatively straightforward provisions in 45 C.F.R. § 164.506, excerpted above and then analyzed in *Citizens for Health*, are hardly representative of the Privacy Rule's complexity. "Administrative simplification" was quite a misnomer here. That said, most of the difficulty arises from the integrated nature of the Rule, and its internal overlaps. The substance of the Rule certainly is less byzantine than many other health care regulations (as anyone who has ever worked on Medicare reimbursement issues can attest). The HHS summary lays out a fairly coherent and understandable set of rules.

2. ***A Data Protection Approach.*** Unlike some US privacy requirements, the HIPAA Privacy Rule is a data protection law, not a consumer protection law [see Chapters 3 and 4]. It is not tied to a commercial interaction—while doctor-patient relationships and insurance reimbursements may, of course, have commercial qualities, the protection of the patient is distinct from the nature of any accompanying transactions. The substantive requirements of the Rule follow the data protection model. The Rule starts with a presumed default of nondisclosure and then defines those situations where disclosure will be permitted. A central pillar of the Rule is its requirement that covered entities request, use, and disclose the "minimum necessary" amount of protected health information to accomplish the purpose at hand. The HIPAA Privacy Rule also grants the subject of the data a right of access to that data. These provisions—a default of nondisclosure, a minimization requirement tied to purpose specification, and access rights for data subjects—all could have been copied directly from the EU Data Protection Directive [see Chapter 4]. In the EU, of course, there is no separate law covering health information, because it falls within omnibus data protection statutes. Article 8 of the EU Data Protection Directive imposes additional conditions on the processing of sensitive information, which explicitly includes all "data concerning health." Even though HIPAA follows the data protection model, do these extra protections in Article 8 make EU law more restrictive than HIPAA, or are they roughly comparable?

3. ***Covered Entities.*** Based on the description above, pause for a moment to consider what health-related actors are *not* covered entities. One example might be a doctor who uses no electronic mechanisms for specified services such as insurance reimbursement. But the number of such medical practices is plummeting and will soon be almost zero. Indeed, as *Citizens for Health* emphasizes, one of the overall purposes of HIPAA is to shift health records to electronic formats for a host of policy reasons including efficiency, cost savings, portability of records, and reduction of errors. More significant examples of "uncovered entities" are health-related web sites that are not directly involved in treatment or insurance. Private sites such as WebMD offer health advice and often call upon users to input significant personal health information. Other sites such as Microsoft Health Vault serve as

personal cloud storage for an individual's medical records. Neither of these types of private internet-based services falls within the definition of a covered entity. Similarly, "personal genetics" services that analyze biological samples to provide information about a customer's disease risks or ancestry are not necessarily covered entities either, absent some extra factor like insurance coverage. The FDA recently authorized the web site 23andme.com to market an at-home test directly to consumers to determine whether a healthy parent has a variant gene that could potentially allow their offspring to inherit Bloom Syndrome, a serious genetic disorder. Consider the tradeoffs at play here: on one side, reducing cost and improving access to health information, but on the other side, more direct service provided outside the boundaries of HIPAA's privacy protections.

4. ***Protected Health Information.*** The applicability of the Privacy Rule also turns on the nature of the data in question and whether it qualifies as protected health information ("PHI"). Note the central place of deidentification in the scope of the definition included in the HIPAA regulations. To qualify as "individually identifiable health information," data must relate to a person's health and also must be linked to an individual through personally identifiable information. Moreover, "deidentified" information is removed completely from the coverage of HIPAA. Data used for medical research, for example, frequently has been deidentified in compliance with the Privacy Rule, taking it out of HIPAA's purview. As technology improves, and particularly as new techniques allow for the prospect of reidentification in an age of Big Data [see Chapter 6], the concept of "personally identifiable information" has become unstable. Are these HIPAA definitions in danger of being overtaken by more sophisticated data mining techniques? If reliable deidentification becomes more difficult, how should regulators like HHS respond?

5. ***Business Associates.*** Under the Amended Privacy Rule (the first one to take effect), covered entities could hire subcontractors for certain services such as claims processing or billing that involved handling protected health information. These subcontractors, known as "business associates," were not themselves subject to the Privacy Rule, but the covered entity was required to include certain data handling provisions in a written contract with the business associate in order to ensure respect for patient privacy. [For more about nondisclosure contracts such as business associate agreements, see Chapter 8.] In 2009, as part of a larger economic stimulus package, Congress passed the Health Information Technology for Economic and Clinical Health ("HITECH") Act. This statute beefed up requirements for contracts between covered entities and business associates. PHI. The HITECH Act added additional required terms, such as a contractual duty for the business associate to report any breach in PHI and assurances that additional subcontractors will also protect PHI. More importantly, the HITECH Act also allowed HHS to enforce HIPAA rules against business associates directly, rather than relying entirely on the contracts and the government's power over the original covered entity. Also, the HITECH Act directly imposed requirements such as recordkeeping and auditing on business associates. Finally, business associates are now obliged, if they

witness any violation of HIPAA duties or a business associate agreement by the covered entity, to cure the breach or report it to the authorities. In general, business associates now have greater obligations under HIPAA than before, although still not quite as many as covered entities have.

6. ***Permitted Uses.*** As noted in *Citizens for Health*, the Privacy Rule includes a number of situations where covered entities are allowed to disclose PHI if they choose (consistent with other applicable law or professional ethical duties). The "routine use" exceptions that the plaintiffs challenged in that case were only some of the multiple permitted uses. Lengthy regulatory language defines each of these situations in detail. Some significant examples of permitted uses include disclosures:

- To the patient;
- For treatment, payment, and health care operations;
- To family, friends, clergy, and similar recipients, provided the individual has a reasonable opportunity to agree or object to those disclosures appropriate to the circumstances;
- For certain purposes for an individual's welfare, such as in reporting indications of child abuse or domestic violence;
- For certain law enforcement or judicial purposes;
- For medical or other research, provided certain safeguards are observed.

More explicit authorization is required in some instances, including most uses for marketing purposes and most disclosures of psychotherapy notes. Does the large number of exceptions and the attention to defining them so carefully suggest problems with this approach? Or would there be equally as much difficulty starting with a default of permitted disclosure and then defining situations where disclosure was forbidden?

7. ***Privacy vs. Efficiency.*** The plaintiffs in *Citizens for Health* clearly disagreed with HHS policy choices, particularly the acceptance of arguments from the health care industry that the Original Rule would interfere unduly with normal operations. A footnote from the court's opinion elaborated on those objections from providers:

> According to the Secretary, some of the "more significant examples and concerns" that commenters raised in connection with the Original Rule were that the prior consent requirement for routine disclosures would bar pharmacists from filling prescriptions and searching for potential drug interactions before patients arrived at the pharmacy, it would interfere with the practice of emergency medicine in cases where it would be difficult or impossible to obtain patient consent before treatment, and it would delay the scheduling of and preparation for hospital procedures until the patient provided the required consent.

How far should the category of "routine uses" extend? Could these examples have been handled with a narrower exception than the one HHS adopted? Is a somewhat broad exception necessary to avoid interfering with patient care?

All these examples concerned negative effects felt directly by a patient. But consider how some "routine uses" may offer systemic benefits rather than individual ones. For example, detailed analysis of copious data may help identify means to reduce costs—a signal goal of health policy today, and a particular objective of the Affordable Care Act, which established various incentives for cost containment. When should we loosen limits on processing of individual data to achieve greater efficiency in our health care system?

8. ***Administrative Requirements.*** The Privacy Rule also includes many requirements for covered entities to observe in the administration of their systems. Some of these concern the individual's rights to notice and access. Most of us have been handed a sheet of paper containing privacy disclosures while checking in at a doctor's office, as required by the Privacy Rule's notice provisions. Covered entities also must provide individuals access to their medical records and, upon request, an accounting of disclosures from those records. These and similar rules trace their origins back to the original 1973 Fair Information Practices—which were, after all, developed by HHS' predecessor, the U.S. Department of Health, Education, and Welfare [see Chapters 4 and 10]. Other administrative obligations imposed by the HIPAA Privacy Rule relate to the maintenance of written policies, employee training, recordkeeping, audits, and similar functions.

9. ***Enforcement.*** There is no private right of action under HIPAA. The HHS Office for Civil Rights (OCR) takes the enforcement lead at the federal level; state attorneys general are also empowered to pursue HIPAA violations. In exceedingly rare cases, OCR refers cases to the Department of Justice for criminal prosecution, but most enforcement is civil. According to data compiled by HHS for 2013, there were 14,300 resolutions of complaints that year, of which 3,470 (24%) involved corrective action by the respondent. These numbers have climbed steadily since the Privacy Rule took effect—they are almost three times those for 2004, the first full year under the Privacy Rule. HHS very rarely imposes fines for HIPAA violations. Critics object that HHS lacks the resources to properly enforce the Privacy Rule and that its enforcement actions are too often "slaps on the wrist." The agency and its defenders suggest that a cooperative regulatory approach is more effective than an adversarial one, that securing corrective action is the most important outcome for protecting patient privacy, and that the prospect of large fines encourages adequate compliance. Even though HIPAA creates a data protection regime, the HHS approach resembles the FTC's consumer protection enforcement techniques [see Chapter 3] in many ways.

10. ***The Politics of HIPAA.*** The plaintiffs' objections in *Citizens for Health* have a political component as well. The Original Rule was finalized in December 2000, during the last weeks in office of a Democratic president, Bill Clinton. Michael Leavitt was appointed HHS Secretary by his Republican successor, George W. Bush, and it was the latter Administration that revisited the HIPAA Privacy Rule. The court ignored this change in political leadership, because the APA assumes broadly nonpartisan policy analysis by administrative agencies—as long as the Amended Rule's departures from the Original Rule could be justified on the record, which the court found they could be.

## 2. HIPAA SECURITY RULE

In addition to implementing HIPAA through the well-known Privacy Rule, HHS later promulgated the less prominent but still extremely important HIPAA Security Rule. This regulation seeks both to prevent data breaches and to help move the health care industry toward more standardized electronic communications. The Security Rule observes the same definitional parameters as the Privacy Rule, including the scope of covered entities and PHI. It similarly imposes additional duties on business associates as a result of the HITECH Act.

# HIPAA Security Rule

45 C.F.R. 164

### SUBPART C—SECURITY STANDARDS FOR THE PROTECTION OF ELECTRONIC PROTECTED HEALTH INFORMATION

### § 164.306 Security standards: General rules.

(a) **General requirements.** Covered entities and business associates must do the following:

(1) Ensure the confidentiality, integrity, and availability of all electronic protected health information the covered entity or business associate creates, receives, maintains, or transmits.

(2) Protect against any reasonably anticipated threats or hazards to the security or integrity of such information.

(3) Protect against any reasonably anticipated uses or disclosures of such information that are not permitted or required under subpart E of this part.

(4) Ensure compliance with this subpart by its workforce.

(b) **Flexibility of approach.**

(1) Covered entities and business associates may use any security measures that allow the covered entity or business associate to reasonably and appropriately implement the standards and implementation specifications as specified in this subpart.

(2) In deciding which security measures to use, a covered entity or business associate must take into account the following factors:

(i) The size, complexity, and capabilities of the covered entity or business associate.

(ii) The covered entity's or the business associate's technical infrastructure, hardware, and software security capabilities.

(iii) The costs of security measures.

(iv) The probability and criticality of potential risks to electronic protected health information. . . .

## SUMMARY OF THE HIPAA SECURITY RULE

## OFFICE OF CIVIL RIGHTS, U.S. DEPT. OF HEALTH AND HUMAN SERVICES

The Privacy Rule, or *Standards for Privacy of Individually Identifiable Health Information*, establishes national standards for the protection of certain health information. The *Security Standards for the Protection of Electronic Protected Health Information* (the Security Rule) establish a national set of security standards for protecting certain health information that is held or transferred in electronic form. The Security Rule operationalizes the protections contained in the Privacy Rule by addressing the technical and non-technical safeguards that organizations called "covered entities" must put in place to secure individuals' "electronic protected health information" (e-PHI). Within HHS, the Office for Civil Rights (OCR) has responsibility for enforcing the Privacy and Security Rules with voluntary compliance activities and civil money penalties.

Prior to HIPAA, no generally accepted set of security standards or general requirements for protecting health information existed in the health care industry. At the same time, new technologies were evolving, and the health care industry began to move away from paper processes and rely more heavily on the use of electronic information systems to pay claims, answer eligibility questions, provide health information and conduct a host of other administrative and clinically based functions.

Today, providers are using clinical applications such as computerized physician order entry (CPOE) systems, electronic health records (EHR), and radiology, pharmacy, and laboratory systems. Health plans are providing access to claims and care management, as well as member self-service applications. While this means that the medical workforce can be more mobile and efficient (i.e., physicians can check patient records and test results from wherever they are), the rise in the adoption rate of these technologies increases the potential security risks.

A major goal of the Security Rule is to protect the privacy of individuals' health information while allowing covered entities to adopt new technologies to improve the quality and efficiency of patient care. Given that the health care marketplace is diverse, the Security Rule is designed to be flexible and scalable so a covered entity can implement policies, procedures, and technologies that are appropriate for the entity's particular size, organizational structure, and risks to consumers' e-PHI.

The Security Rule defines "confidentiality" to mean that e-PHI is not available or disclosed to unauthorized persons. The Security Rule's confidentiality requirements support the Privacy Rule's prohibitions against improper uses and disclosures of PHI. The Security Rule also promotes the two additional goals of maintaining the integrity and availability of e-PHI. Under the Security Rule, "integrity" means that e-PHI is not altered or destroyed in an unauthorized manner. "Availability" means that e-PHI is accessible and usable on demand by an authorized person.

HHS recognizes that covered entities range from the smallest provider to the largest, multi-state health plan. Therefore, when a covered entity is deciding which security measures to use, the Rule does not dictate those measures but requires the covered entity to consider [the factors listed in 45 C.F.R. § 164.306(b)(2).]

Covered entities must review and modify their security measures to continue protecting e-PHI in a changing environment.

The Security Rule require[s] covered entities to perform risk analysis as part of their security management processes. A risk analysis process includes, but is not limited to, the following activities:

- Evaluate the likelihood and impact of potential risks to e-PHI;
- Implement appropriate security measures to address the risks identified in the risk analysis;
- Document the chosen security measures and, where required, the rationale for adopting those measures; and
- Maintain continuous, reasonable, and appropriate security protections.

Risk analysis should be an ongoing process, in which a covered entity regularly reviews its records to track access to e-PHI and detect security incidents, periodically evaluates the effectiveness of security measures put in place, and regularly reevaluates potential risks to e-PHI. A covered entity must designate a security official who is responsible for developing and implementing its security policies and procedures.

[In response to the individualized risk analysis, covered entities must have the following types of safeguards in place:]

**Administrative Safeguards**

***Information Access Management.*** The Security Rule requires a covered entity to implement policies and procedures for authorizing access to e-PHI only when such access is appropriate based on the user or recipient's role (role-based access).

***Workforce Training and Management.*** A covered entity must provide for appropriate authorization and supervision of workforce members who work with e-PHI. A covered entity must train all workforce members regarding its security policies and procedures, and must have and apply appropriate sanctions against workforce members who violate its policies and procedures.

## Physical Safeguards

***Facility Access and Control.*** A covered entity must limit physical access to its facilities while ensuring that authorized access is allowed.

***Workstation and Device Security.*** A covered entity must implement policies and procedures to specify proper use of and access to workstations and electronic media. A covered entity also must have in place policies and procedures regarding the transfer, removal, disposal, and re-use of electronic media, to ensure appropriate protection of electronic protected health information (e-PHI).

## Technical Safeguards

***Access Control.*** A covered entity must implement technical policies and procedures that allow only authorized persons to access electronic protected health information (e-PHI).

***Audit Controls.*** A covered entity must implement hardware, software, and/or procedural mechanisms to record and examine access and other activity in information systems that contain or use e-PHI.

***Integrity Controls.*** A covered entity must implement policies and procedures to ensure that e-PHI is not improperly altered or destroyed.

***Transmission Security.*** A covered entity must implement technical security measures that guard against unauthorized access to e-PHI that is being transmitted over an electronic network.

## NOTES

1. ***Specificity of Guidance.*** The HHS Summary repeatedly emphasizes that it is "flexible and scalable," but then provides a pretty detailed checklist of steps a covered entity must take. Is this inconsistent?

2. ***Comparing HIPAA to Other Security Rules.*** There are regulations for data security covered throughout this book, including the FTC's general guidance for businesses [see Chapter 3], the PCI security rules for handling payment card data [see Chapter 7], and the Gramm-Leach-Bliley Act Safeguards Rule for financial institutions [Chapter 13]. If you have already studied some of these, compare them to the HIPAA Security Rule. How specific are they in comparison to HIPAA? Where does the advice given by different data security rules differ? Which key requirements are the same?

3. ***Breach Notification.*** The HITECH Act also mandated that HHS add a breach notification provision to the Security Rule. Under the resulting regulations, covered entities must provide notice of data breaches to affected patients "without unreasonable delay and in no case later than 60 days following the discovery of a breach." The rules also provide for notice to HHS and, in cases involving records of more than 500 persons, public notice through the mass media. *See* 45 C.F.R. 164, Subpart D. If you read earlier material about state data breach notification statutes [see Chapter 7], how do you think the HIPAA requirements compare to those?

## 3. THE COMMON RULE

### William McGeveran et al., *Deidentification and Reidentification in Returning Individual Findings from Biobank and Secondary Research: Regulatory Challenges and Models for Management*

13 Minn. J. L. Sci. & Tech 485 (2012)

The Common Rule was established in 1991 to create uniform protection for human research subjects. The Rule reaches certain research "conducted, supported or otherwise subject to regulation" by fifteen federal agencies, including the National Institutes of Health, as well as research by any institution claiming federal-wide assurance for the protection of human subjects by adopting the standards and rules articulated in the Common Rule. The Common Rule only attaches when "research involv[es] human subjects." Both "research" and "human subject" have specific definitions under the Rule. "Research" is limited to "systematic investigation[s] . . . designed to develop or contribute to the generalizable knowledge." A "human subject" is defined as "a living individual about whom an investigator . . . conducting research obtains (1) [d]ata through intervention or interaction with the individual, or (2) [i]dentifiable private information." The Common Rule further stipulates that private information "must be individually identifiable," meaning that "the identity of the subject is or may readily be ascertained by the investigator or associated with the information."

The current Common Rule provides three levels of independent review for research protocols based on the level of risk posed. Research studies posing greater than a minimal risk to subjects require review by a fully convened Institutional Review Board (IRB), the highest level of independent review. Studies posing no more than minimal risk are eligible for expedited review, which is typically performed by a single IRB reviewer who can either approve the protocol or find that the protocol poses more than minimal risk and requires full IRB review. Studies exempt from or outside of the Common Rule's reach comprise the lowest risk category and have no IRB requirements at all. [If IRB review is required,] the Common Rule specifically directs the IRB to assess a number of factors, including: minimization of risks to human subjects; reasonability of risks in relation to anticipated benefits, if any; adequacy of informed consent; sufficiency of data monitoring; and protection of human subjects' privacy and the confidentiality of data. The failure to obtain compliant informed consent and IRB approval, or failure to comply with requirements for an exemption, may result in the defunding of the project.

## NOTES

1. ***The Common Rule and HIPAA.*** Why isn't HIPAA good enough protection to govern uses of personal data in medical research? In what ways might research pose greater privacy and security concerns than clinical care? In what ways might it be less troublesome? Note that the Common Rule has been around a good deal longer; in its current basic form it predates the HIPAA regulations by a decade, and precursors to the rule go back further.

2. ***Deidentification.*** Notice that, like HIPAA, the Common Rule only concerns data that is individually identifiable. Deidentified individuals are not categorized as "human subjects" to whom the Common Rule applies. Until recently the two regimes had distinct standards for what was required to deidentify data, but HHS has now harmonized them. HHS considers data deidentified when either (a) an expert has determined it is very unlikely the data will be reidentified or (b) enough identifiers have been removed that no residual information can be used to identify the individual. Reidentification is a major concern for research institutions, which routinely use deidentified data from millions of individuals. If the data is identified at a large scale, the institution could face insurmountable fines. At the same time, it improves an institution's findings to retain certain identifiers. For example, a researcher who knows that an individual was a 45-year-old African-American male who lives in an urban area and has a history of obesity and heart disease could derive more robust findings from that information than the bare-bones fact that an unidentified individual had heart disease. Using analytic techniques across populations, researchers can find important correlations. This is another example of the use of "Big Data" [see Chapter 6] in medical research, but it pulls against an effort to make individual medical data as anonymous as possible.

3. ***The IRB.*** The Common Rule delegates considerable regulatory power to Institutional Review Boards ("IRBs") set up within each establishment sponsoring human subjects research—often universities, hospitals, or research organizations. IRBs must register and there are very significant reporting requirements. Regulations also govern the composition of IRBs; according to HHS guidance an IRB must:

> i. have at least five members with varying backgrounds to promote complete and adequate review of the research activities commonly conducted by the institution;
>
> ii. make every nondiscriminatory effort to ensure that the membership is not composed of entirely men or entirely women;
>
> iii. include at least one member whose primary concerns are in scientific areas and at least one member whose primary concerns are in nonscientific areas;
>
> iv. include at least one member who is not otherwise affiliated with the institution and who is not part of the immediate family of a person who is affiliated with the institution; and
>
> v. not allow any member to participate in the initial or continuing review of any project in which the member has a

conflicting interest, except to provide information requested by the IRB.

Within these types of broad boundaries, however, the internal structure and deliberations of IRBs can vary widely. Some institutions refer IRB decisionmaking to specialized subcontractors, a few of which are for-profit enterprises. What are the advantages and disadvantages of the decentralized and largely self-regulatory structure of the Common Rule?

An IRB is intended to safeguard research subjects against a much broader range of harms than merely invasions of privacy. The IRB structure was originally created to protect subjects of medical experiments from risks to their health, as reflected in the broader discipline of bioethics. They were established in response to the outcry over abuses in some studies, exemplified by the notorious "Tuskegee syphilis experiment," a long-term clinical study in which poor African-American men in rural Alabama were deceived and were not treated for the disease so its progress could be observed. The scope of IRB oversight extends from such strictly medical research to psychological and social science as well. In those contexts, there has been harsh criticism of IRBs as overly cautious, to the point that they are obstructing academic research and even engaging in censorship. See generally *Symposium, Censorship and Institutional Review Boards*, 101 NW. U. L. REV. (2007). When harm to research subjects' privacy interests is the relevant risk, how can IRBs strike the correct balance between promoting research and protecting privacy?

## D. GENETIC INFORMATION

---

### Focus

The Genetic Information Nondiscrimination Act

In 2008, Congress passed and President George W. Bush signed the Genetic Information Nondiscrimination Act (GINA), Pub. L. 110–233. The statute defines "genetic information" as (a) information about an individual's genetic tests; (b) information about genetic tests of that person's family members; and (c) "the manifestation of a disease or disorder in family members of such individual." It does not include sex or age characteristics.

Title I of the statute prohibits use of genetic information by health insurers. (It does not, however, cover other forms of insurance such as life, long-term care, or disability.) Rules enforcing Title I were issued by multiple agencies involved in insurance regulation and codified in several places. The rules are summarized as follows in an HHS fact sheet (available at http://www.genome.gov/27535101):

> [H]ealth insurers may not use genetic information to make eligibility, coverage, underwriting, or premium-setting decisions. Health insurers may not request or require individuals or their family members to undergo genetic testing or to provide genetic information. Further, they cannot use genetic information obtained intentionally or unintentionally in decisions about enrollment or coverage. Finally, the use of genetic information as a preexisting condition is prohibited in both the Medicare supplemental policy and individual health insurance markets.

Title II prohibits discrimination against employees or job applicants on the basis of genetic information. According to regulations promulgated by the Equal Employment Opportunity Commission, 29 C.F.R §§ 1635 et seq., employers cannot consider genetic information in any decisions about "any aspect of employment, including hiring, firing, pay, job assignments, promotions, layoffs, training, fringe benefits, or any other term or condition of employment. An employer may never use genetic information to make an employment decision because genetic information is not relevant to an individual's current ability to work." The regulations also forbid disclosure of genetic information by employers, and they include provisions banning retaliation against employees or applicants for making claims under GINA.

GINA is noteworthy as a relatively unusual example of a privacy statute that clearly intervenes in the use phase of the life cycle of data [see Chapter 6]. The statute does not regulate collection of genetic information. Is this an effective structure? Should other areas of privacy law consider shifting focus from the collection phase to the use phase?

As noted in the next excerpt, there are additional genetic privacy measures at the state level. Why does genetic privacy inspire special treatment distinct from the general privacy law applied to other health information?

---

## Bearder v. State

806 N.W.2d 766 (Minn. 2011)

■ MEYER, JUSTICE.

At issue in this case is the interplay between the newborn screening statutes, Minn. Stat. §§ 144.125–144.128, and the Genetic Privacy Act, Minn. Stat. § 13.386 (2010). The Minnesota Department of Health, as part of its newborn screening program, collects blood samples of newborn children to test for various disorders. The Department has retained the excess blood samples and the test results. The Department has used the blood samples for purposes other than the initial screening of newborn children and has allowed outside research organizations to use the blood samples to conduct health studies. Nine families (the appellants) sued the State of Minnesota, the Department, and the Commissioner of the Department [collectively "the State"] over the Department's practice of collecting, using, storing, and disseminating the children's blood samples and test results without obtaining written informed consent in violation of the Genetic Privacy Act. The district court granted the State's motion to dismiss or, in the alternative, the State's motion for summary judgment. The court of appeals affirmed. We reverse and remand to the district court.

The district court granted the State's motion for summary judgment on all claims. The court concluded (1) that the Genetic Privacy Act did not apply to children born before August 1, 2006, (2) that the blood samples were not "genetic information" under the Genetic Privacy Act, and (3) that the Genetic Privacy Act did not supersede existing laws such as the newborn screening statutes.

On appeal, the court of appeals held that the blood samples qualified as "genetic information" under the Genetic Privacy Act. But the court affirmed the grant of summary judgment, concluding that the Department of Health possesses broad statutory authority to operate the newborn screening program and that the Genetic Privacy Act does not apply. The court concluded that using newborn children's blood samples for purposes other than screening could violate the Genetic Privacy Act but that appellants had not presented specific facts to support their claims that the children's blood samples were being used improperly. The court of appeals, therefore, affirmed summary judgment on all claims. Appellants appeal the decision to affirm summary judgment on the Genetic Privacy Act claim.

I

In 1965 Minnesota began to test newborns for certain metabolic disorders [citing Minn. Stat. §§ 144.125–144.128]. The current program screens newborns for more than 50 disorders. Each year, more than 73,000 Minnesota newborns are screened; approximately 100 are discovered to have a confirmed disorder.

Newborn screening is conducted under the authority of the newborn screening statutes, which (1) require the Commissioner of Health to prescribe the manner of testing, recording, and reporting of newborn screening results; (2) require those who perform screenings to advise parents that the blood samples and test results may be retained by the Department of Health; and (3) permit parents either to decline to have their infants tested or to require destruction of the blood samples and test results following screening.

The newborn screening program requires certain individuals to collect blood samples from newborn children by the fifth day after birth. A sample consists of a few blood drops collected on a specimen card. The blood sample is sent to the Department within 24 hours of collection. Screening tests are then run on the blood sample.

Almost all of the screening tests analyze the blood sample for the presence of substances that indicate the possible presence of a disorder. The only test that analyzes the DNA or RNA of the blood is the second-level test for cystic fibrosis, which is performed only if the first test indicates the presence of a certain substance in the blood. The screening process typically uses 70% of the sample.

If a portion of the blood sample remains after the screening tests are completed, the sample is retained indefinitely unless there is a specific request to have it destroyed. As of December 31, 2008, there were more than 800,000 newborn screening samples in storage, dating back to samples taken as early as 1997. More than 50,000 blood samples have been used in studies for purposes beyond the initial screening of the newborn children. These studies have included developing new tests and assuring the quality of existing tests. Blood samples have also been used for studies unrelated to the newborn screening program. A blood sample is capable of being used for research for up to 20 years.

The State asserts that a federal law requires the Department to retain newborn screening test results for two years. *See* 42 C.F.R. § 493.1105 (2010). After this two-year period, the test results are retained indefinitely unless the Department receives a request to destroy the results. The Department currently has electronic test results dating back to 1986 and "a small amount of paper records dating back to the 1960s." The appellants allege that the Department possesses more than 1.5 million screening test results.

The Department of Health contracts with Mayo Medical Laboratories to perform screening tests on newborn children's blood samples. This contract allows Mayo to use excess blood samples for studies unrelated to the newborn screening program if—in addition to other requirements—the samples have been de-identified or Mayo has received written consent from the children's parent or legal guardian. The majority of the studies performed by outside research institutions use de-identified blood samples.

In 2006 the Legislature [enacted the Genetic Privacy Act, codified at Minn. Stat. § 13.386, subd. 3, which amended the Minnesota Government Data Practices Act to regulate the treatment of genetic information collected by the government. The statute] prohibits the collection, use, storage, or dissemination of a person's genetic information without the written informed consent of that person:

> Unless otherwise expressly provided by law, genetic information about an individual:
>
> (1) may be collected by a government entity, as defined in section 13.02, subdivision 7a, or any other person only with the written informed consent of the individual;
>
> (2) may be used only for purposes to which the individual has given written informed consent;
>
> (3) may be stored only for a period of time to which the individual has given written informed consent; and
>
> (4) may be disseminated only:
>
> > (i) with the individual's written informed consent; or
> >
> > (ii) if necessary in order to accomplish purposes described by clause (2). A consent to disseminate genetic information under item (i) must be signed and dated. Unless otherwise provided by law, such a consent is valid for one year or for a lesser period specified in the consent.

This provision "applies to genetic information collected on or after" August 1, 2006.

Appellants argue that the Genetic Privacy Act requires the Department of Health to obtain informed consent before it may collect, use, store, or disseminate the blood samples that remain after newborn health screening is complete. The State argues that the Genetic Privacy Act does not limit the Department's handling of the samples because (1) blood samples received by the Department of Health are not "genetic information" under the Act, and (2) the newborn screening statutes "expressly provide" that the Department of Health may use, store, and disseminate the genetic information without first obtaining written informed consent.

## II

Our first task is to determine whether the blood samples collected and stored by the Department are "genetic information," as that term is used in the Genetic Privacy Act, requiring the Department to obtain informed consent before it may use, store, or disseminate the blood samples that remain after the newborn health screening is complete. Appellants argue that the Genetic Privacy Act applies to blood samples because those samples contain information in the form of DNA. The State argues that the Genetic Privacy Act does not apply to blood samples because the Act treats those samples as biological specimens, not genetic information.

The language of Minn. Stat. § 13.386, subd. 1, includes two definitions for the term "genetic information":

> (a) "Genetic information" means information about an identifiable individual derived from the presence, absence, alteration, or mutation of a gene, or the presence or absence of a specific DNA or RNA marker, which has been obtained from an analysis of:
>
> > (1) the individual's biological information or specimen; or
> >
> > (2) the biological information or specimen of a person to whom the individual is related.
>
> (b) "Genetic information" also means medical or biological information collected from an individual about a particular genetic condition that is or might be used to provide medical care to that individual or the individual's family members.

Appellants and the State generally agree that genetic information under (a) does not include the blood samples because, by its express terms, the information must have been obtained from "an analysis" of biological information. In other words, definition (a) protects the privacy of the test results, and not the specimen or source of the information. It is self-evident that the biological information being subject to analysis includes blood samples. But the blood samples themselves are not protected under definition (a).

We therefore consider whether the blood samples are "genetic information" under the definition contained in subdivision 1(b). Under subdivision (b), genetic information "also means medical or biological information collected from an individual." Unlike definition (a), definition (b) does not limit its protection to information "obtained" from an analysis of a "biological specimen." Rather, the definition is broader in scope because it encompasses "medical or biological information" about an individual. As noted under our analysis of subdivision 1(a), biological information includes blood samples. Therefore, an individual's blood samples are biological information subject to protection under definition (b).

Aside from the Legislature's unambiguous intent to include blood samples within the ambit of "biological information" that can be analyzed to glean "genetic information," the common understanding of "biological information collected from an individual" is the information contained in blood cells via DNA. The blood samples collected from the appellants in this case unquestionably contain biological information. The blood samples are also "biological information" under definition (b) because the genetic information in the samples may be used to provide medical care to the individuals. It is the DNA within the blood samples that is the information that brings the blood sample within the protection of the Genetic Privacy Act. Thus, the blood samples fit within the common understanding of "medical or biological information collected from an individual."

The State argues that blood samples are not "genetic information" because the "genetic information" comes from analysis of the blood samples. The State's argument is essentially that the Genetic Privacy Act applies only after blood samples have been analyzed. The State relies primarily on two areas of the statutory definition for its argument. First, it relies on subdivision 1(a), which defines genetic information as the result of "an analysis of . . . the . . . biological information or specimen." Second, the State argues that the use of the term "biological information or specimen" in subdivision 1(a) implies that the Legislature intended a "biological specimen" to have a meaning distinct from "biological information."

We conclude that this is not a reasonable interpretation of the language of the statute. Definitions (a) and (b) must be read together, but each definition describes a different type of genetic information. The "genetic information" defined in subdivision 1(a) is information obtained from an analysis of biological samples or from an analysis of information already obtained from biological samples. But the "genetic information" defined in subdivision 1(b) includes "biological information" itself collected from an individual, not just the analysis of the biological information. See Minn.Stat. § 13.386, subd. 1(b). We also do not read into the plain language of subdivision 1(a)'s use of the phrase "biological information or specimen" a distinction between "biological information" and a "biological specimen" that is meant to apply in subdivision 1(b), where the phrase used is "medical or biological information." See Minn. Stat. § 13.386, subd. 1.

We conclude that "genetic information" under Minn. Stat. § 13.386, subd. 1(b), includes the actual blood samples as "medical or biological" information. We also note that even if the Genetic Privacy Act did not define the blood samples themselves as "genetic information," those samples unquestionably contain genetic information. The Act limits the collection, use, storage, or dissemination of genetic information. It would be impossible to collect, use, store, or disseminate those samples without also collecting, using, storing, or disseminating the genetic information contained in those samples.

In sum, because the definition of "genetic information" is not subject to two reasonable interpretations, it is not ambiguous. We hold that the blood samples collected by the Department of Health fit the definition of "biological information collected from an individual" under Minn. Stat. § 13.386, subd. 1(b), and, therefore, the Genetic Privacy Act applies to the blood samples. Unless otherwise expressly provided by law, the Department must have written informed consent to collect, use, store, or disseminate those samples.

### III

Having concluded that the blood samples collected and stored by the Department are "genetic information" and subject to the restrictions of the Genetic Privacy Act, we turn to the question of whether the Department is exempted from those restrictions because they are "expressly provided" with authority to collect, use, store, and disseminate the information. Thus, the Department may collect, use, store, or disseminate blood samples collected as part of the newborn screening program only to the extent expressly authorized by Minn. Stat. §§ 144.125–144.128 (the newborn screening statutes). We examine each of the restrictions of the Genetic Privacy Act to determine the extent to which the newborn screening statutes give the Department the express authority to collect, use, store, or disseminate blood samples without written informed consent.

The Genetic Privacy Act's first restriction is on collection. Minn. Stat. § 13.386, subd. 3(1). Under the Act, genetic information "may be collected . . . only with the written informed consent of the individual." Although the language of the newborn screening statutes [does] not explicitly state that the Department may collect blood samples, the statutes' provisions authorizing the Department to conduct tests and providing for destruction of samples require that the Department be able to collect samples to be tested and destroyed. Despite the fact that this constitutes implied rather than express authorization, we conclude that the newborn screening statutes authorize the collection of blood samples to the extent necessary to allow the Department to conduct the tests expressly authorized by statute.

The Genetic Privacy Act's second restriction is on use. The Act provides that genetic information "may be used only for purposes to which the individual has given written informed consent." The newborn screening statutes authorize the Commissioner to conduct "tests for heritable and congenital disorders," and require the Commissioner to "maintain a registry of the cases of heritable and congenital disorders detected by the screening program for the purpose of follow-up services." The newborn screening statutes therefore expressly authorize the Commissioner to use the blood samples without written informed consent only to the extent necessary to conduct tests for heritable and congenital disorders and conduct follow-up services.

The court of appeals held that the broad authority given to the Commissioner to perform various functions expressly allowed the Department of Health to use genetic information to improve its screening methods. The Commissioner's power to conduct health studies does not include unlimited authority to use the genetic information obtained from newborns for screening purposes in those health studies. Use of genetic information for purposes other than the screening of newborn children and for follow-up services requires written informed consent.

The Genetic Privacy Act also restricts storage. The Act requires that genetic information "may be stored only for a period of time to which the individual has given written informed consent." The newborn screening statutes require the Commissioner to "maintain a registry of the cases of heritable and congenital disorders detected by the screening program for the purpose of follow-up services." This language creates an express exception to the Genetic Privacy Act that allows the Commissioner to maintain blood samples from positive test results unless a child's parents object.

The State argues that the newborn screening statutes provide two other express exceptions to the Genetic Privacy Act. First, it argues that the newborn screening statutes' requirement that the Commissioner "comply with a destruction request within 45 days after receiving it" authorizes the Commissioner to retain information for 45 days. But even if this provision authorizes the Commissioner to retain genetic information for 45 days before complying with a destruction request, it does not expressly provide for indefinite storage when no destruction request is received. [It] is silent on the question of how long genetic information may be retained, and therefore the statute cannot be an "express" exception to the Genetic Privacy Act's opt-in framework.

Second, the State argues that language requiring "responsible parties" to advise parents "that the blood or tissue samples used to perform testing thereunder as well as the results of such testing may be retained by the Department of Health," expressly requires the Department to retain blood samples because if the Department were not allowed to do so, the statement would be false. At best, this language provides only implicit authorization for the Department to retain blood samples. A requirement that "responsible parties" inform parents that blood samples may be retained implies that the Department is in fact authorized to do so, but it does not expressly authorize retention of those samples. Furthermore, the use of the word "may" indicates that blood samples might not be retained.

The Genetic Privacy Act's final restriction is on dissemination. The Act allows genetic information to be "disseminated only: (i) with the individual's written informed consent; or (ii) if necessary in order to accomplish purposes" for which informed consent was given. The newborn screening statutes expressly authorize the "reporting of test results." The Commissioner is also expressly authorized to contract with a private entity to perform the Department's functions. But there is no other source of law authorizing the dissemination of blood samples or genetic information beyond that expressly authorized for the reporting of newborn test results.

We conclude that the newborn screening statutes provide an express exception to the Genetic Privacy Act only to the extent that the Department is authorized to administer newborn screening by testing the samples for heritable and congenital disorders, recording and reporting those test results, maintaining a registry of positive cases for the purpose of follow-up services, and storing those test results as required by federal law. The newborn screening statutes do not expressly authorize the Department to conduct any other use, storage, or dissemination of the blood samples.

**IV**

Because the district court concluded that the Department had not violated the Genetic Privacy Act, the court did not consider the availability of remedies to particular parties or whether any parties had established the facts necessary to show that their children's blood samples had been used, stored, or disseminated in violation of the Act. Because the record is insufficient to allow us to determine whether any of the appellants are entitled to remedies for such violation, we remand to the district court for further proceedings consistent with this opinion.

■ ANDERSON, PAUL H., JUSTICE, concurring in part and dissenting in part.

I concur in part and dissent in part. I agree with the majority that test results generated by the Department of Health's newborn screening program are "genetic information" subject to the requirements of Minn. Stat. § 13.386 (2010), the Genetic Privacy Act, except to the extent otherwise expressly authorized by law. To the extent that this conclusion applies to newborn screening test results, I concur.

But I disagree with the majority's conclusion that the Genetic Privacy Act applies to blood samples obtained in the newborn screening program. The Genetic Privacy Act applies to "genetic information," which, as defined by the statute, does not include specimens. Because newborn children's blood samples are specimens, blood samples do not meet the definition of genetic information and the Genetic Privacy Act does not apply to them.

Subdivision 1(a) does not say that the biological information or specimen itself is genetic information, only that results of certain analyses of either is genetic information. Therefore, I conclude, as does the majority, that the blood sample cannot meet the first definition of "genetic information."

But subdivision 1(a) provides relevant information for our interpretation. Importantly, the definition in subdivision 1(a) uses the phrase "biological information *or specimen*" [emphasis added in opinion]. By using both the terms "biological information" and "specimen," the statute draws a distinction between the two terms, and therefore, specimens cannot be "biological information." As a result, a blood sample, because it is a specimen, cannot be "biological information." If biological information included specimens, the term "specimen" would be rendered superfluous in the statute.

The definition of "genetic information" provided in subdivision 1(b) includes certain types of medical or biological information but omits the term "specimen," which term was included in the definition in subdivision 1(a). This omission leads to the inevitable conclusion that the definition in subdivision 1(b) does not include "specimens."

Because neither definition of "genetic information" applies to the blood samples, I conclude that the Genetic Privacy Act does not apply to the blood samples collected for the newborn screening program. Therefore, I would hold that the Department of Health is not limited by the Genetic Privacy Act's opt-in framework for the collection, use, storage, and dissemination of blood samples.

The majority concludes that the definition of "genetic information" includes the blood samples collected in the newborn screening program. There are numerous problems with the majority's analysis and conclusion.

First, the only way for the majority to reach its conclusion that a blood sample meets the second definition of "genetic information" is to interpret the term "biological information" to have two different meanings when used in the same statute and subdivision. The two uses of "biological information," however, are separated by fewer than 20 words. This conclusion has no foundation and is contrary to settled rules of statutory interpretation.

Second, the majority's conclusion conflicts with the Data Practices Act requirement that copies of the information be made available to the subject of the data. Notably, because the majority concludes that the blood sample itself is "genetic information," the Department would somehow need to copy the physical blood sample, because a copy of a report based on the blood sample would not be a copy of the blood sample.

Third, and more fundamentally, the majority's reliance on the common understanding of the term "genetic information" is flawed. First, when the statute provides an explicit definition of "genetic information," the common understanding of the term "genetic information" is unhelpful. Moreover, the common understanding of the term "information" does not support the majority's conclusion. Information is not a physical object but is an intangible noun. A blood sample is a tangible object that conveys no information without analysis, and therefore, it cannot be "biological information."

Fourth, the majority's conclusion that the Genetic Privacy Act applies to blood samples significantly, or even drastically, complicates the interpretation of the newborn screening program statute. [I]f the blood samples are "genetic information," the newborn screening program statutes would require responsible parties to misinform parents of newborns as to the Department's authority to retain blood samples and whether the parents are required to opt-out of the retention, or required to opt-in. However, if blood samples are not considered "genetic information," as I conclude, this subdivision requires no misleading information be given to parents of newborn children.

In conclusion, the majority repeatedly ignores the narrow definition of "genetic information" and relies instead on what it subjectively believes the term genetic information ought to mean.

At this point, a final comment is in order. The majority appears to be motivated by a policy concern that I share. The Department's assertion that it can use, store, and disseminate the more than 800,000 blood samples it has on file without violating the Genetic Privacy Act is troubling. While the policy implications of this case should not overshadow the plain language of the statute, it should be noted that these policy concerns, while very real, are not as severe as they initially appear.

The newborn screening statutes restrict what the Department may do with the blood samples it collects in the newborn screening program. First, the parties responsible for collecting the newborn blood samples are statutorily required to inform parents of their ability to refuse testing and to have their test results and blood samples destroyed. In other words, parents may receive the testing that is beneficial to their newborns and still have the blood samples and test results destroyed upon request. The parents do not face the dilemma of choosing between testing accompanied by the Department's retention of blood samples or no testing at all. Second, the Commissioner of the Department is statutorily required to destroy blood samples within 45 days of receiving a request. The parents may decide later that they want their child's blood sample to be destroyed, and the Commissioner is obligated to do so. Third, the children are able to request that their own blood samples and test results be destroyed once they reach the age of majority.

In conclusion, I, unlike the majority, would hold that the Department is not violating Minn. Stat. § 13.386 by collecting, using, storing, or disseminating blood samples without written consent, because section 13.386 does not apply to specimens.

[This opinion was joined by Justices Dietzen and Stras; the opinion of the court therefore had a 4–3 majority vote.]

■ STRAS, JUSTICE. concurring in part, dissenting in part.

In my view, the court reaches the correct policy result. If I were a legislator, I would vote for legislation protecting blood samples under the Genetic Privacy Act. However, my role as a judge is not to implement my own policy preferences, but to interpret the law as written.

In this case, the court's conclusion that blood samples are "genetic information" is at odds with the plain and unambiguous language of the Genetic Privacy Act for all of the reasons stated by Justice Paul H. Anderson in his opinion.

## NOTES

1. ***Statutory Interpretation.*** Which opinion has the better argument on grounds of statutory interpretation alone? The majority's view that subdivision 1(a) refers to information generated by analysis and subdivision 1(b) is broader? Or the contrary view that both subdivisions' definitions of "information" exclude specimens?

2. **Bearder *After Remand.*** The *Bearder* court resolved the legal questions concerning the interpretation of the statute, but remanded for factual determinations. After protracted additional proceedings, the lower courts ruled that the state was required to destroy over one million blood samples from newborns that had been stored without the opt-in parental consent required under *Bearder*. This caused national outcry among pediatrics and medical research groups, who bemoaned the loss of a resource for improving future tests and other medical research. The state's Health Commissioner said, "For the first time in almost 20 years, we're going to begin destroying a valuable public health resource." To supporters of the plaintiffs' position, of course, this was just the natural consequence of collecting genetic information without securing legally required consent. The previously obtained blood samples have now been destroyed, but in 2014, the Minnesota Legislature amended the law to reinstate the practices followed before the *Bearder* decision. Perhaps this means the Legislature never intended the Genetic Privacy Act to interfere with the newborn screening program—but if so, the lesson of the incident may be the need for great care in defining terms and scope in genetic privacy legislation. Could the Legislature have done anything to retroactively fix the law and prevent the destruction of the older blood spots?

3. ***A Divergence of Two Professional Cultures.*** The protest against the destruction of blood samples after *Bearder* points to a broad divergence of viewpoints between many medical researchers and public health officials on one side and many privacy advocates and lawyers on the

other. Health care professionals saw the screening program as an essential resource for both treatment and research; the older blood spots helped them improve the testing technology itself and, in some cases, therapies. They characterized the *Bearder* decision and its aftermath as a tragedy, and at times implied pretty strongly that it was based on unscientific ignorance. In contrast, even the justices who thought the blood samples could be retained expressed significant discomfort with that outcome: Justice Anderson called the Department's position "troubling" and the privacy concerns "very real," while Justice Stras went so far as to say he would have voted to include blood samples under the Genetic Privacy Act if he were a legislator, even though as a judge he interpreted the statute as written not to reach them. Of course, the medical researchers care about privacy and the lawyers support medical progress. But in many cases, the basic predispositions of the two professional groups are different. Why is this so? Do you think one of them is closer to the correct attitude?

4. ***Deidentification.*** Regulations like the HIPAA Privacy Rule and the Common Rule rely on deidentification as the linchpin for privacy protection in medical research. Why isn't that the obvious solution here? The majority opinion observed that research conducted using the blood samples by Mayo Labs and other outside institutions was always based on parental consent or conducted on deidentified samples. Is there a privacy harm in either of these situations? If not, where is the harm?

5. ***Genes as Property.*** Twila Brase, a privacy advocate involved in the challenge to newborn screening in Minnesota, characterized their storage as tantamount to a government seizure of property. "It's clearly valuable to the government," she told the scientific journal *Nature*, "but they couldn't do that with your coat or your cat." Genetic privacy issues are a modern example of a debate this book has considered several times before—the extent to which privacy interests should be viewed as property interests as opposed to personal ones [see Chapter 1 for the most extended discussion]. In one famous case you may have read in the first year of law school, *Moore v. Regents of the University of California*, 793 P.2d 479 (Cal. 1990), the plaintiff's genetic material had been used without his permission to develop a cell line that enabled highly profitable medical research. His claims included conversion, lack of informed consent, and breach of fiduciary duty, but much of the analysis in the case turned on his property-based theories, which the court ultimately rejected. In part, the holding in *Moore* was based on the conclusion that physicians' traditional fiduciary duties protect patients effectively, so recognizing individuals' ownership over their biological material would be an unnecessary but dramatic innovation with possible unintended consequences. Does that conclusion hold true for genetic privacy overall? For privacy more broadly? Would the interpretation of the Genetic Privacy Act in *Bearder* give parents property rights over their newborns' blood samples? Or would such a law be better explained as a data protection measure?

## Focus

### Is Genetic Privacy Special?

We have seen throughout this chapter that personal medical information is assumed to have special sensitivity, in part because of its relationship to the body, that most private of spaces. This assumption is much stronger for individual genetic information. Collection of DNA information in law enforcement has been a contentious issue in constitutional law in both the US and Europe, as seen in cases like *S and Marper v. United Kingdom, Maryland v. King*, and *People v. Buza*. [see Chapter 1]. Medical research involving genetics and genomics typically receives much more scrutiny from IRBs and other authorities concerned about respect for privacy and additional individual consequences that could arise from such studies. GINA and the Minnesota Genetic Privacy Act discussed in *Bearder* are just two examples of multiple statutes establishing distinct privacy rules for genetic information. Illinois restricts the use of biometric identification. *See* Illinois Biometric Information Privacy Act, 740 ILCS 14. At least 35 states have statutes that restrict the disclosure of genetic information, with details that vary greatly from one state to the next. In Delaware, for example, informed consent is necessary for any disclosure of genetic information, with some narrow enumerated exceptions. *See* DEL. CODE ANN., tit. 16, § 1205. New York requires specific individual consent for all disclosures of genetic testing results (so that usually a general waiver allowing release medical records, for example, will not suffice). *See* N.Y. CLS Civ R § 79–L. The list of specific state requirements goes on at length.

Before reading further, pause to consider this crucial question: Why is genetic data perceived as special, different from all other types of personal information?

There are many potential reasons. For one thing, genetic information could support conclusions about an individual that would have been impossible to reach before. Many of these conclusions amount only to an increased likelihood or propensity, which further increases discomfort about the disclosure of genetic information and implicates the threat of discriminatory treatment addressed partially in GINA. Second, as our knowledge in this area improves rapidly, there is a strong possibility that any given piece of genetic data will provide even more information about an individual than it does today, as our understanding of the relationship between genes and personal characteristics increases. This unpredictability is a major reason for caution in dealing with genetic information: in life cycle terms, the potential uses for the data may expand greatly after collection has already occurred. These two concerns then combine to intensify the problems they raise: what if we discover later that a particular genetic pattern increases, say, the likelihood of antisocial behavior? If DNA data collected for present purposes could be used in the future to identify persons more prone to commit crimes, is this a result we should welcome? What might be the consequences? What privacy concerns might it raise? Would it upset some of our current assumptions about how anti-social behavior should be addressed? And if all this speculation starts to remind us of the science fiction dystopias depicted in well-known movies such as *Minority Report* or *Gattaca*, then perhaps that helps to underline the deep societal unease about genetic information.

A third aspect of genetic data that may make it different from other types of personal data is the extreme individuality of each person's genetic code. Older techniques of deidentification become very difficult to use when a data point is truly unique, associated with only one person on the planet. Fourth, genetic information may reflect not only on the data subject but on that person's blood relatives, giving rise to possible privacy consequences for individuals who have never given any consent to disclosure of genetic information about themselves. The *Dierickx* decision [see Section A above] illustrated this point.

Fifth, and perhaps most importantly, much of our understanding of genetics is so recent that it disrupts settled models for thinking about privacy. We have seen at many other points in this book how new technology—such as instant photography for Warren and Brandeis, the telephone for wiretapping law, or the internet for commercial privacy and social media—upended previous social and legal models. Because it is so new, it is also unfamiliar to most ordinary people, and fully understood mostly by scientists and other specialists. This novelty helps foster a general sense of suspicion and unease about genetic privacy as well.

Do other aspects of genetic information make it different from personal data studied elsewhere in this book? Must the legal approach change dramatically as a result of all these differences? Why or why not?

---

# CHAPTER 13

# FINANCIAL RECORDS

Rev. Billy Graham, the famous evangelical Christian minister, once said, "Give me five minutes with a person's checkbook, and I will tell you where their heart is." While most people write fewer paper checks than they used to, the sentiment surely carries over to online banking transactions or credit card statements. Financial institutions hold vast quantities of personal data about their customers. Many people consider information about their finances particularly private, especially because, as Graham suggested, financial transactions can reveal so much about a person's preferences, habits, and even physical location. At the same time, the rise of online banking and the advent of modern identity theft heighten concerns about data security in the financial services industry. Not surprisingly, then, Congress has passed several important financial privacy statutes. As you review them in this chapter, note how the regulatory structure in this area is split between many different authorities, and consider the pros and cons of this arrangement. [The same is true of FCRA, discussed in Chapter 6.] In addition, compare privacy and data protection law in the financial services industry to other sectoral regulations you have studied. The laws discussed here generally follow a consumer protection blueprint rather than a data protection one. Why do you think that is so? This chapter begins with the general topic of law enforcement access to financial data [Section A] before turning to some narrower rules applicable to financial institutions: regulations issued under the Gramm-Leach-Bliley Act [Section B] and the Red Flags Rule for detection of identity theft [Section C].

## A. LAW ENFORCEMENT ACCESS TO FINANCIAL RECORDS

Under the third party doctrine in constitutional law, a person's reasonable expectation of privacy typically does not extend to information that he or she has given to another person or entity [see Chapter 1]. In *United States v. Miller*, 425 U.S. 435 (1976), the Supreme Court found that the third party doctrine applies to financial records held by a bank:

> The depositor takes the risk, in revealing his affairs to another, that the information will be conveyed by that person to the Government. This Court has held repeatedly that the Fourth Amendment does not prohibit the obtaining of information revealed to a third party and conveyed by him to Government authorities, even if the information is revealed on the assumption that it will be used only for a limited purpose and the confidence placed in the third party will not be betrayed.

*Id.* at 443. Because a depositor has no reasonable expectation of privacy, the Court held the Fourth Amendment did not apply to bank records and law enforcement may examine them without a search warrant.

Just as Congress had earlier responded to a Supreme Court ruling that allowed warrantless wiretapping [see Chapter 1], so too Congress passed new limitations on access to bank records soon after the *Miller* decision. The Right to Financial Privacy Act (RFPA), 12 U.S.C. §§ 3401 et seq., requires that, at a minimum, the government must (a) secure an administrative subpoena or an equivalent "formal written request" and (b) provide notice to a depositor before examining bank records. The standard for the subpoena or request is considerably less than would be needed under the Fourth Amendment; rather than demonstrating probable cause, the government can get an administrative subpoena as long as "there is reason to believe that the records sought are relevant to a legitimate law enforcement inquiry." *Id.* §§ 3405(1), 3408(3). The RFPA allows the depositor to challenge the subpoena, *id.* § 3410, or to sue a bank for violations, *id.* § 3417. Of course, if investigators get consent or a traditional search warrant, the requirements of both the Fourth Amendment and the statute are fulfilled, and they need not give advance notice to the account holder, *see id.* § 3402. As a result of the RFPA, bank records are subject to a specialized hybrid set of rules for law enforcement access, demanding more than in ordinary third party situations but less than if the Fourth Amendment applied.

## Anderson v. La Junta State Bank

115 F.3d 756 (10th Cir. 1997)

■ BURRAGE, CHIEF DISTRICT JUDGE [sitting by designation].

Plaintiffs Larry O. Anderson and his wife, Alberta, appeal from an order of the district court granting La Junta State Bank's motion for summary judgment. Plaintiffs brought this action pursuant to 12 U.S.C. §§ 3401–3422, the Right to Financial Privacy Act (RFPA), alleging that the Bank had violated their rights under the Act.

In 1993, the Air Force began an investigation of Mr. Anderson, then an active duty lieutenant colonel in the Air Force, for violations of various provisions of the Uniform Code of Military Justice, including theft of nonappropriated funds. An investigating agent met with the Bank's senior vice president and asked him to produce plaintiffs' bank records. The vice president pulled up the information on his computer screen and, without permitting the investigator to view the screen, informed him that plaintiffs' records contained nothing relevant to the investigation as only Mr. Anderson's military pay check was being deposited into their account. The investigators later subpoenaed plaintiffs' bank records.

Plaintiffs thereafter commenced this action. They initially alleged the Bank had violated the RFPA because plaintiffs were not afforded the opportunity to challenge the subpoenas issued pursuant to the RFPA.

However, plaintiffs [eventually relied on an allegation] that the Bank had violated the RFPA when it orally released information in response to the investigator's oral request.

The RFPA was enacted in response to a pattern of government abuse in the area of individual privacy and was intended to protect the customers of financial institutions from unwarranted intrusion into their records while at the same time permitting legitimate law enforcement activity by requiring federal agencies to follow established procedures when seeking a customer's financial records. However, "[t]he most salient feature of the [RFPA] is the narrow scope of the entitlements it creates" by limiting the kinds of customers to whom the RFPA applies and the types of records it protects. *SEC v. Jerry T. O'Brien, Inc.*, 467 U.S. 735, 745 (1984).

Under the RFPA, the government may have access to, or obtain copies of, information contained in a customer's financial records from a financial institution only if the customer authorizes the disclosure, the government obtains an administrative or judicial subpoena or summons, or the records are sought pursuant to a search warrant or formal written request. *See* 12 U.S.C. § 3402. Further, the financial institution may not release the requested financial records until the government "certifies in writing to the financial institution that it has complied with the applicable provisions" of the RFPA, including notice to the customer of the existence of the subpoena, summons, search warrant, or request; the nature of the government's inquiry; and permitting the customer sufficient time to respond to the notice. *Id.* §§ 3403(b), 3405–08.

The RFPA also restricts disclosure of customers' financial records by financial institutions themselves. Financial institutions may not provide "any Government authority access to or copies of, or the information contained in, the financial records of any customer. . . ." *Id.* § 3403(a). One exception has been provided: A financial institution may notify a Government authority if it believes it has "information which may be relevant to a possible violation of a statute or regulation." *Id.* § 3403(c). In such a case, the financial institution may provide only the customer's name or other identifying information and the nature of the suspected illegal activity. *See id.*

The issue in this case is one we have not previously addressed. We must determine whether an oral request by a government investigator which is orally responded to, without permitting visual inspection of the customer's records, violates the RFPA, absent compliance by the Government authority with [RFPA] requirements.

The district court held, and the bank argues, that such a disclosure does not run afoul of the RFPA. The district court held that our decision in *Bailey v. USDA*, 59 F.3d 141 (10th Cir. 1995), permitted the Bank to orally disclose the information provided. We disagree.

In *Bailey*, the bank suspected two of its customers were engaging in questionable banking practices relating to the deposit of food stamps and the immediate withdrawal of a corresponding amount of cash. The bank notified the government. A government investigator went to the bank and interviewed a bank employee who told the investigator the customers' names and the monetary value of the transactions and showed him a log of the transactions. We held this disclosure did not violate § 3403(c) as only the "essence of the suspected illegal activity" was revealed by the disclosure.

The district court held that the disclosure in this case was also valid as the bank revealed even less information than had been revealed in *Bailey*. However, the issue here is not how much information was provided, but who initiated the contact. The Bank did not suspect plaintiffs of any wrongdoing. Rather, the government initiated the contact based on suspicions arising from information obtained from sources outside of plaintiffs' bank records. We agree with the district court that had the Bank suspected plaintiffs of wrongdoing and initiated contact with the government investigators, the information disclosed would not have violated the RFPA. However, the Bank could not respond to the government's inquiry and release information to the government investigator unless the government had properly complied with the procedures set forth in the RFPA. Thus, the Bank violated the RFPA.

The Bank also argues that the RFPA permits oral disclosure of information absent compliance with RFPA procedures. The RFPA prohibits the release of "financial records" unless set procedures are followed. "Financial records" are defined as "an original of, a copy of, or information known to have been derived from" a customer's bank records. 12 U.S.C. § 3401(2). The oral disclosure here by the Bank related information derived from plaintiffs' bank records and was protected by the RFPA. The RFPA does not require that such information be conveyed in writing before its disclosure can violate a bank customer's right to privacy in his records.

We need not consider whether plaintiffs suffered any damages as a result of the disclosure. If the government or a financial institution violates the RFPA, the customer whose financial records were disclosed is entitled to $100, regardless of the volume of records involved. *Id.* § 3417(a). Damages may also be awarded in the form of any actual damages sustained as a result of the disclosure and punitive damages if the violation is determined to have been willful or intentional. *Id.* Further, if the action is successful, costs and reasonable attorney's fees may also be awarded. *Id.* We leave it for the district court in the first instance to determine whether damages are appropriate here.

The judgment of the United States District Court for the District of Colorado is REVERSED, and the case is REMANDED for further proceedings in accordance with this opinion.

## Tabet v. SEC

2012 WL 3205581 (S.D. Cal. Aug. 6, 2012)

■ DAVID H. BARTICK, UNITED STATES MAGISTRATE JUDGE.

Movants Paul Tabet and Jenifer Tabet ("Movants") filed a Motion for Order Pursuant to Customer Challenge Provisions of the Right to Financial Privacy Act of 1978, 12 U.S.C. § 3410. Movants seek an order preventing the U.S. Securities and Exchange Commission ("SEC") from obtaining access to their personal financial records. On July 30, 2012, the SEC filed a verified Opposition to the motion. Having considered the parties' submissions and supporting exhibits, the Court DENIES the motion.

The SEC is investigating whether certain persons or entities have violated, or are violating, federal securities laws by making false and misleading statements to investors, or otherwise engaging in fraudulent conduct, in connection with the offer and sale of pre-initial public offering ("pre-IPO") shares of Facebook, Inc. The SEC proffers that through its investigation, it has obtained evidence that Movants may have been involved in the alleged violations.

As part of its investigation, the SEC sought Movants' bank records through an administrative subpoena. On June 14, 2012, the SEC issued two subpoenas to Bank of America, one for Paul Tabet's bank records and one for Jenifer Tabet's bank records. On June 14, 2012, the SEC also sent Movants a certified letter informing each of them that it intended to subpoena their financial records from Bank of America. The subpoenas request account opening records, account statements, checks, wire transfers, signature cards, and other records, for the time period from January 1, 2009 to present.

On June 28, 2012, Movants timely moved to quash the subpoenas. *See* 12 U.S.C. § 3410(a) (requiring a motion to quash an administrative subpoena or summons to be filed within ten days of service or fourteen days of mailing.) Movants contend the financial records sought are not relevant to a legitimate law enforcement inquiry, that the subpoena is overbroad, oppressive, lacks particularity, and that the request amounts to a warrantless search and seizure under the Fourth Amendment.

On July 2, 2012, the Court ordered the SEC to respond to the motion to quash. On July 30, 2012 the SEC filed its verified opposition.

Under the Right to Financial Privacy Act ("RFPA"), 12 U.S.C. §§ 3401 et seq., a financial institution may disclose a customer's financial records if such records are properly requested by a governmental authority via an administrative subpoena or judicial subpoena. 12 U.S.C. § 3402(2) and (4). If a customer objects to the disclosure of their records, the customer must file a motion to quash the subpoena that includes an affidavit or sworn statement, and timely serve the government entity with the motion. 12 U.S.C. § 3410(a). If the Court orders the government entity to respond to the motion to quash, the government must filed a sworn response. § 3410(b).

In ruling on the motion to quash, the Court must determine whether: (1) Movants are the customers whose financial records are being sought; (2) the law enforcement inquiry is legitimate; and (3) the records sought are relevant to the law enforcement inquiry. 12 U.S.C. § 3410(c).

First, Movants have standing to challenge the subpoena under the RFPA. Movants state in their sworn statements that they are customers of Bank of America whose bank records are being sought. The SEC does not contest their allegations.

Second, there is no dispute that the SEC has established it is involved in a legitimate law enforcement inquiry. The RFPA defines a law enforcement inquiry as "a lawful investigation or official proceeding inquiring into a violation of, or failure to comply with, any criminal or civil statute or any regulation, rule, or order issued pursuant thereto." 12 U.S.C. § 3401(8). In this case, the inquiry is lawful because the SEC is empowered to undertake investigations to determine whether violation[s] of the federal securities laws have occurred. The Court, therefore, concludes that the subpoenas issued to Bank of America are part of a legitimate law enforcement inquiry.

Third, the SEC has demonstrated that there is reason to believe the bank records sought by the subpoenas are relevant to a legitimate law enforcement inquiry. The burden is on the SEC to make a sufficient showing of relevance. To satisfy this burden, the SEC submitted an Opposition to the Motion to Quash and a declaration signed under penalty of perjury by Christopher M. Castano, an attorney with the SEC's Division of Enforcement. The SEC contends the subpoenaed records are relevant because they are likely to provide information about the extent of Movants' involvement in the alleged scheme; what other persons or entities were involved in the scheme, what ultimately happened to the investors' money; the extent to which investor money may have been misused for purposes other than the specific investment purpose for which the funds were purportedly raised; the identity of potential victims; and the amount of any disgorgement that might potentially be owed in the event of an enforcement action.

Movants contend the subpoenas are not relevant because they seek records [dating back to] January 1, 2009 [and that the subpoenas are] overbroad, oppressive, lack particularity, and amount to a warrantless search and seizure. These arguments are unavailing. First, the SEC has indicated it has evidence that the scheme being investigated dates as far back as 2010, and there is other relevant information that dates to well before 2009. Second, even if not every record sought turns out to be relevant, there is reason to believe the records overall contain information relevant to the investigation. Third, the subpoenas do not lack particularity. They provide thorough definitions, identify specific types of records that are sought from Movants' accounts, and they provide a specific time period (January 1, 2009 to present). Finally, Movants' argument that the subpoenas violate the Fourth Amendment lacks merit. In *United States v. Miller*, 425 U.S. 435 (1967), the Supreme Court held that bank customers have no legitimate expectation of privacy in their bank records. Therefore, when a federal agency issues a subpoena for customer records from a bank, the customer cannot successfully challenge the subpoena on Fourth Amendment grounds.

## NOTES

1. ***The "Relevance" Standard.*** The standard articulated in the statute and applied in *Tabet* requires only that law enforcement show there is "reason to believe that the records sought are relevant to a legitimate law enforcement inquiry." This is not an especially demanding standard. The burden is on the government to satisfy it, but typically law enforcement officers will be able to demonstrate *some* legitimate purpose for their inquiry. Other statutes also require less than the "probable cause" showing for a search warrant but more than the zero showing that the Supreme Court has found required by the Constitution when the third party doctrine applies: the Stored Communications Act [see Chapter 5] and the Foreign Intelligence Surveillance Act [see Chapter 9] are two prominent examples. If you have studied those statutes, how do their standards compare with the RFPA? Also consider for a moment this broader question, which is pursued in the notes that follow: what purpose does such a diluted standard serve?

2. ***Shielding the Bank.*** One possible benefit of a standard for law enforcement access to records held by third parties, even a relatively forgiving one such as the one included in the RFPA, is that it changes the position of the financial institution. When you were a teenager, did you ever get out of an unpleasant or boring social obligation by saying your parents would not permit you to go? The RFPA offers the same sort of shield to banks. When law enforcement requests depositor records, the third party doctrine suggests that the bank is free to choose to provide them. And banks are generally eager to stay in the government's good graces. Thanks to the RFPA, they can reply, "Shucks, I would love to give you these records, but I am not allowed." The fact that failure to follow the RFPA's procedural requirements opens the financial institution to the risk of a lawsuit helps justify that refusal even more.

3. ***Fishing Expeditions.*** Another result of a relevance standard like the one in the RFPA and other statutes named above is a curb on "fishing expeditions" through bank records. One danger of broad investigative power is the possibility that the authorities will use that power to target someone for reasons unrelated to any underlying criminal charges. [This issue comes up, for example, in critiques and defenses of the Computer Fraud and Abuse Act, see Chapter 7.] According to this argument, if the federal government wanted to harass the Andersons or the Tabets, it could rummage through their bank records in the hopes of finding some basis to accuse them of wrongdoing. A requirement that the government articulate the existence of a legitimate investigation to a court first—and give notice to the target about

that basis, so that there is an opportunity to respond and argue that it is unjustified—helps to prevent the state from using this power indiscriminately. At the same time, bank records can be a valuable way for investigators to develop the theories that allow them to formulate probable cause, and the RFPA standard gives them access to records for that purpose. Indeed, the RFPA allows the government to procure financial records about people who will not themselves be accused, provided those records are relevant to an investigation.

4. ***Statutory Damages.*** The *Anderson* court does not decide whether the plaintiffs there suffered any damages, leaving the district court to make this fact-specific determination. That case was decided in 1997. We have seen more recent courts hold that Article III standing could depend on the existence of an additional injury beyond a disclosure made contrary to the law. If this case came up today, could the La Junta State Bank argue that the Andersons lacked standing to bring their claim?

5. ***Required Bank Disclosures.*** As a counterweight to the RFPA's requirements that financial institutions may not divulge depositor records without certain safeguards, different laws *require* disclosures to the government in other circumstances. In particular, the Bank Secrecy Act ("BSA"), 31 U.S.C. §§ 5311 et seq., was enacted in 1970 in an effort to combat money laundering. Its best-known provision is the requirement that banks notify the federal government if an individual engages in transactions that exceeded an aggregate of $10,000 in a single day. The scope of the statute has since been expanded several times, so now the law states that its purpose is "to require certain reports or records where they have a high degree of usefulness in criminal, tax, or regulatory investigations or proceedings, or in the conduct of intelligence or counterintelligence activities, including analysis, to protect against international terrorism." *Id.* § 5311. A division of the Treasury Department, the Financial Crimes Enforcement Network (FinCEN), oversees compliance with the BSA and collects numerous reports from banks concerning certain defined transactions. FinCEN has issued complex regulations defining the situations that banks must report. These include "suspicious activity" that appears structured to evade the other reporting requirements, such as multiple transactions just below the reporting threshold. *See* 31 C.F.R. Chapter X. Financial institutions that fail to file required reports with FinCEN can be penalized with significant fines.

## B. THE GRAMM-LEACH-BLILEY ACT

In 1999, Congress passed a comprehensive banking regulation bill that eliminated many restrictions on the operations of financial institutions, in particular allowing the same company to provide a wider range of services under one roof. Because these combined services would increase access to customer information previously held by distinct entities, the changes gave rise to new data privacy and security concerns. At the same time, the commercial internet was beginning to become an extremely important force in daily life, which further increased privacy risks from online financial activity. In response to both of these developments, Congress included provisions in the sprawling bill concerning financial institutions' handling of "nonpublic personal information"—a term agencies have defined broadly in regulations to encompass not only purely financial information, but also accompanying data such as names, addresses, Social Security numbers, and even content a financial institution gathers from a web site cookie [see Chapter 5]. Because of this law, known as the Gramm-Leach-Bliley Act (and also as the "GLBA" or "GLB Act"), as well as regulations issued under it, financial institutions have responsibilities concerning (1) notice provided to customers about data handling practices; (2) disclosure of information to unaffiliated entities; and (3) data security.

## The Gramm-Leach-Bliley Financial Services Modernization Act

15 U.S.C. §§ 6801 et seq.

### § 6801. Protection of nonpublic personal information

(a) Privacy obligation policy

It is the policy of the Congress that each financial institution has an affirmative and continuing obligation to respect the privacy of its customers and to protect the security and confidentiality of those customers' nonpublic personal information.

(b) Financial institutions safeguards

In furtherance of the policy in subsection (a) of this section, [designated agencies] shall establish appropriate standards for the financial institutions subject to their jurisdiction relating to administrative, technical, and physical safeguards—

(1) to insure the security and confidentiality of customer records and information;

(2) to protect against any anticipated threats or hazards to the security or integrity of such records; and

(3) to protect against unauthorized access to or use of such records or information which could result in substantial harm or inconvenience to any customer.

### § 6802. Obligations with respect to disclosures of personal information

(a) Notice requirements

Except as otherwise provided in this subchapter, a financial institution may not, directly or through any affiliate, disclose to a nonaffiliated third party any nonpublic personal information, unless such financial institution provides or has provided to the consumer a notice that complies with section 6803 of this title.

(b) Opt out

(1) In general—A financial institution may not disclose nonpublic personal information to a nonaffiliated third party unless—

(A) such financial institution clearly and conspicuously discloses to the consumer, in writing or in electronic form or other form permitted by [agency regulations], that such information may be disclosed to such third party;

(B) the consumer is given the opportunity, before the time that such information is initially disclosed, to direct that such information not be disclosed to such third party; and

(C) the consumer is given an explanation of how the consumer can exercise that nondisclosure option.

(2) Exception—This subsection shall not prevent a financial institution from providing nonpublic personal information to a nonaffiliated third party to perform services for or functions on behalf of the financial institution, including marketing of the financial institution's own products or services . . . if the financial institution fully discloses the providing of such information and enters into a contractual agreement with the third party that requires the third party to maintain the confidentiality of such information.

(c) Limits on reuse of information

Except as otherwise provided in this subchapter, a nonaffiliated third party that receives from a financial institution nonpublic personal information under this section shall not, directly or through an affiliate of such receiving third party, disclose such information to any other person that is a nonaffiliated third party of both the financial institution and such receiving third party, unless such disclosure would be lawful if made directly to such other person by the financial institution.

(d) Limitations on the sharing of account number information for marketing purposes

A financial institution shall not disclose, other than to a consumer reporting agency, an account number or similar form of access number or access code for a credit card account, deposit account, or transaction account of a consumer to any nonaffiliated third party for use in telemarketing, direct mail marketing, or other marketing through electronic mail to the consumer.

(e) General exceptions—Subsections (a) and (b) of this section shall not prohibit the disclosure of nonpublic personal information—

(1) as necessary to effect, administer, or enforce a transaction requested or authorized by the consumer, or in connection with—

(A) servicing or processing a financial product or service requested or authorized by the consumer;

(B) maintaining or servicing the consumer's account with the financial institution, or with another entity as part of a private label credit card program or other extension of credit on behalf of such entity; or

(C) a proposed or actual securitization, secondary market sale (including sales of servicing rights), or similar transaction related to a transaction of the consumer;

(2) with the consent or at the direction of the consumer;

. . .

(5) to the extent specifically permitted or required under other provisions of law and in accordance with the Right to Financial Privacy Act of 1978, to law enforcement agencies . . .

. . .

**§ 6803. Disclosure of institution privacy policy**

(a) Disclosure required—At the time of establishing a customer relationship with a consumer and not less than annually during the continuation of such relationship, a financial institution shall provide a clear and conspicuous disclosure to such consumer, in writing or in electronic form or other form permitted by [agency regulations], of such financial institution's policies and practices with respect to—

(1) disclosing nonpublic personal information to affiliates and nonaffiliated third parties, consistent with section 6802 of this title, including the categories of information that may be disclosed;

(2) disclosing nonpublic personal information of persons who have ceased to be customers of the financial institution; and

(3) protecting the nonpublic personal information of consumers.

. . .

(c) Information to be included—The disclosure required by subsection (a) of this section shall include—

(1) the policies and practices of the institution with respect to disclosing nonpublic personal information to nonaffiliated third parties, including—

(A) the categories of persons to whom the information is or may be disclosed, other than the persons to whom the information may be provided pursuant to section 6802(e) of this title; and

(B) the policies and practices of the institution with respect to disclosing of nonpublic personal information of persons who have ceased to be customers of the financial institution;

(2) the categories of nonpublic personal information that are collected by the financial institution; [and]

(3) the policies that the institution maintains to protect the confidentiality and security of nonpublic personal information in accordance with section 6801 of this title[.]

. . .

(e) Model forms

(1) In general

The [designated agencies] shall jointly develop a model form which may be used, at the option of the financial institution, for the provision of disclosures under this section.

(2) Format—A model form developed under paragraph (1) shall—

(A) be comprehensible to consumers, with a clear format and design;

(B) provide for clear and conspicuous disclosures;

(C) enable consumers easily to identify the sharing practices of a financial institution and to compare privacy practices among financial institutions; and

(D) be succinct, and use an easily readable type font.

. . .

(4) Safe harbor

Any financial institution that elects to provide the model form developed by the agencies under this subsection shall be deemed to be in compliance with the disclosures required under this section.

### § 6807. Relation to State laws

(a) In general

This subchapter and the amendments made by this subchapter shall not be construed as superseding, altering, or affecting any statute, regulation, order, or interpretation in effect in any State, except to the extent that such statute, regulation, order, or interpretation is inconsistent with the provisions of this subchapter, and then only to the extent of the inconsistency.

(b) Greater protection under State law

For purposes of this section, a State statute, regulation, order, or interpretation is not inconsistent with the provisions of this subchapter if the protection such statute, regulation, order, or interpretation affords any person is greater than the protection provided under this subchapter and the amendments made by this subchapter, as determined by the Bureau of Consumer Financial Protection, after consultation with [other designated agencies].

**§ 6809. Definitions.**

. . .

(4) Nonpublic personal information

(A) The term "nonpublic personal information" means personally identifiable financial information—

(i) provided by a consumer to a financial institution;

(ii) resulting from any transaction with the consumer or any service performed for the consumer; or

(iii) otherwise obtained by the financial institution.

(B) Such term does not include publicly available information. . .

(C) Notwithstanding subparagraph (B), such term—

(i) shall include any list, description, or other grouping of consumers (and publicly available information pertaining to them) that is derived using any nonpublic personal information other than publicly available information; but

(ii) shall not include any list, description, or other grouping of consumers (and publicly available information pertaining to them) that is derived without using any nonpublic personal information.

(5) Nonaffiliated third party

The term "nonaffiliated third party" means any entity that is not an affiliate of, or related by common ownership or affiliated by corporate control with, the financial institution, but does not include a joint employee of such institution.

(6) Affiliate

The term "affiliate" means any company that controls, is controlled by, or is under common control with another company.

## NOTES

1. ***Regulation and Enforcement.*** Regulatory authority under the Gramm-Leach-Bliley Act is divided among many agencies. When Congress created the Consumer Financial Protection Bureau (CFPB), it transferred primary rulemaking authority under both the GLB Act and the Fair Credit Reporting Act (FCRA) [see Chapter 6] from the FTC to the CFPB. But numerous financial regulators also have enforcement powers under Gramm-Leach-Bliley, in relation to the particular types of institutions each one oversees. Agencies with that type of authority under the GLB Act include the Federal Reserve Bank's Board of Governors, the Commodity Futures Trading Commission (CFTC), the Federal Deposit Insurance Corporation

(FDIC), the National Credit Union Administration (NCUA), the Office of the Comptroller of the Currency (OCC), the Office of Thrift Supervision (OTC), and the Securities and Exchange Commission (SEC). Before the creation of the CFPB, these other agencies jointly adopted identical regulations interpreting the privacy provisions of the Gramm-Leach-Bliley Act and codified them separately in portions of the Code of Federal Regulations applicable to each individual agency. *See, e.g.*, 12 C.F.R. Part 40 (codifying the multi-agency regulations for Office of Comptroller of the Currency). Those rules remain in force.

2. ***Model Notice.*** In 2006, Congress amended the statute and directed that eight financial regulatory agencies should cooperatively develop a model privacy notice form. *See* 15 U.S.C. § 6803(e). The form the agencies created is reproduced below. Financial institutions that use the model are automatically deemed in compliance with their notice responsibilities under the Gramm-Leach-Bliley Act, *id.* § 6803(e)(4), so most do just that. The shift to a model form responded to critics who said that previous annual disclosures from banks had been so complicated that they were impossible for consumers to understand, and that as a result only an infinitesimal proportion of consumers exercised their opt-out rights. *See, e.g.*, Edward J. Janger and Paul M. Schwartz, *The Gramm-Leach-Bliley Act, Information Privacy, and the Limits of Default Rules*, 86 MINN. L. REV. 1219 (2001). The model form was influenced by other government-mandated standardized information disclosure formats, such as the nutrition label found on food packaging or the "Schumer Box" spelling out the terms for credit card offers. How well do you think the model form works? How does the information it contains differ from the list in § 6803(c)?

3. ***Comparison with Other Consumer Protection Laws.*** With its default allowing free use of information, its emphasis on notice and choice, and its close ties to commercial activity, the Gramm-Leach-Bliley Act qualifies as a consumer protection law rather than a measure aimed at data protection [see Chapters 3 and 4]. How do the privacy requirements this law places on banks compare to responsibilities of other commercial enterprises under the consumer protection model, such as Amazon.com? One difference can be seen in the rules about notice: the GLB Act requires that banks provide their customers with privacy notices that contain particular information about certain practices, and regulators have also created a model notice to illustrate these. What else differentiates banks from other businesses? Is the different treatment justified? Does it place comparatively too much burden on banks? Do you think the Gramm-Leach-Bliley Act is likely to be more effective than the baseline consumer protection model?

Rev. [insert date]

| FACTS | WHAT DOES [NAME OF FINANCIAL INSTITUTION] DO WITH YOUR PERSONAL INFORMATION? |
|---|---|
| Why? | Financial companies choose how they share your personal information. Federal law gives consumers the right to limit some but not all sharing. Federal law also requires us to tell you how we collect, share, and protect your personal information. Please read this notice carefully to understand what we do. |
| What? | The types of personal information we collect and share depend on the product or service you have with us. This information can include:<br>■ Social Security number and [income]<br>■ [account balances] and [payment history]<br>■ [credit history] and [credit scores] |
| How? | All financial companies need to share customers' personal information to run their everyday business. In the section below, we list the reasons financial companies can share their customers' personal information; the reasons [name of financial institution] chooses to share; and whether you can limit this sharing. |

| Reasons we can share your personal information | Does **[name of financial institution]** share? | Can you limit this sharing? |
|---|---|---|
| **For our everyday business purposes—** such as to process your transactions, maintain your account(s), respond to court orders and legal investigations, or report to credit bureaus | | |
| **For our marketing purposes—** to offer our products and services to you | | |
| **For joint marketing with other financial companies** | | |
| **For our affiliates' everyday business purposes—** information about your transactions and experiences | | |
| **For our affiliates' everyday business purposes—** information about your creditworthiness | | |
| For our affiliates to market to you | | |
| **For nonaffiliates to market to you** | | |

| To limit our sharing | ■ Call **[phone number]**—our menu will prompt you through your choice(s)<br>■ Visit us online: **[website] or**<br>■ Mail the **form** below<br>**Please note:**<br>If you are a *new* customer, we can begin sharing your information [30] days from the date we sent this notice. When you are *no longer* our customer, we continue to share your information as described in this notice.<br>However, you can contact us at any time to limit our sharing. |
|---|---|
| Questions? | Call [phone number] or go to [website] |

✂ - - - - - - - - - - - - - - - - - - - -

**Mail-in Form**

| **Leave Blank OR** [If you have a joint account, your choice(s) will apply to everyone on your account unless you mark below.<br>❑ Apply my choices only to me] | Mark any/all you want to limit:<br>❑ Do not share information about my creditworthiness with your affiliates for their everyday business purposes.<br>❑ Do not allow your affiliates to use my personal information to market to me.<br>❑ Do not share my personal information with nonaffiliates to market their products and services to me. | |
|---|---|---|
| | Name<br>Address<br><br>City, State, Zip<br>**[Account #]** | **Mail to:**<br>[Name of Financial Institution]<br>[Address1]<br>[Address2]<br>[City], [ST] [ZIP] |

**Page 2**

| Who we are | |
|---|---|
| **Who is providing this notice?** | [insert] |

| What we do | |
|---|---|
| **How does [name of financial institution] protect my personal information?** | To protect your personal information from unauthorized access and use, we use security measures that comply with federal law. These measures include computer safeguards and secured files and buildings.<br><br>[insert] |
| **How does [name of financial institution] collect my personal information?** | We collect your personal information, for example, when you<br>▪ [open an account] or [deposit money]<br>▪ [pay your bills] or [apply for a loan]<br>▪ [use your credit or debit card]<br><br>[We also collect your personal information from other companies.]<br>**OR**<br>[We also collect your personal information from others, such as credit bureaus, affiliates, or other companies.] |
| **Why can't I limit all sharing?** | Federal law gives you the right to limit only<br>▪ sharing for affiliates' everyday business purposes—information about your creditworthiness<br>▪ affiliates from using your information to market to you<br>▪ sharing for nonaffiliates to market to you<br><br>State laws and individual companies may give you additional rights to limit sharing. [See below for more on your rights under state law.] |
| **What happens when I limit sharing for an account I hold jointly with someone else?** | [Your choices will apply to everyone on your account.]<br>**OR**<br>[Your choices will apply to everyone on your account—unless you tell us otherwise.] |

| Definitions | |
|---|---|
| **Affiliates** | Companies related by common ownership or control. They can be financial and nonfinancial companies.<br>▪ *[affiliate information]* |
| **Nonaffiliates** | Companies not related by common ownership or control. They can be financial and nonfinancial companies.<br>▪ *[nonaffiliate information]* |
| **Joint marketing** | A formal agreement between nonaffiliated financial companies that together market financial products or services to you.<br>▪ *[joint marketing information]* |

| Other important information |
|---|
| [insert other important information] |

4. ***Opt-out.*** As the Gramm-Leach-Bliley privacy provisions wended their way through Congress, there was heated debate about whether the new law should require banks to secure consent through an "opt-in" or an "opt-out." By choosing the latter, Congress made treatment of financial institutions broadly consistent with the more common American default rule of providing "notice and choice" to the consumer—notice about the details of data handling, and choice not to use the service or, at least under the GLB Act, to intervene and require different treatment. Other laws, particularly data protection regimes, instead demand an opt-in, where a data processor must secure affirmative consent from a consumer approving proposed

downstream uses and disclosures of personal information. Which is better? In a world without transaction costs, it would not matter: "Provided the market for financial privacy works fairly well, it should not make much difference whether we adopt an opt-out law or an opt-in law. Either way, an economically efficient level of information sharing will result." Jeffrey M. Lacker, *The Economics of Financial Privacy: To Opt Out or Opt In*, 88(3) FED. RES. BANK OF RICHMOND ECON. Q., 7 (2002); *see also* Jerry Kang & Benedikt Buchner, *Privacy in Atlantis*, 18 HARV. J.L & TECH. 229, 243–44 (2004) (suggesting differences between the "dignity" model that gives entitlement to individual and "market" model that gives entitlement to data collector are overstated). However, experience has shown that transaction costs make this what economists would call a very "sticky" default rule. The overwhelming majority of consumers do not take any action to opt out or to opt in, so that the underlying default applies. This means the choice of an opt-out or opt-in rule matters a great deal. [For another discussion of the same problem, in efforts to develop a technological "Do Not Track" protocol for web cookies, see Chapter 5.]

Supporters of opt-out, including the financial services industry, point to the high cost of collecting opt-in consent and the extremely low response rates. Data collectors would need to call customers repeatedly trying to secure an opt-in. That might cause more hassle and intrusion for consumers than they would experience from the marketing that is supposed to be the rule's actual target. One study examined the effect that opt-in requirements would have on MBNA Corporation, then a large and growing financial institution and one of the nation's largest issuers of credit cards, which later was acquired by Bank of America. MBNA specialized in "affinity cards"—credit cards cobranded with partners such as professional organizations, university alumni associations, or sports teams—whose success depended on sharing information with the partners. As the authors state their conclusion:

> [W]e found that mandatory opt-in requirements on MBNA's operations would impair MBNA's affinity group business model, raise account acquisition costs and lower profits, reduce the supply of credit and raise credit card prices, generate more offers to uninterested or unqualified consumers and raise the number of missed opportunities for qualified consumers, and impair efforts to prevent fraud and identity theft.

Michael E. Staten & Fred H. Cate, *The Impact of Opt-in Privacy Rules on Retail Credit Markets: A Case Study of MBNA*, 52 DUKE L.J. 745, 783 (2003). Others protest that opt-out regimes simply shift those transaction costs to consumers, discouraging them from exercising control over the use of personal information. Moreover, these critics say, an opt-in structure harmonizes with the incentives of financial institutions to obtain consent:

> [A]n opt-in system is preferable, chiefly because it eliminates the incentive firms have to engage in strategic behavior and thus inflate consumer transaction costs. An opt-in system would permit consumers who wish to protect their privacy to do so without incurring transaction costs. Consumers who permit the use of their personal information should also be able to realize their wish

> easily. Indeed, because firms profit from the use of consumer information, firms would have an incentive to make it as easy as possible for consumers to consent to the use of their personal information.

Jeff Sovern, *Opting In, Opting Out, or No Options at All: The Fight for Control of Personal Information*, 74 WASH. L. REV. 1033, 1118 (1999); *see also* Janger & Schwartz, *supra* Note 2.

5. ***The Scope of Opt-Out Rights.*** A consumer's ability to veto information sharing under the GLB Act is actually rather limited. First, the statutory excerpt above omits numerous exemptions, including many specified in § 6802(e), which goes on for pages. The end result of this long list is to allow disclosures for many purposes, without a legal right for the consumer to opt out. Consumer choices mostly relate to disclosures for marketing and for evaluation of credit. The model form states this in plainer language than the statute. Are these two uses of information in fact the ones that consumers most wish to control? Second, the notice and opt-out provisions only govern disclosures to "nonaffiliated third parties." Recall that the larger purpose of the GLB Act was to allow financial institutions to engage in a broader range of activities. Under this provision, a single company might take information about a consumer derived from, for example, a checking account, and use it in connection with its own businesses offering mortgages, investment services, or insurance. As an executive of the American Bankers Association argued in opposition to an opt-in requirement, this can be beneficial to consumers:

> Let's say you're a bank customer with a checking account and a credit card account. In addition, you financed your mortgage through the same bank. Now you'd like to take out a loan to buy a new car. Ordinarily, the bank would have all your information in one place, making it relatively easy to apply for the new loan. But if you failed to allow the bank's various business lines to share information with one another—if you chose not to "opt in"—the bank would be forced to ask you to fill out a potentially lengthy application for the car loan—even though most of the relevant information probably already existed elsewhere in the bank.
>
> The auto-loan people wouldn't be able to talk to the mortgage people, who couldn't talk to the checking account people, who wouldn't be able to talk to the credit-card people. Your financial information at the bank would be compartmentalized. You might begin to wonder: At what cost have I gained my complete privacy?

Donald G. Ogilvie, *Financial Privacy: The Choice is in the Mail*, NAT'L CENTER FOR POL'Y ANALYSIS (Apr. 27, 2001). Ogilvie's argument resembles those presented by marketers in favor of targeted advertising [see Chapters 3 and 14] and Big Data analysis [see Chapter 6]. In the banking context it may take on special salience: surely, it would suggest, if the whole purpose of the GLB Act was to allow banks to offer many different products, its privacy provisions should not unravel the efficiencies created as a result.

6. ***Preacquired Account Marketing.*** There is only one type of disclosure flatly prohibited by the text of the Gramm-Leach-Bliley Act, rather than made contingent on a consumer opt-out. Look at § 6802(d). Why do you suppose an account number was singled out for this treatment? Under one interpretation, Congress intended to reach a practice known as preacquired account marketing. This occurs when a financial institution, for a fee, provides unaffiliated sales operations with special access to customer lists that include the customers' account numbers. The third parties can then debit the account directly; because they do not have to ask for an account number, they can make a sale without any need to ask that the customer provide it, which is how customers typically expect to authorize an account charge. Preacquired account marketing enables shady practices such as targeting immigrant or elderly customers who may not realize they are making a purchase, or setting up recurring charges for membership clubs or subscriptions that customers do not notice on their statements. When regulators interpreted the provision, however, their definition of "account number" excluded "a number or code in an encrypted form, as long as the bank does not provide the recipient with a means to decode the number or code." *See, e.g.*, 12 C.F.R. 40.12(c)(1). As a result, banks could still provide marketers access that allowed them to debit accounts,without knowing the account numbers themselves. Thus, preacquired account marketing continued. The regulators' interpretation understands Congress to have targeted a data security problem—in which case an encrypted account number is acceptable, because it cannot be misused or hacked in a way that risks theft from the account. Look at § 6802(d) again. Which reading do you consider more likely? *See* Prentiss Cox, *The Invisible Hand of Preacquired Account Marketing*, 47 HARV. J. ON LEGIS. 425 (2010).

7. ***Differences Between Policies.*** One might think that information handling practices would vary little within one highly regulated industry covered by a single privacy law, where most institutions use the same model notice. According to a recent study, one would be wrong. Researchers at Carnegie Mellon University wrote a computer program that automatically crawled the web, locating and analyzing financial institutions' model privacy notices. The program found notices for over 6,000 institutions and discovered significant differences between them, even among banks that were otherwise similar. *See* Lorrie Faith Cranor et al., *A Large-Scale Evaluation of U.S. Financial Institutions' Standardized Privacy Notices* (working paper, under review) (2015), available at http://cups.cs.cmu.edu/bankprivacy/financial notices-UnderReview.pdf. According to the researchers' analysis, large banks and those in northeastern states tended to share more customer data for marketing purposes than other banks. The study also found almost 100 banks that appeared not to comply with Gramm-Leach-Bliley requirements to make opt-outs available, and it identified many errors in model notices. The study results have been converted to a user-friendly web site that allows consumers to search for banks and compare their privacy notices to one another. *See* http://cups.cs.cmu.edu/bankprivacy/. Why do you suppose banks haven't converged around similar data practices?

8. ***Preemption and State Law.*** Unlike some federal privacy statutes, the Gramm-Leach-Bliley Act explicitly states that it does not preempt state law, particularly state law that offers a higher level of consumer protection. *See* 15 U.S.C. § 6807. A number of states have enacted stricter laws including, not surprisingly, California. The California Financial Information Privacy Act ("CalFIPA"), CAL. FIN. CODE §§ 4050 et seq., also known frequently by its original bill number, "S.B. 1," requires an opt-in for information sharing, *id.* § 4052.5. A statute in Vermont, VT. STAT. ANN. TIT. 8, §§ 10201 et seq., contains a similar opt-in rule for financial data. Under the clear terms of the GLB Act, this provision would seem not to be preempted by federal law, but there is a serious complication: FCRA [see Chapter 6] does preempt state law, and some of the information a financial institution might share is the type of credit information covered by that law. After lengthy litigation, a federal appeals court ultimately determined that financial institutions must secure customer opt-ins under CalFIPA for some types of data, but not for those types that are covered by FCRA. *See Am. Bankers Ass'n v. Lockyer*, 541 F.3d 1214 (9th Cir. 2008).

9. ***Online Notices.*** The CFPB issued new regulations in 2014 that allow financial institutions to provide annual privacy notice to customers online instead of by postal mail, under certain conditions. The banking industry had been enthusiastic about this change, given the cost of printing and mailing privacy notices (especially when applied to customers who choose to receive their statements and other communications electronically), but ended up being disappointed in the resulting regulations. The CFPB rule allows the online alternative only when all of the following conditions apply:

- The institution uses the model notice;
- The information in the notice has not changed since the consumer received the previous notice; and
- The information handling practices described in the notice do not trigger consumer opt-out rights under the Gramm-Leach-Bliley Act or the Fair Credit Reporting Act.

The last of these requirements prevents most larger banks, which are the most likely to share information, from being able to take advantage of the online alternative. Why did the CFPB structure its rule this way? Should financial institutions have greater flexibility as to the manner in which they provide notice?

## Standards for Safeguarding Customer Information [The "Safeguards Rule"]

16 C.F.R. Part 314

. . .

### § 314.3 Standards for safeguarding customer information.

(a) Information security program. You shall develop, implement, and maintain a comprehensive information security program that is written in one or more readily accessible parts and contains administrative, technical, and physical safeguards that are appropriate to your size and complexity, the nature and scope of your activities, and the sensitivity of any customer information at issue. Such safeguards shall include the elements set forth in § 314.4 and shall be reasonably designed to achieve the objectives of this part, as set forth in paragraph (b) of this section.

(b) Objectives. The objectives of section 501(b) of the [Gramm-Leach-Bliley] Act [15 U.S.C. § 6801(b)], and of this part, are to:

(1) Insure the security and confidentiality of customer information;

(2) Protect against any anticipated threats or hazards to the security or integrity of such information; and

(3) Protect against unauthorized access to or use of such information that could result in substantial harm or inconvenience to any customer.

**§ 314.4 Elements.**

In order to develop, implement, and maintain your information security program, you shall:

(a) Designate an employee or employees to coordinate your information security program.

(b) Identify reasonably foreseeable internal and external risks to the security, confidentiality, and integrity of customer information that could result in the unauthorized disclosure, misuse, alteration, destruction or other compromise of such information, and assess the sufficiency of any safeguards in place to control these risks. At a minimum, such a risk assessment should include consideration of risks in each relevant area of your operations, including:

(1) Employee training and management;

(2) Information systems, including network and software design, as well as information processing, storage, transmission and disposal; and

(3) Detecting, preventing and responding to attacks, intrusions, or other systems failures.

(c) Design and implement information safeguards to control the risks you identify through risk assessment, and regularly test or otherwise monitor the effectiveness of the safeguards' key controls, systems, and procedures.

(d) Oversee service providers, by:

(1) Taking reasonable steps to select and retain service providers that are capable of maintaining appropriate safeguards for the customer information at issue; and

(2) Requiring your service providers by contract to implement and maintain such safeguards.

(e) Evaluate and adjust your information security program in light of the results of the testing and monitoring required by paragraph (c) of this section; any material changes to your operations or business arrangements; or any other circumstances that you know or have reason to know may have a material impact on your information security program.

## In re R.T. Jones Capital Equities Management, Inc.

SEC Administrative Proceeding File No. 3–16827 (Sept. 22, 2015)

### ORDER

#### I.

The Securities and Exchange Commission ("Commission") deems it appropriate and in the public interest that public administrative and cease-and-desist proceedings be, and hereby are, instituted pursuant to the Investment Advisers Act of 1940 against R.T. Jones Capital Equities Management, Inc. ("R.T. Jones" or "Respondent").

#### II.

In anticipation of the institution of these proceedings, Respondent has submitted an Offer of Settlement (the "Offer") which the Commission has determined to accept. Solely for the purpose of these proceedings and any other proceedings brought by or on behalf of the Commission, or to which the Commission is a party, and without admitting or denying the findings herein, except as to the Commission's jurisdiction over it and the subject matter of these proceedings, which are admitted, Respondent consents to the entry of this Order, as set forth below.

#### III.

On the basis of this Order and Respondent's Offer, the Commission finds that

#### Summary

These proceedings arise out of R.T. Jones's failure to adopt written policies and procedures reasonably designed to protect customer records and information, in violation of [the Safeguards Rule]. From at least September 2009 through July 2013, R.T. Jones stored sensitive personally identifiable information ("PII") of clients and other persons on its third party-hosted web server without adopting written policies and procedures regarding the security and confidentiality of that information and the protection of that information from anticipated threats or unauthorized access. In July 2013, the firm's web server was attacked by an unauthorized, unknown intruder, who gained access rights and copy rights to the data on the server. As a result of the attack, the PII of more than 100,000 individuals, including thousands of R.T. Jones's clients, was rendered vulnerable to theft.

## Respondent

1. R.T. Jones, located in St. Louis, Missouri, is an investment adviser registered with the Commission that has approximately 8400 client accounts and about $480 million in regulatory assets under management. The firm does not have custody of client assets.

## Background

2. Through agreements with a retirement plan administrator and various retirement plan sponsors, R.T. Jones provides investment advice to individual plan participants using a managed account option called Artesys. Artesys offers a variety of model portfolios that range in investment objectives and risk profiles. Plan participants can access the Artesys program through R.T. Jones's public website. Plan participants who elect to enroll in the program are instructed to fill out a questionnaire on the website regarding their investment objectives and risk tolerance. Based on information provided in the questionnaire, R.T. Jones recommends a particular portfolio allocation from among the Artesys models to the client. If the client agrees to the recommended allocation, R.T. Jones provides trade instructions to the retirement plan administrator, which then effects the transactions. R.T. Jones does not control or maintain client accounts or client account information.

3. During the relevant period, in order to verify eligibility to enroll in Artesys, R.T. Jones required prospective clients to log on to its website by entering their name, date of birth and social security number. The login information was then compared against the PII of eligible plan participants, which was provided to R.T. Jones by its plan sponsor partners. R.T. Jones stored this PII, without modification or encryption, on its third party-hosted web server. To facilitate the verification process, the plan sponsors provided R.T. Jones with information about all of their plan participants. Thus, even though R.T. Jones had fewer than 8000 plan participant clients, its web server contained the PII of over 100,000 individuals.

4. R.T. Jones limited access to the PII stored on the server to two individuals who held administrator status. In July 2013, R.T. Jones discovered a potential cybersecurity breach at its third party-hosted web server. R.T. Jones promptly retained more than one cybersecurity consulting firm to confirm the attack and assess the scope of the breach. One of the forensic cybersecurity firms reported that the cyberattack had been launched from multiple IP addresses, all of which traced back to mainland China, and that the intruder had gained full access rights and copy rights to the data stored on the server. However, the cybersecurity firms could not determine the full nature or extent of the breach because the intruder had destroyed the log files surrounding the period of the intruder's activity.

6. Shortly after the breach incident, R.T. Jones provided notice of the breach to all of the individuals whose PII may have been

compromised and offered them free identity monitoring through a third-party provider. To date, the firm has not learned of any information indicating that a client has suffered any financial harm as a result of the cyber attack.

**R.T. Jones Failed to Adopt Written Policies and ProceduresReasonably Designed to Safeguard Customer Information**

8. During the relevant period, R.T. Jones maintained client PII on its third party-hosted web server. However, the firm failed to adopt any written policies and procedures reasonably designed to safeguard its clients' PII as required by the Safeguards Rule. R.T. Jones's policies and procedures for protecting its clients' information did not include, for example: conducting periodic risk assessments, employing a firewall to protect the web server containing client PII, encrypting client PII stored on that server, or establishing procedures for responding to a cybersecurity incident. Taken as a whole, R.T. Jones's policies and procedures for protecting customer records and information were not reasonable to safeguard customer information.

**Violations of the Federal Securities Laws**

9. As a result of the conduct described above, R.T. Jones willfully violated [the Safeguards Rule], which requires registered investment advisers to adopt written policies and procedures that are reasonably designed to safeguard customer records and information.

**Remedial Efforts**

10. To mitigate against any future risk of cyber threats, R.T. Jones has appointed an information security manager to oversee data security and protection of PII, and adopted and implemented a written information security policy. Among other things, the firm no longer stores PII on its webserver and any PII stored on its internal network is encrypted. The firm has also installed a new firewall and logging system to prevent and detect malicious incursions. Finally, R.T. Jones has retained a cybersecurity firm to provide ongoing reports and advice on the firm's information technology security.

11. In determining to accept R.T. Jones's Offer, the Commission considered the remedial acts promptly undertaken by R.T. Jones and the cooperation R.T. Jones afforded the Commission staff.

**IV.**

In view of the foregoing, the Commission deems it appropriate and in the public interest to impose the sanctions agreed to in R.T. Jones's Offer. Accordingly, pursuant to Sections 203(e) and 203(k) of the Advisers Act, it is hereby ORDERED that:

A. Respondent R.T. Jones cease and desist from committing or causing any violations and any future violations of Rule 30(a) of Regulation S–P (17 C.F.R. § 248.30(a));

B. Respondent R.T. Jones is censured; and

C. Respondent R.T. Jones shall pay, within 10 (ten) days of the entry of this Order, a civil money penalty in the amount of $75,000 to the Securities and Exchange Commission.

## NOTES

1. ***Single Rule, Multiple Regulators.*** As with other aspects of the GLB Act, multiple financial regulators cooperated to issue the Safeguards Rule and then it was codified in multiple locations, corresponding to each of the different agencies. The SEC was the agency to take action against R.T. Jones because it has oversight of investment advisors. Congress created this diffused authority in part because of entrenched political power—agencies are loath to surrender any jurisdiction over the entities they regulate. But is it, in fact, a good structure? There are arguments on both sides. Maybe it would be better to have a single regulator with deep expertise about data security in general and the Safeguards Rule in particular. On the other hand, it also might be better for regulators to have deep familiarity with the business activities and the various key actors that are important in their corner of the marketplace—so the SEC oversees security at R.T. Jones while the NCUA does the same with respect to a credit union. Which model do you think is more likely to be effective? This debate is a smaller version of one that divides US and EU privacy law: the FTC is the closest thing to a general-purpose enforcement authority in the US, but it is joined by numerous federal and state agencies from state attorneys general [see Chapter 3] to the US Department of Health and Human Services [see Chapter 12] to the US Department of Education [see Chapter 15], not to mention all the financial regulators involved in overseeing the Gramm-Leach-Bliley Act and FCRA [see Chapter 6]. Most EU countries, in marked contrast, have a single data protection authority and one omnibus law. Is it more important for the regulator to have expertise in privacy and data protection law and associated technology, or in the circumstances of the particular industry sector?

2. ***The Safeguards Rule Compared.*** The Safeguards Rule is one of many sources of regulatory standards for data security discussed in this book. Other important examples include the FTC's oversight of data security [see Chapter 3], data protection law in EU countries [see Chapter 4], the self-regulatory PCI standards for payment cards [see Chapter 7], Massachusetts state regulations mandating certain security precautions [see Chapter 7], and the HIPAA Security Rule for covered entities in the health care system [see Chapter 12]. How does the Safeguards Rule compare to these other data security regulations? Turning to a different comparison, how does the Safeguards Rule compare to the other privacy and data protection requirements imposed by the Gramm-Leach-Bliley Act?

3. ***Avoiding R.T. Jones' Mistakes.*** Exactly what did R.T. Jones do wrong? How much of the problem arose from the lack of a written data security policy? The failure to designate a particular person to be responsible for data security? If you were an attorney for a different investment advisor

after this enforcement action, what questions would you ask your client? What advice would you offer?

4. ***Increased Regulatory Scrutiny.*** The *R.T. Jones* matter was the SEC's first enforcement action under the Safeguards Rule, 15 years after it was first adopted. But this action appears to be part of a general focus on cybersecurity enforcement at the agency in the wake of high-profile system breaches and concern about the state of data security in the investment sector. In 2014, the SEC announced that "cybersecurity compliance and control" would be an enforcement priority, and in 2015 it declared that this initiative was being expanded. The degree of attention to data security issues among other regulators responsible for enforcement of the Safeguards Rule has been uneven.

5. ***Self-Regulation for Financial Industry Data Security.*** In addition to new scrutiny by the SEC, there has been increased attention to cybersecurity at the Financial Industry Regulatory Authority (FINRA) over the last several years. FINRA is a huge nongovernmental organization that licenses securities broker-dealers, conducts audits and inspections in the securities industry, and takes its own enforcement actions against regulated entities. In a 2015 report, FINRA provided detailed guidance to members for satisfying their data security obligations, both under federal and state law and under FINRA's own rules. Its recommendations included "a sound governance framework" for data security, with participation of senior firm leadership; detailed periodic risk assessments; technical controls; incident response plans; vendor management; and staff training. This list resembles more general data security best practices applicable across industries [see Chapter 7].

## C. THE RED FLAGS RULE

In 2003, Congress significantly amended the Fair Credit Reporting Act (FCRA) when it passed the Fair and Accurate Credit Transactions Act (FACTA), Pub. L. 108–159 (2003). Many of FACTA's provisions affected only the portion of the financial services sector directly involved in credit reporting, while others altered broad rules applicable to every entity that uses a "credit report." Those provisions are covered elsewhere in the book [see Chapter 6]. In addition, however, FACTA directed financial regulatory agencies to issue rules to combat identity theft.

The result was the Red Flags Rule, which requires financial services businesses to develop plans for detecting warning signs of identity theft—the "red flags" of the rule's name—and to prevent and mitigate its harms. As with other privacy and data security regulation in the financial services sector, rulemaking and enforcement authority are divided among different agencies based on the types of entities they oversee for other purposes, but the agencies have cooperated to adopt a common regulation. The FTC's version, for example, is found at 16 C.F.R. Part 681; the Federal Reserve's version is at 12 C.F.R. Part 222, Subpart J.

The Red Flags Rule's definitions of covered entities are a byzantine tangle of cross-references. The Rule applies to "financial institutions" and to some "creditors." The definition of financial institutions is found in the statutory text of FCRA, *see* 15 U.S.C. § 1681a(t), and essentially covers most banks and credit unions that offer "covered accounts," which in turn are defined to include any account used "primarily for personal, family, or household purposes, that involves or is designed to permit multiple payments or transactions, such as a credit card account, mortgage loan, automobile loan, margin account, cell phone account, utility account, checking account, or savings account." 12 C.F.R. § 222.90. Originally, regulators interpreted the definition of "creditor" to include professionals such as doctors, accountants, and attorneys who provide services and bill for them later. The American Bar Association challenged this aspect of the Rule in court. *See Am. Bar. Ass'n v FTC*, 671 F. Supp. 2d 64 (D.D.C. 2009). Before that litigation was resolved, Congress intervened, passing legislation to limit the definition of "creditor" largely to financial services businesses that extend credit. *See* Red Flag Program Clarification Act, Pub. L. 111–319 (2010).

For those financial institutions and (now more narrowly defined) creditors covered by the Red Flags Rule, the Guidelines tell them what they need to do—at least, in extremely general terms.

## Interagency Guidelines on Identity Theft Detection, Prevention, and Mitigation

16 C.F.R. Part 681, Appendix A

### I. The Program

In designing its Program, a financial institution or creditor may incorporate, as appropriate, its existing policies, procedures, and other arrangements that control reasonably foreseeable risks to customers or to the safety and soundness of the financial institution or creditor from identity theft.

### II. Identifying Relevant Red Flags

(a) *Risk Factors.* A financial institution or creditor should consider the following factors in identifying relevant Red Flags for covered accounts, as appropriate:

(1) The types of covered accounts it offers or maintains;

(2) The methods it provides to open its covered accounts;

(3) The methods it provides to access its covered accounts; and

(4) Its previous experiences with identity theft.

(b) *Sources of Red Flags.* Financial institutions and creditors should incorporate relevant Red Flags from sources such as:

(1) Incidents of identity theft that the financial institution or creditor has experienced;

(2) Methods of identity theft that the financial institution or creditor has identified that reflect changes in identity theft risks; and

(3) Applicable supervisory guidance.

(c) *Categories of Red Flags.* The Program should include relevant Red Flags from the following categories, as appropriate. . . .

(1) Alerts, notifications, or other warnings received from consumer reporting agencies or service providers, such as fraud detection services;

(2) The presentation of suspicious documents;

(3) The presentation of suspicious personal identifying information, such as a suspicious address change;

(4) The unusual use of, or other suspicious activity related to, a covered account; and

(5) Notice from customers, victims of identity theft, law enforcement authorities, or other persons regarding possible identity theft in connection with covered accounts held by the financial institution or creditor.

### III. Detecting Red Flags

The Program's policies and procedures should address the detection of Red Flags in connection with the opening of covered accounts and existing covered accounts, such as by:

(a) Obtaining identifying information about, and verifying the identity of, a person opening a covered account . . . and

(b) Authenticating customers, monitoring transactions, and verifying the validity of change of address requests, in the case of existing covered accounts.

### IV. Preventing and Mitigating Identity Theft

The Program's policies and procedures should provide for appropriate responses to the Red Flags the financial institution or creditor has detected that are commensurate with the degree of risk posed. In determining an appropriate response, a financial institution or creditor should consider aggravating factors that may heighten the risk of identity theft, such as a data security incident that results in unauthorized access to a customer's account records held by the financial institution, creditor, or third party, or notice that a customer has provided information related to a covered account held by the financial institution or creditor to someone fraudulently claiming to represent the financial institution or creditor or to a fraudulent website. Appropriate responses may include the following:

(a) Monitoring a covered account for evidence of identity theft;

(b) Contacting the customer;

(c) Changing any passwords, security codes, or other security devices that permit access to a covered account;

(d) Reopening a covered account with a new account number;

(e) Not opening a new covered account;

(f) Closing an existing covered account;

(g) Not attempting to collect on a covered account or not selling a covered account to a debt collector;

(h) Notifying law enforcement; or

(i) Determining that no response is warranted under the particular circumstances.

**V. Updating the Program**

Financial institutions and creditors should update the Program (including the Red Flags determined to be relevant) periodically, to reflect changes in risks to customers or to the safety and soundness of the financial institution or creditor from identity theft . . .

**VI. Methods for Administering the Program**

(a) *Oversight of Program.* Oversight by the board of directors, an appropriate committee of the board, or a designated employee at the level of senior management should include:

(1) Assigning specific responsibility for the Program's implementation;

(2) Reviewing reports prepared by staff regarding compliance by the financial institution or creditor . . . and

(3) Approving material changes to the Program as necessary to address changing identity theft risks.

(b) Reports. . . .

(2) *Contents of report.* The report [to management, noted in section (a),] should address material matters related to the Program and evaluate issues such as: The effectiveness of the policies and procedures of the financial institution or creditor in addressing the risk of identity theft in connection with the opening of covered accounts and with respect to existing covered accounts; service provider arrangements; significant incidents involving identity theft and management's response; and recommendations for material changes to the Program. . . .

## NOTES

1. ***A Different Kind of Security.*** Most data security rules discussed in this book are designed to prevent computer hacking and other intrusions and thefts from occurring in the first place; appropriate responses include technical safeguards, such as firewalls, and physical safeguards, such as limiting network access to employees with functional requirements to use

the data stored there. In other words, this form of security tries to prevent the bad guys from obtaining personal data in the first place. The Red Flags Rule instead reacts to the exploitation of previously stolen data in order to commit fraud. How does the response to this distinct threat resemble those other rules, and how does it differ from them?

2. ***Privacy and Security Professionals, Again.*** The Red Flags Rule was another job creator for experts in data security, whether they specialize in law, management, or information technology. In particular, the continual monitoring and reporting called for in Part VI of the Guidelines requires dedicated staff who are directly responsible to senior management. Implementation of the detection and response programs mandated by the Red Flags Rule necessitates considerable policy development work and employee training. The Guidelines also require an active vendor management program [see Chapter 7] covering third parties who handle customer data, to ensure that they are also detecting and responding to identity theft warning signs.

3. ***Examples of Red Flags.*** An appendix to the Guidelines lists specific examples of "red flags," including unusual patterns of account activity, inconsistencies between different sources of information, and indicators of forgery. Some indicators are relatively subtle, such as, "Shortly following the notice of a change of address for a covered account, the institution or creditor receives a request for a new, additional, or replacement card or a cell phone, or for the addition of authorized users on the account." Others are almost funny, for example, "The address on an application is fictitious, a mail drop, or a prison."

# CHAPTER 14

# COMMUNICATIONS AND MARKETING

In every sector examined in Part III of this book, privacy and data protection law has been disrupted by new technology. But perhaps none has seen as much fundamental transformation as the telecommunications, publishing, and marketing industries. These industries have been challenged, even threatened, by developments such as illegal digital copying; the displacement of old intermediaries like editors and record label executives by new tastemakers; novel sources of direct competition such as self-publishing or streaming music; and even the ability of television viewers to skip commercials. But the digital revolution also offers tantalizing promise these businesses. A witticism often attributed to the early 20th century department store magnate John Wanamaker explains why; he reputedly said, "Half the money I spend on advertising is wasted—the trouble is I don't know which half." At last, new methods of tracking and targeting could allow marketers like Wanamaker to reach exactly the right customers and to know exactly who responds to their pitches, instead of simply broadcasting one-size-fits-all messages and hoping the right people see them. One problem, of course, is that gathering and processing this type of detailed personal information can compromise privacy.

Many of the general sources of law discussed throughout this book involve these businesses in particularly significant ways, for example:

- All the privacy torts arise frequently in cases about communications and marketing [see Chapter 2];
- Consumer protection actions often target new media like the iPhone, the Snapchat messaging app, and Comcast cable television [see Chapter 3 for cases about each of these];
- The European Union's application of the "right to be forgotten" to Google has become a central battleground in data protection law [see Chapter 4].
- ECPA is fundamentally a statute about communications technology, with particular effects on telephone companies, internet service providers, and email platforms [see Chapter 5]
- Behavioral targeting and advertising technologies [see Chapter 5] and social media [see Chapter 8], which have upended the communications world, are also frequent targets for regulation of all types.

This chapter considers some more specific US privacy laws, mostly statutory, that were crafted to zero in on issues particular to the communications industries. First, it examines narrow laws aimed at preserving the privacy of defined types of communications records held by private businesses such as cable television services, telephone companies, and video rental providers [Section A]. Then it moves to privacy defined as the right to be let alone rather than the right to control records: law that limits the unsolicited marketing messages that might otherwise inundate us [Section B].

## A. SECTOR-SPECIFIC COMMUNICATIONS PRIVACY

### Cable Communications Policy Act of 1984

47 U.S.C. § 551

#### § 551. Protection of Subscriber Privacy

(a) Notice to subscriber regarding personally identifiable information; definitions

(1) At the time of entering into an agreement to provide any cable service or other service to a subscriber and at least once a year thereafter, a cable operator shall provide notice in the form of a separate, written statement to such subscriber which clearly and conspicuously informs the subscriber of—

(A) the nature of personally identifiable information collected or to be collected with respect to the subscriber and the nature of the use of such information;

(B) the nature, frequency, and purpose of any disclosure which may be made of such information, including an identification of the types of persons to whom the disclosure may be made;

(C) the period during which such information will be maintained by the cable operator;

(D) the times and place at which the subscriber may have access to such information in accordance with subsection (d) of this section; and

(E) the limitations provided by this section with respect to the collection and disclosure of information by a cable operator and the right of the subscriber . . . to enforce such limitations. . . .

(2) For purposes of this section . . . —

(A) the term "personally identifiable information" does not include any record of aggregate data which does not identify particular persons;

(B) the term "other service" includes any wire or radio communications service provided using any of the facilities of a cable operator that are used in the provision of cable service . . .

(b) Collection of personally identifiable information using cable system

(1) Except as provided in paragraph (2), a cable operator shall not use the cable system to collect personally identifiable information concerning any subscriber without the prior written or electronic consent of the subscriber concerned.

(2) A cable operator may use the cable system to collect such information in order to—

(A) obtain information necessary to render a cable service or other service provided by the cable operator to the subscriber; or

(B) detect unauthorized reception of cable communications.

(c) Disclosure of personally identifiable information

(1) Except as provided in paragraph (2), a cable operator shall not disclose personally identifiable information concerning any subscriber without the prior written or electronic consent of the subscriber concerned and shall take such actions as are necessary to prevent unauthorized access to such information by a person other than the subscriber or cable operator.

(2) A cable operator may disclose such information if the disclosure is—

(A) necessary to render, or conduct a legitimate business activity related to, a cable service or other service provided by the cable operator to the subscriber;

(B) subject to subsection (h) of this section, made pursuant to a court order authorizing such disclosure, if the subscriber is notified of such order by the person to whom the order is directed;

(C) a disclosure of the names and addresses of subscribers to any cable service or other service, if—

(i) the cable operator has provided the subscriber the opportunity to prohibit or limit such disclosure, and

(ii) the disclosure does not reveal, directly or indirectly, the—

(I) extent of any viewing or other use by the subscriber of a cable service or other service provided by the cable operator, or

(II) the nature of any transaction made by the subscriber over the cable system of the cable operator[.] . . .

(d) Subscriber access to information

A cable subscriber shall be provided access to all personally identifiable information regarding that subscriber which is collected and maintained by a cable operator. Such information shall be made available to the subscriber at reasonable times and at a convenient place designated by such cable operator. A cable subscriber shall be provided reasonable opportunity to correct any error in such information.

(e) Destruction of information

A cable operator shall destroy personally identifiable information if the information is no longer necessary for the purpose for which it was collected and there are no pending requests or orders for access to such information under subsection (d) of this section or pursuant to a court order.

(f) Civil action in United States district court; damages; attorney's fees and costs; nonexclusive nature of remedy

(1) Any person aggrieved by any act of a cable operator in violation of this section may bring a civil action in a United States district court.

(2) The court may award—

(A) actual damages but not less than liquidated damages computed at the rate of $100 a day for each day of violation or $1,000, whichever is higher;

(B) punitive damages; and

(C) reasonable attorneys' fees and other litigation costs reasonably incurred.

(3) The remedy provided by this section shall be in addition to any other lawful remedy available to a cable subscriber.

(h) Disclosure of information to governmental entity pursuant to court order

. . . [A] governmental entity may obtain personally identifiable information concerning a cable subscriber pursuant to a court order only if, in the court proceeding relevant to such court order—

(1) such entity offers clear and convincing evidence that the subject of the information is reasonably suspected of engaging in criminal activity and that the information sought would be material evidence in the case; and

(2) the subject of the information is afforded the opportunity to appear and contest such entity's claim.

## Pruitt v. Comcast Cable Holdings, LLC

100 Fed. Appx. 713 (10th Cir. 2004)

■ O'BRIEN, CIRCUIT JUDGE.

Former and current subscribers of Comcast Cable Holdings, LLC's ("Comcast") digital cable service filed suit claiming Comcast violated the 1984 Cable Communications Privacy Act ("Cable Act"), 47 U.S.C. § 551 et. seq., by retaining personally identifiable information in its cable converter boxes without notice or consent. The district court granted summary judgment in favor of Comcast on the federal claims, holding the information in the converter boxes was not personally identifiable information and dismissing the state law claims without prejudice. We affirm.

### BACKGROUND

Martin Pruitt, Lucretia Pruitt, David Elgin, Daniel Llewellyn and Cheryl Llewellyn ("Appellants") are past or present subscribers of Comcast's digital cable service. To receive such service, subscribers must have a special converter box installed and attached to their telephone line. The converter boxes, manufactured by Motorola, transmit and store (1) pay-per-view purchase information, (2) system diagnostic information and (3) settop bugging information. Each converter box contains a code displayed in hexadecimal format indicating the date of a pay-per-view purchase and a source identifier for the pay-per-view channel. The converter box stores a maximum of sixty-four purchases. When total purchases exceed that number, the newest purchase information overwrites the oldest purchase. The converter box also contains a code (again displayed in hexadecimal format) signifying the total number of purchases and payments generated through that particular box. Individual subscriber information is not contained within the converter box, but an identifying number known as a "unit address" allows Comcast to match the subscriber's purchases to its billing system. The billing system contains the name and address of the household member responsible for payment.

Appellants filed suit claiming Comcast violated the Cable Act by (1) storing personally identifiable information (47 U.S.C. § 551(e)) and (2) storing that information longer than necessary (47 U.S.C. § 551(a)). After reviewing cross motions for summary judgment, the district court held the coded information in the converter boxes was not "personally identifiable," and therefore declined to consider whether Comcast retained that information longer than necessary. This appeal followed.

### DISCUSSION

We review summary judgment de novo applying the same legal standard used by the district court.

In 1984, Congress enacted the Cable Act to establish national policy and guidelines for the cable television industry. The Cable Act creates a nationwide standard for the protection of subscriber privacy by regulating the collection, use, and disclosure by cable operators of personally identifiable information regarding cable subscribers. In particular, 47 U.S.C. § 551 "establishes a self-contained and privately enforceable scheme for the protection of cable subscriber privacy." *Scofield v. TeleCable of Overland Park*, 973 F.2d 874, 876 (10th Cir.1992). This section responds to Congress' observation that: "[c]able systems, particularly those with a 'two-way' capability, have an enormous capacity to collect and store personally identifiable information about each cable subscriber." H.R. Rep. No. 934, 98th Cong., 2d Sess. 29 (1984). "Subscriber records from interactive systems," Congress noted, "can reveal details about bank transactions, shopping habits, political contributions, viewing habits and other significant personal decisions." *Id.*

Although § 551 regulates cable company practices involving personally identifiable information, exceptions are provided where such information is necessary to render service to the subscriber, § 551(b)(2)(A), or to detect unauthorized reception of cable communications, § 551(b)(2)(B). Even so, such subscriber information must be destroyed when it is no longer necessary for the purpose for which it was collected. § 551(e). Further, § 551(a) of the Cable Act establishes a set of subscriber notice requirements designed to inform subscribers of the operator's information practices that affect subscriber privacy.

The heart of this dispute is whether the information stored within Comcast's converter boxes is personally identifiable information. While the term is not affirmatively defined by the Act, § 551(a)(2) defines what it is not. It provides: "for purposes of this section, the term 'personally identifiable information' does not include any record of aggregate data which does not identify particular persons." 47 U.S.C. § 551(a)(2). "In addition, legislative history [suggests] that personally identifiable information would include specific information about the subscriber, or a list of names and addresses on which the subscriber is included." *Scofield*, 973 F.2d at 876.

Appellants concede the information in the converter boxes does not contain the name, address or any information regarding the customer. However, they maintain the unit address enables Comcast to identify a customer's viewing habits by connecting the coded information with its billing or management system. Because the information in any given converter box is not eradicated when it is recycled to another customer, they conclude the converter boxes contain personally identifiable information which may never be purged.

In granting summary judgment to Comcast, the district court distinguished the information in the converter boxes from that contained in the billing system. It noted the converter box code—without more—provides nothing but a series of numbers. We agree. Without the information in the billing or management system one cannot connect the unit address with a specific customer; without the billing information, even Comcast would be unable to identify which individual household was associated with the raw data in the converter box. Consequently, it is the billing system that holds the key to obtaining personally identifiable information, not the converter box. Appellants made no claim in their briefs or at oral argument that the collection of information in the billing system violates the Cable Act. Moreover, Comcast's privacy notice to subscribers clearly states the retention policies related to information in the billing system:

> Accounting and billing records are retained for ten years for tax and accounting purposes or until the relevant income tax years for which the document was created has been closed for income tax purposes and/or all appeals have been exhausted. Routine paper records necessary to render or conduct legitimate business activities . . . are kept in accordance with the local cable company's voluntarily adopted document retention program. Paper records such as work orders and records of technical maintenance and service . . . are retained for three years. Subject to applicable law, records relating to involuntary disconnects are kept indefinitely by us or [our] affiliates . . . to facilitate collection and evaluation of creditworthiness and are updated as new information is added.

Absent any allegation that the retention of data in the billing or management systems violates the Cable Act, we agree with the district court that the converter boxes contain no personally identifiable information and Comcast's privacy notice to subscribers adequately states its billing information policies. Because we conclude the converter boxes contain no personally identifiable information, we need not consider whether Comcast retained such information longer than otherwise necessary. *See* 47 U.S.C. § 551(e).

## Parker v. Time Warner Entertainment Co., L.P.

631 F. Supp. 2d 242 (E.D.N.Y. 2009)

■ GLASSER, SENIOR DISTRICT JUDGE.

Proposed class representatives Andrew Parker and Eric DeBrauwere (the "Representative Plaintiffs") filed an amended class action complaint on October 30, 1998 (the "Complaint") against defendants Time Warner Entertainment Company, L.P. and its subsidiary, Time Warner Cable (collectively, "Time Warner" or the "defendant"). The Complaint alleges, inter alia, that the defendant violated certain provisions of the Cable Communications Policy Act of 1984, 47 U.S.C. §§ 551 et seq. (the "Cable Act").

The Representative Plaintiffs and the defendant move jointly for approval of a class action settlement agreement. [Attorneys for plaintiffs and for intervening objectors also move for awards of fees and expenses.]

For the reasons stated below, the parties' motion for approval of the settlement agreement is granted. [Motions] for attorneys' fees, expenses and plaintiff incentive awards is granted in part and denied in part.

## I. Background

This order brings to a close a case that has raised compelling questions of law arising at the intersection of consumer protection statutes that provide for minimum statutory damages and the class action mechanism. Each of these tools is intended to encourage the prosecution of cases that would otherwise be too costly for an individual plaintiff to pursue. The combination of the two threatens defendants with the multiplication of statutory damages, possibly beyond the contemplation of Congress and the limits of due process.

The settlement of this case reserves for another day the question of whether a class seeking statutory damages for each of its members, far in excess of the actual harm and ruinous to the defendant, should be certified for trial. However, the proposed settlement itself raises interesting questions about the valuation of settlements involving large numbers of class members and benefits that are difficult to value.

The settlement, while fair, adequate and reasonable—in that it makes a minimal sum available to the purported victims of a minimal harm—is nonetheless unsatisfying because so much time and labor was expended to achieve so little.

### A. Prior Decisions

[The court summarized numerous prior orders extending back to the denial of a motion to dismiss in November 1999. A protracted dispute over certification of the class then produced multiple opinions by the magistrate judge and district judge, and an opinion by the Second Circuit.]

### B. Facts

The Complaint alleges that Time Warner collected detailed personal information about cable television subscribers throughout its nationwide system. Time Warner maintained this information in its list sales database ("LSDB"), which it offered for sale to third parties, including telemarketers, direct marketing services companies, and Time Warner affiliates and divisions. The Complaint alleged that the database included subscribers' names and addresses, premium subscriptions, such as HBO, Disney, and Playboy, credit card information, places of employment, whether subscribers lease or own their residence, and social security and drivers' license numbers. Time Warner enhanced the information that it collected directly from its subscribers with information it had obtained from third parties, including Time Warner affiliates and divisions.

The Complaint alleges that Time Warner violated the Cable Act's substantive privacy provisions by collecting and disclosing its customers' personally identifiable information ("PII") and failing to give proper notice of its practices. Under the Cable Act, cable providers must give notice to their customers of the nature of the PII that they collect, how it is used, the nature, frequency and purpose of any PII disclosures and their retention of such information, all as provided for by 47 U.S.C. § 551(a)(1). The Complaint alleges that Time Warner violated the notice provisions of § 551(a) by failing to adequately notify subscribers of its use and disclosure of their PII, including the nature of the PII collected from subscribers and third party sources, the nature and frequency of the uses and disclosures of such information, and the period during which Time Warner maintained such information.

Subsection § 551(c) of the Cable Act prohibits the disclosure of PII without the prior consent of a subscriber with the exceptions provided for in subdivision (c)(2). This subdivision allows for the disclosure of the names and addresses of subscribers to any cable service or other service, provided that customers are given the opportunity to opt out of such disclosure and so long as the disclosure does not give additional detail pertaining to customer viewing habits. The Complaint alleges that Time Warner violated the disclosure provisions of § 551(c) by disclosing information other than subscribers' names and addresses without their consent.

The Complaint sought minimum statutory damages of at least $1,000 per violation for every subscriber, as provided for by § 551(f), claiming injury by the class "which is, at a minimum, hundreds of millions of dollars."

### C. Procedural History

The parties first reached a proposed settlement in June 2005 (the "Prior Agreement"). The Prior Agreement gave class members whose names appeared in the LSDB the opportunity to claim free Time Warner cable services for their own use, or to transfer that benefit to a third party. After a hearing on May 19, 2006, at which the parties and the Objectors were heard, the Prior Agreement was ultimately rejected by the Court. Chief among the reasons for its rejection was distributional unfairness to class members who were identified as being in the LSDB, but did not at the time of the settlement live in areas of the country where cable television service is provided by Time Warner. Those class members could not personally use the free cable services and could only transfer the benefit to those who did live in such areas. The Prior Agreement was also rejected because the notice provisions failed to provide "the best notice that is practicable under the circumstances."

The Representative Plaintiffs and the defendant filed a new settlement agreement on April 2, 2008 (the "Settlement Agreement").

The benefits made available by the Settlement Agreement differ from those in the Prior Agreement in that Class Members eligible to receive benefits may now opt to receive a $5 check rather than service benefits. All class members who select as their benefit a free month of service may either contact Time Warner to cancel the service at the end of the month or do nothing and be billed for the service at Time Warner's usual rate until such a time as they cancel it.

In addition to the direct benefits to the Class Members, the Settlement Agreement also provides for what is termed "Remedial Relief." This includes revisions to Time Warner's privacy notice and additional revisions to the privacy notice should Time Warner reenter the business of selling customer information that has been enhanced with publicly available data. Furthermore, Time Warner will provide Class Counsel with its privacy notices for a period of three years from the date the Settlement Agreement is approved. Finally, Time Warner will employ a Chief Privacy Officer for an unspecified period of time and will give as cy pres relief $250,000 to each of the Samuelson Law, Technology & Public Policy Clinic at Boalt Hall Law School and the Center for Democracy and Technology's Ronald Plesser Fellowship.

Once the settlement becomes effective, Class Members release "all claims which have been alleged in the Action, and claims which could have been alleged in the Action relating to Time Warner's privacy notices and list sales practices between 1994 and 1998 under 47 U.S.C. § 551 and/or any similar federal or state consumer protection law, privacy law and/or common law." The Settlement Agreement also provides that, subject to Court approval, Time Warner will pay Class Counsel's fees and costs in the total amount of $5 million.

## II. Discussion

[The court provided a lengthy analysis of class certification and settlement under Federal Rule of Civil Procedure 23. In its discussion of the "superiority" requirement, which includes a court's determination that "a class action is superior to other available methods for the fair and efficient adjudication of the controversy," Fed. R. Civ. P. 23(b)(3), the court evaluated the risk of "disproportionate liability."]

[T]his Court denied class certification under Rule 23(b)(3) [in a 2001 ruling in this case], holding that "a class action is not the superior manner of proceeding where the liability defendant stands to incur is grossly disproportionate to any actual harm sustained by an aggrieved individual." The disproportionate liability the Court was referring to was the availability of minimum statutory damages in the amount of $1,000 per violation of the Cable Act pursuant to 47 U.S.C. § 551(f). The Court feared "a misuse of the procedural mechanism provided by a class action suit to turn what is fundamentally a consumer protection scheme for cable subscribers into a vehicle for the financial demise of a cable service provider that failed to comply with technical aspects of that scheme."

Judge Newman, in his opinion concurring in [the appellate decision reversing that order, *Parker v. Time Warner*, 331 F.3d 13 (2d Cir. 2003)], observed that the district court is seemingly forced to choose between granting class certification and exposing the defendant to damages at trial out of all proportion to the alleged harm—potentially running afoul of the Due Process Clause and legislative intent—or denying class certification and "rewarding some law violators with liability for only a slight amount of total damages if, as seems more likely, few suits are filed." Id. at 26 (Newman, J., concurring).

Weighing these choices, Judge Newman suggests a third alternative of "determining that a class will be certified only up to some reasonable aggregate amount of damages," stating his view that "statutes are not to be applied according to their literal terms when doing so achieves a result manifestly not intended by the legislature." *Id.* at 28 The unintended result here being the exposure of a company to billions of dollars in liability for technical violations of a statute resulting in little or no harm. "Even if possible due process concerns or statutory construction to avoid a bizarre result not intended by Congress might not independently require limiting an aggregate statutory damages award, such considerations would seem appropriate to inform the customarily broad discretion of a district judge in the context of class certification." *Id.*

Here, the certification of a settlement class effectively implements Judge Newman's recommendation of setting a limit on damages. However, rather than attempting to set a damages ceiling based on congressional intent, the limits of due process[,] or the Court's own conception of a proper level of damages, the Court here accepts the parties' settlement as being within such limits as these various considerations might impose. Although the threat of class certification for trial—characterized by the defendant as a "very narrow band of very grave risk [ ] that informed the decision to settle the case"—hung over the settlement negotiations, it can nonetheless be fairly said that in a motion for class certification based upon a negotiated settlement, concerns about the disproportionate impact of the class action form are answered so long as the settlement is not unduly punitive and plainly within the defendant's ability to pay.

The Court's concerns pertaining to the disproportionate impact of statutory damages in a class action having been addressed, and the enumerated Rule 23(b)(3) factors having been weighed, the Court finds that the superiority prong is satisfied. For the foregoing reasons, the Class is certified pursuant to Rule 23(b)(3).

[The court then reviewed in detail the fairness of the settlement and the motions for attorneys' fees and expenses.]

For the foregoing reasons, the Court grants certification to the Class and approves the Settlement Agreement as fair, reasonable and adequate. Class Counsel is awarded attorneys' fees in the amount of $3,301,572.97, or approximately 30.85% of the Settlement Value, and reimbursement of reasonable expenses in the amount of $183,898.87. Representative Plaintiffs Parker and DeBrauwere are awarded incentive awards in the amount of $2,500 each. [Counsel for one group of objectors] are awarded attorneys' fees in the amount of $97,915 and reimbursement of reasonable expenses in the amount of $7,903.46. [Other motions for attorneys' fees and expenses and incentive awards are denied.]

## NOTES

1. ***Why Was Cable TV Seen as a Privacy Threat?*** Did you notice that the *Pruitt* court called the statute the Cable Communications *Privacy* Act? It is an understandable error in a case focused entirely on the CCPA's privacy provisions. In fact, § 551 was part of a more comprehensive piece of legislation, the Cable Communications *Policy* Act, which amended telecom law in multiple ways to usher in the modern form of cable TV. There are other prominent examples of privacy requirements piggybacking on more wide-ranging statutes, such as the Health Insurance Portability and Accountability Act (HIPAA) [see Chapter 12], and the Gramm-Leach-Bliley Act deregulating financial services institutions [see Chapter 13]. In both of those examples, legislators believed that the larger changes they were making also increased privacy concerns. HIPAA, for example, encouraged a shift to electronic health records that might have made medical data more vulnerable to privacy and security incursions. Was that the case with the CCPA? It may be difficult to recognize it over three decades later, but at the time cable television was a dramatic departure from traditional broadcasting which—as the name suggests—transmitted a signal broadly, to be picked up by anyone with a receiver (a radio or television set) and an antenna. Cable TV inaugurated wide adoption of the "set-top box"—a signal converter, so named because it sat on top of boxy CRT television sets. Suddenly, and for the first time, a precise record was created of everything a consumer watched. In part to ensure that privacy concerns did not slow adoption of cable, the CCPA included privacy protection measures.

2. ***Personally Identifiable Information.*** The CCPA did not do much to confront the persistently slippery issue in privacy law of defining personally identifiable information (PII), other than excluding aggregate data. How satisfactory was the *Pruitt* court's determination of this issue? It emphasized the fact that the converter box code was no more than a "series of numbers." By this logic, a number string is not PII if it can be linked to other identifiers, such as personal name, only by reference to some form of directory. Does that mean a social security number or a telephone number, standing alone, is not PII? On the other hand, who exactly are the nefarious third parties who would come into possession of a reused converter box and hack it to discover information about its previous owner's viewing habits? They wouldn't have access to the directory, would they? The court seems to suggest that the plaintiffs' failure to allege that Comcast's retention of billing

information violated the statute concluded the analysis. Would that fact, if properly alleged, turn the converter box data into PII?

3. ***Class Actions, Statutory Damages, and Harm.*** The CCPA, like many of the other privacy statutes discussed in this book, raises the issue of privacy harm. The judge in *Parker* certainly doesn't think much of the notion that the plaintiffs were harmed, even assuming that Time Warner's aggregation of data without required notice did contravene the CCPA. Do you agree? Articulate the strongest case you can make for the proposition that Time Warner's failure to follow the rules in the statute harmed its customers. One source of the *Parker* court's skepticism is its observation that Time Warner could lawfully provide customers' names and addresses to an independent entity, which could then do exactly the same data aggregation complained of in the case. Does that miss the point that the CCPA imposed stricter rules on cable operators in particular? Or is it a way of saying that the wrong is not very significant, no matter who commits it? The *Parker* court also suggests that Congress probably did not intend multimillion-dollar statutory damages that would be ruinous for a defendant. But what did Congress expect? Did it think individual plaintiffs would bring independent lawsuits to collect $1,000? All these issues may be addressed from the perspective of Article III standing in the Supreme Court's decision in *Spokeo, Inc. v. Robins*, which is still pending as of this writing in early 2016.

4. ***TV Only.*** Although today the major cable companies are also internet service providers, the CCPA does not apply to their activities as ISPs. It defines cable services as "one-way" transmissions, allowing only user inputs similar to channel selection, not the pervasive two-way interactions of web surfing. *See* 47 U.S.C. § 522(6)(A).

5. ***Consumer Protection or Data Protection?*** Overall, is the CCPA a consumer protection statute, a data protection statute, or a mixture? [See Chapters 3 and 4.] Where does it rely on notice and consent (presumed or affirmative)? Where does it forbid particular data practices as a default rule? Recall that a California consumer protection suit against Comcast recently invoked the CCPA [see Chapter 3].

---

## Focus

Customer Proprietary Network Information

In 1996, as a small part of massive legislation to overhaul telecommunications law, Congress directed the Federal Communications Commission (FCC) to develop regulations governing the disclosure of certain account information by telephone companies (defined in terms which now include local, long distance, wireless, and VoIP carriers). The data, called customer proprietary network information ("CPNI"), includes information about calls such as numbers dialed and time and duration of calls, similar to the metadata at the heart of debates over NSA surveillance [see Chapter 9]. It also includes account information such as data on billing and services purchased. Telecom companies had previously earned revenue by selling CPNI to third parties for marketing purposes., They successfully challenged the first version of the rules, which required a customer's "opt in" consent for all marketing-related disclosures, on First Amendment grounds. *See U.S. West, Inc. v. FCC*, 182 F.3d

1224 (10th Cir. 1999). [For more on First Amendment arguments of this nature, see Chapter 8.] After multiple revisions of the rules by the FCC and additional litigation, the bulk of the current version was upheld by a different court of appeals over a decade after the first regulations had been promulgated. *See Nat'l Cable & Telecomms. Ass'n v. FCC*, 555 F.3d 996 (D.C. Cir. 2009).

Under the current version of the CPNI rules, 47 C.F.R. § 64.2003, companies may use CPNI internally for marketing purposes—such as to sell additional services to existing customers—unless those customers opt out of such uses. They must receive affirmative "opt-in" consent for disclosures of CPNI to third parties, including "joint venture partners." How does this arrangement compare to other information-sharing arrangements you may have studied, such as those under HIPAA [see Chapter 12] or the Gramm-Leach-Bliley Act [see Chapter 13]? The regulations do permit disclosure of aggregate data. They also allow for the provision of call data to law enforcement and intelligence authorities consistent with other legal requirements [see Chapters 1, 5, and 9].

The CPNI regulations also contain data security safeguards. These especially target "pretexting"—a tactic for obtaining an individual's communications records by posing as that person and contacting the service provider. To combat such deceit, the FCC requires that telephone companies arrange for customers to have secure passwords or PINs that they must provide before receiving their own call detail information. (Alternatively, the provider may mail the information to the customer's address of record.) To further combat would-be identity thieves, telephone service providers must inform individuals when their passwords have been changed, in case they did not make the change themselves. The rules also include fairly strict requirements to notify the FCC of a data breach involving CPNI.

In early 2016, FCC Chairman Tom Wheeler announced plans to revise CPNI regulations so that they would also cover internet service providers. He argued that ISPs, because they carry all of a consumer's online traffic, potentially have access to a unique trove of personal data. Broadband providers responded that they bear more resemblance to Apple and Google than to traditional telephone companies, and should be regulated that way to avoid placing them at a competitive disadvantage. At this writing in early 2016, the proposal has just begun the rulemaking process—and given the history of CPNI regulations, debate may continue for some time.

Meanwhile, the FCC has also increased its enforcement of existing CPNI rules. In 2014, it fined Verizon $7.4 million for failure to provide required notice to customers about their rights to opt out of internal marketing uses. The size of that penalty seemed notable until the following year, when the FCC reached a settlement with AT&T for $25 million. In that case, the FCC alleged that employees at AT&T call centers in Mexico, Colombia, and the Philippines were in league with cell phone trafficking rings and misappropriated CPNI for a total of almost 280,000 customers. The settlement also included changes in the company's security practices and systems, and requirements that AT&T file compliance reports with the FCC.

---

## Video Privacy Protection Act

18 U.S.C. § 2710

(a) Definitions.

For purposes of this section—

(1) the term "consumer" means any renter, purchaser, or subscriber of goods or services from a video tape service provider;

(2) the term "ordinary course of business" means only debt collection activities, order fulfillment, request processing, and the transfer of ownership;

(3) the term "personally identifiable information" includes information which identifies a person as having requested or obtained specific video materials or services from a video tape service provider; and

(4) the term "video tape service provider" means any person, engaged in the business, in or affecting interstate or foreign commerce, of rental, sale, or delivery of prerecorded video cassette tapes or similar audio visual materials, or any person or other entity to whom a disclosure is made under subparagraph (D) or (E) of subsection (b)(2), but only with respect to the information contained in the disclosure.

(b) Video tape rental and sale records.

(1) A video tape service provider who knowingly discloses, to any person, personally identifiable information concerning any consumer of such provider shall be liable to the aggrieved person for the relief provided in subsection (d).

(2) A video tape service provider may disclose personally identifiable information concerning any consumer—

(A) to the consumer;

(B) to any person with the informed, written consent (including through an electronic means using the Internet) of the consumer that—

(i) is in a form distinct and separate from any form setting forth other legal or financial obligations of the consumer;

(ii) at the election of the consumer—

(I) is given at the time the disclosure is sought; or

(II) is given in advance for a set period of time, not to exceed 2 years or until consent is withdrawn by the consumer, whichever is sooner; and

(iii) the video tape service provider has provided an opportunity, in a clear and conspicuous manner, for the consumer to withdraw on a case-by-case basis or to withdraw from ongoing disclosures, at the consumer's election;

(C) to a law enforcement agency pursuant to a warrant issued under the Federal Rules of Criminal Procedure, an equivalent State warrant, a grand jury subpoena, or a court order;

(D) to any person if the disclosure is solely of the names and addresses of consumers and if—

(i) the video tape service provider has provided the consumer with the opportunity, in a clear and conspicuous manner, to prohibit such disclosure; and

(ii) the disclosure does not identify the title, description, or subject matter of any video tapes or other audio visual material; however, the subject matter of such materials may be disclosed if the disclosure is for the exclusive use of marketing goods and services directly to the consumer;

(E) to any person if the disclosure is incident to the ordinary course of business of the video tape service provider; or

(F) pursuant to a court order, in a civil proceeding upon a showing of compelling need for the information that cannot be accommodated by any other means, if—

(i) the consumer is given reasonable notice, by the person seeking the disclosure, of the court proceeding relevant to the issuance of the court order; and

(ii) the consumer is afforded the opportunity to appear and contest the claim of the person seeking the disclosure.

If an order is granted pursuant to subparagraph (C) or (F), the court shall impose appropriate safeguards against unauthorized disclosure.

(c) Civil action.

(1) Any person aggrieved by any act of a person in violation of this section may bring a civil action in a United States district court.

(2) The court may award—

(A) actual damages but not less than liquidated damages in an amount of $2,500;

(B) punitive damages;

(C) reasonable attorneys' fees and other litigation costs reasonably incurred; and

(D) such other preliminary and equitable relief as the court determines to be appropriate.

(d) Personally identifiable information.

Personally identifiable information obtained in any manner other than as provided in this section shall not be received in evidence in any trial, hearing, arbitration, or other proceeding in or before any court, grand jury, department, officer, agency, regulatory body, legislative committee, or other authority of the United States, a State, or a political subdivision of a State.

(e) Destruction of old records.

A person subject to this section shall destroy personally identifiable information as soon as practicable, but no later than one year from the date the information is no longer necessary for the purpose for which it was collected and there are no pending requests or orders for access to such information under subsection (b)(2) or (c)(2) or pursuant to a court order.

(f) Preemption.

The provisions of this section preempt only the provisions of State or local law that require disclosure prohibited by this section.

## Sterk v. Redbox Automated Retail, LLC

672 F.3d 535 (7th Cir. 2012)

■ POSNER, CIRCUIT JUDGE.

Redbox, a company that specializes in renting DVDs, Blu-ray Discs, and video games to consumers from automated retail kiosks and is the defendant in this class action suit under the Video Privacy Protection Act, 18 U.S.C. § 2710, asks us to allow it to take an interlocutory appeal. The issue it wants to appeal is whether subsection (e) of the Act can be enforced by a damages suit under subsection (c). The district judge held that it can be; Redbox asks us to rule that it cannot be.

[The court held that it would accept the interlocutory appeal and then moved to the merits.]

The biggest interpretive problem is created by the statute's failure to specify the scope of subsection (c), which creates the right of action on which this lawsuit is based. If (c) appeared after all the prohibitions, which is to say after (d) and (e) as well as (b), the natural inference would be that any violator of any of the prohibitions could be sued for damages. But instead (c) appears after just the first prohibition, the one in subsection (b), prohibiting disclosure. This placement could be an accident, but we agree with the only reported appellate case to address the issue, *Daniel v. Cantrell*, 375 F.3d 377, 384–85 (6th Cir. 2004), that it is not; that the more plausible interpretation is that it is limited to enforcing the prohibition of disclosure. For one thing, the disclosure provision, but not the others, states that a "video tape service provider who knowingly discloses, to any person, personally identifiable information . . . shall be liable to the aggrieved person for the relief provided in subsection [c]," which includes damages. And for another thing, it would be odd to create a damages remedy for "receiv[ing]" information in evidence in an official proceeding; that would make a judge who admitted evidence in violation of subsection (d) liable in damages, erasing the absolute immunity from suit for acts taken in a judge's judicial capacity.

Nor would it make a lot of sense to award damages for a violation of the requirement of timely destruction of personally identifiable information, in subsection (e)—the specific issue presented by this appeal. How could there be injury, unless the information, not having been destroyed, were disclosed? If, though not timely destroyed, it remained secreted in the video service provider's files until it was destroyed, there would be no injury. True, subsection (c)(2)(A) allows $2,500 in "liquidated damages," without need to prove "actual damages," but liquidated damages are intended to be an estimate of actual damages, and if failure of timely destruction results in no injury at all because there is never any disclosure, the only possible estimate of actual damages for violating subsection (e) would be zero. In interpreting [the Privacy Act, 5 U.S.C. § 552a], a statute even less indicative that an actual injury must be proved to entitle the plaintiff to statutory damages (the statute read "actual damages sustained by the individual as a result of the refusal or failure [of a federal agency to comply with the Privacy Act], but in no case shall a person entitled to recovery receive less than the sum of $1,000," 5 U.S.C. § 552a(g)(4)(A)), the Supreme Court held that the plaintiff could not obtain statutory damages without proof of an actual injury. *Doe v. Chao*, 540 U.S. 614 (2004). [For more on injury and the Privacy Act, see Chapter 10.]

This analysis of the unsuitability of subsections (d) and (e) to be predicates for awards of damages lends meaning and significance to the portion of (b)(1) that makes the "video tape service provider who knowingly *discloses*, to any person, personally identifiable information . . . liable to the aggrieved person for the relief provided in subsection [(c)]" (emphasis added)—relief that includes damages. Unlawful disclosure is the only misconduct listed in the statute for which an award of damages is an appropriate remedy, so it makes sense for the damages section to be sited between the disclosure prohibition and the other prohibitions; it belongs with the former.

It is true that subsection (c) authorizes other relief besides just damages, relief less obviously inappropriate to a violation of (d). That is particularly true of equitable relief, authorized in subsection (c)(2)(D). But when all that a plaintiff seeks is to enjoin an unlawful act, there is no need for express statutory authorization; absent the clearest command to the contrary from Congress, federal courts retain their equitable power to issue injunctions in suits over which they have jurisdiction.

We cannot be certain that we have divined the legislative meaning correctly. But since we can't grill Congress on the matter, it is enough that we think our interpretation superior to the district court's, and we are fortified in that belief by the Sixth Circuit's decision.

The ruling by the district court is REVERSED.

## In re Hulu Privacy Litigation

2012 WL 3282960 (N.D. Cal. 2012)

■ LAUREL BEELER, UNITED STATES MAGISTRATE JUDGE.

In this putative class action, viewers of Hulu's on-line video content allege that Hulu wrongfully disclosed their video viewing selections and personal identification information to third parties such as online ad networks, metrics companies (meaning, companies that track data), and social networks, in violation of the Video Privacy Protection Act.

### FACTS

### A. *Procedural History*

[The ]First Amended Consolidated Class Action Complaint ("FAC") defines the class period as March 4, 2011 to July 28, 2011 and defines a "Class" and a "Video Subclass:" (1) Class: "All individuals and entities in the United States who visited Hulu.com during the Class Period;" and (2) Video Subclass: "All individuals and entities in the United States who visited Hulu.com during the Class Period and viewed video content."

### B. *Allegations in Complaint*

#### 1. Hulu's Product

Hulu operates a website called Hulu.com that provides video content, both previously released and posted and originally developed. The programs include news, entertainment, educational, and general interest programs.

#### 2. Plaintiffs' Use of Hulu.com

Plaintiffs and Class Members used their Internet-connected computers and browsers to visit hulu.com and view video content.

#### 3. Plaintiffs' Interests

Plaintiffs value their privacy while web-browsing; they do not want to be tracked online; their web browsing (including their viewing choices) involves personal information that is private; it is their decision to disclose (or not) information when they view a web page; and they expect that the websites they use and "the third parties utilized by those websites will not transmit code that repurposes . . . software . . . to perform unintended functions, such as tracking and circumvention of privacy protection[s]" in Plaintiffs' software.

#### 4. Hulu's Alleged Unauthorized Tracking and Sharing of Users' Video Viewing Details

Hulu allowed a metrics company called KISSmetrics to place code containing tracking identifiers on Plaintiffs' computers in the browser cache, Adobe Flash local storage, or DOM local storage. This code allegedly "respawned" or "resurrected" previously-deleted cookies. This code was "inescapable" and allowed Plaintiffs' data to be "retained . . . so that they could be tracked over long periods of time and across multiple websites, regardless of whether they were registered and logged in." As a result, when Class Members viewed video content on Hulu.com, Hulu transmitted their video viewing choices and personally identifiable information to third parties without obtaining their written consent before the disclosure. The third parties included online ad networks, metrics companies, and social networks such as Scorecard Research ("Scorecard") (an online market research company), Facebook (the online social network), DoubleClick (an online ad network), Google Analytics (an online web analytics company), and QuantCast (an online ad network and web analytics company).

The information transmitted to Scorecard and Facebook included information that identified Plaintiffs and Class Members personally. As to Facebook, Hulu included their Facebook IDs, connecting the video content information to Facebook's personally identifiable user registration information. As to Scorecard, Hulu provided Plaintiffs' "Hulu profile identifiers" linked to their "individual Hulu profile pages that included name, location, preference information designated by the user as private, and Hulu username (which, in the case of many individuals, is the same screen name used in other online environments)." Scorecard stored the Hulu ID information in a cookie named "b.scorecardresearch.com" and stored the video information in a cookie named "beacon. scorecardresearch.com." Scorecard also set its own unique identifier tied to these two cookies. Scorecard's cookies were unencrypted, so any intruder who gained access to a Class Member's computer could "engage in a trivial exploit to view the profile and perform a 'screen scrape' copy of that person's profile page." Hulu's and Scorecard's practice of sharing user profile IDs and storing them in cookies is a severe failure to observe basic security standards in the handling of user information.

Plaintiffs and Class Members "reasonably expected that Hulu would not disclose their video and/or video service requests and their identities to social networks and online ad/metrics networks," and they "did not authorize or otherwise consent to" such disclosures. As a condition of using Hulu, Plaintiffs agreed to Hulu's terms of use and privacy policy.

### DISCUSSION

Plaintiffs allege that Hulu "knowingly and without . . . [their] consent disclosed to third parties . . . [their] video viewing selections and personally identifiable information, knowing that such disclosure included the disclosure of [their] personally identifying information . . . and their requests for and/or obtaining of specific video materials and/or services from Hulu," in violation of the Video Privacy Protection Act ("VPPA"), 18 U.S.C. § 2710(b)(1).

Hulu moves to dismiss under Federal Rule of Civil Procedure 12(b)(6) for failure to state a claim, alleging that (A) Hulu is not a "video tape service provider" and thus is not liable under the Act, (B) any disclosures were incident to the ordinary course of Hulu's business and are not covered by the Act, and (C) Plaintiffs are not "consumers" within the meaning of the Act.

### A. *Video Tape Service Provider*

VPPA defines "video tape service provider" as "any person, engaged in the business, in or affecting interstate or foreign commerce, of rental, sale, or delivery of prerecorded video cassette tapes or similar audio visual materials." 18 U.S.C. § 2710(a)(4).

Hulu does not deal in prerecorded video cassette tapes. Thus, whether Hulu is a "video tape service providers" turns on the scope of the phrase "similar audio visual materials."

Citing dictionary definitions, Hulu contends that "materials" are things "composed of physical matter." Hulu argues that the legislative history confirms a focus on "physical stores selling goods." As drafted, Hulu contends, the VPPA "only regulates businesses that sell or rent physical objects (i.e., 'video cassettes or other similar audio visual materials') . . . and not businesses that transmit digital content over the Internet." This makes sense, Hulu argues, because unlike bricks-and-mortar businesses that can provide videos directly to customers, video-streaming businesses like Hulu necessarily rely on third parties to "facilitate many aspects of their businesses, including in-stream advertising, analytics, and transmission to users." Had Congress wanted to regulate businesses dealing in digital content, it would have defined "video tape service provider" to include businesses that "traffic in audio-visual information or data."

Plaintiffs counter that by focusing on the word "materials," Hulu misconstrues the VPPA to apply only to physical objects and ignores the full statutory language that covers businesses that "rent, sell, or deliver 'prerecorded video cassette tapes or similar audio visual materials.' " "Similar audio visual materials" is a broad phrase designed to include new technologies for pre-recorded video content. ([quoting Senate Report's statement that] "video tape service provider" means a person " 'engaged in the business of . . . delivery of pre-recorded video cassette tapes or similar audio visual materials such as laser discs, open-reel movies, and CDI technologies.' ") Plaintiffs note that Hulu provides only a dictionary definition for the singular, adjective form of the word "material" as opposed to the definition of the plural "materials" used in the VPPA. The singular "material" is "matter" or the composition of something, but the plural "materials" means "the equipment necessary for a particular activity." And, Plaintiffs observe, in its own terms of use, Hulu uses the words "video materials" to mean "content . . . includ[ing] . . . any text, graphics, layout, interface, logos, photographs, audio and video materials, and stills." Plaintiffs conclude that pre-existing video cassettes are obsolete and analogize Hulu's argument that its product is not a "similar audio visual material" to an argument that an e-mail is not a document because it exists only in cyberspace.

Statutory interpretation begins with the plain language of the statute, and it ends there if the text is unambiguous. If the statutory language is unclear, courts consider legislative history and also follow the common practice of consulting dictionary definitions to clarify their ordinary meaning and look to how the terms were defined at the time the statute was adopted.

To this reader, a plain reading of a statute that covers videotapes and "similar audio visual materials" is about the video content, not about how that content was delivered (e.g. via the Internet or a bricks-and-mortar store). Still, the online streaming mechanism of delivery here did not exist when Congress enacted the statute in 1988. A dictionary definition helps some. The undersigned looked at the third edition of Oxford English Dictionary, which defines "material" both as "relating to substance" and as "Text or images in printed or electronic form; also with distinguishing word, as *reading material, etc.*" (Oxford English Dictionary, Third Edition, March 2001). This second definition predates the streaming video content that Hulu offers and comports with the court's ordinary sense of the definition of "audio visual materials."

Also, the Senate Report confirms that Congress was concerned with protecting the confidentiality of private information about viewing preferences regardless of the business model or media format involved. [The court quoted from the legislative history a statement of the VPPA's sponsor, Senator Patrick Leahy: "In an era of interactive television cables, the growth of computer checking and check-out counters, of security systems and telephones, all lodged together in computers, it would be relatively easy at some point to give a profile of a person and tell what they buy in a store, what kind of food they like, what sort of television programs they watch. . . . I think that is wrong, I think that is Big Brother, and I think it is something we have to guard against."]

Congress's concern with privacy and protecting the confidentiality of an individual's choices is relevant context to the Senate Report's discussion of "similar audio visual materials, such as laser discs, open-reel movies, and CDI technologies." Considering both together does not suggest—as Hulu argues—an intent to limit the VPPA to tangible materials but—as Plaintiffs argue—instead suggests Congress's intent to cover new technologies for pre-recorded video content. Indeed, the Senate Report discusses extensively the concept of privacy in an evolving technological world. The court concludes that Congress used "similar audio video materials" to ensure that VPPA's protections would retain their force even as technologies evolve.

### B. *Disclosures "Incident to the Ordinary Course of Business"*

The next issue is whether Hulu's alleged disclosures did not violate the VPPA because they were "incident to the ordinary course of [Hulu's] business." *See* 18 U.S.C. § 2710(b)(2)(E). The VPPA defines "ordinary course of business" as "debt collection activities, order fulfillment, request processing, and the transfer of ownership."

Hulu argues that the section shows that Congress took into account that providers use third parties in their business operations and "allows disclosure to permit video tape service providers to use mailing houses, warehouses, computer services, and similar companies for marketing to their customers. These practices are called 'order fulfillment' and 'request processing.' " Hulu contends that the plaintiffs' allegations—that Hulu shared data with online market research, ad network and web analytics companies—all involve Hulu's use of third-party vendors providing services like internal research, advertising, and analytics that Hulu [cannot] do on its own and thus permissibly can outsource in the "ordinary course of business."

Plaintiffs counter that the "ordinary course of business" is narrowly defined to mean only debt collection, order fulfillment, request processing, and the transfer of ownership. The third parties here—ScoreCard, Google Analytics, Doubleclick, QuantCast, and Facebook—do not perform any of those functions. Market research and web analytics are not in the ordinary course of Hulu's business of delivering video content to consumers. And if Hulu is challenging Plaintiffs' facial allegations about the role of the third parties that Hulu shared information with, those are factual questions that cannot be resolved in a motion to dismiss.

Whatever the merits are to Hulu's contentions that it uses the challenged services to deliver targeted advertisements to its users, Plaintiffs alleged unauthorized tracking of Plaintiffs' data (including video content information). The court cannot resolve this factual issue in a motion to dismiss. Put another way, as pled, the claim survives a Rule 12(b)(6) motion.

### C. *"Consumers" Under the VPPA*

The VPPA defines "consumers" as "any renter, purchaser, or subscriber of goods or services from a video tape service provider." 28 U.S.C. § 2710(a)(1). The terms "renter," "purchaser," and "subscriber" are not defined in the Act and thus are given their ordinary meaning. The parties focus on the term "subscriber" because Plaintiffs did not allege that they rented or purchased content from Hulu.

Hulu argues that the ordinary meaning of "subscriber" implies payment of money. Also, the acts of renting and buying require the exchange of money, and a consistent interpretation of "subscriber" also should require the payment of money. Plaintiffs did not allege that they subscribed to Hulu Plus, a pay-to-watch service. Plaintiffs respond that they signed up for a Hulu account, became registered users, received a Hulu ID, established Hulu profiles, and used Hulu's video streaming services. Hulu counters that even if payment is not required to be a subscriber, being a subscriber requires more than just visiting Hulu.

Plaintiffs pleaded more than just visiting Hulu's website. They were subscribers of goods and services. They visited hulu.com and viewed video content. The resurrected previously-deleted cookies allowed their data to be tracked "regardless of whether they were registered and logged in." Hulu gave Scorecard Research Plaintiffs' "Hulu profile identifiers" linked to their "individual Hulu profile pages that included name, location preference information designated by the user as private, and Hulu username." And while the terms "renter" and "buyer" necessarily imply payment of money, the term "subscriber" does not. Hulu cites no authority suggesting any different result. If Congress wanted to limit the word "subscriber" to "paid subscriber," it would have said so.

The court denies Hulu's motion to dismiss.

## NOTES

1. ***A Drafting Error.*** A portion of *Sterk* that was omitted from the excerpt above identifies a pretty significant and clear drafting error in § 2710(b)(1) of the VPPA. Do you see it?

2. ***The "Bork Bill."*** There is an interesting backstory to explain why Congress passed a statute specially addressing the privacy of "video tape rental and sale records."

> Congress passed the VPPA in 1988. As often happens with legislation to protect privacy, the proponents of the bill acted in response to a particular attention-grabbing incident. During the fervor over the nomination of Judge Robert Bork to the Supreme Court, an enterprising reporter for an alternative weekly newspaper in Washington, DC obtained the judge's borrowing records from his neighborhood video rental store and published an article about them. Members of Congress (perhaps afraid that reporters in their own hometowns would get similar ideas) responded quickly. Displaying much more unity than they had on the Bork nomination itself, both chambers passed the measure by voice vote.

William McGeveran, *The Law of Friction*, 2013 U. CHI. L. FORUM 15, 23 (2013). Because of this history, some old-timers still refer to the VPPA as the "Bork Bill." Can you think of other narrow privacy rules established in response to "horror stories" that grabbed policymakers' attention?

3. ***Eventual Outcomes.*** The plaintiffs lost their argument about data retention in *Sterk*, but continued in the district court with claims that Redbox's disclosures of data to third parties violated § 2710(b), which were similar to the allegations that went forward in *Hulu*. Eventually, however,

the defendants prevailed in both *Sterk* and *Hulu*. The courts found a variety of flaws in the plaintiffs' arguments—can you anticipate them? First, in *Sterk*, the third party recipient was a subcontractor that "provides customer service to Redbox users when, for example, a customer encounters technical problems at a kiosk and requires help from a live person." *Sterk v. Redbox Automated Retail, LLC*, 770 F.3d 618, 621 (7th Cir. 2014). The Seventh Circuit affirmed the district court's summary judgment ruling that this activity was part of "request processing," one of the four categories under the "ordinary course of business" exception. Meanwhile, the *Hulu* plaintiffs voluntarily narrowed their claims to focus on disclosures to the analytics firm comScore and to Facebook. In 2014, the district court granted early summary judgment as to the comScore disclosures, drawing on the *Pruitt* decision about PII under the CCPA [see above]:

> *Pruitt* stands for the proposition that an anonymous, unique ID *without* more does not constitute PII. But it also suggests that if an anonymous, unique ID were disclosed to a person who could understand it, that might constitute PII. Hulu nonetheless argues that the disclosure has to be the person's actual name. That position paints too bright a line. One could not skirt liability under the VPPA, for example, by disclosing a unique identifier and a correlated look-up table.

*In re Hulu Privacy Litig.*, 2014 WL 1724344, at *11 (N.D. Cal. Apr. 28, 2014). The court held, consistent with *Pruitt*, that a unique identifier must be linked to personal identity to violate the statute; it found no genuine issue of material fact that the IDs received by comScore were not linked in this way, but decided there was dispute about whether Facebook could look up individuals using the data it received from Hulu. Finally, in 2015, the *Hulu* court granted summary judgment on those claims too, because even if Facebook could link videos to identity, the plaintiffs did not have proof that Hulu *knew* this was possible, as required for liability under § 2710(b)(1). *In re Hulu Privacy Litig.*, 86 F. Supp. 3d 1090 (N.D. Cal. 2015). These three different rulings, despite the factual similarities, relied on three different provisions: the "ordinary course of business" exception, the definition of PII, and the knowledge requirement.

4. ***Harm, Again.*** In *Sterk*, Judge Posner considers it obvious that the mere retention of personal data, without disclosure, can cause no injury to the individual. Is that obvious? Under a data protection framework such as EU law, retaining data longer than necessary can be an independent violation that is viewed as injurious to the data subject. Is this understanding tied to the European "human rights" conception of personal data—an inherent right to control data about oneself? If so, it might not be consistent with other US assumptions about private data. Might regulation of data retention instead be justified because it increases the risk that the data will be disclosed (or breached)? Or is Judge Posner correct that mere retention of data, "secreted in the video service provider's files until it was destroyed," causes no cognizable harm?

5. ***Enforcement Alternatives.*** The Ninth Circuit has since joined the Sixth and Seventh Circuits in the conclusion that there is no private right

of action for violation of the VPPA's data retention provisions. *See Rodriguez v. Sony Computer Entm't Am., LLC*, 801 F.3d 1045 (9th Cir. 2015). Does this leave any mechanism to enforce the retention rule against companies that violate it?

6. ***Battle of the Dictionaries.*** *Hulu* provides an excellent example of the disputes that sometimes arise over competing dictionary definitions in statutory interpretation cases. Focusing just on textual arguments, who has the better argument concerning the word "materials" in the statute? Is it a problem that the Court relies on a dictionary definition from 2001? Is it a problem that the defendant cites definitions of the singular instead of the plural? How persuasive is the plaintiffs' argument about the way Hulu uses the word in its own written policies?

7. ***"Subscribers."*** The *Hulu* court refused to dismiss the complaint on the basis of an argument that users of Hulu's service were not "subscribers" under the VPPA. Does that mean a user who downloaded a free mobile app and watched videos on it would be a subscriber? In a classs action involving such an app from the Cartoon Network, the Eleventh Circuit—while agreeing that the definition of "subscriber" did not require financial payment—read *Hulu* more narrowly than that:

> Mr. Ellis [the named plaintiff] did not sign up for or establish an account with Cartoon Network, did not provide any personal information to Cartoon Network, did not make any payments to Cartoon Network for use of the CN app, did not become a registered user of Cartoon Network or the CN app, did not receive a Cartoon Network ID, did not establish a Cartoon Network profile, did not sign up for any periodic services or transmissions, and did not make any commitment or establish any relationship that would allow him to have access to exclusive or restricted content. Mr. Ellis simply watched video clips on the CN app, which he downloaded onto his Android smartphone for free. In our view, downloading an app for free and using it to view content at no cost is not enough to make a user of the app a "subscriber" under the VPPA, as there is no ongoing commitment or relationship between the user and the entity which owns and operates the app.

*Ellis v. Cartoon Network, Inc.*, 803 F.3d 1251, 1257 (11th Cir. 2015). The First Circuit, in contrast, thought users of a free downloaded app could be "subscribers" for VPPA purposes:

> To use the App, Yershov [the named plaintiff] did indeed have to provide Gannett with personal information, such as his Android ID and his mobile device's GPS location at the time he viewed a video, each linked to his viewing selections. While he paid no money, access was not free of a commitment to provide consideration in the form of that information, which was of value to Gannett. And by installing the App on his phone, thereby establishing seamless access to an electronic version of USA Today, Yershov established a relationship with Gannett that is materially different from what would have been the case had USA Today simply remained one of

> millions of sites on the web that Yershov might have accessed through a web browser.

Yershov v. Gannett Satellite Information Network, 2016 WL 1719825 (1st Cir. 2016). Which court has the best reading of the *Hulu* decision? Of the statute? When the VPPA was written, nothing existed like Hulu or smart phone apps. How well do these interpretations of "subscriber" correctly perceive the boundaries of the type of relationship Congress sought to regulate?

8. ***Facebook Beacon.*** While the plaintiffs in *Hulu* cited disclosures made *to* Facebook, an earlier class action complaint objected to disclosures made *by* Facebook. Through the social network's Beacon program [also discussed in Chapter 8], Facebook had partnerships with a number of web sites that the plaintiffs alleged were classified as "video tape service providers," including Blockbuster Video, Fandango, Overstock.com, and Gamefly. Facebook users' activities at those sites—including rating videos they had seen—could be divulged in their friends' news feeds, without the users taking any specific action. The plaintiffs invoked several federal privacy statutes, but the VPPA was prominent among them. Facebook very quickly reached a $9.5 million settlement with the class. *See Lane v. Facebook, Inc.*, 696 F.3d 811 (9th Cir. 2012). Of all the disclosures made by Beacon, those involving video viewing habits probably represented the greatest legal vulnerability, thanks to the unique nature of the VPPA.

9. ***VPPA Amendments Act.*** Congress amended the VPPA in 2012, rewriting the consent exception in § 2710(b)(2)(B) to read the way it does in the above excerpt. In the old statute this portion read simply, "to any person with the informed, written consent of the consumer given at the time the disclosure is sought." What did this amendment change? Why do you think Congress passed it?

10. ***The VPPA and Law Enforcement.*** The VPPA has been invoked at times in cases where government investigators sought to gather information about individuals' viewing habits. *See, e.g., Amazon.com LLC v. Lay*, 758 F. Supp. 2d 1154 (W.D. Wash. 2010); *Dirkes v. Borough of Runnemede*, 936 F. Supp. 235 (D.N.J. 1996). An especially notorious case involved *The Tin Drum*, a 1979 German film that won both the top prize at the Cannes Film Festival and the Oscar for best foreign film. In 1997, police and prosecutors in Oklahoma City procured a court order declaring the movie to be child pornography in violation of state obscenity law, confiscated copies of it from video stores and libraries, and demanded information about patrons who had checked out other copies. They then seized the movie from at least one of those customers—who, to their great misfortune, was an ACLU activist named Michael Camfield. Of course, Camfield sued the city. In addition to numerous constitutional claims, he invoked the VPPA, for which he received $2,500 in liquidated damages. *See Camfield v. City of Oklahoma City*, 248 F.3d 1214 (10th Cir. 2001).

11. ***Intellectual Privacy.*** The VPPA and the CCPA both protect intellectual privacy—the principle that personal choices about reading and viewing are closely tied to freedom of thought and deserve special protection

[see Chapter 1]. Strong state laws and the professional ethics of librarians establish similar safeguards for most public library borrowing records. There are, however, few comparable restrictions concerning information about individuals' book or music purchases, magazine subscriptions, web surfing, or music streaming. A new Delaware privacy law, which became effective at the beginning of 2016, is an exception: it imposes similar rules on providers of e-books. *See* Del. Code tit. 6, §§ 1206C; *see also* California Reader Privacy Act, Cal. Civ. Code § 1798.90. Are there principled reasons why cable and video are subject to more privacy restrictions than other forms of media? *See generally* NEIL RICHARDS, INTELLECTUAL PRIVACY: RETHINKING CIVIL LIBERTIES IN THE DIGITAL AGE (2015).

## B. RESTRICTIONS ON COMMERCIAL CONTACTS

---

### Focus

The Do Not Call Registry

The Do Not Call Registry must be one of the most popular federal government programs in US history. The list contains over 222 million residential and wireless phone numbers, registered by individuals who had signed up to refuse most telemarketing calls. One can register a telephone number online simply by visiting www.donotcall.gov.

The FTC's Telemarketing Sales Rule ("TSR"), 16 C.F.R. Part 310, a broader consumer protection regulation governing the conduct of telemarketing, contains the core provisions for the registry. It defines telemarketing as "a plan, program, or campaign which is conducted to induce the purchase of goods or services or a charitable contribution, by use of one or more telephones and which involves more than one interstate phone call." 16 C.F.R. § 310.2(dd). The regulations require that a telemarketer consult the registry at least once every 31 days and bars calls to any number listed there. Nonprofit organizations calling on their own behalf (but not those using subcontractors) are exempt from complying with the Do Not Call list. Businesses may call people with whom they have established relationships as defined in the TSR, *id.* at § 310.2(o), those who have consented in writing to receive calls, or business numbers.

The FCC has complementary regulations requiring telemarketers to consult the registry and honor its opt-out requests. FCC rules also require sellers to maintain their own Do Not Call list for customers who request directly that they not receive further calls; such requests must be obeyed for five years after they are made. *See generally* 47 C.F.R. § 64.1200. About half the states also have their own Do Not Call lists; in recent years many of them have integrated their lists with the national registry, so that we are moving toward a single centralized location for telemarketing opt-outs. Failure to consult the Do Not Call list, and calls made to registered numbers without an applicable exemption, can result in enforcement actions and fines.

The FCC's role in Do Not Call regulation is distinct from another set of telephone-related privacy rules under the Telephone Consumer Protection Act, 47 U.S.C. §§ 227 et seq., and FCC regulations enforcing it. A short excerpt from those regulations follows directly below.

---

## Telephone Consumer Protection Act Regulations

47 C.F.R. § 64.1200

(a) No person or entity may:

(1) Except as provided in paragraph (a)(2) of this section, initiate any telephone call (other than a call made for emergency purposes or . . . with the prior express consent of the called party) using an automatic telephone dialing system or an artificial or prerecorded voice

(i) To any emergency telephone line . . . ;

(ii) To the telephone line of any guest room or patient room of a hospital, health care facility, elderly home, or similar establishment; or

(iii) To any telephone number assigned to a paging service, cellular telephone service, specialized mobile radio service, or other radio common carrier service, or any service for which the called party is charged for the call.

(2) Initiate, or cause to be initiated, any telephone call that includes or introduces an advertisement or constitutes telemarketing, using an automatic telephone dialing system or an artificial or prerecorded voice, to any of the lines or telephone numbers described in paragraphs (a)(1)(i) through (iii) of this section, other than a call made with the prior express written consent of the called party . . .

(3) Initiate any telephone call to any residential line using an artificial or prerecorded voice to deliver a message without the prior express written consent of the called party, unless the call

(i) Is made for emergency purposes;

(ii) Is not made for a commercial purpose;

(iii) Is made for a commercial purpose but does not include or introduce an advertisement or constitute telemarketing;

(iv) Is made by or on behalf of a tax-exempt nonprofit organization; or

(v) Delivers a "health care" message made by, or on behalf of, a "covered entity" or its "business associate," as those terms are defined in the HIPAA Privacy Rule, 45 CFR 160.103.

. . .

(f) As used in this section:

(2) The terms *automatic telephone dialing system* and *autodialer* mean equipment which has the capacity to store or produce telephone numbers to be called using a random or sequential number generator and to dial such numbers.

. . .

(5) The term *established business relationship* for purposes of telephone solicitations means a prior or existing relationship formed by a voluntary two-way communication between a person or entity and a residential subscriber with or without an exchange of consideration, on the basis of the subscriber's purchase or transaction with the entity within the eighteen (18) months immediately preceding the date of the telephone call or on the basis of the subscriber's inquiry or application regarding products or services offered by the entity within the three months immediately preceding the date of the call, which relationship has not been previously terminated by either party.

(i) The subscriber's seller-specific do-not-call request . . . terminates an established business relationship for purposes of telemarketing and telephone solicitation even if the subscriber continues to do business with the seller.

(ii) The subscriber's established business relationship with a particular business entity does not extend to affiliated entities unless the subscriber would reasonably expect them to be included given the nature and type of goods or services offered by the affiliate and the identity of the affiliate.

. . .

(14) The term *telephone solicitation* means the initiation of a telephone call or message for the purpose of encouraging the purchase or rental of, or investment in, property, goods, or services, which is transmitted to any person, but such term does not include a call or message:

(i) To any person with that person's prior express invitation or permission;

(ii) To any person with whom the caller has an established business relationship; or

(iii) By or on behalf of a tax-exempt nonprofit organization

## Davis v. Diversified Consultants, Inc.

36 F. Supp. 3d 217 (D. Mass. 2014)

■ SAYLOR, DISTRICT JUDGE.

[This case] arises out of a series of telephone calls between plaintiff Jamie Davis and various employees of defendant Diversified Consultants, Inc., a debt collection agency. Davis contends that, by the mode and manner in which they called him, DCI and its employees violated the Telephone Consumer Protection Act ("TCPA"), 47 U.S.C. §§ 227 et seq.; the Fair Debt Collection Practices Act ("FDCPA"), 15

U.S.C. §§ 1692 et seq.; and the Massachusetts Privacy Act, Mass. Gen. Laws ch. 214, § 1B.

Davis has moved for partial summary judgment as to the TCPA claim, and DCI has cross-moved for summary judgment on all counts. For the reasons set forth below, defendant's motion for summary judgment will be denied, and plaintiff's motion for summary judgment will be granted in part and denied in part.

## BACKGROUND

Unless otherwise noted, the following facts are undisputed.

### A. The Telephone Calls

On July 9, 2012, DCI acquired an account (that is, an alleged debt) belonging to Rosalee Pagan. It first attempted to collect on Pagan's debt on July 11, 2012. On July 15, 2012, DCI paid a "skip trace" service provider, a company called Innovis, for location information and telephone numbers related to Pagan. Among the data Innovis provided was the telephone number (857) XXX–8596. That number, however, was assigned to Jamie Davis's MetroPCS cellular telephone.

From August 1 to November 15, 2012, Davis received a total of 60 telephone calls at the [XXX–8596] number from DCI collectors. Davis answered five to seven of those calls, and DCI may have left one voice-mail message. When DCI collectors asked about Pagan, Davis stated that he was not Pagan, did not know her, and had never heard of her, and asked the collectors to stop contacting him. At no point in time did he consent to being called. Davis alleges that one of the collectors was rude to him and implied that Davis was lying about not knowing Pagan.

### B. The LiveVox System

During the relevant time period, DCI utilized a telephone system operated by LiveVox in order to place many, if not all, of its telephone calls. Both Mavis-Ann Pye, who was the DCI Vice President of Compliance, and the DCI website refer to the LiveVox system as a "predictive dialer."

Every morning, DCI Director Jamie Sullivan uploaded a file containing telephone numbers into the LiveVox cloud-based server. The LiveVox system then called those numbers throughout the day. If someone answered the call, the system routed that call to a DCI debt collector. The parties dispute whether DCI or LiveVox actually placed the telephone calls.

DCI had the option to store telephone numbers in the LiveVox system for up to 30 days. However, the numbers instead were erased at 1:00 a.m. every night, and DCI uploaded new numbers every morning. Pye stated that DCI had the option for LiveVox to dial numbers sequentially; DCI did not, however, use that function. According to a memorandum written by LiveVox concerning the Telephone Consumer Protection Act, "the LiveVox Application Service, while able to store or produce telephone numbers to be called, does not have the capacity to store or produce numbers to be called using a random or sequential number generator." LiveVox therefore concluded that its system does not constitute an "automatic telephone dialing system" under the TCPA, but noted in the memorandum that one court has disagreed with that conclusion.

Davis contends that DCI used the LiveVox system to call him from August to November 2012. Pye confirmed at her deposition that the LiveVox system called the '8596 number. She nonetheless now states in an affidavit opposing summary judgment that no calls were made using "an automatic telephone dialing system." Pye also states that DCI's standard practice is to "scrub" new accounts for cellular telephone numbers in order avoid calling such numbers.

## CROSS-MOTIONS FOR SUMMARY JUDGMENT

Congress passed the TCPA to protect individual consumers from receiving intrusive and unwanted calls. The TCPA, in relevant part, makes it unlawful for any person "to make any call (other than a call made for emergency purposes or made with the prior express consent of the called party) using any automatic telephone dialing system . . . to any telephone number assigned to a . . . cellular telephone service. . . ." 47 U.S.C. § 227(b)(1)(A). The TCPA is essentially a strict liability statute and does not require any intent for liability except when awarding treble damages.

There are two factual issues under the TCPA that are relevant here: whether a person called another on a cellular telephone, and whether that call utilized an automatic telephone dialing system.

The first issue is relatively straightforward. It is undisputed that plaintiff received calls on his cellular telephone. Defendant argues that LiveVox, not it, actually made the complained-of calls. It emphasizes that LiveVox is an "independent, third-party contractor" and that "the LiveVox system, not DCI's collection agents, places the calls." But that argument ignores several critical facts. Every morning, a DCI employee uploaded telephone numbers into the LiveVox system. Essentially, that instructed LiveVox which numbers to call to the same extent as if a DCI collector himself had typed in the number on a telephone keypad. Then, when a person answered a call, the call was routed to, and the person was greeted by, a DCI employee. Defendant cannot deny responsibility merely because it used a technological intermediary. Even viewing the evidence in a light favorable to defendant, it is clear that defendant "made" the calls to plaintiff's cellular telephone within the meaning of the TCPA.

The second issue, however, poses a slightly more difficult question. The statute defines "automatic telephone dialing system" ("ATDS") as "equipment which has the *capacity*—(A) to store or produce telephone numbers to be called, using a random or sequential number generator;

and (B) to dial such numbers." 47 U.S.C. § 227(a) (emphasis added). To satisfy that definition, the equipment does not actually have to store or produce telephone numbers or to use a random or sequential number generator; it merely must have the capacity to do so.

The FCC has ruled that a predictive dialer qualifies as an ATDS. *See In the Matter of Rules and Regulations Implementing the Tel. Consumer Prot. Act of 1991*, 18 FCC Rcd. 14014, 14091–93 (July 3, 2003). The agency found that predictive dialer hardware, "when paired with certain software, has the capacity to store or produce numbers and dial those numbers at random, in sequential order, or from a database of numbers." It noted that "the evolution of the teleservices industry has progressed to the point where using lists of numbers is far more cost effective" but that "[t]he basic function of such equipment . . . has not changed—the capacity to dial numbers without human intervention." In 2008, the FCC issued a Declaratory Ruling reaffirming that "a predictive dialer constitutes an automatic telephone dialing system and is subject to the TCPA's restrictions on the use of autodialers." *In re Rules & Regulations Implementing the Telephone Consumer Protection Act of 1991*, Declaratory Ruling, 23 F.C.C. Rcd. 559, 556 ¶ 12.

The undisputed evidence here clearly establishes that the LiveVox system has the capacity to store telephone numbers. Pye stated that the system could store numbers for up to 30 days, and the LiveVox memorandum confirms that it is "able to store or produce telephone numbers to be called." Defendant appears to argue that the system fails to meet the statutory definition because it deletes all numbers at the end of the day. But it is undisputed that the system stores numbers for at least the course of a single day. The TCPA, on its face, does not require storage for any length of time. In any event, the system here has the capacity to do so.

Whether the LiveVox system has the capacity for random or sequential number generation is a somewhat murkier question. According to Pye's deposition testimony [when she testified as DCI's corporate representative witness under Fed. R. Civ. P. 30(b)(6)], the answer is yes. She confirmed that LiveVox has the capacity to dial sequentially and that sequential dialing is its default option. Defendant's contrary evidence consists of (1) a statement in [the current operations director's] affidavit that contradicts Pye's deposition testimony and (2) a memorandum issued by LiveVox to its clients that states that its system does not use a random or sequential number generator, but that also notes that a court had found it met the definition of an ATDS.

Ultimately, defendant's evidence is insufficient to raise a dispute of material fact sufficient to prevent summary judgment. Defendant cannot rely on the affidavit to defeat summary judgment on this issue because it directly contradicts the prior statements of defendant's prior Rule 30(b)(6) witness. And even if the LiveVox memorandum correctly states that its system cannot dial randomly or sequentially, it is undisputed that LiveVox is a "predictive dialer" that dials from lists of numbers. The FCC rulings specifically account for the fact that technology has developed such that lists of numbers are more cost-effective than random or sequential numbers. The agency concluded that a "predictive dialer" that relies on lists of numbers qualifies as an ATDS under the TCPA. That ruling is entitled to deference. Here, Pye testified that the LiveVox system was a predictive dialer. The LiveVox memorandum and defendant's own website likewise stated that the LiveVox system was a predictive dialer. In short, the LiveVox system, as utilized by defendant, was an ATDS.

In sum, even viewing the facts in the light most favorable to defendant, the evidence demonstrates that defendant used an ATDS to call plaintiff, without his prior consent. Accordingly, plaintiff is entitled to summary judgment that defendant violated § 227 of the TCPA.

The TCPA provides for damages in an amount totaling the greater of actual monetary loss or $500 for each violation of the statute. 47 U.S.C. § 227(b)(3)(B). However, a plaintiff may recover treble damages if a defendant willfully or knowingly violated the statute or regulations promulgated under § 227(b). While neither the TCPA nor FCC regulations provide a definition for willful and knowing, most courts have interpreted the willful or knowing standard to require only that a party's actions were intentional, not that it was aware that it was violating the statute. Those courts relied, in part, on the fact that the Communications Act of 1943, of which the TCPA is a part, defines willful as "the conscious or deliberate commission or omission of such act, irrespective of any intent to violate any provision[ ], rule or regulation." 47 U.S.C. § 312(f). And "[t]he plain language of 47 U.S.C. § 227(b) makes the sender of an unauthorized [communication] strictly liable, so interpreting 'willfully' as requiring a volitional act does not render the treble damages provision redundant with simple [liability] under the TCPA." *Bridgeview Health Care Ctr. Ltd. v. Clark*, 2013 WL 1154206 (N.D. Ill. Mar. 19, 2013), at *7. The Court finds that reasoning persuasive and will therefore apply that standard here.

The undisputed evidence demonstrates that defendant called plaintiff 60 times. Plaintiff therefore is entitled to at least $500 per call. The only remaining question is whether he is entitled to treble damages.

There is substantial evidence to suggest that defendant may have acted willfully in calling plaintiff. Defendant did not acquire plaintiff's telephone number from its client, as a number associated with the debtor, but instead from a third-party service provider. Even assuming that the subscriber of that number was the debtor, it was not the number she had provided to defendant's client; defendant therefore could not reasonably have believed that it had her consent to call that number. In any event, the subscriber was plaintiff, not the debtor. Even after plaintiff informed defendant that he was not the debtor and did not know the debtor, defendant continued to call him. Moreover, the LiveVox memorandum clearly stated that one court had ruled that its system was an ATDS subject to the TCPA, therefore putting defendant on notice of potential illegality.

On the other hand, defendant has asserted that it acted in good faith. It contends that it relied on LiveVox's statement that its system was not an ATDS, and that it took steps to scrub cellular telephone numbers from its system so as not to violate the TCPA.

Intent is an issue of fact that is rarely decided at the summary judgment stage. The evidence presented here is not so clear and one-sided as to the alleged willfulness of defendant's conduct that reasonable jurors could come to only one conclusion. Accordingly, neither plaintiff nor defendant is entitled to summary judgment as to treble damages for willful conduct.

[The court denied the defendant's motion for summary judgment on claims under the federal Fair Debt Collection Practices Act and under state law.]

## CONCLUSION

For the foregoing reasons, defendant's motion for summary judgment is DENIED, and plaintiff's motion for summary judgment is DENIED as to treble damages [under the TCPA] and otherwise GRANTED.

## NOTES

1. ***Seclusion.*** Unlike the law discussed in Section A of this chapter—or many of the other rules reviewed in this book—the Do Not Call registry and the TCPA do not regulate the flow of personal *information*. Rather, they protect an individual interest in seclusion or solitude. Indeed, you may recall the intrusion on seclusion tort can be invoked against repeated telephone calls that are "hounding" the recipient [see Chapter 2]. Why do they count as privacy law? Are they better understood more generically as a form of consumer protection regulation?

2. ***Texts and Faxes.*** The word "telephone" may be right there in the name of the law, but the reach of the TCPA extends beyond voice telephone calls. Text messages sent via SMS to telephone numbers (or to the shorter SMS codes assigned by wireless providers) are treated the same as other "calls" under the TCPA. *See Satterfield v. Simon & Schuster, Inc.*, 569 F.3d 946, 951–52 (9th Cir. 2009) (affirming FCC interpretation of TCPA to that effect). Another section of the statute (and its attendant regulations) establishes opt-in consent requirements for unsolicited promotional faxes. *See* 47 U.S.C. § 227(b)(1)(C); 47 C.F.R. § 64.1200(a)(4). Some of those provisions were added to the statute by the Junk Fax Prevention Act, Pub. L. 109–21 (2005), so the treatment of faxes differs in certain respects from other communications regulated by the TCPA. For one thing, the fax rules apply to business and residential lines alike, while many of the other limitations in the TCPA apply only to personal or residential customers. The statute and FCC regulations concerning faxes also contain different notice

requirements and other disclosures, and an "established business relationship" exception that is defined somewhat differently than for the rest of the TCPA.

3. ***The 2015 Declaratory Ruling.*** You may have noticed how heavily the *Davis* court relied on decisions and declaratory rulings by the FCC. These regulatory statements carry great weight in private TCPA lawsuits, including class actions. In July 2015, the FCC issued asubstantial declaratory ruling addressing a number of outstanding issues that had divided courts and other observers, several of which are evident in the *Davis* opinion. *See In the Matter of Rules & Regulations Implementing the Tel. Consumer Prot. Act of 1991*, 30 FCC Rcd. 7961 (July 10, 2015). The FCC reaffirmed an expansive definition of autodialers, and in particular sided with the *Davis* court's interpretation that "capacity" refers to a machine's technical potential to store numbers, not to the specific way it has been used by the marketer in question. The FCC also addressed the vexing problem of phone numbers that have been reassigned from one person to another (which could be the reason for the problems in *Davis*, if the XXX–8596 had previously belonged to Pagan, who owed the debt DCI was trying to collect). A number of businesses, noting that there is no centralized national directory of reassigned phone numbers, had petitioned the FCC to clarify that they were not liable for calls made to a number that was previously assigned to a person whom they were lawfully permitted to call. The FCC rejected this request, emphasizing the strict liability standard of the statute and interpreting it to refer to the person called, not the number. *See Osorio v. State Farm Bank*, 746 F.3d 1242, 1251–52 (11th Cir. 2014) (finding that the current subscriber, not the intended recipient, needed to consent to calls under the TCPA); *Soppet v. Enhanced Recovery Co., LLC*, 679 F.3d 637, 639–40 (7th Cir. 2012) (same). The agency said that it would allow "one free call" to a number before attributing constructive knowledge of its reassignment for TCPA purposes—even if the new subscriber did not answer. Finally, the FCC broadly described the ability of a consumer to cancel previously granted consent:

> Consumers have a right to revoke consent, using any reasonable method including orally or in writing. Consumers generally may revoke, for example, by way of a consumer-initiated call, directly in response to a call initiated or made by a caller, or at an in-store bill payment location, among other possibilities.

*In the Matter of Rules & Regulations Implementing the Tel. Consumer Prot. Act of 1991*, 30 FCC Rcd. 7961, 7996 (July 10, 2015). Overall, the ruling was quite friendly to consumers. Two of the five FCC commissioners dissented, and a large number of businesses and trade associations have joined in a challenge to the ruling at the Court of Appeals for the District of Columbia, which remained pending as of this writing in early 2016.

4. ***Class Actions.*** Part of the reason businesses are so upset about what they view as broad FCC interpretations of potential liability is that the TCPA has been a hotbed of class action litigation. Statistics compiled by the law firm of Bryan Cave LLP for a 15-month period in 2013 and 2014 counted 672 privacy-related class actions filed in federal courts, and found that a

whopping 65% of these were based on the TCPA. *See* DAVID ZETOONY ET AL., BRYAN CAVE LLP, 2015 DATA PRIVACY LITIGATION REPORT, *available at* http://www.bryancavedatamatters.com/category/miscellaneous/litigation/. The TCPA's statutory damages, multiplied by the enormous volume of calls made by many telemarketers, results in significant potential awards. Most of these cases end in settlements, some for large total sums. Banks and credit card companies, which rely particularly on telemarketing as a sales technique, have been hit especially hard: in the last few years, Bank of America paid $32 million in one case, HSBC $40 million in another, and a third suit brought against Capital One and three debt collection agencies resulted in a record-breaking settlement of over $75 million. But as an article by three lawyers at WilmerHale explains:

> TCPA lawsuits are no longer limited to the world of debt collectors and telemarketers. Lawsuits have been filed across many industries [in the last few years], including against social networking companies (Twitter Inc., GroupMe), sports franchises (Los Angeles Clippers, Buffalo Bills), pharmacies (CVS Pharmacy Inc., Rite Aid Corp.), travel and entertainment companies (Cirque du Soleil Co.), retailers (Best Buy Co., J.C. Penney Co.), and online service providers (29 Prime Inc.).

Bradley M. Baglien et al., *TCPA Do's and Don'ts: Lessons Learned From the Recent Litigation Wave and FCC Order*, BLOOMBERG BNA PRIVACY & SECURITY LAW REPORT, 14 PVLR 1219 (July 6, 2015). The authors note a string of TCPA settlements "in the $30–40 million range."

5. ***Strict Liability and Treble Damages.*** In addition to the large potential damages awards, class action plaintiffs lawyers have been drawn to TCPA cases because the statute's strict liability standard makes them easier to win. Note that in *Davis*, an individual action, the court granted a contested summary judgment motion on liability *to the plaintiff*—quite an unusual outcome in litigation of any type. But all that had to be proven was the use of an autodialer and lack of consent. Furthermore, although the *Davis* court did not rule on willfulness because it was preserving an issue of intent for consideration by the jury, the opinion clearly suggests that such a finding is likely. ("There is substantial evidence to suggest that defendant may have acted willfully in calling plaintiff.") The willfulness determination requires only intentional action, not any knowledge that those actions were unlawful. The resulting treble damages, multiplying a statutory damages award, can add up fast. Davis, a lone plaintiff, received 60 phone calls; this opinion alone appears to entitle him to $30,000, which would become $90,000 if trebled.

6. ***Standing and Pick-offs.*** What happens to a TCPA class action if the defendant offers to pay the full statutory damages award to the named plaintiff? Does that moot the case and deny standing to the entire proposed class? This defensive maneuver, known as the "pick-off," was used against all sorts of class actions seeking fixed damages, such as the TCPA's statutory damages awards, and it had caused a circuit split. In a recent TCPA case, however, the Supreme Court ruled that "an unaccepted settlement offer or offer of judgment does not moot a plaintiff's case." *Campbell-Ewald Co. v.*

*Gomez*, 136 S. Ct. 663, 672 (2016). Nevertheless, the Court left the door open for a slight variation of the pick-off, where a defendant deposits the offered settlement money in escrow or with the court. *Id.*; *see also id.* at 683 (Roberts, C.J., dissenting) ("For aught that appears, the majority's analysis may have come out differently if Campbell had deposited the offered funds with the District Court.") Presumably that scenario will come to the Court in the near future. In addition, standing in TCPA cases could be affected by a Supreme Court ruling about privacy injury in *Spokeo, Inc. v. Robins*, still pending as of this writing in early 2016.

7. ***Regulatory Enforcement.*** Private suits are not the only mode of enforcement for the TCPA. Both the FCC and state consumer protection regulators may bring actions against violations. The FCC can impose fines of up to $16,000 for *each call* that violates the statute. It has imposed multiple TCPA penalties over $1 million in recent years.

8. ***Self-Regulatory Ethics Guidelines.*** A number of marketing trade associations have developed their own self-regulatory guidelines [see Chapter 3] in this space. The Direct Marketing Association has well-established *Guidelines for Ethical Business Practice* that cover solicitation by telephone, text message, and email. The Mobile Marketing Association (MMA) has published *US Consumer Best Practices* which include some detailed guidance for sending advertisements by SMS or other text message services. The MMA rules span issues such as notice to consumers, a standard of allowing consumers to revoke consent for commercial messages by texting STOP as a reply text message, and parameters for "viral" marketing techniques.

9. ***Avoiding Mistakes.*** Given the strict liability standard under the TCPA, precisely what should DCI have done differently in the *Davis* case? How would you counsel the firm to change its practices to avoid future liability, and what practical objections do you think DCI might have to your recommendations? Overall, is it too difficult and costly to comply with the TCPA, as many businesses suggest, or is the law simply requiring telemarketers to internalize the costs of their practices and take appropriate precautions, as proponents maintain?

---

## Practice

### Mapping the TCPA

The TCPA is a particularly intricate statute involving relationships between many different variables. Try your hand at depicting its provisions visually—in a table or a flowchart, for example. You should incorporate the following considerations into your presentation:

- ***What technology does the caller use?*** Is there an autodialer? A recorded message?
- ***What type of line is being called?*** Residential land line? Business land line? Mobile phone? Fax machine?

- ***What is the relationship between the caller and the recipient?*** Is there an existing customer relationship? Has there been prior express invitation? Is there written consent?

---

## Focus

The CAN-SPAM Act

Of all the jokey acronyms for US privacy statutes, even including the unwieldy USA PATRIOT Act, the one for the law that governs commercial email messages is the silliest (or the cleverest if you really like puns): the Controlling the Assault of Non-Solicited Pornography and Marketing Act ("CAN-SPAM Act"), 15 U.S.C. §§ 7701 et seq. Get it?

The CAN-SPAM Act is closer to a consumer protection than to a data protection model [see Chapter 3]. Its centerpiece is a requirement that recipients of unsolicited commercial electronic messages must be allowed to opt out of them. (Those "unsubscribe" links you see at the bottom of emails from retailers are federally mandated.)

Unlike the TCPA, recipients of messages that violate the CAN-SPAM Act have no private right of action. Service providers who are "adversely affected" by spam do have authority to sue. *See* 15 U.S.C. § 7706(g). The primary enforcement comes from regulatory agencies, however. The FTC can bring actions against CAN-SPAM violations through exercise of its consumer protection powers, *see id.* at § 7706(a), and may impose fines of up to $16,000 per violation, which can multiply quickly. The FTC typically pairs CAN-SPAM enforcement with other authority, such as Section 5 regulation of unfair or deceptive trade practices [see Chapter 3]. The statute also includes a laundry list of other federal agencies that retain jurisdiction over CAN-SPAM enforcement for the entities they supervise (even the Secretary of Agriculture under the Packers and Stockyards Act of 1921, *see id.* at § 7706(b)(8)). The FCC has power over messages sent to wireless domains—in other words, to cell phones—and has written regulations which require an opt-in from the recipient in such cases rather than an opt-out. *See* 47 C.F.R. § 64.3100. Finally, the CAN-SPAM Act also empowers state consumer protection regulators to bring suit under the Act, and to collect statutory damages of up to $250 per individual message, which is ordinarily subject to a cap of $2 million. 15 U.S.C. § 7706(f). The federal statute preempts state laws targeted at email spam, although it does not preempt any state law based on falsehood, deception, or fraud, or broader state claims like those under tort or contract law.

In guidance for businesses, the FTC summarized the requirements of the CAN-SPAM Act as follows:

1. **Don't use false or misleading header information.** Your "From," "To," "Reply-To," and routing information—including the originating domain name and email address—must be accurate and identify the person or business who initiated the message.

2. **Don't use deceptive subject lines.** The subject line must accurately reflect the content of the message.

3. **Identify the message as an ad.** The law gives you a lot of leeway in how to do this, but you must disclose clearly and conspicuously that your message is an advertisement.

4. **Tell recipients where you're located.** Your message must include your valid physical postal address. This can be your current street address, a post office box you've registered with the U.S. Postal Service, or a private mailbox you've registered with a commercial mail receiving agency established under Postal Service regulations.

5. **Tell recipients how to opt out of receiving future email from you.** Your message must include a clear and conspicuous explanation of how the recipient can opt out of getting email from you in the future. Craft the notice in a way that's easy for an ordinary person to recognize, read, and understand. Creative use of type size, color, and location can improve clarity. Give a return email address or another easy Internet-based way to allow people to communicate their choice to you. You may create a menu to allow a recipient to opt out of certain types of messages, but you must include the option to stop all commercial messages from you. Make sure your spam filter doesn't block these opt-out requests.

6. **Honor opt-out requests promptly.** Any opt-out mechanism you offer must be able to process opt-out requests for at least 30 days after you send your message. You must honor a recipient's opt-out request within 10 business days. You can't charge a fee, require the recipient to give you any personally identifying information beyond an email address, or make the recipient take any step other than sending a reply email or visiting a single page on an Internet website as a condition for honoring an opt-out request. Once people have told you they don't want to receive more messages from you, you can't sell or transfer their email addresses, even in the form of a mailing list. The only exception is that you may transfer the addresses to a company you've hired to help you comply with the CAN-SPAM Act.

7. **Monitor what others are doing on your behalf.** The law makes clear that even if you hire another company to handle your email marketing, you can't contract away your legal responsibility to comply with the law. Both the company whose product is promoted in the message and the company that actually sends the message may be held legally responsible.

FTC, *CAN-SPAM Act: A Compliance Guide for Business* (Sept. 2009). Other parts of the statute prohibit certain practices that facilitate large-scale spamming, such as address harvesting, dictionary attacks, and automated creation of multiple email accounts. *See* 15 U.S.C. § 7704(b). As its full name suggests, the CAN-SPAM Act also includes labeling requirements and other rules for "sexually oriented material" in electronic messages. *See id.* at § 7704(d).

The law presents a few definitional challenges. For instance, the FTC has written detailed rules and guidance to demarcate when an electronic mail message is "commercial" and so covered by the Act. *See, e.g.*, 16 C.F.R. § 316.3. The essence of the FTC's test asks whether the "primary purpose" of a message is "advertisement or promotion of a product or service," as distinguished from "transactional or relationship" content and other information.

While directed largely at email, the statute can apply to other types of digital messages. For example, as noted above, the FCC regulates mobile phone messages. Another variation was illustrated when Facebook brought suit (under the right of action for affected service providers) against MaxBounty, a marketer allegedly sending spam within its social networking platform. The court rejected an argument that the CAN-SPAM Act did not apply to those communications:

> [I]n order for the Facebook pages at issue to be considered "electronic mail messages," they must be "sent to a unique electronic mail address," that is, to "a destination . . . to which an electronic mail message can be sent." 15 U.S.C. § 7702(6). In MaxBounty's alleged scheme, a user is instructed to effect transmission of Facebook pages to all of his or her Facebook friends. Based on a number of factors, including individual user account settings, the pages are transmitted to destinations including the user's "wall," the "news feed" or "home" page of the user's friends, the Facebook inbox of the user's friends, and to users' external e-mail addresses.
>
> Significantly, these transmissions require at least some routing activity [by] Facebook. While the routing employed by Facebook may be less complex and elongated than those employed by ISP's, *any* routing necessarily implicates issues regarding volume and traffic utilization of infrastructure—issues which CAN-SPAM seeks to address. A determination that the communications at issue here are "electronic messages" thus is consistent with the intent of Congress to mitigate the number of misleading commercial communications that overburden infrastructure of the internet. 15 U.S.C. § 7701(a). Accordingly, the Court concludes that Facebook's CAN-SPAM Act claim is sufficiently pled.

*Facebook, Inc. v. MaxBounty, Inc.*, 274 F.R.D. 279, 283–84 (N.D. Cal. 2011).

The nuisance of spam email is much less pervasive today than it was in 2003 when Congress passed the CAN-SPAM Act. The primary reason probably is not the law, however. Thanks to the enormous improvement in spam filtering technology provided by ISPs and email providers, the large majority of unsolicited messages that most people receive today end up deleted or placed in a "junk mail" folder, never to be seen. The abusive spammers and phishers who use bots to spew huge numbers of unsolicited messages at arbitrary lists of addresses tend to be defeated by this technology and, failing that, by fraud and hacking laws that may include criminal liabilty. In practice, the CAN-SPAM Act has the greatest effect, not on them, but on more reputable businesses that must design their email marketing campaigns to comply with its opt-out rule and other conditions.

---

## CHAPTER 15

# EDUCATIONAL PRIVACY

Privacy law pays special attention to children. The Children's Online Privacy Protection Act (COPPA) establishes some of the most stringent broadly applicable data protection rules in US law, as a means to protect the youngest data subjects [see Chapter 4]. When exercising its consumer protection authority under Section 5, the Federal Trade Commission is especially likely to intervene when it sees practices that it believes might compromise privacy for younger people [see Chapter 3]. Against that backdrop, it is no surprise that educational institutions—elementary and secondary schools, colleges and universities—are responsible for obeying specialized layers of privacy regulation in addition to the foundational rules applied to other organizations. This Chapter considers two of the most significant of these. Section A examines constitutional rules governing searches in public schools. Section B turns to regulation of students' personal data, particularly under the Family Educational Rights and Privacy Act (FERPA) and its accompanying regulations from the Department of Education.

## A. PUBLIC SCHOOL SEARCHES

As government entities, public schools are bound by the Fourth Amendment. Those strictures are not nearly as tight on educators as on law enforcement officials, however. Because children generally do not enjoy full civil rights, and because schools have a compelling need to maintain discipline and ensure a safe environment for students, the Supreme Court has established a considerably lower threshold for constitutional compliance in elementary and secondary schools. The number of people affected by this particular rule is enormous. Roughly nine out of ten US students in elementary and high school attend public schools, for a total of some 50 million children and teenagers—and that number is growing. For some of them, being called to the assistant principal's office will be their first encounter with government authority.

The Court set out its standard in the leading case of *New Jersey v. T.L.O.*, 469 U.S. 325 (1985), where it held that a warrant was not necessary for school officials to search students or their belongings:

> [T]he legality of a search of a student should depend simply on the reasonableness, under all the circumstances, of the search. Determining the reasonableness of any search involves a twofold inquiry: first, one must consider whether the action was justified at its inception; second, one must determine whether the search as actually conducted was reasonably related in scope to the circumstances which justified the interference in the first place [citing *Terry v. Ohio*, 392 U.S. 1, 20 (1968)]. Under

> ordinary circumstances, a search of a student by a teacher or other school official will be justified at its inception when there are reasonable grounds for suspecting that the search will turn up evidence that the student has violated or is violating either the law or the rules of the school. Such a search will be permissible in its scope when the measures adopted are reasonably related to the objectives of the search and not excessively intrusive in light of the age and sex of the student and the nature of the infraction.

*Id.* at 341–42. The *T.L.O.* standard resembles Fourth Amendment rules for other "special needs" searches in contexts such as traffic stops [see Chapter 1] or workplace searches by government employers [see Chapter 11]. Many unique demands press teachers and administrators to monitor their students, from spitballs and drug dealing to online bullying and school shootings. As you read the following cases, contemplate whether Fourth Amendment doctrine gives school officials the breathing room necessary to make daily judgment calls about discipline while also protecting students from the possibility of overreaching authority.

## Vernonia School District v. Acton

515 U.S. 646 (1995)

■ JUSTICE SCALIA delivered the opinion of the Court.

Petitioner Vernonia School District 47J (District) operates one high school and three grade schools in the logging community of Vernonia, Oregon. As elsewhere in small town America, school sports play a prominent role in the town's life, and student athletes are admired in their schools and in the community.

Drugs had not been a major problem in Vernonia schools. In the mid-to-late 1980's, however, teachers and administrators observed a sharp increase in drug use. Students began to speak out about their attraction to the drug culture, and to boast that there was nothing the school could do about it. Along with more drugs came more disciplinary problems. Between 1988 and 1989 the number of disciplinary referrals in Vernonia schools rose to more than twice the number reported in the early 1980's, and several students were suspended. Students became increasingly rude during class; outbursts of profane language became common.

Not only were student athletes included among the drug users but, as the District Court found, athletes were the leaders of the drug culture. This caused the District's administrators particular concern, since drug use increases the risk of sports-related injury. Expert testimony at the trial confirmed the deleterious effects of drugs on motivation, memory, judgment, reaction, coordination, and performance. The high school football and wrestling coach witnessed a severe sternum injury suffered by a wrestler, and various omissions of safety procedures and misexecutions by football players, all attributable in his belief to the effects of drug use. [In response, the District instituted random drug testing rules for athletes ("the Policy").]

The Policy applies to all students participating in interscholastic athletics. Students wishing to play sports must sign a form consenting to the testing and must obtain the written consent of their parents. Athletes are tested at the beginning of the season for their sport. In addition, once each week of the season the names of the athletes are placed in a "pool" from which a student, with the supervision of two adults, blindly draws the names of 10% of the athletes for random testing. Those selected are notified and tested that same day, if possible.

In the fall of 1991, respondent James Acton, then a seventh grader, signed up to play football at one of the District's grade schools. He was denied participation, however, because he and his parents refused to sign the testing consent forms. The Actons filed suit, seeking declaratory and injunctive relief from enforcement of the Policy on the grounds that it violated the Fourth and Fourteenth Amendments to the United States Constitution and Article I, § 9, of the Oregon Constitution. After a bench trial, the District Court entered an order denying the claims on the merits and dismissing the action. The United States Court of Appeals for the Ninth Circuit reversed, holding that the Policy violated both the Fourth and Fourteenth Amendments and Article I, § 9, of the Oregon Constitution. We granted certiorari.

As the text of the Fourth Amendment indicates, the ultimate measure of the constitutionality of a governmental search is "reasonableness." At least in a case such as this, where there was no clear practice, either approving or disapproving the type of search at issue, at the time the constitutional provision was enacted, whether a particular search meets the reasonableness standard is judged by balancing its intrusion on the individual's Fourth Amendment interests against its promotion of legitimate governmental interests. A search unsupported by probable cause can be constitutional, we have said, when special needs, beyond the normal need for law enforcement, make the warrant and probable cause requirement impracticable.

We have found such "special needs" to exist in the public school context. There, the warrant requirement would unduly interfere with the maintenance of the swift and informal disciplinary procedures that are needed.

The first factor to be considered is the nature of the privacy interest upon which the search here at issue intrudes. Central, in our view, to the present case is the fact that the subjects of the Policy are (1) children, who (2) have been committed to the temporary custody of the State as schoolmaster.

Fourth Amendment rights, no less than First and Fourteenth Amendment rights, are different in public schools than elsewhere; the "reasonableness" inquiry cannot disregard the schools' custodial and tutelary responsibility for children. For their own good and that of their classmates, public school children are routinely required to submit to various physical examinations, and to be vaccinated against various diseases.

Legitimate privacy expectations are even less with regard to student athletes. School sports are not for the bashful. They require "suiting up" before each practice or event, and showering and changing afterwards. Public school locker rooms, the usual sites for these activities, are not notable for the privacy they afford. The locker rooms in Vernonia are typical: no individual dressing rooms are provided; shower heads are lined up along a wall, unseparated by any sort of partition or curtain; not even all the toilet stalls have doors. As the United States Court of Appeals for the Seventh Circuit has noted, there is "an element of 'communal undress' inherent in athletic participation." *Schaill by Kross v. Tippecanoe County School Corp.*, 864 F. 2d 1309, 1318 (1988).

There is an additional respect in which school athletes have a reduced expectation of privacy. By choosing to "go out for the team," they voluntarily subject themselves to a degree of regulation even higher than that imposed on students generally. In Vernonia's public schools, they must submit to a preseason physical exam (James testified that his included the giving of a urine sample), they must acquire adequate insurance coverage or sign an insurance waiver, maintain a minimum grade point average, and comply with any "rules of conduct, dress, training hours and related matters as may be established for each sport by the head coach and athletic director with the principal's approval." Somewhat like adults who choose to participate in a "closely regulated industry," students who voluntarily participate in school athletics have reason to expect intrusions upon normal rights and privileges, including privacy.

Having considered the scope of the legitimate expectation of privacy at issue here, we turn next to the character of the intrusion that is complained of. Under the District's Policy, male students produce samples at a urinal along a wall. They remain fully clothed and are only observed from behind, if at all. Female students produce samples in an enclosed stall, with a female monitor standing outside listening only for sounds of tampering. These conditions are nearly identical to those typically encountered in public restrooms, which men, women, and especially school children use daily. Under such conditions, the privacy interests compromised by the process of obtaining the urine sample are in our view negligible. The other privacy invasive aspect of urinalysis is, of course, the information it discloses concerning the state of the subject's body, and the materials he has ingested. In this regard it is significant that the tests at issue here look only for drugs, and not for whether the student is, for example, epileptic, pregnant, or diabetic. Moreover, the drugs for which the samples are screened are standard, and do not vary according to the identity of the student. And finally, the results of the tests are disclosed only to a limited class of school personnel who have a need to know; and they are not turned over to law enforcement authorities or used for any internal disciplinary function.

Respondents argue, however, that the District's Policy is in fact more intrusive than this suggests, because it requires the students, if they are to avoid sanctions for a falsely positive test, to identify in advance prescription medications they are taking. We agree that this raises some cause for concern.

The General Authorization Form that respondents refused to sign, which refusal was the basis for James's exclusion from the sports program, said only (in relevant part): "I . . . authorize the Vernonia School District to conduct a test on a urine specimen which I provide to test for drugs and/or alcohol use. I also authorize the release of information concerning the results of such a test to the Vernonia School District and to the parents and/or guardians of the student." While the practice of the District seems to have been to have a school official take medication information from the student at the time of the test, that practice is not set forth in, or required by, the Policy. It may well be that, if and when James was selected for random testing at a time that he was taking medication, the School District would have permitted him to provide the requested information in a confidential manner—for example, in a sealed envelope delivered to the testing lab. Nothing in the Policy contradicts that, and when respondents choose, in effect, to challenge the Policy on its face, we will not assume the worst.

Finally, we turn to consider the nature and immediacy of the governmental concern at issue here, and the efficacy of this means for meeting it.

That the nature of the concern is important—indeed, perhaps compelling—can hardly be doubted. School years are the time when the physical, psychological, and addictive effects of drugs are most severe. And of course the effects of a drug-infested school are visited not just upon the users, but upon the entire student body and faculty, as the educational process is disrupted. In the present case, moreover, the necessity for the State to act is magnified by the fact that this evil is being visited not just upon individuals at large, but upon children for whom it has undertaken a special responsibility of care and direction. Finally, it must not be lost sight of that this program is directed more narrowly to drug use by school athletes, where the risk of immediate physical harm to the drug user or those with whom he is playing his sport is particularly high. Apart from psychological effects, which include impairment of judgment, slow reaction time, and a lessening of the perception of pain, the particular drugs screened by the District's Policy have been demonstrated to pose substantial physical risks to athletes.

As for the immediacy of the District's concerns: We are not inclined to question—indeed, we could not possibly find clearly erroneous—the District Court's conclusion that "a large segment of the student body, particularly those involved in interscholastic athletics, was in a state of rebellion," that "[d]isciplinary actions had reached 'epidemic proportions,'" and that "the rebellion was being fueled by alcohol and drug abuse as well as by the student's misperceptions about the drug culture."

As to the efficacy of this means for addressing the problem: It seems to us self evident that a drug problem largely fueled by the "role model" effect of athletes' drug use, and of particular danger to athletes, is effectively addressed by making sure that athletes do not use drugs. Respondents argue that a "less intrusive means to the same end" was available, namely, "drug testing on suspicion of drug use." We have repeatedly refused to declare that only the "least intrusive" search practicable can be reasonable under the Fourth Amendment. Respondents' alternative entails substantial difficulties—if it is indeed practicable at all. Respondents' proposal brings the risk that teachers will impose testing arbitrarily upon troublesome but not drug likely students. It generates the expense of defending lawsuits that charge such arbitrary imposition, or that simply demand greater process before accusatory drug testing is imposed. And not least of all, it adds to the ever expanding diversionary duties of schoolteachers the new function of spotting and bringing to account drug abuse, a task for which they are ill prepared, and which is not readily compatible with their vocation.

Taking into account all the factors we have considered above—the decreased expectation of privacy, the relative unobtrusiveness of the search, and the severity of the need met by the search—we conclude Vernonia's Policy is reasonable and hence constitutional.

We caution against the assumption that suspicionless drug testing will readily pass constitutional muster in other contexts. The most significant element in this case is the first we discussed: that the Policy was undertaken in furtherance of the government's responsibilities, under a public school system, as guardian and tutor of children entrusted to its care. [T]he relevant question is whether the search is one that a reasonable guardian and tutor might undertake. Given the findings of need made by the District Court, we conclude that in the present case it is.

We therefore vacate the judgment, and remand the case to the Court of Appeals for further proceedings consistent with this opinion.

■ JUSTICE GINSBURG, concurring.

The Court constantly observes that the School District's drug-testing policy applies only to students who voluntarily participate in interscholastic athletics. Correspondingly, the most severe sanction allowed under the District's policy is suspension from extracurricular athletic programs. I comprehend the Court's opinion as reserving the question whether the District, on no more than the showing made here, constitutionally could impose routine drug testing not only on those seeking to engage with others in team sports, but on all students required to attend school.

■ JUSTICE O'CONNOR, with whom JUSTICE STEVENS and JUSTICE SOUTER join, dissenting.

One searches today's majority opinion in vain for recognition that history and precedent establish that individualized suspicion is "usually required" under the Fourth Amendment (regardless of whether a warrant and probable cause are also required) and that, in the area of intrusive personal searches, the only recognized exception is for situations in which a suspicion-based scheme would be likely ineffectual. Far from acknowledging anything special about individualized suspicion, the Court treats a suspicion-based regime as if it were just any run-of-the-mill, less intrusive alternative—that is, an alternative that officials may bypass if the lesser intrusion, in their reasonable estimation, is outweighed by policy concerns unrelated to practicability.

But having misconstrued the fundamental role of the individualized suspicion requirement in Fourth Amendment analysis, the Court never seriously engages the practicality of such a requirement in the instant case. And that failure is crucial because nowhere is it *less* clear that an individualized suspicion requirement would be ineffectual than in the school context. In most schools, the entire pool of potential search targets—students—is under constant supervision by teachers and administrators and coaches, be it in classrooms, hallways, or locker rooms.

The record here indicates that the Vernonia schools are no exception. The great irony of this case is that most (though not all) of the evidence the District introduced to justify its suspicionless drug testing program consisted of first-or second-hand stories of particular, identifiable students acting in ways that plainly gave rise to reasonable suspicion of in-school drug use—and thus that would have justified a drug-related search.

In light of all this evidence of drug use by particular students, there is a substantial basis for concluding that a vigorous regime of suspicion-based testing (for which the District appears already to have rules in place) would have gone a long way toward solving Vernonia's school drug problem while preserving the Fourth Amendment rights of James Acton and others like him. And were there any doubt about such a conclusion, it is removed by indications in the record that suspicion-based testing could have been supplemented by an equally vigorous campaign to have Vernonia's parents encourage their children to submit to the District's *voluntary* drug testing program. In these circumstances, the Fourth Amendment dictates that a mass, suspicionless search regime is categorically unreasonable.

## Safford Unified Sch. Dist. No. 1 v. Redding

557 U.S. 364 (2009)

■ JUSTICE SOUTER delivered the opinion of the Court.

The issue here is whether a 13-year-old student's Fourth Amendment right was violated when she was subjected to a search of her bra and underpants by school officials acting on reasonable suspicion that she had brought forbidden prescription and over-the-counter drugs to school. Because there were no reasons to suspect the drugs presented a danger or were concealed in her underwear, we hold that the search did violate the Constitution, but because there is reason to question the clarity with which the right was established, the official who ordered the unconstitutional search is entitled to qualified immunity from liability.

### I

The events immediately prior to the search in question began in 13-year-old Savana Redding's math class at Safford Middle School one October day in 2003. The assistant principal of the school, Kerry Wilson, came into the room and asked Savana to go to his office. There, he showed her a day planner, unzipped and open flat on his desk, in which there were several knives, lighters, a permanent marker, and a cigarette. Wilson asked Savana whether the planner was hers; she said it was, but that a few days before she had lent it to her friend, Marissa Glines. Savana stated that none of the items in the planner belonged to her.

Wilson then showed Savana four white prescription-strength ibuprofen 400-mg pills, and one over-the-counter blue naproxen 200-mg pill, all used for pain and inflammation but banned under school rules without advance permission. He asked Savana if she knew anything about the pills. Savana answered that she did not. Wilson then told Savana that he had received a report that she was giving these pills to fellow students; Savana denied it and agreed to let Wilson search her belongings. Helen Romero, an administrative assistant, came into the office, and together with Wilson they searched Savana's backpack, finding nothing.

At that point, Wilson instructed Romero to take Savana to the school nurse's office to search her clothes for pills. Romero and the nurse, Peggy Schwallier, asked Savana to remove her jacket, socks, and shoes, leaving her in stretch pants and a T-shirt (both without pockets), which she was then asked to remove. Finally, Savana was told to pull her bra out and to the side and shake it, and to pull out the elastic on her underpants, thus exposing her breasts and pelvic area to some degree. No pills were found.

Savana's mother filed suit against Safford Unified School District #1, Wilson, Romero, and Schwallier for conducting a strip search in violation of Savana's Fourth Amendment rights. The individuals (hereinafter petitioners) moved for summary judgment, raising a defense of qualified immunity. The District Court for the District of Arizona granted the motion on the ground that there was no Fourth Amendment violation, and a panel of the Ninth Circuit affirmed.

A closely divided Circuit sitting en banc, however, reversed. Following the two-step protocol for evaluating claims of qualified immunity, the Ninth Circuit held that the strip search was unjustified under the Fourth Amendment test for searches of children by school officials set out in *New Jersey v. T.L.O.*, 469 U.S. 325 (1985). The Circuit then applied the test for qualified immunity, and found that Savana's right was clearly established at the time of the search.

We granted certiorari, and now affirm in part, reverse in part, and remand.

## II

In *T.L.O.*, we recognized that the school setting "requires some modification of the level of suspicion of illicit activity needed to justify a search," and held that for searches by school officials "a careful balancing of governmental and private interests suggests that the public interest is best served by a Fourth Amendment standard of reasonableness that stops short of probable cause." We have thus applied a standard of reasonable suspicion to determine the legality of a school administrator's search of a student, and have held that a school search "will be permissible in its scope when the measures adopted are reasonably related to the objectives of the search and not excessively intrusive in light of the age and sex of the student and the nature of the infraction."

Perhaps the best that can be said generally about the required knowledge component of probable cause for a law enforcement officer's evidence search is that it raise a "fair probability" or a "substantial chance" of discovering evidence of criminal activity. The lesser standard for school searches could as readily be described as a moderate chance of finding evidence of wrongdoing.

## III

### A

In this case, the school's policies strictly prohibit the nonmedical use, possession, or sale of any drug on school grounds, including "[a]ny prescription or over-the-counter drug, except those for which permission to use in school has been granted pursuant to Board policy." A week before Savana was searched, another student told the principal and Assistant Principal Wilson that "certain students were bringing drugs and weapons on campus," and that he had been sick after taking some pills that "he got from a classmate." On the morning of October 8, the same boy handed Wilson a white pill that he said Marissa Glines had given him. He told Wilson that students were planning to take the pills at lunch.

Wilson learned from Peggy Schwallier, the school nurse, that the pill was Ibuprofen 400 mg, available only by prescription. Wilson then called

Marissa out of class. Outside the classroom, Marissa's teacher handed Wilson the day planner, found within Marissa's reach, containing various contraband items. Wilson escorted Marissa back to his office.

In the presence of Helen Romero, Wilson requested Marissa to turn out her pockets and open her wallet. Marissa produced a blue pill, several white ones, and a razor blade. Wilson asked where the blue pill came from, and Marissa answered, "I guess it slipped in when she gave me the IBU 400s." When Wilson asked whom she meant, Marissa replied, "Savana Redding." Wilson then enquired about the day planner and its contents; Marissa denied knowing anything about them. Wilson did not ask Marissa any follow-up questions to determine whether there was any likelihood that Savana presently had pills: neither asking when Marissa received the pills from Savana nor where Savana might be hiding them.

Schwallier did not immediately recognize the blue pill, but information provided through a poison control hotline indicated that the pill was a 200-mg dose of an anti-inflammatory drug, generically called naproxen, available over the counter. At Wilson's direction, Marissa was then subjected to a search of her bra and underpants by Romero and Schwallier, as Savana was later on. The search revealed no additional pills.

It was at this juncture that Wilson called Savana into his office and showed her the day planner. Their conversation established that Savana and Marissa were on friendly terms: while she denied knowledge of the contraband, Savana admitted that the day planner was hers and that she had lent it to Marissa. Wilson had other reports of their friendship from staff members, who had identified Savana and Marissa as part of an unusually rowdy group at the school's opening dance in August, during which alcohol and cigarettes were found in the girls' bathroom. Wilson had reason to connect the girls with this contraband, for Wilson knew that [another student] had told the principal that before the dance, he had been at a party at Savana's house where alcohol was served. Marissa's statement that the pills came from Savana was thus sufficiently plausible to warrant suspicion that Savana was involved in pill distribution.

This suspicion of Wilson's was enough to justify a search of Savana's backpack and outer clothing. If a student is reasonably suspected of giving out contraband pills, she is reasonably suspected of carrying them on her person and in the carryall that has become an item of student uniform in most places today. If Wilson's reasonable suspicion of pill distribution were not understood to support searches of outer clothes and backpack, it would not justify any search worth making. And the look into Savana's bag, in her presence and in the relative privacy of Wilson's office, was not excessively intrusive, any more than Romero's subsequent search of her outer clothing.

### B

Here it is that the parties part company, with Savana's claim that extending the search at Wilson's behest to the point of making her pull out her underwear was constitutionally unreasonable. The exact label for this final step in the intrusion is not important, though strip search is a fair way to speak of it. Romero and Schwallier directed Savana to remove her clothes down to her underwear, and then "pull out" her bra and the elastic band on her underpants. Although Romero and Schwallier stated that they did not see anything when Savana followed their instructions, we would not define strip search and its Fourth Amendment consequences in a way that would guarantee litigation about who was looking and how much was seen. The very fact of Savana's pulling her underwear away from her body in the presence of the two officials who were able to see her necessarily exposed her breasts and pelvic area to some degree, and both subjective and reasonable societal expectations of personal privacy support the treatment of such a search as categorically distinct, requiring distinct elements of justification on the part of school authorities for going beyond a search of outer clothing and belongings.

Savana's subjective expectation of privacy against such a search is inherent in her account of it as embarrassing, frightening, and humiliating. The reasonableness of her expectation (required by the Fourth Amendment standard) is indicated by the consistent experiences of other young people similarly searched, whose adolescent vulnerability intensifies the patent intrusiveness of the exposure [citing Brief for National Association of Social Workers et al. as Amici Curiae]. The common reaction of these adolescents simply registers the obviously different meaning of a search exposing the body from the experience of nakedness or near undress in other school circumstances. Changing for gym is getting ready for play; exposing for a search is responding to an accusation reserved for suspected wrongdoers and fairly understood as so degrading that a number of communities have decided that strip searches in schools are never reasonable and have banned them no matter what the facts may be [citing New York City Dept. of Education policy].

The indignity of the search does not, of course, outlaw it, but it does implicate the rule of reasonableness as stated in *T.L.O.*, that "the search as actually conducted [be] reasonably related in scope to the circumstances which justified the interference in the first place." The scope will be permissible, that is, when it is "not excessively intrusive in light of the age and sex of the student and the nature of the infraction."

Here, the content of the suspicion failed to match the degree of intrusion. Wilson knew beforehand that the pills were prescription-strength ibuprofen and over-the-counter naproxen, common pain relievers equivalent to two Advil, or one Aleve. He must have been aware of the nature and limited threat of the specific drugs he was searching for, and while just about anything can be taken in quantities that will do real harm, Wilson had no reason to suspect that large amounts of the drugs were being passed around, or that individual students were receiving great numbers of pills.

Nor could Wilson have suspected that Savana was hiding common painkillers in her underwear. Petitioners suggest, as a truth universally acknowledged, that "students . . . hid[e] contraband in or under their clothing," and cite a smattering of cases of students with contraband in their underwear. But when the categorically extreme intrusiveness of a search down to the body of an adolescent requires some justification in suspected facts, general background possibilities fall short; a reasonable search that extensive calls for suspicion that it will pay off. But nondangerous school contraband does not raise the specter of stashes in intimate places, and there is no evidence in the record of any general practice among Safford Middle School students of hiding that sort of thing in underwear.

In sum, what was missing from the suspected facts that pointed to Savana was any indication of danger to the students from the power of the drugs or their quantity, and any reason to suppose that Savana was carrying pills in her underwear. We think that the combination of these deficiencies was fatal to finding the search reasonable.

In so holding, we mean to cast no ill reflection on the assistant principal, for the record raises no doubt that his motive throughout was to eliminate drugs from his school and protect students. Parents are known to overreact to protect their children from danger, and a school official with responsibility for safety may tend to do the same. The difference is that the Fourth Amendment places limits on the official, even with the high degree of deference that courts must pay to the educator's professional judgment.

We do mean, though, to make it clear that the *T.L.O.* concern to limit a school search to reasonable scope requires the support of reasonable suspicion of danger or of resort to underwear for hiding evidence of wrongdoing before a search can reasonably make the quantum leap from outer clothes and backpacks to exposure of intimate parts. The meaning of such a search, and the degradation its subject may reasonably feel, place a search that intrusive in a category of its own demanding its own specific suspicions.

## IV

*T.L.O.* directed school officials to limit the intrusiveness of a search, "in light of the age and sex of the student and the nature of the infraction," and as we have just said at some length, the intrusiveness of the strip search here cannot be seen as justifiably related to the circumstances. But we realize that the lower courts have reached divergent conclusions regarding how the *T.L.O.* standard applies to such searches.

We think these differences of opinion from our own are substantial enough to require immunity for the school officials in this case. We would not suggest that entitlement to qualified immunity is the guaranteed product of disuniform views of the law in the other federal, or state, courts, and the fact that a single judge, or even a group of judges, disagrees about the contours of a right does not automatically render the law unclear if we have been clear. That said, however, the cases viewing school strip searches differently from the way we see them are numerous enough, with well-reasoned majority and dissenting opinions, to counsel doubt that we were sufficiently clear in the prior statement of law. We conclude that qualified immunity is warranted.

V

The strip search of Savana Redding was unreasonable and a violation of the Fourth Amendment, but petitioners Wilson, Romero, and Schwallier are nevertheless protected from liability through qualified immunity.

▪ JUSTICE STEVENS, with whom JUSTICE GINSBURG joins, concurring in part and dissenting in part.

In *New Jersey v. T.L.O.*, 469 U.S. 325 (1985), the Court established a two-step inquiry for determining the reasonableness of a school official's decision to search a student.

Nothing the Court decides today alters this basic framework. It simply applies *T.L.O.* to declare unconstitutional a strip search of a 13-year-old honors student that was based on a groundless suspicion that she might be hiding medicine in her underwear. This is, in essence, a case in which clearly established law meets clearly outrageous conduct. The strip search of Savana Redding in this case was both more intrusive and less justified than the search of the student's purse in *T.L.O.* Therefore, while I join Parts I–III of the Court's opinion, I disagree with its decision to extend qualified immunity to the school official who authorized this unconstitutional search.

▪ JUSTICE THOMAS, concurring in the judgment in part and dissenting in part.

I agree with the Court that the judgment against the school officials with respect to qualified immunity should be reversed. Unlike the majority, however, I would hold that the search of Savana Redding did not violate the Fourth Amendment. The majority imposes a vague and amorphous standard on school administrators. It also grants judges sweeping authority to second-guess the measures that these officials take to maintain discipline in their schools and ensure the health and safety of the students in their charge. This deep intrusion into the administration of public schools exemplifies why the Court should return to the common-law doctrine of in loco parentis under which the judiciary was reluctant to interfere in the routine business of school administration, allowing schools and teachers to set and enforce rules and to maintain order. But even under the prevailing Fourth Amendment test established by *New Jersey v. T.L.O.*, 469 U.S. 325 (1985), all petitioners, including the school district, are entitled to judgment as a matter of law in their favor.

Here, petitioners had reasonable grounds to suspect that Redding was in possession of prescription and nonprescription drugs in violation of the school's prohibition of the non-medical use, possession, or sale of a drug on school property or at school events. Thus, as the majority acknowledges, the totality of relevant circumstances justified a search of Redding for pills.

The remaining question is whether the search was reasonable in scope. According to the majority, to be reasonable, this school search required a showing of "danger to the students from the power of the drugs or their quantity" or a "reason to suppose that [Redding] was carrying pills in her underwear." Each of these additional requirements is an unjustifiable departure from bedrock Fourth Amendment law in the school setting, where this Court has heretofore read the Fourth Amendment to grant considerable leeway to school officials. Because the school officials searched in a location where the pills could have been hidden, the search was reasonable in scope under *T.L.O.*

By deciding that it is better equipped [than locally accountable school officials] to decide what behavior should be permitted in schools, the Court has undercut student safety and undermined the authority of school administrators and local officials. Even more troubling, it has done so in a case in which the underlying response by school administrators was reasonable and justified. I cannot join this regrettable decision. I, therefore, respectfully dissent from the Court's determination that this search violated the Fourth Amendment.

## NOTES

1. ***Drug-Testing the Marching Band.*** Seven years after *Vernonia*, the drug testing issue returned to the Supreme Court in *Board of Education v. Earls*, 536 U.S. 822 (2002). There, the school board in rural Tecumseh, Oklahoma applied a drug testing policy to middle school and high school students participating in competitive extracurricular activities other than athletics, including the choir, academic team, and Future Farmers of America. Writing for a 5–4 majority, Justice Thomas presented the case as a straightforward application of *Vernonia*: students' privacy interests were significantly reduced in the school environment; privacy safeguards in the testing program and limits on the use of results were very similar to those in *Vernonia* and limited the degree of intrusion; and student drug use remained a national epidemic. Justice Ginsburg, who had concurred in *Vernonia* on a narrow basis, now found herself writing the principal dissent in *Earls*. Unlike student athletes, she contended, the students tested in Tecumseh did not routinely shower and change clothes in communal locker rooms or undergo physicals as did the athletes in *Vernonia*. She also argued that the

*Vernonia* Court had relied on particular circumstances related to a narrow subset of students:

> The Vernonia district had two good reasons for testing athletes: Sports team members faced special health risks and they "were the leaders of the drug culture." No similar reason, and no other tenable justification, explains Tecumseh's decision to target for testing all participants in every competitive extracurricular activity.

The *Earls* majority disagreed that *Vernonia* relied on the communal locker rooms as anything more than an additional factor reducing students' expectations of privacy:

> This distinction was not essential to our decision in *Vernonia*, which depended primarily upon the school's custodial responsibility and authority. In any event, students who participate in competitive extracurricular activities voluntarily subject themselves to many of the same intrusions on their privacy as do athletes. This regulation of extracurricular activities further diminishes the expectation of privacy among schoolchildren.

As to the argument that athletes were considered particular leaders of the "drug culture" in *Vernonia*, the majority said it would not "second-guess" the Tecumseh board's determination: "Given the nationwide epidemic of drug use, and the evidence of increased drug use in Tecumseh schools, it was entirely reasonable for the School District to enact this particular drug testing policy."

Under *Vernonia* and *Earls*, could a public school subject *all* of its students to a random drug testing policy? If not, how are the privacy interests of students who participate in extracurricular activities different from those of students in the general population?

2. ***Physical Privacy.*** Distinctive protection of the body is an influential first principle in privacy law, everywhere from the constitutionality of genetic testing [see Chapter 1] to differential treatment of medical information [see Chapter 12], among many other examples. This certainly seems to be an important factor in *Safford*, where the Court relies a great deal on the intrusiveness of a search that required a young student to expose her breasts and pelvic area, even if just for a fleeting moment. Why does this factor have so much less salience in *Vernonia* (and *Earls*)—where, after all, school authorities observed students urinate and then seized the resulting waste product? Is the difference that the justification was found to be more significant in *Vernonia*? Was the potentially invasive search conducted more sensitively in the drug testing cases than in *Safford*? Or are there other differences in the surrounding circumstances that account for this different treatment of the students' physical privacy?

3. ***What Would Have Justified the Search?*** Could a school's search of a minor's underwear ever be justified under the Fourth Amendment? Consider some hypothetical variations on the facts of *Safford*. What if the initially incriminating pills were highly addictive OxyContin rather than prescription-strength ibuprofen? What if the drug in question were heroin

instead? Or, what if Kerry Wilson had questioned Marissa Glines somewhat more extensively and effectively first? What if Glines told him that she had obtained the pills from Savana Redding that morning? Or that the pills were concealed in Redding's underpants? What if school authorities had specific information leading them to believe that students at the school commonly concealed contraband in their undergarments? What if Wilson observed Redding furtively touching her hand to the side of her breast when he questioned her about whether she was carrying any additional pills, and believed she was unconsciously revealing their location?

4. ***Universities.*** Cases such as *T.L.O.*, *Vernonia*, and *Safford* apply to elementary and secondary schools, not to higher education. Justifications about the limited rights of children and the need to maintain discipline do not extend to the university setting. Most Fourth Amendment litigation concerning college students arises from searches of dormitory rooms at public institutions, typically after campus police or other authorities have found evidence of criminal conduct in the room. The standards here are quite similar to those applied in other locations where there may be a reasonable expectation of privacy, such as rented apartments or hotel rooms. A warrant usually would be required for entry unless an exception, such as exigent circumstances or plain view, applies to excuse the requirement. Most institutions require students to sign "housing contracts" that often include terms consenting to searches of the premises. Courts may enforce these agreements as waivers of Fourth Amendment expectations of privacy when they are narrowly tied to entries by university authorities for legitimate purposes such as investigating hazards or responding to noise complaints. Courts typically refuse to consider them carte blanche consent to all searches. *See, e.g.*, *Commonwealth v. Neilson*, 666 N.E.2d 984 (Mass. 1996); *Devers v. S. Univ.* 712 So. 2d 199 (La. App. 1998). Similar rules may apply in private universities if public officials such as the police are involved; while private college officials will have greater scope to conduct searches for their own purposes, they cannot necessarily transfer that consent to law enforcement. *See, e.g.*, *People v. Superior Court*, 49 Cal. Rptr. 3d 831 (App. Ct. 2006). Beyond the context of dorm rooms, most other Fourth Amendment rules apply to college and graduate students exactly as they do to other adults.

## G.C. v. Owensboro Public Schools

711 F.3d 623 (6th Cir. 2013)

■ KAREN NELSON MOORE, CIRCUIT JUDGE.

Plaintiff-Appellant G.C. began attending school in the Owensboro Public School District as an out-of-district student in 2005. In September 2009, G.C. was caught sending text messages in class. School officials confiscated his cell phone and read the text messages. Because this was the last in a series of disciplinary infractions, Superintendent Dr. Larry Vick ("Vick") revoked G.C.'s out-of-district status, barring him from attending Owensboro High School. G.C. filed suit, raising both federal and state-law claims [including a Fourth Amendment claim] based on the

September 2009 search, in which he contends that school officials violated his constitutional rights when they read text messages on his phone without the requisite reasonable suspicion.

For the reasons stated below, we **REVERSE** the district court's grant of summary judgment on G.C.'s Fourth Amendment claim based on the September 2009 search. We **REMAND** for further proceedings consistent with this opinion.

**BACKGROUND**

During his freshman year at Owensboro High School, G.C. began to have disciplinary problems. Shortly thereafter, he communicated with school officials that he used drugs and was disposed to anger and depression. [The court reviewed the history of G.C.'s disciplinary problems.]

On March 5, 2009, G.C. walked out of a meeting with Summer Bell, the prevention coordinator at the high school, and left the building without permission. G.C. made a phone call to his father and was located in the parking lot at his car, where there were tobacco products in plain view. G.C. then went to [the office of Assistant Principal Christina Smith ("Smith")], and Smith avers that G.C. "indicated he was worried about the same things we had discussed before when he had told me he was suicidal." She states that she "was very concerned about [G.C.'s] well-being because he had indicated he was thinking about suicide again. I, therefore, checked [G.C.'s] cell phone to see if there was any indication he was thinking about suicide." The record also indicates that G.C. visited a treatment center that day, and the counselor recommended that he be admitted for one to two weeks.

On September 2, 2009, G.C. violated the school cell-phone policy when he was seen texting in class. G.C.'s teacher confiscated the phone, which was brought to [Assistant Principal Melissa Brown ("Brown")], who then read four text messages on the phone. Brown stated that she looked at the messages "to see if there was an issue with which I could help him so that he would not do something harmful to himself or someone else." Brown explained that she had these worries because she "was aware of previous angry outbursts from [G.C.] and that [he] had admitted to drug use in the past. I also knew [he] drove a fast car and had once talked about suicide to [Smith]. I was concerned how [he] would further react to his phone being taken away and that he might hurt himself or someone else."

[In the wake of the September 2 incident, the district revoked G.C.'s privileges to attend Owensboro High School as a resident outside the district. The superintendent explained that G.C. "had violated the condition of his out-of-district privilege to attend Owensboro High School by texting in class." He had been allowed to return to the district for the 2009–2010 school year with a warning that he would be barred if he had any further disciplinary problems.]

On October 21, 2009, G.C. filed an action for declaratory and injunctive relief, as well as compensatory and punitive damages, in the U.S. District Court for the Western District of Kentucky. G.C. alleged violations of his First, Fourth, and Fifth Amendment rights as well as violations of the Kentucky Constitution. [The district court granted defendant's motion for summary judgment on the constitutional claims and G.C. appealed.]

## FOURTH AMENDMENT CLAIM

G.C. argues that the district court erred when it granted summary judgment to the defendants on his Fourth Amendment claim. G.C. conceded at oral argument that the March 2009 search of his cell phone was justified in light of the surrounding circumstances, yet maintains that the September 2009 search was not supported by a reasonable suspicion that would justify school officials reading his text messages. The defendants respond that reasonable suspicion existed to search his phone in September 2009 given his documented drug abuse and suicidal thoughts, particularly under the lower standard applied to searches in a school setting. They argue that the searches were limited and "aimed at uncovering any evidence of illegal activity" or any indication that G.C. might hurt himself.

The Supreme Court has implemented a relaxed standard for searches in the school setting [citing *New Jersey v. T.L.O.*, 469 U.S. 325, 341–42 (1985)]. A student search is justified in its inception when there are reasonable grounds for suspecting that the search will garner evidence that a student has violated or is violating the law or the rules of the school, or is in imminent danger of injury on school premises. "Such a search will be permissible in its scope when the measures adopted are reasonably related to the objectives of the search and not excessively intrusive in light of the age and sex of the student and the nature of the infraction." *T.L.O.*, 469 U.S. at 342. In determining whether a search is excessive in its scope, the nature and immediacy of the governmental concern that prompted the search is considered. In order to satisfy the constitutional requirements, the means employed must be congruent to the end sought.

Because this court has yet to address how the *T.L.O.* inquiry applies to the search of a student's cell phone, the parties point to two district court cases that have addressed this issue. In *J.W. v. Desoto County School District*, No. 2:09–cv–00155–MPM–DAS, 2010 WL 4394059 (N.D. Miss. Nov. 1, 2010), the case relied upon by the defendants and cited by the district court, a faculty member observed a student using his cell phone in class, took the cell phone from the student, and "opened the phone to review the personal pictures stored on it and taken by [the student] while at his home." The district court found the faculty member's actions reasonable, explaining that "[i]n assessing the reasonableness of the defendants' actions under *T.L.O.*, a crucial factor is that [the student] was caught using his cell phone at school." The court further reasoned that "[u]pon witnessing a student improperly using a cell phone at school, it strikes this court as being reasonable for a school official to seek to determine to what end the student was improperly using that phone."

Such broad language, however, does not comport with our precedent. A search is justified at its inception if there is reasonable suspicion that a search will uncover evidence of further wrongdoing or of injury to the student or another. Not all infractions involving cell phones will present such indications. Moreover, even assuming that a search of the phone were justified, the scope of the search must be tailored to the nature of the infraction and must be related to the objectives of the search. Under our two-part test, using a cell phone on school grounds does not automatically trigger an essentially unlimited right enabling a school official to search any content stored on the phone that is not related either substantively or temporally to the infraction. Because the crux of the *T.L.O.* standard is reasonableness, as evaluated by the circumstances of each case, we decline to adopt the broad standard set forth by *Desoto* and the district court.

G.C. directs the panel to *Klump v. Nazareth Area School District*, 425 F. Supp. 2d 622 (E.D. Pa. 2006), a case in which a student was seen using his cell phone, followed by two school officials accessing the student's text messages and voice mail; searching the student's contacts list; using the phone to call other students; and having an online conversation with the student's brother. The court initially determined that the school officials were "justified in seizing the cell phone, as [the student] had violated the school's policy prohibiting use or display of cell phones during school hours." The court found that the school officials were not, however, justified in calling other students, as "[t]hey had no reason to suspect at the outset that such a search would reveal that [the student] himself was violating another school policy." The court further discussed the text messages read by the school officials, concluding that although the school officials ultimately found evidence of drug activity on the phone, for the purposes of a Fourth Amendment claim, the court must consider only that which the officials knew at the inception of the search: "the school officials did not see the allegedly drug-related text message until after they initiated the search of [the] cell phone. Accordingly, . . . there was no justification for the school officials to search [the] phone for evidence of drug activity." We conclude that the fact-based approach taken in *Klump* more accurately reflects our court's standard than the blanket rule set forth in *Desoto*.

G.C.'s objection to the September 2009 search centers on the first step of the *T.L.O.* inquiry—whether the search was justified at its inception. G.C. argues that the school officials had no reasonable grounds to suspect that a search of his phone would result in evidence of any improper activity. The defendants counter that the search was justified because of G.C.'s documented drug abuse and suicidal thoughts.

Therefore, they argue, the school officials had reason to believe that they would find evidence of unlawful activity on G.C.'s cell phone or an indication that he was intending to harm himself or others.

We disagree, though, that general background knowledge of drug abuse or depressive tendencies, without more, enables a school official to search a student's cell phone when a search would otherwise be unwarranted. The defendants do not argue, and there is no evidence in the record to support the conclusion, that the school officials had any specific reason at the inception of the September 2009 search to believe that G.C. then was engaging in any unlawful activity or that he was contemplating injuring himself or another student. Rather, the evidence in the record demonstrates that G.C. was sitting in class when his teacher caught him sending two text messages on his phone. When his phone was confiscated by his teacher pursuant to school policy, G.C. became upset. The defendants have failed to demonstrate how anything in this sequence of events indicated to them that a search of the phone would reveal evidence of criminal activity, impending contravention of additional school rules, or potential harm to anyone in the school.

On these facts, the defendants did not have a reasonable suspicion to justify the search at its inception.

The defendants further argue that G.C.'s claim must fail because he did not suffer any harm as a result of the search; specifically, they point to the fact that he "was not disciplined based on the contents of his phone." However, the issue of injury and compensable damages has not been developed before us. Even if G.C. cannot establish compensable damages, he may be entitled to nominal damages. Moreover, punitive damages sometimes attach to an award comprised solely of nominal damages. Therefore, we remand to the district court to address the issue of injury and damages in the first instance.

We therefore REVERSE the district court's grant of summary judgment as to G.C.'s Fourth Amendment claim based on the September 2009 search.

■ ALAN E. NORRIS, CIRCUIT JUDGE, concurring in part and dissenting in part.

I must dissent from [the] decision with respect to the September 2009 search of G.C.'s cell phone. There is a reason that the Supreme Court in *New Jersey v. T.L.O.*, 469 U.S. 325 (1985), concluded that the legality of a search in the school setting hinges on reasonableness in light of all the circumstances: school officials are acting in loco parentis and, as such, they have a keen interest in student welfare and safety. For that reason, they must be allowed more leeway under the Fourth Amendment than is appropriate outside the school setting.

What happened here? G.C. violated school policy by using his cell phone during class. Under the terms of that policy, his phone was seized, an action that he does not contest. The question then becomes, was a limited search of the phone's text messages permissible? The school official who conducted the search was aware of G.C.'s prior suicidal thoughts and drug use. She also knew that he had a history of disciplinary problems, which included fighting. Her duty as an administrator was to ensure the safety of the students, including G.C. Her subsequent search, which was limited to reading four text messages created that day, strikes me as reasonable under *T.L.O.* I respectfully dissent.

## NOTES

1. ***A Tale of Two Searches.*** G.C. concedes the legitimacy of the earlier search of his cell phone in March 2009, even as he contests the September 2009 search. In a footnote omitted from the excerpt above, the court contrasts the two incidents to illustrate why the September search was not permissible. Prior to the March 2009 search,"there was reason to believe—based on that day's sequence of events—that G.C. was contemplating injuring himself or breaking additional school rules. The defendants, however, can point to no such indications in the hours, weeks, or months leading up to the September 2009 search." Go back and look at the description of the March 2009 events. Precisely which facts from the day's sequence of events justified the cell phone search? Exactly how do they differ from the facts of the September 2009 incident?

2. ***Potential Justifications.*** What if, when called to assistant principal Brown's office, G.C. protested that he had been texting in class only because he was communicating with his grandmother about a family emergency? Would that make an examination of his text messages a search justified at its inception? What if G.C. were texting during an exam? If you think either of these factual variations would justify the search, can you articulate exactly why they are different from the case?

3. **Owensboro *and* Riley.** This decision was issued the year before *Riley v. California*, 134 S. Ct. 2473 (2014) [see Chapter 1], where the Supreme Court unanimously held a warrant was necessary to search the cell phone of a person under arrest, primarily because of the amount and diversity of information that can be found through inspection of a modern smart phone. Those considerations do not seem to have been as important here, especially because Brown only read four text messages in the September 2009 incident. But they certainly could arise under the second *T.L.O.* factor concerning the scope of the search. For example, assume the March 2009 search was justified at its inception, as G.C. concedes, and that G.C. had a modern smart phone. How much of the contents of the phone would school officials be allowed to examine before violating *T.L.O.*? Does *Riley* help in making that assessment? Try to be specific—how would you answer if you were the lawyer for the school board and Smith, the assistant principal in the March 2009 incident, called you and asked for guidance before looking at G.C.'s phone?

4. ***Harm.*** In many varied areas ranging from consumer protection law [see Chapter 3] to national security [see Chapter 9], courts have paid a

great deal of attention to the concrete harm suffered by plaintiffs in privacy cases. What harm did G.C. suffer here? His enrollment privileges were revoked because he was texting, not based on any additional evidence obtained from the phone. There is no criminal proceeding from which he wants to exclude evidence. What remedy could he seek? Why does the court seem so unconcerned about harm and standing in this case when those issues have been so important in other contexts?

5. ***The Remainder of G.C.'s Claims.*** The Fourth Amendment was only a portion of G.C.'s case against the district. He also claimed, based on Kentucky statutes and the Due Process Clause, that he was entitled to a hearing prior to being removed from Owensboro High School, and he alleged that the school violated the Rehabilitation Act by failing to recognize his need for special services and to provide them. The district court had also granted summary judgment on these counts; the appeals court reversed on the issue of G.C.'s entitlement to a hearing but affirmed summary judgment on the Rehabilitation Act claim. Understanding the larger context of the case helps explain why G.C. bothered to bring his Fourth Amendment claims at all; they might not have been worth a lawsuit standing alone.

6. ***Qualified Immunity.*** These three judges do not agree whether the search of the phone in September 2009 was permissible, and the majority explains that existing district court opinions were divided as well. Should Brown receive qualified immunity for her actions, as the school officials in *Safford* did on the basis of divided opinion about the Fourth Amendment boundaries there?

---

## Practice

### Monitoring Students Online

You are a lawyer for a public school district that has experienced serious problems with online gossip and bullying, including one suicide attempt by a student who had been mocked in an online chat group. District officials want you to help develop a policy for appropriate monitoring of students' internet postings by school administrators.

For background, you should know a little bit about a public school's authority to discipline students for speech that occurs outside of school. As discussed above, the Supreme Court has recognized that the needs for education and discipline are "special characteristics of the school environment." *Tinker v. Des Moines Indep. Community Sch. Dist.*, 393 U.S. 503, 513 (1969) (quoting *Burnside v. Byars*, 363 F.2d 744, 749 (5th Cir. 1966)). Thus, schools can regulate student conduct, including speech, if the conduct is reasonably likely to create a "substantial disruption" of school activities. *Tinker*, 393 U.S. at 514. This test applies to off-campus conduct as well as on-campus conduct. *See Morse v. Frederick*, 551 U.S. 393 (2007) (high school principal did not violate student's right to free speech at off-campus, school-approved event by confiscating a banner bearing the phrase "BONG HiTS 4 JESUS" and suspending student). Circuit courts have reached different results when applying this test to off-campus online activity. *Compare Kowalski v. Berkeley Cty. Sch.*, 652 F.3d 565 (4th Cir. 2011) (MySpace page dedicated to alleging a fellow student had herpes created a substantial disruption due to its harmful and defamatory nature) *with J.S. ex rel. Snyder v. Blue Mountain Sch. Dist.*, 650 F.3d 915 (3d Cir. 2011) (fake MySpace profile of school principal, alleging he was a sex addict and pedophile, did not create a substantial disruption because no one could have taken it seriously).

What questions do you ask the school district officials? What advice do you have for them?

---

## B. EDUCATIONAL RECORDS

The Violent Femmes song "Kiss Off" quotes a familiar warning from an authority figure: "I hope you know that this will go down on your permanent record." The band members seem unimpressed. Perhaps it is because they believe their privacy will be protected by the Family Educational Rights and Privacy Act ("FERPA"), 20 U.S.C. § 1232g, sometimes also known as the "Buckley Amendment." FERPA and its accompanying regulations govern the way elementary, secondary, and postsecondary educational institutions handle personal data about their students. It is unquestionably a data protection regime and shares many features with other data protection law discussed elsewhere in this book [see especially Chapter 4]: duties are not tied to commercial activity, data may only be used for purposes specified in the law, and data subjects (or their parents) have rights of access, correction, and deletion in connection with their personal data. The statute is administered by the Department of Education. This Section begins with the statute and the administrative regulations interpreting it, and then turns to some cases about the enforcement of FERPA rights.

### Family Educational Rights and Privacy Act

20 U.S.C. § 1232g

**§ 1232g. Family educational and privacy rights**

**(a) Conditions for availability of funds to educational agencies or institutions; inspection and review of education records; specific information to be made available; procedure for access to education records; reasonableness of time for such access; hearings; written explanations by parents; definitions**

(1)

(A) No funds shall be made available under any applicable program to any educational agency or institution which has a policy of denying, or which effectively prevents, the parents of students who are or have been in attendance at a school of such agency or at such institution, as the case may be, the right to inspect and review the education records of their children. . . . Each educational agency or institution shall establish appropriate procedures for the granting of a request by parents for access to the education records of their children within a reasonable period of time, but in no case more than forty-five days after the request has been made.

. . .

(2) No funds shall be made available under any applicable program to any educational agency or institution unless the parents of students who are or have been in attendance at a school of such agency or at such institution are provided an opportunity for a hearing by such agency or institution, in accordance with regulations of the Secretary, to challenge the content of such student's education records, in order to insure that the records are not inaccurate, misleading, or otherwise in violation of the privacy rights of students, and to provide an opportunity for the correction or deletion of any such inaccurate, misleading or otherwise inappropriate data contained therein and to insert into such records a written explanation of the parents respecting the content of such records.

(3) For the purposes of this section the term "educational agency or institution" means any public or private agency or institution which is the recipient of funds under any applicable program.

(4)

(A) For the purposes of this section, the term "education records" means, except as may be provided otherwise in subparagraph (B), those records, files, documents, and other materials which—

(i) contain information directly related to a student; and

(ii) are maintained by an educational agency or institution or by a person acting for such agency or institution.

(B) The term "education records" does not include—

(i) records of instructional, supervisory, and administrative personnel and educational personnel ancillary thereto which are in the sole possession of the maker thereof and which are not accessible or revealed to any other person except a substitute;

(ii) records maintained by a law enforcement unit of the educational agency or institution that were created by that law enforcement unit for the purpose of law enforcement;

. . .

(5)

(A) For the purposes of this section the term "directory information" relating to a student includes the following:

the student's name, address, telephone listing, date and place of birth, major field of study, participation in officially recognized activities and sports, weight and height of members of athletic teams, dates of attendance, degrees and awards received, and the most recent previous educational agency or institution attended by the student.

(B) Any educational agency or institution making public directory information shall give public notice of the categories of information which it has designated as such information with respect to each student attending the institution or agency and shall allow a reasonable period of time after such notice has been given for a parent to inform the institution or agency that any or all of the information designated should not be released without the parent's prior consent.

. . .

**(b) Release of education records; parental consent requirement; exceptions; compliance with judicial orders and subpoenas; audit and evaluation of federally-supported education programs; recordkeeping**

(1) No funds shall be made available under any applicable program to any educational agency or institution which has a policy or practice of permitting the release of education records (or personally identifiable information contained therein other than directory information . . .) of students without the written consent of their parents to any individual, agency, or organization, other than to the following—

(A) other school officials, including teachers within the educational institution or local educational agency, who have been determined by such agency or institution to have legitimate educational interests, including the educational interests of the child for whom consent would otherwise be required;

. . .

(F) organizations conducting studies for, or on behalf of, educational agencies or institutions for the purpose of developing, validating, or administering predictive tests, administering student aid programs, and improving instruction, if such studies are conducted in such a manner as will not permit the personal identification of students and their parents by persons other than representatives of such organizations and such information will be destroyed when no longer needed for the purpose for which it is conducted;

. . .

(I) subject to regulations of the Secretary, in connection with an emergency, appropriate persons if the knowledge of such information is necessary to protect the health or safety of the student or other persons;

. . .

(2) No funds shall be made available under any applicable program to any educational agency or institution which has a policy or practice of releasing, or providing access to, any personally identifiable information in education records other than directory information, or as is permitted under paragraph (1) of this subsection, unless—

(A) there is written consent from the student's parents specifying records to be released, the reasons for such release, and to whom, and with a copy of the records to be released to the student's parents and the student if desired by the parents, or

(B) . . . such information is furnished in compliance with judicial order, or pursuant to any lawfully issued subpoena, upon condition that parents and the students are notified of all such orders or subpoenas in advance of the compliance therewith by the educational institution or agency.

. . .

**(d) Students' rather than parents' permission or consent**

For the purposes of this section, whenever a student has attained eighteen years of age, or is attending an institution of postsecondary education, the permission or consent required of and the rights accorded to the parents of the student shall thereafter only be required of and accorded to the student.

**(e) Informing parents or students of rights under this section**

No funds shall be made available under any applicable program to any educational agency or institution unless such agency or institution effectively informs the parents of students, or the students, if they are eighteen years of age or older, or are attending an institution of postsecondary education, of the rights accorded them by this section.

**(f) Enforcement; termination of assistance**

The Secretary shall take appropriate actions to enforce this section and to deal with violations of this section, in accordance with this chapter, except that action to terminate assistance may be taken only if the Secretary finds there has been a failure to comply with this section, and he has determined that compliance cannot be secured by voluntary means.

**(g) Office and review board; creation; functions**

The Secretary shall establish or designate an office and review board within the Department for the purpose of investigating, processing, reviewing, and adjudicating violations of this section and complaints which may be filed concerning alleged violations of this section. Except for the conduct of hearings, none of the functions of the Secretary under this section shall be carried out in any of the regional offices of such Department.

. . .

## Family Educational Rights and Privacy Rule

34 C.F.R. Part 99

### § 99.30 Under what conditions is prior consent required to disclose information?

(a) The parent or eligible student shall provide a signed and dated written consent before an educational agency or institution discloses personally identifiable information from the student's education records, except as provided in § 99.31.

(b) The written consent must:

(1) Specify the records that may be disclosed;

(2) State the purpose of the disclosure; and

(3) Identify the party or class of parties to whom the disclosure may be made.

(c) When a disclosure is made under paragraph (a) of this section:

(1) If a parent or eligible student so requests, the educational agency or institution shall provide him or her with a copy of the records disclosed; and

(2) If the parent of a student who is not an eligible student so requests, the agency or institution shall provide the student with a copy of the records disclosed.

. . .

### § 99.31 Under what conditions is prior consent not required to disclose information?

(a) An educational agency or institution may disclose personally identifiable information from an education record of a student without the consent required by § 99.30 if the disclosure meets one or more of the following conditions:

(1)

(i)

(A) The disclosure is to other school officials, including teachers, within the agency or institution whom the agency or institution has determined to have legitimate educational interests.

(B) A contractor, consultant, volunteer, or other party to whom an agency or institution has outsourced institutional services or functions may be considered a school official under this paragraph provided that the outside party—

(1) Performs an institutional service or function for which the agency or institution would otherwise use employees;

(2) Is under the direct control of the agency or institution with respect to the use and maintenance of education records; and

(3) Is subject to the requirements of § 99.33(a) governing the use and redisclosure of personally identifiable information from education records.

. . .

**§ 99.33 What limitations apply to the redisclosure of information?**

(a)

(1) An educational agency or institution may disclose personally identifiable information from an education record only on the condition that the party to whom the information is disclosed will not disclose the information to any other party without the prior consent of the parent or eligible student.

. . .

**§ 99.36 What conditions apply to disclosure of information in health and safety emergencies?**

(a) An educational agency or institution may disclose personally identifiable information from an education record to appropriate parties, including parents of an eligible student, in connection with an emergency if knowledge of the information is necessary to protect the health or safety of the student or other individuals.

(b) Nothing in this Act or this part shall prevent an educational agency or institution from—

(1) Including in the education records of a student appropriate information concerning disciplinary action taken against the student for conduct that posed a significant risk to the safety or well-being of that student, other students, or other members of the school community;

(2) Disclosing appropriate information maintained under paragraph (b)(1) of this section to teachers and school officials within the agency or institution who the agency or institution

has determined have legitimate educational interests in the behavior of the student; or

(3) Disclosing appropriate information maintained under paragraph (b)(1) of this section to teachers and school officials in other schools who have been determined to have legitimate educational interests in the behavior of the student.

(c) In making a determination under paragraph (a) of this section, an educational agency or institution may take into account the totality of the circumstances pertaining to a threat to the health or safety of a student or other individuals. If the educational agency or institution determines that there is an articulable and significant threat to the health or safety of a student or other individuals, it may disclose information from education records to any person whose knowledge of the information is necessary to protect the health or safety of the student or other individuals. If, based on the information available at the time of the determination, there is a rational basis for the determination, the Department will not substitute its judgment for that of the educational agency or institution in evaluating the circumstances and making its determination.

---

## Practice

Applying FERPA and Its Regulations

You are a lawyer for a school district that needs advice about FERPA requirements. Administrators ask you which of the following is exempt from FERPA requirements. If you think a situation is exempt, point to specific language supporting that view. If you think a situation is not exempt, explain what the district must do.

1. A classroom teacher keeping a spreadsheet of student grades on her laptop computer.

2. The district providing students' home address, race, subsidized school lunch eligibility, and standardized test scores to a consultant developing strategies to reduce the district's socioeconomic achievement gap.

3. A principal posting a list of students included in the quarterly honor roll on the school web site.

4. A creative writing teacher using a peer grading system where students swap their draft essays, evaluate them according to a rubric, and call out their partner's mark at the end of the exercise.

5. A school sending information about a former student's poor attendance to her new school in another district.

Now assume you are a lawyer for a university. How should the institution handle the following situations?

6. A parent who pays a student's tuition calls the dean and requests his attendance records.

7. A parent who pays a student's tuition calls the dean and informs her that the student may be suicidal, and requests any information that could be important for mental health professionals to know.

8. A student asks to see the original copy of her exam as graded by her professor.

9. A student who works for the college newspaper and is writing a story about recent vandalism at the science labs requests information about the disciplinary hearing of another student accused of committing the vandalism.

---

## Gonzaga University v. Doe

536 U.S. 273 (2002)

■ CHIEF JUSTICE REHNQUIST delivered the opinion of the Court.

The question presented is whether a student may sue a private university for damages under 42 U.S.C. § 1983 to enforce provisions of the Family Educational Rights and Privacy Act of 1974 (FERPA or Act), 20 U.S.C. § 1232g, which prohibit the federal funding of educational institutions that have a policy or practice of releasing education records to unauthorized persons. We hold such an action foreclosed because the relevant provisions of FERPA create no personal rights to enforce under 42 U.S.C. § 1983.

Respondent John Doe is a former undergraduate in the School of Education at Gonzaga University, a private university in Spokane, Washington. He planned to graduate and teach at a Washington public elementary school. Washington at the time required all of its new teachers to obtain an affidavit of good moral character from a dean of their graduating college or university. In October 1993, Roberta League, Gonzaga's "teacher certification specialist," overheard one student tell another that respondent engaged in acts of sexual misconduct against Jane Doe, a female undergraduate. League launched an investigation and contacted the state agency responsible for teacher certification, identifying respondent by name and discussing the allegations against him. Respondent did not learn of the investigation, or that information about him had been disclosed, until March 1994, when he was told by League and others that he would not receive the affidavit required for certification as a Washington schoolteacher.

Respondent then sued Gonzaga and League (petitioners) in state court. He alleged violations of Washington tort and contract law, as well as a pendent violation of § 1983 for the release of personal information to an "unauthorized person" in violation of FERPA. A jury found for respondent on all counts, awarding him $1,155,000, including $150,000 in compensatory damages and $300,000 in punitive damages on the FERPA claim. [The Supreme Court assumed without deciding that the involvement of the state's teacher licensing agency meant League's disclosure was made "under color of state law," a requirement for liability under § 1983.]

The Washington Court of Appeals reversed in relevant part, concluding that FERPA does not create individual rights and thus cannot be enforced under § 1983. The Washington Supreme Court reversed that decision, and ordered the FERPA damages reinstated.

Like the Washington Supreme Court and the state court of appeals below, other state and federal courts have divided on the question of FERPA's enforceability under § 1983. The fact that all of these courts have relied on the same set of opinions from this Court suggests that our opinions in this area may not be models of clarity. We therefore granted certiorari to resolve the conflict among the lower courts and in the process resolve any ambiguity in our own opinions.

Congress enacted FERPA under its spending power to condition the receipt of federal funds on certain requirements relating to the access and disclosure of student educational records. The Act directs the Secretary of Education to withhold federal funds from any public or private "educational agency or institution" that fails to comply with these conditions. As relevant here, the Act provides:

> No funds shall be made available under any applicable program to any educational agency or institution which has a policy or practice of permitting the release of education records (or personally identifiable information contained therein . . .) of students without the written consent of their parents to any individual, agency, or organization.

20 U.S.C. § 1232g(b)(1).

The Act directs the Secretary of Education to enforce this and other of the Act's spending conditions. § 1232g(f). The Secretary is required to establish an office and review board within the Department of Education for "investigating, processing, reviewing, and adjudicating violations of [the Act]." § 1232g(g). Funds may be terminated only if the Secretary determines that a recipient institution "is failing to comply substantially with any requirement of [the Act]" and that such compliance "cannot be secured by voluntary means." §§ 1234c(a), 1232g(f).

Respondent contends that this statutory regime confers upon any student enrolled at a covered school or institution a federal right, enforceable in suits for damages under § 1983, not to have "education records" disclosed to unauthorized persons without the student's express written consent. But we have never before held, and decline to do so here, that spending legislation drafted in terms resembling those of FERPA can confer enforceable rights.

In *Maine v. Thiboutot*, 448 U.S. 1 (1980), six years after Congress enacted FERPA, we recognized for the first time that § 1983 actions may be brought against state actors to enforce rights created by federal statutes as well as by the Constitution. There we held that plaintiffs could recover payments wrongfully withheld by a state agency in violation of the Social Security Act. A year later, in *Pennhurst State*

*School and Hospital v. Halderman*, 451 U.S. 1 (1981), we rejected a claim that the Developmentally Disabled Assistance and Bill of Rights Act of 1975 conferred enforceable rights, saying:

> In legislation enacted pursuant to the spending power, the typical remedy for state noncompliance with federally imposed conditions is not a private cause of action for noncompliance but rather action by the Federal Government to terminate funds to the State.

*Id.* at 28. We made clear that unless Congress "speak[s] with a clear voice," and manifests an "unambiguous" intent to confer individual rights, federal funding provisions provide no basis for private enforcement by § 1983. *Id.* at 17, 28, and n. 21.

Some language in our opinions might be read to suggest that something less than an unambiguously conferred right is enforceable by § 1983. This confusion has led some courts to interpret [cases such as *Blessing v. Freestone*, 520 U.S. 329 (1997)] as allowing plaintiffs to enforce a statute under § 1983 so long as the plaintiff falls within the general zone of interest that the statute is intended to protect; something less than what is required for a statute to create rights enforceable directly from the statute itself under an implied private right of action.

We now reject the notion that our cases permit anything short of an unambiguously conferred right to support a cause of action brought under § 1983. Section 1983 provides a remedy only for the deprivation of "rights, privileges, or immunities secured by the Constitution and laws" of the United States. Accordingly, it is rights, not the broader or vaguer "benefits" or "interests," that may be enforced under the authority of that section.

With this principle in mind, there is no question that FERPA's nondisclosure provisions fail to confer enforceable rights. To begin with, the provisions entirely lack the sort of "rights-creating" language critical to showing the requisite congressional intent to create new rights. Unlike the individually focused terminology of Titles VI and IX ("no person shall be subjected to discrimination"), FERPA's provisions speak only to the Secretary of Education, directing that "[n]o funds shall be made available" to any "educational agency or institution" which has a prohibited "policy or practice." 20 U.S.C. § 1232g(b)(1). This focus is two steps removed from the interests of individual students and parents and clearly does not confer the sort of "*individual* entitlement" that is enforceable under § 1983.

FERPA's nondisclosure provisions further speak only in terms of institutional policy and practice, not individual instances of disclosure. *See* §§ 1232g(b)(1)–(2) (prohibiting the funding of "any educational agency or institution which has a *policy or practice* of permitting the release of education records" (emphasis added)). Respondent directs our attention to subsection (b)(2), but the text and structure of subsections (b)(1) and (b)(2) are essentially the same. In each provision the reference to individual consent is in the context of describing the type of "policy or practice" that triggers a funding prohibition. For reasons expressed repeatedly in our prior cases, however, such provisions cannot make out the requisite congressional intent to confer individual rights enforceable by § 1983.

Our conclusion that FERPA's nondisclosure provisions fail to confer enforceable rights is buttressed by the mechanism that Congress chose to provide for enforcing those provisions. Congress expressly authorized the Secretary of Education to "*deal with violations*" of the Act, § 1232g(f) (emphasis added), and required the Secretary to "establish or designate [a] review board" for investigating and adjudicating such violations, § 1232g(g). Pursuant to these provisions, the Secretary created the Family Policy Compliance Office (FPCO) "to act as the Review Board required under the Act and to enforce the Act with respect to all applicable programs." 34 CFR §§ 99.60(a) and (b). The FPCO permits students and parents who suspect a violation of the Act to file individual written complaints. § 99.63. If a complaint is timely and contains required information, the FPCO will initiate an investigation, §§ 99.64(a)–(b), notify the educational institution of the charge, § 99.65(a), and request a written response, § 99.65. If a violation is found, the FPCO distributes a notice of factual findings and a "statement of the specific steps that the agency or institution must take to comply" with FERPA. §§ 99.66(b) and (c)(1). These administrative procedures further counsel against our finding a congressional intent to create individually enforceable private rights.

Congress finally provided that "[e]xcept for the conduct of hearings, none of the functions of the Secretary under this section shall be carried out in any of the regional offices" of the Department of Education. 20 U.S.C. § 1232g(g). This centralized review provision was added just four months after FERPA's enactment due to "concern that regionalizing the enforcement of [FERPA] may lead to multiple interpretations of it, and possibly work a hardship on parents, students, and institutions." 120 Cong. Rec. 39863 (1974) (joint statement). It is implausible to presume that the same Congress nonetheless intended private suits to be brought before thousands of federal-and state-court judges, which could only result in the sort of "multiple interpretations" the Act explicitly sought to avoid.

In sum, if Congress wishes to create new rights enforceable under § 1983, it must do so in clear and unambiguous terms—no less and no more than what is required for Congress to create new rights enforceable under an implied private right of action. FERPA's nondisclosure provisions contain no rights-creating language, they have an aggregate, not individual, focus, and they serve primarily to direct the Secretary of Education's distribution of public funds to educational institutions. They therefore create no rights enforceable under § 1983. Accordingly, the judgment of the Supreme Court of Washington is reversed, and the case is remanded for further proceedings not inconsistent with this opinion.

■ JUSTICE BREYER, with whom JUSTICE SOUTER joins, concurring in the judgment.

The ultimate question, in respect to whether private individuals may bring a lawsuit to enforce a federal statute, through 42 U.S.C. § 1983 or otherwise, is a question of congressional intent. In my view, the factors set forth in this Court's § 1983 cases are helpful indications of that intent. I would not, in effect, pre-determine an outcome through the use of a presumption—such as the majority's presumption that a right is conferred only if set forth "unambiguously" in the statute's "text and structure."

At the same time, I do not believe that Congress intended private judicial enforcement of this statute's "school record privacy" provisions. The Court mentions most of the considerations I find persuasive.

I would add one further reason. Much of the statute's key language is broad and nonspecific. The statute, for example, defines its key term, "education records," as (with certain enumerated exceptions) "those records, files, documents, and other materials which (i) contain information directly related to a student; and (ii) are maintained by an educational . . . institution." 20 U.S.C. § 1232g(a)(4)(A). This kind of language leaves schools uncertain as to just when they can, or cannot, reveal various kinds of information.

Under these circumstances, Congress may well have wanted to make the agency remedy that it provided exclusive—both to achieve the expertise, uniformity, wide-spread consultation, and resulting administrative guidance that can accompany agency decisionmaking and to avoid the comparative risk of inconsistent interpretations and misincentives that can arise out of an occasional inappropriate application of the statute in a private action for damages. This factor, together with the others to which the majority refers, convinces me that Congress did not intend private judicial enforcement actions here.

■ JUSTICE STEVENS, with whom JUSTICE GINSBURG joins, dissenting.

Title 20 U.S.C. § 1232g, which embodies FERPA in its entirety, includes 10 subsections, which create rights for both students and their parents, and describe the procedures for enforcing and protecting those rights. Subsection (a)(1)(A) accords parents "the right to inspect and review the education records of their children." Subsection (a)(1)(D) provides that a "student or a person applying for admission" may waive "his right of access" to certain confidential statements. Two separate provisions protect students' privacy rights: subsection (a)(2) refers to "the privacy rights of students," and subsection (c) protects "the rights of privacy of students and their families." And subsection (d) provides that after a student has attained the age of 18, "the rights accorded to the parents of the student" shall thereafter be extended to the student. Given such explicit rights-creating language, the title of the statute, which describes "family educational rights," is appropriate: The entire statutory scheme was designed to protect such rights.

The Court claims that § 1232g(b), because it references a "policy or practice," has an aggregate focus and thus cannot qualify as an individual right. But § 1232g(b) does not simply ban an institution from having a policy or practice—which would be a more systemic requirement. Rather, it permits a policy or practice of releasing information, so long as "there is written consent from the student's parents specifying records to be released, the reasons for such release, and to whom, and with a copy of the records to be released to the student's parents and the student if desired by the parents." 20 U.S.C. § 1232g(b)(2)(A). The provision speaks of the individual "student," not students generally. In light of FERPA's stated purpose to "protect such individuals' rights to privacy by limiting the transferability of their records without their consent," 120 Cong. Rec. 39862 (1974) (statement of Sen. Buckley), the individual focus of § 1232g(b) is manifest.

Although § 1232g(b) alone provides strong evidence that an individual federal right has been created, this conclusion is bolstered by viewing the provision in the overall context of FERPA. Not once in its opinion does the Court acknowledge the substantial number of references to "rights" in the FERPA provisions surrounding § 1232g(b), even though our past § 1983 cases have made clear that a given statutory provision's meaning is to be discerned "in light of the entire legislative enactment,"

Although a "presumptively enforceable" right has been created by § 1232g(b), one final question remains. As our cases recognize, Congress can rebut the presumption of enforcement under § 1983 either "expressly, by forbidding recourse to § 1983 in the statute itself, or impliedly, by creating a comprehensive enforcement scheme that is incompatible with individual enforcement [actions]." *Blessing*, 520 U.S. at 341. FERPA has not explicitly foreclosed enforcement under § 1983. The only question, then, is whether the administrative enforcement mechanisms provided by the statute are "comprehensive" and "incompatible" with § 1983 actions. As the Court explains, FERPA authorizes the establishment of an administrative enforcement framework, and the Secretary of Education has created the Family Policy Compliance Office (FPCO) to "deal with violations" of the Act, 20 U.S.C. § 1232g(f). FPCO accepts complaints from the public concerning alleged FERPA violations and, if it so chooses, may follow up on such a complaint by informing institutions of the steps they must take to comply with FERPA, *see* 34 CFR §§ 99.63–99.67 (2001), and, in exceptional cases, by administrative adjudication against noncomplying institutions, *see* 20 U.S.C. § 1234. These administrative avenues fall far short of what is necessary to overcome the presumption of enforceability.

Since FERPA was enacted in 1974, all of the Federal Courts of Appeals expressly deciding the question have concluded that FERPA creates federal rights enforceable under § 1983. Nearly all other federal and state courts reaching the issue agree with these Circuits. Congress has not overruled these decisions by amending FERPA to expressly preclude recourse to § 1983. And yet, the Court departs from over a quarter century of settled law in concluding that FERPA creates no enforceable rights.

Accordingly, I respectfully dissent.

## Press-Citizen Co. v. University of Iowa

817 N.W.2d 480 (Iowa 2012)

■ MANSFIELD, JUSTICE.

This case requires us to decide where disclosure ends and where confidentiality begins under the Iowa Open Records Act and the Federal Educational Rights and Privacy Act (FERPA). *See* 20 U.S.C. § 1232g; Iowa Code §§ 22.2, 22.7, 22.9. In October 2007, two University of Iowa football players were accused of sexually assaulting another student in a campus dorm room. This incident led to a criminal investigation, criminal charges, and the conviction of one player on a charge of assault with intent to inflict serious injury and the other on a charge of simple assault. This incident also led to internal actions and responses by the University, external criticism of the University, and a special counsel investigation and report. Finally, this incident led to the present lawsuit.

The present litigation concerns Open Records Act requests that the Iowa City Press-Citizen served on the University after reports of the incident surfaced. Dissatisfied with the University's initial response to those requests, the Press-Citizen filed suit. The lawsuit resulted in more documents being produced and others being submitted for in camera review by the district court. The court then ordered additional documents produced, in some instances with redactions.

The University has appealed that order in part. It argues that FERPA prohibits the disclosure of the remaining documents, including even redacted versions of "education records" where the identity of the student is known to the recipient. The Press-Citizen counters that FERPA does not supersede any obligation to produce records under the Open Records Act, and in any event, the University has misinterpreted FERPA. For the reasons discussed herein, we ultimately agree with the University's arguments as to the meaning and force of FERPA, and therefore reverse the district court's judgment in part.

### BACKGROUND FACTS AND PROCEEDINGS

During the early morning hours of Sunday, October 14, 2007, a female student-athlete was allegedly sexually assaulted at the Hillcrest dormitory at the University of Iowa. Two University of Iowa football players who were accused of involvement were suspended and later dismissed from the team. A criminal investigation resulted in both men being charged. One ultimately pled guilty to assault with intent to inflict serious injury, and the other was convicted of simple misdemeanor assault following a jury trial.

Numerous University officials were informed of the incident by Monday, October 15, 2007; however, the parents of the student-athlete believed their response was inadequate. Among other things, concerns were expressed that the University had shown a lack of understanding for the victim, had communicated poorly with her, and had allowed her to be subjected to retaliatory harassment from other students. In 2008, the University's Board of Regents engaged an outside law firm (the Stolar Partnership) to conduct a detailed investigation. Their report (the Stolar Report) criticized some aspects of the University's policies and performance.

Meanwhile, the incident received considerable publicity in the media. Articles appeared in which both football players were named. Beginning November 13, 2007, the Iowa City Press-Citizen served requests on the University under the Iowa Open Records Act. The requests sought, among other things, reports of attempted or actual sexual assaults; correspondence to or from various University officials relating to any such incidents; and e-mail, memos, and other records relating to any such incidents from October 1, 2007 to the present.

The University initially produced only eighteen pages of documents, claiming that any other responsive documents were protected from disclosure under Iowa Code section 22.7(1) (protecting from disclosure "[p]ersonal information in records regarding a student . . . maintained, created, collected or assembled by or for a school corporation or educational institution maintaining such records"). On January 4, 2008, the Press-Citizen filed a petition in district court seeking judicial enforcement of the Open Records Act.

[The University contended that over 2000 pages of documents should be withheld and submitted them to the district court for review. After a "painstaking in camera review," the district court ordered disclosure of certain withheld documents, some in full and some "with appropriate redactions made to remove student-identifying information including students' names, parents' names, addresses including E-mail addresses of students, dormitory and room numbers."]

The University sought and obtained a stay of the district court's order pending appeal. The University now argues to us that the district court erred in ordering the production of some of the documents [the "appealed documents"].

## ANALYSIS

### A. The Iowa Open Records Act

Generally speaking, the Iowa Open Records Act requires state and local entities to make their records available to the public. The University of Iowa, a state institution, is clearly covered by the Open Records Act.

The Open Records Act is subject to a number of listed exemptions, both large and small. Nonetheless, the University does not argue that any of those designated exceptions applies here. Its sole argument on appeal is that federal law, i.e., FERPA, requires the appealed documents to be kept confidential.

## B. FERPA

Congress enacted the Family Educational Rights and Privacy Act or FERPA in 1974 "under its spending power to condition the receipt of federal funds on certain requirements relating to the access and disclosure of student educational records." *Gonzaga Univ. v. Doe*, 536 U.S. 273, 278 (2002).

In light of [FERPA's requirements], the University argues that the appealed documents cannot be produced at all. As it understands the law, "education records" with "personally identifiable information" cannot be released. Further, even if no student is actually identified in the document, either because his or her name and personal identifiers have been redacted or because the original document did not have that information, the regulations prohibit disclosure if the recipient would "know[ ] the identity of the student"—or "a reasonable person" would be able to "identify the student with reasonable certainty" [quoting from the definition of "personally identifiable information" in the regulations, 34 C.F.R. § 99.3]. In short, the University contends that if the Press-Citizen or the student community would know the student being discussed in the education record, the record cannot be divulged—even in redacted form—under FERPA.

For purposes of this appeal, we assume that the appealed documents are in fact "education records" under FERPA. The Press-Citizen does not dispute that if these documents were produced, even in redacted form, it would be able to determine the students to whom the documents refer. However, the Press-Citizen argues that FERPA is merely a funding statute that does not prohibit the disclosure of documents whose production is otherwise required by the Iowa Open Records Act. Alternatively, the Press-Citizen argues that FERPA does not allow the withholding of records, as opposed to their redaction. We now turn to these points of disagreement.

## C. The Interplay Between FERPA and the Open Records Act

The University argues that the relationship between FERPA and the Open Records Act is a simple matter of federal supremacy. *See* U.S. Const. art. VI (providing that the laws of the United States "shall be the supreme Law of the Land"). Iowa law, according to the University, cannot authorize disclosure where federal law requires confidentiality. The Press-Citizen, on the other hand, maintains that FERPA is not a positive law at all, but simply a funding provision, which cannot override the express directives of the Open Records Act.

This debate has been played out in cases from other jurisdictions. Some courts have concluded that FERPA does not prohibit the disclosure of educational records. *See Bauer v. Kincaid*, 759 F. Supp. 575, 589 (W.D. Mo. 1991) ("FERPA is not a law which prohibits disclosure of educational records. It is a provision which imposes a penalty for the disclosure of educational records."); *WFTV, Inc. v. Sch. Bd. of Seminole*, 874 So. 2d 48, 57 (Fla. Dist. Ct. App. 2004) ("FERPA does not prohibit the disclosure of any educational records. FERPA only operates to deprive an educational agency or institution of its eligibility for applicable federal funding based on their policies and practices regarding public access to educational records if they have any policies or practices that run afoul of the rights of access and disclosural privacy protected by FERPA."); *see also Kirwan v. The Diamondback*, 721 A.2d 196, 206 (Md. 1998) [noting the argument without reaching it].

FERPA regulations allow for the possibility that an educational institution "cannot comply with the Act or this part due to a conflict with State or local law." *See* 34 C.F.R. § 99.61. One could argue that the mere recognition of this possibility in the regulations indicates that FERPA does not supersede state law.

On the other hand, other courts have given direct effect to FERPA's provisions, treating them as positive law with binding force on state authorities. In *United States v. Miami University*, 294 F.3d 797, 803 (6th Cir. 2002), a federal court of appeals affirmed an injunction against the release of student disciplinary records covered by FERPA. The court reasoned that the remedies for FERPA violations were not limited to a cutoff of federal funding. Rather, once funds are accepted, "the school is indeed prohibited from systematically releasing education records without consent." *Id.* at 809; *see also Rim of the World Unified Sch. Dist. v. Super. Ct.*, 129 Cal. Rptr. 2d 11, 15 (Ct. App. 2002) (finding that FERPA preempts California law requiring the disclosure of student expulsion records); *Unincorporated Operating Div. of Ind. Newspapers, Inc. v. Trs. of Ind. Univ.*, 787 N.E.2d 893, 904 (Ind. Ct. App. 2003) (stating that "FERPA is a federal law which requires education records to be kept confidential").

In short, as one court has observed, "state and federal courts are sharply divided on this issue." *Caledonian-Record Publ'g Co. v. Vt. State Colls.*, 833 A.2d 1273, 1274–76 (Vt. 2003) (citing cases).

We need not step into this controversy here, however, because we believe a provision of the Iowa Open Records Act already gives priority to FERPA. Section 22.9 of the Act provides:

> If it is determined that any provision of this chapter would cause the denial of funds, services or essential information from the United States government which would otherwise definitely be available to an agency of this state, such provision shall be suspended as to such agency, but only to the extent necessary to prevent denial of such funds, services, or essential information.

Otherwise stated, the first paragraph of section 22.9 suspends the operation of a provision of the Open Records Act if the provision would cause the denial of federal funds to a state agency. This paragraph, we believe, answers the Press-Citizen's argument that FERPA in and of itself is not a positive law. Section 22.9 gives it the effect of a positive law. If the University regularly released educational records pursuant to the Open Records Act, it would be engaging in a "practice" of permitting the release of confidential education records, assuming the records contained "personally identifiable information." *See* 20 U.S.C. § 1232g(b)(1). The sanction for this would be a loss of federal funding. *See* 20 U.S.C. §§ 1232c, 1234c (authorizing the withholding of funds when a recipient "is failing to comply substantially with any requirement of law applicable to such funds"); *see also id.* § 1232g(f).

The Press-Citizen responds that the University has not shown the disclosure of records would "definitely" cause it to lose funds as required by the first paragraph of section 22. This argument, we believe, misreads the statute. Section 22.9 requires that the federal funds be "definitely available." That they are. The University enjoys considerable federal support. The statute does not have similar language requiring that the *loss* be definite.

The Press-Citizen urges, however, that a one-off production of records in this case would not amount to a "policy or practice." *See Gonzaga Univ.*, 536 U.S. at 288 (noting that FERPA's nondisclosure provisions "speak only in terms of institutional policy and practice, not individual instances of disclosure" and "have an aggregate focus"); *see also Achman v. Chisago Lakes Indep. Sch. Dist. No. 2144*, 45 F. Supp. 2d 664, 674 (D. Minn. 1999) (finding that "a solitary violation is insufficient to support a finding that the District has violated FERPA as a matter of policy or practice"). One problem with this argument, however, is that the production would not be accidental or inadvertent and would necessarily set some kind of precedent after having been authorized by the Iowa courts. A "policy or practice" to some extent would be established.

The larger problem with the Press-Citizen's position is that section 22.9 also operates on an aggregate basis. That section asks us to consider not whether a specific production of records in a particular case would result in a loss of funds, but whether a "provision"—e.g., section 22.2(1), the overall legal requirement that public records be made available—would cause such a loss. In other words, section 22.9 requires us to consider whether section 22.2(1), the basic open records "provision," applied consistently to education records at the University of Iowa, i.e., "an agency of this state," would "cause the denial of funds," and if so it "suspend[s]" that provision.

Of course, at the end of the day the federal government might not try to defund the University of Iowa regardless of the circumstances. But we do not think section 22.9 requires Iowa courts to make predictions about policy decisions made in Washington D.C. That would be unworkable. As we read the first paragraph of section 22.9, it requires us to withhold legal effect from a provision of the Open Records Act, such as section 22.2(1), if it appears that provision (not just an isolated application of the provision) would result in a loss of federal funding for a state agency.

### D. FERPA and "Personally Identifiable Information"

Assuming FERPA applies, the next issue is whether its obligations can be met by redaction or whether it requires the withholding of entire records in some instances. The University argues that under the DOE's interpretation of "personally identifiable information," an educational record must be withheld if the recipient would know the student to whom the record refers, even with the redaction of personal information, such as the student's name. *See* 34 C.F.R. § 99.3. Given the notoriety of the October 14, 2007 incident, the University contends that no amount of redaction of personal information would prevent the newspaper from knowing the identity of various persons referenced in records relating to that incident.

The Press-Citizen responds that under the Open Records Act, access is a yes-or-no proposition. It cannot vary based upon the identity of the party making the request. The flaw in this argument, however, is that the relevant legal standards in this case actually come from FERPA, incorporated into Iowa law through section 22.9.

The Press-Citizen also insists that it is not a legally permissible construction of the term "personally identifiable information" for the University to withhold entire documents, rather than redact them. We disagree. The statute forbids federal funding of institutions that have a policy or practice of releasing "education records (or personally identifiable information contained therein . . .)" without parental permission. *See* 20 U.S.C. § 1232g(b)(1). This either-or language, as we read it, is at least subject to the interpretation that an entire record can be withheld where redaction would not be enough to protect the identity of a student. And as long as the underlying statute is ambiguous, we are required to defer to any reasonable and permissible interpretation made by the agency—here DOE. *See Chevron U.S.A., Inc. v. Natural Res. Def. Council, Inc.*, 467 U.S. 837, 842–43 (1984).

Thus, consistent with current DOE regulations, we conclude that educational records may be withheld in their entirety where the requester would otherwise know the identity of the referenced student or students even with redactions.

The Press-Citizen criticizes this position as a matter of policy. In its view: "The University's position boils down to a peculiar argument that FERPA applies on a sliding scale, saving its most vigorous application to records concerning crimes and alleged crimes that are the most notorious." This feature of FERPA, however, derives from earlier determinations by Congress and the DOE that preservation of student confidentiality should be an overarching goal of the statute. It is not our role to reexamine those decisions.

### E. Additional Issues

The Press-Citizen points out that FERPA has an exception when education records are "furnished in compliance with judicial order, or pursuant to any lawfully issued subpoena, upon condition that parents and the students are notified of all such orders or subpoenas in advance of the compliance therewith by the educational institution." *See* 20 U.S.C. § 1232g(b)(2)(B); *see also* 34 C.F.R. 99.31(a)(9)(i) (indicating that an education record may be disclosed "to comply with a judicial order or lawfully issued subpoena"). This exception has been applied in prior cases. *See, e.g., Ragusa v. Malverne Union Free Sch. Dist.*, 549 F. Supp. 2d 288, 293–94 (E.D.N.Y. 2008) (ordering the production of relevant education records in a discrimination case); *Catrone v. Miles*, 160 P.3d 1204, 1210–12 (Ariz. Ct. App. 2007) (holding that education records could be ordered to be produced in a medical malpractice case and noting "the protections afforded to educational records by statute do not prohibit, but rather permit, disclosure pursuant to court order"); *Gaumond v. Trinity Repertory Co.*, 909 A.2d 512, 518 (R.I. 2006) (holding that FERPA does not bar the production of relevant education records pursuant to court order in a personal injury case). But in those instances, the records were relevant to litigation that did not involve the records themselves. It would make no sense to interpret the "judicial order" exception as authorizing disclosure whenever a party chose to bring a separate court action seeking access to education records. This would lead to a highly incongruous situation where FERPA would only have effect until the party requesting records chose to go to court, at which point FERPA would cease to have any effect at all.

The Press-Citizen also argues that the University has been inconsistent in its position. As the Press-Citizen points out, University officials including the president, the athletic director, and the football coach have commented publicly on aspects of the University's response to the alleged sexual assault. In addition, the seventy-two-page Stolar Report that was commissioned by the Board of Regents contains a detailed narrative and critique of the University's response to the incident, replete with references to "Football Player #1," "Football Player #2," and "the Student-Athlete."

We are not persuaded that the University has been altogether consistent. At the same time, commentators have criticized FERPA for permitting institutions to behave inconsistently—revealing student information when it puts the university in a good light and withholding it when it does not. *See* Matthew R. Salzwedel & Jon Ericson, *Cleaning Up Buckley: How the Family Educational Rights and Privacy Act Shields Academic Corruption in College Athletics*, 2003 WIS. L. REV. 1053, 1105–06 (commenting that universities "provide disclosure that is selective in application"). Regardless, the Press-Citizen does not attach any particular legal significance to the University's alleged inconsistency. It provides no legal authority in this section of its brief and, at oral argument, specifically disclaimed any waiver argument. For these reasons, the Press-Citizen's inconsistency argument does not alter our conclusions as to what FERPA requires in this case.

## CONCLUSION

We reverse the judgment of the district court to the extent it orders the production of the appealed documents. We remand for further proceedings in accordance with this opinion.

■ APPEL, JUSTICE (dissenting) [with whom JUSTICES WIGGINS AND HECHT join].

I respectfully dissent.

The Federal Educational Rights and Privacy Act (FERPA) states that federal funds shall not be available "to any educational agency or institution which has a policy or practice" of releasing personally identifiable information without the written consent of parents. 20 U.S.C. § 1232g(b)(1). In my view, compliance with a judicial order pursuant to a generally applicable state public records statute does not amount to a policy or practice of *any educational agency or institution*. The majority opinion repeatedly cites "policy or practice," while omitting the statutory requirement that the "policy or practice" must be one of the "educational agency or institution." In effect, the majority opinion amends the statute to strike the words "agency or institution."

In light of this explicit wording of FERPA and the Iowa Open Records Act, I would not rewrite either statute. While federal law plainly is supreme, I find no conflict between FERPA and the Iowa Public Records Act. As a result, I would require disclosure of the public records in this case.

## NOTES

1. ***Regulatory Enforcement.*** With the end of the private right of action after *Gonzaga*, almost all enforcement of FERPA occurs in the Department of Education, specifically its Family Policy Compliance Office (FPCO), with a staff of about ten people. In principle, the FPCO could withhold all federal funding from a school district or an institution of higher education based on a FERPA violation. In practice, such a draconian penalty is unlikely—indeed, no federal education funding has ever been withheld on the basis of FERPA compliance problems. Parents of minor children or college and graduate students over the age of 18 may file complaints with the FPCO alleging violations of FERPA; if the FPCO investigates the complaint, it does so with the objective of identifying potential corrective actions such as policy changes or improved training. The FPCO devotes much of its energy to technical assistance. It produces FAQs aimed at different audiences (such as parents, principals, or higher education

administrators) and provides model disclosures and policies. It also answers specific inquiries from educators, and it makes the explanatory letter written in response to each question publicly available to serve as a sort of advisory opinion for other institutions to rely upon. Critics have argued that FERPA's enforcement structure after *Gonzaga* is lax: they say Congress has not amended the statute to give students the ability to enforce the law on their own, and the FPCO does not have the resources or the inclination to enforce FERPA aggressively enough or to issue regulations clarifying and strengthening its protections. *See, e.g.*, Lynn M. Daggett, *FERPA in the Twenty-First Century: Failure to Effectively Regulate Privacy for All Students*, 58 CATHOLIC L. REV. 59 (2008). On the other hand, as with FTC enforcement [see Chapter 3] or HIPAA [see Chapter 12], one might conclude that a collaborative regulatory model where the FPCO works with schools to improve their policies is a better option.

2. ***End Runs.*** Despite the apparently clear determination in *Gonzaga* that FERPA confers no private right of action on students, plaintiffs still do attempt creative end runs around the ruling. One court recently expressed skepticism about a plaintiff's use of FERPA as the predicate to a claimed violation of substantive due process rights to information privacy under *Whalen v. Roe* [see Chapter 1], but then proceeded to analyze the case under FERPA anyway and dispose of it on other grounds. *Risica ex rel. Risica v. Dumas*, 466 F. Supp. 2d 434, 441 (D. Conn. 2006) ("Instead of attempting to bring a FERPA claim directly before the court under 42 U.S.C. § 1983, the plaintiff is attempting to circumvent the holding in *Gonzaga University* by using the Fourteenth Amendment as a backdoor."). Another court affirmed summary judgment against a negligence per se tort claim alleging a violation of FERPA requirements. *Atria v. Vanderbilt Univ.*, 142 F. App'x 246, 254 (6th Cir. 2005) (holding that "FERPA imposes administrative requirements and does not define a standard of care"). Could any such suit succeed after *Gonzaga*?

3. ***Spending Statutes, Procedures, and Remedies.*** Why do you suppose Congress originally crafted FERPA as a condition for federal funding of educational institutions rather than simply imposing requirements on them directly? A significant part of the explanation has nothing to do with privacy or the enforcement of individual rights, but a much simpler point: most other federal education law is written that way. Historically, education has been an area of state control, so Congress generally has sought to influence education policy by tying strings to the considerable federal funding given to schools, colleges, and universities. Federal education statutes with sweeping effects on educational institutions, such as the No Child Left Behind Act, 20 U.S.C. §§ 6311 et seq., and the Individuals with Disabilities Education Act (IDEA), 20 U.S.C. §§ 1400 et seq., are also structured as conditions on federal funding. However, the statutory language of IDEA includes an elaborate dispute resolution system, under which parents dissatisfied with a school district's educational plans for their children may demand due process hearings and ultimately may sue in federal court. *See* 20 U.S.C. § 1415, *Bd. of Educ. v. Rowley*, 458 U.S. 176 (1982). Remedies include attorney's fees as well as compensatory financial

awards and injunctive relief. Does the absence of such explicit provisions in FERPA support the Court's conclusion in *Gonzaga*? What about the fact that FERPA does entitle parents to a hearing at the school concerning their rights of access to records, correction, and deletion—but not their rights concerning disclosures? Would it be better if FERPA included broader IDEA-like procedural safeguards for families? Or do differences between special education and student privacy make the IDEA model inappropriate for FERPA? Also note that the very same spending-control character of FERPA is what made the *Press-Citizen* court find that FERPA *did* apply to that case, because of its reading of the Iowa public records law.

4. ***Reading Congress' Mind.*** The majority and dissenting opinions in *Gonzaga* each point to different evidence to support their accounts of congressional intent. The majority, for example, emphasizes the statutory conferral of authority on the Secretary of Education to "deal with violations" and the decision to centralize regulatory enforcement of FERPA in the Department of Education's headquarters to avoid variation of decisions in different regional offices. Couldn't one just as easily read those provisions as indicating that Congress wanted the Secretary to have enforcement power in addition to courts, and to reach uniform decisions to which courts would give deference as a matter of administrative law? In the same way, the dissent stresses the use of language about "rights" in the statute as an indication that Congress created rights enforceable through § 1983 actions, and it relies on congressional inaction in the face of case law allowing FERPA suits under § 1983. But should a reference to rights automatically indicate a decision to provide a judicial remedy? And does congressional inaction carry as much weight as the dissent gives it—particularly in light of the fact that Congress hasn't acted to change FERPA's enforcement mechanisms since *Gonzaga* either? In the end, the correct interpretation in *Gonzaga* depends largely on how clear a statement courts want to require Congress to make about private rights of action, which is a longstanding disagreement among the Justices.

5. ***Discovery.*** Under the reasoning of the *Press-Citizen* majority, if the student-athlete who was sexually assaulted were suing the university over its mishandling of the crime, could she gain access to the appealed documents in discovery? The court acknowledges that many cases have allowed the enforcement of subpoenas that required production of student records covered by FERPA. Why does it conclude those cases are different from the claim in *Press-Citizen*?

6. ***Free Press Arguments in* Press-Citizen.** A coalition of media companies and free press organizations submitted an amicus brief in *Press-Citizen* making arguments based on constitutional free expression protection, but the Iowa Supreme Court largely declined to reach these arguments by amici because they had not been raised by the petitioner in the lower courts. Is the court's holding consistent with the First Amendment [see Chapters 1 and 8]? With the purposes of freedom of information laws [see Chapter 10]? On one hand, FERPA is only a restriction on access to information. As seen elsewhere in this casebook, the First Amendment often places greater constraints on privacy laws that would prevent the press from

disclosing information than on laws that make it more difficult for the press to collect information. On the other hand, the Press-Citizen is a newspaper trying to cover a highly newsworthy event, and the University is a public institution subject to freedom of information laws. Which is the better understanding of the balance between privacy and speech rights here? As the *Press-Citizen* opinion explains, there is little consensus on the issue within the judiciary; the court here avoids the larger dispute by finding Iowa's public records law inapplicable under its own terms. Do you think that was the best resolution?

7. ***Law Enforcement Records and Educational Records.*** The Jeanne Clery Disclosure of Campus Security Policy and Campus Crime Statistics Act ("Clery Act"), 20 U.S.C. § 1092(f), yet another education statute tied to the receipt of federal funds, requires colleges and universities to collect and report specified information about crime on or near their campus and to issue "timely warnings" to students and staff about criminal incidents that could threaten their safety. (As a student, you may have become accustomed to receiving emails and text messages containing these warnings.) Is there any inconsistency between the policy of extensive sunlight about campus crime embodied in the Clery Act and the provisions of FERPA analyzed in *Press-Citizen*? FERPA's definition of "education records" excludes "records maintained by a law enforcement unit of the educational agency or institution that were created by that law enforcement unit for the purpose of law enforcement." Does that resolve the tension? In *Press-Citizen*, the amicus brief also argued that many of the appealed documents were covered by this exception, but the court again said that this contention had been waived below.

8. ***Sensitive Situations.*** Privacy concerns about both student searches and educational records tend to get raised in sensitive situations. Schools can be intense environments, and disputes between school authorities and parents or students can become emotionally charged. It is not surprising that the cases in this chapter involve drugs (*Vernonia, Safford*), risks of suicide (*Owensboro*), and sexual misconduct (*Gonzaga, Press-Citizen*). Those are the types of circumstances when student privacy often arises as a legal issue: an educational institution has extended its police-like powers to a controversial degree in response to some problem it perceives as significant, or upset families are raising every available accusation against the school, or both. (And, an important side note: why does the *Press-Citizen* court keep referring to a sexual assault that gave rise to criminal convictions as an "alleged" "incident"—rather than "the assault" or something similar?) Attorneys advising either side in these situations need to keep their cool and avoid being drawn into the sometimes heightened emotions. Counseling educational institutions to take measured steps during such a crisis can avoid legal violations and simultaneously protect students from privacy invasions and schools from liability.

---

## Focus

Educational Technology and Student Privacy

Educational technology is an $8 billion industry, growing at astonishing speed. Students are more tech-savvy than ever before and companies—both established educational publishers adjusting to a new market and startups sensing opportunity—have created everything from school email services to online textbooks and testing. One consequence of these new technologies is an explosion of student data. Each time a student using one of these products watches a video tutorial, turns an electronic page, or hesitates before answering a question, the provider collects personal information about that student. Some companies say they gather up to 10 million unique data points per child, per day.

This new technology is intended to promote learning. Modern tools may improve student engagement. Better data can diagnose areas where a student is struggling and help teachers provide targeted educational support in response. Some educational reformers also suggest the data could help evaluate teachers and schools, or at least provide feedback about educational methods that would allow them to be improved.

Many privacy advocates and parents nonetheless worry about third parties collecting so much student data. Oftentimes these products track highly sensitive information related to academic performance, disciplinary records, or disability status. One recent example is inBloom, born out of an education nonprofit with funds from the Bill and Melinda Gates Foundation. Parents were concerned to find that inBloom collected over 400 data points on students, including learning disabilities and Social Security numbers. Parents in multiple states began protesting and filing lawsuits, New York passed legislation effectively banning inBloom from operating in the state, and the organization shut down. In addition to collection, there are also concerns about use of student data. In 2014, Google became the target of a lawsuit challenging its practices of data mining student email messages for advertising purposes.

FERPA wasn't designed to include the wealth of student data that third parties directly create, collect, and use without it ever passing through the principal's office. The statute protects information in a student's "education record," which the Supreme Court has compared to the types of records "kept in a filing cabinet in a records room" or on a "permanent secure database." *Owasso Independent School Dist. No. I–011 v. Falvo*, 534 U.S. 426, 433 (2002). Identify the provisions of FERPA and its regulations that might give third parties like inBloom and Google access to information about students. To critics, these provisions are loopholes.

Moreover, because FERPA applies only to educational institutions themselves, its mandates are not directly enforceable against companies; regulators must rely on schools to ensure safeguards are in place. There are indications that, despite clear requirements in the regulations that schools ensure subcontractors preserve FERPA protections, many schools are not maintaining control over student data. A recent national study found that only 6.7% of contracts between educational technology companies and schools ban selling student data for profit, and many agreements allow vendors to unilaterally change the terms of these agreements without notice. *See* JOEL REIDENBERG ET AL., FORDHAM CENTER ON LAW AND INFORMATION POLICY, PRIVACY AND CLOUD COMPUTING IN PUBLIC SCHOOLS (2013). To address this problem, the Department of Education recommended best practices for schools negotiating contracts with third party service providers. *See* U.S DEP'T OF EDUCATION, PRIVACY TECHNICAL ASSISTANCE CENTER, PTAC–FAQ–3, PROTECTING STUDENT PRIVACY WHILE USING ONLINE EDUCATIONAL SERVICES: REQUIREMENTS AND BEST PRACTICES (2014).

[For more general discussion of contracts concerning third party vendors' handling of data, see Chapter 8.]

In response to these controversies, President Obama released a legislative proposal, the Student Digital Privacy Act, in January 2015. H.R. 2092, 114th Cong. (2015); S. 1788, 114th Cong. (2015). The bill attempted to fill FERPA's gaps by explicitly prohibiting companies from disclosing student data to additional parties for purposes such as targeted advertising. Many privacy advocates criticized the legislation, saying it did not go far enough to address what they see as shortcomings in the statute. For example, a number of exceptions permitted vendors to disclose student information for a wide number of purposes, including to future employers or military recruiters, and the bill continued to allow them to make unilateral changes to their policies. After several contentious congressional hearings on the legislation, it was withdrawn by its sponsors for redrafting.

Rather than waiting for Congress, California enacted the Student Online Personal Information Protection Act (SOPIPA), CAL. BUS. & PROF. CODE § 22584, which became effective at the beginning of 2016. Unlike FERPA, California's statute applies directly to companies that receive data about elementary or secondary school students from schools, and it prohibits them from using, sharing, disclosing, or compiling that data for anything other than specified education-related purposes. SOPIPA also imposes security requirements on companies and rules on data retention and deletion. Finally, the statute creates a private right of action for enforcement. A number of states are now considering similar bills. Some observers expect that educational technology companies operating nationwide will simply ensure that they comply with California rules, which may reduce or eliminate the need for additional state or federal measures.

Another nationally applicable shift is a notable increase in self-regulation within the education technology sector. After several of the high-profile controversies described above, the Future of Privacy Forum and the Software and Information Industry Association jointly developed a "Student Privacy Pledge" for educational technology companies. The pledge specifies 12 commitments signatories make to protect the privacy and security of student data, including bans on selling the information, using it for behaviorally targeted advertising, or changing privacy policies without notice and choice. The pledge also defines student data more broadly than the "education record" under FERPA. To date, over 200 companies have signed the pledge, including Apple, Microsoft, and Google. Supporters note that the promises contained in the pledge can be enforced as a matter of consumer protection law [see Chapter 3]. Skeptics still want to see FERPA amended to cover third party vendors unambiguously and to strengthen overall legal and regulatory protection for student data.

---

# INDEX

References are to Pages